America, Britain, & Russia

THEIR CO-OPERATION AND CONFLICT

1941-1946

BY

WILLIAM HARDY McNEILL
Assistant Professor of History
The College, University of Chicago

JOHNSON REPRINT CORPORATION
New York and London
1970

Reprinted with the permission of the Oxford University Press

Library of Congress Catalog Card Number: 71-129286

Printed in the United States of America

INTRODUCTION

This book has had an unusual history. It appeared in 1953 as one in a series of volumes designed to carry the *Survey of International Affairs* across the years of World War II when the production of annual volumes had been suspended. As such it was little noticed; it took its place on a few hundred library shelves as one more red back in a well-known and very bulky series of volumes published by the Royal Institute of International Affairs, London. The Institute's title led many to suppose, quite wrongly, that it held some sort of official or at least semiofficial status in the British government; its publications, because of their handsome appearance, looked official too.

But in 1953 the Cold War had been well and truly joined in Asia as well as in Europe, and Americans, at least, were less interested in how it began than in how to carry it on toward some kind of (dimly conceived) victory while still escaping nuclear disaster. The book had nothing to say to such concerns, nor did it reveal any new secrets about the war years. It therefore remained quietly on library shelves where cataloguers had placed it.

The decent obscurity in which *America, Britain and Russia: Their Cooperation and Conflict 1941–46* thus came to rest deepened when Herbert Feis came out with three volumes between 1957 and 1961 that traced the diplomacy of the wartime Big Three with more detail than I had done. Feis was accorded special access to State Department files which made his work a kind of semiofficial free-lance history. Since the Royal Institute of International Affairs, despite its imposing titulature, does not enjoy any kind of preferential access to British Foreign Office records, it certainly seemed that Feis's books had superseded anything I had been able to do earlier on the basis of published sources. On the other hand, Feis's books revealed almost nothing of importance that had not been made public previously. It seemed clear that main lines of Allied diplomacy, at least as recorded in Washington, had been knowable when I wrote.

Matters took a new turn after 1961 when D. F. Fleming published a book entitled *The Cold War and Its Origins, 1917-1950*. This was the first of the revisionist histories to be published in the United States; revisionist in the sense that it challenged the official United States interpretation of world events by arguing that the Cold War arose in large part from American fears and American aggressiveness. A covey of eager and sometimes angry demythologizers followed, provoking a rival band of "establishment" historians to defend the view that Russian aggressiveness and revolutionary ideology was mainly responsible for the Cold War.

In the second half of the 1960's these academic arguments began to resonate among a small but vocal segment of the American public, especially among college students, who faced the possibility of being drafted into the army and compelled to fight in Vietnam. Many feared and hated such a prospect and asked themselves how the United States had blundered into Vietnam in particular and the Cold War in general. The more mistaken American policy in southeast Asia seemed to these critics, the more live the question of how we had ever been sucked into such a maelstrom became. If in 1968 or 1970 global confrontation between an embattled free world and an expansive Communist conspiracy no longer seemed a plausible interpretation of world events, why had it seemed so convincing to a majority of the American public in 1948 or 1950?

One obvious explanation was the stupidity and/or moral degradation of everyone over thirty; and many youthful rebels felt satisfied with this explanation. Others were attracted to interpretations that cast either big business or American militarism or both in the role of villain. Such historians as William A. Williams, Walter LeFeber, and Gar Alperovitz conveyed the message that powerful special interests had thrown up a smoke screen of propaganda and half-truths, misleading the American public in order to forward their own, narrowly conceived, private advantage. Such a vision of the domestic and international politics of the 1940's was heady stuff for a generation of students who were predisposed to suspect almost every form of constituted authority, and who thought of themselves as having been immorally designated by their elders for the role of sacrificial victim and/or executioner of the no longer Cold War against Communism. In this situation historians who argued that the fault lay with Stalin and revolutionary Russian ideology met with little response.

A third school of historians, however, resorted to the characteristically academic device of finding fault not with the United States nor with the Russians, but with the situation in general. From this "realpolitik" point of view, nuances of motive and consciousness on the part of policy makers, whether in Washington or in Moscow, became less important than the quasi-geometric rules of the diplomatic quadrille itself, which required realignment of the world's surviving powers once Germany and Japan had been removed from the scene by defeat in World War II. In an extreme form, this vision of human affairs portrayed what happened after World War II as occurring almost independently of human will or intent. In accordance with age-old precedent, the changing balance of power, of fear, and of terror broke up the wartime alliance — as it were automatically — and rearranged the states of the earth into new precariously "balanced" camps. Distinguished representatives of this school such as Louis Halle and Hans Morgenthau did not discount human motivation and consciousness entirely. On the contrary, a major theme of their work was criticism of American policy and public opinion for preferring global ideological panaceas to a sober recognition of the more limited national interests of the United States.

As debate over the Cold War and its origins thus came alive in American academic circles, the older literature was combed over for ammunition, suggestions, information. This provoked a sort of resurrection for *America, Britain and Russia: Their Cooperation and Conflict, 1941–46.* Nearly everybody found it useful. Defenders of the idea that Stalin was fundamentally responsible for the beginning of the Cold War because he broke his promises to institute democratic governments in eastern Europe and supported Communist take-over everywhere in the world saw nothing in the record here set forth to contradict their view, and found much to support it. Revisionists who made the United States mainly responsible for the breakdown of the wartime Alliance could and did do the same. But the school that found this book most to its taste was that of the realpolitikers, who felt that the interpretation of events set forth in the following pages confirmed their own opinions.

No author who has read diverse reviews of the same book will be fundamentally surprised to discover that his work can be understood in different ways by different men and used for different purposes. Indeed, it is the nature of all communication among men to be imprecise, and liable to distortion by differential receptivity. If we did not constantly misunderstand one another, all aspects of human life, including international affairs, would be unrecognizably different from the reality we confront and — at least sometimes — also attempt to comprehend.

Perhaps the renewed interest in this book that became apparent in the late 1960's merely or mainly reflected its convenient location on library shelves. And its use by men of widely differing opinions may have reflected, more than anything else, my own lack of any clear and single-minded point of view in interpreting the tangled events of 1941–46. But I prefer to think it was because the book had some virtues and advantages that arose largely from the time and place in which it was written.

Time was surely of the essence. In the years when this book was put together, 1950–52, the Korean War was in progress half a world away from the streets of London where it was composed. An American, living in a foreign land, isolated in large degree from currents of feeling running strong in the

United States, but unable all at once to share the concerns and perturbations of British public life was, therefore, in a position to rework the immediate past without being much affected by the postwar passions and fears that were, and are, so strong. This, I think, is the reason why this book seems largely to escape the partisanship characteristic of many other attempts to deal with the beginnings of the Cold War.

Coming at the theme from the perspective of the World War II years meant asking "How did the Grand Alliance break up?" rather than "How did the Cold War begin?" This, too, probably helped to sustain a more detached, ironic tone than is usual among historians who address themselves to the question in its second form. Detachment, of course, is not always a virtue, but in a book that purports to be a history it has this advantage: a work that achieves a modicum of detachment is likely to age better than others, since it does not necessarily become naive or antiquated at the moment when a particular cause fades from current relevance. And because this book did achieve a relatively high degree of detachment it has survived almost twenty years without requiring any kind of updating.

This longevity depends on a second important fact about the time in which it was written. By 1952 almost all the important facts available from British and American sources had entered the public domain. A flood of official publication supplemented by personal memoirs and by two distinguished memoirs-as-history, Winston Churchill, *The Second World War,* and Robert Sherwood, *Roosevelt and Hopkins,* left remarkably little undisclosed. Russian sources, of course, were and remain dark and mysterious; but until such time as the Soviet Union opens its archives freely, inference and surmise as to Stalin's opinions and motives will remain about as flimsy as they were in 1952. Russian archives have not been opened yet and are not likely to be made available to western scholars in any foreseeable future. Hence the body of information upon which a history of the Grand Alliance and its breakup must be based remains today much as it was in 1952, with the difference that today there are well-defined and rival schools of historical interpretation, whereas twenty years ago no such historiographical tradition had yet come into existence.

No doubt there are perils in trying to come to grips with a large body of information in the absence of well-defined historiographical traditions, which tend, always, to direct attention to certain critical issues and skirt over others or neglect them entirely. The prior existence of a number of points of debate, or a vigorous dissent from some item in the established view of affairs, can give focus and direction to historical research. Yet to look things over freshly, without clear awareness of where the important issues lie, is also advantageous.

It was easy in 1950–52 to see beyond the unpretentious myopia of daily journalism on the one hand and of personal memoirs on the other — not to mention the reticences characteristic of official communiqués, document collections, and more formal histories. Moreover, the experience of reliving in imagination five years whose main events — Pearl Harbor, Stalingrad, Tarawa, D Day, and VJ Day — had been very much a part of my own life as a soldier in the army of the United States meant trying to understand from the top what I had already experienced in a minor and trifling but sufficiently poignant way from the bottom of the command hierarchy.

One can aspire toward a kind of stereoscopic vision in such circumstances — a two-eyed effort at comprehension that may hope to envision men and events in the round. Immediacy of this kind can surely do something to make up for the disadvantage that haunts all efforts at writing contemporary history, namely the author's inability to recognize long-range trends and meanings that become clear only in the context of subsequent developments.

Historians, wise after the event, have as their professional function the task of reworking the record of the past in the light of subsequent as well as of contemporary data. But the experience that fell my lot in writing this book can never be duplicated by others, working in a different context and at a different time. Their advantages do not entirely cancel out the advantages that I enjoyed of simultaneous closeness and detachment: closeness in having lived 1941–46, as it were, twice; detachment in having both times experienced the events of those years as a kind of outsider, a displaced person, a stranger who, whether in Hawaii in 1942, Athens in 1944, or London in 1950–52 was inhibited from making any kind of intense identification with the competing causes and actors of the story by knowing that I did not really belong in the role and location where I found myself, but was a mere wayfarer, en route to some quite different place and future professional role.

Whether these facts account for the value of the book or not, it remains true that in rereading its pages I find much to be pleased with and nothing that seems clearly wrong. This may reflect an insensitivity to change characteristic of men over thirty; it also conveniently justifies reissue of the book without revision.

It remains for others who may read the pages that follow to judge for themselves how well the facts and their interpretation as available twenty years ago stand up in an age when the Cold War has become or is rapidly becoming a thing of the past, just like the Grand Alliance of World War II, whose rise and fall is here recorded.

William H. McNeill
Chicago, April 1970

AMERICA, BRITAIN, AND RUSSIA

THEIR CO-OPERATION AND CONFLICT

1941–1946

SURVEY OF INTERNATIONAL AFFAIRS

1939–1946

EDITED BY

ARNOLD TOYNBEE

Director of Studies in the Royal Institute of International Affairs
Research Professor of International History
in the University of London
(Both on the Sir Daniel Stevenson Foundation)

SURVEY OF INTERNATIONAL AFFAIRS
1939–1946

America, Britain, & Russia

THEIR CO-OPERATION AND CONFLICT

1941–1946

BY
WILLIAM HARDY McNEILL
Assistant Professor of History
The College, University of Chicago

Issued under the auspices of the
Royal Institute of International Affairs

OXFORD UNIVERSITY PRESS
LONDON NEW YORK TORONTO
1953

FOREWORD

THE writing of the history of the Second World War in the Chatham House *Survey of International Affairs* series has had one good point in common with the waging and winning of the war itself by the Allies. It has been done by British and American hands in co-operation. The author of the present volume is an American on the staff of the University of Chicago, and Chatham House is glad of this opportunity of expressing its gratitude to the University for giving Mr. McNeill leave of absence for two years for the purpose of doing this piece of historical work in London, and to the Exchange Organization initiated by the vision of Senator Fulbright for providing financial ways and means.

This volume records the history of the most interesting, as well as the most important, of all the international transactions within the period of the Second World War. The course of the relations, here narrated, between the United States, the United Kingdom, and the Soviet Union during the years 1942–6 decided, first, the issue of this war and then the division of the victors between two opposing camps; and these historic events, which were thus crowded into the short time-span of five years, were both the culmination of a long train of antecedent historical developments and the point of departure for a new chapter of history stretching away into the future beyond the horizon of an observer taking his bearings in the year 1952.

Like the history of the last bout of anarchy before the foundation of the Roman Empire, the history of the years under review in this volume would have been of absorbing interest in virtue of the personalities of the principal actors on the political stage even if the tale of their action had, to all political intents and purposes, signified nothing. Each member of the Anglo-Russo-American triumvirate that captained the winning side in the Second World War was a fascinating object of psychological study in his own right; each of them was piquantly different from either of his two partners; and the encounter between the three was an epitome of the abrupt confrontation, at close quarters, of the diverse tribes of mankind, as the result of a galloping technology's 'annihilation of distance', which was the most characteristic, most dominant, and most awkward feature in the history of this generation.

The English triumvir—who, like Caesar, would have made his fame as a great writer if he had not made it as a great man of action—had already told his story in inimitable words. The American triumvir had been fortunate in the intimacy and the perceptiveness of the records of his acts that had been kept by members of his personal entourage. The Georgian triumvir had exercised his fascination through the antithetical art of keeping himself wrapt in a cloud of mystery. In dealing with these three great figures both severally and jointly, the author of the present work was, of course, writing under the historian's limitation which is at the same time the historian's advantage. To write as an observer and not as an advocate —and, particularly, not as an advocate in one's own cause—puts a distance between a writer and his subject with which the art of biography, and *à fortiori* autobiography, does not have to contend; but this very distance confers the possibility of seeing and presenting events in a perspective which is hardly within the compass of any writer who has himself been one of the principal actors in the scenes that he is describing. While the present volume will assuredly stimulate any reader of it to plunge into Mr. Churchill's book and into the Hopkins papers, if he is not already familiar with these enthralling primary sources, students of this episode of history will also realize that brilliant and persuasive presentations of the story from the standpoint of a single statesman, or of the single Power whose interests were in a particular statesman's charge, require to be supplemented by a narrative which attempts to tell the story as a whole from the standpoint, not of any one individual or one country, but of a human race on whose long history these brief transactions seemed bound to make a marked and enduring effect.

In so far as the history of those five years 1942–6 could yet be seen in perspective in the year 1952, it was by then already manifest that the dramatic events which had occurred within this brief, though crucial, span of time were only intelligible when they were seen as incidents in a longer story which touched the deeper levels of mankind's life below the military and political surface. The two world wars of which the human race had been both the perpetrator and the victim between 1914 and 1945 were evidently part of the price that mankind was paying for a revolutionarily rapid progress towards political, social, and spiritual unification; and this unification itself was evidently the price—or the dividend—of a technological revolution that, by bringing 'Danaan gifts', was forcing the pace of mankind's advance towards unity on every non-technological plane of human activity. This desperate forced march under the prick of technology's apparently inexorable goad might seem, to an observer who found himself living through this twentieth-century revolution, to be the peculiar and distinctive feature of the age into which he happened to have been born; yet, on a second view, this could be seen also to be a feature that was shared by this age with all previous ages of human history of which any record had survived; for there was no known age in which man had not been on the run under pressure from his own technological inventiveness. The most ancient surviving traces of human life were tools, not bones; and, though the pace had become formidably hotter within the last two hundred years immediately preceding the time of writing, the spectacle was perhaps still the same in essence as it had always been since a pre-human creature had become man. It was the spectacle of a biped who united in one person the two natures of a rational and reasonable human being and a perverse and recalcitrant camel, mule, or goat, and who seemed to be condemned all the time to play simultaneously the two roles of the distracting drove and its distracted driver.

This wider horizon and deeper significance of the international transactions of the years 1942–6 need not be enlarged upon in this introductory note, since they are lucidly brought into focus in the reflections and general observations with which the volume closes. The writer of this foreword will take it upon himself merely to suggest to the reader that this closing chapter is just as integral a part of Mr. McNeill's subject as the narrative, leading up to it, which constitutes the greater part of the book.

ARNOLD TOYNBEE

AUTHOR'S PREFACE

THIS book was written between November 1950 and November 1951; then revised and corrected up to June 1952. It is based wholly upon published material, but the manuscript has benefited from the scrutiny of a number of individuals familiar with the events narrated, but who must, according to Chatham House policy, remain anonymous. Their help has saved me from numerous errors both of fact and emphasis, and I am deeply grateful for the time and attention which busy men spared for the improvement of this book. Errors which remain, and all opinions, speculations, and interpretations are, of course, my own; and Chatham House bears no responsibility for any of them.

I must further acknowledge my debt to the United States Educational Commission in the United Kingdom, administrators of the Fulbright exchange programme, and to the Rockefeller Foundation whose combined financial support made it possible for me to write this book; and to the fellowship of the Chatham House staff whose intellectual support was equally indispensable.

Finally, my intellectual debt to Arnold Toynbee, Director of Studies at Chatham House, will be apparent to all those who can read between the lines.

June 1952

Authorization has been obtained for all major quotations, and full reference to the book, the author, and the publisher has been given in each case in a footnote under the first mention of the work

CONTENTS

PART II. CO-OPERATION AS PEACE LOOMED, DECEMBER 1943–FEBRUARY 1945

PART III. BREAKDOWN OF ALLIED CO-OPERATION, FEBRUARY 1945–DECEMBER 1946

MAPS

Explanatory Note on the Three World Maps

The object of these maps is to visualize the change in the shape of the arena of international affairs during and since the Second World War.

Down to 1940 the arena of international affairs was still, for practical purposes, the flat oblong shape that it had been since the beginning of history. Admiral King's achievement of conducting naval operations across the whole breadth of the Pacific transformed this oblong into a continuous belt by sewing together the two ends. The conquest, since then, of the air over the North Pole has expanded this circular belt round the globe, which still had a northern as well as a southern edge, into three-quarters of a sphere, with no edge left to it except one round a still untraversable South Polar circle.

As a result, each of the two surviving Power-groups is now threatened by the other surviving Power-group on *three* fronts, east, west, and north, whereas before 1940 no Power was ever threatened on more than two fronts, and even this only happened to a 'central' Power, such as France was in the sixteenth century and Germany from 1871 to 1945.

This change in the 'geo-political' map is a first-class revolution in international affairs. It is so revolutionary, and has come so suddenly, that it is not easily grasped or taken into account. The purpose of these maps is to make the new shape of the human race's habitat visible to the eye.

ARNOLD TOYNBEE

ABBREVIATIONS

USED IN CITING REFERENCES IN FOOTNOTES

Allen: 'Mutual Aid'	R. G. D. Allen: 'Mutual Aid between the U.S. and the British Empire, 1941–45', *Journal of the Royal Statistical Society*, vol. cix, part iii, 1946, pp. 243–71.
Churchill, i–v	Winston S. Churchill: *The Second World War*, vols. i–v (London, Cassell, 1948–52; Boston, Houghton Mifflin, 1948–51).
Decade (A) of American Foreign Policy	U.S.A., Senate Committee on Foreign Relations, and U.S.A., Department of State: *A Decade of American Foreign Policy, Basic Documents 1941–49* (Washington, U.S.G.P.O., 1950).
Hull: *Memoirs*, i, ii	*The Memoirs of Cordell Hull*, 2 vols. (New York, Macmillan, 1948; London, Hodder & Stoughton, 1948).
Industrial Mobilization for War, i	U.S.A., Civilian Production Administration, Bureau of Demobilization: *Industrial Mobilization for War: History of the War Production Board and Predecessor Agencies 1940–1945*, vol. i. *Program and Administration* (Washington, U.S.G.P.O., 1947).
Kammerer: *Du débarquement africain*	Albert Kammerer: *Du débarquement africain au meurtre de Darlan* (Paris, Flammarion, 1949).
Mountbatten: *Report*	Vice-Admiral the Earl Mountbatten of Burma: *Report to the Combined Chiefs of Staff by the Supreme Allied Commander, South-East Asia* (London, H.M.S.O., 1951).
Occupation of Japan	U.S.A., Department of State: *Occupation of Japan: Policy and Progress*, Pub. 2671 (Washington, U.S.G.P.O., 1947).
Pearl Harbor Attack	U.S.A., Congress: *Hearings before the Joint Committee on the Investigation of the Pearl Harbor Attack*, Part 15 (Washington, U.S.G.P.O., 1946).
Postwar Foreign Policy Preparation	U.S.A., Department of State: *Postwar Foreign Policy Preparation 1939–1945*, Pub. 3580 (Washington, U.S.G.P.O., 1950).
Reports on Lend-Lease Operations	U.S.A., the President: *Reports to Congress on Lend-Lease Operations* (Washington, U.S.G.P.O., quarterly).
Sherwood: *Roosevelt and Hopkins*	Robert E. Sherwood: *Roosevelt and Hopkins: an Intimate History* (New York, Harper, 1948). An English edition with title: *The White House Papers of Harry L. Hopkins* was published in 2 vols. in 1948–9 by Eyre & Spottiswoode. The book will be cited under the American title, but pagination of both U.S. and English editions will be given.
Soviet Supply Protocols	U.S.A., Department of State: *Soviet Supply Protocols*, Pub. 2759 (Washington, U.S.G.P.O., 1948).
United States and Italy	U.S.A., Department of State: *United States and Italy, 1936–1946*, Pub. 2669 (Washington, U.S.G.P.O., 1946).
United States at War	U.S.A., Bureau of the Budget: *The United States at War* (Washington, U.S.G.P.O., 1947).
United States Relations with China	U.S.A., Department of State: *United States Relations with China*, Pub. 3573 (Washington, U.S.G.P.O., 1949).
Woodbridge: *UNRRA*, i, ii, iii	United Nations Relief and Rehabilitation Administration, Office of the Chief Historian, George Woodbridge: *UNRRA: The History of the United Nations Relief and Rehabilitation Administration*, 3 vols. (New York, Columbia University Press, 1950).

NOTE

British Parliamentary Debates (Hansard) are cited in the form suggested in the bound volumes of the Official Reports, preceded by the date (if not given in the text) and followed by the column number, e.g.

(for the House of Commons)
7 June 1944, H.C.Deb. 5th ser., vol. 400, col. 1403;
(for the House of Lords)
9 March 1943, H.L.Deb. 5th ser., vol. 126, coll. 493–4.

PART I

CO-OPERATION TO FIGHT THE WAR

DECEMBER 1941–DECEMBER 1943

CHAPTER I

AMERICAN ENTRY INTO WAR

THE dawn that came peacefully to the American naval base at Pearl Harbour on 7 December 1941 broke almost simultaneously upon a Japanese naval task force poised for attack about 275 miles to the northward. With the dawn Japanese planes took off and winged their way southward over the island of Oahu to deliver their loads of bombs and torpedoes. Their assault transformed what had hitherto been a European and Atlantic war into the first genuinely global conflict of history.

If in imagination we follow the curtain of light which was the Pearl Harbour dawn as it swept round the earth, we may be able to recreate something of the complexity and world-girdling rush of events in which the Japanese attack on Pearl Harbour was only a part. A few hours after dawn had come to Pearl Harbour, the rays of the rising sun crossed the international date line, to begin a new day, 8 December. Sweeping across the Western Pacific, first light discovered Japanese ships crawling the ocean in various directions, prepared or preparing for attacks on Wake Island, Guam, the Philippines, Hongkong. When dawn reached the Malay coast it discovered Japanese troops already ashore at Kota Bharu, where they had begun landing under cover of darkness about an hour and a half before the first planes attacked Pearl Harbour. As the attack on Pearl Harbour meant war with the United States, so this landing meant war with Great Britain; but before either of these countries had time to react the Japanese (at 6 a.m., 8 December, Tokyo time) went through the formality of declaring a war which they had already begun.

As dawn sped westward into Asia, it brought no such startling changes. A powerful Japanese army in Manchuria stood, as it had for years, opposed to a Russian force across the Amur; but to these armies the Pearl Harbour dawn brought—so far as it brought any change at all—a relaxation of tension. Each nation was fully engaged elsewhere. To the south, in China proper, Japanese garrisons occupied, as they had for years, the richest and most developed parts of the country, while the Government and armies of Chiang Kai-shek, lodged in the upper Yangtze basin, waited anxiously for a change in the balance of forces which might permit reconquest of their lost provinces. On this front, too, Pearl Harbour morning brought no great changes.

Still farther west, in Russia, dawn uncovered a vast battle line, extending in a series of irregular loops and curves from the dark Arctic regions of the Kola peninsula southward to the Black Sea. Along the Russian front, great events, high hopes, and desperate fears were at a climax. Just three days earlier, on 5 December, the German attack upon Moscow had been broken off; Russian counter-attacks were launched on 6 December, and when the Pearl Harbour dawn arrived to illumine the battle it found the Germans, harried from flank and rear, retreating towards the hoped-for security of winter quarters. For the first time since the war had broken out in Europe more than two years before, German land armies had failed to win an easy and overwhelming victory; for the first time Hitler had clearly overreached himself and was forced to retreat. In Berlin 8 December brought forth a public acknowledgement of the 'cessation of large-scale operations' in the east. It appeared that the Soviet régime had won respite, if not escape, from what nearly all Western observers had believed to be certain defeat.

In Libya, too, the Pearl Harbour dawn broke upon great events. The British Eighth Army had given battle nearly three weeks before, on 18 November, and, after a number of dramatic reversals and threatened reversals of fortune, on 8 December firm contact with the beleaguered garrison of Tobruk was finally made. As in Russia, the Germans and their allies were in retreat, and the British could, after so many disasters, at last congratulate themselves upon a victory against German ground forces.

In Britain itself the dawn which had launched Japanese planes for the attack on Pearl Harbour saw R.A.F. planes returning from a raid on Aachen. News of Japan's attack had reached the British Government and people during the evening of 7 December. It took time for the appropriate formalities to be accomplished; but by early afternoon, 8 December, within twenty hours of the attack upon Malaya, Britain was officially at war not only with Germany, Italy, and their European satellites, but with Japan as well.

Passing westward over the Atlantic the dawn disclosed ships clustered in convoy, guarded by British, Canadian, and American warships. In Iceland, an American garrison constituted one extreme outpost of President Roosevelt's Western Hemisphere defence. In Newfoundland, Bermuda, and the islands of the Caribbean, other American garrisons occupied new air and naval bases which had been constructed since September 1940 on British territories as a result of the bases-for-destroyers deal between Britain and the United States.

Yet, despite these physical evidences of close collaboration between the British and American Governments, when the dawn which had seen the attack on Pearl Harbour rounded the globe and reached the shores of the United States, it came to a country still nominally at peace. News of the Japanese attack had arrived in Washington early in the afternoon of 7 December; but the American Government moved more slowly than the British, and it was not until 4.10 p.m., 8 December (Washington time), that the United States officially became a belligerent. Three more days elapsed before the major war alignment of the Powers was completed. On 11 December Germany and Italy declared war on the United States. On the same day the American Congress returned the compliment. By these acts the United States came into full war partnership with Great Britain, sharing enemies and friends round the circuit of the globe. The Anglo-American partnership with Russia, however, remained incomplete since the Soviet Government kept at peace with Japan. For the Russians the war continued to be a merely European struggle.

(i) The American Outlook

(*a*) Japan versus Germany as Enemy No. 1

American opinion had long been deeply divided on the question of participation in the European war.[1] Up to the day of Pearl Harbour a small but vociferous group of 'isolationists' had argued that the struggle in Europe was of no immediate concern to the United States. They had criticized President Roosevelt violently for his moves to help Britain and Russia in their struggle against Germany. On the opposite side, many persons felt that war with Germany was sure to come eventually; but very few public figures or private persons had openly championed an American declaration of war. A deliberate decision to embark upon a war seemed too terrible to face. Perhaps a majority of the public vaguely hoped that American supplies delivered to Britain and Russia would be enough.

The Japanese attack on Pearl Harbour changed everything, uniting Americans for war as nothing else could have done. No one had supposed that the Japanese would dare to affront the power of the United States in so flagrant a fashion; and it was some weeks before the full scope, daring, and skill of the Japanese attack could be realized. The immediate reaction to the news was shocked surprise and determination to wreak dire vengeance upon Japan. Many who had wavered in the pre-Pearl Harbour days found the onset of war a relief: events had made up their minds for them and removed a difficult decision from America's own hands. There was an immediate closing of ranks behind Roosevelt, the Commander-in-Chief; and for the moment at least old quarrels between isolationists and interventionists were buried.[2]

Immediately after the Japanese attack, when American indignation was

[1] A fuller account will be found in the *Survey* for 1939–46: *Initial Triumph of the Axis*.

[2] The America First Committee, which had been the most prominent isolationist organization, disbanded after issuing an appeal to its members to support the war effort (*Chicago Daily News*, 8 December 1941).

still at a peak, there seemed a possibility that the war in Europe might be forgotten. But steps were taken to prevent such forgetfulness from going far. Large sections of the press which had previously supported Roosevelt's policies of aid to Britain and Russia stressed the global nature of the struggle, even before Hitler and Mussolini solved the problem by taking the initiative in declaring war. Roosevelt, too, was at pains to identify German, Italian, and Japanese aggression as part of a single whole,[1] and in speeches subsequent to the declaration of war on Germany he repeatedly emphasized Hitler's pre-eminence among America's enemies.[2]

Newspapers which had formerly opposed intervention in the war in Europe found it convenient to concentrate attention on the war in the Pacific, and as soon as the first shock was past, a paper such as the *Chicago Tribune*, which had been one of the most extreme and violent of the isolationist press organs, argued that America's real interest lay in the Pacific, from which it would be an error to divert military forces.[3] It seems fair to say that at first the American public was in general far more hostile towards Japan than towards Germany. The attack on Pearl Harbour affronted American pride directly and deeply. The long succession of Japanese successes in the Pacific and the hard struggle of American troops on Bataan kept the Japanese war in the forefront of the news for months after Pearl Harbour; and, until American forces were actively engaged against Germany in North Africa (November 1942), the war in Europe could not seem to have the same urgency.[4]

[1] 'Remember always that Germany and Italy, regardless of any formal declaration of war, consider themselves at war with the United States at this moment just as much as they consider themselves at war with Britain and Russia': broadcast, 9 December 1941 (*Documents on American Foreign Relations, July 1941–June 1942*, ed. Leland M. Goodrich (Boston, World Peace Foundation, 1942), p. 42).

The fact that Roosevelt made no mention of Germany in his speech to Congress on 8 December in which he asked for a declaration of war was undoubtedly due to his desire not to stir up the embers of the old controversy. He knew that Hitler had promised the Japanese, as recently as 29 November, to declare war on the United States if Japan got into war with the Americans. Roosevelt probably over-estimated the degree of co-operation between Japan and Germany. Actually the Japanese attack came as a most unpleasant surprise to the Germans. Cf. F. H. Hinsley: *Hitler's Strategy* (Cambridge University Press, 1951), p. 188; Samuel Eliot Morison: *History of United States Naval Operations in World War II* (Boston, Little, Brown, 1948), iii. 48; Robert E. Sherwood: *Roosevelt and Hopkins: an Intimate History* (New York, Harper, 1948), p. 441; Eng. edition, 2 vols., *The White House Papers of Harry L. Hopkins* (London, Eyre & Spottiswoode, 1948–9), i. 445. [This book is referred to hereafter under the American title, but pagination of both U.S. and English editions will be given.]

[2] See for example the Annual Message to Congress, 6 January 1942: *Documents on American Foreign Relations, 1941–1942*, p. 47.

[3] 'It is a sound principle of war to concentrate on the principal and proximate enemy. For the United States, that enemy is Japan. . . . If we scatter our strength in a dozen trifling expeditions all over the world, we may succeed only in giving the Japanese the opportunity to strike us at home' (*Chicago Tribune*, 14 January 1942).

[4] Another element in the American attitude which should not be neglected was a sense of race superiority *vis-à-vis* the Japanese. The sovereign superiority of the white man had been challenged; and, at least among the soldiers of the Pacific, it became a commonplace to assert that

Yet despite these facts the public recognized that America was engaged in a global war and would have to deal with Germany and Italy too, and make sure of their defeat. What was not realized was that the grand strategy on which Roosevelt and his military advisers had agreed committed the United States to a generally defensive role in the Pacific while concentrating first upon the defeat of the European Axis. But in the first days of the war, when both the American strategic plan and the power of the Japanese attack were unknown to the public, matters did not really present themselves as a choice between Japan and Germany as enemy number one. Facile hopes of early victory in the Pacific were widespread, and all else was forgotten in a determination to fight and win the war on all fronts.

In retrospect it is clear that the importance of Pearl Harbour lay primarily in the psychological effect it had upon the American public. The long indecision was over once and for all. The United States embarked upon open hostilities with a public opinion fully united. Compared to this transformation of American national psychology, the military consequences of Pearl Harbour were transitory. Whatever Japan's immediate gains, and however acute the emergency which Pearl Harbour created for the Allies, it remains true that the dramatic irruption of Japan into the balance of world war worked amazingly little change in the long-range strategic dispositions and plans of the American high command.[1] The basis of their plans was co-operation with Great Britain and Russia; and it is to American relations with these two countries that we must now turn.

(*b*) American Relations with Great Britain

The intimacy and effectiveness of Anglo-American co-operation was, from many points of view, the most remarkable political and military achievement of the war. What would have been inconceivable in 1936, when the American Congress enacted a Neutrality Act designed to keep the country out of any future European war; what would have been incredible in 1938, when American opinion was generally scornful of the British and French capitulation at Munich; what would have been impolitic in 1940, when the sudden collapse of France upset all calculations of the balance of world power but failed to rid important sectors of

'the Japs are not human'. This in part accounts for the peculiarly bloodthirsty character of the Pacific fighting. Until the very end, Japanese prisoners were very few, not only because of Japanese *bushido*, but also because Americans often refused to take prisoners. Against Germany, of course, no such racial animosity existed.

[1] Morison (*History of U.S. Naval Operations*, iii. 125, 132) argues that an attack on repair, maintenance, and fuel installations at Pearl Harbour would have done more long-range damage to the American fleet than did the actual attack, which was concentrated on battleships. Moreover, had Japan declared war more formally and allowed the U.S. navy to follow its plan of attacking westward towards the Marshall Islands, Morison suggests that equal damage to the U.S. fleet might well have been wreaked on the high seas.

American opinion of long-standing distrust of Britain—became an ever growing reality during 1941 and an accomplished fact by 1942.

The underlying cultural and institutional community between Great Britain and the United States provided the *sine qua non* of Anglo-American war-time co-operation. Language was, of course, the most important link; and indeed the massive scale of the eventual co-operation between the British and Americans would not have been possible if translators had been required at each point of contact between the two nationalities.

But cultural and institutional likenesses by themselves are not enough to account for the effectiveness of Anglo-American co-operation. The pattern of world politics also acted powerfully to bring the two nations together, and, by establishing a real community of interest, provided a setting in which the cultural affinities could bear fruit. During the nineteenth century Britain had stood as a sort of shield between the United States and Europe. British policy helped to prevent any single European state from so consolidating the Continent that a world-dominating centre of power could arise to threaten the New World. Outside Europe, Great Britain won a measure of world hegemony through the exercise of naval and economic power. Such a position inevitably led to a series of disputes and quarrels with the United States; and memories of the eighteenth- and nineteenth-century relationship left a residue of distrust among certain groups of Americans even in the mid-twentieth century. But vestiges of old quarrels held small sway over the public mind of America in comparison with the reaction produced by Britain's failure in the twentieth century to retain her power, single-handed, to act as a shield against a potential European conqueror. In 1917 and again in 1941 the prospect that Britain and her allies might be unable to prevent a victorious Germany from dominating Europe (and from Europe, perhaps, the world) brought the United States into war at Britain's side. High-sounding principles undoubtedly played some part in convincing Americans on both occasions that intervention in Europe was required; but the fear of a new and ruthless German world-master was surely the more potent motive, especially in 1941.

The world balance of power and the community of culture between Britain and the United States did not work with any mathematic exactness to swing American opinion into wholehearted support of the British cause. Indeed the long debate between isolationists and interventionists throughout 1940 and 1941 was in effect a debate as to whether the United States should support Britain, and to what extent.

In the weeks immediately after Pearl Harbour, isolationist spokesmen were, with very few exceptions,[1] eager to forget and forgive; but the im-

[1] Senator Gerald P. Nye, the principal author of the Neutrality Bill of 1936 and a stout

pulses which had moved them in the months preceding Pearl Harbour did not die out altogether. Suspicion and distrust of Great Britain remained latent, and it was not long before overt criticism of the British found place once again in the ex-isolationist press.

In Congress, the isolationists had been an effective minority bloc prior to Pearl Harbour; and Roosevelt had frequently hesitated and even retreated in the face of their opposition.[1] After the beginning of war, however, there was no opposition on the part of Congressmen to an all-out effort, and in this Congress no more than reflected the attitude of the public.

As far as Roosevelt and his top advisers were concerned, co-operation with Great Britain had long been a cardinal point of their policy. The outbreak of war came as a relief to them,[2] for no longer would every step have to be carefully calculated against potential Congressional and public opposition. Roosevelt's attitude was expressed in the words that he spoke to Churchill when the latter telephoned to confirm the first news of the Pearl Harbour attack: 'We are all in the same boat now.'[3]

From the early summer of 1940, when for a few months British defeat seemed a real possibility, the American Government had moved by degrees into an ever closer partnership with Britain. On the military side, by December 1941 the United States was in reality engaged in an undeclared war in the Atlantic,[4] and the United States navy had undertaken primary responsibility for escorting merchant ships as far as Iceland.

The actual military and naval co-operation between the United States and Great Britain 'short of war' was only a part of a much more comprehensive plan which had been drawn up to guide combined Anglo-American operations in case America should become an active belligerent. As early as June 1940 the American army and navy officers responsible for drafting war plans agreed to consultation proposed by the British.[5] Conversations

isolationist, described Pearl Harbour on 7 December as 'just what Britain had planned for us', but voted with the rest of the Senate for the declaration of war next day (*New York Herald Tribune*, 8 December 1941). He was the only prominent isolationist who allowed himself any such public comment.

[1] This was notably true in the matter of sending the American navy on convoy duty all the way to British ports. This had been agreed upon by American naval authorities in March 1941, but was not actually put into effect until after Pearl Harbour (Morison: *History of U.S. Naval Operations*, i. 50, 84). Technical naval considerations also contributed to the change in plans.

[2] Sherwood: *Roosevelt and Hopkins*, pp. 428, 431; Eng. edition, i. 433, 436.

[3] Winston S. Churchill: *The Second World War* (London, Cassell, 1950), iii. 538; (Boston, Houghton Mifflin, 1950), iii. 605. [This work will be referred to hereafter as Churchill, i, ii, &c., and the pagination of both English and U.S. editions will be given.]

[4] Roosevelt announced on 27 October 1941 that orders had been issued to the U.S. navy to 'shoot on sight' at any German vessels within the U.S. security zone in the western Atlantic; and this was only a public announcement of an existing situation. Morison dates *de facto* hostilities from the *Greer* incident of 4 September 1941 (*History of U.S. Naval Operations*, i. 80). Details will be found in the *Survey* for 1939–46: *Initial Triumph of the Axis*.

[5] Morison: *History of U.S. Naval Operations*, i. 40. Details will be found in the *Survey* for 1939–46: *Initial Triumph of the Axis*.

in London and Washington began in August 1940; and formal staff conferences were held in Washington between 29 January and 27 March 1941. From the latter emerged a joint strategic plan known by the short title of ABC–1. It was to be put into effect 'should the United States be compelled to resort to war'.[1] Despite the fact that this plan was drawn up at a time when Russia was not yet a belligerent, and when it was still hoped that Japan might not join battle in the Pacific, the major strategic and administrative principles agreed upon in ABC–1 were those which guided the actual Anglo-American conduct of the war, and provided the basic framework of Anglo-American military co-operation throughout the war period.[2]

The major decision embodied in ABC–1, to attack Germany first, was stated in the following words:

> Since Germany is the predominant member of the Axis Powers, the Atlantic and European area is considered to be the decisive theatre. The principal United States Military effort will be exerted in that theatre, and operations of United States forces in other theatres will be conducted in such a manner as to facilitate that effort. . . .
>
> Even if Japan were not initially to enter the war on the side of the Axis Powers, it would still be necessary for the Associated Powers [i.e. the United States and the British Commonwealth] to deploy their forces in a manner to guard against eventual Japanese intervention. If Japan does enter the war, the Military strategy in the Far East will be defensive. The United States does not intend to add to its present Military strength in the Far East but will employ the United States Pacific Fleet offensively in the manner best calculated to weaken Japanese economic power, and to support the defense of the Malay barrier by diverting Japanese strength away from Malaysia. The United States intends so to augment its forces in the Atlantic and Mediterranean areas that the British Commonwealth will be in a position to release the necessary forces for the Far East.[3]

The 'principal offensive policies' to be employed against the Axis enemy were listed as follows:

(*a*) Application of economic pressure by naval, land, and air forces and all

[1] U.S.A., Congress: *Hearings before the Joint Committee on the Investigation of the Pearl Harbor Attack*, Part 15 (Washington, U.S.G.P.O., 1946), p. 1487. [This volume is referred to hereafter as *Pearl Harbor Attack*.]

[2] The Anglo-American staff planning which produced ABC–1 was guided by two assumptions which the Japanese Pacific offensive of 1941–2 falsified. First, that war, if it came to the United States, would originate in the Atlantic or European theatres, and Japan herself would come in only after the United States had become engaged against Germany. Second, that Japanese military and naval strength was far less than in fact proved to be the case.

Had American military planners been able to foresee more accurately the future course of events, it seems doubtful whether they would have subscribed to the plans actually agreed upon (cf. Morison, op. cit. i. 47). But plans and estimates based upon erroneous foresight are normal in human affairs; and this is only an especially striking instance because of the vast forces affected.

[3] *Pearl Harbor Attack*, pp. 1491–2. In accordance with the proposed disposition of naval forces, command in most of the North Atlantic was to pass to the United States, and in the Western Pacific to Great Britain (ibid. pp. 1505, 1516).

other means, including the control of commodities at their source by diplomatic and financial measures.

(*b*) A sustained air offensive against German Military power, supplemented by air offensives against other regions under enemy control which contribute to that power.

(*c*) The early elimination of Italy as an active partner in the Axis.

(*d*) The employment of the air, land, and naval forces of the Associated Powers, at every opportunity, in raids and minor offensives against Axis Military strength.

(*e*) The support of neutrals, and of Allies of the United Kingdom, Associates of the United States, and populations in Axis-occupied territory in resistance to the Axis Powers.

(*f*) The building up of the necessary forces for an eventual offensive against Germany.

(*g*) The capture of positions from which to launch the eventual offensive.[1]

In view of later disputes, it is interesting to compare the formulation of the offensive tasks assigned to land forces in the United Kingdom with those assigned in the Mediterranean and Middle East theatres. Land forces in the United Kingdom were to 'undertake offensive land operations as opportunity offers, in accordance with joint United States–British plans to be agreed upon at a later date'. In the Mediterranean and Middle East, land and air forces were to 'conduct offensive operations against the Axis Powers on the Continent of Europe'.[2] The more emphatic phrasing of the second assignment seems to reflect a belief that the Mediterranean was the better base from which to invade Europe.[3] Indeed, British military authorities had begun to look forward to an invasion of Sicily as early as January 1941. It seemed one of the most promising offensive possibilities that lay within unaided British power.[4] The clause (*c*) quoted above, proposing an early elimination of Italy from the war, must reflect discussion of this British plan at the staff conferences which produced ABC–1, and one may infer at least a tentative acceptance of the scheme by the Americans.

The general pattern which emerged from the ABC–1 formulation of offensive policies—economic blockade, air attack, peripheral military harassment, especially in the Mediterranean, and an 'eventual' direct offensive against a Germany presumably already much weakened—was one to which British military and political leaders persistently clung, despite subsequent pleas from the Russians and pressure from the Americans for an earlier direct attack upon the centre of German power. It was, moreover, in surprising degree, the path actually followed by the Anglo-American forces when by the last months of 1942 it became possible for them to take the strategic initiative.

[1] Ibid. pp. 1490–1.
[2] Ibid. pp. 1523, 1531.
[3] It should be remembered, however, that ABC–1 was drawn up at a time when British forces were actually engaged in Greece.
[4] Churchill, iii. 8, 90; U.S. edition, iii. 7–8, 102.

ABC–1 not only laid down basic strategy, but also formulated a number of administrative principles which were to be of the greatest importance in the actual conduct of the war. First, continuous joint planning:

The High Command of the United States and United Kingdom will collaborate continuously in the formulation and execution of strategical policies and plans which shall govern the conduct of the war. They and their respective commanders in the field, as may be appropriate, will similarly collaborate in the planning and execution of such operations as may be undertaken jointly by United States and British forces. This arrangement will apply also to such plans and operations as may be undertaken separately, the extent of collaboration required in each particular plan or operation being agreed mutually when the general policy has been decided.[1]

To effect the top-level planning contemplated in the above paragraph, an exchange of military missions was agreed upon. London and Washington were to be entirely equal, each capital becoming the seat of planning for 'the conduct of the war in areas in which that Power assumes responsibility for strategic direction'.[2] Areas of responsibility were described in Annexes II and III to the *Report*. In addition to these provisions for a strictly military co-ordination, the Staff Conference recommended that over-all political-military direction of the war effort should be lodged in a Supreme War Council, and that authoritative agencies should be set up in London and in Washington to supervise all the activities of representatives of each Government engaged in official dealings with the other. Inasmuch as these were considered more political than military matters, they were omitted from the ABC–1 *Report*, and submitted in a separate document as a recommendation to the respective Governments.[3]

Continuous large-scale joint operations (directed by a combined Anglo-American staff) of the sort which actually occurred from 1942 onwards in the European theatre were only dimly foreseen, if at all, and in any case were put off to an indefinite future.[4] The relation contemplated in ABC–1 was much more limited:

In accordance with plans based on joint strategic policy, each Power will be charged with the strategic direction of all forces of the Associated Powers normally operating in certain areas. The areas are defined initially in Annex II.

As a general rule, the forces of each of the Associated Powers should operate under their own commanders in the areas of responsibility of their own Power...

The forces of either Power which are employed normally under the strategic direction of an established commander of the other, will, with due regard to

[1] *Pearl Harbor Attack*, p. 1489. [2] Ibid. p. 1494.

[3] W. K. Hancock and M. M. Gowing: *British War Economy* (London, H.M.S.O., 1949), p. 402.

[4] 'Responsibility for the strategic direction of Military forces engaged in joint offensive action on land will be in accordance with joint agreements to be entered upon at the proper time. In these circumstances unity of command in the theatre of operations should be established' (*Pearl Harbor Attack*, p. 1503).

their type, be employed as task (organized) forces charged with the execution of specific strategic tasks. These task (organized) forces will operate under their own commanders, and will not be distributed into small bodies attached to the forces of the other Power. Only exceptional Military circumstances will justify the temporary suspension of the normal strategic tasks.[1]

A final administrative principle prescribed that 'military bases, repair facilities, and supplies of either nation will be at the disposal of the Military forces of the other as required for the successful prosecution of the war'.[2]

In view of the actual degree of fusion between British and American forces which was achieved in North Africa and Europe during the war years, this document may seem cautious; but when one reflects that it was agreed upon at a time when the United States was at peace, and when there was no certainty that Americans would ever go to war, the radical daring of the American armed services in making such an agreement can perhaps be appreciated. Actually, the document had no legally binding force. It was subject to confirmation by superior military and political authorities in both countries; and although the Secretary of War and the Secretary of the Navy officially approved the plan the President never did so. Moreover, the whole scheme was contingent upon an American declaration of war against Germany. Yet the very fact of such planning carried with it certain moral commitments and practical consequences. The U.S. army and navy governed themselves as though war with Germany impended, which meant, especially for the navy, action in accordance with ABC–1.[3] Such actions 'short of war' were, of course, subject to Presidential approval; but their cumulative force made Anglo-American co-operation in the Atlantic so close that the transition to full-scale belligerency after 7 December made little immediate difference.

In the Pacific, however, this was not true. ABC–1 left details of the Pacific command areas to be settled by a subsequent conference between representatives of the local commanders of American, Dutch, and British Commonwealth (ADB) armed forces. Appropriate consultation took place at Singapore in April 1941. After some rather warm discussion the ADB conversations ended in an agreement. Areas of responsibility were defined, and the twin objects, security of sea communications and of Singapore naval base, were declared to be the 'most important interests' of the Associated Powers in the Far East.[4] In general, Japan's potential strength was seriously underestimated. The men who drew up the agreement assumed that Japan would probably not resort to war if confronted with a solid

[1] *Pearl Harbor Attack*, p. 1493.

[2] Ibid.

[3] In particular, the U.S. navy reinforced the Atlantic Fleet in accordance with the ABC–1 plan (cf. Morison: *History of U.S. Naval Operations*, i. 49–50).

[4] *Pearl Harbor Attack*, p. 1558.

Anglo-Dutch-American political front,[1] and proposed a sort of ultimatum, defining ahead of time the limits beyond which any Japanese advance would become a *casus belli* for all the Powers concerned.[2] The strategic disposition of forces contemplated in the agreement called for concentration upon Singapore as the main base, while holding both Hongkong and the Philippines as advanced bases from which to blockade and harass Japan. The possibility that the advanced bases would be overrun was, however, considered, and plans for withdrawal prescribed.[3]

When the text of this agreement was submitted to General George C. Marshall, U.S. Army Chief of Staff, and to Admiral H. R. Stark, Chief of Naval Operations, they united in rejecting it on 3 July 1941. Stark proceeded to withdraw authorization from the commander of the U.S. Asiatic Fleet to operate under British strategic direction in case of war.[4] The strategic principles of the ADB agreement did not accord with American ideas,[5] and no one, not even Roosevelt himself, could commit the United States to the political provisions of the plan.

American rejection of the ADB Agreement marked a breakdown of the effort to arrive at an over-all plan for the Pacific. Each nation went ahead with plans and preparations of its own, but continuous consultation was maintained in the hope that full agreement could be reached. Through this process important segments of the ADB plan were salvaged. Thus the U.S. navy war plan which was in force at the time of Pearl Harbour contemplated the dispatch of the major part of the U.S. Asiatic fleet from China and the Philippines southward to Malaya and the Netherlands East Indies, where it would come under British command.[6] And, as had been agreed in ABC–1, the British began to strengthen their fleet in Far Eastern waters by dispatching the *Prince of Wales* and the *Repulse* as well as four destroyers to Singapore in the autumn of 1941.[7]

Yet it remained true that co-ordination between American, British, Dutch, and Australian military and naval plans continued to be imperfect. About midsummer 1941 the U.S. army changed its plan for the Philippines. On the basis of optimistic reports from Douglas MacArthur, then Field Marshal of the Philippine army, and of equally optimistic reports of

[1] 'If it is clear to Japan that the united forces of the British Empire, the United States and the Dutch would meet aggression on her part, her immediate intervention in the war is unlikely' (*Pearl Harbor Attack*, p. 1563).

[2] Ibid. p. 1564.

[3] Ibid. pp. 1568–70.

[4] Morison: *History of U.S. Naval Operations*, iii. 55. This meant, of course, retreat from one clause of the ABC–1 agreement which had assigned strategic direction of the Western Pacific to the British.

[5] Difference of opinion between British and American strategists over the importance of Singapore as a base were not new, and had led to an earlier stalemate at the Washington staff conferences of January–April 1941. Australia, too, did not see eye to eye with British plans for Singapore, preferring to keep Australian naval forces at hand for the defence of the home country (ibid. p. 54).

[6] Ibid. p. 154.

[7] Churchill, iii. 524; U.S. edition, iii. 589.

the effectiveness of American heavy bombers, it was decided that the main island, Luzon, and perhaps others of the Philippine archipelago, could be made defensible against Japanese attack.[1] Accordingly, a build-up of American air and ground forces was begun, only to be cut short by the Japanese attack in December. This change of strategy (it had previously been assumed that the Philippines could not be held) led the commander of the U.S. Asiatic Fleet, Admiral T. C. Hart, to suggest a change in the war plan affecting his command. Awaiting reply for a critical three weeks, from 27 October to 20 November, he put off the southward deployment of his forces which was called for by his standing orders when war appeared imminent.[2]

In general, the Japanese attack in December caught the Anglo-American forces unprepared. The U.S. army's reinforcement of the Philippines was scheduled to be completed by April 1942; and it is legitimate to suppose that further efforts to co-ordinate Allied plans for the Pacific, taking into account this new disposition of forces, would have been attempted. But the Japanese cut all such planning and preparation short; and, through their startling successes, they made not only the pre-war planning, but also the efforts at co-ordination undertaken immediately after the outbreak of the Pacific war, quickly obsolete.

Economic co-operation was the counterpart and indispensable underpinning for the strategic co-operation between the British and American nations. The growth of economic interdependence was gradual, and at the beginning quite unsystematic. In the first months of the European war Britain and France set up government missions in the United States to manage war purchasing; but the scale of their buying was relatively small and was conducted through commercial channels without the direct intervention of the American Government. After the fall of France in the spring of 1940 things began to change. The British took over outstanding French orders and greatly increased the scale of their own purchases; simultaneously the American domestic rearmament programme began to get under way. A growing list of shortages resulted, as demand for one item after another outran existing productive capacity. With the appearance of such shortages American officials began more and more to intervene, assigning first advisory and later mandatory priorities.

As 1940 drew towards its close a British shortage of dollars began to

[1] Henry L. Stimson and McGeorge Bundy: *On Active Service in Peace and War* (London, Hutchinson, [1949]), p. 193 [quotations from *On Active Service in Peace and War* in later sections of this volume are made by permission of Messrs. Hutchinson & Co. (Publishers) Ltd., London]; Mark S. Watson: *Chief of Staff: Prewar Plans and Preparations*, series issued by the Department of the Army, Office of the Chief of Military History (Washington, U.S.G.P.O., 1950), pp. 423–6.

[2] Morison: *History of U.S. Naval Operations*, iii. 153–4.

match the shortages in American production. This problem was met by the passage of the Lend-Lease Act in March 1941.[1] As the Lend-Lease machinery came into operation[2] a new and closer administrative integration between the British and American Governments was established. The British Purchasing Mission no longer tried to place orders with manufacturers, subject to the regulation and control of American officials; instead British requirements were presented direct to the American Government,[3] and actual procurement of the items approved was entrusted to various departments of the regular administration.[4] British representatives were frequently invited to sit in on meetings of committees set up within the Departments of the United States Government, where they could defend their requests, fight for priorities, and follow the details of procurement and production.[5]

In this fashion the procurement activities of the American Government were fused with procurement for Great Britain and other countries in receipt of Lend-Lease aid. Governmental demands were united into a single whole which could be adjusted, in theory if not yet in practice, to the physical productive capacity of American industry and agriculture. What was still lacking in 1941, however, was any systematic pooling of actual and potential resources between Great Britain and the United States. Lend-Lease worked in this direction, for the British naturally asked only for what they could not produce themselves; moreover, the demands made by various American officials for 'justification' of British requests meant in fact that the British more and more presented statistical and other information about their total war production for the inspection of American officials.[6] Concerted purchase of raw materials had been

[1] An account of the American background for the passage of the Lend-Lease Act will be found in the *Survey* for 1939–46: *Initial Triumph of the Axis*. See also the study of Lend-Lease, in Appendix II to the present volume, by Sir David Waley, formerly of the United Kingdom Treasury, who played an important personal part in these transactions.

[2] It was several months before Lend-Lease goods became available in large amounts. In the meanwhile Britain continued to pay for munitions and supplies ordered earlier. Indeed, up to Pearl Harbour the British continued to pay in dollars for more than half their supplies from America (cf. Hancock and Gowing: *British War Economy*, pp. 236–7).

[3] At first there was no separate Lend-Lease administration; instead Harry Hopkins acted for the President, receiving requests for Lend-Lease aid, and passing the requests on to appropriate procurement branches of the American Government. On 28 August 1941 Edward R. Stettinius was appointed Lend-Lease Administrator, and on 28 October 1941 Roosevelt set up an Office of Lend-Lease Administration by Executive order.

[4] Edward R. Stettinius, Jr.: *Lend-Lease, Weapon for Victory* (New York, Macmillan, 1944), pp. 95–96, 105–6 [quotations from *Lend-Lease* (copyright 1944 by The Macmillan Company) in later sections of this volume are made by permission of The Macmillan Company, New York].

[5] Hancock and Gowing: *British War Economy*, p. 383. Details will be found in the *Survey* for 1939–46: *Initial Triumph of the Axis*.

[6] Cf. the account in Hancock and Gowing: *British War Economy*, pp. 244–5, of the dispute over British re-export of Lend-Lease supplies. The dispute led to a White Paper's being issued on 10 September 1941 (Great Britain, Foreign Office: *Correspondence respecting the Policy of His Majesty's Government in the United Kingdom in Connexion with the Use of Materials received under the Lend-Lease*

carried quite a long way. Various regions of the earth were recognized as the special preserve of Britain or of America; and any raw material surpluses available to one Government were shared with the other. In case of world shortage, quotas dividing supplies of raw materials were agreed to. These devices for controlling raw material distribution were well developed by 1941 at a time when analogous control over finished industrial products was still rudimentary.[1]

A second, and related, shortcoming of the American and British war economies in 1941 was the absence of any firm relation between production planning and the military obligations envisaged in ABC–1. It must, of course, be remembered that ABC–1 was not a binding agreement; that the United States was not at war; that the strategic plan was a closely guarded secret; and that no one could say for sure whether the American nation would in fact go to war, or when. Under such circumstances, planning for war production on a scale sufficient to assure victory over all potential enemies of the United States could not command universal assent among Americans, the more so as any full-scale war production programme would of necessity involve a considerable sacrifice of civilian consumption. Yet in the course of 1941 conversion of civilian industry to war production began.[2]

It was, of course, obvious that existing American factories were incapable of meeting the multiple demands placed upon them by civilian consumers, the American armed services, and the British, Russian, Chinese, and other Governments. Priorities had to be and were assigned; but until the end of 1941 there was no reasoned basis for their assignment. Instead *ad hoc* empirical decisions, taken largely in ignorance of future military requirements, were resorted to. The fundamental political uncertainty as to the future course of the United States made any other procedure impossible. No American knew exactly what to prepare for, or when.

Perhaps the most important issue in day-to-day administration was the ever present contradiction between the long and the short run. To increase production in the long run required erection of new factories and machinery; but materials and skilled man-power so used had to be subtracted from current war production. One of the most basic decisions in this connexion was taken on 30 September 1941 when the Supplies, Priorities, and Allocation Board authorized an expansion of American steel capacity by 10 million tons. But the new capacity did not come fully into production

Act, Cmd. 6311 (London, H.M.S.O., 1941)). According to this the British Government undertook not to use Lend-Lease goods for export production, save in specified and restricted cases. See also below, Appendix II, iii (*a*).

[1] Hancock and Gowing: *British War Economy*, pp. 381–2.

[2] The pace of American war conversion was reflected in the order issued on 21 August 1941 for the curtailment of passenger automobile production. By 30 November 1941 production was to be reduced by 26 per cent. and by July 1942 by 50 per cent. (Donald M. Nelson: *Arsenal of Democracy* (New York, Harcourt Brace, 1946), p. 146).

until the end of 1943, and in the interim steel mill construction constituted a significant drain on available supplies.[1] In effect, this and similar decisions postponed the peak of American war production until 1944. A smaller expansion of capital plant would have made possible an earlier achievement of peak production, but would have also meant a lower maximum.[2]

The most striking fact about the decisions taken in 1941 was that they were made without any serious effort to correlate economic with military planning. Yet a decision such as that which expanded steel capacity and postponed maximum production until 1944 obviously carried with it enormous military significance. In the course of the summer of 1941 this lack of correlation came to be recognized by many individuals, both in America and in Britain. Many were also convinced that the level of American production would have to be enormously raised if victory was to be assured. In the hope of discovering what would in fact be required, a few men began to try to calculate exactly what munitions and supplies would be necessary to defeat the Axis and where they could come from. The result of their efforts was called the Victory Program.[3]

Actually, the work of compiling the Victory Program—making estimates of requirements and calculating the feasibility of production plans which would meet the requirements—was completed only on 4 December 1941, just three days before Pearl Harbour. This coincidence solved what might otherwise have become a most critical problem. In the heat of war, opposition to the Victory Program evaporated, despite the civilian sacrifices and extraordinary expenditures which it required from the American people and Government. Thus by happy chance, information and rough production plans needful for an all-out war effort were ready at hand when the Japanese struck. Efforts to translate figures into facts were promptly begun.[4]

The planning incorporated in the Victory Program was the economic

[1] Nelson, *Arsenal of Democracy*, pp. 172–3.

[2] An alternative would, of course, have been more severe restriction on civilian consumption in the United States, for the American domestic economy never came near to equalling the Spartan regimens established in Great Britain and in Russia. Such a policy would, however, have had incalculable repercussions on American morale. The American public, accustomed to a higher standard of living and not being so immediately exposed to foreign danger, would have had a more difficult psychological adjustment to make than was the case in either Great Britain or the U.S.S.R.

[3] Details will be found in the *Survey* for 1939–46: *Initial Triumph of the Axis*.

[4] Published accounts of the genesis of the Victory Program differ as to who was primarily responsible for its initiation. The Frenchman, Jean Monnet, certainly played a central role, and individuals from both the American and the British side also contributed. Cf. Hancock and Gowing: *British War Economy*, pp. 384–8; Nelson: *Arsenal of Democracy*, pp. 130–8; Watson: *Chief of Staff: Prewar Plans and Preparations*, pp. 330–66; U.S.A., Civilian Production Administration, Bureau of Demobilization: *Industrial Mobilization for War: History of the War Production Board and Predecessor Agencies 1940–1945*, vol. i: *Program and Administration* (Washington, U.S.G.P.O., 1947), pp. 134–5, 138–40. [This volume is referred to hereafter as *Industrial Mobilization for War*, i.]

counterpart of the military planning embodied in ABC–1, and was at least equally daring. For the United States, the concept of a planned economy was entirely alien to tradition. Personnel required to draw up and administer the plan had to be convinced (perhaps converted better describes the experience of some) before the operation could go ahead. In the course of 1941 a long agitation, working mainly behind the scenes, succeeded in preparing the minds of American administrators (many of them recent recruits from private business) to accept an over-all plan for the war economy. As a result, once war began for the United States, disputes centred round methods of execution rather than round the principle of planning an economic organization for war.

From the British point of view, British advocacy and eager acceptance of the Victory Program were exceedingly rash. By rationalizing production not only within but between the two national economies, the dependence on the United States, which Britain had already been compelled to accept, was increased still further; and American officials came to exercise a potential stranglehold on the whole British economy.

Yet rashness was rewarded by results. The pooling of industrial and raw material resources between the United States and Great Britain raised the war potential of the two nations far above what could have been achieved by each working alone; and the reality of economic interdependence facilitated and indeed required the continuance of close strategic co-operation. After 1942 it would have been almost beyond the power of either nation to disentangle itself from the alliance with the other, even had anyone considered such a step desirable.

From what has been said it is obvious that the density of contact between the American and British Governments had far surpassed anything resembling normal diplomatic relations long before the United States came into the war. Interchange of information, ideas, and attitudes between subordinate officials of the two Governments took place constantly as a result of the military and economic planning which had been done before America became a belligerent.

The net effect of this interchange upon Anglo-American relations can only be surmised. It seems a safe generalization, however, to assert that in both military and economic spheres American officials profited greatly from British experience and practice. The major outlines of ABC–1 seem to reflect more the British than the American planners' hand; and British economic mobilization was by 1941 nearly complete, offering models in detail for many American measures. This does not imply that American officials adopted British practices consciously and wholesale. Rather, as practical problems arose, British representatives in Washington could draw upon their experience in meeting analogous difficulties in their own country, and were able, therefore, to offer useful advice. In drawing up the Victory Program, for example, very close co-operation on relatively subordinate levels was established between American and British officials, who discussed back and forth what each national economy could best contribute to the joint war effort. In this exchange, the longer experience of the British with the new problems of total war mobilization meant that their point of view often prevailed.

The interlacing of American and British officialdom on subordinate levels, however important, necessarily took place privately, and only detailed administrative histories could trace all the ramifications of the partnership between the two Governments. Relations between Roosevelt and Churchill, by contrast, were more dramatic, can be more easily grasped, and were of decisive importance. Indeed, in so far as Roosevelt and Churchill embodied the popular will of their respective nations, the personal contact between the two men became a symbol of the co-operation of the two peoples.

This is no place to attempt an assessment of the characters and historic roles of the two Chiefs of Government, but a few remarks about the relations between them may be ventured. First, from the beginning there was an element of deference in Churchill's dealings with Roosevelt, and growing familiarity never erased it. This arose partly from the fact that Roosevelt combined the functions of Chief of State and Commander-in-Chief with those of Chief of Government, and so by diplomatic protocol outranked Churchill. The second factor, and, of course, the decisive one (Churchill was fully capable of treating the crowned heads of small states with a punctilious courtesy and simultaneous condescension) was that Roosevelt headed a nation which by virtue of geographical and other advantages possessed potential military power far exceeding that of Great Britain; a nation, moreover, on which Great Britain had become economically dependent. As a result, Churchill's freedom of manœuvre was restricted: in case of serious difference of opinion he could argue against the American position, but he could never afford to risk an open break. The very phrase with which Churchill chose to sign his frequent cables to Roosevelt—'Former Naval Person'—constituted a symbol of his sense of disadvantage *vis-à-vis* the President.[1]

If it is correct to ascribe Churchill's diffidence in dealing with Roosevelt to an acute sense of the limits of his personal and national power, it seems equally correct to ascribe a parallel diffidence to Roosevelt, arising from

[1] Churchill's correspondence with Roosevelt began when he was First Lord of the Admiralty, and hence a 'Naval Person'. When he became Prime Minister, Churchill changed his signature to 'Former Naval Person'. This was, of course, a sort of private joke; but Churchill's mock modesty did not fail to reflect something of the real relationship between the two men.

his general distaste for Churchill's political views. Roosevelt had made his name in American history as a champion of social reform; after a chequered political career, Churchill had come to rest as a Conservative. Roosevelt was an optimist, a believer in the essential goodness of mankind and in the possibility of human betterment through the exercise of good-will, intelligence, and persuasion. As representative of a nation whose power was clearly on the increase, he could look to the future of the world without too anxious a concern for the special interests of the United States. American power could be trusted to look after American interests, as it were, automatically. Instead, Roosevelt felt free to dream dreams of future peace, prosperity, and democracy for all mankind. So doing, he was able to stir a warm response in many hearts, in many countries, and among many classes and conditions of men.

Churchill looked more towards the past with all its glories, and conceived himself as the hard-pressed guardian of the far-flung interests of the British Empire. Perhaps, at the bottom of his heart, Churchill believed in the natural right of Englishmen to lead and guide the world; and in the right of a select group of Englishmen, prepared by birth and education and renewed over the generations by freshly recruited talent, to lead and guide the British people. But now all too clearly he saw that such an ideal was no longer capable of realization; and Churchill was quite prepared to welcome the Americans within the pale as a necessary support and supplement to unaided British power.

But Churchill's deep-lying conceptions, if this fairly describes them, clashed with Roosevelt's more generous hopes for mankind. The resulting divergence of view did not often trouble the war-time co-operation which developed between the two men; but discord lay just beneath the surface.

When all due allowance is made for the differences between Churchill and Roosevelt, it remains true that mutual respect, extraordinary frankness, and general sympathy dominated their relationship with each other. Roosevelt's remark: 'It is fun to be in the same decade with you'[1] reflected the sense of their historic role which each felt; and each was so well convinced of the need for mutual co-operation as to remain nearly always responsive to the arguments and considerate of the susceptibilities of the other.

The regular form of communication between the two leaders was by transatlantic cable and telephone,[2] supplemented by visits from Roosevelt's personal representatives, most notably Harry Hopkins. These

[1] Sherwood: *Roosevelt and Hopkins*, p. 364; Eng. edition, i. 365.

[2] Altogether about 1,700 personal messages were exchanged between Churchill and Roosevelt from the time the correspondence began in 1940 until Roosevelt's death in 1945. This meant an average of more than one message per day. Cf. Winston S. Churchill: *Victory* (London, Cassell, 1946), p. 103.

channels quite eclipsed the more usual diplomatic means of communication. Moreover, by the time the United States was catapulted into war, the first of the personal meetings between Roosevelt and Churchill had already taken place at the Atlantic Conference in August 1941. The personal acquaintance which stemmed from this meeting was, indeed, one of its most important products.[1]

(c) American Relations with Russia

The military and economic alliance which existed in all but name between the United States and Great Britain had at least eighteen months' growth behind it at the time of Pearl Harbour; and in the background there were decades of general sympathy and friendship upon which the alliance could feed. Such was by no means the case with Russia. The hostility which had been created in America by the Bolshevik Revolution was matched on the Russian side by doctrinaire Marxist antagonism to that outstanding capitalist stronghold, the United States of America. Diplomatic relations between the two countries had been opened in 1933 for the first time since the Russian Revolution, but a number of small irritations kept relations cool. The Russo-German treaty of 1939, followed by the attack upon Finland in the winter of 1939–40, made Russia very unpopular in the United States; and a number of Communist-inspired strikes in war industries, combined with a strident anti-war propaganda in the Communist press, alienated all but a handful of the liberals who were normally most sympathetic to the Soviet Union. Hitler's attack on Russia was at first regarded with general aloofness. Americans almost universally expected an early German victory after the poor showing Russian troops had made against Finland, and the campaign was welcomed mainly as a diversion of German strength from the British Isles.

By August 1941 the prolongation of Russian resistance began to work a change in newspaper opinion; and, when the American Government decided to permit the Russians to purchase supplies in the United States, the move met with very little public criticism. As the autumn wore on admiration for Russian fighting strength began to gain ground, and exculpatory explanations of the Russian purges (no fifth columnists in Russia) and of the Russo-German Pact (to gain time) won general acceptance among the liberal groups whose sympathy for the Russian experiment had been so rudely shaken by Stalin's policies between 1937 and 1941. Among isolationists and conservatives, however, distrust of

[1] The formal statement of war aims embodied in the Atlantic Charter, useful perhaps more for propaganda than for anything else, was the other main achievement of the Conference. No decisive changes in previous plans or policies resulted from the Conference, a fact which deeply disappointed British public (and perhaps official) expectation. In particular, the military conversations merely led to disagreement. Cf. Watson: *Chief of Staff: Prewar Plans and Preparations*, pp. 400–10.

Russia did not die so easily. Fear of revolution[1] mingled illogically with predictions of a quick Russian collapse or surrender. Roman Catholic opinion, so far as it existed as a separate force in American society, was strongly anti-Communist. Roosevelt was seriously perturbed by an extensive press campaign in the autumn of 1941 which accused the Soviet régime of religious persecution. The campaign was inspired, at least in part, by the Roman Catholic hierarchy. After diplomatic contact with the Vatican, the campaign died down, and this source of overt hostility to Russia weakened.[2]

The sudden outbreak of war in the Pacific precipitated a crisis in American attitudes towards Russia. It had generally been assumed that in the event of war with Japan Russia would come in, at least to the extent of allowing American forces to use bases in eastern Siberia. So responsible and sober a journal as the *New York Times* declared editorially on 11 December: 'If Soviet Russia fails to aid us in our war against Japan, then the United States would be justified for more than one reason in discontinuing its aid-to-Russia policy.' Similar opinions were widely printed in newspapers which had supported Roosevelt's policy of aiding Hitler's enemies.[3]

News of Russian advances against the Germans (with Libya, the only cheerful news for the Allied cause in the weeks just after Pearl Harbour), and the skilful handling of the American press by the new Russian Ambassador, Maxim Litvinov (whose personal reputation as a champion of Allied action against aggression was regarded as something of a guarantee of Russian co-operation), combined to reconcile American newspapers to a prolongation of Russian neutrality in the Pacific. It came to be generally assumed that Russia would sooner or later, and probably sooner than later, join in the war against Japan.[4]

[1] Cf. the remarks of Congressman Hamilton Fish reported in the *New York Times*, 6 December 1941: 'If we crush the German Army, the Russian Army will overrun Germany, this country will be left bankrupt and communism will come, bringing chaos and revolution.' This was an extreme minority view, in its way no less untypical of general attitudes than were the broadsides of the Communist press.

[2] Sherwood (*Roosevelt and Hopkins*, pp. 384, 398; Eng. edition, i. 386, 401) makes much of Roman Catholic influence and Roosevelt's respect for the weight of the hierarchy in American politics. Cf. *Wartime Correspondence between President Roosevelt and Pope Pius XII* (New York, Macmillan, 1947), pp. 57–64; *The Memoirs of Cordell Hull*, 2 vols. (New York, Macmillan; London, Hodder & Stoughton; 1948), ii. 997. [This work is referred to hereafter as Hull: *Memoirs*, i, ii; quotations from the *Memoirs* (copyright 1948 by Cordell Hull) in later sections of this volume are made by permission of The Macmillan Company, New York.]

[3] e.g. *Chicago Daily News*, 11 December 1941; *St. Louis Post Despatch*, 12 December 1941.

[4] See e.g. Anne O'Hare McCormick in the *New York Times*, 15 December 1941, who foresaw the early end of 'the fantastic paradox presented by the spectacle of the United States bearing the brunt of the Japanese attack while Russia, Nippon's historic foe, stands hesitant on the sidelines'. Cf. *New York Herald Tribune*, editorial, 17 December 1941; Walter Duranty in the *Cleveland Plain Dealer*, 29 December 1941.

Official relations with Russia conformed generally to the drift of public opinion. Hitler's attack upon Russia did not come as a surprise to the American Government. The first official reaction was, in the words of Sumner Welles, Acting Secretary of State, to welcome 'any rallying of the forces opposing Hitlerism, from whatever source these forces may spring'. At the same time Welles made it clear that Communist dictatorship was 'as intolerable and as alien to their [i.e. the people of the United States'] own beliefs as are the principles and doctrines of Nazi dictatorship'.[1] Despite such lukewarmness, Russian funds in the United States were promptly unfrozen, and a small trickle of goods began to flow from the United States within the first two weeks of the Russo-German war. War materials were not included, for munitions were all earmarked for American, British, or other use. American military leaders did not expect that Russia could long withstand the German attack, and they felt no enthusiasm for sending large amounts of war material, which might arrive in Russia only to fall into German hands.[2]

Nevertheless, as early as 21 July 1941 Roosevelt ordered 'immediate and substantial shipments of assistance to the Union of Soviet Socialist Republics'.[3] But even with the best will in the world it was impossible to produce the implements of war overnight. Only by taking materials earmarked for Britain, and dispatching them to Russia instead, were the first shipments of such precious things as pursuit planes made possible, and that not before September.[4]

The first Soviet purchases in the United States were paid for in cash; but on 11 September 1941 the Russian Ambassador began negotiation for some form of credit. The outcome of the negotiation was a declaration by the President, issued on 7 November 1941, the anniversary of the Bolshevik Revolution, in which he proclaimed: 'The defense of the Union of Soviet Socialist Republics is vital to the defense of the United States', and ordered the Lend-Lease Administrator, Edward L. Stettinius, 'to transfer defense supplies to the Union of Soviet Socialist Republics under the Lend-Lease Act'.[5]

[1] *Documents on American Foreign Relations, vol. iii, July 1940–June 1941*, ed. S. Shepard Jones and Denys P. Myers (Boston, World Peace Foundation, 1941), p. 365.

[2] Cf. Sherwood: *Roosevelt and Hopkins*, pp. 303–4; Eng. edition, i. 303–4; Stimson and Bundy: *On Active Service*, p. 189.

[3] Stettinius: *Lend-Lease*, p. 122. This may have been intended mainly as a gesture of psychological warfare designed to encourage Russian resistance. Sherwood, who was personally in close contact with Roosevelt at the time, says that the President's policy was 'to make haste slowly' and wait for more information from Russia before sending large quantities of war materials to Stalin (cf. Sherwood: *Roosevelt and Hopkins*, p. 308; Eng. edition, i. 309).

[4] Stettinius: *Lend-Lease*, p. 124. The total value of goods shipped from the United States to Russia before the end of October 1941 (when Russian Lend-Lease went into operation) was only $41 million, although more than twice that amount had been put on order (ibid. p. 128).

[5] Directive of the President to the Lend-Lease Administrator, 7 November 1941, in *Documents on American Foreign Relations, 1941–1942*, p. 607.

The admission of Communist Russia to the benefits of Lend-Lease reflected the rapid shift of public and official opinion which had taken place in the United States. It also reflected the work of two official missions dispatched by the President to Stalin. Since the mould of the war-time relationship between Russia and America, at least until 1943, was set by these two missions, they must briefly be described.

In July 1941 Hopkins went to London in order to confer with the heads of the British Government on matters of supply and strategy. The new situation created by Russia's entry into the war made it hard to take decisions without some estimate of what Russia wanted in the way of war material, and without some estimate of the probable future of Russian military resistance to the Nazis. In the hope of finding answers to these two questions Hopkins flew to Russia at the end of July. After conferences with Stalin he became firmly convinced that the Russians could hold out for a long time, and compiled a list of the arms and supplies which Stalin most urgently required. His impressions and his information he brought back to the Atlantic Conference. Hopkins's report did much to convince Roosevelt of the wisdom of shipping as much war material to Russia as could be spared.[1]

During the Atlantic Conference Roosevelt and Churchill endorsed a cable to Stalin in which they promised to provide the maximum possible amount of war supplies and proposed a conference in Moscow to draw up longer-term plans.[2] Stalin agreed to the suggestion, and a joint British-American mission, headed by Lord Beaverbrook and Averell Harriman, began consultations in Moscow on 29 September 1941. The Russians presented lists of what they wanted, and the representatives of the Western Powers stated what quantities of each product they could promise to provide. The protocol in which the American and British offers of supplies were listed was meant to cover a nine-month period, from 1 October 1941 to 30 June 1942, and came commonly to be referred to as the First Russian Supply Protocol. It did not include any calculation of money costs. That aspect of the transaction was attended to subsequently, as far as the United States was concerned, by an exchange of letters between President Roosevelt and Premier Stalin. On 30 October 1941 Roosevelt wrote:

> In an effort to obviate any financial difficulties immediate arrangements are to be made so that supplies up to one billion dollars in value may be effected

[1] Serious and whole-hearted efforts to send American aid to Russia must be dated from the time of Hopkins's return. The decision was a delicate one for Roosevelt to take, since isolationist sentiment against aid to Britain was still strong and sentiment against aid to Communist Russia was, of course, stronger still.

[2] Text of the message is reprinted in *Documents on American Foreign Relations, 1941–1942*, p. 602. The text of the cable had been drawn up by Hopkins and Sir Stafford Cripps, then British Ambassador in Moscow, while Hopkins was visiting the Russian capital (Sherwood: *Roosevelt and Hopkins*, p. 331; Eng. edition, i. 332).

under the Lend-Lease Act. If approved by the Government of the U.S.S.R. I propose that the indebtedness thus incurred be subject to no interest and that the payments by the Government of the U.S.S.R. do not commence until five years after the war's conclusion and be completed over a ten-year period thereafter.[1]

Stalin accepted the proposal on 4 November. Three days later Roosevelt made the exchange of letters public and proclaimed Russia's eligibility for Lend-Lease aid.

Two things are noteworthy about these negotiations. First, the terms on which Russia was first admitted to Lend-Lease aid were in one sense stricter than were the terms accorded to Great Britain. Repayment was definitely prescribed as it was not for the British.[2] But in another sense, Russia was accorded far greater freedom of action. No detailed figures of Russian production were produced to justify Russian requests for assistance, nor was any effort made to check up on the uses to which Lend-Lease materials were put within the Russian economy. The briefness of the Conference in Moscow stands in sharp contrast to the prolonged calculations and intimate day-to-day exchange of information which knit the British and American economies so thoroughly together.

Undoubtedly the main reason for this difference in treatment was that the Russians were unwilling to share secrets of their war production with the Western Powers.[3] This reticence was, of course, matched by the Russian secretiveness on matters of army strength, deployment, and strategy. In view of the Russian attitude, no combined strategy such as was contemplated in ABC–1 was possible until near the end of the war; and even then the real degree of military co-operation was slight.

One may speculate as to why American and British negotiators did not insist upon more information and a genuine tripartite over-all economic and strategic plan. The personalities of the men concerned—Hopkins, Harriman, and Lord Beaverbrook—may have had something to do with the outcome;[4] but the circumstances under which the first negotiations took place were more important. Russia was then fighting with her back to the wall, and quite obviously needed everything she could get in the way of military supplies. No problem of re-export such as had roiled Anglo-American Lend-Lease relationship in the summer of 1941 arose. Eventual Russian collapse was still regarded as possible when the Harri-

[1] *Documents on American Foreign Relations, 1941–1942*, p. 606.

[2] This discrimination did not last for long, however, for on 11 June 1942 the terms of Lend-Lease aid to Russia were changed to the same basis as Lend-Lease to Great Britain, thus cancelling the arrangement for repayment prescribed in the letter quoted above.

[3] When the question of credits for Russia had first been raised, Roosevelt said that to qualify for Lend-Lease the Russians would have to provide exact statements of their assets. To this the Russian Ambassador replied that he would prefer a direct credit (Hull: *Memoirs*, ii. 977).

[4] Cf. the rather embittered comment of the Polish Ambassador to the United States in Jan Ciechanowski: *Defeat in Victory* (London, Gollancz, 1948), p. 75.

man–Beaverbrook Mission went to Moscow, and few English or American observers expected Russia to be able to hold a line anywhere west of the Urals. When disaster to Russian arms might come at any time, haggling over statistics could not seem worth while, especially as such conduct would complicate or even conflict with the aim of strengthening Soviet military power and morale by generous deliveries and promises of more to come.

Finally an important element, which became more prominent in 1942 but which was probably already present at the time of the first consultations, was the sense among representatives of the Western Powers that the Russians were doing more than their share of the fighting; that the West was at a moral disadvantage in not yet having contributed its full strength to the war; and that it was dangerous to run the risk of angering the Russians by pressing them to lift the veil of secrecy in which their war operations were shrouded. In the back of many minds was the fear that Stalin might make a separate peace if he did not get ready co-operation from his allies; and when for many long months the Western nations were unable to bring their ground and air forces into action on any grand scale, it seemed to many that the least the United States and Britain could do was to supply what the Russians needed and make no onerous or irritating demands in connexion with such supply.

One must, of course, remember that, if some persons among the British and Americans remained fearful of a separate Soviet peace, many if not most Soviet officials reciprocated the distrust, believing that the Western Powers were deliberately holding back in the hope of seeing Russia and Germany bleed one another white. To give detailed information of war production to such dubious allies would merely permit them to calculate more exactly how the Russian side was weakening or gaining in strength, and would allow them to adjust their delivery of war materials accordingly. To many a Russian official any attempt on the part of the United States to demand military and economic statistics as a prerequisite for further aid would have seemed proof of all his suspicions.

The hurried negotiations between Stalin and Hopkins in the summer and the protocol agreed upon by the Harriman–Beaverbrook Mission in the autumn of 1941 set the pattern for the relationship between Russia and the Western Powers which lasted through the first years of the war. In effect, Russia was only half an ally. Nothing remotely resembling the co-ordinated strategy which had developed between Britain and America was achieved; and not far beneath the surface of Anglo-American relations with Russia lay a dark shadow of mutual distrust.

As befitted such a relation, the channels of contact between the American and Russian Governments remained relatively restricted. It is true that Roosevelt and Stalin conducted a personal correspondence, but it was far less bulky and more largely formal in content than was the almost daily flow of communication between Churchill and Roosevelt. A Russian Purchasing Commission enjoyed approximately the same powers as did the corresponding British organization; but with rare exceptions Russian officials maintained a personal aloofness which limited exchanges between them and American administrators to strictly official, supplemented by vacuous social, business. Normal diplomatic channels of communication remained of far greater relative importance in American relations with Russia than was the case with Britain; but in Moscow, too, critical negotiations were usually entrusted by Roosevelt to personal emissaries such as Hopkins and Harriman.

(*d*) Peculiarities of the American Government affecting Allied Co-operation

The war brought a great upheaval to the administration of the American Government. New agencies proliferated, overlapped, and conflicted with one another; and while efforts at reorganization and reshuffling of leading personnel were frequent, it can hardly be said that clear lines of authority and responsibility within the various agencies, not to speak of clear definitions of jurisdiction between them, were ever established. One of the most notable consequences of the mobilization of the economy was the migration of numerous business men to Washington, where they took over many of the key positions in economic administration. These men were generally new to government, a fact which had both advantages and disadvantages. On the one hand, the dead weight of routine and established procedure did not lie heavy upon the newcomers, and at least some of them were willing to meet unprecedented conditions by dismissing administrative precedent. But on the other hand, it was in large part this willingness to cut short the intricacies of red tape that led to the frequent conflicts of jurisdiction between different sub-groups in the governmental machine.

Conflicts took place on all levels. For instance, there was a running battle between the Army Service of Supply and the War Production Board in which the stakes were little less than control of the whole American economy. But in addition the army and the navy frequently collided with one another over supplies, man-power, command responsibilities, &c. Within single agencies of the Government, too, personal battles were sometimes fought out, as for example the long and only half-hidden series of differences between Sumner Welles, Assistant Secretary of State, and Cordell Hull, his immediate superior.

The President's position as head of the executive branch of the Government was often more that of arbiter than administrator. The crushing nature of the President's multiple tasks meant that Roosevelt had little energy to spare for working out a clear-cut system of administration; and in any case his personality was such that he rather shied away from trying to make sharp definition of bureaucratic organization. He preferred to wait until some crisis threatened before intervening as a sort of *deus ex machina*.

Access to the President's ear was one of the most precious of war-time privileges; and it was by virtue of his possession of that advantage that Harry Hopkins was able to play his extraordinary role.[1] The official Cabinet, consisting of the heads of the old-established departments of the Government, did not, and could not, play the role of the British Cabinet, if only because so much of the war administration was entrusted to special and temporary agencies which were quite independent of any Cabinet officer, and responsible only to the President. Crucial decisions were not usually made at formal meetings of the Cabinet. Rather, Roosevelt made them himself after consultation and discussion with a shifting circle of intimate associates.

Government conducted on such lines was highly personal and sometimes erratic. There were no well defined channels by which information about key decisions could be passed down to all the agencies, bureaux, and departments affected. Rumour and gossip became very important, though rather unsatisfactory, antidotes, and the Washington cocktail party became an institution which should find its place in any considered effort to describe the war-time working of the American Government.

Despite the obvious defects of such administration, it did function and achieved truly remarkable results. Roosevelt's personality, with all his magnetism and high vision, dominated the Washington scene in a fashion which a more regular administration would scarcely have permitted. When all key decisions came from him, the constricting, cautionary influence of a regular, hierarchical bureaucracy was minimized. The very conflict and confusion in administration may have contributed something positive to the success of the American war effort by giving more scope to bold and insubordinate spirits than a normal bureaucracy could permit.

Officials of foreign governments confronted with the booming confusion of war-time Washington must frequently have been amazed and more than a little befuddled. In a sense, the administrative system which prevailed made easy the path of co-operation with Great Britain and the U.S.S.R., for to these matters Roosevelt regularly gave personal attention, and the paths of Presidential attention in some degree governed the functioning of the whole machine. *Vis-à-vis* the smaller allies, on the other

[1] Sherwood's book *Roosevelt and Hopkins* is, of course, the best account of the remarkable partnership which existed between the two men.

hand, the effect was less happy. Paying meticulous court to the State Department did not always get an Ambassador much hearing for his case in the circles of government which mattered most; and the small countries, like the small business men of the American nation, generally found the climate of the war-time capital difficult.[1]

The separation of powers, on which the structure of American government theoretically rested, was deprived of much of its reality by the grant of special war-time powers to the President. Congress of course retained its power of appropriation, but the war budgets were not subjected to effective Congressional control. Opposition to any expenditure could too easily be made to appear as half-heartedness in the prosecution of the war. The Congressional power to investigate the conduct of the executive branch was of more significance. It was as chairman of a Senate Committee investigating war contracts that Truman first won national prominence; and the work of his committee and others like it did much to prune away and even more to inhibit abuses and inefficiencies in administration.

Of more importance for relations with other nations was the Senate's power over treaties. According to the Constitution, international treaties must be ratified by a two-thirds vote of the Senate. This provision had led to the rejection of the Versailles Treaty in 1920; and memories of that débâcle were ever present in the minds of leaders of the administration during the Second World War. On more than one occasion Roosevelt was faced with an awkward dilemma in deciding how far he dared to commit the United States without risking the danger of subsequent senatorial repudiation.

The difficulties which the Constitution placed in the path of formal treaties led the administration to fall back upon a series of legal devices by which the Senate's power could be left dormant. Declarations such as the Atlantic Charter, executive agreements such as the Lend-Lease Master Agreements, understandings between special branches of the Government and their equivalents in foreign countries such as the ABC–1 staff agreement, and even less formal memoranda, letters, and verbal undertakings between key figures of the American Government and officials of other nations took the place of formal treaties. Indeed, until the foundation of the United Nations, at San Francisco in 1945, there were no political treaties binding the United States to its principal allies. This departure from old international usage must certainly be attributed in large part to the peculiarities of the American Constitution and party system which made the submission of a treaty to the Senate such a precarious procedure.

The role of the military in American Government was of the highest significance during the war years. As in so many other respects, President

[1] Cf. Ciechanowski: *Defeat in Victory*, pp. 95–102, and *passim*.

Roosevelt's personality had a decisive part in defining that role. Roosevelt recognized his lack of expertness in military affairs, and relied to a very large extent upon the advice of the leading men in the army and navy. When military reasons were advanced for a particular line of action, he seldom was tempted to overrule his advisers.[1] This attitude stands in striking contrast to the President's constant intervention in diplomacy which led him frequently to go behind the back of the State Department and to supersede normal diplomatic channels by resort to special emissaries and personal communication.

Yet Roosevelt was no militarist, and believed that civilians should exercise political authority. His concept, and it was one shared by the leaders of the army and navy as well, was that the military establishment should be a politically neutral instrument whose operations should be guided exclusively by special military rules—strategic, logistical, and tactical.

This doctrine of the sharp separation between military and political matters was a peculiar form of narrow professional specialization, deeply rooted in the traditions of the American army and navy. The non-political officer was an ideal enforced by a rigid *esprit de corps* among the leaders of the regular army; and a non-political officer was expected to organize and command a non-political, technically efficient, socially unbiased campaign. Victory in the field became an end in itself, and consideration of the political or social conditions which might result from a victory won in a particular fashion as against a victory won through pursuit of a different strategy, was considered to be outside the proper province of a military man. Technical military efficiency became the sole criterion by which the choice between alternative policies was to be made.

The historical roots and practical justifications for such attitudes were of course very real. Soldier politicians are a standing threat to any democracy; and from that point of view the determination of the American military to stick to its last had much to recommend it. But in an age of total war there was such a large element of unreality in the position that a systematic refusal to face the political, social, and economic repercussions of military policy perhaps constituted an equal danger. By no stretch of the imagination can one describe many of the decisions taken by the American Joint Chiefs of Staff as non-political, yet they were seldom or never made explicitly on political grounds.

The doctrine of the separability of military from other considerations exercised a pervasive influence on the decisions of American generals and admirals. Some of the conflicts in matters of high strategy between

[1] Sherwood calculates that the President overruled his military advisers only on two occasions during the war (*Roosevelt and Hopkins*, p. 446; Eng. edition, i. 450).

American and British military chiefs arose from the professional rigidity of the American tradition; and the unforeseen manner in which critical political decisions were suddenly thrust upon American generals (for example the Darlan affair in North Africa) led the American Government into some awkward passes.

It is worth noting that no similar doctrine governed the military affairs of either the British or Russian Governments. The British regularly adopted the practice of accrediting political advisers connected with the Foreign Office to generals in the field; and the generals usually deferred to advice they received. Political advisers were often accredited to American military headquarters, too, but an effort was made to limit their sphere to 'civilian' matters. 'Military' considerations ranked apart, and civilians were not expected to meddle with them. American generals often regarded 'politics' as somehow disgraceful, and to say that a plan for military operations was politically motivated damned it in their eyes. In the Russian army the subordination of military to political considerations was very nearly complete. For the Russians, war and politics were inseparably and necessarily connected, being but two aspects of the same struggle.[1]

The unexpressed assumption behind the American doctrine was that, once victory had been won by the most efficient technical means available, the political and social order would revert to normal by itself. In an age when wars were marginal affairs, mainly the concern of professional soldiers, such a doctrine was true enough to fact. But in an age when the distinction between war and peace had blurred and when wars engulfed the whole available energies of society, the doctrine became ludicrously false. The normality of peace disappeared, the very structure of society was beaten into new shapes on the anvil of war, and the decisions of soldiers became irreversible political and social facts, upon which the post-war order had to be built.

It must be recognized that for the United States the older conception of war as an abnormal and limited state of affairs continued to have some validity. The war did not shake the American social order to its foundation, as was the case in European countries, and it was possible quickly to revert to something like pre-war normality after the end of hostilities. Indeed, it was in the hope of such a return to normal that the United States fought the war. The concept of victory as an end in itself, to be won as expeditiously as possible by the soundest military methods, harmonized with a deep-seated feeling among the American people, who believed that intervention abroad was only necessary in exceptional times of emergency. Thus victory could be expected to bring peace, peace normality, and normality an end to American foreign entanglements. From such a point

[1] See below, pp. 85–87.

of view, concern with post-war balance of power and strategic advantage was either irrelevant, if it had no deleterious effect upon the promptest ending of war, or else criminal, if it interfered with military plans.[1]

These ideas and attitudes constituted perhaps the most pervasive difference between Americans and their allies. The Russians, in particular, were acutely aware of the war as only a part of a larger political whole, and never supposed that things would revert to a hypothetically normal state after the end of the fighting. The British, too, with their long experience of international politics and war, were much more responsive to questions of post-war power relations and national interests. From the very desperateness of their situation on the edge of Hitler's Europe, they could not easily fall into the habit of imagining an automatic return to normality after military victory had been secured.

(ii) The British Outlook

(a) Pearl Harbour

By December 1941 Great Britain could look back upon twenty-seven weary months of war. Defeats in Norway, France, Greece, Crete had followed one upon the other; and the successes which had been won were only holding operations, precariously maintaining British power in the home islands, on the Atlantic, and in the Near East. Yet even in Britain's most desperate hour, when to all outward seeming the war had been lost, the British people preserved a sublime self-confidence, and, refusing to conceive the possibility, had been able to ward off the actuality of irremediable defeat.

The parallel with the period of the Napoleonic wars, when Britain had stood often alone and always at the forefront in a long struggle against a conqueror of Europe, was striking; but in the years between Napoleon and Hitler the balance of forces had turned drastically against Great Britain. An island in the throes of rapid industrialization opposed to a continent whose economic organization was markedly less developed was in a position to thrive despite long-drawn-out warfare, and could stand alone for an indefinite period secure behind the English Channel. Hitler's Europe, however, was industrially developed to the point where it outmatched unassisted British power; and the progress of military technology had reduced, though by no means eliminated, the protection given by the Channel.

[1] The fact that many Americans hoped for a brave new world bound into an harmonious whole by a revivified League of Nations did not conflict with the basically 'isolationist' attitude which inspired American popular and military thought. The internationalists, too, wanted an international organization mainly in order to be free to cultivate their own garden in peace. Their aim and the aim of isolationists was essentially the same: the difference was over how best to attain the common goal.

Under the new conditions, Great Britain could not hope for an unassisted victory, and from 1940 onward British eyes turned more and more to the United States as the sole source from which sufficient help might come. American aid short of war was enough to maintain a stalemate with Germany; but by the summer and autumn of 1941 it had become clear that, if eventual victory were to be achieved, American armies and the mobilization of American production for war would both be required. British military strength was spread thinly over the Middle and Far East, and the resources which remained available in the home islands were too small to permit anything but strictly limited operations against the German colossus which had planted itself astride the Continent.

From the autumn of 1940 onward the British watched for signs of America's entry into the war. But, in spite of words and deeds expressing sympathy and support, time after time British hopes for America's final commitment were disappointed. Hope deferred and the hardships of war made many spirits droop while time dragged heavily along. In the last weeks of November 1941, the British offensive in Libya introduced a brighter note into the news; and the prolongation of Russian resistance began to raise images of Napoleon's 1812 campaign in many minds. Thus it was to a somewhat more cheerful Britain that the electrifying news of Pearl Harbour came, and with the news came a thrill of confidence in the certainty of eventual victory.

The immediate reaction of the British press was, however, notably restrained. Obviously it would have been neither politic nor polite to express open satisfaction at Japan's treacherous attack upon a friend and ally. Instead, the newspapers stressed the fact that Britain, the Commonwealth, and the United States were in the war together, all round the world; and many journalists confidently calculated the potentially overwhelming power of an alliance which included Russia and China as well. With such forces operating together ultimate victory was assured. At the same time, the press was at pains to point out the reverse side of the medal. The entry of the United States into the war would mean a temporary diversion of Lend-Lease supplies for the use of America's own forces; and some journalists expected serious initial set-backs in the war with Japan.[1]

Concern lest the United States divert her military strength from the European to the Pacific theatre of war was not openly expressed, but may perhaps legitimately be read between the lines of numerous editorials and news stories which stressed the global unity of the war.[2] On 16 December,

[1] See e.g. *Daily Express*, 'Opinion', 8 December 1941; *The Times*, editorial, 9 December 1941; *Manchester Guardian*, editorial, 10 December 1941.

[2] e.g. *News Chronicle*, 'Hitler Pushed Them over the Brink', 8 December 1941; *Manchester Guardian*, editorial, 9 December 1941; *Daily Mail*, 'Each for All', 10 December 1941.

when the major outlines of American war policy had already become fairly clear, *The Times* published an editorial referring retrospectively to twin dangers brought by Pearl Harbour: the United States might have stopped supplies to her allies in order to build up her own forces more rapidly; and the United States might have turned her strength mainly or solely against Japan. But in fact, said *The Times* with satisfaction, the United States had done neither.[1]

The inner circles of the British Government shared, if indeed they did not inspire, the attitudes of the British press towards the new world situation created by the attack on Pearl Harbour. Churchill has described in vivid language his immediate reaction to the news:

> So we had won after all! Yes, after Dunkirk; after the fall of France; after the horrible episode of Oran; after the threat of invasion, when, apart from the Air and the Navy, we were an almost unarmed people; after the deadly struggle of the U-boat war—the first Battle of the Atlantic, gained by a hand's-breadth; after seventeen months of lonely fighting and nineteen months of my responsibility in dire stress. . . . Once again in our long Island history we should emerge, however mauled or mutilated, safe and victorious.[2]

When there had been time for calm reflection, however, anxieties only hinted at in the press became very lively in Churchill's mind. He began to ask himself whether the United States would turn in its wrath against Japan and leave Hitler for the British and Russians to deal with. Again, would the United States be willing to honour the Lend-Lease contracts which had been entered upon in time of peace? Or would the Americans turn what war materials were at hand to the equipping of their own forces? Finally, what arrangements could be made to fill the gap in Anglo-American co-operation created by failure to ratify the staff conversations in the Pacific area? These questions seemed real and serious; and it was to find answers to them that Churchill undertook his visit to Washington less than a week after Pearl Harbour.[3]

To understand Churchill's anxieties we must briefly survey Britain's military, political, and economic situation as it existed at the end of 1941. Unlike the Russian Government, which ruled a single compact land mass and was engaged in military operations on a single front, the British Government were bound by complex military, political, and economic relations with almost the whole world. One may distinguish, for con-

[1] Until then the British press had almost unanimously maintained a discreet silence on questions of American war policy. Strangely enough, the three-day delay between America's declaration of war on Japan and the declaration of war against Germany elicited almost no editorial attention. An exception was 'Opinion' in the *Daily Express*, 11 December 1941, which called upon 'the people of America to follow the lead of their President and declare the Axis chief [i.e. Hitler] their open enemy'. The remarkable restraint of the press in this matter, which was after all one of life and death for Great Britain, must have been influenced by official policy.

[2] Churchill, iii. 539; U.S. edition, iii. 606–7.

[3] Ibid. pp. 567–71 and 641–3, respectively.

venience, three major problems which continually pressed themselves upon the attention of the British Government: the disproportion between national power and the requirements of victory; relations with the various parts of the Empire; and relations with Europe, in particular with Russia. All these were secondary to the overriding concern of all—relations with the United States; but the status of the Anglo-American alliance has been described above from the American point of view, and need not be considered further here.

(b) The Limits of British Power

During the year between the fall of France and the German attack upon Russia, the British bent every effort towards increasing their military strength. Workmen and farmers in many parts of the world, especially in the United States and Canada, were employed to provide Britain with the sinews of war; British manufacture for export was drastically cut down; and the man-power so set free in the British Isles was used in the military services and in armament production.

Britain's relation to the trans-oceanic world was from one point of view analogous with Germany's relation to Europe. Both nations were able to call upon unrequited services and supplies with which they supported a greatly expanded national military establishment.

After the spring campaigns of 1941 Nazi Germany was the master of almost all Europe west of the Russian frontier. Around the hard core of some eighty million Germans were grouped subject and ancillary populations of more than twice the number. Despite the sullen discontent of most of Europe, the Germans found themselves in a position to use the population and resources of the Continent as a whole to support their war machine and were thus able to build it up on a scale which German national resources alone could not have come near to equalling.

The difference in the methods by which the British and Germans secured the assistance of other peoples and countries was of course important. German use of force and threat reduced the efficiency with which the subject and satellite populations served the Nazis; but the Germans made the subject populations themselves the major sufferers from any decline in productive efficiency by drawing off what they needed regardless of the consequences for local standards of living. British methods of financial inducement and political persuasion did not damage the general productive efficiency of the contributing countries, but, at least from the British point of view, there were other drawbacks. Because the British could not command, they had, accordingly, to cajole. As a result, only marginal production of the trans-oceanic world could be counted on to supply the British war effort. More important, as the British became dependent upon the production of the United States and Canada, American and Canadian officials came to exercise a potential veto over the policy of the British Government. The leaders of the subject and satellite nations of Europe did not exercise any comparable influence over German policy. Thus, despite the much greater geographic extent of the British hinterland, the lower rate of exploitation open to the British made it impossible to equal German military power without the direct and active participation of allies. The basic fact of comparative populations—about 45 million British against about 80 million Germans—gave Germany an enduring margin of superiority.

A second weakness in the British power position arose from the fact that Great Britain was not solely concerned with the European scene. Defence of the Empire required naval and military forces in all quarters of the globe. The potential enmity of Japan (and, prior to June 1941, of Russia) could not be neglected, even when the forces at the command of the British Government were inadequate to cope with Hitler alone. Had the British goal been simply to beat Germany, extensive parts of the Empire might have been sacrificed (e.g. the Middle East) in order to build up more rapidly a strong invasion force with which to attack the centre of German power. But a victory which meant first the loss of the Empire would scarcely have been worth the name; and it seemed best to try to hold on to what could be retained, even sometimes at the risk of the security of the home islands.[1]

In the first half of 1941, when Britain fought with only a few minor allies, strategy was perforce primarily defensive. The impossibility of a frontal attack upon Germany led British strategists to pin their hopes on indirect methods: economic blockade, air bombing, and fomentation of unrest among the subject and satellite peoples of Europe. Only after Hitler's New Order showed signs of cracking under the pressure of these methods was a cross-Channel landing believed possible or wise. These views were, of course, embodied in ABC–1. In the early months of 1941 when that plan was drawn up neither British nor American military leaders were able to contemplate an early invasion of the Continent. American military strength was still a figment of the future, and British strength was insufficient.

The outbreak of the Russo-German war in June 1941 relieved the British of important immediate worries, but at first did not seem to alter fundamentally the general strategic picture. In the short run, equipment sent from Britain to Russia actually postponed the build-up of British military

[1] Cf. Sherwood: *Roosevelt and Hopkins*, pp. 314–17; Eng. edition, i. 313–17: an account of a debate between British and American military leaders as to the best distribution of British forces between the Middle East and the home islands. The initial American scepticism concerning the wisdom of the Middle Eastern campaigns was in part at least a reflection of the divorce between military and political spheres, so common in the thinking of American military men. Cf. above, pp. 29–31.

strength. Russian pleas for a second front began as early as July 1941 in private, and became a matter of public agitation by October. But Britain's relative weakness, the growing threat from Japan, and the continued expectation of a Soviet collapse, made British leaders deaf to all such proposals. A second Dunkirk could scarcely be endured; and, in view of the disparity of military power, that was all a cross-Channel landing seemed to promise, if, indeed, a bridge-head on the hostile shore could be established in the first place.

Reluctance to commit their carefully husbanded military strength to an invasion of the Continent continued to exist among British military leaders after the United States had come into the war, and when long-term Russian resistance was already a reality. This, of course, came to constitute one of the most delicate and difficult elements in the whole Allied war relationship.

Two factors help to explain British reluctance to stake all upon an early invasion of the continent of Europe. One was an over-estimate of the potentialities of air power. At the time of the Atlantic Conference, August 1941, the British Chiefs of Staff had written in a memorandum for the Americans: 'It may be that the methods described above [bombing, blockade, subversive activity among the conquered European populations] will by themselves be enough to make Germany sue for peace.'[1] And an American officer stationed in London reported that the general consensus among British strategists was that Germany could be defeated by prolonged bombing on a sufficient scale; and that in any case 'it is highly improbable that a land invasion can be carried out against Germany proper, at least within the next three years. If the air offensive is successful, a land offensive probably will not be necessary.'[2] The Americans were not convinced. They countered with a document which declared: 'It should be recognized as an almost invariable rule that wars cannot be finally won without the use of land armies.'[3]

A second and much more important consideration which always coloured British thinking about an invasion of the Continent was the memory of the bloody and futile trench warfare of 1915–18. Churchill and his colleagues felt with all the force of their being that no repetition of such a disaster could be tolerated. The cost in terms of human life would be too severe for a nation whose ageing population and relatively low birth-rate made replacement of war losses much more problematic than had been the case even a generation earlier; and, even apart from such calculation, the stupidity of a strategy and generalship which could

[1] Watson: *Chief of Staff: Prewar Plans and Preparations*, p. 403.

[2] Ibid. p. 408.

[3] Ibid. pp. 407–8. It is interesting to see how at this early date, before the United States had become a belligerent, the difference in strategic emphasis which was to divide the two countries throughout the war had already made its appearance.

find no way to fight and win a war save by the painful and expensive methods of trench warfare repelled every British mind.

No comparable fears had been bred into the bones of American military leaders. American participation in the First World War had come only at the end, when the front was in motion, and American strategists generally had full confidence of being able once again to keep a front on the Continent in motion. The British were by no means convinced that the aeroplane and tank and other technical inventions would suffice to prevent static warfare from developing again when armies of approximately equal strength met on a restricted front; and since such conditions never developed during the Second World War (save for a while in Italy) it is impossible to say that they were wrong. What might have happened to an Anglo-American invasion of northern France in 1942 or 1943 can never be known; but it seems certain that such an invasion could not have had the brilliant success actually achieved in 1944 when Anglo-American military power had become greater and German power less than in earlier years.

What is sure is that the British military point of view, which emphasized the dangers of a cross-Channel operation, remained a permanent element of the greatest significance for Allied relations. A policy of attrition—bombing, blockading, attacking the periphery of *Festung Europa*—together with a steadfast guard of the outposts of Empire was the only one which seemed militarily sound to British strategists until such time as German power had been seriously weakened. Then, and only then, did the British wish to attack across the Channel in order to deliver a *coup de grâce* to the German military machine. Their difference with the Americans was thus primarily over timing: Whether to attack across the Channel as soon as possible, as strongly as possible, and with the least diversion of resources to other fronts, as the Americans wished, or whether to wait until other operations had made such an attack surer of success, as the British desired—this was the fundamental theme of all the Anglo-American strategic debates in the first two years of their combined war effort.

(*c*) The Problem of Empire

The British Empire was largely the creation of sea power. As long as the Royal Navy could command the seven seas, the defence of the Empire raised no great difficulties. But such conditions did not outlive the nineteenth century. The disappearance of British naval supremacy on the oceans of the world presented a series of nearly insoluble problems for the maintenance of established imperial relationships. These problems naturally became especially acute during the Second World War when Britain's military strength was so desperately needed at home. Yet, by a peculiarly ironic twist of history, Britain's survival as a Great Power depended in large degree upon the possibility of drawing strength—not merely economic, but also military—from the Empire.

The rise of a new sea power in the Pacific—Japan—took the British navy in the rear. In the nineteenth century, a naval screen thrown against the European coast could in practice assure the far-flung outposts of Empire against any important military threat, which could then come only from the continent of Europe.[1] Japan's development as an important naval Power was first countered by making Japan an ally; but in the 1920s this policy was abandoned, partly as a result of American pressure. Thenceforward the British navy lived under the threat of war on two fronts—against a European conqueror and against Japan. To meet this strategic situation, actually realized in December 1941, the Royal Navy was simply not strong enough.

The development of military aviation and of the submarine worked a parallel change by weakening the sovereignty of ships on the seas. In particular such narrow seas as the Mediterranean could no longer be commanded by a British flotilla as in the days of Nelson. The Mediterranean line of communication to the Middle and Far East was endangered, and with it one of the important links in the Empire.

The strategic problem so presented to the British Government had two distinct facets, according to the nature of the imperial territories concerned. The self-governing Dominions, inhabited in large part by people of British ancestry, felt and acted quite differently from those British territories inhabited mainly by other races; and yet for both parts of the Empire the weakening of the British power to protect caused basic changes.

As far as the Dominions were concerned, Britain had long given up all but ceremonial power over their conduct of affairs; but ties of sentiment and interest remained powerful enough to bring all the dominions (except Eire) into war on Britain's side almost immediately after the outbreak of hostilities in Europe. The help which the Dominions were able and willing to give was substantial, and took both economic and direct military forms. Nevertheless, Britain's strategic weakness introduced the possibility of a real conflict of interest between imperial defence, taken as a whole, and the defence of individual Dominions. This potential division became evident during the efforts at staff planning in the Pacific in the spring of 1941 when the Australians, fearing for the security of their continent, were un-

[1] Occasional American threats to Canada, especially in the years immediately after the Civil War, constitute an exception to this generalization, but such threats were never very serious. Had relations between Britain and the United States been less amicable, the United States might have taken over the role which was actually reserved for Japan; but Americans were engaged in the exploitation of a continent and lacked a militaristic tradition, and so were in general well content to leave to the British the enjoyment of their Empire. British trade policies, more generous to outsiders in the nineteenth than in the twentieth century, made the American attitude much easier to maintain.

willing to send as much of their scanty naval strength to the defence of Singapore as British naval planners wished them to do. After the outbreak of the Pacific war the cleavage became acute, and British efforts to use Australian troops in Burma produced a considerable amount of ill feeling.[1]

The realities of power tended to bring the Dominions into a new relationship with the United States. After 1941 it was to the United States more than to Britain that both Canada and the two Pacific Dominions had to look for help as far as the immediate task of self-defence was concerned. Canada had long belonged simultaneously to the American economic sphere and to the British political family. During the war years Canada kept this position. In the Pacific, however, the war brought rather striking changes. Before 1941 Australia and New Zealand had relatively little contact with the United States, whereas after the Japanese attack it was mainly the Americans who came to their aid. The British, after the fall of Singapore,[2] were almost entirely driven from the Pacific.

As for South Africa, the internal division between Afrikander Dutch and British, and their common fear of the numerically preponderant negro population, made its military contribution to the war effort relatively slight. As in the composition of its population, so in the measure of its contribution to the war, South Africa stood intermediate between the Dominions and the colonial parts of the British Empire.

The colonies and India could not be mobilized for war to the same extent as the Dominions. Native peoples, in varying stages of backwardness, were of military use only after a long period of training; and, lacking any strong political attachment to the British régime, their services were inspired mainly by the mercenary's pride in his profession.[3] The Indian army, blended from British and Indian troops, contributed some excellent divisions to the British military effort; but the state of feeling in India as a whole illustrated the dilemma which faced the British in dealing with the native-inhabited parts of their Empire.

The dilemma might be put thus: as the Indians were trained and educated to a familiarity with Western ideas and techniques, and so became of immediate value for modern war, a major proportion of the educated group became discontented with British political rule and felt no inclination to contribute their efforts to strengthen British military power.

[1] Churchill, iv. 3–17; U.S. edition, iv. 3–19.

[2] On 15 February 1942.

[3] Mercenary pride may under certain circumstances produce very good soldiers; but to achieve that result one must build upon a military tradition indigenous to the native population. Thus the Ghurkas and certain other Indian peoples, man for man, probably equal any European foot soldiers; but the peculiar pride, loyalty, and daring they exhibit as mercenary soldiers cannot be created among men who do not share, at least to some degree, a childhood training in the military virtues.

Large numbers of Indian soldiers were almost or entirely unaffected by anti-British agitation, and the economic attractions of army service for Indian peasants were such that British authorities never had any difficulty in recruiting as many men as they could train and equip. Yet the active opposition of the Congress Party, which reached particularly threatening dimensions in 1942 when the Japanese stood at India's very door, seriously interfered with India's contribution to the British war effort. Men were needed to police India who might otherwise have been available for offensive action against the enemy; and thousands of India's best educated men withheld their services or even languished in gaol.

In the less developed portions of the colonial Empire, discontent with British rule was weaker, but the native populations were also of less military value. The role of such regions as Malaya, the Near East, and the colonies in Africa was largely economic. Various raw materials and semi-finished products were produced by native labour, and in some cases were of key importance to the Anglo-American economy. But it remained true that mobilization for war in these regions was only rudimentary, and when, as in Hongkong, Malaya, or Burma, such regions were exposed to enemy attack, the native population either was indifferent to, or positively welcomed, the overthrow of British control.

The delicate problems of colonial and Indian administration were complicated by the attitude taken by the Americans, many of whom looked forward with approval to the post-war demise of all brands of European imperialism, and to a sort of world-wide new deal for ex-colonial areas. Empire was a word which carried a general connotation of evil and wrongdoing in American ears. This was an issue on which political extremes within the American body politic agreed. Roosevelt's most devoted liberal supporters and his bitterest enemies among the isolationists were united in their distrust of British imperialism; and one of the President's constant fears was that he might be manœuvred into using, or seeming to use, American power to prop up the British colonial Empire.

Roosevelt himself did not believe in either the viability or the desirability of colonial empires. He cherished large visions of a future world in which all peoples might live freely, masters of their own political fortunes; and he imagined an interim period of international trusteeship over such backward nations as could not immediately enter into the family of nations upon a plane of equality. Roosevelt and other Americans who thought as he did undoubtedly underestimated the difficulties which lay in the path of any such programme. They tended to assume that American political patterns could be reproduced almost at will in totally different societies. This is illustrated by Roosevelt's casual suggestion to Churchill that the Indian problem might be solved by modelling new ruling bodies on the example of the American Continental Congress and Articles of

Confederation, to be followed in due course by a Constitution to establish a permanent government.[1]

The difference between British and American views of empire came to a focus in the interpretation placed upon the phraseology of the Atlantic Charter. The Third Article of the Charter stated: 'Third, they respect the right of all peoples to choose the form of government under which they will live; and they wish to see sovereign rights and self-government restored to those who have been forcibly deprived of them.' Roosevelt publicly interpreted this statement as applying to the whole world—including by inference the peoples of Asia living under European imperial rule.[2] Churchill, on the contrary, stated his quite different interpretation as follows:

> . . . the Joint Declaration does not qualify in any way the various statements of policy which have been made from time to time about the development of constitutional government in India, Burma or other parts of the British Empire. . . . At the Atlantic meeting, we had in mind, primarily, the restoration of the sovereignty, self-government and national life of the States and nations of Europe now under the Nazi yoke, and the principles governing any alterations in the territorial boundaries which may have to be made. So that is quite a separate problem from the progressive evolution of self-governing institutions in the regions and peoples which owe allegiance to the British Crown.[3]

The future of the British Empire was one of the principal questions upon which Roosevelt's and Churchill's views clashed head on; and their clash no more than reflected the divergent attitudes of the two peoples.

(*d*) The Problem of Europe

(1) *The Governments in Exile*

British policy towards occupied Europe suffered from a serious contradiction between short- and long-run aims. Basically, the British were trying to conjure up an unrevolutionary revolution. They sought in the short run to encourage unrest, rebellion, and resistance in every possible way. But in the longer run the British hoped to see after the end of the war a general restoration of pre-war political and social arrangements, with, to be sure, various reforms. These two aims frequently clashed, for the groups among the conquered population of Europe most ready to take part in subversive movements were not the groups which supported a restoration of pre-war social conditions.

Before June 1941 resistance movements made very little headway. In the summer of 1940 most Europeans expected to see Britain defeated, and

[1] Sherwood: *Roosevelt and Hopkins*, pp. 511–12; Eng. edition, ii. 516–17.

[2] Radio Address, 23 February 1942, reproduced in *Documents on American Foreign Relations, 1941–1942*, p. 61.

[3] 9 September 1941, H.C.Deb. 5th ser., vol. 374, coll. 68–69.

it seemed necessary to reconcile themselves to life under Hitler's New Order, however distasteful, brutal, and oppressive it might be. With such expectations of the future, few men could be found willing to risk life, property, and the human ties of normal existence in order to make a futile gesture for a lost cause. Britain's survival against German air attack in the autumn of 1940 brought new hope to many Europeans, and various resistance groups formed. Some of them came into clandestine contact with British representatives; but, except in Yugoslavia, these organizations limited their activity to intelligence work and plan-laying for some future rising against the Germans.

The German attack upon Russia served as a signal for the various Communist Parties of Europe to become champions of resistance to the Nazis. The fact that in many European countries the Communists had long lived on the edge of legality, or had existed underground, meant that they had already at hand an organization suited to illegal work. Moreover, the revolutionary ideal attracted dedicated and fanatic men as older creeds could seldom do. Consequently, the Communists became an important factor in European resistance movements almost at once.[1]

The actual extent of Communist influence in the resistance movements is very hard to define. Communist policy was directed towards the formation of 'united fronts' with all groups which were willing to join actively in the fight against the Nazis; and to make the appeal of the resistance as wide as possible Communists systematically avoided conspicuous positions of leadership. A result of this policy was that in countries where substantial non-Communist groups were attracted to the resistance, Communist influence remained marginal. In countries where the pre-war political and social leaders were not willing to risk the perils of illegal activity, on the other hand, Communists came to play a dominating part even though they operated mainly from behind the scenes. In general, apart from Poland, the farther east in Europe the more important was the role of the Communists in the resistance.

Official British policy in 1941 was not seriously concerned with the possible post-war impact of anti-Nazi organizations. The illegal apparatus was embryonic in nearly every part of Europe, and all recruits were welcome. Many persons hoped that the Communists' professions of faith in democratic procedures were genuine; and in any case the military value of guerrilla armies, of acts of sabotage, and of intelligence from underground organizations in Europe was enough to outweigh any other consideration.

The various governments of Europe which had fled before Nazi con-

[1] Poland constitutes the great exception to this generalization. Historical and religious hostility to Russia, memories of the Red Army's invasion in 1939, and the existence of a fiery, romantic Polish nationalism, all discouraged Communist influence in the Polish resistance movement. Cf. Hugh Seton-Watson: *The East European Revolution* (London, Methuen, 1950), pp. 110–15.

querors and taken up residence in London or elsewhere served the British Government in a variety of ways. First of all, they constituted symbols for the population of the conquered countries—symbols of a better past and of hope for a better future. Moreover, the exiled governments were the repositories of legal continuity; and the British Government hoped that they would be able to exercise power in their homeland during the awkward period immediately after liberation before normal constitutional machinery could be set up again. The exiled governments were also able to supply agents for intelligence and sabotage work within Europe; in several instances they continued to exercise political authority in colonial areas which were of value to the British war effort; and, in the case of the Free French Movement and of the Polish Government, significant armies were formed from among escaped nationals.

British officials were not unaware of the many difficulties which beset their policy towards occupied Europe, and for a long time the Government sought to minimize the problem by postponing declarations about war aims and post-war plans. After Churchill and Roosevelt had issued the Atlantic Charter, however, it seemed appropriate to secure the agreement of the various Allied Governments to the principles so proclaimed. Accordingly, in September 1941 a general meeting of representatives of the Allied Governments was held in London. All of them solemnly accepted the provisions of the Atlantic Charter. By far the most significant gesture was that of the Soviet Government, represented by Ivan Maisky, Russian Ambassador to Great Britain. He declared that his Government accepted the 'fundamental principles' of the Charter, and specified that 'the Soviet Union defends the right of every nation to the independence and territorial integrity of its country, and its right to establish such a social order and to choose such a form of government as it deems opportune and necessary for the better promotion of its economic and cultural prosperity'.[1]

By such a declaration Russia came a long way towards meeting British views. But, however reassuring such a pronouncement sounded, the British Government had good reason to know that Russia's use of phrases like 'independence and territorial integrity' was capable of very elastic interpretation to accommodate Russian national and imperial interests.[2] Yet, for what it was worth, the approval of the Atlantic Charter by Russia and the other Allied Governments in September 1941 seemed to cushion and postpone conflict over the post-war future of Europe.

With two of the occupied countries of Europe Britain's relations were

[1] Address, 24 September 1941, reproduced in *Documents on American Foreign Relations, 1941–1942*, p. 215.

[2] Demands for post-war boundary changes had already been presented to the British in secret, and active negotiation on the question was in progress. See below, p. 167.

especially delicate and involved important divergences of policy among the three principal Allies. These two countries were France and Poland.

The collapse of the Third French Republic in 1940 left a bitter after-taste which subsequent events did nothing to alleviate. The British felt that the French could and should have continued the war from North Africa. Many Frenchmen felt that they had been inadequately supported by the British in the 1940 campaign, and some at least looked forward with a certain macabre satisfaction to the impending defeat of their former ally. Such an attitude was especially prevalent among the leaders of the new Government established at Vichy by Marshal Pétain.

After the British attack upon French naval vessels at Oran in July 1940 diplomatic relations were broken off by the Vichy Government. Relations remained bad, and were constantly exacerbated by the fact that the British lent both moral and financial support to what came to be known as the Free French Movement under the leadership of General Charles de Gaulle.[1] De Gaulle's supporters had no shadow of legal claim to represent the legitimate government of France; yet de Gaulle did represent something of the French spirit, and almost from its inception the Movement which he headed strove to win recognition as a legitimate government comparable to the governments in exile from other conquered European countries.

In the desperate time of 1940–1 the niceties of French legality mattered little to the British. What was important was that de Gaulle and his Free French could act effectively in lieu of a French government in exile. In particular, de Gaulle became a symbol and centre of propaganda for a France free from German domination, and he was able to attract a small but valuable armed force to his command. The Free French Movement was also successful in winning over parts of the French colonial empire which were thereby opened to British use; and de Gaulle undertook to administer other areas captured from the Vichy French by force of arms.

To unfriendly eyes de Gaulle appeared simply as a puppet of British policy, and a vain, ambitious, and troublesome puppet to boot. Certainly de Gaulle's personality was not one that made him easy to deal with. He was obsessed with the greatness of France, and easily identified real or imagined slights to his own person with slights to the dignity, power, and glory of his country. In the short run such behaviour alienated many who might have been his friends; but de Gaulle's excessive sensitivity about national honour struck a responsive chord in many French hearts, and one may hazard the guess that here lay the principal secret of his success. At the very least, a man who could so exasperate Churchill and Roosevelt could not be dismissed as a nonentity; and the more he bickered with his

[1] A fuller account of the Free French Movement and its relations with the British Government will be found in the *Survey* for 1939–46: *Hitler's Europe*.

'allies', the more he attracted the support of Frenchmen who felt, like de Gaulle himself, the need for a strenuous reassertion of the national dignity of France.

British policy towards de Gaulle was complicated by the attitude taken by the United States. Although there was a general understanding between the British and American Governments about French affairs,[1] it proved difficult in practice to avoid awkward divergences. Indeed, Cordell Hull, U.S. Secretary of State, came to cherish an almost personal grudge against General de Gaulle. His dislike was echoed though not quite equalled by President Roosevelt, as well as by other leading figures of the American Government. The reasons for the American attitude are hard to understand. Accident, jurisdictional disputes within the American Government, and personal clashes seem to have entered largely into the shaping of American policy, embittering the more tangible issues which did arise.

In the confused days of 1940 when Pétain first came to power, the American Government saw no reason to withhold recognition from the new régime in France. Thus, when the Free French Movement began to challenge the legitimacy of the Vichy Government, American officials were not inclined to take the claims of de Gaulle and his followers seriously. Criticism of the policy of recognizing the Vichy régime in the liberal press of the United States merely had the effect of increasing the stubbornness with which the State Department clung to its original position.[2]

[1] Cf. Hull: *Memoirs*, i. 805–6.

[2] It has been suggested that Secretary of State Hull was unused to public criticism of his conduct of foreign affairs, and that he became mulishly stubborn when an unexpected attack came on the Vichy–Free French issue. Cf. Churchill, iii. 590–1; U.S. edition, iii. 665–7; Sherwood: *Roosevelt and Hopkins*, pp. 482–3; Eng. edition, i. 459–60. Hull's *Memoirs* are generally distinguished by a touch of self-righteousness, and this characteristic is especially notable in the chapters dealing with the Vichy policy. Cf. especially ii. 1045, 1132–3.

In later years Hull became most anxious to clear his name and that of the State Department from accusations of undue sympathy for a semi-Fascist Vichy. Accordingly he asked a leading American historian, Professor Langer of Harvard University, to investigate the whole affair. Official records were made available to him, almost or entirely without let. The result is William L. Langer: *Our Vichy Gamble* (New York, Knopf, 1947), a semi-official history, and, in effect, an apology. Cf. a rebuttal of Langer's judgements in Louis R. Gottschalk: 'Our Vichy Fumble', *Journal of Modern History*, vol. xx, 1948, pp. 47–57.

Langer and Gottschalk continue as historians the contemporary debate between conservatives, who in general sympathized with the State Department's conduct, and liberals, who attacked it. But there was another dimension to the matter which was perhaps the most influential of all in determining the rigidity with which the State Department dealt with de Gaulle. The Vichy question became the occasion for a bitter jurisdictional dispute between the Board of Economic Warfare (which tried to prevent delivery of goods to North Africa) and the State Department (which wanted to send supplies to North Africa in the hope of future political and military gains). With leaders of the State Department assuming the attitude of Horatius at the bridge, striving to repel the incursion of alien bureaucrats into the sacred precincts of foreign policy, conditions were not propitious for a completely neutral decision. Any concession to de Gaulle became in the eyes of some officials of the State Department equivalent to a victory for the outsiders. Since the State Department was for the most part staffed by conservatives, while the Board of Economic

Nevertheless, as the practical importance of the Free French Movement asserted itself, the U.S. Government came into limited official relations with it. On 11 November 1941 Roosevelt proclaimed that territories under the control of the Free French were eligible for Lend-Lease aid, and American consular officials maintained official contact with the Free French authorities of the colonial areas. These gestures did not, however, alter the fact that, in the eyes of the American Government, de Gaulle was an untrustworthy adventurer[1] while Pétain was the official, and to a large extent the real, representative of the French people. The American attitude was hard to reconcile with the British policy of seeking to discredit Pétain and to increase the prestige and usefulness of the Free French Movement.[2]

Soviet policy towards de Gaulle and the Free French Movement was far less grudging. On 27 September 1941 a letter from Ivan Maisky, Russian Ambassador in London, to General de Gaulle accorded the latter recognition 'as the leader of all Free Frenchmen' and promised 'to afford the Free French every possible help and assistance in the common struggle against Hitlerite Germany'.[3] In practice all the Soviet Government could do was to instruct French Communists to support de Gaulle. This was not unimportant for the growth of the Free French Movement, but was something of a mixed blessing since it lent colour to Vichy accusations.

If British relations with France involved a certain awkwardness *vis-à-vis* the United States, the Polish problem created a similar obstacle to good relations with the Soviet Union. Great Britain had gone to war in 1939 as an ally of Poland, and was at least morally committed to the restoration of an independent Polish state, with, presumably, the same or nearly the same boundaries as in 1939. Russia's entry into the war and the consequent conclusion of an Anglo-Russian alliance put an awkward obstacle

Warfare was a stronghold of New Dealers, this jurisdictional conflict was only a special case of the more general division of opinion between conservatives and liberals over the merits of the U.S. policy towards Vichy.

[1] 'De Gaulle was a hireling of the British, who caused the latter no end of trouble in Syria. He had no demonstrable following in France, or even among Frenchmen outside of France. Everywhere he had the reputation of being a man personally vain and ambitious, self-centred and almost impossible to deal with' (Langer: *Our Vichy Gamble*, p. 394).

[2] It is true that Churchill sometimes found occasion to agree that the American connexion with Vichy was of use to the Allied cause (cf. Hull: *Memoirs*, ii. 1132; Churchill, iii. 561; U.S. edition, iii. 631–2). But it would be straining the truth to argue from such remarks that he or the British Government generally liked the American policy towards de Gaulle, which seemed to British eyes unnecessarily unfriendly.

[3] Text of the letter may be found in *Soviet Foreign Policy during the Patriotic War: Documents and Materials*, tr. Andrew Rothstein, 2 vols. (London, Hutchinson, [1946]), i. 99. [Quotations from this work in later sections of this volume are made by permission of Messrs. Hutchinson & Co. (Publishers) Ltd., London.]

in the path of such a programme. The Russians had formally annexed the eastern part of inter-war Poland to the Soviet Union in 1939, and Stalin was not inclined to abandon his claim to the territory he had acquired as Hitler's jackal. The Polish Government in Exile, for their part, were unwilling to surrender their claim to any part of former Polish territory, and indeed Polish patriots dreamed of vast extension of Polish political-military-cultural leadership through all Eastern Europe, to take the form of a federation in which Poland would be dominant.[1]

No compromise between the conflicting territorial ambitions of the Poles and Russians could be found;[2] but the British could hardly remain allies of both without attempting to establish some *modus vivendi* between them. Accordingly, diplomatic conversations opened between Russian and Polish representatives in London on 5 July 1941. The discussion was long and often acrimonious, but in the end an Agreement was concluded (30 July 1941) by which diplomatic relations between the Polish Government in Exile and the U.S.S.R. were resumed. On the territorial issue the Agreement stated: 'The Government of the U.S.S.R. recognizes the Soviet-German treaties of 1939 as to territorial changes in Poland as having lost their validity.'[3] In addition, the Soviet Government agreed to free all Polish prisoners of war in their hands, and to permit the formation of a Polish army on Russian soil by recruitment among the released prisoners.

The Poles were not satisfied with the rather ambiguous wording of this Agreement as far as territorial questions were concerned. The British Government tried to reassure them with an official note declaring that 'His Majesty's Government do not recognize any territorial changes which have been effected in Poland since August 1939'. But the force of this note was largely cancelled by the Foreign Minister's statement in the House of Commons in reply to a question: 'The exchange of Notes which I have just read to the House does not involve any guarantee of frontiers by His Majesty's Government.'[4]

It would in fact appear that some British officials were not unsympathetic to the idea of an adjustment of the eastern Polish boundary to bring it closer to the ethnic frontiers.[5] Churchill felt that postponement of any commitment on post-war Polish boundaries was the only wise course for Great Britain. In that way a head-on collision of the rival Polish-Russian ambitions could be put off to some future peace conference, when the constellation of military and economic power emerging from the war

[1] Ciechanowski: *Defeat in Victory*, p. 29.

[2] An account of Polish-Russian relations from 1941 to 1946 will be found in the *Survey* for 1939–46: *The Realignment of Europe*.

[3] Text of the Agreement may be found in *Documents on American Foreign Relations, 1941–1942*, pp. 260–1.

[4] Churchill, iii. 349–50; U.S. edition, iii. 392–3.

[5] Ciechanowski, op. cit., pp. 46–47; David J. Dallin: *Soviet Russia's Foreign Policy, 1939–1942* (New Haven, Yale University Press, 1942), p. 398.

might be expected to favour the Anglo-Americans as against the Russians.[1] In his advocacy of postponement he was strenuously supported by the United States.[2] At least some of the Poles, too, were well content to leave boundary questions to the future, when, they imagined, a war-weakened or defeated Russia would not be able to oppose the realization of at least a part of Polish ambitions.[3]

Numerous points of conflict arose between the Russian and Polish authorities over the interpretation of the Agreement of 30 July 1941. The Poles ostentatiously interpreted the text to mean that pre-war boundaries had been reinstated; the Russians officially denied that any final determination had been agreed upon. Moveover, the Russians' treatment of Polish soldiers both before and after their release from prison was harsh, and supplies were too scant within Russia to make the formation of a new Polish army easily possible. The Polish Prime Minister, General Wladislaw Sikorski, visited Moscow early in December 1941 in an effort to try to settle some of these difficulties. After some long and frank conversations with Stalin he was able to secure the promise of satisfaction on most points. Stalin tried to raise the boundary issue again, but Sikorski declined to commit himself; and, after a brief insistence, Stalin let the matter drop for the time being.[4] The contact between Stalin and Sikorski on this occasion was on the whole friendly, and their Joint Declaration of Friendship and Mutual Aid, issued on 4 December 1941, marked, as it turned out, the high point of Russo-Polish amity during the war.

Thus by the time of Pearl Harbour what looked like an effective adjustment had been made between rival Russian and Polish ambitions. Britain's position as ally of each began to make sense.[5]

(2) *British Relations with the U.S.S.R.*

On the evening of the day when the German troops attacked Russia, 22 June 1941, Churchill, welcoming the new ally, asserted: 'The past with all its crimes, its follies and its tragedies, flashes away.'[6] But, whatever Churchill may have thought on that summer evening, in fact the past could not and did not cease to exercise its influence. On the contrary, memories and fears based upon the troubled history of relations between

[1] Churchill, iii. 486, 616; U.S. edition, iii. 548, 696.

[2] Hull: *Memoirs*, ii. 1167–8.

[3] Cf. the remark reported to have been made by the Polish Premier, General Sikorski, in March 1942: 'The question of the Polish borders will be settled by the correlation of forces after the war' (Dallin: *Soviet Foreign Policy*, p. 399).

[4] Ciechanowski: *Defeat in Victory*, pp. 63–92.

[5] As far as the United States was concerned, relations with the Polish Government in Exile were largely limited, before Pearl Harbour, to expressions of sympathy. Lend-Lease was extended to Polish forces on 4 September 1941, but the Poles did not profit much immediately. Supplies were already short, and Britain and Russia came first.

[6] Winston S. Churchill: *The Unrelenting Struggle* (London: Cassell, 1942), p. 178.

Russia and Britain continued to disturb the co-belligerency which Hitler had thrust upon the two nations.

To go back no farther than 1917, it was a peculiar irony of history that the Englishman who had been most outspoken in his advocacy of the Allied policy of intervention against the Bolsheviks should be the person who as war-time Prime Minister of Great Britain welcomed Soviet Russia as a new and much needed ally in the struggle against Hitler. But the Russians could not forget what Churchill's policies had been a quarter of a century before, even if Churchill himself was able to do so.

British relations with Russia were crossed by yet another, more recent and therefore more clearly remembered, shadow. In the late 1930s some Englishmen in high position hoped that, if Nazi expansion could not be peaceably bottled up, it could at least be diverted eastward away from their own country and towards Russia. Stalin and his advisers hoped just the opposite, and they had been able by means of the Non-Aggression Pact of August 1939 to turn the main weight of Nazi attack against the two Western nations, France and Britain. Nor was the Russian Government content to remain 'neutral in thought and deed'. Supplies were dispatched to Germany on a considerable scale, and the force of the Communist propaganda machine was turned against the Western 'imperialist warmongers' until the very eve of the German attack upon Russia.

The Western Powers, for their part, fully reciprocated the Soviet dislike; and when the Russians attacked Finland in the winter of 1939–40 France and Britain set about preparing an expeditionary force to come to the Finns' aid. Had the expedition been sent, the Western Powers would obviously have found themselves at war with Russia as well as with Germany. Indeed, French and British war plans took that situation into account, envisioning a bombing attack against the oil-wells of Baku from bases in the Middle East in the hope of thereby cutting off German oil supplies.

Mercifully, the unwillingness of Norway and Sweden to allow free passage for Franco-British troops over their territory and the equal unwillingness of the Turks to allow aeroplanes to fly over their country delayed action until Finland's surrender and the German *Blitzkrieg* in France ended all thoughts of an early Allied offensive. In view of the later course of events, these plans of 1939–40 seem hare-brained; yet they were soberly prepared on the basis of a belief that the Russian social system was tottering on the brink of explosion, and that a relatively slight blow would therefore produce great results. The survival of this underestimate of Russian military strength and internal stability constituted one of the most important elements in Anglo-Russian relations up to (and after) Pearl Harbour.

The fall of France did not produce any palpable public change in

Russia's attitude towards Great Britain; and indeed, up to the very eve, Stalin hoped that by giving no cause of offence to Hitler he could avert or at least postpone the German attack. Ten days before the Russo-German war began, British and American warnings of German preparations against Russia were officially described as 'clumsily concocted propaganda of forces hostile to the U.S.S.R. and to Germany'.[1]

Yet, despite his personal record as an enemy of Communism and despite the unfriendliness of recent relations with Russia, Churchill did not hesitate upon hearing the news of the outbreak of the Russo-German war. In one of the most important speeches he ever made Churchill promised British help, as might be possible, to the Russian struggle against Hitler, and concluded:

> The Russian danger is therefore our danger, and the danger of the United States, just as the cause of any Russian fighting for his hearth and home is the cause of free men and free people in every quarter of the globe. Let us learn the lessons taught by such cruel experience. Let us redouble our exertions, and strike with united strength while life and power remain.[2]

Churchill's generous eloquence set the tone for the immediate reaction of British public opinion to the new phase of the war. Nevertheless, it took some time for British journalists to forget the constant flow of invective which had been so recently directed against Great Britain by the Russians; and the first reception of the new ally was a trifle on the cool side.[3] Hitler's perfidy rather than any virtue of Soviet Russia was the favourite theme. Some journalists feared that the accession of Communist Russia to the anti-Nazi cause might alienate the sympathy of the United States;[4] but an official statement by Sumner Welles, Acting Secretary of State, welcoming any opponent of Hitler as a useful addition to the Allied cause, dispelled most such anxiety.

As news of heavy fighting on the Russian front continued day after day it gradually began to reverberate in British minds; and the fact that their own forces were relatively inactive only underlined Russian courage. As early as July 1941 some newspapers, especially those of the Labour Party and the Beaverbrook press, were expressing dissatisfaction with the inactivity of British arms, and urged more help to the Russians.[5]

[1] Tass communiqué, 12 June 1941, reprinted in Dallin: *Soviet Foreign Policy*, pp. 372–3.

[2] Churchill, iii. 333; U.S. edition, iii. 373. The complete text of this speech may be found in *The Listener*, 26 June 1941, p. 896.

[3] e.g. *The Times*, leading article, 23 June 1941; *Daily Mail*, leading article, 23 June 1941; *Daily Herald*, leading article, 23 June 1941.

[4] *The Times*, leading article, 25 June 1941: 'It is significant that the small but vocal group of isolationists in the United States is using the argument that the new development makes American aid to Britain a less urgent necessity.' Cf. *Manchester Guardian*, 'Britain and Russia', 11 September 1941.

[5] See e.g. *Sunday Express*, 'Where's that Second Front?', 6 July 1941; *Daily Herald*, 'Clean Out anti-Soviet High-ups', 17 July 1941.

The changing temper of public opinion in Britain was manifested by an incident involving the Minister for Aircraft Production, Lt.-Col. J. T. C. Moore-Brabazon. At a private gathering in July Moore-Brabazon expressed his hope that the German and Russian armies would destroy one another while the British Commonwealth in the meantime built up its forces to assure a dominating position in Europe. When this indiscretion was made public at a meeting of the Trades Union Congress in September 1941, indignation was intense, and Churchill was forced to come to the rescue in Parliament, announcing that the Minister had not meant what he had said, and really agreed with Government policy.[1]

This incident exposed a sensitive nerve in Anglo-Russian relations. Moore-Brabazon had voiced an attitude fairly widespread among British Conservatives during the early weeks of the Russo-German war,[2] and it was an attitude which the Russians, with their Marxist indoctrination, suspected the British Government of secretly adopting. Official denials and the intense effort to hush the matter up could only partially quiet suspicion in Britain. One can only speculate upon the impact Moore-Brabazon's words had among the Russians.

Spurred partly by a sense of guilt—for throughout the summer and early autumn British military effort remained predominantly defensive—public admiration and respect for the Russians continued to mount. By November 1941 (when official relations were near their worst) sympathy for the Russians' cause extended to quarters which were normally anything but well disposed towards Russia and Communism.[3]

By the time of Pearl Harbour it would seem, as far as the expression of opinion in the newspapers provided any accurate clue, that the British people had almost forgotten the hostility towards Russia which had been so general a mere six months before. In its place came admiration, mingled in some quarters with a sense of the inadequacy of British effort. But in official circles memories were longer, practical difficulties in the way of aid

[1] 11 September 1941, H.C.Deb. 5th ser., vol. 374, col. 296, and see reports in *New York Times*, 3 September 1941; *Christian Science Monitor*, 4 September 1941. The British papers were obviously under restraint in dealing with this incident, and only the *Daily Herald* took it up prominently, or even gave a full account of what passed. See *Daily Herald*, 4 September 1941, 9 September 1941; the *News Chronicle* (3 September, 11 September 1941) also gave the story a limited play. When the matter came up in Parliament, normal coverage was given for the first time. See *The Times*, 12 September 1941; *Daily Telegraph*, 12 September 1941; *Manchester Guardian*, 12 September 1941.

[2] *New York Times*, 3 September 1941.

[3] See e.g. *The Times*, leading article, 7 November 1941; *New York Times*, 'British Go All Out for Aid to Russia', 6 November 1941; *Manchester Guardian*, 'Britain and Russia', 15 September 1941.

One avenue through which the admiration of the British public for Russia's war against Hitler found expression was the raising of relief funds by various private organizations. A Red Cross drive for Russian relief was opened by Mrs. Churchill in October 1941, and after a little more than two months £1 million had been subscribed by the public. Other agencies were no less active, though on a smaller scale.

to Russia were all too familiar, and the defence of British and Imperial interests was naturally put ahead of any commitment to Russia.

Official relations with the new-found Russian ally were governed by the belief that a serious, if not a total, Soviet defeat was inevitable.[1] The war in the east, by diverting the main strength of the German army and air force from Britain, meant a valuable respite. It offered a chance to strengthen British defences both at home and in the Middle East against the expected resumption of German attack. Assuming such an estimate of the future, the only reasonable policy which the British Government could pursue was to try to lengthen the respite as much as was possible.

To encourage and prolong Russian resistance the British were prepared to send supplies, including such precious things as military aircraft, in considerable quantity. Actually Britain delivered about 450 planes to the Russians before October 1941, when the first Russian Supply Protocol went into effect;[2] and considerable quantities of other supplies were also shipped. As compared with the Americans, the British were considerably prompter in sending war material to Russia, partly because mobilization in Britain was far more advanced and military stock-piles larger, and also partly because British authorities were less reluctant to risk supplies falling into German hands. But the British were confronted with the difficult choice between husbanding material at home for their own forces, and relinquishing what might some day soon be desperately needed for the defence of Britain itself, or of the Middle East. In practice, physical difficulties, especially the shortage of shipping, limited deliveries to Russia from the beginning.

A second method by which the British Government attempted to prolong Russian resistance was political. Very soon after the beginning of the Russo-German war, conversations were begun in Moscow between the British Ambassador, Sir Stafford Cripps, and Stalin and Molotov. Their aim was to formalize the new relationship between the two Governments which had been established by Hitler's attack. The negotiation ended in an Agreement, signed on 12 July 1941. Its text was as follows: '(1) The two Governments mutually undertake to render each other assistance and support of all kinds in the present war against Hitlerite Germany.

[1] British military experts generally believed that the Germans would be able to advance as far as they chose into Russia, and would call a halt, perhaps at the Urals, when their lines of communication had become uncomfortably extended. This was, in fact, the German intention. Cf. Chester Wilmot: *The Struggle for Europe* (London, Collins, 1952), p. 72. The British did not rule out the possibility of an indefinite survival of the Stalinist régime behind the Urals; but under such circumstances they believed that the Russians' resistance would be reduced to little more than a guerrilla war, while Hitler would once again be free to turn his main strength against Britain.

[2] See above, p. 23.

(2) They further undertake that during this war they will neither negotiate nor conclude an armistice or treaty of peace except by mutual agreement.'[1] By the second of these two clauses the British hoped to dispel a danger which was frequently in their minds during the first months of the Russian alliance—fear that the Russians might make a separate peace, and open their resources completely to German exploitation.[2]

The Agreement of 12 July 1941 did not, of course, settle any of the specific questions which arose between the British and Russian Governments. It was more in the nature of a public declaration of solidarity than anything else. The progress of negotiations over supplies and financial relations has been sketched above, and need not be recapitulated here. On the military and political level, however, there was a series of most important exchanges between the British and Russian Governments in the months before Pearl Harbour.

It did not take Stalin long to decide that what he wanted more than anything else from the British was a diversionary attack upon the German rear. In the very first telegram he addressed to Churchill, sent on 18 July 1941, he broached the question of a second front, or rather of two second fronts, one in France and another in Norway. Stalin suggested that these enterprises should be undertaken promptly while the German forces were busy against the Russians, and before Hitler had time 'to consolidate the position occupied by him in the East'. Rather lamely Stalin argued that the invasion of France would be 'popular with the British Army, as well as with the whole population of Southern England', and would be 'in the interests of Great Britain herself'.[3]

To the British, on the contrary, an invasion of France seemed sure disaster; and the interests of Great Britain required instead the careful husbanding of home resources and as rapid a build-up of forces in the Middle East as transport and supply permitted. Anticipating Russian collapse or retreat into Siberia, British military authorities tried to make preparations for facing a German attack on the Middle East from the direction of the Caucasus. But efforts to concert plans with the Russians for common action in case of a German break-through—the British were particularly concerned that the oil-wells of the Caspian and Caucasus region should be destroyed before falling into German hands—merely irritated the Russians, who were not interested in what might happen after their defeat.[4]

One point on which British and Russian military conceptions coincided

[1] Great Britain, Foreign Office: *Agreement providing for Joint Action in the war against Germany*, Cmd. 6304 (London, H.M.S.O., 1941); *Documents on American Foreign Relations, 1941–1942*, pp. 252–3.

[2] Cf. Churchill, iii. 409; U.S. edition, iii. 460.

[3] Ibid. pp. 342–3 and 383–4, respectively.

[4] Cf. ibid. pp. 466 and 525, respectively, where Churchill quotes one of his memoranda, dated 5 November 1941, in which he assumed the certainty of German conquest of the Caucasus.

was the necessity of securing Persia against German infiltration. Accordingly, that country was jointly occupied by Russian and British forces in the months of August and September 1941. In time a new route of supply to Russia was opened through Persia; but, despite this, friction and suspicion between the two occupying Powers were not absent.[1]

Britain's refusal to risk a second Dunkirk in France or a second repulse in Norway led Stalin on 4 September 1941 to propose a landing in the Balkans instead.[2] That, too, the British found impracticable, and Stalin then suggested that a British expeditionary force might either land at Archangel or come over the Caucasus in order to take over a sector of the Russian front.[3] But Stalin's suggestions took little or no account of the enormous difficulties of supply and transport which hampered every British move; and the British Government were not prepared to risk their forces on what seemed certain to become forlorn enterprises such as those which Stalin proposed.

As the Germans drove on into Russia the tone of the telegrams exchanged between Churchill and Stalin became steadily more acrimonious. Stalin said on 4 September that without a second front and a copious supply of aluminium Soviet defeat or partial collapse would surely come to pass.[4] Churchill felt that, however dangerous to Britain, such an outcome could not be prevented by the forces at his disposal. German reserves already stationed in Western Europe were, according to British intelligence reports, quite sufficient to defeat any expedition that the British could launch against the European mainland. Under such circumstances, it seemed clear to Churchill and his advisers that rash dissipation of British military forces would not be likely to delay Russia's defeat and would only make the subsequent situation worse. Replying to Stalin's reproaches Churchill vigorously rejected all insinuations that the British were not doing their share of fighting. He even, on one occasion, embarrassed the Soviet Ambassador by bringing up the subject of Stalin's recent collaboration with the Nazis.[5]

The nadir of cordiality was reached early in November when Churchill telegraphed to Stalin: 'I cannot tell you about our immediate military plans, any more than you can tell me about yours, but rest assured we are not going to be idle.' And Stalin replied:

I fully agree with you that clarity should be established in the relations be-

[1] Churchill was anxious that Russian influence in Persia be 'kept within reasonable bounds', and suggested that the British would be willing to take over responsibility for the whole country, if Stalin needed his troops elsewhere (ibid. pp. 430–1 and 484–5 respectively). The Russians declined to be the accomplice of such an extension of the British sphere of influence, and the matter lapsed.

[2] Ibid. pp. 405 and 455, respectively.

[3] Ibid. pp. 411 and 462–3, respectively.

[4] Ibid. pp. 406 and 456, respectively.

[5] Ibid. pp. 407 and 457–8, respectively. Cf. the statement of Churchill's position in a telegram to Sir Stafford Cripps, quoted ibid. pp. 420 and 472, respectively.

tween the U.S.S.R. and Great Britain. Such clarity does not exist at present. The lack of clarity is the consequence of two circumstances: (*a*) There is no definite understanding between our two countries on war aims and on plans for the post-war organization of peace; (*b*) There is no agreement between the U.S.S.R. and Great Britain on mutual military assistance against Hitler in Europe.

As long as there is no accord on both these questions there can be no clarity in Anglo-Soviet relations. More than that: to be frank, as long as the present situation exists there will be difficulty in securing mutual confidence. Of course the agreement on military supplies to the U.S.S.R. has a great positive value, but it does not settle, neither does it exhaust, the whole problem of relations between our two countries.

Stalin continued, referring ironically to an offer Churchill had made to send two British generals to Moscow for consultation: 'If however the mission of the Generals is confined to the questions of information, and to the consideration of secondary matters, it would not be, I think, worth while to intrude upon the Generals. In such a case it would also be very difficult for me to find the time for the conversations.'[1]

Such a telegram must have raised ominous echoes in the minds of all Englishmen who read it. It sounded too much like the abortive negotiations of 1939, which had been cut short by the conclusion of the Nazi-Soviet pact. Stalin, too, may have felt that the tone of this telegram was too harsh; in any case, the Russian Ambassador called upon the Foreign Minister, Anthony Eden, twelve days later and explained that Stalin had not intended to cause offence by his telegram of 8 November.[2] The British promptly took up the proffered olive branch, and on the next day (21 November 1941) Churchill sent off a telegram to Stalin proposing that Eden should go to Moscow with powers 'to discuss every question relating to the war, including the sending of troops not only into the Caucasus but into the fighting line of your armies in the south'. Discussion of post-war problems was likewise to be included within the scope of Eden's commission.[3] Stalin accepted the proposal, and arrangements for Eden's trip were promptly made. He sailed on 7 December, a few hours after the news of Pearl Harbour had reached Britain.

A subsidiary issue, but one which apparently excited great distrust on the part of Stalin and his advisers, was created by the unwillingness of the British Government to declare war on Finland, despite the fact that the Finns had joined with the Germans in attacking Russia. Churchill finally

[1] Ibid. pp. 468–9 and 528–9, respectively. The date of Churchill's telegram was 4 November 1941; of Stalin's reply, 8 November 1941.

[2] The fact that the British campaign in Libya started on 18 November 1941 may have had a part in mollifying Stalin's mood. It at least showed that the British were not planning to stand idle while Germany and Russia fought to a finish.

[3] Churchill, iii. 471; U.S. edition, iii. 531.

yielded and declared war on Finland on 6 December 1941, to take effect on the following day. At the same time Great Britain also declared war on Hungary and Rumania as a gesture of solidarity with the Russians, who were at war with both.

The distrust which can clearly be seen in the exchange of telegrams between Churchill and Stalin in the autumn of 1941 arose basically from the fact that each man was out to protect the interests of his own country first and last. The very real British interest in lessening Russian distrust could not come into play until British officials became convinced that the Soviet régime would not collapse—for good will is intangible at best and the good will of a vanquished government is not of much value to anyone. The fact that the conduct of the British Government seemed unco-operative to the Russians was certainly unfortunate; yet the only way that Stalin could have been satisfied would have been by a subordination of British national and imperial interests to the interests of Russia, a step which no British Government, least of all one headed by Winston Churchill, could or would consider for a moment.

By the time of Pearl Harbour, the first crisis had passed. The great German drive on Moscow had fallen just short of success; the British offensive in Libya was under way; supplies from Britain and America had begun to arrive at Russian ports; the Finnish and Polish questions had reached a standing more or less satisfactory to both Britain and Russia; and the entry of the United States into full war partnership introduced a third element into the Anglo-Russian relationship which changed it profoundly. In the subsequent years Roosevelt was often able to mediate between the Russian and British points of view; and American power and policy often helped to cushion or postpone collisions between Stalin and Churchill.

(*e*) Peculiarities of the British Government affecting Allied Co-operation

Despite the fact that the war worked more drastic changes in Britain than it did in the United States, the governmental administration of the United Kingdom remained more regular, more nearly normal, than was the case in America. Regular peace-time branches of the Government retained their influence on high policy and were not so nearly snowed under by new bureaucratic growths. In other words, the administrative machine of the British Government exhibited a great flexibility: a capacity to undertake new tasks and absorb new personnel without losing its established character and coherence.

Three major reasons may be suggested for this achievement. One was experience. In Britain the rudiments of modern war mobilization had been painfully evolved during the First World War, and the lessons of that experience had not been forgotten during the inter-war years. Moreover, by the time of Pearl Harbour, Britain had been at war for more than two years, and had had time to adjust administration to the needs of war.

A second major reason was that the structure of British government had evolved over the centuries into a pattern suitable for major war enterprises. The American administration, on the other hand, was frequently embarrassed by the provisions of a written Constitution which had been drawn up under conditions quite different from those prevailing in the mid-twentieth century. Parliamentary supremacy, Cabinet government, and civil service administration constituted, of course, the fundamental basis of British government. This is not the place to attempt any description of the working of war-time administration within that general framework. But it may be worth while to compare the position occupied by the Foreign Office with that of the American Department of State.

Foreign policy had for centuries been of first importance to the British Government. In war, as in peace, the views of senior members of the Foreign Office and of Ambassadors in the field were communicated to the Foreign Minister, who, as an important and respected member of the Cabinet, took direct part in making the key decisions of government and in defending them in Parliament. Thus a clear and effective channel between the Foreign Office and the seat of power was established, as it were automatically, by the Cabinet and Parliamentary systems. Under such conditions, co-ordination of policy between different bodies whose actions touched upon foreign questions was relatively easy. If only because the Foreign Office had secure connexion with the ultimate seat of power, other branches of government were obliged to consult and concert with representatives of the Foreign Office before embarking upon some line of action which might otherwise run the risk of being countermanded. It followed that despite the very great growth of the bureaucracy in the war years, and despite the rise of several new Ministries and sub-Ministries whose functions impinged on foreign affairs, the Foreign Office nevertheless remained in control.

The position of the American State Department was, by comparison, most unhappy. Despite formal precedence accorded by the Constitution to the Department of State, it had by tradition lacked high prestige in governmental circles, mainly because questions of foreign policy were, until relatively recent times, distinctly marginal to American political life. The absence of strong traditional prestige was not easily repaired, even when foreign affairs grew in importance. During the war years the State Department lacked firm and well-established channels of communication with the arcanum of power, which, during Roosevelt's Presidency, lay in his study. Key decisions were taken by the President after consultation with a small and varying group of men; and it was more or less a matter of accident whether or not the views of senior officials of the State Department got serious hearing. Moreover, there was no certainty that the State Department would be speedily and officially informed of Presidential decisions after they had been taken. As a result, the State Department frequently found itself competing with other branches of the Government, each with a foreign policy to press upon the President. The Departments of War, of the Navy, and of the Treasury were particularly prominent as competitors of the State Department. Under such circumstances, the coherence and cohesion which characterized British views in the field of foreign affairs could not be established among American officials.

The third major reason for the regularity of British war-time administration was the existence of the civil service and of the tradition according to which men of good education and high intelligence entered upon careers as government officials. As a result of this tradition, Britain enjoyed a high general level of bureaucratic competence which made it easier for old Ministries to adapt their ways and organization to new conditions. The new Ministries which the war brought forth all began as branches within older Ministries. When they separated from the parent Ministry a number of strategically placed permanent civil servants went into the new Ministry. Consequently no important social or psychological gaps appeared between new and old sections of the bureaucratic machine. All branches of the Government were affected by a great influx of men from academic and business life; but in all of them a core of old civil servants assured a general uniformity in structure and conduct.[1]

Jurisdictional disputes and differences of opinion of course arose within the British Government, and it sometimes happened that different branches pursued conflicting policies. An example of this may be seen in the frequent differences between Foreign Office representatives and the military units charged with intelligence and sabotage work in Europe, especially in the Balkans. Such quarrels and differences were, however,

[1] These conditions did not prevail in the United States, where social and psychological differences between various parts of the governmental machine were marked. One major fission line was between the 'New Dealers' and old line bureaucrats. The New Dealers were, of course, the men who had swarmed to Washington in the early years of Roosevelt's Presidency. In some of the branches of government, and for our purposes most notably in the State Department, the pre-New Deal personnel and traditions survived unbroken; whereas in other branches of the administration New Deal personnel and New Deal social attitudes and beliefs prevailed. New Dealers were dominant in some of the new war-time agencies—especially in Vice President Wallace's Board of Economic Warfare; but in general the top conduct of the war administration fell into the hands of two other groups: ex-business men who had come to Washington 'for the duration', and professional army and navy officers. Among such diverse and often antagonistic groups, a common point of view was often hard to find; and jurisdictional disputes between agencies were often envenomed by the social and psychological differences between their constituent personnel. The clearest example was the dispute over United States policy towards France, mentioned above, p. 45, note 2.

generally settled *in camera* and relatively rapidly. Public display of administrative disputes was always far less common than in America, where official indiscretion sometimes became a weapon in the struggle for power.

The obverse to these characteristics of the British administrative machine should be mentioned. Bureaucracy encourages a certain conservatism and lack of imagination in even the most intelligent of men. The monotony of daily office routine, if nothing else, is likely to blunt the mind and limit thought to habitual paths. It is probably just to detect in some of the behaviour of the British Government during the war the effect of such hardening of judgement among the members of both the civil and military services. The classic instance was the slowness of British mobilization before and during the first year of the war—a slowness dictated in considerable part by Treasury concern for financial solvency.[1] Other later but more problematic instances—for example the tremendous underestimate of Russia's military potential, or the disaster at Singapore—might be cited to illustrate the survival of a routine-bound frame of mind.

But one must not over-stress the point. British mobilization for war was by 1941 far more radical than anything accomplished at any time in the United States. Something like a controlled social revolution took place during the war years as a result of the fiscal, man-power, and rationing policies pursued by the Government. A bureaucracy capable of carrying out such a series of drastic actions cannot properly be called conservative or lacking in imagination.

On the political level, too, the British achieved a remarkably unified common front for presentation to the outer world. No significant public opposition to the Government existed in the country, although criticism of practical performance was sometimes sharp. The superficial reasons for the political solidarity—the existence of a coalition Government after May 1940, and the rigour of party discipline which kept public figures measurably in check—only partly account for the phenomenon. Behind and beneath lay the social structure of Britain itself, a structure which was remarkably close-knit despite the outward differences of class and manners.

Opposition did not miraculously disappear. It found expression not so much in public debate and strictures, as would be normal in peace-time under party government, but rather through private discussion within a small circle of party leaders and Cabinet members. Parliament served in a limited degree as a sounding board and echo of the private discussions among the party big-wigs. The press served the same function, two degrees removed.

[1] Cf. Hancock and Gowing: *British War Economy*, p. 93.

Semi-voluntary war-time censorship, not to mention the shortage of newsprint, restricted the traditional freedom of the British press in a negative way by preventing publication of news. But the most significant relationship between the British Government and the press was not embodied in formal law or regulation. It was rather 'unofficial' and 'off the record': a collaboration between representatives of the Government and of the press whereby delicate issues were handled more or less in accordance with official suggestions. This transformation of the press into a semi-official organ of the Government was not complete. Newspapers were free, and upon occasion found reason to go against the Government's wishes. But the attitude of the British press, especially towards international questions, was generally influenced, if indeed not governed, by private indications of official policy.

This relationship between Government and press may be looked upon as no more than a special instance of the general co-ordination which the British were able to achieve in all sectors of their war effort. In proportion as the press was responsive to official suggestions, the Government enjoyed a somewhat freer field of manœuvre in relations with both friend and foe.[1] But the control was not one of compulsion: only if the Government could convince them with inside information and sound arguments did the journalists comply with the Government's wishes. Consequently, the Government's freedom of manœuvre was not nearly as wide as in the Soviet Union, where any fluctuation of policy would be sure to find welcome and justification in the press. Rather, British journalists were, with the members of Parliament, specially privileged representatives of the public at large, whose approval the Government were in one case practically and in the other case legally bound to seek.[2]

The role of individual personality in modern government is hard to assess; yet just as Roosevelt dominated and gave a distinctive character to the American Government, so Churchill, from the time when he became Prime Minister in May 1940 until his dismissal from office in July

[1] An example of the control of the press has been given above (pp. 32–33) in connexion with the description of British reaction to Pearl Harbour. One can imagine the embarrassment to Anglo-American relations which might have arisen had the British press, or a part of it, begun to clamour loudly for an American declaration of war on Germany in the days between 7 and 11 December 1941.

[2] The status of American journalists was not altogether dissimilar, and during the war years it became more like the British pattern. But the co-ordination of government policy and press opinion was never as close in the United States as in Great Britain, partly owing to a long tradition by which the press considered itself the watchful guardian of the public interest *against* the Government; partly owing to the American party system, which kept certain influential newspapers in systematic and sometimes rather embittered opposition to the policies—any policies—of the Roosevelt administration.

1945, profoundly influenced the conduct of the whole British Government.

The legal limitations of Churchill's position as Prime Minister and Minister of Defence in a coalition Cabinet were greater than the limitations placed upon Roosevelt. By the American Constitution, the President was solely responsible for many decisions whose analogue in Britain had to be taken jointly by the Cabinet as a whole. The need to refer proposals back to the Cabinet in London was a constant feature of the periodic meetings between Roosevelt and Churchill; and, while it is true that Churchill was usually able to persuade the Cabinet to agree to what he recommended, there remained always the possibility that the Cabinet would demand rejection or modification.

It followed from the system of Cabinet government that Churchill's personality could not dominate all branches of the British administration to anything like the degree to which Roosevelt dominated the American administration. Each Minister had his own special sphere; and Churchill's chosen sphere was the military. Here, as Minister of Defence, he kept close and constant contact with the plans and personalities of the navy, army, and air force; and a cursory examination of the memoranda which showered from his hand[1] provides convincing evidence of the extraordinary scope of his activities.

Churchill felt himself fully qualified to direct the activities of British military leaders in drafting war plans, and he collaborated actively and constantly with the Chiefs of Staff. But while Churchill harassed his military entourage with incessant queries and orders, and while he felt free to reach downward through the military hierarchy to correct any small detail which seemed to him not to be going as it should, still it remained true that he carried on his multifarious activity through channels that were fairly well defined by convention and by law. He did not by-pass Ministers or neglect formal channels of administration as Roosevelt regularly did.[2]

In general, if one turns over in one's mind the major outlines of the American, Russian, and British administrations, it seems hard to deny that the British struck a happy medium between the confusion of the American and the lock-step of the Russian bureaucracies. The British

[1] Reprinted as Appendices to Churchill, iii, iv, and v.

[2] The likeness between Roosevelt's irregular administrative methods and those used by Lloyd George during the First World War is striking. Perhaps the fact that both of them came to high office as reformers, more or less systematically opposed to traditional governmental and social practices, accounts for the parallel. Churchill, with his strong sense of tradition, could not so easily cut across normal bureaucratic paths; and, moreover, he found himself in general sympathy with the points of view of senior civil servants who were to no small degree the embodiment of the tradition he sought to sustain.

Government, supported by an almost universal consent to their central aims and policies, were able to perform prodigies of what might be called human engineering without more than token resort to force or compulsion. Populations, property, products, and prices were shifted round, controlled, and regulated as never before. Something approaching the totalitarian power of a police régime was achieved without breaking the thread of voluntary consent which bound the people to the Government. To have carried through such a revolution by consent is surely the greatest war-time achievement of the British Government. Resolution and intelligence on the part of the Government were certainly needed; but the extraordinary solidarity of British society and the obvious mortal danger in which Britain found herself in 1940 were also prerequisites of success.

(iii) The Russian Outlook

(*a*) Enigmatic Russia

Any attempt to describe the Russian outlook at the time of Pearl Harbour must face almost impossible difficulties. First and foremost was the lack of information. In 1952 there were no Russian memoirs analogous to those which had been written by some of the members of the American and British high command. Official history in Russia must be suspect, for it was freely rewritten to serve propaganda ends.[1] Equal suspicion must attach to the Russian newspapers and the official pronouncements made by Stalin and others during the war.[2] It was true, of course, that the propaganda line followed by the Russian Government might sometimes have been of interest in itself, and changes in it might have reflected changes in the plans and intentions of the inner circle of the Kremlin. But one had to guess blindly what was real, what falsified or distorted; or, more prudently, leave the question open.

As far as relations among the Allies were concerned, various accounts from British and American sources allowed glimpses of Stalin's behaviour in negotiation with the Western Powers. But here, too, there was a problem of interpretation. How much of what Stalin said and did was a frank expression of his inner thoughts and wishes? How much was a calculated disguise, put on to impress his foreign visitors? Stalin could hardly be described as trustful, and it would always be rash to assume that at any particular time he was not deliberately misleading his interrogator.

[1] An instance is the systematic playing down of the importance of Marshal Zhukov's part in the war, which went to the length of describing one of his subordinates as commander in the battle of Stalingrad (see I. Deutscher: *Stalin: A Political Biography* (London, Oxford University Press, 1949), p. 483).

[2] No attempt has been made to use Russian documents at first hand in the preparation of this volume. This means that the picture of Russia's part in the war-time alliance is derived from translated and secondary sources.

Indeed, it seemed likely that Stalin was so two-faced as to make it impossible even for himself to say which was the 'real' and which the 'false' front he presented to the world. This state of indecision between roles is normal among politicians who tend to assume whatever guise seems best calculated to appeal to or impress the audience of the moment. But there is variation in the degree of contradiction between successive roles; that is, some politicians are more nearly consistent than others. But Stalin's role as revolutionary Marxist and his role as ruler of Russia—not to mention others he might have assumed—were widely different and often contradictory. To try to decide which was the true and which the false would be to over-simplify the mysteries of individual and political psychology. In these regions, logical consistency does not govern, and should not be used as a guide.

A similar and equally impenetrable difficulty arose when any effort was made to describe popular attitudes in Russia. The Russians themselves had available only official channels of expression, shaped, guided, and controlled. Ordinary human contact with foreigners was systematically and effectively discouraged by the police. Consequently, the reports of foreign journalists were of limited value; the more so, because during the war the censorship imposed upon despatches from Russia was exceedingly severe and sometimes seemingly senseless.

Another difficulty beset anyone writing when tension and hostility between the war-time Allies had become acute. It was almost irresistible to look at the war-time history in the light of what had come after, to search for signs and portents of the strained situation which had prevailed since 1946 or 1947, and to forget or minimize the 'open-endedness' of Allied relationships during the war years. Yet in 1941 and 1942 the defeat of Germany was not a certainty; in 1943 and 1944 the break-up of the Grand Alliance did not seem inevitable; in 1945 and 1946 the lines of division of the world between Communist and non-Communist areas had not been definitely drawn. In the face of these and countless lesser uncertainties, the Allied Governments had to act as best they could; and to suppose either that the outcome as it was known in 1952 was inevitable or that it was 'planned that way' by any of the Allied leaders or Governments was surely fallacious.

Broadly speaking, two antithetical views might be taken of the policy of the Soviet Government. On the one hand, their actions might be interpreted as the application, however tortuous, of Marxian principles. In international affairs this meant first the preservation of the homeland of Socialism, and secondly the fomentation of proletarian revolution round the world. According to such an interpretation of the motive springs of

Russian policy, the only possible relationship between the U.S.S.R. and non-Communist states was one of hostility, sometimes veiled, sometimes open. Circumstances might require alliances or superficial co-operation with other states; but such alignments were temporary and a semblance rather than a reality.[1]

This might be called the plot theory: from the Communist point of view, capitalists were plotting to encircle and overthrow the Soviet state, while anti-Communists saw a cleverly camouflaged Red plot which threatened world revolution. Reduced to such melodramatic terms, the theory was unquestionably an over-simplification. But in proportion as men are prone to see things simply, dramatically, and in terms of plot and counter-plot, such a theory may take on a considerable share of reality. In human affairs men regularly create what they most fear or hope. They act *as if* their sentiments were founded in fact; and presently, as a result of their own acts (and counter-acts of others) what they believe becomes at least in some measure true. One cannot, therefore, dismiss the plot theory of Russian motivation out of hand, nor easily deny that something like it had exercised, and was continuing to exercise, influence over official decisions in Russia and outside it too.

The second general interpretation of the conduct of the Russian Government dismissed ideology and the plot theory as verbal figments, designed to mislead the ignorant and naïve. Instead, *Realpolitik*, the quest for power, and security in the enjoyment of power might be advanced as a fully adequate explanation of the twists and turns of Soviet policy. According to this view, the relations between the U.S.S.R. and other states did not differ in any essential from the relations which normally prevailed between national and imperial states.[2] In proportion as the Russian ruling class or clique felt insecure in its power, it became restless, striving after internal security through self-discipline (i.e. the Party), supplemented by propaganda and police. Simultaneously the rulers pursued external security through alliances, territorial expansion, and armaments.

The peculiarity of the Soviet régime, according to this view, arose from the continued insecurity which disturbed the ruling clique. An acute sense of insecurity had led Stalin and his advisers to make sharp and sudden shifts in policy, both as regards internal administration, and on the international scene. More stable régimes, such as those which prevailed in the United States or Great Britain, having had a longer time to settle down internally and internationally, had not been impelled to make comparably drastic shifts in their policies. But, despite this difference, it

[1] For a learned and impressive presentation of this view see 'Historicus': 'Stalin on Revolution', *Foreign Affairs*, vol. xxvii, January 1949, pp. 175–214.

[2] A presentation of this point of view may be found in Barrington Moore: *Soviet Politics* (Cambridge, Mass., Harvard University Press, 1950), p. 394 and *passim*. Cf. also Hans J. Morgenthau: 'History's Lessons', *The Nation*, vol. clxxi, 1950, pp. 587–91.

might be argued that essentially the same motive was everywhere at work: national self-interest and the self-interest of the ruling class or clique (as understood at the moment) guided all power-wielding groups; and the fact that high-sounding phrases and moral or political principles were appealed to by governmental leaders was merely a device—perhaps used unconsciously in some instances—by which the obedience of the masses was the more easily secured.

It would be wrong to dismiss this theory with a shrug of the shoulders, despite the fact that in an extreme form it, too, was clearly an over-simplification. Governments do, after all, act to protect their power and to increase it when opportunity offers.[1] And when moral principles conflict with what seems to be self-interest, principles seldom prevail.

The policy of every government actually exhibits an ambiguity between professed principle and self-interest, between ideology and expediency, between morality and immorality. A judicious mind will always take both into account in trying to explain official policies. It is impossible in practice to draw any clear line between the two, or to estimate mathematically the vectors of force which enter into the making of any particular decision.

What was peculiar to the Union of Soviet Socialist Republics was the violence of the interaction between ideology and expediency. Communist ideology was a heady brew, able to win powerful emotional support among large numbers of men. On the other hand, Russia's geographical position and the level of Russian social and technical development made her vulnerable to attack. In a world divided among actually or potentially hostile national states, it required nimble footwork and a careful calculation of expediency for such a comparatively weak society to survive.[2] But in proportion as Communist idealism was strong, compromises with the demands of Russian state security were difficult to make.

Fortunately for the peace of mind of the Bolshevik leaders and for their practical effectiveness, resolution of the conflict was possible through an easy rationalization. After all, the centre of Communist idealism was the vision of a future good society; but the vision did not imply a definite

[1] This is true internally as well as externally. For an interesting discussion of the long-range aggression of European governments against private citizens, their subjects and supporters, see Bertrand de Jouvenel: *On Power* (New York, Viking Press, 1949).

[2] The history of Russia reflected this fact. Indeed, one might say that the technical backwardness of Russian society had been compensated for by a relatively great mobilization of social resources by the state. This mobilization had allowed the Tsars, and more recently had allowed Stalin, to meet the military threat presented by more highly developed neighbours in the west. When, in the nineteenth century, the Tsarist régime relaxed its guard and failed to out-do the West in harnessing the wealth and man-power of the Russian Empire to the chariot of the state—allowing, for example, the luxury of private control over natural resources, as Peter the Great had not done—then the relative weakness of Russian society was revealed and the defeat of 1917 resulted.

time-table. Thus it was possible to affirm and reaffirm the ultimate ideal of a stateless, egalitarian, free, and peaceable society while, in the name of socialist self-defence, actually extending the power of the state, establishing sharp differentials between various groups of the population, checking dangerous deeds and thoughts by means of an oppressive police, and building a great army. Marxism, as reformulated by Lenin and Stalin, actually hallowed such a solution of the conflict between principles and expediency. Tactics were sharply differentiated from ultimate ends; and any tactic was thought justified if circumstances seemed to impose it.

The effect of a series of compromises between principle and expediency operating over a period of years or decades is, of course, to reduce ideals to a thin transparency. They may in the end become something to which lip service is paid on ceremonial occasions. But it takes time for ideals imbued originally with a white heat of revolutionary ardour to lose their power over day-to-day action; and it seemed unlikely that any such complete betrayal had yet taken place in Russia. In the meanwhile, a persistent and perhaps an acute tension between principles and expediency might be presumed to exist within the directing circle of the Kremlin.

The two institutions which embodied the opposite poles of Russian policy were the Bolshevik Party and the Red Army. The Party's whole *raison d'être* and the justification for its power were its capacity to perfect the revolution; and young Communists were religiously taught the sacred principles of Marxism from the texts of great revolutionary heroes—Marx, Engels, Lenin, and Stalin. The Red Army, on the other hand, was first and foremost the protector of the Russian state and nation. Its traditions descended directly from the Tsarist army, and Red Army officers had never been completely subjected to Communist domination.[1] It was possible, and perhaps not unilluminating, to regard the internal development of Russia between 1941 and 1950 as an oscillation between dominance by the army and dominance by the Party. There was, of course, no open conflict between the two, but there was a notable shift in public prominence of military and Party leaders; and there was a parallel shift in the propaganda line from the patriotism of the war to the revived Bolshevism of the post-war years.

The disharmony between Communist principles and the interests of the Russian state had to be set within the framework of a wider tension which had long run through Russian history. Russia's attitude towards the countries of Western Europe had been, at least since the days of Ivan the

[1] Trotsky perforce recruited a large proportion of his officers from the ranks of the Tsarist army, since no other technically qualified men could be found: cf. D. F. White: *The Growth of the Red Army* (Princeton University Press, 1944). For evidence of the survival of a non-Party tradition among the Red Army officers cf. Cyrille D. Kalinov: *Les Maréchaux soviétiques vous parlent* (Paris, Librairie Stock, 1950), *passim*; and Ivan Krylov: *Soviet Staff Officer* (London, Falcon Press, 1951), pp. 11–22, and *passim*.

Terrible, a curious mixture of attraction and repulsion, of imitation and rejection, of admiration and dislike.[1] Stalin's government did not escape from this long-standing ambivalence. Bolshevism itself was a Western creed, at least in origin. American efficiency was long held up to the Soviet workers and industrial managers as an ideal to be imitated. The Constitution of 1936 was in large part framed on Western models. On the other hand revulsion against the West took new forms: capitalism and imperialism and all evil was attributed to European and American society, while the superiority of the Soviet system was constantly, sometimes ridiculously, insisted upon. It seemed plausible to believe that some of the stiffness and punctilio with which the Russians carried on diplomatic negotiation arose from their effort to suppress a deep-seated malaise *vis-à-vis* the capitalist–imperialist and more civilized countries of the West.

The differences between Russian society and Western society were sufficiently great to persuade some observers that two associated but separate civilizations here found themselves face to face. In any event, the gap was great enough to make understanding difficult at best. The artificial closure which the Soviet police and censorship put upon ordinary contact between Russians and outsiders, reinforced by the dark secrecy which surrounded governmental decisions on matters of high policy, multiplied the difficulty. But despite the uncertainty which must result, it still seems proper to try to say something of the Russian outlook about the time of Pearl Harbour.

(*b*) Looking Eastward

Russia's easternmost frontier had been the scene of repeated frontier incidents, sometimes approaching the scale of full-dress battles between Japanese and Russian troops during the late 1930s. But by the spring of 1941 the imperial ambitions of Japan had turned towards the islands and coast lands of the South-West Pacific, while Russia was increasingly concerned at German penetration of the Balkan peninsula. The result was

[1] These mixtures were probably to be paralleled in any society which found itself adjacent to a vigorously developing civilization in which it only partially shared. The attitude of Latin America to the United States exhibited many parallels, for instance; so did the attitudes of the Scots and of the Irish to England before the seventeenth and nineteenth centuries, respectively. Incidentally, Scotland and Ireland represented two strikingly divergent resolutions of such ambivalence. The Scots developed towards a full partnership in English civilization, and lost the earlier sense of inferiority while preserving a mild and inoffensive conviction of their own superiority. The Irish, on the other hand, rejected (or at least were trying to reject) English civilization, and had turned inward, but still nursed almost sub-consciously a sense of loss, of inferiority. The programme of the Social Revolutionaries in Russia—land to the peasants and the preservation of the *mir*—would have perhaps produced a situation in Russia analogous to that prevailing in Ireland; and the prime factor in preventing such a solution was surely the need for a military organization of the Russian state to protect it from without. Bolshevik control of Russia after all had been riveted into place by the civil war and intervention of 1918–22.

that both Governments were prepared to come to agreement. A Neutrality Pact, signed on 13 April 1941, formalized the new relationship.[1]

Despite the persistence of very real divergences of interest between Japan and Russia, the Neutrality Pact of 1941 continued as the formal basis for relations between the two countries until April 1945. The major divergences of interest were two: in China, where the Russians continued to support the Chinese against the Japanese; and in Europe, where before the year was out the Russians were fighting in alliance with Japan's enemies, America and Britain.

In China, Russian policy was complicated by the existence of a vigorous and powerful Chinese Communist Party which, in effect, exercised governmental control over a fluctuating area in North China adjacent to the Russian border. Suspicion, breaking out into sporadic hostilities, had long existed between the Kuomintang Government and the Chinese Communists. The Russians, however, were anxious to prevent this internal quarrel from interfering with Chinese resistance to the Japanese, for the consolidation of Japan's control over China might have freed Japanese troops for adventures in Siberia. Thus, in accordance with world-wide Communist policy, the Chinese Party continued to adhere at least nominally to a 'united front' with the Kuomintang. The U.S.S.R. recognized Chiang Kai-shek's Government as the legitimate authority in China, and in fact had concluded a Non-Aggression Treaty and a trade agreement with the Kuomintang régime.[2] In accordance with the policy of encouraging resistance to the Japanese, the Soviet Union sent considerable military supplies to Chiang Kai-shek until the outbreak of war with Germany.[3] After June 1941 the Russians had few or no military supplies to spare for the Chinese. Relations cooled, and renewed conflicts between the Kuomintang and the Chinese Communists broke out. Nevertheless

[1] The parallel between the Russo-German pact of 1939 and the Russo-Japanese pact of 1941 is worth mention. In April 1941 Stalin was still no friend of 'capitalist war-mongers' like Britain or the United States, and he was well aware of the alternatives before Japanese imperialists—Siberia or the South Pacific. He cannot have doubted that, by signing the Neutrality Pact, he was encouraging Japanese expansion southward, preparing the way for a further extension of the war, just as the Non-Aggression Pact of 1939 had prepared the way for the beginning of the war in Europe. In each case Stalin was probably primarily concerned with deflecting danger from the U.S.S.R., but he may also have been influenced by Leninist principles which saw in international war the best opportunity for the spread of revolution and class war.

[2] The Non-Aggression Treaty was signed on 21 August 1937 and ran for a term of five years; the Trade Agreement was signed on 16 June 1939. Texts may be found in Harriet L. Moore: *Soviet Far Eastern Policy, 1931–1945* (Princeton University Press, 1945), pp. 187–99.

[3] Supplies delivered to China from Russia during this period were considerably greater than were the supplies that came to Chiang Kai-shek from the United States (Moore, op. cit. p. 118). This arose partly from the great difficulties of transport between America and Chungking; partly from the fact that there were clamorous demands for American supplies from other directions; and also partly from the policy of the American Government, which was seeking a diplomatic settlement with Japan and hesitated to provoke any irreparable antagonism. At various times in 1941 the Chinese were afraid of being 'sold down the river' by the Americans.

the Russians did not withdraw their formal support from Chiang Kai-shek.[1]

The importance of the Russo-Japanese Neutrality Pact was officially minimized in the United States and was interpreted privately as an effort on Stalin's part to secure his eastern flank in the face of Hitler's threat.[2] As long as Japan remained at peace with the United States and Great Britain, the pact raised no particular problem for Soviet relations with the Western Powers. But after Pearl Harbour matters became rather awkward. Could Russia, Britain, and America be allies in Europe and strangers to one another in the Pacific? Or would continued Russian neutrality towards Japan lead the Americans and perhaps even the British to stop delivery of supplies or refuse co-operation? On the other hand, was the pact worth anything? Would the Japanese in spite of the treaty decide to help the Germans by attacking Siberia? Probably the most burning question of all was this: Would American strength be diverted from the war in Europe in order to fight a separate war in the Far East?[3]

Until the answers to these questions became clearer, it behoved the Russians to step warily, and to try to avoid antagonizing either the Americans or the Japanese. Russian newspapers and official pronouncements fully reflected this need for caution. News of the Japanese attack on Pearl Harbour and of Japan's victories in the Pacific were at first published without comment. Equal prominence was given to the communiqués of the American and Japanese Governments.

Within a week, however, the situation cleared. The German and Italian declarations of war against the United States (11 December 1941) assured the Russians that the war in Europe would not cease to concern the Americans; and, as the scale of Japanese operations was revealed, fear for Siberia may well have been allayed.[4] Meanwhile, American opinion

[1] The contradiction between Russian neutrality towards Japan and continued assistance to China must be understood to result from the fact that in the negotiations leading up to the conclusion of the Neutrality Pact it was the Japanese who took the initiative and who were most anxious to come to terms. To secure Russian agreement, the Japanese were in fact willing to promise to surrender their oil concession on the island of Sakhalin. In Japanese eyes the hoped-for oil of the Dutch East Indies no doubt seemed worth the loss.

[2] Hull, U.S. Secretary of State, announced on 14 April 1941: 'The agreement would seem to be descriptive of a situation which has in effect existed between the two countries for some time past' (Hull: *Memoirs*, ii. 993).

[3] There is no reason to suppose that the Americans and British shared with the Russians the information which came to their Governments from the decoding of Japanese cables. But it was only information so secured that forewarned the Western Powers of Hitler's promise to declare war on the United States.

[4] The Russian secret service may, of course, have been able to secure information about Japanese troop movements or even about Japanese military plans. This one cannot know; and lacking the information it is impossible to know whether serious concern for the security of the Soviet eastern provinces was felt by the Russian Government in the period of Pearl Harbour. American intelligence, which may have been as incorrect in 1941 as it was in 1944–5 about Japanese strength in Manchuria, estimated the Japanese Manchurian army at nearly a million men (see John R.

showed signs of restiveness at Russia's failure to declare war on Japan.[1] Accordingly steps were taken both in Moscow and in Washington to define and explain the Russian position.

On 12 December 1941, the day following the German declaration of war on the United States, *Pravda* published an editorial on the Pacific war. The tone of the article was anti-Japanese, and its theme was the certainty of eventual Japanese defeat, despite initial advantages gained by a treacherous attack. A clear implication of the article was that the help of the U.S.S.R. was not needed to bring about Japan's overthrow.[2] On the next day, the newly arrived Russian Ambassador to the United States, Maxim Litvinov, issued a statement to the American press in which he said: 'We are proud and happy to count ourselves the allies of your great country. I am quite sure that complete understanding exists or will be arrived at among these three allies [U.S.S.R., U.S.A., and Great Britain] as to which of them should concentrate its greatest efforts and energy on which sector, and that they will be ruled in this by the interests of the common cause.'[3] During these same days in mid-December 1941 correspondents in Russia sent back to British and American papers a series of stories explaining and justifying the Russian decision to concentrate against Hitler alone.[4] The result of these moves, combined of course with the official policy adopted by the American and British Governments and the trend of the news (Russian victories on the eastern front and Japanese victories in the Pacific), was to reduce or even eliminate public pressure in America and Britain for Russian intervention in the Japanese war. Thus little more than a week after the opening of hostilities in the Pacific Russia's role was defined and accepted by her Anglo-American allies.[5] As for the Japanese, they were too deeply engaged elsewhere to do more

Deane: *The Strange Alliance* (New York, Viking, 1947), p. 223). General Deane was secretary to the Combined Chiefs of Staff before going to Moscow in 1943, and so was in a position to know the exact authoritative American estimates of Japanese strength.

[1] See above, p. 21.

[2] A translation of the text of this editorial may be found in Moore: *Soviet Far Eastern Policy, 1931–1945*, pp. 254–6.

[3] Complete text of Litvinov's statement may be found in the *New York Times*, 14 December 1941. Litvinov emphasized in his statement the parallel between Russia's need for a second front and the Anglo-American need for Russian help against Japan. Each would be desirable, but just as Russia had 'never made any demands upon our ally, England, that she should create such a front', so, he implied, the Americans should not demand Russian participation in the war against Japan.

[4] See e.g. *Daily Mail*, 'Russia will Keep Out for Present, Fully Occupied with Germany', 11 December 1941; *Daily Express*, 'Russia Fights Hitler First', 12 December 1941; *Chicago Daily News*, 'No Pressure on Russia', 13 December 1941.

[5] A curious incident was the publication of an editorial in *Pravda* on 31 December 1941 which scathingly attacked the American action of declaring Manila an open city. Such conduct, the writer declared, was simple cowardice. On the following day it was officially denied that the article was anything but the expression of an individual's opinion. In general, the Russian press continued to be very chary of comment on the Pacific war throughout the first month. Cf. *Chicago Daily News*, 'Russian Policy in Pacific War?', 8 January 1942.

than take note of Russia's formally correct, though unfriendly, attitude towards their country.

One may say that the Russians were able to enjoy the best part of two worlds in the Far East. The pact with Japan safeguarded Siberia, at least on paper; while the involvement of Japanese troops in war with the Anglo-Americans and in China safeguarded it in fact. Yet, at the same time, Stalin was able to remain on reasonably good terms with the Chinese, both Communist and non-Communist; and persuaded the Americans and the British that Russian participation in the war against Japan was not practicable. This was no mean achievement, and was of incalculable importance for the general course of the war. The success of Russia's eastern policy revealed the lack of any real solidarity in the Axis. Had Germany and Japan genuinely co-operated, a Japanese attack on the Russian defences of Siberia might have been the straw to break the back of Russian resistance.

(*c*) Looking Westward

In the grim days of the first winter campaign, when the fate of Leningrad and Moscow hung in the balance and the whole future of the Soviet régime was threatened, the Far East could only rank as a side-show in Russian eyes. What really mattered was the struggle with Germany. Russia's own military strength in comparison with Germany's was clearly the primary determinative of the course of events. But the rulers of Russia must also have counted upon two other—and in a measure conflicting—factors. The possibility of revolution in the German rear could never be absent from a good Marxist's mind; on the other hand, the possibility of help from Britain and America could not escape the attention of practical politicians and diplomats. The principal steps by which co-operation between the Western Allies and the Russians was initiated up to the time of Pearl Harbour have been described above.[1] What concerns us now is the Russian attitude towards the war, towards the possibility of revolution in Hitler's rear, and towards Britain and America.

Despite warnings of impending German attack sent to Stalin by both the British and American Governments,[2] there seems no doubt that the Soviet Government were caught by surprise when Hitler's armies attacked on 22 June 1941. Stalin was on vacation far from Moscow, the Red Army was not fully mobilized,[3] and the economic plans by which the Soviet Government guided their domestic policy were based upon the assumption that war would not interrupt industrial development during 1941.[4]

[1] See above, pp. 22–26, 48–56.

[2] Churchill, iii. 319–23; U.S. edition, iii. 357–61; Hull: *Memoirs*, ii. 1174.

[3] Sherwood: *Roosevelt and Hopkins*, pp. 333, 335; Eng. edition, i. 335, 336.

[4] N. A. Voznesensky: *The Economy of the U.S.S.R. during World War II* (Washington, Public Affairs Press, 1948), p. 21.

Stalin's tremendous miscalculation of Hitler's intentions can only be attributed to the deep distrust with which he viewed warnings that came from the Western Powers, and to a serious defect in his own intelligence system.[1]

There seems good reason to suppose that popular opinion in Russia was dismayed at the course of events during the first days and weeks of the war with Germany. Propaganda had led most Russians to believe that the Red Army was the most powerful on earth,[2] and Stalin found it necessary to explain at some length why the Red Army had suffered such reverses.[3] On the other hand, the Russian Government's rather ignominious efforts to please and appease Hitler after the collapse of the Balkan front in the spring of 1941, and Molotov's attempt to negotiate with the Nazis to the very last,[4] suggest that in the inner circles of the Russian Government the relative weakness of the Red Army was recognized or perhaps even exaggerated.

The great question must have been one of morale. After the purges of 1936–8, when a large number of the officers of the army had been arrested and some had been executed,[5] no one could be entirely sure of the reaction of the Red Army and of the general population to war under the leadership of the Stalinist régime. It seems altogether probable that Stalin was aware of the doubtful loyalty of his subjects;[6] and the large-scale surrender of Ukrainian and other Red Army troops in the first months of the war made the problem obvious.[7]

As the events of the German campaign unfolded themselves, and as

[1] Kalinov (*Les Maréchaux soviétiques vous parlent*, pp. 28–35) says that the intelligence services of the Red Army foresaw German attack, but were overruled by the M.V.D. [i.e. the Ministry for Internal Affairs, at that time called N.K.V.D.—i.e. People's Commissariat of Internal Affairs], whose foreign intelligence branch believed that German troop concentrations on the Russian borders were only a bluff intended to wring greater economic concessions from the Russians.

[2] Cf. Henry C. Cassidy: *Moscow Dateline* (Boston, Houghton Mifflin, 1943), p. 50, for an interesting account of the immediate reaction to the outbreak of the war in a Black Sea resort town, where he happened to be on vacation at the time.

[3] J. V. Stalin: *The Great Patriotic War of the Soviet Union* (New York, International Publishers, 1945), pp. 9–10, 24–25. Texts of Stalin's war-time speeches in different translations may also be found in Rothstein: *Soviet Foreign Policy during the Patriotic War*, and in J. V. Stalin: *Stalin's War Speeches* (London, Hutchinson, 1946).

[4] Cf. the German Ambassador's account of a conversation with Molotov on the evening of 21 June 1941, only a few hours before the invasion began (U.S.A., Department of State: *Nazi-Soviet Relations*, Pub. 3023 (Washington, U.S.G.P.O., 1948), pp. 355–6).

[5] Erich Wollenberg (*The Red Army* (London, Secker & Warburg, 1940), p. 253) says that about 25 per cent. of the Red Army officers were eliminated by the purges. On the purges, see also *Survey* for 1938, iii. 393–400.

[6] It is part of the nature of a secret political police to report, and in reporting to exaggerate, the threat of political dissent. Without lively dangers the justification for a political police is removed; hence, in the policeman's corporate and individual interest, it becomes important to stress dangers, real or imagined.

[7] Kalinov: *Les Maréchaux soviétiques vous parlent*, p. 273; Krylov: *Soviet Staff Officer*, pp. 112–18.

fertile and productive parts of Russia were overrun by the invading armies, Stalin and his advisers may sometimes have doubted the ability of the Red Army to withstand the blows to which it was subjected. The decline in military production continued throughout 1941. By November 1941 gross industrial production was less than half what it had been in June, five months before.[1] Supplies from Britain and the United States were, of course, far from adequate to replace such losses; but, unless and until industrial production could be restored, the long-range powers of resistance of the Red Army were threatened by impending shortages of equipment. In 'this more than unfavourable situation'[2] Stalin predicted to Churchill that 'the Soviet Union will either suffer defeat or be weakened to such an extent that it will lose for a long period any capacity to render assistance to its Allies'.[3]

But such gloom may have been exaggerated in the hope of stirring the British to action. To other audiences, Stalin expressed quite different sentiments. For example, a month before writing the sentences quoted above, Stalin expressed to Harry Hopkins his belief that German morale was low and near the breaking-point.[4] And two months later, at a time when nothing but more disasters had yet come to Russian arms, Stalin said in a speech delivered on the anniversary of the Bolshevik Revolution:

> Hunger and poverty reign in Germany. In four and a half months of war Germany has lost four and a half million soldiers. Germany is bleeding white: her manpower is giving out. A spirit of revolt is gaining possession not only of the nations of Europe under the German invaders' yoke, but of the Germans themselves, who see no end to the war.
>
> The German invaders are straining their last forces. There is no doubt that Germany cannot keep up such an effort for any long time. Another few months, another half year, one year perhaps—and Hitlerite Germany must collapse under the weight of its own crimes.[5]

If the report to Churchill may be suspected of exaggerated pessimism, this speech palpably exaggerated whatever cause for optimism Stalin may then have had.

What did Stalin himself really believe? With such contradictory evidence, it is of course impossible to know. Perhaps he was too busy with day-to-day supervision of the Russian war effort to be able to spare much time for speculation on the course of future events. There is, however, one

[1] Voznesensky: *The Economy of the U.S.S.R. during World War II*, p. 24.

[2] Stalin's words in a telegram to Churchill, dated 4 September 1941, in Churchill, iii. 405; U.S. edition, iii. 456.

[3] Ibid. pp. 406 and 456, respectively. Cf. Deutscher: *Stalin*, p. 465, for a report of a conversation between the British Ambassador to Moscow, Sir Stafford Cripps, and Stalin in the course of which Stalin foresaw the possibility of the loss of Moscow and retreat beyond the Volga.

[4] Sherwood: *Roosevelt and Hopkins*, pp. 339, 342; Eng. edition, i. 340, 343.

[5] Stalin: *Great Patriotic War*, p. 37.

of Stalin's published utterances which has the ring of sincerity to it. In 1945, while proposing a toast to the Russian people at a banquet given in the Kremlin to honour the commanders of the Red Army, he described the first months of the war in these words:

> Our Government made not a few errors, we experienced at moments a desperate situation in 1941–1942, when our Army was retreating, abandoning our villages and towns . . . because there was no other way out. A different people could have said to the Government: 'You have failed to justify our expectations. Go away. We shall install another government which will conclude peace with Germany and assure us a quiet life.' The Russian people, however, did not take this path because it trusted the correctness of the policy of its Government, and it made sacrifices to ensure the rout of Germany. This confidence of the Russian people in the Soviet Government proved to be the decisive force which ensured the historic victory over the enemy of humanity—over fascism.[1]

In vino veritas? Perhaps. His unaccustomed admission of error in high places and his emphasis upon the decisive importance of morale sound authentic and frank. From what we know of the course of the struggle in Russia, it seems almost sure that Stalin must more than once have stared defeat in the face, and almost singly, by the strength of his will, stared it down.

Indeed, Stalin's personal conduct was a factor of the greatest importance in maintaining Russian morale. He never gave any public hint of faltering, even when the situation seemed most desperate; and the fact that in 1941, when foreign diplomats and some of the branches of the Soviet Government had been evacuated from Moscow, Stalin remained in the Kremlin, and even made a public appearance at a parade held as usual to celebrate the anniversary of the Bolshevik Revolution, symbolized for the Russian population his resolution and their own fortitude.

An important element in Stalin's estimate of the situation must have been his assessment of the likelihood of revolution springing up in the German rear. Doctrinaire Marxism would have required the Russians to put their whole war propaganda upon a revolutionary foundation. Stalin did not do so, yet appeal to the workers of the world was not entirely abandoned. In Allied countries it took the form of agitation for a second front and more war production. In German-occupied lands it took the form of 'popular fronts' whose programme was reformist and patriotic: throw out the Germans and then build a better world, in short. As for Germany itself, Stalin made repeated efforts in his speeches during the first year of the Russo-German war to distinguish between the Hitlerite Government and the German people;[2] and the Moscow radio followed a similar line.

[1] Stalin: *War Speeches*, p. 139.
[2] Stalin: *Great Patriotic War*, pp. 12, 16, 31, 37, 44, 48–50, 69.

But revolution did not come in Germany, and resistance movements had only limited success. At a later stage of the war Stalin tended to drop the distinction between German people and government, and instead condemned the 'fascist beasts' *en masse*. In 1941 Stalin perhaps thought that revolution might come to Germany; but when the initial German failure before Moscow in December 1941 and the first German retreats which followed did not produce the hoped-for results, it seems that Stalin dropped whatever faith he had earlier had in the possibility of separating the German people from Hitler.[1] It was no doubt too difficult to fight wholeheartedly against the Germans while regarding them as potential proletarian brothers.

One may perhaps guess, from the scanty evidence at hand, that the Russian high command experienced three successive moods in the first six months of the war, passing from initial stunned surprise to a state approaching panic, and then, about November 1941 when the Russian counter-offensive in the Moscow region began to take shape, to excessive optimism. When the worst did not happen, when the Red Army survived the first shock of attack and proved able to withdraw before the Germans and yet retain discipline, it became possible to believe that the Germans would quail before the prospect of prolonged battle in the Russian snows with a hostile Britain on the westward flank. After all, the earlier Nazi campaigns had all been brief, and the avoidance of a two-front war had long been the foremost principle of German military and political thinking. Moreover, would the German workers prove loyal to a Hitler who for once had failed to win easy victory? And how could German industry supply a two-front war of indefinite duration? Hope of an early end to the struggle, such as Stalin more than once publicly voiced in the winter of 1941–2, fed on considerations such as these.

Yet, while Stalin and his advisers may have suffered sharp reversals of mood, all the while they were able to initiate most strenuous and unbending efforts to save and re-establish war industry by transporting whole factories to the east; and the building up of the Red Army, requiring a ruthless mobilization of every resource of man-power and production, was never relaxed. Tumultuous hopes and fears did not paralyse the most vigorous action.

Communist theory had long foreseen a time when the Soviet Union

[1] It was not solely Marxian dialectic which supported the early faith in the possibility of sudden German collapse. The fate of Napoleon's *Grande Armée*, which after one campaign was compelled to retreat from Russia's inhospitable plains, was very much in the foreground of men's minds. The name which from the first was given to the struggle—the Patriotic War—echoed the name traditionally accorded to the struggle against Napoleon. Molotov, in the speech which first informed the Russians of the outbreak of war, drew the parallel explicitly. Stalin did so implicitly in his first speech of the war (*Great Patriotic War*, p. 9). But cf. his refutation of the parallel in a speech of 6 November 1942, when it had become clear that the Germans were not going to collapse as easily as had Napoleon's invading army (ibid. p. 63).

would be attacked from without; and it can be argued that the whole policy of Stalin's Government from the time when he first consolidated his control over the Party and administrative machine had been directed primarily towards preparing Russia for such an assault. But Communist theory had not seriously considered the possibility of alliances with bourgeois-imperialist states in time of war. Stalin had often emphasized the inevitable hostility between two rival economic systems: socialist Russia versus capitalist West. According to this view, Britain and America were the natural allies of fascist Germany in war against the Soviet Union, since all three nations had at bottom identical, capitalist economic systems.[1]

Under the special circumstances in which the war with Germany came to the 'Motherland of Socialism' in 1941, orthodox Marxians presumably expected that Britain and the United States would stand on the sidelines of the new struggle, seeking by judicious intervention to balance the forces of Germany and Russia against one another so that they would mutually exhaust their strength and leave the Anglo-American Powers in a position to dictate a new peace settlement. The role of *tertius gaudens* was, in fact, exactly the part which Stalin had tried to assure for Russia in 1939,[2] and he may well have been taken aback by the impetuosity with which Churchill hailed the Russians as allies as soon as they had been attacked.[3] The sudden propaganda reversal—from heaping opprobrium upon Britain for prolongation of the war to hailing her as an ally—was unquestionably difficult, even with the help of the thoroughly disciplined Russian press;[4] and Stalin may have felt it wise to make the transition easier by making it slower, waiting first to see how valuable British support might prove to be. Mere words did not impress him,[5] and the whole weight of a life-long Marxist indoctrination resisted the thought that British and American capitalists could for their part be really sincere in offering help to the land

[1] In 1947 Stalin affirmed in an interview with Harold Stassen that Nazi Germany and the United States had essentially the same economic systems (*Soviet News*, 9 May 1947; *New York Times*, 4 May 1947). Stalin's most striking references to the final and inevitable conflict between Socialism and capitalism are conveniently assembled in 'Historicus': 'Stalin on Revolution', *Foreign Affairs*, vol. xxvii, January 1949, pp. 175 seqq.

[2] As early as 1925 Stalin had defined the proper role of the Soviet state in time of war as follows: 'The banner of peace remains our banner as of old. But, if war begins, we shall hardly have to sit with folded arms. We shall have to come out, but we ought to be the last to come out. And we should come out in order to throw the decisive weight on the scales, the weight that should tilt the scales.' (Speech to the Plenary Session of the Central Committee of the Bolshevik Party, January 1925, quoted in Deutscher: *Stalin*, p. 411).

[3] Stalin made no immediate move to acknowledge Churchill's offer of help and friendship, nor did Churchill's speech receive much publicity within Russia. 'The silence on the top level was oppressive', says Churchill (iii. 340; U.S. edition, iii. 380).

[4] Cassidy (*Moscow Dateline*, p. 67) reports that as late as 12 July 1941, when the Soviet-British alliance was announced, he overheard a Russian remark: 'I thought we were signing with honest people'.

[5] Sherwood: *Roosevelt and Hopkins*, p. 309; Eng. edition, i. 311.

of the Soviets.[1] The troubled history of relations between Britain and America on the one hand and Bolshevik Russia on the other gave neither party ground for trust or mutual confidence.

Yet from the practical point of view, Stalin's aim in 1941 must have been to prevent Marxist predictions from coming true. Help from the West in the form of supplies and still more in the form of a second front against Germany was desperately needed by the Russians, and ideological differences were certainly not going to prevent Stalin from accepting all the aid he could get and asking for more. This called for a drastic reorientation of the official Soviet interpretation of the nature of the war and of the character of British and American society. Without such a shift from traditional Communist views, relations with the Western Allies would have been difficult to justify to the peoples of the Soviet Union, and American and British co-operation with Russia would have been almost if not entirely impossible.

Stalin's speeches provide the most authoritative as well as the most accessible guide to the new line of Soviet propaganda. In his first war-time speech, delivered on 3 July 1941, Stalin declared that the struggle was a 'national war in defense of our country', and continued:

> In this war of liberation we shall not be alone. In this great war we shall have loyal allies in the peoples of Europe and America, including the German people who are enslaved by the Hitlerite despots.
>
> Our war for the freedom of our country will merge with the struggle of the peoples of Europe and America for their independence, for democratic liberties. . . .
>
> In this connection the historic utterance of the British Prime Minister Churchill regarding aid to the Soviet Union and the declaration of the United States government signifying its readiness to render aid to our country, which can only evoke a feeling of gratitude in the hearts of the peoples of the Soviet Union, are fully comprehensible and symptomatic.[2]

The war, then, was to be fought for national independence, freedom, and democracy, not to defend Socialism or to revolutionize the world. This remained the cornerstone of Soviet war propaganda throughout the following years; and it was not until 1944 that a troublesome ambiguity in the meaning of the word 'democracy' became evident.

[1] While translation interrupted negotiation with the Beaverbrook-Harriman Mission, Stalin occupied himself by drawing 'numberless pictures of wolves on paper and filling in the background with red pencil' according to Lord Beaverbrook (ibid. p. 390; Eng. edition, i. 391). Surely, these must have been capitalist wolves? The paper wolves of Marxian mythology? Here, almost for the first time in Stalin's experience, sitting with him face to face and negotiating a matter of high importance, were the capitalist wolves of reality—Beaverbrook, a newspaper tycoon, and Harriman, scion of a wealthy banking family. But they failed to bare their fangs. Was it a ruse? Did Beaverbrook, who was to become a leading champion of all-out aid to Russia, protest too much? Who can tell what thoughts passed through Stalin's mind as his fingers idly sketched and the interpreter droned on?

[2] Stalin: *Great Patriotic War*, pp. 15–16.

Stalin's second war speech, delivered on 6 November 1941, was more explicit in rejecting traditional Marxian analysis. He said that the Germans had believed they would be able to frighten the ruling classes of Britain and America by the spectre of Communist revolution, thus persuading them to join forces against the U.S.S.R. 'But the Germans gravely miscalculated. In spite of Hess's efforts, Great Britain and the United States not only have not joined the campaign of the German fascist invaders against the U.S.S.R.; on the contrary, they are in one camp with the U.S.S.R. against Hitler Germany.'[1]

Later in the speech he argued, in a way which at first sight seems curiously unnecessary, that the Germans were not nationalists and were not socialists as they claimed to be. He went on:

> To cover up their reactionary, blackguard essence, the Hitlerites are branding the Anglo-American internal regime as a plutocratic regime. But in England and the United States there are elementary democratic liberties, there are trade unions of workers and employees, there are labor parties, there is a parliament, whereas the Hitler regime has abolished all these institutions in Germany.[2]

In this part of his speech Stalin was answering the pseudo- or semi-revolutionary appeal which German propaganda made to the world. He rejected the opposition between Socialism and plutocracy, which had for so long been a feature of Soviet propaganda, and which Goebbels had borrowed for his own purposes. Instead Stalin pictured the war as a struggle between reaction ('Actually the Hitler regime is a counterpart of the reactionary regime which existed in Russia under tsarism')[3] and democracy; and he admitted the Western Powers within the fold as possessing at least elementary democratic liberties. Patriotism, which in the days of Lenin had been regarded in Bolshevik circles as a bourgeois superstition, was now to be glorified. Stalin even took over the patriotic heroes of the tsarist régime and officially beatified them. From lackeys of the Russian ruling class they were abruptly transformed into figures fit to inspire the men of the Red Army.[4]

A war fought for ends such as these could not offend British or American susceptibilities. There was, however, another problem which exercised the attention of the Russian rulers from the start. They hoped to win the assent of their new-found allies to the annexation of the border-lands—the Baltic states, eastern Poland, Bessarabia—which had been acquired in 1939–40 as a by-product of alliance with Hitler. This was a matter on which no easy agreement with the Western Powers was possible. Stalin was not prepared to give up his claim; but he was most chary of making the claim public. In fact, in his speeches he took a rather different tack;[5]

[1] Stalin: *Great Patriotic War*, p. 21.
[2] Ibid. p. 27.
[3] Ibid. pp. 27–28.
[4] Ibid. p. 38.
[5] Cf. speech of 6 November 1941: 'We have not and cannot have such war aims as the seizure

and in September 1941, as we have seen, the Soviet Union officially subscribed to the Atlantic Charter. Public disquiet in the West could be allayed by such gestures, and Stalin was content to register his claim in private while refraining from pressing it at a time when the Nazis were deep within Russian territory, and when the whole matter was merely academic as far as the immediate future was concerned.

If one asks the blunt question: Did Stalin and his circle of advisers believe that the war was being fought for the purposes he defined in his speeches? the answer must surely be in the negative. Stalin believed not at all in the democracy of the West. He and his fellow Communists had for too long harped upon the hollowness of political democracy when based upon private ownership of the means of production. But Stalin was content to cling for the moment to the propaganda line he had worked out as the most effective one he could use to win support at home and abroad. Alliance with the bourgeois West was required by the situation in which the Soviet Union found itself; and if in the long run the inevitable conflict between capitalists and socialists had to come, it would come. In the meanwhile, the help of the West was of great importance and it would be folly to do anything to endanger that help. When the situation changed it would be time enough to change Soviet policy in whatever direction circumstances might seem to dictate.

If this fairly describes the attitude of the Soviet leaders towards Britain and America in the latter months of 1941, it should also be remembered that such conduct could be justified on doctrinaire grounds easily enough. The conflicts of interest within the capitalist-imperialist camp had split the encirclement of the U.S.S.R.; and it was elementary good sense to do everything to maintain the split as long as the relative weakness of the world's first socialist state required it. Whether the U.S.S.R. had 'honest people' or merely short-sighted 'capitalists' as allies would be determined by the future course of events.

(*d*) Peculiarities of the Soviet Government affecting Allied Co-operation

The concentration of authority in the person of Stalin was the dominant characteristic of the Soviet system. In effect, negotiation with anyone else was impossible, for Stalin alone had the power to make binding decisions.

of foreign territories, the subjugation of foreign peoples. . . . We have not and cannot have such war aims as imposing our will and our regime on the Slavs and other enslaved peoples of Europe who are awaiting our aid. Our aid consists in assisting these peoples in their liberation struggle against Hitler tyranny and then setting them free to rule on their own land as they desire. No intervention whatever in the internal affairs of other peoples!' (*Great Patriotic War*, p. 33). Stalin, of course, counted the Baltic states, eastern Poland, and Bessarabia as integral parts of the Soviet Union, and so was not contradicting himself. But by such declarations as that quoted above he certainly was trying to divert public attention in the West away from his territorial ambitions.

Even very high-ranking officials of the army and government were unwilling to say or do anything which had not already been authorized by Stalin.[1] The resulting paralysis among the lesser officials of the Russian Government in dealings with representatives of the Western Powers was frequently exasperating[2] and certainly did not help to make smooth the path of co-operation between them. On the other hand, top-level negotiations were handled with extraordinary dispatch, even though it often happened that the concessions Stalin made were subsequently nullified by the failure of his subordinates to translate agreements into deeds.

Nevertheless, the limits of Stalin's power were real. Some Western observers came to believe that he was in reality more a spokesman for the invisible Politburo than a completely independent agent.[3] It is, indeed, inherent in human affairs that there should be limits to the most absolute power. A dictator is always in some sense the prisoner of his subordinates who supply him with information, and carry out, or fail to carry out, his decisions. More than this, Stalin appears to have adopted the practice of soliciting advice from the men around him. Only after hearing various arguments and proposals did he make the decision.[4] Inasmuch as the decision came not solely from Stalin's own brain, but took into account the ideas and attitudes expressed by his advisers, choosing and perhaps compromising between them, it would be just to surmise that Stalin's behaviour reflected in part at least the influence of the Politburo, of his generals, and perhaps of other associates.

But it was also true that the Politburo and the army high command were creatures of Stalin. In the years before 1939 he had systematically killed or otherwise rid himself of men who dared in any way to oppose his leadership. By the time the war came to Russia, Stalin's personal ascendancy was unchallenged and unchallengeable. There is no reason to suppose that the members of the Politburo ever tried to overrule their leader by majority vote or anything of that sort. Stalin was far more than a spokesman for the Politburo, however much he depended upon its members for advice.

A problem much more delicate and difficult for Stalin was his relationship with the leaders of the Red Army. Nurtured as they were on the

[1] Harry Hopkins, when he first visited Moscow, discovered that it was all but useless to deal with anyone but Stalin and Molotov. Cf. the interesting description of his interview with General Yakovlev of the Red Army in Sherwood: *Roosevelt and Hopkins*, p. 330; Eng. edition, i. 331.

[2] Deane in his *Strange Alliance* records repeated failures of efforts to concert plans for American and Russian co-operation.

[3] This theory, based upon the apparently contradictory moods which Stalin showed in successive meetings with Western negotiators, was held by Harry Hopkins and, less definitely, by Churchill (Sherwood: *Roosevelt and Hopkins*, pp. 345, 621; Eng. edition, i. 346, ii. 621; Churchill, iv. 440; U.S. edition, iv. 489).

[4] Deutscher: *Stalin*, pp. 495–6; Kalinov: *Les Maréchaux soviétiques vous parlent*, p. 202; Krylov: *Soviet Staff Officer*, pp. 123–30.

history of the French Revolution, the Bolsheviks had always been aware of the danger of Bonapartism rising in the rear of revolution. The Great Patriotic War seemed to offer the opportunity for an ambitious general to emulate Napoleon, if precautions were not taken in advance. Stalin and his Party colleagues did take precautions which turned out to be markedly successful. Soon after the outbreak of hostilities, supreme direction of the war was placed in the hands of a new body, the State Defence Committee. Stalin acted as chairman, and its members were all drawn from the Politburo. But this device did not seem enough to assure the Party and Stalin against the danger of a military *coup d'état*. Early in 1942 Stalin personally took over day-to-day direction of the campaign; and at the same time military commands were divided into relatively small armies each directly subordinated to Stalin.[1] This organization was adopted expressly to prevent the rise of some general to a position of power and prestige from which he could endanger Stalin's dictatorship.

But relatively small independent armies meant that large-scale strategic action was difficult. Personal rivalries among adjacent commanders and the awkwardness of liaison through Moscow interfered with military efficiency. Accordingly, towards the end of 1942 the system was modified. Larger commands were reinstituted—the so-called 'fronts'—and Stalin relied upon his personal day-by-day contact with the generals to keep them in their proper place.[2]

The system which was thus evolved worked smoothly throughout the rest of the war. Almost daily telephone conversations between Stalin and the chief commanders in the field helped them to feel that Stalin was indeed one of themselves, the ultimate authority from whom orders and help both came. As long as he exercised active personal command Stalin could not easily become the target for a military *coup d'état*, since a sense of psychological separation and opposition between the military and the supreme civilian authorities could not develop. Stalin's assumption of the military rank of Marshal of the Soviet Union in March 1943 symbolized and helped to confirm this psychological solidarity between military and civil leadership which he was so anxious to preserve.[3]

Stalin's role as Commander-in-Chief of the Red Army was only a part of his war-time duties. A few weeks before the war began he assumed the post of Chairman of the Council of People's Commissars, i.e. Premier of the Soviet Government. In addition he was Secretary-General of the

[1] Kalinov: *Les Maréchaux soviétiques vous parlent*, pp. 24–25.

[2] According to Kalinov, Stalin did not hesitate to tell Zhukov to his face that generals who thought of *coups d'état* would not be tolerated in the Red Army (ibid. p. 26).

[3] Cf. Deutscher: *Stalin*, p. 496, and the sample of Stalin's telephone conversations with his generals reproduced in Kalinov, op. cit. p. 196, also p. 79. Kalinov, a colonel on the General Staff of the Red Army during the war, claims to have overheard several such conversations, some from Stalin's command-post in the Kremlin, others when visiting headquarters in the field.

Bolshevik Party. Thus all threads were now at last openly gathered in his hands. The Government, the army, and the Party all were directly subordinated to him; and Stalin's power, which in the 1930s had been half disguised, was now openly acknowledged and consecrated by office.

The adulation—one might almost say worship—which was accorded to Stalin in Soviet publications, demonstrations, public speeches, radio broadcasts, &c., was another important element in his power. It accorded strangely with Stalin's lack of theatrical mannerisms or eloquence. His model was not the mass-demagogue of the West but the remote, fatherly tsar of the peasant imagination. The parallel between Stalin's myth and the tsarist myth may have been generated partly by conscious intent,[1] but the apparent success and fulsome extravagance of the cult could only arise because the Russian people were peculiarly receptive to it.[2]

Stalin's personality was one which Westerners found difficult to understand.[3] Sometimes bland and polite, at other times deliberately rude, and always suspicious; perhaps, too, genuinely puzzled as to why the Westerners did not behave as representatives of a capitalist régime should—Stalin's myth confronted in the flesh with Stalin's reality made an awkward package for Westerners to handle. His personal capacity and industry were easily apparent; but what passed in the inner recesses of his mind, what he really felt and thought, could never be more than guessed. An enigmatic leader of an enigmatic people, Stalin fittingly symbolized the ambiguity which underlay the war-time co-operation between Russia and the West.

The traditions of the Russian bureaucracy (or bureaucracies, since the Party, Government, and army each constituted a bureaucracy in its own right) in one sense exalted Stalin's power and in another sense limited it. The bureaucracies were each characterized by a rigid authoritarianism: orders were orders and punishment for any failure to obey was likely to be

[1] When Stalin first met Lenin in 1905 he was surprised and disappointed at the lack of aloofness in Lenin's conduct. He wrote: 'I will not conceal from you that at that time this [i.e. Lenin's unassuming conduct] seemed to me to be rather a violation of certain essential rules' (Deutscher: *Stalin*, p. 78).

[2] It is an interesting speculation in the field of mass psychology to suggest that the Russian peasant family system, characterized by the despotic power of the father, prepared the ground for the popular reception of tsar or Stalin as a sort of super-father of all the Russians. The ambivalence which such relationship arouses among the sons can be paralleled in Russian history easily enough—an alternation of heroic dedication on the battlefield with wild revolt against authority. If this psychological analysis is well founded, one might expect changes in the Russian attitude towards authority in the course of a generation or two, since the revolution had done much to free the youth and womenfolk of Russia from the mujik's power; and conditions of family life in the new industrial centres could hardly reproduce very accurately the conditions of the village *isba*.

[3] Roosevelt after first meeting Stalin declared: 'I don't understand the Russians' and complained that he found 'nothing human to get hold of' in Stalin's personality (Frances Perkins: *The Roosevelt I Knew* (London, Hammond, Hammond & Co. [1947]), p. 72).

drastic. An unbroken chain of command reached from the humblest functionary to the very top of the Russian Government, Party, and army: and it was this that gave Stalin such tremendous power.

But just as Stalin was dependent upon his personal circle of advisers and colleagues for help in making up his mind and for access to the information upon which to do so, in a similar fashion the Soviet dictator was a prisoner of the administrative machines which wielded power at his command. They were clumsy, blood-stained juggernauts, incapable of fine adjustments to local situations: and this awkwardness of Russian administration resulted from its internal structure and traditions. When failure to get results or to show enthusiasm might be punished by death, exile, or imprisonment, subordinates at every level of authority were driven to try to out-do their superiors, to over-fulfil instructions, and to ride roughshod over opposition in a frantic effort to make a good impression on those who held authority over them.[1] But such obedience by subordinates must often have failed to realize the original intention of the man at the top. Men deprived of all personal initiative could not adjust action to local situations or to unforeseen new circumstances until, perhaps, serious damage had been done by foolish and frantic efforts to fulfil inapplicable orders.[2] It is certainly reasonable to suppose that Stalin did not always foresee nor perhaps did he always approve some of the acts of his agents both at home and abroad; yet he could hardly disown their deeds publicly save on very serious occasions, nor could he prevent recurrence of occasionally disastrous over-fulfilment of instructions.

Fear and sycophancy are no doubt powerful motives, but they do not make for wisdom and flexibility in administration. In particular, there must be a great likelihood that subordinates will systematically disguise from their superiors any failure to fulfil orders, and thus mislead them as to the facts of the case. Inspectors and journalists serve as a check against such practices; but they too can be corrupted in their turn, requiring inspectors of the inspectors and so on in an infinitely receding chain.

These ills were inherent in any bureaucratic organization to greater or

[1] Anyone familiar with army administration as it existed in America or Britain during the war will recognize how a general's lightest word might precipitate endless hurry and scurry among his aides and subordinates, sometimes quite out of proportion to the general's original intention. A factor in creating this phenomenon was the personal afflatus which an eager aide enjoyed when as agent for the general he clothed himself temporarily in the general's authority. This was a position which many men found intoxicating, to a point where they might take it upon themselves to anticipate the general's wishes or even to distort them by preparing things which he did not want or even disapproved. For an example of this sort of thing cf. Harry C. Butcher: *My Three Years with Eisenhower* (New York, Simon & Schuster, 1946), pp. 536–7, and *passim*. Sycophantic busybodies presumably existed in Russia too, and must have helped to make the Russian Government the violent, jerky machine it was.

[2] The most obvious example of this phenomenon was, of course, the disastrous over-fulfilment of the collectivization plan in 1930 which Stalin found necessary to check publicly with his speech 'Dizzy with Success'.

lesser degree. But the Russian bureaucracy, both under Tsardom and under Bolshevism, had been peculiarly liable to them, and for the following reason. If individual officials have a chance to make a career elsewhere in private life, they can afford to talk back to their superiors upon occasion, and can always afford to approach higher authority in a spirit which reflects a certain sense of human equality. Such quasi-independence may permit a fruitful exchange of opinion and information up and down the bureaucratic hierarchy. In Russia, however, officials had never had alternative careers, and this was truer under Bolshevism than it was before the Revolution. As a result, everything depended on staying in the good graces of established authority—and a slavish obedience to even the most foolish order was the almost inevitable consequence. Taken in the mass, the resulting attitude of mind among officials established a maddeningly irresponsible machine—a machine which could not be adequately controlled from the top since no single mind could comprehend all the circumstances or foresee all the difficulties which might arise when a particular order was given; nor, as has already been suggested, could the individuals at the top prevent their original intentions from being sometimes betrayed in the act by exaggeration and over-fulfilment on the part of mindless and consciencelesss subordinates.

Nevertheless, however clumsy and erratic the Russian bureaucracies were, it must be recognized that their rigid authoritarianism and ruthless disregard of human feeling had their compensations. Just as military discipline in the West proved itself capable of organizing human energies into instruments of vast power otherwise unattainable, so the Russian administration proved itself capable of organizing the energies of all Russian society to achieve hitherto unparalleled changes in traditional social and economic relationships. The achievement of the Bolsheviks should be compared to the achievement of the French revolutionaries of the late eighteenth century. Just as the French in their day proved to a reluctant Europe that government was a creature of men's will and habit and not something established by God, so the Russians in the twentieth century seemed well on the way to demonstrating to a reluctant world that economic and social relations were man-made, capable of transformation in accordance with a deliberate plan. In both France and Russia the resort to violence and bloodshed by the revolutionaries appalled outsiders; yet, to meet the challenge created by each revolutionary régime, it proved necessary to imitate in principle, while changing in detail, the central innovations of the revolution. Thus it was a nationalized and in some essentials a liberalized Europe that defeated Napoleon; and in the mid-twentieth century Western nations were hard at work transforming their economies into planned, governmentally directed instruments of policy, after the pattern first consciously and deliberately created by the Bolsheviks.

The major advantage of economic and social planning as developed by the Bolsheviks was the relatively enormous concentration of the total resources of the society which could be directed towards any desired end. Since the early 1930s, the overriding end towards which the Bolsheviks worked was military strength; and the course of the Second World War amply demonstrated the new-found military effectiveness of the régime.

Success in grandiose socio-physical engineering such as the Bolsheviks undertook required first of all a capable and hard-working group of managers in whose hands control and planning might be lodged. Through the Communist Party the Russians were able to create such an *élite*. Success also required a compliant population. This prerequisite, too, the Russians created, partly by persuasion, partly by compulsion. The relations between the managers and the mass was one of artificer to his materials. Callousness towards human life inevitably resulted—a callousness which had long roots in Russian tradition but which Bolshevik doctrine reinforced and made morally respectable. The original Marxian ideal became oddly inverted. Self-appointed rulers acted on the principle that they knew better than the masses themselves what was good for them; and this doctrine gave the Bolsheviks a moral sanction for horrible deeds against their own people and against neighbouring peoples—all in the name of the greater good of the larger whole in the indefinitely distant future. This moral attitude might perhaps be counted as a third prerequisite for the Bolsheviks' success in socio-physical engineering. Without it the nerve of the ruling clique would almost certainly have failed,[1] and the acquiescence of the mass would have been much harder to win.

However repulsive some of the manifestations of the Bolshevik transformation of Russia might be to Western minds, it must be admitted that their example had been indirectly influential upon the policies of all the leading Governments in the world. By demonstrating how the sphere of governmental control within human societies might be expanded, the Bolshevik example had transformed the nature of international relations. This was particularly manifest in the methods of mobilization which were developed by all the belligerent nations during the Second World War.[2]

[1] Cf. Stalin's most enlightening remarks to Churchill comparing the strain of war with the strain of collectivization (Churchill, iv. 447–8; U.S. edition, iv. 498–9).

[2] The likenesses between war economies as developed in the West in the First and Second World Wars and the peace-time Bolshevik economy as developed in Russia between the wars would be worth detailed study. It has been suggested that part of the Bolshevik blueprint in the early days was borrowed from or inspired by German war mobilization in 1914–18 (Deutscher: *Stalin*, p. 341); and, whether consciously or not, both British and American war mobilization in 1939–45 took something like Russian forms. Instead of relying upon price to direct and control production, physical controls, manipulated to achieve production goals assigned in advance, became characteristic of British and American as well as of Russian economic practice.

Indeed one of the most significant aspects of Bolshevism was its doctrine and practice of war. From its inception, Bolshevism was a warlike creed. The Bolsheviks first came to power in time of war, and they consolidated their rule over Russia as leaders in a civil and foreign war. Conceived in war and dedicated to the proposition that war was inevitable and universal until the world revolution should change the basis of human society, it was hardly an accident that Bolshevik language was shot through and through with military metaphors. The production front, the battle of industrialization, the wheat-gathering campaign, revolutionary cadres, &c., dominated the Russian newspapers of the 1930s as the battles of Moscow and of Stalingrad dominated them in 1941 and 1942.

Indeed, one might say that the Soviet régime destroyed the traditional distinction between war and peace. Class war within nations and between nations became, by orthodox doctrine, the normal relationship short of the millenary world revolution. Overt 'legal' war, in such a view, was merely an unusually active phase of chronic hostility. Instead of regarding war as a temporary and exceptional extension of politics, using forcible means, politics became merely an expression of class war, whether within or between nations.

In the actual conduct of war, the most striking characteristic of the Russians was their willingness to suffer enormous losses with apparent equanimity. 'When we come to a mine field', Marshal Zhukov said to General Eisenhower in 1945, 'our infantry attacks exactly as if it were not there. The losses we get from personnel mines we consider only equal to those we would have gotten from machine guns and artillery if the Germans had chosen to defend that particular area with strong bodies of troops instead of with mine fields.'[1] The hardihood, fatalism, and brutality of the Soviet troops, resulting from the rough and difficult life led by nearly all citizens of the U.S.S.R., were indispensable for the success of the policy adopted by the Russian generals.

The peculiarities of Russian practice with respect to warfare did not help to smooth Allied relations during the war years. Russian leaders could not easily understand the squeamishness of British and American generals when it came to losses. This became particularly prominent in debates over a second front. British protests against the terrible loss of life which a landing might entail sounded hollow in Russian ears. The temptation to interpret the British attitude as a thin disguise for a basic unwillingness to fight on the side of the Soviet Union was immeasurably strengthened by the basic Marxian tenets, according to which the British

[1] Dwight D. Eisenhower: *Crusade in Europe* (New York, Doubleday, 1948), pp. 467–8. Eisenhower comments: 'Americans assess the cost of war in terms of human lives, the Russians in the over-all drain on the nation.' [An English edition of *Crusade in Europe* was published in London by William Heinemann in 1948.]

and Americans should have behaved in just such a fashion, playing Germany off against Russia, and husbanding their own strength in the meanwhile.

When one considers how fundamentally different Russian society and government were from those of Britain and America, how inimical the ideology of Marxist-Leninism was to co-operation with the West, and how divergent were the national interests of Russia from those of her Allies—when one considers all this, the wonder is not that co-operation soon broke down, but that it was possible for co-operation to become as effective as it was during the later war years. Restraint and compromise on both sides—not only on Roosevelt's and Churchill's but on Stalin's too—made possible what was achieved; but the principal architect of the Grand Alliance was not any Allied leader, but Hitler himself. When his sustaining hand was removed, the Alliance soon fell to the ground.

But however vital Hitler's role was in shaping the Alliance that brought him to ruin, much depended on how the Allied nations responded to his challenge. The pages that follow will attempt to trace the history of the American, British, and Russian response.

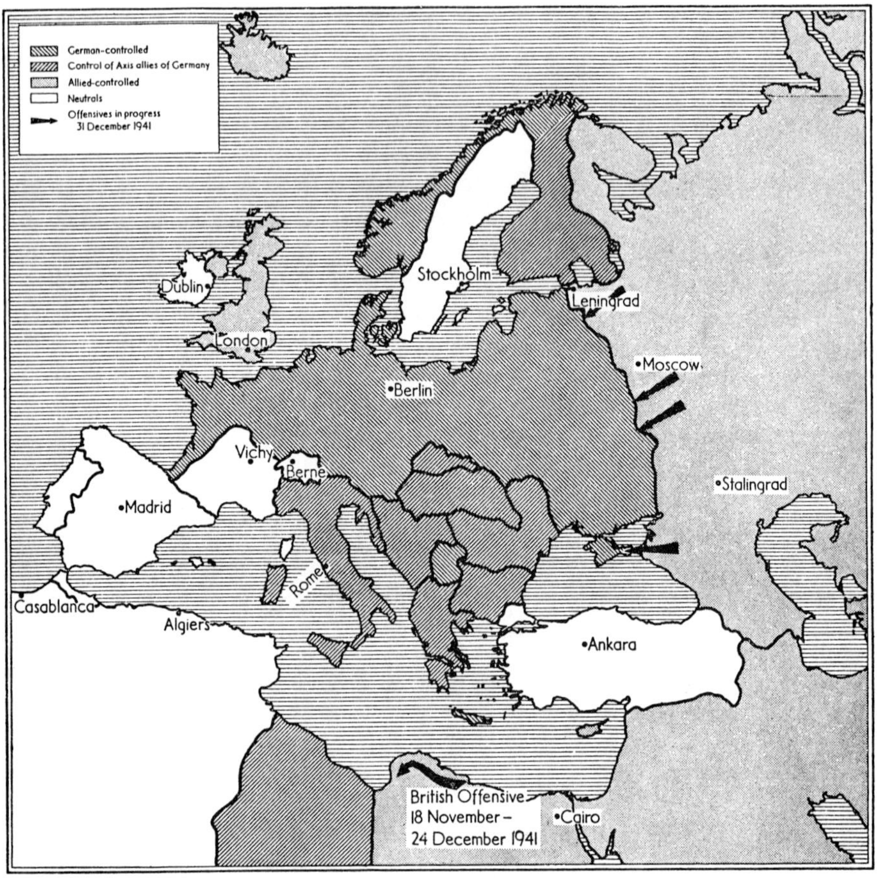

MAP I. EUROPEAN FRONTS, 31 DECEMBER 1941
(ARCADIA CONFERENCE)

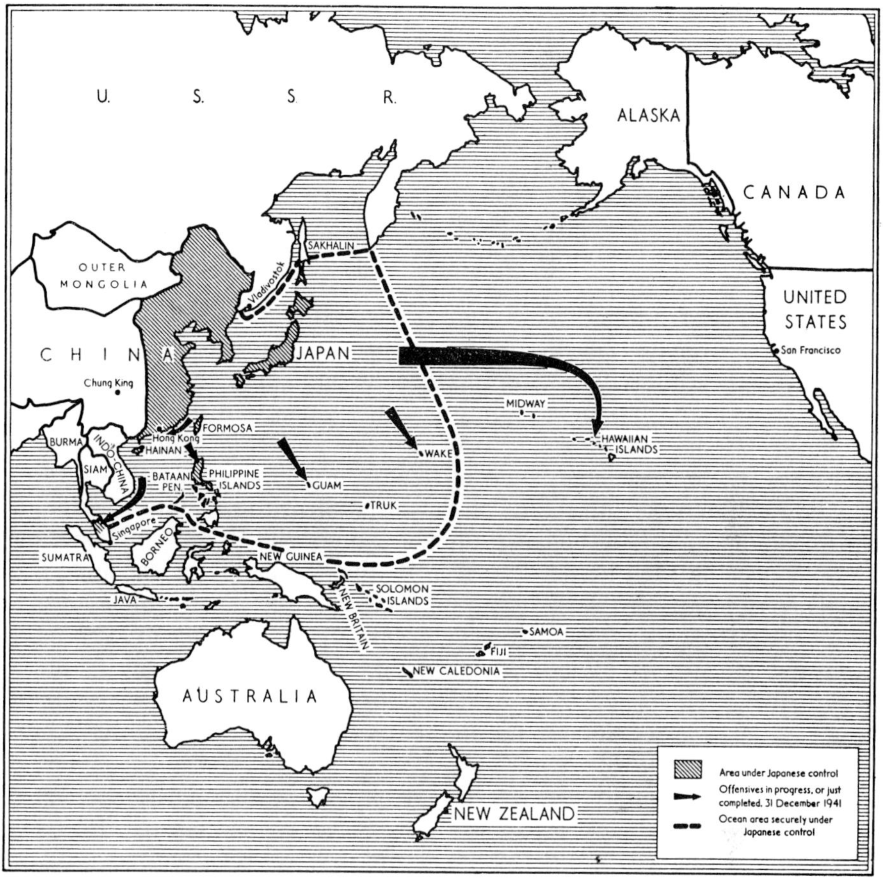

MAP 2. PACIFIC THEATRE, 31 DECEMBER 1941
(ARCADIA CONFERENCE)

CHAPTER II

RECOIL AND ADJUSTMENT TO GLOBAL WAR

DECEMBER 1941–NOVEMBER 1942

(i) The Arcadia Conference, Washington, 22 December 1941–14 January 1942

It did not take Churchill more than a few hours to decide that the new state of affairs created by Japan's Pacific attack required a top-level conference between himself and Roosevelt. The immediate military question of how to meet the Japanese assault was only a part of the problem which faced the 'Associated Powers'.[1] Of primary importance in Churchill's eyes were the longer-range issues of how to organize, how to distribute, and how to increase the forces at the disposal of the Allies in order to ensure victory. Thus in the telegram which he sent to Roosevelt proposing a conference he mentioned a review of 'the whole war plan' and 'the problems of production and distribution' as the subjects on which consultation would be desirable.[2] Roosevelt was not at once enthusiastic, and expressed concern for Churchill's personal safety; but Churchill brushed that consideration aside. On 11 December the conference was agreed upon, and eleven days later Churchill was installed as a guest in the White House for the first time.

Diplomatic punctilio was largely done away with. The fact that Churchill lived in the White House introduced a personal, private relation of host and guest into the political and military relation between the two chiefs of government. This both symbolized the peculiarity of Anglo-American relations and greatly simplified the business of getting things done. Informal contact at meals and even, on one famous occasion, in the bath, multiplied the opportunities for what diplomats call 'exchange of views'. What had been an acquaintanceship after the Atlantic Conference in August 1941 became, by the end of the Arcadia Conference in January 1942, something approaching friendship.

Churchill did not come to the Arcadia Conference single-handed. The British Chiefs of Staff[3] and Lord Beaverbrook, Minister of Supply, as well

[1] This was the term used until 29 December 1941 to designate the nations fighting against the Axis. It was thereafter replaced by the term 'United Nations'; but common usage retained the terminology of the First World War, and referred to the 'Allies' despite the fact that there was no formal treaty of alliance binding the United States to the other enemies of Hitler and Hirohito. There seems no reason not to follow usage even though it is technically incorrect.

[2] Churchill, iii. 541; U.S. edition, iii. 609.

[3] Field Marshal Sir John Dill replaced the Chief of the Imperial General Staff, General Sir Alan Brooke, in Churchill's entourage. Dill had recently retired from the post of Chief of the

as numerous assistants, secretaries, and subordinates, journeyed with the Prime Minister to Washington. These men promptly entered into conferences with their American opposite numbers so that the Arcadia Conference became the occasion for an intimate mingling of top-level British and American strategists. Procedure was not formalized in any rigid fashion, but the pattern which was to be followed at later conferences emerged clearly enough from the rush and confusion of those days in the White House.

Military discussion was the most formalized part of the Conference. The prior existence of a clear definition of military authority and responsibility within each Government made orderly procedure a relatively easy matter. Thus the American and British Chiefs of Staff held twelve meetings during the Arcadia Conference, and their intimate contact laid the ground for the future working of the famous Combined Chiefs of Staff Committee. Political questions were largely dealt with through personal discussion between Churchill and Roosevelt. When economic matters came up, the fact that the United States did not have any clear analogue to the British Ministry of Supply meant that consultation took a much less regular path. Hopkins was perhaps the chief figure with whom Beaverbrook had to deal; but Hopkins's activities were not confined to economic questions,[1] nor did he have any direct authority to carry out decisions which were reached.

Conclusions or disagreements, after they had been thrashed out on one or another of these consulting grounds, were brought before general sessions at which their advisers gathered with the President and Prime Minister. Through a process of continued discussion the whole group tried to weave various special plans into a workable, harmonious whole. When conflicts existed either within the specialized staffs, or between the proposals of one group of specialists and another, the discussion process could be slow, devious, and inconclusive.[2] But in general American and British points of view were remarkably harmonious. The persistent diffi-

Imperial General Staff, and Churchill preferred to leave the newly appointed C.I.G.S. in London (ibid. pp. 555–6 and 625–6 respectively).

[1] Nor were Beaverbrook's for that matter. Cf. Sherwood: *Roosevelt and Hopkins*, p. 457; Eng. edition, i. 470.

[2] The American record of the first plenary session of the Arcadia Conference is reproduced in Sherwood: *Roosevelt and Hopkins*, pp. 460–6; Eng. edition, i. 473–9. It opens: 'The President suggested that the status of Super-Gymnast [i.e. the project for landing in North Africa] be discussed.' And several hours later, the record concludes: 'Mr. Churchill then stated that the Staff is to check up on the actual impact of the plan on Gymnast and establish the earliest date on which it would be possible; and also what would be available for the expedition if an invitation arrived suddenly.' In one sense, nothing had been decided; but discussion had ranged all round the globe, and if a firm plan for a landing in North Africa was not agreed to, the reasons why it could not be undertaken at once were made clear.

Part of the apparent confusion embodied in this record may result from inexpertness on the part of the American secretarial staff, which was recruited at a moment's notice, and whose members in some instances continued to carry on normally full-time jobs in the Pentagon and thus had no time for careful preparation of the record.

culties arose not over questions of what should be done, but rather over the question of how the means could be found for doing what was agreed to be desirable.

The Americans approached the Arcadia Conference with no single, thoroughly prepared set of proposals. The lack of smooth and continuous consultation between branches of the administration was and continued to be characteristic of the American Government. Moreover, the frantic efforts required to meet the sudden emergency of war did not give high American officials any time to prepare themselves systematically for the Conference. Among the British, on the other hand, administrative conversion to war had long since been effected; and the week-long semi-isolation which Churchill and his staff enjoyed during their passage across the Atlantic gave them time to prepare for the forthcoming encounter with the Americans. Another factor should be mentioned. The outcome of the Conference meant everything to the British. If American effort and supplies had been turned away from Europe towards the Pacific, as Churchill feared might happen, British war strength would have been seriously undermined, and, despite everything, Britain would have been back in the desperate position of 1940. No parallel anxieties existed among the Americans. The Conference could not therefore appear as vital to them as it did to the British, nor did careful preparation for it seem so necessary.

As a result, the State Department, the War Department, the Navy Department, and President Roosevelt each came to the Arcadia Conference with more or less distinct points of view. State Department proposals were embodied in two documents. One was a declaration to be signed by all the nations fighting against the Axis. This document, subject to some modifications, became the Declaration of the United Nations. The other State Department document proposed the establishment of a Supreme War Council on which Russia, China, Britain, America, and perhaps the Netherlands[1] would be represented. Despite Hull's earnest efforts on behalf of this second proposal, nothing came of it.[2]

The U.S. Army General Staff in the person of its Chief, General George C. Marshall, sought one thing above all else from the Arcadia Conference: an agreement on the principle of unity of command in the field. This meant unity of command as among the different armed services and unity of command as among different nationalities in cases where the forces of different nations were active side by side. The only part of the world where the issue as between nations was of immediate practical importance

[1] The inclusion of the Netherlands as a possible fifth suggests that the men who drafted the document were thinking primarily of the war in the Pacific. Hull omits the Netherlands from his account, but the official publication (U.S.A., Department of State: *Postwar Foreign Policy Preparation 1939–1945*, Pub. 3580 (Washington, U.S.G.P.O., 1950), p. 62) mentions this part of the proposal. [This volume is referred to hereafter as *Postwar Foreign Policy Preparation*.]

[2] Hull (*Memoirs*, ii. 1114–24) explains the origin and the fate of these documents in some detail.

was South-East Asia, where American, British, Dutch, Australian, and—one degree removed—Chinese forces were all fighting against the Japanese. But the issue between the army and navy of the United States was present and very much alive wherever American forces were stationed. Long-standing disharmony and petty jealousy between the armed services made the U.S. navy suspicious of the principle of unity of command. The admirals feared they might lose their autonomy.[1]

On questions of general strategy, Marshall was content to build upon the basic decisions of ABC-1. This meant, first and foremost, the concentration of American offensive power against Germany and a holding operation against Japan until Germany had been defeated. But in December 1941 the problem of holding Japan within a fixed perimeter was not an easy one; and serious, detailed plans for the employment of American power against Germany had not been drawn up by the U.S. General Staff.

The view-point of the U.S. navy was less clearly and less forcibly presented at the Arcadia Conference. A new Commander-in-Chief, Admiral Ernest J. King, took over only two days before the Conference opened,[2] and the operational problems which beset him and his staff were even more harassing than those which faced General Marshall. But this only partly accounted for the navy's reticence. As has been said above, the navy suspected the principle of unity of command, but could offer no good military arguments against it; hence reluctantly agreed. On the issue of general strategy, the navy found itself similarly embarrassed. Prior agreements and convincing arguments could be advanced for the decision to concentrate first on Germany; but, by long tradition, the enemy against whom the U.S. navy had prepared itself was Japan. Most naval officers could not help feeling unhappy when asked to concentrate first against an enemy who could only be defeated on land, while leaving the humiliation of Pearl Harbour unavenged, certainly for months and perhaps for years. Thus after Pearl Harbour the navy's agreement to the general strategy of the war was never wholehearted. American admirals were always ready to lend a willing ear to arguments for the postponement of the wholesale commitment of American troops to Europe, for, once such an effort had been undertaken, it would automatically take top priority for all supplies, and postpone the building up of American naval strength in the Pacific for the war against Japan.

[1] Sherwood: *Roosevelt and Hopkins*, pp. 455–7; Eng. edition, i. 469–70; Churchill, iii. 597–8; U.S. edition, iii. 674–5.

[2] Admiral King's predecessor, Admiral H. E. Stark, had been active in preparing U.S. naval plans for co-operation with the British in case of war, and his long experience in this negotiation was not discarded. Both Stark and King took active part in the Arcadia Conference, and it was not until 26 March 1942 that Admiral Stark was removed from the post of Chief of Naval Operations.

Bureaucratic jealousy was an important element in these divergences between the State, War, and Navy Departments. The Supreme War Council recommended itself to the men in the State Department partly because the Council would include political (i.e. State Department) as well as military representatives.[1] The generals of the U.S. army were naturally gratified that sound military considerations dictated the formation of a large American army and its prompt use against Germany. The realization that pursuit of such a policy would give the army a relative priority over the navy in competition for man-power and supplies certainly did nothing to weaken their conviction that the policy was correct. The contrary pressure of the U.S. navy's ambitions upon its conceptions of strategy has been suggested already.

Roosevelt was of course the only person in a position to adjudicate such rival departmental ambitions. He approached the Arcadia Conference without any very clearly thought-out personal plans. But he was sure he wanted big goals, rapid action, noble ideals. As between the army and the navy he personally was sympathetic with the latter. He had been Assistant Secretary of the Navy in Wilson's administration, and was himself an enthusiastic amateur sailor. But in the strategic issue between the army and navy, Roosevelt's sympathies lay with the army view-point. Germany seemed to him intrinsically a greater menace than Japan, as it did to General Marshall.

The British point of view was, by comparison, single and definite. Churchill and his advisers wanted a reaffirmation of the strategic policy of ABC-1, decisions on the steps by which German defeat could be encompassed, and reassurance as to the continuation of the flow of American supplies. In the Pacific, they contemplated primarily a naval war, and hoped to be able to win American help in the defence of Singapore. Initial strategy against Japan was to be strictly defensive, aimed at holding the key bases of Hawaii, Australia, and Singapore. Against Germany the British proposed joint Anglo-American offensive action as soon as possible. The first step, they argued, should be to close the ring round *Festung Europa* by actions in the Mediterranean and, perhaps, elsewhere.[2]

Available records do not permit any day-to-day chronicle of the proceedings of the Conference. In fact military, economic, and political con-

[1] Hull: *Memoirs*, ii. 1118.

[2] While on board ship *en route* to Washington, Churchill composed three memoranda which he presented to Roosevelt upon arrival. The basic proposal of these documents was that in return for British naval help in the Pacific the Americans should send substantial ground and air forces to Europe as soon as possible. Sections from these memoranda are reproduced in Churchill, iii. 574–84; U.S. edition, iii. 646–58. Roosevelt presumably read them, but they did not become the basis for formal military deliberations at the Conference.

versations proceeded simultaneously, and constantly criss-crossed one another in the general sessions. It seems best to discuss the achievements of the Conference systematically even though any such arrangement disguises the informality and intermingling which actually characterized the procedure.

The major political outcome of the Conference was the United Nations Declaration. This document, after being drafted in the State Department, was discussed by the American Cabinet before Churchill's arrival. Roosevelt liked the idea of making such a declaration and broached the proposal to Churchill at the beginning of the Conference. He gave the Prime Minister the State Department text and asked him to suggest emendations. Roosevelt simultaneously made changes himself, and on Christmas Eve their two revised versions were compared and blended into one. The result was as follows:

> The Governments of the United States of America, the United Kingdom of Great Britain and Northern Ireland, the Dominion of Canada, the Commonwealth of Australia, the Dominion of New Zealand, the Union of South Africa, Belgium, China, Czecho-Slovakia, Greece, Luxemburg, the Netherlands, Norway, Poland, the Union of Soviet Socialist Republics, and Yugo-Slavia,
>
> Having subscribed to a common programme of purposes and principles embodied in the Joint Declaration of the President of the United States of America and the Prime Minister of Great Britain dated August 14th, 1941 and known as the Atlantic Charter,
>
> Being convinced that the complete and world-wide victory of all the Governments is essential to defend and preserve life, liberty, and independence as well as the righteous possibilities of human freedom, justice, and social security not only in their own lands but throughout the world, and that the struggle in which they are now engaged is the common defence of human decencies everywhere against savage and brutal force seeking to subjugate the world, declare:
>
> 1. Each Government pledges itself to employ its full resources against the Axis forces of conquest and to continue such employment until these forces have been finally defeated;
>
> 2. Each Government pledges itself to the other Governments associated in this Declaration to effect the full coordination of its military effort and the use of its resources against the common enemies;
>
> 3. Each Government pledges itself to continue war against, and not to make a separate peace with, the common enemies or any of them.
>
> Other Governments desirous of associating themselves with this Declaration are hereby privileged to accede to it.[1]

Roosevelt conceived the idea of signalizing the New Year by the issuance of the Declaration. This raised a number of difficulties, since the agreement of a large number of governments had to be secured in a very short period of time. There was a series of further changes in the text which in

[1] Sherwood: *Roosevelt and Hopkins*, p. 447; Eng. edition, i. 451.

their turn had to be agreed to; and the project of securing the signatures of all the nations at war with the Axis raised delicate questions of precedence and eligibility. In practice, active consultation as to details of the text was confined to three Governments: those of the U.S.S.R., Britain, and the United States. When the Big Three had reached agreement, the text was submitted to the other Allied Governments on a take it or leave it basis. Nevertheless, after some hasty telegraphy round the world, no less than twenty-six nations adhered to the Declaration by 2 January 1942.

The points which arose in negotiation with the British Government were three. First, what was the status of India? The British War Cabinet at first objected to the inclusion of India among the signatories of the Declaration, but by 29 December the British changed their stand and agreed that an invitation should be sent to India along with the Dominions.[1] The second issue was more complex. What of the Free French? The British Government urged that the text be amended to read 'Governments and authorities' in order to allow the Free French to sign the Declaration without obtaining recognition as a government.

This issue arose at a peculiarly unfortunate time. On Christmas eve 1941 small Free French forces landed on the islands of St. Pierre and Miquelon which lie just south of Newfoundland.[2] These islands had been under Vichy control, and, though the population enthusiastically rallied to the Gaullist cause, Secretary of State Hull was outraged. The expedition had been undertaken without the knowledge and indeed despite the disapproval of the Canadian, British, and American Governments. Moreover, de Gaulle's coup violated an agreement which had just been reached between American and Vichy officials for the maintenance of the *status quo* in all French possessions in the Western Hemisphere. Hull felt that the whole basis of American relations with the Vichy Government was endangered. He was therefore in no mood to make any concessions to the Free French. Roosevelt was by no means so angry, and in private conversation with the Russian Ambassador, Litvinov, apparently he argued in favour of the British proposal to admit the Free French signature. But Litvinov had to get authorization from Moscow, and by the time that Stalin's agreement had been secured it was too late to amend the text.[3]

[1] Churchill, iii. 590; U.S. edition, iii. 666; Hull: *Memoirs*, ii. 1120, 1123; Sherwood: *Roosevelt and Hopkins*, pp. 447, 453; Eng. edition, i. 451, 454.

[2] Details will be found in the *Survey* for 1939–46: *Hitler's Europe*.

[3] This negotiation offers a striking example of the manner in which Roosevelt carried on personal diplomacy behind Hull's back without fully and frankly informing the Secretary of State as to the position he took. Thus Hull in his *Memoirs* is emphatic in claiming that he had Roosevelt's support for his violent and, indeed, petty reaction to the St. Pierre and Miquelon incident (ii. 1130, 1132). But the records left by Harry Hopkins show the President in a very different light, agreeing in general with the British position (Sherwood: *Roosevelt and Hopkins*, p. 449; Eng. edition, i. 453). It seems clear that Roosevelt was anxious to conciliate Hull, who

The third issue that arose with the British Government was trivial. The phrase 'social security', which occurred in the draft of 24 December quoted above, was struck out in the course of revision. The British War Cabinet asked that it be reinserted; but someone, presumably Roosevelt, objected and the change was not made.[1]

The American Government, too, had an afterthought about the text. Religious freedom had been omitted from the phraseology of the Atlantic Charter, and some critics in the United States had objected to its absence among the goals for which the war was to be fought. This touched upon the delicate matter of religious, particularly Roman Catholic, opposition to co-operation with godless Russia, a matter to which Roosevelt had directed considerable personal attention in the preceding months. Consequently, Roosevelt raised the matter on 27 December with the British and Russians. The British had no objection, but Litvinov was at first considerably perturbed. However, he succeeded in getting the change approved by Moscow in time for its inclusion in the final text.[2]

On 27 December the Ambassadors of the various nations at war with the Axis were summoned in successive groups to meet the President and the Prime Minister. They were acquainted with the fact that a United Nations Declaration was in process of preparation, and were told that its text would be made available to them in a few days. This procedure ruffled a few diplomatic feathers in Washington, the more so because the Russians had been singled out for special treatment.[3]

On or before 27 December the preliminary text of the Declaration was communicated to Moscow, and on 29 December the Russian reply arrived. Soviet leaders had not apparently been informed that they were being consulted in advance of other Allied Governments, and proposed to withhold their signature. A separate Russian statement was instead prepared for release simultaneously with the Anglo-American declaration.[4] The difficulty lay in the fact that the Soviet Union was not at war with Japan, and was most anxious not to sign anything that would imply a commitment to fight the Japanese. But what Hull and Roosevelt wanted was a declara-

at one time considered resigning over the issue (*Memoirs*, ii. 1137). A change in the American Cabinet at the very beginning of the war would have been awkward for Roosevelt, and, moreover, he undoubtedly felt a sincere respect for Hull. But the method the President used to escape a showdown over the Vichy issue with his stubborn Secretary of State simply made things worse in the long run and introduced a profound confusion into the administration of American foreign policy.

[1] Sherwood: *Roosevelt and Hopkins*, p. 453; Eng. edition, i. 454; Hull: *Memoirs*, ii. 1123.

[2] Churchill (iii. 604–5; U.S. edition, iii. 682–3) records that Roosevelt thought it worth while amid all the press of business to speak privately and at length with Litvinov 'about his soul and the dangers of hell-fire'. It would be interesting to know what the Old Bolshevik thought of the President's effort on his behalf.

[3] '. . . we have been invited here today as "poor relations", whom rich and powerful uncles have to see from time to time' was the comment of the Polish Ambassador (Ciechanowski: *Defeat in Victory*, p. 101).

[4] Hull: *Memoirs*, ii. 1122.

tion that would unite all the nations fighting against the Axis, not separate declarations. By altering the original text they were able to provide Stalin with adequate escape clauses *vis-à-vis* the Japanese, and in the end the Russians agreed to sign a common document.[1]

The problem of precedence among the signatories was apparently settled between Roosevelt and Churchill themselves, with advice from their Governments. At the suggestion of the Americans, all the countries of Latin America which had declared war on the Axis were added to the list of those invited to sign the Declaration. Despite the request of the British Government that the Dominions be grouped together, as in the draft of 24 December, this was not done. Instead the principle of alphabetical arrangement was used to determine the order of appearance of the names of all the lesser Powers.

But the alphabet was not allowed to determine everything. Grouped at the head of the list were the United States, Britain, the U.S.S.R., and China—the first formal appearance of the 'Big Four' among the United Nations. There seems never to have been any question among the Americans that the United States should lead all the rest; and Churchill 'gladly accorded the first place' to his powerful ally.[2] Putting the Union of Soviet Socialist Republics among the first signatories of the Declaration was proposed as a gesture recognizing the military role played by Russian armies.[3] China was added to the topmost group as a result of American advocacy. The principle used to justify China's inclusion was that the nations 'actively engaged in war in their own countries'[4] should be separated from the others, though taken seriously such a principle would surely have excluded the United States from top billing.

These matters of precedence may at first sight seem trivial. But details of diplomatic protocol do reflect real distinctions sometimes. What is notable in the United Nations Declaration is the precedence assumed by the United States. Indeed, it appears that the whole initiative and driving force behind the Declaration came from Roosevelt and the American Government; and the calm way in which the Americans assigned precedence to themselves was acceded to by the other parties to the Declaration without remonstrance.

This reflected the real balance of forces behind the new United Nations alliance. Of the Great Powers, only the United States enjoyed a significant latitude of choice as to where and how to engage its forces. It followed

[1] The changes made to accommodate Russian susceptibilities may be seen in the facsimile text reproduced in Sherwood: *Roosevelt and Hopkins*, pp. 450–1 (not included in Eng. edition).

[2] Churchill, iii. 590; U.S. edition, iii. 666.

[3] 'I have a feeling', Roosevelt wrote to Hull, 'the U.S.S.R. would not be pleased to see their name following some of the countries which are realistically making a minor contribution' (Hull: *Memoirs*, ii. 1120).

[4] Sherwood: *Roosevelt and Hopkins*, p. 448; Eng. edition, i. 452.

that the extent to which the new association of nations would become an operative military alliance depended very largely upon American decisions. Both the Russian and the British Governments were willing to accept and indeed to welcome any American initiative which promised to bind the U.S. Government more closely to an Allied line of policy and action. Formal precedence in the signing of joint documents was a small price to pay for the help which America could and did give to both Britain and Russia.

China was, of course, never more than a courtesy member of the Big Four. It is a curious question why the Americans backed China's claim to rank as a Great Power. Sentiment had something to do with it perhaps.[1] There was also a wish to turn the page of European imperialism and begin a new era of world history; and in such a new era a country with the population, geographic extent, and potential resources of China might become a Great Power. It is also true that American army strategists entertained the project of building up the Chinese army in order to bring the full weight of Chinese man-power against Japan.[2] Had these plans been realized, and had a powerful, well-equipped, and well-trained Chinese army emerged from the war, some substance might have been lent to China's claim to rank with the Big Three. In view of these plans, it could be argued that an early 'courtesy' recognition of China's equality with the other three principal allies would be the best way to assure Chinese co-operation during and after the war. Finally, many Americans felt that China could be depended on to follow the lead of the United States, since they believed that both Russia and Great Britain had alienated the Chinese by past acts of imperialist aggression or exploitation. The prospect of a grateful, friendly, and dependent Chinese protégé with a secure seat in the counsels of the mighty appealed both to the chivalrous impulses and to the economic and political self-interest of Americans.[3]

The question of what the alliance against the Axis should be called had excited the attention of the President from the time of Pearl Harbour. During the initial stages of the drafting of the Declaration, the phrase 'Associated Powers' was used. This was designed to avoid the awkward

[1] Roosevelt himself had a family connexion with China of which he was very conscious (Sumner Welles: *Seven Major Decisions* (London, Hamish Hamilton, 1951), p. 78), and generations of missionary enterprise in China had made a deep impression on many millions of Americans.

[2] As late as 16 January 1943 the Combined Chiefs of Staff stated: 'It should be our basic policy to provide the man-power resources of Russia and China with the necessary equipment to enable them to fight'; and this they decided on the ground that those two countries were the 'most advantageously placed' to fight Germany and Japan respectively (Ray S. Cline: *Washington Command Post: The Operations Division*, series issued by the Department of the Army, Office of the Chief of Military History (Washington, U.S.G.P.O., 1951), p. 335).

[3] Churchill's private view was expressed as follows in a minute to Eden, 21 October 1942: 'As to China, I cannot regard the Chungking Government as representing a great world Power. Certainly there would be a faggot vote on the side of the United States in any attempt to liquidate the British overseas Empire' (Churchill, iv. 504; U.S. edition, iv. 562).

legal question of the limits of Presidential power. Treaties, of course, had to be submitted for ratification by the American Senate, but Roosevelt did not want to submit the proposed declaration to the risks of Senate debate.[1] A treaty of alliance—the normal name for an engagement such as that embodied in the Declaration—was thus out of the question. But the colourless term 'Associated Powers' seemed to emphasize the looseness of the ties between the nations at war with the Axis. On 29 December, Roosevelt hit upon the phrase 'United Nations' to take its place. When Churchill returned, on 1 January 1942, from a brief visit to Ottawa, time had run very short and Roosevelt intruded upon him in order to see what he thought of the phrase. The Prime Minister was taking a bath at the time, but emerged from the tub to ratify Roosevelt's idea.[2] No one else seems to have been consulted before the new title was announced; and indeed 'United Nations' appears only in the heading of the official text.

The phrase 'United Nations' opened up large vistas. A new world order and long years of future collaboration among the nations of the world was suggested by the parallel between United Nations and United States; and Roosevelt may be presumed to have had such a parallel in mind when he chose the name for the war-time alliance.

The text of the United Nations Declaration when it finally emerged from the tangle of telegraph wires was as follows:

A Joint Declaration by The United States of America, The United Kingdom of Great Britain and Northern Ireland, The Union of Soviet Socialist Republics, China, Australia, Belgium, Canada, Costa Rica, Cuba, Czechoslovakia, Dominican Republic, El Salvador, Greece, Guatemala, Haiti, Honduras, India, Luxemburg, Netherlands, New Zealand, Nicaragua, Norway, Panama, Poland, South Africa, Yugoslavia,

The Governments signatory hereto,

Having subscribed to a common program of purposes and principles embodied in the Joint Declaration of the President of the United States of America

[1] A legal opinion written by a State Department official assured Roosevelt that in signing an instrument such as the proposed Declaration he was not trespassing upon the Senate's powers. The argument was this: As Commander-in-Chief the President is empowered to prosecute the war as seems best to him; to prosecute the war successfully may require pledges from allies not to give up the struggle before victory has been achieved; but to secure such a pledge it must be reciprocated. Therefore the President is justified in making such a pledge (see Hull: *Memoirs*, ii. 1119).

[2] The three authorities upon which this account is based disagree as to the birth date of the United Nations. Churchill (iii. 605; U.S. edition, iii. 683) gives 1 January 1942; Hull (*Memoirs*, ii. 1124) gives 31 December 1941, and Sherwood (*Roosevelt and Hopkins*, p. 458; Eng. edition, i. 470) gives 29 December as the day on which the new name was adopted. Hull is clearly wrong, since Churchill left for Ottawa on 28 December and returned to Washington on 1 January 1942. It is, however, possible to reconcile Sherwood's and Churchill's chronology by assuming that Roosevelt conceived the new name on 29 December and sprung it on the Prime Minister only after his return. Hull's error may arise from the fact that he was first informed of Roosevelt's idea on 31 December.

and the Prime Minister of the United Kingdom of Great Britain and Northern Ireland dated August 14, 1941, known as the Atlantic Charter,

Being convinced that complete victory over their enemies is essential to defend life, liberty, independence and religious freedom, and to preserve human rights and justice in their own lands as well as in other lands, and that they are now engaged in a common struggle against savage and brutal forces seeking to subjugate the world, Declare:

1. Each Government pledges itself to employ its full resources, military or economic, against those members of the Tripartite Pact and its adherents with which such government is at war.

2. Each Government pledges itself to cooperate with the Governments signatory hereto and not to make a separate armistice or peace with the enemies.

The foregoing declaration may be adhered to by other nations which are, or which may be, rendering material assistance and contributions in the struggle for victory over Hitlerism.

Done at Washington
January First, 1942.[1]

On New Year's day 1942 Roosevelt, Churchill, Litvinov, and T. V. Soong (the latter newly appointed as Chinese Foreign Minister) signed this document in the White House. On the following day, 2 January 1942, the Declaration was deposited in the State Department where the Ambassadors of the other nations in due course added their signatures.[2]

Hull hailed the publication of the United Nations Declaration warmly: 'The Declaration by the United Nations joins together, in the greatest common war effort of history, the purpose and will of twenty-six free nations, representing the overwhelming majority of the inhabitants of all six continents. This is a living proof that law-abiding and peace-loving nations can unite in using the sword when necessary to preserve liberty and justice and the fundamental values of mankind.'[3] Churchill's retrospective comment was more measured in its enthusiasm. 'The Declaration', he wrote, 'could not by itself win battles, but it set forth who we were and

[1] *Documents on American Foreign Relations, 1941–1942*, pp. 203–8; Great Britain, Foreign Office: *Declaration by United Nations, Washington, January 1, 1942*, Cmd. 6388 (London, H.M.S.O., 1942). It does not appear from the available records who it was that boiled down the verbiage of the Declaration from its lengthier form of 24 December. Nor is it clear what version was originally submitted to the Russians for approval. Roosevelt himself may have been the man who rephrased the Declaration and reduced the three points to two. Facsimiles of his handwritten changes are published in Sherwood: *Roosevelt and Hopkins*, pp. 450–1 (not included in Eng. edition), from which it appears that in conferences with Churchill, at least, Roosevelt acted as secretary, writing in agreed modifications.

[2] Sherwood mistakenly says that all twenty-six nations signed on 1 January (*Roosevelt and Hopkins*, p. 453; Eng. edition, i. 455). Cf. Churchill, iii. 605; U.S. edition, iii. 683; and Hull: *Memoirs*, ii. 1125.

On 4 January 1942 the State Department declared that it would receive statements of adherence to the principles of the United Nations Declaration from 'appropriate authorities which are not governments'. This was intended to satisfy the Free French; but in fact de Gaulle did not avail himself of this back door which had been rather grudgingly opened to him (Hull: *Memoirs*, ii. 1125–6).

[3] Ibid., p. 1125.

what we were fighting for.'[1] Stalin's comment, if any, was not publicly recorded. In point of fact the immediate significance of the Declaration was wholly psychological. A Grand Alliance, the United Nations, was publicly arrayed against the Axis for the first time. The number of small nations that signed the document made an impressive list, and as other countries declared war on Germany and Japan the list grew longer still. Only the Americans perhaps took the statement of principles in the preamble to the Declaration very seriously as a programme for future international relations; but American ideas were, of course, far from being a negligible factor. Though the principles of the Declaration did not in fact govern future international relations, and from that point of view one might consider it empty rhetoric, yet from another point of view the Declaration did have important practical results. The grouping of Great and Little Powers implied by the order of signatures to the Declaration was preserved throughout the war years as the legal-diplomatic framework of the Alliance, despite the unreality of the position accorded to China. Moreover, the United Nations Organization, when in due course it emerged, bore marks of its origin in this Declaration.

The Declaration may be regarded as the first post-Wilsonian fruit of active American diplomacy on the stage of world politics. As a reflection of American thinking, replete with both high principle and easy optimism, it was symptomatic of a new departure in international affairs.

The text of the United Nations Declaration was released to the press on the day of its final signature, 2 January 1942. Comment in Britain and America was almost universally favourable, but the Russian press maintained a discreet silence. American journalists were on the whole more inclined to take the Declaration at face value than were the British. Thus, for example, the *New York Times* declared in an editorial (4 January 1942): 'The agreement . . . may prove to be as important a political document as any signed in human history'; whereas the *Sunday Express*, one of Lord Beaverbrook's papers, was more cautious: 'The Grand Alliance is a fact—signed, sealed, and delivered. . . . On paper the Grand Alliance is its [victory's] cast-iron guarantee. But figures won't bring it. Paper won't bring it. Orations won't bring it.'[2]

The preparation of the United Nations Declaration was only a small part of the activity of the Arcadia Conference; and in the British view it was hardly more than marginal. For Churchill and his advisers, the main thing was agreement on military strategy, and in fact questions of strategy, deployment, and military administration did occupy most of the time at the Conference meetings. The British fear lest the impact of events in the

[1] Churchill, iii. 605; U.S. edition, iii. 683.

[2] Editorial, 4 January 1942.

Pacific should have altered American military plans was dissolved at the start, when the Americans presented to the first meeting of the Chiefs of Staff a memorandum which read in part: 'Much has happened since February last, but notwithstanding the entry of Japan into the War, our view remains that Germany is still the prime enemy and her defeat the key to victory. Once Germany is defeated, the collapse of Italy and the defeat of Japan must follow.'[1] When they heard these words the British Chiefs of Staff must have heaved a sigh of relief, for their fears had been lively.

A second British apprehension was that the Americans would insist upon diverting their military production wholesale to the task of equipping the American armed forces. 'What will harm us', Churchill wrote in one of his memoranda prepared for the Conference, 'is for a vast United States Army of ten millions to be created which for at least two years while it was training would absorb all the available supplies and stand idle defending the American continent.'[2] This fear, too, proved ungrounded. Roosevelt was as anxious as anyone to see American troops in action, and welcomed proposals for their speedy deployment against the Germans.

It was, however, one thing to propose and quite another to dispose. Shortage of shipping, which proved to be the major preoccupation of Allied strategists during the ensuing two years, constituted the main bottle-neck. The immediate problem which faced the Conference was defensive deployment of ships and troops in the Pacific in order to assure communication with Australia and the Far East. General Marshall had prepared a plan for garrisoning New Caledonia as the principal way station *en route* to Australia; but shipping for this and other projects in the Pacific could only be found by diverting vessels from other urgent assignments. In the Atlantic theatre the Americans agreed to send troops to Northern Ireland where they could complete training. These troops not only would help to secure the safety of the British Isles but also would make it possible to use overseas some fully-trained British divisions which would otherwise have been required for the home security of Great Britain. Action was speedy. Before the Arcadia Conference ended American troops had started on their way to Ireland. The move was publicized as a propaganda stroke against both German morale and whatever lingering isolationist sentiment there was in the United States.

The pressure of the immediate emergency was so great that no firm, definite, and detailed agreement about long-range offensive strategy could be reached at the Conference itself. Nevertheless, the British proposed a definite plan. It was based on the assumption that the offensive in Libya then in progress would lead to the complete destruction of the Axis armies

[1] Sherwood: *Roosevelt and Hopkins*, p. 445; Eng. edition, i. 449.

[2] Churchill, iii. 581; U.S. edition, iii. 655.

in North Africa. When this had been achieved, they wished to see an American and British expeditionary force land in French North Africa, preferably with, but if necessary without, the prior agreement of Vichy authorities. This plan, known by the code-word Gymnast,[1] was tentatively scheduled for the spring of 1942; but the time-table was not definitely fixed. The unknown variable of Vichy policy made Churchill anxious to be able to send at least a token force at any moment, should a sudden invitation from French authorities arrive.

Success in North Africa would 'close the ring' round Germany and open the way for a landing in force on the Continent in 1943. Churchill's conception of the final operation against Germany was that several landings should be made simultaneously by relatively small, but very well equipped, armoured forces. 'It need not be assumed', he wrote, 'that great numbers of men are required. If the incursion of the armoured formations is successful, the uprising of the local population, for whom weapons must be brought, will supply the corpus of the liberating offensive.'[2]

The U.S. General Staff had not had time to prepare any detailed long-range plans of its own for the employment of American troops against Germany. Thus Marshall had no specific counter-proposal to present to the Conference. Nevertheless, he was unenthusiastic if not positively opposed to the plan, and other high American officers shared the same view.[3]

Roosevelt was personally attracted to the North Africa scheme. Dakar had loomed large in his pre-Pearl Harbour thinking as a threat to the security of the American hemisphere, and the occupation of French North Africa would remove that danger. Moreover, the opening of the Mediterranean would greatly shorten supply routes and relieve some of the pressure upon shipping. The most important military consideration was, of course, that no other plan seemed to provide a chance for the active employment of large numbers of American soldiers against the enemy in the near future. Yet Anglo-American offensive action in the near future seemed vitally necessary to relieve some of the pressure on the Russians.

[1] 'Gymnast' had first been applied to an American plan for seizing Casablanca. At the Arcadia Conference the enlarged scheme for combined Anglo-American action to occupy the whole of French North Africa was dubbed 'Super-Gymnast', but on both sides of the Atlantic the new proposal was nevertheless usually referred to simply as 'Gymnast'. (Cf. W. F. Craven and J. L. Cate, edd.: *The Army Air Forces in World War II*, Office of Air Force History, United States Air Force (Chicago, University of Chicago Press, 1948), i. 240–1). This is only one instance of the sort of confusion in the exact use of code-names which was frequent in the early stages of combined Anglo-American planning, when changes occurred rapidly and repeatedly.

[2] Churchill, iii. 583–4; U.S. edition, iii. 657. Sherwood (*Roosevelt and Hopkins*, 459; Eng. edition, i. 472) says that the British estimate was that Germany's final defeat would come as a result of a British attack from the west, an American attack from the south (i.e. from North Africa), and a Russian attack from the east.

[3] Joseph W. Stilwell: *The Stilwell Papers* (New York, Sloane Associates, 1948), pp. 20, 25; Eisenhower: *Crusade in Europe*, p. 22.

A final consideration which always bulked large in Roosevelt's mind was the precarious state of American public opinion. In the days immediately after Pearl Harbour American attention was largely fixed upon the Pacific, and in particular upon the defence of the Philippines; and it was not difficult to imagine circumstances in which overwhelming public pressure would require the diversion of major American strength to the Pacific against the Japanese. This, as we have seen,[1] was in fact demanded by leading newspapers which had been isolationist before Pearl Harbour. The surest and best way of preventing such concentration of public attention on the Pacific was to start operations in the European theatre. The balance of news would then be shifted away from exclusive pre-emption by the Japanese front, and the American public could be depended on to support an offensive already under way. There seems little doubt that this consideration underlay Roosevelt's insistence upon the earliest possible engagement of American troops in the European theatre.

The upshot of the deliberations of the Conference was an agreement to study the logistical and other requirements of Gymnast. No one denied that the operation would be advantageous to the Allied cause. The question was rather the availability of the necessary ships, men, and equipment. Even before the end of the Conference it had become clear that the hope for a complete victory in Libya would not be realized, and with that hope the original basis of the Gymnast plan disappeared. A victorious British army would not be on hand at the border of French Tunisia for some time to come; and lacking that *point d'appui* any landing would have to be undertaken on a larger scale than had first been conceived. Thus, in spite of Roosevelt's favourable attitude to the British plan, no firm commitment to Gymnast, much less a definite schedule of operations, could be agreed to. The pressing requirements of defensive deployment in the Pacific and the unexpected power of enemy counter-strokes in the Mediterranean made Anglo-American offensive planning premature.

Though General Marshall had no clearly formulated long-range strategy to present to the Conference, he did have some very definite ideas about the principles of military administration which should govern Allied operations. The agreements which were reached in these matters proved to have the greatest importance for the general conduct of the war and for the shaping of Anglo-American co-operation. On Christmas Day Marshall put his position before the British and American Chiefs of Staff. His remarks appear in the official record as follows:

I express these as my personal views and not those as a result of consultation with the Navy or with my own War Plans Division. As a result of what I saw

[1] See above, pp. 3–4.

in France and from following our own experience, I feel very strongly that the most important consideration is the question of unity of command. The matters being settled here are mere details which will continuously reoccur unless settled in a broader way. With differences between groups and between services, the situation is impossible unless we operate on a frank and direct basis. I am convinced that there must be one man in command of the entire theater—air, ground, and ships. We cannot manage by cooperation. Human frailties are such that there would be emphatic unwillingness to place portions of troops under another service. If we make a plan for unified command now, it will solve nine-tenths of our troubles.

. . . I am willing to go the limit to accomplish this. We must decide on a line of action here and not expect it to be done out there. I favor one man being in control, but operating under a controlled directive from here. We had to come to this in the first World War, but it was not until 1918 that it was accomplished and much valuable time, blood, and treasure had been needlessly sacrificed.[1]

It is important to realize the radical nature of Marshall's proposal. In view of the later successes which attended Allied enterprises in the war, it is easy to think that combined staffs and unified theatre commands necessarily and naturally resulted from the Anglo-American war relationship. But in 1941 such had not been the intention or expectation of the strategists of either Britain or America. In ABC-1 the principle of separate national responsibility for definite areas was laid down: one nation was to assume command in each theatre, and, when needed, troops or ships or aeroplanes from the forces of the other nation would serve under alien command. But Marshall now proposed a step farther. He wished to see in each theatre of war the forces of the different nations and services placed under the control of a single commander, assisted by a joint or combined staff incorporating into a single body representatives of the nations and services concerned. Such a proposal involved a reduction in the control exercised over the armed forces by their respective national governments and by the separate services. In so far as joint staffs and unified commands were realized in practice, they marked the beginning of the emergence of a supra-national armed force, not of course independent of ultimate national control, but none the less in significant degree and for day-to-day administration insulated from normal national direction.

It is probable that neither Marshall nor those who disagreed with him at the time of the Arcadia Conference saw the matter in such a light. The U.S. navy was reluctant to accept the proposal, and the British, too, found it hard to swallow. British plans had looked to a retention of the principle of separate areas of responsibility, even for the massive operation of invasion of the continent of Europe. It may be supposed that Churchill at least had thoughts of the long-range future of the British Empire and of

[1] Sherwood: *Roosevelt and Hopkins*, pp. 455–7; Eng. edition, i. 469.

British influence in such regions as the Far East.[1] Combined staffs and unified command over British, American, and other Allied contingents would at the least blur British control in such areas, and might lead to the substitution of American for British influence in important and extensive regions of the world.

The theatre where decision was most urgent—South-East Asia—was one in which practical obstacles to Marshall's proposal were peculiarly great. Not only British and American, but also Dutch, Australian, New Zealand, Chinese, and Indian forces were all engaged there against the Japanese, and the lack of adequate communications in a little-developed part of the world made the establishment of a single command additionally difficult. Practical obstacles such as these were urged, and urged emphatically, by Churchill and others against Marshall's proposal. 'The situation out there', Churchill was recorded as saying, 'was that certain particular strategic points had to be held, and the commander in each locality was quite clear as to what he should do. The difficult question was the application of resources arriving in the area. This was a matter which could only be settled by the Governments concerned.'[2]

Harry Hopkins arranged a private meeting between Marshall and Churchill to discuss the matter. During a long conversation the Prime Minister was able to assess the depth of Marshall's determination; and despite misgivings Churchill decided to yield. Roosevelt played his part in assuring this outcome by backing Marshall's arguments to the full. Characteristically, once he had been won over Churchill entered wholeheartedly into the project and lost no time in urging the War Cabinet to give approval to what he described as a 'war-winner'.[3]

By 29 December the matter was settled, and General Sir Archibald Wavell had been chosen to take over the Allied command in South-East Asia. It was the Americans who proposed that the supreme command of what was called the A.B.D.A. (i.e. American, British, Dutch, Australian) area should be given to a British general. The first reaction of the British Chiefs of Staff was one of pleased surprise, but they realized that under the proposed arrangement Wavell would take public blame for future defeats which clearly lay ahead. This they felt might be dangerous for Anglo-American amity. Churchill, however, resolutely quashed such fears and determined to accept the arrangement as proposed.[4]

[1] The paragraph in Churchill's telegram to the War Cabinet of 29 December 1941 which speaks of 'safeguarding the residuary interests of various Governments involved' must reflect discussion of this problem, though it does not make clear what decision was made (Churchill, iii. 599; U.S. edition, iii. 676).

[2] Ibid. pp. 597 and 674, respectively.

[3] Ibid. pp. 599 and 676, respectively.

[4] Another incident reflecting the opposition to Marshall's scheme was an effort, inspired presumably by American and/or British admirals, to exempt the naval command from Wavell's jurisdiction. This was prevented by Marshall, Hopkins, and Roosevelt at the last minute (Sher-

In theatres of war where combined Allied operations were not in progress, no changes in the existing arrangements were made. In China, however, after consultation with the Chinese Government, a second Allied theatre was set up. Chiang Kai-shek became 'Allied' Commander-in-Chief, and an American general was to be appointed as his 'Chief of Staff'. Obviously, an arrangement whereby an American became second in command in China, where almost no American troops were on the ground, was a very different sort of 'allied' command from one in which American, British, Dutch, and others contributed troops, ships, planes, *and* commanders. Events were to emphasize this difference by making plans for large-scale dispatch of American troops to China vain; but the differences were less apparent at the beginning of January 1942 when the two new Allied commands were announced to the world.

Agreement upon the principle of unity of command in the field raised the even more important question of unity in the high command itself. This confronted the Conference more directly than before with the question of limiting national authority over the armed forces. At first the general question was not faced. Rather, discussion was directed to the question: What shall be the chain of authority over General Wavell in his new command? On 29 December 1941 the Chiefs of Staff proposed that no special body should be set up to supervise Wavell. Such a body, they argued, would be ineffective. It would have to incorporate representatives of all the lesser nations concerned in the theatre; and such representatives would be unable to arrive at decisions without consultation of their home governments.

After discussing the question with Hopkins, Roosevelt rejected this advice. Instead he proposed a new committee, comprising three American and three British representatives of the respective national armed services, with an Australian, a New Zealand, and a Dutch representative attached in an advisory capacity. It is instructive to see how piecemeal and unforeseen was the origin of what came to be called the Combined Chiefs of Staff Committee, one of the most powerful bodies in the world during the latter years of the war. For this was its beginning, in the President's emendation of a memorandum dealing with the arrangements to be made in a single theatre of operations.

When Roosevelt's new proposal was put before the Conference, it 'kicked up a hell of a row', in Harry Hopkins's words.[1] The British speedily broadened the issue. An international military authority whose power was limited to a single theatre of operations would, they pointed out, become meaningless unless it had authority to decide what men and

wood: *Roosevelt and Hopkins*, pp. 458, 467; Eng. edition, i. 470, 480). American army leaders believed that the Royal Navy was the prime mover in this affair: cf. *The Stilwell Papers*, p. 18.

[1] Sherwood: *Roosevelt and Hopkins*, p. 469; Eng. edition, i. 481.

supplies should be sent to the scene of action. But decisions of that sort could not be taken without consideration of all the rival claims upon war production which every Allied country and every theatre of operations was making.

Among the proposals which the British had brought with them to the Conference was one for the establishment of a permanent military planning organization upon which each of the British and American armed services would be represented.[1] The British plan called for each nation to take control over definite sectors of the battle front; and the planning organization was conceived as a means whereby the military undertakings of each nation could be concerted. But power to decide upon any action would be reserved to the respective national governments and their separate military commands. Obviously the establishment of Allied and unified commands in the Far East interfered with the neat working of any such scheme; yet Roosevelt's piecemeal proposal for the establishment of a special committee to control the 'allied' commanders in each theatre begged the question of how to distribute the resources available to the two Governments between theatres.

In the discussion that followed, the two initial proposals were merged and blended until the concept of a Combined Chiefs of Staff Committee emerged as the only logical method of dealing with the problem. The Combined Chiefs differed from Roosevelt's original concept in having a world-wide jurisdiction; it differed from the British proposal in having more than mere planning powers.

The authority assigned to the Combined Chiefs of Staff at the Arcadia Conference was, however, primarily logistical. The Committee was authorized to 'settle broad programmes of requirements based on strategic policy', to 'issue general directives laying down policy to govern distribution of existing weapons', and to 'settle the broad issues of priority of overseas movement'.[2] The relatively limited scope thus assigned to the Combined Chiefs of Staff Committee reflected both the original British proposal and the unwillingness of the British Government to sign away too much of their national independence of military action to an untried body. But it soon became obvious that control of the materials for waging war was inseparable from control of operations themselves, since nothing could be undertaken without supplies. Hence it was not long before the Combined Chiefs of Staff were impelled to ask for a broadening of their authority to cover the entire 'strategic conduct of the war'. This new definition of the Committee's function was approved on 21 April 1942.[3]

[1] Hancock and Gowing: *British War Economy*, p. 389.

[2] Cline: *Washington Command Post: The Operations Division*, p. 100.

[3] Ibid. A most important fact which helps to explain the power which the Combined Chiefs of Staff came to exercise was the personal friendship and constant companionship which established itself between President Roosevelt and Admiral William D. Leahy from July 1942 until

The manner in which the Combined Chiefs of Staff came into existence, and the gradualness with which the new body asserted its power over the conduct of the war, minimized what might otherwise have become a troublesome problem. Lesser Allied nations could not be expected to approve an arrangement which in effect excluded them from the inner counsels of the High Command; and at the time of the Arcadia Conference there was much talk of the establishment of an all-embracing Allied body on the model of the Supreme Allied War Council of 1918. Expecting the establishment of such a council, the lesser nations missed the boat, which at its first launching seemed destined to freight only a limited cargo of military technicalities.

The agreement to establish the Combined Chiefs of Staff Committee raised the question of where the new body should meet. American primacy in supplies and man-power was obvious, and the Committee's initial assignment was to supervise their distribution. This provided a good reason for locating the Combined Chiefs in Washington; and the fact that the American capital was also midway between the European and Pacific theatres of war could be adduced as a second argument. The British therefore agreed that the normal site for the new Committee's operations would be Washington.

In actual fact the Combined Chiefs of Staff Committee did not come formally into existence until after the Arcadia Conference had ended. One reason for this was that some preliminary adjustment of American military administration was necessary. A body analogous to the British Chiefs of Staff had not existed in the United States before Pearl Harbour. A War Council, comprising the President, the Secretaries of State, War, and the Navy, the Army Chief of Staff, and the Chief of Naval Operations, had met at irregular intervals; and there was also a Joint Army-Navy Board which considered special problems assigned to it by the President. But no regular, continuous, day-to-day machinery for consultation among the top-level commanders of the U.S. army and navy existed, and it was not until February 1942 that the American Joint Chiefs of Staff came formally into existence.[1]

The decision to hold the meetings of the Combined Chiefs of Staff Committee in Washington implied that deputies would represent the British Chiefs of Staff at most meetings. The first British representatives

Roosevelt's death. Leahy became the President's personal representative with the Combined Chiefs of Staff and was able to gain access to Roosevelt's office at almost any time when a critical matter came up for decision. No other organ of the American or Anglo-American administration could so regularly secure Presidential attention to its proposals; yet on countless issues the President's ruling was final and, in case of dispute, necessary. Hence from July 1942 onward the U.S. Joint Chiefs of Staff and the Combined Chiefs of Staff had something of an inside track in any and all disputes with other governmental agencies, thanks to Admiral Leahy's unique personal position. Leahy's own book, *I Was There* (London, Gollancz, 1950), is the best evidence of his special role; but cf. Cline, op. cit. p. 105.

[1] Leahy: *I Was There*, p. 125.

on the Committee were recruited from among men already on hand in Washington. Sir John Dill, who had come with Churchill to the Arcadia Conference in place of the C.I.G.S., remained behind, and became the senior British member of the Combined Chiefs Committee. He represented Churchill personally, rather than any one of the British armed services. His appointment at first raised some question among the Americans who were not used to the idea that military matters should be mixed up in politics. It was objected that Dill had a political capacity; and the problem was solved only by the subsequent appointment (July 1942) of Admiral William D. Leahy as personal representative of the President on the Committee.[1] As it turned out, Dill's appointment was a peculiarly fortunate one. He succeeded in winning the personal confidence and friendship of General Marshall, and indeed of all his American colleagues to a degree that no other British representative ever did. The other British deputy members representing the Royal Navy, the R.A.F., and the army changed frequently, and did not have anything like the personal influence that Dill exercised.

From January 1942 throughout the war the Combined Chiefs of Staff Committee met once a week, and upon occasion more frequently. Normally, the British Chiefs of Staff and the American Joint Chiefs of Staff considered outstanding questions separately ahead of time, and then proceeded to compare and reconcile their distinct national views at the Combined Chiefs' sessions. However, it would be a mistake to suggest that differences in the Combined Chiefs Committee always or even usually developed along national lines. Divergences between the Services often eclipsed national differences; and such 'domestic' differences were aired freely enough in the meetings of the Combined Chiefs.

The great decisions of strategy were taken during the periodic meetings between Roosevelt and Churchill which punctuated the war years. On these occasions the British Chiefs of Staff were always on hand, and replaced their deputies on the Combined Chiefs of Staff Committee. Only what might be termed the routine of Allied administration was entrusted to the Combined Chiefs in Washington. But routine administration is the essence of government; and the Committee gave a substance and continuity to Anglo-American military co-operation which could hardly have been achieved in any other way. Since the British representatives were in constant telegraphic contact with their superiors in London, they could

[1] This solution simultaneously solved the problem which had arisen between the U.S. army and navy over numerical preponderance on the Combined Chiefs Committee. To match the British arrangement and to satisfy the *amour propre* of the army air force, an air representative had to be placed on the Committee. But the U.S. navy demanded (and got) equal representation, despite the absence of any logical reason for the arrangement. Leahy's appointment in another capacity neatly solved the problem by providing a real function—liaison with the President—for a second naval member of both the U.S. Joint Chiefs of Staff and the Combined Chiefs of Staff.

from day to day present with authority the latest thinking of the British high command to the Americans and, equally, inform the British of American plans and opinions. As circumstances shifted, the Committee was able to make adjustments in the disposition of Anglo-American resources within the framework of the general strategy which had already been agreed to. In addition, the Committee kept Anglo-American war plans under constant review, and on all major questions drafted recommendations for the approval of Roosevelt and the British War Cabinet. A secretariat and numerous sub-committees appointed to give expert advice on special aspects of the military effort greatly extended the practical importance of the Combined Chiefs Committee by assuring its members access to the best available information upon which to base their recommendations and decisions.

The most prominent of the legal powers which the Combined Chiefs of Staff Committee came to exercise was its right to supervise Allied commanders, such as General Wavell in 1941–2 or General Eisenhower in 1943–5. In proportion as such combined commands became important in the war, the Combined Chiefs Committee encroached upon the separate national military administrations. The overlapping of personnel between the national high commands and the Combined Chiefs Committee avoided any possibility of conflict; and, indeed, men like Marshall or Dill must sometimes have forgotten whether they were acting as a member of a Combined or of a national Chiefs of Staff Committee.

The advantages of operational co-ordination between Britain and America both sustained and helped to create the Combined Chiefs of Staff Committee. Yet it seems fair to say that its power came to rest more on its ability to control the flow of war materials to the various theatres of action than upon its right to order Allied commanders to undertake a particular operation or campaign. Indeed the logistical and the operational sides of warfare were so intimately connected that it is really false to try to distinguish: supplies, shipping, troops, planes, and naval vessels were the determinants of every campaign, and it was as the Combined Chiefs of Staff agreed to dispose these over the globe that one or another military enterprise became feasible.

No effort was made at the Arcadia Conference to bring the Russians into the Combined Chiefs of Staff Committee. There is no published evidence to suggest that the Russians ever wanted to join regularly in the Committee's deliberations. The Soviet system did not lend itself to committee work, since Stalin was unwilling to delegate powers of strategic decision; nor was the Soviet dictator prepared to put the operations of the Red Army under any sort of combined command. Even more important was the fact that Russia was not at war with Japan. The *raison d'être* of the new combined committee was the need to balance and direct the Anglo-American war effort against the two ends of the Axis, and in this enterprise the Russians could have no share as long as their whole effort was directed to a single front against a single enemy. By the time when the Russians were preparing to enter the war against Japan, the Combined Chiefs of Staff Committee was a going concern, and there seemed every reason to keep its smoothly working organization in being without risking disruption through attempting to include men who spoke a different language and whose national interests were so distinct from those of Britain and America.

By the time of the Arcadia Conference Britain had come to depend upon the United States for essential war supplies; and one of Churchill's primary purposes in visiting Washington was to assure some sort of satisfactory system for dividing American war production between American, British, and other needs. This became the next item of business at the Conference after the Combined Chiefs of Staff Committee had been agreed to.

As usual, the British had definite proposals to present. According to their scheme a series of Anglo-American boards should be set up, of which the military planning committee, mentioned above, was only one. The others were listed as a Supply Board, to handle procurement and allocation of raw materials as well as to supervise munitions production itself; a Munitions Assignment Board; a Shipping Control Board; and, as a possible supplement, a board to co-ordinate measures of economic warfare.[1] President Roosevelt jibbed at the proposal to set up a Supply Board with such sweeping responsibilities; and in the end it was agreed that only a Combined Raw Materials Board would be set up immediately, leaving responsibility for the planning and expansion of production to the respective national authorities. The proposal for a Combined Shipping Adjustment Board met with no dissent; but the suggestion for a combined economic warfare organization was abandoned.

It did not prove difficult to come to agreement on these points; but a prolonged and at times bitter struggle arose over the organization of a Munitions Assignment Board. The underlying issue was, of course, who would get what and when. American officers were clamorous in their demands for military and naval equipment of all sorts. Many felt that their needs should be met first, and only surplus items should be given to the British or other allies.[2] But in the months just after Pearl Harbour,

[1] Sherwood: *Roosevelt and Hopkins*, p. 470; Eng. edition, i. 482; Hancock and Gowing: *British War Economy*, p. 389.

[2] Stilwell's remarks about the diversion of supplies to the 'Limeys' reflect an attitude quite widespread among Marshall's immediate subordinates (*The Stilwell Papers*, pp. 16, 22–23).

there was no surplus. Had any such principle been accepted, American deliveries to Britain and Russia would have stopped or been reduced to a trickle. Actually, the responsible heads of the United States army and navy never disallowed Allied claims upon American war production point-blank, but they were under considerable pressure from their subordinates, who needed everything, and more than everything, that could be produced. The British, of course, felt that it was essential that American supplies coming to them should not be cut off nor much reduced, and they were prepared to bend every effort to that end.

The debate that took shape round the question of the powers and organization of the proposed Munitions Assignment Board was therefore tense and prolonged. The original British proposal was based upon the principle of separate spheres of military responsibility. They proposed that definite portions of American war production should be allotted to Britain in much the same fashion as had already been done for Russia by the First Russian Supply Protocol. Then a British Munitions Assignment Board would allocate all the supplies available to the British Government among the various nations and armies within their sphere of military responsibility, while an American Board did likewise with the remnant of American production left after British and Russian needs had been supplied. According to their original proposal the British sphere of military responsibility would have included the occupied countries of Europe, the Near East, and the British Dominions and colonies; while Latin America and China were to be entrusted to the Americans.

This idea failed to appeal to any of the Americans present at the Conference. They were determined to control the distribution of all American war production themselves, but were willing to allow the British a voice in arguing over particular cases and to recognize the general principle that supplies should be sent where need was most urgent. Specifically, the Americans advocated the establishment of a single Munitions Assignment Board which would distribute the combined Anglo-American production all round the world in accordance with strategic directives from the new Combined Chiefs of Staff Committee. Such a proposal, given the potential bulk of American production and the fact that the Combined Chiefs were to sit in Washington, would in effect have assured the Americans a predominant voice in the military planning for every theatre of war. This the British were most reluctant to accept, for it would have meant a general sacrifice of their autonomy in military matters.

The dispute was not concluded until the last day of the Conference, on 14 January 1942. In the end an uneasy compromise was reached. Twin boards were set up, one in Washington and another in London, headed respectively by Harry Hopkins and Lord Beaverbrook. The Washington Board was to deal with the allocation of all American-made munitions, the London Board with that of all British-made munitions; and, although it was not clearly stated in the agreed text, Harry Hopkins declared that his Board was to be regarded as a sub-committee of the Combined Chiefs of Staff.

The British accepted this proposal with the greatest reluctance, and their acceptance was only conditional. They agreed to try the arrangement for a month. In practice it remained in force throughout the war. Friction between British and Americans over the distribution of munitions did not come to an end, but no better scheme for dividing what was available could be agreed upon. In general the system worked out well enough and it provided the Combined Chiefs of Staff Committee with the most potent basis of its influence. Since the Combined Chiefs disposed of American munitions production through the Munitions Assignment Board in Washington, their decisions could be and were translated into military action. The London Board, in comparison, played a minor role. It proved in practice to be something like a branch office of the Washington Board rather than the co-ordinate body which had been agreed to on paper at the Arcadia Conference. The reason was that British munitions production was smaller than American, and depended for essential raw materials upon allocation from Washington. Thus by granting or withholding raw materials and finished munitions, the Washington Board could in effect control much of British war production, whereas the London Board had no comparable lever over the American economy.

Nevertheless, within its own sphere the London Board had real power. The European Governments in Exile were in much the same relationship to the British as were the British to the Americans; indeed, their dependence on British bounty was even greater. Also the British Dominions, except Canada, depended in very considerable degree for their military equipment upon British production and allocation of supplies. Yet as compared with the American colossus Britain was indeed puny; and the effect of the decisions taken at the Arcadia Conference was to create a machinery for Anglo-American combined military administration which lodged the supreme direction of the war securely in Washington. Given the balance of resources between the two countries, no other result of a combined effort could easily be imagined.

A constant source of conflict in the months of scarcity that followed was caused by the unwillingness of American military leaders to place their demands on the same basis as those of other Allied nations. The British felt that American military requirements should be 'justified' with statistics and careful calculations of the use to be made of the material in the same way that they had to justify each demand they made on American bounty. The American army and navy, on the other hand, naturally felt that they had first claim on home production, and that the

British and other Allies should be content with material that in their own judgement could be spared from American military needs. No paper agreement could eliminate the diversity of American and British views on this point; but friction never became so serious as to endanger the major outlines of administrative co-operation and integration which had been drawn up by the Arcadia Conference.

Just as the establishment of the Combined Chiefs of Staff Committee required preliminary adjustment of American military administration at home before it could function smoothly, so also the economic administration of the combined British-American war effort required changes in American domestic economic administration. In both spheres the Americans profited extensively from British advice and the model available in British practice. Thus Lord Beaverbrook played a leading part in stimulating American officials to set their sights high for the production of munitions. The War Production Board, established on 13 January 1942 just before the Conference came to an end, was entrusted with broad powers to carry out the enlarged programme of production which Roosevelt had put before the nation. The achievements of American economic mobilization and its integration into the Allied war effort will be described separately,[1] and need only be mentioned here as another question taken up during the Arcadia Conference.

A major aspect of the Arcadia Conference was the impact it had upon public opinion, especially in the United States. Churchill's arrival was announced at once, and he and Roosevelt interviewed the press on the second day of the Conference. Christmas festivities at the White House provided the occasion for public appearances and announcements by both Roosevelt and Churchill; and, indeed, the American newspapers were fed with a steady stream of human interest stories. The ingenuity of journalists padded out the bare bones of official communiqués with abundant speculation and surmise upon the course of deliberations, but nothing of the strategic decisions was revealed.

The first announcement issued from the White House after Churchill's arrival contained the following sentence: '. . . the present conferences in Washington should be regarded as preliminary to further conferences which will officially include Russia, China, the Netherlands, and the [British] dominions.'[2] This provoked a flood of speculation and comment, and most journalists expected the establishment of an all-embracing Allied War Council. Such speculation did much to obscure the significance of the actual achievements of the Conference in the direction of strictly Anglo-American co-operation, and it was not until some time later

[1] See below, pp. 124 seqq.

[2] *New York Times*, 23 December 1941.

that expectation of an extension of the machinery of inter-governmental co-operation to include other nations ceased to agitate the newspaper commentators.[1]

During his stay on the western side of the Atlantic, Churchill made two public speeches. On 26 December 1941 he addressed a joint session of the Senate and House of Representatives; and four days later he addressed the Canadian Parliament in Ottawa. Both speeches were well received, and were given the widest publicity through radio and newspapers.

The net effect of all this publicity upon the state of mind of the American public cannot be accurately assessed, but it seems clear that the liberal policy of the White House publicity staff in giving out titbits of news was intended at least in part to remind Americans of the British role in the war and to consolidate Anglo-American good feeling. Newspaper comment on the Conference proceedings was uniformly laudatory, both in the United States and in Great Britain; and no hint of the differences of opinion which arose in the course of the Conference leaked into the public prints.

By the end of the Conference, both British and American participants had much to congratulate themselves upon. The British were assured that American forces would be directed primarily against Germany and that American munitions supply would not be cut off. As for the Americans, they had been able to get their way on nearly all disputed points. More than that, the groundwork for the most intimate and effective war-time alliance of history had been well and truly laid. The marriage of Britain to America was to be closer than either partner had expected before the Conference began; and, while American predominance on most of the Combined Boards was unmistakable, yet it remained true that both nations had surrendered a portion of their sovereign control over the separate national armed forces by subordinating them to a combined over-all direction.

Retrospectively, it is easy to recognize the tremendous importance of the decisions taken at the Arcadia Conference for the future of Anglo-American co-operation. In general, one may say that the basic institutions through which the co-operation was to be carried on were established or took new forms during the Conference.

[1] The White House announcement of 22 December reads strangely in the light of information which has since been published. In view of the fact that Roosevelt brushed off Hull's proposal for the establishment of an Allied War Council without giving it serious consideration (Hull: *Memoirs*, ii. 1121) it is hard to believe that he really looked forward to the establishment of any all-embracing Allied framework of co-operation. It is much more probable that Roosevelt chose to announce Churchill's visit in the way he did in the hope of warding off criticism from persons who distrusted too much British influence in Washington. He may also have wished to avoid giving the Russians, Dutch, and Chinese the impression that the war was to be an Anglo-American enterprise.

Other important consequences flowed from the Conference. The prolonged and intimate contact between British and American top-level administrators stimulated the Americans to overhaul their domestic administration in the direction of the war mobilization pattern already worked out in Britain. The failure of Secretary Hull to get on personally with Churchill, and his petty dudgeon over the St. Pierre and Miquelon incident, sealed the fate of the State Department as far as influence on the high decisions of the war were concerned. From that time on Hull was excluded from the inner counsels of the American Government, and American foreign relations came to be administered in a curiously ambiguous fashion, formally through the regular channels of diplomacy, and in all important matters informally through the President's own office.

As far as Britain was concerned, the Arcadia Conference showed up clearly the impossibility of a truly independent policy. For better or for worse, Britain depended on America; and American influence in the united counsels of the two Powers proportionately increased. It is true that the British plan for a landing in North Africa was accepted in principle, but in the other matters that came under discussion American preponderance was clearly manifest.

Finally, the Conference, as it turned out, set the pattern for Anglo-American military relations—or rather lack of relations—with Russia. In effect two separate wars were being fought. The Russian war with Germany had only a tenuous connexion with the Anglo-American war with Germany, Italy, and Japan. Supplies which the Western Allies shipped to Russia, and the common subscription to declarations such as that produced at the Conference itself, formed the only connecting link. The task of trying to establish real and effective co-operation between the Russians and the West in their war against Germany was to prove difficult. Yet efforts were made, some of them not totally in vain. It is the story of these efforts which will constitute one of the central threads of this history.

(ii) Economic Mobilization and Integration of Allied Effort during 1942

(a) The Allied War Economies in 1942

The hesitation and half-measures which had characterized American economic policy in the months before Pearl Harbour were quickly transformed into an all-out effort for increased war production when the United States suddenly found herself under attack. Far-reaching changes were necessary. Factories had to be converted to munitions work. New methods of administration had to be developed to control and direct production into channels most useful for the war effort. Shortages of material, of plant, and, at a later stage, of man-power had to be met. Jurisdictional quarrels between different branches of the Government had to be kept within tolerable limits. Conflicting claims upon the product of American factories had to be adjudicated. And, overriding all other considerations, production had to be increased at a rate and to a level that had hardly been dreamed of before. The simultaneous impact of so many demands upon the American economy inevitably produced confusion on a grand scale, and indeed it was not until the last months of 1942 that the main outlines of war-time economic administration attained definition.

American war production was of such central importance for the entire Allied war effort that it will be discussed more at length below.

In Great Britain, the new demands of war in the Pacific made no such drastic change. Britain had already converted production to a war basis, and after more than two years of war had developed techniques of organization and control which endured for the rest of the war period. New problems of course arose, especially shortages of such critical raw materials as rubber and tin resulting from the Japanese conquest of Malaya. An even more critical problem was the shortage of shipping which became more acute than ever after Japan opened a new front in the distant Pacific. In 1942 the total tonnage of British imports had to be cut down to just 42 per cent. of pre-war averages because there were no available ships; but, despite considerable anxiety lest industrial stocks and food run short, no important ill effects were felt.[1] Actually munitions production continued to increase, though at a relatively modest rate; and no one went seriously short of food.

Upon Churchill's return from the Arcadia Conference, he made an important change in the administrative set-up of the Government. A new Ministry of Production was announced on 5 February 1942, but owing to special problems of personnel and party politics the Ministry did not become a functioning reality until mid-March when Oliver Lyttelton assumed its direction. The Ministry of Production was intended to have three main functions. At home, a general supervisory control over all the Ministries concerned with war production was entrusted to it. This was designed particularly to prevent unregulated 'raiding' by, for example, the Ministry of Aircraft Production, which in the past had seized man-power and materials from other Ministries. In general the new Ministry was expected to assure a balance between different production programmes by controlling the application of resources according to a general plan. A second main function of the Ministry of Production was the correlation

[1] Hancock and Gowing: *British War Economy*, p. 434. Owing to a number of devices to reduce the bulk of imports, the total value did not decrease so drastically. The index figure for the value of British imports in 1942 was 70 (1938 = 100).

of military strategy with schedules of production. A third duty was the integration of British with American production programmes. In the original conception of the job, this third aspect was the most prominent; but, before Lyttelton took over the new Ministry, he was assured of rather wider powers over domestic production than Churchill had at first been prepared to delegate to him. Actual administration of the production programmes, however, was left in the hands of the Ministries already in the field, subject only to the 'general direction of the Minister of Production'.[1]

The establishment of a Ministry of Production met a criticism of the Government's economic policies which had been widespread, especially among Labour members of Parliament. They had argued that over-all co-ordination and central, balanced production planning were required, and could not be achieved by the co-ordinating committees which the new Ministry displaced. In the months after the establishment of the Ministry of Production, munitions and other war production did increase in Great Britain and a greater measure of division of labour between American and British economies was established. In this achievement the Ministry of Production played a part. But it would be easy to exaggerate the degree of integration and balanced planning that was really achieved. Strategic uncertainties, which persisted throughout 1942, made long-range production planning on a secure military basis impossible. Moreover, the apportionment of production between the United States and Great Britain was influenced at least as much by accident—success or failure in a squabble over raw materials or finished goods—as it was by any over-all rational plan. But when almost every muniment of war was desperately short what mattered most was an increase in production, and that was achieved.

In comparison with the United States the British war effort in 1942 was both greater in intensity and smoother in its administration.[2] Many factors contributed to this result—in particular, the longer time that Britain had been at war. Moreover, the task which confronted the Americans in 1942 was greater than that which the British had faced in 1939. The very size of the United States and the complexity of its industrial plant was not all. The main lever by means of which the British Government directed the economy was control over imports and shipping. But in the United States governmental control of imports and shipping brought no parallel control over the economy as a whole. A far greater proportion of the raw materials of industry originated within the boundaries of the United States itself than was the case with Great Britain. As a result, supply points were dispersed, totals could not easily be calculated, and

[1] Great Britain: *Office of the Minister of Production*, Cmd. 6337 (London, H.M.S.O., 1942).

[2] Hancock and Gowing: *British War Economy*, pp. 366–70.

distribution according to a single, central plan was much more complicated. In cases where raw materials had to be imported into the American economy, control not much less effective, if at all, than the control exercised so widely by the British Government was speedily established in the United States.

The Russian economy in 1942 was, like the American, in the throes of adjustment to war conditions; but in almost no other respect was there much likeness. A centralized economic planning organization had been set up in Russia more than a decade before the war began. In the first months of war, some new Commissariats were established to direct phases of the munitions programme (e.g. People's Commissariat of Tank Industry); and a new directing body, the State Defence Committee, was entrusted with 'operational control' over the fulfilment of war production plans.[1] But these were changes in detail. The major principles of state economic planning which had been developed during the successive Five-Year Plans continued to operate throughout the war years.

The problems Russia faced were not so much those of organization and control as those of physical production. German conquest of the western parts of the U.S.S.R. deprived the Soviet Government of access to the most developed part of the country; and it was only with the utmost difficulty that the losses were made good. In 1942, indeed, the losses were not made good. Total production remained much lower than in 1940, but large-scale conversion to munitions work made it possible by March 1942[2] to equal the 'war output' of 1940. But 1940 was a year of peace for the Soviet Union, and it was not until the autumn of 1942 that supplies for the Red Army became adequate to sustain offensive operations for more than a few weeks at a time.[3]

The problems of conversion to war production were complicated for the Russians by the geographical shift which the German invasion made necessary. The regions of the Urals, Volga, and to a lesser degree, Transcaucasia, Siberia, and Central Asia, became the seats of much new war

[1] Voznesensky: *The Economy of the U.S.S.R. during World War II*, p. 21.

[2] Voznesensky: *The Economy of the U.S.S.R. during World War II*, pp. 16, 25. The basis and general reliability of official Russian statistics are always something of a mystery to outsiders. The statistics in Voznesensky's book are frequently misleading, and are nearly all expressed in percentages which have no definite quantitative base. A figure such as that quoted in the text was presumably calculated in roubles, which introduces another variable—monetary inflation—which may distort the result. Unless war output was exceptionally low in 1940—a possibility, since the Russians were in the course of introducing new models of such items as aeroplanes and tanks when the war broke out (ibid. pp. 46–47)—it is hard to believe that production could have been restored by March 1942 to the pre-war *physical* volume.

[3] Kalinov: *Les Maréchaux soviétiques vous parlent*, pp. 125, 260. According to Kalinov, one of the reasons why the Soviet offensive in the winter of 1941–2 was not more successful was the shortage of munitions.

industry. Many plants were successfully transferred from the Ukraine, Moscow, or Leningrad to new sites in the east; but the process of transplantation was not an easy one, and it often took a long while for a factory to get back into production.[1] An especially difficult problem was the supply of power to the factories transplanted and built anew in the eastern parts of the U.S.S.R. The supply of fuel was a closely connected and scarcely less difficult problem. Metals, particularly aluminium, were also seriously short, as one would expect in war-time.[2]

It is not clear from the official account how much trouble the Russians had in regulating the flow of materials through the industrial system. This was the most difficult problem which American administrators had to face, and one that never arrived at an altogether perfect solution. Nicolai Voznesensky, the head of the State Planning Commission during and after the war, mentions incidentally that the Russian economy exhibited a marked seasonal fluctuation during the war years. Production declined as much as 12 per cent. during winter months, owing to difficulties with respect to transportation of raw materials and fuel.[3] From this it is evident that the flow of materials was not always smooth; but how much production lines may have been held up even during summer months by irregularity in delivery of materials or parts cannot be stated.

As compared with Great Britain or even the United States, Russian war economy was remarkably self-contained. Deliveries from the Allies were small compared with the total Russian industrial production.[4] However, the bulk or even the value of Lend-Lease and Mutual Aid supplies hardly does justice to their importance to Russia. Some of the items, e.g. rubber and ball-bearings, were crucial to Russian production and helped to relieve critical shortages which might otherwise have immobilized large sectors of the Russian industrial plant. Likewise the finished munitions delivered to Russia filled critical gaps in home production.

In general, the Russian war economy retained a far greater degree of independence than did the British war economy. Political considerations as well as the obstacles of geography contributed to this result. Another factor was the comparative simplicity of Russian war production. The whole range of naval supplies was not produced in Russia, and relatively little radar and other electronic equipment was manufactured for the use

[1] Thus 55 plants had not resumed production in the Urals region by the end of 1942 out of a total of 455 which had been transferred thither (Voznesensky: *The Economy of the U.S.S.R. during World War II*, p. 29).

[2] Ibid. pp. 40–43.

[3] Ibid. p. 92; cf. p. 67.

[4] Voznesensky says that supplies from Britain and America amounted to only 4 per cent. of Russian production (ibid. p. 44). This figure is really meaningless, since there was no real common basis for valuation between Russian and Anglo-American products; and, while Voznesensky does not say how the figure was calculated, one can assume that it was done in such a way as to minimize the Anglo-American contribution to Russian victory.

of the Russian armies. Russian tanks, artillery, and rockets were as good as any in the world. On the other hand, Russian aeroplanes were nearly all short-range, tactical machines, less complex than the big bombers used by British and American air forces for strategic attack. The net effect of these limitations on Russian war equipment was to simplify production very considerably; and the relatively simpler production schedule made self-sufficiency easier to attain.

A final factor, and one of great importance in the Russian war effort, was the extraordinary hardihood and toughness of the population. Being accustomed to a much lower standard of living than the people of Britain or of America, the Russians were able to endure a reduced civilian supply that would have proved intolerable to the nations of the West. Correspondingly, a greater proportion of total industrial production could be diverted to military uses; and imports necessary to sustain a higher level of consumption could be and were dispensed with.[1]

The same parsimony was exercised in the ranks of the Red Army. Troops in the field were supplied on a much more Spartan scale than was done by Great Britain and, especially, the United States. The direct saving in consumption was multiplied by savings in transport and in rear area supply and administrative personnel. A far higher proportion of the total strength of the Red Army entered directly into combat than was the case with the British or American armies. Because Russian soldiers would accept and could withstand extreme privation, the frequent inadequacies of the Russian supply system did not destroy the army's fighting capacity as similar breakdowns and shortages would surely have done with British or American soldiers. Private poverty, if it can be dissociated from ignorance and technical incompetence, is one of the greatest military assets a country can have. Russia approached that optimum condition in the Second World War.

Gaps in Russian statistics and the general differences between Russian and Anglo-American society make any detailed comparison of the intensity or efficiency of the respective war efforts impossible. There can be no doubt that the war hurt the Russians more than it hurt either of the Western Powers. Human and capital losses in Russia were far more severe; and these losses were felt especially in 1942, the period now under consideration. The question of Russian efficiency is one of peculiar interest, but it cannot be answered with any assurance. Labour productivity fell below pre-war levels in 1942 in many important industries. Military discipline and compulsory overtime work were imposed upon the labour force in 'war industry and industries connected with it'.[2] Women and children

[1] Cf. Alexander Werth: *The Year of Stalingrad* (London, Hamish Hamilton, 1946), pp. 63–65, and *passim* for an account of semi-starvation in the northern region of Russia in 1942.

[2] Voznesensky: *The Economy of the U.S.S.R. during World War II*, p. 20; cf. pp. 64 seqq.

were brought into industry on a large scale by financial and other means of compulsion. On *a priori* grounds one would expect such forcible methods to reduce labour efficiency; but, when morale was sustained by patriotism and flaming hate of the invading Germans, it is possible that no widespread or serious resentment, with consequent loss of efficiency, was aroused. Similar compulsion in Great Britain, though used far more sparingly than in Russia, had little deleterious effect, for it was sustained by popular opinion. The same may well have been true in Russia.

(*b*) Reorganization of the American Economy

One of the important results of the Arcadia Conference was the establishment of greatly expanded goals for American war production. Urged on by Lord Beaverbrook in particular, American officials began to think in almost astronomic terms. On 6 January 1942, in his annual message to Congress,[1] Roosevelt made public a part of the new goals which he had set for the American economy in 1942. He announced that orders had been sent to the appropriate agencies of the Government directing them to take steps to assure the production in 1942 of the following:

60,000 planes
45,000 tanks
20,000 anti-aircraft guns
8 million tons of merchant shipping.

These figures were derived in part from the calculations of the men who had drawn up the Victory Program,[2] but the President himself rounded off the figures and revised them upward arbitrarily.[3] The corresponding figures for items actually produced in 1942 were as follows:

47,836 planes
25,000 tanks
14,400 anti-aircraft guns
8·09 million tons of merchant shipping.[4]

Thus, except for ship-building, achievement lagged a long way behind the President's announced goals.

One reason for this apparent shortcoming was that production pro-

[1] *Documents on American Foreign Relations, 1941–1942*, pp. 45–53.
[2] See above, pp. 16–17.
[3] Sherwood: *Roosevelt and Hopkins*, pp. 473–4; Eng. edition, i. 486–7.
[4] These figures are taken from *Industrial Mobilization for War*, i. 534–9. There is considerable discrepancy between the figures published in this and other official documents. Thus a pamphlet, *War Production in 1942*, issued (presumably early in 1943) by the Division of Information, War Production Board, uniformly gives higher figures than those quoted—in the case of AA guns the difference is as much as 20 per cent. Figures in U.S.A., War Production Board: *Wartime Production Achievements and the Reconversion Outlook: Report of the Chairman, October 9, 1945* (Washington, U.S.G.P.O., 1945) differ only slightly from those given above, and in some instances are the same.

grammes were shifted, and shifted several times, in the course of the year. The President's round figures were early abandoned. In any case they covered only a small part of the total variety of munitions which had to be produced; and it soon became apparent that it would be the height of folly to produce all the tanks Roosevelt had called for if there would not be ships to carry them to the scene of battle, nor trained men to use them. Indeed, the multiple problems of balancing production as between end products, adjusting them to the expected demands imposed by strategic plans, and, finally, pooling production between America and the Allies in the most efficient possible fashion soon became inextricably intertwined with the simple engineering problem of meeting physical production goals.

In the first months of 1942 the full complexity of war-time economic administration had not been fully grasped by anyone in Washington. The first impulse was to expand production as fast as possible. Everything was short, and everything was needed. On 13 January 1942 Roosevelt entrusted the job of expanding production to a new agency, the War Production Board (W.P.B.). It differed from its predecessors in having a single responsible head, Donald M. Nelson, with full powers of decision and of execution. The grant of authority to the W.P.B. was very broad, and all branches of the federal government were instructed to comply with the decisions of the W.P.B. in matters of war procurement and production.[1] In fact, however, the W.P.B. had to make its way gingerly amid the tangled skein of jurisdictional disputes which constituted the American Government. In particular the army and navy were impatient of civilian control over their purchasing activity, and were in a position to bring their complaints before the President. As a result, the concentration of control over the economy was not nearly as great in practice as the original grant seemed to indicate.

During the first six months or so of the War Production Board's existence, the primary aim of all concerned was to increase war production. This meant large-scale conversion of factories to munitions work; but before such change-over could be made factory managers had to have orders, specifications, and contracts. Placing munitions orders was itself a formidable task, for many factories had never worked on munitions before and many factory managers could not easily find their way through the maze of Washington officialdom. The matching of need with productive capacity thus became in large degree a hit or miss affair.[2]

[1] The text of the Executive Order No. 9024 which set up the W.P.B. may be found in *Documents on American Foreign Relations, 1941–1942*, pp. 161–3. Owing to disputes over the exact definition of the W.P.B.'s authority, the executive order was not issued until 16 January, three days after Roosevelt had announced the news of the establishment of the W.P.B.

[2] Small firms were at a particular disadvantage in the scramble. It was easier for procurement officers to sign a contract with a great corporation for millions of dollars than to break up the order into small parts which could, perhaps, be produced by a dozen or more small factories.

In the first rush to place war contracts little or no attention was paid to over-all balance and feasibility. Nelson early agreed to delegate contract-drawing power to the hands of the army and navy officers who had been doing that sort of work before. Until 1940 the limit which confronted military purchasers was shortage of funds appropriated by Congress. After Pearl Harbour, Congress in effect removed this control altogether by making vast appropriations. Instead of a pecuniary limit, the physical limit of the productive capacity of American industry now imposed itself upon the activities of military procurement officers.

Neither by training nor by the organization of the purchasing agencies were the American services prepared to adapt themselves to this new situation. Separate offices, charged with procurement of one or another type of war supplies, went ahead and placed orders with factories regardless of what might happen to other, complementary production programmes. Whichever military office happened to get to a particular factory first could, in effect, pre-empt its product. Taking the economy as a whole, vastly more was put on order during the first months of 1942 than could possibly be produced. Such a procedure created a dangerous lack of balance in production. For example, enormous quantities of small arms ammunition were ordered and the construction of new factories for its manufacture was begun before anyone discovered that the ammunition supply, if the programme were completed, would be far in excess of any immediate need.

The priority system which had been inherited from pre-war months proved entirely inadequate to meet the new strain. The power to assign priorities was divided between W.P.B. and the Army–Navy Munitions Board; and soon so many priorities were handed out to factories working on war contracts that they became meaningless. When there were enough A-1 priorities in circulation to absorb or more than absorb available supplies of raw materials, the system lost significance. And this is nearly what happened during the first six months of 1942. The situation was seriously complicated by shortages of rubber and tin resulting from the Japanese conquest of Malaya, and by a shortage of oil along the east coast which resulted from the success of German submarines in sinking tankers which normally supplied that region.

The net consequence of all these disbalances was that in the autumn months of 1942 the rate of expansion of American munitions production began to fall off alarmingly. Numerous individuals had foreseen the difficulties that arose, and there were various proposals to remedy them.

Moreover, large corporations were able to maintain contact men in Washington who steered war contracts into their hands. The result was a great concentration of orders in relatively few hands, while some small enterprises found it hard to keep man-power or obtain supplies. This became the occasion for Congressional investigation, and some conscious efforts, only partially successful, were made to counteract the concentration of war contracts in the hands of big corporations.

The leading spirits of the Army Services of Supply pressed for extension of their control over the economy, believing that chicken-hearts among the civilians of the W.P.B. stood between them and the full realization of their production schedules. In their turn, Nelson and other officials of W.P.B. criticized the army for economic *naïveté*, and in particular defended civilian claims for supplies which the soldiers would gladly have cut off. The struggle between W.P.B. and the army lasted throughout the war years and flared into spectacular public quarrels from time to time.[1]

Three devices were tried during 1942 to remedy the disorganization of the American war economy. Special 'czars' were appointed to push through capital developments designed to solve the rubber and oil shortages. This device was perhaps an effective way to meet a crisis—at any rate synthetic rubber plants were built and a pipe-line was constructed to bring oil to the east coast. But in the long run such special organizations merely added another element to the existing confusion of economic administration. Rational solution of the difficulties could only be found by a broad over-all system of control that would be able to channel the productive capacity of the nation to the tasks judged to be most urgent, and do so without sacrificing the necessary balance between competing programmes.

The first attempt at such over-all control was a rather blunt instrument. Statisticians pointed out that the total of outstanding orders was simply more than the factories could possibly handle in the course of 1942. Consequently, W.P.B. recommended, and the President eventually ordered, the armed services to cut down their contracts to a total money value that was estimated to be within the capacity of the nation's factories.[2] This procedure did not by itself assure balance among the things actually produced, though by eliminating marginal projects it did relieve some of the pressure upon the productive capacity of the nation. Other and more precise controls were needed to assure that (1) the production programmes planned within the over-all financial limit would not break down for want of critical raw materials, and (2) the end products would be reasonably well adjusted to the current needs of army, navy, Lend-Lease, and the civilian economy.

The first attempt to establish such control was known as the Production

[1] Cf. the rather pointed remarks in Nelson: *Arsenal of Democracy*, pp. 388–90.

[2] There were not one but several such blanket reductions. Thus the army supply programme in February 1942 called for the delivery of supplies worth $62 milliard in that year; on 6 April this was cut to $45 milliard, on 29 May to $38 milliard, and on 12 November to $31 milliard—approximately the value of goods actually delivered. See U.S.A., Bureau of the Budget: *The United States at War* (Washington, U.S.G.P.O., 1947), p. 301. [This volume is referred to hereafter as *United States at War*.]

Requirements Plan. It had been in operation on a voluntary basis and on a small scale before Pearl Harbour. On 10 June 1942 Nelson announced that the plan would be made compulsory for all but the smallest consumers of metal after 1 September 1942. The plan called for an enormous statistical and clerical effort. Each plant was asked to report orders on its books, stocks of raw materials on hand, and to estimate future requirements month by month. Simultaneously, total national supplies of raw material and semi-manufactured goods were estimated. Then the two schedules of requirements and supplies had to be balanced. Finally, manufacturers whose programmes survived the scrutiny were to be issued with chits of paper entitling them to given quantities of the materials they required at specified delivery times.

Given time, perhaps the plan could have been made to work well enough. As things were, however, the complexity of the necessary calculations and paper work proved overwhelming. Adequate information and experienced personnel both were lacking. Moreover, there was an important group of persons in W.P.B. and outside it who opposed the scheme, and urged its abandonment.[1] The period during which the plan first went into effect coincided with the slowing down in the rate of munitions expansion, and this was taken as a rough and ready indication of its failure. Personal and bureaucratic ambitions and jealousies entered into the picture to an important degree. Finally, the plan was open to a theoretical objection in as much as it made no direct provision for a systematic apportionment of industrial capacity between the various claimants—army, navy, civilian economy, and Lend-Lease.

These pressures led to the abandonment of the Production Requirements Plan. Its successor was known as the Controlled Materials Plan. In November 1942 the new plan was announced, but a period was allowed for manufacturers and government officials to become acquainted with its provisions before it was put into effect. As a result, the new scheme became operative only in June 1943. It thus falls outside the period here under consideration, and will be described below.[2]

In spite of the confusion which attended American economic mobilization, the physical accomplishments in 1942 were most impressive when measured by any standard except that of the President's January goals. The total value of 'war output' in the United States in 1941 was \$18·5 milliard; in 1942 the corresponding figure was \$46.6 milliard, more than a threefold increase. Of the 1942 total, \$32.5 milliard was the value of munitions manufactured, and \$14.1 milliard was the cost of war construc-

[1] For a detailed account of the debates on the best method for controlling the flow of materials, see *Industrial Mobilization for War*, i. 457–85.

[2] See below, pp. 226–7.

tion—new factories, army camps, and the like.[1] The increase in munitions output was proportionately greater than the total increase, being almost fourfold over 1941.

Despite such great successes, the military demand for equipment and supplies was still far short of satisfaction by the end of 1942; and at the planning and control level there remained two important unsolved problems. One was the co-ordination of production schedules with strategy. In October 1942 a Joint Requirements Group was set up in the hope that it would remedy this obvious shortcoming. But the Group died a paper death, partly because of jealousies between the armed services, partly because the Chiefs of Staff were extremely reluctant to permit any civilian to penetrate into the secrets of military strategy, and partly because such a large element of uncertainty still existed among the military leaders themselves as to the future course of Allied strategy.[2]

A second unsolved, or, more correctly, incompletely solved problem was the efficacious pooling of productive resources among the Allies—or, as was in practice the case, between America, Britain, and Canada. For this purpose, Churchill and Roosevelt had agreed at the Arcadia Conference to set up three Combined Boards; and in June 1942, following a visit of Oliver Lyttelton, British Minister of Production, to Washington, two more Combined Boards were established. These were intended to be the principal instruments by means of which British and American economic effort could be united into a larger and more efficient whole. We must next consider briefly how much these Boards were able to accomplish.

(*c*) The Anglo-American Combined Boards

On 26 January 1942 Churchill and Roosevelt announced the establishment of the Combined Munitions Assignment Board, the Combined Raw Materials Board, and the Combined Shipping Adjustment Board. As with the Combined Chiefs of Staff Committee, the word 'combined' signified inter-national combination. This terminology was preserved when two additional boards were set up on 9 June 1942; the Combined Production and Resources Board and the Combined Food Board. There was, however, no uniformity in the powers assigned to these Boards, and even less was there any uniformity in the scope and success of their activity.

In general, the Board that worked most effectively was the Combined Raw Materials Board. It was composed of two men (with supporting staffs), one representing the British Ministry of Supply, the other representing the 'United States Government'.[3] Its seat was in Washington. Accord-

[1] *Industrial Mobilization for War*, i. 202–5. [2] Ibid. pp. 450–2.

[3] This vagueness in its original charter threatened to create trouble between the Board and W.P.B., whose chairman was anxious to exercise control over raw materials in the United States. In practice, however, this potential difficulty was largely overcome by the choice of the individual who filled the post on the Combined Raw Materials Board: William L. Batt. Batt

ing to its original charter the Board had the task of planning the best and speediest possible development, expansion, and use of the raw materials available to the two Governments. The agreement which established the C.R.M.B. declared that its recommendations 'shall be carried out by all parts of the respective Governments'.[1] Such wording implied mandatory powers, and, had the Board insisted upon their exercise, a bitter jurisdictional dispute might well have arisen. In fact, however, the C.R.M.B. adopted the policy of relying upon the statistical and other services of W.P.B. and of the Ministry of Supply (later, the Ministry of Production); and it depended upon persuasion and argument to convince the national administrators of the need for sharing raw materials in short supply.

Indeed, an important element in the Board's success was the modesty of its undertakings. Only materials critically short drew the Board's attention. In each such case an estimate of the world supply available to Britain and the United States was made. On the basis of this information various measures were devised by which available supplies could be most effectively distributed between the two Governments. In some instances, allocations from one nation's supplies were made to the other—for instance, the United States made quarterly allotments of copper to Great Britain. In other cases, available sources of supply were apportioned between the two countries in what seemed the most equitable manner. Thus rubber-producing areas were divided between the two nations, and, within the areas assigned, each Government undertook preclusive buying.[2]

In addition to allocation of scarce materials, the Board recommended methods for the increase of supply by development of various potential producing regions; it recommended methods for economizing the use of scarce materials by substitution, changes in specification, &c.; and it tried to relieve the pressure upon shipping space by suggesting various shifts and changes in established trade patterns (e.g. refined phosphorus instead of phosphate rock was shipped to Great Britain).

The Board's many recommendations were nearly always accepted. This was partly a reflection of the tactful personalities of the Board's two members. But a factor perhaps of greater importance was the fact that in

simultaneously occupied a leading position in W.P.B. Cf. *Industrial Mobilization for War*, i. 222–3. When the Ministry of Production was established in Britain (February 1942) the British representative on the C.R.M.B., Sir Clive Baillieu, was transferred from the jurisdiction of the Ministry of Supply, and came under the Ministry of Production.

[1] Text of the agreement may be found in Great Britain: *Agreements between the Prime Minister and the President of the United States of America*, Cmd. 6332 (London, H.M.S.O., 1942), and in *Documents on American Foreign Relations, 1941–1942*, p. 248.

[2] In the case of rubber, actually, the methods were combined, for Great Britain made a small allocation of Ceylon rubber to the United States. Cf. Great Britain, Ministry of Production: *Report on the Work of the Combined Raw Materials Board to January 26th, 1943* (London, H.M.S.O., 1943), p. 5.

the field of raw material supply the British Empire and the United States were more or less on a plane of equality. The British colonies and Dominions had much to offer the United States in return for American raw materials; and, when the give and take were about equal, each partner could easily recognize not only the general Allied benefit but also the national advantage which pooling arrangements could and did bring.

Raw materials were the only sphere in which anything like over-all equality existed between British and American contributions to the common economic effort. In other fields the relationship was one-sided: America giving and the British receiving. Under such conditions, Americans often found it hard to understand why they should relinquish something that they needed themselves. This recurrent strain did much to undermine the effectiveness of the other Combined Boards. American veto power was too close to the surface to make joint deliberation easy, while the British position was always on the verge of becoming that of suppliant rather than partner.

This distortion of the Anglo-American relationship was particularly apparent during 1942 in the fields of shipping and munitions. Both were desperately short; and the build-up of American military forces conflicted directly with the demands made by British representatives for allocation of shipping and munitions for the support of their own troops and civilian population.

In the circumstances, nothing could prevent many American officials from viewing British appeals to the principle of Allied community as sophistical, while British representatives often found Americans absurdly short-sighted or stubbornly selfish. Only the determination of men at the top to maintain and develop mutual helpfulness prevented friction at lower levels from exceeding tolerable bounds.

Something has already been said of the Munitions Assignment Board, and of the manner in which it was originally set up on a trial basis at the Arcadia Conference.[1] Unlike the Combined Raw Materials Board, the Munitions Assignment Board was divided into two parts, one sitting in London, to distribute British munitions, and one in Washington, to distribute American munitions. Each branch was composed of American and British officers representing the armed services, but each operated under a civilian chairman: Harry Hopkins in Washington and Lord Beaverbrook (and later Oliver Lyttelton) in London. The Board had only advisory power; recommendations had finally to be approved by the Combined Chiefs of Staff.

The manner in which the Board functioned was this. Claims for muni-

[1] See above, pp. 113–16.

tions were lodged in the first instance with either London or Washington, according to whether the claimant was equipped with American-type or British-type weapons. (Russian claims were a special case, being handled through protocol agreements which specified what items would be provided from Britain and what from America.) Since British production could not supply all the claims put upon it, unsatisfied requirements were forwarded to the Washington Board; and in practice, the major conflicts over munitions distribution were fought out in Washington.[1]

Throughout 1942 the struggle for equipment was severe. The personal role played by Harry Hopkins was of great importance in preventing British and other Allied requests from being neglected. When disputes over the disposition of munitions reached a particularly acute stage, Hopkins could always get an authoritative ruling from Roosevelt on short notice. The effect was in many instances to override the imperious demands made by American generals and admirals for equipment they badly needed; but, without such overruling, Britain, Russia, and the other Allied countries might well have been thrown back almost entirely upon their own resources in 1942.

Looked at from an over-all Allied view-point, the basic conflict between British and American members of the Washington Munitions Board was a form of the perennial conflict between short- and long-range advantage. The Americans were anxious to create and train a great army and navy; the British tried to convince their colleagues that the first task was to maintain and complete the equipment of existing forces engaged in active theatres of war.[2] In practice no clear principle was followed. Shortages were too great, and sudden emergencies regularly arose to upset whatever long-range plans had been agreed to. Thus, after the British defeat in Libya in the summer of 1942, the Americans agreed to send a fleet of Sherman tanks to Egypt, despite the fact that these tanks had been tentatively assigned to an American armoured division then on the point of completing its training.[3] This sort of emergency action, rather than apportionment of munitions according to a future Order of Battle and a firm strategic plan, was the usual manner in which decisions were made by the Munitions Assignment Board in 1942.

The Combined Shipping Adjustment Board faced the most difficult of all the problems which beset Allied planners in 1942. Until August merchant shipping losses exceeded new construction; and, despite a net

[1] In the early months of 1942 there were some instances in which Britain was able to supply American forces with special items, such as barrage balloons, AA guns, anti-submarine corvettes, and radar equipment. Cf. Hancock and Gowing: *British War Economy*, p. 395; Stettinius: *Lend-Lease*, p. 163.

[2] Hancock and Gowing: op. cit. p. 396.

[3] Churchill, iv. 344; U.S. edition, iv. 383.

gain of 738,000 deadweight tons in the last quarter of the year, the losses incurred during the first part of 1942 were not offset. Instead of the 44,390,000 deadweight tons with which the Allied nations began in 1942, only 42,421,000 tons were on hand at the end of the year.[1] Such losses were especially serious for Great Britain. The very existence of the British nation was at stake. Imports were a necessity, not only to fight but to live. An especial hardship arose from the fact that losses to British shipping were not replaced. New ships built in American ship-yards were put under the control of the War Shipping Administration; while British ship-yards concentrated upon repair and naval construction.[2]

These facts did not make the path of Anglo-American co-operation with respect to shipping easy. The Combined Shipping Adjustment Board in practice had only slender influence. The agreement which established the Board specified that 'executive power will be exercised solely by the appropriate shipping agency in Washington and by the Minister of War Transport in London'. This statement effectively annulled the principle enunciated at the beginning of the same document: 'The shipping resources of the two countries will be deemed to be pooled.'[3]

The Board was divided into two co-ordinate bodies, one in each of the capitals. But as in the case of the Munitions Assignment Board, and for the same reason, important negotiations centred in Washington. The major question at issue in 1942 was the future of the British merchant marine. The British representative on the Washington branch of the Combined Shipping Adjustment Board, Sir Arthur Salter, argued that the first call upon new construction should be replacement of losses. Had this been accepted, it would have assured the British of the maintenance of their merchant marine at something near its existing level. American shipping authorities did not reject, but also did not accept the British argument. Even after American shipbuilding caught up with losses to the American shipping pool in May 1942 the issue was not decided.

Meanwhile anxiety mounted in Great Britain. The import programme for 1943, after it had been reduced as much as the Cabinet believed possible, could not be met by the shipping which remained under British control. Accordingly, Churchill sent a letter to Roosevelt in November 1942 asking that the Americans transfer enough ships to British registry to replace losses which had been suffered (and would be suffered in the

[1] Morison: *History of U.S. Naval Operations*, i. 403.

[2] This division of labour had been informally agreed upon by Churchill and Roosevelt. Cf. *United States at War*, p. 36; Hancock and Gowing: *British War Economy*, p. 431. In spite of demands made by naval construction and repair of merchant shipping upon the facilities of British ship-yards, new merchant tonnage was built in substantial quantity throughout the war years. Cf. Great Britain, Central Statistical Office: *Annual Abstract of Statistics, No. 84, 1935–1946* (London, H.M.S.O., 1948), table 164, p. 157, which shows that construction during the war years generally equalled construction rates in the immediately preceding years of peace.

[3] Cmd. 6332; *Documents on American Foreign Relations, 1941–1942*, pp. 249–50.

future) up to a total of two and a half million deadweight tons. Roosevelt did not agree to transfer so much shipping to British control, but he did accept the principle that the minimum British import programme should be met in 1943 by allocation of American-built ships to Britain. This, however, did not end the matter. Negotiation, angry at times, continued until June 1943, when Roosevelt ordered a large-scale transfer of ships to the British under what was known as bareboat charter.[1]

Churchill's irruption into the negotiations which had been in progress among the members of the Combined Shipping Adjustment Board took the matter more or less out of the Board's hands. The understandable anxiety of the British Cabinet lest imports fell to such a point that the British economy could no longer continue to function led the British to give up the principle of a real Anglo-American shipping pool. Instead they began to negotiate for, and were in the end successful in assuring, transfer of ships to British control on a scale sufficient to assure Britain of at least a bare minimum of food and raw material. In effect, then, the British Ministry of War Transport and the War Shipping Administration in Washington managed two separate fleets of ships. Anglo-American pooling of resources was limited to the occasional lending of a ship from one to the other for some particular voyage or series of voyages.[2]

The Combined Production and Resources Board, established on 9 June 1942, was originally conceived as the keystone of the Combined Board structure. It was intended to provide a link between the Raw Materials Board on the one hand and the Munitions Assignment Board on the other, planning and co-ordinating the processes of production on an international scale. A board with some such responsibility had been among the recommendations which the British had brought to the Arcadia Conference, but it was not until the summer of 1942 that Roosevelt was willing to accept the idea. Donald Nelson, chairman of the War Production Board, and Oliver Lyttelton, Minister of Production, were the two members of the Board; but in practice it functioned through deputies. In November 1942 a Canadian representative was given a third place on the Board.[3] The seat of its operations was Washington.

[1] See below, p. 234. See also Hancock and Gowing: *British War Economy*, pp. 428–31; S. McKee Rosen: *The Combined Boards of the Second World War* (New York, Columbia University Press, 1951), pp. 126–30. After a quarrel between the British and American members of the Combined Shipping Adjustment Board in Washington, lasting from November 1942 to May 1943, the Board for all practical purposes ceased to function altogether. It retained a paper existence until the end of the war, however.

[2] An early example of this sort of co-operation was the use of the *Queen Mary* and the *Queen Elizabeth* as transports for the American troops sent to Ireland at the beginning of 1942.

[3] Canada's place in the Anglo-American scheme of things was anomalous. Before Pearl Harbour a number of U.S.-Canadian committees had been set up to co-ordinate defence and

The instructions given to the Combined Production and Resources Board were most sweeping. 'The Board shall: (*a*) Combine the production programs of the United States and the United Kingdom into a single integrated program, adjusted to the strategic requirements of the war, as indicated to the Board by the Combined Chiefs of Staff, and to all relevant production factors.'[1] It proved, however, far easier to assign such duties than it was to carry them out. Integration and balancing of a national programme of production had proved a difficult thing; and at the time that the Combined Production and Resources Board was set up nothing resembling an effective over-all control had yet been devised for the American economy. Actually, one of the services that the Board was able to perform was to assist in bringing British experience to bear upon the American administrative problem.[2]

Integration of the two economies could only be attempted in a rough and ready fashion. The absence of standardization of parts—even in such an elemental matter as the pitch of screw threads—made impossible any detailed intermeshing of the production processes of the two nations. The further fact that the national administrative organizations controlling production were well dug in by midsummer 1942 and naturally resisted outside control made the Board's task as conceived in the original grant of powers a practical impossibility.[3]

A very considerable degree of national specialization in munitions production did develop, but the critical decisions were nearly all taken by direct negotiation between the Governments without reference to the Combined Production and Resources Board. Thus, for example, the Canadians undertook to build corvettes for anti-submarine work, relieving British ship-yards of that task, while the British undertook the job of supplying American troops in Britain with barracks and other facilities. But for the most part such agreements ran in the other direction. The United States undertook production of a large number of items on a scale

other activities; and many of these continued to function after the United States came into the war. On the Raw Materials Board, for example, Canada was represented through the U.S. member, whereas all the rest of the British Commonwealth was represented through the British member. The growing importance of Canada's contribution to Allied war economy was recognized by admission as a third partner in the Combined Production and Resources Board and the Combined Food Board, but the other Combined Boards, set up earlier, continued to function without direct Canadian representation. It was not deemed wise to upset organizations already in operation merely to achieve symmetry.

1 *Documents on American Foreign Relations, 1941–1942*, p. 250.

2 British advice was one element in shaping the Controlled Materials Plan, for example (cf. *United States at War*, p. 306).

3 The first blow to the high hopes with which the Board was launched came from the American army which refused, in effect, to set before the Board the strategic requirements which Anglo-American production would have to meet (cf. Rosen: *The Combined Boards of the Second World War*, pp. 145–8). After this set-back the Board lost any but marginal significance, and serious Anglo-American negotiation over production matters tended to follow other channels.

to supply all the Allies. Merchant shipping, transport aeroplanes, and the atomic bomb are the most obvious and important examples.

There was, however, a limit to the degree to which such international specialization could be carried without seriously affecting post-war economic prospects and the balance of the respective national economies. This problem was peculiarly pressing for the British. On more than one occasion British representatives resisted American proposals to undertake manufacture on their behalf. An instance of this was the American proposal that tank production be stopped in Britain entirely. More efficient American production lines, it was argued, could supply both British and American needs. On strictly economic grounds the American proposal was thoroughly sound. Man-power and other resources could be more efficiently brought to bear in the United States. But the dispersal of skilled workers, managerial talent, and machinery used for tank production would have had a damaging effect upon post-war British production of such things as automobiles. Given the prospect of a post-war interruption of the war-time intermeshing of the British with the American economy, it is easy to understand why British officials steadily rejected the plan.

In practice the success of the Combined Production and Resources Board was limited to statistical and other investigations that pointed out bottle-necks and wastes in the combined economies. The physical Balance Sheet which had been first drawn up in the summer and autumn of 1941 in connexion with the planning of the Victory Program,[1] was kept up to date by the Board. Combined Allied production of munitions, and estimates of future production, were plotted in the balance sheet, and against such totals were placed estimates of future needs. This procedure often showed up shortages and sometimes indicated present or future surpluses; and the national production programmes could be and often were adjusted in the light of such figures.

The prestige of the Combined Production and Resources Board was not very great. This was partly because its operation was left to deputies; and partly because the tasks which had been assigned to it were so vital and so complex that neither the American nor the British Governments were really prepared to allow the Board to exercise the powers nominally assigned to it. Advice, warnings, suggestions did come from the Board, and sometimes led to appropriate top-level decisions. But the Board never attained a position from which it could address the Combined Chiefs as an equal, despite a charter which nominally endowed it with powers of decision and control comparable to those exercised by the military leaders.

The Board's main practical role was to serve as a sort of court of appeal to which the British Government could refer disputes which arose over

[1] See above, pp. 16–17.

economic policy. As a member of the Combined Production and Resources Board Britain could appear as a partner, not as a claimant for crumbs from the American table, and could get a hearing as an equal rather than as a mendicant in the topmost levels of administration. As such, the Board was of especial value to the British. The Americans tended to minimize its role and reduce its scope, preferring to act through the channels of their own economic administration.[1]

The fifth of the Combined Boards, established at the same time as the Production and Resources Board, was concerned with the production and distribution of food. It was composed of the American Secretary of Agriculture and the Head of the British Food Mission in the United States. It operated from Washington. The Board served as a means by which the food needs of Britain and of both American and British armed forces were brought before the U.S. Department of Agriculture; but as long as a food surplus existed in the United States no great problems, except for those of delivery, arose. Consequently the Board's activities were not of much importance until 1943.

In general, the power and effectiveness of the Combined Boards was a good deal less than was contemplated by the men who drafted the agreements which set them up. They served as a useful device for bringing British and American views into touch, and in many instances were able to bring important considerations to the attention of the national administrators. But the locus of power and final decision remained in the hands of national authorities despite the seeming transfer of mandatory power to the Boards presiding over Raw Materials and Production and Resources. Persuasion, negotiation, argument, and adjustment were the methods by which the Boards functioned, not command.

(*d*) Lend-Lease and Mutual Aid

The Lend-Lease Act had been passed by the U.S. Congress at a time when many Americans hoped that their country would not become an active belligerent. When that hope was disappointed adjustments in the administration and in the theory of Lend-Lease became either necessary or desirable. During 1942 both were made. From the side of Great Britain and the Dominions the Lend-Lease principle was extended by what was called Mutual Aid or reverse Lend-Lease; but Anglo-American economic relations with Russia remained on a special protocol basis as before. The quantities of supplies and services exchanged between the Allies increased

[1] Cf. R. Warren James: *Wartime Economic Co-operation* (Toronto, Ryerson, 1949), p. 264.

sharply from the levels of 1941. This exchange served as a very powerful cement to the alliance, since every party clearly benefited, and the military power of the whole was enlarged far beyond the sum of what each nation could have mounted separately.

The first American reaction to the news of Pearl Harbour was to embargo Lend-Lease shipments, an act which created consternation in Great Britain and, presumably, though there is no record to show it, in Russia also. As soon as American military and naval authorities had checked through the cargoes ready and waiting for shipment, and had repossessed certain items which were judged necessary for the defence of the United States, Lend-Lease shipments were resumed. The total delay was not great. Despite the interruption a larger quantity of Lend-Lease goods was delivered in December 1941 than in the preceding month.[1]

The vast expansion of American home demand for munitions after Pearl Harbour meant that Lend-Lease orders faced intense competition from the U.S. army and navy. One consequence was a blurring of conventional property rights. By the time items originally ordered for Lend-Lease had been manufactured, they might be needed more urgently by the American forces, and vice versa. When such was the case, transfers were made. We have already paid some attention to the administrative devices which were introduced in order to make such flexibility possible. The Munitions Assignment Board and the Combined Raw Materials Board effected transfers of this sort from the time they began to operate.

After Pearl Harbour no more appropriations were made directly to Lend-Lease; instead, the Congress authorized the use of part of the funds appropriated to the American armed services for Lend-Lease purchases. This amounted to a recognition on the financial plane of the integration of Lend-Lease and domestic armaments programmes which the powers of the Munitions Assignment Board made real in practice. Thereafter, the financial duties of the Office of Lend-Lease Administration became simply to tot up the value of materials supplied to the Allied nations and report the figures regularly to Congress.

The Office of Lend-Lease Administration was the branch of the U.S. Government before which Allied requests for supplies were first lodged. The main job from the American point of view was to make sure that the requests were well-founded, i.e. that the country in question could not pay in dollars, that the need for the things requested was urgent, and that their supply would contribute directly to the progress of the war. This task of inspection involved many demands for statistical and other information to justify requests, and British officials were sometimes nettled by the American supervision and interference which resulted.[2]

[1] Stettinius: *Lend-Lease*, p. 155.

[2] Cf. Hancock and Gowing: *British War Economy*, p. 245. The fact that the Office of Lend-

Once the Office of Lend-Lease Administration had satisfied itself of the legitimacy of a request, the task of actual procurement was passed on to one or another branch of the American Government, and in due course, if nothing arose to interfere in the meanwhile, the goods were delivered to an American port. The Office took some responsibility for helping Allied requests through the mill, arguing before committees which assigned priorities or divided up available supplies. Neither Britain nor Russia, however, refrained from coming directly into contact with officers and officials who controlled American production in order to argue on their own behalf.

Another and quite important aspect of the activity of the Lend-Lease administration was its advocacy of the cause of the Allies before the Congress in particular and before the American people in general. Particularly in 1942 when munitions were so short, Americans were prone to think that their own needs should take absolute priority. The reports made by the Office of Lend-Lease to Congress were drawn up in part to counteract this habit of mind. They carefully laid emphasis upon the advantages received by the United States in return for her Lend-Lease programme.[1]

The Lend-Lease Act prescribed that in return for Lend-Lease supplies 'the benefit to the United States may be payment or repayment in kind or property, or any other direct or indirect benefit which the President deems satisfactory'. Almost at once, negotiations were begun with Great Britain in order to define more explicitly the benefits which the United States would receive in return for Lend-Lease. These negotiations were entrusted to the State Department. The major goal which the officials of the State Department set before themselves was this: that in return for Lend-Lease the British should agree to give up Empire trade preference when the war was over. Freer international trade had long been a cardinal element in Cordell Hull's political creed. He regarded flourishing international trade as an indispensable prerequisite for any stable peace between nations; and he conceived his mission as Secretary of State to be, at least in part, the removal of obstacles to the exchange of goods between nations.

The negotiation of a Lend-Lease Master Agreement with Great Britain thus seemed to him a golden opportunity. In July 1941 the State Department drafted an agreement committing the British to liberal trade policies after the war; but the proposal met with resistance. At the Arcadia Conference Hull brought the question up with Churchill, but the Prime

Lease Administration took it upon itself to 'police' observance of the White Paper of September 1941 (in which the British Government had promised not to use Lend-Lease material for export manufacture) was a particularly sore point.

[1] Cf., for example, U.S.A., the President: *Report to Congress on Lend-Lease Operations from the Passage of the Act, March 11, 1941 to December 31, 1942* (Washington, U.S.G.P.O., 1943), *passim.*

Minister put him off, saying that he was too busy with other matters. Pressed a second time, Churchill roundly affirmed that he would never give up Empire preference. But Hull was persistent, and, after a telegram from Roosevelt, the British Cabinet at length yielded and agreed to the American proposal.[1]

Accordingly, a Lend-Lease Master Agreement was signed on 23 February 1942.[2] This document was only preliminary. Final determination of the benefits to be received by the United States was deferred until the end of the war. Pending such a settlement, however, the Agreement recognized a number of principles which were to govern the administration and final settlement of Lend-Lease. Three of the articles of the Agreement were of special importance.

> Article II. The government of the United Kingdom will continue to contribute to the defense of the United States of America and the strengthening thereof and will provide such articles, services, facilities or information as it may be in a position to supply.

This constituted the first formal acknowledgement of reverse Lend-Lease. Actually the British had already transferred certain facilities and munitions to the United States for which payment had not been demanded. This article (and Article VI) made clear that the practice would be extended, and that settlement of the resulting obligations between the two Governments would be postponed until the end of the war.

> Article V. The Government of the United Kingdom will return to the United States of America at the end of the present emergency, as determined by the President, such defense articles transferred under this Agreement as shall not have been destroyed, lost or consumed and as shall be determined by the President to be useful in the defense of the United States of America or of the Western Hemisphere or to be otherwise of use to the United States of America.

This article affirmed the lend part of Lend-Lease. As far as return of material was concerned, it was generally recognized at the time that the United States would have little if any use for reclaimed munitions. It was rather the other element—the recognition that what was consumed in the course of the war was *not* returnable—that was significant. One of Roosevelt's central ideas in connexion with Lend-Lease was the necessity of avoiding war debts of the sort that had emerged from the Allied financial dealings of the First World War, and had embittered post-war relations.[3]

[1] Hull: *Memoirs*, ii. 1151–3.

[2] Text may be found in Great Britain, Foreign Office: *Agreement between the Government of the United Kingdom and the United States of America on the Principles applying to Mutual Aid*, Cmd. 6341 (London, H.M.S.O., 1942) and in *Documents on American Foreign Relations, 1941–1942*, pp. 235–7.

[3] It was only slowly that Roosevelt came to believe that no repayment for Lend-Lease and other aid would be possible. In May 1942, for example, he spoke to Molotov of long-term repayment of capital, without, however, levying interest charges on the debt (Sherwood: *Roosevelt and Hopkins*, p. 572; Eng. edition, ii. 576).

The rather oblique language of the Article quoted above was designed to relieve the British from what would otherwise be overwhelming indebtedness.

> Article VII. In the final determination of the benefits to be provided to the United States of America . . . the terms and conditions thereof shall be such as not to burden commerce between the two countries. . . . To that end, they shall include provision for agreed action . . . directed to the expansion, by appropriate international and domestic measures, of production, employment, and the exchange and consumption of goods, which are the material foundations of the liberty and welfare of all peoples; to the elimination of all forms of discriminatory treatment in international commerce, and to the reduction of tariffs and other trade barriers. . . .

This was the article to which Churchill objected and his acceptance of this part of the Agreement was at best half-hearted.[1]

The British leaders realized something at least of the post-war economic difficulties that would confront them in any free competition with American industry. It may be presumed that the Cabinet's acceptance of this Article was intended not to close the issue, but rather to appease Hull and avoid what might have been a very embarrassing dispute over Lend-Lease policy. Roosevelt was far less doctrinaire than Hull on the subject of free trade, and he privately assured Churchill that the first rather than the second part of Article VII would predominate in the final accounting for Lend-Lease.[2]

This Agreement with Great Britain served as a model for similar agreements with other countries. On 11 June 1942 Ambassador Litvinov signed an identical agreement on behalf of the U.S.S.R., the more lightly, perhaps, because the provisions about tariff reduction and free trade were almost meaningless when applied to the Russian economy. Agreements with other countries followed, so that by mid-1943 thirteen of the principal Allies had accepted identical terms.[3]

The result of this network of agreements, supplemented and supported by the growing physical interpenetration of the armed forces of all the Allies (except Russia), was to expand the original one-way concept of Lend-Lease into multilateral Mutual Aid. American forces stationed in the United Kingdom, in Australia, New Zealand, and India needed a wide variety of products which could most easily be supplied locally. Food

[1] Hull remarked: 'Thereafter, however, it frequently became apparent to me that Prime Minister Churchill, despite this pledge, was determined to hold on to imperial preference' (*Memoirs*, ii. 1476).

[2] 13 December 1945, H.C.Deb. 5th ser., vol. 417, col. 723. Cf. Sherwood: *Roosevelt and Hopkins*, p. 507; Eng. edition, ii. 512.

[3] By 1945 thirty-five Master Agreements had been concluded (see Appendix II, p. 780 below).

and clothing, for example, were available or could easily be manufactured in the two southern Dominions for the use of American troops and naval detachments fighting in the South-West Pacific. The growing American garrison of the British Isles, too, could be and was supplied with a wide variety of things—barracks, aerodromes, transportation, &c.

Mutual Aid was not confined to the United States and Great Britain. On the same basis, supplies were made available without financial obligation to the various expatriated armies—Polish, Free French, &c. And British supplies of munitions to Russia were delivered under the same arrangement.

Mutual Aid was given a legal basis when a series of agreements between the United States, Great Britain, Australia, New Zealand, and the Free French were signed on 3 September 1942. These agreements all followed a similar pattern. The Anglo-American Agreement[1] stated the principle upon which Mutual Aid was to be extended as follows: '... the war production and the war resources of both Nations should be used by the armed forces of each and of the other United Nations in ways which most effectively utilize the available materials, manpower, production facilities, and shipping space.' The Agreement further declared that: 'While each Government retains the right of final decision, in the light of its own potentialities and responsibilities, decisions as to the most effective use of resources shall, so far as possible, be made in common, pursuant to common plans for winning the war.' And '. . . as large a portion as possible of the articles and services which each Government may authorize to be provided to the other shall be in the form of reciprocal aid so that the need of each Government for the currency of the other may be reduced to a minimum'. The Agreement also listed the classes of supplies which Great Britain would offer to the United States. Raw materials were left out, for at the time American payment for raw materials originating in the British Empire was the only important source of dollars available to Britain. These were needed to complete payment on munitions which had been ordered before the Lend-Lease Act came into force. With this exception, the list was almost all-inclusive.[2]

The Master Lend-Lease Agreements and the Mutual Aid Agreements hinted at, if they did not fully express, a new theory of Lend-Lease. The original act prescribed repayment, whether in goods, services, money, or other benefit. But in the course of 1942 American spokesmen, most notably

[1] Text may be found in Great Britain, Foreign Office: *Exchange of Notes between the Governments of the United Kingdom and the United States of America on the Principles applying to Reciprocal Aid*, Cmd. 6389 (London, H.M.S.O., 1942), and in *Documents on American Foreign Relations vol. v, July 1942–June 1943*, ed. Leland M. Goodrich and Marie J. Carroll (Boston, World Peace Foundation, 1944), pp. 234–6.

[2] See Appendix II, p. 781 below.

President Roosevelt, developed a quite different idea. In the President's Fifth Report to Congress on Lend-Lease, 11 June 1942, occurred the following passage:

> The real costs of the war cannot be measured, nor compared, nor paid for in money. They must and are being met in blood and toil. But the financial costs of the war can and should be met in a way which will serve the needs of lasting peace and mutual economic well-being.
>
> All the United Nations are seeking maximum conversion to war production, in the light of their special resources. If each country devotes roughly the same fraction of its national production to the war, then the financial burden of war is distributed equally among the United Nations in accordance with their ability to pay.[1]

This may be called the fair shares theory of Lend-Lease. It was never directly confronted with the earlier repayment theory in official declarations or agreements. Some influential members of Congress and various newspapers[2] detected a plot to cancel Lend-Lease debt; but administration spokesmen, and most American newspapers, accepted the new theory of Lend-Lease as essentially just.[3]

The American public, however, found such a doctrine hard to understand. International debts were habitually viewed as analogous to private debts, and most Americans felt that the morality which prescribed private repayment of debt applied with equal force to international finance. Thus in March 1942 a public opinion poll discovered that no less than 75 per cent. of the persons asked: 'Should Britain and the U.S.S.R. pay us for the war materials we have sent them under the Lend-Lease Bill?' answered in the affirmative.[4] But this was early in 1942; by the end of the year the public had partly come round to the view advanced by Roosevelt and the administration. Nevertheless, an ambiguity in Lend-Lease theory persisted in the American mind, and it was not until the end of the war when a final settlement was negotiated that the ambiguity was fully resolved.

Canada's position in the Mutual Aid system was peculiar.[5] Because Canada exported a number of valuable raw materials to the United States, she never ceased to accumulate a dollar supply which was sufficient to cover all or nearly all of Canada's imports from the United States. Thus the financial disbalance which had originally caused the Lend-Lease Act to be put into operation did not exist between Canada and the United

[1] *Documents on American Foreign Relations, 1941–1942*, p. 234.

[2] See e.g. *Chicago Tribune*, 12 and 18 July 1942; *New York Journal American*, 3 March 1942.

[3] See e.g. *Christian Science Monitor*, 27 May 1942; *Washington Post*, 7 July 1942; *Baltimore Sun*, 2 November 1942.

[4] *New York Herald Tribune*, 30 March 1942.

[5] See also Appendix II, p. 786 below.

States; and in its absence the provisions of Lend-Lease were not extended to Canada. The trade between the two countries remained on a cash basis throughout the war.

But in relation to Great Britain, Canada occupied a position quite similar to that of the United States herself. Exports of raw materials and of munitions from Canada far outbalanced imports from Great Britain. This situation was met by a series of grants from Canada to Great Britain, the first of which, made in April 1942, extinguished the existing British debt and extended $1 milliard credit for the future. This credit just covered exchanges during 1942.[1]

Russia's position was also unique. The physical facts of the war fronts made any large-scale reciprocal aid to the Anglo-Americans impossible. Only the presence on Russian soil of large Anglo-American forces would have offered the occasion for the Soviet Government to provide supplies and services analogous to those provided by the British or Australian Governments to Americans. Thus Mutual Aid was almost entirely a one-way street as far as the Russians were concerned.

Until the end of June 1942 deliveries to Russia from America and Britain were governed by the Protocol which had been agreed to after the Beaverbrook–Harriman mission to Moscow at the end of September 1941. Actually, some important changes were made in the original agreement. Particularly, the amount of rubber and tin which the Western Allies had agreed to send to the Russians was drastically reduced. This alteration, necessitated by the loss of Malaya, was agreed to by Russian representatives, who also initiated other changes themselves as one or another shortage in the Soviet economy became specially critical.

Difficulties of delivery as well as of production and supply interfered with the fulfilment of the Russian Supply Protocol. In the months after Pearl Harbour the United States fell seriously behind the delivery schedule that had been agreed to. When this situation was called to Roosevelt's attention in March 1942 he issued special orders assigning overriding priority to supplies destined for Russia.[2] As a result, the scale of shipments to Russia rose sharply in April. Unfortunately this effort coincided with the lengthening of the daylight hours in the Arctic, so that the convoys sent to Murmansk and Archangel had to run a gauntlet of German sea and air

[1] Canada's economic contribution to the United Kingdom was considerably above that made by the United States when calculated on a *per capita* basis. In addition, the methods of international accountancy between Canada and Britain were especially favourable to Britain. Thus, for example, the Canadians met the cost of maintaining their army in England from the Dominion Treasury, paying for items supplied to them from British sources. Similar services to American troops were charged up to reverse Lend-Lease, i.e. were paid by the British Treasury.

[2] Stettinius: *Lend-Lease*, p. 205.

attack as they rounded North Cape and headed into Murmansk, a bare twenty miles from German-held territory. Losses were heavy: of eighty-four ships dispatched from U.S. ports alone between April and June 1942 only forty-four delivered their cargoes. Twenty-three were sunk. The rest were off-loaded in Scotland to await better conditions, for such a rate of loss seemed intolerable when shipping was already critically short.[1] The decision to unload in Scotland led the Russians to accuse the British of stealing Lend-Lease goods consigned to them.

By the end of June 1942, when the first Protocol expired, both Britain and America had lived up to the letter of the original agreement, which had only provided that materials should be made available to the Russians, and had left the question of transport unresolved. But, though supplies had been made available, only about four-fifths of the total had been shipped, and of that much had failed of delivery.

Strenuous efforts were made to develop alternative and safer routes to Russia. Transport through Persia from ports on the Persian Gulf was one route; another was transport across the Pacific in Russian bottoms.[2] But these routes involved very long sea and land travel, and it was not until the second half of 1942 that they became of much importance.

The Second Russian Supply Protocol was signed in Washington. It ran from 1 July 1942 to the end of June 1943; and, despite the fact that negotiations were begun as early as May, the Protocol was not finally signed until October 1942. The delay was partly occasioned by a difference between the British and American Governments as to the policy to be adopted in their economic relations with Russia, and partly by bargaining with Russia over the amount of tonnage which could be assigned to the Murmansk–Archangel run.

The British wished to bring the Russian supply operation into conformity with the relation which prevailed between the United States and their own country. They saw no reason why the Russians should not be required to justify their requests by supplying facts and figures in the same fashion as they did themselves; and they proposed that the allotment of Russian supplies should be handled through the Combined Boards already in existence, modified, perhaps, by the addition of Russian members. The Americans, however, resisted and in the end vetoed the whole idea.[3]

The shortage of shipping became a more and more serious problem for the Allies during 1942. As plans for offensive operations began to loom

[1] Morison: *History of U.S. Naval Operations*, i. 165; Sherwood: *Roosevelt and Hopkins*, p. 544; Eng. edition, ii. 548.

[2] Even when this route became quite important as a result of the transfer of American-built ships to the U.S.S.R., the Japanese did not molest the traffic, though they could easily have closed the narrow waters between Japan and Vladivostok had they been willing to risk the Russian reaction to such an act.

[3] Hancock and Gowing: *British War Economy*, p. 363.

large, it became obvious that one of the ways in which shipping could be saved was by cutting down on the amount of supplies delivered to the Russians. When Molotov visited Washington in May 1942 an effort was made to persuade him to agree to a smaller allocation of shipping in exchange for a promise of a second front. Molotov, however, would not agree.[1] It was not until the Western Allies had settled their own plans for the invasion of North Africa that this bargaining with Russia could be completed. What happened in the end was that America and Britain agreed on paper to send the full amount of 4,400,000 tons originally fixed upon. This agreement was influenced by the need to mollify Russian displeasure at the cancellation of the project for landing in France in 1942.

Actually, the delay in concluding the Second Russian Supply Protocol did not significantly affect deliveries to Russia. The day-to-day activities of the Russian supply missions in both Britain and America, co-operating with officials of the two Governments, governed the flow of materials. In practice the provisions of the Protocols were frequently altered as new Russian needs arose, and as unforeseen shortages or fresh sources of supply appeared in the American and British economies. Shipments were not interrupted therefore when the First Protocol expired, even though the second had not yet been signed.

What did interrupt deliveries were the physical difficulties of transport, and enemy action. Early in July 1942 a convoy, numbered PQ17, was dispersed and nearly destroyed while trying to round North Cape. As a result of this disaster the next convoy was suspended. A further attempt to brave German submarine and air attack was made early in September 1942; but, when preparations for the landing in North Africa began to absorb American and British naval strength, convoys were once again suspended. Some single ships attempted to run the gauntlet unescorted, but few of them got through safely. As a result, it was not until the beginning of 1943 that regular convoys were resumed. These difficulties meant that the rate of delivery fell far behind the schedule of the Second Protocol. Things went better in 1943 owing in part to the expanding capacity of the Persian roads and railways; but the deficit was not made good before the end of the Second Protocol period.

Despite the efforts of the Lend-Lease administration to keep records of the value of goods and services transferred to other countries, it is not easy from the official statistics to get an accurate picture of actual physical transactions. One reason for this is that, when last-minute switches in the assignment of munitions were made during 1942, diversions from Lend-

[1] Sherwood: *Roosevelt and Hopkins*, p. 574; Eng. edition, ii. 579. See below, p. 182.

Lease were not always entered in the records. Items subtracted from Lend-Lease were, at least theoretically, replaceable at some future date, and recipient countries were anxious to keep the record of transfer on the books, even when physical delivery had been postponed, because it served as a sort of entitlement on the basis of which future claims could be lodged. Thus items were regularly entered on the Lend-Lease record as soon as an assignment was made, sometimes months before actual delivery could be effected. As a result, the official statistics can only be expected to give a rough indication of the scale of supplies delivered under Lend-Lease during any particular period of time.

Mutual Aid records were even more imperfect. This was partly because the British and Dominion Governments, the principal suppliers of Mutual Aid, did not at first try to keep records of the value of services and goods given to the Americans. They began to do so in the autumn of 1942 only after the Americans urged it. The defects of the record of Mutual Aid also resulted from the nature of the assistance, some of which (e.g. radar designs) could hardly be assigned any cash value, and most of which, from the nature of the relationship between British and American forces, was supplied not through any central office where accounts could easily be kept, but locally on airfields and army camps scattered over the British Isles and throughout the Empire. Mutual Aid to other Allies and from other Allies made the accounting still more complex; and since the major advantage which the system of Mutual Aid gave was escape from financial limitation on Allied economic co-operation, it is perhaps foolish to try retrospectively to cast up the balance.[1]

Nevertheless a few figures will give some idea of the magnitude of the exchange which took place. In 1941, from 11 March when the Lend-Lease act went into operation to the end of the year, the United States assigned goods and services to the British Empire valued at $1,082 million, of which more than three-quarters went to the United Kingdom herself. Goods and services worth only $20 million were provided for Russia during the same period. In 1942 the comparable figures were as follows:

Aid to British Empire	$4,757 million
Aid to Russia	$1,376 million.

Thus the total increase in Lend-Lease deliveries was more than 300 per cent.[2] A general rise in the U.S. price level, and the fact that prices for

[1] See also Sir David Waley's analysis of Mutual Aid in Appendix II, pp. 782–4 below.

[2] These figures are derived from R. G. D. Allen: 'Mutual Aid between the U.S. and the British Empire, 1941–45', *Journal of the Royal Statistical Society*, vol. cix, part iii, 1946, table 4, p. 250. [This paper is referred to hereafter as Allen: 'Mutual Aid'.] These figures incorporate an effort to correct some of the defects mentioned in the text. They are thus somewhat lower than those published in U.S.A., the President: *Report to Congress on Lend-Lease Operations from the Passage of the Act, March 11, 1941 to December 31, 1942*, pp. 36–37. Lend-Lease to other countries was by comparison almost negligible. For 1941–2 together it totalled less than $360 million.

munitions newly brought into production were often high, should be borne in mind when trying to translate these dollar figures into physical terms.

Aid extended by Great Britain to the United States and Russia cannot be broken down into the same periods. Direct comparison is therefore impossible. British supplies and services transfered to the United States were of small account before the middle of 1942 in any case. Up to 30 June 1943 their value was officially calculated at £229,700,000; during the same period aid to Russia totalled £187,700,000. Differences of price level and the incomparability of goods exchanged make translation of these figures into dollar terms (or of the dollar figures into pounds) a more or less fruitless sleight of hand.[1]

Indeed, it would be a great mistake to take such figures as these very seriously. The great fact was that by means of the system of Mutual Aid established during 1942 the Allies could substitute for financial the far more relevant physical and strategic criteria by which to control the flow of goods and services between their national economies. The absurdity of Lend-Lease accountancy can best be appreciated by recollecting that an aeroplane made in America flown by British pilots from an airfield in Britain would appear as a debit against Great Britain; whereas an identical aeroplane flown by American pilots from the same airfield, if its supply of petrol came from Haifa, would appear as a debit against the United States—if, indeed, anyone bothered to keep track.

As the system of unified commands, combined staffs, and combined operations developed, the old concept of national 'ownership' of the weapons and supplies used to fight the war became obsolete. Lend-Lease accounts were in reality a vestige of the time when the Act was passed, before the United States had become a full-scale war partner. Many men recognized this transformation at the time, especially those at or near the fronts where American and British units were operating side by side. But fear of Congressional or public disapproval in the United States prevented anyone from openly and officially abandoning the Lend-Lease accounting procedure, even when innumerable small transactions went unrecorded.

From the figures quoted above, it becomes clear that the major axis of Mutual Aid ran between the United States and the British family of nations. Russia's contribution took the form of death on the battlefield; and other nations played only marginal roles. The division of labour between the United States and the British Commonwealth was fairly simple.

[1] Allen ('Mutual Aid') makes the attempt for the entire period, and uses the ratio of \$7:£1 for munitions and \$4:£1 for other goods. These ratios were chosen to adjust for the high cost of munitions in the United States. Under war conditions the rate of exchange as fixed officially was nearly meaningless.

America sent munitions in ever growing quantity to Great Britain, Australia, India, New Zealand, &c.; and in addition sent food and industrial raw materials to Great Britain. In return the United States received a variety of services, and enjoyed the use of various military installations in Great Britain and throughout the Empire. In addition, Australia and New Zealand provided important quantities of food for U.S. forces operating in the Pacific. One may conceive the added power which such division of labour conferred upon the Allies by imagining the waste of shipping which would have resulted had Great Britain drawn food from the Southern Dominions while the United States shipped food to American forces in the Pacific. Yet, if financial barriers had been allowed to stand in the way of the common war effort, such would have been an obvious (indeed, a necessary) way to help maintain the sterling balance.

The Mutual Aid system was an indispensable prerequisite for the sort of combined operations which were undertaken first on a small scale in New Guinea and India, then in North Africa. Under the system American tanks could stock up on British petrol or vice versa; spare parts could be exchanged as need arose; food stocks could be drawn upon freely regardless of which army needed rations, &c. Without such flexibility, the duplication of rear services and delay in supplying urgent wants would have made Anglo-American combined operations almost if not altogether impossible.

It is, however, worth pointing out that the system of Mutual Aid was not universal among the Allies. Canada's peculiar position has already been mentioned; in addition, no financial eraser was employed in British dealings with such countries as Egypt or India. Consequently, the British piled up enormous indebtedness to these and other countries during the war years as a result of military purchases and the hiring of local labour for military construction work. In Britain's relation with Russia, too, Mutual Aid was incomplete. Munitions were 'free' and so were medical supplies. But other items, classified as civil, were delivered under an agreement by which the Soviet Government undertook to pay 40 per cent. of the cost in gold or dollars while contracting an interest-bearing debt for the balance.[1] Since no such restrictions were put upon civil supplies from the United States it is not surprising that items delivered under this agreement were of small amount.

When one considers the success which attended American industrial mobilization despite the early confusion, the extraordinary efforts of the British and the Russian industrial, agricultural, and transportation systems, the rationalizing effort of the Combined Boards, and the effectiveness

[1] Hancock and Gowing: *British War Economy*, p. 364.

of the Mutual Aid arrangement, it seems fair to assert that the Allies showed unusual daring and imagination in departing from traditional forms of international and domestic economic relations in order to work together more effectively in waging a common war. Nothing comparable was achieved during the First World War; nothing comparable was achieved by the Axis nations; nor had anything comparable been conceived in advance even in 1941.

By the end of 1942 the administrative machinery for the direction of the Allied war effort had been successfully developed and only a few changes proved necessary during the rest of the war. The new administrative machinery of inter-Allied co-operation had also begun abundantly to justify itself. Munitions and supplies, produced on a scale scarcely dreamed of before, were distributed to Allied forces all round the globe according to military and political rather than to financial criteria. This fact constitutes one of the greatest innovations of the Second World War. The compartmentation of national economies was breached and broken through. An Allied control, centred in Washington, became strong enough to affect vitally each national economy and, in doing so, brought them all into a more or less well co-ordinated whole. The Grand Alliance became an economic even more than a political and military fact.

(iii) Shakedown in the Pacific, December 1941–May 1942

(*a*) Military Adjustments to Japan's Conquests

The first three months of 1942 saw an amazing series of Japanese victories in the South-West Pacific and in South-East Asia. Japanese forces were superior to anything the Allies could bring to bear in those regions; and even when, as at Singapore, Japanese troops were locally outnumbered, their tactics, morale, and training for tropic warfare proved so far superior as to assure relatively easy victories.

The only bright spot for the Allies in the Pacific was Bataan peninsula in Luzon, the main island of the Philippine archipelago, where a desperate defence successfully stood off Japanese attacks for four months. Retreating before superior Japanese forces, American and Filipino troops withdrew from Manila (captured on 2 January 1942) and established a continuous defence line across Bataan. The Japanese found this line hard to penetrate. General Douglas MacArthur, who was in command, rapidly acquired a great reputation. His men were the only ones who seemed able to stop the Japanese. But the brave resistance could not go on indefinitely without relief from outside. The distances of the Pacific and Japanese command of the sea and air made reinforcement impossible. Only a few ships, submarines, and aeroplanes succeeded in getting through to the Philippines bringing a handful of supplies. As the Japanese conquests extended southward, hope of relief dwindled; and with hope, supplies and fighting man-power dwindled too. On 9 April 1942 the troops in Bataan surrendered; and on 6 May the American flag on Corregidor, an island fortress in Manila Bay, was hauled down when the last remnant of the garrison of the Philippines surrendered.

Before the bitter end came, General MacArthur escaped on 11 March by motor torpedo-boat and aeroplane, travelling south to Australia to take up a higher command. He was personally much affected by the defeat in the Philippines. MacArthur's feeling for the Philippines, and his vehement desire to return as soon as possible, had an important influence on later strategic decisions in the Pacific war; but in the dark times of 1942 the significance of the defence of Bataan was psychological. Americans had something they could feel proud of in the way their own and the Filipino troops had fought.[1]

From a general point of view, however, the rear-guard action on Bataan was only a side show. Japan's principal efforts were made farther south and east; and at the Arcadia Conference the Allies had entrusted the defence of the threatened region to General Wavell. But the unified Allied Command which he was supposed to establish hardly had time to begin functioning before the weight of Japanese attack broke it up. Wavell arrived in Batavia in Java to take up his new duties on 10 January 1942. There was, however, all too little for him to command. Allied naval forces were markedly inferior to the Japanese; Allied air forces were at an even greater disadvantage; and with superiority in these two arms, the Japanese could strike almost at will, landing at one point after another in the Netherlands East Indies, in the islands of the South-West Pacific, outflanking British lines in Malaya, and threatening Australia.

Wavell had also to face complicated frictions within his own camp. The Dutch had not been consulted before the decision to set up the A.B.D.A. Command had been made at the Arcadia Conference, and were understandably nettled.[2] Soothing explanations from Roosevelt and Churchill secured Dutch consent to the arrangement, but for all that a residue of hard feeling remained. Success would have quickly dispelled it, but disaster had the opposite effect. Dutch admirals chafed at finding the defence of their islands in the hands of British and American officers, and there was

[1] The effectiveness of Filipino soldiers stood in contrast to the behaviour of the Malay, Indonesian, and Burmese populations, most of whom either welcomed or passively accepted Japanese conquest (or liberation, depending on how one viewed it). To be sure, the Filipino civilian population accepted Japanese conquest in much the same fashion as did the peoples of Malaya, Indonesia, and Burma, and the Japanese had no difficulty in finding political figures to co-operate with them. But the conduct of the Filipino units under MacArthur's command seemed to nearly all Americans a striking justification of American policy towards the islands, and helped to convince Americans generally that they had something to teach the European colonial Powers.

[2] Sherwood: *Roosevelt and Hopkins*, p. 458; Eng. edition, i. 471; Morison: *History of U.S. Naval Operations*, iii. 311–12.

little or no time to work out differences in staff procedures, signal arrangements, and the like. As a result, the Supreme Headquarters never worked very well, especially after the fall of Singapore had seriously discredited British military prestige and with it General Wavell's authority.

It was not only the Dutch who were restive. The Australians, too, developed a lively fear for the security of their homeland and were not willing to see Australian troops or ships used to shore up sagging defences in other parts of the front. Four Australian divisions were stationed in the Middle East when the Japanese attack began. Naturally enough, the Australian Government wanted these experienced troops at home, and wanted them home as soon as possible.[1] The loss of the greater part of an Australian division at Singapore convinced many people in Australia that British commanders were bungling and incompetent. The contrast between the American resistance on Bataan and the British collapse at Singapore made them turn more and more towards the United States in hope of succour.

As soon as shipping could be found, two of the four Australian divisions in the Middle East started for home. The leading division was just rounding the tip of India when a new crisis broke out. As Supreme Commander of the A.B.D.A. Area, Wavell decided that Burma was the place where the homeward bound Australians would be most useful. Japanese forces had begun the conquest of that country and were threatening to cut off the Burma Road; but timely reinforcements, it seemed, might stop their advance or even turn it back. Churchill, too, arrived at the same conclusion and hoped to be able to persuade the Australian Government to agree. His idea was that if American troops arrived in Australia itself to protect that continent and stop the Japanese advance on the eastern flank, Australian troops could do the same on the western flank in Burma. American troops were actually *en route* to Australia across the Pacific just as the Australians were *en route* across the Indian Ocean.

From a military point of view the plan seemed eminently sound, if risky. No one could be sure that the Australians would arrive in Burma soon enough, nor that their numbers would suffice to stop the Japanese. But Churchill's plan took no account of the state of feeling in Australia. Consequently, when on 20 February 1942, just five days after the fall of Singapore, Churchill asked the Australian Government to approve the diversion of one of their divisions to Burma, he met with a stony refusal. The situation was embittered by Churchill's hasty action. Realizing that time was of the essence, he ordered the ships with the Australians on board to turn northward towards Burma without waiting for reply from the Aus-

[1] A change in government which had brought the Australian Labour Party to power in October 1941 was an important factor in the crisis. The Australian Labour Party was not empire-minded, and the Prime Minister, John Curtin, did not get on well with Churchill. Cf. Churchill's remarks (Churchill, iv. 8, 13; U.S. edition, iv. 9, 15).

tralian Government. This only angered the Australians. They remembered Greece and Singapore, and felt that the British were once again prepared to throw Australian troops into a desperate gamble, a gamble that might expose Australia herself to the risk of invasion. The Prime Minister, Curtin, emphatically reiterated his demand for the return of the Australian divisions, and Churchill had no choice but to concur. He did so on 23 February in a curt telegram.[1]

This affair not only put a severe strain upon Australia's loyalty to Great Britain, but marked an important step in the break-up of the A.B.D.A. Command and of effective Allied co-operation in the war against Japan. Theoretically, the Australian Government had accepted Wavell as Supreme Commander; but when it came to the pinch they were not willing to accept his plan for the defence of the area assigned to him. It should be made clear that the Australians were in no sense breaking their obligations. The troops Wavell and Churchill wanted in Burma had not been formally assigned to the A.B.D.A. Command. They were homeward bound; and Wavell and Churchill had no legal power to order them on any mission. Nevertheless, the Australian refusal deprived Wavell of his sole remaining hope of forming a land front against the Japanese.[2]

The Australian refusal of land reinforcement for the A.B.D.A. Command was soon followed by naval disaster. The battle of the Java Sea on 27 February 1942 destroyed or dispersed Allied naval strength. Remnants of the fleet retired westward to Ceylon or southward to Australia. Naturally enough, it was British ships that went west, Australian and American that went south. The Dutch tried vainly to stay on and defend Java, but the task was impossible, and only a few Dutch submarines escaped. The Japanese landed on Java on 1 March and just a week later the Dutch surrendered the island.

Before this final scene, the A.B.D.A. Command had fallen apart. With Australians intransigent, the Dutch discontented, without any sizeable body of troops, and with only a smattering of an air force at his command, Wavell decided that the effort to exercise a unified Allied Command in the vast area which had originally been entrusted to him was vain. As early as 16 February he contemplated the loss of Java; by 20 February British forces began their evacuation from the island; and on 25 February Wavell himself departed for Ceylon.

Nominally, the A.B.D.A. Command was retained in being after Wavell's departure, with the Dutch Governor General as Supreme Commander. But he was helpless. On 1 March the British naval commander, who had

[1] Texts of some of the telegrams exchanged between the principals of this negotiation are reproduced in Churchill, iv. 138–46; U.S. edition, iv. 157–66.

[2] One Australian division remained in the Middle East until the end of 1942 and saw notable service in the battle of Alamein. Thus the Australians did not cease to contribute to the defence of the Empire, despite the dangers at home.

remained in Java, decided that withdrawal was imperative, his American colleague concurred, and the Allied A.B.D.A. Command was formally dissolved.[1]

So ended, ingloriously enough, the first experiment in Allied combined command. It had been a resounding failure. Under the conditions which Wavell and his subordinates had to face, success would have been most difficult. Only if Singapore had held could the A.B.D.A. Command have become an operational reality. The fall of Singapore seems in retrospect to have been avoidable: but avoidable only with better preparation, different tactics, and, perhaps, more modern equipment which could only have been provided at the expense of other war fronts. The preparation, at least, was beyond the control of the A.B.D.A. Command: to be effective it would have had to start months if not years before Wavell took over. Altogether, the brief career of the first Allied Command was not a happy one; and its failure left a mark upon Allied co-operation in the Pacific which endured throughout the war.

Obviously the situation which had so unexpectedly developed in the Far East and in the South Pacific called for reorganization. On 9 March 1942 Roosevelt telegraphed a proposal to Churchill. The key sentences were as follows:

> The whole of the operation[al] responsibility for the Pacific area will rest on the United States. The Army, Navy, and Air operating decisions for the area as a whole will be made in Washington by the United States Chiefs of Staff, and there will be in Washington an Advisory Council on operational matters, with members from Australia, New Zealand, Netherlands East Indies, and China, with an American presiding. . . .
>
> The middle area, extending from Singapore to and including India and the Indian Ocean, Persian Gulf, Red Sea, Libya, and the Mediterranean, would fall directly under British responsibility. All operating matters in this area would be decided by you. . . .[2]

In a third zone, the Atlantic and European area, joint Anglo-American responsibility was to continue.

The President's proposal became the basis for some weeks of negotiation. Australian and Dutch feelings were inflamed, and they distrusted the men and methods that had been used against the Japanese. They wanted to have a greater voice in Allied counsels, but with the loss of the East Indies,

[1] Morison (*History of U.S. Naval Operations*, iii. 376–7) reproduces the American participant's recollection of the final scene. Dutch resentment against the British was intense.

[2] Churchill, iv. 175; U.S. edition, iv. 197–8. Cf. Sherwood: *Roosevelt and Hopkins*, pp. 509–10; Eng. edition, ii. 514–15. This proposal, of course, represented an acceptance of the principle of separate spheres of military responsibility which the British had urged at the Arcadia Conference. It seems likely that Wavell's failure discredited the idea of Allied commands, at least in the extra-European and Atlantic theatres.

the Dutch had lost their role in the Far East as far as active warfare was concerned. Australia, on the contrary, was very much in the forefront, for many persons expected Japan's next move would be to invade that continent. Accordingly, the Australians made a determined effort to win a place in the inner circle of Allied war deliberation. Herbert Evatt, Foreign Minister of the Australian Government, made a trip to Washington and London in order to force his Government's views upon the reluctant British and undecided Americans. Details of the negotiation cannot be reconstructed from the information which had been published in 1952, but it is possible to outline the result which emerged by the beginning of April 1942.

First of all, two Pacific War Councils were set up, one in London, one in Washington. The London Council had been established on 10 February 1942, largely in the hope of stilling the rising dissatisfaction of the Australians at the conduct of the war in Malaya.[1] From its inception, however, the Council was of little importance.[2] The Australians were not satisfied to have London direct the war in the Far East. It was in large part their insistence which led to the establishment on 1 April 1942 of a second Pacific War Council with its seat in Washington. Roosevelt himself acted as chairman, and China, Great Britain, the Netherlands, Australia, New Zealand, and Canada were all represented. Later the Philippines and India were added. The public announcement said that the new Pacific War Council would maintain 'intimate contact with a similar body in London';[3] but in practice this body, too, exercised little influence on the course of events in the Pacific.

The two Pacific War Councils were, in fact, concessions to the indignant smaller nations of the Pacific area, especially to Australia. Neither Britain nor America was desirous of submitting the difficult decisions of high strategy to examination, criticism, or obstruction by the smaller nations. In particular, the American armed services resented civilian efforts to control or direct military strategy, in the Pacific or anywhere else.[4] The fundamental decision—to fight Germany first—had already been taken by Britain and America; and in face of that fact Australian hopes for early massive action against Japan were doomed to disappointment. In so far as the lesser members of the Pacific Council tried to call into question this and other decisions of the Combined Chiefs of Staff, their efforts were repulsed.

[1] Cf. the Australian Foreign Minister's statement to the Australian Parliament, 25 February 1942, in *Documents on American Foreign Relations, 1941–1942*, pp. 579–82.

[2] It died a quiet death in 1943, long before the Pacific war was near a close (cf. Churchill, iv. 16–17; U.S. edition, iv. 18–19).

[3] *Documents on American Foreign Relations, 1941–1942*, p. 244. The establishment of the Pacific War Council in London did not directly affect political and military liaison between the British and Dominion Governments, which continued as before through regular channels. However, the inability of Great Britain to help Australia and New Zealand in their hour of danger did change relationships significantly. For remarks on this subject see above, pp. 37–39.

[4] Sherwood: *Roosevelt and Hopkins*, p. 515; Eng. edition, ii. 520.

As a result, the Pacific War Council became little more than a means of airing grievances.

The establishment of the two Pacific War Councils marked the high water mark of efforts to put the direction of the war into the hands of a widely representative body. The inherent unwieldiness of any committee on which divergent interests were fully represented, and the opposition of the British and American Governments, defeated the plan. Australia and all the other smaller Powers were condemned to the exercise of only marginal influence upon high strategy, speaking as it were from the wings. Inasmuch as the Anglo-American monopoly of strategic decision reflected the realities of military and economic power, the system worked well enough; and it seems clear that any body on which such nations as Australia, China, and the Netherlands had equal voice with Britain and America could not in practice have made the key decisions. Powerful nations have never yet been willing to submit their actions to majority vote of small Powers.

The reorganization of military commands in the Pacific and Far Eastern areas was of more practical importance for the conduct of the war than were the two Pacific Councils. In place of the A.B.D.A. and China combined commands, four independent but interlocking war theatres were established. The principle of unity of command was discarded or disregarded in the new arrangement. The Americans set up three commands: the Pacific, the South-West Pacific, and China–Burma–India. In India the British retained their traditional military organization. The set-up was awkward on paper, especially in India, and proved even more awkward in practice.

One may speculate on the reasons why Marshall's principle of unity of command was abandoned, but the records which might substantiate speculation had not been published in 1952. A.B.D.A.'s failure must have been one factor, and the ruffled state of feeling between the national groups which had been associated under Wavell must also have played a part. The whole arrangement was obvious makeshift, but, once agreed to, the commands froze for the duration of the war. Later efforts to improve command relationships were never more than superficially successful.

In the Pacific, the new arrangements were established by a directive of 4 April 1942. The Pacific Ocean area was placed under the command of Admiral Chester Nimitz of the U.S. navy. His headquarters in Hawaii was a joint army–navy affair, but the navy of course predominated. Subordinate commands for the north, central, and south Pacific were set up, the latter including New Caledonia and New Zealand. In this theatre the only Ally of any importance was New Zealand; and New Zealand's part was almost restricted to supply and the provision of base facilities, &c. Most of the New Zealand troops remained in the Mediterranean. As a result, for all practical purposes, Americans found themselves in undisputed control; and, in accordance with Roosevelt's suggestion of 9 March, quoted above, the American Joint Chiefs of Staff, not the Combined Chiefs of Staff, exercised supreme operational direction in this theatre.[1]

The South-West Pacific Area, including Australia, the Solomons,[2] the Dutch East Indies (except for Sumatra), and the Philippines, was put under the command of General MacArthur. MacArthur arrived in Australia from Bataan on 17 March 1942. It was immediately announced that he would take command of the then undefined South-West Pacific area. Negotiations with the Australians and other interested parties took quite a long time, and it was not until 19 April 1942 that public announcement of the scope of MacArthur's authority was made.[3] The South-West Pacific was an Allied command, with British, Dutch, Australians, and Americans all officially contributing to it. In practice, however, only the Australians and the Americans could send significant forces, and the participation of the other two nations was little more than nominal.

The Australians, however, put all their troops (except for one division which remained in the Middle East until after Alamein), ships and aeroplanes under MacArthur's supreme command. At first an Australian, General Blamey, exercised command of the ground forces, while navy and air force were put under American commanders. Later MacArthur split the army command, and created an independent American army to undertake operations northward towards the Philippines. Despite its Allied character, MacArthur's headquarters, like that of Nimitz, was placed directly under the American Joint Chiefs of Staff, and was exempt from any but indirect control by the Combined Chiefs.

The principle of unified command was explicitly violated in the South-West Pacific. In March 1942 it was decided that Nimitz should exercise strategic control of naval operations everywhere in the Pacific, even within the limits of MacArthur's command; but in the South-West Pacific theatre MacArthur was given exclusive control of ground forces and land-based

[1] Morison: *History of U.S. Naval Operations*, iv. 249. The Combined Chiefs, of course, still controlled the allocation of forces among the various theatres of war, and thus exercised an important limiting influence on the Pacific campaigns. The independence of the American Joint Chiefs of Staff in the Pacific was reaffirmed and made more definite at the Casablanca Conference in January 1943 (ibid. vi. 7).

[2] The Solomons were transferred to Nimitz's command at the time of the Guadalcanal operation in August 1942.

[3] *Documents on American Foreign Relations, 1941–1942*, p. 245. It has been intimated that MacArthur expected to take supreme command of the entire war against Japan at the time of his escape from Bataan. This would help to account for the very bad personal relations which later prevailed between him and the leaders of the U.S. navy. Cf. Sherwood: *Roosevelt and Hopkins*, note to vol. ii, pp. 84–85 of paper-board edition only (New York, Bantam Books, 1950).

aircraft.[1] Many of the unfortunate results which Marshall had foreseen flowed from this separation of naval from ground and air commands. When operations in the Solomon Islands and in New Guinea called for combined naval and air force action—as they regularly did—co-ordination was not good; rival claims and recrimination over failures developed to a serious degree; and personal, strategic, and service differences of opinion were allowed relatively free scope. Relations between the two commands were consequently embittered throughout the war.

It is easy to understand why the Chiefs of Staff gave Admiral Nimitz control over naval forces in the whole Pacific. It would have been most wasteful to have maintained a separate fleet, under separate command, in the South-West Pacific area, especially in 1942 when American naval weakness required skilful shuttling of aircraft carriers from the Coral Sea to Midway and back again to meet Japanese thrusts. When MacArthur took command in Australia it looked as though the Japanese might invade that continent and establish a major land front. In such a situation, MacArthur's ground and air command would have made sense. But, as it turned out, MacArthur's operations began in the jungles of New Guinea, where the absence of roads and the nature of the terrain made armies wholly dependent on supplies brought by sea and air. When, later, MacArthur was able to start on his island-hopping campaigns, the anomalies of his relationship to Nimitz became a standing source of trouble. He depended on naval support and ship transport, but had to conduct negotiations of a semi-diplomatic character with U.S. naval authorities before appropriate naval support could be assured for operations he planned to undertake.

The logical solution of these difficulties would have been to establish a single supreme commander for the entire Pacific area. But this raised insuperable difficulties. The U.S. navy would not even consider giving such a command to MacArthur, a mere soldier and no friend of the navy; yet the alternative, subordinating MacArthur to Nimitz, would have raised serious political difficulties in the United States,[2] and perhaps also in Australia. As a result, nothing was done, and the makeshift arrangement of April 1942 survived until almost the end of the war.

Command arrangements in China, Burma, and India were even more

[1] Morison: *History of U.S. Naval Operations*, iv. 13.

[2] After Bataan, MacArthur became a great hero, especially celebrated in the section of the American press which was most hostile to Roosevelt. As early as May 1942 MacArthur was touted as presidential timber (*The Times*, 19 May 1942) and in 1943 an organized 'MacArthur for President' campaign was begun. Consequently, any diminution of his authority would have been interpreted as a political move on Roosevelt's part, and would undoubtedly have stirred up loud protests.

confused than in the Pacific. While the A.B.D.A. Command was breaking up, defeats in Burma had a similar effect upon the second 'allied' command which had been set up in China at the Arcadia Conference. It will be recalled that Chiang Kai-shek accepted supreme command, and agreed that an American general should become his Chief of Staff. General Joseph W. Stilwell was appointed to that post and arrived in China on 3 March 1942. By that time the Japanese had already begun to invade Burma and four days later, on 7 March, the British were compelled to evacuate Rangoon. The loss of Rangoon meant the loss of the only port through which supplies for China could easily come.

Three Chinese divisions had already taken stations in northern Burma and Stilwell strove to bring them into action against the advancing Japanese. But ill feeling between the British and Chinese was acute, and Chiang Kai-shek was not willing to entrust untrammelled command over his troops to the American general. At the same time no definite legal relationship had been established between the British commander in Burma, General Sir Harold Alexander, and Stilwell; and the geographic boundaries of the 'allied' command in which Chiang Kai-shek exercised authority were not clear. Plans laid at the Arcadia Conference had not envisaged Burma as a threatre of war, and the Allies were not prepared either militarily or administratively to conduct a campaign there.

These difficulties were not relieved by defeat. Towards the end of March 1942 the Japanese renewed their offensive and by May the whole of Burma had been conquered. The southern terminus of the Burma Road fell into Japanese hands, and thereafter communication between China and India was limited to air routes.

The physical separation of the Indian from the Chinese fronts added a new complication to the already tangled lines of authority. A new American theatre was established—China–Burma–India—and Stilwell became its commander. In practice he had at his disposal mostly air force personnel who manned a new airline over the 'Hump' from India to China, which now became the sole source of outside supplies available to Chiang Kai-shek. But at both ends of the Hump, Stilwell's relationship with the established authorities was exceedingly awkward.

In China, Stilwell and Chiang bickered constantly. The basic difficulty was this: Stilwell's formal title as 'Chief of Staff' to Chiang Kai-shek had been intended by the Americans to justify his assumption of operational control over the armies of the Kuomintang Government. Roosevelt and Marshall had hoped that Chiang as an Allied Commander-in-Chief would busy himself with political or other tasks, and leave the job of reforming, training, and deploying the Chinese armies in Stilwell's hands.[1] But when

[1] One should remember that General Marshall's official title was Chief of Staff to Roosevelt, the American Commander-in-Chief. As a matter of course, Roosevelt left the supervision of

Chiang accepted Stilwell as his 'Chief of Staff' he had no intention of falling in with any such plan. He was quite unwilling to turn his army over to a foreigner, and yet he felt it hardly safe to defy the Americans openly. Instead he resorted to devious methods, secretly countermanding Stilwell's orders, or delaying decisions he disliked. What Chiang did want from Stilwell and the Americans was an abundant flow of supplies; and to get them he was prepared to soothe Stilwell with flattering words. He was not, however, prepared to give him any more power over Chinese soldiers than could be helped. Such a situation was in the nature of things a trying one, and only a supreme diplomat could have negotiated the obstacles which lay in the path of effective utilization of the Chinese forces. Stilwell was not a diplomat: quite the contrary, he fully earned his nickname of 'Vinegar Joe'.

Physical obstacles to the delivery of war material to China were enormous after the Burma Road had been cut. Since the Americans were able to deliver only a trickle of supplies by air over the Himalayas, Chiang saw little reason to give more than lip service to Stilwell's demands for reform of his army. General Stilwell was therefore unable to do much to transform the Chinese army. He did, however, establish a training camp in India, and before 1942 was over he managed to begin training a small Chinese force there for a future campaign to recover northern Burma and reopen land communications from India to China.

American and Chinese activities in India, however, meant co-ordination and co-operation with the British. And Stilwell was as unable to get on well with the British as he was with the Chinese Government. The British, for their part, had small faith in the fighting qualities of Chinese troops, and tended to think that supplies assigned to them were wasted. Their own Indian army took precedence; and the defence of India, including the maintenance of civil order in that troubled land, seemed more important than reconquest of Burma—the aim towards which Stilwell steadily bent all his efforts.

With such differences of view, it is not surprising that there was friction between the Americans and the British. Supreme military command in India was entrusted to Wavell immediately after he had been forced to abandon Java. Wavell's command was entirely separate from Stilwell's,

military training and troop deployment to Marshall, and took a hand only in the determination of general strategy. This was the model the Americans had in mind for Stilwell in China. In supposing that Chinese social, political, and military conditions could be assimilated to those prevailing in the United States by a simple act of will or through an agreement on paper, the Americans were surely naïve, as Roosevelt also showed himself when he tried his hand at constitution-building for India (see above, p. 40). The delicate relation between civil authority and military command in China had no analogue in the stable constitutional system of the United States, and it appears that Roosevelt and his advisers never realized how impossible it was for Chiang Kai-shek to abdicate personal control over his armies and generals without undermining his civil authority at the same time.

but since Stilwell operated partly in India, he inevitably trespassed, or seemed to trespass, upon Wavell's authority.[1]

The jurisdictional tangle was exacerbated by the shortage of all sorts of supplies—a shortage which in turn reflected the over-all assignment of priority to other theatres of war. In the Pacific the U.S. navy was a powerful claimant; but Europe and the Mediterranean took precedence in British and in U.S. army thinking. China, Burma, and India ranked a poor third; and the vast distances which separated that theatre from Britain and America made everything doubly difficult. The lack of supplies combined with Stilwell's prickly personality made Allied co-operation in the Far East at best a guttering flame.

The one sphere in which effective Allied co-operation might have been possible was on the seas. The British fleet in the Indian Ocean and the American in the Pacific might well have co-ordinated their activities against the Japanese. Yet little was done. The British Admiralty felt that they were excluded from a proper share in American naval planning. Admiral King's irascible temper often led him to disagree violently with the British, and made relations on the topmost level somewhat strained.[2] In the first part of 1942, relations between the fleets in the Indian and Pacific Oceans were not very cordial. In May when the Japanese attack on Midway Island was looming, the Americans asked that a British aircraft carrier which was operating in the Indian Ocean be sent to join the U.S. Pacific Fleet. The request was refused on 19 May 1942, so that the Americans had to face four Japanese carriers with only three of their own.[3] It was incidents such as this that led Churchill to complain to Hopkins in April that 'our two Fleets were acting as though they were two totally independent forces'.[4]

Later in the year a modicum of co-operation was established. At the time of the American landing on Guadalcanal,[5] for example, the British fleet made a diversionary manœuvre in the Indian Ocean.[6] But such actions fell far short of large-scale combined operations and, as the war progressed in the Pacific and as the U.S. fleet increased in size, the Americans showed less and less interest in getting British help. Some American admirals seemed to feel that the Japanese war was a private feud between Japan and the U.S. navy and did not want third parties mixing in. This

[1] By all odds the most illuminating account of the situation in India and China is embodied in *The Stilwell Papers, passim.* The book is composed of diaries, notes, and jottings made by Stilwell himself, and vividly reveals his personality and his harsh judgements of the men with whom he had to work.

[2] Leahy: *I Was There*, pp. 128–9.

[3] Morison: *History of U.S. Naval Operations*, iv. 81.

[4] Sherwood: *Roosevelt and Hopkins*, p. 525; Eng. edition, ii. 530; cf. ibid. pp. 510 and 515 respectively.

[5] See below, pp. 216–17.

[6] Morison, op. cit. iv. 276–7.

attitude, combined with the British caution lest the fleet in the Indian Ocean be weakened too much, kept naval co-operation to a minimum. Ships of the Australian and New Zealand navies did fight side by side with the U.S. navy in the Pacific, but they were not numerous and could not play a major part in the war.

(*b*) Political Obstacles to Allied Co-operation in the War against Japan

The contrast between the level of Allied co-operation attained in the Pacific and Far East with that attained in Europe was very striking. Some of the reasons for the difference have been suggested above. The personalities of Stilwell and MacArthur did not encourage co-operation; lack of supplies doomed all ambitious plans to discard or postponement. Inter-service rivalries assumed a peculiarly acute form within the American forces. And finally, geographic obstacles made the Japanese war into two separate wars: one fought in Asia, supplied from America and Britain to the west; the other fought in the Pacific, supplied from America to the east.

In addition to these military factors, there were fundamental political difficulties in both India and China which did much to obstruct Allied co-operation. In China, a half submerged civil war between the Kuomintang and the Communists continued to distract Chiang Kai-shek from single-minded fighting against the Japanese. Indeed, Chiang may have felt, as his critics alleged, that his primary enemy was no longer the Japanese. Japan's eventual defeat could be counted upon as a result of American efforts, but his domestic rivals for power, the Chinese Communists, could not be counted out so easily, and required careful watching. Such an attitude invited clashes with Stilwell, who was much impressed by the military effectiveness of the Chinese Communists and of their Russian mentors.[1] In 1942, when the end of the war was clearly still far in the future, this aspect of the Chinese problem was not prominent. It became crucial later.

The political situation in India in 1942 was, however, of the greatest importance. The Japanese threat to India, which seemed especially acute in the early months of the year, raised for Indian leaders the question of what attitude to take towards their fellow Asiatics, conquerors of a great empire in a short three months. Some Indian leaders hated British rule so much as to welcome the prospect of Japanese liberation. Such extremists were not, however, very numerous or very influential. Gandhi took a

[1] *The Stilwell Papers*, pp. 181, 210, 262, 317, 321; cf. Sherwood: *Roosevelt and Hopkins*, p. 759; Eng. edition, ii. 756.

pacifist position. He disapproved of violence in any form and declared that Indians should abstain from the war, neither helping the British nor opposing the Japanese. Gandhi's great personal prestige made his voice an important one in India, and some Indians hoped that, if somehow British rule in India could be broken, the Japanese would respect Indian neutrality. In rough accord with Gandhi's ideas, the Congress Party, representing the politically active fraction of the Hindu population, demanded Indian independence and the prompt establishment of an Indian national government which would be free from British control.

The British Government, however, were by no means disposed to give up their control over India while the world was still at war. Friction and distrust between the Hindu majority and the Muslim minority in India were, as post-war events later proved, a real obstacle to the establishment of Indian independence. The British were particularly sensitive to Muslim pressure, partly because a large part of the Indian army was recruited from among Muslims, partly because the British had a delicate position to defend in the Middle East and needed Muslim support there, and partly because the conflict between Muslims and Hindus constituted the best justification for the continuation of British rule in India. In addition to the difficulties in India itself, any programme of immediate and unqualified independence for India had to face opposition in England. An important group in the Cabinet and in Parliament disliked the idea of surrendering British control over India; and Churchill himself should perhaps be numbered among them.[1]

Nevertheless, in the spring of 1942 some step to appease Indian disaffection seemed imperative. The British Cabinet sent Sir Stafford Cripps to India in March to see whether a settlement satisfactory to both British and Indian leaders could be reached. Cripps took with him a definite proposal which had been approved by the British Government, offering India the promise of Dominion status after the end of hostilities. The proposal fell far short of what Gandhi and other Indian leaders desired, and the negotiation ended in failure.

The progress of the Cripps mission to India was followed with eager attention by Roosevelt. Louis Johnson arrived in India while negotiations were in progress as a special representative of the President, and he was not backward in expressing the hope that Indian self-government would be established forthwith, at least in preliminary form. His activities roused deep suspicion among British officials in India, to whom it appeared that the Americans were intent upon undermining British rule. When, in private correspondence with Churchill, Roosevelt urged drastic action to

[1] Churchill (iv. 184; U.S. edition, iv. 207) says he 'was of course committed' to Indian self-government; but his mind dwelt upon the obstacles to self-government, and his commitment was to a rather distant and undefined future.

establish Indian independence, he was pointedly rebuffed. This was one of the few cases in which Churchill flatly refused to accept American suggestions. He was intensely irritated by Roosevelt's idealism at British expense.[1]

Americans tended to plume themselves upon the example of their administration of the Philippines; but British administrators were not willing to take lessons in colonial administration from the United States. The British saw rank intervention in what appeared to Americans as a necessary step to bring about India's wholehearted participation in the war against Japan; but the more the Americans talked of the mobilization of India's man-power for war the more the British emphasized the internal problems of India and the dubious loyalty of the Congress Party to the Allied cause. This difference in attitude proved a fruitful source of mistrust. Efforts by Chiang Kai-shek to act as mediator between Indian and British points of view did nothing to make the British more receptive to outside suggestions.[2]

After the failure of Cripps's mission, Indians and British remained deadlocked. Gandhi and the Congress Party launched a campaign of civil disobedience, and in August 1942 the Mahatma was gaoled along with a few thousand members of the Congress Party. After that, tension continued to be acute, and widespread disorder broke out. By the end of 1942, however, police and army had largely restored public order, and as the prospect of Japanese invasion receded the intensity of the political crisis decreased.

It was by no means true that all the population of India shared the Congress Party's point of view. The Muslims certainly did not; and in fact it was only a small group of the Hindu population that would do more than engage in an occasional riot against the British. The peasant majority had only the vaguest conception of the political programmes and demands put forward by the Congress Party. Yet the situation in India was explosive. For long months in 1942 the sub-continent seemed to tremble on the verge of revolutionary disorder, and had the Japanese been able to attack, a great victory seemed easily theirs.

The British tried hard to establish stability and security. Police methods, sometimes harsh, checked open manifestations of discontent; and an ambitious programme for creating a great Indian army was speeded up. By the end of 1942 more than a million men had been enlisted into the Indian army, and the number was later raised to over two million. But this vast force required long training before it could take equal part in a

[1] Parts of Roosevelt's correspondence with Churchill about India are reproduced in Churchill, iv. 185–90, 192–6; U.S. edition, iv. 208–14, 217–21. For the collision of British and American views on India see Hull: *Memoirs*, ii. 1482–97; Sherwood: *Roosevelt and Hopkins*, pp. 511–12, 524–5; Eng. edition, ii. 515–16, 529–30.

[2] Churchill, iv. 183, 456; U.S. edition, iv. 206–7, 507.

technically complex war, for most of the recruits were simple peasants. And by the time the army had been trained up to reasonable efficiency, new obstacles—the shortage of shipping and other forms of transport—arose to limit its deployment against the enemy. As a result, a large proportion of the Indian army, so painfully built, never saw action.

Nevertheless, by the end of 1942 the first crisis created by the Japanese threat had been surmounted. Civil disorder in India ceased to be a serious danger to the rear, and a large army had been created to repel any Japanese attempt at invasion of India itself. But behind the façade, friction and distrust remained, not only between British and Indian political leaders, but between British and American and between British and Chinese leaders as well. Allied co-operation in India remained superficial, deeply troubled by fundamental cross purposes. Each group was inclined to put the worst possible interpretation on the others' actions and motives. Americans accused the British of inactivity and half-heartedness in the war against Japan; the British suspected the Americans of seeking to overthrow British rule in India; and the Chinese intrigued among themselves and with both Americans and British for private and party advantage.

A final deficiency in Allied co-operation in the war against Japan needs only to be mentioned. The Soviet Union stood resolutely apart from the struggle and continued to maintain diplomatically correct relations with Japan. In China, the Russians maintained ambiguous relations with the Kuomintang Government and with the Communists; but in 1942 Russia's attention and strength were fastened on the German war, and she did not pursue any very active policy in China.

(iv) Planning a Second Front, April–November 1942

(*a*) Anglo-American Relations with Russia

Relations between the Western Allies and Russia were always deeply influenced by the progress of military operations on the Russian front. In November 1941 when the German advance towards Moscow had not yet been checked, Britain's inability to start a second front or to send large forces to fight in Russia led to sharp exchanges between Stalin and Churchill.[1] When at the beginning of December the German drive halted short of Moscow and a Russian counter-offensive began, relations took on a less urgent, less acrimonious tone. This was the state of affairs when Anthony Eden, British Foreign Minister, undertook a visit to Moscow. He left Britain on 7 December 1941. The sudden extension of the war to the Pacific and America's entry into full-fledged belligerency on the very eve of his departure obviously called for readjustment of British policy;

[1] See above, pp. 48–56.

but Eden proceeded on his way to the Soviet capital without waiting for the new shape of world affairs to become clear.

Eden had two purposes. First, he hoped to be able to formalize the alliance between Britain and Russia which had been established in a preliminary fashion by the Cripps–Molotov agreement of 12 July 1941. A treaty of alliance such as the British Cabinet hoped to sign would commit both parties to fight until Hitler's overthrow. It would help to exorcize the spectre of a separate peace. Such a treaty also implied the settlement of outstanding differences between the two Governments. By all odds the most immediate of these was military; and Eden's second purpose in going to Moscow was to review with Stalin the military picture as a whole in the hope of impressing upon the Soviet leader the potentialities of and the obstacles to British military deployment against Germany.

The British Cabinet seriously considered the possibility of sending troops to fight on the southern Russian front; but such plans were contingent upon first defeating the Axis in Libya. On 5 December 1941 Churchill authorized Eden to promise the Russians ten squadrons of the R.A.F. for service in southern Russia; but all calculations were upset by the Japanese attack, and five days later Churchill telegraphed to Eden to say that for the present at least the offer of R.A.F. help should not be made.[1] The result was that when Eden arrived in Moscow he had more obstacles than offers to present to the Russians.

The Russians, for their part, were anxious to assert their right to be consulted as an equal partner in any and all negotiations between the Allies, especially in those concerning post-war settlements. The way in which the Atlantic Charter had been concluded without reference to Russia had offended Stalin; and he was anxious lest the Western Powers should try to keep even a defeated Germany strong as a military counterweight to the Soviet Union.[2] Stalin's concern with post-war arrangements seems rather strange when one remembers that three and a half years of hard fighting lay ahead before Germany would be beaten. In December 1941, however, Stalin may have thought that the end of the war was much closer. References to ending the war in 1942 which appeared repeatedly in Stalin's speeches and in the Russian press between December 1941 and June 1942 do not prove, but certainly suggest, that Stalin thought Hitler would come to terms with the Allies, singly or together, before German power had been completely overthrown. If this was his judgement of the situation, post-war agreements were obviously of pressing importance, and it especially behoved the Russians to forestall, if possible, over-generous terms to Germany which might allow Hitler or his successors again to threaten the Soviet state.

On the military side, Stalin still professed to want a second front. But

[1] Churchill, iii. 475, 554; U.S. edition, iii. 535, 624.

[2] Hull: *Memoirs*, ii. 1165.

by the time Eden reached Moscow, the Japanese attack on British possessions in the Far East made it obvious that Britain would have little to spare for the next few months; and Stalin was not ready to join in the war against Japan in return for greater British military aid against Germany. Moreover, the Russian counter-offensive had just been launched. Stalin seems to have pinned high hopes upon it, thinking that German morale might crack and the German army be forced to withdraw from Russia entirely.[1] Consequently, Stalin did not really press Eden for an immediate invasion of France. He may, indeed, have preferred to continue alone, in a position to reap the glory and profit from any German collapse himself, without having to consider British or American wishes. In any case, neither side was able to offer any direct military help to the other immediately, so that aspect of Eden's conversations was unimportant.

Discussion instead centred upon the shape of post-war Europe. In the first conversation, Stalin set forth his ideas for a European settlement. He wanted to partition Germany and to collect reparations in kind from German industry. In general, he suggested restoration of pre-war frontiers, with minor modifications. There was, however, an important question as to what pre-war meant. To Stalin, pre-war meant before the Soviet Union was attacked; and he claimed that the pre-war boundaries of 1941 should be re-established. This meant that the territories he had annexed in 1939–40 would be recognized as legitimately and permanently a part of the Soviet state. In return, Stalin said he would support any British plans for securing bases in Western Europe. On the other hand, if the British would not agree to recognize his annexation of the Baltic states, and parts of Finland, Poland, and Rumania, Stalin declared that he would not sign the treaty of alliance which Eden wished to conclude.

The British Government were not surprised by these territorial demands. Stalin's ambitions had been made at least partially evident in preliminary conversations before Eden undertook his trip to Moscow.[2] The British attitude on the question was equivocal. Influential persons in the Foreign Office were convinced that some territorial concessions should be made; and Eden himself inclined to that view.[3] Churchill, however, stoutly opposed any agreement which would commit Great Britain to supporting the transfer of territory to Russia in advance of a future peace conference.[4] Churchill's reasons were twofold. First, and undoubtedly most important,

[1] Stalin: *Great Patriotic War*, pp. 42, 55. Cf. Werth: *Year of Stalingrad*, pp. 80, 92, 98, for samples of Russian press comment during these weeks.

[2] Hull: *Memoirs*, ii. 1166.

[3] Hull says that Eden 'indicated to Stalin he would endeavor to obtain a favorable decision from his Government' (ibid. p. 1168). Churchill's telegram of 8 January 1942 (quoted in Churchill, iii. 615–16; U.S. edition, iii. 685–6) is obviously an answer to a telegram recommending some concession to Russian territorial claims. Churchill, however, skates over the matter, without making it clear who had recommended what.

[4] Churchill, iii. 559–60, 615–16; U.S. edition, iii. 630, 685–6.

was the fact that the United States had taken a strong line against secret agreements and territorial settlements made in advance of a general peace conference. If Britain did not back up the American position, a fruitful source of friction between the two nations would arise at the very beginning of their war partnership. A second reason why Churchill refused to agree to territorial concessions to Russia was this: he thought that Russia would probably emerge greatly weakened from the war, and would be in no position to take what Stalin now demanded.[1] The full power of the Soviet Union had not yet been revealed.

The American stand and Churchill's vigorous veto of territorial concessions to Stalin temporarily stalemated Anglo-Russian negotiations for a treaty of alliance. During the following five months complex fears and hopes played upon the wills of the British and of the Russian Governments. The eventual outcome was the signature on 26 May 1942 of a formal treaty of alliance between the U.S.S.R. and Great Britain; but before that consummation was achieved military events and military plans had gone far towards transforming the situation as it had existed at the time of Eden's visit to Moscow.

When Stalin failed in December 1941 to win British endorsement for his territorial claims along the western frontier of Russia, it appears that the Soviet dictator turned his thoughts once again towards the possibility of securing similar or greater advantages from Germany. There were, from Stalin's point of view, two possibilities. Either Germany might collapse from within as a result of the Wehrmacht's winter losses in Russia,[2] or, failing that, Hitler might be persuaded to withdraw from his misadventure in the east by seeking a negotiated settlement of some sort. Stalin must have decided to test these possibilities when on 23 February 1942 he published an Order of the Day in commemoration of the anniversary of the establishment of the Red Army. In it he clearly adumbrated the possibility of a diplomatic settlement with Hitler. His words were as follows:

> Occasionally the foreign press engages in prattle to the effect that the Red Army's aim is to exterminate the German people and destroy the German state. This is, of course, a stupid lie and a witless slander against the Red Army. The Red Army has not and cannot have such idiotic aims. The Red Army's aim is

[1] Churchill, iii. 616; U.S. edition, iii. 696. The Americans, too, calculated on a greatly weakened Russia, and thought that one reason why Stalin insisted was that he expected not to be strong enough to take what he wanted when the war had ended (Hull: *Memoirs*, ii. 1169).

[2] After all, Hitler had until the winter of 1941–2 experienced an unbroken series of successes, and it may have seemed plausible to suppose that revolutionary discontent—perhaps exaggerated to Stalin by Comintern informants—might break out in his rear when the magic of victory deserted the Nazi standards.

to drive out the German occupants from our country and liberate Soviet soil from the German fascist invaders.

It is very likely that the war for liberation of the Soviet land will result in ousting or destroying Hitler's clique. We should welcome such an outcome. But it would be ridiculous to identify Hitler's clique with the German people and the German state. History shows that Hitlers come and go, but the German people and the German state remain.[1]

What interpretation should be put upon these words? Out of context one may be tempted to put too much emphasis upon the passage; yet the Order of the Day as a whole was conspicuously lacking in denunciation of the Germans. It seems certain that Stalin meant his words to be heard not only in Berlin but in London and Washington as well. In effect he was saying to Hitler: 'Are you interested in a negotiated peace?', and to the German people: 'Are you interested in peace, even if Hitler is not?'. In either case, withdrawal of German troops from Soviet soil was all that Stalin asked. Whether Hitler and his clique were overthrown or whether they remained in power was left an open question.[2]

At the same time, Stalin was undoubtedly trying to bring pressure upon Britain and the United States. To them he was saying in effect: 'If you will not come to terms with me, I always have an alternative course open: agreement with Hitler.' Stalin's words were so interpreted in important Western diplomatic circles.[3]

It is probable that this speech did much to persuade the British Government that territorial concessions to Stalin should be agreed to. At any rate, by March 1942 the British were ready to recognize the Baltic states as part of the Soviet Union, but continued to boggle at Stalin's claims upon Poland.[4] Britain, after all, had declared war when Poland was attacked by the Germans, and it seemed impossible to assign to the Russians, without the consent of the Polish Government, territory which had been under Polish rule between the end of the First World War and the outbreak of the Second. But giving up their claim to the eastern marches of inter-war Poland was the last thing that the Polish Government in Exile would consider. Hence on the Polish question Anglo-Russian negotiations stuck fast.

Meanwhile, the American Government took their stand on the principles of the Atlantic Charter. Both Hull and Roosevelt remembered the secret treaties and territorial bargains between the allies of the First World

[1] Stalin: *Great Patriotic War*, p. 44.

[2] It is worth remembering in this connexion that the German-Soviet *rapprochement* which resulted in the Ribbentrop-Molotov Agreement of 1939 started with a similar hint embodied in Stalin's speech of 10 March 1939. Cf. Deutscher: *Stalin*, pp. 429–30.

[3] Ciechanowski: *Defeat in Victory*, p. 110.

[4] Churchill, iv. 293; U.S. edition, iv. 327; Hull: *Memoirs*, ii. 1170; Ciechanowski, op. cit. pp. 107–13.

War which had, they felt, done much to spoil the Versailles peace settlement. They were determined to try to prevent any repetition of the experience. The Americans hoped to be able to convince the Russians, once Germany had been defeated, that an international organization of all the victorious Powers would suffice to ensure security for every state in the world. Such assurance, coupled with the disarmament and perhaps the dismemberment of Germany, might persuade Stalin to abandon his territorial ambitions. So Hull argued.[1]

American pressure, of course, acted as a powerful restraint upon the British; but the decisive factor was Hitler's refusal to take up Stalin's proffered olive branch. The Germans had not yet lost hope of decisive victory in Russia, and with the spring Hitler could look forward to launching a new offensive in the east. The Red Army's counter-attack died away in March 1942, and a three months' lull set in on the Russian front; but it was clear to all that the Germans were using the time to prepare themselves for a renewal of the battle.

Stalin's speech on May Day 1942 reflected the new view of the future which the progress of events had brought home to him. He now declared that the overthrow of Hitler was a necessity. 'It is becoming increasingly clear to the German people', he said, 'that the only way out of the present situation is the liberation of Germany from the Hitler-Goering adventurist clique.'[2] Moreover, Stalin eulogized hatred, filling 'every fibre of one's soul', as requisite for victory over the invading fascists.[3] The theme of hate was extensively developed in the Soviet press during the following months. Denunciation was harsh, brutal, blood-curdling. The full force of Soviet invective was turned against the Germans and all their works. German cruelty gave the Soviet propagandists abundant and often entirely authentic material for their barrage and helped to erase earlier efforts to distinguish Hitler and his clique from the German people as a whole. More and more Russian propaganda condemned all Germans without exception.[4]

A second development which smoothed over relations between Britain, America, and Russia was the decision, pressed especially by the American General Staff, to embark upon an invasion of continental Europe at the earliest possible moment. Such plans now seemed music to Stalin's ears. If they could be realized, the Red Army would be relieved of a part of the weight of the impending German attack, and good grounds for hope of an early victory would be restored despite the relative failure of the Russian counter-offensive of the winter of 1941–2.

[1] Hull: *Memoirs*, ii. 1170.

[2] Stalin: *Great Patriotic War*, p. 50. [3] Ibid. p. 53.

[4] Cf. Werth: *Year of Stalingrad*, pp. 80–81; also Molotov's long and detailed account of German atrocities issued as a diplomatic note on 27 April 1942, translated in Rothstein: *Russian Foreign Policy during the Patriotic War*, i. 134–57.

We must now turn our attention to the planning and negotiation which led to preliminary agreement upon a second front in 1942.

(*b*) Second Front in 1942?

At the time of the Arcadia Conference the American General Staff had not worked out its own plans for the defeat of Hitler. The British proposal for the clearance of North Africa as a preliminary to direct attack on the Continent had been tentatively accepted at the Conference; but that plan had been based upon the hope that Axis troops would be driven out of Libya by the offensive which had been started in November 1941. When the British Eighth Army failed to win decisive victory in Libya, the plan for the occupation of French North Africa in the spring of 1942 lapsed. The field was clear for American military planners to propose a substitute strategy.

The officer directly in charge of planning was the still obscure General Dwight D. Eisenhower. As Chief of the Operations Division of the War Department General Staff, a position which he occupied from 9 March 1942,[1] Eisenhower was responsible to General Marshall for drawing up plans for the deployment of American troops against the German and Japanese enemies. The various possibilities for offensive action, proposed by British staff planners, had been under consideration more or less continuously since early in 1941, but it was not until March 1942 that a new planning team, assembled after the outbreak of war, could spare much attention from immediate stop-gap measures in order to think of longer-range offensive action.

By March the immediate adjustments necessitated by the outbreak of war had been made. Eisenhower and his subordinates were able to direct their minds more consistently towards the problems of how best to seize the initiative from the enemy, how soonest and cheapest to defeat Germany. One by one they eliminated alternatives: attack through Norway, attack through Spain, attack through the Mediterranean, attack through the air alone—all were rejected in favour of a cross-Channel landing in France. Their reasons for the decision were strictly military. The direct route to the heart of Germany seemed the shortest way to victory. Moreover, only by attacking directly from the British Isles could the entire strength of Anglo-American air and ground forces come into play. Any other operation would be weakened by the need for keeping the garrison

[1] Eisenhower had been summoned to the General Staff on 12 December 1941; and from 16 February 1942 had headed its planning section. On 9 March 1942 the above title was introduced as a part of a general reorganization of the General Staff; but Eisenhower had been responsible for drawing up operational plans for more than three weeks before that date (cf. Eisenhower: *Crusade in Europe*, pp. 16, 31; Cline: *Washington Command Post: The Operations Division*, pp. 145–7).

and air defence of Great Britain strong. Finally, the shortage of shipping, which became more and more serious during the first five months of 1942, set narrow limits to Allied undertakings. But, by a fortunate coincidence, the transatlantic route to Great Britain and from there to France was the shortest possible path to the enemy; and the shorter the sea haul, the more troops and supplies could be carried from America with the shipping which was available. These were the considerations which convinced Eisenhower and Marshall that a cross-Channel landing was the proper strategy for the Anglo-American forces to pursue.[1] The fact that a landing in France would relieve the Russian front was a subordinate, but not unimportant, consideration. That the soundest military plan would simultaneously satisfy Stalin's demand for help seemed to the American military planners a happy coincidence, but Stalin's wishes were not a determining factor.[2]

On 1 April 1942 the American plan was ready. Marshall, the American Joint Chiefs of Staff, and the President had all been consulted as the plan was drawn up, and were thus prepared to act quickly. Within the day all three authorities gave their approval to Eisenhower's proposals. Roosevelt at once decided to send Marshall and Hopkins to London in order to present the plan to the British. The day was April Fool's; so, as it turned out, was the plan.

The general war situation at the beginning of April 1942 was not very bright from the Allies' point of view. Japan's expansion had not yet come to a halt. The conquest of Burma was in full swing, India was in turmoil, and on the day after conversations began in London the American and Filipino forces on Bataan surrendered. On the Russian front things were relatively quiet, but it was recognized on every side that this was merely a lull before the storm. The Germans were busy preparing to launch their second and what might be their final offensive against the Red Army. The most disquieting news of all came from the Atlantic, where German submarines were sinking ships faster than they could be built. It was against the background of these military defeats that the strategic deliberations of April took place.

Churchill and the British Chiefs of Staff were well aware of the direction which American military thinking had taken. Through the Combined Chiefs of Staff the British Government had been kept up to date. Churchill was also very acutely conscious that the Americans might still decide to turn their main attention towards the Pacific. It therefore behoved the

[1] Eisenhower: *Crusade in Europe*, pp. 43–45.

[2] Cf. Sherwood: *Roosevelt and Hopkins*, pp. 519–20; Eng. edition, ii. 524–5.

British military chiefs to watch their step. Disagreement with the Americans was difficult, indeed dangerous; agreement was imperative.[1]

Yet the British were by no means convinced that the American plan was sound. Two things bothered them. The first was India, where it looked in April 1942 as if British power might entirely disintegrate. The prospect of the loss of the Empire was bad enough; the prospect that Japanese and German forces might join one another somewhere in the Middle East was even more appalling. Yet this was the fear that haunted British minds. It led them constantly to emphasize the Japanese danger in conferences with the Americans and to insist that Japan must be checked before offensive moves against Germany could be undertaken.[2]

The second consideration which weighed heavily on British strategists' minds was their fear that a cross-Channel operation might not succeed. They had themselves made a plan for a landing in France in 1943,[3] and the British warmly welcomed the American proposal to mount a large-scale cross-Channel attack in that year. But there was another part to the American plan which did not win British approval. The Americans foresaw the possibility of a small-scale landing in 1942. Such an operation would be launched only in one of two opposite circumstances, described in these words:

> This Limited Operation Would Be Justified Only in Case (1) The Situation on the Russian Front Becomes Desperate, i.e., the success of German arms becomes so complete as to threaten the imminent collapse of Russian resistance unless the pressure is relieved by an attack from the west by British and American troops. In this case the attack should be considered as a sacrifice in the common good.
>
> (2) The German Situation in Western Europe becomes Critically Weakened.[4]

The second of these two hypothetical circumstances soon dropped out of consideration. Germany was obviously not yet ready to give up the war.

The 1942 operation was known by the code-name Sledgehammer. From the time it was first proposed details of the plan underwent constant modification. One may, however, distinguish two general variants. Either the landing in France would be a sacrifice operation, involving the loss of most of the troops engaged and the abandonment of the coast after full-scale German counter-attack had been mounted; or, if Allied air power and supply lines proved equal to the strain, a small beachhead might be seized and retained until the main landings of 1943 could be launched. In either case, the major strategic purpose of Sledgehammer was to draw

[1] Churchill, iv. 289–90; U.S. edition, iv. 324.

[2] Ibid. pp. 283, 288 and 317, 322, respectively.

[3] This plan was submitted to the U.S. Joint Chiefs of Staff on 16 March 1942 (cf. Cline: *Washington Command Post: The Operations Division*, p. 153).

[4] Sherwood: *Roosevelt and Hopkins*, p. 520; Eng. edition, ii. 525.

off the strength of the Luftwaffe from the Russian front and thus deprive the German troops in Russia of air superiority. It was believed that great and decisive air battles would develop over the Anglo-American beach-head; and that in a matter of a few days German air power might be largely destroyed.[1]

The pinch, from the British point of view, was that any attack mounted in 1942 would have to be largely a British undertaking. American troops could not be trained, equipped, and brought across the Atlantic soon enough to undertake a share proportionate to the resources and population of America; and the American air force, too, could not build up its strength in Great Britain soon enough to take part on any large scale in the expected air battles.[2] It may readily be imagined that a deliberate sacrifice of British troops and aircraft that would be so disproportionate to the ratio between the two Powers' respective reserves of strength did not much appeal to British military leaders. The security of the British Isles and of the Empire had but precariously been maintained through 1940 and 1941. To risk hard-won security on a reckless throw seemed to Churchill and the British Chiefs of Staff the height of folly.

Their problem in April 1942 was that they did not dare to say so openly. The Americans might bridle at an outright refusal to consider offensive operations on the Continent in 1942. They might even decide to attack the Japanese instead. As Churchill said afterwards: 'But I had to work by influence and diplomacy in order to secure agreed and harmonious action with our cherished Ally, without whose aid nothing but ruin faced the world. I did not therefore open any of these alternatives at our meeting on the 14th.'[3]

Churchill's diplomacy took the form of agreeing with calculated enthusiasm to *parts* of the American plan, while discreetly passing over those other parts of which he disapproved. Thus Churchill and the British Chiefs of Staff sincerely accepted the proposal for a rapid build-up of American ground and air forces in Britain in preparation for a grand assault upon the French coast in 1943. They believed that before such an assault could be successful Germany would have to be much weakened; but they most sincerely hoped that such a weakening could be brought about before the great force contemplated by the Americans had been assembled and equipped.

[1] Eisenhower: *Crusade in Europe*, pp. 46–47; Churchill, iv. 297–8; U.S. edition, iv. 333; Sherwood: *Roosevelt and Hopkins*, pp. 564, 569; Eng. edition, ii. 567, 573.

[2] A memorandum which Marshall and Hopkins brought with them stated: '. . . the chief burden would fall on the U.K. For example, on September 15 the U.S. could find two and a half divisions of the five needed, but only seven hundred combat aircraft; so that the contribution required from the U.K. might amount to five thousand aircraft' (Churchill, iv. 282; U.S. edition, iv. 315).

[3] Ibid. pp. 289–90 and 324, respectively. Churchill refers to 14 April 1942 and the main alternative he had in mind was North Africa.

Thus there was no disagreement either on the immediate steps to be taken—an American build-up in Britain, or on the ultimate goal—invasion of France. The British did from the start refuse to take seriously any proposal for a 'sacrifice' landing in France in 1942; but this, after all, was a subordinate matter. Successive estimates of the situation would in any case alter plans, and Churchill had no doubt that, unless Germany showed sudden signs of collapse, good and compelling reasons for the abandonment of Sledgehammer would be found.[1] If worst came to worst, he could always refuse to embark British forces on the expedition, thus automatically ending it; but in April 1942, when the fundamental pattern of American deployment against the enemy was still in the making, there seemed to him no advantage and great risk in emphasizing these potential points of difference.

Churchill's manœuvre did not entirely escape the Americans. Hopkins knew Churchill fairly well by now, and he was struck by the light-heartedness with which Churchill agreed to Marshall's proposals. He guessed shrewdly enough that Churchill did not intend to initiate land operations on the Continent for at least a year. The British Chiefs of Staff spoke more frankly on the subject; they emphasized Germany's strength and the dangers of premature attack. As a result, General Sir Alan Brooke, C.I.G.S., made a rather poor impression on General Marshall. Hopkins privately tried to impress Churchill with the seriousness of the American proposal. The British Prime Minister was polite but reserved, and did not bring forward the objections he felt towards Sledgehammer. Hopkins was apparently convinced after this exchange that the British did indeed accept *in toto* the proposals which Marshall and he had presented to them. Marshall, for his part, was inclined to take the British simply at their word, and tried to meet their objections by assurances about supplies for India and the Middle East.[2]

Another dimension to be considered was the effect of the proposed Anglo-American military plan upon Russia. Hopkins talked with Eden about the progress of negotiations for the Anglo-Russian treaty of alliance, and emphasized the disapproval with which the American Government viewed territorial concessions to Stalin. He also pointed out that a second front in 1942 would 'take the heat off' Britain. Russia could be expected to give up territorial claims, at least for the time being, if a second front could be offered instead.

The upshot of the discussions was the formal acceptance of the American plan at a meeting on 14 April 1942. It should be emphasized that what

[1] Cf. Churchill's memorandum to the Chiefs of Staff dated 8 June 1942: 'No substantial landing in France unless the Germans are demoralized by another failure against Russia' (Churchill, iv. 311; U.S. edition, iv. 348).

[2] Sherwood: *Roosevelt and Hopkins*, pp. 523, 526, 534–6; Eng. edition, ii. 528, 531, 540–2.

the British accepted on 14 April was a plan for preparing a major attack on the French coast in 1943. The only operations definitely scheduled for 1942 were air and commando raids. Sledgehammer was only an emergency measure, to be undertaken if either Russia or Germany seemed on the point of collapse.[1] The British made only one qualification: safeguarding India against the Japanese must take precedence over the attack on Germany in case of conflicting demands for supplies or man-power. But Marshall expressed the conviction that enough supplies to stop the Japanese from invading India could be provided without interfering with the build-up of American and British armies and air forces for an attack upon the European continent.[2]

The apparent meeting of minds vastly encouraged Marshall; and Hopkins, too, felt that at last plans which could reasonably be expected to lead to victory had been agreed upon. But the real differences in outlook were much greater than appeared on the surface during the London conversations. Churchill's idea from the beginning had been to encircle Germany on land and sea; and then gradually to throttle German war power by air attack, subversive activity among the conquered populations, and commando-type raids along exposed coasts. Invasion on a grand scale he believed could only be prudently attempted after the main power of the German war machine had been broken by these methods.[3]

The Americans, especially Marshall, Eisenhower, and their superior, Secretary of War Henry L. Stimson, were convinced that a direct crushing blow would be necessary before the German war machine could be broken. Not the dispersed landings of armoured forces which Churchill imagined, but a single landing by a balanced army with overwhelming power: this was what the Americans thought would be needed. They realized that no such force could be assembled before 1943, and were prepared to subordinate everything to its speedy creation.

The Sledgehammer operation was an essential part of their conception. If the Russian front should collapse in 1942, the Germans would be able to concentrate their full power against the West in 1943. If that happened the great landing operation might not be possible, or would at best become very hazardous. Therefore to keep the Russian front in being was of prime importance, and a preliminary small-scale landing in 1942 might turn out to be the only way to assure Russian survival. In April, when the general American plan was accepted, the problem was still

[1] Cf. Cline: *Washington Command Post: The Operations Division*, p. 157.

[2] Churchill, iv. 286–7; U.S. edition, iv. 320.

[3] Cf. the memorandum Churchill wrote for the Arcadia Conference in which his long-term strategic conceptions were clearly presented (Churchill, iii. 582–5; U.S. edition, iii. 655–9; also ibid. iv. 316–18; U.S. edition, iv. 353–5).

academic. Neither Germany nor Russia was at the moment in danger of sudden collapse, so that the pre-conditions for the American Sledgehammer were still absent. During the weeks that followed, however, opinion among American strategists moved in an opposite direction from that followed by British military minds. More and more the Americans convinced themselves that Sledgehammer would be both necessary and possible in 1942;[1] while detailed staff studies confirmed the British in their original opinion that any immediate attack on France would be folly. This divergence of views set the stage for a very awkward passage in Anglo-American relations which reached its crisis in the second half of July 1942.

Another difference of opinion which was not fully expressed in April but which became clear later was the question of the battle-worthiness of American troops. Churchill was convinced that longer training than the Americans had scheduled was necessary before it would be safe to pit American against German forces. Marshall and his subordinates were far more sanguine, and indeed feared that American troops might grow stale if held off from action for any prolonged period of time.[2]

Yet there was a core of agreement between the British and American military leaders. The American decision to concentrate first upon Germany stirred the warmest concurrence among the British; and the idea of a great offensive in 1943 appealed to them too. Differences as to the exact form the final attack should take were real but subordinate to the central conception of an attack in force. All the discords which were to arise in the following months between British and American strategists did not shake this fundamental core of agreement. Its existence made possible the solution of disputes by genuine compromises.

It is really impossible to pass retrospective judgement upon the wisdom of Sledgehammer. It would almost surely have been a disaster, and both Eisenhower and his principal American lieutenant, General Mark Clark, have since agreed that their advocacy of the plan was a mistake.[3] But the decisive factor which made Sledgehammer seem foolish to them in retrospect was the fact that the Russians held at Stalingrad. Had the

[1] The drift of American military opinion towards stronger support of Sledgehammer during the late spring and early summer of 1942 was influenced by Roosevelt's vehement insistence upon the need to engage American troops against the Germans before the year was out. The only way American officers believed such an engagement could be achieved without interfering fatally with the preparation of the great invasion of 1943 was Sledgehammer. Any alternative operation seemed sure to divert men and resources from the build-up in Great Britain. As late as June 1942, therefore, Eisenhower believed that Sledgehammer should be attempted (cf. *Crusade in Europe*, p. 70).

[2] Churchill, iv. 288; U.S. edition, iv. 323: Sherwood: *Roosevelt and Hopkins*, pp. 591–2; Eng. edition, ii. 594–5.

[3] Eisenhower: *Crusade in Europe*, p. 71; Mark W. Clark: *Calculated Risk* (New York, Harper, 1950), p. 34. [An English edition of *Calculated Risk* was published in London by Harrap in 1951.]

Russians collapsed, judgement would be clouded by wondering whether they would have fought on successfully if a landing, even a disastrous landing, had been attempted in 1942. There can be no profit in embarking on such doubly hypothetical speculation; but it is worth remembering the many and almost incalculable uncertainties which beset the men who addressed themselves to the task of planning offensive Anglo-American action in the spring of 1942. Events, as always, made and unmade decisions for them.

(c) Molotov's Visits to London and Washington

It was not only the British who were concerned with an offensive against Germany from the west. Roosevelt waited only until his emissaries had arrived in Britain and had been able to sound out the British reaction before broaching the question to the Russians. He did so only in general terms. He telegraphed to Stalin on 10 or 11 April 1942: 'I have in mind very important military proposals involving the utilization of our armed forces in a manner to relieve your critical western front. This objective carries great weight with me. Therefore, I wish you would consider sending Mr. Molotov and a General upon whom you rely to Washington in the immediate future.'[1] A day or two later the Russian Ambassador called upon Roosevelt to ask for fuller information about what the President had in mind.[2] Presumably Roosevelt must have told Litvinov enough to make it clear that a second front was in the offing. Stalin soon decided that to secure such a prize would be well worth Molotov's time, and he agreed to send him to both London and Washington. There was, moreover, the still unsettled negotiation for an Anglo-Soviet treaty which could perhaps be brought to a head at the same time. A third matter was the question of supplies. The first Russian Supply Protocol was due to expire on 1 July 1942, and negotiations for a second Protocol could conveniently begin at the highest level while Molotov was in London and Washington.

Molotov's departure was several times postponed and he did not arrive in London until 20 May 1942. On arrival he began conversations with Eden about the treaty and with Churchill about the second front. The British had a draft of the proposed treaty ready in which they recognized the Baltic states as a part of the Soviet Union. This did not satisfy Molotov, however, and he reasserted all Stalin's original territorial demands. Eden flatly refused to prejudge the question of the Russo-Polish boundary. For a few days it looked as though the stalemate would continue as before.

American diplomacy now entered actively into the picture. Hull sent

[1] Sherwood: *Roosevelt and Hopkins*, p. 528; Eng. edition, ii. 533.

[2] Ibid. p. 534; Eng. edition, ii. 540.

a telegram to London stating that if a treaty were signed with territorial clauses the United States might issue a statement explicitly dissociating the American Government from any responsibility for its terms.[1] This threat carried great weight with both British and Russian negotiators. On 23 May Eden proposed a new text, omitting territorial questions altogether. Ambassador Winant had a long conversation with Molotov on the following day in which he emphasized America's interest in a second front and America's opposition to territorial settlements before the general peace conference could be held. Molotov obviously weighed in his mind the advantages of territorial promises against second front promises and concluded that the second front was worth more. Accordingly, on 25 May he telegraphed to ask Stalin's approval for abandoning the territorial clauses. Stalin agreed, suggesting a few minor modifications in the draft Eden had originally presented. The next day, 26 May 1942, the treaty was signed.

Both the American and British Governments regarded Molotov's decision to withdraw territorial demands as a hopeful sign for future co-operation between Russia and the West. The attitude of the Russian Government was not revealed. It seems quite certain that Stalin never abandoned his intention of building a protective glacis on his western frontier, and of uniting all the White Russians and Ukrainians under Soviet rule. But he was ready to postpone the issue if it seemed likely to embitter America and endanger the second front.

The text of the treaty was divided into two parts. The first part was valid for the duration of the war with Germany. It prescribed that the two Governments would lend each other all possible aid and would not conclude any separate peace or armistice except by mutual consent. The second part was valid for twenty years, and thereafter would remain in force until one party gave twelve months' notice of intention to terminate it. It provided for post-war economic assistance, renounced territorial aggrandizement[2] and interference in the internal affairs of other states, and declared that in case of any future hostilities with Germany, each Government would immediately come to the aid of the other. One of the most interesting articles was the following: 'Article III. (1) The High Contracting Parties declare their desire to unite with other like-minded States in adopting proposals for common action to preserve peace and resist aggression in the post-war period.'[3] Thus for the first time a sug-

[1] Hull: *Memoirs*, ii. 1172.

[2] This provision did not imply the abandonment of Stalin's territorial claims, for in his view the territory which had been incorporated in the Soviet Union in 1939 and 1940 was still a part of the U.S.S.R. This point was made plain during the ceremony of ratification when delegates to the Supreme Soviet from the Baltic provinces were among those who spoke on behalf of ratification.

[3] For text of the treaty see Great Britain: *Treaty for an Alliance in the War against Hitlerite*

gestion of the future United Nations Organization was officially and publicly proclaimed.[1]

Molotov's conversations with Churchill on the subject of a second front were not conclusive. The Russian Foreign Minister began by inquiring what prospect there was of drawing forty German divisions from Russia by a landing in France. This was what he calculated would be necessary to eliminate the margin of German superiority against the Red Army. Churchill replied by emphasizing the obstacles to amphibious attack, especially the shortage of suitable landing craft. He then outlined plans and preparations in progress. Churchill made it clear that the best the Russians could hope for would be the withdrawal of a large proportion of the Luftwaffe from the Russian front. The German divisions already stationed in Western Europe were quite numerous enough to oppose any landing that the British and Americans could hope to make in 1942.

Molotov then asked what would happen if Russian armies were defeated in 1942, to which Churchill stoutly replied that Britain and America would then continue the battle alone, and, after air power had sufficiently weakened the Germans, they would make landings on the Continent and bring about the final overthrow of Hitler's power.[2] Churchill carefully avoided any firm commitment to a second front in 1942. It was agreed that, after talks with Roosevelt on the subject, Molotov would stop a second time in London for further discussion of the military question.

On 29 May 1942 Molotov arrived in Washington. On the day before, Churchill had forwarded an account of his conversation with the Russian Foreign Minister, and in a covering cable had included the sentences:

> Dickie [i.e. Lord Louis Mountbatten, British Chief of Combined Operations] will explain to you the difficulties of 1942 when he arrives. I have also told the Staffs to study a landing in the north of Norway, the occupation of which seems necessary to ensure the flow of our supplies next year to Russia. . . .
>
> We must never let 'Gymnast' [the code name for the landing in French North Africa] pass from our minds. All other preparations would help, if need be, towards that.[3]

This cable was the first definite indication to the Americans that the British were boggling at their Sledgehammer plan. The news was not welcome in Washington. It probably had the effect of hardening

Germany . . . between the United Kingdom and the U.S.S.R., London, May 26, 1942, Cmd. 6368 (London, H.M.S.O., 1942); *Documents on American Foreign Relations, 1941–1942*, p. 256.

[1] The first official American statement advocating a post-war international organization came from Secretary of State Hull on 23 July 1942 in a radio broadcast (Hull: *Memoirs*, ii. 1177).

[2] Churchill (iv. 297–9; U.S. edition, iv. 332–5) reproduces an official minute of the conversation of 22 May 1942.

[3] Ibid. iv. 303–4; U.S. edition, iv. 340.

Marshall's determination to go ahead with plans for a landing in France in 1942.

Obviously one of the best ways to force the British into a commitment to a landing in France in 1942 was to bring the Russians into the agreement. Roosevelt from the beginning had been anxious that the Big Three should arrive at a concerted strategic plan for 1942,[1] and Molotov's visit seemed to provide the chance to transform a shaky two-Power agreement on strategy into a firm three-Power commitment. Such at any rate was the American hope.

Molotov presented the same questions to Roosevelt and Marshall that he had earlier put to Churchill. He wanted forty German divisions withdrawn from the Russian front and asked what would follow from Russian defeat in 1942 if such a diversion did not take place. He further suggested that if a landing were postponed until 1943 the Americans and British would probably find themselves facing a more difficult military problem, since it could not be assumed that the Russian front would hold. The official record of the conversation then continues: 'The President then put to General Marshall the query whether developments were clear enough so that we could say to Mr. Stalin that we were preparing a second front. "Yes", replied the General. The President then authorized Mr. Molotov to inform Mr. Stalin that we expect the formation of a second front this year.'[2] The general's laconic answer was what Molotov had travelled so far to hear. Marshall was, however, at pains to point out that he could not guarantee to divert forty or any other definite number of German divisions from the Russian front. Transport, he explained, was the principal limiting factor on any offensive operation which the Americans and British could undertake. Admiral King seized the opportunity to point out that the necessity of using ships for deliveries to Archangel and Murmansk cut directly and inevitably into preparations for an invasion of France.

It is difficult to reconstruct from the official records any vivid picture of the state of opinion among the dozen or so top leaders of the United States who were directly concerned in the conversations with Molotov. The question as to Molotov's sincerity in suggesting that the Russian front might collapse was brought up at a meeting between the President and the American Joint Chiefs of Staff on 31 May. Roosevelt believed that Molotov's report was reliable, and had not been put forward in order to force the American and British hand. According to Hopkins's personal record, Marshall, too, had become convinced that a landing in 1942 would prove to be inevitable 'merely by force of circumstance'.[3] The

[1] Churchill, iv. 280–1; U.S. edition, iv. 313–14.

[2] Sherwood: *Roosevelt and Hopkins*, p. 563; Eng. edition, ii. 567.

[3] What Marshall had in mind can be seen from a cable Roosevelt sent to Churchill on 31 May 1942 immediately after this meeting. It ran in part:

'After discussion with the Staffs, I believe that the German air forces cannot be destroyed

desire to arrive at a firm understanding with the Russian representative was certainly lively on all sides; and it is also clear that Marshall had become impatient with what he thought to be British half-heartedness and was anxious to pin the British down irrevocably to Sledgehammer in 1942.

In subsequent conversations the Americans tried to get Molotov to agree to a reduction in the amount of supplies to be delivered to Russia. They pointed out that this sacrifice on Russia's part would be required to make the second front possible on a big enough scale. Roosevelt suggested that instead of 4,400,000 tons, as tentatively agreed, the amount of supplies to be delivered under the new Russian Protocol should be cut to 2,500,000 tons. The saving was to be made by eliminating nearly all the general supplies scheduled for delivery to Russia, while maintaining the scale of munitions undiminished. When Molotov was confronted with this proposal, he refused to accept it. What, he asked, would happen if the Russians agreed to the lower scale of deliveries and no second front eventuated? Roosevelt hastened to assure him that detailed plans for a second front were in preparation, and that the Americans fully expected to invade France in 1942.[1]

Molotov and the Americans did not reach any final agreement about the scale of deliveries to Russia after the expiry of the First Supply Protocol, and indeed, as we have seen,[2] the matter was not finally settled until October 1942. Nor was the question of the second front definitely disposed of. When it came to preparing a communiqué for the press, Molotov insisted that the following sentence be included: 'In the course of the conversations full understanding was reached with regard to the urgent tasks of creating a Second Front in Europe in 1942.' General Marshall felt that this statement was too definite, and that mention of 1942 should be suppressed. Roosevelt, however, decided to let it stand.[3] A parallel sentence was inserted in the communiqué describing Molotov's visit to London with, of course, the approval of the British Government. The communiqués and the text of the Anglo-Soviet treaty were published on 12 June 1942 after Molotov had returned safely to Moscow.

The British were not, however, prepared to let the communiqué commit them irrevocably to Sledgehammer or any similar plan. When Molotov stopped in London on his way back from Washington, Churchill personally handed him an *aide-mémoire* which read as follows:

We are making preparations for a landing on the Continent in August or

unless they have been forced to take the air by preliminary or temporary actions by ground forces. If we can start this phase early in August we can produce one of the following results:

1. Divert German air forces from the Russian front and attempt to destroy them.

2. If such air forces are not moved to the west, we can increase our operations with ground forces and determine on the establishment of permanent positions as our objective' (Sherwood: *Roosevelt and Hopkins*, p. 569; Eng. edition, ii. 573).

[1] Ibid. pp. 574–5; Eng. edition, ii. 578–9.

[2] See above, p. 145.

[3] Sherwood: *Roosevelt and Hopkins*, p. 577; Eng. edition, ii. 582.

September, 1942. As already explained, the main limiting factor to the size of the landing-force is the availability of special landing-craft. Clearly however it would not further either the Russian cause or that of the Allies as a whole if, for the sake of action at any price, we embarked on some operation which ended in disaster and gave the enemy an opportunity for glorification at our discomfiture. It is impossible to say in advance whether the situation will be such as to make this operation feasible when the time comes. *We can therefore give no promise in the matter*, but provided that it appears sound and sensible we shall not hesitate to put our plans into effect.[1]

Molotov's visit to London and Washington was the first occasion on which Churchill and Roosevelt came into contact with the top level of Soviet officialdom. Roosevelt took the occasion to expound to Molotov many of his personal hopes for the post-war world: disarmament, economic agreements, international trusteeships for backward areas of the world (including areas formerly under British and Dutch rule in Asia and the Pacific), and control of the post-war world by the Big Four. These and other ideas he put before Molotov for his consideration. Molotov was non-committal, but polite. He talked a different language from the President; and his dreams of the future were assuredly very different from those Roosevelt cherished. The two men were aware of the gap between them, and Roosevelt found it hard to understand how Molotov could be so different from any man he had known before. The problem of translation also cramped the President's usual loquaciousness and introduced an irritating barrier between the two.[2]

Molotov's visit had a second significance. Up to that time the United States had on the whole been less sympathetic to the Russians than had the British Government. The Americans, for instance, had been far more emphatic in their opposition to Stalin's territorial ambitions than had the British, and at first had been more hesitant about sending supplies to Russia. But, as champions of a second front, the Americans appeared to the Russians as their great and good friends. British lukewarmness stood in sharp contrast. From this time until his death, Roosevelt was able to occupy a position intermediate between Britain and Russia on nearly all disputed points. From such a position he could often act as mediator and moderator—a role which he found personally agreeable and which appealed most strongly to his conception of America's proper place in the world.

The publication of the Anglo-Soviet Treaty and the two communiqués describing Molotov's visits to London and Washington provided the

[1] Churchill, iv. 305; U.S. edition, iv. 342.

[2] Cf. Sherwood: *Roosevelt and Hopkins*, p. 561; Eng. edition, ii. 564.

occasion for a burst of Allied good feeling. In Moscow a special session of the Supreme Soviet was called on 18 June 1942 in order to ratify the treaty with full and extraordinary pomp. Molotov made the principal speech on the occasion, full of cordiality towards the Western nations. The passage in his speech which excited most attention was his reference to the second front. He said: '. . . the creation of a second front in Europe will bring about insuperable difficulties for Hitler's armies on our front. Let us hope that our common enemy will soon experience to his cost the results of the ever-growing military co-operation of the three Great Powers.'[1] Molotov's expression of hope was something less than an assurance of fact, but no one in Russia wanted to emphasize the conditional mood of Western promises for a second front. In the enthusiasm of the moment all reservations were forgotten, and the Russian public came to believe that a second front in 1942 on the continent of Europe had been definitely promised. All the resources of the Soviet Government were brought to bear in spreading the news. Emphasis was especially put upon the military help which could now be expected against the Germans. The treaty, according to *Pravda* (20 June 1942), was a 'bombshell in the enemy's camp'.

Newspaper reaction in Britain was also highly enthusiastic, and emphasized the long-term implications of the treaty. *The Times* (12 June 1942) declared that 'the solid foundations of Anglo-Soviet friendship and collaboration are securely laid'. The *Daily Telegraph* (same date) said: 'With the United States and the British Commonwealth working in accord with Russia on the lines laid down in this treaty Europe could look forward to a period of greater security than it has known for a hundred years and the whole world might be brought into a happier order.' The *Daily Herald* (same date) pointed out: 'The tremendous import of the Treaty itself lies in its pledge of collaboration in the rebuilding of Europe after victory is achieved.'

In the United States newspaper comment was more restrained. The *New York Herald Tribune* (12 June 1942) said: '. . . here is a firm, genuine and realistic meeting of minds all around'. The *New York Times* (same date) asserted that the treaty 'forecasts one of those fundamental shifts in the balance of forces which may have immense consequences in the future of Europe'. The *Chicago Tribune* (13 June 1942) admitted: 'At any rate the Governments of the two peoples feel that they have a community of ideas which will make it possible for them to act together in reasonable harmony for a generation.' The *Christian Science Monitor* (12 June 1942) emphasized ideological differences between Britain and Russia, and observed: 'It would be folly to expect from this change any such fundamental partnership as exists between English-speaking and democratic

[1] Rothstein: *Soviet Foreign Policy during the Patriotic War*, i. 174.

peoples.' The *Chicago Daily News* (13 June 1942) remarked: 'As for the Russo-British twenty year mutual aid pact that is a matter which need give us no concern. . . . So long as it is not directed against us it is their affair.'

Treaties and alliances, one may surmise, still carried somewhat sinister connotations to many Americans. Public attention remained focused largely upon Japan, and many commentators noticed the omission of any definite undertaking against that country in the communiqué describing Molotov's visit. Hope that Russia might soon join battle against the Japanese was not dead in America; and the idea that Germany should be attacked first had not spread far beyond official circles.[1]

(*d*) Second Thoughts about the Second Front

After the agreement upon Anglo-American strategy had been reached in London in April, detailed planning was at once begun. At first British staff officers were primarily engaged on this task. It was not until 11 June 1942 that the European Theatre of Operations, U.S.A., was established with General Eisenhower in command; and he did not arrive in London until 24 June. His command extended to all American land, air, and naval forces in Britain, Northern Ireland, and Iceland. British forces remained entirely separate. No over-all Allied commander for the proposed landing in France had been appointed, so that all planning for that operation took on the character of negotiation in committee.

Before Eisenhower arrived in England in the hope of pushing Sledgehammer through to a successful conclusion, the British had made their position much clearer. Lord Louis Mountbatten arrived in the American capital at the beginning of June immediately after Molotov's departure, and in his conversations with the American Joint Chiefs of Staff he explained some of the practical difficulties which British staff planners had encountered. He conveyed the impression that important changes in the strategy agreed to in April would have to be made, but was not specific and categorical in rejecting Sledgehammer. The decisive effort to bring British and American strategic thinking into harmony was reserved for Churchill himself, who arrived in Washington on 18 June 1942 to present the British arguments. He began conversations with Roosevelt on the following day at Hyde Park.

Churchill had two matters of prime importance on his mind: what to do about the second front, and what to do about atomic energy. Physicists in many countries had been aware even before 1939 that extremely powerful atomic explosives might be capable of manufacture. In the years after 1939 laboratory work in both Britain and America had gone forward rapidly with the help of Government funds. Formal exchanges

[1] Cf. Sherwood: *Roosevelt and Hopkins*, p. 536; Eng. edition, ii. 542.

of information and views between the scientists of the two countries had begun in September 1940 when the British sent a scientific mission to the United States under the leadership of Sir Henry Tizard. As the prospect of making a uranium bomb which would unleash the power of atomic energy became more and more promising, the desirability of a systematic pooling of British and American theoretical and practical work became obvious. In October 1941 Roosevelt suggested to Churchill that work on this project should be conducted jointly, and some British scientists came to the United States soon afterwards for the purpose. Americans in the same way visited Britain.[1]

Large uncertainties still persisted. No one could be sure that money and talent expended on further work with uranium would not end in a blind alley so far as producing anything useful for the prosecution of the war was concerned. But what if the Germans succeeded first? Atomic bombs in German hands would almost surely paralyse Britain and bring resounding victory to the Nazis in Russia. With such a possibility in the background it could not be safe to suspend any effort that promised results.

By midsummer 1942 the American atomic programme had already reached a very substantial scale. The erection of pilot plants for the separation of uranium isotopes had been authorized, and it was hoped to produce the first bombs by July 1944.[2] British resources were not sufficient to permit parallel development without the gravest strain. Consequently Churchill proposed to Roosevelt on 20 June 1942 that efforts to make atomic bombs in Britain should be abandoned, and all engineering and factory production be concentrated in America. He offered the help of British scientists, and asked in return that Britain share fully in the technical information which might be gathered from the American experience. Roosevelt agreed that atomic production should be undertaken in the United States, and, in Churchill's words, 'settled a basis of agreement' as to how information should be shared.[3]

Atomic research and production promised important long-term results, but in the immediate situation the most pressing strategic decision was when and how to invade the European continent. On 20 June 1942 Churchill gave Roosevelt a memorandum in which he pointed out that British staff officers had been unable to draw up any plan for an invasion in 1942 that seemed to offer a reasonable chance of success. He wanted to know whether the American staff had been able to do so; and, if (as he knew well enough was the case) the Americans had no detailed opera-

[1] James Phinney Baxter: *Scientists Against Time* (Boston, Little, Brown, 1946), pp. 420–4; Churchill, iv. 340; U.S. edition, iv. 379.

[2] Baxter, op. cit. pp. 428–35.

[3] Churchill: iv. 342; U.S. edition, iv. 381. Churchill does not explain details of the agreement. Whatever form it took cannot have been perfectly clear, since friction later developed between British and American authorities over the question of just what sort of information the British were entitled to have.

tional plan for Sledgehammer, he asked: What other operation could be launched in 1942 in order to relieve some of the pressure from the Russian front and bring Anglo-American forces into action against Germany? He suggested re-study of the possibility of landing in French North Africa. In this memorandum Churchill explicitly stated that the British Government would not approve any sacrifice operation which involved the loss of most or all of the troops embarked. Only if the beach-head could be held permanently would the British go ahead. On the other hand, when a satisfactory plan was found, Churchill promised to share fully all risks and losses.[1]

The fact of the matter was that the American General Staff had not worked out a detailed plan, but Marshall and his assistants were loath to believe that one could not be prepared if every ounce of will and energy were bent to the one end of making a landing in France. Marshall looked upon Eisenhower, then on the point of departure for London to take up command in the European Theatre of Operations, as the man who would and could draw up and carry through such a plan. Consequently the American military chiefs were not ready to give up Sledgehammer until American brains had tried to solve the difficulties.

Before formal discussion could begin, however, shattering news arrived from Egypt. Rommel had attacked the British lines in Libya on 26 May 1942. Auchinleck's first reports of the battle were encouraging, and, indeed, the British expected to win a victory. Their forces in the Middle East had been augmented during the preceding months, and preparations were already far advanced towards a new British attack when Rommel struck. The event was very different. On 12–13 June a decisive tank battle was fought near a ridge which had been nicknamed 'Knightsbridge', and most of the British armour was destroyed. A week later, on 21 June, British troops which had been cut off in Tobruk, numbering altogether 33,000 men, surrendered to a force inferior in numbers. Rommel was free to press onward towards the Delta. British units retreated precipitously and by 30 June the remnants of the British Eighth Army were dug in at Alamein. It was not until Rommel had been repulsed in his attack upon this position (15–20 July 1942) that anyone could be sure that the Afrika Korps would not be able to press on victoriously into Egypt and beyond.

This defeat, and the totally unexpected surrender of Tobruk, coincided with the beginning of the second great German offensive in Russia. By the end of June German tanks were rolling once more across the plains of southern Russia, heading for the Volga and the Caucasus. It was

[1] Churchill: iv. 342; U.S. edition, iv. 381–2.

indeed, as General Marshall said, 'a very black hour' for the Allied cause.[1] Only in the Pacific was there good news. The naval battles of the Coral Sea (7–8 May 1942) and of Midway Island (4–7 June 1942) had checked Japanese expansion, though it was still too soon to say that naval supremacy in the central Pacific had passed from Japanese hands.

The disastrous news from Egypt caused Churchill to break off his conversations with Roosevelt and the American Chiefs of Staff before any decision had been reached. Tobruk morning was not a propitious time to talk of future offensive operations. Emergency measures were called for. Everyone agreed that it was of the highest importance to prevent the Germans from overrunning the Middle East. Such an event combined with a Japanese attack upon India might have led to the dreaded junction of the two Axis Powers. Accordingly, the Americans agreed to send 300 of the new Sherman tanks as well as 100 self-propelled anti-tank guns to the Middle East to replace the losses of the battle of Knightsbridge. These weapons arrived in time for the battle of Alamein, and gave the British troops for the first time equipment equal in quality to German armour and anti-tank guns.[2]

Nevertheless, before Churchill departed hastily for England, he found time to argue vigorously against Sledgehammer. He pictured the Channel running red with blood and recalled the carnage of the trenches in 1915–18. He was convinced that a landing on a restricted front in 1942 would re-create the conditions of trench warfare which had prevailed in the First World War. But Roosevelt and his advisers were not ready to accept Churchill's opinion. The upshot was merely an agreement to study the various offensive possibilities: landings in France, North Africa, Norway, or the Iberian peninsula. Meanwhile the American build-up in Great Britain was to proceed at the fastest possible rate.[3]

When the British Prime Minister returned to London he had to face a vote of censure in Parliament. Despite all the disasters which had befallen British arms in the months since he had assumed office, the party leaders in the Cabinet supported him, and only twenty-five back benchers voted for the censure. It was a great Parliamentary victory and, under

[1] *The War Reports of General of the Army George C. Marshall, General of the Army H. H. Arnold, Fleet Admiral Ernest J. King* (Philadelphia, Lippincott, 1947), p. 154.

[2] The major cause of British ill-success against Rommel in the desert battles was the inferiority of British tanks and guns to German models. German tanks out-ranged the British and proved more sturdy in action. On the other hand, the R.A.F. proved itself superior to the German air force; and it was largely command of the air which saved the British troops from complete disaster after the defeat of 13–14 June. Rommel's supply difficulties were, of course, another factor of the first importance in checking the German advance just short of the Delta.

[3] Churchill, iv. 344–5; U.S. edition, iv. 384; Stimson and Bundy: *On Active Service*, pp. 219–20.

the circumstances, a remarkable expression of confidence in the man who headed the British Government.

But the question of what should be done by British and American troops had still to be settled. It was not until 25 July 1942 that a definite decision was reached. The weeks between Tobruk and the decision to land in North Africa were, indeed, the most critical of the war. Allied fortunes had reached their lowest ebb. Egypt was on the verge of panic, and the garrisons of the Middle East had to be stripped in order to plug the gap at Alamein. Civil disturbances threatened in India, and no one could be sure that the Japanese would not be able to walk through that great sub-continent, and be welcomed as liberators by many among the population.

The crisis in the Middle East led the Americans to divert aeroplanes which had been destined for China to that theatre. In addition, the heavy bombers of the U.S. Tenth Airforce were sent from India (where they had been expected to support the Chinese armies) to Egypt on 25 June. These decisions stirred Chiang Kai-skek to bitter anger. He felt that China had been abandoned in her hour of greatest need. When, with the Burma Road cut, air support was all that the Allies could give, it had been drastically reduced. He demanded to know whether the United States was interested in keeping China in the war. Early in July he presented three minimum demands to General Stilwell and the U.S. Chiefs of Staff: dispatch of three American divisions to India to support an effort to reconquer Burma, delivery of 500 combat planes to China itself, and a monthly delivery of 5,000 tons of supplies over the Hump. If these demands were not met, Chiang declared that China would 'make other arrangements'. The other arrangements were obviously some sort of understanding with Japan. Rumours of peace feelers on the part of the Chinese Government soon spread in Chungking, and were taken seriously by General Stilwell, who by this time thoroughly distrusted the Kuomintang Government.[1]

In the Atlantic, the sinking of Allied ships by U-boats continued at an ominously high rate. In the week of 7–14 July the Allies lost a total of 400,000 tons. If this had been maintained, it would have more than doubled the rate at which new ships could be turned out. A large proportion of this loss was incurred by the ill-fated convoy PQ-17 which, *en route* to Archangel, suffered dispersal and was nearly destroyed. This disastrous experience led Churchill to cancel the Russian convoy scheduled for August. He so informed Stalin by telegram on 17 July. Six days later he received a sharp reply. Stalin said:

> Our naval experts consider the reasons put forward by the British naval experts to justify the cessation of convoys to the northern ports of the U.S.S.R. wholly unconvincing. . . . With regard to the second question, i.e. the question

[1] *The Stilwell Papers*, pp. 119–26.

of a second front in Europe, I am afraid it is not being treated with the seriousness it deserves. . . . I must state in the most emphatic manner that the Soviet Government cannot acquiesce in the postponement of a second front in Europe until 1943.[1]

Churchill thought it wise not to answer Stalin's reproaches and so kept silence.

The news that convoys to Russia would be suspended must have come as a severe shock to Stalin. The relentless German advance in the south was then in full swing, and Russian morale was already strained to the limit. By mid-July hope of succour from the West was gone, at least in any near future; and it now appeared that the promised supplies and munitions would not be forthcoming on schedule. The Soviet Government took steps to break the news to the public in a curiously indirect fashion. On 23 July 1942 all the Moscow papers featured an interview which Sir Stafford Cripps had given to the American magazine *Life* in March. The interview stressed the long-standing mutual distrust between Britain and Russia and the fear of Bolshevism which existed in Great Britain. The curious resurrection of this interview was obviously intended to undermine whatever confidence the public still felt in the imminence of a second front. It implied that the Russians would have to save themselves by their own efforts; that Britain could not really be trusted as an ally.[2]

While these blows were falling upon the Russian Government and people, a serious crisis developed on the fighting front. On 27 July 1942 the loss of Rostov was announced. This in itself was not especially significant; what was significant was the fact that it had been surrendered almost without a fight. It looked as though the morale of the Red Army might be on the point of collapse. From every point of view except the economic, July 1942 marked the lowest point of the Soviet war against Hitler. By August and September a new spirit began to spread—the heroic spirit of Stalingrad; and as this mood seized the soldiers and civilians the danger of immediate collapse disappeared. Rostov was not enough: the Germans would have to win a greater victory than that before Red Army morale would again be in danger of cracking.

During these same weeks, the differences between American and British military leaders reached the most critical phase of the entire war. In London, Eisenhower found the British unwilling to spend more time debating the merits and demerits of Sledgehammer. Just two weeks after Eisenhower had arrived to take up his new command, on 5 July 1942,

[1] Churchill, iv. 241–2; U.S. edition, iv. 270–1.

[2] Cf. Werth: *Year of Stalingrad*, pp. 152–3, for an interesting account of this episode.

Churchill invited him and his principal subordinate, General Mark Clark, to Chequers for a weekend's strategy. The Prime Minister lost no time in telling the Americans that he felt an invasion of France in 1942 was foolhardy and would in any case fail to help the Russians significantly. He proposed the invasion of North Africa instead as the most fruitful use of American and British power which could be made in 1942.[1] In the following week a series of conferences with British military leaders brought Eisenhower face to face with the obstacles which would have to be overcome if a landing in France were to be attempted in 1942. By 10 July he had become convinced that an invasion on a scale large enough to bring reasonable hope of victory over Germany could not be made before the autumn of 1943 or perhaps even 1944.[2]

These opinions were accepted by Eisenhower and his fellow staff officers most reluctantly. They felt a lively suspicion of British intentions, and believed that the British might be exaggerating the difficulties of invasion in order to disguise the fact that they had decided never to attempt a major cross-Channel attack. This suspicion made Eisenhower unwilling to agree to any substitute such as Churchill's North African proposal, for he thought that once such an enterprise had been launched it would divert men and supplies from the invasion of France, and so give the British fresh ground for baulking at that enterprise when the time came in 1943 or 1944.[3] Having come to realize that the British had not been entirely frank in April, the American military leaders were now dubious of British frankness in June and July. They consequently discounted assurances that a great cross-Channel invasion would be mounted eventually. Churchill's April pigeons were coming home to roost.

While these exchanges were in progress in England, the U.S. Joint Chiefs of Staff began to discuss the possibility of turning the major American military effort to the Pacific in 1942. This was an idea which always had a strong appeal to the U.S. navy; and Marshall, who had long been convinced that sound military strategy required concentration on Germany first, was so disgusted with what seemed to him to be British obstruction and half-heartedness that he too turned his mind to consider what could be done against Japan.

The critical days were 8–15 July. On 8 July the British Chiefs of Staff officially informed their American colleagues that Sledgehammer would have to be abandoned as a hopeless enterprise. When this unwelcome news had been digested by the American Chiefs of Staff they formally recommended to President Roosevelt on 10 July that the major American effort

[1] Clark: *Calculated Risk*, pp. 27–28.

[2] Eisenhower: *Crusade in Europe*, p. 68.

[3] Ibid. p. 70.

should be diverted from Europe to the Pacific.[1] Two plans for a Pacific offensive had already been advanced, one by General MacArthur and another by Admiral King. On the very day that Churchill left Washington (25 June 1942), King had proposed to General Marshall an offensive against the Japanese beginning with the occupation of the Solomon Islands. A week later, on 2 July 1942, the U.S. Joint Chiefs of Staff approved a plan which combined features of both MacArthur's and King's proposals. On that day they ordered the occupation of 'Tulagi and adjacent positions' as a first step in reconquest of the vast New Britain–New Ireland–New Guinea area.[2] The difficult and long drawn out battle of Guadalcanal (one of the 'adjacent positions' to Tulagi) was the outcome of this order. The operation began on 7 August 1942. With the exception of the Doolittle raid on Tokyo (18 April 1942) it was the first American offensive in the Pacific.

The decision of the U.S. Joint Chiefs of Staff to undertake the Solomons campaign was not in itself decisive. The operations ordered on 2 July were on a relatively small scale and did not commit the major strength of American ground or air forces. Decision still lay in the balance on 10 July when the matter was brought before Roosevelt. In the last analysis it was he alone, as Commander-in-Chief, who could determine American strategy. The Joint Chiefs of Staff were merely his military advisers.

It is impossible to reconstruct fully the thoughts and feelings of the time. The U.S. Joint Chiefs of Staff were by no means united solidly behind the Pacific proposal. Sir John Dill, who was personally close to Marshall, reported to Churchill on 15 July:

> There is no doubt that Marshall is true to his first love, but he is convinced that there is no real drive behind the European project. Meetings are held, discussions take place, and time slips by. Germany will never again be so occupied in the East as she is today, and if we do not take advantage of her present preoccupation we shall find ourselves faced with a Germany so strong in the West that no invasion of the Continent will be possible. We can then go on pummelling each other by air, but the possibility of a decision will have gone.

On the other hand, he added: 'King's war is against the Japanese.'[3]

Long-standing professional jealousies entered into the picture: the U.S.

[1] The critical sentence in the U.S. Joint Chiefs' memorandum of 10 July was: 'If the United States is to engage in any other operation than forceful, unswerving adherence to full Bolero plans [i.e. build-up in Great Britain in preparation for invasion across the Channel in 1943], we are definitely of the opinion that we should turn to the Pacific and strike decisively against Japan' (Gordon A. Harrison: *Cross-Channel Attack* (Washington, Office of the Chief of Military History, Department of the Army, 1951), p. 27). Thus there was still an element of hypothesis in the recommendation to turn first against Japan.

[2] Morison (*History of U.S. Naval Operations*, iv. 260–1) reproduces the Joint Chiefs of Staff directive of 2 July 1942 in summary.

[3] Churchill, iv. 396; U.S. edition, iv. 439.

navy would predominate in Pacific operations; the army in European operations. Each service, realizing these facts, tended to favour the course of action which would exalt its own role.[1] Quite apart from these jealousies, the strategy originally accepted by the Americans—to attack Germany first—had at least three arguments in its favour. First, U.S. concentration upon the Pacific would mean surrender of any effective co-operation with Britain and Russia. Second, the argument that Germany was more dangerous than Japan could not well be gainsaid. Third, large-scale offensive action in the Pacific could hardly be initiated until naval supremacy had been won by the American fleet; but to win such supremacy first required the construction of hundreds of warships, and in 1942 they had not yet been built. Large ground forces would have to remain idle waiting for the navy to carry forward its building programme if the decision to attack first in the Pacific were maintained.

It was, indeed, the irritation of the moment which persuaded the Joint Chiefs of Staff to recommend the Pacific offensive. It is quite possible that General Marshall thought of the Pacific plan partly as a means of bringing new pressure to bear on the British; but it seems alien to his straightforward character to believe that such a calculation was the only reason why he swung over to the Pacific plan in mid-July. He probably thought more like this: 'Without the British nothing can be done in Europe in 1942; let us then do what we can by ourselves in the Pacific rather than remain on the defensive indefinitely.'[2]

Roosevelt, of course, stood more or less above the service rivalries which coloured the judgement of his military advisers. He also was more responsive to Churchill's fears of disaster if a cross-Channel offensive were attempted, and he valued the alliance with Britain even more highly than did his military chiefs. In addition, Roosevelt's interest and concern with Europe usually outweighed his concern for the Pacific. All these and doubtless other elements—probably including regard and admiration for Churchill personally—entered into the making of the great decision which had been thrust upon him. For five days Roosevelt debated what should be done. On the evening of 15 July he talked matters over with Hopkins, turning over in his mind one last time the recommendation

[1] The air force was still a part of the U.S. army, but so far as there was a separate and distinct air point of view it coincided with the army bias in favour of Germany first. A large-scale strategic bombing offensive could not be mounted against Japan until bases within air range of the Japanese islands had been won by the navy; but in Europe Great Britain offered a suitable base for such an attack immediately. Therefore the professional interest of the air forces lay in directing the major effort against Germany first.

[2] Secretary of War Stimson recorded in his diary on 15 July 1942 that in conversation with Roosevelt he had argued for the use of the threat to turn to the Pacific in order to 'get through the hides of the British'. Writing retrospectively he described the whole thing as a bluff to force the British to take more active measures against the Germans (Stimson and Bundy: *On Active Service*, pp. 219–21).

which his Chiefs of Staff had made to him on 10 July. Hopkins recorded Roosevelt as saying:

> I cannot agree . . . that we should turn our faces away from Germany and toward Japan.
>
> In the first place I am not content with the British Cabinet position. I want to know what our men on the ground—Eisenhower, Spaatz, Clark and Stark—think. Do they agree with the British Cabinet? Can you get a confidential report from them?
>
> Even though we must reluctantly agree to no Sledgehammer in 1942, I still think we should press forward vigorously for the 1943 enterprise. I see nothing in the message from England to indicate any luke-warmness on their part for the 1943 enterprise. I am somewhat disturbed about this readiness to give up 1942. Will they also give up 1943?
>
> But my main point is that I do not believe we can wait until 1943 to strike at Germany. If we cannot strike at Sledgehammer, then we must take the second best—and that is not the Pacific. There we are conducting a successful holding war. Troops and air alone will not be decisive at once—it requires the increasing strength of our Navy—which takes time.[1]

The second best is not the Pacific: with those words Roosevelt passed judgement against the recommendation which had just been made to him.

It was surely a fateful decision upon which the whole course of the war depended. The picture of two men deep in perplexity—the one crippled, the other chronically ill—talking things out after dinner in the White House on a hot summer evening is one which should be remembered in every history of the Second World War.

Alone among the three great Allied Powers, the United States had a choice of how and where to fight. Upon the American decision depended whether the war would be fought by a genuine alliance or separately by each nation. Roosevelt's decision of 15 July 1942 was, in effect, a decision to try once more to make the alliance effective in action. Seldom in history has a choice so important for the fate of nations and peoples presented itself so sharply, so urgently, so personally.

Another decision, or series of decisions, taken about two weeks later in the secret recesses of the Kremlin, deserves, with this of Roosevelt's, to be considered the turning-point of the war. About the end of July 1942, immediately after the fall of Rostov, Stalin introduced drastic new disciplinary measures in the Red Army, shifted many of his commanders, launched a tremendous propaganda drive, and by a combination of all these steps saved the wavering morale of the army and people of Russia. At the same time he began to accumulate reserves behind the Volga for

[1] Sherwood: *Roosevelt and Hopkins,* p. 602; Eng. edition, ii. 603–4.

the counter-attack which was eventually unleashed at Stalingrad.[1] It was November before the effects of these twin decisions manifested themselves on the battlefields. But the landing in North Africa on 8 November and the Stalingrad counter-offensive which began on 19 November both stemmed directly from the two decisions taken in July.

(*e*) The Resolution of Allied Differences

Roosevelt's refusal on 15 July to accept the advice of the Joint Chiefs of Staff did no more than set the scene for another effort to arrive at an understanding with the British. He decided on that same evening to send Hopkins, Marshall, and King to London for one more attempt. They left on the following day, and arrived in England on 18 July 1942. From the ensuing consultations a genuine meeting of minds at last emerged.

The three American emissaries carried with them written instructions from the President. In this document Roosevelt laid down a number of principles of the highest significance. 'Absolute coordinated use of British and American forces is essential', he said. Further: 'It is of the highest importance that U.S. ground troops be brought into action against the enemy in 1942.'[2] With regard to Russia, Roosevelt said that the promised deliveries must be made; and he instructed Hopkins, Marshall, and King to investigate fully the possibility of supporting the Russians by launching Sledgehammer in spite of all that had been said against it. If they became 'completely convinced' that Sledgehammer was impossible, they were to inform the President, and turn to a consideration of where else American troops could be used in 1942. Roosevelt further declared that defence of the Middle East was of the greatest importance, whether or not Russia collapsed. He envisaged two methods by which it might be held: the dispatch of American troops to Egypt, Syria, or the Persian Gulf, or 'a new operation in Morocco and Algeria intended to drive in against the back door of Rommel's armies'. Thus Roosevelt officially acknowledged Gymnast—the operation in North Africa—as a possibility. The President ended his instructions with the following injunction: 'Please remember three cardinal principles—speed of decision on plans, unity of plans, attack combined with defence but not defence alone. . . . I hope for total agreement within one week of your arrival.'

Agreement came exactly seven days after the three Americans arrived. Their first step was to confer with Eisenhower and his assistants. Eisenhower urged that Sledgehammer be attempted. He believed that any other operation would make the big cross-Channel landing in France impossible until 1944 at earliest, and he wished to subordinate every other

[1] Cf. Deutscher: *Stalin*, pp. 478, 480.

[2] The directive is quoted in full in Sherwood: *Roosevelt and Hopkins*, pp. 603–5; Eng. edition, ii. 604–6; and Churchill, iv. 398–400; U.S. edition, iv. 441–4.

consideration to a landing in force in 1943. But when Marshall and King discussed the question with the British Chiefs of Staff they met with a blank refusal to accept Sledgehammer in any of its variant forms. After three meetings the deadlock remained unbroken. On 22 July the Americans telegraphed to Roosevelt according to their instructions, informing him that the British would not undertake Sledgehammer. Roosevelt replied that he was not surprised, and instructed them anew to proceed to find some other offensive plan that would bring American troops into action before 1942 came to an end.

There was little doubt as to what the substitute operation would be. Churchill and the British Chiefs of Staff had agreed among themselves on 18 July that 'the only feasible proposition appeared to be "Gymnast"'.[1] Roosevelt himself had been much attracted by the idea of a landing in North Africa when it was first suggested to him at the Arcadia Conference—so much so that Secretary of War Stimson had long regarded the Gymnast plan as 'the President's great secret baby'.[2] In the face of these facts, the American negotiators soon accepted North Africa as the best substitute for Sledgehammer.[3] By 24 July discussion had turned to questions of the scale and timing of the invasion of North Africa. On 25 July Roosevelt endorsed the decision and urged that the target date for the landing be set no later than 30 October 1942.

It was agreed on both sides that the landing in North Africa—rechristened 'Torch' on 24 July—should be primarily an American affair. The main reason for this was the belief that the French in North Africa would not be likely to resist an American landing, whereas memories of former clashes at Oran and in Syria might be expected to make them fight hard against the British. Thus it was agreed that the supreme commander of the expedition should be an American. On 26 July, before he left London, Marshall informed Eisenhower that he would command Torch. It took considerable time, however, for formal agreement about command appointments to be reached, mainly because the British, as a token of their sincerity, proposed at the same time to appoint Marshall Commander-in-Chief for 'Round-up'—the landing in France, still hopefully scheduled for 1943. Roosevelt, however, was not yet ready to designate a commander for the main operation against Germany, and the

[1] Churchill, iv. 400–1; U.S. edition, iv. 443–4.

[2] Stimson and Bundy: *On Active Service*, p. 221.

[3] Marshall and King first wished to keep Sledgehammer as a possibility until 15 September 'in case the Russian situation were to become desperate' (Wilmot: *Struggle for Europe*, p. 110; Craven and Cate, edd.: *The Army Air Forces in World War II*, i. 573. Cf. Harrison: *Cross-Channel Attack*, pp. 28–31). Wilmot also says that even after their return to Washington the two American Chiefs of Staff tried to persuade Roosevelt to go back to the original American plan for a direct invasion of France. Wilmot gives no authority for this statement, and it may reflect an uncharitable interpretation of the motives which inspired the U.S. Chiefs of Staff to hesitate over the venture into North Africa and to put obstacles in its way during the months that followed.

matter was settled by appointing Eisenhower Allied Commander-in-Chief for Torch on 14 August.[1]

The decision to invade North Africa was undoubtedly a great success for Churchill personally and for the British point of view generally. Disagreement and friction between American and British military leaders did not disappear after the decision had been taken, but never again did such differences seriously threaten the continuance of combined operations. One reason for this was the success with which Eisenhower built up a combined British-American staff to plan and execute Torch. Eisenhower's own personality must unquestionably be held responsible for much of the harmony with which combined staff work proceeded in the following months. It is also true that the British Government and military leaders showed a good deal of forbearance, subordinating themselves willingly and in good faith to the supreme direction of an untried American general. Having scored on the major point of strategy, the British felt it both politic and proper to give the Americans the top place in the combined operation. The larger the American stake in North Africa and Europe, the more surely was the ghost of diversion to the Pacific laid.

Apart from the vast difficulties of detail which had to be settled before the invasion of North Africa could begin—the physical assemblage of ships, planes, and men which must precede assault, the alarums and excursions incident to secret negotiation with the French military leaders of North Africa and of France itself, the choice of landing beaches, and the co-ordination of preparations in Britain with those in America—apart from all these difficulties, there remained one which loomed far greater: breaking the news to Stalin. Only if the Russians accepted the decision to invade North Africa instead of France would the rift in Allied relations be healed.

Churchill himself undertook this delicate task. On 28 July 1942 the War Cabinet approved the proposal that he should go to the Middle East to look into the situation there, and, if the Russians agreed, go on from Cairo to some meeting place with Stalin in order to make the Russian leader privy to the plans which had been newly agreed upon. Stalin welcomed the prospect of a meeting, but said he could not leave Moscow. Churchill accordingly agreed on 1 August 1942 to fly from Cairo to the Russian capital.[2]

[1] Churchill, iv. 405–6; U.S. edition, iv. 449–50; Eisenhower: *Crusade in Europe*, pp. 71–72.

[2] Churchill, iv. 410; U.S. edition, iv. 454. It is worth noting that Stalin's more cordial attitude followed notification from Churchill that convoys to north Russia would be resumed in September 1942.

While in Cairo, Churchill came to the decision to change commanders in the Middle East. General Auchinleck was relieved, General Sir Harold Alexander was appointed to succeed him, and General Bernard Montgomery was made commander of the Eighth Army. Thus was formed the team which was to win victory in the desert and go on triumphantly into Italy. After making these changes and inspecting much of the British army in the desert, Churchill flew on to Moscow. He arrived on 12 August, accompanied by Averell Harriman as special observer for the President.

Discussions started on the same day. Churchill began abruptly by informing Stalin that there would be no landing in France in 1942, but held out the prospect of invasion in great force the following year. Stalin was not, perhaps, surprised at the news; but he was glum and somewhat brutal in his comments on the caution exhibited by the Western Allies. He seemed to discount the reality of the promises for 1943. Churchill next turned the conversation to bombing operations, which had been greatly stepped up during the summer. This was a subject which did something to warm Stalin's heart; and, borne along on the somewhat more friendly atmosphere, Churchill then proceeded to tell of the plan for Torch. After a little while Stalin began to show some enthusiasm for the idea and took the lead in pointing out advantages which might be expected to flow from a successful landing in North Africa. Before the end of the conversation an atmosphere of cordiality had been established. Good feeling was strengthened when Churchill offered to send an Allied air force to the southern part of the Russian front as soon as Rommel had been defeated in the desert. Stalin said he would welcome such help, and receive it 'gratefully.'[1]

On the next day a second meeting took place. The atmosphere was entirely changed from the cordiality which had prevailed at the close of the meeting the night before. Stalin handed Churchill and Harriman an *aide-mémoire* which stated that a second front in Europe in 1942 had been 'pre-decided during the sojourn of Molotov in London'.[2] Churchill denied that a second front had been definitely promised and quoted from the *aide-mémoire* which he had given Molotov at the time. But nothing could soften the head-on collision. Stalin wanted a second front in Europe and made it clear that nothing else would satisfy him. He insulted the British army by impugning its bravery; Churchill retorted with angry oratory, defending the good faith and military prowess of Great Britain in particular and of the West in general. The interview ended, however, on

[1] Churchill, iv. 429–35; U.S. edition, iv. 476–83. Harriman's report of the conversation, in which he took no active part, is reproduced in Sherwood: *Roosevelt and Hopkins*, p. 617; Eng. edition, ii. 616–17.

[2] Ibid. pp. 619, respectively; Churchill, iv. 440; U.S. edition, iv. 490.

a more agreeable note. Stalin described Russian rocket artillery, and asked for an exchange of information about military inventions. Churchill agreed with only slight reservations. Churchill next asked about the defence of the Caucasus; Stalin described the forces available and declared himself entirely confident that the Germans would not get across the mountain range before snow blocked the passes.

On 14 August Churchill attended a state banquet at the Kremlin; on the following day conferences between the top Russian generals and their British counterparts (whom Churchill had brought with him) took place. Once again the futility of trying to deal with anyone in the Soviet Government except Stalin and Molotov was demonstrated: the conversations got nowhere.

The most remarkable incident of the whole visit occurred on the last night, when, at the close of a farewell call by Churchill, Stalin asked him to come to his private quarters in the Kremlin and have a few drinks. Informal chitchat and more serious talk about the possibility of a landing in northern Norway occupied no less than six hours. Conviviality lasted until 2.30 a.m. Stalin and Churchill had, at least for the moment, established personal, human contact with one another.[1]

By the end of his visit, Churchill felt that Stalin was 'entirely convinced of the great advantages of Torch'. For his part, Churchill had been persuaded that the Russian military position and prospects 'seemed very encouraging'.[2] In strictest secrecy, Stalin had told him of the preparation for the great Stalingrad counter-offensive; and Churchill reported to the War Cabinet and to Roosevelt that he believed there was now an even chance that the Russians would hold. General Sir Alan Brooke, Chief of the Imperial General Staff, was more doubtful, for he had flown low along the shore of the Caspian and had not seen the fortifications which the Russians assured him were ready to stop the German advance in the foothills of the Caucasus.[3] It was another three or four months before British military leaders ceased to worry about what would happen when the Germans broke through to the Middle East over the Caucasus mountains.

The curious alternation of Stalin's mood during these interviews puzzled Churchill and Harriman at the time, and their record of what passed does not remove the puzzlement. Churchill thought that in the

[1] The most interesting incident in this conversation was the question put to Stalin about collectivization. The Prime Minister asked whether the strain of the war had been as severe as that of the early 1930s. Stalin replied in the negative: 'It was fearful. Four years it lasted. It was absolutely necessary . . .', he said. Churchill's account of this conversation provides almost the only glimpse of Stalin's personal emotions available to those who were not his personal intimates (Churchill, iv. 447; U.S. edition, iv. 498).

[2] Ibid. pp. 450–1 and 501–2, respectively.

[3] Ibid. pp. 445 and 495, respectively.

second interview, when Stalin was so hostile and so insistent upon a second front in Europe, his behaviour may have been influenced by advice from the Council of Commissars.[1] But such a theory imputes the powers of the British Cabinet to the Russian Council of Commissars—a most unlikely thing. It seems possible that Stalin was testing Churchill's personality—his ability to stand up under attack: and when Churchill stuck to his guns and vigorously turned back all Stalin's reproaches and imputations, Stalin is reported to have thrown back his head, laughed, and said, before the translator had time to get a word in edgewise: 'I do not understand your words, but I like your spirit.'[2]

It does indeed appear that Churchill made a real impression on Stalin; and it is possible that Stalin respected and 'understood' Churchill the better because they held such diametrically opposite social views and defended divergent national interests with an equal tenacity. Churchill, after all, fitted fairly well the Marxian picture of what a capitalist statesman should be, whereas Roosevelt's idealism and easy optimism were puzzling and entirely alien to Stalin's mind. The President did not fit the Marxian stereotype, and it is doubtful whether Stalin ever felt secure in dealing with him, or 'understood' him any more than Roosevelt 'understood' Stalin. At any rate, the President never reached so easy an intimacy with the Russian dictator as Churchill did on this occasion. Nor, for that matter, did Churchill in his subsequent meetings with Stalin.

While these conferences in London and Moscow were bringing about a firmer strategic agreement among the American, British, and Russian Governments as to how the war against Germany should be fought, the crisis which had arisen in China when news of the diversion of aircraft to the Middle East reached Chiang Kai-shek simmered on through the summer, but never came to a head. Roosevelt sent Lauchlin Currie, one of his special administrative assistants, out to China in order to try to smooth things over. Currie was not successful in ending friction between General Stilwell and Chiang. On the other hand, China did remain in the war. The Japanese offensive against China which many had expected in the latter part of 1942 did not materialize; Stilwell's plan for the reconquest of Burma proved equally impossible. On 27 September 1942 the Americans answered the three demands which Chiang had made in July. They promised 265 combat planes instead of the 500 Chiang had demanded, and offered a hundred transport planes to bring supplies over the Hump. But no ground troops were to be sent. With this half satis-

[1] Churchill, iv. 440; U.S. edition, iv. 489. Cf. Sherwood: *Roosevelt and Hopkins*, p. 621; Eng. edition, ii. 621.

[2] Ibid. pp. 620, respectively.

faction Chiang had to be content.[1] China's war remained a side show and Anglo-American co-operation with the Chinese Government remained precarious and uneasy.

(*f*) Preparations for the Offensive

At the time of the summer battle in Libya, two British divisions were on the seas headed eastward with destination open: India, Australia, or the Middle East all were possibilities. Auchinleck's defeat decided the British Government to turn the transports towards Suez.[2] Thus in a few weeks British strength was restored after the losses at Tobruk, and in the following four months new reinforcements of armour and aeroplanes arrived. Equally important, Malta was reinforced and became a serious thorn in Rommel's side. During the following months aeroplanes and submarines operating from Malta sank a large proportion of his supply ships in the Mediterranean. Preparations for a decisive attack went smoothly ahead under the new commanders, Alexander and Montgomery. Except for Free French and Greek units, the desert battle was almost entirely a British show. United Kingdom, Australian, New Zealand and Indian divisions all were engaged. The only American contribution (apart from supplies and the precious Sherman tanks) took the form of air support offered by units of the 14th U.S. Air Force.

Torch, by contrast, required everything to be done from scratch. A combined American-British staff had to be created, and the hitherto unexplored difficulties of combined operations between Anglo-American forces and between the naval, air, and ground forces of both nations had to be solved. Given the short time available between the decision of the end of July to embark upon Torch and the time when bad weather would make the venture precarious if not foolhardy, these obstacles were formidable enough. But Eisenhower and his colleagues had to struggle with additional difficulties. The decision of 25 July had left all details unsettled. Moreover, the American army and navy high command found it hard to pin their faith upon the new strategy and were inclined to emphasize dangers and obstacles. It was a reversal of roles, for the British had behaved in exactly the same manner about Sledgehammer. The U.S. navy was reluctant to divert any of its strength from the Solomons campaign, which had developed into a more arduous undertaking than had originally been envisaged. As a result, it was only late in the game that Eisenhower was able to get from Admiral King a firm statement of what American warships would be available for Torch.[3]

A major difference of opinion arose between the American and British General Staffs as to where the landings should take place. Eisenhower

[1] *The Stilwell Papers*, p. 152.
[2] Churchill, iv. 325; U.S. edition, iv. 363.
[3] Eisenhower: *Crusade in Europe*, p. 77; Wilmot: *Struggle for Europe*, pp. 111–14.

and the British both thought that it was important to land as far eastward as possible, in order to give the Allies a good chance to occupy Tunisia at the waist of the Mediterranean before the Germans could establish themselves there. But operations far inside the Mediterranean seemed perilous to the men in Washington. They feared what might happen if Spain admitted the Germans and thus cut the Allied force off at Gibraltar. Consequently, they insisted that a landing be made on the Atlantic coast near Casablanca so that everything would not depend on communications through the straits.[1]

The matter was debated throughout the month of August. On 25 August the United States Chiefs of Staff telegraphed to Eisenhower, instructing him that no attempt should be made to land in the Algiers–Bône area; on 29 August Eisenhower and Clark received a message telling them that Roosevelt had decided that British troops should not take part in Torch, and that landings should be made only at Casablanca and Oran. A barrage of such cables from Washington deeply disturbed the American commanders on the spot. As General Clark said to his staff officers: 'Some of you men are less confused than others about TORCH. Let's all get equally confused.'[2]

The British, too, were distressed and confused. After receipt of the two cables from Washington during the last week of August, the loading of ships had to be suspended, and as a result preparations suffered a three weeks' delay. Clearly this sort of shilly-shallying could not go on for long if Torch were to be a success. Churchill leaped into the breach: on 1 September he telegraphed to Roosevelt:

> Orders were given to suspend loadings yesterday in order that, if necessary, all should be recast. . . . In spite of the difficulties, it seems to us vital that Algiers should be occupied simultaneously with Casablanca and Oran. . . . We have accepted an American command and your leadership. . . . We must however say quite plainly that we are sure that the best course is to persevere along the general lines so clearly set out in the agreed directive handed to General Eisenhower on August 14.[3]

There was talk of sending Eisenhower or Clark to Washington to force things to a definite decision; and Churchill composed (but never sent) an emphatic letter to Hopkins protesting against the sudden changes in plan.[4] But drastic action proved not to be necessary. On 3 September

[1] Eisenhower: *Crusade in Europe*, pp. 77–80. This decision raised another problem, for the surf on the beaches near Casablanca was usually so high as to make a landing hazardous. In the event all went well. By extraordinary luck D-day happened to be relatively calm.

[2] Mark W. Clark: *Calculated Risk* (New York, Harper, 1950), p. 51. [Quotation made by permission of Messrs. Harper & Brothers, of New York, and of Messrs. George G. Harrap, of London (publishers of the English edition).]

[3] Churchill, iv. 479–80; U.S. edition, iv. 535.

[4] Ibid. pp. 483–5 and 538–41 respectively.

Roosevelt modified his stand, and agreed to a landing at Algiers. Two days later, after some further minor adjustments, full agreement was reached. But time had been lost, and it was clear that it would not be possible to invade North Africa before the end of October. Not until 22 September was D-day finally fixed for 8 November.[1]

The Americans' desire to limit Torch to Oran and Casablanca was due not only to fears about the military security of an expedition inside the Mediterranean. Political considerations weighed very heavily with Roosevelt and his military advisers. The great problem was to know what reaction could be expected from the French commanders on the spot. It was widely believed that a purely American enterprise would not meet with serious resistance, whereas a landing carried out by British or Free French troops would, according to the information provided by American intelligence agents, be resisted bitterly. On the basis of this estimate, it seemed wise to make Torch exclusively American. This was the reason why Roosevelt sent the telegram of 29 August proposing that no British troops should take part in the first landings. But, if American troops only were used, the scale of the proposed operation would have to be reduced. There were not enough trained American troops to carry through three landings without British help; and the landing to be sacrificed was obviously the most easterly, at Algiers. The decision of 5 September was a compromise: American troops were to form the assault wave at Algiers, but the main force there was to be British. At Oran and Casablanca, the Americans were to constitute almost the whole force, supported, however, at Oran, by British naval and air detachments.

The whole question of the French reaction to Torch was extremely complex and confused. At the same time, it was of the highest importance for the success or failure of the entire enterprise. From a legalistic point of view, the invasion of North Africa was an act of aggression against a neutral Power; and French officials were nothing if not legalistic. The officers and men of the French army in North Africa had all sworn allegiance to Marshal Pétain, and were bound by their oaths of obedience to him. Many of the officers felt sympathy for the conservative, authoritarian ideals which Pétain had come to embody. At the same time, every French officer hoped for a regeneration of French glory and greatness. The agonizing question from their point of view was how such a rebirth could come about: whether through loyalty, faith, and obedience to the Marshal or whether by renewed intrigue and eventual revolt against the Germans. The majority of French officers and officials were in 1942 quite unwilling to make such a difficult choice. Even those who began to

[1] Churchill, iv. 478–88; U.S. edition, iv. 534–45.

intrigue against the Germans did so in the name of Marshal Pétain, believing or pretending to believe that they were doing what he really wished them to do.

The frame of mind which prevailed among official and military circles in North Africa and in France was peculiar and very difficult for an outsider fully to understand. Failure to do so led the Allies into a rather awkward pass. Equally important was the wide gap between official and military attitudes and those of the public at large, especially the public in metropolitan France. But the Frenchman or Arab in the street had little influence upon events in North Africa at first: what mattered initially were the attitudes and actions of officials, and particularly of the handful of men who commanded the garrisons and naval detachments safeguarding French possessions in North Africa.[1]

A small number of French army officers in North Africa, associated with some civilians, had long cherished the hope that some day a rising could be arranged against the Germans so that France could again enter the war and avenge the disaster of 1940. General Charles Mast, commander of the XIX Army Corps stationed at Algiers, was the most prominent among this group. In May 1942 Mast had made contact with Giraud, whose name had rocketed to fame in France after his dramatic escape to Vichy France from a German prison in April. Mast offered Giraud the headship of the rather flimsy organization he and others had formed in North Africa. Giraud, for his part, had amused his prison hours by planning how France itself could be freed from German domination through a sudden revolt led by army officers and aided by the Allies. He therefore welcomed the news from Mast and his friends, accepted the leadership they offered, and formally appointed Mast as his representative in North Africa.

American diplomats in North Africa made it their business to follow the currents of opinion among French officials. Leaders of Mast's group had come into touch with Robert D. Murphy, the senior American representative in North Africa, and told him something of their plans. Murphy made a trip to America in August 1942 to inform Roosevelt of the state of opinion in French North Africa. Roosevelt in turn told him in strict confidence of the plan for Torch. Hence, upon his return to Algiers, Murphy was able to make guarded offers of American help. He was, however, in a very delicate and difficult position. The success of Torch depended very largely upon secrecy, and it was feared that if full information of Anglo-American plans were given to the French some fatal leak might occur. Hence all

[1] For an interesting analysis of French official attitudes cf. Albert Kammerer: *Du débarquement africain au meurtre de Darlan* (Paris, Flammarion, 1949), pp. 11–27 [referred to hereafter as Kammerer: *Du débarquement africain*]; also Winston S. Churchill: *Secret Session Speeches* (London, Cassell, 1946), pp. 81–82.

details, including the date of D-day, were kept secret from the French conspirators until almost the last moment.

Giraud, Mast, and their colleagues conceived of the operation as fundamentally their own. Revolt in North Africa and in southern France was to coincide with an invasion of northern France from England and with a Russian offensive against Germany on the east. The Americans were to be called in to help the French in Africa and southern France; but they were to come at French bidding, and naturally would be under French command. Giraud calculated that preparation for the revolt he was planning could not be completed before the spring of 1943. It was therefore with fundamentally divergent plans in mind that Giraud and Murphy attempted to come to a definite agreement after the latter's return to North Africa on 10 October 1942.

The wide differences between Torch and the plans Giraud had made soon became evident. The major point of difficulty which first arose was that of command. Giraud believed he had been promised the right to command Allied forces fighting on French territory;[1] but General Eisenhower was by no means prepared to yield his authority to Giraud or to any other Frenchman. Still less was he ready to adjust the plans for Torch and regulate the timing of D-day according to the desires of the French conspirators and the state of Giraud's preparation for a rising.

When the breadth of disagreement had become clear to Murphy, he arranged that an American general should come secretly to North Africa in the hope that he would be able to smooth over some of the difficulties. General Mark Clark, deputy to Eisenhower, was assigned this task. Travelling from England by plane and submarine, Clark arrived off the North African coast, not far from Algiers, on the night of 22–23 October

[1] Giraud had come directly into touch with American agents in metropolitan France early in July 1942 and had then undertaken to work with them for the liberation of France. However, he made certain conditions. The most important of these was the following: 'General Giraud will take supreme command of the Allied troops where French forces are engaged.' According to his own report, Giraud's memorandum in which he set forth his conditions was returned to him in August 1942 marked 'O.K. Roosevelt'. On the basis of this document, Giraud believed that he had a promise from the highest authority to the effect that he would have supreme command of any Allied force sent to help the French to revolt against Hitler. Cf. Henri Giraud: *Un Seul But: la victoire* (Paris, Julliard, 1949), pp. 16–17, 335. The question of authenticity and of dates becomes crucial here. In other connexions, Giraud was reported to have said that the document was returned to him at the end of July with the notation 'accepted' but without signature (cf. Kammerer, op. cit. p. 112). Moreover, it was during the second half of July that Torch was decided upon. Roosevelt's decision at a time when American aid to a French rising may have seemed a remote and marginal undertaking would presumably have been different from his reaction after a large-scale Anglo-American expedition had been agreed to. If Giraud's document was in fact genuine and Roosevelt did in fact 'O.K.' his plan, one can only assume that the President did so before Torch had been agreed to.

These are matters that cannot be decided on the basis of published information. What is important was that Giraud believed he had been promised supreme command by no less a person than Roosevelt; and this belief remained unshaken up to and after his rude awakening during his first interview with Eisenhower at Gibraltar on the very eve of the landing.

1942. After some misadventures, he met General Mast and Murphy in a seaside villa. Mast gave valuable last-minute information about troop dispositions, supplies, communications, &c.; but on the political level the meeting was inconclusive. Clark was bound by his instructions to keep the French in the dark on all important military details. Thus he did not tell Mast when the landings would take place, despite the fact that the time was only two weeks away. Indeed, Clark left the impression that the operation would not take place for at least a month. He did make clear that a landing in southern France could not take place simultaneously with the North African invasion, despite the fact that this was a cardinal element in the French plan. Clark also said that the Allies would turn over command to the French as soon as possible, but he would not be more precise. It was agreed that further negotiation should be carried on with General Giraud to see whether he, as the recognized commander of Mast's group, would agree to the conditions Clark had so vaguely outlined.[1]

Giraud's reaction was to demand clarification. In a letter of 27 October sent to Murphy he accepted Clark's proposals 'in principle' but reserved the right to set the date for the landing himself, and reasserted his desire that a landing be made simultaneously in southern France. Receipt of this letter, revealing the full gap which still existed between Giraud's plans and those of the Allies, put Murphy into something of a panic. He had visions of what might happen if the French fought to the death against the American troops which were so soon to come ashore in North Africa. Accordingly, he sent off a telegram to Eisenhower suggesting that the date of D-day be postponed for a few days until things could be straightened out. But the time for postponement was already past, even had Eisenhower shared Murphy's alarm. Ships were already under way; events would have to take their course. Murphy was left to make the best of what promised to be a very unpleasant situation.

In the hope of winning Giraud over, Murphy sent a studiously vague reply to his letter of 27 October. Giraud received it on 2 November. Murphy said that the Allies would transfer command in North Africa to French hands as soon as possible, but American command would be necessary 'during those phases of the operation involving the landing, establishing the security of North Africa, and providing the necessary base'.[2]

Meanwhile events were moving rapidly toward their climax. On

[1] Langer: *Our Vichy Gamble*, pp. 329–31; Kammerer: *Du débarquement africain*, pp. 165–73. Cf. Clark: *Calculated Risk*, pp. 78–89, for an account which gives fuller details of the adventure than of the political aspect.

[2] Texts of the exchange between Murphy and Giraud are conveniently gathered together in Kammerer: *Du débarquement africain*, pp. 650–9. Cf. a less complete collection in Giraud: *Un Seul But: la victoire*, pp. 348–52; also Langer: *Our Vichy Gamble*, p. 333.

2 November Giraud received cryptic notification of the date of D-day, then only six days in the future. He was aghast. His cherished plan for a French rising in the spring of 1943 had been unceremoniously brushed aside. Instead of arriving as invited guests, the Americans were coming when they were not yet wanted, and were proposing to take over control of French territory for an indefinite length of time. Under the circumstances, Giraud and the French officers who had entered into his plans were understandably distraught and hardly knew what to do.

Giraud's day, which began with notification of the date of D-day and which had been further complicated by receipt of Murphy's ambiguous letter, was crowned by the news that a submarine would soon be waiting off the French coast to take him to the Allies. This confronted the French general with a hard choice. Should he refuse to have anything to do with an enterprise which, from his point of view, had gone so lamentably awry? Or in spite of all should he cast in his lot with the Allies, trusting that when he took over supreme command (as he thought had been promised) he would be able to set things at least partially straight?

At first Giraud declared the whole thing an insult to the honour of France and to himself, but in the end he decided to embark in the submarine and go to Gibraltar in order to clear up the matter with Eisenhower. He was not reconciled to, nor even fully informed of, the Allied plan for Torch; Eisenhower for his part imperfectly appreciated Giraud's state of mind, and was unaware of the promise of supreme command which Giraud believed had been made to him.[1] No real understanding had been reached between the French and the Americans. Confusion was the inevitable result. It was not reduced by the unexpected presence of Admiral François Darlan in Algiers on D-day.

There was still another aspect of the tangled skein of French affairs which the Allies had to take into account. What of de Gaulle and his following? The group of officers who had nourished plans for a rising against the Germans under Giraud were all conservatives and quite out of sympathy with French Left-wing parties and groups. During 1942 these groups had more and more rallied to General de Gaulle and the Fighting French. They were weak in North Africa, where the colonial atmosphere of French settlement did not encourage Left-wing sentiment; but in metropolitan France Left-wing attitudes were widespread. Various resistance organizations had begun to form and grow stronger, nourished and guided by radical and even revolutionary ideals; and in the course of 1942 these organizations came into contact with de Gaulle's followers in London. Thus the influence and importance of the Free French was

[1] For the meetings between Eisenhower and Giraud on 7–8 November see below, pp. 245–7.

definitely on the up grade. De Gaulle was no longer an isolated figure who could be dismissed as a man with no significant following in France.[1]

Early in July 1942, before Torch had been agreed upon and when the prospect of a landing in France itself was still in the forefront of military planning, the British Government had recognized de Gaulle formally as the 'symbol of resistance to the Axis'. Even the American Government relented somewhat. On 9 July the Americans handed de Gaulle a note in which it was stated that the United States would lend 'all possible military assistance and support to the French National Committee as a symbol of French resistance in general against the Axis powers'.[2] De Gaulle hoped to convert this acknowledgement into full recognition of his organization as the French Government in Exile; but in this he was disappointed. The American attitude was unbending. The future government of France, Hull and Roosevelt argued, should be established by the French people themselves after liberation from the Germans and not before.

The decision on Torch obviously introduced a new element into the picture of Allied relations with de Gaulle and his French rivals. A new and most important reason for maintaining diplomatic relations with the Vichy Government came into play. Only by maintaining relations could American consular and diplomatic officials find easy access to intelligence which was desperately needed for the military planning of Torch.[3]

It was Torch, too, that brought Giraud and the officers of French North Africa into the forefront of Allied plans for France. De Gaulle no longer enjoyed a monopoly of 'resistance' in the eyes of the American Government. Indeed, one of the points upon which Roosevelt was most insistent was that de Gaulle should have no part in the proposed operation. General Mast in North Africa asserted emphatically that any landing by Free French forces would be strenuously resisted by the garrisons there; and this information, coupled with the suspicion of de Gaulle which the American Government had long felt, convinced Roosevelt that under no

[1] Even de Gaulle's most unsympathetic critics admit the growth of his movement in 1942. Cf. Hull: *Memoirs*, ii. 1162–3; Langer: *Our Vichy Gamble*, p. 291. The rise of de Gaulle's reputation in France was connected with the return of Pierre Laval to power in the Vichy Government in April 1942, and with the beginning of labour conscription for work in German factories. (Details will be found in the *Survey* for 1939–46: *Hitler's Europe*.)

[2] Hull: *Memoirs*, ii. 1162–3.

[3] After the United States Government had made an agreement with Vichy in March 1941 to send supplies to North Africa, a large force of consular officials was sent to the scene to check the use made of the materials delivered under the agreement. Their main task was to make sure that supplies were not allowed to pass into the hands of theGermans (ibid. pp. 951–2). These officials were ideally placed to collect the thousand and one items of information needful for detailed military planning; and in the summer of 1942 they sent Eisenhower voluminous reports about landing beaches, communications, the attitudes of French officials, troop dispositions, &c. Without this intelligence Torch would have been a far more hazardous undertaking than it was. Neither British nor American military intelligence concerning North Africa was in any sense adequate at the time the expedition was decided upon.

circumstances should the Free French leader be allowed to participate. Even when Churchill proposed to cushion the blow to de Gaulle's pride by telling him of the plan a day before the landings took place, Roosevelt vetoed the idea. Consequently, de Gaulle was first officially informed of Torch when American and British troops were already ashore.[1]

The British attitude towards de Gaulle was, as before, more friendly than the American. It followed that on the eve of the North African landings the Allies found themselves in the awkward position of seeming to back two different French leaders. Giraud was the American candidate for supreme military leadership, and, presumably, for political authority in liberated areas; de Gaulle was the British candidate for the same role. The differences were not so great as appeared publicly. Both British and Americans were primarily interested in the military success of Torch and were prepared to take whatever political steps seemed best calculated to advance that end. The situation was completely fluid, misunderstanding rife on all sides; and all calculations were suddenly upset by Admiral Darlan.

The inevitable risks of Torch were indeed very great. Had the French resisted the landing seriously and for a long time, the military effect would have been rather to strengthen than to weaken the Germans. Had the Spaniards adopted a hostile attitude, or passively permitted German troops or air forces to traverse Spain, a serious threat to the Allied flank would have been created, and the march to Tunisia might well have stopped in its tracks. The whole operation was indeed amazingly audacious—far more so than any subsequent Allied undertaking in Europe. Yet, in the event, audacity was well rewarded.

(g) Difficulties with the Russians

The preparation for Torch strained Allied shipping to the limit. U-boat sinkings had scarcely been checked at the time the enterprise was launched. Anglo-American naval forces had to be spread very thin. It soon became clear to the men planning Torch that every available warship would be required to protect the Torch convoys and cover the landings. This meant that convoys to Russia, which had been resumed in September, would have to be interrupted again. The large convoy which sailed to Archangel early in September lost twelve ships by enemy action, but twenty-seven arrived safely. No less than seventy-seven warships had helped to cover the convoy's passage.[2] It was obvious that no similar effort could be made during the period when the Torch convoys required naval protection. As early as 22 September Churchill wished to inform Stalin that the October

[1] Churchill, iv. 543–4; U.S. edition, iv. 605–6.
[2] Ibid. iv. 244, 508, 519–20; U.S. edition, iv. 273, 567, 579.

convoy to Russia would have to be postponed; but Roosevelt felt that such unwelcome news could do no good and might seriously embitter relations with Russia. Instead of cancelling the convoy entirely it was decided to try and run individual ships into the Russian ports from Iceland without escort.[1] Stalin was informed of this decision on 9 October. He replied with a non-committal 'Thank you'. In the following weeks a stony silence from Moscow troubled Churchill's mind.

The silence was the more perplexing because the British and American Governments had initiated negotiations for establishing an air force on the southern part of the Russian front, in accordance with the promises Churchill had made to Stalin in August. The matter had gone ahead slowly, and now the Russians seemed to be dragging their feet, despite the fact that the battle of Stalingrad was at its height.[2]

Another matter of concern between the Western Allies and the Soviet Union was the development of the Persian Gulf route for delivery of supplies to the Russian war front. When Churchill was on his way back from Moscow in August he had made arrangements for the Americans to take over responsibility for operating the railway and port facilities of Persia.[3] It was, however, several months before American personnel and equipment arrived in large amount, and not before 1943 did the Persian Gulf route begin to carry a large proportion of the supplies delivered from the United States to Russia.

The British and Americans hoped that their proposal to establish an air force in southern Russia and their efforts to develop the Persian Gulf route would cushion the blow dealt by the interruption of regular convoys to northern Russia. From the point of view of the Russians, however, they were being asked to exchange promises about the future for present and much needed help. The fact that Torch D-day had been postponed beyond the date which Churchill had set when he was in Moscow may also have excited a certain amount of suspicion among the Russians. Whatever the causes, the Russian Government went out of their way during October 1942 to suggest in the public press that the Western Allies were not faithful to the Soviet Union.

The principal events marking the decline in Soviet confidence in the West were the following. On 17 August, the day after Churchill left Moscow, came news of the commando raid on Dieppe. Many Russians at first thought the long awaited second front had come. The next day's news was all the more crushing. The repulse and re-embarkation seemed to end all hope of speedy relief from the West.[4]

[1] Thirteen ships tried to make the run; only five arrived (Churchill, iv. 518, note; U.S. edition, iv. 578, note). [2] Ibid. pp. 521 and 581, respectively. [3] Ibid. pp. 461 and 513, respectively.

[4] Werth: *Year of Stalingrad*, pp. 159, 184; Sherwood: *Roosevelt and Hopkins*, p. 626; Eng. edition, ii. 623–4. The Russian newspapers did not interpret the Dieppe raid as the second front; but many individual Russians nevertheless felt for a few hours that this was it.

A second chilling experience from the Russian point of view was the withdrawal of the Polish army which had been formed on Russian soil from among the prisoners taken in 1939–40. The withdrawal of the Poles to the Middle East had been under negotiation since July 1942,[1] but the actual evacuation did not get under way until August and September. To the Russians, inevitably, the Poles looked like rats abandoning a sinking ship, for the battle of Stalingrad was then just beginning.[2]

The desperate position of Stalingrad was in every Russian mind throughout the last weeks of August and the months of September and October that followed. Tempers naturally and inevitably mounted against the Western Allies, who were still apparently doing nothing. This was the psychological background for the reception of Wendell Willkie's famous statement about the second front. Willkie had started on a good-will trip round the world. As the defeated Republican candidate for the presidency, his position was a peculiar one. He had no place in the American Government, and was not informed of Anglo-American plans. Yet in the eyes of most of the world his pronouncements carried semi-official weight. When he was in Moscow, Willkie was mightily lionized, conversed with Stalin, and was even allowed to visit a quiet part of the front. Before his departure, on 26 September 1942, he met press correspondents in Moscow and said to them: 'Personally, I am now convinced that we can help them [the Russians] by establishing a real Second Front in Europe with Great Britain at the earliest possible moment our military leaders will approve. And perhaps some of them will need some public prodding.'[3]

This statement, of course, revealed how little Willkie knew of the plans for Torch; but at the time the public not only of Russia but of all the world was equally ignorant of what was being prepared. Willkie's remark was promptly spread on the front pages of nearly every Allied newspaper, and what he had said was taken, in Russia especially, as proof that the Anglo-Americans could, if only they would, start a second front at once. Roosevelt was very angry at what had happened,[4] and Churchill found it hard to understand how a leading American public figure could be allowed to travel semi-officially and make public statements without at the same time being permitted at least a glimpse of the inside plans which

[1] Churchill, iv. 241; U.S. edition, iv. 269.

[2] It was, of course, only with the consent of the Russian Government that the Poles departed, and, indeed, Stalin may have been glad to be rid of an alien and potentially hostile military body. The Russian Government had not been able (or perhaps willing) to assign equipment or even adequate food to the Polish ex-prisoners, and when they arrived in 'Irāq and came under British military administration they were in no condition to fight. The profound suspicion which divided the Russians and Poles made real military co-operation between them impossible; but the withdrawal in the autumn of 1942 when Russia's agony was approaching its height served to dramatize the lack of mutual confidence.

[3] Werth: *Year of Stalingrad*, p. 262.

[4] Sherwood: *Roosevelt and Hopkins*, pp. 634–5; Eng. edition, ii. 632–3.

his Government were maturing. Stalin, too, must have been puzzled at the strange, irresponsible ways of Americans.[1]

The net effect of Willkie's statement was to reinforce newspaper clamour for a second front, both in Russia and in the Western nations. The agitation was stirred up further by Stalin himself a week later. Henry Cassidy, representative of the United Press in Moscow, conceived the idea of interviewing Stalin by mail. He asked three questions: 'What place does the possibility of a second front occupy in Soviet estimates of the current situation?' To which Stalin replied: 'A very important, one might say, a prime place.' Second, 'To what extent is Allied aid to the Soviet Union proving effective and what could be done to amplify and improve this aid?' Stalin's reply was: '. . . the aid of the Allies to the Soviet Union has so far been little effective. In order to amplify and improve this aid, only one thing is required: the full and prompt fulfilment by the Allies of their obligations'. This, of course, came when the postponement of Torch from October to November had just been announced to Stalin; but to the uninformed public such a statement could only be interpreted as a demand for a second front such as had been promised by the communiqué after Molotov's visit to Washington and London in May and June. Cassidy's third question dealt with Soviet capacity for resistance, and Stalin answered reassuringly, but without any definite prediction of victory. Stalin's remarks, like Willkie's, echoed round the world, and provided a text for the numerous journalists who were demanding a second front in no uncertain terms.[2]

Excitement over Stalin's answers to Cassidy had scarcely died down before a new controversy with Great Britain was given great play in the Russian press. On 14 October Molotov published a statement on German atrocities in occupied areas. Near the end, he said: 'The Soviet Government considers essential the immediate trial before a special international tribunal, and the punishment with all the severity of the criminal law, of any of the leaders of Fascist Germany who have already in the course of the war fallen into the hands of the authorities in States fighting against Hitlerite Germany.'[3] This could only refer to Rudolf Hess;[4] and the reference was made clear by a vitriolic editorial in *Pravda* which appeared five days later. *Pravda* declared that England had become a sanctuary for gangsters and accused the British Government of regarding Hess not as a criminal, but 'as the representative of another state' enjoying all diplo-

[1] On 5 October he referred to Russian need for aeroplanes which had been explained 'in great detail to Mr. Wendell Willkie' (Churchill, iv. 518; U.S. edition, iv. 577). In view of the strained personal relations which now arose between Willkie and Roosevelt, it is safe to assume that Stalin's message did not directly reach the ears it was intended for.

[2] For a detailed account of Cassidy's coup see Cassidy: *Moscow Dateline*, pp. 275–80.

[3] Text in Rothstein: *Soviet Foreign Policy during the Patriotic War*, i. 186.

[4] Details of Hess's flight to England will be found in the *Survey* for 1939–46: *Hitler's Europe*.

matic immunities.[1] The demand that Hess be brought to trial was played up prominently in the whole Soviet press for the following week. The affair made a deep impression on the Russian public whose feelings against the Germans had been fanned to white heat.[2]

On top of the Hess affair came a public lecture by a leading interpreter of Marxian dialectics, Professor Yudin, delivered on 28 October 1942. Yudin declared that the delay in the second front was due to political causes alone; that powerful social groups—the Astor clique supported by coldly calculating capitalists—were influencing the British Government to put off the second front until Russia had been thoroughly weakened if not defeated. Yudin went so far as to throw doubts upon Churchill's motives, quoting with approval a statement to the effect that Churchill regarded the alliance with Russia as an unpleasant necessity.[3]

This speech, which so bluntly reasserted familiar Marxist suspicions, was widely publicized in the press. It marked the low point in Russian cordiality towards the Western nations. On the same day the 'November slogans' commemorating the Bolshevik Revolution were published, and among them was one acclaiming the fighting alliance with Britain and America. On the anniversary itself Stalin spoke as usual. He rather soft-pedalled the second front issue. His speech contained several cordial references to the Western Allies. 'Facts and events', Stalin said, 'point to the steadily growing friendship among the members of the Anglo-Soviet-American coalition and to their amalgamation into a united fighting alliance.'[4] At the time when Stalin spoke D-day in North Africa was only two days ahead. When the news of the landing reached Russia, it made a good impression. The West was moving at last, though many felt that North Africa was a poor substitute for a real second front in France.

It is, of course, impossible to know what calculations or motives lay behind the rather erratic course of the Russian press in its dealings with the Western Allies. One thing that immediately strikes the eye is the degree to which Britain was singled out as the villain, while America was treated far more politely. The agitation against Britain may have been designed

[1] Translation of excerpts from this editorial appear in Cassidy: *Moscow Dateline*, pp. 284–6; Werth: *Year of Stalingrad*, pp. 269–70.

[2] A curious footnote to the agitation was added when the British propaganda magazine distributed in Russia, *Britansky Soyuznik*, chose this occasion to print a photograph of Madame Hess giving a piano recital in London. The Madame Hess in question was of course Myra Hess, but no Russian could be convinced that she was not Rudolf Hess's wife. Cf. Werth: *Year of Stalingrad*, p. 316.

[3] Ibid. pp. 320–2.

[4] Stalin: *Great Patriotic War*, p. 67. In contrast to his hint of the possibility of an understanding with Hitler in the speech of February 1942, this time Stalin declared that 'our first task is to destroy the Hitler state and its inspirers'. But he went on: 'We do not pursue the aim of destroying the entire organized military force in Germany, for . . . this is not only impossible . . . but also inadvisable from the point of view of the victor. But we can and must destroy Hitler's army' (ibid. p. 69). This may plausibly be interpreted as a bid for the support of the professional army against Hitler and his reckless generalship.

primarily for home consumption—to provide the Russian public with a convenient scapegoat to blame for the hardships which the war brought to them. On the other hand, the Soviet Government may have believed that agitation for a second front would influence the policies of the British and American Governments. If so, their success was slight. Churchill was greatly annoyed at the treatment his Government received from the Russian press during the autumn of 1942, and Roosevelt declared in a telegram to the Prime Minister: 'I have decided they [the Russians] do not use speech for the same purposes as we do.'[1]

These difficulties with Russia did not directly impinge upon Eisenhower and the men under him who planned Torch.[2] Despite all obstacles and amid a vast confusion, preparation for Torch went rapidly ahead. Under Eisenhower's benign influence a growing confidence and mutual understanding arose among the members of the combined staffs working under him. It was a happy portent for the future of Anglo-American military co-operation, beside which all the earlier frictions and disappointments shrank to trivial proportions.

From the point of view of Allied co-operation, the three months from

[1] Churchill, iv. 521; U.S. edition, iv. 582; Sherwood: *Roosevelt and Hopkins*, p. 641; Eng. edition, ii. 639. Another consideration which may help to account for the behaviour of the Russian press is this. A few journals and magazines in America and Britain gave vent to anti-Russian sentiments during the war as before it, and their remarks were, of course, disowned by the Governments. The Russians may have felt that if the Western nations could allow their press such freedom, there could be no legitimate objection if Russian newspapers indulged in occasional anti-Western diatribes. By doing so they could give vent to what must have been a very real and deep-seated irritation at the relative inactivity of the Western Allies during Russia's long summer agony. The fact that the Russian press was far more strictly controlled by officials of the Soviet Government made Western leaders interpret the newspaper broadsides as official manœuvres in a game of psychological warfare; yet it is at least possible that in reality the control from the top was far looser than appeared. Some of the articles and editorials may not have fitted into any concerted official scheme but may have risen more or less directly from the feelings of the writers themselves. Even Stalin could not be omnipresent, and his subordinates must sometimes have gone ahead on their own, subject only retroactively to control from above.

[2] It was mainly Churchill who was worried by the strain with Russia. Roosevelt was less concerned. Indeed, at almost the last minute the Russian complication made Churchill doubt whether he had decided rightly for Torch as against a landing in Norway, since Norway would bring more direct help to Russia than any operation in North Africa could do. Cf. Clark: *Calculated Risk*, p. 59. During these same days, Churchill had to face discontent within his Cabinet. Sir Stafford Cripps had worked out a scheme for directing the whole British war effort, but Churchill disapproved of it, and the two men fell into serious disagreement. Cripps, however, agreed to withhold his resignation from the Government until after the invasion of North Africa, and he later agreed to take over the Ministry of Aircraft Production instead of leaving the Government entirely (Churchill, iv. 501–3; U.S. edition, iv. 558–60). Cripps's behaviour during these weeks was very high-minded. His position as a leading advocate of aid to Russia and as the favourite of the Leftish element in the British political arena would have made any open break with Churchill at this juncture extremely damaging to the Prime Minister's position as a truly national leader.

25 July to 8 November 1942 were perhaps the most pregnant of the whole war. It was during this time that the first combined staff and combined force were assembled and brought to life. Their cross-national and cross-service functioning provided a model for future, larger-scale military co-operation between the two nations. Details of staff organization need not be described here, but it is worth emphasizing what an innovation was involved in trying to work out plans and to conduct operations with a group of men drawn from the military services of two separate nations. Each nation and each service had its own peculiarities and traditions in which professional officers had been trained from youth. Much of this tradition had to be scrapped. Even such matters as terminology presented minor but in the aggregate serious difficulties. Only through a spirit of eager compromise and willing resort to innovation were these and far more basic differences overcome.[1] Torch became a genuine Allied enterprise as perhaps no previous military undertaking of history had ever been.

[1] Another interesting innovation was the establishment of Anglo-American psychological warfare teams equipped to carry on propaganda right up to the enemy in the front lines. This involved not only the merging of national propaganda 'lines' in North Africa—a task not easy in view of the de Gaulle–Giraud problem—but also required the integration of civilians into a military headquarters. Combined psychological warfare survived all the pitfalls of divergent national policies in the Mediterranean until the end of the war.

CHAPTER III

'TORCH' TO TEHRĀN: THE ALLIED SEIZURE OF STRATEGIC INITIATIVE

NOVEMBER 1942–NOVEMBER 1943

(i) The Turning-Point of the War

FROM the outbreak of the Second World War in 1939 until the autumn of 1942 Germany and then Japan had enjoyed the strategic initiative. They had been able to choose when and where to strike, and had gained great military and psychological advantages from being able to do so.

But the six months from August 1942 to February 1943 brought a fundamental change. In one theatre after another the Allies successfully took the initiative away from the Axis forces and won a series of brilliant victories. Taken together, these victories clearly constitute the turning-point of the Second World War. Although German and Japanese resistance proved tenacious, after Midway, Guadalcanal, Alamein, Torch, Stalingrad, and, not least, the failure of German submarines to sink ships as fast as they were built, there could no longer be much doubt that victory would rest with the Allies. Only the rupture of the Grand Alliance could have seriously endangered its victory; and the realization of that fact both in Russia and in Britain and America helped to keep Allied differences within manageable proportions.

It was in the Pacific that the Allies first took the initiative. On 7 August 1942 American troops landed on Guadalcanal, one of the southernmost of the Solomon Islands. A long and bitter struggle resulted, in which the Americans only slowly won the upper hand. Late in January 1943 the Japanese began to evacuate Guadalcanal when they found it too costly to maintain their forces there; and by 9 February American troops had occupied the whole island. About 800 miles to the west, only a few weeks after the battle for Guadalcanal began, Australian and American troops first stopped and then painfully began to repel the Japanese from New Guinea.

These two campaigns, conducted under extremely difficult climatic and geographical conditions, set the pattern for the fighting in the Pacific during the following year. Two 'fronts' came into being. One was in the Solomons, where a series of operations pushed the Japanese northward through the archipelago; the second was in New Guinea, where Australian and American troops laboriously reconquered the northern coast. Both in the Solomons and in New Guinea air power operating from land bases was of key importance. In New Guinea troops were transported and supplied by air on a hitherto unprecedented scale. This overcame some of the supply difficulties created by the roadless, mountainous jungle, but the size of the forces that could be maintained was nevertheless severely limited. After what had happened to the *Repulse* and *Prince of Wales* off the Malay coast, no fleet was prepared to risk itself within the range of hostile land-based aeroplanes without the cover of friendly fighters. Consequently the forward movement of the Americans and Australians was limited by the effective range of fighter aeroplanes operating from bases already captured. In the vast spaces of the Pacific, advances on such a scale were bound to eat up distance very slowly. Tokyo was very far away.

In the central Pacific there were no island stepping-stones to connect Hawaii with the Japanese strongholds in the Marshall and Caroline Islands. Hence land-based air cover could not be provided for offensive operations against this sector of the Japanese defence periphery. Before the Americans could take the direct path to Tokyo it was necessary to construct a fleet capable of meeting and defeating land-based aeroplanes and coast defences. This meant first of all the construction of aircraft carriers in unparalleled numbers. In addition a host of supply and maintenance ships, landing barges, amphibious tanks, and standard fighting ships all had to be built. The creation of such a fleet required many months. It was only on 20 November 1943 that the assault upon Tarawa and neighbouring atolls in the Gilbert Islands proved that a water-borne force without direct support from land-based planes could overcome Japanese defences. The conquest of Tarawa marked the beginning of a new main thrust against the Japanese across the central Pacific. Until then the ocean distances of the central Pacific safeguarded the Japanese outposts and confined active battles to the remote south-west.

In Burma military difficulties analogous to those of the central Pacific prevented any successful attack upon the Japanese in 1943. Mountain and jungle separated the Allied ground forces in India and China from the Japanese in Burma, and normal supply methods could not cope with the difficulties of the terrain and climate. (Heavy rains during the monsoon months made military movement almost impossible between May and October each year.) Only the use of aeroplanes for supply and troop transport on a vast scale, and the abandonment of normal lines of communication, could make effective attack upon the Japanese garrison of Burma possible. Not until 1944 was this done. In addition to strictly military difficulties, there were important political obstacles to the success of Allied operations in Burma.[1] Between them, the military and political factors made Allied operations on the Burma front ineffective throughout 1943.

[1] See above, p. 159.

As a matter of fact, relatively small forces were actually engaged in combat with the Japanese in 1943. It was against Germany and her allies that the major strength of the Grand Alliance was directed. Terrain and distance did not offer such obstacles as they did in the war with Japan; moreover, the decision of the Americans, and the necessities of the British and Russians, made Germany the main target.

The first great and irreversible defeat which the Germans suffered came in the Egyptian desert. The British Eighth Army attacked from its position at Alamein during the night of 23–24 October 1942. Ten days later the Germans began their long retreat westward, leaving behind most of the Italian troops who had taken part in the battle. Skilful organization of supply and the rapid reopening of ports recovered from the Axis permitted the Eighth Army to press its pursuit of Rommel's army thousands of miles along the North African coast. On 12 November Tobruk was reoccupied; eight days later British troops entered Benghazi again. A month later they passed on beyond Agheila, the point at which earlier advances had twice halted. On 23 January 1943 the Eighth Army entered the port of Tripoli, and soon thereafter came up against the Mareth Line on the border of Tunisia.

Although the numbers of men engaged in this campaign were not very large on either side owing to difficulties of maintenance in the desert, the Eighth Army's victorious campaign was of the highest importance. For one thing it proved that German tanks could be outfought, given enough artillery, air superiority, and new American and British tank models. The campaign had political importance through its repercussions upon Italian morale;[1] and psychologically the knowledge that a great victory had at last been won buoyed up the British public and imparted new confidence to the British army.

Two weeks after the beginning of the battle of Alamein, on 8 November 1942, American and British troops landed in French North Africa. Resistance in the Algiers area was little more than nominal and ended within twenty-four hours. At Oran and Casablanca the French fought longer, but on 11 November, just three days after the landings, French resistance ceased. The campaign then turned into a race for Tunisia, where the Germans had begun to send in aeroplanes and to land troops within forty-eight hours of the Anglo-American invasion. The British First Army spearheaded the drive for Tunisia; but mud, the absence of strong air support, and German resistance first slowed and then brought the advance to a halt. It was, however, not until 24 December that Eisenhower gave up hope of an early entry into Tunis. The winter months gave the Germans a chance to strengthen their forces in Tunisia, so that when British, American, and French troops resumed the offensive in the spring

[1] A fuller account will be found in the *Survey* for 1939–46: *Hitler's Europe*.

they found a formidable army opposing them. But naval and air attack in the Mediterranean seriously interfered with German supplies and the weight of the veteran Eighth Army was added to the Allied forces in Tunisia when it successfully outflanked the Mareth Line in April. A final assault led to the surrender of all German and Italian troops in North Africa on 13 May 1943. It was a great victory. More than a quarter of a million prisoners were taken.

Long before the North African campaign came to an end, the Germans suffered an even more disastrous defeat in the east. Just eleven days after the Allied landing in North Africa, the Russians launched an offensive on the southern part of their front. Powerful armies attacked both north and south of Stalingrad on 19 November 1942, and after four days' rapid advance the Russians succeeded in encircling the German troops which had fought so long for Stalin's city on the Volga. For reasons of prestige, Hitler refused to sanction withdrawal when a breakout might still have been possible. Instead the Germans tried to organize a relief force to break the Russian ring from the west. The German counter-attack began on 12 December. It was stopped after hard fighting about twenty-two miles short of the beleaguered German force attacking Stalingrad. Fresh encircling Russian attacks compelled the relieving force to retreat westward in haste in order to avoid the fate of the troops cut off at Stalingrad. Simultaneously, the Germans began to evacuate the area north of the Caucasus which they had overrun during the summer. The battle line moved steadily westward toward Rostov (recaptured on 14 February 1943) and Kharkov (recaptured on 16 February 1943). The long German retreat doomed the Nazi forces at Stalingrad. They surrendered on 2 February 1943. It is true that the campaign ended with a German riposte which led to their reconquest of Kharkov on 12 March;[1] but this was a small set-back for the Russians after the great victories of the second winter campaign.

The Red Army had dealt the Wehrmacht a blow from which it could never recover. Germans could no longer look forward to a complete military victory unless some revolutionary secret weapon suddenly changed the balance of forces. Russian morale rose as German morale sank. Victory seemed sure. Moreover, it would be a Russian victory, for the contributions of the Western Allies to Russia's success were not very obvious. Supply deliveries had lagged during the summer and autumn of 1942[2] and it was not until 1943 that large amounts of weapons, food, and military transport from the West became available for the day-to-day support of

[1] See below, p. 274.

[2] Nevertheless, according to Kalinov (*Les Maréchaux soviétiques vous parlent*, p. 281) no fewer than 750 Sherman tanks arrived in time to take part in the Stalingrad offensive. Such a number would equip about two armoured divisions.

Russian troops. Indirectly, by diverting part of the German strength to North Africa and by pinning other reserves in Western Europe, the British and American war effort did, of course, affect the course of events in Russia profoundly; but this the Russian public and, indeed, the Russian high command were naturally inclined to discount.

Alamein, Torch, and Stalingrad were each telling blows against the Germans; no less telling was the victory over the U-boats. This battle was won on the Atlantic and in American shipyards during the last half of 1942 and the first months of 1943. Until August 1942 Allied shipping losses exceeded new construction. But the rate of construction rose rapidly and losses decreased from the war-time peak reached in June 1942. As a result, in August 1942 new construction for the first time surpassed losses by a small margin. Thereafter, the margin widened, except for November 1942 when extraordinary losses connected with Torch and Guadalcanal offensive operations temporarily reversed the balance. This success was won despite the fact that more U-boats were at large in the Atlantic during the early months of 1943 than ever before. By August 1943, the balance had been so far shifted that new tonnage amounted to more than nine times the tonnage lost from all causes.[1]

Apart from the achievements of American shipbuilders, the main explanation of this great success lay in the use of radar-equipped search planes which were able to harass U-boats when they lay on the surface recharging their batteries. These planes, working in combination with other anti-submarine weapons, effectively blunted the U-boat attack. The result was a steadily increasing trans-oceanic mobility for the Anglo-American forces. Supplies and troops could be sent where needed on an ever increasing scale. A massive Anglo-American offensive against Germany became merely a matter of time and preparation.

As the Allies won the strategic initiative in the war the problems of co-operation among them took on new forms. The most important change came in Anglo-American relations with Russia. During the first eighteen months of the Russo-German war, the leaders of both Britain and America had believed that the Red Army would either be defeated or find itself compelled to withdraw far to the east where an inadequate industrial base would make its offensive power relatively slight. After Stalingrad and the triumphant advance of Russian armies to the Donetz river at the border of the Ukraine, the picture changed. Russian armies had proved themselves capable of a great offensive despite all the losses they had suffered. The power of the Soviet Union exceeded by far the previous calculations of Western generals and statesmen; and as the certainty of

[1] Statistics are conveniently assembled in Morison's *History of U.S. Naval Operations*, i. 404–12.

victory grew the question of Russia's part in the post-war world became more and more pressing. The earlier expectation of a settlement in which the Soviet Union would be no more than a passive partner to Britain and America, restored to pre-war boundaries by the victory of its Western Allies, became ludicrously inapplicable. What was needed was an active co-operation between the Soviet rulers and the West. Throughout 1943 the Americans and, to a less extent, the British tried to reach a meeting of minds with the Russians in the hope that a basis for active post-war co-operation could be found. The Moscow Conference of Foreign Ministers in October 1943, and the Tehrān meeting of Roosevelt, Churchill, and Stalin at the end of November 1943 were the first fruit of these attempts.

The emergence of post-war problems did not eclipse the more immediate military question between the Soviet Union and the West. The familiar agitation for a second front in Europe still cast a long shadow. The Russians had demanded it in 1941, they had been half promised it in 1942, and Stalin and his fellows expected it in 1943. But things turned out otherwise, and the Russians had to wait until 1944. The decisions which led to this postponement were not well received in Russia; but the more hopeful shape of military events and the growing volume of supplies delivered to Russia from the West prevented any open break.

Anglo-American success in Africa raised the immediate military question: Where do we go from here? Two alternatives offered themselves. Tunisia could be made to serve as a springboard for assault upon Sicily and Italy; and from there attack could be extended either to the Balkans (perhaps with the co-operation of Turkey) or to southern France. On the other hand, forces could be concentrated in England for an invasion of northern France in the hope of shattering German power by a single overwhelming blow. Anglo-American resources would hardly permit both at once; some sort of choice had to be made.

The choice was further complicated by the demands of other theatres. In particular, the precarious state of China seemed to require powerful and speedy succour. The Americans were particularly concerned with this problem, and tried repeatedly to arrange for a campaign that would reconquer northern Burma and open land communication with China once more. But in the Asiatic theatre, too, there were strategic alternatives open to the Allies. Japanese garrisons in Burma and Malaya could be cut off from home bases by successful landings in their rear. In particular, the recovery of Singapore or of Sumatra would sever the sea routes which alone could carry any large quantity of supplies to the Japanese in Burma. Such an operation, if successful, might make the recovery of Burma a relatively easy matter. There seemed to be still a third possibility. If a powerful long-range bombing force could be assembled in China itself, supplied by air from India, it might be possible to bomb Japan and interdict the Yellow Sea to Japanese shipping. Such an achievement would sever the tap root of the Japanese Empire, and at one blow cut off all the Japanese garrisons in Asia and the Pacific from their homeland. But in Asia just as in Europe a choice had to be made. Everything could not be done at once, and, moreover, the decision in Asia would affect the decision in Europe and vice versa.

Offensive operations in the Pacific did not enter into the balance in quite the same way. The U.S. Joint Chiefs of Staff exercised jurisdiction in that theatre without direct British participation in strategic decisions. Allocation of supplies and man-power to the Pacific was of course of key importance, and the Combined Chiefs of Staff together with the President and the Prime Minister did have the final voice in making these decisions. In practice, however, the Pacific was the special province of the U.S. navy; and the navy took on all comers in its Washington battles for allocation of men and material to the Pacific. The Pacific was assigned its share, so to speak, absolutely: indeed the British tended to regard assent to the demands made by the U.S. navy as a sort of blackmail paid to keep Admiral King among the Allies.[1] Supplies destined for Russia were in a somewhat similar position; though their sacrosanctity was not so great since the Russians had not the same influence with the Combined Chiefs of Staff as the U.S. navy. It was only after allocations to the Pacific and to Russia had been subtracted from the total of Allied resources that really flexible apportionment between the various theatres of war came into play. China, India, the Middle East, the Mediterranean, and the British Isles were all candidates: how Anglo-American resources were to be divided between them depended on the strategic decisions made during 1943.

As usual, unforeseen contingencies powerfully affected the outcome. The disappointing delay before the completion of the conquest of Tunisia made a powerful cross-Channel landing in France in 1943 impossible. The season of good weather was too far advanced before the German surrender in North Africa freed Allied troops for any such undertaking. After the invasion of Sicily, on the other hand, Mussolini's overthrow and the peace negotiations initiated by the new Italian Government[2] opened an inviting path for invasion of Italy. Neither of these circumstances could be clearly or certainly foreseen at the beginning of 1943 when preliminary strategic decisions were made at the Casablanca conference.

The general pattern which emerged from the strategic deliberations of

[1] Cf. Churchill, iv. 484; U.S. edition, iv. 540: 'I thought . . . that King had been paid off with what he needed for his Pacific war.'

[2] Details will be found in the *Survey* for 1939–46: *Hitler's Europe*.

the two Governments during 1943 was the result of compromise and repeated adjustments to new circumstances. A vigorous offensive in the central Mediterranean took Allied forces into Sicily and Italy; on the other hand, projects for attack in the eastern Mediterranean came to nothing. In England great emphasis was put upon the development of an air offensive against Germany. Bombing attacks began to assume serious dimensions in the summer of 1943 for the first time. In addition, a build-up of forces for the following year's invasion of France was begun, though it did not reach full scale until the early months of 1944. In Asia, on the other hand, plans for the reconquest of Burma, agreed to at the beginning of the year, petered out as supplies and man-power were assigned to other theatres.

Perhaps the most important development of 1943 was the consolidation of Anglo-American partnership in the war against Germany. The political, military, and economic bases for the partnership had taken form during the first year of America's participation in the war. But it was only as co-operation developed weight and mass on the battlefields of North Africa, Sicily, and Italy, in the air attack upon Germany, and in naval action on the Atlantic, that co-operation reached downward from the highest levels of government and military administration to embrace the rank and file. The partnership so formed was without precedent in history.

No similar partnership with the Russians arose. The project for putting an Anglo-American air detachment on the southern part of the Russian front, which Stalin had welcomed in August 1942,[1] did not seem so attractive to him after victory at Stalingrad had removed the urgency of Russia's need. He suggested that America and Britain should send the planes without their crews for the use of the Russian air force; but this proposal was not acceptable to the British and American Governments.[2] The project sank from sight, and the Russians continued to fight alone on their front. The war against Germany thus remained really two wars, and Russian strategy bore only tangential relation to the strategy of the Western Allies. Economic rather than military or political ties connected the Russian with the Western war effort. These ties grew stronger during 1943; and on their basis partially successful efforts were made to establish closer political relations between East and West.

[1] See above, p. 198.

[2] The Americans had offered to provide a group of heavy bombers, and the ground on which Stalin's suggestion was rejected by the American Government was that it would take too long to train Russian crews to use a type of plane which was unknown in the Russian air force (cf. Deane: *Strange Alliance*, p. 144).

(ii) Economic Co-operation, November 1942–November 1943

The institutional framework of economic co-operation among the Allies had been constructed during 1941 and 1942. Lend-Lease, the Combined Boards, and Mutual Aid underwent only minor changes in the period from Torch to Tehrān. But the scale of their operation enlarged as American war production swelled to its full capacity by the end of 1943, and internal changes in the war economies of the principal Allies affected the type and quantity of supplies and services exchanged between them. Moreover, plans for post-war relief and economic rehabilitation began to assume importance along with plans and policies for the administration of conquered and liberated areas.

(*a*) Internal Economic Changes

By all odds the fact which dominated Allied economic relations was the expansion of American war production. In 1942 factory after factory had been converted from civilian to war use, and extensive building programmes for new factories, barracks, and other military installations had been initiated. Despite the widespread administrative confusion which prevailed in Washington, these efforts were markedly successful. By the beginning of 1943 conversion to war production was substantially complete, and during that year nearly all the new factories came into production. Month after month the output of munitions rose until it reached its war-time peak in November 1943. By that time the great bulk of the initial equipment of the U.S. army and navy had been provided, and cuts in the production of certain items became possible. The task of the American war economy was now a simpler one: maintenance and replacement of equipment already in being and in the hands of the armed forces. As a result, more and more war material became available for Britain, Russia, and the smaller Allies. The acute struggle for allocation of war supplies faded, though of course differences between rival claimants never entirely disappeared.

The administration of the American economy underwent a number of important changes. The War Production Board introduced two new major devices for directing the war economy: the Controlled Materials Plan and what was known as component scheduling. Difficulties arose at the beginning with both procedures, but by the end of the year a reasonably accurate, flexible, and successful system had been worked out for the over-all direction and step-by-step integration of American war production.

This success was made possible not only by the work of the W.P.B. itself, but also by the fact that the needs of the U.S. army and navy and of the Allies had become definite and, within limits, predictable over future periods of as much as one year. The definition of military requirements itself depended on firm strategic decisions as to future operations, upon the ability of the Allies to retain the initiative and thus translate their strategy into action, and, not least, upon a definite calculation of the balance to be aimed at between military and civilian use of man-power. Indeed, a leading characteristic of American economic administration during 1943 was the emergence of man-power as the basic limit to the war effort. It was not until the summer of 1943 that a ceiling for the size of the American army and navy was fixed at 15 million men;[1] a figure which was chosen in the light both of estimated strategic requirements for victory and man-power needs for production at home. Once this basic figure had been determined, the amount of equipment required could be calculated with fair accuracy, and the over-all balance of the economy between war and civilian production and between production for American armed forces and for Allied forces could be estimated in advance.[2]

As such estimates took on exactness, a nicer adjustment of raw materials, production facilities, and man-power could be and was made. Thus by the end of 1943 the unplanned profit-regulated American economy had been transformed into a managed economy, adjusted to fulfil goals set in advance by government officials. Profits did not of course disappear, but they ceased to exercise decisive influence over the economy. Calculations of physical productive capacity and assignment of value according to military criteria replaced pecuniary calculation as the dominant guide for economic activity. It was a striking transformation which surely justified itself in the record of production established by American farms and factories in 1943 and 1944.

The administrative patterns by which this transformation was effected were developed mainly from two sources. The example of British war

[1] *The War Reports of Marshall, Arnold, and King*, pp. 264–6. This figure was never realized. The peak strength of the U.S. armed forces was 14 million (ibid. p. 266); but this level of mobilization lasted for only a few months. The annual averages of American armed forces in 1944 and 1945 were only 11,260,000 and 11,280,000 men respectively (cf. U.S.A., The President: *The Economic Report of the President, January 1952* (Washington, U.S.G.P.O., 1952), table B–11, p. 177). These statistics reflect the comfortable man-power margin the United States enjoyed in comparison to a country like Great Britain, where the peak mobilization was attained earlier and lasted longer. Victory came before the United States had to scrape the bottom of the barrel as far as man-power was concerned, despite the fact that troublesome local shortages of labour did occur.

[2] In April 1942 the British Government had been able to submit a calculation of the British Order of Battle for 1943, with estimates of the quantity of munitions which would be needed from the United States to complete the equipment of the British forces. It was not until 1943 that American needs achieved a similar definition (Hancock and Gowing: *British War Economy*, p. 397). Russian requirements were, of course, defined from 1941 by the series of Supply Protocols. Hence both British and Russian needs were known long before the requirements of the American armed forces were defined; but until the over-all needs could be calculated, plans for war production were inevitably imprecise and liable to sudden changes.

economy contributed directly to the Controlled Materials Plan[1] and, less spectacularly, American action was affected by British experience throughout the whole range of economic administration. On the other hand, the procedures for the control of production which had been developed by large American corporations served as a most important example for national production planning. Thus, the scheduling of critical components, introduced largely by Charles E. Wilson, whose prior experience had been with the General Electric Corporation, may plausibly be regarded as the application of the rationalized production methods of a great industrial corporation to the entire American economy.

The Controlled Materials Plan was first announced on 2 November 1942, but it was not until 1 April 1943 that it went into partial operation, nor until 1 July that it entirely superseded the Production Requirements Plan which had been tried in 1942.[2] This delay was deliberate, designed to permit the collection of necessary data and the education of government officials and of industrial managers in the details of the proposed system. As a result it went into effect fairly smoothly and won general approval.

The detailed application of the plan was inevitably complex, but the general lines were simple enough. The overriding aim was to secure an effective adjustment of production to military needs. To accomplish this end, the plan depended on allocation of the available supply of three metals: steel, aluminium, and copper. Supplies of these metals were calculated month by month into the future. At the same time, requirements were calculated month by month for the steel, aluminium, and copper which would be needed to fulfil the contracts which war agencies had let or intended to let to manufacturers. Requirements, of course, exceeded supply; and the problem then became one of cutting down on proposed orders in the way which would agree best with military expediency. When the elimination of marginal projects had brought demand into balance with estimated supplies, W.P.B. committees then made definite allotments of tons of metal to the various contracting agencies of the Government—army, navy, war shipping administration, &c.—and these agencies were left free to apportion their allotments among contractors producing for them.

In this way it became impossible for the programme of, say, the air forces to pre-empt all the aluminium of the country without regard for alternative needs which might be equally or more urgent. Not only was a balance between competing programmes enforced, but the over-all demand placed upon the economy was kept within the physically possible limits.[3] Thus calculation of physical quantities replaced the rough

[1] *Industrial Mobilization for War*, i. 485.
[2] See above, pp. 127–8.
[3] For a fuller account of the Controlled Materials Plan see *Industrial Mobilization for War*, i. 485–501, 663–82.

measurement in terms of dollars which had been resorted to in 1942 when the first effort to adjust the demand of the armed services to national productive capacity was made.[1]

It was not easy to calculate the amount of aluminium or copper or steel required for constructing 1,000 tanks or 10,000 aeroplanes; and it was especially difficult to predict the time at which definite amounts of each metal would be needed. At first manufacturers played for safety by over-estimating their requirements systematically; and it was not until 1944 that this practice ceased to constitute a serious obstacle to the effectiveness of the plan. A greater difficulty, and one that could never be solved satisfactorily, arose from the fact that other materials were not subject to parallel control. Yet there could be no guarantee that the supply of rubber, oil, chemicals, &c., would balance the supply of the basic metals. It was, however, judged to be too cumbersome to try to allocate all the raw materials which entered into manufacturing processes. In practice, control of the three basic metals proved to be enough to regulate and balance the whole war economy effectively if not quite perfectly.

In February 1943 another problem drew the attention of W.P.B. officials. The completion of a number of instruments of war was held up by shortages of certain component parts such as valves, pumps, ball bearings, gears, &c. These components were simultaneously in demand for many different end-products; and it was a clear absurdity to have a newly built ship, for example, waiting idly in dock for a few vital parts, while stocks of the same parts lay in the inventory of some factory waiting to be used for the construction of something else.

Component scheduling was introduced to avoid this sort of waste. Charles E. Wilson, Nelson's newly appointed second in command of W.P.B., issued a general scheduling order on 25 February 1943 to become effective on 1 April. He subjected only a limited number of critically short component parts to this new control. The principle was much the same as that of the Controlled Materials Plan. Production of the component parts was calculated in advance, and future requirements were also calculated. Then the best possible division of the limited supply was made by W.P.B. officials in consultation with representatives of the various government procurement agencies; and manufacturers of the scarce components were required to deliver their finished product to the user indicated by a W.P.B. order.[2]

It is not fantastic to think of this procedure as analogous to the planning and control that keeps a factory assembly line running smoothly. But in this case not a single factory but the whole American economy was treated as a series of parallel assembly lines. Parts in critically short supply were shuffled back and forth from one stockroom to another in order to keep

[1] See above, p. 128.

[2] *Industrial Mobilization for War*, i. 682–93.

all the assembly lines moving with a minimum of interruption or delay. The general scheduling order of 25 February helped to solve some production snags and presumably prevented others from arising. Within a fairly short time, increased supply of parts solved most of the difficulties.

W.P.B.'s success in balancing and expanding war production did not solve all economic problems. As all-out economic mobilization became a reality, the question of civilian needs became more and more pressing, not perhaps absolutely—the standard of consumption in America remained throughout the war far higher than in the other principal belligerent countries[1]—but certainly as a matter of practical politics. By mid-1943 man-power shortages in certain districts of the country had also become critical. A third problem was the continual bickering between W.P.B. and the army services of supply, and within W.P.B. itself.

Roosevelt decided that an effort to cope with these problems would have to be made. What he wanted was a man who could adjudicate some of the administrative quarrels and exercise a general control over the entire breadth of the economy. For this job the President picked James E. Byrnes, a long-time member of Congress and former Justice of the Supreme Court. On 27 May 1943 Roosevelt appointed him head of a new agency called Office of War Mobilization.[2] Byrnes's functions were best described by the unofficial title bestowed upon him: 'Assistant President'. The O.W.M. remained a small organization, but exercised general control over the man-power, industrial, and agricultural policies of the Government. More important, Brynes personally had ready access to the President's ear, and could argue with the Joint Chiefs of Staff on equal terms—a thing which Nelson, the head of W.P.B., had never succeeded in doing.

Jurisdictional confusion and squabbles among the branches of the American Government engaged in economic dealings with foreign countries led to a further change in the administrative organization. In the hope of clearing up these difficulties Roosevelt set up the Foreign Economic Administration on 25 September 1943. It took over the activities of the Office of Lend-Lease Administration, as well as economic warfare, relief activities, and foreign purchasing on behalf of the Government.[3] Actually, the new agency simply incorporated the personnel of its predecessors, and,

[1] Actually, personal consumption expenditure in the United States, calculated at 1939 prices, rose from $67,500 million in 1939 to $86,300 million in 1945 (*Economic Report of the President*, table B–2, p. 168). This indicates a remarkable rise in the standard of living, but did not prevent certain shortages from exciting complaint.

[2] For text of the executive order establishing O.W.M. see *The Public Papers and Addresses of Franklin D. Roosevelt*, ed. S. I. Rosenman, 1943 volume (New York, Harper, 1950), pp. 232–4.

[3] For text of the executive order defining the functions of F.E.A. see Rosenman, op. cit. pp. 406–8.

apart from changes in the topmost administrators, the consolidation made relatively little difference. With the establishment of these two over-all agencies—O.W.M. for domestic and F.E.A. for foreign matters—the major outlines of American economic administration achieved a form which lasted throughout the rest of the war.

In spite of all the publicity which was given to the friction generated between the various branches of the Government, it must be recognized that America's economic mobilization was very successful, indeed amazingly so. Success became clearly apparent during 1943. Production of munitions rose steadily until November, and reached a level that would have seemed beyond the bounds of possibility two years earlier.

The total value of munitions produced in 1943 was \$51·7 milliard as compared with \$30·1 milliard in 1942. Except for merchant shipping, achievements fell considerably short of the goals which Roosevelt had set in January 1942, as is indicated in the following table:[1]

Article	*President's goals*		*Actual production*	
	1942	*1943*	*1942*	*1943*
Military aeroplanes .	60,000	100,000	47,836	85,898
Tanks . . .	45,000	75,000	23,884	29,497
Merchant shipping .	8 million tons	10 million tons	8,090,000 tons	19,296,000 tons

The divergence between the President's goals and actual production reflected in part a better calculation of military requirements. Thus the relatively small increase in tank production during 1943 was the result not of shortages but of a surplus: the Allies by mid-1943 had all the tanks they wanted. Tank production was actually throttled down somewhat, and the Americans found themselves in the novel position of offering to the Russians tanks which the Red Army did not want.[2] On the other hand, the extraordinary expansion of ship-building reflected the special efforts made to overcome the shipping shortage which so greatly plagued Allied war plans throughout 1942.

The crude figures quoted above hardly do justice to the almost endless variety of munitions turned out by American industry during 1943. Weapons and shipping were only a part of the complex whole which included such diverse objects as acres of steel landing mats for use on airports and the complex proximity fuses which multiplied the effectiveness of anti-aircraft fire manyfold. With the conspicuous exception of landing

[1] Data taken from War Production Board: *Wartime Production Achievements*, pp. 106–9. The discrepancy between the figure for tank production in 1942 cited above with the figure cited on p. 124 is a discrepancy in the sources used. At best, the figures are only approximate.

[2] U.S.A., Department of State, Wartime International Agreements: *Soviet Supply Protocols*, Pub. 2759 (Washington, U.S.G.P.O., 1948), p. 57. [This publication is referred to hereafter as *Soviet Supply Protocols*.]

craft,[1] production had been reasonably well adjusted to the very complex demands of the armed forces, and the finished products flowed in approximately the right proportions and with satisfactory promptitude into the hands of the men who were to use them on the battlefields of Europe and the Pacific.

Internal changes in the British economy during 1943 were by comparison slight. The administrative control of British war production had been completed in 1942 when the Ministry of Production was established to provide over-all balance and co-ordination, and no important new departures were made thereafter. Production difficulties of course persisted, turning in most cases upon shortages of man-power. Calculation showed in mid-1943 that, if the size of the armed forces were to be maintained at the figure already achieved, withdrawal of labour from munitions industries would be necessary.[2] The Cabinet decided to withdraw the necessary number of men from munitions work in order to be able to exert the maximum military power in 1944. This decision was taken with the confidence that American production would be available to fill in the gaps, and thus maintain the equipment of British forces at the necessary level.[3]

In effect the British nation found itself poised like a wave on the point of breaking. The crest of military preparation which had been slowly built up over four years of war could not be long maintained, and had to be nourished constantly from across the Atlantic; but by careful calculation, the high point of British military striking power was made to coincide with D-day in Normandy.

In economic terms, however, the maximum of British war production came in 1943. For the year as a whole, munitions production in 1943 showed an increase of about 15 per cent. over 1942. But this did not nearly

[1] The construction of landing craft was the responsibility of the navy, but they were used mainly by the army. This division of authority proved most unfortunate, for the navy chose to use the material and man-power at its disposal for other forms of ship construction. Thus the naval schedule for 1943 did not provide for an expansion of landing craft construction over the relatively small numbers constructed in 1942; and it was only late in the year that small increases were made. This situation was brought home to Roosevelt at the time of the Second Cairo Conference (December 1943) when a shortage of landing craft turned out to be the main limiting factor upon the proposed future military offensives in Europe and Burma (see below, pp. 368–71). Landing craft were promptly given the first priority in naval construction work, but sufficient quantities were barely ready in time for the landing in Normandy in 1944. Cf. *Industrial Mobilization for War*, i. 603, 607–8.

[2] This necessity reflected in large part the difficult demographic position in which Great Britain found herself. A population in which new adult age-groups did not equal in numbers the older groups whose productivity was nearing an end meant that the total labour force would decrease in the future. Thus it was calculated that normal wastage, not considering battle losses, would reduce the labour force by 150,000 in 1944 from the total of 1943 (Hancock and Gowing: *British War Economy*, p. 449).

[3] Ibid. p. 450.

match American expansion. British munitions production was about a quarter of American munitions production in 1943, whereas in 1942 British munitions production had amounted to more than a third of the American total.[1] This inelasticity reflected the fact that the British economy no longer had any slack. Man-power, plant, materials all were fully employed, and an increase here required a decrease there. As the war shifted towards the offensive, new weapons and equipment were needed. Most of this new production had to be provided by the United States. Thus such items as landing craft, self-propelled guns, transport aeroplanes, &c., were not made in Great Britain.[2]

Information about the Russian war economy is too inadequate for comparison to be possible. The recovery of industrial production which had taken place during 1942 continued in 1943, but at a slower rate. At the beginning of 1943 the upward trend was reversed for a while,[3] owing to disruptions in the flow of raw materials, fuel, and other supplies. This was partly a result of weather, and may partly have been due to the extraordinary strain put upon the transport system by the great Stalingrad offensive. Despite this slow start, the year's total production was 17 per cent. higher than in 1942; but it still stood far below pre-war production figures.[4]

It appears that by the end of 1943 Russian production of tanks, guns, and ammunition was generally adequate to supply the needs of the Red Army.[5] The expansion of munitions production was achieved only at the cost of enormous civilian sacrifice. Many consumer goods became unobtainable. Working hours were extended to the limits of physical en-

[1] These ratios are derived from Combined Production and Resources Board: *The Impact of the War on Civilian Consumption in the United Kingdom, The United States, and Canada* (London, H.M.S.O., 1945), p. 11.

[2] Hancock and Gowing: *British War Economy*, p. 373.

[3] Voznesensky (*The Economy of the U.S.S.R. during World War II*, p. 92) says that gross industrial output in the first quarter of 1943 decreased by 12 per cent. in comparison with the output of the last quarter of 1942.

[4] Ibid. p. 26. If one assumes that production in January 1942 was not more than a trifle above the nadir reached in November 1941—a not unreasonable assumption since the winter weather must seriously have interfered with production—it appears from the ratios Voznesensky has published that the rate of Russian industrial production in 1943 was 0·83 as great as in June 1940 (ibid. p. 24). The meaning of the ratios—whether they are derived from monetary or physical indices, and how production was divided between munitions and other production, &c.—is not clear, and it would be foolish to put much faith in their reliability as an index of what really happened in Russia.

[5] Voznesensky, in his chapter on the planning of production (ibid. p. 84), cites percentage increases of production of a considerable list of such munitions. Thus output of aircraft was 37 per cent. greater in 1943 than in 1942; of small arms ammunition 45 per cent.; of 122 mm. shells, 90 per cent., and of self-propelled guns no less than 71 times greater in 1943 than in the preceding year. Without a numerical base these figures are treacherous, for if only one self-propelled gun was produced in 1942 it would be a relatively easy matter to multiply its production 71 times in 1943 by producing only 71 such weapons.

durance; overtime work in factories was made compulsory, and eleven-hour working shifts were apparently not uncommon.[1]

Food shortage had been acute in parts of Russia during 1942, but large government grain reserves had made it possible to maintain the ration of bread in most parts of the country. By the end of 1942, however, reserves were running low, and the import of food from America became a prime necessity, even taking priority over steel.[2] Only slight agricultural recovery was possible in 1943. The total sown area increased by only 7 per cent. in comparison with 1942;[3] but when tractor plants were busy turning out tanks, or, as at Stalingrad, had been wrecked by the battle, when the best agricultural land of the Soviet Union was still in German hands, and when man-power had to be taken from the fields to fill out the ranks of the army, food production inevitably decreased seriously.

What is amazing is not the failure of the Russians to restore or maintain their pre-war levels of production, but rather the fact that they were able to keep going at all. Consumption was cut to bare survival level; heart-breaking and back-breaking burdens were put upon the working population; yet, despite grim conditions, the Russian Government were able to demand and to get sufficient war production to keep the Red Army strong. It was an achievement quite as great as any British or American record.

(b) Intermeshing of the War Economies

Between Torch and Tehrān the growth of American war production made the United States more and more the arsenal of the Grand Alliance. Munitions, food, and supplies of all kinds flowed from the United States to Great Britain and to Russia in growing quantities.

The increasing scale of American Lend-Lease to Britain and Russia can be seen from the following table.[4]

U.S. Lend-Lease

$ million

	1941	*1942*	*1943*
United Kingdom (excluding services)	662	2,391	4,579
British Empire (goods and services)	1,082	4,757	9,031
Russia (goods and services)	20	1,376	2,436

[1] Cf. Werth: *The Year of Stalingrad*, p. 330 and *passim*, for a vivid account of life in Moscow in 1942–3.

[2] Stettinius: *Lend-Lease*, p. 227.

[3] Voznesensky: *The Economy of the U.S.S.R. during World War II*, p. 85.

[4] Derived from Allen: 'Mutual Aid', p. 250. These figures differ considerably from those published in the Presidential *Reports to Congress on Lend-Lease Operations* (Washington, U.S.G.P.O.). This reflects revisions made retroactively by the F.E.A. accountants in June 1945. Detailed accuracy in period analysis of Lend-Lease deliveries cannot be expected (see above, pp. 146–7). Cf. the table (also based on R. G. D. Allen's analysis) in Appendix II, p. 778, and Sir D. Waley's comments on the figures. This table shows in greater detail the development of Lend-Lease aid to the British Empire between 1941 and 1945.

Equally significant was the growing proportion of munitions in the Lend-Lease total. In 1941 only 31·7 per cent. of all the aid provided to Great Britain by the United States under Lend-Lease took the form of munitions; in 1942 the proportion rose to 53·6 per cent., and in 1943 to 70·3 per cent.[1] The obverse of these figures was the growing proportion of the total munitions supply of the British Empire which came from American Lend-Lease. In 1941 the percentage was only 2·4; but in 1942 the figure rose to 12·2, and in 1943 to 24·5 per cent.[2] These statistics reflect not only the great expansion of American war production, but also the growing inability of Great Britain to supply from home production the military forces which she had raised.

Britain's economic dependence on America gave rise to a few uncomfortable moments. Lend-Lease officials sometimes acted rather like a rich uncle putting a nephew through school. Thus when the Lend-Lease Administrator, Edward R. Stettinius, visited Great Britain, he looked askance at the iron fence surrounding Grosvenor Square, and told the British that it should come down for use as scrap metal.[3] A more serious matter was a dispute over tyres. In mid-1943, when tyres had become short in the United States, U.S. army authorities reported that the British had accumulated millions of tyres in Middle East stockpiles. On the strength of this report, shipments of tyres to Great Britain were temporarily suspended. The British retaliated by threatening to stop production of tyres for U.S. Eighth Airforce planes. The matter was, however, amicably settled by the establishment of a special committee under the Combined Production and Resources Board which assembled authoritative information as to the international supply of and requirements for tyres.[4] Tiffs like this were trivial in one sense, for they were easily settled by higher authorities in the two Governments. But they serve to illustrate how easily hasty judgement could touch national feeling and stir up misunderstanding. On the whole it is strange that disputes of this sort were not more common than in fact they were.

Three matters of more serious import arose between Britain and the United States in the course of 1943: the control of shipping, the exchange of information on atomic development, and the methods of book-keeping to be used in keeping track of the exchanges of goods and services between the two nations.

We have already seen how the original British hope of laying claim to a proportion of the ships produced in American shipyards was disappointed.[5] The heavy losses suffered by the British merchant marine during 1942

[1] Allen: 'Mutual Aid', p. 263. [2] Ibid. p. 268.

[3] Stettinius: *Lend-Lease*, pp. 251–2. The British in reply informed him that the railings had already been requisitioned for scrap, but that shortage of man-power and transport had prevented their removal up to date.

[4] *Industrial Mobilization for War*, i. 627. [5] See above, pp. 133–4.

made the British Government doubly anxious to find some way of keeping their merchant fleet strong. Long tradition and consideration of the competitive post-war shipping position no doubt played a part in determining the British attitude. But the weakening of the British merchant marine was also a matter of grave concern in the immediate war situation. The Government were determined to keep enough ships under British control to assure at least the minimum of imports into the United Kingdom without which the nation could not long survive. To be completely at the mercy of some Combined Board, or, still worse, at the mercy of the American War Shipping Administration, seemed intolerable.

As long as shipping was seriously short, however, the American authorities were not willing to hand over ships which had been built in their yards to British control. They were willing to assign ships to the task of supplying Britain, but wished to retain the ultimate right of reassignment. But this was just what the British did not feel they could tolerate. Some rather warm interchanges resulted.[1] The matter was brought up by Churchill when he visited Washington in May 1943. He argued that the British had ships' crews ready and waiting, while the Americans were hard pressed to find and train the necessary men. Under the circumstances, Churchill asserted, economy of man-power and resources dictated a transfer of American-built ships to British hands. Roosevelt accepted the argument and promised to do something about it. On 7 June 1943 he directed the War Shipping Administration to transfer fifteen to twenty ships a month for the ensuing ten months to British control.[2] This decision relieved British anxiety for the immediate future; but, since the Americans kept legal title to the ships, a problem of post-war settlement loomed ahead. This was highlighted by a speech made on 7 July 1943 by Admiral Emory Land, War Shipping Administrator, in which he recommended a vast post-war expansion of the American merchant marine and argued for 'our present policy of holding title to new ships'.[3]

Atomic research was the occasion for a similar contest of wills which rose to the highest level of the two Governments before reaching solution. In June 1942 Churchill and Roosevelt had agreed that atomic development should be concentrated in the United States and that the British

[1] The fact that the United States transferred no fewer than sixty-four ships to the Russian flag between July 1942 and July 1943 made the British the more determined. This transfer was, of course, a legal dodge to permit Lend-Lease goods to cross the Pacific to Vladivostok passing under the guns of Japanese warships without molestation. Cf. Hancock and Gowing: *British War Economy*, p. 361.

[2] Churchill, iv. 723; U.S. edition, iv. 809; Hancock and Gowing: *British War Economy*, pp. 430–1. Text of Roosevelt's letter may be found in *Documents on American Foreign Relations, vol. vi, July 1943–June 1944*, ed. Leland M. Goodrich and Marie J. Carroll (Boston, World Peace Foundation, 1945), pp. 404–6.

[3] An extract from Admiral Land's speech is reproduced in *Documents on American Foreign Relations, 1942–1943*, pp. 657–8.

should share in the project to some degree.[1] Work went ahead rapidly, and on 2 December 1942 the first self-sustaining atomic chain reaction took place on the campus of the University of Chicago. This success paved the way for the transfer of atomic development from the laboratory to the industrial scale; and as this transfer took place the share of the U.S. army in supervision of the project increased. On 1 May 1943 the Army Corps of Engineers took over responsibility for the whole enterprise, disguising it under the code name Manhattan District.[2]

Army officers were more security-minded than were the scientists who had previously managed atomic work. As a result, more and more stringent regulations were put into force to maintain secrecy. These regulations cut down, and after 1 May 1943 practically cut off, the flow of information to the British. From the point of view of the men in charge of 'Manhattan District', there could be no justification for spreading information about their doings beyond the narrowest circle of persons directly engaged in the work; and, of course, British Government officials in distant London fell outside the pale.

This state of affairs troubled the British. Churchill protested at Casablanca in January 1943 against the lack of full Anglo-American co-operation in atomic development, but did not press the matter. At the beginning of February he took the question up with Hopkins in a series of cables; but Hopkins could not resolve the differences. At the end of February Churchill hinted in one of his telegrams to Hopkins that if the Americans persisted in maintaining secrecy the British would have to embark upon a rival atomic project in Canada or elsewhere.[3] Such a procedure would have involved a prodigal use of precious materials and man-power; moreover, Churchill was very reluctant to surrender the British claim to share in American work on the atomic bomb.

When he visited Washington in May 1943 this, as well as the shipping dispute, came up for settlement. In both cases Churchill was able to convince the President that a more generous policy would be wise. Roosevelt agreed that exchange of atomic information should be resumed.[4] Published accounts do not make it clear what terms Roosevelt accepted. Certainly, in the following months individual British scientists took part in the American atomic project on a basis of full equality with individual American scientists. Whether security regulations were altered, as a result of Churchill's protest, to allow the British Government access to atomic secrets cannot be said, but seems unlikely.

A third important Anglo-American problem was financial. Under the arrangements of 1942, raw materials supplied to the United States from

[1] See above, p. 186.
[2] Baxter: *Scientists Against Time*, p. 436.
[3] Sherwood: *Roosevelt and Hopkins*, pp. 703–4; Eng. edition, ii. 700–1.
[4] Churchill, iv. 723; U.S. edition, iv. 809.

British possessions were excluded from Mutual Aid. Instead they were paid for with dollar credits. This procedure had been instituted in order to permit the British Government to pay off debts for munitions and other supplies which had been ordered before Lend-Lease went into operation. By the summer of 1943, however, the credits for raw materials had extinguished all such indebtedness. As a result, British dollar balances began to mount.[1] American officials objected to this situation. They pointed out that Lend-Lease had been started in the first place because Britain had run out of dollars, and demanded that now, when a dollar surplus began to appear in British accounts, steps should be taken to prevent any further rise. The British Government had little choice but to agree. Accordingly, in September 1943 raw materials supplied from British sources to the United States were brought under Mutual Aid accountancy.[2] In October a number of items—mainly capital goods which would be of value for post-war production—were removed from eligibility for Lend-Lease. If the British wished to receive such goods thenceforward they would have to pay for them with dollars. As a result of these changes, the rate of increase in British dollar balances was reduced.[3]

Lend-Lease to the Soviet Union not only became greater in amount during 1943, but the rudimentary outlines of a division of labour between American and Russian war economies began to appear. In 1942 Russia's most urgent need had been for finished implements of war which could be thrown directly into the battle. Britain, with a larger stockpile of weapons, was able to supply a larger proportion of what could be delivered in 1942—roughly half. In 1943 the situation changed fundamentally. Imminent collapse no longer threatened the Red Army. Problems were longer-term: how could the Russian armed forces be maintained at full fighting strength over a prolonged period—perhaps for years? By mid-1943 Russian factories proved able to supply the Red Army adequately, or very nearly so, with ammunition, tanks, artillery, &c. But this effort could not have been long maintained without help from outside. Industrial materials were short; so was food; so were replacement and maintenance parts for industrial machinery.

Russia had not the means and the skilled man-power to supply these

[1] See Appendix II, p. 773 below. [2] See Appendix II, pp. 781–4 below.

[3] Hancock and Gowing: *British War Economy*, p. 526. A powerful counter agent was the increase in payments made to American forces stationed in Britain (see also Appendix II, p. 773). In so far as their pay was spent in Britain, it added to British dollar holdings; and, since the number of U.S. troops in the British Isles rose rapidly in the first six months of 1944, this source of dollars became very important until some months after D-day, when the dollar irrigation was transferred, with the troops, to France.

lacks without aid from the West. Only the United States could easily spare men and machinery to make the things the Russians required. Consequently, the Americans undertook to supply a wide variety of machinery and component parts, semi-manufactured products (such as steel shapes, copper tubing, &c.), chemicals, tools, and, in some instances, even complete factories. Deliveries of such materials helped to relieve what had been a critical problem for the Russian economy not only during the war, but ever since the Five-Year Plans had begun. Skilled workmen who could turn out accurate machine parts from blueprints had always been scarce in Russia; now, in 1943, large-scale importation of machinery and component parts allowed the Russians to concentrate their skilled labour force upon assembly and maintenance of machinery. Less skilled workmen could then work the machines and produce the armaments needed by the Red Army in quantity. In addition, the Russians concentrated enormous efforts upon mining, transport, and gross construction (of such things as railways, new factory buildings, power lines, &c.), where unskilled labour could be used extensively. Thus in effect the Russians were able through Lend-Lease to avail themselves of the long accumulated skill and machine capital of the United States, and could concentrate their own less skilled labour force upon the immediate job of producing munitions and delivering them to the front lines.

The relationship which thus emerged between the Soviet economy and the American economy was not unlike that which had been established between Britain and America in 1940–1. Both Britain and Russia concentrated their man-power and productive capacity upon building up a munitions industry and armed forces at the expense of a rounded, self-sufficient economy; and both countries depended upon the United States to supply the things which they could not economically or conveniently produce themselves.

The parallel between the economic position of Great Britain and that of Russia meant that after 1942 the British could offer relatively little aid to the Russians. The British continued to ship to Russia aeroplanes and various munitions as well as raw materials which originated in the Empire; but the amounts promised by the Protocol of 1943 were smaller than those promised in 1942, and actual deliveries were less than one-third as great as in the previous year.[1] After February 1943 convoys to northern Russia were once again suspended and were not resumed until November, when winter darkness returned to shelter the ships from German attack.[2]

[1] Churchill, v. 231; U.S. edition, v. 261.

[2] Stalin felt that the British Government were altogether too slow about starting convoys up again in the autumn of 1943, and he exchanged some rather rough words with Churchill on the matter in October (ibid. pp. 231–44; U.S. edition, pp. 261–74). Stalin had some ground for complaint since, when the convoys were suspended in March, their resumption in September had been, if not promised, at least expected (cf. ibid. iv. 675–6; U.S. edition, iv. 754–5).

The decrease in the amount of British aid to Russia was only partly a consequence of the difficulties of delivery. The major reason was that Britain needed more than she could produce at home to supply her own armed forces. To send things to Russia on a large scale would thus mean simply an extended dependence on the United States. Obviously, when a direct, single trip from American ports could supply what Russia needed, it would have been a waste of shipping to send raw materials to Britain, fabricate them there, and export the finished or semi-finished material thence to Russia. Moreover, if British industry had devoted a large proportion of its effort to supplying the Red Army, maximum concentration of man-power upon the British war effort itself would not have been possible. Britain would have been equipping others to do the fighting; and the political and moral consequences of a victory won solely or largely by Russian soldiers would have been, to say the least, distasteful to the British Government and public.

The change in the nature of American Lend-Lease aid to Russia may be seen from the following statistics.[1]

Lend-Lease Exports to U.S.S.R. 1942–3

$ million

	1942	*1943*	*Per cent. increase*
Ordnance and ammunition	214	368	72
Aircraft and parts	303	502	65
Tanks and parts	177	75	−58
Motor vehicles and parts	149	406	172
Industrial materials and products	313	853	173
Agricultural products	185	592	220

Perhaps the most striking thing in the table is the decline in tanks—a reflection of the fact that the Russians no longer needed to import them on a grand scale. The rise in food shipments was necessitated by the loss of the Ukraine and the exhaustion of stockpiles of grain which had been accumulated before the war. The rise in shipments of motor vehicles was the result of an interesting division of labour between the Russian and the American economies. The Red Army traditionally depended mainly on railways for supply, supplemented by animal transport and man-portage from rail-heads. Roads were in any case both few and bad in Russia. Nevertheless the uses of jeeps and lorries were evident, especially when the Russian armies took the offensive and had to move into areas where the Germans had destroyed rail communication. It was not possible to

[1] U.S.A., the President: *Fourteenth Report to Congress on Lend-Lease Operations* (Washington, U.S.G.P.O., 1944), p. 31. [These reports are referred to hereafter as *Reports on Lend-Lease Operations*.] These figures, like those previously cited, are not accurate in detail.

improvise a great industry to produce motor vehicles in large numbers; consequently the Russians came to depend to a considerable degree upon American-made motor transport. Thus, by the end of the war, the field mobility of the Red Army was in good part American,[1] while the weapons and ammunition with which the Russian soldiers fought were nearly all home-produced.

The close integration of the Soviet war economy with the American was promoted by the improved regularity of delivery which became possible in 1943. In 1942, twelve out of every hundred ships that sailed for Russia were sunk; in 1943 the proportion was reduced to 1 per cent. This great saving was largely the result of shifting deliveries to the Persian Gulf and trans-Pacific routes. As we have seen, convoys to the northern ports of Archangel and Murmansk, which had been so costly in 1942, were interrupted again in the summer of 1943. When Stalin was first informed of the decision to suspend the Arctic convoys he complained to Churchill on 2 April 1943 of what he expected would turn out to be a 'catastrophic diminution of supplies of arms and military raw materials to the U.S.S.R.'. But, instead of diminishing catastrophically, deliveries to Russia increased month by month (with the exception of a trough in May and June), and by the end of 1943 they were running at more than twice the monthly rate which had prevailed at the beginning of the year.[2] Transfer of ships to the Russian flag permitted extensive use of Vladivostok; the work of U.S. army engineers greatly expanded the carrying capacity of the Persian ports, roads, and railways, and, with the clearance of North Africa, it became possible to fly even fairly short-range aircraft from the British Isles to Russia under their own power. Other air ferry routes to Russia (which, however, could be used only by longer-range planes) began to operate across the Atlantic. Together, these routes more than compensated for the interruption of the Murmansk and Archangel convoys. Thus the hazardous bridge of ships which had united the Russian with the Western war economies in 1942 was replaced by much more solid structures in 1943.

Schedules of deliveries remained as before on a Protocol basis; but the negotiation leading to the Third Soviet Supply Protocol did not become a matter of direct concern to the topmost political leaders. It was, like other aspects of Lend-Lease administration, becoming a matter of routine.

[1] Even the shoes worn by the Red Army infantry were in large part American-made (cf. Deutscher: *Stalin*, p. 512). Although Kalinov (*Les Maréchaux soviétiques vous parlent*, p. 512) cites what he claims to be official Russian statistics to show that less than one-third of the Red Army's motor vehicles were American-made, it seems hard to credit his accuracy.

[2] Monthly deliveries from the United States are tabulated in *Fourteenth Report on Lend-Lease Operations*, p. 58. The writer has not been able to find comparable figures for British deliveries; but if they were added the effect would be to accentuate the drop in midsummer and to increase the rise at the end of the year when convoys to the North were resumed.

Negotiation was begun as early as 6 January 1943; the Third Protocol came into effect on 1 July 1943; but it was not finally signed until 19 October 1943 owing to a number of minor adjustments.

Two points about the Third Protocol are worthy of special note. First, Canada for the first time appeared as a signatory. This was a recognition of the fact that Canada had a considerable surplus of munitions and food which she was willing to transfer to Russia; at the same time, it was a concession to Canada's new-found self-consciousness as a 'Middle Power'. Second, the principle of tripartite (or with Canada, quadripartite) pooling of resources was made much more explicit than in earlier Protocols. Under the first two Protocols, changes had been made fairly freely in practice, depending on availability of material and unexpected Russian needs. But the wording of the two Protocols promised the allocation of certain quantities of supplies to Russia, subject only, in the words of the Second Protocol, to 'unforeseen developments in the progress of the war'.[1] In the Third Protocol a more sweeping principle was asserted:

> The list of supplies in the schedules annexed hereto shall be subject to reallocation between the three supplying countries as they may decide between themselves in order to meet strategic, supply, or shipping exigencies. They shall, too, be liable to variation to meet unforeseen developments in the war situation. If shipping losses, production failures, or the necessities of other operations render their fulfilment prohibitive, it may be necessary to reduce them. On the other hand, if conditions permit, the Governments of the United States, the United Kingdom, and Canada will be glad to review the schedules from time to time for the purpose of increasing the quantities to be provided and delivered.[2]

This was no more than putting on paper what had been the fact before, when shipping shortages and the necessities of the North African operation had prevented the complete fulfilment of Allied promises to Russia.

Moreover, Russia was not quite on the same basis as the supplying Powers. Exchange of information with the Russians always remained a difficult matter; and the Third Protocol was drawn up as before without requiring detailed 'user justification' for the requests made by the Russians. Still, the principle that the Russian supply schedules should reflect over-all Allied strategy and supply had been formally asserted. Russia no longer appeared on the point of collapse. The Soviet Union was no longer, from the Western point of view, an expendable asset in the war against Hitler; nor could the consignment of supplies to the Russians any longer be regarded as a gamble undertaken to prolong a desperate resistance to the Nazis. Economic relations had to conform to the new political-military relations between the principal Allied Powers.

This was not pure gain for Russia. Soviet economy, willy-nilly, came

[1] *Soviet Supply Protocols*, p. 17. Cf. a similar proviso in the text of the First Protocol, ibid. p. 8.
[2] Ibid. p. 52.

to be part of a larger whole, dependent upon the United States for essential supplies and upon a day-to-day process of inter-governmental negotiation and planning for their delivery. Thus Russia became, during 1943, more nearly a partner sharing in the gains and losses of the Western Powers, and was compelled to adjust her economy not solely to her own but to Allied resources and policies. This was a great change from the 1930s and should be borne in mind when we turn attention to Russia's political attitudes towards the West as they developed during 1943 and 1944.

When Congress passed the Lend-Lease Act in March 1941, it was valid for only two years. Consequently, in March 1943, it became necessary to renew the Act. As a preliminary, committees of both the House and Senate held hearings to investigate the uses and abuses which the Administration had made of the powers conferred by the Lend-Lease Act. Congressional and public opinion in general supported renewal of Lend-Lease,[1] but some Congressmen wanted to know what benefits the United States would get in return. They feared that the President would be too generous. The doctrine that, if each nation contributed an equal proportion of its national income to the war, no balance of indebtedness should remain—a doctrine which Roosevelt had tentatively advanced in his *Fifth Report to Congress on the Operations of Lend-Lease* in June 1942—was not universally acknowledged. Many members of Congress, as well as private persons outside it, felt that when the time came to settle Lend-Lease accounts the United States should get military bases and air rights as a part of the benefit to be received in return for Lend-Lease goods.[2]

The enthusiastic endorsement of Lend-Lease by Congress in March 1943 convinced some members of the President's circle—and probably persuaded Roosevelt himself—that now was a good time to clarify the theory of Lend-Lease. Every economist realized that there could be no large-scale reimbursement for Lend-Lease. Accordingly, on 25 August 1943, the *Eleventh Report on Lend-Lease Operations* was submitted in the name of the President. The covering letter stated:

The United Nations are growing stronger because each of them is contributing to the common struggle in full measure—whether in men, in weapons, or in

[1] The House Committee on Foreign Affairs reported, for example, that 'the Lend-Lease Act has operated with brilliant effectiveness', and when it came to a vote, the line-up in the House of Representatives was 407 to 6 and in the Senate 82 to 0 in favour of renewal. For the texts of House and Senate Committee reports on Lend-Lease renewal, see *Documents on American Foreign Relations, 1942–1943*, pp. 123–30.

[2] Ibid. pp. 125, 130. Assistant Secretary of State Dean Acheson suggested in a part of his testimony that the United States might try to acquire bases in return for Lend-Lease (ibid. p. 121).

materials. Each is contributing in accordance with its ability and its resources. . . . The Congress in passing and extending the Lend-Lease Act made it plain that the United States wants no new war debts to jeopardize the coming peace. Victory and a secure peace are the only coin in which we can be repaid.[1]

This assertion stirred up some protest among the newspapers which had long been opposed to Roosevelt and his New Deal policies,[2] and some members of Congress took exception to the President's remarks.[3] On the other hand newspapers which supported Roosevelt's foreign policy welcomed the statement quite enthusiastically.[4]

At the time when the *Eleventh Report* was submitted to Congress Roosevelt was in Quebec, conferring with Churchill once again. Upon his return, at a press conference on 7 September 1943, he repudiated the last two sentences of the section quoted above, denying that he had approved them. In his remarks to the correspondents he implied that, while money repayments would not be expected, other forms of repayment would.[5] The theory of Lend-Lease remained as uncertain as it had been before.

Spokesmen for the American administration had emphasized in their testimony before the Congressional committees investigating Lend-Lease the advantages which the American Government received through Reverse Lend-Lease, or, as the British more accurately called it, Mutual Aid. The American Government were anxious to have statistics of the amount of this aid with which to impress public and Congressional opinion, and, when such data as could be gathered had been assembled, Roosevelt devoted his *Twelfth Report on Lend-Lease Operations* (11 November 1943) to presenting an account of British contributions to the American war effort.

From the nature of the British contribution to the support of the American armed forces, accountancy was bound to be difficult. Transfers which took place in such zones of combat as North Africa were never

[1] *New York Times*, 26 August 1943.

[2] e.g. *Chicago Tribune*, 2 September 1943: 'The American people shall permanently have placed on their back the burden of rehabilitating, supporting, and defending in their possessions the present lend-lease clients.'

[3] Senator Revercomb of West Virginia was quoted as saying: 'The other nations have an obligation to us that should be repaid value for value' (*Daily Express*, 28 August 1943).

[4] See e.g. *New York Times* and *Christian Science Monitor*, 27 August, *Chicago Daily News*, 30 August 1943.

[5] The President's words were: 'It is perfectly true that in the narrow technical sense we want no new war debts, but at the same time . . . other Nations . . . will repay us as far as they possibly can. Now that doesn't mean necessarily *dollars*, because there are all kinds of other repayments which can be made' (Rosenman: *The Public Papers and Addresses of Franklin D. Roosevelt*, 1943 volume, p. 375). To set the record straight, the *Report* was withdrawn and a new page printed and pasted in with the offending lines struck out.

recorded.[1] Until the build-up for Normandy began in the late autumn of 1943, the rate at which the United Kingdom gave aid to American forces was not high, since there were few American troops stationed in Britain at the time. The major development of Mutual Aid thus falls outside the period here under consideration. Australia and New Zealand, on the other hand, contributed food and other supplies at or near their full capacity during 1943.

The Combined Boards which had been set up in the course of 1942 did not undergo any fundamental alteration in 1943. Canada made a vigorous effort to gain separate representation for herself on them; and despite the reluctance of both Britain and the United States—who feared that the Boards would become hopelessly clumsy if all the United Nations secured places for themselves—Canada was accorded a seat on the Combined Food Board on 19 October 1943, and on the Combined Production and Resources Board on 10 November 1942.[2] There was talk of adding Russia to the Combined Boards, but it all came to nothing; and, except for the two Boards to which Canada was admitted, the system remained bi-national.

In fact, as the supply situation became easier, the work of the Combined Boards became somewhat less controversial. Much of what had been a matter of keen bargaining in 1942 settled down to a routine division of materials and production capacity in 1943; and it was as new

[1] British contributions to American war activities began on a significant scale during the summer of 1942, and records were kept by fiscal years ending 30 June. Consequently the official figures do not match with those for American Lend-Lease cited above, nor do they fit into the periodization adopted here. Allen ('Mutual Aid', p. 255) has compiled the following figures:

U.K. Reciprocal Aid (£ million)

	to June 30, 1943	*to June 30, 1944*
To United States .	229·7	420·9
To Russia . . .	187·7	93·3

The *Twelfth Report to Congress on Lend-Lease Operations* calculated the money value of supplies and services received from the British Empire up to 30 June 1943 as follows:

	$ million
From U.K.	871
From Australia	196
From New Zealand . . .	51
From India	56·9
Total	1,174·9

The official rate of exchange was used to convert from local to American currency in making these calculations. Owing to differing price levels, this basis of conversion generally undervalued the British contribution.

[2] C. C. Lingard and R. G. Trotter: *Canada in World Affairs, September 1941 to May 1944* (Toronto, Oxford University Press, 1950), iii. 233.

shortages showed up, mainly in the field of civilian supply, that the sphere of the Combined Boards expanded. Thus the Combined Production and Resources Board established a series of commodity committees to study and make recommendations about the supply of textiles, tyres, and coal; the Combined Food Board investigated various shortages which manifested themselves in the supply of such things as butter; and the Combined Raw Materials Board reported upon supplies of leather and recommended an equitable division of what was available between competing purchasers.[1] The expansion of the activities of the Combined Boards in this direction reflected both the fact that they were largely excluded from control over military production by the respective national authorities, and the fact that civilian shortages became apparent in the United States almost for the first time in the course of 1943. To avoid serious repercussions, the sort of planning and foresight which had earlier been developed to direct military production was needed for a growing range of civilian soft goods. As always, the Boards had only advisory power. Even when on paper their powers were mandatory, they were not used in practice.

As planning for post-war relief and the conduct of economic operations in liberated and conquered areas became realities, the Combined Boards were given a new part to play. When the United Nations Relief and Rehabilitation Administration was established on 9 November 1943, it was decided that its requests for supplies for liberated areas would be lodged in the first instance with the Combined Boards, which would make decisions as to the sources and amounts of supplies that could be made available.[2] Since, however, the major part of UNRRA's activities was reserved for 1945 and 1946, it seems best to postpone consideration of Allied co-operative planning and action in the sphere of relief work until later.[3]

The central phenomenon in the sphere of economic co-operation between the Allies in 1943 was the growing dominance of the United States of America. Not only Great Britain but Russia, too, came to depend to a significant degree upon American production. The resulting international division of labour unquestionably enhanced the combined military power of the alliance, and was justified thereby. At the same time, economic dependence or semi-dependence carried with it political and other consequences which could not be wholly agreeable to either Britain or Russia. But as long as the overriding political aim of all three nations was the same—to defeat Hitler—these latent difficulties hardly manifested them-

[1] *Industrial Mobilization for War*, i. 625–9. [2] Ibid. i. 627.
[3] See below, pp. 313–15.

selves openly; indeed, on the contrary, economic co-operation strengthened the political and military alliance.

(iii) Offensive in the Mediterranean

(*a*) Political Settlement in North Africa

When American and British troops began to land near Algiers, Oran, and Casablanca in the early hours of the morning of 8 November 1942, they rushed into a complicated military and political situation. The Allied troops were invading neutral land, nominally to prevent its occupation by the Germans. At best, the Allies hoped that the French would actively come to their support, and that Allied troops would be able to pass eastward without let through Tunisia into Libya, where the remainder of the Afrika Korps could be ground to pieces between the British Eighth Army striking westward from Egypt and the new armies advancing from French North Africa. At worst, the Allies feared that the French would resist bitterly, and lay down their arms only after military defeat. Such an event would put a heavy strain upon the expeditionary force not only during the fighting itself, but afterwards as well, for the administration of North Africa in the face of sullen French resentment and native unrest would not be an easy thing. German attack through Spain and Spanish Morocco was also seriously feared by the men who planned Torch; and at first most of the American troops were stationed near the border of Spanish Morocco to guard against this danger.

Among the French confusion reigned. Very few Frenchmen found it in their hearts to prefer the Nazis to the Allies; but it was the Allies who attacked, and Pétain's Government in Vichy, which was recognized by the army and administration of North Africa as the legitimate authority over French North Africa, lost little time in denouncing the Allied invasion and instructing local French officials to resist to the uttermost.

The Allies hoped that General Henri Giraud by his personal authority and prestige would be able to win over the leading military and civilian officials of North Africa to their side.[1] The plan was that he should arrive in Algiers shortly before the invasion, activate the conspirators who had already recognized his leadership, and, as the Allied troops came ashore, issue a proclamation welcoming them and instructing all French authorities to aid and assist them in the drive for Tunisia. Inasmuch as Giraud did not leave France until the night of 5–6 November and did not arrive at Gibraltar until the afternoon of 7 November, only the smoothest and most rapid action could have brought him to Algiers in time.[2]

[1] For an account of Allied negotiation with Giraud down to the eve of his interview with Eisenhower, see above, pp. 204–7.

[2] The embarkation had been scheduled for 4–5 November; but rough weather made it impossible until the following night (Giraud: *Un Seul But: la victoire*, p. 20). The original plan

The necessary speed could not be achieved for the simple reason that no firm agreement between Giraud and the Allies had been reached. Giraud arrived in Gibraltar still nursing his plan for a rising in France and North Africa which would be assisted by the Americans. He expected to take command of the rising and of the American troops which might be assigned to support it. He was aware that the Americans had some reservations about putting their troops under his command. He was also aware that the Americans did not agree with his plan for operations in southern France. But in Giraud's eyes these two points were central to the whole enterprise. It was up to him to convince the Americans; if they would not agree he felt that he could simply call the whole thing off.

When Giraud presented his demands to General Eisenhower (who had taken over Gibraltar as a command post for the invasion), he met with blank refusal.[1] Giraud, who already felt that the Americans had been less than frank with him in hiding the date of D-day until the last minute, felt that he was being used as a cat's-paw, and refused to have anything to do with the affair. The landings began that same night with Giraud far from the scene and in a state of high exasperation against the Allies. The exasperation was reciprocated by Eisenhower and Clark, who felt that their plans were being endangered by the stubborn foolishness of an old man who had no understanding of modern war. Thus the original Allied plan went all awry.

In North Africa itself, the scene was no less confused. In Algiers, the conspirators under the leadership of General Charles Mast[2] were able to take control of the city for a few hours, on 8 November. Before the Allied troops appeared in Algiers itself, however, the regular authorities under Admiral Darlan and General Alfonse Juin had re-established themselves, and arrested most of the conspirators, including, for a few hours, the American Consul-General, Robert Murphy. Nevertheless, Darlan and Juin did not really want to fight against the Allies, and resistance was light and disorganized. In the late afternoon of 8 November negotiation

had been to send Giraud direct to Algiers, but this plan was dropped because it seemed first necessary to establish an understanding between Giraud and Eisenhower (cf. Butcher: *My Three Years with Eisenhower*, p. 163).

[1] According to General Clark, Eisenhower's Deputy Commander, the two American generals were taken completely by surprise when Giraud made his demand for the supreme command (Clark: *Calculated Risk*, p. 96; but cf. Eisenhower: *Crusade in Europe*, pp. 99–101, and Butcher: *My Three Years with Eisenhower*, p. 163). If Eisenhower did not understand Giraud's point of view, it must be attributed to a strange failure of communication between Robert Murphy, who had conducted the negotiation with Giraud, and the Allied Supreme Commander. Julius C. Holmes, who acted as translator during part of the interview, described the American reaction to Giraud's demands as one of fright (cf. Kammerer: *Du débarquement africain*, p. 239). Indeed, Eisenhower's political advisers believed that Giraud's help was so necessary to the success of Torch that at one time they recommended that the French general be placed in nominal command of the Allied forces (Eisenhower: *Crusade in Europe*, p. 100).

[2] See above, p. 204.

for an armistice began, and at 6.45 p.m. Juin surrendered the city of Algiers to the American general commanding the landing force. At Oran and Casablanca, however, French resistance was stronger and more prolonged, and came to an end only after further negotiations had quite changed the political aspect of affairs.

Meanwhile at Gibraltar on the morning of 8 November Giraud showed himself willing to compromise with Eisenhower on the question of the supreme command. The Americans and British, for their part, were anxious to assuage Giraud's wounded feelings and get his co-operation. Agreement was reached, apparently on the basis that the Allied and French military commands would be equal and independent of one another. Co-operation would be established at the top by agreement between Giraud and Eisenhower; and the command of subordinate units would rest with whichever side had the larger number of troops on the spot. Eisenhower at the same time promised to recognize Giraud as the head of the civil administration and the commander-in-chief of all French forces in North Africa.[1]

On the strength of this agreement, Giraud flew to Algiers on the following day, 9 November. General Clark followed him a few hours later. Upon arrival in Algiers, each discovered that the military-political situation bore little relation to their expectations. The central fact was this: the military commanders in French North Africa were with few exceptions quite unwilling to recognize General Giraud's authority; and some of them regarded him as a traitor or at best as guilty of insubordination. A second fact, of almost equal import, was that Admiral François Darlan, Commander-in-Chief of all French Armed Forces for the Vichy Government, was in Algiers; and by virtue of his office exercised legal authority over the French army and navy in North Africa.[2]

When Giraud discovered his powerlessness over the commanders of French forces in North Africa he retired to the house of one of the members of the circle that had conspired to bring him to Africa. There he brooded in silence while his supporters reproached him for not having arrived in time to take the command away from Darlan.[3] Giraud's position was

[1] Kammerer: *Du débarquement africain*, p. 243; Langer: *Our Vichy Gamble*, p. 340. The text of this agreement has not been published. It was subject to rather diverse interpretation by the two generals in retrospect. Eisenhower (*Crusade in Europe*, p. 101) says that his promises to Giraud were contingent upon his winning support in North Africa. Giraud (*Un Seul But: la victoire*, p. 27) says that it was agreed that he would take command of the Allied forces as soon as French troops equalled in number the Allied troops engaged in the theatre of operations.

[2] Darlan had come to Algiers in order to visit his son who was suffering from an attack of infantile paralysis. Whether he may also have had some inkling of Allied plans for invasion is not certain. Darlan had come into touch with Murphy in October 1942, offering, under certain circumstances, to join the Allied side; but nothing definite was arranged (cf. Langer: *Our Vichy Gamble*, pp. 321–3; Butcher: *My Three Years with Eisenhower*, pp. 145–6; Kenneth Pendar: *Adventure in Diplomacy* (New York, Dodd Mead, 1945), pp. 92–93).

[3] Kammerer, op. cit. p. 382.

indeed a difficult one, for he shared the respect for Pétain's constituted authority which ruled the behaviour of most of the French officers in North Africa, and he could not easily forgive the Americans for the manner in which they had forced his hand and disregarded his plans.

Meanwhile General Clark was trying desperately to find someone who would be able to end the hostilities which were still in progress at Oran and Casablanca. His idea was to leave the French to settle their own affairs so far as possible.[1] First of all, he wanted an armistice to cover the whole of French North Africa. Secondly, he wanted some sort of agreement among the French which would establish a civil and military authority with whom the Allied Commander-in-Chief could deal. If possible, Clark wanted to put Giraud into the saddle, according to the agreement just made at Gibraltar; but he had little respect for Giraud's military or political judgement, and, in accordance with the principle of letting the French settle things among themselves, he was quite willing to deal with someone else if French officials so wished. Under the circumstances, someone else could only be Darlan.

Darlan's mind was apparently swept with contradictory impulses. On 8 November he approved an offer of help from German aeroplanes; later in the same day he authorized the surrender of Algiers.[2] Like the other French officials, he was anxious to act in the name of Pétain; at the same time he was anxious to come out on the winning side. By the morning of 10 November, when he first interviewed Clark, Darlan was still uncertain of what to do, but, after first refusing, he at length agreed to order cessation of hostilities in the whole of North Africa.[3]

At Oran, the local French commander surrendered on 10 November after notifying Darlan of his intention by telephone, but before Darlan's order for a general armistice in North Africa had been received.[4] The military situation of the French was such that, with or without Darlan, surrender would have been made; but his authority gave a suitable legal cover for the decision of the French commander on the spot. At Casablanca hostilities lasted for a few hours longer. It was not until the morning of 11 November that General Auguste Noguès, the senior French official in Morocco, acted upon Darlan's order of 10 November, and suspended hostilities. The official explanation of the delay was that the French officials in Morocco were doubtful as to the authenticity of the message from Darlan ordering cease fire. Only after a messenger delivered the order personally did Noguès agree to accept it.[5]

Whether this version truly represents Noguès's thoughts is very doubtful. On 10 November Pétain officially disavowed Darlan and appointed

[1] Clark: *Calculated Risk*, pp. 70–71.
[2] Kammerer: *Du débarquement africain*, pp. 268–9, 282.
[3] Clark, op. cit. pp. 106–16.
[4] Kammerer, op. cit. p. 424.
[5] Ibid. pp. 400, 455.

Noguès as Commander-in-Chief in North Africa in his stead.[1] Noguès may well have chosen to disregard the order from Darlan until he saw how military and political events turned out. A successful American naval bombardment of Casablanca on 10 November, the approach of tanks from the south, and news of the surrender of Oran must have served to convince Noguès that further resistance in Morocco would not long be possible. Thus it seems probable that his decision to surrender was not so much in obedience to Darlan as a recognition of the inevitable.[2] This point is of importance only because the main argument used to justify the agreement later concluded with Darlan was that he alone had been able to end hostilities. To know the truth one would have to penetrate into the inner recesses of Noguès's mind, and that is obviously impossible. The important point, however, was that Clark in Algiers came firmly to believe that it was Darlan's order that ended French resistance. It seems sure that Darlan's order made the surrender more palatable to the French commanders at Oran and Casablanca; but to assume that they would not have surrendered without the cover of Darlan's authority is, at the least, dubious.

At this stage of negotiation, no promises had been made to Darlan about the future government of North Africa; and Clark was still free to offer the supreme civil and military authority to Giraud. He did so about noon on 10 November, almost immediately after Darlan had signed the armistice order. But Giraud, much bruised in spirit by the events of the past three days, refused. He asserted that all he wanted was the supreme military command, without making it clear whether he meant Allied or only French supreme command.[3]

A meeting between Darlan and Giraud was arranged for the afternoon of the same day, 10 November. Just before the meeting began a telegram from Pétain arrived, disowning Darlan for his decision, taken that same morning, to order a cease fire in all French North Africa. Darlan's reaction to this news was to abdicate all authority and responsibility and refuse further co-operation with General Clark. Clark countered by ordering Darlan's house arrest.[4] A few hours afterwards Darlan's situation was restored when he received a second telegram from Vichy by a private cipher which disavowed Pétain's public actions and assured him of

[1] This news reached Algiers in the early afternoon of 10 November, about three hours after Darlan had issued his order for cease fire. Presumably the conflicting orders from Pétain and Darlan reached Noguès at nearly the same time.

[2] Cf. the telegram Noguès sent to Vichy justifying his surrender (Kammerer, op. cit. p. 420).

[3] Ibid. p. 404. The accounts of these negotiations written later by Giraud and Clark say nothing of this offer, but it is clear that neither of them could particularly wish it to be remembered: Giraud because of his refusal and subsequent change of mind; Clark because he was concerned to prove that the deal with Darlan was necessary and inevitable. Kammerer's authorities, which seem unimpeachable, were Giraud's supporters in Algiers, some of whom were present at the time Clark made his offer.

[4] Ibid. p. 415; Clark: *Calculated Risk*, p. 113.

Pétain's secret support and sympathy. Darlan thereupon resumed command in Pétain's name, and proceeded to co-operate willingly enough with General Clark.[1]

Something like a game of blind-man's-buff continued in Algiers for the next two days. Fortified by his secret telegram, Darlan proceeded to act as Pétain's representative *vis-à-vis* Clark and Murphy. Giraud, for his part, changed his mind about accepting civil authority, and on 11 November prepared a proclamation in which he declared that he would provisionally take over the government of North Africa in the name of Marshal Pétain.[2] But Giraud's bid for power came too late. Clark was disgusted with Giraud's vacillation, and he knew that French resistance in Morocco and Algeria had ended, apparently as a result of Darlan's orders. Moreover, there was the question of the French fleet. On 10 November Darlan had sent a telegram to the commander of the fleet in Toulon inviting him to sally forth and join the Allies; and on 11 November he sent a second and more urgent telegram to the same effect.[3] It seemed to Clark that a break with Darlan when the future action of the French fleet was still uncertain would simply invite failure. Accordingly when Clark and Murphy visited Giraud again on 11 November they informed him that Darlan was to remain in charge of French affairs in North Africa. Giraud accepted without protest, saying that all he wanted was a military command. Clark was pleased, for he thought the basis of an agreement between Darlan and Giraud had now been laid.

On that same day, 11 November, the Germans began to invade Vichy France, thus definitely breaking the terms of the armistice of 1940. This worked a deep change in the psychology of the French officers of North Africa, who could now tell themselves that Pétain was no longer a free agent, and that in disobeying his command to fight against the Allies they were in fact obeying his secret wish.

Such a line of thinking might justify resistance to the Germans in Tunisia and agreement with the Allies; but it did not pardon the insubordination of Giraud and his supporters. Consequently, when the first full-dress conference between Giraud, Darlan, Noguès and other leading

[1] Kammerer, op. cit. p. 409. This secret telegram was sent from Vichy not quite an hour after Pétain's official repudiation of Darlan in the afternoon of 10 November. Cf. Admiral Auphan: *Les Grimaces de l'histoire* (Paris, Plon, 1951), p. 282; Kammerer, op. cit. p. 408; and Mme Chamine: *La Querelle des généraux* (Paris, A. Michel, 1952), pp. 53, 119. When exactly Darlan received the repudiation of the repudiation cannot be said definitely; but it seems probable that by the evening of 10 November Clark had been informed of the reversal and knew that Darlan had resumed military and political authority in French North Africa (Kammerer, op. cit. p. 417). Clark's own account, however, dates Darlan's resumption of co-operation with him only from noon, 11 November (*Calculated Risk*, p. 115). Details of this episode will be found also in the *Survey* for 1939–46: *Hitler's Europe*.

[2] Kammerer, op. cit. p. 446.

[3] Ibid. p. 394; Clark: *Calculated Risk*, p. 116.

French officials took place on 12 November the atmosphere was strained. Noguès in particular refused to have any dealings with Giraud. Nevertheless, a tentative agreement was reached. Darlan was to have political power; the existing authorities were to remain in office in French North Africa; and Giraud was to be permitted to raise a free corps of men to fight against the Germans, while the regular French forces remained neutral.[1]

News of this tentative agreement persuaded Eisenhower that it was time for him to come to Algiers to ratify the work that his deputy, Clark, had accomplished. He arrived the next day, 13 November. That morning a second meeting of the French leaders took place at which they modified their agreement of the previous day. Giraud accepted three conditions put to him by Noguès: that de Gaulle should not be admitted to North Africa; that Giraud should accept the orders of Darlan; that Giraud should command in the name of Pétain. Having thus brought Giraud within the pale of Vichy legality, Noguès and Darlan were willing to accept Giraud as French Commander-in-Chief and to abandon the neutrality upon which Noguès had insisted the day before. The French in North Africa were henceforth openly at war with Germany. The first hostile contact between French and German troops occurred four days later on 17 November, and something like a front took form by 19 November in Tunisia.[2]

When this agreement had been reached, General Eisenhower was introduced to the meeting. He accepted the proposed arrangement, declaring that it harmonized with the instructions which had been given him to leave to the French the choice of their leaders. Details were to be settled by continued negotiation with Clark. No written record was made; and Eisenhower specifically stated that any agreement would be subject to ratification by the American and British Governments at a later time.[3] He departed for Gibraltar in haste, leaving Clark once more in charge.

In the following days, Clark was concerned principally with three things: Tunis, Dakar, and the French fleet stationed at Toulon. At Clark's prompting, Darlan sent several more messages to the French fleet urging that it should join the Allies; but the admiral in command refused to obey and, when the Germans marched into Toulon, the French ships were scuttled in the harbour on 27 November. Against this failure could

[1] Clark: *Calculated Risk*, p. 120; Kammerer: *Du débarquement africain*, pp. 474–5.

[2] Kammerer, op. cit. pp. 481–2. It was during this same day—13 November—that Noguès and Darlan received another secret telegram from Vichy approving the policy of co-operation with the Allies. This provided Darlan with documentary proof of his claim to be acting in Pétain's name—proof which apparently helped to persuade some important French officers to come over to the Allied side, most notably the Governor of French West Africa. Cf. Auphan: *Les Grimaces de l'histoire*, pp. 293–4. The secret communication between Darlan and Vichy ended only on 14 November (ibid. p. 296).

[3] Kammerer, op. cit. pp. 483–4; Eisenhower: *Crusade in Europe*, p. 108; Clark: *Calculated Risk*, p. 122.

be put the adhesion on 23 November of French West Africa to the Allied cause, along with the naval forces stationed at Dakar. In Tunis to the east the situation was even more complicated. The first German troops arrived within forty-eight hours of the Allied landing, coming by air. On 12 November the first shiploads of Germans arrived. The French authorities admitted them to the harbours of Tunis and Bizerta without offering any resistance. The French army in Tunisia, however, withdrew to the westward, and after a period of indecision and uncertainty began to resist the advancing Germans on 19 November.

While these military events unrolled themselves, negotiations to define the relationship between French and Allied authorities in North Africa were carried on, largely by Murphy who was acting in the name of Clark and Eisenhower. The outcome was the so-called Clark–Darlan Agreement, signed on 22 November 1942. This Agreement declared that the French and the Allies were united in three aims: to drive the Germans and Italians from North Africa, to liberate France, and to restore the integrity of the French Empire. It gave the Allied commanders the right to use airfields, ports, communications, and military installations freely, and authorized the American Commander-in-Chief to declare any part of French North Africa a military region within which he would assume direct control of civil administration. With this exception, however, the existing French officials in North Africa were to remain in office, subject to the authority of Darlan. An article provided that persons imprisoned or subjected to restrictions of any kind as a result of having expressed sympathy for the United Nations should be freed upon orders from the American Commander-in-Chief; but no blanket amnesty, still less a repeal of Vichy legislation, was provided for.[1]

The key figure in these complex negotiations was General Clark, a man whose only qualifications for the job were self-confidence and determination.[2] Three considerations seem to have governed Clark's decisions. First, he did not respect Giraud. As a general, Clark thought he was professionally incompetent, living in a world which had vanished with 1918 if not earlier; and as a politician, Giraud ranked even lower in Clark's estimation.[3] As a result Clark made no serious effort to back Giraud's claims to primacy in North Africa. Indeed he used the figure of Giraud mainly as a bogyman to bring Darlan to terms.

[1] Text of the Agreement may be found in Kammerer: *Du débarquement africain*, pp. 681–6.

[2] Murphy was always present at the important meetings and often acted as interpreter; but when it came to decisions as to American action he regularly shifted responsibility to the military (cf. Eisenhower: *Crusade in Europe*, p. 107). His legal position as Civil Affairs Officer, under the orders of the Supreme Allied Commander, may account for Murphy's relatively passive role.

[3] Cf. Clark: *Calculated Risk*, p. 230; Eisenhower: *Crusade in Europe*, p. 130.

Second, Clark was impressed by results and thought that, since Admiral Darlan's orders seemed to have brought French resistance to an end, he was obviously the man to deal with. Clark hoped that Darlan's value to the Allies was just beginning; that he would be able to bring over the French fleet at Toulon and persuade the admiral in command in Tunisia to resist the Germans. These hopes were in due course disappointed, but on 13 November, when the decisive agreement with Darlan was made, the chance of success seemed far from negligible. French West Africa, with Dakar, did come over to Darlan and the Allies without a shot having been fired.[1]

Third, Clark felt that a soldier's job was to keep out of politics and let French officials settle political questions for themselves according to their own pleasure. If they chose to act under Darlan and in the name of Marshal Pétain, it was a matter of indifference to Clark. It was here, surely, that Murphy failed Clark, and that the doctrine of the separability of military from political affairs acted adversely upon the wisdom of American policy. Neither Murphy nor Clark seemed to be sensitive to the political smell Darlan brought with him as a result of his acts as a member of the Vichy Government.[2] They both seemed to feel that their decisions should properly be guided by purely military considerations—the establishment of a secure base in North Africa and the hoped-for extension of Allied control to Dakar, Tunis, and the French fleet. Both Clark and Murphy were taken aback by the criticism and doubt which arose when news of their deal with Darlan reached Britain and America. They had acted according to their best lights for strictly military ends, and were accused, quite unjustly, of harbouring ulterior political motives.[3]

In looking back upon the events of the crowded week of 8 to 13 November 1942 one may doubt the wisdom of the decision which Clark took; but it would be unfair to lose sight of the haste, uncertainty, and apparent

[1] The argument used so regularly afterwards to justify the deal with Darlan—that thousands of American and British lives were saved as a result—has only a limited validity. As argued above, it is an open question whether Darlan's orders of 10 November shortened French resistance in North Africa. But Eisenhower and Clark had great hopes on 13 November that Darlan would be able to bring the French fleet and Tunisia into the Allied camp. Had Darlan succeeded in this, Allied lives spent in the Tunisian campaign would have been saved.

A second consideration of importance was the fear that the French might resume hostilities and attack the Allies in the rear (cf. Butcher: *My Three Years with Eisenhower*, p. 213). Considering the attitudes of the French soldiers and of the population, this fear cannot seem in retrospect very well founded; but in view of the extreme stress and the marked fluidity of political and military relations at the time, it was impossible to be sure. In this sense, the deal with Darlan may be said to have saved Allied lives from what was probably an imaginary danger.

For Eisenhower's argument justifying the agreement with Darlan in a telegram to Washington on 14 November 1942 see Langer: *Our Vichy Gamble*, pp. 357–60; Sherwood: *Roosevelt and Hopkins*, p. 652; Eng. edition, ii. 648–9.

[2] Details will be found in the *Survey* for 1939–46: *Hitler's Europe*.

[3] Cf. Clark: *Calculated Risk*, p. 125; Pendar: *Adventure in Diplomacy*, p. 19.

lack of alternatives which surrounded the whole negotiation. If Tunisia and the French fleet had accepted Darlan's lead and joined the Allies, the agreement would have justified the hopes Clark put in it at the time. On the other hand, if Clark had been able to find some figure to put in Darlan's place as head of the French administration in North Africa in whom he had real confidence, it is hard to believe that the deal with Darlan would have been made. Giraud was completely unsuited to the role which had been assigned to him in the preliminary planning. Political incapacity, occasional sulkiness, and sudden changes of mind ruined Giraud's chances. He was in an essentially awkward position. He was not willing to break outright with Pétain, with whose social and political views he generally sympathized; but the other men in North Africa who supported Pétainism were unwilling to recognize him. Those who were openly in revolt against Vichy legality in North Africa were few and weak; and most of them were also personally distasteful to Giraud. Realizing how greatly he had been deceived first by the Americans and secondly by his own supporters in Algiers, Giraud cut the ground from under himself in the first hours after his arrival in Algiers by his passive attitude.

De Gaulle was not a practicable alternative to Darlan in North Africa in November 1942, even if American high policy had not been so much opposed to his claims.[1] The French commanders in North Africa were bitter in their dislike of de Gaulle, and made it perfectly clear that they would never accept his leadership. No other prominent French politician or general was on the spot. Clark was, therefore, without any promising alternative to Darlan.

The fault lay partly with chance. Giraud's tardy arrival in Algiers and Darlan's presence could not have been foreseen. But a faulty estimate of the situation, in particular the incorrect assessment of Giraud's prestige and character, must also be blamed for the confusion that developed after the landings.[2] Good policy would surely have found a better leader than Giraud proved himself to be; and would have determined in advance upon a definite break with Vichy legality and a return to republicanism. Instead, the Americans first accepted Giraud without really knowing anything about him, and then, not without reason, turned their backs upon him and, in deference to a rather farcical doctrine of non-interference in domestic political affairs, allowed the Vichy régime to continue in North Africa under Allied auspices. Despite real and hoped-for military gains, the agreement with Darlan cannot be regarded as a triumph of Allied statesmanship.

[1] See above, pp. 208–9.

[2] This weakness of American policy, too, must be laid primarily at Murphy's door, for he was the key figure on the American side in the negotiation before the landing.

The establishment of Darlan's political authority in North Africa did not bring an end to political difficulties; but, as the immediate pressure of an uncertain military situation gradually relaxed, more normal channels for dealing with political issues were re-established. Clark and Eisenhower gladly concentrated their attention upon the progress of the campaign in Tunisia. Political dealings with the French became the responsibility of civilian officials, and ultimately of Roosevelt and Churchill.

Roosevelt felt at first that Eisenhower and Clark had blundered in making the agreement with Darlan,[1] but on 14 November a long telegram from Eisenhower convinced him that the immediate advantages which had been secured justified what had been done. Churchill's doubts were more pronounced, but he felt that he had no choice but to accept General Eisenhower's arrangements.[2] Stalin, on the other hand, expressed warm approval of the deal with Darlan in telegrams to Churchill and Roosevelt.[3]

A rigorous political censorship prevented detailed information about what had happened in North Africa from reaching the American and British publics during the first six weeks of the campaign. Distracted by the excitement of military events, the press expressed only rather mild dissent from the political arrangement that had been made.[4] But political censorship and military distraction could not last for long. Hoping to make the American position clear and to head off serious criticism, Roosevelt made a statement on 17 November 1942 in which he reaffirmed his basic view about French affairs. He said: 'The future French Government will be established, not by any individual in Metropolitan France or overseas but by the French people themselves after they have been set free by the victory of the United Nations.' In the light of this principle, Roosevelt declared that the agreement with Darlan was a 'temporary expedient, justified solely by the stress of battle'. His statement concluded with an account of the military advantages which Darlan's co-operation had brought.[5] In private, Roosevelt hoped that Darlan could soon be removed from power,[6] but until the fighting in Tunis had been ended it was judged unwise to upset the arrangement that had been made.

Distrust and dislike of Darlan were far more intense in Great Britain than in the United States, but Churchill was able to argue that the whole

[1] Leahy: *I Was There*, p. 163.

[2] Churchill, iv. 567; U.S. edition, iv. 631.

[3] Ibid. pp. 598 and 667, respectively.

[4] Cf. *Manchester Guardian*, 18 November, *Daily Telegraph*, 19 November, *New York Times*, 17 November 1942.

[5] Text of the statement may be found in *Documents on American Foreign Relations, 1942–1943*, pp. 550–1.

[6] Sherwood: *Roosevelt and Hopkins*, p. 654; Eng. edition, ii. 651.

affair was an American responsibility and that nothing should be done right away by the British Government to change the situation.[1]

These efforts by Roosevelt and Churchill helped to prevent public opinion from turning violently against the Darlan deal. But an after-taste of dislike and distrust remained among many persons who felt that no compromise with men tainted by fascist records should be tolerated. This feeling later came into the open in connexion with the jockeying for power between de Gaulle and Giraud in North Africa.[2]

In North Africa, Roosevelt's statement of 17 November helped to undermine Darlan's position. The French admiral had originally hoped and intended to preserve the Vichy régime unchanged, and he regarded himself as acting in place of Pétain until the aged Marshal could free himself from the Germans and resume his rightful place as head of the French state. Such a conception implied that Darlan's authority would cover all parts of the French Empire which remained loyal to Vichy. But neither the American nor the British Government were willing to allow such an extension of his authority.[3]

Even in North Africa it became more and more difficult for the Americans and the British to accept Darlan's policy. From the beginning the idea that the French could be left to settle their own political affairs proved unworkable in practice. As early as 20 November Roosevelt intervened by ordering Eisenhower to release all political prisoners in North Africa with or without Darlan's consent.[4] At the end of December 1942 Allied supervision of French policy was regularized by the appointment of Murphy and a British M.P., Harold Macmillan, as special political advisers to Eisenhower, with power to veto acts of French administrators.[5] But French officials were, almost to a man, quite unwilling to accept foreign dictation. Many of them began to play a double game, agreeing facilely to much of what was urged upon them, but failing to put Anglo-American recommendations into practice. They pleaded special knowledge of local conditions and dilated upon the dangers of Arab discontent if Vichy laws such as those disfranchising the Jews were withdrawn.[6] As a result, Allied pressure failed to make any very notice-

[1] The argument was most fully developed in a speech to the House of Commons in secret session on 10 December 1942. For text see Churchill: *Secret Session Speeches*, pp. 76–96.

[2] The position of the American State Department was peculiar. Secretary Hull seized the occasion of the landing in North Africa to gloat over critics of American policy toward Vichy. Partly as a result, the State Department was generally accorded responsibility for what had happened in North Africa, although in fact, as we have seen, the key negotiations were wholly in military hands.

[3] Leahy: *I Was There*, p. 164.

[4] Churchill, iv. 571; U.S. edition, iv. 636. Eisenhower had already acted on similar lines on his own authority (cf. Butcher: *My Three Years with Eisenhower*, p. 193).

[5] Leahy: *I Was There*, pp. 166–7; Langer: *Our Vichy Gamble*, p. 378.

[6] Eisenhower: *Crusade in Europe*, pp. 128–9; Pendar: *Adventure in Diplomacy*, pp. 124–5.

able changes in the existing policies of the French administration of North Africa.

Giraud on principle took no part in political manœuvres. His attention was directed wholly to military questions, and in practice he largely dissociated himself from the groups which had used his name in their secret planning before the Allied landing. The conspirators were naturally bitter. The attempted *coup d'état* in Algiers on the night of 7–8 November had failed; the Americans and Giraud himself had turned their backs. Darlan removed from office most of the conspirators who had been in official position, including General Mast. They were all subjected to a rigorous social ostracism by loyal Pétainists. Some of them promptly turned their thoughts to de Gaulle, hoping that he might be able and willing to support them. An emissary from de Gaulle's headquarters arrived in Algiers on 19 November and came into contact with some of the malcontents. An understanding was quickly reached.

De Gaulle had first reacted to the news of the Anglo-American landing in North Africa by making a speech on the radio welcoming the Allies. The agreement with Darlan, however, roused his ire, especially when it appeared that he and his followers were to be excluded from North Africa. To get to the root of the matter, de Gaulle decided that it would be useful for him to visit the United States and try to come to an understanding with Roosevelt. He was on the point of departure for Washington when news of Darlan's assassination arrived in England, and his trip was promptly called off.

On the day before Christmas 1942 a young man who had taken part in the 7–8 November *coup d'état* in Algiers shot and killed Darlan. The political background of this deed was complex, and attempts were made to hush up the full story so that only incomplete and distorted versions of what occurred were made known at the time. It seems certain, in the light of later investigation, that the assassination was plotted by some of the same men who had planned the rising in support of the Allied landing. The two most directly implicated were Henri d'Astier and a rather mysterious figure, the Abbé Cordier. D'Astier and Cordier were both de Gaullists and royalists—a combination at first sight strange, but logical enough at the time. Their hope was that the pretender to the French throne, the Comte de Paris, would be able to unite all French factions under his banner if once Darlan could be got out of the way. Nothing came of the scheme, for the Comte de Paris backed out when he discovered that the American authorities would not approve of the plan.[1]

At the time none of this was known. The official communiqué suggested that Axis agents were responsible for the murder of Darlan; and various French officials hid essential evidence from one another and from

[1] Kammerer: *Du débarquement africain*, pp. 610–15; Pendar: *Adventure in Diplomacy*, pp. 127–8.

the public.[1] As a result an air of mystery surrounded the assassination; and the rather indecent haste with which the French authorities executed the murderer on 26 December after a very sketchy trial did nothing to remove the suspicions and rumours that quickly spread abroad in Algiers.

Darlan's death put the political future of French North Africa into the melting pot. The high French officials who constituted what was known as the Imperial Council wanted to pass Darlan's authority on to Noguès; but Eisenhower, acting under instructions from Roosevelt, declared that Giraud was the only acceptable candidate. Giraud himself did not want the position, but after a little persuasion he agreed to take over Darlan's office.[2]

Giraud's assumption of political and military leadership opened anew the question of the future relationship between the French authorities in North Africa and de Gaulle. More important, the whole question of the validity of Vichy legality and of Pétain's 'National Revolution' had to be decided. Nevertheless, the removal of Darlan from the North African scene at first promised to smooth the way to reconciliation between the two French factions.[3]

Even before 8 November de Gaulle had expressed his willingness to come to an agreement with Giraud, and, when news of Darlan's assassination reached him, de Gaulle offered to meet Giraud in order to establish a single French authority. But Giraud remembered his promise to Noguès that he would never permit de Gaulle to come to North Africa, and so did not take up the offer. Indeed, Giraud still considered himself the vice-gerent for Pétain and would not agree to the radical purge of Vichy officials which de Gaulle demanded.

Roosevelt and Churchill had been anxious almost from the first to bring about a reconciliation between the two Frenchmen, and they made an effort in this direction at the time of the Casablanca Conference in January 1943.[4] De Gaulle at first refused an invitation to come to Casablanca, and though he changed his mind as the result of strong British pressure, the interview which was arranged between him and Giraud did not lead to an agreement.

During the following four months Giraud's position in North Africa was gradually undermined. Allied pressure restricted his freedom of action in both the political and military spheres. As the campaign in Tunisia settled down to a long winter of mud and immobility, the original idea

[1] In particular, a police officer suppressed the confession made by the murderer (cf. Kammerer: op. cit. pp. 621–4).

[2] Clark: *Calculated Risk*, p. 129; Langer: *Our Vichy Gamble*, p. 380.

[3] A fuller account of French affairs will be found in *Survey* for 1939–46: *Hitler's Europe*.

[4] See below, p. 261.

that French North Africa would quickly cease to be a theatre of operations lost its reality. In response to the new situation, French troops were put directly under Allied command about the middle of January, in violation of the agreement which Eisenhower had made with Giraud at Gibraltar.[1]

The Gaullist movement, on the other hand, was expanding and growing stronger in North Africa during these months, as de Gaulle's prestige increased in the French world as a whole. De Gaulle's relations with the French resistance in metropolitan France greatly strengthened his position *vis-à-vis* Giraud. He also had greater political sagacity than his rival, and a better propaganda machine, which took full advantage of the opportunities presented by Giraud's attitude to accuse him of protecting fascists and enemies of democracy. The support given to de Gaulle by the British Foreign Office helped to counterbalance American support for Giraud.[2] De Gaulle was also strengthened by the support of the Russians and of the French Communists, although it was partly this fact that confirmed American opposition to him.[3]

The American Government watched the growth of de Gaulle's influence in North Africa without enthusiasm, and the topmost officials did what they could to bolster up Giraud's sagging prestige. But in the United States, following the relaxation of political censorship in North Africa (coming at a time when military stagnation in Tunisia disappointed popular hopes), a widespread outburst of criticism arose against the political policies which were being followed in North Africa.[4] Even within the State Department there were some who felt that agreement with de Gaulle would be wise; and various branches of the American Government worked at cross purposes on the spot in North Africa, some supporting and others opposing de Gaulle.[5] As a result, American opposition was ineffective in preventing the growth of Gaullism; and after the victory in Tunisia (on 13 May 1943) the need for military security could no longer be invoked as a reason for keeping de Gaulle at arm's length.[6]

Despite their liking for Giraud, the American Government had no liking for his policy of trying to maintain Vichy legality, and American officials put steady pressure upon Giraud to persuade him to modify his

[1] See above, pp. 246–7.

[2] Friction between British and American officials on the spot in North Africa was frequently rather acute. The Americans felt that the British were trying to undercut their influence. What the British felt has not been made public (cf. Leahy: *I Was There*, p. 170; Pendar: *Adventure in Diplomacy*, p. 177).

[3] Leahy, op. cit. p. 175; Pendar, op. cit. pp. 159–75.

[4] The *New York Herald Tribune* was the prime mover in this outburst. Cf. article by Geoffrey Parsons, 13 January, and editorials of 14, 20, 22, and 29 January 1943. Other papers echoed the attack; cf. *Chicago Daily News*, article by Helen Kirkpatrick, 27 January 1943; *New York Times*, editorial, 15 January 1943.

[5] Pendar, op. cit. p. 170.

[6] Eisenhower, acting no doubt on instructions from Washington, had used this pretext to prevent de Gaulle from coming to North Africa at the end of March 1943, though Giraud had by then agreed to meet de Gaulle in order to discuss an agreement (*New York Times*, 6 April 1943).

political principles. But Giraud was stubborn and gave way only slowly. It was not until after the French National Committee in London had proposed a new basis for reconciliation at the end of February 1943[1] that Giraud belatedly accepted liberal and republican principles in a radio speech of 14 March 1943.[2]

These steps removed all ostensible ideological barriers to fusion and marked the final decision against Pétain's National Revolution; but progress towards an agreement between de Gaulle and Giraud was hampered by personal friction and suspicions of bad faith on both sides. It was not until 30 May 1943 that de Gaulle arrived in Algiers to negotiate directly with his rival. After several meetings, they agreed on 3 June 1943 to establish a French Committee of National Liberation under their joint presidency. Nominally Giraud and de Gaulle each was to have equal representation on the Committee, but from the beginning some of Giraud's appointees tended to support de Gaulle on disputed issues.[3] Giraud gladly confined his attention to military matters, and allowed himself to be shunted off to the United States for a long official visit while de Gaulle consolidated his position in North Africa.[4] Thus almost from its inception the French Committee of National Liberation in Algiers accepted de Gaulle's leadership.

In one sense, the long-standing problem of French disunity had been solved. The allegiance of nearly all resistance organizations in France and control over all but a few Caribbean French possessions was now concentrated in the hands of the Committee. In fact, however, factionalism persisted almost as virulently as before within the Committee itself. De Gaulle was not content to share even nominal leadership with Giraud. He speedily set out to depose Giraud, and within a year he had succeeded. Giraud resigned from the Committee on 9 November 1943; and was induced to resign as Commander-in-Chief of the French army on 9 April 1944.

The establishment of the French Committee of National Liberation in Algiers raised the question of its international status among the Allies. De Gaulle was most anxious to win recognition as a Government in Exile. Neither Roosevelt nor Churchill was willing to accord such status, although the British Government were, as always, more friendly. Despite efforts to reach a common phraseology, it proved necessary to issue different

[1] *Documents on American Foreign Relations, 1942–1943*, pp. 571–4.

[2] Ibid. pp. 560–5.

[3] Pendar: *Adventure in Diplomacy*, pp. 173–4.

[4] Giraud's purpose in visiting the United States was to hasten the arrival of American equipment for the French army. He got promises, but while he was enjoying a round of official entertainment in America his practical power was systematically undermined in North Africa (cf. Leahy: *I Was There*, pp. 202–4).

texts defining the relationship of each Government to the French Committee.[1]

The American statement, issued on 26 August 1943, baldly recognized 'the French Committee of National Liberation as administering those French overseas territories which acknowledge its authority'. The British Government stated: 'They take note with sympathy of the desire of the committee to be regarded as a body qualified to ensure the administration and defense of all French interests. It is the intention of His Majesty's Government to give effect to this request as far as possible. . . .' The Soviet Government had no reservations. On 26 August, a Soviet statement declared: 'The Government of the Union of Soviet Socialist Republics . . . has decided to recognize the French Committee of National Liberation as the representatives of the State interests of the French Republic, and leader of all French patriots fighting against Hitlerite tyranny. . . .'[2]

The victory in Tunis, followed by the establishment of the Committee and its recognition by the three principal Allied Governments, brought a settlement to the tangled political situation in French North Africa. Despite or perhaps because of American opposition and the frequently lukewarm support accorded to him by the British, de Gaulle had won his way to leadership over nearly all Frenchmen outside occupied France itself. De Gaulle's further relations with Roosevelt and Churchill turned not upon North Africa but upon policies to be pursued in metropolitan France after the liberation. North Africa became a backwater, no longer of much importance for Allied co-operation or lack thereof.

(b) Strategic Decisions

(1) *The Casablanca Conference, 14–25 January 1943*

Despite the failure of French forces in Tunisia to resist the invasion of German air and ground forces, the Allies had high hopes of being able to occupy the whole of Tunisia before German strength could be built up to significant dimensions. As late as 1 December 1942 Eisenhower's Chief of Staff estimated that Tunisia would be conquered before the end of the year and that all North Africa would be clear of Axis forces by the end of January 1943.[3] It was not until 24 December that these hopes were definitely abandoned. On that date Eisenhower reluctantly decided to call off further efforts to advance on Bizerta and Tunis until more supplies, troops, and air cover could be assembled. This delay gave the Germans

[1] Hull: *Memoirs*, ii. 1232–3, 1241–2.

[2] Texts of these three documents may be found in *Documents on American Foreign Relations, 1943–1944*, pp. 668–70.

[3] Leahy: *I Was There*, p. 166; cf. Sherwood: *Roosevelt and Hopkins*, p. 658; Eng. edition, ii. 654.

a chance to send reinforcements to Tunisia on a fairly large scale, so that the campaign began to take on quite new proportions.

In November and early December 1942, however, this set-back was not foreseen. Assuming a quick and easy victory in North Africa, Anglo-American strategists were confronted with the need to decide what they would undertake next. The problem which faced them was not an easy one. Except in North Africa there were no large concentrations of American troops ready for an attack on Germany. The build-up of American forces in Great Britain, which had been agreed to in April 1942, had halted abruptly when the decision to undertake Torch was made in July. General Marshall opposed committing large numbers of troops to prolonged idleness in the British Isles, and he had come to believe that the British were not willing to undertake the cross-Channel assault on northern France. Even the U.S. Eighth Airforce, destined to lead the American bombing attack on Germany, had grown slowly. It had not dropped a single bomb on Germany at the year's end, though there had been some relatively small-scale American raids on France and the Low Countries.[1]

The slowing down in the deployment of American troops disappointed and somewhat alarmed the British. Churchill was afraid that, if the Americans were not firmly and irrevocably committed to operations against Germany, diversion to the Pacific might once again become a serious possibility. He knew that General Marshall had been overruled when the decision to undertake Torch had been made; knew also that Marshall was the strongest American advocate of the basic Germany-first strategy. Having seen his plan for an invasion of France in 1942 discarded, there seemed the danger that Marshall might come to the conclusion that nothing could be done against the Germans in 1943 either, and as a substitute might send American divisions to the Pacific.

To forestall such a development, Churchill began to insist strongly upon the possibility of invading France in 1943. On 9 November 1942, the very day after the first landings had been made in North Africa, he began to urge upon the British Chiefs of Staff the necessity for engaging the Germans on the mainland of Europe in 1943.[2] The British Chiefs of Staff were reluctant to agree to any such undertaking. They advocated the exploitation of Torch in the Mediterranean through attacks upon Sicily, Sardinia, and Italy, combined with an intensified bombing offensive against the heart of Germany. Such cautious strategy, Churchill

[1] Churchill, iv. 608–9; U.S. edition, iv. 679. In 1942 the R.A.F. as a whole and many Americans, too, thought that daylight raids such as the Americans wished to make would prove impossibly costly. The controversy helped to slow up the American air effort from Britain, and the matter was not settled until the Casablanca Conference, when it was decided to try large-scale daylight raids and see what happened. Cf. Craven and Cate, edd.: *The Army Air Forces in World War II*, i. 591–611.

[2] Churchill, iv. 582–3; U.S. edition, iv. 649–50.

foresaw, would fail to appeal to the Americans, and would rouse the most strenuous distrust and disappointment among the Russians.[1]

British fears seemed to be confirmed when on 24 November 1942 information was received that preparation for the reception of no more than 427,000 American troops should be made in Great Britain in 1943. Such a figure implied that little more than air force troops would be sent across the Atlantic during the coming year. Churchill immediately sent off a cable to Roosevelt to ask whether 'Round-up'—the code name for invasion of the Continent—had been abandoned. Roosevelt replied on 26 November, saying that the Americans had no intention of abandoning Round-up, but that North Africa must take precedence. His telegram ended on what must have seemed to the Prime Minister an ominous note: 'We are far more heavily engaged in the Southwest Pacific than I anticipated a few months ago. Nevertheless we shall continue with "Bolero" [the build-up of American forces in Great Britain] as rapidly as our shipping and other resources permit.'[2] This sounded as though the Pacific might take precedence over the European theatre of operations.[3]

The attitude of the American high command in November 1942 was one of indecision and bafflement. Admiral King, as well as most of the U.S. navy, remained mainly interested in the Japanese war, where the battle for Guadalcanal had not yet passed its critical phase. U.S. naval judgement of strategy against Germany was largely guided by the question: 'Will this permit a bigger effort in the Pacific in 1943?' Hence the U.S. navy was benevolently disposed to any proposal that postponed an all-out effort in Europe until 1944. Leaders of the American air force wanted a chance to demonstrate the possibilities of strategic bombing, and, in their more expansive moments, hoped to bring Germany and Japan down in ruins by bombing alone.[4] Thus General Arnold, too, was open to arguments for postponement of the major cross-Channel offensive.

Marshall, for his part, had come to believe that a landing in France in 1943 would be impossible. The British reluctance to undertake the plan, the diversion of men and material to North Africa, and the prospect that the Russians would be driven back to the Urals and lose a large part of their military effectiveness (thus allowing Hitler to concentrate greater strength against any possible landing in France) all combined to make him feel that Round-up was out of the question until 1944 at the soonest. In

[1] Ibid. pp. 582–3 and 650–1, respectively.

[2] Ibid. pp. 586 and 653, respectively.

[3] Churchill's fears may well have been reinforced by the arrival of Madame Chiang Kai-shek in the United States on 27 November. She came nominally for medical treatment, but lost no time in urging concentration of all American strength against Japan and in criticizing the British. She was a diplomatic rival of whom Churchill had some reason to be afraid, and her arguments for emphasis on the Japanese enemy had of course the support of the U.S. navy (cf. Sherwood: *Roosevelt and Hopkins*, pp. 660–1; Eng. edition, ii. 657–8; Morison: *History of U.S. Naval Operations*, vi. 3–4).

[4] Leahy: *I Was There*, p. 187.

the meanwhile he was determined not to embark on any new offensives in the Mediterranean. He thought that any such enterprises, by consuming men and material, might make it necessary to postpone the attack across the Channel still farther into the future. His strategy implied nearly a year's hiatus in the Anglo-American assault upon Germany; on the other hand it would permit the diversion of a larger proportion of American strength to the Pacific in 1943, as the U.S. navy so much desired.[1]

Marshall was also much concerned about the Chinese. The difficulties American troops were meeting when they came into battle against the Japanese in the jungles of Guadalcanal and New Guinea served to confirm the American General Staff's original view that the only economical way to defeat the Japanese was to mobilize the enormous man-power of China against them. But before a great Chinese army could be equipped and trained it was necessary to re-establish land communication through Burma; and this seemed to Marshall a more urgent task than anything that offered in the Mediterranean. Consequently, he wished to divert a large proportion of the landing craft which had been used for the landing in North Africa to Burma for use there against the Japanese as soon as the monsoon lifted in October 1943.[2]

Roosevelt's personal views do not seem to have been definite, but he was, as in the midsummer of the year, rather more inclined to agree to operations in the Mediterranean than was Marshall, and he apparently never wavered in his conviction that attack upon Germany should come first.[3]

About the beginning of December two new elements encouraged Marshall to believe that his great plan for invasion of France might be salvaged for 1943. One was the Russian victory at Stalingrad, which upset the earlier conviction so widely held that the Red Army would be seriously weakened by the end of 1942. The other change was in Churchill's attitude towards invasion of the Continent.

With all his native optimism, Churchill was quick to react to the new strategic outlook. He sensed Marshall's bruised and baffled mood, and was very anxious to swing him and the whole American high command round to support an ambitious offensive against Germany. He was also quick to believe in Russian strength, and ceased to fear a German break-

[1] Morison, loc. cit.; Churchill, iv. 583; U.S. edition, iv. 651; Sherwood: *Roosevelt and Hopkins*, p. 659; Eng. edition, ii. 656.

[2] Wilmot: *Struggle for Europe*, pp. 119–20. One must remember that at this stage of the war no one had solved the problem of making an amphibious attack on enemy-held beaches beyond the reach of friendly land-based fighter air cover. This assured the Japanese in the central Pacific of virtual immunity from attack; and the long chain of islands stretching northward from Australia to Japan seemed a much harder route after experiences in Guadalcanal and New Guinea than did the alternative via Burma and China.

[3] Sherwood: *Roosevelt and Hopkins*, pp. 658–9; Eng. edition, ii. 654–5; Churchill, iv. 606; U.S. edition, iv. 676.

through over the Caucasus some weeks before his Chiefs of Staff were willing to agree that the troops stationed in Persia against such a disaster were no longer needed there.

Churchill vigorously set out to develop a strategy that would take full advantage of the successes won in North Africa and at Stalingrad and which would bring the Americans fully into the war against Germany. His plan, as set forth in two memoranda dated 25 November and 3 December 1942, was threefold. In the central Mediterranean, he advocated an attack upon Sicily and Italy, with, perhaps, Sardinia thrown in as well. This would employ the forces already assembled in North Africa and might well drive Italy from the war entirely. In the eastern Mediterranean, he hoped to be able to persuade the Turks to come into the war. The British troops in Persia could then be used to strengthen the Turkish army and to establish a front in the Balkans, while the opening of the Straits to Allied shipping would allow delivery of supplies to Russia by a new and shorter route. Finally, he hoped that the Americans would agree to send large numbers of troops to the British Isles, ready to descend upon the Continent when the strength of the German army had been dispersed by the peripheral attacks through the Mediterranean, on the eastern front, and through a stepped-up bombing offensive. Large-scale risings by the conquered populations of Europe supported by British and American armies might, he believed, bring the whole structure of Nazi Europe tumbling down by the end of 1943.[1]

Marshall welcomed Churchill's emphasis upon the possibility of invasion of Europe in 1943 and began to hope that with the new situation on the Russian front and with the new, or apparently new, attitude of the British the major obstacles to his cherished plan had been removed.[2] He did not, however, change his opinion about operations in the Mediterranean, which were, of course, an essential part of Churchill's proposals; nor did his conception of an invasion in overwhelming force conform to Churchill's idea of invasion in the form of multiple, relatively small-scale attacks, which would depend for their success upon the prior weakening of German power and on the support of the subjugated peoples of Europe.[3]

[1] Churchill (iv. 586–90; U.S. edition, iv. 654–8) reproduces parts of his two memoranda. Cf. ibid. pp. 624–5; U.S. edition, pp. 697–8 for his Turkish plan. The British Chiefs of Staff were, as usual, less sanguine than Churchill, and believed that the best possibility for 1943 was a vigorous prosecution of advantages won or about to be won in the Mediterranean. Invasion of France, they calculated, would not be feasible before 1944 (cf. Wilmot: *Struggle for Europe*, pp. 118–19).

[2] Sherwood: *Roosevelt and Hopkins*, p. 674; Eng. edition, ii. 671; Leahy: *I Was There*, p. 174.

[3] In fact, the Prime Minister had not changed his conception of the best basic strategy at all. He still clung to the programme he had first outlined for the Americans at the Arcadia Conference in 1941. Churchill's own account (iv. 583 seqq.; U.S. edition, iv. 651 seqq.) is rather misleading, for he emphasizes his hope of a landing in 1943 but soft-pedals the prerequisite condition—that the Germans should first be drastically weakened. This Churchill and the British Chiefs of Staff still felt to be necessary if a cross-Channel landing were not to be a far too risky operation. Thus

The problems of future strategy which had thus been made apparent required decision at the top level. Roosevelt was most anxious to bring the Russians, and preferably Stalin himself, into conference with American and British strategists in order to settle outstanding differences of opinion. He hoped that face-to-face contact with Stalin would lead to the establishment of better feeling between the Russian leader and himself. He was already thinking of the problems of a post-war settlement, and thought that while the war was still at a critical state, with the Russians obviously needing the help of the United States, it would be wise to broach his hopes and plans to Stalin and get the Russian leader to commit himself at least along general lines.[1]

Churchill was far less anxious to bring the Russians into the conference. In the event, he was spared any embarrassment the Russians might have caused him, for Stalin refused to come to any conference outside the borders of the Soviet Union, declaring that he could not lose direct contact with the front, even for a short time. He made his own position clear by inquiring pointedly for information about Anglo-American plans for the invasion of France.[2]

As soon as Stalin's refusal had been received, Churchill and Roosevelt quickly settled details of time and place. Casablanca was chosen as the scene of their conference, and the time was set for mid-January 1943. The Chiefs of Staff, with subordinate advisers, met a few days beforehand in order to sound out their differences. Churchill appeared on the scene on 12 January and Roosevelt arrived two days later, on 14 January. A series of conferences and informal exchanges of view followed, lasting until 25 January when the President departed by air for the United States.

Full details of the Conference had not been published in 1952, but the principal decisions which eventuated are known, and the general line of compromise which was effected is clear enough. Generally speaking, the Americans agreed to the first step in the British plan for a Mediterranean offensive and the British agreed to American plans for the Pacific and Far East. The basic strategy of Germany first was reaffirmed, and top priority was assigned to the battle of the Atlantic against U-boats, a battle which at the time of the Conference was far from won. Second priority was assigned to delivery of supplies to Russia. In Europe, a triple offensive against Germany was agreed upon: one by air and two by sea. Sicily was to be invaded as soon as possible after the Tunisian campaign came to an end, with the aim of opening the Mediterranean sea to Allied shipping. In Great Britain, American air force strength was to be built up to join with the R.A.F. in the heaviest possible bombing assault upon Germany.

whatever change in British views there was was a change in emphasis and mood, not in essentials. This became clear at Casablanca.

[1] Churchill, iv. 625; U.S. edition, iv. 699.

[2] Ibid. pp. 597 and 666 respectively.

At the same time ground forces were to be assembled in Britain with the aim of landing in August or September 1943 on the Cotentin peninsula. This was not to be the all-out invasion Marshall had hoped for; rather it was a revived Sledgehammer, designed to prepare the way for a larger effort in 1944, unless, of course, Germany collapsed from within before the end of 1943, in which case all available forces would be sent to the Continent.[1]

Preparation for an invasion of the Continent in 1943 partook of the nature of a pious hope rather than of a firm and definite plan. It was certainly as such that the British viewed the commitment, and their attitude was not hidden from the Americans.[2] The fact that things were not going very well in Tunisia made ambitious plans for invasion of Europe tentative at best and no effort was made to agree upon a commander. Soon after the conference, however, a group of staff officers under Lieut.-General Sir Frederick Morgan was set up in London to plan the proposed operation in detail.

The victorious advance of the British Eighth Army was bringing the fronts directed by Generals Eisenhower and Alexander closer and closer together. A new definition of their future relationship was therefore necessary. Despite the fact that the British had a clear preponderance in numbers, Churchill willingly agreed at Casablanca that Eisenhower should remain in supreme command; but Alexander was appointed his Deputy, and took over the operational control of all ground forces. Command of the sea and air forces operating in the Mediterranean and North Africa were also assigned to Britons.[3] The decision to retain Eisenhower in supreme command was made partly to keep up American interest in the Mediterranean, and partly to avoid offending the French, who were unwilling to come directly under British command.

As far as the war against Japan was concerned, the British accepted American proposals all along the line. It was agreed that a series of parallel offensives should be started against the periphery of Japan's dominion. The attacks already under way in the Solomons and along the coast of New Guinea were to be carried forward towards Rabaul and Timor respectively; in addition, an offensive across the central Pacific against Truk and Guam, and another in the North Pacific against the two Aleutian Islands which had been occupied by the Japanese, were to be undertaken. Finally, a combined operation, involving Chinese, British, and American forces, was to be mounted in Burma with the aim of re-opening land communication with China.[4]

[1] Churchill, iv. 612; U.S. edition, iv. 683.

[2] Ibid. pp. 620 and 692 respectively; Sherwood: *Roosevelt and Hopkins*, p. 689; Eng. edition, ii. 686.

[3] Churchill, iv. 606–7; U.S. edition, iv. 677. The eastern Mediterranean remained a separate theatre of war under a British general and the British Chiefs of Staff.

[4] Morison: *History of U.S. Naval Operations*, vi. 6–7. Morison's source is presumably a document

Not only did the British agree to this multifold attack upon Japan, but they also confirmed the principle that strategic decisions for the Pacific should be made solely by the American Joint Chiefs of Staff. The jurisdiction of the Combined Chiefs of Staff was limited to the allocation of additional fighting strength to the Japanese war.[1]

The strategic decisions taken at Casablanca did not bring general satisfaction. The Russians felt that the postponement of a landing in France until August or September 1943 was a device to put the main strain of the war on the Red Army and allow Anglo-American troops to reap the major rewards of victory. When the fighting in Tunisia became bogged down in mud Stalin was quick to suspect half-heartedness on the part of the Anglo-Americans.[2] The Americans felt that British agreement with their plans for France and for the Pacific was an agreement in words only, and that little of real value had been achieved by the long debates over future strategy.[3] The British, however, felt that they had been able to open American eyes to some of the realities of the European theatre of operations and believed that the strategic tasks which had been scheduled for 1943 matched Allied resources fairly well.[4]

There were three major political questions which came up at Casablanca. One was the French problem. As we have seen, Roosevelt and Churchill attempted to bring Giraud and de Gaulle to an agreement concerning French affairs in North Africa, but failed to secure any tangible result.[5]

A second and most important political question was, however, given

preserved in the files of the U.S. navy, and he may report as definite agreements which were, in the eyes of the British at least, only tentative. Cf. Churchill, iv. 612; U.S. edition, iv. 683, where he reproduces a telegram sent to the Cabinet part way through the Conference in which the attack on Truk is described as subject to re-examination later in the year.

[1] King and Marshall had come to the Conference armed with a document which asserted that only 15 per cent. of the total Allied war effort was being directed against the Japanese. They wished to double this figure; but in the end no determination of the over-all balance of forces between the European and the Japanese wars was attempted at the Conference (Morison: *History of U.S. Naval Operations*, vi. 4–5).

[2] Churchill, iv. 667; U.S. edition, iv. 745.

[3] Leahy: *I Was There*, p. 174. The Americans came away from Casablanca with the feeling that superior British staff organization had been an important factor in blunting their own arguments and sharpening those of the British Chiefs of Staff. A great effort was made, consequently, to improve American staff organization in the following months, and at future conferences the Americans arrived with an elaborately organized series of 'briefs' for each proposal they wished to argue for (cf. Cline: *Washington Command Post: The Operations Division*, pp. 218–21). This is an interesting example of how the Americans even in detail found it prudent or necessary to imitate the British organization for war.

[4] Churchill does not say anything of his reactions to the outcome of the Conference; but cf. Hopkins's report of a conversation with the Prime Minister, according to which Churchill was satisfied with what had been decided (Sherwood: *Roosevelt and Hopkins*, p. 688; Eng. edition, ii. 685).

[5] See above, p. 258.

a decisive turn, namely, the formulation of the terms of surrender that would be acceptable to the Anglo-Americans. Roosevelt came to Casablanca with the idea of launching a ringing slogan—'Unconditional Surrender'—as the only terms the Allies would offer to their enemies. As early as 7 January 1942, before he left Washington for the Conference, the President had informed his military advisers of his intention;[1] and when he met Churchill at Casablanca the President proposed the slogan to the Prime Minister fairly early in the proceedings. On 20 January, Churchill asked his Cabinet whether it would approve of Unconditional Surrender for Germany and Japan; and on the following day he received a reply approving the principle, but arguing that Italy, too, should be included in the list.[2] Churchill himself was anxious to entice Italy into suing for peace (seeing therein the best of all possible chances to enlarge the Mediterranean offensive) and hoped to exclude Italy from any demand for Unconditional Surrender. Consequently, he let the matter drop;[3] but Roosevelt was thinking along different lines, and at the press interview arranged at the end of the Conference, he said:

> . . . Peace can come to the world only by the total elimination of German and Japanese war power. . . . The elimination of German, Japanese, and Italian war power means the unconditional surrender by Germany, Italy, and Japan. That means a reasonable assurance of future world peace. It does not mean the destruction of the population of Germany, Italy, or Japan, but it does mean the destruction of the philosophies in those countries which are based on conquest and the subjugation of other people.[4]

This announcement came as a rather unwelcome surprise to Churchill, who thought the President had dropped the idea, at least for the present. However, he made no public dissent and later associated himself with the formula, while at the same time explaining, as Roosevelt had done in the original announcement, that no unjust punishment would be meted out to the vanquished populations.[5]

There are two questions in connexion with this step which can be answered only by speculation. First, why did Roosevelt use the phrase and stick to it afterwards to the time of his death? Second, what was the effect upon the German, Italian, and Japanese will to resist?

[1] Cf. Cline: *Washington Command Post: The Operations Division*, p. 217. This point is of importance only because Roosevelt later professed that the phrase had just popped into his head at the time of the Casablanca press conference at which he first uttered the phrase publicly. For remarks on Roosevelt's penchant for pretending to frivolity in high affairs, see Sherwood: *Roosevelt and Hopkins*, p. 696; Eng. edition, ii. 693.

[2] Churchill, iv. 613–15; U.S. edition, iv. 684–6.

[3] One may perhaps surmise that Churchill was dubious of the wisdom of the slogan from the beginning. He tried at Yalta, though rather half-heartedly, to persuade Roosevelt to modify the formula of Unconditional Surrender (cf. Cline, op. cit. p. 341).

[4] Rosenman: *The Public Papers and Addresses of Franklin D. Roosevelt*, 1943 vol., p. 39.

[5] Churchill, iv. 614–16; U.S. edition, iv. 686–8.

Roosevelt's motives were probably threefold. He was anxious to avoid making detailed and generous promises to the Germans analogous to the promises made by his predecessor, Wilson, in the Fourteen Points. He wished to avoid all possibility that some future German leader might claim, as Hitler had claimed, that Germany had never been really defeated, but that false promises had disarmed the trusting German people. A second and perhaps more important consideration was this: the deal with Darlan had led some journalists in the United States to anticipate (and castigate) similar deals with men like Göring, Badoglio, or Konoye. Roosevelt was anxious to disperse fears that the Allies would deal with men tainted by Nazism, Fascism, or Japanese imperialism; and the demand for Unconditional Surrender seemed one way of doing so. Finally, Roosevelt may have been concerned to prove dramatically to the Russians that the Western Allies were in the war to the end and would never consider the possibility of a separate peace, leaving the Germans free to fight Communism.[1]

But though Unconditional Surrender made a good war cry for the Allied camp and conveniently postponed awkward problems of post-war policy and power relations, it had serious disadvantages too. For one thing, the phrase was meaningless. When in due course Italy, Germany, and Japan did surrender, it was not unconditionally: on the contrary, the instruments of surrender and connected documents prescribed a whole series of conditions, ranging from immediate steps to be taken by each of the armed forces concerned to long-term political and administrative definitions of Allied occupation prerogatives. Surrender involving millions of soldiers and the whole apparatus of modern government cannot in the nature of things be unconditional in any strict sense. Administrative arrangements between victor and vanquished have to be made, whether the victor wishes it or not. This objection is perhaps a quibble, and unimportant in itself. It was important, however, in as much as the phrase 'Unconditional Surrender' tended to disguise from the public and even, to some degree, from officials, not least of whom was Roosevelt himself, the need to foresee and plan for arrangements to be made in conquered countries after fighting ended.[2]

More important was the question of the effect of the slogan on the enemy's will to resist. Certainly the phrase 'Unconditional Surrender' was much used by Axis propagandists in their efforts to whip up public

[1] Cf. the speculations of Sherwood in *Roosevelt and Hopkins*, pp. 696–7; Eng. edition, ii. 693–4. Reassurance to the occupied countries of Europe against any deal with Germany at their expense may have been another factor, but probably not an important one. Cf. Daniel Lerner: *Sykewar, Psychological Warfare against Germany, D-Day to V-E Day* (New York, George W. Stewart, 1949), p. 18.

[2] As we shall see, Roosevelt refused, at a critical time, to bother with attempts to work out surrender terms for Germany. See below, p. 491.

resolution. It is quite impossible to estimate with any assurance what success they may have owed to the uninviting overtones of the Allied demand.[1] It is easy to believe that a *camarilla* of German generals might have displaced Hitler and sued for peace at almost any time after the Normandy landing, had they not been disheartened (among other things) by the stony bleakness of Unconditional Surrender. But, in a real sense, part of Roosevelt's design in formulating the phrase was to prevent such a situation from arising. After the experience with Darlan (and later Badoglio) the President did not want to have dealings with any group such as the German officer corps. He was not willing to accept the only alternative wielders of power within Hitler's Germany, preferring to put off the reconstitution of German society and the selection of a new ruling *élite* to a more distant future. Thus it was not so much Unconditional Surrender as such but the attitude behind it that can be blamed for any prolongation of the war in Europe which may have occurred.[2]

Japan's case provides fairly definite evidence that the demand for Unconditional Surrender delayed the end of the war by a few days.[3] When it came to the moment of decision, Truman refrained from following the policy Roosevelt had pursued towards Germany. Instead, he came to terms with the Emperor of Japan and made use of the imperial authority to facilitate the occupation and administration of Japan.

Differences between German and Japanese social structure and traditions make direct comparison of the two unwise, and it is perhaps equally foolish to try to pass any sort of judgement on the wisdom or unwisdom of Roosevelt's slogan. Various important persons, including Stalin, Churchill, and Eisenhower, tried at various times to persuade the President to modify the demand originally made at Casablanca, but he always refused to do so.[4] Unconditional Surrender, from the time the words were uttered by Roosevelt at Casablanca, became the predominant, immediate

[1] Public opinion surveys in Germany after defeat suggest that by that time, at any rate, many Germans did not react strongly against the demand for Unconditional Surrender. Cf. Wallace Carroll: *Persuade or Perish* (Boston, Houghton Mifflin, 1948), p. 336. But such surveys after the surrender prove nothing about the contemporary effect of the slogan on German morale.

[2] One may argue that total war, in which the mass attitudes of home populations play an important part, can only be fought on the basis of simple slogans such as Unconditional Surrender. To try to set definite and limited war aims introduces complications, subtleties, difficulties, which can hardly win strong emotional support at home. A war fought by an alliance is even more ticklish, since sharp definition of post-war intentions may split the alliance before the war is won.

[3] On 21 July 1945 (over three weeks before Japan surrendered) the Japanese Government cabled their Ambassador in Moscow: 'We cannot consent to unconditional surrender under any circumstances. . . . So long as the enemy demands unconditional surrender we will fight as one man . . . in accordance with the Emperor's command' (James E. Byrnes: *Speaking Frankly* (New York, Harper, 1947; London, Heinemann, 1947), p. 211). In point of fact it was only when the Allies had retreated from the original rigour of Unconditional Surrender that Japan did yield.

[4] Sherwood: *Roosevelt and Hopkins*, pp. 783, 903; Eng. edition, ii. 778, 892; Carroll: *Persuade or Perish*, pp. 306–34; Cline: *Washington Command Post: The Operations Division*, p. 341; *The Roosevelt Letters*, ed. Elliott Roosevelt (London, Harrap, 1952), iii. 492, 498–9.

war aim of the Grand Alliance, and tended to eclipse and supplant such earlier definitions of Allied intentions as the Atlantic Charter.

A third political issue which came up at the Casablanca Conference was Turkey's future role in the war. Churchill's strategic plan required the Turks to join with the Allies, but the Americans were reluctant to do anything positive to bring this about. Marshall and others feared the dissipation of men and resources which the opening of a Balkan front would entail; and some Americans also suspected that Churchill was trying to use American men and material to build up a British sphere of influence in the Mediterranean as a make-weight against the Russians.[1] Nevertheless, the real gain which the help of the Turkish army and the opening of the Straits would bring to the Allied cause could hardly be gainsaid; and it was agreed at Casablanca that the British should have a free hand in Turkey to do whatever seemed possible to bring the Turks into the war.[2]

Churchill at once decided that he should himself try to persuade the Turks to play his game. He was able to wring a reluctant agreement from the British Cabinet, and as soon as the Casablanca Conference had broken up, he set off eastward to Egypt and Adana, where an interview with the President of Turkey, Ismet Inönü, was arranged. The conference took place on 30–31 January 1943. Churchill offered Inönü military supplies, the prospect of immediate support by specialist troops, and ultimate support from the British armies in Persia and Syria when Turkey went to war. Inönü and his fellow Turks were glad to accept military supplies, but despite Churchill's efforts to convince them that a post-war international organization would secure Turkey against any possible Russian threat, and despite his efforts to prove to them that the safest place for Turkey to be in the post-war world was among the victors with her own and British armies planted firmly in the Balkans, the Turks refused to commit themselves to war. Churchill had to go away with his great scheme unrealized; but he did have the satisfaction of establishing a Joint Anglo-Turkish Military Commission which could be depended upon to strengthen the Turkish army with supplies and to increase British influence in the councils of the Turkish Government.[3] The agreement was less than he had hoped,

[1] Sherwood: *Roosevelt and Hopkins*, p. 748; Eng. edition, ii. 744; cf. Leahy: *I Was There*, p. 190.

[2] Sherwood: *Roosevelt and Hopkins*, p. 691; Eng. edition, ii. 688; Churchill, iv. 625–6; U.S. edition, iv. 699. A part of the bargain was that the Americans would have a similar monopoly in dealings with China. The American State Department was not informed of this arrangement, a fact which led to a trifling but symptomatic dispute between the diplomatic representatives of Britain and America in Turkey at a later time (cf. Hull: *Memoirs*, ii. 1376).

[3] Churchill, iv. 630–40; U.S. edition, iv. 705–14.

but Churchill refused to abandon the project of enticing Turkey into belligerency.

Only a part of the military decisions taken at the Casablanca Conference ever came into effect. In the Mediterranean, the attack upon Sicily was made on schedule; in the Pacific, the Japanese proved more tenacious than had been hoped; and in Burma the attempt at reconquest failed dismally. The differences between British and American strategic views had not been really resolved at Casablanca, and plans for the balance of 1943 to which both parties firmly adhered had not been drawn up. The outcome was a compromise, a compromise which was much more extensive on paper than in the minds and wills of the men who had conferred. Nevertheless, there was agreement on the immediate future: Sicily was to be invaded and the offensives already under way in the Solomons and New Guinea were to continue. Until the shipping shortage had been relieved and the outcome in Tunisia had become clear, any longer-range plans would, in the nature of things, have been subject to such wide uncertainties that nothing could have been decided definitely. Thus it seems fair to say that as much had been done as could have been sensibly done at the time.

(2) *Concert or Quarrel with the U.S.S.R.? November 1942–July 1943*

As before, the warmth of Russian relations with the Western Allies turned mainly on military events and strategic decisions during the first six months of 1943. What Stalin wanted was a second front in Europe; what he feared was that the British and Americans would stand aside from all-out participation in the war, waiting while Germany and Russia exhausted one another on the field of battle. Stalin's conduct towards Roosevelt and Churchill varied as the military acts and policies of the Western nations seemed to conform to the pattern of his wishes or of his fears. All the major changes in Soviet cordiality toward the Anglo-Americans can be quite directly related to changes in the military outlook.

Stalin greeted the news of the invasion of North Africa with a statement in which he described it as:

> . . . an outstanding fact of major importance demonstrating the growing might of the armed forces of the Allies and opening the prospect of the disintegration of the Italo-German coalition in the very near future. . . .
>
> It is yet too soon to say to what an extent this campaign has been effective in relieving immediate pressure on the Soviet Union. But it may be confidently said that the effect will not be a small one. . . .

But Stalin did not miss the opportunity of returning to the theme of a second front. Among the advantages which he foresaw from the North

African landing was '. . . that the campaign creates the prerequisites for establishment of a second front in Europe nearer to Germany's vital centers. . . .'[1]

The decisions of the Casablanca Conference were announced to Stalin in a telegram of 26 January 1943 sent jointly by Roosevelt and Churchill. The wording was distinctly vague. Stalin was simply informed that the immediate intention was to clear North Africa, then to launch 'large-scale amphibious operations in the Mediterranean at the earliest possible moment'. As far as the second front was concerned, the telegram merely said that British and American forces would 'prepare themselves to re-enter the continent of Europe as soon as practicable'.[2]

Not unnaturally, Stalin asked for more detail. In reply Churchill informed him early in February of the decision to attack Sicily, and described the plan to invade Europe in these words:

> We are also pushing preparations to the limit of our resources for a cross-Channel operation in August, in which both British and United States units would participate. Here again shipping and assault landing-craft will be limiting factors. If the operation is delayed by weather or other reasons it will be prepared with stronger forces for September. The timing of this attack must of course be dependent upon the condition of German defensive possibilities across the Channel at that time.[3]

Stalin observed in reply on 16 February 1943:

> It seems to me that the present situation demands the greatest possible speeding up of the action contemplated—i.e. of the opening of the second front in the West at a considerably earlier date than indicated. In order not to give the enemy any respite it is extremely important to deliver the blow from the West in the spring or in the early summer. . . .[4]

This exchange coincided with the defeat suffered by American troops in the Kasserine pass in Tunisia—a defeat which led some British journalists and others to make severe criticisms of the greenness of American troops, and suggested to Stalin that the Western Allies were holding back and were not really trying to wind up the Tunisian campaign in a hurry. Moreover, on 21 February the Germans launched a counter-attack on the southern Russian front which led to the recapture of Kharkov on 12 March. Stalin blamed for this reverse the arrival of German reinforcements from France, Belgium, and Holland. He felt that it could not

[1] Reply to a letter from Henry C. Cassidy, 13 November 1942, reproduced in Stalin: *Great Patriotic War*, pp. 164–5.

[2] Churchill (iv. 664–6; U.S. edition, iv. 742–3) reproduces the complete telegram.

[3] Ibid. p. 666; U.S. edition, p. 744; cf. Sherwood: *Roosevelt and Hopkins*, p. 701; Eng. edition, ii. 698.

[4] Churchill, iv. 667; U.S. edition, iv. 745; cf. Roosevelt's reply in Sherwood: *Roosevelt and Hopkins*, p. 705; Eng. edition, ii. 702.

have happened if a more active Allied offensive had pinned down German troops in the west.[1]

The Order of the Day which he published on the occasion of the twenty-fifth anniversary of the founding of the Red Army, 23 February 1943, reflected his displeasure and distrust. The Order did not mention the Western Allies directly, but did contain the significant sentence: 'In view of the absence of a second front in Europe, the Red Army alone bears the whole burden of the war.' In a later passage, Stalin referred to the task of the Red Army as the pursuit of the Germans 'to the western frontiers of our country'.[2] This phrase, combined with the conspicuous lack of cordiality to the West in the Order as a whole, led some in Britain and America to fear that the Russians might make peace with Hitler as soon as the German army had been driven from Russian soil.[3]

In the following weeks, however, relations became more friendly. The German counter-offensive ended in mid-March and a period of quiescence came to the Russian front. The respite lasted until 5 July. At the same time, the activities of Western statesmen and of the Allied armies in Tunisia reassured Stalin. Churchill promised him on 11 March that, if the Germans weakened sufficiently, the Western Allies would strike across the Channel before August 1943.[4] Moreover, the British Eighth Army offensive which broke the Mareth Line in southern Tunisia started on 20 March, and the less spectacular but equally important progress of Allied armies in northern Tunisia showed that the Western Powers were not planning to remain inactive in North Africa, while watching the Russians and Germans bleed each other white.

The mellower mood of March was reflected by the way in which the Russians reacted to the criticism of their failure to publicize Lend-Lease aid, which was made by the American Ambassador, Admiral Standley. Standley told press correspondents on 8 March 1943 that it was unfair 'to mislead Americans into giving millions from their pockets, thinking that they are aiding the Russian people, without the Russian people knowing about it'.[5] This reproach promptly produced results. On 11 March Ambassador Litvinov made a speech in Washington in which he praised the help Lend-Lease had provided to Russia. His speech was given a full spread in the Russian press, as was also a report by Stettinius, Lend-Lease Administrator, listing the amounts of goods which had been delivered to Russia and other countries.[6]

When on 30 March 1943 Churchill informed Stalin that convoys to northern Russia would have to be suspended until the autumn, Stalin's

[1] Churchill, iv. 667; U.S. edition, iv. 745.
[2] Stalin: *Great Patriotic War*, pp. 76, 80.
[3] Leahy: *I Was There*, p. 177.
[4] Churchill, iv. 671; U.S. edition, iv. 749.
[5] *Documents on American Foreign Relations, 1942–1943*, p. 523.
[6] *New York Times*, 15 March 1943.

reply was moderate in tone; and the news of the Allied advance in Tunisia, of heavy bombing raids on Germany, and assurances about increased deliveries through Persia, produced a cordial note once again in Stalin's communications with the British Prime Minister.[1]

The restored cordiality was reflected in Stalin's Order of the Day issued on May Day 1943. He referred to the Allied advance in Tunisia and to the bombing offensive against Germany as 'foreshadowing the formation of a second front in Europe', and declared that blows from east and west had for the first time merged into one joint Allied effort against Hitler. In a later passage of the Order, Stalin followed the example set by Roosevelt and Churchill and demanded unconditional surrender of Hitlerite Germany as the only basis for European peace.[2]

The outbreak of a new, public quarrel between the Poles and the Russians at the end of April 1943 did not at the time seriously affect the newly cordial relations between the Allied Great Powers. This was at least partly due to the fact that the German radio and propaganda services played a critical role in precipitating the Russo-Polish dispute. When the Germans announced that they had discovered a mass grave at Katyn where several thousand Polish officers had been slaughtered by the Russians, the Poles in London could not resist the temptation to ask the International Red Cross to investigate. The Poles had long missed large numbers of officers who had been taken prisoner by the Russians in 1939 and who had not reappeared when the Polish prisoners were released to form a Polish army on Russian soil. Hence the Polish authorities had good reason for wishing to discover what had happened to the missing men; but in British and American eyes it seemed that the Poles were falling victim to German propaganda, and in doing so were inviting a serious disturbance of Allied relations. As a result, when the Russian Government broke off diplomatic relations with the Poles on 26 April 1943, the American and British Governments not only refused to intervene on behalf of the Poles, but felt a real displeasure against them for breaking Allied ranks so flagrantly.[3]

The restraint of the Western Allies on the Polish question may have encouraged Stalin to believe that conciliatory gestures on his part might win him important concessions in Eastern Europe—concessions which had been denied at the time when the Anglo-Soviet alliance was under negotiation in 1941 and 1942. In any event, the month of May 1943 brought forth two new friendly Russian moves.

[1] Churchill, iv. 674–8; U.S. edition, iv. 753–7. [2] Stalin: *Great Patriotic War*, pp. 84, 86.

[3] At the time there was a strong tendency in America and Britain to discount the Katyn affair as the work of German propaganda, but, in the light of post-war records and reticences on the part of the Russians, there seems much less doubt that the Russians were in fact responsible for the slaughter. A fuller account of the Katyn affair will be found in the *Survey* for 1939–46: *The Realignment of Europe*.

On 22 May the Comintern was dissolved. Lest anyone should miss the point, six days later Stalin issued a statement explaining that this act, among other advantages, facilitated 'the work of patriots in all countries for uniting all freedom-loving peoples into a single international camp'.[1] Official circles in the West were cautious in assuming that the formal abolition of the Comintern would effect any real change in Communist activity round the world,[2] but the move was generally interpreted as intended to eliminate a chronic irritant to good relations between Russia and other nations.

At the time when the Comintern's dissolution was announced, Joseph E. Davies was in Moscow as a personal representative of President Roosevelt.[3] He had been sent to urge upon Stalin the desirability of a personal meeting with Roosevelt. The President had the idea that the establishment of warm personal relations might be easier if he could see Stalin without Churchill being also present.[4] Roosevelt thought that Churchill could then be brought into the picture at a later meeting of the Big Three. When Davies broached the question of a personal meeting, Stalin was at first suspicious; but in the end he agreed to meet the President on 15 July 1943, or within two weeks of that date if unforeseen military events compelled postponement.[5] This was a great relief to Roosevelt, who had been trying to arrange a meeting with Stalin since the spring of 1942. Churchill was apparently kept in the dark until later,[6] but it was not difficult to imagine what his reaction to such a proposal would have been.

The friendliness of Russian relations with the West was suddenly blighted at the beginning of June 1943 when Stalin received word of the decisions which had been reached at the Trident Conference in Washington[7] postponing the invasion of France until 1944. This news led him to accuse the Western Powers of bad faith, and an acrimonious exchange of cables between Stalin and Churchill ensued. Stalin withdrew his Ambassadors from London and Washington, and the meeting between Roosevelt and Stalin was postponed.[8] The establishment of a Free Germany Committee

[1] Reply to a letter from Harold King, correspondent of Reuter's News Agency, 28 May 1943, reproduced in Stalin: *Great Patriotic War*, p. 167.

[2] Hull: *Memoirs*, ii. 1252; Ciechanowski: *Defeat in Victory*, pp. 180–1.

[3] Davies had been the U.S. Ambassador to Moscow from 1936 to 1938 and in 1942 published an account of his tour of duty, *Mission to Moscow* (London, Gollancz, 1942), which was an impressive apology for the great purges and for Soviet policy in general.

[4] Roosevelt suggested a meeting-place in Alaska or in Siberia near Behring Straits in the letter he sent with Davies (cf. Elliott Roosevelt, ed.: *The Roosevelt Letters*, iii. 464–5).

[5] Sherwood: *Roosevelt and Hopkins*, pp. 733–4; Eng. edition, ii. 729; Hull: *Memoirs*, ii. 1249–50.

[6] Roosevelt sent Averell Harriman to Churchill on 30 June 1943 to explain his project for a tête-à-tête with Stalin (Sherwood: *Roosevelt and Hopkins*, pp. 737–8; Eng. edition, ii. 733–4).

[7] See below, p. 286.

[8] Sherwood: *Roosevelt and Hopkins*, p. 734; Eng. edition, ii. 730. There are some grounds for

in Russia on 13 July 1943 did nothing to improve relations, for it looked as though the Russians might be preparing a puppet régime for a defeated Germany. The opening of the long-awaited German summer offensive on 5 July added to Russian ill will. Once again the Red Army faced the Germans unassisted and without the prospect of prompt succour from the West.

(3) *The Trident and Algiers Conferences, 12–31 May 1943*

The decision to invade Sicily had been made at Casablanca at a time when the outcome of the Tunisian campaign was still unforeseeable. The task of planning an attack upon Sicily while simultaneously fighting in Tunisia was a difficult one, and serious differences of opinion arose between the various commanders and services concerned. At one time Eisenhower recommended postponement or abandonment of the enterprise, but Churchill convinced Roosevelt that no other operation could engage German and Italian troops and assist Russia in the coming summer, and so Eisenhower's doubts were not allowed to prevail.[1]

The difficulties in planning the attack on Sicily arose in part from the fact that the basic difference between British and American views of future strategy had not been fully and frankly settled at Casablanca. Marshall and Eisenhower still felt that operations in the Mediterranean should be kept to a small scale and that major effort should be concentrated on preparing a great invasion of northern France as soon as possible. Churchill and the British Chiefs of Staff, on the contrary, felt that the campaign in Sicily should be a preliminary to an attack on Italy, with a converging assault on the Balkan peninsula through Turkey and across the Adriatic as a further goal. The Mediterranean campaign, they felt, should take priority over preparation for a cross-Channel invasion.

A similar unresolved difference existed in the Asiatic theatre. At Casablanca it had been agreed to begin driving the Japanese from Burma in 1943. The first part of this operation was to be a limited offensive down the coast of the Bay of Bengal towards the port of Akyab; but when British and Indian troops began to advance in January 1943 they ran into difficulties, and by May the Japanese had succeeded in driving them back to approximately the original battle line. This failure was matched by the cancellation of a Chinese offensive in northern Burma, which had originally been scheduled to coincide with the later stages of the battle for Akyab.

The failure to get the Burma campaign off to a successful start in the

believing that the Russians entered into new peace negotiations with Germany during the summer of 1943. See below, p. 324.

[1] Sherwood: *Roosevelt and Hopkins*, p. 701; Eng. edition, ii. 698. For the difficulties in planning the invasion see Eisenhower: *Crusade in Europe*, pp. 163–4; Admiral of the Fleet Viscount Cunningham of Hyndhope: *A Sailor's Odyssey* (London, Hutchinson, 1951), pp. 535–9.

spring of 1943 exacerbated the conflicts which already resounded throughout that theatre. The British under General Wavell, the Americans under General Stilwell, and the Chinese under Chiang Kai-shek all distrusted and disliked one another. Moreover, the American air force commander in China, General Claire Chennault, was at daggers drawn with Stilwell. Chennault believed that, if the limited supplies which could be delivered to China by air were devoted to building up a strong bombing force, the war against Japan could be won without the need of costly and difficult land campaigns in the Burmese jungles. Stilwell on the contrary believed that as soon as a bombing offensive, based on China, began to hurt Japan, Japanese ground troops would overrun the airbases. Only after Chinese ground forces had been trained and equipped to fight Japanese troops on equal terms did he believe that a big air offensive could be successfully launched. For that, the reconquest of northern Burma and reopening of land communications with China seemed to Stilwell as essential as before.[1]

As the campaign in Tunisia moved towards its close, Churchill became concerned over the lack of firm agreement between himself and the Americans. His first move was to try to arrange a conference of the Combined Chiefs of Staff in Algiers when they could consult Eisenhower and the other Mediterranean commanders face to face. But the Americans refused to agree[2] and so Churchill decided that he must once again go to Washington. The Conference was given the code name Trident, and lasted from 12 to 25 May 1943.

Churchill's strategic plans were, as usual, clearly worked out in collaboration with the British Chiefs of Staff before the meetings began. Negatively, the British wanted to persuade the Americans to call off the Burma offensive and to abandon the hope of mounting an attack in strength across the Channel in 1943. These were Marshall's most cherished projects, and Churchill realized that too blunt a refusal on his part would create a very bad impression. On the other hand, events had already done much to remove the possibility of either operation being prepared in time. The battle in Tunisia had taken longer than was originally expected, and there was neither time nor shipping available to bring a great American force to the British Isles for an invasion of the Continent in 1943 before

[1] Leahy: *I Was There*, pp. 188–9; Sherwood: *Roosevelt and Hopkins*, p. 730; Eng. edition, ii. 726; *The Stilwell Papers*, pp. 203–4.

[2] Sherwood: *Roosevelt and Hopkins*, p. 727; Eng. edition, ii. 723. In proposing Algiers, Churchill no doubt calculated that the local commanders in the Mediterranean would be more willing to press for an extension of the campaign in their theatre than would the men in Washington. The Americans probably refused to go to Algiers for the same reason. From the point of view of at least some of the American Chiefs of Staff, Eisenhower seemed at this time to be taking a somewhat British view (Leahy: *I Was There*, p. 162).

bad weather set in. Similarly, in Burma preliminary failures had made the project of clearing the Japanese from that country impossible without far larger assignments of supplies and troops.

Churchill's positive plan was to pursue the offensive in the Mediterranean by invading Italy and by taking active steps to bring Turkey into the war. His argument was a good one; there was nothing else that could be done in 1943 with the large concentration of forces which the Allies had on hand in North Africa and the Middle East; and to halt operations after the conquest of Sicily would leave the Russians to bear the whole brunt of the war against Germany through the late summer and autumn.

In Asia, Churchill had worked out a quite new strategy. Instead of trying to drive the Japanese from Burma by fighting on land, he proposed that amphibious attacks be made on Sumatra and the Malay peninsula. The advantage of this plan, according to the Prime Minister, was that it avoided meeting the Japanese in their own best element—the jungle; and would deprive Japan of valuable resources. But before such a campaign could be launched, naval reinforcement of the British fleet in the Indian Ocean would be necessary; and that could come only from the Mediterranean after the Italian fleet had been destroyed or compelled to surrender.[1]

The collision between the British proposals and the plans of the Americans was a sharp one. As had not been the case in earlier conferences, the Americans came to Trident well prepared and united in their views. A Pacific Military Conference had met in Washington in March 1943 to draft a master plan for the defeat of Japan, and this was ready for presentation to the British at Trident. The plan was in essence a great pincers movement, converging on Hongkong. The Americans would drive across the Pacific, island-hopping towards the south China coast; the British in conjunction with the Chinese would clear Burma, and then conduct harassing operations in Malaya and the Dutch East Indies. Meanwhile, supplies for the Chinese armies would be delivered over the reopened Burma Road; a great strategic air force would be created in China; then a powerful Chinese land offensive would drive the Japanese into the sea in the region of Hongkong. After American naval and Chinese ground forces had thus made a junction at Hongkong, the final invasion of Japan would be launched from that vantage point.[2]

As for the war against Germany, the Americans reaffirmed their faith in a massive cross-Channel invasion, but recognized that no such attack

[1] Churchill (iv. 702–9; U.S. edition, iv. 786–93) presents an unusually frank and extremely interesting pair of documents. One is a memorandum he prepared for the British Chiefs of Staff in preparation for the Trident Conference; the second is a record of his remarks at the first plenary session of Trident. The differences between what Churchill privately wished and what he thought it diplomatic to say can be studied by comparing the two.

[2] Morison: *History of U.S. Naval Operations*, vi. 7–8.

could be prepared until the spring of 1944. It was decided at a conference between the American Joint Chiefs of Staff and Roosevelt that the primary objective of the American Government at the Trident Conference would be to pin the British down to a definite and irrevocable commitment to a cross-Channel invasion 'at the earliest practical date and to make full preparations for such an operation by the spring of 1944'.[1] Acceptance of the Pacific plan was a secondary but almost equally important objective.

When the Conference met, there was no disagreement on a number of lesser points. It was agreed without dissent that use of the Azores as a naval and air base should be acquired from Portugal by diplomacy or, if necessary, by force. This project was assigned to the British, who secured the desired result by negotiation in October 1943.[2] It was agreed similarly without demur that the bomber offensive against Germany should be stepped up tremendously, and that a special effort should be made to bomb the Ploeşti oilfields in Rumania.[3]

On the major strategic issues, however, discussion was long and sometimes heated. The Americans were not willing to agree to an offensive in the Mediterranean which, they feared, might postpone the cross-Channel attack yet again. The British were equally stubborn in refusing to agree to further efforts in Burma in 1943, and made it quite clear that they thought the American faith in the potential effectiveness of Chinese soldiers was illusory. Nevertheless, by 23 May 1943 an indecisive compromise had been reached. The Americans agreed to an ambiguous paragraph defining policy in the Mediterranean as follows:

> . . . the Allied Commander-in-Chief North Africa will be instructed, as a matter of urgency, to plan such operations in exploitation of 'Husky' [the invasion of Sicily] as are best calculated to eliminate Italy from the war and to contain the maximum number of German forces. Which of the various specific operations should be adopted, and thereafter mounted, is a decision which will be reserved to the Combined Chiefs of Staff.[4]

This meant almost nothing. Eisenhower was to make plans, but whether the plans would be acted upon was left to future decision. Nevertheless, it was an opening wedge for British Mediterranean plans. Circumstances and the passage of time were on Churchill's side, as he well knew. Most of the troops in the Mediterranean were British, and it was natural that the wishes of the British Government should play a preponderant part in

[1] Leahy: *I Was There*, p. 189.

[2] Sherwood: *Roosevelt and Hopkins*, pp. 731–2; Eng. edition, ii. 727; Churchill, v. 146–8; U.S. edition, v. 165–6.

[3] It was during the Trident Conference that Churchill was able to settle the shipping dispute and the differences over sharing information on atomic development which had arisen between the British and American Governments. See above, pp. 234–5.

[4] Churchill, iv. 724; U.S. edition, iv. 810.

deciding the use to which they would be put. Moreover, it was hard for Marshall and his colleagues to defend a strategy which required that Allied forces in the Mediterranean should stand idle through the late summer and autumn of 1943 while Italy lay under Allied guns, waiting to be invaded.

In Burma, the plan for a land campaign was postponed until 1944. Instead, effort was to be concentrated on building air bases from which bombers could harass the Japanese garrison of Burma, and from which air transport to China could be organized on a vastly increased scale. This, the Americans hoped, would be enough to keep the Chinese in the war; and would also make it possible to create a powerful strategic air force in China which could attack the Japanese homeland itself.[1]

Thus the British conceded something in Burma while the Americans conceded something in the Mediterranean. But the key issue in American eyes was to win British agreement to a landing in France in the spring of 1944. Planning for such an operation had been advanced in the months since the Casablanca Conference, but there were still great uncertainties as to what would be needed in the way both of man-power and equipment if a landing in northern France were to be successful. Nevertheless, General Marshall and his American colleagues pressed hard for a firm decision and wished to set a definite target date for invasion across the Channel. The British Chiefs of Staff objected on principle to making unduly long-range commitments, and preferred to concentrate attention upon the new opportunities which were about to open in the Mediterranean. The upshot was a compromise. It was agreed to assemble troops and supplies in Great Britain 'with the object of mounting an operation with target date 1 May 1944 to secure a lodgement on the Continent from which further offensive operations can be carried out'.[2] A total of twenty-nine divisions were assigned to this task, seven of which were to come from those already on hand in the Mediterranean.[3] The operation, thus conceived, was soon thereafter dubbed Overlord, a code name which survived all the subsequent shifts and changes in plan up to the day of final invasion in June 1944.

It was, however, with serious reservations that the British Chiefs of Staff accepted the plan for Overlord. They believed that before an invasion of France could be successfully undertaken, the Anglo-American forces would have to win unquestioned superiority in the air and would have also to defeat the U-boats decisively. Neither of these things had yet been done

[1] The decision to rest Allied hopes on air attack and air transport to China was, in part, a victory for Chennault's point of view over Stilwell's. Stilwell attributed his defeat to the British (cf. *The Stilwell Papers*, p. 205).

[2] Harrison: *Cross-Channel Attack*, p. 69.

[3] Leahy: *I Was There*, p. 193; Sherwood: *Roosevelt and Hopkins*, p. 732; Eng. edition, ii. 728; Lt.-General Sir Frederick Morgan: *Overture to Overlord* (London, Hodder & Stoughton, 1950), p. 75; Harrison, op. cit. pp. 63–70.

in May 1943. In the meanwhile, the British thought it would be better to exploit opportunities which might open in the Mediterranean, rather than to concentrate all effort on preparing for a great invasion which might, in the end, prove impossible unless German strength had first been dispersed by harassing attacks on the southern flank of *Festung Europa*. The British feared that, without a vigorous prosecution of the Mediterranean campaigns, the American plan for invasion would become dangerous, rash, and premature; yet they could not evade Marshall's stubborn insistence on a promise to invade at a fixed date, and the British Chiefs of Staff therefore reluctantly signed on the dotted line, agreeing to give the build-up for Overlord priority over any further Mediterranean operations.

These decisions were far from satisfying the British Prime Minister. On 24 May, when the Combined Chiefs of Staff presented their conclusions to a plenary session of the Conference, Churchill pleaded eloquently for invasion of Italy and pictured the repercussions of such a step in the Balkans in his usual optimistic colours. But the Americans were stubborn and refused to budge from the agreement that had been reached by the Combined Chiefs. On the following day, 25 May, Churchill conceded defeat for the time being and the Conference concluded with the acceptance of the strategic decisions of 23 May.[1]

American unwillingness to agree to the invasion of Italy was, of course, motivated by the belief that such a step would prevent Overlord from coming off on schedule; and Marshall pinned all his military faith upon Overlord as the best and shortest way to win the war against Germany. Any other strategy, he believed, would prolong the war unnecessarily. British insistence upon action in the Mediterranean (and Churchill's plan for amphibious action in Sumatra and Malaya too) seemed to the American Chiefs of Staff to be inspired by political rather than military aims.

The fact that the British had real military objections to Overlord, fearing a repetition of the slaughter and a lapse into the futile trench warfare of 1915–18 such as dominated the Western campaigns of the First World

[1] Leahy: *I Was There*, p. 194. Churchill's account of Trident decisions (iv. 722–3; U.S. edition, iv. 808–9) is misleading. He omits any mention of the decision for Overlord, and quotes only the vague 'Basic Undertakings' including one which reads as follows: 'Concentrate maximum resources in a selected area as early as practicable for the purpose of conducting a decisive invasion of the Axis citadel.' This wording may have been designed to give the British an escape clause if conditions for the invasion did not develop as they hoped by the spring of 1944; but from other accounts of the Trident Conference it is certain that in other papers a definite plan—Overlord—was accepted. The British did not hide their distrust of Overlord; and when the Chief of the Imperial General Staff (Sir Alan Brooke) visited Eisenhower immediately after Trident he told the American general that he would be glad to eliminate the whole project of a cross-Channel attack from Allied strategy (Eisenhower: *Crusade in Europe*, p. 167). The Americans in Washington, however, chose to interpret the Trident agreement as a binding commitment (cf. Leahy: *I Was There*, p. 193).

War, made little impression on the American strategists. They were inclined to discount such fears as a false façade, used to hide the real, political motives of British strategy. The suspicion that British diplomatic skill might hoodwink the Americans into using their men and supplies to support and extend British empire and influence was constantly in the background of American strategic planning, and this fear helped to make the Americans unbending in their insistence upon the plans they had drawn up. Needing American help, Churchill and his colleagues regularly had to yield at least nominal assent to the American proposals; but they could and did make obstacles to plans of which they disapproved, while forwarding others of which they did approve, and in this somewhat indirect manner were able to exercise a very large influence on the actual course of events.

The crabwise manner in which the Allies advanced into the Italian campaign provides one of the best instances of this somewhat uncomfortable relation between British and American strategists. Despite his rebuff at Trident, Churchill was not ready to abandon his plan for an invasion of Italy. He wished above all to convert General Marshall to his view, for Marshall was the principal figure on the American side who opposed adventures in the Mediterranean. Accordingly, Churchill invited Marshall to come with him to Algiers for conferences with the Allied commanders in the Mediterranean. Marshall accepted, and travelled with the Prime Minister by air to North Africa. They arrived on 29 May 1943.

As he had no doubt expected, Churchill found that the American commanders in the Mediterranean were far more willing to embark upon an invasion of Italy than were their superiors in Washington. Eisenhower's view was that, if the conquest of Sicily proved relatively easy, the campaign should continue on across the Straits of Messina into southern Italy without a stop. Marshall, however, was not to be rushed into agreement. He argued that nothing should be decided until the outcome of the attack on Sicily was known, and felt that an alternative to the invasion of Italy would be the seizure of Sardinia and Corsica in the later months of 1943. From his point of view these island operations had the advantage that once they were completed, only small garrisons would be needed to hold what had been won, whereas an Italian campaign would result in a front which would have to be maintained steadily at the expense of maximum concentration on the cross-Channel assault.[1]

Churchill and the British, for their part, were very circumspect. Any intention of extending Mediterranean operations to the Balkans was disclaimed,[2] and Churchill presented the invasion of Italy as a campaign

[1] Churchill, iv. 732–3; U.S. edition, iv. 818–19.

[2] Thereafter, Eden, who had been summoned to join the Conference, referred incidentally on 31 May to the Turkish reaction 'when our troops had reached the Balkan area', but Churchill

which would be entirely subsidiary to Overlord, limited to objectives in the south of the peninsula. At the same time, British spokesmen held out the hope that Italy might surrender. In such a case the front might leap northward at one step to the Po or even to the Alps.[1]

No definite decision was reached. Eisenhower agreed that he would work on plans for the exploitation of victory in Sicily, and, when the moment arrived, would send to the Combined Chiefs of Staff not only plans but specific recommendations, based upon the situation as it had developed. Churchill felt reasonably satisfied with this conclusion. He sensed the desire of the Mediterranean commanders to push on into Italy, and, as he reported to London, 'with a little patience, we British being all agreed, will probably obtain the desired solutions'.[2]

As far as Europe was concerned, the outcome of the Trident and Algiers Conferences turned out to be much more solid than the agreements reached at Casablanca. One reason was the background of victory in North Africa, and the increasing abundance of supplies, shipping, and trained man-power at the disposal of the Allies. Under such circumstances, firmer plans could be prepared, the Germans could be kept on the defensive, and the Allies could more and more strike at will against their enemies. The British were no longer seriously afraid lest the Americans withdraw their main forces from Europe to fight Japan. They hoped that circumstances, their own military diplomacy, and their sounder estimate of future capabilities and obstacles would enable them to bend the Americans to accept the major outlines of the strategy they had worked out. The Americans for their part felt that British reluctance to agree to their strategic plans could be overcome by sufficient bluntness; and while they still stood very much on guard lest British wiles lead them into sidepaths, they recognized the solidarity of ultimate aims which united the two nations.[3]

In Asia and the Pacific, however, the situation was not much different from what it had been at the time of Casablanca. No very effective meet-

intervened to state that he did not advocate an expedition into the Balkans in the near future (ibid. pp. 739 and 826 respectively).

[1] Ibid. pp. 732–40 and 818–28 respectively; Eisenhower: *Crusade in Europe*, pp. 167–8.

[2] Churchill, iv. 730; U.S. edition, iv. 816; Eisenhower: *Crusade in Europe*, p. 168. The agreement which established the French Committee of National Liberation and merged de Gaulle's and Giraud's forces into one was reached while Churchill and Eden were in Algiers. A part of their attention was devoted to forwarding this step towards French unity.

[3] Leahy: *I Was There*, pp. 195–6. Marshall's estimate of Trident was as follows: '. . . The Trident Conference may prove to be one of the most historic military conclaves of this war, for here the specific strategy to which the movements of the land, sea, and air forces of the American and British Allies conformed was translated into firm commitments' (*The War Reports of Marshall, Arnold, and King*, p. 157).

ing of minds had been achieved in Washington, and quarrels between British, Chinese, and Americans continued to flourish on the spot. The grand plan for Japan's overthrow which had been accepted at Trident was destined to undergo fundamental modification through the omission of the Chinese half of the pincers.

The Trident decisions put a severe strain upon relations between Russia and the Western Allies. Despite the margin of disagreement which persisted concerning Overlord, British and Americans were both agreed that no second front in France could be established in the remaining months of 1943. To break this news to Stalin was certainly a delicate task. Churchill and Roosevelt found it very difficult to prepare a telegram that would put the decision in the best possible light. In the end the final draft was made by Marshall.[1] Despite verbal efforts of the Allied leaders to make the news palatable, Stalin received it with indignation, and, as we have seen, a period of estrangement ensued.[2]

(c) THE ADVANCE INTO ITALY

(1) *Allied Reaction to Mussolini's Overthrow*

British, American, and Canadian troops invaded Sicily on the night of 9–10 July 1943. The Italian soldiers, despite the fact that they were defending the soil of their homeland, did not put up much resistance, and the local population generally welcomed the Allies. However, German troops which were in Sicily fought with all their usual skill, and were able to retreat to the north-east corner of the island. There they defended themselves in a series of stubborn rear-guard actions until 17 August, when the last of them crossed the Straits of Messina to the mainland of Italy.

The invasion of Sicily presented the Allies with the problem of administering a part of the enemy homeland. In North Africa civil administration had been complicated by the ambiguous status of the French officials: neutrals before the landing, enemies at the time of the landing, and friends a few days later. No such complexities faced the Allies in Sicily, and it was determined ahead of time that there should be a clean sweep of fascist office holders. Roosevelt was anxious to prevent a repetition of the embarrassment which he had suffered as a result of the retention of Vichy French officials in office. He fell back upon the idea which he had vainly attempted to apply to French affairs: suspension of political activity until after the war.[3]

The instrument which was designed to exercise Allied control over the civil population was called Allied Military Government of Occupied

[1] Churchill, iv. 726–7; U.S. edition, iv. 812–13. [2] See above, pp. 277–8.

[3] Carl J. Friedrich and others: *American Experiences in Military Government in World War II* (New York, Rhinehart, 1948), pp. 29–30.

Territory, or AMGOT. Its duties were originally conceived as narrowly military. Teams of army officers were expected to secure peace and order in the rear of the combat troops, keep lines of communication in good order, and govern local affairs generally in such a way as to promote 'political and military objectives of the Allied Forces in connection with future operations'.[1] The commander of the Sicilian campaign, General Alexander, was designated as Military Governor of Sicily, and AMGOT itself was commanded by a British officer with an American deputy.

In Sicily AMGOT was able to work fairly smoothly during the first days. As the Allied armies advanced through the island, they moved into what in truth amounted to a political vacuum, and the problems which confronted the military government teams were mainly of a technical nature—food, sanitation, looting, &c. The surrender of the Italian Government at the time of the invasion of mainland Italy, however, introduced political complications analogous to those which had plagued the Allies in French North Africa.

Anglo-American strategic intentions were less well defined. According to the decision reached at the Trident Conference in May 1943, Eisenhower had the task of preparing plans to 'eliminate Italy from the war', but he had no authority to act upon such plans until after they had been approved by the Combined Chiefs of Staff. Moreover, political decisions were removed entirely from Eisenhower's province. Roosevelt and Churchill wished to keep policy with respect to Italy in their own hands, leaving a minimum of discretion to their military representatives in the field.[2] The result, inevitably, was confusion and uncertainty among the Allied commanders in the Mediterranean, who could not go ahead with any assurance that their superiors would approve their proposals.

The confusion in the Allied camp, however, was as nothing compared with the turmoil in Italy itself. The war had gone badly for the Italians almost from the beginning. Large numbers of men had been lost in North Africa. Hatred of the Germans was widespread; but at the same time there were enough German troops in Italy itself to make it difficult and dangerous for the Italians to take matters into their own hands and break away from Hitler. Yet this was what the Allies demanded. On 16 July

[1] *AMGOT Operational Order, 1 May 1943*, quoted in Allied Commission in Italy: *Review of Allied Military Government and the Allied Control Commission* (U.S. Army, n.d.), p. 9.

[2] Churchill, v. 51, 58–59, 89; U.S. edition, v. 55, 63, 99. They were presumably intent upon avoiding a repetition of the dubious advantages which had come from entrusting political decisions to General Clark in North Africa. Eisenhower's political sagacity was generally held in low repute as a result of the Darlan episode, with the result that his every step in the negotiation for the surrender of Italy was carefully scrutinized from Washington and London.

1943 a joint message from Churchill and Roosevelt was broadcast to Italy. It said in part:

> The sole hope for Italy's survival lies in honorable capitulation to the overwhelming power of the military forces of the United Nations. If you continue to tolerate the Fascist regime which serves the evil power of the Nazis, you must suffer the consequences of your own choice. . . .
>
> The time has come for you to decide whether Italians shall die for Mussolini and Hitler—or live for Italy, and for civilization.[1]

'Honorable capitulation' sounded a good deal better than 'Unconditional Surrender'; and was, of course, designed to do so. The low state of Italian morale, the difficult military situation (half of the Italian army was stationed in the Balkans and Hitler refused to let the troops come home to help defend their homeland), and the Allied psychological offensive all contributed to the *coup d'état* of 25 July 1943 which drove Mussolini from power and set up Marshal Pietro Badoglio in his place as head of the Italian Government.[2]

Badoglio announced the dissolution of the Fascist Party on 27 July, put Italy under martial law, and prohibited all political activity until the end of the war. He likewise announced that the war would go on; but no one in Italy, Germany, or among the Allies believed him. The Germans began to send reinforcements into northern Italy at once and did not hide their distrust of the new Italian Government.[3]

The Allies were likewise distrustful, but sought to take full advantage of Mussolini's fall. Churchill, speaking in the House of Commons on 27 July, expressed his satisfaction at the overthrow of one European dictator, but reserved any judgement upon Badoglio's new régime. Nevertheless, he held forth an unmistakable olive branch. 'It would be a grave mistake', he said, 'when Italian affairs are in this flexible, fluid, formative condition, for the rescuing Powers, Britain and the United States, so to act as to break down the whole structure and expression of the Italian state.' And again: 'It is the interest of Italy, and also the interest of the Allies, that the unconditional surrender of Italy should be brought about wholesale and not piecemeal.'[4]

On the following day, 28 July, Roosevelt made a speech in which he referred to Italian affairs in a much more uncompromising fashion. The President said:

> Our terms to Italy are still the same as our terms to Germany and Japan—'unconditional surrender'.
>
> We will have no truck with Fascism in any way, shape, or manner. We will permit no vestige of Fascism to remain.

[1] *Documents on American Foreign Relations, 1943–1944*, p. 164.

[2] Details will be found in the *Survey* for 1939–46: *Hitler's Europe*.

[3] Pietro Badoglio: *Italy in the Second World War* (London, Oxford University Press, 1948), p. 55.

[4] 27 July 1943, H.C.Deb. 5th ser., vol. 391, coll. 1399–1400.

Eventually Italy will reconstitute herself. It will be the people of Italy who will do that, choosing their own government in accordance with the basic democratic principles of liberty and equality. . . .

Meanwhile the war in Sicily and Italy goes on. It must go on, and will go on, until the Italian people realize the futility of continuing to fight in a lost cause—a cause to which the people of Italy never gave their whole-hearted approval and support.[1]

The obvious difference in the tone with which Churchill and Roosevelt greeted the formation of Badoglio's Government reflected a considerable divergence in their views. Partly it was a matter of strategy. Churchill had long been convinced that the Allies should fight a campaign in Italy, and he therefore welcomed the prospect of winning the passive or even the active support of the Italian Government. Such support would make the campaign much easier, and, with luck, a front might be formed against the Germans somewhere north of Rome. Moreover, a rupture between Italy and Germany would open inviting prospects in the Balkans and the Aegean. If the Americans could be persuaded to withdraw their opposition to operations in the eastern Mediterranean, Churchill's cherished plan for drawing German reserves from the west by means of multiple attacks from the south would be realized.

Roosevelt was not insensitive to the military advantages which Badoglio's defection to the Allied camp might bring.[2] But he was surrounded by military advisers who distrusted Mediterranean operations, thinking that they merely interfered with prompt and vigorous attack across the Channel. Marshall and his colleagues could not, indeed, neglect the military gain which might come from Italian surrender, and so on 16 July 1943 the Combined Chiefs of Staff approved a plan for the invasion of Italy, which aimed, initially, at seizing the Naples area.[3] But the American members of the Combined Chiefs of Staff approved the invasion of Italy without enthusiasm, and any suggestion from the British that Allied forces should be dispersed still further by attempting operations farther east met with stony refusal. From the American point of view, the new advance into Italy already endangered the concentration of maximum force for an invasion of northern France in the spring of 1944; any further dissipation of resources seemed to them altogether inadmissible. The resultant effect upon Roosevelt was to dim his first enthusiasm for Mediterranean adven-

[1] *Documents on American Foreign Relations, 1943–1944*, p. 165.

[2] On 26 July 1943 he telegraphed to Churchill: 'If any overtures come we must be certain of the use of Italian territory and transportation against the Germans in the north *and against the whole Balkan peninsula*, as well as use of airfields of all kinds' (Churchill, v. 51; U.S. edition, v. 55). This telegram was sent when Roosevelt first received the news of Mussolini's fall, and very likely before he consulted Marshall and his other military advisers. Certainly Roosevelt later repudiated the idea of large-scale action in the Balkans.

[3] Harrison: *Cross-Channel Attack*, p. 87. Final determination of the forces to be allotted to the venture was not made until 26 July.

tures and to reduce his estimate of the military advantages which Badoglio's surrender might bring to the Allies.

Another consideration was perhaps even more important for the President. Badoglio might well turn out another Darlan, difficult to get rid of once the Allies had made a deal with him, and yet, through his close identification with the fascist régime, unacceptable among the ranks of the United Nations.[1] Churchill was restrained by no such scruples. As he wrote to Roosevelt on 31 July:

> I am not in the least afraid for this purpose of seeming to recognize the House of Savoy or Badoglio, provided they are the ones who can make the Italians do what we need for our war purposes. Those purposes would certainly be hindered by chaos, Bolshevisation, or civil war. We have no right to lay undue burdens on our troops. It may well be that after the armistice terms have been accepted both the King and Badoglio will sink under the odium of surrender and that the Crown Prince and a new Prime Minister may be chosen.[2]

Roosevelt saw that there was no immediate alternative to Badoglio and the King on the Italian political scene, and did not wish to force Italy into political chaos.[3] Indeed, it appears that the President was in a profound state of indecision, hesitating over the strategic advantages and liabilities opened by Italian surrender and, equally, hesitating over the question of what attitude to assume towards the turn-coat Badoglio. Churchill's will was by contrast single and resolute; and it is therefore not surprising that he prevailed. Circumstances as well as Churchill's own diplomatic address were on his side.

Events moved rapidly in the days after Mussolini's overthrow. On 4 August the first Italian peace feelers were extended to the Allies through the Italian Embassy in Lisbon; two days later more definite negotiations were started at Tangier.[4] Meanwhile, the British and American Governments hastily set out to draft terms of surrender for Italy. The task was assigned to a sub-committee of the Combined Chiefs of Staff, the Combined Civil Affairs Committee. Important differences arose between the British, who wished to maintain the power of the Italian Crown indefinitely and to build up the prestige of the Badoglio Government, and the Americans, who felt that the Italian King had forfeited all right to his prerogatives by his behaviour under the fascist régime and that the powers and prestige of Badoglio's Government should be severely limited.[5]

[1] Cf. Hopkins's attitude on the question (Sherwood: *Roosevelt and Hopkins*, p. 744; Eng. edition, ii. 740). Roosevelt's speech of 28 July suggests that he felt sympathy for the arguments of men like Hopkins, but no adequate record of the President's state of mind had been published by 1952.
[2] Churchill, v. 59; U.S. edition, v. 64.
[3] Ibid.
[4] Ibid. pp. 88–92 and 98–103, respectively; Badoglio: *Italy in the Second World War*, pp. 66–67.
[5] Hull: *Memoirs*, ii. 1550.

Churchill's personal bias towards monarchy as a political institution played a part in this divergence of views; more fundamental was his fear that, if the framework of monarchy and conservatism, represented by men like Badoglio, once gave way, Italy would soon turn towards Communist revolution. The Americans, on the contrary, were by their own national tradition biased in favour of republicanism, and did not believe that Communism was the only alternative to monarchy in Italy. These differences in national outlook were deep-lying and could not be settled once and for all.

What could be and had to be settled were the steps to take in the immediate situation. It was decided to draw up two documents: a 'short' armistice (as it came to be called) which laid down military terms of surrender, and a fuller document (the 'long' armistice) in which political and economic as well as more detailed military demands were advanced. The reason for this procedure seems to have been the need for haste. When it had become clear that British and American representatives would find difficulty in agreeing upon some of the provisions of the long armistice, it seemed wise to prepare a document upon which they could agree promptly in order to have specific terms in hand to submit to the Italians. In any event, the short armistice was ready by 31 July, and on 2 August 1943 Eisenhower was empowered to offer the agreed terms to any future Italian emissary.[1] Agreement on the text of the long armistice, on the other hand, was not reached until Churchill and Roosevelt had conferred once again, this time at Quebec; and it was not until 28 August that the Soviet Government indicated their approval of the instruments of surrender which had thus been prepared.[2]

While the Allied Governments were getting ready to receive Badoglio's surrender, preparations for the invasion of Italy went ahead in the Mediterranean. The plan that Eisenhower submitted to the Combined Chiefs of Staff called for an invasion of Italy at two points. The British Eighth Army was to cross the Straits of Messina into the toe of Calabria, and an Anglo-American army, under General Clark, was to land on the beaches near Salerno on the shin of the Italian boot. The operation was planned to take place only after Sicily had been completely conquered, and this took longer than Eisenhower and Alexander originally had hoped. Indeed, the skill and determination of German resistance in the north-east corner of Sicily gave the German high command time to recover from the first shock of Mussolini's overthrow by bringing new German troops over the Alps. As a result, by the time Badoglio and the Allies had arranged for Italian

[1] Churchill, v. 55–59; U.S. edition, v. 59–63; Butcher: *My Three Years with Eisenhower*, p. 378. For the negotiations with the Italians on the terms of the short armistice, see below, pp. 297–300.

[2] Hull: *Memoirs*, ii. 1549. For the signature and terms of the long armistice, see below, pp. 303 seqq.

surrender, the chance of winning most or all of Italy had already vanished, and the Germans were able to form a battle line in the south.[1]

(2) *The First Quebec Conference, 14–24 August 1943*

The critical development of Italian affairs which was signalized by the overthrow of Mussolini on 25 July 1943 convinced Churchill that the time had come for another Anglo-American Conference. The Americans agreed and Quebec was fixed upon as the place of meeting. The Conference was given the code-name Quadrant.

Obviously, the sudden change in Italian affairs called for an adjustment of Allied strategy. Churchill wished to take every possible advantage of Italy's weakness, even if it meant modifying plans for Overlord and for operations in Burma which had been agreed to at the Trident Conference in May. It seemed self-evident to the Prime Minister that these earlier plans, which required substantial weakening of the Allied forces in the Mediterranean, should now be changed when brilliant opportunities for great gains, not only in Italy but in the Aegean islands and in the Balkan peninsula as well, had suddenly opened up. If the Italian garrisons of Greece, Yugoslavia, and of the islands of the Aegean could be induced to surrender (or even to join the Allies) the whole German flank in southern Europe would become exposed to devastating assault. With such gains in view, Churchill came to feel that a few weeks' or even months' delay in Overlord would be well worth the price.[2] At the same time, he was acutely aware of the distrust which Marshall and other American military leaders felt for Mediterranean commitments, and did not feel it prudent to propose, at least for the present, any but minor operations in the Balkans.[3]

[1] The slowness with which the Allies exploited the collapse of the Italian will to resist was criticized at the time, and Eisenhower himself chafed at the delays which the nature of his plans imposed (cf. Butcher, op. cit. p. 372). In retrospect, it is hard to see why the Sicilian attack could not have been broken off about 1 August, and landing operations on the Italian mainland prepared two to three weeks earlier than they were actually carried out. Such attacks, if launched somewhere along the coasts of Calabria, would have taken the Germans in Sicily in the rear and the Allies would have reached the mainland before the Germans had much time to reinforce their strength in central Italy. The major obstacle to such flexibility was a shortage of landing craft, some of which were being or about to be withdrawn from the Mediterranean, while others had to be repaired and refitted after the Sicilian landing. A second obstacle was the uncertainty which still prevailed as to the intentions and power of the Badoglio Government. Nevertheless, it seems possible to accuse the Allied command of a certain mechanical adherence to prepared plans in this instance. The necessity of clearing every proposal with the Combined Chiefs of Staff and ultimately with the American and British Governments contributed to the rigidity with which the Allied commanders responded to the situation. Having with difficulty managed to get one plan approved, it perhaps seemed unwise to reopen the issue of proposing a change. The leading-strings imposed upon him irked Eisenhower, who felt that, given the necessary authority, he could deal more speedily and effectively with the Italians than could the men in Washington and London (ibid. pp. 372, 406).

[2] Churchill, v. 188; U.S. edition, v. 211–12.

[3] Churchill (v. 114, 121; U.S. edition, v. 128, 136–7, and *passim*) strives to minimize his advocacy of active operations in the Balkan peninsula. In an extremely fluid situation, it was

Churchill and the British Chiefs of Staff arrived in Canada on 9 August 1943. The American Joint Chiefs of Staff met them at Quebec and began staff discussions on 14 August; but Churchill travelled down to Hyde Park where he spent two days with Roosevelt before the plenary sessions of the Conference began. After the formal end of the Conference the critical state of Italian affairs persuaded Churchill to stay on in the United States, where he could easily confer with Roosevelt and exert his personal influence on the American military authorities in the hope of pressing them to accept a more vigorous line of action in the Mediterranean. He therefore remained in and about Washington until 12 September, by which time the immediate crisis in Italy had passed.

At the Quadrant or First Quebec Conference, the clash between British and American strategists was almost the same as it had been in May at the Trident Conference in Washington. The major stakes, clearly, were in Europe where immediate action in the Mediterranean had to be balanced against future action across the Channel. But the arguments on European strategy were already familiar and the lines clearly drawn. Perhaps partly as a result, discussion of the strategic alternatives in Europe took less time at Quadrant than did debate over the Far East. Churchill revived his proposal for an amphibious attack against Sumatra, and could now offer the prospect of a speedy reinforcement of the fleet in the Indian Ocean with ships drawn from the Mediterranean.[1] The Americans, however, still demanded operations to clear northern Burma and reopen land communications with China. They had earlier commitments on their side, and the British Chiefs of Staff did not support Churchill's project for Sumatra, recognizing that the needful equipment could not be found without trenching upon more vital theatres. The upshot was reaffirmation of the decision of Trident: first priority should go to restoring land communication with

true that Churchill had no fixed and definite plan for large-scale use of Anglo-American troops in that peninsula in the immediate future; but the Americans certainly believed that his whole policy was designed to open up both an Italian and a Balkan front against Germany as speedily as circumstances would permit, even if it meant a postponement of Overlord (cf. Sherwood: *Roosevelt and Hopkins*, pp. 746–7; Eng. edition, ii. 742–3; Leahy: *I Was There*, p. 228). The Americans were probably too suspicious, refusing to take Churchill's military arguments as more than camouflage for political goals. At the same time, if Churchill had been able to bend events to his will, and had brought Turkey into the war in 1943 or early 1944, a Balkan front would have been opened, and it might have developed, as the Americans feared would be the case, into as large an operation for Anglo-American forces as in fact the Italian campaign became. American suspicions were therefore not groundless, however exaggerated they may have become in the minds of certain individuals.

[1] When strategy in South-East Asia was discussed, from 19 to 23 August, the future surrender of the Italian fleet could not confidently be predicted; but definite Italian offers had already reached the Conference (Leahy: *I Was There*, p. 210; Churchill, v. 77–82; U.S. edition, v. 87–92).

China, while amphibious campaigns in the Bay of Bengal were left for future study.[1]

In discussing Burma, the American members of the Combined Chiefs of Staff tended to assume the attitude that a contract had been made which required the British to engage in offensive operations in northern Burma according to the letter of the agreement. The Americans tended to view British efforts to change earlier decisions as evidence of bad faith. This stiff legalism was even more apparent during the discussion of European strategy. The American attitude became extremely irritating to the British, who wished to introduce flexibility into the allocation of Anglo-American resources in order to take full advantage of Italy's impending collapse.

But the Americans insisted stubbornly on going ahead step by step with the preparations which had been worked out in accordance with the agreements reached in Washington at Trident, even though this required the transfer of troops and such precious articles as landing craft from the Mediterranean to England (and to Burma) exactly at a time when glittering opportunities opened in Italy and the Aegean. Meetings of the Combined Chiefs of Staff on 14 and 16 August explored these differences, and after forceful statements by Marshall and King giving their views on the sanctity of previous agreements the British Chiefs of Staff refrained from pressing the matter further. That task was left to Churchill personally and, perhaps, to the developing pressure of circumstance.[2]

From the American point of view, the detailed plan for Overlord which had been drawn up in London by an Anglo-American group of staff officers under General Sir Frederick Morgan[3] was the most important matter up for discussion at Quebec. The operation was conceived on a very big scale; and calculation of the resources available showed that, after the first few weeks, nearly all the build-up of forces on the Continent would have to come from American sources.

After examining the plan, the Combined Chiefs of Staff approved it. They made one important addition, however, by deciding that a supplementary invasion of the south coast of France should be launched from the Mediterranean in order to support the main effort across the Channel. This operation—code-name Anvil—had a number of advantages, of which perhaps the chief was economy of shipping. Troops already stationed in the Mediterranean could bring their weight to bear directly on the battle for France by landing on the Riviera; and they could do so without putting as much strain on Allied shipping as would have been the case if the men had first to be transported from the Mediterranean to England before join-

[1] The question of British participation in the naval campaigns of the Pacific was also discussed in general terms, but indecisively.

[2] Leahy: *I Was There*, pp. 208–9, and below, pp. 303–4.

[3] C.O.S.S.A.C., as this planning headquarters was called, had been established after the Casablanca Conference to plan the great cross-Channel invasion. See above, p. 267.

ing battle. In addition, a landing in southern France promised to open the port of Marseilles as an additional supply point for the immense armies which were to be deployed against Germany.[1]

As between Overlord and any new undertakings in the Mediterranean, the Combined Chiefs of Staff agreed to accord priority to Overlord.[2]

There were three important conditions attached to the plan for the great invasion as presented and approved: German fighter aircraft strength would have to be reduced 'substantially', not more than twelve mobile German divisions should be stationed in northern France, and the technical problems connected with the creation of two artificial harbours would have to be solved before the plan could be successfully acted upon.[3] These were weighty and serious reservations, and it was impossible to be sure in August 1943 that they would be satisfactorily met when D-day came round. Nevertheless, it was decided to go ahead with full-scale preparations and further detailed planning on the assumption that all difficulties could be overcome. Churchill's only comment, when the plan came up for ratification before the plenary session of the Conference on 19 August, was to urge that the scale of the initial assault be increased.[4]

The Combined Chiefs of Staff supplemented these decisions about future operations by reorganizing the command arrangements in both the European and Far Eastern theatres of war. At Casablanca, an informal understanding had been reached to the effect that a British general would command the invasion of France in order to balance the assignment of the supreme Allied command in the Mediterranean to Eisenhower. But by the time of the First Quebec Conference neither party was pleased with this arrangement. The Americans had come to feel that if Overlord were to be a success, it was necessary to appoint as commander a man who wholeheartedly believed in the wisdom of the operation. The attitude of British military leaders to the American plan had never been enthusiastic, and the Americans drew the inference that only an American general

[1] Sherwood: *Roosevelt and Hopkins*, p. 747; Eng. edition, ii. 743; Churchill, v. 77; U.S. edition, v. 86. Churchill accepted Anvil originally not so much because he liked the project in itself, as because it promised to provide a reason for keeping landing craft in the Mediterranean where they could be made to forward his other enterprises before being used against the Riviera (ibid. pp. 358 and 405 respectively). It was only when his other projects failed of realization, or were only partially executed, that he began to oppose Anvil.

[2] Ibid. pp. 75 and 84 respectively. The priority accorded to Overlord was not, however, absolute. The official record ran: 'As between operation Overlord and operations in the Mediterranean, where there is a shortage of resources, available resources will be distributed with the main object of insuring the success of Overlord. Operations in the Mediterranean theater will be carried out with the forces allotted at Trident except as these may be varied by decision of the Combined Chiefs of Staff' (Harrison: *Cross-Channel Attack*, p. 98).

[3] Churchill, v. 70; U.S. edition, v. 77.

[4] Ibid. pp. 76 and 86 respectively.

could be trusted to bring it finally to a successful issue.[1] In addition, it had become clear that the major part of the men and resources for Overlord would have to come from the United States, and this gave a second basis for an American claim to the supreme command.

The British, for their part, were fully prepared to accord the command of Overlord to an American. Indeed, Churchill took the Americans by surprise when he proposed that General Marshall should command the attack on France.[2] It seems a reasonable inference to believe that Churchill and the British Chiefs of Staff were more interested in assuring a vigorous prosecution of the Mediterranean campaigns than they were in safeguarding British claims to command Overlord. If by according to the Americans command in France they could put supreme command in the Mediterranean in British hands there seemed a better chance of influencing events in the direction that seemed wise to the British strategists.

Thus no difficulties arose. By mutual consent, it was agreed that American command of Overlord should be balanced by the transfer of supreme command in the Mediterranean from Eisenhower to a British general.[3] For the time being, however, no changes were made. The invasion of Italy was about to begin; Overlord was still only a plan; the timing of the actual transfer of authority could be left for future decision in the light of the development of the Italian campaign.

These agreements about command arrangements in Europe were matched by analogous adjustments in the Far East. Now that Japanese invasion of India no longer seemed imminent, the British had come to the conclusion that command of operations against the Japanese in Burma should be separated from the military administration of India. They proposed that a new Allied command for South-East Asia should be created, to operate under the strategic direction of the British Chiefs of Staff in a fashion analogous to the manner in which Nimitz's and MacArthur's commands came under the strategic direction of the U.S. Joint Chiefs of Staff. The Americans were willing enough to agree with the proposal, the more so because the man chosen for the new post, Lord Louis Mountbatten, seemed likely to infuse a new energy into British operations in Burma.[4] They were, however, not prepared to adjust their own anomalous command set-up in the China–Burma–India theatre to accord with the geographic boundaries or chain of command which Lord Louis Mountbatten

[1] Stimson and Bundy: *On Active Service*, pp. 228–30.

[2] Churchill, v. 76; U.S. edition, v. 85; Stimson and Bundy: *On Active Service*, p. 231; Sherwood: *Roosevelt and Hopkins*, p. 758; Eng. edition, ii. 755. Churchill was no more than repeating an offer he had made originally in July 1942 at the time the decision to invade North Africa had been taken. See above, p. 196.

[3] In addition, the eastern Mediterranean, previously separate from Eisenhower's command, was now to be brought under Allied Force Headquarters.

[4] Leahy: *I Was There*, pp. 210–11.

was about to inherit.[1] Instead, General Stilwell was made Deputy Commander to Mountbatten in the new South-East Asia theatre of operations, thus adding yet one more complication to Stilwell's already divided loyalties. The arrangement was obviously makeshift, and did nothing to relieve the quarrels which from the start had disfigured Allied operations in Burma.

Nevertheless, Mountbatten's appointment as Supreme Allied Commander, South-East Asia, completed a neat global balancing of responsibility between British and American commanders. The agreements reached at Quebec entrusted the subordinate theatres of war against both the Germans and the Japanese to British supreme commanders, while command of the major enterprises in the Pacific and in Northern Europe alike was assigned to Americans. The principal commands were all, at least in name, Allied; in fact, however, it was only in the two European theatres that Anglo-American combined command proved genuinely effective.

(3) *The Surrender of Italy*

The First Quebec Conference took up a number of important political issues connected with post-war international organization which will be discussed elsewhere.[2] In addition, it was at this Conference that the American and British Governments drew up their respective formulae for the recognition of the French Committee of National Liberation after failing to reach agreement between themselves;[3] and on 25 August, just as the sessions at Quebec were drawing to a close, Stalin agreed to a meeting of the British, American, and Russian Foreign Ministers as a preliminary to a meeting of the Big Three themselves.[4]

These matters were important, but for the time being they were put in the shade by the political problems presented by developments in Italy. On the day Roosevelt arrived in Quebec, 17 August, the Sicilian campaign ended. The day before, the British Government received news from the

[1] The anomalies of command no more than reflected divergences of strategic view. The British had come to regard the campaign in Burma as the only way they could bring the vast Indian army into operation against the Japanese. The Americans, on the contrary, always put China first, viewing the Burma campaign as a means of re-establishing land communication with that country. Hence, however illogical in fact and unworkable in practice, there were stubborn reasons why Mountbatten's command excluded, while his deputy Stilwell's command included, China.

[2] See below, pp. 323, 326, 330–1.

[3] See above, pp. 260–1.

[4] Stalin had suggested in a telegram of 10 August that a meeting of 'responsible representatives of our states' should take place as a preliminary to a full-dress meeting between himself and Roosevelt and Churchill (Churchill, v. 248; U.S. edition, v. 278). When the First Quebec Conference began, Roosevelt and Churchill tried to persuade Stalin to come to Fairbanks, Alaska, to meet them. Churchill proposed to stay on the American side of the Atlantic until such a meeting could be held, if Stalin would agree to come quickly. But Stalin replied that he could not abandon day-to-day control of the front at a critical time, and proposed instead a meeting of Foreign Ministers (ibid. pp. 248–9 and 278–80 respectively).

Rumours that Stalin had been invited to the Quebec Conference spread widely enough to provoke denials by Tass on 13 August (Rothstein: *Soviet Foreign Policy during the Patriotic War*, i. 271; cf. Ciechanowski: *Defeat in Victory*, p. 208; Hull: *Memoirs*, ii. 1252).

British Ambassador in Madrid that a new Italian envoy, General Castellano, had come to offer Italian help against the Germans. Churchill forwarded this news to Roosevelt as soon as he received it himself, and on 18 August Roosevelt and Churchill authorized Eisenhower to deliver the terms of the 'short' armistice to Castellano.[1] Accordingly, General Bedell Smith and General Kenneth W. D. Strong arrived at the appointed rendezvous in Lisbon on the night of 19 August.[2] The meeting lasted all through the night of 19–20 August.

Castellano's mission was to propose that Italy should change sides in the war and join with the Allies in fighting against the Germans. This offer caught the Anglo-Americans unready. Their surrender terms envisaged Italy as a conquered enemy, not as a future ally. The somersault that Badoglio proposed from one camp to the other presented obvious psychological difficulties not only for the Italians but for the Allied publics as well. Moreover, the problem of securing Allied consensus—in particular, the difficulty of getting Russia's agreement to each step—hampered the negotiation from the Allied side. Confusion, indecision, and a strangely dilatory conduct of affairs on the part of the Italian Government hindered the negotiation even more.

Yet the prospect of Italy's military help against Germany was not something to be lightly cast aside. Churchill and Roosevelt attempted to make the best of the situation by instructing Eisenhower to insist upon the acceptance of the terms of surrender which had been drawn up in advance, but at the same time they sent off a telegram to be shown to General Castellano in which they said: 'These terms do *not* visualise the active assistance of Italy in fighting the Germans. The extent to which the terms will be modified in favour of Italy will depend on how far the Italian Government and people do in fact aid the United Nations against Germany during the remainder of the war.'[3]

At the meeting of 19–20 August, General Smith first declared that he was authorized only to negotiate a military armistice which must be accepted unconditionally. Castellano replied that there was a misunderstanding: he had come not to surrender but to discuss how Italy could join the United Nations against the Germans. This fundamental difference

[1] Churchill, v. 92–95; U.S. edition, v. 103–6.

[2] Castellano travelled nominally as a member of an official party sent from Rome to greet the Italian Ambassador returning from Chile. He merely took advantage of a stop-over in Madrid to inform the British Ambassador of his mission before going on to Lisbon. Castellano's ostensible errand impeded his return to Rome, for the Italian Ambassador from Chile was delayed and Castellano could not plausibly leave Lisbon until he arrived. This was only one of several small incidents which delayed the negotiations; but each obstruction roused suspicion among the Allied negotiators, who feared that the whole affair was a ruse designed to uncover the secret of when and where Allied troops would land in Italy. For a detailed narrative from the Italian side, see Giuseppe Castellano: *Come firmai l'armistizio de Cassibile* (Milan, Mondadori, 1945).

[3] Churchill, v. 94; U.S. edition, v. 105.

could not be resolved, since each was bound by his instructions. The upshot was that Castellano agreed to communicate the terms of surrender to Badoglio together with the mitigating telegram from Churchill and Roosevelt; means for secret radio communication were established; and a second meeting in Sicily was arranged for 31 August.[1]

Castellano returned to Rome on 27 August. After a series of agitated debates the Italian Government—or rather those members of the Cabinet and of the Italian General Staff who were privy to the secret negotiations—drew up a counter-proposal and sent Castellano off to Sicily on 31 August to present it to the Allies. The Italians asked that no less than fifteen Allied divisions be landed in Italy before they announced an armistice, and proposed that most of these troops should land north of Rome. In view of the fact that the Allied plan called for the participation of only five divisions in the initial landings, two in Calabria and three at Salerno, such a proposal was clearly impossible without long preparation and a complete recasting of Allied military plans.[2] Eisenhower was not willing to postpone and transform his plans in accordance with the wishes of the Italian Government; but the Italians clung to their scheme, hoping desperately that Allied arms would safeguard their country from German retaliation and from the devastation of a long war fought over Italian soil.

The Allied negotiators continued to insist upon acceptance of the terms of surrender, but as a result of the conversations of 31 August Eisenhower made an important concession. He agreed that an airborne division might be sent to airfields near Rome in order to help the Italian troops to defend their capital against German units in the neighbourhood.[3] Except for this, however, details of the Allied plan for attacking Italy were kept secret, and no definite indication of the time at which the landings would take place was given to the Italian representatives. In fact, Castellano was given to understand that the Allied attack would be on a much larger scale than was planned for the first assault.[4] Such bluffing and reticence as to timing resulted from the distrust of the real intentions of the Italian Government which still lingered in Allied minds. It had the unfortunate effect of encouraging Badoglio and his advisers to do what they were in any case inclined to do: sit back and wait for the Allies to come and save

[1] Castellano (op. cit. pp. 211–18, Appendix 1) reproduces official minutes of the meeting.

[2] Eisenhower: *Crusade in Europe*, p. 184; Castellano, op. cit. p. 131.

[3] Churchill, v. 97–98; U.S. edition, v. 109; Clark: *Calculated Risk*, pp. 180–1. A statement in the U.S. edition of Churchill (v. 96) that the airborne operation against Rome was part of the original plan for invasion is corrected in the English edition (see p. 85).

A second last-minute change in plans was the decision to embark a division on board naval vessels and land in Taranto harbour, despite the risk of mines and of Italian coastal batteries. This decision was taken only after it had become clear that the Italian fleet would come over to the Allies (cf. Cunningham: *A Sailor's Odyssey*, pp. 563–4).

[4] Howard McGaw Smyth: 'The Armistice of Cassibile', *Military Affairs*, vol. xii, Spring 1948, pp. 12–15; Castellano, op. cit. pp. 142–3; Badoglio: *Italy in the Second World War*, pp. 70–71.

them from the consequences of their double dealing and internal weakness. Expecting a great landing at some indefinite time in the future, the Italians allowed the days to drift past without making preparations to bring their forces to bear against the Germans.

Castellano returned to Rome in the evening of 31 August with the new proposal for an Allied airborne landing. On the following day, 1 September, Badoglio, the King, and the circle of high officials who had taken part in the negotiations agreed that it was necessary to accept the terms which the Allies had offered. A telegram was sent off to Allied Headquarters announcing their decision, and on 2 September Castellano took off by aeroplane again in order to concert Allied and Italian military measures. When he arrived at Allied headquarters General Smith asked whether he was authorized to sign the armistice; Castellano said he was not, and argued that the telegram had provided the necessary basis for co-operation between the Allied Commander-in-Chief and the Italian Government. This immediately roused all the latent suspicion of the Allied negotiators. They wanted a formal, signed document of surrender before they would proceed. Castellano sent a radio message asking for the necessary authority, but Badoglio first replied that the armistice terms had already been 'implicitly' accepted. A few hours later, on 3 September, however, he changed his mind and accorded Castellano formal authority to sign the armistice.[1]

The armistice, accepting the Allied terms of surrender, was signed at once by Castellano on behalf of the Italian Government and by General Smith on behalf of the Allied Commander-in-Chief. It was agreed that the armistice should remain secret until the Allies were ready to land in force on the mainland. (A few hours before the ceremony of signing the first British troops had crossed the Straits of Messina and invaded Calabria; but it was the Allied plan to make the announcement of the armistice coincide with the Salerno landings). The coded radio signal for the announcement of the armistice was to come from General Eisenhower's headquarters; and Castellano promised that Badoglio would announce the armistice at the time indicated by the Allied Commander-in-Chief.

In Sicily, Castellano and Allied officers worked feverishly to prepare the details of the airborne operation. By 5 September the plan had reached Rome. Instructions were also sent for the movement of Italian ships and aircraft after the armistice had been announced. The landing at Salerno was by then only three days in the future. Time for preparation was at best very short. The Italian Government, however, did not realize

[1] Castellano, op. cit. pp. 152–7. Presumably Badoglio's effort to avoid signing the armistice terms was inspired by a hope that he would be able to wring from the Allies more favourable conditions, in accordance with the promise contained in the telegram from Churchill and Roosevelt of 15 August.

how soon the decisive day would come. Castellano had guessed from an ambiguous remark made to him by General Bedell Smith that the Allies did not plan to make their main landing before 10 September, and he estimated that it would come on 12 September. Badoglio and his generals took this guess as gospel, and as a result were most disagreeably surprised when on the morning of 6 September they received intelligence of Allied convoys at sea off Palermo. The location, size, and direction of the convoys soon made it clear to the Italian General Staff that the Allied assault would be smaller and would come farther to the south than they had expected; indeed they were in some doubt as to whether this was the main landing or a second, subsidiary assault of which they had not been told.[1]

The Italians had scarcely begun their preparations to resist the Germans, and the generals in command of the Italian army were by no means united in believing that the Government's turncoat policy was wise, honourable, or practicable. When it became clear that Allied operations were not going to conform to the pattern the Italian high command had expected, when it became obvious that the Allies would land long before the Italians had made ready and would come ashore far to the south of Rome, the Italian Government decided that the armistice announcement would have to be postponed. But Badoglio was in no great hurry to inform Eisenhower of this decision, and refrained from using the radio channels which lay at his command.

Meanwhile, frantic preparation for the airborne landing went ahead in Sicily. In the evening of 7 September, General Maxwell Taylor, second in command of the airborne division which was designated for the landing at Rome, arrived in the Italian capital to concert last-minute plans. To his consternation he discovered that the Italian military authorities were now blandly affirming that the armistice would have to be postponed and the airborne operation put off until Allied troops had arrived within striking distance of Rome. The fact that this violated the terms of surrender which General Castellano had signed on behalf of the Italian Government just four days earlier did not seem to bother the Italians. Indeed Badoglio tried to persuade General Taylor to become his advocate before General Eisenhower. When the American refused, Badoglio reluctantly prepared a telegram himself, as follows:

> Due to changes in the situation brought about by the disposition and strength of the German forces in the Rome area, it is no longer possible to accept an immediate armistice as this could provoke the occupation of the capital and the violent assumption of the Government by the Germans. Operation Giant Two [the airborne attack] is no longer possible because of lack of forces to guarantee the airfields.[2]

[1] Smyth: 'Armistice of Cassibile', loc. cit. pp. 29–30.
[2] Ibid. p. 33.

This telegram, together with another from General Taylor which countermanded the airborne operation, arrived at the Allied headquarters on 8 September, on the morning of the day when Eisenhower had planned the announcement of the armistice. It seemed a clear and unmistakable double cross. Eisenhower, of course, cancelled the airborne attack upon Rome; and replied to Badoglio's telegram with a threat of 'grave consequences' if he did not make a public announcement of the armistice as had first been agreed. In any case, Eisenhower informed him, the Allied radio would broadcast news of the armistice on the afternoon of 8 September, a step which would deprive Badoglio of any hope of keeping peace with the Germans.[1]

Eisenhower's telegram and the progress of events, so rapid, so unforeseen, and so catastrophic for Italy, completely destroyed the morale and effective power of the Italian Government. After Eisenhower's announcement of the armistice agreement had been made on the radio, Badoglio had no choice left. If he kept silent, the Germans would surely get rid of him and deal with him as a traitor. His only hope lay with the Allies. As a result, an hour and a half after Eisenhower's proclamation had been released, Badoglio spoke over the Rome radio to confirm the armistice. His words were no stirring call to arms against the Germans, but bore on their surface the mark of his half-heartedness. He said:

> The Italian Government, recognizing the impossibility of continuing the unequal struggle against the overwhelming power of the enemy . . . has requested an armistice. . . . This request has been granted. The Italian forces will therefore cease all acts of hostility against the Anglo-American forces whereever they may be met. They will, however, oppose attack from any quarter.[2]

Badoglio's words must have sounded strangely contradictory to the Italian troops who heard them. Who exactly was the enemy? And what were the orders of the Italian Government? Except for the Italian navy, which sailed, as instructed, to Allied ports as soon as the armistice was announced, it appears that the Italians had no effective plan of action. Individual commanders were left to decide for themselves what to do in the crisis which suddenly faced them.

A few hours after Eisenhower and Badoglio had announced Italy's surrender, the first Allied troops under the command of General Mark Clark reached the Salerno beaches. They found themselves opposed by alert German forces. At first the landings went well, however, and it was not until 12 September that German counter-attacks were launched in strength. Long before that Italian military might on the mainland of Italy had disintegrated. By the early hours of the morning of 9 September,

[1] Eisenhower: *Crusade in Europe*, p. 186.

[2] Texts of the armistice proclamations may be found in *Documents on American Foreign Relations, 1943–1944*, pp. 169–70.

it became apparent that Italian troops were nowhere able to hold their own against the Germans. Indeed, with a few exceptions, the Italians did not even try to resist German threats and demands but meekly allowed themselves to be disarmed or herded into barracks.[1]

Realizing that Rome would soon be occupied by German troops, Badoglio and the King fled from the capital about 4.30 a.m. on 9 September. They succeeded in making their way safely to Brindisi, where they came within Allied lines. But whatever reality the Badoglio Government had once had evaporated in the course of the twenty-four hours following the armistice announcement. Few of the Ministers escaped with Badoglio and the King; the army dissolved, or was captured by the Germans; and the administration became utterly disorganized. Badoglio and his sovereign arrived in Brindisi more as refugees than as rulers of anything or anybody.

While these momentous events were taking place in Italy, Churchill was at work in Washington trying hard to mollify American opposition to the full exploitation of the new military opportunities opened by Badoglio's volte-face. He had high hopes not only of taking Rome and establishing a battle line against the Germans somewhere in northern Italy, but also of compelling the Germans to withdraw from the southern part of the Balkan peninsula to the Save and Danube river line. If the twenty-four Italian divisions then stationed in the Balkan area joined the Greek and Yugoslav guerrilla forces, and if Turkey could be persuaded either to declare war on Germany or to allow British air forces to use bases on Turkish soil, it seemed unlikely that the Germans would be able to maintain their position in the Balkans, however vehemently Hitler might wish to do so. Defection of German satellites like Bulgaria, Rumania, and Hungary might well be expected if all went well and if the Allies seized the immediate opportunity resolutely.[2] But full exploitation of the Italian collapse depended upon winning American approval for a more active policy in the Mediterranean. In particular, withdrawals of forces and landing craft according to the agreed schedule would have

[1] Away from the mainland of Italy, where German counter action could not in the nature of things come so rapidly, some Italian units resisted (in Cephallonia, for example) or even succeeded in overpowering German detachments (as in Sardinia). It was more than a month before the Germans were able to stabilize the situation in Greece and Yugoslavia where Italians had provided the main Axis garrisons. Some of the Italian divisions in that area surrendered not to the Germans but to Allied liaison officers assigned to guerrilla headquarters. The windfall of arms and supplies which the surrender of Italian units thus brought to Tito and to the Greek guerrillas greatly enlarged the scale of their subsequent activity. The Germans could no longer spare adequate forces for garrison duty, and as a result day-to-day control over large sections of both Greece and Yugoslavia passed permanently into guerrilla hands.

[2] Churchill, v. 114–15, 120–1; U.S. edition, v. 128–9, 135–6.

to be cancelled; and this, of course, implied postponement of Overlord by a few weeks or months.[1]

The showdown came on 9 September 1943. On that day Roosevelt arranged a meeting with the Combined Chiefs of Staff[2] in order to hear Churchill's arguments for a revision of the agreements which had been made at Trident and confirmed (with modifications) at Quebec. Clearly it was a time for decision. Events were moving very rapidly in Italy, and if the Allies were to seize all the advantages which Churchill's sanguine imagination spread before them, then action would have to be both resolute and rapid. At the same time, Churchill knew that the more spacious the opportunities, the more suspicious Marshall would become. The Prime Minister therefore presented only his minimum programme for exploitation of the Italian surrender. Thus Churchill was at pains to repudiate any thought of 'whittling down Overlord' and refrained from challenging afresh the agreement whereby seven divisions were to be withdrawn from the Mediterranean in order to strengthen the invasion of France. Churchill suggested that the advance into Italy should stop short of the Po valley in order to avoid lengthening the front, and he placed any possible Balkan operations far in the future, arguing that when once a defence line had been set up across northern Italy it might prove possible to spare some troops for action east of the Adriatic.[3]

These proposals did not add up to any very drastic change in plans already agreed upon. But the Americans were highly suspicious, fearing that any change in plan might prove an opening wedge for a complete reversal of Anglo-American strategy such as had come in 1942 when Churchill's Torch was substituted for the American Sledgehammer. Hence

[1] Churchill, v. pp. 188–9, 254–5; U.S. edition, v. 211–12, 286.

[2] Except for Lord Ismay, the British Chiefs of Staff had returned to England. Their place was therefore taken by their regular deputies. But the men who really mattered, Marshall, Leahy, King, and Arnold, were all on hand (ibid. pp. 118 and 133, respectively).

[3] Ibid. pp. 119–21 and 134–7, respectively. The American Chiefs of Staff, of course, believed that by insisting upon Overlord they were advocating a strategy that would shorten the war and lessen the cost of victory. To their minds, any and all operations in the Mediterranean still left the heart of German power untouched, and thus merely postponed decisive action.

Two points should be borne in mind when trying to understand the collision of views which occurred. For one thing, the Americans regularly suspected ulterior, i.e. political, motives in Churchill's strategy, and this almost automatically damned his proposals in their eyes, since the American Chiefs of Staff felt that they should not allow themselves to use American resources to buttress British imperial interests in the Mediterranean or anywhere else. A second important point is this: American resources were so ample that American military tradition tended to support a policy of taking the war to the enemy according to a definite plan, more or less without regard to local helps or hindrances. A tradition of improvisation, taking advantage of any and every opening that might turn up, found a far warmer welcome in British military thought. This was no more than appropriate to a nation whose resources had long been incommensurate with its world-wide interests. The divergence made the Americans seem sometimes stupidly rigid to their British colleagues, while the British occasionally seemed devious and undependable to the Americans.

Marshall and his colleagues were not to be moved. For them Overlord came first, and they would not agree to any change in the scheduled build-up for that operation. Nothing needed for Overlord, according to Marshall's view, should be retained in the Mediterranean, no matter how enticing the newly opened opportunities might seem. As far as he and his American colleagues were concerned, the exploitation of the Italian collapse would have to be limited to what the forces already earmarked for the Mediterranean could accomplish. The only new enterprise which was approved as a result of the meeting of 9 September was a British effort to take the Dodecanese Islands; and even for this the Americans would not agree to delay the departure of landing craft or in any other way to trench upon men and resources assigned to Overlord and Burma by their earlier plans.[1] A second meeting, which took place in Roosevelt's absence on 11 September, had an almost equally unsatisfactory result from Churchill's point of view. Marshall did agree that the rate at which reinforcements were being brought up for the battle in Italy should be increased,[2] but he continued to resist any departure from the plans for the disposition of Anglo-American resources which had been agreed to before the surrender of Italy had so dramatically changed the balance of forces in the Mediterranean.

After this rebuff, Churchill's bolt was spent, at least for the time being. The Allied commanders in the Mediterranean would have to do what they could with the diminishing forces already under their control. The Prime Minister fell back upon urgent injunctions to Generals Wilson and Alexander to be bold, even rash, in the hope of winning great advantages with relatively small forces; and he promptly set in train arrangements for his return to London. He departed from Halifax, Canada, on 14 September.[3]

[1] Churchill, v. 102; U.S. edition, v. 114. The Americans even opposed making a new effort to bring Turkey into the war, believing that the Turks would need help on a scale to endanger the preparations for Overlord (General Sir H. Maitland Wilson [afterwards Field Marshal Lord Wilson of Libya]: *Eight Years Overseas, 1939–1947* (London, Hutchinson, 1950), pp. 179–80; Leahy: *I Was There*, p. 225).

[2] Churchill, v. 122; U.S. edition, v. 138.

[3] Churchill glosses over the friction between himself and the Americans during this period, and even interprets the second session with the Combined Chiefs of Staff at which he presided on 11 September as a compliment paid him by Roosevelt. Yet Roosevelt's decision to depart for Hyde Park instead of staying in Washington should probably be interpreted as signifying his unwillingness to hear more of Churchill's arguments. The President had come more and more to the opinion that Marshall was right in pressing for Overlord at all costs (Stimson and Bundy: *On Active Service*, p. 231). Indeed, Roosevelt seems to have felt a growing suspicion of Churchill's political motivation in arguing for Balkan and Mediterranean operations, and may also have felt that the British were not quite playing the game in seeking to reopen questions which the Americans regarded as already settled. There are indications in Churchill's own account of strain between himself and Roosevelt during this time (v. 78, 188–9; U.S. edition, v. 88, 211–13). On the eve of Tehrān, however, Roosevelt veered once again towards a more sympathetic view of possible Balkan operations; but seems to have done so under the impression that the Russians desired such a course. See below, p. 341.

(4) *Political Settlement in Italy*

Churchill's failure to convince the Americans of the wisdom of his military plans was a severe blow to the Prime Minister, but he could find some comfort from the fashion in which he and Roosevelt agreed to manage Italian political affairs. In the first days of confusion after the armistice, political and civil questions received scant attention. Everything turned on the battle at Salerno, which, for a few days, seemed to threaten disaster for the Allies. After some difficult moments, however, air superiority, naval supporting fire, and the approach of General Montgomery's Eighth Army from Calabria (where it had landed on 3 September) restored the situation for General Clark's Fifth Army. On 16 September the Fifth and Eighth Armies made contact with each other; two weeks later Naples fell and the Germans withdrew northward to form a front across the peninsula. The port of Naples and the air bases near Foggia, which had been the two first goals of Allied strategy, were thus won by the beginning of October. But the larger hope of winning all Italy south of the Appenines, or at least as far north as Rome, had not been realized.

When the military crisis of the first days passed, the problem of what to do with Badoglio and his Government became a matter for decision at the highest Allied level. Badoglio had three things on his side. One was the armistice itself. The Allies had thereby entered into official relations with him and could not easily repudiate his services. A second point in Badoglio's favour was the fact that nearly the whole of the Italian fleet had surrendered upon his orders. This quite changed the world balance of naval forces, freed British and American ships from duty in the Mediterranean for service elsewhere, and added a number of useful vessels of war to the Allied command. Finally, a factor of great importance was Churchill's conviction that monarchy was best for Italy; and support of the monarchy could only take the form of support of the King's choice as first Minister, Marshal Badoglio.[1]

The armistice of 3 September was limited to military matters. It bound Italy to withdraw her armed forces from the war, gave the Allied Commander-in-Chief authority to establish military government over any part of Italy, and specifically stated that at a later time political, economic, and financial conditions would be prescribed with which the Italian Government would be bound to comply.[2] The collapse of Badoglio's Government

[1] Churchill, v. 167–8; U.S. edition, v. 189. For comments on Churchill's attitude, see Sherwood: *Roosevelt and Hopkins*, p. 743; Eng. edition, ii. 739; Hull: *Memoirs*, ii. 1550.

[2] Text of the armistice may be found in Great Britain, Foreign Office: *Documents relating to the Conditions of an Armistice with Italy (September–November 1943)*, Cmd. 6693 (London, H.M.S.O., 1945); U.S.A., Department of State: *United States and Italy 1936–1946*, Pub. 2669 (Washington, U.S.G.P.O., 1946), pp. 51–52. [This volume is referred to hereafter as *United States and Italy*.]

made it impossible for him to fulfil all the terms of the armistice, and, had the Allies wished, they would have been able on that ground to repudiate him.

But the Allies did not so wish. On 10 September Churchill and Roosevelt sent a very friendly and encouraging joint message to Badoglio from Washington. The language has a clear Churchillian ring:

> It has fallen to you in the hour of your country's agony to take the first decisive steps to win peace and freedom for the Italian people and to win back for Italy an honourable place in the civilization of Europe.
>
> You have already freed your country from Fascist servitude. There remains the even more important task of cleansing the Italian soil from the German invaders. . . . Strike hard and strike home. Have faith in your future. All will come well. March forward with your American and British friends in the great world movement towards Freedom, Justice, and Peace.[1]

This message was sent before the full extent of the collapse of Badoglio's Government had become clear; but it arrived at the time when Badoglio's fortunes were at their lowest, and had the effect of confirming Allied support for his claim to head the Government of Italy.

But vague recognition of the King and Badoglio as heads of the Government of Italy did not solve the many problems of Italian administration. What would be the status of military government? What would Russia's part in Allied direction of Italian affairs amount to? What should be done with the 'long' armistice which had been so painstakingly drawn up by advance consultation between the three Allied Governments?

The prime factor in the development of Allied policy towards Italy in the weeks immediately after the armistice was an agreement reached privately between Churchill and Roosevelt according to which the British would take the lead in Italian affairs. This agreement was made either at the First Quebec Conference, or in the days immediately afterwards when Churchill stayed on in Washington in order to concert Italian policy with Roosevelt.[2] This arrangement was a counterpart to the agreement which had entrusted the lead in French North Africa to the Americans, but in neither case did the agreements assign complete and exclusive control of affairs to one of the Allies. Consultation still preceded every important move.

The Russians, of course, were not directly concerned with what happened in Italy, but Stalin nevertheless wished to have some part in Allied counsels. From the beginning Churchill and Roosevelt made an effort to

[1] Text may be found in *United States and Italy*, p. 68.

[2] Hull (*Memoirs*, ii. 1557) merely says that the agreement was made 'in their [i.e. Roosevelt's and Churchill's] early discussions concerning Italy'; but it seems clear that the joint message of 10 September quoted above was the fruit, perhaps the first fruit, of the agreement (cf. Leahy: *I Was There*, p. 311). Churchill himself does not refer to any such agreement directly, but some of the phrases in his telegrams to Roosevelt imply it (e.g. Churchill, v. 440; U.S. edition, v. 498).

keep him informed of their dealings with the Italians, and his approval of major steps was regularly solicited. In general, Stalin accepted Anglo-American proposals without quarrelling. He did, however, insist upon Russia's right to rank among the victors over Italy.[1] Yet it was not a part of Churchill's plans for Italy to accord the Russians an equal share with British and American officials in directing Allied policy in that country. British and American arms had won the victory. It seemed no more than right that Britain and America should exercise a corresponding preponderance.

The upshot of these cross pressures was an essentially awkward compromise. On 29 September 1943 Eisenhower presented the 'long' armistice to Badoglio for signature. Badoglio resented its terms, but he was helpless and had to conform to the demand made upon him. Despite the fact that the document was largely obsolete, it did serve to establish a legal basis for the authority of the Allied Commander-in-Chief in Italy.[2] This was perhaps the major reason why the Allied Governments insisted upon the solemn enactment of the farce whereby Badoglio was made to sign undertakings respecting the whole of Italy which he could not possibly honour.[3]

The terms of the 'long' armistice were certainly harsh. The Allied Commander-in-Chief was given sweeping legislative and economic powers. For example, he had the right to invalidate existing laws and to demand any payment of reparations and occupation costs which pleased him. The arrest of war criminals and the removal of all Fascists from office was also prescribed, along with the dissolution of fascist organizations. By these and like provisions, the Italian Government were bound hand and foot, and made completely subject to the will of the Allied Governments as expressed through the Allied Commander-in-Chief.[4]

The question of the machinery through which the will of the Allied Governments would be enforced was not made clear by the 'long' armistice. Article 37 merely said: 'There will be appointed a Control Commission representative of the United Nations charged with regulating and

[1] Churchill, v. 83–84, 98, 99, 171–5; U.S. edition, v. 93–94, 110, 111, 192–7.

[2] Article 21 provided that 'the United Nations will exercise all the rights of an occupying power' and declared that 'personnel of the Italian administrative, judicial, and public services will carry out their functions under the control of the Allied Commander-in-Chief unless otherwise directed'.

[3] Churchill, v. 168–9; U.S. edition, v. 190.

[4] Two gestures were made to remove a part of the sting. As soon as Badoglio had signed the 'long' armistice, Eisenhower handed him a letter which said, in part: 'It is to be understood that the terms both of this document and of the short military armistice of September 3rd may be modified from time to time if military necessity or the extent of co-operation by the Italian Government indicates this as desirable' (*United States and Italy*, p. 64).

The first such change was the elimination of the phrase 'Unconditional Surrender' from the official text of the 'long' armistice. Badoglio had particularly objected to the inclusion of these words, and on 9 November 1943 the Allies met his wishes while salvaging the slogan by inserting 'unconditionally' in the preamble, when it appeared in a context less obnoxious to Italian feeling.

executing this instrument under the orders and general direction of the Allied Commander-in-Chief.' This obviously left the matter of Russian participation in Allied control of Italy entirely open. Negotiation over the question took considerable time, and it was only on 10 November that an Allied Control Commission was formally constituted. This Commission was Anglo-American; and the Russians agreed to its establishment only after place for a second body, the Advisory Council for Italy, had been found.[1] The original members of the Council were Britain, America, Russia, and the French Committee of National Liberation; but provision was also made for the subsequent admission of Greece and Yugoslavia to membership.[2]

As a result of these agreements three distinct bodies divided Allied responsibility in Italy: Allied Military Government, the Control Commission, and the Advisory Council. Of the three, the Control Commission was from the start the most important as far as relations with Badoglio's Government were concerned. But in the early days Badoglio's Government was largely a legal figment. Day-by-day local activities of Allied Military Government were of more importance for Italians. The problem of the relationship between Military Government and the Control Commission was solved in January 1944 by the merger of the top personnel of the two organizations. Thereafter it became impossible for the two to follow divergent policies as had happened at first; and in practice the division of function between them became fairly clear and simple. Military Government controlled civilian affairs immediately behind the battle line, while the Control Commission supervised the Italian Government's administration of areas farther in the rear.[3]

The Advisory Council for Italy was powerless and of negligible importance from the start. For one thing, its seat was at Algiers, where information about events in Italy could only be had at second-hand; for another, it was the policy of the British and American Governments to keep the Advisory Council far out on the wings of all real decisions and debates. It did not take the Russians and French long to grasp the facts. Accordingly, new demands for their participation in Allied control of Italy were lodged with the British and American Governments. In January 1944 a minor concession was made. A Russian and a French General were accorded the rights of 'observers' on the Control Commission, thus at

[1] The agreement to establish an Advisory Council for Italy was reached during the meeting of Foreign Ministers in Moscow at the end of October 1943 (see below, p. 332). A communiqué of 1 November 1943 announced the establishment of the Advisory Council *before* the Control Commission formally came into existence. For Russian objections to the proposed set-up in Italy see Deane: *Strange Alliance*, p. 300.

[2] The Foreign Ministers' communiqué may be found in *United States and Italy*, pp. 72–74.

[3] Hajo Holborn: *American Military Government, Its Organization and Policies* (Washington, Infantry Journal Press, 1947), p. 20.

least assuring their respective home authorities of access to information about what was done in Italy. But executive power remained securely in British and American hands.[1]

The pattern of Allied control over Italy which thus finally emerged lasted until the end of the war. It was of importance not only for Italy itself, but as a model for other armistice régimes in ex-enemy countries of Eastern Europe. Having excluded Russia from any but nominal participation in Italian affairs, the Western Powers prepared the way for their own exclusion from any but a marginal share in the affairs of Eastern Europe. No other arrangement, of course, conformed to the real distribution of military power and responsibility, or could have been compatible with the mutual distrust which lay close to the surface in Anglo-Russian and, less obviously, in the background of Russo-American relations.

A cardinal element in Churchill's policy towards Badoglio and the King was his desire to build up their power and prestige in Italy. Immediately after Italy's surrender, the Allies, and particularly Churchill, were anxious to persuade the Italian Government to declare war on Germany. The reason was that Churchill believed a declaration of war in the name of the King of Italy would rally the support of Italian army officers to the Allied side against Germany. Since important Italian garrisons continued to exist in such places as the Dodecanese Islands, Sardinia, Corsica, and the Ionian Islands, there was a good deal to be gained if the local Italian commanders could be persuaded to join wholeheartedly in war against Germany.[2]

Accordingly, on 23 September 1943 the Combined Chiefs of Staff instructed Eisenhower to admit Italy to 'co-belligerency' if the King would declare war on Germany. But the King and Badoglio hung back. They hoped to wring various concessions (e.g. the cancellation of the 'long' armistice, which had not yet been signed) in return for a declaration of war.[3] In the end, however, the Italian Government were persuaded that any future concessions would come only after a declaration of war. Accordingly on 13 October 1943 the King and his Government declared war against Germany. Badoglio issued a proclamation to the Italian people in which he ordered all Italian forces to fight the Germans 'to the

[1] Nominally British and American participation in the Control Commission was equal; in fact the British, in accordance with the Churchill–Roosevelt agreement, tended to predominate. This was partly because with the turn of the year Eisenhower relinquished his command to a British general. It was also partly due to the British practice of appointing higher ranking officers (or promoting them if they lacked seniority over their American counterparts) to the Control Commission and its connected organizations.

[2] Wilson: *Eight Years Overseas*, p. 178.

[3] Churchill, v. 168–9; U.S. edition, v. 190–1; Leahy: *I Was There*, pp. 216–17.

last man'—an order which they conspicuously failed to obey—and continued: 'The Government headed by me will shortly be completed. In order that it may constitute a true expression of democratic government in Italy, the representatives of every political party will be asked to participate. The present arrangement will in no way impair the untrammelled right of the people of Italy to choose their own form of democratic government when peace is restored.'[1] Simultaneously a joint statement by Roosevelt, Churchill, and Stalin was published which accorded the Italians the rather nebulous status of co-belligerent, but warned them that 'the relationship of co-belligerency . . . cannot of itself affect the terms recently signed, which retain their full force and can only be adjusted by agreement between the allied governments in the light of the assistance which the Italian Government may be able to afford to the United Nations' cause'.[2]

When Badoglio attempted to bring representatives of liberal and leftist Italian political groups into his Cabinet, in accordance with his proclamation of 13 October, he ran into difficulties. Republicanism was strong among these groups, and they demanded the abdication of the King. But the King was unwilling to resign his powers, and the British Government, equally, did not wish to see the monarchy abolished, though at least some British officials thought that Crown Prince Umberto was a more promising bearer of royal responsibility than was his father, King Victor Emmanuel. As a result of the impasse on the question of the monarchy, *pourparlers* came to nothing and were broken off on 31 October.[3] Badoglio fell back upon a Cabinet of technicians. This was regarded as a temporary expedient, subject to revision as soon as Rome had been taken. When Rome did not fall, growing agitation among the politicians of Italy, centring round the question of the future status of the King, could not be repressed. The result was that issues of internal Italian politics became an irritation to Allied relations in 1944 just as French political feuds in North Africa had troubled Anglo-American co-operation in 1943.

(5) *Repulse in the Aegean*

The net results of Allied action and negotiation in Italy conformed reasonably well to what Churchill had desired. His best hope of pushing the front far to the north of Rome had been disappointed; on the other hand, Anglo-American troops were firmly committed to a major campaign in Italy which could be counted upon to weaken German strength in North-Western Europe. But the partial success of his plans in Italy

[1] *United States and Italy*, p. 70. For an account of some of the Allied negotiations which produced this action by the Italian Government see Churchill, v. 167–75, 177–8; U.S. edition, v. 189–97, 200–1.

[2] *United States and Italy*, p. 71.

[3] This failure led Roosevelt to consider getting rid of Badoglio, but Churchill came to the rescue (Churchill, v. 178; U.S. edition, v. 201).

was not matched farther east. Instead, Churchill's hopes for the eastern Mediterranean and the Balkans went sadly askew.

As soon as the Combined Chiefs of Staff had approved an attack on the Dodecanese Islands (9 September)[1] General Wilson, Commander-in-Chief, Middle East, was ordered to attack them boldly with the makeshift forces at his disposal. Rhodes appeared to be too formidable to seize without larger resources than Wilson could spare, but small parties of British troops were put ashore on Cos and Leros and other nearby islands in the Aegean on 18 September 1943. The position of these troops was very precarious. Without the use of Turkish airfields on the mainland, it was impossible for the Royal Air Force to provide satisfactory air cover, whereas the Germans could easily dominate the air from bases in Crete and Greece. The British, therefore, found themselves fighting under the conditions of 1940 all over again, and with the same result. On 3 October the Germans recovered Cos by means of a parachute attack—a feat which was not very difficult since the Italians displayed a fine impartiality, failing to resist the Germans as they had failed to resist the British battalion two weeks earlier. On 7 October, however, a British naval detachment intercepted and destroyed an armada of German troop-carrying vessels near the island of Stampalia. This severe set-back to the Germans established a precarious balance between British and German forces in the eastern Aegean which lasted for the next few weeks.

It was clear that, if disaster were to be averted, additional forces were needed in the Dodecanese. The only place they could come from was the central Mediterranean. Accordingly Churchill vigorously set out to try to persuade Eisenhower to divert some of the troops earmarked for Italy to the Dodecanese, where he hoped to be able to capture Rhodes and thus make Leros secure. To explore this possibility, a conference was held on 10 October 1943 between General Wilson and the commanders of the Mediterranean theatre of operations. The meeting came at an inopportune moment, for it had just become apparent that the Germans were willing and able to maintain themselves in southern Italy indefinitely. As a result, it was decided that no forces could be spared from Italy.[2]

Even this set-back did not entirely daunt the Prime Minister. One last card turned up in October, when the Russians took the lead in suggesting, at the meeting of the Foreign Ministers in Moscow, that steps should be taken to bring Turkey into the war.[3] Here was a last chance to get succour to the isolated British force on Leros, and, after some hesitation,

[1] See above, p. 305.

[2] Eisenhower: *Crusade in Europe*, pp. 190–1; Wilson: *Eight Years Overseas*, pp. 176–8; Churchill, v. 192–4; U.S. edition, v. 216–18.

[3] Churchill, v. 254; U.S. edition, v. 285. For the Moscow Conference see below, pp. 328–30.

Churchill decided to take advantage of it.[1] On or before 4 November Roosevelt acceded to the combined Russian and British pressure and agreed to support efforts to get the Turks to declare war on Germany before the end of 1943.[2] But it was already too late. Eden's efforts to persuade the Turks to allow British planes to use their airfields were unsuccessful, and the British forces in the Dodecanese Islands were left without air support.[3] As a result, the Germans were able on 12 November to attack the principal British force in the area, stationed on the island of Leros. Four days later the island was theirs. In the following days remnants of the British troops which had been committed to the enterprise were evacuated or made their way to the Turkish mainland. Thus by the middle of November 1943 the Germans had been able to recover from the blow dealt them by the Italian collapse, and had restored their south-eastern flank. Churchill's hopes for the Balkans and eastern Mediterranean had come to disaster.

(iv) Post-War Planning and Preparation in 1943

After the battles of Alamein, Stalingrad, Guadalcanal, and the landing in North Africa, the Allies could confidently look forward to a victorious end of the war, even though the time and circumstances of German and Japanese surrender were still hidden in the future. In 1942 the problem of how to put together the pieces into which the world had been shattered by war had been more or less academic; but by 1943 it assumed a growing urgency. There were two aspects to the problem. One was short-range: post-war relief and rehabilitation could hardly be left to chance, individual initiative, and the operations of the free market. The economic activity of all the combatant nations had been so harnessed to war that no normal, automatic return to the economic relations of peace time could be expected; moreover, wide areas of Europe and Asia had suffered or might soon be expected to suffer devastation at the hands of warring armies. With communications disrupted, monetary systems discredited, raw materials unavailable, and factories destroyed, it seemed obvious that economic breakdown and widespread starvation would follow upon the victory of the Allies unless systematic relief and rehabilitation were promptly provided by the victors.

This problem had long been foreseen. As early as August 1940 Churchill had promised that the British Government would undertake relief in liberated Europe, and he set up a special inter-departmental committee under the headship of Sir Frederick Leith-Ross to buy up agricultural and other

[1] Churchill, v. 256–7; U.S. edition, v. 288–9. Churchill's hesitation arose from the unfavourable turn of the battle in Italy, which now seemed to require all available resources.

[2] Hull: *Memoirs*, ii. 1369; Leahy: *I Was There*, p. 225.

[3] Hull, loc. cit.; Wilson: *Eight Years Overseas*, p. 181.

surpluses for future relief distribution. As the war spread and intensified, however, surpluses mostly disappeared, and with the change in the situation which resulted from American and Russian entry into the war, a new approach to post-war relief and rehabilitation was obviously called for. In November 1942 the United States established an organization similar to the Leith-Ross Committee to plan post-war relief. This organization, known as O.F.R.R.O. (Office of Foreign Relief and Rehabilitation Operations), was headed by Herbert Lehman, former Governor of the state of New York.

But a national approach to relief problems was clearly inadequate, if only because competitive buying would unnecessarily raise prices. As early as February 1942 preliminary plans for the establishment of an international body to administer relief were advanced. Various suggestions were made by the British, Russian, and American Governments. In August 1942 efforts to harmonize them produced the first of a series of draft constitutions for an international relief agency. By May 1943 the three principal Allies and China had reached preliminary agreement, and the text of the proposed constitution for UNRRA was then distributed to forty other Allied and associated nations for comment and criticism. By September 1943 some minor modifications had been made in the light of suggestions from the smaller Powers, and the result, the Draft UNRRA Agreement, was made public on 24 September 1943. It was duly signed by representatives of all the United Nations on 9 November 1943 in the White House.[1]

The UNRRA Agreement provided for the establishment of an international administrative body to distribute relief supplies in the post-war period; but many points, including the all-important question of finance, were left to be decided at the First Session of the UNRRA Council. This took place at Atlantic City, New Jersey, 10 November–1 December 1943. No fewer than forty-four nations were represented, making it by far the most impressive international conference which had assembled since the beginning of the war.[2] The UNRRA Council was able to arrive at a series of important agreements. It decided that each contributing nation should make approximately one per cent. of the national income available to UNRRA for procurement of relief supplies. It decided that distribution within the nations receiving benefits should not be regulated by the length of private individuals' purses, and that any discrimination on the basis of

[1] United Nations Relief and Rehabilitation Administration, Office of the Chief Historian, George Woodbridge: *UNRRA: The History of the United Nations Relief and Rehabilitation Administration*, 3 vols. (New York, Columbia University Press, 1950), i. 3–14. [This work is referred to hereafter as Woodbridge: *UNRRA*, i, ii, iii.] An account of the establishment and activities of *UNRRA* will be found in the *Survey* for 1939–46: *The Realignment of Europe*.

[2] It was not the first such gathering, however. The United Nations Conference on Food and Agriculture was held at Hot Springs, Virginia, from 8 May to 3 June 1943. As a result of its deliberations, that Conference recommended the establishment of a permanent international body in the field of food and agriculture.

creed, race, or political belief would not be allowed. Countries that had foreign exchange sufficient to pay for UNRRA supplies would be required to do so; those which could not pay were to receive supplies just the same without incurring debt. Finally, Herbert Lehman was elected Director-General of the new organization.[1]

A point of some difficulty was the relationship which should exist between UNRRA and military authorities in the field. In the areas where American forces would operate, Roosevelt decided on 10 November 1943 that military organizations would be responsible for relief work for approximately the first six months after the liberation of any particular district or country, and that UNRRA would only take over responsibility afterwards. The British concurred, and, as a result of these decisions, all Anglo-American Headquarters established a Civil Affairs division (actually a similar set-up had already been developed in North Africa under Eisenhower) which undertook responsibility for relief and other dealings with the civilian populations of liberated and conquered countries.[2]

The establishment of UNRRA and of military organizations for relief work could reasonably be expected to cope with the immediate post-liberation problems of Europe and Asia. But the other aspect of the post-war problem lay far outside their scope. What would be the future relationship between the members of the United Nations? In particular, what would be the future of the Grand Alliance? What would be done with Germany, Italy, and Japan, the defeated enemies? What safeguards could be created to prevent a future war? Questions such as these touched upon conflicts of interest and policy among the Allies themselves—conflicts which were largely submerged for the time being by the overriding necessity of co-operating against Hitler, but which nevertheless remained, sometimes not far below the surface, to trouble Allied harmony.

Both the Russian and the American Governments treasured an ideal pattern for the establishment of a peaceful, productive, and happy world. The American scheme called for a world composed of liberal, independent, and democratic states, modelled roughly upon parliamentary democracy as it had developed in America, Britain, and Western Europe. Many Americans believed that such a world would exhibit a natural harmony of interests. Since no people liked war, if the people could *really* control their governments, there would be no more war, and disputes as they arose could be settled by legal procedure and publicity through a new and improved League of Nations. When a people were misled by evil leaders, men like Roosevelt and Hull argued, force would have to be used—a police force which by its very existence might well discourage potential aggressors and

[1] Woodbridge: *UNRRA*, i. 28–32.

[2] Ibid. pp. 23–24.

could therefore assure peace, if not for ever, at least for a long time to come.

The Russian Government's blueprint for a good world prescribed proletarian revolution and the abolition of capitalist exploiting classes. The Revolution would, according to Marxian doctrine, establish world peace, since the sole cause of war was capitalist wickedness. But the Communist world crusade was already somewhat shopworn; and Stalin had found it prudent to suppress revolutionary propaganda during the war. Russian leaders may still have hoped for revolution in parts of Europe and Asia, but they probably no longer expected world revolution in the near future.[1] Certainly they made no serious attempt in 1943 to act upon the Communist blue-print. The Russians therefore left the field of post-war planning on the grand scale to the Americans.

Great Britain could not accept the American scheme wholeheartedly, for it involved the early liquidation of the British Empire. Still less could the British accept the Russian Communist remedy for the ills of the world. The power of the two vast nation-states, America and Russia, each newly aware of its strength and full of self-confidence, clearly surpassed Britain's unaided strength; and the British Government saw their post-war problem primarily in terms of salvaging as much of Britain's influence, wealth, and power as circumstances would permit. As in the United States, many people in Britain hoped that world-wide co-operation within a liberal framework would be possible in the post-war period; but, as a second best, senior officials of the Foreign Office and men like Churchill always kept in mind the alternative of agreement among the Great Powers to divide the world into spheres of influence.

British foreign policy was thus directed to two principal goals. The first was an effort to come to a global understanding with America and, if possible, with Russia; the second, an effort to consolidate British influence in Western Europe and the Mediterranean. British support for de Gaulle was motivated largely by the wish to see a strong government ready to take over the administration of France as soon as it was liberated from German control: a government which might be expected to show a modicum of gratitude to Great Britain and which might help to provide a counterweight on the Continent to the Russian colossus.[2] Similarly, the persistent penchant for operations in the Mediterranean, which the British Chiefs of Staff and the Prime Minister so regularly evinced, was no doubt connected with their wish to see British forces and friendly governments established round its shores.[3]

[1] Cf. Molotov's statement to Hull at the Moscow Conference (Hull: *Memoirs*, ii. 1289).

[2] Churchill, iv. 717; U.S. edition, iv. 803; Sherwood: *Roosevelt and Hopkins*, p. 721; Eng. edition, ii. 719; Pendar: *Adventure in Diplomacy*, p. 171.

[3] Churchill, iv. 642; U.S. edition, iv. 716; Hull: *Memoirs*, ii. 1231; Leahy: *I Was There*, pp. 176, 190; Eisenhower: *Crusade in Europe*, p. 194. This is not to say that the British strategists did not have purely military objections to alternative employment of their forces. They did; but

For all the faith that Roosevelt and Hull put in a global understanding with Britain and Russia as the fundamental key to a satisfactory post-war settlement, the United States, too, devoted considerable attention to building for herself a sphere of influence. The fact that Americans did not call their activities by such a name obscured from their own eyes much of what they did. Secretary of State Cordell Hull found it possible to say, quite sincerely, in a speech to Congress upon his return from the Moscow Conference of Foreign Ministers: '... There will no longer be need for spheres of influence, for alliances, for balance of power, or any other of the special arrangements through which, in the unhappy past, the nations strove to safeguard their security or promote their interests.'[1] Such words must have seemed hypocritical to the Russians, and perhaps also to the British. They had the actions of the United States in Latin America and China before their eyes. But the fact remained that to most Americans the Good Neighbour policy in Latin America and the Big Brother policy towards China seemed nothing less noble than the practical application of liberal, democratic principles to international relations.

Yet American policy in Latin America bore a suspicious likeness to European practices which American statesmen so much deplored. To be sure, the United States gave up coercive methods in Latin America after Roosevelt's introduction of the Good Neighbour policy, but economic domination was a good substitute, and made the American republics, with the exception of Argentina, almost always obedient to the diplomatic leadership of the United States.

America's war-time policy toward China was clothed in similarly idealistic garb, but outsiders could reasonably be pardoned for interpreting America's policy as designed to bring China within the sphere of American influence.[2] An American officer was appointed as Chief of Staff to the Chinese army; emissaries from the President bombarded Chiang Kai-shek with good advice; and American pressure compelled Russia and Britain to accord China a courtesy seat among the Great Allied Powers. Madame Chiang Kai-shek privately assured Roosevelt in February 1943 that he could be sure China would support American policy at a peace conference after the war, and the President believed he could count upon China as a friend and supporter of the United States.[3]

The Russians, similarly, had given unmistakable signs of their intention to create a sphere of influence for themselves along their western border. In December 1941 Stalin had demanded that Great Britain should recognize the annexation of the Baltic states and parts of pre-war Poland, Fin-

political considerations were not on principle excluded from British military calculations as they were from American.

[1] Hull: *Memoirs*, ii. 1314–15.

[2] Cf. Churchill, iv. 504; U.S. edition, iv. 562.

[3] Sherwood: *Roosevelt and Hopkins*, pp. 706, 718; Eng. edition, ii. 703, 715. Cf. Hull: *Memoirs*, ii. 1257.

land, and Rumania to the U.S.S.R.;[1] and, though the issue had been postponed upon American insistence, the Russian Government never wavered in their stand and took numerous occasions to indicate the fact that Latvia, Lithuania, Estonia, Moldavia, Karelia, and the Ukrainian and White Russian sections of the pre-war Polish state were now officially a part of the Soviet Union.

In the course of 1943 it became apparent that Russian ambitions extended farther. After the breach of diplomatic relations with the Polish Government in Exile (26 April 1943),[2] a Union of Polish Patriots was established in Russia and a new Polish division was formed to fight with the Red Army. The Union of Polish Patriots was under Communist domination, and in its initial public proclamation, on 17 June 1943, it took open issue with the Polish Government in Exile by assuring Stalin that 'we will not allow those people who are trying to drive a wedge between the Polish people and the Soviet Union to disturb our relations'.[3]

At the end of 1943 Soviet activity was publicly extended to Yugoslavia and Czechoslovakia. On 14 December the Russian Government announced that a Russian Military Mission would be sent to Tito's headquarters;[4] and on 12 December a Treaty of Friendship, Mutual Assistance, and Post-War Collaboration between Russia and the Czech Government in Exile was signed in Moscow. These steps could not in themselves be construed as anything more than friendly gestures; but suspicious Westerners could and did see in them a revival of pan-Slavism and Russian expansion. Within Russia the Government permitted, indeed encouraged, a revival of pan-Slav feeling, particularly during the latter years of the war.[5] Similarly, the reinstatement of the Russian Orthodox Church on 4 September 1943 could be interpreted not simply as a concession to the stubborn religiosity of some Russians, but also as a device which the Bolshevik Government might use, as the Tsars had used it, to win influence and support among the orthodox peoples of the Balkan peninsula.

Thus each of the three principal Allies seemed to be intent upon building for itself a geographic sphere of special influence where friendly governments would accommodate their actions to the policies of one or another of the Allied Great Powers. The great difficulty in the way of any amicable division of the world on such principles as these was Germany. No one of the Allies was ready to consign the whole of Germany to the sphere of the

[1] See above, p. 167. [2] See above, p. 276.

[3] The manifesto is translated in Rothstein: *Soviet Foreign Policy during the Patriotic War*, i. 231–3.

[4] This step was taken with British approval, in accordance with decisions taken at the Tehrān Conference. See below, pp. 358–9.

[5] Cf. Stalin's Order of the Day, 1 May 1944: 'And while pursuing the enemy we must deliver from German bondage our brothers, the Poles and Czechoslovaks, and others allied with us, the peoples of Western Europe, who are under the heel of Hitlerite Germany' (Stalin: *Great Patriotic War*, p. 125). For other manifestations of pan-Slav sentiment, see Deutscher: *Stalin*, pp. 479, 492.

others; but all were equally opposed to leaving Germany as a no man's land, intact and uncontrolled, with potential power capable of revival as it had revived after 1918. The problem of how to deal with a defeated Japan was not as important an issue among the three great Allies, partly because Russia was not at war with Japan and Great Britain was unable to devote much of her strength to the Japanese war, and partly because the inherent strength of that country was less than that of Germany.

As guides to Allied post-war policy the declarations which had been made in 1941 and 1942 were vague at best. The Atlantic Charter of August 1941 and the United Nations Declaration of January 1942 were the principal documents in which the intentions of Britain, Russia, and the United States had been formally and publicly stated. But the language of these declarations was general, and, as prospects of victory improved, the diplomats of the three Great Powers began to concern themselves with particular instances and with the difficult matter of harmonizing national interest with the high principles which had been promulgated in time of adversity.

In March 1943 Anthony Eden visited Washington for the purpose of sounding out American officials on post-war issues. In the course of conversations with Roosevelt, Hopkins, Hull, and others, a number of differences between the attitudes of the two Governments became apparent. The most important conflict concerned American plans for a system of United Nations trusteeship. Roosevelt, in his more expansive moments, hoped to see international trusteeship applied to all the colonial and backward regions of the world, replacing pre-war imperial control of such regions by single nations.[1] Eden saw in the trusteeship scheme a device which would be difficult to work in practice owing to the divergent national loyalties of the future United Nations trustees; a device, moreover, which would undermine and eventually destroy the British Empire.

With respect to Europe, there were no fundamental differences between British and American wishes and expectations, though there were disagreements in detail. Roosevelt was reluctant to face the fact that Russia would demand extensive territorial expansion along her western frontier; Eden was inclined to accept at least the more modest of the Russian demands without cavil.[2] Concerning Germany, both agreed that it would be wise to divide the Reich into separate states; and the Americans argued that an effort should be made to decide ahead of time what part of Germany should be occupied by which of the three great Allied armies.[3]

[1] Sherwood: *Roosevelt and Hopkins*, pp. 716; Eng. edition, ii. 713; Hull: *Memoirs*, ii. 1234–8, 1596.

[2] Sherwood: *Roosevelt and Hopkins*, pp. 708–10; Eng. edition, ii. 706–8.

[3] Ibid. pp. 711, 714–15; Eng. edition, ii. 708, 712.

With respect to France, however, a considerable difference of opinion was revealed. Roosevelt had the idea that, once Germany had been disarmed, there would be no reason for the French or any other continental European Power to build up its military strength. Indeed, he conceived the idea that various key strategic points of the French Empire should be converted into United Nations military bases, garrisoned by troops provided by the three great Allies—for example, the British might hold Bizerta, the Americans Dakar. Eden, on the other hand, hoped to see France once more a strong military state, capable of serving in conjunction with Great Britain as a makeweight against Russia.[1]

With respect to Poland, Eden and Roosevelt agreed that territorial changes would have to be made. They both thought that Poland should be given control of East Prussia and that the eastern boundary of Poland should approximately follow the Curzon Line. Eden revealed his irritation at the unrealistic and extravagant ambitions which Polish nationalists in the Government in Exile constantly exhibited; and Roosevelt agreed that the determination of post-war Polish boundaries should be made by the Great Powers without too tender a regard for Polish chauvinist sentiment.[2]

The question of the form and powers of a post-war successor to the League of Nations was one with regard to which neither the American nor the British Government had as yet worked out definite policies. Various committees had been established by the U.S. State Department to consider the possibilities of international organization, but they had not yet reached definite conclusions. Hull was convinced that only a world-wide organization would suit the interests of the United States and be able to attract the support of public opinion. When the matter came up for discussion with Eden, the British Foreign Secretary remarked that he personally favoured a single world-wide international organization.[3]

But the Prime Minister's mind was running in a quite different direction in the first months of 1943. Churchill was not convinced that any international body could eliminate the springs of war, and he believed strongly in the inescapable reality and necessity of a balance of power. Churchill saw two possible dangers. On the one hand, he feared that the United States might, as in 1919–21, withdraw from active participation in European affairs after the end of the war. If that should happen, Britain would be left to face the overwhelming might of the Soviet Union, and the

[1] Sherwood: *Roosevelt and Hopkins*, pp. 712, 716, 721; Eng. edition, ii. 709, 714, 719. Eden did not apparently state his reason for wanting to see France restored as a military Power, but it is not difficult to deduce his reasoning from the initial statement he made in conversation with Roosevelt: that Britain was probably 'too weak to face Russia alone diplomatically' (ibid. p. 709; Eng. edition, ii. 706; cf. Churchill, iv. 717; U.S. edition, iv. 803). The Anglo-American difference about France was tied up with the long-standing rancour between de Gaulle and the Americans. The prospect of a strong France led by de Gaulle offended Hull and Roosevelt personally (cf. Hull: *Memoirs*, ii. 1213–16).

[2] Sherwood: *Roosevelt and Hopkins*, p. 710; Eng. edition, ii. 706.

[3] Ibid. p. 718; Eng. edition, ii. 716.

balance of power in Europe would be endangered. On the other hand, Churchill was keenly aware that, in a world dominated by America and Russia, Great Britain would be likely to find herself in a most uncomfortable position, ground between two vast millstones.

As an answer to both these unpleasant possibilities, he conceived the idea of establishing an instrument of European government which would bind together the European nations into an economic, political, and military unit capable of meeting the continent–nations of the east and of the west on more or less equal terms. He visualized something like a United States of Europe, whose constituent parts would be the major European Powers (including Great Britain) and regional federations of the smaller Powers—for example, in Scandinavia, the Danubian area, and the Balkans.[1] Churchill projected the integration of such a European unit into a larger world organization. In a speech on 21 March 1943, made while Eden was in Washington, he suggested the creation of a Council of Europe and a Council of Asia subordinated to a world organization embodying the war-time United Nations.[2]

When he was in Washington for the Trident Conference in May 1943, Churchill found occasion to expatiate upon his ideas for the post-war world. In conversation with leaders of the American Government he outlined his conception of a world organization subdivided into Regional Councils. This time he proposed three councils: one for the Pacific, one for the Americas, and one for Europe. In addition, the Prime Minister proposed that all the nations of the world should divide their armed forces into two parts, one to serve as usual, the other to be constantly at the disposal of the Regional Councils for use against any aggressor who might arise in their sphere of responsibility. Moreover, he dwelt upon the desirability of close bonds between Britain and the United States, proposing some form of common citizenship, continuation of the Combined Chiefs of Staff Committee in the post-war period, and systematic procedures to concert foreign policy between the two nations.[3]

Churchill's ideas about the post-war organization of the world were not of necessity those of the British Government. It does not appear that the Cabinet arrived at any formal agreement in 1943 as to what Britain wanted in the way of international organization. As far as the British public was concerned, it was in general far less inclined to calculate in terms of balance of power and national interest than was the Prime Minister. Hopes for a better world were quite as widespread in Great Britain as in America, and the forms which this idealism took were similar in the two countries. Feel-

[1] Churchill, iv. 504, 636–7; U.S. edition, iv. 561–2, 710–12.

[2] Churchill: *Onwards to Victory* (London, Cassell, 1944), pp. 36–37.

[3] Churchill, iv. 717–21; U.S. edition, iv. 802–6. Churchill later made public his three proposals for the consolidation of Anglo-American relations in a speech made at Harvard University on 6 September 1943 (Churchill: *Onwards to Victory*, pp. 181–6).

ing, as most people in Britain did, deeply grateful to the Russians for their heroic fight against Hitler, the British public did not see why the war-time alliance should break down after victory, and hoped devoutly that it would not. A world in which goodwill and common sense might prevail through some form of international association did not seem a fantastic vision to those who had suffered so much from two world wars within a generation. Knowing that the people of Russia had suffered even more from war, it did not seem unreasonable to expect that similar attitudes would prevail in the Soviet Union and that the popular will to peace would bridge the gaps of doctrine and practice which separated Russia from Britain, and America from both.

During the spring and summer months of 1943 American officials devoted much thought to the problems of the post-war international order and America's place in any future international organization. Roosevelt was at first inclined to accept Churchill's plan for establishing regional organizations; but Secretary of State Hull mustered his arguments against such a proposal and by degrees converted the President to his way of thinking. Hull's objections to regional organizations were twofold. On the one hand he feared that the practical result of regional organizations would be to create spheres of influence for the various Great Powers. This he thought bad in itself, a breeding-ground for future wars. In addition, he believed that Britain and Russia might use regional organizations to raise trade barriers which would exclude American trade from important segments of the world, and thus damage the national interest of the United States.

His second principal objection was that he believed the American public would not support United States participation in a European or Asiatic regional council, but would instead insist upon a modified form of isolationism, limiting America's active participation in international affairs to the Western Hemisphere.[1]

These arguments convinced Roosevelt, and by August 1943 he had definitely changed his mind, and now favoured the creation of a single world-wide international organization which would be so constituted as to give predominant voice to the Big Four—America, Britain, Russia, and China. Meanwhile, Churchill had lost his faith in the possibility of creating an effective European political unit which could hold a balance between Russian and American power. Two reasons for his change of mind may be surmised. The most important was the tension and ill feeling which had arisen between the Russian and British Governments in the months between the Trident (May 1943) and Quadrant (August 1943) Conferences. With-

[1] Hull: *Memoirs*, ii. 1643–6.

out Russia's consent, a plan for federating Europe could hardly hope to succeed; and the Russians made it quite clear that they opposed any project for federation which extended to Central and Eastern Europe.[1]

A second reason which impelled Churchill to abandon his hope for a powerful, independent, and federated post-war Europe was the rejection of regionalism by the American Government. From Churchill's point of view, there was much that seemed unrealistic in American attitudes, but acceptance of American leadership in post-war planning had the great advantage of committing the United States to an active part in post-war international affairs. The more difficulties there were in Anglo-Russian relations, the more necessary it seemed to Churchill to consolidate Anglo-American policy and plans. Thus the sacrifice of a scheme which, while far more attractive to Great Britain, was in all probability unworkable, seemed a small price to pay for active American collaboration in the post-war world.

The scene was thus set at the First Quebec (or Quadrant) Conference in August 1943 for British acceptance of American post-war plans. On 21 August Secretary of State Hull submitted a draft declaration which proposed the establishment at the earliest practicable time (presumably before the end of the war) of a world-wide international organization. Eden approved the declaration as a basis for negotiation with Russia; and, before the Conference ended, Churchill, too, accepted it.[2]

In accepting the American draft, Churchill in effect surrendered whatever hopes he had once had of pursuing an independent post-war policy. Instead of relying on Britain's own strength and the support of a friendly and consolidated Europe, Churchill decided to pin his hope upon America. The United States, rather than a revived and reorganized Europe, would have to counterbalance Russian power.

Russian attitudes towards post-war organization of the world must remain a matter for conjecture. The period between the Trident and Quadrant Conferences (May–August 1943) was characterized by severely strained relations between Russia and the two Western Allies. The decision made at Trident to postpone invasion of northern France until 1944 had aroused all Stalin's suspicions of the West. Were Churchill and Roosevelt really playing Germany off against Russia? Were they waiting until the

[1] Ibid. pp. 1298–9; Sherwood: *Roosevelt and Hopkins*, p. 714; Eng. edition, ii. 711; Ciechanowski: *Defeat in Victory*, pp. 152, 184. In the first years of the war, Britain had encouraged projects for post-war federation between the Poles and Czechs and between the Greeks and Yugoslavs. Despite formal agreements reached between the Governments in Exile, these projects had never attracted much support, and by the end of 1943, after the Russians had rebuffed proposals for federating the smaller East European states at the Moscow and Tehrān Conferences, the British Government ceased to hope for the success of such plans.

[2] Hull: *Memoirs*, ii. 1238–9.

two countries had exhausted themselves before intervening in force on the European continent in order to dictate a peace settlement which would once again, as in 1919, exclude Russia from any part in European affairs? It must have seemed so to the Russians, who refused to recognize the physical difficulties of a cross-Channel attack, and who did not share Western squeamishness at the sacrifice of soldiers' lives. Moreover, Marxian teaching made it clear that there could be no real friendship between predatory capitalists and the Soviet Union. What could be more probable than that the wicked and clever capitalists of Britain and America would use the Germans to fight one battle for them while simultaneously using the Russians to fight another? As for Lend-Lease, it could be interpreted as a device for equalizing the struggle in order to assure mutual exhaustion of Russia and Germany, twin enemies of the Western Allies. On the other hand, Lend-Lease deliveries increased in scale during the summer of 1943 despite the fact that Russia's most bitter need had passed. Could this be simply because the Americans miscalculated and were inadvertently making the Red Army too strong?

It is, of course, impossible to know what thoughts and fears dictated the actions of Stalin and his advisers during these months. It seems altogether probable, however, that the Russian leaders did weigh in their minds the alternatives of separate peace with Germany as against a continuation of the alliance with the West—an alliance which had so far led to little but the shedding of Russian and German blood. Scattered but convincing evidence has been published to show that Russian agents entered into conversations with subordinate German officials in Stockholm during the summer of 1943, in an effort to see whether a mutually agreeable basis for peace could be found.[1] Hitler, however, was not seriously interested in negotiations which might be taken as a sign of weakness or despair on his part; and, since the agents involved had no authority to commit their respective Governments, nothing came of the Russian initiative. Instead, intensive fighting was resumed when, on 5 July 1943, the Germans broke the lull which had followed the Stalingrad offensive by starting a large-scale attack on the central part of the front; within a week the Russians had stopped the Nazi advance and launched a counter-attack which continued successfully during the rest of the summer.

By 24 August 1943, when Stalin agreed to the proposed meeting of the

[1] Peter Kleist (*Zwischen Hitler und Stalin, 1939–1945* (Bonn, Athenäum Verlag, 1950), pp. 235–84) purports to give an account of this negotiation as remembered by the principal German go-between. His story seems quite plausible. At the time, newspaper rumours of secret Russo-German peace negotiations provoked Tass denials on 18 June and again on 17 July 1943. Cf. Rothstein: *Soviet Foreign Policy during the Great Patriotic War*, i. 269–70. Exaggerated reports of the affair reached Western intelligence agents, and formed the basis for Robert M. W. Kempner's 'Stalin's "Separate Peace" in 1943', *United Nations World*, vol. iv, March 1950, pp. 7–9; and for Donald B. Sanders's [pseud.] 'Stalin Plotted a Separate Peace', *American Mercury*, vol. lxv, November 1947, pp. 519–27.

Foreign Ministers of Britain, America, and Russia,[1] it may be assumed that the Russian Government had decided definitely to continue the war in alliance with the two Western Powers. By that time, the notable achievements of Russian industry in producing armaments, and the growing confidence and skill of the massive Red Army, opened the prospect of total victory over Germany. Even without the help of winter weather, the Russian army had shown itself able to advance against the Germans; even without a second front in France in 1943 Hitler's troops could not stand fast against Russian attack. Victory over Germany, secured with or without the direct help of Allied armies in the west, would mean that Stalin could reasonably hope to remove permanently the danger to Soviet security which a strong Germany inevitably constituted: something that no negotiated peace with Hitler could ever bring. The elimination of German military power would also make it possible for the Russians to establish friendly governments in Eastern and Central Europe; indeed, with the help of the various national Communist parties, Russian influence might be able to make itself powerfully felt throughout the whole of the Continent.

If it is correct to infer that Stalin took the decision to fight the war to the bitter end sometime in late July or in August 1943, he had a second and equally momentous decision to make at about the same time: how far to play a lone hand, how far to concert policy and post-war planning with Britain and America? Obviously, from Stalin's point of view, an open rupture with the Western Allies could not be risked as long as the war with Germany continued. Not only was Lend-Lease an important supplement to Russian war production, but also the military aid of the Anglo-American forces was of actual and still more of potential value in helping the Red Army to tumble Hitler's power down to ruins. Yet on the face of things it does not seem that it was necessary for Stalin to accept American plans for post-war international organization or to agree to a formula about the establishment of democratic governments in the liberated countries as he did at the Moscow and Tehrān Conferences in October and November 1943.

In the absence of all evidence, it is foolish to speculate on the calculations that persuaded the Russian Government to work out verbal agreements on post-war questions with the American and British Governments. Whatever the reasons, this was the direction in which Russian policy moved; and even before the Foreign Ministers assembled at Moscow in October 1943 the Russians had given evidence of their intention to cooperate. Thus the Russians concurred in the steps taken with respect to Italy, and the Russian press refrained from criticizing the support which the British and American Governments gave to Badoglio.[2] On 3 September

[1] See above, p. 297.

[2] Cf. the article in *Pravda*, 12 November 1943, by Palmiro Togliatti, the Italian Communist

Persia adhered to the United Nations Declaration without any objections from Russia. This seemed to indicate that Stalin had renounced any immediate intention of seeking an outlet to the Persian Gulf.[1] Again, on 16 September 1943, the Soviet Government officially informed the Western Allies of an attempt by Japan to mediate between the Russians and Hitler, an offer which Stalin had rejected out of hand.[2] Yet not everything was smooth sailing. The Russians did not accept the American draft declaration about post-war international organization and security when it was first submitted to them, objecting to the American intention of associating China with the other Great Powers as co-sponsor of the declaration;[3] and an American offer to mediate between the Polish Government in Exile and the Russians was, after long delay, turned down.[4]

By the time the Quadrant Conference had ended, the British and American Governments were fairly well aware of each other's hopes and plans for the post-war world; and both were hopeful that Russia could be persuaded to join with them to make and maintain a peace settlement.[5] It was the Americans who took the lead in opening negotiations with the Russians about post-war plans. In doing so, there were two persistent threads which governed their approach to Stalin in 1943. The first of these was Roosevelt's belief that if he could see Stalin and talk to him as man to man he would be able to break down some of the barriers of suspicion between Russia and the Western Allies. Roosevelt put much faith in his own personal charm; but he also believed most profoundly that his proposals were so patently sensible that no one, not even Stalin, could turn them down.

He was prepared to be generous to the Russians in small things—the Italian navy for example[6]—and thought that such generosity should not be spoiled by bargaining. Once he had proved to Stalin that the United States was really ready to be friendly and co-operative, he hoped (and he was willing to stake everything upon his hope) that the Russian leader would abandon the Communist world crusade and come to the support of Roosevelt's plan for a liberal, democratic, and peaceful world order. After all the Russians had much to gain. They surely needed time and the help of other countries to rebuild their own shattered economy. Moreover, Roosevelt had a deep-seated conviction that all men were potentially good and well-intentioned; and he did not believe there were any conflicts of national interest which could not be solved if an atmosphere of goodwill prevailed.

leader, in which he called for national unity of all Italians and made no mention of the question of the monarchy.

[1] Hull: *Memoirs*, ii. 1253.
[2] Ibid. pp. 1263–4.
[3] Ibid. p. 1256. See also below, pp. 330–1.
[4] Hull: *Memoirs*, ii. 1270–1.
[5] Sherwood: *Roosevelt and Hopkins*, pp. 709, 748–9; Eng. edition, ii. 706, 744–5; Churchill, iv. 635; U.S. edition, iv. 710.
[6] See below, p. 364.

When the alternative was new and even more devastating war, who could be so reckless or so blind as not to prefer compromise and peaceful adjudication by an international body?

The central problem seemed to be relatively simple: to break through the distrust which past events had created between the Soviet Union and other countries. And the way to do that most quickly and efficaciously was to convert Stalin from an ally into a friend through personal contact and frank discussion. That Stalin might approach such a meeting in an entirely different spirit, that he might view Roosevelt not as an open-hearted and open-handed friend but as a strangely irrational representative of predatory capitalism or as an impenetrably devious agent of American imperialism perhaps never occurred to the President; or, if it did, such a caricature of his real self seemed so implausible that he brushed it aside, confident that after five minutes face to face Stalin would see how mistaken he had been. As a result, Roosevelt lost no opportunity to try to arrange a personal meeting with Stalin, and persisted despite repeated rebuffs and postponements.

A second important consideration which affected the American attitude towards Russia was the wish to have Russian help in the war against Japan. The American Joint Chiefs of Staff were much concerned with the danger that even after Japan herself had been conquered the Japanese army in Manchuria might be able to maintain itself and fight on.[1] Even should this eventuality not develop, it would obviously be a help to the United States in the war against Japan if Russian armies attacked the Japanese in Manchuria and if the Russians would agree to allow American air forces to base themselves in Siberia. Russia's military co-operation in the Far East would certainly save American lives and shorten the war; and these were the criteria by which the American Chiefs of Staff evaluated policy.

Thus despite the growing military and economic power of the United States, throughout the first ten months of 1943 the American Government played the role of suitor to Stalin's coy mistress. Without Stalin's assent all Roosevelt's bright hopes for the future would be dashed to the ground. Moreover, many people in both Britain and America felt uneasy at the manner in which the Western Powers had treated the Bolshevik Government of Russia during the years between the wars, and felt vaguely at fault because Russian sacrifices in the war surpassed those which had been made by Britain and America. Liberals and Leftists felt that the Western nations had much to learn from Russia in matters of social and economic policy; and conservatives found it possible to interpret events in war-time Russia as an abandonment of revolutionary folly and a return to the traditions of Old Russia. Threads of feeling, hope, and belief such as these all influenced the

[1] Deane: *Strange Alliance*, pp. 41, 225.

attitudes assumed by the United States, and less pronouncedly by Great Britain, towards the Soviet Union during 1943.[1]

As soon as Stalin had agreed to a meeting of the three Foreign Ministers, negotiations were started to determine the agenda and time and place of the meeting. Efforts were made to persuade the Russians to agree to a meeting in England or in some neutral place, but Stalin insisted upon Moscow. On 10 September the Western Allies conceded the point.[2] Accordingly, on 18 October 1943, Molotov, Eden, and Hull met in the Kremlin to discuss preliminary formalities, and the first full-dress Conference session took place on the following day.

The first question brought before the Conference was how to shorten the war. The Russians wished to know whether Anglo-American plans to invade France in 1944 held firm, and proposed that the Big Three should bring immediate pressure on Turkey to enter the war and on Sweden to allow the Allies to use air bases against Germany. The Americans proposed that arrangements be made for 'shuttle bombing', i.e. that American air bases should be set up in Russia in order to allow American planes to attack targets in eastern Germany, and then refuel and rearm in Russia before attacking other targets on the return trip. In addition, the Americans wanted to set up weather stations in Siberia and proposed an agreement to facilitate air transport between the United States and Russia.

Hull took the position that military questions lay outside his sphere of authority, and left these matters to General John R. Deane, who had accompanied him to Moscow. Deane and General Sir Hastings Ismay, Churchill's personal representative with the British Chiefs of Staff, were able to assure the Russians that the invasion of northern France was planned for the spring of 1944 and outlined the preparations that were under way. They did, however, emphasize the provisos which had been

[1] The British public was perceptibly warmer in its feelings towards Russia than was the American public, among whom repugnance to socialism and consciousness of Russia's failure to join in the war against Japan were far greater than in Britain. On the other hand, the American Government in general assumed a more indulgent attitude towards Russia on current questions (for instance Lend-Lease), combined with a more rigid attitude on long-range issues (for instance, the question of the Baltic states) than did the British Government. The secret of this curious contradiction lay mainly in the fact that Churchill and Eden, thinking largely in terms of a balance of power, wanted to bargain with Stalin, whereas Roosevelt and Hull thought in terms of abstract principles to which they hoped Stalin could, if treated indulgently enough by his war-time allies, be committed.

[2] Churchill, v. 251; U.S. edition, v. 281. The negotiation was complicated on the American side by Roosevelt's desire to send Sumner Welles, Assistant Secretary of State, in place of Hull. Hull, however, was then thoroughly distrustful of Welles and insisted upon attending the Conference in person despite his advanced age and dislike of air travel. The quarrel between Hull and Welles led to the resignation of the latter shortly before Hull's departure for Moscow. Cf. Leahy: *I Was There*, p. 219.

accepted at Quebec: the invasion could not occur unless German air strength were substantially reduced, unless German reserves in France and the Low Countries were not more than twelve divisions, and, a new one, unless the Germans could not bring more than fifteen divisions into action against the invading troops in the first two months after D-day. The Russians professed themselves satisfied with the information, even though they were kept in the dark as to the exact date at which the proposed invasion would take place.[1]

The Russians agreed 'in principle' to the American proposals for shuttle-bombing, weather stations, and improved air transport, but the approval was a grudging one and many obstacles were later put in the way of their practical realization. Indeed, Molotov tried to exclude these matters from the official record of the Conference, and agreed to their inclusion only after Hull had personally intervened.[2]

The question of Turkey and Sweden was referred to the Combined Chiefs of Staff, and to Roosevelt and Churchill. On 28 October, as the Conference was drawing near an end, a negative answer arrived in Moscow. The Combined Chiefs of Staff felt the Soviet proposals for Turkey and Sweden would require the diversion of resources from Overlord and Italy; but the Russians were not convinced, and appeared to resent the rejection of their proposal.[3] After the Conference had formally come to an end, but while the British and American Foreign Ministers were still in Moscow waiting for flying weather to allow their departure, the Dodecanese affair brought Turkey once more to the forefront. On 2 November the British and Russian Governments agreed that Eden should try to get immediate use of air bases in Turkey and that both Governments should later bring pressure on the Turks to enter the war on a full scale.[4]

While these tripartite military negotiations took place through the formal channels of the Conference, far more significant negotiations also took place in private between Eden and Stalin. The situation which had developed in Italy worried the British and irritated the Americans. Instead of capturing Rome and moving rapidly north to the Appenines, Allied armies were becoming bogged down in the south, facing potentially superior German forces. Churchill had already begun efforts to increase the allotment of landing craft and troops to Italy in order to permit flank attack by amphibious forces in the rear of the German defence line; but the Americans as always were loath to agree to anything that threatened to interfere with the build-up for Overlord.[5]

[1] Deane: *Strange Alliance*, pp. 18–19; Churchill, v. 255–6; U.S. edition, v. 287.

[2] Deane, op. cit. p. 23.

[3] Hull: *Memoirs*, ii. 1301; Deane, op. cit., pp. 21–23; Churchill, v. 261; U.S. edition, v. 294.

[4] Churchill, v. 265–6; U.S. edition, v. 298; Hull: *Memoirs*, ii. 1312. As we have seen, Roosevelt agreed later (see above, pp. 312–13).

[5] Churchill, v. 215–24; U.S. edition, v. 243–51.

In the course of an interview with Stalin, Eden presented these facts to the Soviet dictator, and explained that the new situation might make it necessary to postpone the date of Overlord for a month or two. Stalin was surprisingly sympathetic, and went out of his way to acknowledge the assistance that the Red Army was already receiving from Anglo-American operations.[1] Stalin's attitude encouraged Churchill to think that perhaps the Russians could be persuaded to back his military policy against that of the Americans. After all, at the Moscow Conference of Foreign Ministers it was the Russians who had raised the question of Turkish participation in the war, and Stalin seemed not to be indignant at the prospect of Overlord's postponement in favour of larger-scale operations in Italy and the eastern Mediterranean. Russia stood to profit enormously from the opening of the Turkish straits, for then a new and shorter supply line could be established which would bring Lend-Lease goods right up to the Russian front.

This new hope of winning Stalin's support for his Mediterranean strategy was a key element in Churchill's thinking on the eve of the Tehrān Conference; and when Roosevelt heard of Stalin's attitude, he too cooled in his advocacy of Overlord, hesitating between Marshall and Churchill until he had heard from Stalin direct.

However important military matters appeared to the Russians and to the British, the American delegation at the Conference was interested primarily in other things.[2] What Hull had most at heart was to lay the basis for post-war co-operation between the Great Allied Powers; and as soon as the preliminary military discussion had ended, the Conference turned to consider the Four-Power Declaration on General Security. This was a document which had been drawn up by the State Department, approved by the British at the Quadrant Conference in August 1943, and submitted to the Russian Government immediately thereafter.[3] The principal stumbling-block in this connexion was American insistence upon associating China with Britain, Russia, and America as co-sponsor of the Declaration. Eden

[1] Stalin's tone may have been influenced by Churchill's stern gesture of refusing to accept a note of protest from Stalin on the Arctic convoys. This occurred on 18 October, just as the Moscow Conference opened, and must have given Stalin pause. He could not afford to risk an open break with Britain (cf. Churchill, v. 241–2, 259–62; U.S. edition, v. 271–2, 291–4).

[2] After the rejection of his proposal for the establishment of a Supreme Allied War Council at the Arcadia Conference (see above, p. 92), Hull systematically and ostentatiously dissociated himself and the State Department from all things military, thus abdicating much of the authority which fell naturally to the British Foreign Office and exacerbating the separation in American policy between 'military' and 'political' considerations. Actually, Hull and his subordinates in the State Department were in large part making the best of a situation which arose from Roosevelt's unwillingness to entrust matters of high policy to their hands.

[3] See above, pp. 323, 326.

was willing to accommodate the Americans, but Molotov at first flatly opposed the inclusion of China. Hull, however, insisted. Molotov first yielded so far as to leave the question of China's place open, and a few days later, on 26 October, he conceded the point.[1]

Discussion of the text of the Declaration led to numerous changes in phraseology, and at Molotov's insistence one of the original articles, providing for the establishment of a technical military commission, was omitted. As soon as the text had been agreed to, the concurrence of the Chinese Government was requested; and, after some nimble radio-telegraphy, the Chinese Ambassador to Moscow was empowered to sign on behalf of the Chinese Government. Formal signatures were affixed on 30 October 1943.

The Declaration solemnly stated that the four Powers would co-operate in fighting the war to its end, and would continue to co-operate afterwards 'for the organization and maintenance of peace and security'. Three practical steps were promised:

> . . . They [i.e. the Governments of the United States of America, the United Kingdom, the Soviet Union, and China] recognize the necessity of establishing at the earliest practicable date a general international organization, based on the principle of the sovereign equality of all peace-loving states, and open to membership by all such states, large and small, for the maintenance of international peace and security. . . .
>
> After the termination of hostilities they will not employ their military forces within the territories of other states except for the purposes envisaged in this declaration and after joint consultation.
>
> . . . They will confer and cooperate with one another and with other members of the United Nations to bring about a practicable general agreement with respect to the regulation of armaments in the post-war period.[2]

This declaration had momentous implications. The signature of the Russian Government seemed good evidence of the willingness of the Soviet leaders to co-operate with Britain and America in the post-war period. The signature of the American Government seemed equally to indicate the abandonment of a traditional policy of isolation from European and world politics. A further gesture which confirmed this view was the passage of the Connally Resolution by the U.S. Senate on 5 November 1943 by an overwhelming 85–5 vote. This resolution declared that the Senate 'recognized the necessity' of establishing an international organization for the maintenance of peace which the United States should join.[3] Its

[1] Hull: *Memoirs*, ii. 1280–2, 1299.

[2] Text of the Declaration may be found in *Documents on American Foreign Relations, 1943–1944*, pp. 229–30.

[3] Text of the resolution may be found ibid. p. 318. In the House of Representatives the Fulbright Resolution, passed on 21 September 1943 by a vote of 360 to 29, put the lower House on record as approving American participation in 'appropriate international machinery' to maintain peace. Text, ibid. p. 315.

passage seemed to forestall the possibility of a repetition of the events of 1920, when the Senate rejected President Wilson's project of the League of Nations.

In Hull's eyes the Four-Power Declaration was the most important achievement of the Conference. Other political issues which came under discussion were all, in his view, subsidiary to the general affirmation of post-war co-operation embodied in the Declaration.

The British had less confidence in the value of statements of general principles, and it was left to Eden to introduce most of the specific issues which were discussed at the Conference. Thus it was at Eden's suggestion that the Foreign Ministers agreed to set up a European Advisory Commission with headquarters in London.[1] The Commission was intended to consider all specific questions pertaining to terms of surrender and their execution which might arise between the principal Allies. It was empowered to make recommendations for common action, but had no mandatory authority. Similarly, the Advisory Council for Italy was agreed to, again at Eden's suggestion.[2]

The Foreign Ministers agreed that Austria should be re-established as an independent state when Germany had been defeated. They likewise accepted Eden's suggestion that no separate spheres of influence should be carved out in Europe, but that joint responsibility should be the basis of their policies in the liberated and conquered countries of the Continent. On two other issues, however, Eden was not so successful. Molotov sharply rejected his proposal for sanctioning federations of the smaller European states; and his effort to persuade the Russians to resume diplomatic relations with the Polish Government in Exile was fruitless. In effect, though not in so many words, Molotov made it clear that his Government expected to have the predominant voice in affairs of Eastern and South-Eastern Europe.[3]

The Russians introduced two items into the discussion. On 22 October Molotov presented a list of measures for the elimination of Fascists and fascist influence from Italian affairs. Most of his points were incorporated in a declaration on Italy which the Foreign Ministers issued at the close of their Conference. In addition, the Russians asked that a part of the Italian navy and merchant fleet be turned over to their control. This matter was referred back to the American and British Governments, and on 30 October Molotov was informed that for the moment no such transfer

[1] The establishment of such a body had been first proposed by the British in July 1943. The Americans had opposed the original suggestion which would have assigned to the Commission responsibility for drafting plans for European security and economic relations in the post-war era (Hull: *Memoirs*, ii. 1642).

[2] See above, p. 309.

[3] For Eden's suggestions and their fate see Hull: *Memoirs*, ii. 1283–4; 1297–9, 1305–6. Eden also introduced a discussion of Allied policy in Persia, but conversation was presumably inconclusive (cf. Churchill, v. 253; U.S. edition, v. 284).

could be made, since Italian ships should be used where they would best serve the general Allied cause.[1]

These questions of detail did not seem of primary importance to the American delegation. Their idea was to approach all the problems of the post-war world and of the immediate present only after arriving at general agreement upon sweeping principles. The Four-Power Declaration was only one of four basic documents they had brought to the Conference. The others were a memorandum on the treatment of defeated Germany, a statement of the principles which should govern post-war economic relations between nations, and a statement on trusteeship for 'dependent peoples'.

The American memorandum on Germany was presented to the Conference on 23 October. It declared that Germany should be totally disarmed and should be required to make reparations in the form of goods and services for physical damage done by the German troops. The memorandum proposed that an inter-Allied Commission for Germany should be set up to enforce the terms of surrender. On the question of the dismemberment of Germany, Hull reported that the American Government were undecided whether forcible division of Germany into several states would be wise, but he felt that decentralization should in any event be encouraged. All three Foreign Ministers agreed that Germany should be compelled to surrender all territory acquired since 1938, and that East Prussia should be separated from Germany. Eden felt more strongly than Hull that Germany should be partitioned; Molotov contented himself with remarking that the Russians were behindhand in their study of the treatment to be accorded to Germany after Hitler's defeat. It was decided to refer the whole question to the European Advisory Commission for further study.[2]

On the day before the Conference came to an end Hull brought up the questions of post-war economic principles and the post-war status of dependent peoples. On both these issues American policy ran directly athwart British interests. Hull was by long conviction a free trader, and hoped to see liberal trade practices take root in the post-war world. Indeed, he believed that only with freer trade could the economic basis for peace be assured. This meant that Great Britain should abandon Empire preference; but what liberal trade principles could mean when applied to a socialized economy such as that of the Soviet Union was hard

[1] Hull: *Memoirs*, ii. 1283–4, 1301–2; Leahy: *I Was There*, pp. 217–18. Roosevelt, when the matter was first raised, expressed his willingness to transfer a third of the Italian navy and merchant fleet to Russia, but Hull persuaded the President to take second thought and postpone settlement for the time being. Churchill agreed 'in principle' to recognize the Russians' right to some share in the Italian fleet, but wished to postpone decision until the meeting of the three Heads of Government (Churchill, v. 262–3; U.S. edition, v. 294–5).

[2] Hull: *Memoirs*, ii. 1284–7.

to say. Nevertheless, Molotov declared that he viewed Hull's proposals with favour. Probably what he meant was that he approved of reparations and the establishment of an international bank which were included as parts of the American proposal.[1] Eden's position was delicate for while the British Government most certainly did not approve of an unconditional removal of trade barriers after the war—a step which would expose British industry to the full impact of American competition—yet the British had officially committed themselves to liberalization of trade as a *quid pro quo* for Lend-Lease. This commitment had been incorporated in the Master Lend-Lease Agreement of 1942, and Eden could not repudiate that agreement. At the same time he could not approve Hull's suggestions without making embarrassing qualifications. In the dilemma he presumably was non-committal.[2]

The American plan to transfer responsibility for the tutelage of dependent peoples from individual nations to international trustees was even more directly a challenge to the traditional power and interests of Great Britain. Eden bluntly said at the Conference that his Government could not accept the principles set forth in Hull's memorandum on the question. Molotov merely remarked that the matter deserved further study and that his Government were much interested in the question.[3]

What sort of punishment should be meted out to individual Germans who were responsible for acts of violence and atrocity in the various occupied countries of Europe had been under discussion among the Allied Governments for some time prior to the Foreign Ministers' Conference. Churchill drafted a text on 12 October, and, after it had been slightly modified in the light of discussion at Moscow, a Declaration on German Atrocities was published, with the other public documents of the Conference, over the signatures of Roosevelt, Churchill, and Stalin. This declaration was drawn up in the hope of deterring future acts of cruelty. It declared that the Allied Governments would search out individuals responsible for massacres, executions, and other atrocities and send them back to the countries where their deeds had been done, there to be judged and punished by local authorities. Major criminals at and near the summit of the German Government, whose acts had no single geographic locality, would be punished by joint decision of the Allied Governments. Discussion revealed that the British were inclined to observe the legal formalities of trial, whereas the Russians and the Americans favoured summary and drastic action against Hitler and his colleagues. The Declaration dodged this issue. It did not say anything about how the

[1] Hull: *Memoirs*, ii. pp. 1303–4.

[2] Neither Hull nor Churchill says anything of Eden's reaction to the American economic proposals.

[3] Ibid. pp. 1304–5.

major criminals would be punished, whether by summary execution or after formal trial.[1]

On the last day of the Conference, 30 October 1943, Stalin gave a formal banquet in the Kremlin. In the course of table conversation he told Hull that when Germany had been defeated Russia would join in fighting Japan.[2] Satisfaction prevailed all round the table, and the Conference broke up in a blaze of vodka and good feeling.

The official communiqué referred to the 'atmosphere of mutual confidence and understanding which characterized all the work of the Conference'; and the four Declarations—on General Security, Italy, Austria, and German Atrocities—which accompanied the communiqué provided public evidence of the scope of agreement which had been achieved. The great fact was that Russia had joined with Britain and America in declaring a common intention to continue to co-operate after the war. The only sour note was Poland. The Russo-Polish dispute had not been ended nor were there any signs of a spirit of compromise on either side. But the complaints of the Polish Government in Exile were quite lost sight of in the general acclaim which greeted the reassuring news of fundamental agreement on post-war co-operation among the great Allies.

Secretary of State Hull was invited to address a joint session of the American Senate and House of Representatives when he arrived back in Washington. He spoke with unqualified optimism:

> . . . The Soviet Union, Great Britain, the United States, and China have laid the foundation for cooperative effort in the post-war world toward enabling all peace-loving nations, large and small, to live in peace and security, to preserve the liberties and rights of civilized existence, and to enjoy expanded opportunities and facilities for economic, social, and spiritual progress. No other important nations anywhere have more in common in the present war or in the peace that is to follow victory over the Axis powers.[3]

Eden was more subdued but still optimistic in his estimate of the accom-

[1] Ibid. pp. 1289–91. Text of the Declaration on German Atrocities may be found in *Documents on American Foreign Relations, 1943–1944*, pp. 231–2. Churchill (v. 264–5; U.S. edition, v. 296–7) reproduces his original draft.

[2] Hull: *Memoirs*, ii. 1309. This was the first time Hull had heard any such promise, and he naturally thought it a matter of the utmost importance. In fact, however, Stalin had at least twice before spoken to American representatives of his intention to fight Japan in due course: once to Harriman in August 1942 at the time of the Harriman–Beaverbrook mission, and a second time to General Patrick Hurley (cf. Harriman's statement on U.S.-U.S.S.R. relations, dated 17 August 1951, *Congressional Record*, 27 August 1951, p. 5665; Deane: *Strange Alliance*, p. 226; Leahy: *I Was There*, pp. 177, 246–7).

[3] Speech delivered to Congress, on 18 November 1943, reproduced in *Documents on American Foreign Relations, 1943–1944*, p. 14.

plishments of the Conference. In a speech to the House of Commons on 11 November 1943 he said:

Let me say at the outset that the results of the Conference exceeded my hopes. As we worked, the sense of confidence grew, and this, in turn, seemed to give an added momentum to our progress. . . . I am not going to pretend for a moment that we were agreed on every point. That would indeed be the international millennium and we are nowhere near that yet. But what I can say is that we do now know each other's points of view on all these subjects . . . and I could not help reflecting, as we flew over Stalingrad: is it not possible that out of it all we shall be able together so to order the world that these cities that have been utterly shattered shall live again and that this time they can live their lives in lasting peace?[1]

The Russians, too, hailed the achievements of the Conference with satisfaction. In a speech delivered in Moscow on the occasion of the twenty-sixth anniversary of the Bolshevik Revolution, 6 November 1943, Stalin said:

The victory of the Allied countries over the common enemy has come nearer, while the relations among the Allies, the fighting partnership of their armies, far from weakening have, contrary to the expectations of their enemies, grown stronger and more enduring.

Eloquent evidence of this also are the historic decisions of the Moscow conference of representatives of the Soviet Union, Great Britain and the United States of America recently published in the press.[2]

Newspapers in all three Allied countries gave great prominence to the news of the Moscow Conference, and were unanimous in praising the outcome. American newspapers generally seized upon the Four-Power Declaration as the most important decision of the Conference;[3] British newspapers tended to emphasize the value of the European Advisory Council as a means for settling disputes and arriving at common decisions;[4] while the Russian newspapers put the greatest emphasis upon the military repercussions which would flow from the Moscow decisions.[5]

[1] 11 November 1943, H.C.Deb. 5th ser., vol. 393, coll. 1323–32. Cf. Eden's private report to Churchill (Churchill, v. 261–2; U.S. edition, v. 293–4).

[2] Stalin: *Great Patriotic War*, p. 102.

[3] See e.g. *New York Times*, editorial, 2 November 1943: 'The reaffirmation of inseparable unity and the pledge of united action in war and peace is so important that for the present it overshadows all the details of the agreements reached.' Cf. *Chicago Daily News*, *New York Herald Tribune*, editorials, 2 November 1943.

[4] See e.g. *The Times*, leading article, 2 November 1943: 'By far the most important operative decision of the conference is that which establishes a "European Advisory Commission". . . .' Cf. *Manchester Guardian*, *Daily Herald*, leading articles, 2 November 1943. The *News Chronicle*, leading article, 2 November 1943, was almost alone in emphasizing the pre-eminent value and importance of the Four-Power Declaration.

[5] *Pravda* said on 2 November 1943: 'The conference has accepted the speedy termination of the war as the first task, a task which the Soviet people regarded, and still regards, as of paramount importance. The decision adopted by the conference deals a heavy blow to the plans of

These divergences of emphasis reflected the divergent attitudes of the three Governments; but the divergences were, after all, slight. Every part of the communiqué and accompanying documents was accepted in all three countries as a worthwhile contribution to Allied co-operation and the winning of the war. Allied cordiality had never been so great. American sentiment seemed definitely reconciled to continued participation in world affairs. In particular the United States as never before seemed ready to join an international organization.[1] British reaction was certainly more subdued, though optimistic; while in Russia a sense of enthusiasm for the Western Allies penetrated to the man in the street—or at least to those with whom Western newspaper correspondents talked.[2]

Roosevelt's long wooing of Stalin seemed to be making progress. The next step was to arrange a meeting between the three principals, for one of the main purposes of the Conference of Foreign Ministers in Moscow had been to lay the groundwork for such an encounter. The success of the Foreign Ministers was attested by the fact that within a month of the conclusion of their Conference, the Big Three met at Tehrān.

(v) The Cairo and Tehrān Conferences, 22 November–6 December 1943

(*a*) Preliminaries

Periodic conferences between Roosevelt and Churchill had proved, during the two years after Pearl Harbour, to be one of the pillars of Anglo-American co-operation. Roosevelt had long hoped to bring Stalin into the Anglo-American circle, and spared no effort to entice the Soviet dictator away from his capital for a conference. But Stalin was unwilling to lose telephonic contact with his front-line commanders, while for reasons of prestige and convenience Roosevelt was not willing to go to Russia. On 8 September 1943 Stalin suggested that the three Heads of Government might meet in Persia, where each nation had armed forces already on the ground;[3] but, though Churchill was willing to go to Tehrān, Roosevelt was not, and negotiations dragged along for several weeks until on, or shortly before, 10 November Roosevelt yielded and agreed to go to the Persian capital.[4]

the Hitlerite strategists who are staking all on a protracted war' (quoted from *Manchester Guardian*, 3 November 1943). *Izvestia*, while also emphasizing the immediate military gain, remarked: 'The great democratic powers, comrades in arms today, tomorrow will become comrades in the struggle for the security of all peace-loving nations' (quoted from *New York Times*, 3 November 1943, article by W. H. Lawrence).

[1] It was on the crest of the wave of internationalist feeling which the news of the Moscow Conference generated that the Connally Resolution passed the Senate on 5 November 1943.

[2] Cf. *The Times*, *News Chronicle*, *New York Herald Tribune*, 3 November 1943.

[3] Churchill, v. 250; U.S. edition, v. 281.

[4] Ibid. pp. 273–83 and 307–19 respectively; Hull: *Memoirs*, ii. 311–13; Leahy: *I Was There*,

Roosevelt's long negotiation with Stalin was further complicated by the President's wish to bring Chiang Kai-shek and the Chinese to the conference along with the Russians. But one of the conditions Stalin made when agreeing to meet in Tehrān was to demand that representatives of all other Powers should be 'absolutely excluded'.[1] This, of course, meant China; and Roosevelt was forced to fall back upon two separate conferences: one with the British and Chinese at Cairo, 22–26 November 1943 (code-name Sextant), and a second at Tehrān with the British and Russians, 28 November–1 December (code-name Eureka). A third conference, to dispose of unfinished business, was arranged at Cairo after the meeting in Tehrān, 3–6 December.[2]

Despite the cross purposes and haggling that preceded the fixing of firm arrangements for the Cairo and Tehrān Conferences, Roosevelt set out on his journey with 'the enthusiasm of a boy'.[3] No other international gathering of the war years was engendered in such youthful ardour or surrounded by such spring-like freshness, though in truth neither Stalin nor Churchill shared much of Roosevelt's faith in the all-powerful virtue of goodwill and friendly personal contact. Still, they both judged it worth a try; and each delegation journeyed to Tehrān with high, though disparate, hopes for their first common meeting.

The Americans came to the Cairo and Tehrān Conferences with three things uppermost in their minds. The most important object which Roosevelt set before himself was the achievement of a firm understanding

p. 229. Roosevelt's reason for objecting to Tehrān was that communications were so undependable that it would not be possible for him to be sure that he could receive and return Congressional Bills within the constitutional ten-day period. But this was probably at least partly a mere debating point. Beneath the surface lay a contest for prestige: Roosevelt did not want to appear to be coming to Stalin's back door for a conference, but when Stalin made it clear that he was prepared to forgo any meeting rather than travel farther afield than Tehrān, Roosevelt decided to give in.

Before he did so, however, he greatly alarmed Churchill by trying to arrange a tripartite meeting in Cairo at which Molotov would take Stalin's place, and Russian military representatives would sit in with the Anglo-American Combined Chiefs of Staff. Indeed, on 27 October Roosevelt suggested that Russians should become regular members of the Combined Chiefs of Staff; but Churchill's remonstrance apparently nipped this project in the bud (Churchill, v. 279–80; U.S. edition, v. 314–15). In the end, the unwillingness of the Russians to join in a conference with the Chinese, whom Roosevelt had also invited to Cairo, prevented the President's plans from reaching maturity. So far as records published down to 1952 show, this was the only occasion upon which a serious effort was made to expand the Anglo-American Combined Chiefs of Staff Committee into a three- or four-Power partnership.

[1] Churchill, v. 284; U.S. edition, v. 320.

[2] This arrangement differed substantially from what Churchill desired. He would have liked a preliminary Anglo-American conference to concert global strategy anew; then a meeting with Stalin; and finally a second Anglo-American discussion to settle details of the war against Japan. He saw no reason for admitting Chiang Kai-shek to the inner sanctum of Allied deliberations at all (ibid. pp. 282–3 and 318 respectively).

[3] Hull: *Memoirs*, ii. 1313.

with Stalin on post-war co-operation. In addition, the American Chiefs of Staff were resolved to defend the two basic strategic decisions which had been made earlier in the year: against Germany, they desired a massive cross-Channel attack to be launched in May 1944; against Japan, they clung to the concept of a vast pincers envelopment designed to converge on Hongkong, preparatory to an assault on Japan itself.

In the Pacific, where the American Joint Chiefs of Staff exercised strategic direction, there were no special difficulties. Progress was slow both in the Solomon Islands and in New Guinea; and relations between General MacArthur and the U.S. naval authorities were not always amicable;[1] but these problems were American and did not enter significantly into dealings with Great Britain or China. The pinch was Burma. According to the decisions of the Casablanca, Trident, and Quadrant Conferences, northern Burma was to be reconquered in order to reopen land communications with China. American air forces and supplies had been assigned to the Burma campaign, but the ground battle was left to British and Chinese troops. Difficulties of terrain, climate, and communications were enormous; to them were added personal and political conflicts. The result was that up to the time of the Cairo Conference little or no progress had been made in Burma. The Japanese were still in possession of almost the whole country and still cut off any but air communication between China and the Western world. This situation was profoundly disquieting to American military leaders. They had planned their grand strategy against Japan on the assumption that Burma would be cleared in the course of 1943; and they had hoped that when land communication with China had been restored, a powerful Chinese army could be equipped and trained to take a significant part in the final overthrow of Japan.[2]

The Americans reacted to the failure of their plans for Burma by insisting all the more strongly that what had not been accomplished in 1943 should be undertaken in 1944. They suspected the British of half-heartedness in the field, the more so since Churchill had made it perfectly clear that the British High Command disliked the whole plan and had agreed to it only under pressure from the Americans.[3]

At the same time, the U.S. navy began to think of alternative ways of defeating Japan. The American Pacific fleet had grown rapidly in 1943 as new ships had come from the dockyards; and on 20 November 1943, just before the Cairo Conference opened, American troops attacked the atolls of Tarawa and Makin in the Gilbert Islands. Five days later

[1] Leahy: *I Was There*, pp. 182–4.

[2] Ibid. p. 239.

[3] Churchill, too, was ill pleased at the conduct of the British war effort in India and Burma (Churchill, v. 80; U.S. edition, v. 89).

After these preliminaries, Roosevelt came to the heart of the matter he had travelled so far to try to settle. He asked Stalin whether he would be willing to talk about the future peace of the world. Stalin was willing, and Roosevelt embarked on a description of an international arrangement which he hoped would assure peace. The President outlined a tripartite organization: an assembly in which each nation belonging to the United Nations would have a representative; an executive committee composed of the Big Four and representative nations drawn from the various regions of the world; and a third body, whose membership would be limited to the Big Four, and whose duties would be to police the world and prevent or, if necessary, combat aggression.[1]

Stalin centred attention on this last proposal which Roosevelt dubbed the 'Four Policemen'. He remarked that the smaller European nations would not like the plan, and questioned China's right to act as a world policeman. He thought that instead of a single world-wide organization it might be more practical to set up two bodies, one to exercise jurisdiction in Europe and a second in the Far East. Roosevelt replied that this was like the proposal Churchill had made in May. The great difficulty was that Congress and American public opinion would probably not support any arrangement which involved America in a purely European organization.[2] Stalin was perhaps puzzled by an opinion so illogical as to prefer world-wide commitment to European commitment, and observed that if Roosevelt's scheme were acted upon American troops might have to be sent anywhere in the world. Roosevelt replied, and his words must have etched themselves into Stalin's consciousness, that American troops would not be available for such service; American naval and air forces could be used to help police the world, but any land armies needed to quell aggression would have to be provided by Russia and Britain.

To this, so far as the published record goes, Stalin made no reply. He shifted the discussion to a more immediate and practical level by saying that the first and greatest problem was control of Germany. To this end he argued that military bases would have to be permanently held in Germany and round its borders, garrisoned by United Nations troops. Similar steps, he said, should be taken against Japan. Roosevelt expressed complete agreement. The rest of the conversation dealt with China—whose potentiality as a Great Power the President emphasized—and the danger of secret German rearmament, which Stalin feared and Roosevelt rather discounted.[3]

[1] Roosevelt's plan (as reported in Sherwood: *Roosevelt and Hopkins*, p. 785; Eng. edition, ii. 779–80) was rather different from the proposals which had been drawn up by the State Department, though it bears certain resemblances to a plan dated 14 July 1943. Cf. *Postwar Foreign Policy Preparation*, pp. 472–85.

[2] Roosevelt was not perfectly candid. He did not mention the other argument against regionalism which Hull had impressed upon him: the danger of rival spheres of influence and trade discrimination against the United States.

[3] Sherwood: *Roosevelt and Hopkins*, pp. 784–7; Eng. edition, ii. 779–82.

Two points deserve emphasis in connexion with this interview. First, Stalin made clear how deeply he feared German power, and how little he trusted military defeat alone to end the threat which a strong Germany inevitably constituted for the Soviet Union. He asserted that in a mere fifteen or twenty years Germany might again find herself able to attack Russia; and at a later stage of the Conference he observed that any confederation of European states which could be devised would in time be dominated by the Germans if any part of Germany were admitted to membership in it.[1] It seems reasonable to suppose that Stalin's main reason for deciding to co-operate with the Western Powers in setting up what became the United Nations was his fear that, if he did not, Germany would be able to seize the opportunity offered by division between the victors to restore her strength. It is even probable that he did not want to see the whole of Germany go Communist, believing that in such an event the Germans might well supplant the Russians as the dominant Soviet group.[2]

The second point to consider is this: what effect did Roosevelt's casual statement that American ground troops would not be available for police duty abroad have on Stalin's calculations? Stalin was a man who greatly respected military force. If America were in truth getting ready to withdraw militarily from Europe and Asia after the end of the war, obviously the only rival to his political influence would be Great Britain. America could be counted out as an actual, physical force so far as any immediate Russian post-war plans were concerned. If Stalin thought in terms such as these, it is probable that Roosevelt's statement encouraged him to raise his sights higher and made the Russians more unbending than before in claiming territorial and other concessions for themselves in Eastern Europe.

Roosevelt's second private interview with Stalin ended at 3.30 in the afternoon, when Churchill ceremoniously presented the Sword of Stalingrad to Stalin on behalf of King George VI. As Stalin received the sword he bowed to kiss it, and, according to Roosevelt's report, there were tears in his eyes as he did so.[3] It was a dramatic moment but did not change the realities of conflict between Churchill and Stalin. After the ceremony, photographs of the assembled dignitaries were taken before they sat down to a second plenary session.

The Combined Chiefs reported on their discussion of the morning and

[1] Ibid. p. 798; Eng. edition, ii. 789.

[2] This was Eden's opinion in March 1943 (ibid. p. 709; Eng. edition, ii. 706). Cf. Barrington Moore: *Soviet Politics*, p. 370.

[3] Perkins: *The Roosevelt I Knew*, p. 71; Churchill, v. 321; U.S. edition, v. 363–4.

their failure to reach agreement. Stalin then asked a question which had long troubled Roosevelt: Who was to command the invasion of France? The President replied evasively to the effect that the choice of a supreme commander would depend on decisions yet to be made at the Conference. Churchill next took the floor and argued once again for operations in the eastern Mediterranean. He developed his plan for successive use of the landing craft available for the Mediterranean: first for an amphibious assault upon the coast of Italy in order to capture Rome, then for an attack on Rhodes, in conjunction with Turkey's declaration of war, thirdly for an assault upon the beaches of southern France, to coincide with the main landing in Normandy. Churchill admitted that his proposals would mean either the postponement of Overlord by six to eight weeks or a cancellation of the amphibious operations in Burma to which Roosevelt had just agreed in Cairo. But he asserted emphatically that only by exploiting the opportunities now open in the Mediterranean could the Allies make the most effective use of the resources at their disposal.

Stalin remained in opposition. He did promise Churchill that, if the Turks came into the war and were consequently threatened by the Bulgars, Russia would declare war against Bulgaria. But Stalin went on to say that in the eyes of the Soviet Union all that really counted was Overlord. Side-shows in the Mediterranean should not be undertaken if they involved any postponement of Overlord beyond May 1944. He recommended that the three Heads of Government should take three immediate steps: fix a date for Overlord, organize an attack on southern France if possible two months before Overlord D-day, and appoint a commander for Overlord.[1] Until these things had been done, he averred, the Russians could not feel sure that Overlord was really on its way.

Roosevelt then intervened to say that all agreed upon the overriding importance of Overlord, and that the only disagreement concerned timing. He pointed out that some of the projects Churchill championed so vigorously might require more forces than foreseen, with the consequence that they might delay Overlord even more than the six to eight weeks which Churchill expected.

Conversation next turned briefly to the situation in Yugoslavia and Greece. Churchill took the initiative in proposing that Allied support should be transferred from Mihailović to Tito, proposing to increase deliveries of supplies and to make commando raids in support of the Partisans. Roosevelt and Stalin both agreed; and Eden later made arrangements for the Russians to send a military mission to Tito to supplement

[1] Stalin made it clear that the choice of a commander lay solely with the American and British Governments, but he wanted the man to be designated before the conference at Tehrān came to an end.

the British Mission already with his headquarters.[1] Stalin then brought the debate back to the problem of fixing a date for Overlord, saying that he would not agree to any postponement of that operation beyond the month of May 1944. Churchill replied that he would not subscribe to any such rigid time-table. He once again painted a glowing picture of the advantages to be won in the Mediterranean, and concluded by emphasizing the three conditions which would have first to be met before Overlord, according to present plans, could be undertaken. Only by engaging in active operations in the Mediterranean in the coming months, he said, could these conditions be realized. They would not delay Overlord, but would rather make Overlord possible as nothing else could do.

By drawing attention to the limiting conditions which had been written into the Overlord plan, Churchill suggested to Stalin's suspicious mind that perhaps the British were trying to play a colossal trick upon him, and really meant not to invade northern France at all. He asked Churchill what would happen if the Germans had thirteen mobile divisions in France instead of the twelve fixed as the maximum by the Overlord plan. But Churchill replied that in such a case Overlord would not be ruled out—thereby taking the edge off his earlier argument.

Churchill next returned to the advantages that would accrue to Russia and the Allies if Turkey came into the war and opened the Straits for supply ships to Russia. He also pointed out that if agreed withdrawals of landing craft from the Mediterranean were rigidly adhered to there would be no possibility of invading southern France in support of Overlord as Stalin had recommended.

The argument, in which Stalin and Churchill were playing the role of protagonists, had become tense, and Roosevelt decided that it was time to break things off. He suggested that the three Heads of Government should refer the strategic question to their military advisers, instructing them to make recommendations for any practicable subsidiary operations in the Mediterranean (or elsewhere) that could be carried out without delaying Overlord. This was accepted; but before the meeting broke up Stalin decided to beard the British lion direct. He asked Churchill whether the British really approved of Overlord, or were only pretending to accept the plan in order to cozen the Russians? Stalin's tone was not friendly and

[1] Churchill, v. 324, 413; U.S. edition, v. 367, 467. Churchill was aware that the Russians might question British activities in the Balkans on political grounds, and sought by this gesture to head off serious conflict. The decision to transfer British support from Mihailović to Tito took place by degrees between June and December 1943 after efforts to establish some sort of working compromise between the rival guerrilla leaders had failed (ibid. pp. 409–14 and 463–8 respectively). For a detailed, though biased, account of relations between Mihailović and the British see Constantine Fotitch: *The War We Lost* (New York, Viking Press, 1948), pp. 219–29. Details will also be found in the *Survey* for 1939–46: *Hitler's Europe*.

the challenge was direct. Churchill angrily replied that, when the conditions which were set forth in the plan for Overlord were met, Britain would hurl her full strength across the Channel.

This cannot have been altogether reassuring to Stalin; but the direction in which the debate had moved was even less reassuring to Churchill. With Russian support, the Americans seemed to be rushing into a commitment which might bring untold disaster to Britain and to America as well. But Churchill had done his best. After this second plenary session, there was little more he could do to resist the decisions which were being pressed upon him.[1]

At dinner Stalin took his turn as host. He was irritated that no decision had been reached during the afternoon and showed his displeasure by deliberately baiting Churchill. The Prime Minister, for his part, was feeling the strain, though he was, perhaps, more irritated by Roosevelt's failure to support him than by Stalin's opposition. At one point in the dinner conversation, Churchill belligerently announced that Great Britain was not going to surrender any of her rightful possessions, whether Hongkong, Singapore, or any other colony, under compulsion from any outsider whomsoever. This remark was, of course, aimed principally at Roosevelt, whose hopes for international trusteeships and United Nations bases in former colonial territory were well known to the British; but it was Stalin who suavely answered, saying that he personally favoured extension of the British Empire. He mentioned Gibraltar as a point where enlargement could appropriately take place. Churchill promptly asked what territorial ambitions Stalin might have for himself, but the Russian dictator turned the question aside, replying that this was not the time to talk of such matters.

At one point in the evening, Stalin remarked that after Germany had been beaten it would be necessary to root out the German military organization entirely. He said that it would be necessary to execute 50,000 German army officers and technicians; and if this were done Germany's war organization would be crippled for generations to come. Churchill took violent exception to such barbarity, and when Roosevelt intervened to ask jocularly whether, if 50,000 was too many, 49,000 would please him, Churchill failed to think it funny. At this juncture the President's son, Elliott Roosevelt, rose from his place at the table to applaud Stalin's proposal. Churchill lost his temper and left the room; but Stalin quickly followed and strove to reassure him that it had all been jest. Churchill

[1] Churchill, v. 411–19; U.S. edition, v. 364–73; Sherwood: *Roosevelt and Hopkins*, pp. 787–8; Eng. edition, ii. 782–3; Leahy: *I Was There*, pp. 245–6. At some time, before or during this second plenary session, Stalin accepted the proposal which Roosevelt had made to him the day before about shuttle bombing by American planes. But he said that he would have to consult Moscow before agreeing to the other proposals Roosevelt had made for co-operation preparatory to Russia's entry into the war against Japan.

was soon mollified and returned to the banquet.[1] This incident, unimportant in itself, was symptomatic of the state of feeling between the three men who were deciding the fate of a large part of the world together at Tehrān.

The next day, 30 November, was the decisive one. Churchill and his military advisers came to the conclusion that it was useless to resist any longer the combined American and Russian pressure for a definite commitment to an early date for Overlord. Consequently, when the British and American Chiefs of Staff met in the morning of 30 November, the British agreed to set Overlord D-day at 1 May 1944. They also agreed that a supporting attack on the coast of southern France should be made 'on the largest scale that was permitted by the landing craft available at that time.'[2] This no more than reaffirmed the decisions made at Quebec in August; but this time the Russians became a party to the agreement and British efforts to emphasize the tentative nature of the decision more or less ceased. This agreement at Tehrān thus marked the final stage in the long debate over the second front.

At this same meeting the Combined Chiefs of Staff came to a second important decision. During the weeks before Tehrān, the Americans had developed a plan to establish a single supreme Anglo-American commander for the entire European theatre of operations. Such a commander would have been directly superior to local commanders for the Mediterranean and for Overlord. The post was in a sense tailor-made for General Marshall, but the Americans were willing to assign the topmost position to Sir John Dill whom they had come to trust completely.[3] The British resisted this proposal, wanting to keep the Mediterranean and the Overlord commands separate, subordinate only to the Combined Chiefs of Staff.

After some discussion, the Americans accepted the British arguments. Two Supreme Allied Commanders were agreed upon, one for Overlord, and one who would command the entire Mediterranean.[4] In addition, the decision first taken at Quebec, that a British general should command the Mediterranean theatre to balance American command of Overlord, was reaffirmed. Such an arrangement obviously gave the Mediterranean command a greater autonomy than could have been the case under the system of command which the Americans had advocated. This undoubtedly

[1] Sherwood: *Roosevelt and Hopkins*, p. 790; Eng. edition, ii. 784; Churchill, v. 329–30; U.S. edition, v. 373–4. Cf. Elliott Roosevelt's rather different account, *As He Saw It*, pp. 245–6.

[2] Churchill, v. 337; U.S. edition, v. 382.

[3] Leahy: *I Was There*, p. 247; Churchill, v. 270–2, 296–300; U.S. edition, v. 304–6, 335–40.

[4] Previously the eastern Mediterranean had been separated from Eisenhower's command, coming directly under the British Chiefs of Staff. The decision to extend the jurisdiction of Allied Force Headquarters (A.F.H.Q.) to the entire Mediterranean had already been taken at the First Quebec Conference; it was simply reaffirmed at Tehrān (cf. pp. 295–6 above).

helped to soothe Churchill for his defeat on the central strategic issue. With a British general in command, subject to his influence as an American could not be, the Prime Minister could still hope that great things might come from a vigorous prosecution of the war in the Mediterranean.[1]

Although he had yielded by accepting a fixed date for Overlord, Churchill was not yet ready to give up his plans. If resources could not be subtracted from Overlord, they could be withdrawn or withheld from Burma instead. In order to try to gain Stalin's support for this move, Churchill arranged for a private interview with the Russian dictator during the morning when the Combined Chiefs of Staff were in session (30 November). He explained that the Americans wanted the British to embark upon an amphibious operation in Burma in March; explained also that the decision to appoint a supreme commander for Overlord rested solely on Roosevelt. He pointed out that the one thing that prevented full exploitation of opportunities in the Mediterranean was the shortage of landing craft; and that the Americans might well supply some from their hoard in the Pacific to help with Overlord. If they would do that, there would be enough for all the proposed operations against Germany. Churchill declared that he favoured the landing in southern France, and wanted to launch an amphibious attack on the Italian coast in the neighbourhood of Rome in the immediate future in order to push the battle line up to the Appenines. Stalin was apparently non-committal, contenting himself with repeating that for the Russians Overlord came first, and pressing Churchill to tell him when the Overlord D-day would come.[2]

This Churchill could not do, for he had agreed with Roosevelt that the President should be the man to impart the news of the decision to fix D-day during the month of May 1944.[3] This Roosevelt did at lunch, shortly after Churchill's private conversation with Stalin came to an end. Stalin was gratified, and promised that a big Russian offensive would be prepared to support Overlord. He recurred to the question of who would command the attack, but Roosevelt put him off, saying that he needed a few more days to make his decision. Despite this evasion, which meant that one of Stalin's three demands had not yet been met, the decisions taken on the morning of 30 November clearly constituted the turning-point of the Tehrān Conference. Stalin had received the assurances he most wanted; and the mood of the Conference, which had been tense and nervous in the first two days, abruptly mellowed. An easy cameraderie and even gaiety came to prevail in the final meetings. Once the immediate military prob-

[1] Churchill, v. 334; U.S. edition, v. 378.

[2] Ibid. pp. 332–6 and 376–81 respectively.

[3] Roosevelt and Churchill did *not* tell Stalin that the target date for D-day had been set at 1 May. By merely mentioning the month they preserved a measure of flexibility against unforeseen obstacles to their plans. As it turned out this was a very prudent act. D-day did not actually come until 6 June 1944.

lem had been decided, the Big Three could converse informally about political and other questions, and in the mood of the moment it seemed that no great disagreements would arise between them. Thus during the latter part of the luncheon meeting on 30 November, Roosevelt and Churchill discussed with Stalin Russia's need for access to ice-free ports—west to the Baltic, south through the Turkish Straits, and east to the Pacific. Perhaps to Stalin's surprise, neither Roosevelt nor Churchill expressed anything but sympathy for Russian ambitions in these directions. No definite undertakings were made, however.[1] A short plenary session was held in the afternoon to ratify the strategic decisions of the morning, and in the evening it was Churchill's turn to act as host. It was also his sixty-ninth birthday. Cordiality prevailed, and complimentary toasts were exchanged round the banquet table. The most striking remark was Stalin's statement that without American production Russia would have lost the war. The strained relations which had characterized the preceding day seemed to have vanished. Stalin relaxed and played the part of good friend and good fellow to Roosevelt's intense satisfaction. Everything seemed to have turned out all right in the end. Military agreement and personal friendship had been achieved. The Russians had at last been brought within the family circle. Churchill's thoughts were doubtless less satisfactory; but he took his defeat in good spirit, consoling himself with the thought that the Turks had yet to be heard from; and he joined with a will in the hilarity of the occasion.[2]

The Anglo-American Combined Chiefs of Staff left Tehrān for Cairo on the following day, 1 December, but the Big Three stayed on for another day. There were still some political matters to be settled, or at least discussed; and Churchill had not given up hope of securing agreement to his plan for an attack upon Rhodes to coincide with a Turkish declaration of war against Germany.

The three Heads of Government met with the Foreign Ministers and Hopkins at lunch on 1 December. The first question was what to do to bring Turkey into the war. Both Roosevelt and Stalin were wary lest they open the door to commitments that would interfere with Overlord. When Churchill mentioned the possibility of bringing landing craft from the Pacific to fill up any shortfall in the requirements for Overlord, Roosevelt promptly and definitely vetoed the idea. The President was also unwilling to change the plan for amphibious attack in Burma in order to

[1] Churchill, v. 336–7; U.S. edition, v. 381–2; Sherwood: *Roosevelt and Hopkins*, pp. 791–2; Eng. edition, ii. 786.

[2] Churchill, v. 339–43; U.S. edition, v. 384–8; Sherwood: *Roosevelt and Hopkins*, pp. 792–3; Eng. edition, ii. 786–7.

allow an assault upon Rhodes. In the end it was agreed that when Churchill and Roosevelt were in Cairo on their way home from Tehrān they should make another effort to persuade the Turks to declare war in spite of the fact that no amphibious operation could be mounted against Rhodes. The only support Churchill was authorized to offer to the Turks was twenty squadrons of fighter planes, supplemented perhaps by some American bombers. But this, Churchill hoped, might be enough to win the Turks over, especially since he planned to use threats against them—threats of cutting off all supplies and of refusal to support Turkey against any future Russian claims for special rights in the Straits area.[1]

A second question then came up: when and how should the Russians take possession of their share of the Italian navy and merchant marine? Churchill and Roosevelt had already agreed in principle that Russia should share in the spoils, but they asked for time to arrange matters with the Italians, suggesting that after a month or two it should be possible to transfer some of the Italian ships to Russian control.[2]

After lunch Stalin came to see Roosevelt privately for a third time. The President took the opportunity to try to acquaint Stalin with some of the intricacies of American politics. Among other things, he mentioned the fact that American citizens of Polish and Lithuanian extraction constituted an important voting bloc, and that their opinions had consequently to be taken seriously into account in determining American foreign policy. Stalin's reply was to suggest that some propaganda work should be undertaken to bend their minds to accord with state policy. Stalin probably did not take Roosevelt's remarks seriously. It is likely that he regarded the President's appeal to Polish-American opinion as a curiously devious trick to justify a policy of opposition to the Soviet Union. It is certain that the Soviet dictator had not the slightest intention of deferring to the sensibilities of Polish-Americans or any other such group in determining his own policy in Eastern Europe.[3]

Later in the afternoon, a final plenary session of the Conference was held. The Foreign Ministers and Hopkins were present as well as the three Heads of Government. Roosevelt began by saying that he hoped the Russians would be able to resume diplomatic relations with the Polish Government in Exile;[4] but Stalin would make no such promise. He declared that the Polish Government in Exile had joined with Hitler in slanderous propaganda against the Soviet Union and that he would

[1] Churchill, v. 344–7; U.S. edition, v. 389–93.

[2] Ibid. pp. 347–8 and 393–4, respectively. This later became a source of embarrassment to Britain and America. In the end it was arranged to transfer some British and American warships to Russia in place of the Italian vessels; and the division of the Italian fleet took place only after the war (ibid. pp. 402–7 and 454–60 respectively).

[3] Sherwood: *Roosevelt and Hopkins*, p. 796; Eng. edition, ii. 788.

[4] For the breach of Russo-Polish relations in April, see above, p. 276.

resume relations only with a Polish Government that put fighting the Germans ahead of all else. The Conference soon dropped this prickly subject and turned instead to consider Polish boundaries. Churchill and Stalin agreed that Poland should acquire German territory to the Oder river; and they accepted the Curzon Line as the eastern Polish boundary after some exchanges over the question of exactly where the Curzon Line ran. Roosevelt took no part in these discussions, but did not indicate any opposition to the arrangements proposed. Stalin said that he did not want to annex any regions predominantly Polish, and accepted the suggestion that in mixed areas exchanges of population might be a solution. Just before the end of the meeting, Churchill brought the matter of the post-war Polish frontier up a second time, and tried to reduce the agreement to a written formula. Stalin took the occasion to say that he wanted to annex Königsberg, in order to secure an ice-free port on the Baltic. This provoked no demur from either Churchill or Roosevelt, but Churchill failed to secure the formal written statement of the Allies' intentions with respect to Polish boundaries which he had sought.[1]

The Polish question was thus left in the air, and the same thing happened when the Conference turned to discuss the possibility of persuading Finland to make peace with Russia. Stalin made it clear that he did not think the Finns were ready to make peace, and outlined his conditions: restoration of the 1940 frontier, a Soviet naval base at either Hangö or Petsamo, reparations amounting to half the damage done to Russia by the Finns, an open break with Germany, the expulsion of all Germans from Finland, and, finally, demobilization of the Finnish army. At the same time he denied any intention of making Finland into a Russian province.[2]

The final matter for discussion was the future of Germany. Roosevelt sketched a plan for dividing Germany into five separate states; Churchill countered with the suggestion that the south German states, or some of them, should be incorporated into a Danubian confederation. But Stalin was against confederation and said so. He did not feel that Roosevelt's ideas were adequate either, and it was decided that the whole matter should be referred to the European Advisory Commission which had been set up by the Foreign Ministers a month before during their meeting in Moscow.[3]

In the course of this last day of the Conference, a Declaration on Persia was signed by Roosevelt, Stalin, Churchill, and by the Persian Prime Minister. Roosevelt was the moving spirit behind this declaration, which

[1] Churchill, v. 348–51, 356–7; U.S. edition, v. 394–7, 403; Sherwood: *Roosevelt and Hopkins*, p. 797; Eng. edition, ii. 789.

[2] Churchill, v. 351–4; U.S. edition, v. 397–400. An account of the Finnish-Russian peace negotiations will be found in the *Survey* for 1939–46: *The Realignment of Europe*.

[3] Sherwood: *Roosevelt and Hopkins*, pp. 797–8; Eng. edition, ii. 789; Churchill, v. 354–6; U.S. edition, v. 400–3.

promised economic aid to Persia both during and after the war, and declared that all concerned were united in desiring 'the maintenance of the independence, sovereignty, and territorial integrity of Iran . . . in accordance with the principles of the Atlantic Charter, to which all four governments have continued to subscribe'.[1] The Declaration was designed primarily to reassure the Persians and all the world that the military occupation of that country, which had been undertaken in defiance of the will of the Persian Government, would not endure after the end of the war.

Stalin acted as host at the final dinner. It was a much less elaborate and lengthy affair than those which had preceded it during the Conference, for Roosevelt was anxious to depart that evening. Nothing of note transpired, and the Big Three bade one another farewell about 10 o'clock on 1 December 1943.

The long-expected meeting of Roosevelt and Churchill with Stalin thus passed into history. The most notable thing about the Conference was the apparent solidarity of Russian and American military views and the corresponding isolation of Great Britain. Churchill found himself in an unexpected and highly embarrassing position. He based his arguments for expanded Mediterranean campaigns on military grounds alone; and it would be hasty, perhaps wrong, to say that his personal ideas about what should next be done were not primarily fixed by purely military considerations. But the Americans suspected that he was thinking primarily of the post-war balance of political power, and wanted to head off Russian domination of the Balkans.[2] As a result of this suspicion, Churchill's military arguments were largely shrugged aside as mere rhetoric, designed to hide his real motives in a garb of plausible words.

At the same time, Roosevelt undoubtedly felt a measure of sympathy for the Prime Minister. Consequently, when conversations were resumed in Cairo to decide finally what should be done in Burma, Roosevelt was in a mood to defer to Churchill's point of view even if it meant disappointing Chiang Kai-shek. After all it would not do to win Russia and China and at the same time alienate the British. That would be to fail in the great task Roosevelt had set himself—the consolidation of the Grand Alliance for war and for the peace to follow.

Roosevelt saw his future role as that of arbiter, conciliator, and teacher: he was the man who would have to raise both the British and the Russians from their old-fashioned concern for national advantage and persuade them to regulate their international dealings by the moral principles

[1] *Documents on American Foreign Relations, 1943–1944*, pp. 235–6.

[2] For an extreme statement of this view cf. Elliott Roosevelt's report of the President's private remarks (*As He Saw It*, pp. 184–6).

professed in the Atlantic Charter and in the United Nations Declaration. Roosevelt believed that only on the basis of such principles could an enduring peace be established. The President did not think the task he set himself would be easy, but he did believe it possible. That compromises between principle and old-fashioned habits of thought (i.e. power politics) might be necessary did not trouble him unduly. After all, his whole political career in the United States had been based on such compromised idealism. His great hope was a new Holy Alliance, to defend and enforce democratic rather than monarchic ideals. The great prerequisite was to convert the leaders of the most powerful Allied Governments to his way of thinking; and Roosevelt felt he could congratulate himself on the heartening progress that had been made in that direction at Tehrān. He believed that the final words of the communiqué which he, Churchill, and Stalin had just signed spoke naked truth. 'We came here with hope and determination. We leave here, friends in fact, in spirit, and in purpose.'

Indeed, the whole communiqué, published to the world on 6 December 1943, was eloquent of the optimism which Roosevelt had come to feel. It declared:

> We express our determination that our nations shall work together in war and in the peace that will follow.
>
> As to war—our military staffs have joined in our round table discussions, and we have concerted our plans for the destruction of the German forces. . . .
>
> And as to peace—we are sure that our concord will win an enduring Peace. We recognize fully the supreme responsibility resting upon us and all the United Nations to make a peace which will command the goodwill of the overwhelming mass of the peoples of the world and banish the scourge and terror of war for many generations.
>
> With our diplomatic advisors we have surveyed the problems of the future. We shall seek the cooperation and active participation of all nations, large and small, whose peoples in heart and mind are dedicated, as are our own peoples, to the elimination of tyranny and slavery, oppression, and intolerance. We will welcome them, as they may choose to come, into a world family of Democratic Nations.[1]

Stalin's views can only be surmised. He was certainly pleased at the strategic decisions which had been made, and was probably delighted to discover the manifest differences which had appeared between the British and American points of view. A united capitalist front against the Soviet Union did not seem a serious danger for the immediate post-war years. Very likely he interpreted Roosevelt's talk about trusteeship for dependent peoples as a clever device for opening the markets of the colonial world to American trade by disrupting the French and British Empires. But he must have found much that was profoundly puzzling in Roosevelt's atti-

[1] *Documents on American Foreign Relations, 1943–1944*, p. 235.

tudes: they did not fit into any of the patterns with which he was familiar; and to believe that Roosevelt meant no more than he said probably surpassed Stalin's strictly limited credulity.

From his own point of view, Stalin had successfully avoided any commitment of Soviet post-war policy. Territorial and other questions in Eastern and Central Europe had been left open; and while he must have realized how widely his intentions differed from Roosevelt's hopes and expectations and from Churchill's wishes, he could congratulate himself on the thought that the strategy which had been agreed to would result in giving the Red Army a free hand to create whatever sort of régime pleased him in such countries as Poland, Rumania, Bulgaria, or even farther west. It had been a thoroughly successful if at times a puzzling or even disturbing encounter.

Churchill cannot have been pleased with the results of the Tehrān Conference, but he was too hardened a campaigner to bear a grudge for long. He still saw a chance of salvaging at least a part of his Mediterranean plans, and, if that could be done, all might yet be well and the ground be truly and properly laid for the success of Overlord in 1944. Everything turned (1) on being able to persuade the Turks to come into the war, or at least to allow British use of Turkish air bases to establish air superiority over the Aegean; and (2) on being able to persuade the Americans to cancel the amphibious operation against the Andaman Islands which Roosevelt had promised to Chiang Kai-shek. Only in this way could enough landing craft be retained in the Mediterranean to allow the realization of his plan for amphibious attack in Italy to take Rome; and, if that were successful, other opportunities to harass the Germans by attacks upon Rhodes and, perhaps, along the Adriatic coast of Yugoslavia, might present themselves before the time came for the landing in southern France. Thus it was in good heart that he approached the further conferences with the Turks and with the Americans in Cairo.[1]

(*d*) The Second Cairo Conference, 2–6 December 1943

Upon their arrival in Cairo, Roosevelt and Churchill dined together on the evening of 2 December and compared their impressions of Stalin. Churchill was particularly at pains to bury past differences. The mood was one of relaxation, a recess after the intensive work at Tehrān.[2] On the following day the meetings of the Combined Chiefs of Staff were resumed. The problem before them was Burma, and discussion was long and bitter. The British as before wanted to cancel the proposed amphibious assault on the Andaman Islands and to use the landing craft to attack Rhodes instead.[3] The Americans insisted that a promise had been made

[1] Churchill, v. 358, 361; U.S. edition, v. 405, 408.
[2] Leahy: *I Was There*, p. 251.
[3] On the shortage of landing craft, see above, p. 230, note 1.

to Chiang Kai-shek and that if it were not fulfilled, China might collapse or make peace, thus prolonging the Japanese war and making the task of the American forces in the Pacific more difficult. The collision of views was direct, and neither side would budge. The British felt that they had already given way quite enough and that it was time the Americans did a little yielding; the Americans felt that China was at stake, and that, if they did not insist, the British would in effect leave the whole weight of the war against Japan on their shoulders.

In the evening of 3 December Roosevelt and Churchill dined together once more, and went over the dispute which their military advisers had debated earlier in the day. Churchill exhausted the armoury of argument. His most telling point was that Stalin's promise to join in the Japanese war as soon as Germany had been defeated quite changed the strategic picture. China would no longer be indispensable: air bases to bomb Japan could be set up in the eastern provinces of Siberia more easily than in China, and the Red Army would be on hand to take care of Japanese troops on the mainland of Asia.[1] A second important consideration which told in the British favour was the difficulty which shipping shortages still presented. Shipping was adequate, but only adequate, for Overlord, the Mediterranean, and the Pacific. To launch a large-scale operation from India required more shipping than could be found; and the great length of the voyage meant that the value of a single ship was greatly reduced. Three trips could easily be made across the North Atlantic in the time required for a single trip to the Bay of Bengal and back. In addition, the detailed plans for the Andaman Islands attack which had now been submitted to the Combined Chiefs of Staff called for an unexpectedly large force which it would be difficult in any case to find, and Churchill made much of the necessity of subordinating everything, even the war against Japan, to Overlord. This was turning the Americans' own argument against them, and one can imagine how Churchill may have taken peculiar pleasure in doing so.[2]

Roosevelt at first seemed as stubborn as his Chiefs of Staff, and no decision was reached. Conversation turned to the question of zones of occupation in Germany, and once again conflict arose. Both Americans and British wanted to occupy north-western Germany, leaving south-western Germany to the other. Again, no decision was reached.[3]

[1] In arguing thus Churchill was in effect turning the Americans' a-political approach to military issues to his own account. It is reasonable to suppose that the prospect of a weak and disunited China, open to Russian influence, displeased the Americans, who cherished the vision of a China warmly grateful to the United States for war-time help and dependent on American economic aid for post-war reconstruction. But they could hardly say so openly, any more than Churchill had felt it possible to argue for his Mediterranean and Balkan projects on the political level.

[2] Sherwood: *Roosevelt and Hopkins*, p. 800; Eng. edition, ii. 792; Churchill, v. 361–4; U.S. edition, v. 408–11.

[3] Leahy: *I Was There*, pp. 251–2.

On the following day, 4 December, the struggle among the Combined Chiefs of Staff continued without any sign of agreement. That evening President Inönü of Turkey arrived in Cairo, and Roosevelt entertained him at dinner. Churchill came in after the meal and began to try to persuade Inönü to declare war on Germany. Roosevelt backed Churchill up, but left most of the talking to the Prime Minister. Inönü listened non-committally.

The first sign of a break in the deadlock came on 5 December after the Combined Chiefs had spent still another day in fruitless argument. Despite the unbending attitude of Marshall and the other members of the American Joint Chiefs of Staff, Roosevelt decided that a concession would have to be made to the British point of view. He prepared a telegram to be sent to Chiang Kai-shek which said:

> Conference with Stalin involves us in combined grand operations on European continent in the late spring giving fair prospect of terminating war with Germany by end of summer of 1944. These operations impose so large a requirement of heavy landing craft as to make it impracticable to devote a sufficient number to the amphibious operation in Bay of Bengal. . . .[1]

The telegram went on to ask whether Chiang would go ahead with the attack on northern Burma anyway, or whether he preferred to wait until November 1944, when the projected amphibious operation could once again be promised. Churchill approved the telegram, and, when the American Joint Chiefs reported to the President in the late afternoon of 5 December, he told them of his decision. They were chagrined and angry and felt that in breaking his word to Chiang Kai-shek the President was risking the unnecessary prolongation of the Japanese war.[2]

As a result of Roosevelt's action, it became relatively easy to reach agreement when the Combined Chiefs met on the following morning, 6 December. It was decided that the Andaman Islands attack should be cancelled, and that Mountbatten should be instructed to work out an alternative operation on a smaller scale. In compliance with these instructions, Mountbatten proposed a landing on the coast of Burma itself in the rear of the Japanese lines; but Chiang Kai-shek refused to accept this proposal as adequate, and declared that he would not send his troops from Yunnan to take part in the general offensive. In view of Chiang's non co-operation and Churchill's pressure for action in Italy, the Combined Chiefs of Staff finally, on 7 January, a month after the Cairo Conference had ended, decided that all amphibious operations in South-East

[1] Sherwood: *Roosevelt and Hopkins*, p. 802; Eng. edition, ii. 792; Churchill, v. 364–5; U.S. edition, v. 411–12.

[2] Leahy: *I Was There*, p. 252; Sherwood: *Roosevelt and Hopkins*, p. 800; Eng. edition, ii. 791. Sherwood says that this was the single occasion during the war upon which Roosevelt definitely overruled his military advisers.

Asia should be cancelled. They ordered the landing craft which had been assembled in the Bay of Bengal to return to the Mediterranean and to England,[1] and instructed Mountbatten to do what he could with the ground and air forces left under his command.

Agreement about Burma left only one item to be decided. Roosevelt had so far yielded to Churchill's pressure that on 5 December he instructed his Chiefs of Staff that every effort should be made to find eighteen to twenty landing craft for an attack on Rhodes; but such an operation was contingent upon Turkish belligerency. Accordingly, on the evening of 5 December Churchill and Roosevelt once more took up the effort to persuade the Turks that their true interests lay in joining the Allies by 15 February 1944.[2] Churchill as before did most of the talking. Inönü was more definite in his replies than he had been on the preceding evening. He asked for supplies and time to train the Turkish troops in the use of modern weapons; but Roosevelt would not agree to the diversion of large quantities of supplies to Turkey and Churchill could not afford more time. It was now or never for his Aegean project. Words alone could not coerce the Turks, and they chose to refrain from risking war. Churchill made one final attempt on the following day, but without any success. The Americans were relieved rather than disappointed. Marshall and the American Chiefs of Staff feared that if the Turks came in they would have to be supplied on a scale that might well interfere with Overlord.[3]

While these debates were in progress, Roosevelt was turning over in his mind another important decision. The time had come to determine who should command Overlord. At Quebec in August it had been agreed that an American should have the supreme responsibility, and there were only two men to be considered: Marshall and Eisenhower. The President tried to get General Marshall to say what he himself judged best; but Marshall, who secretly wished to command in the field rather than in the halls of the Pentagon, refused to give any indication of his preference or judgement. It was on 5 December that Roosevelt finally took the decision. Marshall would remain in Washington; Eisenhower would go to London as Supreme Commander, Allied Expeditionary Force. Churchill first

[1] Mountbatten: *Report*, pp. 263–5.

[2] This was the date by which Churchill hoped the Anzio operation in Italy would have won success, freeing landing craft for Rhodes. For the date at which Turkish belligerency was requested see Hull: *Memoirs*, ii. 1369.

[3] Leahy: *I Was There*, p. 253; Sherwood: *Roosevelt and Hopkins*, pp. 799–800, 802; Eng. edition, ii. 790–1, 793. Churchill (v. 367; U.S. edition, v. 415) says that it had been arranged that Vyshinsky should be present for the Turkish conversations; but he did not come to Cairo and took no part in the negotiations. Cf. Eden's report to the House of Commons, 14 December 1943, H.C.Deb. 5th ser., vol. 395, coll. 1425–8. Obviously the Russians had decided that they should not themselves do anything to help bring the Turks into the war.

heard the news on 6 December; General Eisenhower received notice of his new appointment from Roosevelt's own lips on 7 December 1943, the second anniversary of Pearl Harbour, when the President stopped in Tunis on his way back to Washington.[1] Public announcement of the appointment was postponed until after Roosevelt's return to the United States. It was made on Christmas Eve in the course of a radio broadcast in which Roosevelt reported upon the Cairo and Tehrān Conferences.

(*e*) The Significance of the Conferences

From the time of the First Quebec Conference in August 1943 the newspapers of America and Britain had been full of rumours of an impending meeting of the Big Three, and many journalists allowed themselves to speculate freely upon what decisions would emerge from such a meeting. A favourite idea, reflecting one of Roosevelt's early proposals,[2] was that the Russians would be associated with the Anglo-American Allies on the Combined Chiefs of Staff and other combined boards. During the weeks when the Cairo and Tehrān Conferences were actually under way, unsubstantiated reports of the proceedings reached eager newspaper editors through various neutral channels; and the German radio likewise announced that a meeting of the Big Three was in progress.

As a result, when the official communiqués were released, the news came as something of an anti-climax. The agreements described in the communiqués fell a good deal short of some journalistic expectations; and the fact that newspapermen had been excluded from the scene at Tehrān cut down the amount of local colour that appeared in the press. Nevertheless, the communiqués were received with almost universal approbation by the newspapers of all three Allied countries. The Russian press gave the story of Tehrān extraordinary prominence, and for days after the original announcement the columns of *Pravda* and *Izvestia* were filled with comments and resolutions pertaining to the Tehrān decisions. Stalin's prestige was fully committed. *Pravda* commented:

> Only a short time separates us from the Moscow Conference of the three Foreign Ministers of the Allied Powers, the decisions of which not only demonstrated the strengthening of friendly co-operation between Great Britain, the U.S.S.R., and the U.S.A. in the war period, but laid the basis for fruitful work together after the war. But what a tremendous step forward has now been taken along this path.[3]

Izvestia remarked: 'The greatest statesmen of our epoch met round the table and achieved the fullest understanding on problems of the prosecu-

[1] Eisenhower: *Crusade in Europe*, pp. 206–7; Sherwood: *Roosevelt and Hopkins*, pp. 802–3; Eng. edition, ii. 793; Churchill, v. 369–70; U.S. edition, v. 418. [2] See above, p. 337, note 4.

[3] Quoted by Anthony Eden in a speech to the House of Commons in which he reported on the Cairo and Tehrān Conferences (14 December 1943, H.C.Deb. 5th ser., vol. 395, col. 1429).

tion of the war and the important problems after the war. . . . Anyone who ponders the declaration will understand that the fate of the war has been decided once and for all.'[1]

In the United States, a few senators, who were confirmed opponents of Roosevelt, pointed out that the communiqué said nothing of Russia's intentions with respect to Poland and other countries neighbouring the Soviet Union; but the general reaction was to stress the new certainty of victory and hope of permanent peace. As the *Chicago Daily News* (7 December 1943) expressed it: 'The real meaning of Teheran, as we see it, is that Russia is willing to become a genuine partner, not only in the prosecution of a common war strategy, but in a common peace strategy, in a common interest, for the common good. United in war, united in peace—the United Nations!'

British papers were almost equally enthusiastic, although some, like the *Manchester Guardian* (10 December 1943), pointed out that the breakdown of war-time alliances had been all too common in times past, but took some comfort in reflecting that the outlook was better than it had been in 1918. No hint of the disappointments which Churchill had suffered appeared in the British papers. New confidence that at last the end of the war was clearly in sight dominated British comment.

Roosevelt arrived back in the United States on 17 December 1943 and on Christmas Eve he broadcast to the world. In his speech he said:

> We [i.e. Churchill, Stalin, and himself] did discuss international relationships from the point of view of big, broad objectives, rather than details. But on the basis of what we did discuss, I can say even today that I do not think any insoluble differences will arise among Russia, Great Britain, and the United States. . . .
>
> To use an American and somewhat ungrammatical colloquialism, I may say that I 'got along fine' with Marshal Stalin. He is a man who combines a tremendous, relentless determination with a stalwart good humor. I believe he is truly representative of the heart and soul of Russia; and I believe that we are going to get along very well with him and the Russian people—very well indeed.[2]

The President went on to emphasize the need of keeping the peace by force if necessary and to ridicule 'cheerful idiots' who thought that isolation was a practicable policy for the United States.

Churchill fell ill in North Africa before his return from the Conferences, and Anthony Eden deputized for him in reporting to the House of Commons. On the question of future peace, he said:

> This recurrent threat of war can only be met if there is an international order firmer in strength and unity than any enemy that can seek to challenge it. Is

[1] Quoted in *Evening Standard*, 7 December 1943.

[2] Rosenman: *The Public Papers and Addresses of Franklin D. Roosevelt*, 1943 volume, p. 558.

there or is there not the possibility of creating such an order? Do the foundations exist?

Six months ago I could not have given any certain answer. It might have been so; it might not have been so. But today I can give the answer. It is an emphatic 'Yes'. The foundations do exist, and I am truly confident that there is a possibility, and more than a possibility, a desire, among the three Powers for continued co-operation not only during the war, not only in reshaping Europe when the Armistice comes, but also, thereafter, in maintaining in the world an orderly progress and continuing peace.[1]

In retrospect, it is clear that the hopes for enduring harmony among the three Allies were illusory. Indeed the real significance of the Tehrān Conference lay in the fact that Allied co-operation could be and was founded upon agreement on military strategy. Agreement on post-war issues was not genuinely achieved. All important decisions were left for the future after only vague exploration of the issues involved. The great achievement of the Tehrān Conference was to fix the final strategy against Germany. Earlier Anglo-American conferences had centred round military problems in the same way; subsequent meetings centred round the problems of peace. On these issues agreement proved far less easy to achieve. In this sense, the Tehrān Conference constitutes a very real turning-point in the nature of Allied relations. After Tehrān peace began to loom, and with it the difficulties created by divergent national interests among the Allies came to the forefront. Co-operation became proportionately more difficult, conflicts clearer and less subject to compromise.

The significance of the two Cairo Conferences was quite different. The decisions with respect to the Far Eastern war resulted, during the early months of 1944, in a drastic revision of basic strategy against Japan. China ceased to be pivotal, and with that change Chiang's chance of emerging from the war with an army that could make his Government a power seriously to be reckoned with disappeared.

Taken as a whole, the Cairo and Tehrān Conferences were the most important for the future of the world of any international gathering of the entire war years. The conferences were genuine turning-points from the military point of view. From the political view-point future difficulties did not emerge clearly; optimism could thus flourish on the strength of military agreement, and good feeling between Russia and the West reached its all-time height. Between Britain and America, however, rifts which became more pronounced in 1944 had shown themselves. The British Chiefs of Staff, who had been overruled in the Mediterranean, and the American Chiefs of Staff, who had been overruled in Burma, each found it hard to forget the stubborn contest of wills which had divided them at Cairo and Tehrān. Impending victory cast its shadow far ahead

[1] 14 December 1943, H.C.Deb. 5th ser., vol. 395, coll. 1429–30.

to trouble the military and political co-operation which had been far smoother and more heart-felt in 1942's days of hard adversity. But these things were not made public. From the point of view of the man in the street, allied unity, Anglo-American as much as Anglo-Russo-American, had never seemed more perfect.

PART II

CO-OPERATION AS PEACE LOOMED

DECEMBER 1943–FEBRUARY 1945

CHAPTER I

TEHRĀN TO NORMANDY: PREPARING VICTORY

DECEMBER 1943–AUGUST 1944

(i) Military Problems

(a) Introductory

At the time of the Tehrān Conference and for eight to ten months after it, Allied planners and strategists expected victory over Germany in 1944, and calculated that Japan would be defeated from twenty-four to thirty-six months after the end of the war in Europe.[1] This estimate was influenced by the memory of Germany's sudden collapse in 1918 and by the similarly abrupt end of Axis resistance in Tunisia in 1943. Over-estimate of the effect of bombing was another factor which contributed to the belief that the Nazi state would collapse suddenly and perhaps before much of Germany itself was in the hands of Allied armies. The opposite error was made in calculating Japan's power and will to resist. Until after the end of 1944 only a relatively small part of the Japanese army could be engaged in battle. The main Japanese armies in China and in Japan lay beyond the reach of the Allies, and, if the skill and fanaticism displayed by the island garrisons were indicative of the general state of Japanese fighting potential, it seemed clear that the war would be long drawn out, and could be ended only by overwhelming superiority of material. Before victory over Japan could be assured it seemed obvious that men and equipment would have to be transported from European battlefields half-way round the world—a task which would require months.

Anglo-American plans were prepared with these assumptions very much in mind. Man-power and supplies were assigned for a European campaign in 1944, and on a lavish scale; but when the war against Germany continued into 1945 there were some awkward moments when infantry replacements and supplies of ammunition became short. In addition, political relations between the Big Three were fundamentally affected by

[1] Churchill, v. 370; U.S. edition, v. 419; Leahy: *I Was There*, p. 306; Butcher: *My Three Years with Eisenhower*, pp. 462, 591, 621; Hancock and Gowing: *British War Economy*, p. 517.

the Anglo-American calculation of the length and severity of the Japanese war. Roosevelt and his advisers were willing to pay a stiff price for Russian help against the Japanese, help which they believed would greatly shorten the war and save large numbers of American lives.

After Tehrān, the military problem in Europe was a straightforward though far from simple one. Plans had to be transformed into deeds, and the ruffled feelings of the British and American Chiefs of Staff had to be smoothed over by effective co-operation in the field. From the Anglo-American point of view, a vast work of planning and preparation had to be undertaken, involving agreement on a multitude of details and bi-national co-operation at all levels of the military hierarchy. These tasks, combined with the maintenance of an active front in Italy, were promptly undertaken. From the Russian point of view, the war went on as before with new hope and assurance of victory.

The war against Japan, however, was at a quite different stage. The grand strategy which had been agreed to in 1943—a strategy which assigned a major role to the Chinese—proved more and more incapable of realization in 1944. Instead of growing stronger, China weakened and the Japanese proved able to keep China's back door in Burma firmly closed. But, counterbalancing these failures, American amphibious attack in the Pacific proved itself more and more powerful, able to confine the Japanese navy and air force to an ever narrowing circle in the Western Pacific; and at Tehrān Stalin had promised to fight Japan when the war in Europe had ended. Under these circumstances, a reassessment of strategy against Japan was obviously called for. In the course of the first seven months of 1944 the Americans worked out a new master plan which was agreed to by the British in September and by the Russians in October 1944.

(*b*) The War in Europe

(1) *The Russian Front*

Until 1944 the war on the Russian front consisted of a series of fairly distinct campaigns, separated from one another by periods of relative quiet. By the beginning of 1944, however, the pattern had changed. The Red Army now had sufficient man-power, equipment, and mobility to be able to keep up continuous attack, shifting the offensive from one section of the front to another almost without a break. Thus the great Russian advance on the central front, begun in mid-July 1943, came to a halt in January 1944, having reached the Pripet marshes in the eastern part of inter-war Poland. Then, without giving the Germans any chance to rest, re-group, and re-equip, the Red Army began a new attack in the north which drove the Germans back from Leningrad. This attack ended late in February 1944; at the beginning of March, just ten days later, the Red

Army began a far more massive attack in the south which carried the Russian forces to the Pruth River where they reached, and in places crossed, the 1940 boundary between the U.S.S.R. and Rumania. This great success was followed by the reconquest of the Crimea in April and May 1944. As a result of these campaigns, all but a small portion of pre-war Soviet territory (in the neighbourhood of Pskov) was liberated from the Germans.

But Stalin had no intention of stopping at the boundaries of 1939, and, in accordance with his promise at Tehrān, the Anglo-American landing in Normandy on 6 June 1944 was supported by a renewal of heavy fighting on the Russian front four days later. The Red Army was now strong enough to carry on several offensives simultaneously. The first attack, in Finland, was still in progress when a second Russian offensive began on the White Russian front on 23 June; and, while the Red Army was still advancing on this front through Minsk and Vilna towards the frontier of East Prussia, parallel attacks to the north (towards Pskov and Narva) and to the south (towards Lublin, Lwów, and Brest-Litovsk) were launched. In July these various offensives merged into a general advance on a thousand-mile stretch of the central and northern fronts. By 15 August the Red Army reached Praga, a suburb of Warsaw on the eastern side of the Vistula, where the offensive finally came to a halt.

The extraordinary success which came to Russian arms in the second half of 1943 and the first half of 1944 had, of course, a technical basis. For one thing, the Red Army enjoyed a heavy preponderance of numbers over the Germans; for another, Russian artillery, tanks, and rocket weapons were both highly efficient and available in large numbers. But the decisive factor, which permitted long-continued advances and rapid shifting of the main axis of attack from one section of the front to another, was the improved mobility of the Red Army. When the Russians could move men and supplies as rapidly or more rapidly than could the Germans, they became able to bring the full weight of their numerical superiority to bear, choosing their own points of attack, and driving the Germans steadily back.

As the Russians moved westward, opportunities for military co-operation between the Red Army and Anglo-American forces opened up. Arrangements were made to exchange intelligence and weather information, and to improve communications between Moscow and the Western capitals. Russian authorities seemed frequently to move with exasperating slowness in these matters, but in the end some solid results were achieved.[1]

[1] For a detailed account of the American part in these negotiations see Deane: *Strange Alliance*, pp. 64–86.

At Tehrān Stalin had agreed to provide landing fields for American bombers in Russia in order to permit attack on targets in eastern Germany and in the eastern part of occupied Europe which were too far distant from bases in Italy and Great Britain to permit round-trip attack. The Russians were slow to act on this agreement despite the eagerness of the American air force to get the project under way; nevertheless in April 1944 American personnel began to arrive to set up three bases in the Ukraine, and on 2 June the first shuttle raid was successfully completed.

A second shuttle raid was undertaken on 21 June; but it proved far less successful. The Germans had discovered the new airfields, and attacked the American planes as they lay on the ground. Defence of the airfields was a Russian responsibility, but the Russians failed to bring down a single German plane while no fewer than forty-three Flying Fortresses were destroyed. This event created bad feeling between the American and Russian soldiers on the spot. The Americans tried to persuade the Russians to allow American anti-aircraft artillery and fighters to take over protection of the bases; but the Russian high command took this to imply a reflection upon Russian capacities, and they refused to agree. As a result, only three further shuttle raids were attempted. The airfields remained in American hands until April 1945, serving as bases for the repair of American planes forced down in Russian territory and as concentration points for American airmen whose planes could not be salvaged.[1]

This incident has a peculiar interest, since it was almost the only case during the entire war when military co-operation between the Russians and the Anglo-Americans was attempted at an operational level. According to General Deane, who as Head of the American Military Mission to Russia was directly in charge of the negotiation which surrounded the project, Russian officials, particularly at the higher levels, were generally reluctant and suspicious, and put obstacles in the way at every opportunity. On the other hand, relations between the American and Russian personnel on the bases were friendly at first; but after the disastrous German attack of 21 June petty friction quickly obscured the earlier friendliness, and by 1945 political differences, centring round Russian policy towards Poland, made relations veiledly hostile. Certainly, the results bore no relation to the hopes with which the Americans had first embraced the project. The paralysing difficulties of co-operation with the Russians on a day-to-day operational level were vividly brought home to every American directly connected with the affair. Differences of language and, even more, of habits of thought and conduct made anything like the co-operation which existed between British and American units and staffs entirely impossible.

[1] Ibid. pp. 107–25; Craven and Cate, edd.: *The Army Air Forces in World War II*, iii. 312–18.

The advance of the Red Army into Polish territory during the spring and summer of 1944 raised in acute form the problem of military co-operation between the Russians and the underground Polish Home Army. The Polish Home Army recognized the authority of the exiled Polish Government in London, and had achieved a remarkable degree of organization despite the handicaps of German occupation. The Poles of the Home Army were at once bitterly hostile to the Germans and deeply suspicious and fearful of the Russians. As a result, when the battle line moved into territory where the Polish Home Army was organized, its members found themselves caught between two fires. Their orders were to co-operate militarily with the Russians while retaining full independence of action. This proved impossible. The Russians simply would not permit a potentially hostile force to exist in the rear of their armies; and the Poles could not stand in open fight against either the German Wehrmacht or the Red Army. As in 1939, they lacked the military means to defend their independence.

Russian policy towards the Polish Home Army was to co-operate with its units at the front, but when the battle had passed on, the Red Army commanders demanded that the Polish Home Army detachments should join the Polish division which had been created under the aegis of the Union of Polish Patriots, and which fought as an integral part of the Red Army. This contradicted the orders which had been given to the Polish Home Army by the London Government and by its Commander-in-Chief, General 'Bor'. When local commanders proved loyal to their instructions, they were arrested, and their men conscripted into the Red Army, or else disarmed and interned. The first such incident occurred in April 1944, and the pattern was repeated several times in the following months, especially after the Russian advance into central Poland got under way in July.[1]

The military events in Poland were inextricably intertwined with the political problem of the future of Poland. Both the Poles and the Russians kept this question in the forefront of their minds; and it became a matter of high concern between the British and Russian Governments during the first half of 1944. In effect, the progress of the Red Army across Poland marked the extinction of the Polish Home Army as an independent force; and with its destruction the main hope of the Polish Government in Exile disappeared. All that remained to the London Poles when the Red Army had finished its work was a legal claim and the somewhat ambiguous diplomatic support of the British and American Governments. These were inadequate counterweights to the unwavering resolve of the Russian Government to see a friendly, that is to say a subservient, government established in post-war Poland.

[1] Details will be found in the *Survey* for 1939–46: *The Realignment of Europe.*

Thus the military co-ordination between Russia and the Western Allies which had been achieved on the highest levels at Tehrān did not in practice extend very deep. Stalin pursued political aims which were not identical with those of the other Allies, and the Soviet bureaucracy conducted its affairs in a spirit of jealous isolation. Mere military advantage was not allowed to interfere with Soviet aims and practices, and as a result the efforts of the American and Polish Governments to establish military co-operation with the Red Army on an operational level met with little or no success.[1]

(2) *The Mediterranean Theatre*

The decisions of Tehrān and Cairo made the Mediterranean a subsidiary battle front. Yet Churchill, who from the beginning had been the most ardent and determined advocate of military operations in the Mediterranean, was not ready, even after his repeated rebuffs from the Americans, Russians, and Turks, to give up all hope of making the Mediterranean an important and active theatre of war. Turkey had to be left out of his immediate calculations;[2] but it was still possible to hope that bold and decisive action in Italy would bring speedy results, drive the Germans back to the Appennines, and, perhaps, open a path for Allied armies into the north-western Balkans and Danubian Europe.

Churchill's immediate aim in December 1943 was to stir the Allied commanders in Italy to bolder action. He therefore remained in the Mediterranean area for several weeks after the close of the second Cairo Conference.[3] There were several important decisions to make with respect to the distribution of commands among the British generals, and he wished to exert his authority and persuasive powers in order to shape events more to his liking. By 18 December 1943 Churchill had decided that General Sir Henry Maitland Wilson should succeed to Eisenhower's (enlarged) command in the Mediterranean, and that General Sir Harold Alexander should retain command of the battle in Italy. At the same time General Sir Bernard Montgomery was assigned to Overlord.[4]

[1] American efforts to concert military operations with the Russians in Europe and in the Far East were certainly innocent of ulterior political motives, even though the Russians may have found it hard to believe that the Americans could habitually and honestly separate military convenience from the political aims of war. The same was of course not true of the Polish Government in Exile, whose military co-operation with Russia was intended as a tactical move dictated by geographic and political circumstance.

[2] Churchill was a stubborn optimist, and did not give up hope of Turkish belligerency, according to his own report, until about 23 December 1943 (Churchill, v. 381; U.S. edition, v. 430).

[3] He fell ill with pneumonia on 12 December, but never entirely relaxed his control of affairs, even from the sickbed.

[4] Ibid. pp. 374–5 and 422–5 respectively. The choice of Montgomery instead of Alexander for Overlord came as a disappointment to the American Chiefs of Staff and to Eisenhower himself (cf. Eisenhower: *Crusade in Europe*, p. 211; Sherwood: *Roosevelt and Hopkins*, p. 811; Eng. edition, ii. 803).

Having made these decisions, the Prime Minister turned his attention to the problem of accelerating operations in Italy. After the initial battles at Salerno in September, the Germans had withdrawn to a defensive position extending across the peninsula, and Allied efforts to advance on Rome met with serious difficulties. Terrain and weather handicapped the attack, and the numerical strength of the Allied armies was scarcely more than equal to that of their German opponents. The only hope for rapid and dramatic success lay in utilization of Allied dominion over the sea. An amphibious attack could threaten the Germans from the rear, and if successful might compel them to retreat precipitously northward. The problem was to find the landing craft necessary for such an operation. Unless an amphibious assault were undertaken promptly and were immediately successful, it might trench upon landing craft assigned to Overlord and force the postponement of that operation. On the other hand, Churchill believed that if vigorous and successful action in Italy did not compel the Germans to draw their reserves from France and Northern Europe, then Overlord might fail. After Tehrān, he accepted the sacrosanctity of a May (or early June)[1] target date for Overlord, but believed that careful calculation would permit the use of landing craft for an amphibious attack on the Italian coast before they were transferred to England for use against Normandy.[2] It was on this basis that he now set to work.

On Christmas Day 1943 the Prime Minister called a conference of the senior commanders in the Mediterranean to discuss the situation. All agreed that the Allied armies in Italy should not surrender the initiative; and Churchill argued that the only way to achieve this end was to attack from the sea. The proposal before the conference was to put two divisions ashore at Anzio, nearly one hundred miles behind the German battle line. The target date for the attack was set at 20 January. Supported by Wilson and Alexander, Churchill argued that this threat in their rear would compel the Germans to retreat north of Rome; Eisenhower was not so confident. He pointed out difficulties of supply and reinforcement, and argued that a force of two divisions might not be enough to compel the Germans to withdraw from their positions in southern Italy.

Nevertheless, since Eisenhower was about to give up his Mediterranean command, he did not feel that his should be the deciding voice. He did think that he had the right to demand the delivery of landing craft from the Mediterranean for use in Overlord at a date which would allow adequate overhaul and training in England before the great invasion was attempted. In the end he agreed to accept a promise that the landing craft in question would be turned over to him by 5 February 1944 instead of 15 January as had been agreed to at Tehrān; and he recommended

[1] Churchill, v. 386; U.S. edition, v. 436.

[2] Ibid. pp. 381–7 and 431–7 respectively.

approval of this change in plan to the American Chiefs of Staff.[1] Simultaneously, Churchill took the matter up with Roosevelt. Despite a certain irritation at finding that Churchill would not leave the Mediterranean alone, Roosevelt and the American Chiefs of Staff accepted the new proposal, with the proviso that no Mediterranean undertaking should be allowed to interfere with the schedule for Overlord.[2]

The landing at Anzio took place on 22 January; but the Germans chose to bring up reinforcements instead of retreating. They were able to coop up the invading forces in a small beachhead and at the same time turned back the offensive by the Fifth Army which, it had been hoped, would break through and link up with the troops ashore at Anzio. By the end of January it had become clear that the Anglo-American armies in Italy had once more been baulked. Unless the Allies chose to withdraw from Anzio, it was necessary to build up the strength of the garrison and to maintain a flow of supply over open beaches. Withdrawal from Anzio would have been a serious psychological blow; but to maintain the beachhead General Wilson found it necessary to keep landing craft past the time they had been promised for Overlord.[3]

The failure to win prompt success in Italy complicated Allied planning and did not improve feeling between the British and American members of the Combined Chiefs of Staff. The Americans, of course, still wished to subordinate everything to Overlord; but in the meanwhile changes had been made in the plans for the invasion of France which made it easier for them to agree to the retention of landing craft in the Mediterranean. In January 1944, when Eisenhower and Montgomery began to examine the plans for Overlord which had been drawn up by General Sir Frederick Morgan and his staff in London, they both decided that the initial assault would have to be made on a larger scale.[4] The two generals agreed that, instead of three divisions, five divisions would be needed for the first lodgement. But such an enlargement required more landing craft and other supplies. Additional time for preparation seemed inescapably necessary. Accordingly on 31 January 1944 the target date for the landing in Normandy was put off from the beginning to the last day of May.[5]

[1] Eisenhower: *Crusade in Europe*, pp. 212–13; Wilson: *Eight Years Overseas*, pp. 188–9.

[2] Leahy: *I Was There*, p. 256; Churchill, v. 390; U.S. edition, v. 440–1. The decision of 7 January 1944 whereby all amphibious operations in the Burma theatre were cancelled helped to persuade the Americans to accept Anzio. Any craft lost at Anzio could now be replaced from those to be brought back from Mountbatten's South-East Asia Command.

[3] Wilson: *Eight Years Overseas*, pp. 193–7.

[4] Churchill had urged this change at Quebec in August when the plan was first discussed and approved (see above, p. 295).

[5] Sir Francis de Guingand: *Operation Victory* (London, Hodder & Stoughton, 1947), p. 346;

This change in plan made it possible to postpone the departure of landing craft from the Mediterranean without undue interference with the revised Overlord schedule. As a result, no special difficulty arose over Wilson's inability to surrender his landing craft at the time originally agreed upon. However, the larger problem of what to do in the Mediterranean to support Overlord provoked a long-drawn-out contest of wills between American and British strategists. The British wanted to abandon Anvil, as the landing in southern France was code-named; the Americans viewed it as an essential part of Overlord.[1] It is not possible to follow all the intricacies of proposal and counter-proposal which this divergence of view occasioned. An almost incessant stream of communication flowed between London, Washington, AFHQ (Wilson's headquarters), and SHAEF (Eisenhower's headquarters) during the months from February to August 1944 touching upon this question; and it was not until almost the last minute that the landing was firmly accepted by all parties.

In February and March Americans and British were agreed that the first requirement was to rescue the forces isolated in the Anzio beachhead, and a directive was sent to General Wilson to that effect on 26 February.[2] Their reasons were, however, diametrically opposed. The Americans wanted to escape from an awkward situation and release men and landing craft for Anvil and Overlord; the British believed that the Italian campaign was worth pursuing for its own sake. In the short run this difference did not matter. A second attempt was made to break the German defences and relieve the Anzio beachhead in March 1944; but that, too, failed completely.

By now, time was running short. If forces were to be withdrawn from the battle in Italy for a landing in southern France in support of Overlord, preparations could not be long postponed. The British urged the abandonment of the whole Anvil project in order to concentrate upon the capture of Rome; the Americans, on the contrary, advocated abandonment of the offensive in Italy in order to prepare for Anvil. It had become clear that there would not be enough landing craft available to make simultaneous attacks on the coasts of northern and southern France on the scale which was now judged to be necessary; but the American Chiefs of Staff proposed that Anvil should be launched on 10 July, or as

Eisenhower: *Crusade in Europe*, p. 230; Butcher: *My Three Years with Eisenhower*, pp. 475, 476, 491; Harrison: *Cross-Channel Attack*, pp. 167–8.

[1] Churchill originally approved of Anvil because it provided a good reason for keeping landing craft in the Mediterranean with which to launch other enterprises (Churchill, v. 358; U.S. edition, v. 405). When these went awry at Anzio, he no longer wanted to divert landing craft from Italy and the Adriatic to southern France. As early as 23 December 1943 he cabled to the British Chiefs of Staff: 'In no case can we sacrifice Rome for the Riviera. We must have both' (ibid. pp. 381 and 431 respectively).

[2] Wilson: *Eight Years Overseas*, p. 196: Butcher: *My Three Years with Eisenhower*, p. 497.

soon after Overlord D-day as landing craft could be delivered to the Mediterranean from the Channel.[1]

The British objected vigorously to this suggestion, arguing that no firm date for any attack on southern France could be set until Rome had been captured;[2] the American Chiefs of Staff countered by declaring that no landing craft could be sent to the Mediterranean for an action to which a date could not be assigned and which might never come off. The result was something of a stalemate. On 19 April Anvil was reduced from the status of a scheduled operation to that of a mere feint; and the American Chiefs of Staff gave reluctant approval to one more attempt to break through the German defences in Italy and capture Rome.[3]

Accordingly, on 11 May 1944, a third attack was launched against the German lines. This time success crowned the Allied effort; link-up with Anzio forces occurred on 25 May; and on 4 June 1944 Allied troops entered Rome. This success once more put a new complexion on affairs. The Americans felt that now the aim of the Italian campaign had been accomplished, and ten divisions should be earmarked for a postponed Anvil. The British wished to continue to exploit the success already won with all the troops that were available.

The upshot was an attempt to do both. The Combined Chiefs of Staff instructed General Wilson on 14 June to continue to press the campaign in Italy until the beginning of July, and in the meanwhile to make plans for amphibious attacks either along the Bay of Biscay coast, at the head of the Adriatic, or on the Riviera. Wilson and his staff preferred the Adriatic. They wished to press on with the land battle in Italy, and to use the landing craft which the Combined Chiefs of Staff had allotted to them to make a landing on the Istrian peninsula, with the object of moving through the Ljubljana gap into the Hungarian plain.[4]

When this proposal came to the attention of Generals Marshall and Eisenhower they reacted strongly, seeing in it one more attempt by the British to subordinate military to political aims.[5] Marshall, who was then in England where he had come to observe the first days of the Normandy attack, made a special trip to Wilson's headquarters in order to scotch

[1] Churchill, v. 453; U.S. edition, v. 513; Butcher: *My Three Years with Eisenhower*, p. 509.

[2] One of the assumptions made at Tehrān was that the battle line in Italy would have moved to the neighbourhood of Pisa-Rimini before Anvil was launched. Thus the British could point to an approved plan to support their insistence upon putting the capture of Rome ahead of the attack on southern France.

[3] Wilson: *Eight Years Overseas*, pp. 206–7; Churchill, v. 453–4; U.S. edition, v. 513–14.

[4] Wilson: *Eight Years Overseas*, p. 216; Wilmot: *Struggle for Europe*, pp. 449–52. This proposal undoubtedly reflected Churchill's politico-military ideas (Churchill, v. 358; U.S. edition, v. 405). Cf. Butcher: *My Three Years with Eisenhower*, pp. 608, 638–9. In addition, the Mediterranean commanders, naturally enough, supported a plan which would keep the troops in the Mediterranean united under their command. Plans for Anvil envisaged the transfer of command over the troops assigned to that operation from Wilson to Eisenhower as soon as they had moved north of Lyons.

[5] Eisenhower: *Crusade in Europe*, pp. 283–4.

the idea. He argued that Anvil was necessary in order to open a port for the supply of troops which were waiting in America to join the battle in France; and he asserted roundly that no American troops would under any circumstances enter the Balkans. American reinforcements would only be sent to the Mediterranean for an attack on southern France.[1]

General Wilson found himself caught between two fires. Two months earlier, Churchill had accused him of failing to find good reasons for abandoning Anvil, as British strategists wished to do;[2] and now Marshall trained his big guns upon him for the opposite reason. In the circumstances, General Wilson recommended the Istrian landing as best 'from the Mediterranean point of view' but deferred judgement of over-all strategy to his superiors, the Combined Chiefs of Staff. In spite of Churchill's best efforts, the Americans had their way. On 1 July the Prime Minister telegraphed to Roosevelt agreeing to a landing in southern France, and two days later Wilson was instructed to prepare for the operation, renamed Dragon, by diverting ten divisions from his forces for that purpose. D-day was to be 15 August.[3]

Despite this decision, the British continued to hope for a change of plan. Just a week before the landing took place, Churchill returned to the proposal that the troops and landing craft should be brought all the way round Spain and set ashore on the Bay of Biscay coast.[4] But this last diversionary effort was as vain as its predecessors, and when the American and French troops[5] finally went ashore on the Riviera coast on 15 August, Churchill was on hand to watch their debarkation.

[1] Wilson: *Eight Years Overseas*, pp. 216–17. [2] Ibid. pp. 197–8.

[3] Butcher: *My Three Years with Eisenhower*, p. 603; Leahy: *I Was There*, p. 285.

[4] Eisenhower: *Crusade in Europe*, p. 281; Wilson: *Eight Years Overseas*, p. 221; Wilmot: *Struggle for Europe*, pp. 456–7. It appears that two quite contrary calculations entered into British thinking when they made this proposal to divert forces from the Riviera to the French Atlantic coast. The British Chiefs of Staff, when they first made the suggestion, were afraid of a new Anzio in southern France, and argued that after the break-out at St.-Lô (which had just occurred) a landing in Brittany would be unopposed, or nearly so, thus bringing reinforcement to the Allied armies in northern France. At that time the full scope of the victory in Normandy had not become evident, and the British Chiefs of Staff still feared that the Germans might stabilize a line somewhere in France and restore trench warfare of the 1915–18 type. Reinforcement at a critical time might then make all the difference, and permit a second and decisive break-through.

Churchill, on the other hand, being by nature an optimist, had come to feel by 5 August that the Germans would not be able to recover, and that the end of the war was a matter of weeks or, at most, a few months. He wanted the troops in the Mediterranean to drive through Istria into the Danubian plain; and presumably backed the suggestion of a diversion to the French Atlantic coast because it seemed a device for postponing definitive commitment of forces which he felt could be better used elsewhere. If he could delay the landing in the Riviera by a few weeks, the situation in Normandy might remove the most telling of Marshall's and Eisenhower's arguments—the need for an additional port to supply the great Allied armies in France. Brest, St. Nazaire, and Le Havre would replace Marseilles and Toulon, and the troops in the Mediterranean could then be used in Istria.

[5] One of the weaknesses of Churchill's position was that the margin of disposable strength in

The prolonged and frequently bitter struggle between British and American strategists over the use to be made of the troops in the Mediterranean during the first seven months of 1944 was matched by friction over political issues which arose with respect to Italy and France. Some account of these problems will be given below;[1] but in the Balkans, where politics rested almost nakedly upon the shifting balance of armed force, military and political issues were so inextricably tangled that it seems best to describe the situation in Turkey, Greece, and Yugoslavia under the military heading. In these countries Great Britain played the hand for the Allies, while the United States and the U.S.S.R., from their different points of view, remained relatively passive and upon occasion critical of what the British did.

After the Second Cairo Conference, when the Turks refused to declare war on Germany immediately, conversations were held in Ankara between British and Turkish officials to determine exactly what the Turks required in the way of supply before they would fight.[2] The conversations did not go smoothly, and early in February 1944 the British decided to break them off. They withdrew the head of the British Military Mission, and suspended all deliveries of war supplies to the Turks. But despite these steps, and despite ostentatious diplomatic coolness on the part of both British and American Ambassadors, the Turks refused to budge from their neutrality.[3]

In Greece and Yugoslavia, the effect of the collapse of Italy in September 1943 had been to transfer considerable quantities of arms from the Italian garrisons in those countries to the various guerrilla bands which already disputed the ground. The Germans were able to recover control of the main cities and lines of communication; but from that time onwards the guerrillas controlled substantial though shifting stretches of territory, and their military and political importance greatly increased.

In Greece,[4] fighting broke out between ELAS (Greek initials for National People's Liberation Army) and EDES (Greek initials for Greek Democratic National League), the two principal guerrilla organizations, in October 1943; but a peace was patched up in February 1944

the Mediterranean was American and French. British troops did not take part in the attack on southern France; but the British forces which remained in the Mediterranean theatre (and after 15 August the British enjoyed an overwhelming preponderance there) were inadequate to achieve the goals Churchill so ardently wished for. Thus in effect, the long debate had turned on what use should be made of American strength in the Mediterranean; and under such circumstances it is not strange that Marshall should have had his way.

[1] See below, pp. 411 seqq., 417–18, 420, 425–7.

[2] General Wilson maintained during this time an air reserve ready at short notice to come to the assistance of the Turks (*Eight Years Overseas*, p. 196). Churchill had not entirely given up hope of bringing the Turks round, and wished to be able to support them in the air at very short notice.

[3] Hull: *Memoirs*, ii. 1370–1.

[4] A fuller account will be found in the *Survey* for 1939–46: *Hitler's Europe*.

through the initiative of British liaison officers. The issue at stake was control of the post-war government of Greece. ELAS was under strong Communist influence, and had adopted a republican platform; EDES, although originally also republican, opposed the Communists and gradually assimilated conservative and royalist elements. British policy was by no means unambiguous. Maximum sabotage and military pressure against the Germans were a real object; on the other hand, the British did not wish to see a republican Greek government under Communist influence emerge from the war. Since ELAS was by far the largest guerrilla army, the British found themselves supporting its military activities and opposing its political aims.[1]

Matters became acute in March 1944 when ELAS and its supporting political organization, known as EAM (Greek initials for National Liberation Front), established a Provisional Government which implicitly challenged the legitimacy of the Greek Government in Exile. The British feared that something like the Polish problem might arise with rival governments, one supported by the Russians, the other by themselves. In an effort to head off such a situation, the British took steps to bring about a reconciliation. After a mutiny in the Greek forces stationed in the Middle East, the Government in Exile was remodelled in April; and in May 1944 a conference of Greek political leaders—exiles, guerrilla representatives, and politicians brought out from Greece itself—was arranged under British auspices in Lebanon. From this conference emerged a compromise on the question of King versus republic: King George undertook not to return until after a plebiscite had been held to determine the future form of government. But for several months it remained uncertain whether the Communists and their fellow travellers in Greece would accept or reject the compromise. In the meanwhile, the British did what they could to support the military strength of EDES, and tried to prevent ELAS from becoming overwhelmingly powerful.[2]

In Yugoslavia[3] the situation bore many likenesses to what was happening in Greece. Two rival guerrilla organizations, Tito's Partisans and Mihailović's Chetniks, engaged in sporadic civil war, and the question of King versus republic and of Communism versus royalism divided the population into mutually distrustful parts. An additional complexity was the national diversity of the peoples of Yugoslavia: Serbs, Montenegrins, Macedonians, Croats, and Slovenes all exhibited a sense of separatism in greater or less degree, and old and new grudges divided them from one another.

[1] Wilson: *Eight Years Overseas*, p. 179; Churchill, v. 474–6; U.S. edition, v. 537–9.

[2] Churchill, v. 476–88; U.S. edition, v. 539–52. For a detailed account of British policy in Greece see C. M. Woodhouse: *Apple of Discord* (London, Hutchinson, 1948).

[3] A fuller account will be found in the *Survey* for 1939–46: *Hitler's Europe*.

The great difference between affairs in Greece and in Yugoslavia, however, was in British policy. In Churchill's words: 'In one place we support a king, in another a Communist'.[1] During the first months of 1944 an increasingly close connexion was established between Tito's Partisans and AFHQ. Not only were substantial quantities of supplies delivered to Tito, but a number of joint operations along the Dalmatian coast and inland were arranged between Partisan units and various British Commando and other special troops. In May 1944 a German airborne attack drove Tito from his headquarters in Bosnia. He escaped by air to Italy, and from there he went to the Yugoslav island of Viš where Allied naval and air protection made him secure against further German attack. Relations on the personal and operational level between British authorities and the Partisans were on the whole quite friendly.[2]

In proportion as the British warmed towards Tito they cooled towards Mihailović. In December 1943 the British military mission was ordered to withdraw from Mihailović's headquarters;[3] and this rupture in the field was matched by strenuous efforts made in London to persuade King Peter to disclaim Mihailović and come to terms with Tito. Not until 1 June 1944 did the Yugoslav King defer to British pressure by appointing Ivan Šubašić Prime Minister. Šubašić was a Croat like Tito, and he felt confident that he would be able to bring about a reconciliation between King Peter and the Partisan leader. This was likewise the prime aim of British policy; and a series of conferences did produce a semblance of agreement on 16 June not unlike the agreement reached among the Greeks in the preceding month.[4]

Thus in spite of apparently divergent military policies, the British were in reality pursuing the same goal in both Yugoslavia and Greece. Churchill hoped that in both countries an acceptable compromise could be arrived at between remodelled governments in exile and the leaders of the resistance movements; and that the governments emergent from such a compromise would be well disposed toward Great Britain.[5]

American policy generally supported British action, but Marshall and Roosevelt remained always slightly suspicious, fearing that the British might somehow entangle American forces in unwelcome Balkan adventures.

The Russians showed signs of their interest in the Balkans by sending

[1] Speech in the House of Commons, 24 May 1944, H.C.Deb. 5th ser., vol. 400, col. 778.

[2] Wilson: *Eight Years Overseas*, pp. 204, 212–13, 224–7.

[3] Churchill, v. 413; U.S. edition, v. 467. Actually, owing to difficulties of transport, the British Mission did not leave Mihailović until May 1944.

[4] Fotitch: *The War We Lost*, pp. 238–59.

[5] It is worth remembering that the Russian offensive which brought the Red Army into the Balkans and middle Danube did not begin until 20 August 1944. If German resistance had ended in the autumn of 1944, as was widely expected, the military-political situation in those regions would have been far more favourable for Churchill's aims than it was by May 1945.

military missions to Tito in January 1944 and to ELAS in July 1944. In Yugoslavia Churchill's efforts to concert policy with Stalin met with a modicum of success when the Soviet Government on 21 December 1943 officially stated that they were in agreement with the British in seeking to forward co-operation between Tito and the Royal Yugoslav Government in Exile.[1] Some of Tito's later acts suggest that the Russians may have brought some pressure to bear on him to conform to this policy.[2] In Greece, however, when the British found it prudent to seek Stalin's concurrence and support for their policy at the beginning of May 1944, the Russians at first refused to co-operate.[3]

(3) *Preparation for 'Overlord'*

The military problems of the Mediterranean were all subordinated to the tremendous task of preparation which went on in Great Britain during the first six months of the year. Eisenhower arrived in London to take up his new command on 14 January 1944, less than six months before D-day in Normandy was to occur. His instructions from the Combined Chiefs of Staff were simple: 'You will enter the continent of Europe and, in conjunction with the other Allied Nations, undertake operations aimed at the heart of Germany and the destruction of her Armed Forces.'[4] The task of planning and preparation had already begun, but there remained a tremendous amount of detailed work before the Allied forces could be made ready for the assault. There was also a series of delicate decisions involving conflicting national and service loyalties which Eisenhower had to make, or persuade his superiors to make.

One of the first of these decisions was the place of the air forces in his command. Eisenhower and Marshall were both determined that the whole striking power of the air arm should be made available to the Supreme Commander for the invasion. Churchill and some high officers of the R.A.F., however, felt that strategic bombing attack was more important than any direct support of ground forces. They believed that, if the heavy bombers were put under Eisenhower, they would almost surely be misused. It was only after long discussion that agreement was finally reached in April. Eisenhower won his major point by compromising on details. Thus SHAEF took command of the British and American strategic air forces from April until the 'critical phase' of the Normandy

[1] Churchill, v. 414; U.S. edition, v. 468.

[2] For example on 9 February 1944 Tito offered to co-operate with King Peter, though on terms that could not appeal to the exiled monarch (ibid. pp. 419–20 and 474 respectively).

[3] Ibid. pp. 487 and 551 respectively; Russia's refusal to support British efforts to pacify civil strife in Greece came on 5 May. This presumably provided the stimulus for Eden's first informal soundings aimed at the division of the Balkans into definite spheres of influence, assigning Greece to the British. Cf. Hull: *Memoirs*, ii. 1453, and below, p. 422.

[4] Eisenhower: *Crusade in Europe*, p. 225.

landing had passed; but Eisenhower's orders were to pass through the established Bomber Command channels, and, in the absence of definite orders from SHAEF, Bomber Command was to be free to employ its forces for its own strategic bombing attack.[1]

A similar problem arose in connexion with the chain of command over the ground forces. At Casablanca it had been agreed tentatively that the Supreme Allied Commander for the invasion of France would be assisted by three subordinate commanders for naval, air, and ground forces. This was the system which had been actually employed in the Mediterranean from the time when the Eighth Army broke through the Mareth Line into Tunisia. The British believed that the same pattern should be applied again, and, in accordance with the principle of alternating nationality between successive levels of authority, they argued that the three subordinate commanders should be British. This proposal was acceptable to the Americans as far as naval and air command was concerned, but they were not willing to accept a British commander for ground forces which, after the initial stages of the battle, would be predominantly American.[2]

Debate over this question was prolonged, and involved a mixture of national feeling and personal rivalry as well as administrative principle. In the end an essentially awkward compromise was reached. Montgomery was appointed commander of all ground forces for the initial period, when British and American troops would be fighting in approximately equal numbers and on a relatively narrow front; but it was understood that as soon as the beachhead had been firmly won, a separate American army command, subject directly to Eisenhower, would be set up, and Montgomery's responsibility would be confined to a single sector of the front.[3] Such a change-over in the midst of a campaign was necessarily delicate, for the alteration of Montgomery's status could easily be interpreted as demotion, as indeed, in some quarters, it was.

Despite the national rivalries which lay behind these and similar less important disputes, SHAEF proved able to function with remarkable smoothness on a bi-national basis. Eisenhower made a systematic effort to balance British and American staff officers equally, an American normally having a British assistant and vice versa. In dealing with the innumerable technical problems which arose in planning and preparing the invasion, national considerations almost disappeared. The SHAEF staff developed an *esprit de corps* of its own which survived all the disputes, military, political, and economic, which troubled relations between the British and

[1] Ibid. pp. 221–3; Butcher: *My Three Years with Eisenhower*, pp. 498–9; Craven and Cate, edd.: *The Army Air Forces in World War II*, iii. 79–83.

[2] Butcher: *My Three Years with Eisenhower*, p. 474; cf. Eisenhower (*Crusade in Europe*, p. 223), who argues rather lamely that his opposition to the appointment of a commander-in-chief for ground forces was based upon a wish to avoid administrative confusion.

[3] Eisenhower: *Crusade in Europe*, p. 223.

American Governments in 1944. This remarkable phenomenon was at least in part due to the beneficent influence of General Eisenhower's firmness, tact, and personal example.

Oddly enough, Eisenhower's position as an Allied commander was helped rather than hindered by the fact that he found himself at odds with the American Government over a number of political issues, especially the question of how to deal with France and de Gaulle, while differing simultaneously with Churchill and the British Chiefs of Staff on military and strategic questions. The arguments and cabled confusion which resulted from this situation certainly distracted Eisenhower from the straightforward military problem of planning and preparation for which he was responsible; but at the same time the fact that he found himself at odds with both Governments on certain points conferred upon him a supra-national status which could hardly have been achieved had he agreed all along the line with one or the other.

During the first months of Eisenhower's career as SHAEF commander, Churchill and the British Chiefs of Staff remained somewhat sceptical of the soundness of the basic plan for Overlord. Old fears of disastrous repulse from the beaches of Normandy had not disappeared. Churchill still adhered to his original view, that sound strategy would make the invasion of northern France little more than a *coup de grâce*, to be delivered only when Germany was already verging on collapse. The Americans, on the other hand, believed, as always, that an overwhelmingly powerful invasion was the quickest and cheapest way to shatter Germany's still unbroken military power.

Eisenhower, Marshall, and Roosevelt seem never to have fully understood the British point of view, mainly because Churchill felt it necessary, from May 1943 onwards, to pay lip service to American plans for Overlord, while trying in the act to work out his own strategic purposes step by step. In the six months after Tehrān, matters came to a head. Churchill saw Overlord, the American Overlord, shaping up irresistibly. But it seemed to him too soon. The situation in Germany which he judged prerequisite for success had not yet appeared. The fevered and impassioned note which began to appear in Churchill's relations with the Americans in the first months of 1944 resulted from his realization that time was running out. The Americans were riding roughshod over his artifices and objections, following their chosen path and risking, in Churchill's view, irreparable disaster. But the Americans brusquely dismissed Churchill's arguments as political in inspiration and therefore militarily disreputable.

By May Churchill's attitude to Overlord began to change. On 15 May, after attending a formal conference at which final plans were set forth in considerable detail, Churchill found it in his heart to say: 'Gentlemen, I am hardening toward this enterprise.'[1] By the end of that month the situation seemed even better. The Germans were on the run in Italy, the Russians were driving forward uninterruptedly on the northern part of their front, and the impressive scale of the preparations for the invasion seemed such as to assure if not success at least the avoidance of disaster.

Churchill's growing confidence in the success of Overlord did not cause him to abandon his Mediterranean plans and hopes, but it did give them a different basis. In proportion as victory loomed near, questions of the post-war political arrangement of Europe became urgent; and the best bulwark against the spread of Russian influence and of Communist revolution to any or every part of the Continent was the speedy establishment of British and American armies in disputed or dangerous areas. From military-political his motives shifted to politico-military; and the penetration of Danubian Europe which he had earlier championed mainly on military grounds now seemed to him equally or even more needful on political grounds.

But the Americans were quite insensitive to such arguments; indeed they were openly suspicious, and insisted on sharply distinguishing military from all other considerations. They were quite prepared to forgo possible political advantages of the sort Churchill had in mind, regarding them basically as illusory. Was not the post-war world to be populated by democratic, free, independent, and peace-loving nations, united under the leadership of the Great Allied Powers into a pacific and harmonious whole? The Americans' confidence in Stalin's good intentions, and their impatience with Churchill's efforts to deflect them from their chosen strategy, reduced the Prime Minister to tears on at least one occasion.[2]

While Eisenhower found himself occupying a prominent place as target for divergent British and American strategical arguments, preparations went steadily and rapidly ahead for the attack upon Normandy. On 8 April Eisenhower informed the Russians that D-day would come two or three days before or after 1 June; three weeks later the Russians

[1] Eisenhower: *Crusade in Europe*, pp. 244–5. As early as March, Churchill found it possible to say to Marshall that he wished 'to strike if humanly possible, even if the limiting conditions we laid down at Moscow are not exactly fulfilled' (Churchill, v. 521; U.S. edition, v. 590). The mention of Moscow referred to the meeting of the Conference of Foreign Ministers in October 1943, when General Ismay first told the Russians the details of Overlord (see above, p. 328).

[2] Butcher: *My Three Years with Eisenhower*, p. 644. In conversation with Americans Churchill never admitted to any shift in the motives for his advocacy of his Mediterranean strategy, but the writer finds it impossible to believe that after May 1944 Churchill was not thinking largely in political terms. He certainly feared the bolshevization of Europe. Cf. references in Churchill, v. 422, 475; U.S. edition, v. 477, 537; Eisenhower: *Crusade in Europe*, pp. 283–4; Wilson: *Eight Years Overseas*, p. 218.

responded with the assurance that they would start an offensive about the same time. It was not until 8 May that the exact choice was fixed for 5 June, when tides and moon would fit the requirements for the proposed attack.[1]

As with any amphibious operation, much depended on the weather, for heavy surf would hinder or even prevent successful beaching of landing craft. As everything became ready, Eisenhower and his senior commanders gathered at Portsmouth to watch the weather before giving the final order to attack. It was a dramatic moment. Final decision rested directly and solely upon Eisenhower. For much of the work of modern war, effective control of operations is widely diffused through staff and subordinate commanders so that the individual significance of the Supreme Commander is reduced to little more than symbolic value. But this was one occasion upon which command was genuinely individual; and the fate of millions of men and many nations hung upon Eisenhower's decision. The weather forecast was unfavourable, and on the night of 3 June Eisenhower ordered a postponement of at least twenty-four hours. Ships already at sea had to turn back; but the possibility of postponement had been foreseen and there was no irreparable confusion. On the next day the weather forecast remained uncertain, but in the early hours of the morning Eisenhower gave the order to start. About twenty-six hours later the first landing craft touched the French shore and British and American soldiers rushed on to the beaches of Normandy.

The battle developed approximately as had been planned. A serious storm in the latter part of June interfered with the delivery of supplies and reinforcements, and the Germans fought long and stubbornly. As a result, the first progress of the Allied armies was slower than had been hoped, and particularly to the east, in the district of Caen, the forward movement of the battle line was painfully slow. The battle took on a new character after 25 July when an American army broke through the German lines at St. Lô and, reaching undefended country, was able to sweep rapidly across the base of the Cherbourg peninsula, and then turn northward to take the German defenders of Normandy in the rear. This manœuvre, conducted with striking speed and power, compelled the Germans to withdraw in disorder beyond the Seine, and for some weeks in August it seemed to many people that the Germans could not recover, even temporarily, from the blow they had suffered.[2] High British and American officials

[1] Butcher: *My Three Years with Eisenhower*, pp. 515, 526, 534.

[2] On 20 July 1944, just before the situation in Normandy had turned into a disastrous rout for the Germans, an attempt had been made to assassinate Hitler. High officers of the Wehrmacht were implicated. This unmistakable proof of discontent within Germany might have presaged almost any sudden dénouement to the war, and Allied hopes were high. If Hitler himself fanatically refused to consider capitulation, it was always possible that an assassin or a well-engineered *coup d'état* would open the path to Unconditional Surrender.

and officers believed that the war in Europe would be over by Christmas, and official plans were made on that basis.[1]

(c) The War against Japan

By November 1943 the United States fleet in the Pacific had fully recovered from the losses of Pearl Harbour, and had more than tripled the aircraft carrier strength with which it began the war. The Japanese navy, on the other hand, had barely been able to maintain itself at the strength of 1941, and had actually suffered some diminution in certain classes of vessels.[2] As a result, American naval supremacy in the Pacific became more and more palpable. The Japanese navy was compelled to avoid sea battles, and took shelter behind the far-flung arc of island bases which remained in Japanese hands. From the islands and atolls of the Western Pacific, Japanese land-based planes could menace the American fleet. Therefore, before attack could be brought directly to the shores of Japan the Americans had to capture enough of the Pacific islands to set up bases of their own. It was not necessary to capture all the Japanese-held islands. Once the defence perimeter had been broken through, American planes could neutralize nearby Japanese bases and protect the fleet as it advanced farther westward against Japan. The Japanese garrisons left behind could thus be cut off from effective contact with their homeland, and their offensive power reduced to negligible proportions.

Before the American navy could advance in this fashion across the Pacific, it was necessary to develop new methods and new forms of equipment for amphibious assault. Seaborne air power had to meet and overcome land-based air power; and landing craft had to be transported over long sea distances before being launched against defended beaches. Warfare of this type had never been attempted before, and the Americans had many difficult technical problems to solve and serious doubts to overcome before they mastered it.

The first such attack was directed against Tarawa and some neighbouring atolls in the Gilbert Islands in November 1943. American losses were heavy, but the attack was successful. In January 1944 a similar attack was made on Kwajalein in the Marshall Islands and in February against Eniwetok, 600 miles west of Kwajalein. These attacks successfully breached the outermost Japanese defence line.

By June 1944 advanced bases had been constructed on the newly won islands and sufficient forces had been assembled to permit a further penetration into the Japanese sea domain. On 15 June 1944 American troops

[1] Hancock and Gowing: *British War Economy*, p. 517. Cf. Butcher: *My Three Years with Eisenhower*, pp. 591, 620, 639.

[2] A graphic comparison of the two fleets may be found in Admiral King's Third Official Report to the Secretary of the Navy: *The War Reports of Marshall, Arnold, and King*, p. 657.

went ashore on Saipan, one of the Mariana Islands. Fighting on Saipan was bitter, and the island was not entirely won until 9 July. Later in the same month the Americans captured two other islands in the Mariana group: Guam and Tinian. This brought them within, though only barely within, air striking range of Japan[1] and penetrated the second ring of Japan's imperial defences.

These giant steps across the central Pacific were accompanied, and indeed made possible, by a series of air strikes by carrier planes against the main Japanese bases at Truk and elsewhere. The attacks were so successful as almost to eliminate Japanese air power from the central Pacific. Thus within a period of seven months Admiral Nimitz's forces had advanced about 3,000 miles from Midway to Guam, and come within 1,400 miles of Japan herself. Japan's sea defences had proved inadequate. Japanese sea and air power, which had been so formidable in 1942, could no longer match American strength. The set-back to Japan was immensely serious, and General Tojo's Cabinet was so greatly discredited by the inability of Japan's forces to stop the Americans that it resigned on 18 July 1944.

American success in the central Pacific was matched by almost equally spectacular victories in the South-West Pacific. General MacArthur's American and Australian forces advanced along the coast of New Guinea in the direction of the Philippines, while naval forces under the command of Admiral Halsey moved northward through the Solomon Islands. By the beginning of 1944 the two offensives had come close enough to the great Japanese stronghold at Rabaul in New Britain to neutralize that base as far as offensive action against the Allied forces was concerned. It was decided to by-pass Rabaul where about 100,000 Japanese troops were concentrated. During the following months MacArthur and Halsey co-operated in a series of combined sea, air, and land operations which gave Australian and American troops possession of key points along the entire northern coast of New Guinea by 30 July 1944.

When Halsey's carriers thus joined in operations with MacArthur's troops, the character of the war in the South-West Pacific abruptly changed. It was no longer necessary for MacArthur's forces to keep within the range of land-based fighters when aircraft carriers, instead, could give air support. As a result, distances shrank, and MacArthur was able to leap-frog 400, 600, or 1,000 miles at a time.[2]

[1] Only the new B-29s, then just beginning to come off the American production lines, were capable of the long flights from the Marianas to Japan and back. This of course handicapped air attack seriously.

[2] The first time MacArthur cut loose from land-based air support was when he attacked Hollandia in New Guinea on 22 April 1944, taking the Japanese completely aback. They had weakened this, one of their main bases, in order to strengthen forward garrisons against expected attack, and in the absence of practicable ground communications could not bring their troops

These great successes in the Pacific contrasted with continued disappointment elsewhere in the war against the Japanese. In Burma, as a result of the decisions taken at the Second Cairo Conference,[1] Mountbatten had to give up plans for an amphibious landing in the Japanese rear. He nevertheless got his truncated campaign under way in January 1944 with an advance along the coast aimed at Akyab once again.

Simultaneously in northern Burma General Stilwell took over direct command of the Chinese forces he had trained in India. His plan was to drive the Japanese back from the projected path of the Ledo (or as it was later named, the Stilwell) Road. This road was designed to connect with the old Burma Road at Myitkyina. Construction had already been started on the portion of this road that lay within the territory controlled by Allied troops. Stilwell's forces were supported by two raiding parties: a small American group known as Merrill's Marauders and a larger British unit under General Orde Wingate. These raiders entered central and northern Burma and succeeded in disrupting Japanese communications in front of Stilwell's advance. They abandoned any attempt to retain land connexion with friendly territory, and instead depended on airdrops for needful supplies. The experiment was risky and costly, but in the end successful. As before, Japanese resistance was extremely stubborn, and it was not until 3 August 1944 that Myitkyina finally fell. By then the monsoon had come to hamper movement on the ground, and it was not until 1945 that the Ledo Road was finally opened and land communication between India and China, the original goal of the Burmese campaign, could be restored. By that time the shift in the pattern of the Japanese war and the intrinsic difficulty of the terrain over which the route passed, deprived the achievement of most of its significance. Only small amounts of supplies were ever delivered to China over the road so painfully won.[2]

Meanwhile, the Japanese did not await Mountbatten's attack idly. In central Burma they took the offensive in March 1944, invaded India, and for a period of two months succeeded in cutting off important British forces in the plain around the town of Imphal. Only extraordinary efforts, including the transport of an entire division from southern Burma by air to the Imphal region, succeeded in turning the Japanese back; but the need for this reinforcement on the central front removed the possibility of winning decisive results in the south. By June 1944 the Japanese were

back to defend Hollandia when the Americans struck. It was a daring manœuvre, made possible only by American command of the sea and of the air. From this time on the pace of MacArthur's advance equalled the giant strides of the central Pacific.

[1] See above, p. 370.

[2] The failure of the Ledo Road to fulfil the role which the U.S. Joint Chiefs of Staff had projected for it was, perhaps, a justification for the British point of view. The British had never believed that concentration on northern Burma in order to re-establish land communication with China was sound strategy.

in full retreat from Imphal; and, since the monsoon had begun, the retreating troops suffered great losses from disease and starvation.

These partial successes in Burma in 1944 did not bring much relief to China. On the contrary, occasional diversion of aeroplanes from the 'Hump' to supply troops fighting in Burma interfered with deliveries to Chiang Kai-shek's forces. The Chinese troops that fought under Stilwell in northern Burma conducted themselves with reasonable efficiency, and proved that with training and equipment the Chinese could meet the Japanese on more or less even terms. But this did not help the situation in China itself, where the armies of Chiang Kai-shek conspicuously lacked both training and equipment.

In accordance with the decision of the Trident Conference in May 1943,[1] during the second part of the year more than half of the military supplies delivered to China over the Hump had been assigned for the building-up of a powerful long-range bombing force. Great landing fields were constructed in southern China close enough to Japan to bring that country within the range of the new B-29s. By the spring of 1944 preparations were almost complete; but the Japanese, recognizing this threat to the security of their homeland, began a series of ground attacks aimed at overrunning the newly built airfields. Chinese troops were unable to stop the Japanese, and between April and September 1944 the airfields were overrun almost before they could be used.

This Japanese success in China was a serious blow to American hopes. From the early days of the war American plans in the Pacific had assigned a key role to the Chinese. The Americans had believed that the Chinese, properly trained and equipped, could be depended on to defeat a major part of the Japanese ground forces. Now it appeared in the spring and summer of 1944 that such a hope was illusory. Chinese military efficiency had not improved; if anything, it had deteriorated. Chiang kept a large proportion of his army deployed as a barrier against the Chinese Communists operating in northern China, and he resisted American efforts to change traditional methods of army administration and training. American dreams of making China into a powerful ally against Japan were proving empty indeed.

A final factor in the war against Japan was the promise of Russian help which Stalin had renewed at Tehrān. The Americans were eager to begin preparation for co-operation in the Far East. Their principal project was the establishment of American bomber bases in eastern Siberia from which attack could be made on Japan. As we have seen,[2] at Tehrān Stalin had told Roosevelt that he would have to consult with his subordinates before answering definitely whether such an arrangement could be made. On 2 February 1944 he informed the American Ambassador that an American

[1] See above, p. 281.

[2] See above, p. 360, note 1.

strategic air force could be established in Siberia as soon as Russia declared war on Japan. In the meanwhile it would be necessary to construct airfields capable of receiving heavy bombers. In April Stalin added a new condition: the Soviet air force, too, should take part in the strategic bombing of Japan, using planes to be provided from the United States. The Americans agreed, but tried to make the delivery of heavy bombers to the Russians contingent upon definite and detailed agreements about the establishment of American air bases in Siberia. The Americans proposed that they should operate six air groups to the Russians' four. This disproportion apparently offended the *amour propre* of the Russians, who felt that they were to be relegated to a secondary position in operations from their own territory. As a result, no detailed agreement could be reached during the summer of 1944; but the Americans continued to hope that something would come of it all eventually.[1] The threatened loss of the Chinese air bases made the Siberian bases seem all the more vital; and, even after Saipan had been conquered in July, that island did not seem to offer a sufficient base for the devastating air attack upon Japan which the Americans believed would be necessary to bring that country down to defeat.

The development of operations against Japan during the first months of 1944 made it more and more obvious that a fundamental revision of the strategic plan would be necessary. Russia was a new factor; China was clearly going to be unable to play the part assigned to her in the plan of 1943; the British advance in Burma had not achieved rapid success; and the American attack across the Pacific began to show unexpected promise of decisive results.

The general question of basic strategy against Japan came acutely to the attention of the American Joint Chiefs of Staff when proposals for future operations coming from General MacArthur conflicted with proposals coming from Admiral Nimitz. On 11 and 12 February 1944 the rival plans were presented and discussed by the Joint Chiefs of Staff, but no definite long-range decisions were made.[2] Early in March matters came to a crisis. The immediate issue was a quarrel between MacArthur and Admiral Halsey. Each commander wanted to control the newly conquered Manus Island.[3] Besides this personal quarrel, there was the

[1] Deane: *Strange Alliance*, pp. 226–33. [2] Leahy: *I Was There*, pp. 263–4.

[3] The command relationship between Halsey and MacArthur was a delicate one which could have worked smoothly only by virtue of personal give and take—a characteristic of neither of the commanders concerned. Halsey was under Nimitz's command, but, after the completion of the Solomons campaign, his naval forces became an essential complement to MacArthur's ground and air forces. Manus lay within the South-West Pacific theatre which had been assigned to MacArthur in 1942; but it was an island, and the base that was to be built there was essential for

still unsolved basic issue of strategy. MacArthur and Nimitz still backed their divergent plans: MacArthur desiring to aim at the Philippines as a principal station on the way to Japan itself; Nimitz arguing that the Philippines should be by-passed.

Many strands of feeling were woven into this dispute. MacArthur had developed a cult of Bataan, and wished vehemently to redeem his farewell words: 'I shall return.' A sense of national obligation to the Filipinos was also a real factor in the debate. Moreover, a campaign in the Philippines would of necessity be a large-scale affair, requiring considerable ground forces, which could best be staged through the South-West Pacific. Thus the army and MacArthur would play the predominant role. On the contrary, Nimitz's plan implied the use of bases in the central Pacific as the staging areas. Some naval men believed that the capture of small islands near the Japanese coasts would make it possible to choke Japan to death by naval blockade and air attack without recourse to any large-scale land operations. In such a campaign, of course, the navy would play the leading part, and Nimitz would command.

On 11 March 1944 the dispute was brought before Roosevelt, but the President declined to intervene. He declared that the Joint Chiefs of Staff should be able to settle the quarrel over Manus Island themselves and, as experts, should likewise be able to pick the best strategy. On the following day, 12 March, the Joint Chiefs of Staff agreed upon a compromise. They decided that while MacArthur's troops invaded the Philippines from the south, the forces under Nimitz should continue the axis of their advance across the central Pacific, and head either for Luzon (the northernmost of the Philippine islands) or for Formosa. In addition, the dispute over Manus Island was settled in the navy's favour.[1]

The outbreak of ill-feeling in the Pacific between MacArthur and Nimitz may have helped to persuade Roosevelt that he should visit that theatre of war and confer with the rival commanders personally. On 21 July 1944 he sailed for Hawaii, and a week later (28–29 July) Roosevelt held a series of conferences with Nimitz and MacArthur. The discussion proved quite peaceable. Nimitz agreed that reconquest of the

further naval operations. Apart from personal rivalry, jealousy between the U.S. army and the U.S. navy entered prominently into the picture, enlarging and expanding the dispute among the subordinates of the two commanders. Cf. Morison: *History of U.S. Naval Operations*, vi. 433–4.

[1] Leahy: *I Was There*, pp. 268–71. Churchill (v. 507; U.S. edition, v. 575) says that the main attack was to be against Formosa; but this seems to overstate the definiteness of the decision of 12 March.

It is interesting to observe that, as the war moved towards victory, relations between the U.S. army and the U.S. navy in the Pacific became more and more strained, just as relations between Britain and America in Europe became less easy than they had been in the days of adversity. In May 1944 the question of a unification of all three branches of the U.S. armed forces was first brought before the Joint Chiefs of Staff; and this became a more and more important irritant to good relations between the admirals and generals in the months that followed.

Philippines would be worth while, and promised to use some of the ships at his disposal to support and transport MacArthur's troops for the attack. MacArthur conceded a point to the navy by agreeing that a full-fledged invasion of the Japanese home islands by ground forces would probably not be necessary. Plans for such an attack had already been drawn up, and the U.S. army in Washington had insisted that invasion would almost surely be necessary before Japan's defeat could be assured. Now in Hawaii the army plan was put on the shelf for use only if naval blockade and air attack proved insufficient to force a Japanese surrender.[1] The chief problem which remained was whether MacArthur's attack upon the Philippines or Nimitz's attack upon Formosa should come first. This was left for later decision, since neither operation, it then seemed, could be undertaken before 1945.[2]

These agreements upon future Pacific operations left the question of British participation in the final stages of the war against Japan still unsettled. Neither MacArthur nor Nimitz wanted British help. They told Roosevelt that they had everything they needed for the future operations which had been agreed to. MacArthur expressed his suspicion that the British would try to take over control of the Dutch East Indies if once they landed troops there. He declared that, since it would be American action in the Philippines and elsewhere that would make the Dutch East Indies ripe for the plucking, the British should not be allowed to get the credit nor the material advantages which liberation of those islands would bring. The Americans, however, did not know exactly what the British would propose for their share in future operations against Japan, so that no decision was reached in the matter.[3] After visiting Alaska, the President returned to the United States on 12 August 1944.

American plans for the Pacific were now firm. The role which the Americans wished the Russians and Chinese to play had been made clear to the two countries: between them they were to take care of Japanese

[1] These decisions were, of course, subject to ratification by the Joint Chiefs of Staff and required at least some concurrent action by the Combined Chiefs of Staff in assigning material and men to the Pacific. But, when the theatre commanders and the President agreed, these presented no great obstacle.

[2] Leahy: *I Was There*, pp. 293–7, 306.

[3] Ibid., pp. 294–6, 299–300. There was, indeed, good reason for not knowing what British intentions with respect to the Japanese war might be, for a vigorous and prolonged debate was simultaneously going on in British circles between Churchill and the Foreign Office on the one hand and the Chiefs of Staff on the other as to future British strategy against Japan. Churchill did not wish to play second fiddle to the Americans in the Pacific, and preferred to make a separate attack on Malaya and the Dutch East Indies; but his military and naval advisers argued that at the Second Cairo Conference the British had undertaken to send a fleet to the Pacific in 1944 and pointed out that nothing of any magnitude could be undertaken in the Bay of Bengal until six months after the end of the war in Europe (cf. above, pp. 368–71). This debate was temporarily settled on 20 March 1944 when Churchill ruled that the main British effort against Japan would be confined to the Indian and Bay of Bengal areas until the summer of 1945. But the issue would not stay buried, and various alternative proposals continued to be made during the following months (cf. Churchill, v. 366–7, 504–13; U.S. edition, v. 414–15, 571–81).

forces on the mainland of Asia. The future relationship between the Russians and Chinese remained to be clarified, as did the role of Great Britain in the final stages of the war against Japan. These problems were to be met later at the Second Quebec Conference (September 1944) and at Yalta (February 1945).

These matters were not unimportant; but from a strictly military point of view the final shape of strategy against Japan had in effect been worked out in Washington and in Hawaii by the end of July 1944. The future course of the Japanese war had achieved a definition comparable to that achieved at Tehrān for the war against Germany; and if the Allied character of the planning was almost unimportant, that no more than reflected the real balance of military forces which were employed and were to be employed against the Japanese. From its outbreak at Pearl Harbour, the war against Japan had been felt to be a peculiarly American concern; and some Americans in high places wished to keep it a private affair. Americans tended to feel that they had a personal score to settle with the Japanese and wanted no outside interference in settling it. Failures and disappointments in China and in Burma helped to confirm this frame of mind; yet it was curiously (and illogically) interwoven with reproach, directed especially against Great Britain, for failure to do what men like MacArthur, Stilwell, or Leahy felt to be their fair share of the fighting.[1] Geography, personalities, and this American attitude combined to make Allied co-operation in the war against Japan a tenuous and incomplete affair in comparison with the co-operation which had been achieved against Germany.

(ii) Political Problems

(a) Basic Policy of the Big Three

The Tehrān Conference had explored many of the political questions that victory was sure to bring, but had settled none of them. During the months that followed these problems became more and more pressing, and, since each of the principal Allies followed a different line of policy, they became also more divisive. Britain and Russia differed over Poland, and watched one another suspiciously in the Balkans. In these matters, the United States generally stood on the sidelines, trying to postpone awkward decisions. Britain and the United States differed over France and Italy, Near Eastern oil, and the future of India; and in these matters the Soviet Union remained, for the most part, enigmatically aloof.

What kept the Grand Alliance together was, first of all, the continued necessity for military co-operation against Germany during and perhaps also after the war. In addition, the war had helped to create a widespread

[1] Cf. Leahy: *I Was There*, p. 301; *The Stilwell Papers*, pp. 207, 321, and *passim*.

popular opinion which hoped for and, in Britain and America, demanded continued co-operation among the great Allies during the post-war period. Against this background of fellow feeling, recurrent clashes of national policy in the first months of 1944 were like pin pricks, creating a sense of irritation sometimes verging on exasperation—but no more than that. The Alliance had lost some of its first bloom, but the full disenchantment of 1946 and 1947 lay still in the future.

Behind the various local conflicts which began to interfere with Allied harmony lay a general issue: what was the political geography and character of the post-war world to be? American and Russian answers to this question were almost antithetically opposed, while the British Government took a middle position.

The American Government and a large section of the American people pinned their hopes on the establishment of a world organization whose member states, accepting the principles of democratic self-government, would abstain from intervention in one another's affairs. Sustained by this hope, the American Government felt justified in refusing to take part in the old-fashioned scramble for power and influence in Europe which seemed to have started between Great Britain and the Soviet Union. In general, the American Government tried to postpone decisions on frontiers and forms of government until the end of the war. By then Roosevelt and Hull hoped that a new international organization would be in operation, and by its operation quite transform international relationships, substituting law and majority rule for the anarchy of traditional power politics. In such an atmosphere they hoped and believed that particular problems in Poland, Italy, and elsewhere would become easily soluble in a fashion that could satisfy all reasonable demands for national security, liberty, and justice.

There were a number of special factors which affected American policy in the first half of 1944. One was Roosevelt's health. After his return from Tehrān in December 1943, until May 1944 the President suffered from a persistent respiratory infection which dragged his physical power down to a low ebb. In April he was obliged to leave Washington for a prolonged period of rest; during this time the normal flow of business across the President's desk was slowed down, and his subordinates sometimes found it hard to get decisions from him.[1]

The fact that 1944 was an election year also hampered American diplomacy. Groups like Italian-Americans and Polish-Americans were a far from negligible factor in the balance between the Democratic and Republican parties; and Roosevelt felt that he could not risk offending such bodies of voters. American pressure on Great Britain to modify the

[1] Cf. Stettinius's complaints about the difficulties of dealing with an ill President reported in Butcher: *My Three Years with Eisenhower*, p. 518.

Government of Italy was, at least in part, intended to appeal to American voters of Italian origin. As far as Poland was concerned, the easiest way of avoiding trouble was to do nothing, minimize the problems which had arisen, and postpone any decisions which might prove unpopular until after the election was over in November 1944.[1]

Another facet of the problem was this: Roosevelt felt sure that American public opinion would not permanently support participation in European affairs. He expected a reaction after the end of the war like that which had occurred after 1918, and he believed that, if the American Government tried to take an active part in the post-war settlement of political problems of Europe, such a policy would be repudiated at the first post-war election. With such repudiation American participation in any new international organization might also be threatened. A modest policy, pinning all hope on the formation of a more effective League of Nations and on continued co-operation with the principal Allies, seemed therefore wiser, more likely to ensure continued American participation in international affairs, and less liable to provoke a revulsion of public feeling. After all, places like Poland and the Balkans still seemed a very long way away from the United States.[2]

Finally, during the war years American diplomacy had been largely taken out of the hands of the Department of State. Roosevelt himself, advised by personal confidants like Hopkins and by the members of the Joint Chiefs of Staff, had conducted the principal negotiations with America's allies. After Tehrān Hopkins fell ill, and, even after his recovery, for nearly a year he lost the President's confidence. Meanwhile, the Joint Chiefs of Staff turned their primary attention to Pacific strategy and eschewed post-war political problems as a matter of principle. Secretary of State Hull was himself ailing, and spent much time in hospital. His subordinates were quite unable to gain the President's ear on a regular day-to-day basis, and, lacking instructions from the highest levels of Government, could not easily, even when they wished to do so, pursue any active line of policy. They did not often wish to do so. The pre-war attitude of mind among American diplomats had not been fundamentally disturbed by the war. Observation, criticism of other nations' deeds, and hesitancy to act or to recommend action could be justified on the ground of non-intervention in other nations' affairs; and for men who were quite unaccustomed to the executive responsibilities involved in active diplomacy undertaken by a Great Power, the natural and easy way was to remain passive and wait for instructions which seldom came.

[1] Roosevelt was quite frank in admitting this motive in private conversation (cf. Ciechanowski: *Defeat in Victory*, pp. 308, 317).

[2] For Roosevelt's fears see Sherwood: *Roosevelt and Hopkins*, pp. 786, 827; Eng. edition, ii. 781, 819. Cf. Hull: *Memoirs*, ii. 1656–7.

Thus it happened that in the first months of 1944 the men round Roosevelt who had conducted America's war-time foreign policy were in general uninterested in European political problems, or were unavailable or partially incapacitated by sickness; and there was no organization or group of individuals ready to take their place. The irruption of Secretary of the Treasury Morgenthau into international relations at the Second Quebec Conference is symptomatic of the vacuum which the approaching end of the war had created round the President. For the first ten months or so of 1944 Roosevelt had no advisers seriously interested in specific post-war political problems whom he personally liked and trusted; and it was a part of the President's temperament to depend mainly upon such friends for stimulus to help him to make up his mind on difficult questions. Without such stimulus, Roosevelt habitually tended to let things drift along in the vague hope that something would turn up.[1]

From early in 1942 the American Government had repeatedly proclaimed the principle that no final decisions on matters of post-war frontiers or systems of government should be made until the end of the war. The theory that a political vacuum could be maintained in Europe was absurd on its face; but this principle helped to hide from American officials the daily necessity of making decisions. They could solace themselves with the thought that everything was temporary; that all would come up for re-examination at the peace conference; that *faits accomplis* could be undone; that liberal democratic ideas would yet prevail. This principle also helped to lend respectability to the indecision which other factors, suggested above, had created in the inner circle of the American Government.

The aims of Russian policy in the first half of 1944 were much more specific than those of the American Government; and the Russian Government suffered from none of the indecision or passivity which so prominently characterized American conduct of affairs during this period. It seems plausible to assume that Stalin kept firmly in the front of his mind one principal goal: Russia should be somehow made secure against a repetition of attack from Germany such as she had suffered in 1914 and in 1941. He was convinced that if preventive steps were not taken German power would revive within a generation to threaten Soviet security once again, just as it had revived after the defeat of 1918.[2] Stalin had been deeply

[1] Cf. Sherwood's most illuminating story of how Hopkins returned to the President's intimate circle in October 1944 as a result of saving Roosevelt from just such drifting (*Roosevelt and Hopkins*, pp. 832–4; Eng. edition, ii. 824–6).

[2] Stalin said this to both Churchill and Roosevelt during the meeting at Tehrān (ibid. pp. 786–7 and 781–2 respectively). He said the same thing to the Polish Premier, Mikolajczyk, on 9 August 1944 (cf. Stanislaw Mikolajczyk: *The Pattern of Soviet Domination* (London, Sampson

impressed by German military prowess and by the energy, skill, and discipline of the German people. He was profoundly sceptical of the possibility of changing the German national character or of the chances of Communist revolution in German lands. 'Communism on a German is like a saddle on a cow', he said to the Polish Premier, Mikolajczyk, in August 1944.[1]

Thus the problem as Stalin saw it was simple. Germany must be kept militarily weak; the Soviet Union must be kept militarily so strong that no future German government could ever dream of renewing the struggle. Two things seemed necessary to achieve this aim. First, the establishment of governments in the countries lying between Germany and Russia which could be depended upon to side with Russia in any future quarrel with Germany; second, a sufficiently cordial relationship with Britain and America to prevent any possibility of those Powers siding with Germany against the Soviet Union.

It is, of course, not certain that Stalin thought in these terms. He may still have hoped for a Communist revolution in Europe as an aftermath of the war; but his actions in 1944 do not suggest that he thought revolution likely, or that he was prepared to risk a break with the West by using Russian power to foment it. On the whole, it seems correct to say that in so far as Stalin kept his Bolshevik faith, he applied it to an indefinite future when, perhaps, the internal contradictions of capitalism would have prepared the way for revolution, and Soviet power would have had time to recover from war losses. Waiting for objective conditions to mature the revolution was, after all, the purest of pure Marxist orthodoxy. In the meanwhile, the Russian Government maintained a stable of Communist exiles from most of the countries of Europe, ready, like Lenin in 1917, to take over the leadership of local Communist Parties whenever the time came.

Whatever doubts there must be about Stalin's attitude to European revolution, there were none about his territorial claims. Throughout the war he had asserted that the territories he had annexed in 1939 and 1940 from Poland, Rumania, and Finland were permanently and legally his; and that the countries of Lithuania, Latvia, and Estonia, annexed in 1940, had become member republics of the Soviet Union. Improvement of the military security of Russia's western frontier was no doubt an important consideration which persuaded Stalin to take this position. Prestige was another factor. Stalin was no more than reasserting Russian authority over territories which had long recognized Tsarist rule, and which had been torn away from Russia at the time of her revolutionary weakness

Low, Marston & Co., 1948), p. 87). He said it publicly in a speech on 6 November 1944 (Rothstein: *Soviet Foreign Policy during the Patriotic War*, ii. 31).

[1] Mikolajczyk: *Pattern of Soviet Domination*, p. 87. Cf. Sherwood: *Roosevelt and Hopkins*, p. 782; Eng. edition, ii. 777.

after the First World War. Finally, as far as the eastern provinces of pre-war Poland were concerned, Stalin may well have felt the need to pacify Ukrainian and White Russian national feeling.[1] At least he said so;[2] and, in view of the rather delicate relationship which had existed between the Ukraine and Great Russia since the days of the Bolshevik Revolution, Stalin may have been speaking honestly.[3]

Unfortunately for Stalin's political programme, there was a potential contradiction between his purposes in Eastern Europe and his hope of remaining on good terms with America and Britain. In 1940, and again in 1942, the United States had made clear her opposition to his annexation of the Baltic states, and had never officially altered this stand.[4] More critical was the question of Poland. Stalin wanted a friendly government in Poland which could be depended on to oppose Germany and support Russia. He hoped to obtain such a government by transferring German territory to Poland and by encouraging the Poles to expel the German inhabitants from their new domain. This would both compensate them for the loss of their former eastern provinces to Russia and create an enduring and unbridgeable enmity between the new Poland and Germany. Fearing German revenge, the Poles would be compelled willy-nilly to support and be supported by Russia.[5]

What Stalin conceived to be the future role of the Communist parties in the countries neighbouring Russia cannot be stated with any certainty. The Soviet Government disclaimed on several occasions any intention of revolutionizing the social order, in Poland or in other adjacent countries.[6]

[1] The ethnic distribution of population in the eastern provinces of inter-war Poland has been the subject of heated controversy. In many regions the Poles were a small minority; and outside the towns ethnic Poles were mostly land-owners, while the peasantry was White Russian or Lithuanian in the north, Ukrainian in the south. On ethnic grounds, the Russians had a good case for annexation of these regions; Polish counter-claims were historical and sentimental, not statistical—and the ethnic statistics bore witness that history, too, had not originally been on Poland's side.

[2] Mikolajczyk: *Pattern of Soviet Domination*, p. 69.

[3] Stalin's concern to unite the Ukrainian and White Russian populations may have been partly motivated by a wish to check separatist national agitation which, especially among the Ukrainians, had won considerable success during the war years. A Polish Government unfriendly to Russia might conceivably encourage propaganda among the latter's Ukrainian subjects aimed at reuniting the Ukraine under Polish rather than Russian hegemony, and such propaganda might strike a sympathetic chord among the Ukrainian peasants of Russia. The Germans had won considerable success with similar propaganda in the first months of the Russo-German war. On the other hand, if Stalin could present the Ukrainian and White Russian Soviet Republics with new territory wrested from Poland, the gesture could be interpreted as satisfying their nationalist claims; and separatism could be handled by the Soviet police more effectively if all Ukrainian and White Russian lands were within its power.

[4] Roosevelt's compliant attitude at Tehrān might, perhaps, be counted as an official abandonment of the Baltic republics to Stalin's good pleasure. Certainly the matter of their future was dropped by the State Department thereafter.

[5] Mikolajczyk, op. cit. p. 70.

[6] Cf. proclamation of 26 July 1944: 'The Soviet Government states that it does not pursue the aim of acquiring any part of Polish territory or of changing the social order in Poland . . .' (Roth-

Stalin told Mikolajczyk in October 1944: 'Communism does not fit the Poles. They are too individualistic, too nationalistic. . . . Poland will be a capitalist state.' He went on to inform his startled interlocutor that he would order the Polish Communist Party to refrain from attempting to win power through a revolution.[1] It is impossible to be sure that Stalin was frank in making such statements as these; but his day-to-day policy suggests that throughout 1944 he hoped to come to satisfactory terms with non-Communist groups in Poland, Rumania, and other countries similarly situated. The policy had, up to the time of writing in 1952, proved successful in Finland, and for a while seemed to be so in Czechoslovakia.[2] Perhaps Stalin hoped that Communist Parties would be sufficiently strong after the war to check by a sort of internal veto any anti-Russian tendencies that might arise in the governments of Europe, and wished no more than that for the immediate future.

If this is a fair statement of Stalin's aims—and in the nature of the case it is highly speculative—he no doubt hoped that they would prove acceptable to the Western Powers. Indeed, Britain and America might well have agreed to Stalin's programme if he had been able to persuade the Poles, Rumanians, and others to accept the role he had assigned to them; but as it turned out he was not able to do so without resort to high-handed intervention and brutal disregard of the niceties of democratic government.

As between the friendship of the Western Powers and a secure politico-military position on his western frontier, Stalin chose the latter. He probably never made the choice in any deliberate and cold-blooded manner. Rather, insisting upon the security of his frontiers, he little by little sacrificed the sympathy of Britain and America, without clearly recognizing what he was doing until it was too late.

Stalin, we may assume, felt perfectly free to violate the canons of liberal, democratic government professed by the West. He presumably regarded bourgeois democratic principles as mere shibboleths, employed by Roosevelt and Churchill when it suited their convenience, just as he himself used or conveniently overlooked the slogans of Bolshevism. Indeed,

stein: *Soviet Foreign Policy during the Patriotic War*, ii. 93). A similar proclamation was made with respect to Rumania on 2 April 1944 (ibid. pp. 65–66).

[1] Mikolajczyk: *Pattern of Soviet Domination*, p. 112. Cf. ibid. p. 69 for a report of similar remarks by Stalin made to Professor Oscar Lange in May 1944.

[2] Stalin's unfortunate experience with the Finnish Communists in 1939–40 may have played a part in persuading him to follow a more cautious policy in 1943 and 1944. The puppet Government set up under the Communist Kuusinen had proved quite unable to win perceptible support among the Finns, and Stalin in the end, under the pressure of military and international events, had quietly dissolved it in order to make peace with Mannerheim and Paasikivi. The memory of this fiasco may have convinced Stalin that Communism was not easy to export. Moreover, Stalin must have realized that a policy of spreading Communism would be sure to antagonize the Anglo-Americans, and he was counting on maintaining tolerably good relations with them in the immediate post-war period.

as a Marxist, Stalin may have discounted the validity of Western democratic professions even more: did he not know that Western democracy was a false façade for capitalist exploitation? Did he not see that in Britain and America public opinion was manipulated by the ruling class to forward its selfish interests?

If Stalin did discount the validity of Western democratic professions in the fashion suggested above, he may well have been genuinely taken aback at the Western reaction to his conduct in Poland and Rumania in 1944 and 1945. Britain and America had both solemnly declared that they wished to co-operate with Russia; yet they supported Russia's enemies in Eastern Europe in the name of democratic liberty and civil rights. How could such conduct be explained as anything but a thinly camouflaged propaganda attack upon the Soviet state? How could it be interpreted as anything but another case of capitalist perfidy?

These developments, however, came slowly, and the split between Russia and the West was only fitfully evident in 1944. The passivity of American policy, particularly in questions affecting Eastern Europe, perhaps encouraged Stalin to believe that as far as America was concerned he would continue to enjoy a free hand. It was Great Britain and Winston Churchill who appeared in 1944 as the only serious obstacle to the realization of Russian plans.

The role which the British Government attempted to play in European politics in 1944 was a very difficult one. On the one hand, British public opinion and the British Government took seriously the hope, so freely expressed in the United States, that a new and better world would emerge from the war; a world in which the harmony of the great Allies and the legal powers of an international organization would make traditional forms of international politics obsolete. Moreover, it was a cardinal principle of Churchill's policy to do everything possible to keep the support and friendship of the United States firmly behind Great Britain.

But the Prime Minister distrusted Russia profoundly, and was doubtful whether Stalin would ever in practice co-operate with the rest of the world on terms such as Roosevelt hoped for. Meanwhile, he saw Stalin preparing to set up a sphere of influence in Eastern Europe, and feared that Russian influence might spread farther into Western Europe itself. The only sure way to prevent such an outcome would be to create a counterbalancing group of nations under Anglo-American or (since the Americans steadily refused to show any interest in the project) under British influence. Military security, economic interests, prestige—these and perhaps other considerations must have entered into Churchill's mind when he considered the state of Europe, emergent from the years of Nazi occupation.

He deemed it imperative to establish in France, Italy, and in the lesser countries of Western Europe governments which would be strong, stable, and non-Communist, inclining rather to Great Britain than to Russia. Only so could a balance of power between Russian land and Anglo-American sea and air strength be achieved; and Churchill was profoundly convinced that only on the basis of such a balance of power could reasonably good terms with Stalin be preserved.[1]

In the non-European world, the British Government sought to retain or regain what they had possessed before the war. Suggestions for the future dissolution of the British Empire roused Churchill's fury. American meddling in the relationship between the Mother Country and various parts of the Empire he received with undisguised resentment.

At the beginning of 1944 Churchill hoped that by conceding Bessarabia, eastern Poland, and the Baltic States to the Soviet Union, it would be possible to create governments in Poland and Rumania and other East European countries which would be fully independent of Russia. He certainly did not want an anti-Russian bloc of states along the Soviet frontier; he did hope, however, that non-Communist groups would retain predominance in the whole of Europe outside Russia herself.

The British Government were looking for political leaders from Eastern and South-Eastern Europe who would be non-Communist and yet acceptable to the Russians. In Greece and in Yugoslavia Churchill hoped he had found such persons after the reorganization of the Governments in Exile which took place in May and June.[2] In Beneš the Czechs seemed to have discovered such a figure by themselves. But no individual or group in Poland or Rumania could be found to fit the bill. The Russians feared a revival of a *cordon sanitaire* like that of the 1920s; the British feared Communist revolution and the establishment of satellite governments or even outright annexation to the Soviet Union. In 1952 it was ironic to think that in large part the fears of each had been realized, the hopes of neither.

Germany remained as the main element binding the Grand Alliance together. Neither Russia nor Great Britain felt able to undertake alone the task of warding off German revival and revenge. To prevent such a nemesis seemed to require co-operation after the war. But none the less Great Britain and Russia differed on how to handle defeated Germany. Churchill was concerned lest the peace be too vindictive. He did not want to see the Germans so impoverished and hopeless as to become ripe

[1] Churchill, v. 115; U.S. edition, v. 129–30. Churchill foresaw the possibility of antagonism between Russia and the West, but did not believe it would inevitably arise (cf. ibid. iv. 636–7; U.S. edition, iv. 711–12).

[2] See above, pp. 388–90.

for Communism. Stalin, on the other hand, did not care what the Germans might suffer. In the short run he wanted German machines, man-power, and production to help restore the Russian economy. In the long run, he wanted Germany so weak economically and militarily as not to endanger the Soviet Union.

Again, Churchill's greatest fear was that the United States would abandon Europe after the war, leaving Great Britain to face Soviet Russia with nothing more than her own resources and whatever continental allies could be created. Stalin on the contrary can only have welcomed any signs of American withdrawal from European affairs, so long as the military arrangements he regarded as necessary were maintained against Germany by British and Russian if not by British, Russian, and American troops.

The net effect of these cross currents of high policy among the Big Three was to put Great Britain in a painfully isolated position. On the issue of the second front, the Americans and Russians saw eye to eye, and in the Far East the Americans were ready to make concessions in order to gain Russian help against the Japanese. In political matters, the Americans became irritated at the failure of Britain and Russia to settle their differences, and blamed both parties for the new rifts in Allied unity. Roosevelt tended to think that, if only the British would abandon their efforts at making a sphere of influence for themselves in Europe and play the game with Stalin according to the American plan, then it would become possible to win Stalin over, and liberal democratic principles would prevail.

Since Britain was infinitely closer to the United States in every way, Britain's refusal to conform to American ideas provoked more displeasure than did Russia's uncompromising pursuit of her own special interests in Eastern Europe. After all, what could one expect from the Russians if the British could not be persuaded to pin their faith upon the brave new world of Roosevelt's dreams? Thus the very closeness of Anglo-American association tended to focus American resentment upon the British. All in all, Churchill found himself in a very trying position, anxious to forestall the Russians and to convert the Americans to his view of the post-war political problem, and unable to do either.

(*b*) Europe on the Verge of Liberation

Divergences of basic policy among the Allies were not slow to manifest themselves. On 4 January 1944, scarcely more than a month after the Tehrān Conference had ended, the Russian army crossed the pre-war frontier of Poland. The Russians, of course, did not admit that they had reached any frontier, blandly assuming that the Polish frontier still lay a hundred or more miles ahead of their advancing troops. From the point of view of the Polish Government in Exile, however, the situation had become urgent. They could not afford to admit the Russian claim if they were ever to regain the eastern provinces lost to the Soviet Union in 1939.

Consequently, on 5 January 1944 the Polish Government in London issued a statement claiming for themselves the right to administer the liberated territories.[1] The Russians were not slow to reply. On 11 January Tass issued a statement affirming the validity of the annexation of what it styled western White Russia and the western Ukraine. At the same time, the Tass statement said that the Soviet Government did not regard the frontiers of 1939 as 'immutable'. It suggested the desirability of a Russo-Polish alliance for mutual aid against the Germans and held out the prospect of compensation at Germany's expense for the losses in the east.[2] Despite the fact that this statement included some compliments to the Union of Polish Patriots and attacked the 'émigré Polish Government' for its inability to establish friendly relations with the Soviet Union, Stalin was still hoping that the London Poles would come to terms. At the beginning of January 1944 he made use of Beneš's good offices to transmit to the Poles in London his proposals for future frontiers—proposals which allowed certain deviations from the Curzon Line in Poland's favour in the north. Churchill and the British Government did what they could to persuade the Poles to accept the new Russian offer, which accorded well with the proposal worked out at Tehrān.[3]

The London Poles, however, were adamant and would not agree to surrender what amounted to more than a third of their inter-war territory. On 14 January the Government in Exile replied to the Russians with an uncompromising refusal to recognize 'unilateral decisions or accomplished facts which have taken place, or might take place, on the territory of the Polish Republic'. The statement went on to appeal for British and American help in settling the dispute between themselves and the Russians.[4]

Three days later, on 17 January, the Russians came back with a blistering reply which stated categorically that 'the Soviet Government cannot enter into official negotiation with a Government with which diplomatic relations are interrupted'. The statement further accused the London Poles of rejecting the Curzon Line and of not wishing to establish neighbourly relations with the Soviet Union. With this statement, the door to direct negotiation seemed to be closed.[5]

[1] *Documents on American Foreign Relations, 1943–1944*, pp. 647–8.

[2] Text in Rothstein: *Soviet Foreign Policy during the Patriotic War*, ii. 39–40.

[3] Churchill, v. 398–9; U.S. edition, v. 450–2. See also above, pp. 364–5.

[4] Text may be found in *Polish-Soviet Relations, 1917–1945*, ed. H. W. Henderson (Glasgow, no publisher or date indicated), p. 38.

[5] Text of Soviet reply may be found in Rothstein: *Soviet Foreign Policy during the Patriotic War*, ii. 201.

This was the immediate background for one of the most curious and mysterious incidents of war-time relations between Russia and Great Britain. On 17 January 1944 *Pravda* published a brief despatch under the heading 'Rumours in Cairo' purporting to come from *Pravda*'s Own Correspondent and dated 12 January. The despatch said:

> According to the information of Greek and Yugoslav sources, which are trustworthy, a secret meeting of two leading British personalities with Ribbentrop took place not so long ago in one of the coastal towns of the Iberian peninsula. The purpose of the meeting was to clarify the conditions of a separate peace with Germany. It is supposed that the meeting was not without results.[1]

The British Government promptly and categorically denied the rumour, and after a day's silence Moscow radio broadcast the denial, which was later published in Russian papers. But the denial was accompanied by an account, quoted from a London paper, of German offers of peace to Great Britain coming through Ankara. The effect was to weaken the force of the British Government's denial, leaving a substantial margin of doubt as to their good faith.

The publication of this despatch aroused intense resentment in Great Britain, excited wide attention in the Soviet Union, and provided American journalists with the stimulus to much speculation as to possible Russian intentions. It was speedily established that no such despatch had in fact originated in Cairo through normal journalistic channels, for the censorship in Cairo had not passed the story. The German press picked up the news eagerly as evidence of Allied disunity; and on 22 January the German Overseas News-agency published a story originating from a Swiss correspondent in Turkey which set forth eight points of a supposed peace proposal made by Germany to Great Britain.[2] The Germans neither affirmed nor denied the accuracy of the report. Still another element was added when reports from Stockholm and Basle suggested that Germany was trying to negotiate a separate peace with Russia.[3] It seems clear that strenuous efforts were made in Britain and America to discourage the playing-up of this affair; and within a week the newspapers of all the Allied countries abandoned it.

What purpose lay behind the original publication of the Cairo despatch in *Pravda* is impossible to know. Three hypotheses were made at the time: perhaps the Russians took the rumour seriously and wished to smoke out any truth that there might be in it; perhaps they took this curiously indirect way to put Great Britain at a disadvantage in further negotiation over the Polish question; or, thirdly, perhaps the Russians were

[1] *New York Times*, 18 January 1944.
[2] *News Chronicle*, *New York Times*, 22 January 1944.
[3] *Daily Herald*, *Daily Mail*, 20 January 1944.

preparing the ground for a separate peace between themselves and the Nazis.[1]

A fact unknown to journalists at the time was that the British were then arguing that it would be better to postpone D-day in Normandy from 1 May to the beginning of June.[2] The Russians were not officially informed, but it seems plausible to believe that they may have received news of what Churchill was proposing through intelligence channels of their own. Such unwelcome information may have played a part in deciding Stalin or one of his subordinates to take the psychological offensive.

Whatever the motives, the effect of the *Pravda* despatch upon Anglo-Russian relations was unhappy. The era of good feeling stemming from the Tehrān agreements came abruptly to a close, and the stubborn Polish issue remained to roil the waters. Churchill decided that the time had come to settle relations between Stalin and the Polish Government in Exile if it were humanly possible to do so. On 20 January, while the furore over the *Pravda* despatch was still at its height, he personally took up the cause which Eden had argued during his illness and absence in the Mediterranean. Churchill urged the Polish Premier, Stanislaw Mikolajczyk, to accept the proposals he and Stalin had talked over at Tehrān, at least as a basis for negotiation with the Soviet Government. Mikolajczyk asked for time to consult leaders in Poland and the American Government. As might have been expected, the leaders of the Polish underground state rejected all compromise, and the American reply was equivocal.[3] Sustained by the hope of American help and by their own

[1] See e.g. *Chicago Daily News, Christian Science Monitor,* 18 January 1944; *New York Post, New York Sun,* 20 January 1944, &c. British newspapers conspicuously refrained from speculating on Russian motives. They were, presumably, reflecting the directives of the Government which from the beginning tried to minimize the whole affair.

There is a possibility that Russo-German peace negotiations were under way in January 1944. Cf. Donald B. Sanders, pseud.: 'Stalin Plotted a Separate Peace', *American Mercury,* vol. lxv, November 1947, pp. 519–27. This article states that agreement on peace terms between Russia and Germany was reached on all but three issues, and that negotiations broke down only at the last minute. The article purports to be based upon unspecified official documents.

[2] Churchill, v. 385–6, 391, 396–7; U.S. edition, v. 435–6, 442, 448–9.

[3] Ciechanowski: *Defeat in Victory,* pp. 284–7; Hull: *Memoirs,* ii. 1438–9. Roosevelt refused to back Churchill's proposals in any unambiguous manner, contenting himself with amiable sentiments about 'freely negotiated' and 'friendly' settlement of the Soviet-Polish dispute. Clearly Roosevelt did not wish to grasp the nettle, hoping that Stalin and the Poles would come to terms of their own accord. But his attitude only confirmed the Poles in their obstinate disregard of the realities of their situation, and allowed them to cling to the belief that Roosevelt would come to their rescue. In this instance, and throughout the following year, Roosevelt tried to avoid the responsibilities of the new American power, and by not making himself clear to the Poles he stored up trouble for the future.

Yet one should not blame him too much. Domestic political considerations were important in an election year, and even more influential was the pervasive atmosphere of American public

passionate nationalism, the London Poles decided to stand fast. They flatly refused to accept the Curzon Line as a basis for any future eastern boundary of their homeland.

When they informed Churchill of this decision on 15 February he became thoroughly angry with the quixotism of the Polish exiles. A week later, on 22 February 1944, he made a speech in the House of Commons in which he publicly advocated the Curzon Line as the Polish eastern frontier and expressed the opinion that Russian demands for the annexation of the former Polish territory lying east of that Line were both reasonable and just.[1]

Churchill's irritation over the Polish problem was certainly not diminished by the concurrent difficulties which had arisen in Italy. In November 1943 it had been agreed all round that political decisions affecting the Italian Government should be postponed until after the capture of Rome. This agreement was reached at a time when the Allies still hoped to take Rome before Christmas. When that possibility began to fade away into an indefinite future, agitation among the Italian political groups which opposed the King and Badoglio began to intensify. On 28–29 January 1944 a congress of political figures met at Bari and unanimously resolved that the King must abdicate. Three days earlier the U.S. State Department had reopened the whole political question when Secretary Hull informed the American member of the Advisory Council for Italy that a reorganization of the Italian Government was due, and that Victor Emmanuel should be persuaded to abdicate.[2]

This move roused Churchill's strenuous opposition. He distrusted the men who were attempting to unseat the King, the more so because Communists were prominent among them. He hoped to see Italy emerge from the war as a constitutional monarchy, with a strong conservative element in her political and social life. But in debate with the Americans he could not freely express his views. Instead he pitched his argument on the military plane: to unseat the King and overthrow Badoglio, he argued, would risk disaffection among the Italian officers and soldiers who had followed the King into the Allied camp. Thus a change such as the Americans had suggested might hurt the Allied war effort. He proposed that matters should be allowed to stand until Rome had been conquered, when there would be leisure to look round and decide what was best to do. On 10 February 1944, after a lengthy exchange of cables, Roosevelt

thought which still regarded European affairs as essentially alien, a matter to be handled by Europeans. But the trouble was that the Poles would not give up an almost pathetic faith in American help, and their attitude inevitably dragged the American Government into the problem, but only after it had been irremediably exacerbated by the passage of time (see below, pp. 429–30).

[1] 22 February 1944, H.C.Deb. 5th ser., vol. 397, coll. 697–8.

[2] Hull: *Memoirs*, ii. 1552. Hull was probably influenced by advance reports of the mood of Italian political figures who were preparing for the Bari Conference.

accepted Churchill's argument and instructed the State Department to refrain from any action that might bring about a change in the Italian Government in the immediate future.[1]

As the Polish and Italian issues were approaching this impasse Churchill decided that the only way matters could satisfactorily be straightened out between himself and the Americans would be to meet once more face to face. The military problem, Mediterranean versus Overlord, had become acute after the failure of Anzio to bring the results Churchill had so confidently hoped for;[2] and this was at least as important in Churchill's view as more strictly political questions. On 7 February he proposed to Roosevelt an early meeting to discuss all these matters; but the President refused. The Americans considered the military question closed after Tehrān and refused to reopen it. Roosevelt was unwell, and the U.S. Joint Chiefs of Staff were directing most of their attention to the Pacific. As a result, nothing came of Churchill's proposal. The unsympathetic hearing it received in Washington was symptomatic of the strains which had arisen in Anglo-American relations.[3]

Despite the Roosevelt–Churchill agreement of 10 February 1944 to put off changes in the Italian Government for the time being, the question refused to die. In the latter part of February, the committee or, as it was called, the Junta, which had been set up by six Italian parties opposed to Badoglio and the King, submitted to the Allies its programme for political change in Italy. The main points were a demand for the abdication of the King and a change in government so that all non-fascist political groups would be represented in the Cabinet. Churchill came publicly to the support of the King and Badoglio on 22 February, praising them in a speech to the House of Commons and pouring scorn on the Italian opposition.[4] But on the very next day the American Government approved the plan which had been set forth by the Junta for the reorganization of the Italian Government.[5]

This put the fat once more into the fire. During the following three

[1] Hull: *Memoirs*, ii. 1554; Churchill, v. 439–40; U.S. edition, v. 496–7.

[2] See above, pp. 384 seqq.

[3] Leahy: *I Was There*, pp. 262–3. A minor but not unimportant matter which came to a head at this time between Britain and America concerned the Middle East. On 6 February the American Government announced a plan to build an oil pipe-line from the Persian Gulf to the Mediterranean. This had been preceded and was followed by open rivalry between British and American oil companies in Persia, Sa'ūdi Arabia, and elsewhere over concessions for drilling rights, &c. In January 1944 Roosevelt also approved a recommendation that Lend-Lease goods destined for Middle Eastern countries should not be distributed by British agencies, but by Americans. All this seemed to the British to be a deliberate effort to crowd them out of the Middle East economically; and, as a result, considerable hard feeling arose. Cf. Hull: *Memoirs*, ii. 1507–23; *Survey* for 1939–46: *The Middle East in the War*, pp. 360–3.

[4] 22 February 1944, H.C.Deb. 5th ser., vol. 397, coll. 690–2.

[5] Hull: *Memoirs*, ii. 1554. General Wilson, the new Mediterranean Commander-in-Chief, also supported the Junta's proposals (Churchill, v. 446; U.S. edition, v. 503).

weeks Roosevelt and Churchill indulged in a protracted and at times acrimonious exchange of cables about Italy. Roosevelt pointed out that the original agreement to support Badoglio until Rome had been taken was made when the early capture of the Italian capital had been expected. When the second attempt to break through to Anzio and Rome failed (15 February–March 1944) he argued that action could not further be postponed. Churchill reproached the President for not abiding by the agreement to give him the lead in Italy, pointing out that he had loyally supported the Americans when they found themselves in a comparable position with Darlan.[1]

Churchill was indeed hard pressed between the Americans, the Italian opposition, and his own Commander-in-Chief; but temporary relief came suddenly and from a most unexpected source. On 13 March 1944 the Soviet Union extended formal diplomatic recognition to Badoglio's Government, and this was followed on 2 April by a remarkable about-face in the policy of the Italian Communist Party. The Italian Communists had been associated with the opposition to the King and Badoglio in the first months after the Italian surrender; but when Palmiro Togliatti arrived from Moscow and took over the direction of the Party, he completely reversed the Communist line by offering support to the Badoglio régime and suggesting that the question of the monarchy should be left to a future constitutional convention. The former associates of the Communists in the Junta were thus left gasping, and to all appearance the Badoglio Government received a new lease of life.[2]

The establishment of diplomatic relations between the Soviet Union and Badoglio's Government took Britain and America by surprise. Neither had been consulted ahead of time and both felt that Stalin had rudely short-circuited the Advisory Council for Italy which had been set up to satisfy Russian, French, Greek, and Yugoslav claims to a voice in Italian affairs.[3] Diplomatic remonstrance in Moscow was matched by emphatic protests to Badoglio; but despite legal arguments about the limits of Badoglio's powers to enter into relations with other governments, there was nothing the Western Allies could do to alter the new arrangement.

What may have been the reasons for these actions of the Russian Government in Italy cannot be known for sure. To the Americans, Molotov justified the extension of diplomatic recognition to Badoglio on the ground that Russia had been excluded from the deliberations of the Western Allies touching upon Italy;[4] and since the Advisory Council for Italy was in fact removed from direct control of affairs, this may have helped to make

[1] Churchill, v. 445–6; U.S. edition, v. 503–4; Hull: *Memoirs*, ii. 1555–6.

[2] Badoglio: *Italy in the Second World War*, pp. 128–30, 147–8.

[3] See above, p. 309.

[4] Hull: *Memoirs*, ii. 1557.

the Russians act as they did. But there is also another possibility. By implication the Russians may have intended to offer a deal to Great Britain: if Britain would support Russian policy in Poland the Soviets would return the compliment in Italy.[1]

That some such arrangement may have been in Stalin's mind seems at least possible. After Churchill's speech of 22 February, when he came out for the Curzon Line as Poland's eastern frontier, there seemed to be no insuperable obstacle to Anglo-Russian agreement over Poland. All that seemed necessary from Stalin's point of view was for Churchill to browbeat the London Poles into agreement. But the Poles in London were by no means wholly subject to Churchill's will. No mere argument could convince them that their claims to the eastern provinces of inter-war Poland were not right and just; and Churchill was not willing to resort to extreme measures of compulsion.

Instead he tried to explain the Polish view-point to Stalin and proposed that final settlement of the dispute over Polish boundaries should be left to the future peace conference.[2] Stalin interpreted this as an effort to go back on the agreement reached at Tehrān. On 23 March 1944 he sent a very stiff cable to the Prime Minister, accusing him of bad faith. 'I do not doubt', he said, 'that if you had continued to stand firmly on your Teheran position the conflict with the Polish emigrant Government would have already been solved.' He added:

> In your message of March 21, you say you intend to make a statement in the House of Commons that all questions regarding territorial changes should be postponed until peace conferences of the victorious powers are held, and that until then you cannot recognize any transference of territory *effected by force*. . . .
>
> You are free to make any speech in the House of Commons. That is your affair. But if you make such a speech, I shall consider that you have committed an act of injustice and unfriendliness toward the Soviet Union.[3]

In the face of such a threat, Churchill decided to break off for the time being the effort to bring the Russians and Poles to an understanding.[4] Publicly he returned a soft answer, referring in a radio broadcast on 26 March to Stalin as a great 'warrior leader' who had imparted 'a unity and a concert to the war direction in the East which has been very good for Soviet Russia and for all her Allies'.[5]

[1] This was not the way British officials on the spot in Italy interpreted the move; but Churchill or someone else in London may have detected this possibility. Just four weeks later, the British Government extended feelers for a deal on similar lines affecting the Balkans (see below, p. 422). Churchill (v. 446; U.S. edition, v. 504) merely says that the Soviet move 'complicated the situation'.

[2] This, of course, accorded with the American position, championed more vigorously by the State Department and Secretary Hull than by Roosevelt, but approved by the President none the less.

[3] Leahy: *I Was There*, pp. 274–5.

[4] Mikolajczyk: *Pattern of Soviet Domination*, p. 63.

[5] Winston S. Churchill: *The Dawn of Liberation* (London, Cassell, 1945), p. 41.

It was after Churchill had thus backed down on the Polish issue that the Italian Communists made their surprising about-face; and, although the timing of their offer to support Badoglio may have had no connexion with Polish affairs, it is at least possible that Stalin intended to show the British how easily things could be arranged if only Churchill would, in Stalin's words, 'stand firmly on your Teheran position' and bring the London Poles to heel.

Meanwhile the Russians, in view of the repulse of their overtures to the Polish Government in Exile made through Beneš in January 1944, advanced a more radical plan for dealing with the problem presented by Polish intransigence. Their scheme was to enlist the support of the American and British Governments in an effort to change the personnel of the Polish Government in such a way as to make agreement on Stalin's terms possible. On the day following the publication of the Soviet statement of 17 January, which had so summarily closed the door to direct negotiations with the London Poles,[1] Molotov sent a cable to the American Government in which he declared that the reorganization of the Polish Government to include 'democratic elements' would create the necessary conditions for settlement of the dispute which had arisen; and on 24 January he suggested that Polish leaders from the United States, Britain, and Russia should be brought together to form such a government.[2]

In pursuance of this aim, at the beginning of March 1944 Stalin invited two Polish-Americans, Professor Oscar Lange and a Catholic priest, Stanislaw Orlemanski, to come to Moscow for consultation. They arrived at the end of April, and interviewed Stalin and Molotov. Stalin talked reassuringly to both of them. He told Lange that he had no intention of intervening in Polish domestic affairs, but did intend to assure himself that the future government of Poland would follow a foreign policy friendly to Russia.[3] He informed Father Orlemanski that he supported religious liberty, and believed that co-operation with the Pope would be possible.[4]

But no positive results came from Stalin's effort. The American, and presumably also the British, Governments were not interested in recruiting a new Polish Government from among individuals such as Lange and Orlemanski. And the Polish Government in Exile would have nothing to do with them, considering the two emissaries to be either dupes or traitors.

Churchill's difficulties were enhanced by the fact that just as his negotiation with Stalin over Poland was reaching an impasse (23 March) his

[1] See above, p. 414.

[2] Hull: *Memoirs*, ii. 1437, 1442. It is not clear whether the Russians had in mind a Polish Government established *de novo* by the Big Three, or hoped that some figment of legal continuity with the Government already established in London could be maintained.

[3] Ciechanowski: *Defeat in Victory*, p. 327; Mikolajczyk: *Pattern of Soviet Domination*, p. 69.

[4] An official text was released by Tass on 12 May 1944 describing Orlemanski's trip (cf. Rothstein: *Soviet Foreign Policy during the Patriotic War*, ii. 78–80).

relations with Roosevelt became even more strained. As we have seen, the President failed to support Churchill on the Polish issue and disagreed with him over Badoglio. Dispute over strategy was simultaneously acute, the British urging and the Americans opposing a third attempt to break the German line in Italy and take Rome at the expense of preparing for the landing in southern France.[1] To these grounds of friction was added in March an acute disagreement over policy towards France and de Gaulle.

The question immediately at issue was how to draft instructions for Eisenhower concerning the administration of liberated France. Churchill, and Eisenhower too,[2] wished to rely on de Gaulle and the French Committee of National Liberation, entrusting that body with authority to conduct the civil administration of France. Roosevelt, however, retained his distrust and dislike of de Gaulle. He wished to instruct Eisenhower to make arrangements with any French group, except the Vichy Government, which seemed to attract the support of the local population. Roosevelt argued that it was not certain whether the French liked or trusted de Gaulle and his Committee, and that it would be wrong to tie Eisenhower's hands in advance until the real sentiments of the liberated population could be authoritatively discovered.[3]

Since Eisenhower was an American general, the first drafting of his instructions was entrusted to the American Government. The draft was ready on 15 March; but Churchill would not accept it, and held out for a firmer recognition of the French Committee of National Liberation. This was the situation when Churchill attempted once again to arrange a personal meeting with Roosevelt. The French, Polish, and Italian issues were all acute; and the military question of whether to land in southern France or not was still being hotly debated. Churchill felt his isolation more and more acutely. He much preferred to come to an understanding with the Americans, but, if that was not possible, he was prepared to see what could be done with the Russians.

Accordingly, towards the end of March he sent off a cable to Roosevelt proposing a conference in Bermuda to assemble on 5 April. The President again refused. Roosevelt was then near the end of his tether physically, and on 8 April left Washington to rest in privacy in South Carolina, and try to regain his health. It was while resting there that Admiral Leahy, one of Roosevelt's closest friends and confidants, wryly suggested that an historical tablet should be erected saying that in the year 1944 Roosevelt had, like his predecessor President Madison in 1814, fled Washington to escape from the British.[4] The joke was not pointless. Roosevelt was peevish and ill and did not want to be bothered by Churchill or anyone

[1] See above, pp. 384–5.

[2] Eisenhower: *Crusade in Europe*, p. 249; Stimson and Bundy: *On Active Service*, pp. 310–11.

[3] Hull: *Memoirs*, ii. 1427.

[4] Leahy: *I Was There*, pp. 272–3, 278.

else; but as his health improved so did his spirits, and, by 6 May, when he returned to Washington, the President was more nearly himself again.

Allied cordiality, which had steadily decreased since Tehrān, reached its nadir in the latter part of March and the first days of April 1944. Thereafter things began to pick up a bit. For one thing, Eisenhower was able to inform the Russians officially on 8 April of the date for D-day; and the advanced state of military preparation in Britain must have helped to convince the Russians that this time there would not be further delay.[1] Russian action in Italy and British inaction on the Polish issue relieved some of the tensions between the two Governments; and similarly with respect to France, the Russians and the French Communists both lent their support to de Gaulle as did the British Government.[2]

Some progress was also made in April towards smoothing over the quarrels which had arisen between the American and British Governments. As a substitute for another Churchill–Roosevelt conference, Edward Stettinius, recently appointed Under Secretary of State, came to London with a retinue of State Department officials on 7 April, in order to discuss the political and economic differences which had come to divide the two Governments. He did not return to Washington until 4 May. Although few definite results were achieved, nevertheless Stettinius's mission provided an opportunity for key officials of the State Department to talk things over with the British. A clearing of the atmosphere resulted, even when the upshot was an agreement to differ.

Nevertheless, American and British policy remained badly out of step in Italy, France, and Poland. The British Government had been able to arrive at more far-reaching accord with Stalin than with Roosevelt and the State Department. This situation was dramatically brought to the attention of the American Government at the end of May when Hull and Roosevelt for the first time were informed of an Anglo-Russian agreement for dividing the Balkans into separate 'spheres of action'.

This arrangement arose from the rapid change in the military situation which resulted from the Red Army's victorious drive to and beyond the borders of the Ukraine. On 29 March the Russians, having overrun Bessarabia, reached the Pruth river, thus attaining the 1940 boundary between the Soviet Union and Rumania. Without stopping, the Red Army crossed the river and proceeded, before the impetus of their offen-

[1] Butcher: *My Three Years with Eisenhower*, p. 515.

[2] On 4 April 1944 the alliance between de Gaulle and the French Communists was consummated by the admission of two Communists to the French Committee of National Liberation. This was quite in tune with the British efforts in Greece and Yugoslavia, where Churchill was then seeking to secure Communist support for non-Communist Prime Ministers. It also accorded with the situation in Italy.

sive died away, to occupy a small area of Rumanian soil round the town of Jassy. Molotov signalized this achievement by telling a news conference on 2 April 1944 that the Soviet Union had no intention of annexing Rumanian territory or of 'changing the existing social order of Rumania'.[1] This statement was designed to accomplish two purposes. On the one hand, it notified the world at large that Bessarabia was a part of the Soviet Union, and that the Pruth and not the Dniester would be the boundary of Rumania for the future. On the other hand, it must have been intended to reassure the Western Allies about Soviet intentions, and was perhaps aimed also at the Rumanian Government and people, whose willingness to fight on at Germany's side was already open to doubt.[2]

But statements such as this were not enough to reassure Churchill. He did not want to see Russian influence spread throughout the Balkans with the help of Russian bayonets. He knew ahead of time that the American Government would refuse to interest itself in the question, and so decided to do what he could by himself. Churchill decided there were two things to do: first, redouble his efforts to remodel the Greek and Yugoslav Governments in Exile in such a way as to head off the danger of civil war or a Communist *coup d'état* after the liberation of those countries; and second, come to an understanding with the Russians which would define the respective spheres of action for the two Powers in the Balkans. As we have seen,[3] Churchill succeeded by high-handed pressure in bringing about a reorganization of the Greek Government in May and of the Yugoslav Government in June—reorganizations which gave him some ground for hope that an open clash between the Communist-led resistance armies and the Governments in Exile could be avoided.

As these moves were coming to completion, Eden broached the question of a delimitation of zones of activity in the Balkans to the Russian Ambassador in London on 5 May 1944.[4] In this and following conversations the line of division that was worked out was simple enough: Rumania and Bulgaria were to be Russia's, Greece and Yugoslavia Britain's, sphere of operations. On 18 May 1944 the Russians accepted the British proposal tentatively, but inquired whether the United States had been consulted, and, if so, what was the American view. Churchill had not taken the matter up with Roosevelt ahead of time, and was in no hurry to do so

[1] Rothstein: *Soviet Foreign Policy during the Patriotic War*, ii. 65–66.

[2] The Rumanians had shown signs of wishing to abandon Hitler even before the Tehrān Conference (Churchill, v. 311, 325; U.S. edition, v. 353, 368). In March 1944 negotiations took a more definite form. In that month a Rumanian envoy travelled to Cairo in order to sound out British and American officials about the possibility of changing sides; but the negotiation came to nothing because he demanded the dispatch of British or American troops to Rumania to counterbalance the Red Army. The Western Powers would not or could not agree to such a proposal. Details will be found in the *Survey* for 1939–46: *Hitler's Europe*; cf. Leahy: *I Was There*, p. 267.

[3] See above, pp. 388, 389.

[4] This followed Soviet refusal to endorse British policy in Greece. See above, p. 390.

even after the Russians had raised the question. He was no doubt disgruntled by the repeated rebuffs and opposition he had met from the Americans in the months just past, and realized that the proposed arrangement would not easily win American endorsement.

However, on 30 May 1944 he instructed Lord Halifax, the British Ambassador in Washington, to raise the question with Hull. Lord Halifax mentioned only Greece and Rumania on this occasion, and he was at pains to explain that the proposed agreement would be merely a temporary expedient, applicable only to military operations and their immediate corollaries in the civil sphere. Hull objected strongly to the whole idea, seeing in the proposal the cloven hoof of power politics and spheres of influence. After this rebuff, Churchill took the question up with Roosevelt directly. On 31 May he explained a little more of what was in his mind. He again stressed the temporary nature of the arrangement; and he underlined the fact that the Russians had accepted the proposal.

Roosevelt did not at once agree. He turned Churchill's cable over to the State Department, but, while the officials of that department were working over their reply, Churchill sent another cable on 8 June in which for the first time he mentioned the fact that Yugoslavia and Bulgaria, as well as Greece and Rumania,[1] were to be apportioned between Britain and Russia. On 10 June the American reply was finally ready. It proposed the establishment of a consultative committee for Balkan affairs instead of the Anglo-Russian arrangement. This time it was Churchill's turn to say 'No'. On the following day, 11 June, he rejected the American proposal as too clumsy, and appealed directly to the President's vanity by suggesting that he and Roosevelt could handle matters much better by keeping them in their own hands than by entrusting decisions to mediocre officials sitting on a committee. He suggested that the arrangement he had worked out with the Russians should have a three months' trial, and if it proved unsatisfactory it could then be abandoned.

Hull was at the time ill and away from Washington; and Roosevelt decided to go ahead and accept Churchill's proposals. But, realizing how deeply Hull felt on the question of spheres of influence, he dodged the uncomfortable task of informing his Secretary of State of what he had done. As a result, when Hull returned to Washington he proceeded to draft a further note of remonstrance to the British Government, and actually sent it off before he heard on 26 June, through the American Ambassador to the Greek Government in Exile (who had been informed by his British colleague), that the American Government had agreed to the spheres of influence deal. Hull then took the matter up with Roosevelt,

[1] It is possible that this extension of the agreement had only been negotiated after 30 May, though Hull's account seems to imply that the British deliberately withheld the full scope of the proposal at first (*Memoirs*, ii. 1451–4).

and was informed belatedly and by letter of what Roosevelt had done.[1] This was one of the more egregious instances of the failure of normal communication within the American Government, arising from Roosevelt's unwillingness to share high politics with the State Department and his distaste for telling unwelcome news to personal friends.

The confusion within the American Government must have seemed almost incredible to the British. When the State Department's note criticizing the Balkan arrangement reached Churchill, he replied vigorously, defended the propriety of his action in going first to the Russians before consulting the Americans, and accused Roosevelt of having gone over his head in dealings with Stalin on certain occasions. In this Churchill was on firm ground, for early in June Roosevelt had communicated directly with Stalin about the Polish problem, and had not informed the British of what he was doing. On 26 June, accordingly, Roosevelt sent a contrite message to the irritated Prime Minister, asserting that it was essential for their two countries to maintain accord on all questions connected with the war effort.

Meanwhile, echoes of the confusion between Washington and London had reached Moscow. On 1 July the Russians asked Washington point-blank what the Americans had decided. By 15 July the State Department had ready a reply, acknowledging that the American Government had endorsed the arrangement for the Balkans, but emphasizing the three-month time limit, and reaffirming the general principle of no spheres of influence. Moreover, the note declared that American interests in the Balkans would be in no way affected by the Anglo-Russian agreement.[2]

This reply obviously deprived the agreement of much of its value. If the Americans reserved the right to put a spoke in both the British and the Russian wheel in any Balkan country, then a division into operational spheres could have only an insecure foundation. What was needed was a tripartite agreement; and desultory efforts to persuade the Americans to play the British and Russian game in the Balkans continued throughout the summer and autumn of 1944. It was, however, not until October that the Americans had been won round to the point of accepting, reluctantly, a definite, written delimitation of separate spheres of operational responsibility in the Balkans.[3]

Nevertheless, neither Britain nor Russia repudiated the tentative agreement of May, and, indeed, on some critical occasions each Government acted in the spirit of its terms. Thus the British declined to intervene actively in Rumanian and Bulgarian affairs when in the summer of 1944 envoys from those two countries attempted to bring Anglo-American forces on to the scene as a makeweight against the Red Army; and in

[1] Hull: *Memoirs*, ii. 1454–6.
[2] Ibid. pp. 1457–8.
[3] See below, p. 495.

August 1944 the Russians returned the compliment when they advised the Greek Communists to join a British-sponsored Government for Greece.[1] Despite American objections, which prevented any formal agreement, Britain and Russia acted as though they had divided the Balkan nations between them from May 1944 onwards, Greece and Yugoslavia falling to Britain, Rumania and Bulgaria to Russia.[2]

The new prominence of Balkan questions in April, May, and June did not call a halt to political manœuvres in Italy and France, where British and American policy continued as before to work at cross-purposes. Russian policy with respect to both countries was generally passive. The dramatic action in Italy of March and April, when the Russians had accorded diplomatic recognition to Badoglio, and the Communist Party had come openly to his support, did not suffice to counterbalance the pressure for changes in the Italian régime which came both from the American Government and from the Italians themselves.[3]

Following the about-face of the Italian Communists at the beginning of April, Badoglio began conversations with leaders of the various Opposition Parties, and with the Allied authorities as well. The upshot was that on 12 April 1944 an Allied communiqué announced that King Victor Emmanuel would transfer his powers by appointing the Crown Prince 'Lieutenant of the Realm' as soon as the Allied armies captured Rome; and on 21 April Badoglio became head of a new Cabinet in which the Opposition Parties were all represented.[4]

The British hoped that this concession to the Americans and to the Italian Opposition would keep Italian politics on an even keel after Rome's capture, and that Prince Humbert would be able to take over his father's role successfully. But it did not turn out so. The Allies took Rome on 5 June 1944; and Victor Emmanuel, in accordance with the agreement of 12 April, promptly resigned his constitutional powers to his son. Humbert then asked Badoglio to form a Cabinet again; but the Italian politicians of Rome refused to accept him. Instead Ivanoe Bonomi became Prime Minister on 9 June.[5]

Churchill felt outraged at this turn of events. He feared that the con-

[1] See below, p. 477, note 1.

[2] Hull simply says that the Anglo-Russian arrangement for the Balkans 'duly entered into effect following the President's acquiescence' (*Memoirs*, ii. 1458). This describes the reality but not the legality of the situation.

[3] Thus, if Stalin's action in Italy had been intended as a concession in return for British support of Russian policy in Poland, in the end the bargain failed of consummation. The British were compelled by other influences to yield in Italy; and in Poland Stalin in the end got his way only by defying the Western Powers and the people of Poland themselves.

[4] Badoglio: *Italy in the Second World War*, pp. 143–60; Hull: *Memoirs*, ii. 1558–60; Churchill, v. 455; U.S. edition, v. 515.

[5] See below, p. 478.

servative elements in Italian society would be excluded from the new Government. In a cable to Roosevelt on 10 June he denounced the 'group of aged and hungry politicians' who had taken over the Italian Government, and argued that, since the Advisory Council for Italy had not been consulted in the matter, the new Cabinet should not be recognized by the Allies. To this the American Government replied that it would be a serious mistake not to permit the prompt installation of the Bonomi Cabinet in office; and Churchill was compelled to agree since there seemed no way of undoing what had been done.[1]

While this outcome of the Italian embroglio might well appear as a victory for the American point of view, French affairs moved in quite the opposite direction. In spite of Roosevelt's distrust of him, General de Gaulle went from strength to strength. On 26 March 1944 de Gaulle publicly referred to the French Committee of National Liberation as a Provisional Government for France; and this was followed on 15 May by a formal resolution which changed the name of the French Committee of National Liberation to Provisional Government of the Republic of France. In the meanwhile, de Gaulle's personal leadership of the Committee was confirmed by the elimination of General Giraud, who resigned on 14 April after a dispute over his powers as military commander of the French forces.[2]

The British Government did what they could to strengthen de Gaulle's position, making available to his organization the means of communicating with resistance groups in France and arguing on his behalf with the Americans. General Eisenhower had no other French authority with which to deal, and made arrangements for military liaison with representatives of the Provisional Government. Roosevelt steadily vetoed any agreement about civil administration, however, and on D-day Eisenhower had no arrangement ready. At the last minute before D-day Roosevelt's refusal to accept de Gaulle as head of a French Provisional Government almost precipitated a rupture in the military arrangements Eisenhower had made; and after D-day, on 10 June, de Gaulle publicly announced that he had been unable to reach any agreement with the Allies about the administration of France.[3]

The American Government only reluctantly climbed down. On 6 July de Gaulle arrived for a formal visit in Washington, and so conducted himself as to impress some of his most inveterate enemies favourably.[4] Moreover, it had become clear that de Gaulle had no effective rivals within France itself. The Communists had accepted his leadership, and

[1] Hull: *Memoirs*, ii. 1563–5.

[2] Details will be found in the *Survey* for 1939–46: *Hitler's Europe*.

[3] Eisenhower: *Crusade in Europe*, p. 248; Butcher: *My Three Years with Eisenhower*, pp. 562–3, 570; Stimson and Bundy: *On Active Service*, pp. 311–14.

[4] Leahy: *I Was There*, pp. 287–8; Hull: *Memoirs*, ii. 1433.

so did the other resistance groups as well as the population at large. As a result, Roosevelt and Hull agreed on 11 July 1944 to recognize de Gaulle and his committee as *de facto* representatives of the French people.[1] De Gaulle was at long last within sight of the accomplishment of his ambition to become head of a recognized French Government.

Allied relations with the European neutrals provided still another source of Anglo-American friction. In general, the Americans wanted to use stronger methods to persuade such countries as Eire, Spain, Sweden, and Turkey to break off trade and other relations with Germany than the British Government thought wise; and in the Western Hemisphere the British were not inclined to support high-handed pressure against Argentina which the American Government wished to employ.[2] Such differences were, however, minor matters, turning not on divergences of ultimate purpose but on questions of tactics.

With respect to the smaller countries of Western Europe, and the problems of their liberation, no serious difficulties arose in 1944. The Governments in Exile from Belgium, the Netherlands, and Norway had clear title to legality in Allied eyes, and the resistance movements within those countries, too, recognized the exiled leadership. Hence the problems of liberation were technical rather than political. The relationship between Allied military authority and the Governments in Exile of Belgium, the Netherlands, and Norway was defined by agreements signed by Eisenhower on 16 May.[3]

When D-day came on 6 June 1944 the military success in Normandy did much to mend Allied relations. The long waiting and anxiety was at last over. As the Anglo-American armies went into action and their attack was co-ordinated with the renewed Russian offensive, a profound feeling of relief, pride, and confidence in early victory spread among the Allies everywhere. Roosevelt's mood improved with his health, and by June he perhaps began to feel that he had treated Churchill rather shabbily, especially over the French question, in the months just past. Churchill, for his part, was enormously relieved to find that the military disaster he had so much feared had not come, and, viewing the weight of the Allied attack, he felt so optimistic as to predict in public that victory in 1944 was assured.[4]

Stalin, too, was pleased. On 13 June he said: 'One cannot but recognize that the history of warfare knows no other similar undertaking in the breadth of its conception, in its giant dimensions, and in the mastery of its performance. . . . History will record this event as an achievement of the

[1] Ibid. pp. 1430–4. See also below, pp. 476–7.

[2] Cf. Hull: *Memoirs*, ii. 1324–89.

[3] Butcher: *My Three Years with Eisenhower*, p. 541.

[4] *New York Times*, 19 June 1944.

highest order.'[1] Two other Soviet gestures deserve notice. On 11 June the Russian Government published an official account of the supplies which had been delivered to the Soviet Union by America, Britain, and Canada since the beginning of the war. The statement not only listed the amounts received of a wide variety of articles, but said: 'In supplying the Soviet Union with the above-mentioned valuable materials, the United States, Great Britain and Canada are contributing to the successes of the Red Army in the liberation of its native soil from the Fascist invaders, and in hastening the common victory of the Allies. . . .'[2] This was one of the rare occasions on which the Soviet Government officially and publicly acknowledged the scope and value of the supplies they had received from the West.

A similar gesture was the elaborate celebration of United Nations Day, 14 June 1944, which was ordered by the Council of Peoples' Commissars throughout the Soviet Union.[3] These gestures were evidence, if evidence were needed, of the satisfaction Stalin and his fellows felt when the long awaited second front in Europe at length materialized. Victory now seemed certain, and might, it seemed, come soon.

This interval of good feeling and relief at the success in Normandy set the background for a further effort to arrange a second meeting of Stalin, Churchill, and Roosevelt. Victory would obviously raise the question of how to treat Germany, and how to mobilize maximum force in the shortest time against Japan; and Roosevelt, at least, wanted to handle these problems on a tripartite basis. Stalin, however, was as usual reluctant, and by the end of June it had become apparent that he would not agree to a meeting in the immediate future.[4]

Churchill meanwhile pressed repeatedly for another Anglo-American conference; but Roosevelt was not sure that such a meeting would accomplish what he had in mind. Some of his advisers were afraid that if he consulted Churchill without Stalin it would appear that the Anglo-Americans were trying to exclude Russia from their deliberations. It was also suggested that too close a relation with the minions of King George III would not help Roosevelt's campaign for re-election.[5]

Despite these arguments, when Churchill urgently requested another conference with Roosevelt on 16 July 1944, the President decided that he should agree to meet the Prime Minister in Scotland about the middle of September to discuss, among other things, the question of Germany and the Japanese war.[6] The meeting was later transferred to Quebec, and opened on 11 September 1944.

[1] Rothstein: *Soviet Foreign Policy during the Patriotic War*, ii. 25.

[2] Ibid. ii. 86.

[3] Ibid. p. 88.

[4] Sherwood: *Roosevelt and Hopkins*, p. 812; Eng. edition, ii. 804.

[5] Leahy: *I Was There*, p. 289.

[6] Ibid. p. 292.

The rosy glow which D-day brought to Allied relations did not long endure. By the end of June 1944 the problem of Poland once more came to the fore when the Red Army, resuming its offensive on the central front, began to move into undisputedly Polish territory. At almost the last minute before this offensive began, the Russians made a final attempt to come to an understanding with the London Poles. Following Stalin's fruitless interviews with Lange and Orlemanski in April and May, Soviet representatives put forth unofficial feelers in London to the Polish Premier, Mikolajczyk. But Stalin's terms, like those of the Roman sibyl, had been raised from those he had offered in January. He now wanted not only the recognition of the Curzon Line but also the dismissal of certain key figures in the Polish Government, including the President. Edvard Beneš, President of the Czechoslovak Government in Exile, was again pressed into service by the Russians to act as intermediary, but without any success. Neither the Russians nor the Poles would give way.[1]

In dealing with the Czechs, the Russians met with none of the difficulties which faced them in Poland. The Czechs by national tradition dating from the nineteenth century treasured pan-Slav feeling as a sort of bulwark against the *Deutschtum* which so nearly surrounded Bohemia. Moreover, the historical injustices which divided the Russians from the Poles were absent from Czechoslovak history; their enemy was Germany, and before that had been Austria. Hence it was relatively easy for the Czechs to accept the Russians as friends and fellow-Slavs.

On 12 December 1943 the two Governments signed a Treaty of Friendship, Mutual Assistance, and Post-war Collaboration, which not only promised mutual support in any future war against Germany but also promised mutual 'non-intervention in the internal affairs of the other State'.[2] This treaty was supplemented on 8 May 1944 by an agreement to define the relation between Red Army commanders and the Czech civil administration which would take effect as soon as the Russians reached Czech territory. According to this agreement, military operations were to be exclusively under Russian control, but 'as soon as any part of liberated territory ceases to be a zone of direct military operations, the Czechoslovak Government shall take over complete authority in the management of public affairs. . . .'[3]

Thus the path was cleared for Red Army operations in Czechoslovakia;[4] but naturally nothing similar could be arranged with the Polish Government in Exile while the dispute over the boundary of Polish jurisdiction remained unsolved.

Meanwhile, the London Poles were seeking Roosevelt's succour.

[1] Ciechanowski: *Defeat in Victory*, p. 309.

[2] Rothstein: *Soviet Foreign Policy during the Patriotic War*, i. 250–2; *Documents on American Foreign Relations, 1943–1944*, pp. 642–4.

[3] Rothstein, op. cit. ii. 75–77.

[4] See below, p. 475.

Churchill, they felt, had betrayed them by his open support of the Curzon Line; Stalin was their enemy; only Roosevelt could be their friend and champion. But the President was very unwilling to try to handle so prickly a problem, and for a long time nimbly dodged the issue. At length, however, after he had rebuffed two earlier attempts, Roosevelt agreed to receive an official visit from the Polish Premier, Stanislaw Mikolajczyk. The visit began on 5 June, the day before D-day, and lasted for nine days.

Roosevelt held three conversations with Mikolajczyk. The President urged that Mikolajczyk should try to settle matters by meeting Stalin face to face; and he hinted repeatedly that the Poles should be ready to make concessions to the Russians' demands. But Roosevelt did not dare to be frank; or perhaps it would be fairer to say that the President refused to give up hope that agreement could yet be reached on terms that would satisfy both Stalin and the Poles.

The Polish problem had a growing importance on the American domestic political scene. The presidential election campaigns were about to begin. An open dispute with the Polish Government in Exile would risk alienation of the Polish-American vote—a thing to be reckoned with when, as on the nationalist issue, it was almost solidly united. On the other hand, Roosevelt had pinned his whole international programme upon agreement with Russia, and there were many people in the United States who felt that good relations with Russia should be maintained at almost any cost. As a result, Roosevelt was very cautious, and did not make his views so clear that Mikolajczyk could not over-estimate, as he so eagerly wished to do, the extent of American support for the position taken by the Polish Government in Exile. After hesitating, Roosevelt decided to send a cable to Stalin urging him to see Mikolajczyk and telling him of the conversations he had had with the Polish Premier. Stalin's reply, received in Washington on 15 June, disappointed the President. It said:

> You are familiar with the point of view of the Soviet Government and its endeavour to see Poland strong, independent and democratic and the Polish-Soviet relations good-neighbourly and based upon durable friendship.
>
> . . . It is necessary to say, however, that from the statement of Mr. Mikolajczyk in Washington it is not seen that he makes in this matter any step forward. That is why it is difficult for me, at the present moment, to offer any opinion about Mr. Mikolajczyk's trip to Moscow.[1]

When the Red Army began to move forward into Poland during the last days of June, matters became urgent. Churchill stepped into the breach, and pleaded with Stalin to see Mikolajczyk and try once more for a settlement. Stalin agreed, and on 27 July 1944 the Polish Premier started on his way to Moscow. By that time, the Red Army was within a few miles of Warsaw. The problem of how to administer Polish territory

[1] Mikolajczyk: *Pattern of Soviet Domination*, p. 71; Ciechanowski: *Defeat in Victory*, pp. 305–32.

in the rear of the Red Army could not be easily postponed, and Stalin did not await Mikolajczyk's arrival before taking steps towards solving it. On 26 July, the day before Mikolajczyk left London, the Soviet Government issued a statement which said, in part:

> . . . The Soviet Government does not intend to establish its own administrative bodies in the territory of Poland, considering this to be an affair of the Polish people. It has decided in view of this to conclude with the Polish Committee of National Liberation an Agreement on relations between the Soviet Command and the Polish Administration.
>
> The Soviet Government states that it does not pursue the aim of acquiring any part of Polish territory or of changing the social order in Poland, and that the military operations of the Red Army in the territory of Poland are dictated solely by military necessity and by the desire to afford the friendly Polish people aid in its liberation from German occupation.[1]

The Committee had, in fact, already established its seat of government in Lublin. Simultaneously, an agreement defining the relations between the Soviet military commander-in-chief and the Polish administration was published. It followed almost exactly the model of the Czechoslovak agreement which had been signed in May, with this difference: the Polish Committee of National Liberation was not referred to as a Government.[2]

This technicality was perhaps intended to leave a loophole for agreement with the London Poles. But, in effect, Stalin's terms to Mikolajczyk and his Government had risen yet again. Recognition of the Curzon Line and dismissal of certain members of the London Government would not now suffice: Mikolajczyk would also have to accept some if not all of the members of the Polish Committee of National Liberation as colleagues before Stalin would recognize his Government. The personnel of the Committee was not entirely Communist, but it was certainly dominated by Communists; and in the eyes of the London Poles the Committee was a completely servile group bent on betraying the Polish people in the interests of Russia and Communism.[3] On the other side, the members of the Committee freely accused the Polish Government in Exile of fascist sympathies and of pro-German acts and attitudes. Under the circumstances, anything like voluntary agreement between the two groups was out of the question.

Mikolajczyk was in Tehrān *en route* to Moscow when he first heard the full details of Stalin's agreement with the Polish Committee of National Liberation. For a while he hesitated as to whether to go on or turn back. Telegrams from Churchill and Roosevelt urged him to go to Moscow anyhow, and in the end he decided to do so. He arrived without any real

[1] Rothstein: *Soviet Foreign Policy during the Patriotic War*, ii. 93.
[2] Text of the Agreement may be found ibid. pp. 93–96.
[3] Mikolajczyk: *Pattern of Soviet Domination*, pp. 77–78.

hope of reaching agreement, as unready as ever to yield to Russian demands or to recognize *faits accomplis*.

Mikolajczyk saw Stalin on 3 August 1944. His situation was an anguished one, for on 1 August the Home Army in Warsaw had risen against the Germans in the expectation of freeing it before the Red Army reached the city. But the Polish Home Army could not hold out indefinitely against the full power of the Germans; help from the Russian troops which were then only a few miles to the east of Warsaw was urgently needed if the rising were not to end in disaster. Consequently, when he saw Stalin Mikolajczyk urged and pleaded for military help for Warsaw. Stalin professed to have no information about the rising and was non-committal about helping the Poles. He made it quite clear that what he wanted was a political agreement and acceptance of the Curzon Line; military matters came second.

Mikolajczyk consented to talk things over with members of the Polish Committee of National Liberation. But he could agree with them on nothing. When Boleslaw Bierut offered him the post of Prime Minister if Mikolajczyk would join forces with the Committee and recognize Bierut as President of Poland, Mikolajczyk indignantly rejected the offer. With that, all hope of positive results was gone. On 9 August Mikolajczyk saw Stalin a second time before departing, and wrung from him a promise (or what Mikolajczyk interpreted as such) to investigate the situation in Warsaw and do his best to help the Polish army fighting so heroically and so vainly in that city.[1] Stalin's investigation evidently did not reassure him. By 12 August the Russian Government had definitely come to the conclusion that the Warsaw rising was led by men antagonistic to the Soviet Union, and decided to leave the insurgents to their fate.[2]

Mikolajczyk's visit had done nothing to heal the breach; his unyielding demand for Polish rights as he and his fellows saw them had only deepened the antagonism between the Poles of London and of the Home Army on the one hand and the Russians on the other. It seems clear that Stalin resolved to crush utterly and permanently the organization which the Polish Government in Exile had created within Poland, and he chose to use the situation which had developed in Warsaw as a means towards his end. The Germans, fighting the Poles, were doing his bloody work for him; and Stalin was well content to have it so.

The crisis in Polish affairs which had thus developed in the first part of August deserves a place in the history of the Second World War like that

[1] Mikolajczyk: *Pattern of Soviet Domination*, p. 86. Only Polish accounts of these dealings with Stalin have been published; they may be either deliberately or unconsciously distorted.

[2] Hull: *Memoirs*, ii. 445–6. See also below, pp. 464–6.

which Thucydides gave to the Athenian attack on Melos. The affair had all the elements of tragedy, not only for Poland but for the world at large. Stalin's cold-blooded decision to destroy the Polish Home Army, to deprive the London Government of all effective power in Polish affairs, and to disregard the feelings of the population of Poland herself meant sacrificing much of the sympathy of the British and American public in favour of what he believed to be the security of his Western frontier. Polish nationalism and folly had helped to bring the disaster to its climax; Russian brutality and ruthlessness, Roosevelt's failure to make his opinion about the Curzon Line clear to the Poles, and the bloodthirst of German revenge all united to make this passage of Polish history into unmitigated tragedy.

Indeed the tragedy moved with the inevitability of Greek drama. Poland's fall, like that of Oedipus, came as a result of the defects of Polish virtues. Courage, pride, stubbornness, and impetuosity became folly and recklessness, and brought dire catastrophe.

Catastrophe it was, for Russia as much as for Poland, and for the Western Powers as much as for Russia. The failure of Allied policy to achieve a peaceable settlement of the Polish problem in the first seven months of 1944 may well be considered the turning-point in the history of the Grand Alliance. Although a semblance of harmony was re-established at Yalta in February 1945, that harmony was never translated from words into deeds. Despite all later efforts to mend the breach between East and West, the bad blood created in Poland in 1944 proved the beginning of the end. The streets of Warsaw had been sown with dragons' teeth; the world had yet (in 1952) to reap the whole harvest.

(iii) Economic Co-operation and Conflicts

(*a*) Changes in the Internal Economies of the Big Three

During the eight months that followed the Tehrān Conference, the economic problems which faced the Allies underwent a fundamental alteration. In general, the problems of war production, which had dominated the efforts of each of the great Allies during the first years of the war, had been solved. Changes in production schedules could now be made more or less as matters of routine. Instead, the Allies, at least the Western Allies, found by 1944 that their main worry was man-power. Other factors of production had become available in satisfactory quantity to meet military and other demands: but adequate man-power for the armed forces and for industry proved more and more difficult to find.[1]

[1] Data from Russia are too fragmentary to allow one to say whether man-power or other difficulties were the most important limits on the Russian war effort. Shortage of skilled man-power had been a chronic difficulty for the Bolsheviks since 1917, and the war must have enhanced the problem; but one can hardly say more than that.

A second novelty in the economic picture of 1944 was the growing attention which the managers of the American, British, and, presumably, Russian economies paid to the problems of reconversion and reconstruction. Even at the beginning of the year, the peak of war production had passed; and as the prospect of victory over Germany came closer, men in all the Allied countries began to consider just how and by what stages the war-time pattern of economic life could or should be returned to a peace-time basis. For each country, this problem was both internal and international. The future volume and nature of international trade and the availability or non-availability of international loans was bound to affect the internal economic life of America, Britain, and Russia profoundly.

In the short run, the success with which relief and reconstruction was to be handled meant almost life or death to large areas of Europe. Preparation for the work required elaborate adjustment between the newly established UNRRA (United Nations Relief and Rehabilitation Administration) and the various war-time agencies of the Allied countries on the one hand, and arrangements between UNRRA and the governments of the countries in which it proposed to operate on the other.

In the United States, the month of November 1943 saw the peak of war production. Thereafter, cuts in certain production programmes more than counterbalanced increases in others, so that there was a small net decrease in the over-all rate at which military goods were turned out.[1] The principal reason for this throttling down of war production was that by the end of 1943 the great task of providing initial equipment for the armed forces had been almost completed. The new requirements were less onerous: to manufacture replacements, to adjust production to improved models, and to satisfy special needs (e.g. landing craft) which had not been adequately foreseen. This was a sufficiently formidable task, but the administrative machinery which had been worked out in 1942 and 1943, combined with the new factories which had come into production during the same years, proved able to meet the demands put upon them with great success. The confusion which had been so pervasive in the earlier war years diminished. Military requirements could be predicted with a degree of definiteness which allowed advance scheduling; and this in turn was possible because strategy and the ultimate size of the armed forces had been definitely decided upon.

Debate and confusion focused instead on a different problem: whether

[1] This did not mean that total war production for 1944 was less than the total production of 1943, since in the early part of 1943 American war production was still far below its ultimate capacity. Thus munitions produced in 1943 were valued at $51·7 milliard; in 1944 the figure was $57·6 milliard (cf. U.S.A., War Production Board: *Wartime Production Achievements*, p. 105).

and how to begin relaxing war-time controls over production in order to permit resumption of manufacture for the civilian market. This question was inextricably tangled with the problem of man-power. By the end of 1943 shortages of factory hands had become acute in several parts of the United States where war factories were especially numerous. In other regions, however, where cuts in military production were made, surplus labour was suddenly thrown on the market. There were, in general, two ways of looking at this situation. Attempts might be made to compel or induce labour to move from areas of surplus to the areas of shortage; or manufacturers might be permitted to employ labour which had newly become available to produce various scarce civilian consumption goods.

The head of the War Production Board, Donald Nelson, adopted the second of these positions. On 18 June 1944 he published an order which authorized W.P.B. regional offices to permit production of various items for civilian use which had previously been prohibited, if, in the judgement of the local W.P.B. officials, materials and labour were available for the purpose without interfering with local war production programmes.[1] This, known as the 'Spot Authorization Plan', was originally scheduled to come into force on 1 July 1944; but, after protests had been lodged against it by the armed services and by the War Manpower Commission, its operation was postponed until 15 August, and the War Manpower Commission was given a definite veto power over the decisions of W.P.B. regional offices.

Nelson's action was based upon the assumption that the war in Europe would soon be over. Important groups in Congress, among the public, and in W.P.B. supported his move; on the other hand, the armed services and the War Manpower Commission vigorously opposed any relaxation of control over the economy until man-power shortages in 'tight' areas had been relieved. The debate was brought before Byrnes, 'assistant President' and head of the Office of War Mobilization. When he proved unable to effect a compromise Roosevelt himself was brought into the arena in mid-August, when he returned from his trip to the Pacific.

Roosevelt's sympathies lay on the whole with the military. In January 1944 he had asked Congress to pass legislation requiring 'National Service' of the whole working population, arguing that only so could the sacrifices of war be equably shared by all. Roosevelt's proposal was intended to solve growing man-power problems by authorizing legal measures to compel men to work in war plants; and it was expected that the very existence of such a law on the statute books would go far towards solving the problem automatically.[2] National Service had been proposed

[1] *Industrial Mobilization for War*, i. 739; *The United States at War*, p. 487.

[2] For text of Roosevelt's message to Congress, see Rosenman: *The Public Papers and Addresses of Franklin D. Roosevelt, 1944–45 volume*, pp. 37–39.

to the President by the armed services, and was modelled largely upon the National Service Acts of Great Britain. But such conscription of civilians was highly distasteful to Congress and to the public at large, and the proposal never was acted upon.

When, therefore, the issue between Nelson and the armed services came before him in August 1944, Roosevelt was disposed to view even a limited reconversion of industry as something potentially if not actually damaging to the war effort of the nation. The President solved the problem in a characteristic fashion. He did not dismiss Nelson, but decided to send him on a mission to China, and proposed to leave his principal subordinate, Charles E. Wilson, as acting head of W.P.B. during Nelson's absence.

Wilson had opposed Nelson and sided with the military services in the reconversion dispute. Thus Roosevelt's action indirectly seemed to endorse the position which had been taken by the armed services. However, matters did not work out as the President had hoped, for Wilson and Nelson quarrelled violently, and on 24 August Wilson resigned. Roosevelt therefore appointed a new acting head for W.P.B., and bundled Nelson off to China. After a month's visit to Chungking and Moscow, Nelson in his turn resigned. Meanwhile, the war had not gone so well in Europe as had been hoped, and the whole issue was shelved in favour of newly stepped-up war production of such items as ammunition, which had threatened to run short.[1]

Apart from providing a spectacular example of how personal and policy disputes within the American Government could be fought out in public with free resort to innuendo and rumour,[2] this quarrel marked the eclipse of W.P.B. as the premier agency of war-time economic control. Byrnes's Office of War Mobilization, the War Manpower Commission, and the armed services took on more importance in deciding questions of economic policy and in controlling economic activity, while W.P.B. sank to a rather subordinate level. This development resulted partly from the new importance of man-power, control over which lay outside W.P.B.'s jurisdiction. It must also partly be attributed to personal frictions and shortcomings of the heads of W.P.B. itself.

Despite the disputes which arose over reconversion policy, it should be emphasized that in the United States nearly all the men who had been recruited to manage the economy on behalf of the Government during the war believed it would be possible to return automatically to 'normal' when the war had ended. The temporary and extraordinary

[1] Nelson: *Arsenal of Democracy*, pp. 409–15; *Industrial Mobilization for War*, i. 739–41.

[2] A major aspect of the affair was the accusation made by some of Nelson's partisans that Wilson, as chairman of General Electric, was defending the interests of Big Business by trying to prevent small firms from getting into civilian production before the great corporations had completed their war contracts.

nature of war-time economic controls was constantly in their minds; no idea of maintaining a managed economy on a permanent basis found serious lodgement with any important segment of the American public.

Plans for internal economic reform in the post-war era were not very widely welcomed. Roosevelt, to be sure, had proclaimed an 'economic bill of rights' in January 1944,[1] and referred to it frequently in the course of the election campaign of the summer and autumn. But this was political rhetoric rather than a definite and detailed plan for the future reorganization of the American economy. It remained on that level throughout the remaining war years, and after. To have fully satisfied the economic rights which Roosevelt proclaimed would have required the prolongation of a managed economy, directed to new ends, into peace-time; but neither the President nor those who accepted his vision of a bright and secure economic future readily recognized this implication of their goals.

Instead, the American public and American business men alike looked forward to a prompt return after the war to the good old times, and believed that economic life could start anew where it had left off in 1940 and 1941. The public thought in terms of new motor-cars; business men in terms of reduced taxes and freedom from government forms and regulations; but, despite this difference, for practical purposes both agreed that the war-time administrative machine directing the American economy should be dismantled as soon as possible.

This attitude stood in contrast to the attitudes of the British public and of British officials and business men; for them the war had clearly destroyed any norm to which return could be made automatically; and for many in Britain such a return, even if it had been possible, did not seem desirable. In spite of its unprecedented scale and duration, the war for the United States seemed still at bottom an episode; for Britain it had been, and was recognized as being, a revolution.

The relaxation of pressure for more and ever more war production did not prevent American industry from turning out an impressive volume

[1] The rights he mentioned were:

The right to a useful and remunerative job;
The right to earn enough to buy adequate food, clothing, and recreation;
The right of farmers to good prices;
The rights of business men to freedom from monopolies and unfair competition;
The right to a decent home;
The right to adequate medical care;
The right to protection from economic fears of old age, sickness, accident, and unemployment;
The right to a good education. (Cf. Rosenman: *The Public Papers and Addresses of Franklin D. Roosevelt, 1944–45 volume*, p. 41.)

of military goods in 1944. The following table shows something of the accomplishment:[1]

	1942	*1943*	*1944*
Combat aeroplanes	47,836	85,898	96,318
Tanks	23,884	29,497	17,565
Merchant shipping (million tons)	8,090	19,296	16,447

So simplified a table fails, even more than in earlier years, to do justice to American production in 1944. Manufacture of such complicated things as electronic fire-control devices continued to increase rapidly in 1944; the atomic bomb was beginning to absorb a significant proportion of engineering brains and material as it passed from experimental to production stages; and such a heading as 'combat aeroplanes' changed its real value as emphasis shifted to heavier, longer-range types, such as the new B-29 which first went into mass production in 1944. The complexity of armaments and the variety of weapons had increased notably since 1941; and the United States undertook production for all the Allies of many of the newer, more complicated, weapons which could not easily be produced in Britain, Russia, or elsewhere. Roosevelt's boast, that America would become the arsenal of democracy, was a fact by 1944. From the abundance of American production larger and ever larger quantities could be and were spared for the use of the other Allies.

The British economy in 1944 showed the effects of the long strain of war. The only way in which the strength of the armed services could be maintained was by reducing the numbers of men at work in the munitions industries and in civil defence; and this was done regardless of the fact that it further overbalanced an already precarious economy.[2] Gaps in home production were filled by Lend-Lease; but even with that support the British army could not find the man-power to replace battle losses, and had to resort to 'cannibalization' of reserve units in order to maintain the fighting strength of the divisions committed to the campaign in Europe.[3] The shortage of man-power, which was a troublesome local problem in the United States, was nearly absolute in Britain and set an iron ceiling to the war effort of the nation.

The impact upon the British economy of the six-months' military build-up before D-day was very great. Accommodation for more than a million American soldiers had to be found in the crowded British Isles. The

[1] U.S.A., War Production Board: *Wartime Production Achievements*, pp. 106–9. The reduction in tank and ship construction reflected the fact that the need for them, so urgent in the first years of the war, had in large part been met.

[2] Hancock and Gowing: *British War Economy*, p. 515.

[3] Butcher: *My Three Years with Eisenhower*, p. 622; Eisenhower: *Crusade in Europe*, pp. 289, 328.

communications and transport systems of the country had to be placed almost entirely at the disposal of the military during the last weeks before and just after D-day. Millions of men and mountains of material had to be moved to ports of embarkation on a fixed schedule. The strain upon the railways was especially severe, but it was borne successfully.

The extreme disbalance achieved by the British economy about the time of D-day created a series of very difficult problems for the future. How could a catastrophic tumble be avoided? How could some new balance be gracefully attained? The mobilization of men and resources for war could not be kept to the pitch which had already been achieved without growing American subvention in the form of Lend-Lease; but the approach of victory brought with it the approach of an end to Lend-Lease. It therefore behoved British economic managers to begin preparation for a return to economic independence as soon as possible.

The problems to be faced in the early months of 1944 were threefold. For one thing, the capital plant of the country was seriously run down. Housing had become critically short as a result of bomb damage and the failure to maintain old or build new homes. Many mines and factories and the transportation system needed extensive capital maintenance, replacement, or improvement if economic and efficient peace-time production were to be resumed when the war ended. A second problem was the international trading position of the country. During the war exports had declined, and amounted in 1944 to only about 30 per cent. of the 1939 level. At the same time, the foreign obligations of the British Government had risen to staggering proportions. Vast debts had been piled up with countries like Egypt and India, and they could only be paid off by the export of goods on a grand scale after the war. The problem was enhanced by the fact that many of the foreign investments, which in previous decades had helped to cover the standing deficit in the British export-import balance, had been sold during the early years of the war to pay for munitions and food. If Britain were once again to be able to pay for the imports she needed for her industry and for current consumption while simultaneously paying off the foreign debt incurred during the war, it would first be necessary to raise the level of exports far above pre-war figures. A third problem was the need to increase the standard of civilian consumption above the austere levels of the war years.[1]

While having to face these difficulties which the approach of victory entailed, there was also an extensive and fairly concrete programme of internal economic and social reform to which the Government was officially committed, and which required attention. Plans for a wide extension of social insurance, for a health service, for improvement of education, and for guaranteeing full employment had been advanced by various

[1] Hancock and Gowing: *British War Economy*, pp. 518–22.

official committees during the early years of the war; and the Government had accepted in principle if not in detail the recommendations which had been made to it.[1]

Planning and preparation for the adjustment of the British economy to peace-time conditions faced two main obstacles, apart from the intrinsic difficulties of the problems themselves. One was the unresolved question of what part Great Britain would play in the war against Japan when the European war had ended. Strategy against Japan had become almost entirely an American affair, and until the Second Quebec Conference in September 1944 there was no definite agreement between the American and British Governments as to what the British would do in the final stages of the war. Until this decision had been made, however, it was impossible to calculate what resources would be available for reconstruction at home after victory in Europe; and what would have to be assigned to the Far East.

A second, and rather more delicate, obstacle to post-war adjustment was the commitment, which had been entered into in September 1941 by the British Government, not to export anything which incorporated Lend-Lease materials or which was identical with or substantially similar to things supplied on Lend-Lease.[2] The British Government had accepted this principle in order to avoid criticism from the United States to the effect that British industries were using American materials to compete with American exporters. But by 1944 the British felt that it had become imperative for them to do just that. If exports were to recover, and more than recover, pre-war volume it seemed necessary to begin soon. If nothing were done until the war had ended and Lend-Lease came to a stop, Britain would find herself unable to pay for the necessities of life, and something very like complete internal collapse would surely follow.

But the Americans were most unwilling to admit the British argument. Conversations on an expert level were held almost constantly during the first months of 1944 without positive results.[3] Many American officials recognized the bitter problem facing the British; but they felt that any change in the terms on which Lend-Lease aid was extended, any move

[1] Hancock and Gowing: *British War Economy*, pp. 538–42.

[2] See above, p. 14, n. 6. The effect of this policy, together with the exigencies of the war, was to displace British firms from a number of markets which had traditionally been theirs. In many cases American exporters were able to supply goods their British competitors no longer could, and eagerly built up new trading connexions with such parts of the world as South America, the Middle East, and even Australia. Having won such an advantage during the war, American export firms were unwilling to lose it in time of peace, and they were able to bring a considerable pressure to bear upon American officials against any action that seemed likely to damage their new trading position or help British enterprises to regain their pre-war customers. This special interest conflicted with the more general American interest in seeing a stable and prosperous post-war Britain; and while the general interest usually prevailed, in countless special instances it was the special interest that controlled or at least affected American official action.

[3] Hancock and Gowing, op. cit. p. 527.

which would allow British exports to begin competing with American exports while Britain was still in receipt of Lend-Lease goods, any reconversion of British industry which was not matched by parallel reconversion in the United States—in short, any positive step which would cushion the shock to the British economy that the end of the war threatened to bring would excite serious criticism in Congress and in the American press. In an election year, the administration was unwilling to expose itself to the charge of helping British at the expense of American commercial interests; and, it must also be recognized, many highly placed Americans did not realize the full precariousness of Britain's economic position, nor take at their face value the arguments which British officials set before them. As a result, nothing could be decided until the matter was brought up for top-level consideration at the Second Quebec Conference in September.[1]

The victories of the Red Army on the eastern front in 1943 and 1944 were, from the strictly economic point of view, a mixed blessing to the Soviet Government. The territories evacuated by the Germans were thoroughly devastated,[2] so that an enormous task of reconstruction was thrust upon the Russian Government as the Red Army advanced. So far as can be judged from the very fragmentary information which has been published, it seems that the Russians limited their efforts in 1944 largely to the repair of such things as railways, which had an immediate military value. Industrial rebuilding of the Donbas and other centres of heavy industry had not made much progress by the end of 1944;[3] and state collections of grain from formerly occupied territory were less than one-third of the pre-war total.[4] Industrial effort continued as in earlier years to be concentrated in the new or newly expanded centres in the Ural region and in Siberia. By 1944 the heroic efforts which had been made in these regions earlier in the war began to bear their full fruit. New factories, mines, and furnaces had come into production, and old ones had been enlarged so that in 1944 the output of pig iron had increased by 46 per cent. and of steel by 44 per cent. as compared with the production of the same regions in 1940.[5]

Statistics such as these are so fragmentary as to be almost meaningless.

[1] See below, pp. 488–90.

[2] The average rate at which the Russians advanced was not great, and the Germans nearly always had time enough before retreating to carry out systematic destruction of whatever capital installations had survived the earlier stages of the war. It was officially estimated after the war that two-thirds of the national wealth of the occupied portions of the Soviet Union had been destroyed (cf. Voznesensky: *The Economy of the U.S.S.R. during World War II*, p. 97).

[3] Industrial output in 1944 from the reconquered regions of the U.S.S.R. was less than one-fifth of the pre-war level; coal production was a quarter, and electric power production one-sixth of the pre-war levels (ibid. p. 98).

[4] Ibid.

[5] Ibid. p. 48.

The significant fact was this: that in 1944 even more than in 1943 Russian industry proved able to equip the Red Army with the munitions it required. But as the battle line moved westward, through devastated country, transport and delivery of supplies to the front line inevitably became a more and more difficult problem. By 1944 it was this factor more than the production of munitions itself which limited the speed and power of Red Army advances.

Agricultural expansion in the eastern regions of the U.S.S.R. was more difficult and it was only after the recovery of the Ukraine that the Russians were able to reduce their dependence on food supplies from the United States. Favourable weather made the harvest of 1944 a good one, and state grain collections in that year were 1,100 million poods greater than in 1943.[1] Since the war-time average of grain collections amounted to 4,300 million poods,[2] the increase in 1944 over 1943 amounted to between a quarter and a third. This obviously made an enormous difference to the feeding of Russian city-dwellers. The semi-starvation of the civilian population, which had been prevalent in 1942 and 1943, came to an end with the 1944 harvest. The Red Army, however, continued to depend in very considerable degree upon food supplied from the United States and Canada, partly at least because it arrived packaged in easily transportable form, whereas the Russians lacked the means to pack and preserve the food produced at home in a form that would easily survive the rigours of military transport and distribution.[3]

Thus it seems that by 1944 the munitions and food supply of Russia was generally adequate to maintain the Red Army and to feed the civilian population. On the other hand, man-power and material for reconstruction of the devastated areas may be presumed to have been painfully short, and a serious inflation demanded official attention.

The problem of inflation could only be permanently solved by a reduction of the currency in circulation or by an increase in the supply of civilian goods. Neither alternative was easy for the Russian Government. Currency circulation had risen 2·4 times during the years 1941–4, and the supply of civilian goods had fallen drastically during the same period.[4] War bond drives did something to absorb surplus purchasing power, but this did not prevent the development of more or less openly tolerated dealings on a free market, especially in foodstuffs, between peasants who

[1] Voznesensky: *The Economy of the U.S.S.R. during World War II*, p. 57. A pood equals 36·07 pounds, approximately six-tenths of a bushel of wheat. The increase in collections thus amounted to about 660 million bushels.

[2] Ibid. p. 53.

[3] No less than 1,802,000 tons of food was scheduled under the Fourth Soviet Supply Protocol for delivery from the United States and Canada (*Soviet Supply Protocols*, pp. 95, 156). It has been calculated that for the war years as a whole the amount of food delivered from the United States was enough to supply each man in the Red Army with an average of more than half a pound of fairly concentrated food per day (Deane: *Strange Alliance*, p. 94).

[4] Voznesensky, op. cit. p. 82.

had food and industrial workers, into whose pockets most of the surplus currency had gone. By 1943 prices on the free market were more than twelve times above similar prices in 1940;[1] and peasants who happened to live near large towns were able to accumulate relatively large stocks of currency, as well as receiving goods in kind for the food they could spare. The improved harvest and increased state grain collections of 1944 changed this situation markedly. First of all, civilian rations became more nearly adequate; secondly, the Government entered into direct competition with the peasants by opening stores in which non-rationed food and other goods were sold at high prices. By this means the free market price was reduced by more than half in 1944, but still remained at about six times the 1940 level.[2] Until civilian goods could be produced in greater quantity, this was about all the Government could do to control inflation.

It does not appear that Russian officials had much time to spare from the urgent tasks of keeping the economy going month by month in order to dream dreams or plan plans for the post-war period. Officially the third Five-Year Plan had been suspended when the Germans attacked in 1941, and it was not until 1946 that Stalin announced a new one. The general frame of mind of the managers of the Soviet economy was like that of the Americans in the sense that they looked forward to a return to pre-war economic patterns when the immediate crisis of war and reconstruction had passed. But, of course, this meant the retention of government ownership of industry and the maintenance of the full war-time rigour of governmental control over economic processes, not, as in the United States, their relaxation or abolition.

The principal question that remained open was the end which would be pursued by government economic policy after the war. An increase in civilian goods was urgently necessary, for the level to which Soviet consumption had been depressed could not permanently be maintained without sacrificing the health and morale of the population. But there seems no reason to suppose that Soviet planners had decided in 1944 what balance should be aimed at between heavy and light industry, between capital construction and the production of consumption goods, between armaments and other products.

An important consideration among Soviet officials was the amount of relief for the stricken Russian economy they could hope to wring from the defeated enemy. Soviet officials clearly felt that one of the best ways to restore the damaged capital plant of their country was to seize machinery and other usable items from German factories in order to set them up again in their own land. They probably also hoped that loans from the United States or elsewhere would help to finance purchases of capital goods and other necessities; but it is not clear how confidently they

[1] Ibid. p. 76. [2] Ibid.

expected such help to be forthcoming when the emergency of the war had passed. In the meanwhile, they tried hard to get everything they could under Lend-Lease.

The limited information available about the Russian economy in 1944 leaves much to the imagination. It seems certain that the country was impoverished to a degree which it is hard for Englishmen or Americans to believe. The losses in the western part of the country were not equalled by the gains which had been painfully won in the eastern regions; and, more than this, the concentration of resources upon munitions production had deprived the civilian population of what in the west were deemed essentials of bare existence. The pent-up wish for better food, clothing, housing, and for rest from the extra labour and stern discipline of war-time factories must have been tremendous; but, in spite of all, the Russians kept going throughout 1944. Under the circumstances, this was a great achievement.

(*b*) Pooling Resources for War and Relief

As the war moved to its climax in Europe, Lend-Lease shipments reached their peak. Lend-Lease goods delivered to the United Kingdom increased in value from $4,579 million in 1943 to $6,212 million in 1944; during the same period Lend-Lease aid to Russia increased from $2,436 million to $4,074 million.[1] The pattern of economic interdependence which these figures reflect was much the same as in 1943. Since the munitions output of British factories declined slightly (owing to the withdrawal of labour into the armed services) a slightly larger proportion of the total munitions consumption of the British forces had to come from the United States.[2] This merely accentuated a relationship which had been well established in 1943.

Similarly, the Russians continued, as in 1943, to depend upon Lend-Lease for food for their armies and for many of the vehicles with which to supply them in the field. A notable shift in the pattern of Lend-Lease shipments to Russia was the increase in the amount of industrial machinery and equipment sent from the United States.[3]

The Lend-Lease Act came up for renewal in the American Congress once again in 1944; but there was, as the official report put it, 'no controversy with respect to the necessity for passing this Bill', nor was there much

[1] These figures are taken from Allen: 'Mutual Aid', p. 250. They are based on corrected figures issued after the end of the war by the American Foreign Economic Administration, and differ somewhat from the figures published in the periodic reports to Congress made by the President.

[2] The change in 1944 from 1943 was not very great when measured in percentages, but since vast totals were concerned the change in physical amounts was none the less great. It has been calculated that British home production supplied 62·4 per cent. of the total munitions supplied to British forces in 1943 and 61·2 per cent. in 1944. Correspondingly, Lend-Lease supplied 24·5 per cent. of the total in 1943 and 27·2 per cent. in 1944 (ibid. p. 268).

[3] Deane: *Strange Alliance*, pp. 92–93; *Soviet Supply Protocols*, p. 112.

Congressional anxiety, as there had been in 1943, about the benefits which would accrue to the United States in return for Lend-Lease. The Bill passed Congress on 8 May 1944 and the President signed it into law on 17 May.[1]

One reason why the members of Congress were better content with Lend-Lease in 1944 than they had been the year before was that, with the build-up of American forces in the British Isles, the quantity of Reverse Lend-Lease (as the Americans called it), or Mutual Aid (as the British called it), rose rapidly. By June 1944 no less that 31 per cent. of all the supplies and equipment required by the U.S. Army in the European Theatre of Operations came from British sources;[2] and some of the things provided—for example, the artificial harbour which was manufactured in Britain and assigned to American use on the beaches of Normandy—were of an irreplaceable nature. Official efforts were made to publicize the help that U.S. forces received from Britain and the other Allies. The President's *Seventeenth Report to Congress on Lend-Lease Operations*, submitted in November 1944, was devoted entirely to an account of Reverse Lend-Lease up to the end of June 1944.[3]

On the other hand, while British Mutual Aid to the United States was thus swelling to very substantial proportions, British aid to Russia shrank still further from the level of 1943, and indeed became almost negligible save for a few special categories of supplies—petrol from Abadan, rubber from Ceylon, industrial diamonds from South Africa, and Spitfires and medical supplies from the United Kingdom.[4] The money value of aid supplies by Great Britain to Russia in the year ending 30 June 1943 was £187·7 million; in the year ending 30 June 1944 it had shrunk by half to £93·3 million.[5] This, too, continued a development which had been evident in 1943. It was no more than a rational adjustment to the position in which Great Britain found herself, needing all she could produce for her own forces and for the American troops stationed in the British Isles.

The administration of Lend-Lease and Mutual Aid had reached a level of official routine by 1944. Relative abundance of supply and of shipping made it a fairly simple matter to apportion the shares among the different theatres of operation and the different national claimants. The difficulties which arose in 1944 between British and American officials in connexion with the restrictions on British exports did not interfere with the smooth and cordial operation of Lend-Lease from month to month.

A minor change in the legal relationships of the system was made in February 1944 when Canada concluded a Mutual Aid agreement with

[1] *Documents on American Foreign Relations, 1943–1944*, p. 119.

[2] *Seventeenth Report on Lend-Lease Operations*, Chart 1 and Table 4.

[3] See Appendix II, p. 782 below.

[4] *Soviet Supply Protocols*, pp. 148–54.

[5] Allen: 'Mutual Aid', p. 255.

affair, diluted to be sure by the participation of other nationalities, but at bottom dependent upon the goodwill of the American Congress and subject in innumerable matters to the veto power of officials of the American Government. By refusing to make supplies available from American sources except under conditions approved by themselves, the Americans were in a position to affect all UNRRA's operations. As a result, relations with the Foreign Economic Administration in the United States were far more important for UNRRA than any other day-to-day matter; and relations with Congress fixed the long-term scope of UNRRA's work. The reality of international co-operation for relief work was thus little more than what the American Government chose to make it; and in 1944, while the war was still in full swing, the reality was slight. War needs took precedence, and UNRRA could only plan and plead.

Nevertheless, the core of an international administrative body was created, and principles to govern the distribution of relief were worked out on paper. Minimum food requirements of liberated countries in Europe were calculated in detail, and other needs were estimated as best they could be in advance. The principal agency which developed these plans was the Committee of the UNRRA Council for Europe, with headquarters in London. A similar body for the Far East hardly began functioning until 1945.[1] In July an effort was begun to divide UNRRA funds among the various European countries which needed help; and by November 1944 a tentative apportionment had been fixed upon.[2] On such a basis, the assignment of personnel, detailed planning of national relief programmes, and allocation of supplies could proceed. Despite all the difficulties, a beginning had been made.

(c) Long-range Economic Planning

Relief and rehabilitation were obviously only a first step towards rebuilding the world economy which had been so thoroughly distorted by the war. But the question of how and according to what blue prints international economic relations should be reconstructed was not an easy one to answer. Secretary of State Cordell Hull and officials of the American Government generally were convinced that an enduring peace could only be built upon a world in which trade was free, or nearly free, from the obstacles of national tariffs, quotas, and blocked currencies. In deference to this point of view, a clause had been inserted into the Atlantic Charter which promised that efforts would be made to assure 'access, on equal terms, to the trade and raw materials of the world'; but this promise had been qualified, at Churchill's insistence, by the words 'with due respect to . . . existing obligations'. The Master Lend-Lease Agreement with Great Britain had made matters more specific. Article VII committed

[1] Woodbridge: *UNRRA*, i. 62–67. [2] Ibid. pp. 345–7.

the two Governments to 'the elimination of all forms of discriminatory treatment in international commerce, and to the reduction of tariffs and other trade barriers'. Similar provisions had been made in the Master Lend-Lease Agreements concluded with other countries. At the Moscow Conference Hull had presented a more detailed programme for international economic organization after the war, but it was not acted upon at that time. His proposals included the establishment of an international bank, and of a commission which would supervise the gradual elimination of all barriers to international trade and production.[1]

Despite the fact that Britain and Russia, as well as the other United Nations, had formally adhered to the Atlantic Charter and had signed Master Lend-Lease Agreements which committed them to the acceptance of liberal trade policies in the post-war period, there was no real agreement among the Allies on the issue. Britain and Russia had signed on the dotted line to appease the Americans, but neither country was ready to adapt its post-war economic policy to American ideas. The harsh fact of the matter was that while free trade promised to benefit American industry and agriculture, it seemed likely to damage both British and Russian national interests. At the least, the introduction of anything like free trade would have required a radical transformation of the domestic economies of Russia and Britain; and this neither Government were prepared seriously to consider. This became evident in the course of 1944. Conversations between British and American officials on post-war commercial policy came to an impasse in mid-1944 when the British Cabinet refused to agree to a programme of tariff reduction, abolition of export subsidies, import quotas, &c.[2]

This check to American plans led Secretary Hull and his fellows in the State Department to concentrate their efforts more and more upon the political side of things. They allowed their liberal economic ideals to sink more or less into the background as far as immediate action was concerned. Instead, the U.S. Treasury Department took the lead in negotiations concerning post-war economic policy, focusing attention on monetary questions.

After elaborate preparatory conversations, beginning early in 1943, an International Monetary and Financial Conference met at Bretton Woods from 1 to 22 July 1944, under the chairmanship of Henry Morgenthau, Secretary of the U.S. Treasury. The Bretton Woods Conference recommended that an International Monetary Fund and an International Bank for Reconstruction and Development should be established with funds

[1] Hull: *Memoirs*, ii. 1303–4.

[2] Hancock and Gowing: *British War Economy*, p. 545.

subscribed by the various national governments. Detailed constitutions for both institutions were accepted by the Conference.

The main aim of the Monetary Fund was to prevent any recurrence of the sort of international fiscal war which had prevailed so widely in the 1930s. Competitive devaluation of currencies in order to win trade advantages was to be prohibited; restrictions on the convertibility of national currencies were to be abolished; so was the use of special currencies for export trade and all similar discriminatory practices.[1] The force of these undertakings was, however, modified by a general provision which recognized a 'post-war transitional period' during which it would be permissible for members to 'maintain and adapt to changing circumstances . . . restrictions on payments and transfers for current international transactions'.[2] This, in effect, put off the application of the new monetary rules until some day when the international balance of payments had reached stability.

The Fund's purpose, apart from checking up on the monetary policies of its member nations, was to provide stocks of currency which could be sold to any member which found itself temporarily in need of foreign exchange in order to make payment for goods or services received. The idea was that, by making such a service available to the nations of the world, short-range fluctuations in exchange rates could be minimized; and with stable currencies world trade could develop on a more secure basis.

It seems fair to say that the authors of this plan were locking the door, or trying to lock it, upon the international trade and fiscal practices of Dr. Schacht. They certainly had little idea of the vastness and the persistence of the 'dollar shortage' which was to plague the post-war world; nor did the scheme take into account the devices for economic exploitation of neighbouring countries which the Soviet Government were to develop in the immediate post-war period. The plan for an International Monetary Fund was, like so much of American economic planning for the post-war period, a backward-looking affair, imperfectly suited to the situation which actually confronted the world after the war. This was not evident in 1944, however; and to hopeful eyes the Fund seemed to promise powerful support for its professed aim: 'To facilitate the expansion and balanced growth of international trade.'[3]

The International Bank for Reconstruction and Development was intended to provide a source from which nations could borrow funds for long-range capital improvements. Economically backward nations, and nations suffering from the devastation of war, were regarded as especially likely to need the assistance of the Bank. At the same time, the Bank was

[1] See Article VIII (General Obligations of Members) of Articles of Agreement of International Monetary Fund (*Documents on American Foreign Relations, 1943–1944*, pp. 349–50).

[2] Article XIV (ibid. p. 360).

[3] Article I (ibid. p. 338).

not supposed to replace private foreign investment; indeed among its basic purposes, as set forth in the Agreement, was the promotion of private investment by offering guarantees to investors and by taking a share in loans undertaken by them when circumstances seemed to require such encouragement to private capital ventures. But when private capital was, for whatever reason, not forthcoming, the Bank was authorized to make loans itself.

The Bank's capital was set at $10 milliard to be subscribed by the Governments which were members of the International Monetary Fund.[1] The Bank's role was conceived as twofold. In the shorter run, it would supplement and complete the rehabilitation begun by UNRRA and by the separate national governments which were able to pay for relief themselves. In the longer run, the Bank would assist in making the capital transfers which would have to underlie stable monetary relations as conceived in the International Monetary Fund Agreement. Thus the Bank was designed to play a positive part in supporting the 'balanced growth of international trade and the maintenance of equilibrium in balances of payments' to match the essentially negative and palliative role of the Monetary Fund. That the limited resources of the Bank and the slowness of its procedure would prove inadequate to meet the drastic disbalances of international economic life emerging from the war was not foreseen in 1944.

The Agreements reached at Bretton Woods of course required ratification by the various national governments of the United Nations, and neither the International Monetary Fund nor the International Bank was intended to begin operations until after the temporary and extraordinary post-war difficulties had been surmounted. The two institutions were rather intended to shape the long-term pattern of international economic relations in the post-war period. They were conceived as cornerstones of a more liberal, stable, and prosperous economic order than that which had prevailed in the 1930s.

In general, the ideas and ideals of American economists and financial experts dominated the deliberations which led to these Agreements;[2] and American economic preponderance was reflected in the large share assigned to the United States as her contribution to the Fund and the Bank.[3] But the assumptions underlying the deliberations at Bretton Woods

[1] *Documents on American Foreign Relations, 1943–1944*, pp. 373–97.

[2] Plans conceived in the fertile brain of John Maynard Keynes, the famous British economist, played a large part in the first stages; and Keynes played a prominent part in the entire negotiation. Nevertheless, when his plans or those of his British colleagues conflicted with American ideas, it nearly always happened that Keynes had to give way. For an account of Keynes's part in Bretton Woods and preliminary negotiations, see Roy F. Harrod: *The Life of John Maynard Keynes* (London, Macmillan, 1951), p. 525.

[3] The United States was assigned a quota of $2,750 million for the Fund out of a total sub-

were hardly adequate to the occasion. That the temporary and extraordinary difficulties of international trade and finance would prove enduring, and of a magnitude that the Fund and Bank could not cope with, was not envisaged. Instead, the experts imagined a return to conditions such as had prevailed in the 1930s, and designed the new institutions to meet the needs of such an era.

The monetary planning at Bretton Woods was paralleled by the effort of an Interim Commission of Food and Agriculture to set up a permanent international organization which would advise and help the governments of the world on technical agricultural problems. The Commission had been established by the United Nations Conference on Food and Agriculture in June 1943;[1] and by 1 August 1944 it had completed its work of drawing up a constitution for the proposed organization. The food and agriculture Organization (FAO) was conceived as primarily an advisory body. It was to collect and disseminate information, recommend international action with respect to food production and marketing when it seemed advisable, and was authorized to organize technical assistance for governments which requested such help so far as the budget of the Organization permitted.[2]

Like the agreements reached at Bretton Woods, this document required ratification by its signatories; and, like the International Monetary Fund and the International Bank, the proposed Organization was largely the result of American initiative.[3] As was the case with the monetary agreements, the presuppositions underlying the deliberations on food and agriculture in 1944 were ill-adjusted to the realities of the post-war period. A main concern among the Americans was fear lest agricultural surpluses, such as had burdened American farmers and the Government in the 1930s, should reappear when the extraordinary demands of the war period had ceased. This concern led the American Government in 1944 to remove all restrictions on consumption of such commodities as meat, and to urge farmers to reduce production of hogs. The result was a marked

scription of $8,900 million. The American subscription to the Bank was set at $3,175 million out of a total of $9,100 million. Thus the American share was roughly one-third.

[1] See above, p. 314, n. 2.

[2] *Documents on American Foreign Relations, 1943–1944*, pp. 434–42.

[3] Actually the decision to begin organizing technical international bodies such as the FAO, taken early in 1943 by the American Government, reflected Roosevelt's opinion. At that time the President distrusted schemes for the establishment of broad over-all international bodies in either political or economic fields, preferring regional political associations and separate technical international bodies (Hull: *Memoirs*, ii. 1643). When Roosevelt later changed his mind, the ponderous international machinery had already begun to move, and the FAO and the monetary agreements emerged; but in each case provision was explicitly made for association of these new international institutions with any future general world organization.

rise in civilian consumption and a serious meat shortage on the American domestic market in 1945.[1] Nevertheless, when the demand for food did not collapse as had been expected, the FAO was in a position to adjust itself to the situation and could suggest appropriate policies to national governments. Having no binding authority, it did not, like the Monetary Fund and International Bank, have to face unforeseen conditions with inadequate resources and powers.

Quarrels between British and American oil companies over concessions in the Near East had become a disturbing problem for the two Governments early in 1944. A series of negotiations by experts led up to conversations on Cabinet level in July and August. The result was that on 8 August 1944 Stettinius, Acting Secretary of State, and Lord Beaverbrook, Lord Privy Seal, signed a special Petroleum Agreement. This provided for the establishment of an Anglo-American International Petroleum Commission with advisory powers, and declared that as soon as practicable other countries should be consulted and asked to join a permanent International Petroleum Council.[2] This Agreement, however, was abortive. When it was submitted to the American Senate for approval, it met with serious criticism, and early in 1945 Roosevelt withdrew it and reopened negotiations with the British. Oil, far from calming, continued to trouble the waters. Where British and American national and commercial interests were directly opposed, agreement on a bilateral basis proved hard to reach; and neither was anxious to bring other nations into consultation before an Anglo-American agreement had been reached. As a result, efforts at international regulation of the oil business failed to become more than a hope for the future.

[1] Rosen: *The Combined Boards of the Second World War*, pp. 240–1.

[2] *Documents on American Foreign Relations, 1944–1945*, pp. 678–82.

CHAPTER II

NORMANDY TO YALTA

AUGUST 1944–FEBRUARY 1945

(i) Efforts to concert Allied Policy in the Autumn of 1944

(a) The Situation in August 1944

Festung Europa seemed everywhere on the point of collapse during the last two weeks of August 1944. In the west, Anglo-American forces under General Eisenhower had broken out of the Normandy bridgehead, and were in full pursuit of the Germans across the fields of northern France. In the south, Franco-American troops landed on the Riviera on 15 August and began to move westward and northward with heartening speed. In Italy, too, Allied pursuit of the Germans proceeded, though more slowly. Across the Adriatic, the operations of Tito's Partisans, assisted by small parties of British troops, had cleared most of the Yugoslav coast, and inland German lines of communication were subject to constant harassment.

In the east, the Red Army began a powerful offensive into Rumania on 20 August. Just three days later King Michael engineered a *coup d'état*, with the result that by 25 August Rumanian troops found themselves fighting against the Germans in co-operation with the Red Army. On the central part of the Russian front relative quiet prevailed except in the city of Warsaw where the Polish Home Army was locked in desperate battle against the Wehrmacht. On the Finnish front, too, no large-scale operations were in train. Nevertheless on 25 August the Finns opened negotiations for an armistice. On 26 August the Bulgarian Government announced that it would henceforth be neutral in the war and on 29 August the Germans were compelled to intervene in Hungary and change the Government in order to prevent a similar act of desertion.

Thus in a period of only ten days, Hitler's most valuable allies in Eastern Europe deserted him. German defences were shattered in the south-east, leaving a gaping hole through which the Red Army could plunge forward into the Balkans and over the Carpathians into Central Europe. France, too, had been lost and the frontiers of Germany stood in imminent peril. Under the circumstances, it seemed possible, indeed probable, that complete German collapse would come before the end of the year.[1]

[1] Wisdom after the event has tended to obscure the extent to which Anglo-American leaders placed their confidence in German defeat in 1944. But cf. Butcher: *My Three Years with Eisenhower*, pp. 637, 639, 656, 659–70, for samples of the optimism which prevailed in high quarters in August and September 1944. It was only on 2 October that the British Cabinet formally judged that Germany would not be defeated until the spring of 1945 (Mountbatten: *Report*, p. 83); and the Cabinet did not adjust its economic plans to the new prognosis until near the end of the month (Hancock and Gowing: *British War Economy*, p. 517).

Such a prospect raised more problems for the Allies than it solved. Despite the labours of the European Advisory Commission, established in London according to the decision reached at the Moscow Conference of Foreign Ministers in October 1943,[1] no agreement had been reached as to the policy which should be pursued by the Allies with respect to Germany; and, while an important measure of agreement had been achieved concerning the machinery of Allied control, a prolonged dispute between Roosevelt and Churchill over the zones of occupation to be assigned to their respective countries had prevented detailed preparation for the administration of a defeated Germany.[2]

In addition to the weighty question of Germany's future, the Allies had already discovered how difficult it was to agree on policy towards the various liberated countries of Europe. The long-standing Polish question had reached a new urgency as a result of the Warsaw rising; and, although the embers of the Anglo-American dispute over France had turned to ashes, some heat still lingered, especially among the French themselves. In Italy and the Balkans American and British policies continued to diverge; and throughout Europe the Russians and British watched one another's moves uneasily.

As the German war seemed to approach its end, problems connected with the war against Japan became more important. As far as the Grand Alliance was concerned, the great question was how, in what strength, and under what system of command Britain and Russia would turn their forces from Europe to the Far East. Allied co-operation in the Pacific, in Burma, and in China had never been as smooth and effective as in Europe; and efforts to improve matters had not put things right. Despite the appointment of a Supreme Allied Commander for South-East Asia, Lord Louis Mountbatten, in November 1943[3] friction between British, American, and Chinese leaders continued. In the Pacific, the Americans so completely dominated the scene that problems of Allied relationships sank to second importance, but rivalry between the U.S. navy and U.S. army took the spotlight instead.

As we have seen,[4] the question of the British role against Japan after the end of the war in Europe was inseparably tied up with economic problems. The end of the fighting in Europe threatened to bring at least a partial break-up of Anglo-American economic integration, and Great Britain was ill prepared to stand the shock. This confronted the British with a serious dilemma. The more men and resources the British Government assigned to the war against Japan, the less could be done to prepare the British economy for independence and post-war stability; but, at the same time, the smaller their contribution to victory over Japan, the less

[1] See above, p. 332.
[2] See below, pp. 480–2.
[3] See above, p. 345.
[4] See above, p. 440.

help and sympathy could they expect from the United States during the difficult economic transition that lay ahead. The Soviet Union faced a similar dilemma, though in a less acute form since the Russian economy had never become so completely dependent upon the United States as had the British. Nevertheless, the scale and the speed with which the Russians could intervene in the war against Japan depended, among other things, on Lend-Lease deliveries; and the larger the effort against Japan, the less could be done to restore the damaged economy of the Soviet Union.

A final problem which challenged the goodwill and wisdom of the Allies was the shaping of a long-term international settlement which could promise peace and prosperity for the world after the defeat of Germany and Japan. Everyone recognized that the Great Allied Powers would have to agree on major policy if peace were to be preserved. Britain, America, and Russia were all prepared for such co-operation, but each only on her own terms. Herein lay the seeds of future trouble. But in August 1944, when Germany was not yet beaten and the surge of popular sympathy was still strong among the great Allies, the potential rifts in the Grand Alliance were more or less hidden.

The Allies undertook to meet the problems which approaching victory in Europe brought in its train in the same manner as they had faced their problems earlier in the war. Day-by-day exchanges between Roosevelt, Churchill, and Stalin were supplemented by three important conferences during the autumn of 1944. At Dumbarton Oaks, from 21 August to 28 September, representatives of Great Britain, the Soviet Union, and the United States discussed future international organization; and from 29 September to 9 October British and American representatives went over the same ground with the Chinese. Roosevelt and Churchill, together with their respective staffs, met at Quebec from 11 to 16 September (Second Quebec or Octagon Conference) to try to settle some of the issues which had arisen between them; and after the formal Conference had ended Churchill remained with the President at Hyde Park for an additional week, before returning to London on 25 September. Almost at once he started for Moscow and a conference with Stalin (from 9 to 20 October), in an attempt to do for Anglo-Soviet relations what the Second Quebec Conference had done for Anglo-American relations. Churchill's travels were not in vain. His efforts and the progress of events eliminated some and smoothed over or postponed other points of friction among the Great Allies so that by the end of October the Grand Alliance seemed firmer and more harmonious than it had been at any earlier time in 1944. This happy situation did not last long, however, and by the end of the year the Alliance once again needed mending. The Yalta Conference (from 4 to 11 February 1945) was devoted to this task.

(*b*) The Progress of the War

August 1944 brought a fundamental politico-military shift in the European theatre of war. After the diversion of troops from Italy to southern France, it was clear that Anglo-American operations in the Balkans or in Central Europe could not assume any large scale. The dramatic collapse of German defences in Rumania simultaneously opened the path for the Red Army into Hungary and the northern Balkans. The Russians were not slow to take advantage of the opportunity which thus came to them. Russian troops entered Bucharest on 31 August; on 5 September the Soviet Union declared war against Bulgaria and on 9 September, after a new Bulgarian Government had come into office and declared war on Germany, hostilities were suspended.[1] The Red Army was able to march unopposed into Sofia (16 September) and promptly turned westward towards the Yugoslav frontier. On 1 October the Russian vanguard crossed into Yugoslavia and established contact with Tito's Partisans.[2] Two weeks later, on 15 October, Belgrade was liberated. Meanwhile, Russian and Rumanian troops had crossed the Carpathians and advanced into Hungary. On 11 November the Red Army reached the outskirts of Budapest, and at the end of the month a powerful Russian column struck northward from Yugoslavia, crossing the Danube to take the German garrison of the Hungarian capital in the rear. None the less, the Germans fought on with skill and determination, and Hitler brought up reinforcements which, together with supply difficulties, temporarily halted the Russian offensive about the end of the year.[3]

This check in the neighbourhood of Budapest did not alter the fact that the Russian summer offensive on the southern front had, in scarcely more than three months, completely altered the map of Europe. Rumania, Bulgaria, Yugoslavia, most of Hungary, and part of Slovakia had come within the Russian sphere of operations, with important consequences for the internal politics of each of these countries. In proportion as Russian power and prestige mounted, Western and particularly British influence in these regions of Europe sank; and a peculiar sort of semi-revolution spread throughout South-Eastern Europe.

Farther north, the Russians were not idle. On 15 September 1944 they launched a major offensive in Estonia and on 3 October began an attack in Lithuania. By 10 October the Red Army had reached the Baltic coast near Memel, cutting off a large German force in Latvia; but an attack upon East Prussia, begun on 16 October, ran into fanatical German opposition and was broken off after just ten days. This check, followed two months later by a similar check in the neighbourhood of Budapest, proved

[1] See below, pp. 470–2.
[2] See below, pp. 472–4.
[3] Budapest was not finally captured by the Russians until 14 February 1945.

that the Germans were not yet demoralized or unable to put up stiff and effective resistance when their own homeland and central strategic defence lines were threatened.

The stabilization of the eastern front in November and December had been preceded by a similar German recovery in the west. By the end of August 1944 Eisenhower's supply lines were stretched to such a point that it had become impossible to meet the demands of all the army commanders under him. Two possibilities opened themselves. Either the pace of pursuit could be slowed down all along the front until supplies could be once again assembled for a further offensive, or one section of the front could be pushed ahead at full speed, while all the other armies stood still in their tracks.

To decide between these two possible courses was both difficult and delicate. General Montgomery, who had commanded the entire front during the first stage of the invasion of northern France, had on 1 September 1944 been made co-ordinate with General Omar Bradley. Each commanded an Army Group directly subordinate to Eisenhower. This change in the chain of command had been planned long in advance, but it seemed to some journalists and others that Eisenhower had demoted General Montgomery,[1] whose British and Canadian armies had not met with the same spectacular success as had the Americans in the first days of the Normandy break-out. News of the impending change in Montgomery's status leaked out on 19 August. It was at first denied officially, but on 31 August Eisenhower made a formal announcement with full explanation of the reasons for the change. This incident, combined with some rather chauvinistic newspaper comment on the relative fighting ability of American and British troops, and a certain amount of caustic feeling between the troops and officers of the two nationalities in the field, made it almost impossible for Eisenhower to divert all available supplies and transport either to Montgomery or to Bradley without provoking serious recrimination.[2]

Both Montgomery and Bradley argued and pleaded with the Supreme Commander for more supplies which could only be provided at the expense of the other's forces. Eisenhower resisted them both, and decided to order a general advance on all fronts, aimed at reaching the Rhine along its whole length. In reaching this decision Eisenhower was not only seeking

[1] Eisenhower: *Crusade in Europe*, pp. 298–9.

[2] Ralph Ingersoll: *Top Secret* (New York, Harcourt, Brace, 1946), and Omar Bradley: *A Soldier's Story* (New York, Holt, 1951), present the American point of view with some asperity. British memoirs, e.g. Field Marshal the Viscount Montgomery: *From Normandy to the Baltic* (London, Hutchinson, 1947), pp. 118–19, and de Guingand: *Operation Victory*, pp. 410–13, are by comparison exceedingly discreet. Montgomery left the work of arguing his case to be done by a journalist, Chester Wilmot. Wilmot's book, *Struggle for Europe*, centres round a detailed and vigorous argument for the wisdom of British strategy as against the American; but any discussion that turns on what would have happened if only something that was not done had been done is bound to be inconclusive.

a compromise between his rival subordinates which would not offend national susceptibilities: he also apparently believed, with nearly everyone else in SHAEF Headquarters, that the Germans could not possibly recover from the blows they had suffered in August and that an uninterrupted advance on all fronts would therefore be possible.[1]

Hope that German collapse was near at hand was so strong among the Anglo-American commanders that on 10 September, when Eisenhower and Montgomery met for a conference, they decided to make a daring effort to establish a bridgehead across the lower Rhine. This was a very risky operation. The supply position of the Anglo-American troops was precarious, for the French ports were only beginning to come into use and it was still necessary to deliver supplies over the Normandy beaches and by air. When Montgomery's troops captured Antwerp intact on 4 September it seemed that a solution of the problem lay at hand. The question at issue on 10 September was whether first to direct the British and Canadian forces against the Germans who still held the north bank of the Scheldt estuary and so blocked access to Antwerp, or whether to drive ahead towards the Rhine in the hope that the whole structure of Nazi Germany would tumble down in ruin. Montgomery's enthusiasm for continuing the pursuit to the limit won Eisenhower over, and he agreed to assign his major strategic reserve—an airborne army of three divisions—to Montgomery for the attempt.[2]

The plan was to drop the three divisions in echelon ahead of the advancing British and Canadian troops in order to seize critical river crossings in Belgium and the Netherlands. The divisions were dropped on 17 September, but bad flying weather interfered with their reinforcement and supply. After a week of hard fighting, Montgomery's ground forces successfully linked up with two of the airborne divisions and reached the south bank of the Lower Rhine. But the foremost division, 1st British Airborne, was compelled to withdraw from its position at Arnhem. Only remnants of the division succeeded in crossing safely to the south bank of the Lower Rhine (25–26 September).

The battle of Arnhem introduced a new phase of the campaign. Headlong pursuit was succeeded by slow and difficult slogging against increasing German resistance and in the face of worsening weather. The demoralization of the German forces, so general in August and early September, had been checked short of complete collapse. Allied hopes of early victory were disappointed. The Germans fought with the courage of desperation, and were even able to launch counter-attacks in the Ardennes against the Americans (16 December–26 January)[3] and in Hungary against the Russians (15 February–15 March).

[1] Wilmot: *Struggle for Europe*, p. 490.
[2] Eisenhower: *Crusade in Europe*, pp. 306–7.
[3] See below, pp. 520–1.

While the Germans were thus staging a recovery in Europe, the war against Japan was moving unevenly on the three major fronts—the Chinese, Burmese, and Pacific. In China, the Japanese offensive which had started in April 1944 continued to make steady progress, and the American air bases which had been so laboriously constructed for the bombing of Japan were one by one overrun. The most important of these, at Kweilin, was abandoned to the Japanese on 14 September 1944. Soon after, the Japanese advance into China came to a halt.

The inability of the Chinese forces to defend the air bases was attributed by the Americans largely to the fact that Chiang Kai-shek kept a large proportion of his troops on guard against the Communists in northern China. The cure seemed obvious. A unification of the military forces of the Kuomintang and of the Chinese Communists, combined with a political settlement between the two rival parties, seemed the only way in which China could contribute significantly to the war or emerge from it with the prospect of peaceful and democratic development.[1] As a result, from the summer of 1944 onwards, American policy in China began more and more consciously to put political aims ahead of narrowly military considerations.[2] The faith which the American Joint Chiefs of Staff had put in China's military help against Japan dwindled slowly; and as it dwindled the primary *raison d'être* for the Burma campaign, as the Americans had originally conceived it, likewise dissolved.

Nevertheless, the instructions given to the Supreme Allied Commander, South-East Asia, Mountbatten, were not modified. His first task was still to reopen land communications with China through Burma and at the same time to safeguard the airfields in India which provided a base for the airline over the 'Hump'. The campaign in mountainous jungle therefore went ahead. As we have seen,[3] Myitkyina, in northern Burma, was finally captured on 3 August 1944, and soon after, by 20 August, the last of the Japanese forces which had invaded India at Imphal in the spring were driven back across the border into Burma. The tide had turned at long last, and British-Indian troops were able to prove that the problems of fighting in pathless jungle, which had so baffled them in the first years of the war, had been solved. The key to their success was air transport and extensive medical measures which cut down the incidence of tropical diseases to a fraction of what it had been earlier.[4]

[1] U.S.A., Department of State: *United States Relations with China*, Pub. 3573 (Washington, U.S.G.P.O., 1949), pp. 71–73. [This volume is referred to hereafter as *United States Relations with China*.]

[2] See below, pp. 516–18, for an account of American dealings with China.

[3] See above, p. 397.

[4] Mountbatten (*Report*, pp. 246–51) presents interesting statistics showing that casualties from sickness always far outnumbered losses from enemy action. The proportions were: 120 : 1 in 1943; 20 : 1 in 1944; and 10 : 1 in 1945. In 1942 the sickness rate was 185 per cent. (i.e. each man was, on the average, ill nearly twice in the year); in 1945 it had been reduced to 50 per cent.

The monsoon, lasting from May to October, had always paralysed military movement in previous years, but in 1944 Mountbatten refused to give up the attempt to press on after the retreating Japanese. Nevertheless, the rate of advance was painfully slow. When the monsoon ended, the pace of operations picked up. British and Chinese troops pressed southward towards Mandalay in central Burma; and far to the south a new drive along the coast started on 12 December 1944 in the direction of Akyab. But, though the Japanese in Burma were everywhere on the defensive, Allied arms had succeeded in reconquering only a small part of that country by the end of the year. Decisive victory in Burma had to wait until 1945.[1]

In contrast to the set-backs in China and the slow progress in Burma, the war in the Pacific went unexpectedly well. By the summer of 1944 the forces under General MacArthur in the South-West Pacific and those under Admiral Nimitz in the central Pacific had come within supporting range of one another. Nimitz's fleet and carrier air force had won such ascendancy over the Japanese navy that it could move almost at will over the wide Pacific. Advance bases in the Marianas (seized in July) brought both Japan and the Philippines within range of the U.S. navy's action. MacArthur's forces had simultaneously reached the eastern tip of New Guinea (30 July), within 400 miles of the southernmost islands of the Philippine archipelago.

On 15 September 1944 the possibilities of this strategic position were demonstrated, when the forces under the two commanders co-operated to invade Morotai and Peliliu, islands lying between New Guinea and the Philippines. The fleet, which covered these twin operations by attacking Japanese positions in the Philippines, met with such small opposition that Nimitz and MacArthur agreed to modify their earlier plans. Instead of approaching the Philippines by stages they decided to invade the island of Leyte in the centre of the archipelago without further delay. Accordingly, American troops went ashore on Leyte, on 20 October 1944. This attack precipitated a vast naval action, the Battle of Leyte Gulf, 22–25 October. The Japanese assembled nearly their whole naval strength, but were unable to drive the Americans from the scene and suffered heavy losses in making the attempt.

After this sea battle the Japanese could no longer hope to meet American sea power on anything like equal terms. Without the support of a fleet, the Japanese garrisons left on various Pacific islands, and even in such

[1] In spite of the criticism Americans frequently made of the British effort in Burma, it is a fact that the Burma campaign engaged a larger number of Japanese than were engaged in any single campaign by the Americans at any time in the war. The difficulties of terrain, climate, and communications were so great, and Japanese resistance so formidable, that the campaign was in fact a technical military *tour de force* to be compared with the American feat of conquering the distances of the Pacific.

areas as Burma and Malaya, were in effect stranded, cut off from all but sporadic contact with Japan itself, and compelled to depend on stockpiles and whatever could be found locally for essential supplies. To mop up these garrisons might prove difficult in the face of Japanese tenacity and bravery; but it was none the less clear that the shield of Japanese naval power, which alone could bind the isolated outposts of the Japanese Empire together, had been dashed to the ground.

Indeed, Japan was already feeling the weight of American air attack. Beginning in November 1944, B-29s, based on Saipan, began to drop bombs on Tokyo and other Japanese cities. Thus the loss of the Chinese air bases was made good by the successes of the American navy. From a strictly military point of view, the Americans could afford to neglect China, but in fact they did not abandon their protégé: instead they transformed their primary interest in Chinese affairs into a political one. Simultaneously, in very much the same fashion, the campaign in Burma, with its projected extension to Malaya and the Netherlands East Indies, likewise transformed itself bit by bit into an effort to restore British and Dutch empire over the regions which had been wrested from the European Powers by the Japanese in 1942. This double transformation did nothing to improve Allied harmony in China and Burma.

(*c*) The Meaning of Victory in Europe

As Allied forces closed in on Germany and Japan in the autumn of 1944 multiple problems of how to deal with the liberated countries of Europe closed in upon the Allies. It was easy to profess democratic principles, and declare that in due course liberated populations should be permitted to choose a Government to their liking, freely and without any outside intervention. To such formulas the Soviet Union, Britain, and America all subscribed. But in the immediate present there was a war to be fought. Military communications inevitably ran through the newly liberated areas, amid destitution, confusion, and political upheaval. Interim measures had to be taken to maintain public order, restore communications, and meet essential civilian needs; and interim measures, as always, tended to become permanent facts in the social and political landscape.

The progress of military events thus created two distinct spheres of influence in Europe. In the east, the Red Army operated through Rumania, Bulgaria, parts of Yugoslavia, Hungary, Slovakia, Poland, and Finland. This fact gave the Russians a predominant voice in the political and civil arrangements made in these countries. In the west, British and American forces operated similarly through France and Belgium and through parts of Italy and the Netherlands. In addition, a small British force landed in Greece on 5 October 1944, and token detachments moved northward after the retreating Germans throughout the rest of that month until the whole country had been liberated. Anglo-American military operations were so intermingled that distinct national spheres of influence hardly emerged from the military facts; but informal agreement between the two Governments gave the British a leading role in Greece, Italy, Belgium, and the Netherlands; while France, at least from an economic and military supply point of view, came mainly under American influence.

Had there been no divergences between the American and British Governments about the policies to be pursued towards liberated Europe, the lack of precision in their respective military spheres of action would not have been important. But in fact there were constant and considerable differences of opinion between the two Governments, and the situation thus gave rise to recurrent friction. Various political groups within each liberated country could and did play upon the discrepancies in Anglo-American policy, and by doing so made firm and effective action the more difficult.

Two general differences between the Russian and the Anglo-American spheres of military operation should be mentioned. First, the fact that Eastern Europe was predominantly agricultural meant that the damages of the war were on the whole less crippling than the damages wrought in the more industrialized West. It is in the nature of things that the disorganization of communication and supply, which war inevitably brings, hurts a peasant far less than an industrial worker. It was this fact which permitted the Red Army not only to neglect to provide relief supplies to the liberated populations within its sphere of operations, but even to live off the country it had overrun by requisitioning food and other commodities from the local population. Such a policy undoubtedly created hardship and even occasional famine, but it enormously simplified the Russians' administrative task and materially assisted their armies.

A second important advantage which the Russians enjoyed as against the Anglo-Americans was this: in each country to which their armies penetrated a Communist Party could be found which was willing to take orders from the Russians without hesitation. Communists could provide key personnel for the task of civil administration in the rear of the Red Army, and, camouflaged as national political parties, they could disguise the extent of Russian control over internal policy in each country, not only from local populations but from the Western Allies as well. Neither the British nor the Americans could command any such useful and pliant tool for the enforcement of their wishes within liberated countries.

Nevertheless, the Russians did not at first set out to revolutionize the countries they had liberated. They were, moreover, willing to make certain outward concessions to the cause of Allied co-operation by associating British and American representatives with themselves on Allied Control Commissions in ex-enemy states, just as the Anglo-Americans had accorded the Russians a nominal role in Italian affairs by giving them a seat on the Advisory Council for Italy.[1] In the two Allied countries which came within the Russian sphere, Yugoslavia and Poland, the situation was, of course, entirely different. The ticklish problem in these two countries was to secure some sort of reconciliation between the Governments in Exile and the Communists and their fellow travellers.

(i) *Russia's Sphere of Operations in the Autumn of 1944*

The situation in Poland during the autumn of 1944 severely strained Allied cordiality. The struggle of the Polish Home Army in Warsaw from 1 August to 3 October 1944 received considerable publicity in the Anglo-American press, and the heroism of the Poles excited a mounting pity and admiration among officials and among the general public. But Stalin did not share such sentiments. From his point of view the rising in Warsaw was an annoying and potentially dangerous demonstration of the power exercised in Poland through clandestine channels by the Polish Government in Exile.[2]

Stalin's attitude was made public in a Tass communiqué of 13 August which declared that 'the responsibility for what is going on in Warsaw falls exclusively on the Polish emigrant circles in London'.[3] Such a statement sounded cold-blooded enough to Western ears, but worse was to follow. On 14 August the American Government asked Stalin to approve the use of Russian air bases by American planes assigned to deliver supplies to the Warsaw insurgents. The request was refused. This provoked further remonstrance from the Americans. On 17 August Molotov relented so far as to inform the American Ambassador in Moscow that the Russian Government would not object to the delivery of supplies to Warsaw by British and American planes, but he remained adamant in refusing the use of Russian airfields.[4] Parallel British telegrams were equally unavailing.

A personal and joint appeal to Stalin from Churchill and Roosevelt, sent on 20 August, failed to change the Soviet policy. Churchill felt so angry that on 25 August he urged the President to order the American planes (which were then waiting in readiness to make the flight from Italy as soon as permission to land in Russia had been secured) to fly to Warsaw and land in Russia with or without Soviet permission.[5] But Roosevelt was not willing to defy Stalin so directly, and the waiting planes were assigned other missions.

Meanwhile the R.A.F. had made several flights over Warsaw to deliver arms and ammunition to the Polish Home Army. Small-scale deliveries

[1] See above, p. 309. [2] See above, pp. 432–3.
[3] Rothstein: *Soviet Foreign Policy during the Patriotic War*, ii. 204.
[4] Hull: *Memoirs*, ii. 1446. [5] Mikolajczyk: *Pattern of Soviet Domination*, p. 91.

were made successfully on 4 and 8 August, and a larger-scale operation was conducted each night from 11 to 14 August. But losses were heavy, and after 14 August the R.A.F. commander decided that deliveries to Warsaw could no longer be made. Drops were directed instead to a forest area near the city where German anti-aircraft fire was less of a danger.[1]

By the end of August the heroism of the Poles in Warsaw had created widespread sympathy in Britain and America, and the cold-blooded refusal of the Russians even to facilitate British and American efforts to bring aid to the insurgents excited a growing criticism.[2] The situation was obviously an embarrassing one for Stalin. Probably he had initially expected the insurrection to last only a few days; instead it had lasted a whole month without any help from Russia and with only small assistance from Britain. Stalin found himself playing a peculiarly brutal and morally indefensible role in the eyes of almost all the world, and because of the Poles his relations with Roosevelt and Churchill were once more undergoing a strain. Stalin may have also been concerned about the reaction of the Lublin Committee, some of whose members could not stand as onlookers at the tragedy of Warsaw without feeling restive.[3] Finally, there is some reason to suppose that the Red Army's strategic plan called for an early advance into Warsaw.[4] If the policy of non co-operation with the insurgents were to be maintained, any advance upon Warsaw would have to be delayed until the rising collapsed; and there seemed no immediate signs of such an event.

Whatever the reasons which may have influenced the decision, on 10 September Stalin changed his policy. He informed Roosevelt that Soviet landing fields would be made available for shuttle sorties sent for the relief of Warsaw, and on the same day the Red Army began to advance

[1] T. Bor-Komorowski: *The Secret Army* (London, Gollancz, 1950), pp. 262, 266; Mikolajczyk: *Pattern of Soviet Domination*, p. 89.

[2] On 29 August Vernon Bartlett in the *News Chronicle* broke the news of Russian refusal to allow R.A.F. or American planes to use Russian bases; this precipitated a spate of articles (e.g. *Manchester Guardian, Daily Herald, Christian Science Monitor, Chicago Daily News* on 30 August 1944), all critical of the Russian action. The issue was, however, speedily damped down, no doubt by official suggestion; and when on 5 September the Polish Commander in Chief, General Sosnkowski, issued a public criticism of Allied failure to bring aid to Warsaw, it was ill received in the press and may have dimmed somewhat the sympathy for the Polish position.

[3] On 6 August, when Mikolajczyk met the members of the Committee in Moscow, he had been able to stir some of them to active concern for events in Warsaw (Mikolajczyk: *Pattern of Soviet Domination*, pp. 82–84). It is impossible to say what currents of feeling may have run among the members of the Committee during the following month, but it seems likely that sympathy for the Warsaw insurgents did not disappear. If the Lublin Committee showed any signs of disintegrating over the issue, Stalin must have been seriously concerned. A Provisional Government composed solely of Communists was not what he had in mind for Poland. All his efforts to shape a post-war Polish régime that would be satisfactory from the Russian point of view would, if the Lublin Committee broke up, have come to grief.

[4] On 3 August Stalin told Mikolajczyk that Warsaw would be liberated by the Red Army after a short delay (ibid. p. 82).

towards Praga, the suburb of the city lying on the east bank of the Vistula. It was captured by 15 September. Russian planes began to drop supplies to the insurgents, beginning on the night of 13 September.[1] When Praga had been cleared of the Germans, two battalions of Poles from the Kosciusko Division (an integral part of the Red Army owing political allegiance to the Lublin Committee) crossed the Vistula and fought for several days side by side with the Home Army detachments in Warsaw proper. Finally, after delays due to bad weather, on 18 September a great force of American planes came over the city and dropped supplies, most of which, however, fell outside the areas in the control of the insurgents.[2]

These changes naturally heartened the Poles fighting in Warsaw and helped to relieve the strain between Stalin and the West. But the aid which had reached Warsaw was not enough to prevent the final act of the tragedy. The Soviet offensive stopped at the Vistula. Unable to maintain their lodgement on the west bank of the river, remnants of the two battalions which had crossed the Vistula were withdrawn after a few days. German attacks on the isolated regions of the city still in Polish hands continued relentlessly, and shortages of food and ammunition crippled the defenders. At length, when hope of speedy relief by the Red Army had disappeared, the insurgents surrendered to the Germans on 3 October 1944. Warsaw was in ruins, the morale of the Home Army was shaken to its roots, and it thenceforth ceased to play an active military role, being equally torn between fear of the Russians and hatred of the Germans. Thereby the Polish Government in Exile lost its most valuable basis of practical power in Poland, and a serious obstacle to the assertion of the authority of the Lublin Committee was, if not removed, at least reduced.

The Warsaw rising[3] with all its terror and grandeur was thus of decisive importance for the future of Poland. It was of equal importance on the larger world scene. The glimpse of Stalin's Moloch-face which had been fleetingly accorded to the West could not be forgotten easily. Distrust of Russian intentions in Eastern Europe could never afterwards be entirely overcome even by Roosevelt, much less by Churchill.

While these events were taking place in Poland, Stalin had a new opportunity for testing his diplomacy in the Balkans. The rapid advance of the Red Army into Rumania, Bulgaria, Yugoslavia, and Hungary called for definition of the relationships between the Allies and the newly conquered and liberated countries in general, and between the Red Army and local authorities in particular.

Rumania came first. That country was legally at war with each of the

[1] Bor-Komorowski: *Secret Army*, pp. 338–44. [2] Ibid. pp. 349–50.

[3] A full account will be found in the *Survey* for 1939–46: *The Realignment of Europe.*

Big Three, but in practice Rumanian troops had fought only against the Russians. When the Red Army first crossed the Pruth River on to Rumanian soil in April 1944, the Russians announced to the world the conditions upon which they would grant an armistice. But the Rumanian Government hesitated, fearing complete Russian domination of their country. Efforts to persuade the British or the Americans to drop parachute troops into the country as a makeweight against the Red Army proved fruitless,[1] and, when the Russians resumed their offensive in August, King Michael, with the help of army officers and a few political leaders who had made their reputations before the war, carried through a *coup d'état* on 23 August 1944. A new Government was set up under General Constantin Sanatescu, and leaders of the National Peasant, Liberal, Socialist, and Communist Parties joined the Cabinet.[2]

The new Government lost no time in accepting the preliminary conditions which the Russians had prescribed in April. The Germans had only relatively small forces stationed in Rumania at the time, and the Rumanian army was able to drive them back to the Carpathians. Meanwhile, on 27 August the Russians announced that hostilities against the Rumanian army had been suspended; and as soon as the Red Army could advance far enough to regain contact with the Germans, the erstwhile enemies fought side by side through the passes of the Carpathians and then westward until the whole of Transylvania had been reconquered.

As we have seen,[3] the Russians announced in April that they had no intention of disturbing the independence, territorial integrity, or social order of Rumania; and on 25 August the statement was officially reaffirmed.[4] This suited the situation which developed immediately after the *coup d'état*. It had been a palace revolution in the literal sense of the word, leaving the Rumanian army and administration intact. The preliminary conditions for an armistice which the new Government accepted dealt mainly with military and territorial questions. The Rumanians agreed to join in fighting the Germans, to recognize the annexation of Bessarabia by Russia, to pay reparations to the Soviet Union, to permit the free movement of the Red Army through Rumanian territory, and to repatriate prisoners of war. In return, the Soviet Government 'consented' to the return of the portion of Transylvania which had been annexed by Hungary in 1940.[5]

[1] Henry L. Roberts: *Rumania, Political Problems of an Agrarian State* (New Haven, Yale University Press, 1951), p. 259.

[2] The National Peasant and Liberal Parties were old and relatively conservative organizations; the Socialists and Communists had been small and unimportant in pre-war years. The Communists had also been illegal. Parliamentary government had been in suspension since 1938, and the parties consisted of little more than a handful of leaders gathered in Bucharest who had no real organization at their command (ibid. p. 261).

[3] See above, p. 422.

[4] Rothstein: *Soviet Foreign Policy during the Patriotic War*, ii. 103.

[5] For text of the preliminary conditions for an armistice with Rumania see ibid. pp. 104–5.

These preliminary conditions did not fix the relationship between the Allies and the Rumanian Government. This problem was taken up in Moscow, from 10 to 12 September, when Rumanian plenipotentiaries negotiated an armistice agreement with representatives of the Russian, British, and American Governments, who were, according to the official communiqué, 'acting in the interests of all the United Nations'.[1]

The Rumanian Armistice Agreement was signed on 12 September 1944.[2] In general, the negotiations over the surrender of Italy set the pattern of procedure. Thus, as Eisenhower had signed the Italian armistice, so General Malinovski signed the Rumanian armistice on behalf of all three Allied Governments. Continued tripartite participation in Rumanian affairs was provided for by the following article: 'An Allied Control Commission will be established which will undertake, until the conclusion of peace, the regulation of and control over the execution of the present terms under the general direction and orders of the Allied (Soviet) High Command, acting on behalf of the Allied Powers.'[3] The awkward wording of this article scarcely defined the powers of the Control Commission precisely, and this vagueness was later to give rise to dispute. Yet at the time there seems little doubt that both British and Americans agreed with the Russians in expecting that the only important outside influence upon Rumanian affairs would come from the Soviet Union. In Italy, Russia had effectually been excluded from active participation in Allied decision-making, and the Western Allies could hardly expect to be treated differently by the Russians in Rumania. Moreover, in May 1944 the British Government had tentatively recognized Russia's controlling influence in Rumania in exchange for their own controlling influence in Greece,[4] and, although the agreement had not been formalized, it had not been repudiated either.

The text of the Rumanian Armistice Agreement reaffirmed the preliminary conditions which had been accepted on 27 August, and made some of the obligations of the Rumanian Government more specific. Reparations to the Soviet Union were fixed at $300 million, payable in commodities over a period of six years; but the Soviet High Command was at the same time given unlimited authority to draw upon Rumanian resources for the support of the Red Army. This made the fixing of the amount of reparations almost meaningless. The Russians could legally demand unlimited supplies and services for their military uses.[5] The

[1] Rothstein: *Soviet Foreign Policy during the Patriotic War*, ii. 122.

[2] For text of the Armistice see ibid. pp. 123–7; cf. Cmd. 6585 (1945).

[3] Rothstein, op. cit. ii. 125.

[4] See above, p. 422.

[5] The exact obligation was phrased as follows: 'The Rumanian Government must make regular payments in Rumanian currency required by the Allied (Soviet) High Command for the fulfilment of its functions and will in case of need ensure the use on Rumanian territory of industrial and transportation enterprises, means of communication, power stations, enterprises and installa-

Soviet High Command was also accorded the right to censor all public communications and to arrest persons accused of war crimes. Rumanian armed forces were to conduct their operations 'under the general leadership of the Allied (Soviet) High Command'. The Western Powers received the guarantee that 'all legal rights and interests of the United Nations and their nationals on Rumanian territory as they existed before the war' would be restored. The principal interests at stake were, of course, the oil-wells and refineries at Ploeşti which had been owned by Western companies.

In return, civil administration was 'restored' throughout the country save in a zone of 50–100 kilometres immediately behind the front lines; but it was also provided that Rumanian authorities would carry out the 'instructions and orders of the Allied (Soviet) High Command issued by them for the purpose of securing the execution of these armistice terms'.

It is clear that the terms of this Armistice Agreement gave the Soviet military authorities very extensive powers over Rumanian affairs, and that the Rumanian Government would have little chance of resisting any policy which the Soviet High Command wished to enforce. Little reality was left to the formula of respecting Rumanian independence. This, however, was equally true in Italy, where the armistice terms gave the Allied military commander similarly sweeping powers. In both cases the extraordinary powers accorded to the military were presumably limited to the duration of the war; but such temporal limits did not prevent either the Western Allies in Italy or the Russians in Rumania from fundamentally affecting the régime which emerged by the time of the peace treaties.

As early as May 1944 the British Government had shown a readiness to sacrifice influence in Rumania in order to assure a free hand in Greece. The American State Department, however, was not yet reconciled to a division of the Balkans into separate national operational spheres and accordingly registered a protest against the manner in which the Rumanian armistice had been drawn up and against some of its clauses. In particular, the Americans objected to the assignment of specific sums for reparations payments; to the vagueness of the powers accorded to the Allied Control Commission; and to the manner in which the European Advisory Commission had been by-passed in drawing up the armistice terms.[1]

Yet the behaviour of the Russian authorities in Rumania during the first months of the occupation of that country did not excite serious question in either Britain or America. The Red Army did not bring revolution in its train, even though it did bring new leaders for the Rumanian Communist Party—persons who had long been exiles in Moscow. During

tions of public utility, stores of fuel, fuel oil, food and other materials, services in accordance with instructions issued by the Allied (Soviet) High Command' (Rothstein, op. cit. ii. 124).

[1] Hull: *Memoirs*, ii. 1461.

the first few months the Communists accepted a subordinate position in the Rumanian Government; and the King, army, and old political leaders retained the outward trappings of power and influence in the shadow of the Red Army.

The situation in Bulgaria was quite different. The Bulgars were linked to Russia by strong ties of sentiment, going back to the days of San Stefano (1878) and earlier. Hitler had not been able to persuade the war-time Bulgarian Government to send even a token detachment to the Russian front, or even to declare war on the Soviet Union.[1] Thus at the beginning of September 1944 an anomalous situation arose. Russian troops were nearing the Danube, but Bulgaria was at war only with Britain and the United States. If the Bulgars wished to withdraw from their association with the Nazis, it was, presumably, with the Western Powers that they had to settle accounts.[2] Yet the new military situation made it obvious that it was with the Russians that the Bulgars must come to terms.

This curious legal position was untangled when, on 5 September 1944, the Russians declared war on Bulgaria. Immediately upon receipt of this news the Bulgarian Government asked the Russians for an armistice, and on 8 September the Bulgars declared war against Germany. The next day the Russians suspended military operations against Bulgaria almost before they had begun. At the same time, the Soviet Government officially announced that it was working out the conditions of an armistice jointly with Britain and the United States.[3] This time the European Advisory Commission was entrusted with the task of drawing up the armistice as a concession to American protests against the manner in which the Rumanian armistice negotiation had been conducted.

Agreement proved difficult to achieve. A main stumbling-block arose over the reluctance of the Bulgars to evacuate Greek and Yugoslav territory which they had occupied during the war. The Russians were not anxious to coerce the Bulgars in this matter, since it meant surrender to Greece of an outlet on the north Aegean. But when the Russians suggested that the Bulgars should be allowed to keep at least a part of the territory in question, American and British members of the European Advisory Commission objected strenuously to the idea of allowing an ex-enemy to

[1] Details will be found in the *Survey* for 1939–46: *Hitler's Europe*.

[2] As early as July 1944 the Bulgars had begun negotiations for an armistice with British and American officials, but the Western Powers stalled until the Russian declaration of war transformed the legal situation. Cf. Michael Padev: *Dimitrov Wastes no Bullets* (London, Eyre & Spottiswoode, 1948), pp. 34–35. This, together with the rebuff of similar Rumanian overtures, was at least partly due to British unwillingness to do anything that might seem to call Russia's right to a 'sphere of operations' in Rumania and Bulgaria in question.

[3] Text of the communiqué may be found in Rothstein: *Soviet Foreign Policy during the Patriotic War*, ii. 120–1.

retain territory seized from Allied states.[1] A long stalemate ensued, and it was not until 11 October, and after Churchill's personal intervention had taken the negotiation entirely out of the hands of the European Advisory Commission, that the three Allied Governments formally notified the Bulgarian Government

> that the essential pre-requisite for beginning negotiations for an armistice is an undertaking by the Bulgarian Government to evacuate all Bulgarian troops and all Bulgarian officials from Greek and Yugoslav territory. Such evacuation must commence immediately and must be completed within fifteen days of this communication. For the purpose of supervision and control over this evacuation the three Allied Governments will send their representatives to Bulgaria, who will act as a Joint Allied Military Mission, with the Soviet representative as chairman.[2]

The Bulgarian Government accepted on the same day, and the evacuation was duly carried out.

Another difficulty arose over the use to be made of the Bulgarian army. Should it advance from its positions on Yugoslav soil in order to attack the Germans? Or should Bulgaria be treated as a defeated enemy and disarmed at once? In the end it was agreed that Bulgarian forces should serve under the Soviet High Command, but would not be used on the territory of any Allied state without the prior consent of that state.[3]

Another complication which disturbed the Western Allies in their dealings with Bulgaria was the fact that something approaching revolution swept over the country in September 1944. Unlike the Rumanian Communist Party, the Communists in Bulgaria were a considerable force, and did not have to reckon with the inveterate nationalistic distrust of Russia which had paralysed the Rumanian Communists before and during the war. Certain small Partisan bands had formed under Communist leadership in the mountains of Bulgaria during the spring and summer of 1944, and on 8–9 September a *coup d'état* installed what was known as the Fatherland Front in power in Sofia. The Fatherland Front was an association of political parties and groups in which the Communists were prominent, though they did not completely dominate it. Nevertheless, when the Fatherland Front Government took power the Partisan bands invaded the towns and villages of Bulgaria where they carried through local and sometimes bloody purges of old officials, replacing them with

[1] Hamilton Fish Armstrong: *Tito and Goliath* (London, Gollancz, 1951), p. 197, note 1.

[2] Rothstein: *Soviet Foreign Policy during the Patriotic War*, ii. 156.

[3] The fundamental issue at stake was the future relationship between Yugoslavia and Bulgaria, especially the future status of Macedonia which was in dispute between Tito and the new Bulgarian Government (cf. Elizabeth Barker: *Macedonia, its Place in Balkan Power Politics* (London, Royal Institute of International Affairs, 1950), pp. 97–99). Tito did not want the Bulgars to remain in Macedonia and use it as a base for operations against German troops, since such action might strengthen Bulgarian claims to the disputed Macedonian territories.

Committees, on which Communists were usually able to secure a dominant position. Moreover, a militia was speedily organized round the core of the Partisan bands. The militia not only supplanted the old police but adopted for its own ends the brutal and violent methods which had distinguished its predecessor.

These developments probably reflected the impetus of Bulgarian internal political pressures rather than any directives sent down to the Bulgarian Communists from Moscow. They gave the Bulgarian political scene a character quite different from that in Rumania, where the Communists were far too weak to exert much influence at first; yet it would be an exaggeration to describe what occurred as thorough-going revolution. The Agrarian Party, in particular, continued to exert real influence in the central Government. The coalition of the Fatherland Front in the autumn of 1944 was not merely a fraud.[1]

Despite these differences between Bulgaria and Rumania, the armistice agreement, which was finally signed on 28 October 1944,[2] followed very closely the pattern of the Rumanian armistice. Reparations payable to Greece and Yugoslavia were left undetermined in amount, and none were demanded by the Soviet Government. On the other hand, the Soviet High Command secured the right to demand unlimited supplies and services 'for the discharge of its functions', the right of censorship, of free movement through Bulgarian territory, and the 'general direction' of Bulgarian armed forces in the war against Germany and her satellites. An Allied Control Commission was established to

> regulate and supervise the execution of the armistice terms under the chairmanship of the representative of the Allied (Soviet) High Command and with the participation of representatives of the United Kingdom and the United States. During the period between the coming into force of the Armistice and the conclusion of hostilities against Germany the Allied Control Commission will be under the general direction of the Allied (Soviet) High Command.[3]

The wording of this clause was a good deal more precise than in the case of the parallel clause in the Rumanian armistice.[4] Perhaps partly as a result, no important misunderstanding among the Allies arose in Bulgaria until after the end of the war against Germany.

The problem presented by the advance of the Red Army into Yugoslavia was entirely different, if only because Yugoslavia ranked as an ally. Between the time of the Tehrān Conference, when the British definitely

[1] Elizabeth Barker: *Truce in the Balkans* (London, Percival Marshall, 1948), pp. 44–47.

[2] For text see Rothstein: *Soviet Foreign Policy during the Patriotic War*, ii. 170–3; cf. Cmd. 6587 (1945).

[3] Rothstein, op. cit. ii. 172–3.

[4] These differences were of course largely a result of American criticism of the Rumanian armistice. See above, p. 469.

decided to assist Tito in preference to Mihailović, and about September 1944, it was the British Government which played the most active part in Yugoslav affairs. Indeed, until several weeks after the Russian breakthrough in Rumania (in late August 1944) Yugoslavia belonged rather to the Mediterranean than to the Russian sphere of operations so far as the militant parochialism of the Partisan movement admitted of any external influence at all. As we have seen,[1] Churchill was able to bring about the remodelling of the Yugoslav Government in Exile on 1 June 1944. The new Prime Minister, Ivan Šubašić, proceeded to conclude an agreement with Tito on 16 June. By its terms, Tito agreed not to press the question of the future status of the monarchy for the time being; and Šubašić recognized Tito's 'temporary' administration of the country, and promised to reorganize the Yugoslav exiled Government further so that it would include only 'progressive democratic elements'.[2]

All did not go smoothly, however. In August 1944 Churchill made a trip to the Mediterranean in the course of which he not only watched the American disembarkment on the Riviera (15 August), but set about mending his political fences in Greece and Yugoslavia. On 12 or 13 August the British Prime Minister met Tito for the first time. Churchill asked him whether he planned to communize Yugoslavia after the war; Tito replied, rather truculently, in the negative.[3] Although the conversation was cordial, Tito's general attitude cannot have been very reassuring to Churchill. Nevertheless, the British continued to support Tito and, indeed, the scale of their military assistance to the Partisans was increased.

By September 1944 the rapid advance of the Red Army through the Balkans after the collapse of German resistance in Rumania and Bulgaria put a quite new complexion on the situation. Tito's friendliness towards the British cooled markedly.[4] On or about 20 September he flew secretly to Moscow, landing on the way at Russian headquarters at Craiova; on 29 September 1944 a Tass communiqué announced that an agreement had been reached for the temporary entry of Russian troops into 'Yugoslav territory bordering on Hungary'. The communiqué further stated that 'the civil administration of the National Committee of Liberation of Yugoslavia would continue to function in those districts of Yugoslavia where Red Army units were operating'. But perhaps the most remarkable part

[1] See above, pp. 389–90.

[2] The text of the agreement will be found in *Documents* (R.I.I.A.) for 1939–46, ii: *Hitler's Europe*; cf. Armstrong: *Tito and Goliath*, p. 52.

[3] Stephen Clissold (*Whirlwind, an Account of Marshal Tito's Rise to Power* (London, Cresset Press, 1949), pp. 194–8) reproduces a record of the conversation. Clissold was present as interpreter at the meeting and his report may be presumed to be accurate in spite of its popularized style.

[4] General Wilson attributed the change in Tito's attitude to the Anglo-Soviet dispute over Poland (*Eight Years Overseas*, pp. 227, 233–4). The advance of the Red Army, which promised to make him less dependent on the British for military assistance, was probably of greater importance.

of the announcement was the following: 'The Soviet Command stated ... that the Soviet forces on completion of their operational tasks would be withdrawn from Yugoslavia.'[1]

This communiqué made it clear that the powers and authority of the Red Army in Yugoslavia were to be far different from those enjoyed in Rumania and Bulgaria. Two factors probably contributed to Stalin's restraint. The *pourparlers* of May and June 1944 had tentatively placed Yugoslavia in the British sphere of operations, and it is reasonable to suppose that Stalin wished to minimize the infraction of that understanding by indicating in public his intention to withdraw Red Army forces from the country as soon as the Germans had been driven out. It is also likely, in view of the later development in Yugoslav-Russian relations, that even as early as 1944 Tito insisted that his control over Yugoslavia should not be infringed by a Russian military administration or by a prolonged occupation of any part of the country.

In any case, Tito's relations with Stalin were entirely different from the subserviency of the Rumanian and Bulgarian Governments, bound as they were hand and foot by the armistice provisions. The difference was scant comfort to Churchill and the British, however. As soon as he had the chance, the Yugoslav leader had rushed into Stalin's arms while spurning the British and criticizing them for failure to help his Partisans on the scale they deserved.[2] From Churchill's point of view, the Tehrān decision against a greater Anglo-American effort in the central and eastern Mediterranean areas was beginning to bear bitter fruit.

It was not only in the Balkans and Poland that Russia's newly demonstrated military prowess led to important political shifts. In Hungary, decisive upheaval came on 15 October 1944 when the Regent, Admiral Horthy, publicly announced his intention of surrendering to the Red Army. The Germans were able to carry through a *coup d'état* before this decision could be fully acted upon. Horthy was seized and deported into Germany, and German troops took over control of Budapest and the western part of the country. But part of the Hungarian army, under the leadership of General Miklós, acted on Horthy's pronouncement and joined the Russians. On 23 December General Miklós became head of a provisional Government under Russian sponsorship; and the Allies began negotiations with this new authority for the conclusion of an armistice. It was signed on 20 January 1945. Its provisions reproduced those of the Bulgarian armistice almost exactly, with this addition: Hungary's reparations debt was fixed at $300 million, payable in commodities over

[1] Rothstein: *Soviet Foreign Policy during the Patriotic War*, ii. 141.
[2] Wilson: *Eight Years Overseas*, pp. 233–4.

a period of six years. Of the total, $100 million were designated for Yugoslavia and Czechoslovakia; $200 million for Russia.[1]

Russian troops liberated only a small part of eastern Czechoslovakia during the autumn of 1944. In August, when the Polish rising in Warsaw began, the Slovaks likewise revolted against the Nazi puppet Government which was ruling their country.[2] The revolt collapsed in September when the Red Army failed to arrive in time to prevent German military occupation of Slovakia. But despite the outward likenesses between what happened in Warsaw and what happened in Slovakia, the consequences were altogether different. Beneš in London recognized the authority of the Slovak National Committee which led the revolt, and the Russians recognized the authority of the Beneš Government. Indeed, in accordance with the Soviet-Czechoslovak Treaty of December 1943,[3] a delegation of Czech officials was sent in August from London to Moscow, ready to undertake the civil administration of liberated portions of Czechoslovakia. The military reverse in Slovakia made the arrival of the delegation a little premature, but the set-back did not create ill-feeling or recrimination such as followed in the wake of the Warsaw rising. Alone of the countries which came within the Soviet sphere of military operations, Czechoslovakia presented no awkward problems to Allied diplomats in 1944. Beneš and his colleagues seemed well on the way to accomplishing the difficult feat of retaining good relations with both West and East.[4]

Finland, also, came to terms with the Russians successfully. The Finnish Government sued for an armistice on 25 August; hostilities were suspended on 5 September; and an armistice was signed on 19 September 1944. The armistice provisions were similar to those prescribed for Rumania and Bulgaria. The frontier of 1940 was re-established, with the exception of the far north, where Finland ceded a region, including the valuable nickel mines of Petsamo, to Russia. An Allied Control Commission was set up;[5] reparations to the Soviet Union were fixed at $300 million; and the supremacy of the Soviet High Command was made fully explicit. One thing was different: the Finns were compelled to cede certain military bases to the Russians permanently.[6]

[1] Text of the armistice may be found in *Documents on American Foreign Relations, vol. vii, July 1944–June 1945*, ed. Leland M. Goodrich and Marie J. Carroll (Princeton University Press for World Peace Foundation, 1947), pp. 244–8.

[2] Details will be found in the *Survey* for 1939–46: *Hitler's Europe*.

[3] See above, p. 429.

[4] *Central and South East Europe, 1945–1948*, ed. R. R. Betts (London, Royal Institute of International Affairs, 1950), pp. 168–9.

[5] Since the United States was not at war with Finland, only Great Britain and the Soviet Union were concerned directly with the armistice negotiations, or found a place on the Control Commission. British participation was, for that matter, nominal.

[6] Text of the armistice may be found in Rothstein: *Soviet Foreign Policy during the Patriotic War*, ii. 128–32; cf. Cmd. 6586 (1945).

From this brief survey of the political changes which followed in the wake of the Red Army in Eastern Europe two facts emerge clearly. First, the Russians showed no signs of trying to establish exclusive Communist control. Instead, 'popular fronts' of varying composition were everywhere called into being which associated Communist with socialist, agrarian, and other political parties. Second, the armistice terms gave the Russians untrammelled control over the economic life of the ex-enemy countries, and potential Russian influence on their political affairs was almost as great, since failure to co-operate militarily or economically could be used as an excuse for any sort of intervention. What had not become clear, and very probably had not been firmly decided by Stalin himself, was the use which would be made of the Russians' commanding position. For the moment, Stalin's interest seemed to be mainly military. He sought and received food and other supplies and services for the Red Army; and he sought and received direct military help from the armies of the countries which had been overrun. It is not unreasonable to suppose that Stalin's plans for Eastern Europe had scarcely gone farther than that in 1944. Everything had happened very fast, and it is at least possible that Stalin had not expected to meet with such sudden and extensive success and could not at once decide how best to exploit his gains.

From the point of view of Allied co-operation, two sore spots made themselves felt. No settlement had been reached over Poland; and the sudden upsurge of Russian power in the Balkans upset Churchill, even though Roosevelt seems not to have been much, if at all, concerned over the eclipse of Western influence in South-Eastern Europe.

(2) *The Anglo-American Sphere of Operations*

The victories in France and Italy in the summer of 1944 brought in their wake a temporary relaxation of the Anglo-American political differences which had been so prominent in the earlier part of the year. Churchill's policy in Italy had suffered a set-back in June, when Badoglio was replaced as head of the Italian Government by Bonomi;[1] and Roosevelt's policy towards France suffered a drastic rebuff when the French people proved in general willing and even anxious to support General de Gaulle and the French Committee of National Liberation.[2] As Churchill and Roosevelt each accepted the new situation, the disputes which had earlier divided them as to the best policy towards France and Italy largely disappeared.

After de Gaulle's visit to Washington in July 1944 the Allies recognized the French Committee of National Liberation as the *de facto* civil authority in France. Negotiations were thereupon started to define the relationship between the Committee and the Allied military authorities. By 25 August agreements had been reached concerning such matters as

[1] See above, p. 425. [2] See above, pp. 426–7.

civil administration and jurisdiction, currency, censorship, civilian relief, and the disposal of captured war material. Nevertheless, the United States Government were very cautious.[1] An official statement, issued at the time when these agreements were concluded, emphasized that Eisenhower had been authorized to deal with the members of de Gaulle's Committee 'so long as they continue to receive the support of the majority of Frenchmen who are fighting for the defeat of Germany and the liberation of France'. The old distrust felt by Hull and Roosevelt was reflected in the further stipulation that 'as soon as the military situation permits, the French people will be given the opportunity freely to exercise their will in the choice of their government'.[2]

But such qualifications were little more than a smoke screen of words to cover the retreat of the American Government from a position which had become untenable. As events unfolded themselves, no reasonable doubt could remain of de Gaulle's popularity. He had become the pre-eminent symbol of French resistance, and was welcomed as such by the people of France. Accordingly, on 23 October the United States, Great Britain, and the Soviet Union formally extended recognition to General de Gaulle as head of the Provisional Government of France; and simultaneously a zone of the interior was established, including Paris, within which the authority of the Provisional Government was recognized as sovereign.[3] Shortly thereafter, on 11 November, France was invited to become a member of the European Advisory Commission. This gesture was a recognition of French claims to rank as a European Great Power. An even more unmistakable step in this direction was the agreement reached at the Dumbarton Oaks Conference (August–September) that France should become a fifth permanent member of the proposed Security Council, along with Britain, America, Russia, and China.[4]

The political problems of liberated Belgium were of a different order from those which arose in France. After the Belgian capital had been liberated, the Belgian Government returned from their London exile to Brussels on 8 September 1944. They had to face an awkward problem almost at once. King Leopold had not left the country with the exiled Government in 1940, and his enemies had accused him, not without some

[1] The deployment of Eisenhower's forces put the Americans on the right of the British, and the French on the right of the Americans. As a result, American armies operated through France on a much larger scale than did the British, who soon after the August break-out crossed into Belgium. This fact, combined with American military and economic assistance to France, gave the United States a certain primacy in Allied dealings with France, though the primacy was less definite than it had been in North African days and by no means prevented the French from acting independently of American or any other sort of outside advice.

[2] *Documents on American Foreign Relations, 1944–1945*, p. 867.

[3] Ibid. pp. 867–8; Rothstein: *Soviet Foreign Policy during the Patriotic War*, ii. 163–4. For the public statement by the British Government on French recognition see *The Times*, 24 October 1944.

[4] Hull: *Memoirs*, ii. 1434–5. See below, p. 507, note 1.

apparent basis in fact, of collaborating with the Nazis. The question of whether he should be allowed to retain his throne quickly became a burning one. The issue was complicated by Walloon-Flemish rivalries and by conservative-Leftist struggles, all of which tended to crystallize around the person of the King. The matter was postponed for the moment when a regency was set up on 20 September 1944; but the issue would not remain quiet, and continued to trouble Belgian politics in the months that followed.[1]

In Italy, the Bonomi Cabinet, which assumed office immediately after the liberation of Rome (June 1944), began its career by trying to secure a relaxation of the armistice terms. When Churchill visited Italy in August he concluded that some sort of gesture should be made to lighten the economic and other disabilities under which the Italians were labouring; and he issued a public message of 'encouragement and hope' to the Italian people upon his departure.[2] But definite action could only come with the concurrence of the United States. Consequently relief for Italy became an item on the agenda for the Second Quebec Conference in September.

Greece, on the other hand, was left entirely to the British. Indeed, the Americans pointedly dissociated themselves from Greek affairs, and refused to permit the use of any American forces in that country except for a small group to administer relief.[3] When Churchill visited the Mediterranean in August 1944 he took the occasion to interview George Papandreou, the newly appointed Prime Minister of the Greek Government in Exile. As a result of this meeting Churchill seems to have concluded that Papandreou was the man for the role assigned to him by British policy. He, if anyone could, would be able to conciliate the Communist-led resistance movement without allowing it to take power in the country.[4]

At the time Churchill interviewed Papandreou, the representatives of the Communist-led popular front, EAM, had just joined the Greek Cabinet after a prolonged period of hesitation. This augured well for the success of British plans.[5] Only the question of the relationship between Allied mili-

[1] An account of Belgium after the liberation will be found in the *Survey* for 1939–46: *The Realignment of Europe.*

[2] He said little more than that British authorities in Italy would do what they could to relieve the difficulties in which Italy found herself. Text may be found in Churchill: *Dawn of Liberation*, pp. 169–70.

[3] Wilson: *Eight Years Overseas*, p. 231.

[4] As in Belgium, the question of the future of the King was the burning question of Greek politics which tended to draw diverse causes of discontent to a focus. Papandreou had been a republican in pre-war times, but his enemies accused him of having promised Churchill that he would support the King. Details of what passed between the two men in August 1944 had not been published up to 1952, but it seems likely that Papandreou made it clear that he intended to resist any effort by EAM to dominate the Government of post-war Greece. Cf. Wilson's reference to the possibility of a *coup d'état* in Athens in September (ibid. p. 230).

[5] The EAM representatives joined Papandreou's Cabinet only after receiving the advice of the Russian Minister in Cairo to that effect (cf. W. H. McNeill: *The Greek Dilemma: War and Aftermath* (London, Gollancz, 1947), p. 121). This Russian action corresponded to the restraint

tary authorities and the two rival guerrilla armies, EDES and ELAS, remained to be settled. This was done by an agreement signed on 26 September 1944 at Caserta. By the terms of this agreement, both of the Greek guerrilla forces and the Greek Government in Exile recognized the military authority of the Supreme Allied Commander in the Mediterranean, General Wilson, and accepted his appointment of a British general to exercise command in Greece.[1]

As a result of these preliminary arrangements, when the Germans began to evacuate Greece small British detachments landed without meeting any opposition and pursued the retreating German forces to the Yugoslav border. EAM, with its military arm ELAS, had it within its power to seize political control, but did not do so. Instead it accepted the authority, though at times grudgingly, of representatives of the Greek Government in Exile and made no move to resist the re-establishment of the Cabinet in Athens on 18 October 1944. Nevertheless ELAS remained by far the most numerous armed force in the country, and the possibility of a *coup d'état* from the Left could not be ruled out as long as fundamental problems of political and social policy remained in dispute between the various Greek factions.

The British were acutely aware of this possibility, and set out to strengthen as rapidly as possible the armed force at the disposal of the non-Communist part of the Government. The first step was to bring a Greek brigade which had been fighting in Italy back to Athens, where it arrived on 9 November 1944. The second step was to disband the guerrilla forces, replacing them with a new National Guard. The effort to carry through this action precipitated a political crisis at the beginning of December 1944. Rather than surrender their dominant position peaceably, EAM and ELAS resorted to arms. The fighting which resulted lasted more than a month, to Churchill's intense dismay and embarrassment.

If one compares events in the countries under Anglo-American influence with those in the countries under Russian influence, the most striking difference was the far greater scope for the expression of indigenous political movements and sentiments manifested in the Western sphere. This was not simply the result of Anglo-American policy, though policy was no doubt partly responsible. Two other factors were also at work. One was the political tradition of countries such as France, Belgium, or even Italy—countries in which political parties had a long past and could command

shown by British and American diplomats in their dealings with Bulgarian and Rumanian envoys who tried to make terms with them in the summer of 1944. It seems clear that the Russians, like the British, were prepared to act in the spirit of their tentative division of the Balkans into separate 'spheres of operation'.

[1] Details will be found in the *Survey* for 1939–46: *Hitler's Europe*. For text of the Caserta Agreement see Woodhouse: *Apple of Discord*, pp. 306–7.

widespread public participation; countries, moreover, with a proud national tradition which compelled respect. A second difference was that, with the exception of Italy, the Western Powers had to deal with governments officially classed as allies whose sovereign rights had to be more or less respected. The Russians were dealing with ex-enemies in Rumania, Bulgaria, Hungary, and Finland, where their powers of legal intervention were vastly extended by the armistice terms. In Poland and Yugoslavia, the two Allied countries that fell to the Russian sphere of operations, the Russians faced difficulties and obstacles to their policy comparable to those that faced Britain and America in Western Europe, though in the case of Yugoslavia the difficulties remained well hidden until 1948.

(3) *The Future of Germany*

The problems of liberated Europe were all connected with and in a sense dwarfed by the question of what should be done in Germany after victory had been won. Hitler had given good evidence of German capacity to organize and dominate the Continent, and each of the Great Allies was anxious to make a repetition of the feat impossible. But it was much easier to agree on this general goal than to decide what exact punitive and preventive steps should be taken, particularly at a time when the war had not yet been won and when the military and political situation within Germany at the time of surrender could not accurately be foreseen.

The Allies, nevertheless, made an attempt to foresee and to agree. The Conference of Foreign Ministers in Moscow (October 1943) had decided to establish a European Advisory Commission;[1] and at Tehrān the Big Three decided to refer the question of future policy towards Germany to that body.[2] The problem of Germany proved so difficult, and the discretionary powers of the Commission were so slight,[3] that other problems of Allied policy towards Europe were generally dealt with through other channels.[4] The European Advisory Commission began its career with a first formal meeting on 14 January 1944. Two distinct problems faced it. First was the task of drawing up an instrument of Unconditional Surrender for Germany; second was the more difficult problem of agreeing upon the policy which should be pursued towards Germany by the victorious Powers after the surrender had taken place.

At the first meeting of the Advisory Commission an issue arose which was to paralyse detailed planning on the part of American and British author-

[1] See above, p. 332. [2] See above, p. 365.

[3] For an authoritative account of some of the difficulties that surrounded the operations of the Commission, written by the political adviser to the American member of the European Advisory Commission, see Philip E. Mosely: 'Dismemberment of Germany', *Foreign Affairs*, April 1950, xxviii. 487–98; and 'The Occupation of Germany', ibid. July 1950, xxviii. 580–604.

[4] The European Advisory Commission had some part in negotiating the armistice agreement with Bulgaria (cf. above, p. 471 and Mosely: 'The Occupation of Germany', loc. cit. pp. 581–2).

ities for many months. The British presented a proposal for the division of Germany into three zones of occupation: an eastern Russian zone, a north-western British zone and a south-western American zone. In addition, Berlin was to come under joint occupation by all three Powers.[1] This proposal did not satisfy President Roosevelt. He wished the Americans to occupy the zone in north-western Germany which the British had earmarked for themselves; the British on the other hand clung stubbornly to their original scheme.[2] Eisenhower proposed that no separation into national zones should be attempted. He thought that the addition of Russian and French representatives to a combined staff would not create insuperable obstacles; and that more would be gained by such co-operation than by any other method of controlling Germany.[3] If full quadripartite co-operation should prove too difficult, he thought a continuation of the Anglo-American partnership in defeated Germany would be desirable;[4] but this proposal was rejected by the Americans, presumably because it smacked too much of Anglo-American collaboration against Russia and all the rest of the world.

Dispute over the allocation of zones of occupation was not the only problem which dogged the steps of the European Advisory Commission. It was also seriously handicapped by the fact that a veiled contest for authority over policy towards defeated Germany was going on within the American Government itself. Representatives of the War Department blandly asserted that occupation and military government of Germany were 'military matters' which should be dealt with only by soldiers. Consequently, efforts to concert policy between the various departments of the American

[1] Ibid. pp. 589–90.

[2] Roosevelt and Churchill had already explored this conflict at the Second Cairo Conference (see above, p. 369). The motives which underlay this dispute are not entirely clear. The British scheme had the advantage that it conformed roughly to the anticipated distribution of British and American troops which would exist on V-E day. It also put the main industrial area of Germany and the principal German ports in British hands. Another thing that recommended it to the British was that the American zone, as proposed, was contiguous to France; and if the Americans insisted upon withdrawing from the occupation after a year or two (as Roosevelt at Tehrān had suggested they would do) then the French might be available to take over occupation duty from the departing Americans.

Roosevelt's counter-arguments centred round the need for German ports so that American troops could be rapidly redeployed against Japan—on the face of it a not very convincing argument. In addition, the President seems to have been influenced by his exasperation with de Gaulle. He feared disorder in post-war France, which might involve American troops if they found themselves stationed in south-west Germany, dependent on supply lines coming through France (cf. Leahy: *I Was There*, p. 398; Stimson and Bundy: *On Active Service*, p. 332). On 21 February 1944 Roosevelt wrote a memorandum to the State Department in which he said: 'I do not want the United States to have the postwar burden of reconstituting France, Italy, and the Balkans' (Hull: *Memoirs*, ii. 1612). Such a burden seems to have been connected in Roosevelt's mind with the acceptance of the south-western zone of Germany.

[3] Eisenhower: *Crusade in Europe*, p. 218.

[4] Hull: *Memoirs*, ii. 1613. Eisenhower made the first suggestion in January 1944 before taking up his command in Europe; the second in April 1944.

Government concerned with the future of Germany ran head on into stubborn sabotage by military representatives.[1] Because of the deadlock in Washington, the American member of the European Advisory Commission frequently could not get any instructions from his Government, even on minor points.

Despite these handicaps, some progress was made. In April 1944 Roosevelt agreed to accept the British proposal for the demarcation of the Soviet zone of occupation, and by the end of July details of all three zonal boundaries had been agreed upon, leaving open only the question of which of the two western zones would be assigned to Britain and which to America. During the same month, an agreement on the terms of German surrender was reached, largely on the basis of an American draft.[2]

The agreements thus painfully reached left entirely open the larger problem of Allied policy towards Germany. A first step was clearly for each government to decide what it wanted to do with Germany. How much or how little progress in this direction had been made by the British and Russian Governments in the summer of 1944 had not been made public by 1952; but as it turned out their preparation or lack of it was not the critical factor. Instead, the American Government, because of its internal disputes and indecision, prevented even the discussion of a common Allied policy for Germany. President Roosevelt's irregular methods of administration and the low prestige of the State Department within the American Government must be held responsible for what happened.

It was certainly not for lack of trying that the Americans proved unable to arrive at a firm decision on policy for Germany. Various bodies of experts had studied the problem meticulously and at length within the State Department,[3] but the recommendations which emerged from these labours had to compete with other plans issuing from other departments of the Government, most notably from the Treasury. In order to try to resolve the confusion which resulted, Roosevelt set up a Cabinet Committee on 25 August 1944 which was assigned the task of looking over the various plans then in existence and preparing recommendations for the President. The members of the Committee were the Secretaries of State, War, and the Treasury; and Roosevelt's personal friend and general assistant, Harry Hopkins, was added later.[4]

[1] Mosely: 'The Occupation of Germany', *Foreign Affairs*, July 1950, xxviii. 587–9.

[2] Ibid. pp. 594–5. These zonal boundaries were later shifted substantially, first to allow for Austria's separation from Germany, and then again later to accommodate the French claim to share in the occupation of Germany. See below, pp. 488, 548–9.

[3] For an account of the various groups concerned with planning for post-war Germany within the State Department, see *Postwar Foreign Policy Preparation*, pp. 39, 223, 271, 367–71, 393.

[4] Stimson and Bundy: *On Active Service*, p. 327.

The members of this Committee were not able to reach agreement. The main issue was whether or not to regard Germans as incurable militarists, who could be made peaceable members of the world community only by removing from their control the industrial basis for the conduct of modern war. All agreed that Germany should be demilitarized, that the Nazi Party and all associated organizations should be dissolved, war criminals punished, reparations paid to injured countries, and that Allied authorities should control education and communications for an indefinite period after the conclusion of hostilities. But Henry Morgenthau, Secretary of the Treasury, believed that as long as Germany possessed a formidable industrial plant, the danger of renewal of German aggression would remain; and he argued that the Allies should dismantle the factories and close the coal mines of the country, converting Germany into an agricultural nation.[1] This programme excited the strenuous opposition of Henry L. Stimson, Secretary for War. He argued that to destroy German industry would disrupt the European economy, and would so poison German feeling as to breed not peace but future wars.

A meeting with the President on 6 September 1944 failed to resolve the dispute. Roosevelt pointed out that Great Britain would find herself in dire economic straits after the war, and suggested that perhaps the raw materials of the Ruhr could be diverted to Britain for processing into steel. This was by way of modifying Morgenthau's proposal for the destruction of the mines of the Ruhr, but it did not signify that the President had accepted the line of argument Stimson had put before him. In general, Roosevelt felt that the Germans should be made to suffer for their misdeeds, and with a sublime disregard of economics he was prepared to drag all Europe down with defeated Germany.[2] When Morgenthau argued that by destroying the industrial potential of the Ruhr an important competitor to English industry would be removed, thus assisting British recovery, Roosevelt seems to have accepted the argument as valid.[3] But as far as Hull

[1] Morgenthau explained and defended his views in *Germany is Our Problem* (New York, Harper, 1945). The Treasury 'Program to Prevent Germany from starting a World War III' is reproduced as a frontispiece to this book. It proposed making the Ruhr area into an international zone, from which 'all industrial plants and equipment not destroyed by military action shall be completely dismantled and transported to Allied Nations as restitution. All equipment shall be removed from the mines and the mines closed'. A specific attraction of the plan was that 'under this program United States troops could be withdrawn within a relatively short time'.

[2] Stimson and Bundy: *On Active Service*, pp. 328–31, 335; Hull: *Memoirs*, ii. 1604–10. A subordinate point which also came into dispute at this time was whether or not Germany should be forcibly partitioned. The Treasury plan called for partitioning into north and south German states; the State Department, however, opposed partition unless some spontaneous separatism manifested itself in Germany.

[3] The question of Morgenthau's motives and the good faith of his arguments cannot be dissociated from the fact that he was a Jew, and could not forget what the Nazis had done to his co-religionists. His book, *Germany is Our Problem*, argues in detail that with intensive farming the German population need not starve even after industry had been eliminated from their economy; and the figures he adduced, plausible enough on the surface, may have convinced Morgenthau

and Stimson could tell, Roosevelt had not made up his mind between the rival proposals which had been presented to him at the time when he left Washington to go to meet Churchill at Quebec.

(*d*) Conferences at Quebec and Moscow

The summer and autumn of 1944 were anxious months for Churchill. Looking eastward he saw Russian power spreading over the Balkans and towards Central Europe, moving like some majestic and gigantic glacier, freezing as it advanced the genial warmth of Western influence in the peasant countries of Eastern Europe. Looking westward he saw the United States at an undreamed of pinnacle of power, too startled by the novelty of her new-found strength to know what to do with it. Worse still, he saw at home how seriously British power and the national economy had been eroded by the war, and realized that if hardship or disaster were to be avoided it would be necessary to have help from the United States even after the end of the fighting in Europe and Asia.

In the circumstances, skilful statecraft was called for. He could try to come to terms with the Russians, setting an agreed-upon limit to their expansion; he could try to put the benefit of British insight and experience in international politics at the service of the Anglo-American alliance, opening American eyes, as far as could be, to the realities of world affairs as he saw them; and he could summon his powers of persuasion to try to convince Roosevelt of the wisdom of supporting Britain and the British Empire economically and otherwise during the difficult transition from war to peace which lay ahead. Churchill set busily about these tasks. The results were his Conferences with Roosevelt at Quebec and Hyde Park (11–19 September) and with Stalin at Moscow (9–20 October).

(1) *The Second Quebec Conference, 11–19 September 1944*

When Churchill and Roosevelt, with their military and other advisers,

that he was not advocating mass starvation. Yet it is hard to believe that a man familiar with economics and finance did not appreciate the disastrous repercussions for the European economy as a whole which his programme would have brought had it been put into force; and one may suspect that Morgenthau was prepared to see Germans starve with a degree of equanimity, remembering what they had done in the extermination camps in Poland.

Another factor which cannot be wholly discounted was the influence of Communist-sympathizers in the American Government. It is true that if the Morgenthau plan had been followed, Russia would have received more reparations from Western Germany than actually she did, and that the military power of continental Europe would have been nearly destroyed, leaving Russia supreme. Moreover, the economic suffering and dislocation which would have followed a destruction of the Ruhr might well have created revolutionary discontent. Morgenthau himself must certainly be exempt from any suspicion of working secretly for the Russian interest; but it is not impossible that some of his subordinates had such ends in view. In any such speculation, one should of course remember that in 1944 the interests of Russia and the United States did not seem to be opposed; and that a man could then argue in good conscience that a policy which confirmed Russian predominance in Europe would also be to the interests of the United States, permitting an early withdrawal of American occupation forces.

met at Quebec in September 1944, the air was still electric with hope of an early German collapse. Indeed, Churchill thought it worth while to linger at Hyde Park with the President after the conclusion of the formal Conference until 19 September 1944, thinking that some startling new development might occur analogous to Badoglio's surrender of Italy which had taken place a year before in the wake of the First Quebec Conference. Instead, the repulse at Arnhem (17–25 September) disappointed his hopes. But this came after the Conference had completed its tasks; and the prevailing mood at Quebec was one of brilliant optimism as far as the war against Germany was concerned.

From the British point of view, the two most critical matters to be taken up at the Second Quebec Conference were to decide what should be the nature and scale of British participation in the war against Japan after Germany's surrender; and, intimately connected with the first point, what would be the nature and scale of Lend-Lease deliveries after the end of the German war during the period of hostilities against Japan. Two secondary but important questions were the settlement of the long dispute over the assignment of zones of occupation in Germany, and a modification of the terms of the Italian armistice which would encourage the moderate and conservative elements in Italian society and attach them to the Western Allies.

The Americans wished primarily to fix future strategy against Japan. Roosevelt was eager to settle the German problem and felt concern for Britain's economic future. He was, however, preoccupied with American internal politics. An election campaign was then in full swing, and it was important for the President to avoid any act which could be turned to account against him by the Republican candidate, Governor Thomas E. Dewey of New York. The constitutional limitation upon the presidential powers made it difficult for Roosevelt to agree to any long-range political settlements, since such matters, especially when territorial questions were concerned, were subject to approval by the Senate.[1] Moreover, it was important for Roosevelt not to appear too generous to the British or to any other foreign Power, especially when it came to giving away money. At the same time, the President had to avoid any act which could alienate any important bloc of foreign-born voters (e.g. the Poles), and, if he could present any such group with a decision which promised to help their ancestral homeland, Roosevelt was eager to do so. Hence he found himself entirely in accord with Churchill's idea of lightening the burden

[1] The accusation that he was side-stepping the prerogatives of the Senate by entering into executive agreements dealing with matters that should take treaty form was a telling one: Roosevelt had long been pilloried as a dictator, or would-be dictator, by his political opponents. The indecision of American policy, especially during the period when the war was drawing to its close, must partly be attributed to the vagueness of the limits to the President's power of making international commitments without seeking formal approval by the Senate.

placed on Italy by the armistice terms, and indeed wished to go farther than Churchill in extending economic aid to the Italians.

The military discussions at Quebec proceeded smoothly without any important Anglo-American differences of opinion. At the first plenary meeting on 13 September, Churchill offered the main British fleet for operations against Japan in the Pacific. This was something of a surprise to his own military advisers, for until almost the last minute Churchill had argued that British sea power would be much better employed in regaining the lost British possessions in Malaya.[1] Roosevelt accepted the offer at once. This, too, was rather a surprise, since Admiral King, the American Chief of Naval Operations, had frequently let the British know that he wanted no part of the British navy operating in the Pacific.[2] On the following day, King wished to reconsider the question of British naval participation in the Pacific war, but he was overruled by his colleagues, and contented himself with asserting that the British fleet would have to operate with its own supply train and bases, getting no help from the Americans on the spot.[3]

The British let the Americans take the lead as far as operations and strategy in the Pacific were concerned. The differences which arose were therefore for the most part differences between the U.S. army and navy. Marshall still thought that an invasion of Japan would be necessary before victory could be secured; Admiral Leahy believed that naval and air attack would suffice to force the Japanese to surrender. No decision was reached. Similarly, as far as immediate operations were concerned, the U.S. navy wished to attack Formosa, while the U.S. army argued that Nimitz should assault the main Philippine island, Luzon, instead. These variant plans were discussed, and in the end the army plan was approved.[4] The problems of redeployment against Japan as soon as the war in Germany ended also came up before the Combined Chiefs of Staff. Ship-

[1] Cunningham: *A Sailor's Odyssey*, pp. 568, 598, 611; Churchill, v. 504 seqq.; U.S. edition, v. 571 seqq. [2] Cunningham, op. cit. p. 611. See also above, pp. 161–2, 401–2.

[3] Cunningham, op. cit. p. 613. Admiral King's uncooperative attitude arose not from national or political motives so much as from an intense pride in his navy, with which he hoped to finish off the Japanese single-handed. His hostility to outside help was not shared by Admiral Nimitz, and, when the British fleet arrived in the Pacific, it was treated far more generously by the Americans than King's remarks had augured (ibid. pp. 613–14).

[4] Actually the progress of events quickly made this decision obsolete. As we have seen above (pp. 461–2), the unexpected weakness of Japanese resistance to naval task forces raiding the Philippine coast in mid-September persuaded Nimitz and MacArthur to alter and accelerate their plans, so that instead of attacking the Philippines from extreme north and south they united their forces to assault Leyte in the middle of the archipelago. This operation had not been conceived at the time of the Second Quebec Conference in September, yet the landing on Leyte was made on 20 October. The flexibility of amphibious attack, as it had been developed in the Pacific, was never better demonstrated than by the rapidity with which this operation was planned and carried through.

ping promised to be the factor which would limit the rapidity and scale of redeployment, and it was calculated that nearly a year would be required to bring the full weight of Anglo-American resources to bear against the Japanese.

As far as the scale of British effort against Japan was concerned, the naval question had been settled at the start. It was agreed that the British would study the question of what the Royal Air Force could do most usefully, while British ground forces were to continue the campaign in Burma, with the expectation that when that country had been reconquered, Malaya and Singapore would come next. The target date for the end of the Japanese war was put eighteen months after the conclusion of hostilities in Europe, so that the Combined Chiefs felt able to leave open detailed planning for future campaigns until later meetings.[1]

In Europe, the Combined Chiefs of Staff found relatively little to worry about. The British raised two questions. One was the transfer of the strategic air force from under Eisenhower's command.[2] This was agreed to. For the war against Japan a similar American air force, comprising the B-29s which were bombing Japan from far distant bases, had recently been established with its command headquarters in Washington. These decisions were victories for the airman's point of view, which regarded air power not as an adjunct to land forces but as a separate and properly autonomous mode of warfare.[3]

The second matter which the British raised was more delicate. They proposed that even at this late date landing craft and other resources should be assigned to the Mediterranean in order to allow a landing in Istria or along the Yugoslav coast.[4] The Americans, however, persisted in their earlier refusal to countenance Balkan operations. This was old ground to the members of the Combined Chiefs of Staff, and it does not appear that dispute was very long. Finding that the Americans would not budge, the British yielded without reviving old bitterness. It was decided that no forces would be withdrawn from Italy until the outcome of the pursuit then in progress had become clear; and that no additional forces for new operations should be assigned to the Mediterranean theatre. American participation in the liberation of Greece was expressly refused, and operations along the Yugoslav coast were to be limited, as before, to commando raids.[5]

[1] Leahy: *I Was There*, pp. 305–7.

[2] The R.A.F. had resisted Eisenhower's demand for control over the heavy bombers in the spring of 1944, and a compromise had been effected whereby Eisenhower's orders had to pass through Bomber Command. See above, pp. 390–1.

[3] Leahy: *I Was There*, pp. 307–8. Eisenhower was not pleased with the decision, but regarded it as unimportant (cf. *Crusade in Europe*, p. 307).

[4] Wilson: *Eight Years Overseas*, p. 239; Cunningham: *A Sailor's Odyssey*, p. 611.

[5] Leahy: *I Was There*, p. 308.

The question of zones of occupation in Germany was also a matter with which the Combined Chiefs of Staff were concerned. By the time Roosevelt came to Quebec he had apparently reconciled himself to accepting the zone which the British had originally proposed for American occupation in south-western Germany. The political grounds for his refusal to agree to this zone had weakened if not disappeared since the beginning of the year. Revolution seemed far less likely in France, where de Gaulle and the Committee of National Liberation had planted themselves firmly in authority; moreover, responsibility for the Balkans and South-Eastern Europe was clearly going to be primarily in Russian hands. There remained the military argument of the need for access to German ports. When the British agreed to guarantee such access by transferring Bremen and Bremerhaven to the Americans, Roosevelt accepted the south-western part of Germany as the American zone of occupation.[1] It was, however, decided to treat Austria as a separate entity (the original proposal had lumped that country with south-western Germany into a single zone) and certain changes were made in the British-American zonal boundaries to balance this diminution of the American zone.[2]

Two other questions of prime importance remained: Britain's future economic relationship with the United States and the policy to be pursued by the Allies in Germany. Roosevelt decided to avail himself of Secretary of the Treasury Henry Morgenthau's advice on both points, and accordingly summoned him unexpectedly to join the Conference at Quebec.[3] Morgenthau's technical qualification as a financial expert may have had something to do with the President's decision; it also seems probable that Roosevelt sympathized with his draconic programme for punishment of Germany and had decided to see what Churchill would think of Morgenthau's proposals.[4]

[1] Philip E. Mosely: 'The Occupation of Germany', *Foreign Affairs*, July 1950, xxviii. 597–8. Final details were not settled until February 1945 (see below, p. 538).

[2] Mosely, op. cit. p. 596.

[3] Roosevelt had first arrived in Quebec without any top-level political advisers. Hopkins was not invited, owing to a cooling off in his relations with the President (Sherwood: *Roosevelt and Hopkins*, p. 819; Eng. edition, ii. 811). Hull had been invited, but declined (*Memoirs*, ii. 1602). But Roosevelt by habit felt the need of a personal confidant and adviser. Morgenthau, an old family friend of Roosevelt's, was thus invited at least partly to fill the gap created by Hopkins's absence.

[4] For these proposals see above, pp. 482–4. The conviction that Germany should be made to suffer for the wrongs done to the world by the Nazis was in a sense the obverse of Roosevelt's belief in the goodness and rationality of mankind at large. If a nation somehow failed to exhibit goodness and rationality, thus challenging Roosevelt's general belief about human nature, it endangered its claim to belong to humanity and deserved, Roosevelt came to feel, the severest sort of punishment. The inhumanity of idealists, particularly when their ideals show signs of failing to fit the situation, is proverbial, and Roosevelt seems to have fallen into this trap for a few weeks in the autumn of 1944. For evidence of his peculiar vindictiveness towards Germany see Elliot Roosevelt, ed.: *The Roosevelt Letters*, iii. 498.

Morgenthau arrived full of ardour for his plan to destroy German industry. He was also prepared to offer the British the prospect of a large American loan to help with economic recovery and reconversion to peacetime patterns of production. When he first expounded his plan for Germany to Churchill the Prime Minister reacted violently, declaring, according to one report, that what Morgenthau proposed would chain England to a dead body.[1] Subsequently, however, Churchill changed his mind. Two things may have led to this result. One was Morgenthau's argument that destruction of German industry would help Britain by eliminating a dangerous economic competitor. Another was the loan which Morgenthau suggested. He proposed that Britain should receive Lend-Lease aid to the amount of $3,500 million during the period between the end of the war in Europe and the surrender of Japan; and, in addition, should be granted a credit of $3,000 million for other, non-military purposes. With such a sum the British could hope to maintain their home economy while building up export trade to a point where self-sufficiency could be once again attained.

After his return from the Quebec Conference, Morgenthau denied that the offer of such a loan and acceptance of the Morgenthau Plan for Germany were in any way connected.[2] One may assume that Morgenthau and Roosevelt did not present the two proposals as dependent on one another; but it is not certain that Churchill did not make the connexion in his own mind. He may have believed that Morgenthau was about to inherit Hopkins's old position as friend and confidant of Roosevelt; and in any case he must have been impressed with the importance of reaching friendly terms with the Secretary of the Treasury, who would, presumably, have a leading voice in deciding future American financial policy towards Britain. If acceptance of his scheme for Germany were necessary to win Morgenthau's support, Churchill may have felt that at worst a desert in the Ruhr was preferable to a smokeless Britain.

Whatever his calculations, Churchill on 15 September 1944 set his initials to the following memorandum which he himself had drawn up:

> The ease with which the metallurgical, chemical, and electric industries in Germany can be converted from peace to war has already been impressed upon us by bitter experience. It must also be remembered that the Germans have devastated a large portion of the industries of Russia and other neighbouring Allies, and it is only in accordance with justice that these injured countries should be entitled to remove the machinery they require in order to repair the losses they have suffered. The industries referred to in the Ruhr and in the Saar would therefore be necessarily put out of action and closed down. It was felt that the two districts should be put under some body under the world organization which would supervise the dismantling of these industries and make sure that they were not started up again by some subterfuge.

[1] Hull: *Memoirs*, ii. 1615.

[2] Ibid.

This programme for eliminating the war-making industries in the Ruhr and in the Saar is looking forward to converting Germany into a country primarily agricultural and pastoral in its character.

The Prime Minister and the President were in agreement upon this programme.

This memorandum was initialed 'O.K., F.D.R., W.S.C.'[1] When Eden arrived in Quebec on the day after this memorandum had been initialed, he was flabbergasted and argued heatedly against it. But he arrived too late to do anything at the time.[2]

As for the matter of American credits and the continuation of Lend-Lease, Morgenthau's proposals remained merely tentative. It was agreed that an Anglo-American committee of experts should work out details; and Roosevelt and Churchill initialed a brief memorandum which defined the general basis upon which the Committee should work. The most important principle affirmed in this memorandum was that after Germany's defeat Lend-Lease supplies should continue on a scale which would make it possible for the British Government to use labour and other resources for rebuilding exports and raising home living standards.[3]

When the news reached Washington of what Morgenthau had accomplished at Quebec, Hull and Stimson were as angry and amazed as Eden had been. They each refused to regard the matter as closed, and proceeded to draw up memoranda for the President putting forth their views. Roosevelt himself did not return to Washington at once. When the formal meetings at Quebec ended on 16 September, he and Churchill went to Hyde Park, and it was there that the first bombardment from Stimson and Hull reached Roosevelt. Stimson appealed to Roosevelt's idealism. 'It would be just such a crime as the Germans themselves hoped to perpetrate upon their victims—it would be a crime against civilization itself', he declared.[4] Hull pointed out that the Soviet Government might have other views; and in a later interview with the President reproached him for having disregarded regular State Department channels. Hull also argued that if the proposal became public it would prove injurious to Roosevelt's humane reputation and might prove politically damaging.[5]

On 21 September the news did leak out, apparently through Treasury channels.[6] Public reaction to the news was generally critical,[7] and perhaps

[1] Stimson and Bundy: *On Active Service*, p. 333. [2] Hull: *Memoirs*, ii. 1615.

[3] Hancock and Gowing: *British War Economy*, pp. 527–8.

[4] Stimson and Bundy: *On Active Service*, p. 334. [5] Hull: *Memoirs*, ii. 1616–18.

[6] Ibid. p. 1620. Roosevelt at first assumed that the leak had occurred in the State Department, part of a campaign to discredit the Morgenthau Plan; and Stimson took some pains to prove that such was not the case.

[7] e.g. *New York Herald Tribune*, editorial, 27 September, Arthur Krock in *New York Times*,

for the first time Roosevelt saw how monstrous the Morgenthau proposals were. By 27 September the President had decided that the Plan was a mistake, and he told Stimson that he did not really mean to turn Germany out to pasture. When Stimson interviewed him on 3 October and showed him the wording of the memorandum he had initialed, Roosevelt showed signs of surprise, and declared that he must have signed it without much thought.[1]

Having burnt his fingers with the Morgenthau Plan for Germany, Roosevelt reacted by refusing to consider any alternative policy. He wrote to Hull on 20 October: 'I dislike making detailed plans for a country we do not yet occupy.'[2] And a few days later another memorandum from the President, addressed to the War Department, put a stop for a period of about six months to all efforts to make plans for Germany.[3] This ostrich attitude towards the future prevented whatever chance there may have been for arriving at Allied agreement upon policy towards Germany through the European Advisory Commission or in any other way, and left the subordinate American officials who were charged with the task completely at sea. In the absence of foresight and agreement matters were left to drift, and tripartite agreement of a sort was not reached until the time of the Potsdam Conference in July 1945.[4]

29 September, Edwin Lahey in *Chicago Daily News*, 2 October 1944. In a campaign speech on 4 November Governor Dewey attributed the prolongation of the war against Germany to the Morgenthau Plan. Text in *New York Herald Tribune*, 5 November 1944.

[1] The question of the state of Roosevelt's health was one which had been the subject of considerable gossip throughout the autumn of 1944. Roosevelt himself believed that such talk was part of a deliberate campaign against him conducted by the Republicans (cf. Sherwood: *Roosevelt and Hopkins*, pp. 820, 824, 829; Eng. edition, ii. 812, 816, 821). But his friends were privately worried. Stimson wrote in his diary at the time of the Quebec Conference: 'I have been much troubled by the President's physical condition. He was distinctly not himself Saturday [September 9]. He had a cold and seemed tired out. I rather fear the effects of this hard conference upon him. I am particularly troubled . . . that he is going up there without any real preparation for the solution of the underlying and fundamental problem of how to treat Germany. So far as he had evidenced it in his talks with us, he has had absolutely no study or training in the very difficult problem we have to decide. . . .' (Stimson and Bundy: *On Active Service*, pp. 331–2.) Cf. Sherwood: *Roosevelt and Hopkins*, p. 821; Eng. edition, ii. 813.

It seems, indeed, that Roosevelt never entirely threw off the effects of the prolonged bout of influenza and sinus infection which descended upon him after his return from the Tehrān Conference; and that as physical weakness and fatigue closed in upon him he relied more and more upon spur of the moment decisions, without always considering the full implications of his acts or even remembering in detail what he had done. Cf. Byrnes's account of his failure to prepare himself for the Yalta Conference (Byrnes: *Speaking Frankly*, p. 23). The occasional petulance of Roosevelt's behaviour, so alien to his normal personality, cannot be understood without bearing in mind his physical condition. That his decline coincided with a time when decisions of the highest moment had to be made cannot be regarded as anything but unfortunate, and to the highest degree.

[2] Hull: *Memoirs*, ii. 1611.

[3] Philip E. Mosely: 'The Occupation of Germany', *Foreign Affairs*, July 1950, xxviii. 596.

[4] Churchill's reaction to this episode had not been made public in 1952; nor was it possible to say whether the Quebec memorandum ever came up for Cabinet discussion in London. In any case, when once the Americans had turned their backs upon the Morgenthau Plan in its original

Acceptance of the Morgenthau Plan was surely a monstrous and unmitigated mistake of statecraft. The publicity it received and the timing of the whole affair multiplied the damage to the Allied interest enormously. When the news broke in the American press on 21 September, the critical battle of Arnhem was at its height, and in so far as the German soldiers heard what Roosevelt and Churchill proposed to do to their country it must have helped to steel them for the battle. Indeed everything about the Plan—its provisions and the fact that Morgenthau was a Jew as well as a banker and capitalist—lent itself to Nazi propaganda. It is impossible to escape the conclusion that many thousands of German soldiers decided it was better to face death in battle than undergo the slower death by starvation which was the alternative the Morgenthau Plan seemed to offer. From the German point of view, the words of the Anglo-Americans now threatened a fate as desperate as that they already feared the Russians would visit upon them in retribution for their own crimes. There no longer seemed any reason to prefer the West to the Bolsheviks, and Goebbels made the most of it.[1]

Roosevelt's aberration and Churchill's acceptance of the Morgenthau Plan were the more strange since at almost the same time the two men discussed the steps by which Italian economic and other disabilities could be lightened. While they were staying at Hyde Park a formal declaration was drawn up, and after it had been approved by the British Cabinet, it was made public on 26 September 1944. The declaration promised that an increasing measure of power would be entrusted to the Italian Government in domestic matters; and as token of the change the name of the Allied Control Commission was altered by the omission of the word Control. In addition, the Italian Government were invited to exchange diplomatic agents with the Western Powers; and Roosevelt and Churchill informed the world that they would instruct their delegates at the Second UNRRA Council meeting to press for the inclusion of Italy among the nations entitled to receive a certain measure of assistance from that organization.[2] The Roosevelt-Churchill declaration on Italy also pro-

form, it was dead; but the punitive principle which underlay Morgenthau's proposals did not vanish from American official thinking until more than a year had passed.

[1] Wilmot (*Struggle for Europe*, p. 550) says that letters captured from German soldiers proved the impact of the Morgenthau Plan on German morale so impressively that Eisenhower was impelled to seek for a modification in the Unconditional Surrender slogan in order to undo some of the damage to the Allied cause. Eisenhower's effort was, of course, vain. Yet in spite of the Morgenthau Plan and the unmitigated demand for Unconditional Surrender, when German strength finally reached the point of collapse, German soldiers much preferred Anglo-American to Russian captivity. See below, p. 569.

[2] The combined American and British voice was sufficient to cause the UNRRA Council on 26 September 1944 to approve the dispatch of medical supplies to Italy, and the provision of

mised Anglo-American help in the reconstruction of the Italian economy, primarily to serve military aims, and offered to repeal restrictions on Italian foreign trade.[1] As these promises were acted upon, Italy escaped from the most galling shackles of the armistice agreement, though the damages of the war with attendant distress and unrest lingered on.

On the last day before Churchill departed from Hyde Park for London he once again discussed with Roosevelt the question of atomic research and the exchange of information between British and American authorities. Roosevelt promised that Britain, Canada, and the United States should share information concerning industrial uses for atomic energy, but apparently he was more reserved about undertaking to satisfy all British curiosity concerning the military secrets of the atomic bomb.[2]

(2) *The Conference in Moscow, 9–20 October 1944*

While Churchill could legitimately feel that he had accomplished much at the Second Quebec Conference towards defining the relationship between Britain and America during the period between the defeat of Germany and the defeat of Japan, he had not made much progress towards concerting Anglo-American policy in Eastern Europe. It does not appear that the situation in Poland and the Balkans came up for any formal discussion at Quebec; but the President had already made it quite clear that he would take no active steps to intervene in Eastern Europe, at least not until after the election in November. The Polish question in particular was too explosive, since any step Roosevelt could take would be almost sure to antagonize most of the Polish-Americans.

Without American support, Churchill felt he would have to do what he could alone. On his return to London on 25 September he found the situation sufficiently critical to warrant prompt consultation with Stalin. Churchill first hoped that a meeting of the Big Three could be arranged to handle the problems which had arisen as a result of the rapid advance of the Red Army into the Balkans;[3] but Roosevelt felt he could not leave the United States until after the election, and Stalin as usual refused to venture from his capital. Consequently, Churchill decided to go to Moscow without Roosevelt. He arrived on 8 October,[4] accompanied by Eden.

welfare services for children and expectant mothers. Text of the UNRRA Council resolution may be found in *Documents on American Foreign Relations, 1944–1945*, pp. 375–6.

[1] Text of the declaration may be found ibid. pp. 165–6. Limiting Italian reconstruction to the service of military aims was a concession to Churchill, who naturally did not want to see Italy better off than Britain, where reconstruction still had to be postponed until the war's end.

[2] Leahy: *I Was There*, p. 312.

[3] Cf. his remarks to the House of Commons, 28 September 1944, H.C.Deb. 5th ser., vol. 403, coll. 497–8; Hull: *Memoirs*, ii. 1705.

[4] There is reason to suppose that Churchill decided to make this trip at very short notice, and

The U.S. Ambassador, Averell Harriman, was, at the suggestion of the President, invited to attend the meetings between Churchill and Stalin as a personal observer for Roosevelt. He was, however, not given the power to commit the United States to anything, and apparently remained silent throughout the meetings.[1]

The British had two political matters which they hoped to be able to settle with Stalin.[2] One was to define the limits of Russian influence in Balkan and Danubian Europe; the other was to bring a final quietus to the Polish problem if that were humanly possible. In addition, Churchill wished to exchange opinions about the political settlement of Europe at large, the future of Germany, France's place in the Grand Alliance, &c.[3]

One of the first issues, and perhaps the one which brought Churchill in such haste to Moscow, was the question of the Bulgarian armistice. The Russians had suggested that the Bulgars should be allowed to keep some or all of the territory in Thrace and Macedonia which they had occupied during the war; and it was not until Churchill had been in Moscow for three days that the Allied Governments presented an ultimatum to the Bulgars requiring the prompt evacuation of these territories.[4] It is reasonable to detect Churchill's hand in bringing about this reversal of the earlier Soviet position.

But Stalin's compliance was secured only at a price. The negotiations which had been dragging on between the British, American, and Russian Governments since May 1944 concerning the division of the Balkan countries into Russian and British spheres of operation had not led to formal written agreement. Churchill was now anxious to pin the Russians down, believing that without some definite understanding the Russians might take advantage of the armistice agreements and of their military position to exclude British (and American) influence from the whole of South-Eastern Europe.[5]

had not anticipated going to Moscow so soon when he bid Roosevelt adieu at Hyde Park (cf. Sherwood: *Roosevelt and Hopkins*, p. 832; Eng. edition, ii. 824; Mikolajczyk: *Pattern of Soviet Domination*, p. 103).

[1] Sherwood: *Roosevelt and Hopkins*, p. 834; Eng. edition, ii. 826. Incidentally, it was during the exchanges of telegrams preparatory to this Conference in Moscow that Hopkins came back into Roosevelt's favour. The fiasco of the Morgenthau interlude may have helped to convince Roosevelt that he needed Hopkins's advice and companionship; and a bold action by Hopkins by which he stopped a telegram which seemed to give Churchill authority to speak on behalf of the United States at the forthcoming meeting in Moscow marked Hopkins's full reinstatement as Roosevelt's Man Friday. Sherwood tells the story vividly (ibid. pp. 832–4; Eng. edition, ii. 824–6). It provides an interesting and somewhat dismaying insight into Roosevelt's careless methods in the conduct of high affairs—at least at this period of his life.

[2] For the military discussions which accompanied this Conference, see below, pp. 518–19.

[3] Only the Polish side of the negotiations had been made public by 1952, and that from the point of view of the Polish Government in Exile. Hence it was impossible to describe the conversations in any detail or with full confidence in the accuracy of the information that was available up to the time of writing.

[4] See above, pp. 470–1.

[5] When Churchill journeyed to Moscow, the main British landing in Greece had not yet

In May 1944 the Russians had tentatively accepted a division of the Balkans which assigned both Greece and Yugoslavia to the British sphere of operations.[1] But by October the situation had fundamentally changed. The Red Army was firmly established in Rumania and Bulgaria, and had recently entered Yugoslavia and Hungary as well. On the other hand, British influence in Greece and Yugoslavia was still confined to what military liaison missions could exercise over the guerrilla organizations of those countries, supplemented, potentially, by British control over the Greek and Yugoslav Governments in Exile.

The agreement which emerged from Churchill's discussion with Stalin reflected the new military balance in the Balkans. Russia was guaranteed pre-eminent influence in Rumania, Bulgaria, and Hungary; Britain was to exercise a comparable control over Greek affairs; and influence in Yugoslavia was to be divided equally between Britain and Russia. Indeed, a curious effort was made to reduce the matter to percentages. According to reports sent to Washington by American diplomats, Russian influence in Rumania, Bulgaria, and Hungary was fixed at 75–80 per cent., while influence in Yugoslavia was to be divided 50–50.[2]

Such pseudo-mathematics, of course, neglected whatever indigenous political impulses might develop within the countries concerned, and the only sort of meaning that can be attached to it is this: the percentages might serve as a guide to the numerical division between pro-British and pro-Russian Cabinet members in the Governments to be formed in the various Balkan states. It seems possible that this is what Churchill and Stalin actually had in mind, and helps to explain, for example, the curious efforts the Russians made to bring non-Communist 'Western' representatives into the Rumanian Cabinet which they installed in March 1945.[3]

It is possible that Churchill raised with Stalin the question of what would happen if the British found it necessary to take military action in Greece against ELAS. The Americans, at any rate, believed that an informal understanding had been reached, according to which, in return for Stalin's acquiescence in any action the British might find necessary in

occurred. EAM/ELAS was without question the predominant military and political organization in the country, and if ELAS had elected to resist the British landing parties and refused to admit the Greek exiled Government, there would have been little Churchill could do. As it was, the British found it hard to scrape together the handful of troops actually assigned to the landing in Greece.

[1] See above, pp. 422–3.

[2] Hull: *Memoirs*, ii. 1458.

[3] Cf. Roberts: *Rumania*, p. 271, for an alternative interpretation of Russian motives. Hull does not say whether influence in Greece was also apportioned by percentages, but it is an interesting coincidence, if nothing more, that the EAM members of Papandreou's Cabinet held just 25 per cent. of the seats, leaving 75 per cent. for pro-British political leaders. It seems likely that Churchill took the Greek 'Government of National Unity' as his model and persuaded Stalin to accept it as a sort of prototype for the Governments to be established in other Balkan countries.

Greece, the Russians were accorded a similar free hand in 'maintaining order' in Rumania.[1]

Finally, Churchill once again broached the question of a British landing at the head of the Adriatic or elsewhere on its eastern side. The Americans had vetoed such a proposal at the Second Quebec Conference just a month earlier, but Stalin showed no hesitation in agreeing that the operation would be desirable.[2]

From Stalin's point of view the bargain he had struck with Churchill seemed highly satisfactory. By abandoning Greece and the Greek Communists to Churchill's mercy he had secured Russian predominance in Rumania, Bulgaria, and Hungary against British (or American)[3] diplomatic harassment. In a speech delivered in celebration of the anniversary of the Bolshevik Revolution, on 6 November 1944, Stalin went out of his way to express his satisfaction. He said: 'The recent talks in Moscow with Mr. Churchill, the head of the British Government, and Mr. Eden, the British Foreign Secretary, are to be viewed as an even more striking indication of the consolidation of the United Nations front, held as these talks were in an atmosphere of friendship and a spirit of perfect unanimity.'[4]

Churchill, too, could feel that he had made the best of a ticklish situation, setting an agreed limit to Russian expansion into the Balkans, and securing a British foothold in Greece and in Yugoslavia. With Stalin's approval of a landing at the head of the Adriatic, he could hope to break down the stubborn American resistance to such operations;[5] and, by planting British troops in both Greece and Yugoslavia, he could hope to secure

[1] Byrnes: *Speaking Frankly*, p. 53.

[2] Wilmot (*Struggle for Europe*, p. 630) says that Stalin 'strongly advocated' such a landing. This may be true, for Stalin's plans called for the Red Army columns which had penetrated into Yugoslavia to turn northward into Hungary, and a British landing on the Adriatic coast would help to prevent any German flank attack. On the other hand, Stalin may have agreed to Churchill's proposal simply because he felt that the British were resolved to land in Yugoslavia anyway in order to create the military basis for the 50–50 division of influence to which he and Churchill had just agreed.

[3] It cannot be said whether Churchill had secured Roosevelt's approval for a deal along these lines in advance of his journey to Moscow. The U.S. Ambassador, Harriman, was an observer at the meetings; and the American Government did accept the formal agreement which resulted, despite the stern disapproval of Hull and others in the State Department (cf. Hull: *Memoirs*, ii. 1458).

[4] Stalin: *Great Patriotic War*, p. 138.

[5] For Churchill's renewed efforts to persuade the Americans see Wilmot: *Struggle for Europe*, p. 543. Pending American approval for an attack at the head of the Adriatic—a question which was argued for the last time at the Malta Conference at the end of January 1945 just before Yalta—the British attempted to enlarge the scale of their operations in Yugoslavia. In November 1944 General Wilson proposed to land an armoured regiment and some artillery at Zara in order to support the Partisans and harass the Germans in Bosnia more effectively. But Tito was thoroughly suspicious of British political motives, and refused to admit British forces, suggesting instead that their equipment be handed over to his own men (Wilson: *Eight Years Overseas*, p. 239). It seems likely that Tito was acting on his own initiative in this matter, rather than on any instructions or advice from the Russians. The effect of his decision was to prevent Churchill from establishing a military basis upon which his claim to equal influence in Yugoslav affairs could stand.

the Aegean and Adriatic coasts for the West in any post-war balance of power. The Mediterranean 'life line' of the British Empire would thus be reasonably secure.

Since each found the bargain to his advantage Churchill and Stalin had little difficulty in reaching agreement over the Balkans. Poland, however, proved a more intractable matter. Churchill was not prepared to abandon his support of the Polish Government in Exile, partly because he felt morally obliged to support the Poles on whose behalf Great Britain had originally, in form if not in fact, gone to war; and partly because he wished to see Poland 'a champion of Europe' against, or at least independent of, the Soviet Union.[1] Probably Churchill hoped to reach an agreement with Russia about Poland analogous to the agreement he had made about Yugoslavia: foreign influence in that country, he may have hoped, would be about evenly divided between East and West. The way to such a solution was obviously to arrange a fusion between the Polish Government in London and the Lublin Committee, like the parallel fusions for which Churchill had successfully laboured in Greece and Yugoslavia in the summer of the year.

When Churchill went to Moscow in October he had with him a proposal, aimed at that result, which Mikolajczyk had drawn up in August. Mikolajczyk's plan called for the formation of a Polish Cabinet in which the Communists would have a fifth of the seats—a proportion which was not likely to appeal to them or to the Russians. Moreover, Mikolajczyk could not bring himself and his colleagues in London to accept the Curzon Line, upon which Stalin had so frequently insisted. His proposal declared that the centres of Polish culture in the east and the sources of raw materials there would have to remain within Poland. Given the interpretation of Polish cultural centres which prevailed among the Poles in London, this provision meant that the Poles were not willing to make more than minor adjustments of their inter-war frontier with Russia.[2]

Nevertheless, Mikolajczyk's plan was an opening wedge and could provide a basis for renewed negotiation. Upon their arrival in Moscow Churchill and Eden presumably urged Stalin to see Mikolajczyk once again, and, when Stalin consented, they sent off urgent requests to the Premier of the Polish Government in Exile to come and join them. Mikolajczyk, accordingly, arrived in Moscow on 12 October 1944 and on the following day met with Stalin, Molotov, Churchill, Eden, Harriman, and others. Mikolajczyk went over the main points of his proposal. When

[1] W. Anders: *An Army in Exile* (London, Macmillan, 1949), p. 210.

[2] Text of Mikolajczyk's plan may be found as an appendix to his book, *Pattern of Soviet Domination*, pp. 328–31.

he had finished, Churchill opened the discussion by submitting that the Lublin Committee should have a larger representation in the new Cabinet. Stalin then declared that the plan had two defects: it neglected the Lublin Committee and it failed to recognize the Curzon Line which was the only acceptable Russo-Polish frontier. Churchill then seconded Stalin's demand for the Curzon Line, while offering the prospect of new territory in the west as compensation.

Mikolajczyk, however, refused to agree to any such curtailment of Polish territory in the east. Molotov intervened in the argument that ensued to remark that at Tehrān all the Big Three had agreed on the Curzon Line as the proper frontier for the new Poland. This came as a great shock to Mikolajczyk, who had pinned his hopes upon what he understood to be Roosevelt's assurances of support for Polish claims to the eastern provinces of pre-war Poland.[1] No one contradicted Molotov's statement, but Mikolajczyk remained stubbornly defiant. After this head-on collision, there was little more to be said, and the meeting broke up without reaching any agreement.[2]

On the next day, 14 October, Churchill and Eden interviewed representatives of the Polish Committee of National Liberation, whose idea for the formation of a satisfactory fusion Government was to give only a quarter of the Cabinet seats to representatives of the London Government in Exile.[3] This was a far cry from Mikolajczyk's offer, and no compromise could be reached.

But it was not this issue that led to final failure. In conversation with Churchill, Stalin expressed his disrespect for the Lublin Committee. He did not insist upon making the Committee the basis for a new Polish Government, merely that it should be an equal partner with the London Government.[4] What Stalin did insist upon was that any remodelled Polish Government should recognize the Curzon Line as the fixed boundary of Poland on the east, and to this Mikolajczyk steadily refused to agree. However, towards the end of the negotiation, Mikolajczyk did make an important concession. He stated to Churchill that, if the Soviet Government would deviate slightly from the Curzon Line to allow Lwów and neighbouring oilfields to remain under Polish sovereignty, he would try to persuade the other members of his Government in London to accept

[1] See above, p. 430.

[2] Mikolajczyk: *Pattern of Soviet Domination*, pp. 104–8; Anders: *An Army in Exile*, pp. 237–8; Ciechanowski: *Defeat in Victory*, pp. 346–8. Differences in detail between these accounts make it clear that exact accuracy cannot be expected, but all agree on the main lines of the conversation.

[3] Ciechanowski: *Defeat in Victory*, p. 354.

[4] Ibid. pp. 350, 353. If there is any truth in the suggestion that Churchill, too, was willing to settle for a 50–50 deal in Poland like the deal he had made with Stalin over Yugoslavia, there was no real conflict between the two. This might account for Stalin's remarkably friendly tone in his speech of 6 November 1944, quoted above.

the settlement.[1] When Churchill reported this promise to Stalin, the Soviet dictator was not impressed. He refused to offer Lwów to the Poles, and refused also to agree to Churchill's proposal that Mikolajczyk should become Premier of a future Government of National Unity.

The final effort to come to an agreement was made when Mikolajczyk went to see Stalin privately, seeking to persuade him at least to grant Lwów to Poland. But Stalin was inflexible. He did take pains to assure the Polish Premier that he had no intention of making Poland into a Communist state after the war. He also suggested that, as soon as Mikolajczyk had persuaded his Cabinet in London to accept Russian territorial demands, he would be free and welcome to go to Poland and take part in the formation of a new Government with the Lublin Poles.[2]

This appeared to be the sole remaining hope for agreement, but it did not seem an empty one. Mikolajczyk had shown signs of waking up to the harsh realities of his position, and perhaps he could persuade his fellow exiles in London to yield before it was too late. Or so Churchill hoped. The official communiqué, issued on 21 October 1944, expressed a spirit of optimism. It said:

> Important progress was made towards the solution of the Polish question, which was closely discussed between the Soviet and British Governments. . . . These discussions have notably narrowed the differences and dispelled misconceptions. The conversations are continuing on the outstanding points.
>
> The march of events in south-east Europe was fully considered. Agreement was reached on remaining points in the Bulgarian Armistice terms. The two Governments agreed to pursue a joint policy in Yugoslavia designed to . . . bring about a solution of Yugoslav internal difficulties by a union between the Royal Yugoslav Government and the National Liberation Movement. . . .[3]

A communiqué issued simultaneously by the Lublin Committee was notably conciliatory in its tone. It said, in part:

> At the Conference, which took place in a spirit of mutual understanding and friendship, the delegation of the Polish Committee of National Liberation declared its readiness to come to an agreement with the representatives who had arrived from London. . . . The delegation . . . emphasized in doing so that it always considered its basic task to be the achievement of the unification of the Polish people, and that for the sake of this principle it is prepared to facilitate all sincere efforts to reach this goal. . . .[4]

Although the Polish and Balkan questions dominated the Moscow Con-

[1] In making this concession, Mikolajczyk obviously had his conversation with Roosevelt in mind. In June 1944 the President had dwelt upon his confidence in being able to persuade Stalin to give Lwów to the Poles (see above, p. 430), and Mikolajczyk had probably come to feel that this was the best he could hope for in view of Churchill's vehement efforts to persuade him to agree to the Soviet territorial demands.

[2] Mikolajczyk: *Pattern of Soviet Domination*, pp. 111–12; Ciechanowski: *Defeat in Victory*, p. 354.

[3] Rothstein: *Soviet Foreign Policy during the Patriotic War*, ii. 162.

[4] Ibid. pp. 162–3.

ference, Churchill and Eden found time to run over with Stalin other outstanding problems of European affairs.[1] The question of the future of Germany was discussed; the British raised the matter of finding a place for France on a future Allied Control Commission in Germany; they also agreed upon the advisability of revising the Montreux Convention which defined Turkey's powers over the Dardanelles and Bosporus. In the absence of President Roosevelt, however, no final decisions could be taken on such matters as these.[2]

Despite the fact that the Americans were suspicious of the agreements which Churchill and Stalin had reached concerning the Balkans,[3] Churchill himself declared to the House of Commons, on 27 October 1944, that 'the results achieved on this occasion at Moscow have been highly satisfactory'. He continued: 'I am very glad to inform the House that our relations with Soviet Russia were never more close, intimate and cordial than they are at the present time. Never before have we been able to reach so high a degree of frank and friendly discussions, of the most delicate and often potentially vexatious topics. . . .'[4] With respect to the Polish problem, Churchill said that solution of the many difficulties had come a great deal nearer, and he expressed the hope that Mikolajczyk would soon be able to return to Moscow, and to complete negotiations for his return to Poland as head of a Polish Government that would be recognized by all the Great Powers.[5]

In view of what had passed at Quebec and Moscow, Churchill had indeed much to feel proud of. The strain which had arisen early in 1944 between himself and Roosevelt had been relieved; Britain had been assured of economic assistance; her part in the Japanese war had been more precisely defined; and the long divergence between American and British policy with respect to France and Italy seemed to have come to an end. Much the same could be said of relations with Russia. An understanding in the Balkans had been reached, and what promised to be a satisfactory solution of the Polish issue seemed to be close at hand. Everything depended on Mikolajczyk and the Poles in London: if they would now at last accept the conditions that Stalin had laid down, the most persistent sore spot in Allied relations might begin to heal. Unfortunately for Churchill's hopes, however, matters did not go smoothly among the Poles; and within six weeks of his return from Moscow fresh discord had

[1] See below, pp. 518–20, for an account of the negotiations about Russian participation in the war against Japan.

[2] Cf. Stettinius: *Roosevelt and the Russians*, pp. 117, 123, 238.

[3] Hull: *Memoirs*, ii. 1458.

[4] 27 October 1944, H.C.Deb. 5th ser., vol. 404, col. 491.

[5] Ibid. coll. 494–5.

broken out between Britain and America over events in Italy, Belgium, and, above all, Greece.

(ii) Post-war Plans: Dumbarton Oaks, 21 August–9 October 1944

The Four-Power Declaration produced by the Conference of Foreign Ministers in Moscow (October 1943) had officially committed the United States, Great Britain, the Soviet Union, and China to the establishment 'at the earliest practicable date', of an international organization for the maintenance of peace. This declaration had been made largely upon the initiative of Secretary Hull, and, during the intricate negotiations which followed, the Americans remained the most eager of the Great Powers to press on with the task of forming a new international body to inherit the functions of the League of Nations.

There were two reasons for this. Men who remembered what had happened after 1918 in the United States feared that a similar reaction against foreign entanglements might develop after the end of the Second World War. If such a reaction should come, American opinion might turn against participation in any proposed form of international organization, as in 1920. To prevent such an outcome seemed vitally important to Hull and Roosevelt; and the best way to avoid the danger seemed to be to act before reaction could set in, that is, before the war ended. Accordingly the Americans did everything they could to hurry negotiations along, and took a leading part in suggesting procedure, making proposals, organizing conferences, &c.

A second reason why the Americans were peculiarly active in the negotiations which led finally to the signing of the United Nations Charter at San Francisco in June 1945 was that they tended to think of the establishment of an international organization as a sort of talisman which would possess a powerful virtue to heal disputes among the nations. Instead of regarding international politics as essentially and necessarily an affair of clashing interests and struggle for power, Americans, both officials and the general public, tended to think that international politics were, or at least should be, a matter of legal right and wrong,[1] and that the common interest of all men and nations in the maintenance of peace was so obvious and so compelling that only hardened criminals would think of transgressing against it. Most Americans agreed with Secretary Hull's heartfelt remarks to a group of Senators:

> All these principles and policies [of international co-operation] are so beneficial and appealing to the sense of justice, of right, and of the well-being of free peoples everywhere that in the course of a few years the entire international machinery should be working fairly satisfactorily. Of course, some years will

[1] Cf. George F. Kennan: *American Diplomacy, 1900–1950* (University of Chicago Press, 1951), pp. 95–103, for some interesting remarks on this American penchant.

be necessary to perfect and broaden and otherwise develop such a political, economic, and peace structure.[1]

The British public quite generally shared these hopes and convictions. Churchill, familiar as he was with the history of past wars and with the practice of diplomacy, hoped that some good might come of a new international organization; but he was not prepared to abandon more traditional methods of protecting the power and security of Great Britain on the strength of such a hope. In the House of Commons Churchill was cautious in referring to post-war international organization, seeking, perhaps, to discourage extravagant expectations.[2] Yet, whatever Churchill's personal reservations and doubts, the British Government as a whole were willing and eager to attempt to establish an effective international legal order, and approached the problem in much the same spirit as did Americans.

Stalin, too, wanted an international organization. But the aims and nature of the organization he conceived were notably different from those advocated in the West. He believed that a desirable international organization would be fundamentally a device for extending the Grand Alliance into the future. Hence its membership should not be universal, but rather should be limited to the states which had fought on the Allied side in the war. And the aim of the organization should be primarily to keep Germany and Japan weak and harmless, not to create and enforce some system of abstract legal justice among nations.[3]

As a presupposition for the smooth working of such an organization, Stalin may have believed that each of the Big Three would agree, tacitly or explicitly, not to interfere with one another's spheres of influence. That his own arrangements might violate American and British concepts of democracy and national self-determination must have seemed irrelevant

[1] Hull: *Memoirs*, ii. 1665.

[2] 24 May 1944, H.C.Deb. 5th ser., vol. 400, coll. 782–6; 2 August 1944, ibid. vol. 402, coll. 1486–7.

[3] Stalin made his point of view quite clear in a speech on 6 November 1944, delivered when the Dumbarton Oaks Conference had adjourned after reaching a deadlock on two key issues. He said:

'. . . What means are there to preclude fresh aggression on Germany's part, and, if war should start nevertheless, to nip it in the bud and give it no opportunity to develop into a big war?

There is only one means to this end, in addition to the complete disarmament of the aggressive nations: that is, to establish a special organization made up of representatives of the peace-loving nations to uphold peace and safeguard security; to put the necessary minimum of armed forces required for the averting of aggression at the disposal of the directing body of this organization, and to obligate this organization to employ these armed forces without delay if it becomes necessary to avert or stop aggression and punish the culprits. . . .

Can we expect the actions of this world organization to be sufficiently effective? They will be effective if the great powers which have borne the brunt of the war against Hitler Germany continue to act in a spirit of unanimity and accord. They will not be effective if this essential condition is violated' (Stalin: *Great Patriotic War*, pp. 141–2.)

to the Soviet dictator. After all, Roosevelt's conduct in connexion with the Balkans could certainly be interpreted as an effort to yield tacitly to Russia what Churchill had yielded explicitly. Yet if this was Stalin's belief it was almost the opposite of the truth. In 1944 Roosevelt went to great lengths to avoid offending the Russians, not with the idea of yielding them a sphere of influence in Eastern and Central Europe, but in the hope of disarming suspicion as a preliminary to persuading them to adopt American conceptions of democracy and morality in their dealings with other countries.

In this radical difference of mind lay the seeds of future troubles, but in 1944 it was possible for both Stalin and Roosevelt to persist in their misunderstanding of one another's intentions and convictions. As a result, the negotiations between the Big Three in the months after the Moscow Conference appeared to show an encouraging amount of agreement among them as to the powers and functioning of a new international organization. Exchanges of views between the three Governments began in February 1944.[1] By 24 April the Americans had ready a tentative draft of a charter for the organization, and on the strength of this Hull decided on 30 May 1944 to invite Britain and Russia to begin formal talks. He wished China also to be admitted to the preliminary discussion, but the Russians objected. A compromise was arranged whereby the Conference was divided into two parts: first Britain and America agreed to meet with Russia to work through their diverse proposals for an international organization, and when this phase of the Conference had completed its task Britain and America undertook to go over the same ground with China.[2] On 9 July 1944 the Soviet Government signified their willingness to proceed on this basis, and the Conference was scheduled for August.

Each Government drew up its own proposal. The British, Russian, Chinese, and American drafts were exchanged in advance of the opening of the Conference so that when the delegates met at Dumbarton Oaks on 21 August 1944 each knew what the others had in mind.[3] The first or Soviet phase of the Dumbarton Oaks Conference lasted from 21 August until 28 September 1944. The negotiation was exceedingly complex, since agreement on the phrasing as well as upon the sense of the various articles of the proposed charter had to be attained, and frequent reference to the home Governments was necessary.

[1] Hull: *Memoirs*, ii. 1650. [2] Ibid. pp. 1671–2.

[3] The American draft of 24 April underwent revision before the Conference opened. This second draft became the basic text upon which further revisions agreed at the Conference were made. Texts of the successive American drafts are published in *Postwar Foreign Policy Preparation*, pp. 582–91, 595–606. The draft proposals presented to the Dumbarton Oaks Conference by the British, Russian, and Chinese Governments had not been published up to 1952.

Because the initial proposals of all three Governments were similar on many points, progress at first was rapid. All agreed that the new international organization should have four basic elements: a General Assembly in which all member states would be represented; a Security Council upon which the Great Powers would have permanent seats and to which representatives of smaller nations would be elected by the Assembly; a secretariat; and an International Court of Justice.[1] The model of the League of Nations was an obvious and primary influence in fixing this arrangement, and indeed the experience and the failures of the League exerted a compelling force upon all the discussions at Dumbarton Oaks.[2]

The failure of the League—in so far as it was due to defects in its constitution, and not to defects in its membership—could be attributed to four weaknesses: the requirement of unanimity before action could be taken; the fact that League decisions did not automatically bind member states to definite action; the failure to include economic and social problems within the League's direct jurisdiction; and, most critical of all, the absence of any definite and immediately available military force to carry out the League's decisions. The men who set out in 1944 to create a new international organization to keep the peace had these points in the forefront of their minds, and were resolved to remedy these defects so far as agreement on paper could do so. But a problem which had not been adequately faced was how to assure continued co-operation among the Great Powers themselves—a point which touched directly upon the basic divergence between Russia and the West in their assumptions about the aims and nature of the new organization. When this difficulty came into the open, the Dumbarton Oaks Conference could do nothing to solve it.

Nevertheless, it proved possible to arrive at agreement on a number of important points. All three Governments agreed that unanimous votes should not be required to reach decisions, either in the Council or in the Assembly, and that all members should bind themselves in advance to accept the decisions of the Security Council and to act upon them without further ado. All agreed, further, that the primary responsibility for keeping the peace should be lodged in the hands of the Security Council, upon which the Great Powers—and, this time, all the surviving Great Powers in the world—would have permanent representation. Only so, it seemed, could the duty of keeping the peace and the power to do so be united, as they had never been united in the League of Nations.

But the realities of national power imposed an important qualification

[1] The matter of terminology was one which had to be settled at Dumbarton Oaks. Thus the name Security Council was accepted; this followed the Soviet suggestion and replaced the name Executive Council in the American draft. The name of the organization as a whole, too, was a matter of debate. In the end United Nations was fixed upon.

[2] Charles K. Webster: 'The Making of the Charter of the United Nations', *History*, 1947, xxxi. 17.

upon the rejection of the principle of unanimity. The Americans, as much as the Russians, insisted that the Great Powers should have the right to veto a decision of the Security Council. Only so, Hull and Roosevelt believed, could the obligations entailed by membership in the new international organization be made compatible with American constitutional requirements and palatable to the American public.[1] Thus, in effect, annulment of the principle of unanimity applied only to the smaller Powers.

When the Conference began, the Russians argued that the proposed international organization should confine itself to the task of maintaining security. They advocated a separate body to deal with social and economic questions. The Americans and the British, on the contrary, argued that social and economic conditions might easily become important causes of wars; and that the problems of national and international security could not be dissociated from the conditions under which the peoples of the world lived. As Marxians, the Russians could hardly controvert the argument; and on 8 September the matter was arranged when the Russians agreed that a special Social and Economic Council, responsible to the General Assembly, should be created to carry out any recommendations which the Assembly might make touching these fields.[2]

The military problem, too, was an occasion for difference of opinion. The Russians proposed that an international air force should be created, ready at a moment's notice to spring into action whenever the Security Council gave the word of command. The British, on the other hand, put their main reliance upon the creation of a Military Staff Committee which would be, in effect, an expansion of the Anglo-American Combined Chiefs of Staff Committee that had functioned so successfully during the war. The Americans were unwilling to accept the Russian proposal. They preferred a series of special arrangements between each Government and the Security Council by which each state would designate some part of its armed forces for service under the orders of the Security Council in case of need. The Russians withdrew their proposal for an international air force on 12 September, but, as a concession to their point of view, a clause was inserted in the draft approved by the Conference which declared that national air detachments should be held 'immediately available . . . for combined international enforcement action'. Detailed study and action in the military field was referred to a Military Staff Committee as proposed by the British. This committee was to comprise the Chiefs of Staff (or their representatives) of each of the permanent members of the Security Council.[3]

[1] Hull: *Memoirs*, ii. 1662, 1683.

[2] Ibid. pp. 1677, 1684.

[3] Ibid. pp. 1682, 1684, 1698; *Postwar Foreign Policy Preparation*, pp. 322, 616; Webster: 'The Making of the Charter of the United Nations', loc. cit. p. 28.

An interesting example of the detailed process whereby the final text of the Dumbarton Oaks

The place of the British Commonwealth and of the Pan-American Union in a new international organization was a matter of high concern for Britain and America. The Russians, too, already had in mind the possibility of creating a group of satellite states in Eastern Europe which would respond to the leadership of the Soviet Union as the Latin American republics did to that of the United States. There was thus no discord. A section of the Dumbarton Oaks proposal expressly sanctioned regional arrangements for maintaining peace and security, but provided that no action to enforce peace should be undertaken by any such organization without the authorization of the Security Council.

With such an area of agreement, optimism was easy. Yet the underlying differences in concept between Russia and the West did not fail to come out. The first occasion upon which this showed itself was when the matter of membership in the organization was discussed. The United States wished that all nations which had signed the United Nations Declaration of January 1942 should become members, together with eight other nations which were not at war with the Axis. Six of these were Latin American republics; and to the Russians this proposal must have seemed like a device for packing the Assembly with American puppets. The principle upon which the Russians wished to base the new international organization—a continuation of the war-time Grand Alliance—would have excluded states which had taken no part in the war. Consequently they opposed the admission of non-belligerents. When the Americans showed signs of insisting, Andrei Gromyko, the head of the Russian delegation, announced that each of the sixteen Soviet Republics, too, should have separate representation in the Assembly.[1]

This proposal, advanced on 28 August, created consternation among the American and British delegations. They foresaw the possibility of a complete breakdown of the negotiations. Public opinion in the West, they believed, would never accept the Soviet claim. Roosevelt insisted that the matter should be kept a deep secret, and hastily sent off a telegram of remonstrance to Stalin on 31 August. Stalin's reply on 7 September said that he hoped to be able to explain to the President face to face the 'political importance' of the question. By mutual agreement, the matter was thereupon dropped.[2]

The second point upon which an irreconcilable difference of opinion

proposal was drawn up may be seen in *Postwar Foreign Policy Preparation*, pp. 610–11, where four successive drafts of the clause defining the duties of the Military Staff Committee are reproduced.

[1] On 1 February 1944 the Supreme Soviet had formally amended the Constitution of the U.S.S.R. as follows: 'Each Union Republic has the right to enter into direct relations with foreign states, to conclude agreements with them and to exchange diplomatic and consular representatives with them' (Rothstein: *Soviet Foreign Policy during the Patriotic War*, ii. 50). This, of course, provided a legal basis for the proposal Gromyko made at Dumbarton Oaks.

[2] Hull: *Memoirs*, ii. 1678–80; *Postwar Foreign Policy Preparation*, pp. 317–18.

between Russia and the Western Powers arose concerned voting procedure on the Security Council. Since the Security Council was to be the real centre of the organization, the question of how it should make its decisions was of the greatest importance.[1] There was no dissent from the general principle that the permanent members of the Security Council should have the right to veto a decision; but the British delegation, supported after initial hesitation by the Americans, insisted that an exception should be made in cases when one of the Great Powers was party to a dispute. In such a situation, they argued, it was contrary to all the principles of justice that a nation should be able to act as judge in its own case. The Russians, however, emphatically refused to agree to any abrogation of the veto power. They wished to make unanimity among the Great Powers a *sine qua non* of any action.

The basic differences between Russian and Western concepts of the aims of international organization lay immediately behind this dispute. Was the organization to be a device whereby the Great Powers would act in concert to impose their will upon any refractory small nation, while settling their own differences through other channels of negotiation? Or was the organization to pretend to authority over the Great Powers themselves? Put in another way, was the organization to serve as a disguise for the exercise of control over all the world by the Great Powers, or was it to regulate the relations of all the nations in accordance with the principles of universal justice, recognized, presumably, by all mankind?

The question was connected, of course, with the Russians' haunting sense of their isolation in a capitalist and potentially hostile world. A Marxian could only scorn the bourgeois sense of justice, and a Russian could never forget that his nation was a peculiar people, alone and isolated in the world. Without the safeguard of an absolute veto, what use might not the capitalist nations make of the Security Council to justify intervention in Russia's foreign relations, passing judgement upon Russia's actions in accordance with false bourgeois principles?

On 8 September Roosevelt took the matter up with Stalin by telegram. Stalin replied on 14 or 15 September, suggesting that a special procedure should be worked out for handling any dispute in which a Great Power was involved. He emphasized that no departure from the principle of unanimity could be allowed, and pointed out that the Soviet Union had

[1] Membership of the Council was also an important matter. The British took the lead in championing the claims of France to rank as a Great Power, and with American support they won their point. It was agreed that in due course France should become a fifth permanent member, along with China and the Big Three. An American effort to secure the same status for Brazil was overruled (Hull: *Memoirs*, ii. 1678). Non-permanent seats were set at six, giving the small Powers a numerical preponderance on the Council. This meant that consent of at least some of the small Powers would be required for any decision.

to take into account certain 'ridiculous prejudices' against Russia which other nations frequently exhibited.[1]

In an effort to escape from the impasse which thus presented itself, a compromise formula was devised whereby unanimity of the permanent members was required for any decision involving enforcement, while the principle that a nation should not judge its own case was applied only to preliminary investigation and the making of recommendations for peaceful settlement of disputes. But the British delegation refused to accept this modification, and Roosevelt could not make up his mind. Some of the members of the American delegation favoured giving in to the Russians; others wished to hold fast to the British principle. In the end, it was decided to leave the matter open. The text of the Dumbarton Oaks proposal simply declared that voting procedure of the Security Council was 'still under consideration'.[2]

Two points were conspicuously omitted from consideration at the Dumbarton Oaks Conference. One was the nature and jurisdiction of the International Court of Justice. This was left for subsequent discussion by legal experts. At Dumbarton Oaks it was merely agreed that the court should be like or identical with the Permanent Court of International Justice established at The Hague. The other omission was any consideration of the status of dependent territories. International trusteeships for such territories had long been a favourite project with men like Hull and Roosevelt.[3] But the United States Joint Chiefs of Staff had ideas of their own which conflicted with the trusteeship principle. In particular, American military authorities wanted to gain undisputed sovereignty over at least some of the islands of the Pacific conquered from Japan: and, yielding to their pressure, the American delegation to Dumbarton Oaks put the question discreetly aside.[4]

Officially the Dumbarton Oaks Conference was conducted in secrecy, but in fact the American newspapers found it possible to report most of what transpired.[5] This was the result partly of an effort by the American Government to stir up public sympathy for the idea of joining a new League of Nations. Hull and Roosevelt felt that a tremendous task of public education would have to be undertaken before American membership in a new international organization could be assured of effective support; and to forward such a process they adopted the policy of issuing as much information about the progress of the negotiations at Dumbarton Oaks as possible.

A second source for newspaper information was more irregular, but

[1] Hull: *Memoirs,* ii. 1700–1; Stettinius: *Roosevelt and the Russians,* pp. 27–30.

[2] Hull: *Memoirs,* ii. 1701–5; *Postwar Foreign Policy Preparation,* pp. 324–7, 614.

[3] See above, pp. 319, 333–4, and below, p. 597, note 1.

[4] Hull: *Memoirs,* ii. 1706; Leahy: *I Was There,* p. 304.

[5] Cf. particularly the reports in the *New York Times* by James Reston.

highly characteristic of the American political system. Hull had undertaken to keep key Congressmen informed of the thinking of the administration concerning the future international organization, and, despite the fact that an election campaign was in full cry at the time of the Dumbarton Oaks Conference, the Secretary of State took leaders of the Republican Party into his confidence and solicited their approval and comments upon what was being done. But in these circumstances secrecy could not be maintained. Diligent reporters were able to garner much inside information about the progress of the Conference from talkative Congressmen and others who had been consulted by Hull or his subordinates.[1] As a result, the proceedings at Dumbarton Oaks were surrounded by a blaze of publicity. More important, the Republican candidate for the Presidency, Governor Dewey, in general supported American participation in a new international organization, thus removing one of the main factors which had led in 1920 to the rejection of the Versailles Treaty by the U.S. Senate.

By the third week in September, the stalemate which had been reached on the question of Security Council voting procedure, and the unresolved problem of what states should be admitted to membership in the organization, raised considerable doubt as to what should next be done. Until the Great Powers could agree on these points it seemed futile to summon a general conference of nations to discuss and adopt a charter for the organization. Nevertheless, on 27 September the Soviet, British, and American delegations agreed to the wording of a communiqué (issued only on 9 October after the conclusion of the Chinese phase of the Conference) which said: 'The Governments which were represented in the discussions . . . have agreed that after further study of these proposals they will as soon as possible take the necessary steps with a view to the preparation of complete proposals which could then serve as a basis of discussion at a full United Nations Conference.'[2] The ponderous language of the communiqué reflected the decision that further efforts to resolve the conflict of views which had arisen at Dumbarton Oaks would have to wait until Roosevelt, Churchill, and Stalin could take the problems up personally at a second meeting of the Big Three.

The Soviet phase of the Conference thus came to an end on 28 September 1944, and, as had been pre-arranged, the Chinese phase began immediately. The discussions which followed were of slight significance, since the Chinese delegates had been on hand in Washington from the beginning of the Conference and had been consulted from time to time by the Americans. Certain defects in the drafting of the proposals which

[1] Hull (*Memoirs*, ii. 1657–70, 1686–99) offers a detailed account of his efforts to make the preparation of a new and improved League a non-partisan undertaking.

[2] *Postwar Foreign Policy Preparation*, pp. 328, 335.

had emerged from the Soviet phase of the Conference were noticed,[1] but no very important changes were suggested by the Chinese, and none were incorporated into the approved text. Instead, the modifications which seemed desirable on the basis of the discussions with the Chinese were left for detailed consideration at the full dress Conference promised by the communiqué.

The publication of the Dumbarton Oaks proposal for the establishment of an international organization excited wide attention in the press of all the Allied countries. It did not excite wild enthusiasm; but it did provoke general if cautious approval.[2] The memory of the high hopes and dismal failure of the League of Nations could not altogether be exorcized.

Roosevelt made a rather cautious public statement at the time when the communiqué was released, expressing 'extreme satisfaction' at the progress which had been made; and on 21 October he made a campaign speech in which he came out emphatically for an organization with 'the power to act quickly and decisively to keep the peace by force, if necessary'.[3] Churchill was busy with other matters in Moscow when the announcement of the outcome of the Dumbarton Oaks Conference was made, and so failed to comment; but Stalin, in his speech on 6 November 1944, commemorating the anniversary of the Bolshevik Revolution, declared:

> An equally striking indication of the solidity of the front of the United Nations is to be seen in the decisions of the Dumbarton Oaks Conference on post-war security. There is talk of differences between the three powers on certain security problems. Differences do exist, of course, and they will arise on a number of other issues as well. Differences of opinion are to be found even among people in one and the same party. They are all the more bound to occur between representatives of different states and different parties.
>
> The surprising thing is not that differences exist, but that there are so few of them and that as a rule in practically every case they are resolved in a spirit of unity and co-ordination among the three great powers.[4]

These remarks, and the cordial and accommodating attitude exhibited by the Soviet delegation at the Conference, certainly suggested that Stalin intended and expected to make the new international organization an important element in his foreign policy. This sustained the bright hopes for the future of the world which inspired Roosevelt and which governed, more than any other single factor, his policy towards the Soviet Union.

[1] Webster: 'The Making of the Charter of the United Nations', *History*, 1947, xxxi. 26.

[2] See e.g. *Izvestia*, 10 October 1944, reported in *Daily Worker*, 11 October; *New York Herald Tribune*, 10, 12, 13, 14 October 1944; *New York Times*, *Daily Herald*, *News Chronicle*, 10 October, *The Times*, 12 October 1944.

[3] Rosenman: *Public Papers and Addresses of Franklin D. Roosevelt, 1944–45 volume*, p. 350.

[4] Stalin: *Great Patriotic War*, pp. 137–8.

Differences there might be; but neither Roosevelt nor Stalin, from their opposite points of view, believed them to be insuperable.

(iii) From Moscow to Yalta, October 1944–February 1945

(*a*) Economic Negotiations

At the Second Quebec Conference Roosevelt and Churchill had agreed that American economic help to Great Britain should be adjusted during the period after the end of the war in Europe to permit the beginnings of a conversion of British economy from war to peace.[1] Details were left for settlement by a committee of experts; and, since the problem was a pressing one for the British Government, no time was lost in starting the negotiation. A British Committee headed by Lord Keynes arrived in Washington on 5 October and began consultation with an American group headed by Secretary of the Treasury Henry Morgenthau. The negotiation lasted for several weeks, and was not completed until 23 November 1944.[2]

The British came with four goals definitely in mind. They hoped to be able to persuade the Americans to accept the following principles: (1) to supply Lend-Lease munitions on such a scale as to permit the transfer of some labour in Britain from munitions production to other work; (2) to supply food and other items of civilian consumption on Lend-Lease in sufficient quantity to permit some improvement in British living standards; (3) to remove restrictions on British export trade which had been imposed by the White Paper of September 1941; and (4) to adjust Lend-Lease and other forms of international accountancy in such a way as to forestall a decrease in British holdings of gold and dollars.[3]

The American negotiators heard the British arguments in a generally sympathetic spirit, but they felt themselves bound by Congressional objections to any use of Lend-Lease for purposes not directly connected with the prosecution of the war, and so did not agree to everything the British asked. Neither the British nor the Americans actively explored the possibility of a loan (such as had been mentioned at Quebec) to facilitate Britain's transition from war to peace. That was instead left for some future time.[4]

The British representatives came to Washington with detailed lists of

[1] See above, pp. 489–90.

[2] In addition to the technicality and complexity of the matters to be negotiated, it is likely that the length of the conversations resulted from an American desire to postpone matters until after the election at the beginning of November.

[3] Hancock and Gowing: *British War Economy*, pp. 528–9.

[4] Getting such a loan through Congress at a time when the Japanese war was still to be fought would have been almost or quite impossible. An effort to do so would have convinced many Americans that the British were quitting short of victory.

materials which they wished to have delivered on Lend-Lease during the year starting 1 January 1945.[1] They also hoped to put Lend-Lease deliveries to Britain upon a protocol basis, similar to that which had prevailed from the beginning with respect to Russia. In this they failed. The Americans insisted that deliveries should remain contingent upon unforeseen developments, and that existing administrative bodies should continue to direct the flow of supplies as seemed best. However, there was relatively little difficulty in reaching agreement on a tentative allocation of munitions and non-munitions supplies on a large enough scale to allow the start of British reconversion. Because the British contribution to the war against Japan was set at a relatively low figure, the total value of Lend-Lease supplies even when planned on this basis came much below the levels of 1944—about half for munitions and about 70 per cent. of 1944 totals for non-munitions items.[2]

The question of removing restrictions on British export trade was a more difficult one.[3] American business men and members of Congress were fearful lest the British should steal a march on them in competition for post-war markets. In particular, Americans did not like the idea that Lend-Lease materials might be used by the British to facilitate the revival of their export business: that seemed an abuse of Lend-Lease and a competitive absurdity—financing a business rival with taxpayers' money.

Yet, for the British, revival of exports was a life and death matter. Without a start in that direction, hope of attaining a stable post-war economy was gone. Experts in the American administration recognized this fact, and agreed that economic collapse in Britain at the end of the war would be a disaster to the United States and to the world. The problem was how to avoid offending American public and Congressional feelings and still extend a helping hand to the British export drive.

The upshot was a piece of legerdemain. Publicly American officials affirmed that no change in policy would be made.[4] At the same time, the Americans announced that, after the defeat of Germany, there would be no obstacle to Britain's export of goods 'which are no longer supplied under lend-lease, and are obtained out of their own production or pur-

[1] During most of 1944 this date had been assumed as the probable time of the end of the war against Germany. When the Conference met in October, however, it had become clear that Germany would probably resist into the spring of 1945, though the British Cabinet did not officially decide to put its plans upon this basis until 25 October 1944 (Hancock and Gowing: *British War Economy*, p. 517).

[2] Ibid. pp. 529–31.

[3] See above, pp. 440–1, 489–90.

[4] Cf. the official American statement which signalized the conclusion of the conversations: 'Since lend-lease aid is made available to our allies only when it contributes directly to the winning of the war, lend-lease articles have from the beginning not been available for reexport commercially. That policy will also be continued without change' (*Documents on American Foreign Relations, 1944–1945*, pp. 140–1). Churchill made a statement to parallel effect in the House of Commons, 30 November 1944, H.C.Deb. 5th ser., vol. 406, coll. 69–73.

chased from this country for cash'.[1] Privately, however, the Americans assured the British that full export freedom would be accorded to them from the beginning of 1945 'by administrative action'.[2] The extent of this apparent duplicity was minimized by the fact that a number of classes of goods—metals, minerals, chemicals, and manufactured articles for civilian consumption, &c.—were excluded from the list of Lend-Lease deliveries for 1945. It followed that articles made from these materials or others similar to them were freed from the restrictions of the White Paper of 1941, and that as soon as man-power and factory space could be found the British could begin to export such goods without let or hindrance from the United States.

The exclusion of these items from Lend-Lease, however, meant that whatever American supplies of these goods the British needed would have to be paid for with gold or dollars. As dollar expenditure for the maintenance of American troops in Great Britain decreased when the troops moved on to the Continent, the British Government could not easily lay hands on an adequate supply of dollars. A number of expedients were suggested to relieve this problem; and by various accounting devices the Americans increased British dollar reserves by about $300 million. This sum, large though it was, fell short of the figure which both American and British experts agreed was an optimum. It was, however, the best that legal and political restrictions seemed to allow.[3]

Rumours, sometimes badly distorted, of what had been agreed to in the Washington conversations reached Congressmen and others who suspected the Roosevelt administration of being altogether too generous with American money. As a result, when the Lend-Lease Act came up for renewal once again in April 1945, a number of searching questions were put by the Congressional Committees which sat upon the Bill, and spokesmen for the administration found it prudent to emphasize their intention of stopping Lend-Lease deliveries as soon as the war came to an end. Lest there should be any doubt as to the intentions of Congress concerning the future of Lend-Lease, an amendment was made which expressly prohibited the use of Lend-Lease funds for 'postwar relief, postwar rehabilitation or postwar reconstruction'.[4] This provision had the effect of binding the hands of the administration; and, when the war against Japan came to an unexpectedly early end, the agreements which had been worked out in October and November 1944 in consultation with the British were scrapped.

This outcome was, of course, quite unforeseen at the time the negotia-

[1] *Documents on American Foreign Relations, 1944–1945*, p. 141.

[2] Hancock and Gowing: *British War Economy*, p. 532.

[3] Ibid. pp. 531–2. For a more personal account of this negotiation see Harrod: *Life of John Maynard Keynes*, pp. 586–91.

[4] *Documents on American Relations, 1944–1945*, p. 138.

tions took place. Nevertheless, a gradual break-up of the Siamese-twin relationship between the American and British economies was foreseen and intended by the two delegations which met in October–November. Their efforts were designed to make the separation as gradual and painless as possible. The most notable thing about the conversations, perhaps, was the fact that American experts were prepared to extend the concept of American self-interest to embrace British economic well-being in the post-war period. The conversations of October–November 1944 thus rank as important precursors of the American loan to Britain of 1946 and of the Marshall Plan of 1947.

Economic co-operation between Britain and America was, however, not nearly as easy when peace began to seem close at hand as it had been during the years when economic efficiency for war was the sole criterion of policy. This was very evident in the field of international civil aviation. A Conference of fifty-two nations met at Chicago from 1 November to 7 December 1944 to try to draw up rules to govern international air traffic under peace-time conditions. After first signifying their intention to take part in the Conference, the Russians suddenly refused to attend.[1] The Conference was consequently dominated by the American and British representatives, who soon exhibited radically different ideas as to how post-war aviation should be managed. The British hoped to establish a world organization empowered to assign national traffic quotas to each country; the United States wanted free competition between airlines, and an international body empowered only to establish technical rules.[2]

After prolonged negotiation, the Conference drew up four conventions which on the whole reflected the American position.[3] This, like the conflict over oil concessions in the Middle East,[4] evidenced the new and commanding economic position which the United States had won during the war years.

American economic negotiations with the Russians were similarly entangled by the approach of peace in the summer and autumn of 1944. The Third Russian Supply Protocol expired on 30 June 1944. When the Russians submitted lists of the materials they wished to have delivered under Lend-Lease during the following fiscal year, the Americans dis-

[1] The pretext for Soviet refusal to participate in the Conference was that Switzerland, Portugal, and Spain had been invited. Cf. Tass communiqué of 30 October 1944 in Rothstein: *Soviet Foreign Policy during the Patriotic War*, ii. 210; and cf. p. 101.

[2] An important consideration in this connexion was the tremendous advantage American airlines could be expected to enjoy as a result of the fact that British aircraft factories had ceased to produce transport aeroplanes during the war, while the Americans produced transport planes for all the Allied world.

[3] Texts of the conventions may be found in *Documents on American Foreign Policy, 1944–1945*, pp. 572–617.

[4] See above, p. 453.

covered that the value of industrial equipment and machinery requested by the Russians had more than tripled as compared with the preceding year. Obviously, the Russians had begun to turn their attention seriously to the problem of reconstructing their damaged industrial plant and hoped to be able to get Lend-Lease help in doing so.

According to accepted theory, Lend-Lease was intended only to assist with the prosecution of the war, but many of the items the Russians asked for would have taken more than a year to produce, and, even if the war against Japan should last into 1946, the major part of the usefulness of such industrial machinery would clearly extend into the post-war period. To meet this situation the Americans suggested that certain things, the principal value of which would probably be for peace-time reconstruction, should be bought by the Russians on credit. They suggested that the loan so made by the United States should be paid off over a period of twenty-five to thirty years, and that it should bear interest at the rate of $2\frac{3}{8}$ per cent. But the Russians tried to get better terms, suggesting an interest rate of 2 per cent.[1]

Haggling over the interest rate and other questions resulted in a long delay in the conclusion of the Fourth Russian Supply Protocol. Although it covered the period from 1 July 1944 to 30 June 1945, the Protocol was not finally signed until 17 April 1945, when its period was nearly over and the war in Europe had reached its final stages. By its terms, the United States undertook to make available industrial machinery and equipment to a value of more than $1,000 million; but of this total $481 million was classified by the Americans as ineligible for Lend-Lease.[2] The Protocol simply declared that the items ineligible for Lend-Lease 'may be purchased by the U.S.S.R. if it so elects',[3] leaving the question of credits and interest rate for further discussion.

In actual fact, no agreement was reached between the two countries before the end of the Japanese war or after it, so that the materials in question were never delivered. Trying to drive a shrewd bargain, the Russians overreached themselves.[4] Yet despite this fact the Russians did receive large quantities of goods under Lend-Lease in 1943, 1944, and 1945 which were of long-term value for the industrial rehabilitation of their economy. Value for war and value for peace could not, after all, be sharply distinguished; and in general the Americans pursued a rather generous policy in interpreting what would serve to help the prosecution of the war.

[1] Deane: *Strange Alliance*, pp. 92–93.

[2] By way of comparison: the value of industrial machinery and equipment offered by the Third Protocol was $454 million, of which only about $300 million was actually delivered during the period of the Protocol (*Soviet Supply Protocols*, p. 71; Deane: *Strange Alliance*, pp. 92–93).

[3] *Soviet Supply Protocols*, p. 112.

[4] Deane, loc. cit.

(*b*) American Efforts to Co-operate with China and Russia in the Far East, July 1944 to February 1945

The military and political problems of China reached a new intensity in the second half of 1944. The Japanese offensive overran a considerable part of the country which had until then remained under Chiang Kai-shek's control, and before the enemy advance halted the Americans lost all the air bases from which they had hoped to be able to bomb Japan.[1] Meanwhile, relations between the Chinese Communists and the Kuomintang threatened to degenerate into open civil war as each side made ready for a struggle for power after the defeat of Japan.

American officials in Chungking and Washington were seriously perturbed by these developments. When the scope of the Japanese offensive became clear, and Chiang's troops proved quite unable to offer more than sporadic resistance to it, Roosevelt decided that the only way in which Chinese armies could be made fully efficient was to place them directly and entirely under American command. Accordingly on 7 July 1944 Roosevelt telegraphed to Chiang to suggest that General Stilwell should take command of all Chinese and American forces in China with the ultimate object of uniting Chinese Communist troops under his leadership also.[2] To this drastic proposal Chiang returned a soft answer. He agreed in principle but asked that a high-ranking American official should visit Chungking in order to explore the political and military implications of what the President had proposed. On 10 August Roosevelt suggested General Patrick J. Hurley for this assignment and Chiang gave his approval at once.

Hurley travelled via Moscow, and took the occasion to sound out Molotov's views on Chinese affairs. The Soviet Foreign Minister disclaimed any special interest in Chinese internal problems, and denied that the Chinese Communists were really Communists at all or had any connexion with the Soviet Government. Hurley left Moscow with the impression that the Russians 'would be glad to see the United States taking the lead economically, politically, and militarily in Chinese affairs'.[3]

The President's special emissary arrived in Chungking on 6 September 1944 full of enthusiasm for his task. One of the first things he decided was that the personal relationship between Chiang Kai-shek and General Stilwell had reached such a pitch of bitterness that there was no use in trying to insist upon their co-operation. Stilwell had also quarrelled long and sharply with Admiral Mountbatten, his superior in S.E.A.C. In the face of these facts, Roosevelt decided on 19 October 1944 to recall Stilwell from all his commands. This decision provided an opportunity for sorting

[1] See above, pp. 398, 460.

[2] *United States Relations with China*, p. 66.

[3] Ibid. p. 72.

out the extraordinary confusion of responsibilities which had clustered round Stilwell's person. His military duties were divided into three. As deputy to Mountbatten in command of S.E.A.C. he was succeeded by General R. A. Wheeler; a new India-Burma theatre for American troops was created under General Daniel Sultan; and a new China theatre was created under General A. C. Wedemeyer. No effort was made, however, to persuade Chiang Kai-shek to give Wedemeyer command over Chinese troops. By October, when Stilwell was relieved, the Japanese offensive had stopped and the immediate crisis had passed.[1]

As the military danger of the Japanese offensive faded, the political problem of bringing about some sort of reconciliation between the Communists and the Kuomintang came more and more to dominate American policy in China. Hurley set out to convince Chiang that the Communists had no affiliation with Moscow, and, in his own opinion at least, he was partially successful.[2] On 7 November 1944 he went to the Communist headquarters in Yenan and there negotiated an agreement with Mao Tse-tung defining the terms upon which the Communists would agree to unite their forces with Chiang's armies in order to fight the Japanese. The key point in this agreement was the second, which prescribed:

> The present National Government is to be reorganized into a coalition National Government embracing representatives of all anti-Japanese parties and non-partisan political bodies. A new democratic policy providing for reform . . . shall be promulgated and made effective. At the same time the National Military Council is to be reorganized into the United National Military Council consisting of representatives of all anti-Japanese armies.[3]

This seemed to Hurley an eminently satisfactory basis for agreement, but Chiang rejected it, and proposed instead that the Communist troops should be incorporated in his own armies, and that the Communist Party should, in return for recognition as a legal organization, undertake to support his Government.[4] There followed a prolonged period of negotiation. Chiang reluctantly agreed to alter the composition of his Government, and promised to take steps towards adopting a new Constitution for China. These political issues were, however, not the main stumbling-blocks. The point on which Chiang and the Communists found it most difficult to agree was who should control the military forces of the country. A series of conferences between representatives of the

[1] Ibid. p. 69; Leahy: *I Was There*, p. 319.

[2] *United States Relations with China*, p. 73. Cf. Hurley's testimony before the U.S. Senate Committee on Armed Services and the Committee on Foreign Relations (*Hearings on Military Situation in the Far East* (Washington, U.S.G.P.O., 1951), Part 4, p. 2409).

[3] *United States Relations with China*, p. 74. The parallel between American policy in China and British policy in Greece and Yugoslavia is worth noticing; likewise the almost identical Communist terms for co-operation with the established authorities in each of the three countries is striking.

[4] Ibid. p. 75.

Chinese Communist Party, the Chinese Government, and General Hurley failed to settle this crucial question, and on 16 February 1945 the Communists broke off the negotiation.[1] By this time Hurley's original belief that the Chinese Communists were reasonable people had evaporated, and he reported to Washington that he was now convinced that the only policy for the United States to follow was to support Chiang.[2]

A few days after the breakdown of the negotiation, Hurley returned to Washington for consultations as to what should next be done. Meanwhile matters hung fire in China. The prospect of civil war loomed ever closer. Instead of emerging from the war strengthened and united, ready to assume a place among the Great Powers, China seemed to be sinking into helplessness and anarchy. It was not a situation which corresponded to the hopes which Roosevelt had long cherished for China's future, but to decide what should be done was difficult and became a matter of dispute among American officials in China and a source of much uncertainty of mind in Washington.[3]

The question of Russia's part in the Japanese war had been answered in general terms at the Tehrān Conference[4] when Stalin promised his allies that he would fight the Japanese as soon after the end of hostilities against Germany as troops could be brought into position on the Manchurian border. When it came to making detailed arrangements, however, many delays and difficulties were put in the way of eager American planners. During the ten months that followed the Tehrān Conference very little progress had been made towards settling in detail what Russia's share in the Japanese war would be. Still less had the Americans been able to begin preparations for setting up an American air force in eastern Siberia as they hoped to do.

When Churchill and Eden came to Moscow in October 1944[5] General Deane, the Head of the American Military Mission in Moscow, judged the occasion propitious to try to bring matters into sharper definition. He accordingly participated in the military discussions which took place

[1] *United States Relations with China*, pp. 76–83. The situation was complicated by an abortive plan for sending American supplies and paratroopers to the Communist armies in north China to assist them against the Japanese. When Hurley discovered this plan he promptly vetoed it. The Communists felt aggrieved by this act, while Hurley felt angered at the actions of some of the subordinate American authorities in China who were inclined to take a more friendly view of the Communists than he did (Leahy: *I Was There*, pp. 339–40).

[2] *United States Relations with China*, p. 82.

[3] It is worth noting that the two countries for which the United States had assumed a special responsibility, France and China, had 'gone sour' in 1944. Even in the New World, relations with Argentina were peculiarly strained at the same time. Roosevelt and Hull had thus personal reason to distrust the concept of spheres of influence when events in their own sphere had so greatly betrayed their hopes.

[4] See above, pp. 352, 355–6.

[5] See above, pp. 493 seqq.

during the Conference; and, with British approval, undertook the task of presenting Anglo-American plans for the Japanese war to Stalin. After doing this, he put three questions to the Soviet dictator: How soon after the end of the war against Germany would the Red Army be ready to fight Japan? How long would it be before the Russians could take the offensive? How much of the carrying capacity of the Trans-Siberian railway would be made available for supplying an American air force in eastern Siberia?[1]

On the next night, 15 October 1944, Stalin gave his answers. He said it would take three months after V-E day for him to prepare for war in the Far East, and that the Red Army would take the offensive at once. He calculated that sixty divisions would be needed for the task. The Trans-Siberian railway could not supply so great a force, so that a stock-pile of supplies would have to be built up in eastern Siberia ahead of time. Consequently, he said, the Red Army's offensive against Japan would depend upon the delivery of supplies from America in addition to the amounts previously asked under the Fourth Protocol. He also said that the 'political aspects' of Russia's participation would have to be clarified, i.e. the Allies would have to agree to territorial and other claims which the Russians wished to make in Sakhalin, Manchuria, &c.[2] As for supplying an American air force, that would be impossible over the Trans-Siberian railway: anything necessary would have to come by sea.[3]

At a subsequent meeting, on 17 October, General Deane met Stalin without the presence of the British. The purpose of the meeting was to agree upon an exact list of materials to be delivered from the United States for the supply of the Red Army in the Far East. The upshot was that Deane undertook to deliver two months' supply for sixty divisions, a total of over a million tons, before 30 June 1945. This was all in addition to materials previously requested by the Russians for the German war. During the same meeting, Stalin outlined the strategy he proposed to pursue against the Japanese in Manchuria, and accepted the definition of the Red Army's tasks which had been drawn up by the American Joint Chiefs of Staff.[4]

This seemed to be a great step forward, and when Stalin publicly bracketed Japan with Germany as an aggressor nation in his speech of 6 November 1944[5] he provided a hint of the new definiteness of his commitment against Japan. Nevertheless, in the months that followed the Russians showed much the same spirit of delay and obstruction which had

[1] Deane: *Strange Alliance*, p. 246.

[2] The political question was left open, and Stalin did not even say in detail what his political demands in the Far East would be. It was not until December 1944 that Russian claims were made clear to the American Ambassador. Cf. Harriman's statement, *Congressional Record*, 27 August 1951, p. A5666.

[3] Deane: *Strange Alliance*, p. 247.

[4] Ibid. pp. 248–9.

[5] Stalin: *Great Patriotic War*, p. 141.

characterized their dealings with General Deane earlier.[1] Plans for sending out parties of American soldiers to survey prospective airfield sites in Siberia and to prepare in other ways for the establishment of a strategic bombing force on Russian soil met with persistent delaying tactics.

Eventually Deane decided that the whole project would have to be called off. This, however, was disapproved by the American Chiefs of Staff, who instructed him to persevere.[2] This decision reflected a strictly military calculation of the advantages of air bases in the Maritime Provinces of Siberia for the war against Japan. Indeed, the key to American Far Eastern policy in both China and Russia up to and after the time of the Yalta Conference was almost wholly military. The American Chiefs of Staff believed that the war against Japan would probably last for eighteen months after victory in Europe; they also believed that a strong army would have to be found to subdue the Japanese troops on the mainland of Asia; and since the Chinese were, by the end of 1944, clearly not shaping up for such a task, the American military leaders turned to the Red Army as the most easily available substitute. A Russian campaign in Manchuria would save American lives and shorten the war: and that was all the U.S. Chiefs of Staff and the American Government cared to know.

(c) Allied Difficulties in Europe, September 1944–February 1945

(1) *Military Problems*

Between September 1944 and February 1945 the war in Europe did not go so well for the Allies as it had in the summer and early autumn of 1944. On the east, the Germans had been able to hold both Budapest and Warsaw, and on the west the Anglo-American troops found the border of Germany hard to cross. Difficulties of supply held up progress on both fronts while bad weather deprived the Allies of some of their advantage in the air.

In mid-December 1944 the Germans surprised Eisenhower by mounting a large-scale attack in the Ardennes region. German troops succeeded in breaking through a lightly held sector of the front, and divided General Bradley's Twelfth Army Group into two unequal parts. To meet this situation, Eisenhower on 19 December transferred command of all the troops to the north of the German break-through to Montgomery, while Bradley became responsible only for the southern flank of the 'bulge'.[3] By the end of January the two generals had succeeded in driving the Germans back to approximately the original starting line of their offensive.

[1] See above, p. 378. [2] Deane: *Strange Alliance*, pp. 249–52.

[3] Eisenhower: *Crusade in Europe*, p. 355; de Guingand: *Operation Victory*, p. 428.

When their main forces made contact on 16 January, General Bradley resumed command of part of the troops which had been transferred to Montgomery the month before.[1]

Eisenhower's moves had been dictated by convenience and common sense, but they became the occasion of a rather unpleasant expression of national rivalry between British and American commanders, troops, and journalists. On 7 January 1945 Montgomery gave an interview to the press which seemed to imply that he had taken over complete control of a bad situation and set it right.[2] His remarks were bitterly and vociferously resented by the Americans, who did not like Montgomery's patronizing tone.[3] Mutual charges flew back and forth, and the newspapers picked up enough of them to make the matter a serious one for a few days.

This incident was in itself almost trivial, though it showed how close beneath SHAEF's surface harmony volcanoes of chauvinistic feeling lay. It provided fresh fuel for an old controversy:[4] whether or not Eisenhower should appoint a deputy commander for ground force operations to correspond with his air and naval deputy commanders. The British Chiefs of Staff argued, as always, that such an officer was needed, since Eisenhower was too busy with political and administrative problems to give full and adequate attention to the battle front. Montgomery was the British candidate for the post; but, after the recriminations which the Battle of the Bulge had aroused between Bradley and Montgomery, any such appointment would have certainly had explosive consequences among the Americans. Nevertheless, the debate smouldered on until the time of the Malta Conference, British persistence merely arousing American stubbornness.[5] Some British journalists took up the argument about command arrangements publicly, and this did nothing to smooth over the feelings which had already been so ruffled between American and British officers and men.[6]

[1] Eisenhower: *Crusade in Europe*, p. 364. Montgomery retained the command of the U.S. Ninth Army and so did not lose all the new strength that had been given him.

[2] *The Times*, 8 January 1945. Montgomery paid some high compliments to American soldiers in this interview, but it was sentences like the following that ruffled the Americans: '. . . when I was brought in and told to take over . . . I got reserves into the right places and got balanced—and you know what happened. I regrouped the American and British armies. . . .' And, 'I said to Bradley, they can come back with all honour. They [82nd U.S. Airborne Division] came back to the more secure positions. They put up a wonderful show'.

[3] According to Wilmot (*Struggle for Europe*, p. 611) the initial report of Montgomery's interview reached Bradley's Headquarters in an edited form put out by the German radio. If this is correct, one can better understand the burst of ill-feeling, and the affair must be counted a victory (even though abortive) for German propaganda.

[4] See above, pp. 390–2.

[5] At the Malta Conference Churchill made a last attempt when he proposed to bring Alexander from Italy to act as Deputy Commander for Eisenhower in place of Air Marshal Tedder. When the American Chiefs of Staff made it clear that in such a case Alexander would have no greater scope than that already given to Tedder, the matter was finally dropped (cf. Wilmot: *Struggle for Europe*, pp. 666–7).

[6] Eisenhower: *Crusade in Europe*, pp. 356–7.

The French added their bit to Eisenhower's difficulties. In order to bring his forces to bear against the German salient in the Ardennes area, Eisenhower was compelled to thin out his line in the south; and at one time he proposed to yield ground in Alsace, if need be including Strasbourg. French troops were holding Strasbourg, and when de Gaulle heard of Eisenhower's intention he felt that such a retreat would have serious repercussions on French morale. On 3 January 1945 in an interview with Eisenhower he threatened to countermand Eisenhower's orders to the French troops in Strasbourg and said he would even withdraw them from the Allied Command if Eisenhower did not change his plan. After a somewhat heated interview, Eisenhower yielded the point and changed his orders so as to provide for the retention of Strasbourg.[1]

A more serious problem arose early in January when the British Chiefs of Staff challenged the wisdom of Eisenhower's plans for the resumption of the offensive. Eisenhower wished to make a general advance to the Rhine as a preliminary to a great pincers movement which would isolate the Ruhr. The main thrust was to be north of the Ruhr, commanded by Montgomery; the subordinate thrust was to come on the south under Bradley. The British, however, believed that Allied strength was not sufficient to permit two such attacks to be successfully mounted, and argued that everything available should be concentrated north of the Ruhr. Eisenhower countered by arguing that communications were so limited that no more than thirty-five divisions could be maintained north of the Ruhr; whereas if a double offensive were mounted no less than seventy-five divisions could be brought into action simultaneously against the Germans.[2]

A question which lay in the background of this dispute was whether or not the Allies could break through the Siegfried Line without long and costly battles. Eisenhower's plan required such penetration before the Rhine could be reached in its middle course; the British plan would have run round the northern end of the Line just as the Germans had avoided the Maginot Line in their famous offensive of 1940. The British were constantly afraid that the battle would degenerate into stabilized trench warfare of the sort which had characterized the First World War; and they believed that only a maximum concentration of air power and armour on a sector of the front not defended by fixed fortifications could prevent such a result.

Still another factor was nationalistic rivalry. The British naturally liked to imagine Montgomery as the commander of the final thrust into Germany, and the Americans equally liked the thought that Bradley would

[1] Eisenhower: *Crusade in Europe*, pp. 362–3. [2] Ibid. pp. 369–71.

lead them into the heart of Hitler's homeland. After the recriminations which had followed the Battle of the Bulge, Montgomery and Bradley felt themselves open rivals, and each commander was eager to persuade Eisenhower to give him the supplies and forces for a great attack while starving the other. Thus professional and nationalistic differences of opinion came to coincide. The coincidence set the scene for one of the most tense debates which ever occurred among the Combined Chiefs of Staff when they met at Malta on 31 January 1945, just before the Yalta Conference.[1]

(2) *Political Problems*

While these military differences were coming to the fore, events on the political scene did nothing to make Anglo-American co-operation easier. On 6 December 1944 fighting between British troops and Greek guerrillas broke out in Athens, and at once most of the newspapers of the Western world began to interpret British actions in a very unfavourable light. The deal with Stalin by which the British were accorded a free hand in Greece[2] was, of course, secret, but even had it been known the edge of public criticism against British actions would scarcely have been dulled. To many observers it seemed as though the British were reverting to nineteenth-century methods of imperialism, directing their arms without adequate justification against men who had fought bravely against the Germans, and, in attacking Communists, risking the stability of the Grand Alliance and endangering the brave new world planned at Dumbarton Oaks. Protest in Britain was almost as widespread as in the United States; but the Russian press maintained a discreet silence.[3]

Simultaneously, a political crisis blew up in Italy. On 26 November 1944 the Bonomi Government[4] resigned. On the following day a new Cabinet was tentatively arranged under Bonomi's leadership with Count Carlo Sforza as Foreign Minister. Sforza, however, was *persona non grata* to Churchill. The Prime Minister believed that Sforza had betrayed his word in failing to support the King of Italy, as he had told Churchill he would do before his return to Italy in 1943. Consequently, the British representative in Rome made it clear on 28 November that the British Government disapproved of Sforza's appointment. This, like the affair in Greece, seemed to many people an unwarranted intervention in the domestic affairs of another country—intervention which made mockery of such documents as the Atlantic Charter.

[1] See below, pp. 537–8.
[2] See above, pp. 495–6.
[3] See e.g. editorials and leaders in *New York Post*, 6 December, *Christian Science Monitor*, 9 December, *Manchester Guardian*, 4, 8, and 9 December, *Daily Herald*, 5 December, *The Times*, 7 December 1944. The *Daily Telegraph* and Lord Beaverbrook's press were almost the only London newspapers which supported the Government's policy. In America, the *New York Times* supported British action editorially on 6 and 12 December.
[4] See above, pp. 425, 478.

Still a third sore spot was Belgium. On 29 November 1944 British military authorities received word that a great demonstration was planned in Brussels. Communist elements were prominent among the organizers of the demonstration, and there were fears that it might result in a full-blown Government crisis. Accordingly, British troops were called upon to prevent the demonstrators from assembling. They did so successfully. As in Greece, the question of the future of the monarchy was mingled with the question of disarming ex-resistance organizations: and underneath lay a thinly disguised struggle for power between conservatives and radicals.

Thus in three European countries—Greece, Italy, and Belgium—where the British exercised a special primacy serious political crises broke out in the last days of November and the beginning of December 1944. In each country British action seemed to be designed to support monarchy and the more conservative elements against republicans and radicals. Conditions, of course, were such that normal methods for determining the balance of political forces within each country were impossible; but British action could be and was interpreted in many quarters as directed against the free expression of the popular will, while supporting unpopular kings and men who had collaborated with the Nazis.

Such views met with a particularly ready acceptance in the United States. Roosevelt won his fourth election to the Presidency on 7 November 1944, and the Congress which was returned showed a definite shift towards the special brand of American Liberalism which Roosevelt symbolized to all the world. But British policy in Greece, Italy, and Belgium did not accord very well with Roosevelt's principles, and the American Government took steps to dissociate themselves publicly from British actions. On 5 December, the new Secretary of State,[1] Edward Stettinius, made a formal statement, as follows:

> The position of this Government has been consistently that the composition of the Italian Government is purely an Italian affair except in the case of appointments where important military factors are concerned. This Government has not in any way intimated to the Italian Government that there would be any opposition on its part to Count Sforza. Since Italy is an area of combined responsibility, we have reaffirmed to both the British and Italian Governments that we expect the Italians to work out their problems of government along democratic lines without influence from outside. This policy would apply to an even more pronounced degree with regard to governments of the United Nations in their liberated territories.[2]

Under the circumstances, this was a thinly veiled attack upon British

[1] Cordell Hull had long been ailing, and Roosevelt had with difficulty persuaded him to remain in office until after the election of November 1944. His resignation became official on 27 November 1944.

[2] *Documents on American Foreign Relations, 1944–1945*, p. 172.

policy. Churchill felt deeply offended. He sent off a cable to Roosevelt which, according to one authority, 'may well have been the most violent outburst of rage in all of their historic correspondence'.[1] But Roosevelt refused to disown his Secretary of State. Feeling between the two leaders was very strained, perhaps more than it had ever been before.

In Britain itself, doubt as to the wisdom of Churchill's policy in Belgium, Italy, and Greece was widespread, especially in Labour and Liberal circles. A motion of censure in the House of Commons came up for debate on 7–8 December 1944. Churchill was exposed to some biting criticism. British action in Greece provoked most opposition and was the main subject of debate, but in his reply Churchill took affairs in Belgium, Italy, and Greece all into account. He argued that, far from 'using His Majesty's Forces to disarm the friends of democracy in Greece and in other parts of Europe', as the motion of censure had declared, the British Government was really trying to safeguard democracy and prevent the establishment of Left-wing totalitarian rule. Ballots, not bullets, he declared, should decide the future form of government in all the liberated countries of Europe.

Churchill did not apologize or retract. He denied that the British Government had done anything improper in making known their distrust of Sforza. This was a direct rebuttal to Stettinius's statement of 5 December. He described British action in Greece and Belgium as designed to head off planned *coups d'état* on the part of armed Communists, and disclaimed any intention of forcing any country to accept any particular form of government which was not desired by a majority of the people.

Some part of his irritation at the attitude of the Americans appeared in Churchill's speech. He appealed directly to the American public to take warning from what had happened in Belgium and Greece, and gave vent to some of his anger in the following passage:

> Poor old England! . . . We have to assume the burden of the most thankless tasks and in undertaking them to be scoffed at, criticized and opposed from every quarter; but at least we know where we are making for, know the end of the road, know what is our objective. It is that these countries shall be freed from the German armed power and under conditions of normal tranquillity shall have a free universal vote to decide the Government of their country—except a Fascist régime—and whether that Government shall be of the Left or of the Right.[2]

Churchill made the vote a question of confidence, and was sustained by 281 votes to 32. This was, however, a hollow victory. Of the 172 Labour members, only 23 voted for the Government, while 24 voted against and the rest abstained or intentionally absented themselves. Even in

[1] Sherwood: *Roosevelt and Hopkins*, p. 839; Eng. edition, ii. 830–1.

[2] 8 December 1944, H.C.Deb. 5th ser., vol. 406, coll. 929–30.

Churchill's own party not all the Conservatives voted for him, although none voted against. The vote showed how deeply British opinion was disturbed by the direction events had taken. The Coalition Government had not faced such a crisis since its establishment in 1940; but while the war lasted no responsible political figures wished to endanger Churchill's leadership. Nevertheless, some of his moral authority was destroyed: on the Greek issue at least Churchill could not count upon the support of a united nation.

In Belgium and Italy the crisis did not last for long. On 10 December 1944 Bonomi formed a new Cabinet from which Sforza was excluded, but which did include the Communists. Similarly in Belgium, after the dispersal of the demonstration of 28 November, matters quieted down and ceased to disturb the relations of the Great Powers. But in Greece events took a different course. ELAS proved more resolute and powerful than anyone had expected, and the British found it necessary to bring reinforcements from Italy before they could drive the guerrilla troops from Athens.[1]

As the battle in Athens prolonged itself from day to day, Churchill began to feel that strenuous efforts should be made to bring about some sort of political settlement that would end the fighting and remove what had become a thorn in his flesh. On Christmas Day 1944 he and Eden flew to Athens and summoned a meeting of Greek political leaders, including Communists and other representatives of EAM. The Greeks failed to reach an agreement that would put an end to the battle; but they did agree to appoint Archbishop Damaskinos as Regent. This helped to undercut the charge that the British were seeking to return King George to his throne by force. A few days later, Papandreou resigned from the post of Prime Minister, and General Nicholas Plastiras, an old republican, succeeded him. Plastiras was a figure well calculated to appeal to republican and liberal elements which had supported EAM; at the same time, a widespread public reaction against terroristic measures which ELAS had taken in Athens helped to undermine their power. But what finally was decisive was British armed strength, reinforced from Italy. A general offensive, beginning immediately after Churchill's abortive attempt to settle the matter by negotiation, led to the defeat of the guerrilla insurgents. They were compelled to abandon

[1] The Allied Commander-in-Chief in the Mediterranean, General Wilson, proposed to use American ships to bring the reinforcements to Greece. Admiral King at first ordered the U.S. admiral in the Mediterranean to refuse to permit American ships to be employed for this purpose; but before this became a matter of high dispute, King was persuaded to withdraw his order, which certainly violated the established chain of command (cf. Sherwood: *Roosevelt and Hopkins*, pp. 840–1; Eng. edition, ii. 832–3).

Athens, and on 14 January 1945 a cease fire was negotiated, more or less on the British terms. Further consultation among the Greeks led on 12 February to the conclusion of a definite peace, whereby ELAS agreed to disband and surrender its arms in return for a guarantee of amnesty.[1]

These events in Greece, Italy, and Belgium put a severe strain on Anglo-American relations, but, so far as there is evidence, Stalin looked benignly enough upon British action. He presumably regarded these countries as falling within the British sphere, and may have welcomed the precedent set by British action in Greece for intervention which he foresaw might become necessary on the part of his own forces in such countries as Rumania and Poland. Indeed, the behaviour of the Greek and Italian Communist Parties can only be interpreted as reflecting instructions from Moscow to co-operate with the British-sponsored Governments of those countries.[2] In his own way, Stalin was seeking to honour the agreements he had made with Churchill in October 1944.

Churchill, too, tried hard to make the agreements work. He brought all the pressure he could on the Poles to make them come to terms with Stalin. Private argument he supplemented by public statement. On his return from Moscow, when Churchill reported to Parliament (27 October 1944), he declared:

> I hope Monsieur Mikolajczyk will soon return to Moscow, and it will be a great disappointment to all the sincere friends of Poland if a good arrangement cannot be made which will enable him to form a Polish Government on Polish soil—a Government recognised by all the great Powers concerned. . . .
>
> These are critical days and it would be a great pity if time were wasted in indecision or in protracted negotiation.[3]

But indecision and protracted negotiation was exactly what came. Mikolajczyk found that all the Polish parties represented in his Government, except his own, were unalterably opposed to acceptance of the Curzon Line. In desperation he decided to appeal to Roosevelt in the hope of some powerful intervention. But at the time Roosevelt was engaged in the last stages of the election campaign. He felt he could not risk alienating the Polish vote at home by coming out for the Curzon Line, nor did he wish to offend Stalin by openly opposing it. Consequently Mikolajczyk's appeal went unanswered until after the election had been

[1] McNeill: *The Greek Dilemma*, pp. 153–62.

[2] In Greece the leadership of the Communist Party was shifted to new hands in May 1945, and for a few months the Communists co-operated with the Government, even to the point of betraying to government forces a small ELAS band which refused to surrender its arms in accordance with the agreement of February. At the same time, not all of ELAS arms were handed over; some were hidden away in caches for possible future use.

[3] 27 October 1944, H.C.Deb. 5th ser., vol. 404, col. 494.

won; and even then the President was evasive. While stating that the American Government stood 'unequivocally for a strong, free and independent Polish State' he also declared that if the Polish, Russian, and British Governments could agree upon mutually satisfactory boundaries for Poland 'this Government would offer no objection'.[1] The American Ambassador to Russia, Averell Harriman, delivered this letter personally to Mikolajczyk *en route* from Washington to Moscow. When presenting it he offered, on Roosevelt's authority, to act as mediator between the Poles and the Russians in an effort to secure the concession of Lwów to Poland. But the Poles were disgusted, and they refused the offer on the ground that they would be tacitly yielding the claim to their eastern provinces if they entrusted their cause to Harriman.[2]

Meanwhile, internal friction among the London Poles had reached an acute stage. Mikolajczyk's apparent willingness to compromise on the territorial question isolated him from most of his fellow exiles, and on 24 November 1944 he decided to resign. Thomas Arciszewski succeeded him as Premier of the Government in Exile; and the Peasant Party, of which Mikolajczyk was the head, remained outside the new Government.

On 15 December 1944 Churchill made public his reaction to this trend of events in a speech to the House of Commons. He did not hide his disappointment at the failure of the London Poles to accept the Curzon Line. The new Polish Government, he said, had been constituted 'in a form which in some respects I certainly am not able to applaud', and he described Mikolajczyk as 'the only light which burns for Poland in the immediate future'.[3] American reaction remained indecisive. On 18 December Stettinius issued a statement which in effect repeated the letter that Roosevelt had sent to Mikolajczyk a month earlier.

The Red Army had remained quiet in Poland since September 1944; but Stalin was planning to renew his advance on that sector of the front early in January. Mikolajczyk had clearly failed to persuade his colleagues to accept the Curzon Line, as he had seemed willing to do at Moscow in October. Stalin therefore decided to dismiss the London Poles from further consideration. On 31 December the Polish Committee of National Liberation formally declared itself to be the Provisional Government of Poland; and on 5 January 1945 the Soviet Government recognized it as such, and appointed an ambassador at once.[4] The American Government reacted by announcing on 1 January 1945 that they proposed to continue to recognize the Polish Government in London; and the British Government did likewise.[5]

[1] Text of Roosevelt's letter, dated 17 November 1944, may be found in Mikolajczyk: *Pattern of Soviet Domination*, pp. 116–17; Ciechanowski: *Defeat in Victory*, pp. 358–9.

[2] Mikolajczyk, op. cit. p. 117. [3] 15 December 1944, H.C.Deb. 5th ser., vol. 406, col. 1481.

[4] Mikolajczyk, op. cit. p. 119.

[5] Arthur Bliss Lane (*I Saw Poland Betrayed* (Indianapolis, Bobbs-Merill, 1948), pp. 73–75)

These manœuvres in Poland were preliminary to the opening of the new Russian offensive, which came on 13 January 1945. The Red Army made rapid progress, and by 17 January the Germans had been driven from Warsaw. The newly christened Provisional Government transferred its seat to the old Polish capital within a few days and took up the task of administering Polish territory in the rear of the Red Army. Meanwhile the Poles in London protested to the American and British Governments, but did not receive a very sympathetic hearing. Neither Government was willing to accept the Communist-dominated Provisional Government of Poland; but how to arrange some satisfactory compromise was hard to see. Like so much else, the question was held over for personal settlement by the Big Three at Yalta.

During the months between the Moscow and Yalta Conferences, Yugoslav affairs dragged on inconclusively. Tito and Šubašić, despite their agreements of the summer,[1] found it hard to come to terms with one another; and Churchill's 50–50 agreement with Stalin[2] remained a will-o'-the-wisp. The main immediate issue was the future of the monarchy. On 1 November 1944 Šubašić and Tito agreed that a three-man regency should be set up, pending a plebiscite to decide whether the people of Yugoslavia wanted King Peter to come back; but the King was at first unwilling to accept such an arrangement. Instead he asked Šubašić to resign on 22 January 1945. The British Government thereupon brought pressure to bear on the young King to persuade him to change his stand, and by the end of January he had yielded and agreed to the proposal for a regency. This, however, did not lead to a settlement, for when Šubašić presented the names of three men to act as Regents, Tito found two of them unacceptable. Things had reached this impasse when the Yalta Conference met.[3]

Territorial questions had meanwhile arisen to trouble Yugoslavia's relations with the Allies. In September 1944 Tito publicly stated his intention of annexing Trieste to Yugoslavia, and later he voiced claims to the

summarizes exchanges which took place between Roosevelt and Stalin between 16 December and 29 December in which the President asked Stalin to refrain from recognizing the Lublin Committee as a Provisional Government. The fact that Stalin disregarded the President's request may have stung Roosevelt. The promptness of the American reaction to the proclamation of the new régime in Poland suggests something of that sort. It is possible that Stalin's brusque unilateral action in Poland was taken partly with a view to improving his bargaining position at the Yalta Conference, which was then in the final stages of preparation.

[1] See above, p. 473. [2] See above, p. 474.

[3] Fitzroy Maclean: *Eastern Approaches* (London, Cape, 1949), pp. 518–20; Armstrong: *Tito and Goliath*, p. 54; *Yugoslavia*, ed. Robert J. Kerner (Berkeley, University of California Press, 1949), pp. 378–9. Text of the November Tito-Šubašić Agreement may be found in *The Times*, 24 January 1945.

Austrian province of Carinthia also. During the same months Tito conducted complex and obscure negotiations with the Bulgarians in connexion with Macedonia. There is ground for believing that Tito cherished the project of forming an all-inclusive federation of the south Slavs which would unite the Bulgars with the Serbs, Croats, Slovenes, Montenegrins, and Macedonians into a federal state. Russian policy was of critical importance in this connexion, since both Tito and the dominant faction in the Bulgarian Government were Communists and as such were at least generally responsive to Stalin's instructions. Balkan Federation had long been a plank in the Comintern programme for South-East Europe, but it may perhaps be doubted whether Stalin himself ever welcomed the idea of seeing a great south Slav state emerge even under Communist leadership. In any case, despite the eagerness of both Tito and Dimitrov (who, however, differed as to the form the proposed federal state should assume), nothing was done.[1]

In France, de Gaulle as head of the Provisional Government found frequent occasion to take offence at the actions of the American and British Governments. In particular, he resented the continued exclusion of the French Government from the inmost Allied counsels. When he was not invited to join the Big Three at Yalta he considered himself to have been slighted and the dignity of France impugned.[2] His domestic position *vis-à-vis* the Communists was strengthened when he made a trip to Moscow in December and was received with all honours by Stalin. As a result of this visit France and Russia signed a treaty of Alliance and Mutual Assistance on 10 December 1944. It was aimed explicitly against Germany, and was to endure indefinitely.[3] By this gesture de Gaulle showed the Western Allies that he and his Government had passed beyond the stage of tutelage, a relationship which had long chafed the proud French spirit. He did not, however, make a very favourable personal impression on Stalin.[4]

Throughout the autumn of 1944 Churchill and Roosevelt had made efforts to fix upon a time and place at which to meet Stalin for a second

[1] Barker: *Macedonia*, pp. 98–101; Stettinius: *Roosevelt and the Russians*, pp. 228–9.
British policy was not of central importance, but it is worth noting that it had come full circle. In the early years of the war, the British Government had attempted to forward federation; by the end of 1944 they opposed any south Slav federation, fearing to see a powerful Communist state emerge as a potential core for a still wider Balkan federation.

[2] See also below, p. 539.

[3] Text in Rothstein: *Soviet Foreign Policy during the Patriotic War*, ii. 194–5.

[4] Stettinius: *Roosevelt and the Russians*, pp. 97–98.

tripartite conference. But Stalin refused to leave Russian territory, and Roosevelt was seriously handicapped by the requirements of the election campaign. At various times arrangements seemed on the point of conclusion; but they always broke down.[1] Finally, Roosevelt decided to postpone the meeting until after the ceremonies of opening the new Congress (6 January 1945) and his fourth inauguration as President (20 January). On the matter of the place of meeting, Roosevelt and Churchill gave in to Stalin and somewhat reluctantly (especially on Churchill's part) agreed to journey to Yalta in the Crimea. Roosevelt's commitments set the date at the beginning of February. A preliminary meeting of the Anglo-American Chiefs of Staff was arranged at Malta immediately preceding the Yalta Conference; and Roosevelt sent Harry Hopkins on an advance tour of the main European capitals to lay some of the groundwork for the forthcoming top-level meetings.[2] After these preliminaries, the second and last meeting of Stalin, Churchill, and Roosevelt began on 4 February 1945 at Yalta.

(iv) The Yalta Conference, 4–11 February 1945

(*a*) The Problems to be Faced

The Yalta Conference, 4–11 February 1945, was probably the most important war-time meeting of the Big Three. It came at the time of transition from war planning to peace planning, at a critical moment when the mould of post-war relations between the great Allies was still malleable by words. At Tehrān, military strategy had dominated the discussion; by the time of the Potsdam Conference, on the other hand, the relations between the Russians and the West had so hardened that there was little to be done but ratify the existing fact by agreeing to disagree. At Yalta, on the other hand, the Big Three seemed (though the seeming may have been illusory) to have a wider margin of choice. They met at a time when each country's post-war role was yet to be clearly formulated; at a time when it seemed possible to turn their respective policies either towards agreement or towards conflict with one another. For the first time, Roosevelt, Churchill, and Stalin met with a full retinue of political

[1] Wilmot (*Struggle for Europe*, pp. 628–31) suggests that Stalin waited until the Ardennes offensive in the west and his own offensive in Poland gave him an important vantage over the Anglo-Americans before agreeing to the Yalta Conference. Evidence for this is dubious. The main factor that held up the Yalta Conference was the unwillingness of Roosevelt and Churchill to go to Russian soil to meet Stalin. Had they swallowed their scruples in the autumn of 1944 it is possible that the meeting might have been held after the American elections of November and before Roosevelt's inauguration for a Fourth Term in January (cf. Sherwood: *Roosevelt and Hopkins*, pp. 844–5; Eng. edition, ii. 836–7).

[2] Hopkins's main task *vis-à-vis* Churchill was to try to damp down some of the wrath which had been generated in the Prime Minister's breast by Stettinius's statement of 5 December about Italian and Greek affairs.

and military advisers; and the atmosphere as well as the organization of the conference was that of a full-dress international gathering. By comparison, Tehrān had been an informal, personal encounter between the three chiefs of government, supplemented by military staff conversations.

The United States, Britain, and Russia each approached the Yalta Conference with definite goals in view. For the Americans, two aims took precedence over all others. First, Roosevelt and his advisers wished to smooth out the obstacles to agreement with the Russians which had arisen at Dumbarton Oaks[1] in order to assure the speedy establishment of a United Nations organization. Secondly, the Americans hoped to settle future strategy in both Europe and the Far East. The strategic problem in Europe hinged upon the dispute between British and American Chiefs of Staff as to how best to invade Germany;[2] in the Far East it centred upon Russia's part in the war against Japan.[3]

In comparison, local European political problems took second rank.[4] The Americans still looked forward to a rapid withdrawal of their troops from Europe as soon as Germany had been beaten. Roosevelt told Stalin and Churchill at Yalta that it would be impossible for the American Government to keep any troops in Europe for more than two years after Hitler's overthrow;[5] and, long before that, plans called for the transfer of combat units to the Pacific as fast as ships could be found to carry them. Moreover, many of Roosevelt's most trusted advisers did not expect that public opinion would support an active American policy in Europe after the end of the war.[6] Roosevelt certainly had no desire to repeat President Wilson's fiasco of 1918–20. The spectacle of a new American arbiter of Europe repudiated by his own country could only lead to confusion and misunderstanding. It would be much better if Europeans settled their own affairs to suit themselves, so long as they did so within the general world framework envisaged by the proposals of Dumbarton Oaks, and paid more or less respectful attention to the principles of the United Nations Declaration and the Atlantic Charter.

According to this line of reasoning, the first thing Americans should try to achieve was to secure an agreement with the Russians about the United Nations organization. That done, European disputes could be

[1] See above, pp. 505–8. [2] See above, p. 522. [3] See above, pp. 518–20.

[4] Even on the question of Poland—the problem about which most words were shed at Yalta—the Americans tended to subordinate the rights and wrongs of the case to a consideration of the effect that Big Three action would have on the United Nations organization. Thus when the discussion had reached a seeming stalemate, Stettinius's ultimate plea for some sort of agreement was backed by the observation that, without an agreement acceptable to American opinion, American participation in the future world organization might be endangered (Stettinius: *Roosevelt and the Russians*, p. 199).

[5] Ibid. p. 121. [6] Ibid. p. 88.

left to the Europeans, with a little helpful advice and perhaps some prodding from the United States. It is true that the experts of the State Department came to Yalta with some definite ideas as to how the outstanding disputes in Europe should be solved, but Roosevelt was not inclined to take their advice very seriously.[1] In the debates at the Conference, the President in general preferred not to act as champion of any particular formula. Instead he assumed the role of mediator between Churchill and Stalin whenever he could, leaving the positive initiative for settlement of the tangled affairs of Europe largely to the British and Russians.

On the military side, the British were as anxious as the Americans to settle the dispute over European strategy which had arisen between the two countries; and as usual they were prepared to leave to the Americans the problems of war in the Pacific. But the facts of geography, if nothing else, reversed in British eyes the priority among the political issues to be solved. The problem of Allied policy towards Germany and Poland; the role of France in the post-war balance of power on the Continent; the future of British influence in the Balkans and Persia—these were pressing and important matters, and only after they had been amicably settled by the Great Powers did it seem sensible to go ahead with the formation of a world-wide United Nations organization. High principles and professions of friendship would, after all, mean next to nothing if they could not be translated into detailed agreements about the future fate of particular countries and regions.

Stalin approached the Yalta Conference in a somewhat similar spirit. It seems reasonable to impute to him three general aims. He wanted what help he could get for the economic reconstruction of the Soviet Union. This meant reparations from Germany and, if possible, loans from the United States.[2] Secondly, in return for his intervention against Japan in Manchuria, Stalin wished to acquire the territories and special rights which the Tsarist Government had lost in the Far East after the Russo-Japanese war of 1904–5. Thirdly, and this was by all odds the most important of his aims, Stalin wished to lay the basis for the future security of his country against Germany. This, he probably believed, required the continuation of the general understanding which the war had brought about among the Big Three. To maintain that understanding he was prepared to make concessions, and he did make several that must have seemed to him very great indeed.

But Stalin also believed that the future security of the Soviet Union required the establishment of governments friendly to Russia in the East

[1] Ibid. pp. 84–86. Roosevelt did not even bother to read the dossiers prepared for his guidance by the State Department in advance of the Conference (cf. Byrnes: *Speaking Frankly*, p. 25).

[2] He was not prepared to press for loans from America at the time of the Yalta Conference itself, and contented himself with a couple of casual mentions of the possibility.

European countries that lay between Russia and Germany. It is possible, even probable, that Stalin had not yet come fully to realize the dilemma which this very natural wish created for him. As later events were to show, a government which satisfied the Soviet definition of friendliness could hardly at the same time satisfy the Western Powers' definition of a democracy. But the forcible imposition of 'friendly' governments in countries like Poland or Rumania was likely to offend, even antagonize, Britain and America. Thus the two basic requirements for Soviet security as Stalin saw them in February 1945 were to prove mutually incompatible in the long run.

In February 1945, however, this dilemma had not become clear. Stalin seems to have hoped that it would be possible to create 'people's democracies' in the states of Eastern Europe whose governments would, in effect, perpetuate the 'popular fronts' which local Communist Parties had created during the war. In such governments, the Communist Parties would, of course, play an important though not an exclusive role; and 'fascists' and 'collaborators' would be legally excluded from political activity. By extending the definition of these terms to include anyone actively anti-Russian or anti-Communist, it might prove possible to assure the establishment of friendly governments which at the same time would not offend the democratic shibboleths of the West.[1] Who, after all, in Britain or America, would care to defend the right of a 'fascist' to make trouble in Russia's zone of influence, especially if Stalin took steps to restrain Communists from embarrassing Britain and America in Western Europe and in the other parts of the world where Anglo-American influence predominated? How far he was prepared to go in this direction had been recently and dramatically proved in Greece, and Churchill was both aware of and grateful for Stalin's extraordinary restraint.[2]

It thus appears probable that at the time of the Yalta Conference Stalin felt that if he refrained from interfering in British and American zones of influence he could expect the Western nations to do the same in the Russian zone in Eastern Europe. The problem was merely to fix amicably the limits of the Russian zone; and the recent agreement reached by the European Advisory Commission[3] which defined the Russian zone of occupation in Germany, combined with the agreements which he had made with Churchill at Moscow in October 1944 with respect to the Balkans and Danubian Europe,[4] seemed already to have solved a large part of that problem. There remained the Far East and, most difficult of all, Poland.

[1] Cf. Deutscher: *Stalin*, pp. 542–3.

[2] Cf. the verbal fencing over Greece between Stalin and Churchill reported in Stettinius: *Roosevelt and the Russians*, pp. 194, 218; and Churchill's praise: 'I know of no Government which stands to its obligations, even in its own despite, more solidly than the Russian Soviet Government' (Speech to House of Commons, 27 February 1945, H.C.Deb. 5th ser., vol. 408, col. 1284).

[3] See above, p. 482. [4] See above, p. 494.

In each area Stalin had what must have seemed to him good bargaining counters. In the Far East he could offer the help of the Red Army against Japan and an agreement to recognize the Government of Chiang Kai-shek at the expense of the Chinese Communists. As for Poland, there were hints that he considered France a sort of equivalent. The bargain he hoped to make was simple. In return for his recognition of and support for de Gaulle's Provisional Government (sealed by the Treaty concluded in December 1944)[1] he felt he could demand British and American recognition of and support for the new Provisional Government of Poland.[2]

But neither Britain nor America saw things in such a light. Churchill was anxious to rescue Poland from Russian domination; and what seemed to Stalin a friendly Polish Government seemed to Churchill to promise a mere puppet show. Roosevelt, for his part, hoped that the whole problem of spheres of influence could be transcended by basic agreement upon the principles of international relations—an agreement which would obviate the need for unilateral intervention by any one of the Great Powers in any part of Europe. For practical purposes, his view coincided with Churchill's: Poland, he felt, should be genuinely free to run her own affairs and the Polish people should be permitted to elect whatever sort of government they preferred.

Neither Roosevelt nor Churchill seems frankly to have faced the fact that, in Poland at least, genuinely free democratic elections would return governments unfriendly to Russia—certainly by Stalin's definition, and, indeed, by any definition of international friendliness. Stalin's dilemma—his wish at once to maintain harmony with the Western Powers and to create a belt of friendly governments between himself and Germany—was matched by a similar dilemma in the policy of the West. The democratic process upon which so many eulogies were expended could not produce governments in Eastern Europe (or in many other parts of the world) that would further the harmony of the Great Powers and prove acceptable to all of them. Men were not so uniform, so rational, nor possessed of such good will, as the democratic theory presupposed; and in talking of East European governments which would be both democratic and friendly to Russia the Western Powers were in large part deluding themselves.

In February 1945, however, these truths had yet to be demonstrated by the progress of events. Stalin, as much as Roosevelt, and Churchill, as much as Stalin, talked of the importance of free democratic elections

[1] See above, p. 530.

[2] Cf. Stalin's remark, twice repeated, that the Provisional Government in Poland was just as 'democratic' as de Gaulle's Government in France (Stettinius: *Roosevelt and the Russians*, p. 147).

to determine as soon as possible the future form of government in the various countries of Europe which had been liberated from the Nazis; and the identity of their phrases disguised the divergence of their hopes and intentions. It was because the Big Three failed to cut through the smoke-screen of words and face frankly the differences that existed among them that the agreements reached at Yalta in so many cases were no more than verbal and did not long endure the test of practice. In the course of the long discussions over the formation of a Polish government—the topic which took more time than anything else at Yalta—the real differences between Russia and the West were often very near the surface, but neither side dared to grasp the nettle.

Reading the record in retrospect one is tempted to scorn the pious phrases which were used so freely on all sides; but it is perhaps over-hasty to do so. War-time propaganda and military co-operation had obscured the great differences between Russian and Western ideas of democracy; and it seemed imperative to many good, honest, and intelligent men to retain the common slogans in the hope that the reality of agreement might gradually grow up under the shelter of an identity of verbal formulae. Deliberately to uncover the disagreements which a common profession of faith in democracy hid might have made things worse, might even have fractured the Grand Alliance before Germany and Japan had been defeated. With a war yet to win, such an alternative was rejected out of hand by all the participants in the Yalta Conference. Hence the persistence with which they refused to examine the real hopes and fears which they attached to phrases like 'free democratic elections'.[1]

(*b*) Preliminary Discussions at Malta, 31 January to 3 February 1945

The Combined Chiefs of Staff met at Malta on 31 January 1945 in order to agree upon Anglo-American strategy in advance of their encounter with the Russians. The shipping problem, which had been so acute in 1942 and 1943, had become critical once again. The unexpectedly rapid advance of American forces in the Pacific combined with anticipated requirements for redeploying troops from Europe to the Far East, put an unprecedented strain upon the Allies' shipping resources. At the same time, relief supplies for liberated Europe had to be considered; and, to make matters more difficult, new and more formidable types of German

[1] It is most instructive to read Stettinius's account of the one occasion on which Churchill ventured to pull back something of the curtain of double-talk which enveloped the whole debate over Poland. On 9 February he pointed out that in some countries the government which organized elections automatically won; Stalin replied by denying that Poland was such a country because the population was not illiterate; and a few soothing words from Roosevelt closed the matter (Stettinius: *Roosevelt and the Russians*, pp. 214–16). No one, not even Churchill, really wished to explore the antagonism which lay behind their common praises of democracy.

submarines threatened a renewal of the Atlantic war if Germany's defeat were long delayed. The American military authorities wished to transfer all U.S. shipping from the Atlantic to the Pacific as soon as victory had been won in Europe; but British arguments, supported by Harry Hopkins, persuaded them to agree to the assignment of some ships for civilian uses.[1]

A second debate centred round the future of the Italian campaign. The British once again proposed that an expedition across the Adriatic should be prepared in the hope of driving the Germans from Yugoslavia and into Austria; the Americans instead argued that additional troops should be withdrawn from the Mediterranean in order to reinforce the western front. This was an echo of the old dispute which had reached such intensity at Cairo and Tehrān fourteen months earlier;[2] and as before the Americans had their way. It was decided that five divisions and some aircraft should be withdrawn from Italy and be sent to join Eisenhower's forces. Plans for an amphibious operation in the Adriatic were abandoned.[3] Churchill made one further effort to reverse this decision at the first plenary session of the Yalta Conference, but when his plea for a landing in Yugoslavia met with Russian disapproval, he at long last conceded the issue.[4]

These matters were far overshadowed, however, by a very sharp debate over the best strategy for the western front itself. The British argued for a single thrust across the Rhine; the Americans defended Eisenhower's plan for a frontal advance to the Rhine, to be followed by twin attacks north and south of the Ruhr designed to isolate that industrial area from the

[1] Sherwood: *Roosevelt and Hopkins*, pp. 848–9; Eng. edition, ii. 840–1.

[2] See above, pp. 346, 352–3, 359–60, 368–70.

[3] Wilson: *Eight Years Overseas*, p. 248; Leahy: *I Was There*, p. 346.

[4] Churchill had both military and political goals in view when he urged an amphibious operation in the Adriatic. Militarily, an amphibious attack in the German rear at the head of the Adriatic would have been likely to compel the Germans to withdraw from Italy, thus bringing an end to the slow and difficult fighting which had continued in the high Appenines through the winter of 1944–5. Politically, Churchill was anxious to establish Anglo-American forces in Vienna before the Red Army reached that city; and he may also have thought that should British troops operate in and through Yugoslavia he would be in a better position to turn his October deal with Stalin to account. Tito's undisguised suspicion of British motives, and his repulse of British offers of military aid which had been made in November 1944 (see p. 496, note 5), must have disheartened Churchill. He may, indeed, have written Yugoslavia off as a bad bargain by the beginning of 1945. Certainly he was not prepared to fight Tito to enforce a British share in Yugloslav affairs as he had fought ELAS in Greece; and after November 1944 it must have looked to Churchill as though nothing less would make any impression on the Yugoslav Partisans.

A very important element in the situation was the fact that three of the five divisions scheduled for withdrawal from the Mediterranean were Canadian. The Canadian Government and military authorities were anxious to unite all their forces into a single (and more nearly autonomous) army by withdrawing from Italy and concentrating all Canadian troops on the western front. This, of course, very much weakened Churchill's position, and the combined American and Canadian pressure was too much for him. On the Canadian attitude cf. Lingard and Trotter: *Canada in World Affairs*, pp. 166–70.

rest of Germany.[1] The debate was stubborn on both sides, and at one time Marshall stated that if the British plan were approved he would tell Eisenhower that he should ask to be relieved of his command.[2] No one wished to push matters to such an extreme. Moreover, it seemed absolutely imperative to reach agreement before the coming meeting with the Russians. Hence the discussion was brief despite its warmth; and in the end the British yielded a reluctant endorsement of Eisenhower's plan.

No comparable difficulties existed as far as the war against Japan was concerned. Plans for attack upon Iwo Jima and Okinawa were approved. The longer-range strategy of the war came under general consideration, including preliminary discussion of plans for the invasion of Japan itself, for the liberation of Malaya, and for co-operation between the Royal Navy and the U.S. navy in the Pacific.[3]

For planning purposes, the end of the war in Europe was set between 1 July 1945 and the end of the year. Japan, it was calculated, would hold out for eighteen months after V-E day, i.e. until 1947. It was in the light of these estimates that Roosevelt made his bargain with Stalin about the Far East at Yalta. Mistaken as they proved to be, they were the latest and most authoritative guesses available to him at the time.

Another matter of considerable importance which was settled at Malta by the Combined Chiefs of Staff pertained to the question of zones of occupation in Germany. At the Second Quebec Conference it had been decided that the Americans would accept a zone in south-west Germany on condition that access to the German North Sea ports of Bremen and Bremerhaven be guaranteed by the British.[4] But the American military authorities refused to accept the definition of their rights over the ports which the British drew up, and a long deadlock ensued. In the meanwhile formal approval of the entire zonal agreement had to wait.[5] This situation seemed alarming to the American and British members of the European Advisory Commission. The Russians were already far into Germany, and they feared that failure to ratify the zonal agreement might give the Russians an excuse to disregard the zonal boundaries which had been set and simply keep on going westward while Anglo-American forces battered against the Siegfried Line. In view of these fears, the Americans finally yielded and accepted the British definition of their rights of access and control over Bremen and Bremerhaven. This removed the last obstacle to formal tri-

[1] For an account of the rival plans see Eisenhower: *Crusade in Europe*, pp. 369–72. See also above, pp. 522–3.

[2] Sherwood: *Roosevelt and Hopkins*, p. 848; Eng. edition, ii. 840.

[3] Wilson: *Eight Years Overseas*, p. 248; Cunningham: *A Sailor's Odyssey*, p. 628.

[4] See above, p. 488.

[5] Philip E. Mosely: 'The Occupation of Germany', *Foreign Affairs*, July 1950, xxviii. 597–9.

partite approval of the zonal agreement which was signed on 6 February,[1] just two days after the Yalta Conference began.

While the Combined Chiefs of Staff were thus concerting Anglo-American military policy, Secretary of State Stettinius and Foreign Secretary Eden engaged in parallel discussions of political issues.[2] They discussed the disputes which had recently divided American and British policy in Italy and Greece—by then both things of the past. Policy towards France, the Balkans, Poland, Persia, and China also came under discussion; and Stettinius presented his hopes for the future of the United Nations organization to a rather sceptical Churchill. These discussions were exploratory and led to no formal agreements.[3]

On 2 February Roosevelt arrived at Malta in time to approve jointly with Churchill the decisions reached by the Combined Chiefs of Staff. He had informal conversations with Churchill at lunch and dinner in the course of which Roosevelt informed the Prime Minister that he planned to meet Ibn Saʿūd, Haile Selassie, and Faruq of Egypt on his return journey from Yalta. The President also hoped to see de Gaulle in Algiers *en route* for home, but de Gaulle was so piqued at not being invited to Yalta that he refused to leave Paris to meet Roosevelt.

(c) Negotiations and Decisions at Yalta

The next day, 3 February, the American and British delegations flew to the Crimea. Since the airfield was about ninety miles from the palaces appointed to receive the delegates, they did not arrive until evening, and the Conference began only on 4 February 1945.

The routine was very strenuous. Actually, there were four formal levels of discussion at which the business of the Conference took place. Each afternoon, from 4 to 11 February, a plenary session was attended by the Heads of Government, the Foreign Secretaries, Chiefs of Staff, and various other advisers, experts, and interpreters. The Chiefs of Staff met daily, usually in the mornings, and the Foreign Ministers met in the early afternoon. Finally, various private conversations between Stalin, Roosevelt, and Churchill took place at irregular intervals. In addition to these official channels, there was much informal consultation at all levels, both within and between the various national delegations. Moreover, banquets were given in rotation by Roosevelt, Stalin, and Churchill, featured by multitudinous toasts and informal but sometimes enlightening sallies. By

[1] Philip E. Mosely: 'The Occupation of Germany', loc. cit.; Stettinius: *Roosevelt and the Russians*, pp. 65–66.

[2] Churchill was also on the spot and took part in both the military and political deliberations on an informal basis.

[3] Stettinius: *Roosevelt and the Russians*, pp. 63–71.

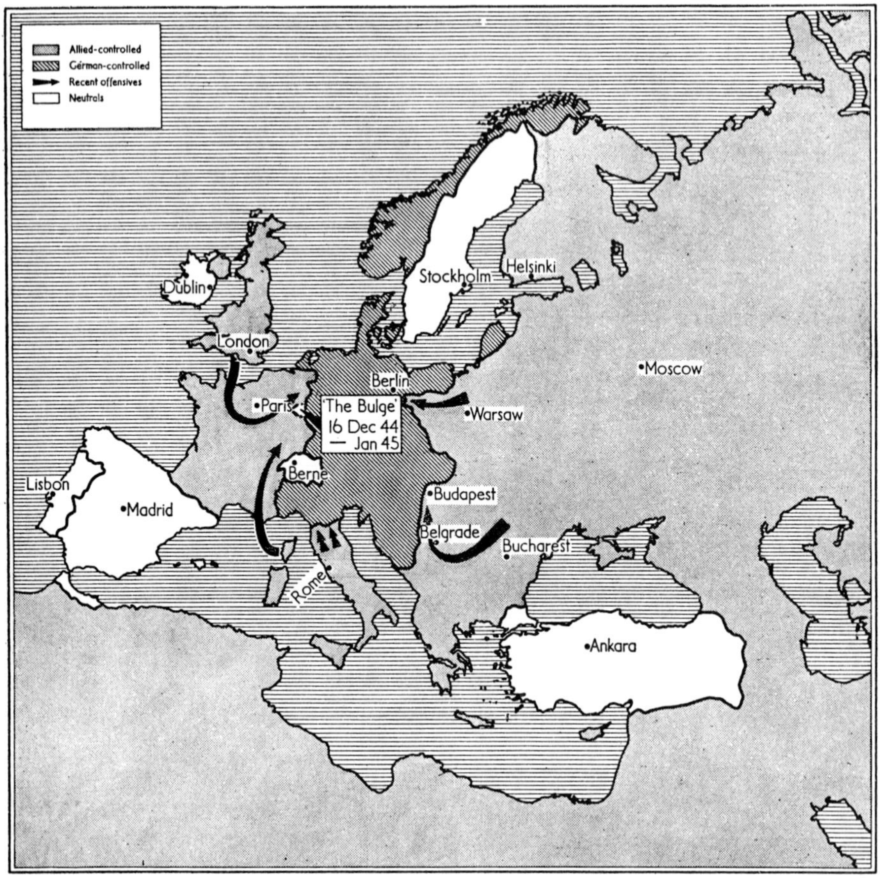

Map 5. EUROPEAN THEATRE, FEBRUARY 1945 (YALTA CONFERENCE)

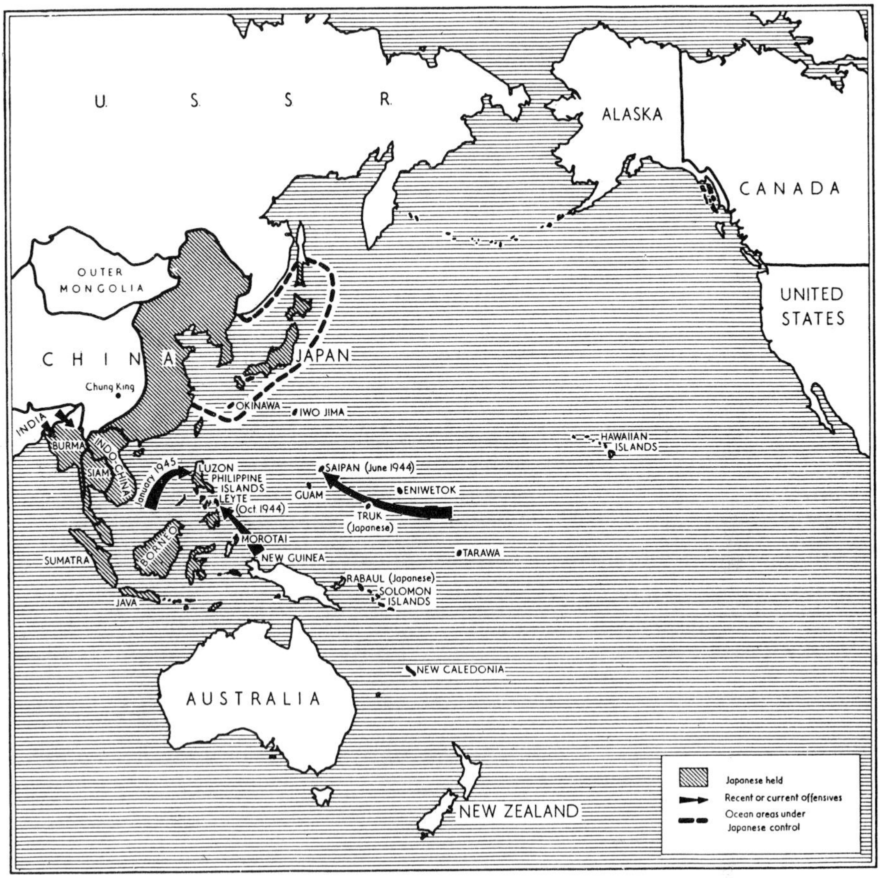

Map 6. JAPANESE THEATRE, FEBRUARY 1945 (YALTA CONFERENCE)

the time the Conference ended, everyone who had taken part in it was thoroughly tired out, not least Roosevelt, whose health at the time gave various of his associates cause for concern.[1] That the President's physical condition had any bearing on the results of the Conference cannot be proved. It is, however, a fact that he was anxious to break off the meeting before either Churchill or Stalin felt that everything had been satisfactorily settled. Roosevelt's attitude rushed the final stages of the Conference and led to the exclusion of certain items from the agenda which might otherwise have been considered.[2]

The Yalta Conference began, as had the Tehrān Conference, with a private interview between Roosevelt and Stalin, at which Molotov also was present. Roosevelt's first remark, after preliminary courtesies, showed, if half in jest, something of the mistaken estimate of the military balance of forces which the Americans brought with them to the Conference. He told Stalin that on the way over the Americans had placed various bets as to whether the Russians would capture Berlin before the Americans took Manila. Stalin replied that those who bet on Manila would win. After some further discussion of the progress of the campaign against Germany, Roosevelt asked Stalin how he had fared with de Gaulle when the French leader had visited Moscow in December.[3] Stalin replied that de Gaulle was unrealistic in his pretensions. Finally, the question of whether or not France should be granted a zone of occupation in Germany was touched upon. Stalin opposed the idea, while Roosevelt declared that perhaps it would be a good idea 'out of kindness' for the French. On this note the interview was broken off in order to begin the first plenary session.[4]

Stalin opened the proceedings by suggesting that Roosevelt should take the chair, as he had done at Tehrān. The first topic for discussion was the military situation. General Antonov, Chief of the Russian General Staff, began with a circumstantial and detailed account of the progress of the recent Russian offensive through Poland; General Marshall followed with a description of the Battle of the Bulge and of Anglo-American plans for resuming the offensive; and Admiral Cunningham concluded with some remarks about the anticipated resumption of German U-boat warfare. In the course of these talks, Stalin, Churchill, and Roosevelt interposed ques-

[1] Reports of the state of Roosevelt's health at the time of the Yalta Conference are conflicting, and much apparently depended on the mood and moment at which one or another observer encountered the President. Cf. Stettinius: *Roosevelt and the Russians*, pp. 73–74; Cunningham: *A Sailor's Odyssey*, p. 627; Byrnes: *Speaking Frankly*, pp. 22–23; Harriman Statement regarding War-time Relations with the Soviet Union, *Congressional Record*, 27 August 1951, p. A5666.

[2] Stettinius: *Roosevelt and the Russians*, pp. 229, 246; Leahy: *I Was There*, p. 374.

[3] See above, p. 530.

[4] Stettinius: *Roosevelt and the Russians*, pp. 97–99; Sherwood: *Roosevelt and Hopkins*, p. 851; Eng. edition, ii. 843.

tions and remarks freely; and at the end of the meeting it was agreed that the Chiefs of Staff of the three countries should meet on the following morning to co-ordinate their future plans in detail.

The military conversations which ensued were cordial and, on the whole, unimportant. The Russians and the Anglo-Americans explained to one another the plans each had prepared for future operations. Two tripartite meetings of the Chiefs of Staff sufficed to explore first the European and then the Japanese war in adequate detail. At a third meeting the Americans pressed their Soviet colleagues for agreements concerning the use of Russian bases by American forces in the Far East and the establishment of shuttle airfields in Hungary to facilitate bombing of eastern Germany, and sought permission to send teams to survey bomb damage in areas held by the Red Army. But the Soviet Chiefs of Staff could not answer until Stalin had passed judgement. Instead, they stalled. They had no independent power to commit themselves to anything. Under such circumstances, the military conversations of necessity were limited to exchange of information.[1] From these conversations one decision did, however, emerge. The Anglo-American Combined Chiefs suggested that Eisenhower should be empowered to communicate directly with Moscow on matters of mutual concern. The Russians acceted the proposal pwillingly enough.[2]

Really important issues of military policy had to be settled by Stalin, in consultation with Roosevelt and, to a lesser extent, with Churchill. In the afternoon of the day when the Soviet Chiefs of Staff declared themselves unable to reply to the American requests concerning bases (8 February), Stalin took up the points in question with Roosevelt, and agreed out of hand to everything the Americans asked, except for the establishment of air bases in Kamchatka, where the presence of a Japanese Consul would, he declared, make it impossible to keep the operation secret.[3] Stalin's assurances seemed to remove the obstacles to Russo-American military collaboration; but, as in previous instances,[4] the Americans entrusted with carrying out the agreements found one delay after another blocking their path. Thus the Americans never used the promised airfields near Budapest, nor, in the end, did American planes fly from Soviet bases in the Far East.[5]

[1] Leahy: *I Was There*, pp. 353, 355–6, 360–1. Actually the most significant military consultations at Yalta on the Chiefs of Staff level were those conducted between the Americans and the British. Various points not fully settled at Malta were agreed to, and a formal report, setting forth the decisions reached, was prepared for Churchill and Roosevelt to approve. This work was not finished until 9 February, two days before the end of the Conference.

[2] Eisenhower: *Crusade in Europe*, p. 367; Wilson: *Eight Years Overseas*, p. 249.

[3] Leahy: *I Was There*, pp. 361–2.

[4] See above, pp. 378–9, 519–20.

[5] Deane: *Strange Alliance*, pp. 157, 251–4, 265. See also below, p. 579. A similar fate befell an agreement concluded by General Deane at the Yalta Conference which defined the methods and procedures to be followed in returning liberated prisoners of war to the Russian and American armies (cf. Stettinius: *Roosevelt and the Russians*, p. 274; Deane, op. cit. pp. 188–91).

These were, however, essentially minor questions. One of Roosevelt's prime purposes in coming to Yalta was to pin down firmly and finally Stalin's promise, given at Tehrān,[1] to join in the Japanese war as soon as he could gather his forces together after victory had come in Europe. Details of the scale and timing of Russian intervention against Japan had largely been settled during Churchill's visit to Moscow in October 1944;[2] but what had not been settled was the price to be paid for Stalin's intervention. The Soviet dictator had mentioned in October political prerequisites for his intervention; and in December 1944 he explained to the American Ambassador, Averell Harriman, exactly what he wished to gain in the Far East. Thus Roosevelt came to Yalta with a clear knowledge of what would be demanded of him.[3] He came also, it is safe to surmise, with the definite intention of accepting Stalin's major demands in order to gain Russian military assistance which the U.S. Joint Chiefs of Staff assured him would be vital for shortening the war against Japan.

As a matter of fact, Stalin's political terms for participation in the Japanese war were well calculated to conform to Roosevelt's way of thinking. Except for the Kurile Islands, the Russians did not ask for anything new. They asked only for the restitution of old rights and territories seized from the Tsarist Government as a result of the Russo-Japanese war of 1904–5. This demand, it could be argued, simply conformed to the principle enunciated after the First Cairo Conference when Roosevelt, Churchill, and Chiang Kai-shek had solemnly declared that Japan would be forced to disgorge all the fruits of past aggression.[4] Roosevelt very probably viewed the matter in this light; and, if he did, one can understand why he accepted Stalin's demands so readily.[5]

Nevertheless, there was a serious difficulty. In Manchuria Chinese and Russian claims for restitution of old rights came into conflict. Stalin wanted to renew Russian leases on the ports of Dairen and Port Arthur and to re-establish Russian control over the Manchurian railways. He also wished for an international guarantee of the maintenance of the autonomous status of Outer Mongolia. These were things which no Chinese Government could be expected to accept with enthusiasm. Roosevelt hoped he would be able to soften Stalin's terms and make them more palatable to the Chinese.

[1] See above, p. 352. [2] See above, p. 519.

[3] Harriman Statement regarding War-time Relations with the Soviet Union, *Congressional Record*, 27 August 1951, p. A5666.

[4] See above, pp. 347–8.

[5] Roosevelt was not well acquainted with the history of the Far East, and may well have failed to realize that Stalin was claiming the restitution of rights which had been won by the imperialistic methods he decried, and which had been enjoyed only fleetingly under the Tsars—in the case of Port Arthur for only six years.

On 8 February he met Stalin to discuss the question. Roosevelt indicated that he saw no difficulty at all in accepting the other Russian demands—the retrocession of southern Sakhalin and the cession of the Kuriles. With regard to Manchuria, Roosevelt informed Stalin that Chiang Kai-shek would probably be willing to make Dairen and Port Arthur into free ports under an international commission of some sort, and suggested that an agreement along these lines would be better than simply to renew the old Tsarist leases. The President also indicated that he thought joint Russo-Chinese operation and ownership of the Manchurian railway would be a better arrangement than outright Russian control.[1]

During the following two days Harriman and Molotov carried on the negotiation and succeeded in drawing up a draft agreement. On 10 February Stalin and Roosevelt met again to go over what their subordinates had done and to settle the points still in dispute. Two matters caused the main difficulty. Stalin insisted that Port Arthur would be needed by the Soviet Union as a naval base, and could therefore not be made an international port; he also wished to deny Chiang Kai-shek any power to revise or reject the agreements he and Roosevelt had reached. Roosevelt was reluctant to agree to these demands, but in the end he yielded on Port Arthur. Stalin conceded a point by allowing the following sentence to be inserted into the text: 'It is understood that the agreement concerning Outer Mongolia and the ports and railroads referred to above will require concurrence of Generalissimo Chiang Kai-shek. The President will take measures in order to obtain this concurrence on advice from Marshal Stalin.' But the force of this clause was nullified by the paragraph immediately following: 'The Heads of the three Great Powers have agreed that these claims of the Soviet Union shall be unquestionably fulfilled after Japan has been defeated.'[2]

As a result of their interview of 10 February 1945, Roosevelt and Stalin agreed upon a text defining the gains which Russia should have from Japan's defeat. On the next day, 11 February, the text was shown to Churchill, and his concurrence requested. Despite the fact that he had taken no active part in drawing it up, the Prime Minister decided to sign the document,[3] which accordingly took the form of a tripartite agreement.

In its final form, the agreement read as follows:

The leaders of the three Great Powers—the Soviet Union, the United States

[1] Harriman Statement regarding War-time Relations with the Soviet Union, *Congressional Record*, 27 August 1951, p. A5667. Roosevelt had sounded Chiang out on the question of making Dairen a free port at the First Cairo Conference.

[2] Harriman Statement, loc. cit. The text of the Agreement was published exactly a year after its signature, on 11 February 1946 (*Department of State Bulletin*, 24 February 1946, xiv. 282; *Documents on American Foreign Relations, 1944–1945*, pp. 355–6).

[3] Eden advised against this move (cf. Stettinius: *Roosevelt and the Russians*, p. 93; Wilmot: *Struggle for Europe*, p. 653).

of America and Great Britain—have agreed that in two or three months after Germany has surrendered and the war in Europe has terminated, the Soviet Union shall enter into the war against Japan on the side of the Allies on condition that:

1. The status quo in Outer-Mongolia (the Mongolian People's Republic) shall be preserved;
2. The former rights of Russia violated by the treacherous attack of Japan in 1904 shall be restored, viz.:
   (*a*) the southern part of Sakhalin, as well as all the islands adjacent to it shall be returned to the Soviet Union;
   (*b*) the commercial port of Dairen shall be internationalized, the preeminent interest of the Soviet Union in this port being safeguarded and the lease of Port Arthur as a naval base of the U.S.S.R. restored;
   (*c*) the Chinese–Eastern Railroad and the South Manchurian Railroad which provides an outlet to Dairen shall be jointly operated by the establishment of a joint Soviet–Chinese Company, it being understood that the preeminent interests of the Soviet Union shall be safeguarded and that China shall retain full sovereignty in Manchuria;
3. The Kurile Islands shall be handed over to the Soviet Union.

Then followed the two paragraphs, quoted above, concerning Chiang's concurrence. The agreement concluded: 'For its part the Soviet Union expresses its readiness to conclude with the National Government of China a pact of friendship and alliance between the U.S.S.R. and China in order to render assistance to China with its armed forces for the purpose of liberating China from the Japanese yoke.'

Of all Roosevelt's war-time acts, this agreement has most often been attacked. At the time, he felt well content with the bargain he had struck. Stalin had promised to fight Japan, thus helping America; he had also promised to aid the Chinese National Government and to recognize its sovereignty over Manchuria, thus helping Chiang. Yet Roosevelt found himself in a profoundly awkward position. He was surrendering Chinese claims in Manchuria and Outer Mongolia without consulting the Chinese themselves. Such an act certainly smacked of the imperialistic bargains among Great Powers of which Americans had often been critical in the past, and which Roosevelt himself had often attacked.

Yet it is easy to see why Roosevelt acted as he did. Partly it was because secrets could not be trusted in Chungking; partly it was because Roosevelt had confidence in his ability to win Chiang's willing endorsement of what was after all a good bargain for the Chinese National Government; partly it was because neither Stalin nor Churchill, but especially the former, wished to accept Chiang Kai-shek and the Chinese as equals in negotiation; and partly it was because the military failures of the Chinese Government in the war had done much to dissolve Roosevelt's earlier confidence in China's right and capacity to act as a Great Power.

The whole affair was shrouded in the deepest secrecy. Admiral Leahy was the only member of Roosevelt's entourage who was entrusted with knowledge of the text of the agreement, and so responsible an official as the American Secretary of State was kept in ignorance of what had been decided.[1] It appears that Stalin formally announced to the plenary session, either on 10 or 11 February, that Russia would enter the war against Japan within two or three months after V-E day, and outlined in very general terms the agreement he had just reached with Roosevelt about political changes in the Far East. This seems to be the closest the deal came to any sort of general airing at the Yalta Conference.[2]

Military problems did not take a prominent place in the Yalta discussions. The secret Roosevelt–Stalin conversations did of course exercise a very important influence from behind the scenes, setting much of the tone of Russo-American relations at the Conference. No similar link between British and Russian policy existed, and in the debates over the political future of Europe, which occupied by far the largest part of the attention of the Conference, the opposing wills of the two Governments became clearly apparent. Both Britain and Russia had much at stake in Europe and could not subordinate their differences to considerations of military co-operation in the Far East, still less to plans for the establishment of an international organization. The American Government, on the other hand, could and did do just this. Hence in the debates over Europe's future Roosevelt generally played a relatively passive part, and fell naturally into the role of mediator between Churchill and Stalin.

The first subject that came up for decision was the question of Allied policy towards Germany. The labours of the European Advisory Commission had provided a blue print for occupation administrative machinery, and, as we have seen,[3] while the Yalta Conference was in session, on 6 February, a protocol which defined the three zones of occupation was finally ratified. This protocol provided for the establishment of an Allied Control Council, comprising the Commanders-in-Chief of each national occupation force; and it recognized Berlin, the seat of the Allied Control Council, as a special zone, jointly under the control of all three Allied Powers.

This still left unsettled the general problem of Allied policy towards defeated Germany The eradication of the Nazi Party, of Nazi laws and institutions, and of 'militarism' were goals that won general acceptance.

[1] Sherwood: *Roosevelt and Hopkins*, p. 866; Eng. edition, ii. 854; Leahy: *I Was There*, p. 364; Stettinius: *Roosevelt and the Russians*, pp. 90–94.

[2] Leahy: *I Was There*, p. 373; Sherwood: *Roosevelt and Hopkins*, p. 867; Eng. edition, ii. 855. Oddly enough, Stettinius's day-by-day account of the Conference makes no mention of this announcement. This omission may arise from Stettinius's desire to disclaim all responsibility for the Agreement. As it stands, Stettinius's record leaves a very different impression from Leahy's. Sherwood's book is not clear, but seems to imply that the general terms of the Agreement were put before the Conference.

[3] See above, p. 538.

In the communiqué issued at the close of the Yalta Conference the Allies reaffirmed their intention to extirpate these things. But there were other matters of economic and political policy upon which it was not so easy to agree. The discussion at Yalta centred round three points. (1) Should Germany be dismembered, and if so, should the terms of surrender, as drawn up by the European Advisory Commission, be amended to say so explicitly? (2) What part should France play in occupying and controlling Germany? And (3) what amount and form of reparations should be imposed upon Germany, and how should the total be divided among claimant nations?

Churchill accepted dismemberment of Germany in principle, but wanted to put off a definite decision until after expert study. He also felt that mention of dismemberment should be kept out of the surrender instrument. Stalin wanted a decision; but the matter was referred to the Foreign Ministers. After two meetings at which the matter was discussed, the Foreign Ministers agreed that a mention of dismemberment should be inserted in the surrender terms for Germany, and that a special commission, composed of Eden and the Russian and American Ambassadors in London, should be entrusted with working out a specific recommendation as to how dismemberment should be brought about.[1]

The question of French participation in the occupation and control of Germany was an even more difficult matter. The British were anxious to bring France in on a plane of full equality since they felt they could not count, for any long time, upon American help in the task of occupying Germany. Roosevelt, indeed, said once again[2] that American troops would be withdrawn from Germany within two years of the end of the war. In view of Roosevelt's statement, the British felt that it was imperative to have French participation in Allied Government of Germany from the beginning. Who else could take over part or all of the American zone so soon to be vacated? Roosevelt was willing enough to give the French a zone of occupation in western Germany; but, when Stalin objected to French participation in the Allied Control Commission (which, according to the proposals accepted by the European Advisory Commission, would be charged with the determination of over-all Allied policy towards Germany), Roosevelt, too, stated that he saw no reason for giving the French equality with the victorious Powers.

The question was referred to the Foreign Ministers. Agreement proved difficult, and it was only after private conversations among the three Heads of Government that a final decision was reached. On 10 February, Roosevelt announced to the plenary session that he had changed his mind, and

[1] For a detailed account of the confusion of cross purposes which ensued from this decision, see Philip E. Mosely: 'Dismemberment of Germany', *Foreign Affairs*, April 1950, xxviii. 487–98.

[2] For his earlier statement to this effect at Tehrān see above, p. 356.

now advocated the admission of the French as equal members of the Allied Control Commission for Germany; Stalin responded with a laconic 'I agree'.[1] It is impossible to reconstruct the situation which led to this turn of events. The Conference was nearing its end. Decisions on contentious points were coming thick and fast; and on this question the arguments of the British and of some of Roosevelt's expert advisers prevailed.[2]

Reparations presented an equally difficult problem. The Russians came to the Conference with a definite proposal. They wished to fix the total of German reparations at $20 milliard, and claimed half of this sum for themselves. They proposed that reparations worth $10 milliard should be seized within two years of the end of hostilities in the form of movable capital—machinery, rolling-stock, &c. The balance they wished to take from current German production over a period of ten years. The Soviet plan was calculated to reduce the capital plant of German heavy industry by 80 per cent. Heavy industries remaining in the country as well as all secondary industries useful for war production were to be 'internationalized', i.e. put under the control of Allied boards of directors.

The Russian proposal was less drastic than the Morgenthau Plan which Roosevelt and Churchill had accepted at Quebec five months earlier.[3] Instead of total destruction of German heavy industry, 20 per cent. of it was to remain operative; and there was no talk of making Germany an agricultural and pastoral nation. The Russians may, therefore, have felt themselves moderate and eminently reasonable in putting forward the figure of $20 milliard for reparations.[4] They were certainly indignant when the British argued that the total was too great.

But British and American views had undergone a very considerable change since the Second Quebec Conference. Churchill in particular had begun to consider what might be the effect upon German society if the Allies imposed heavy reparations payments upon an impoverished and distracted nation. Might not economic suffering and despair provide a fertile ground for revolution? Might not Britain and America even find themselves compelled, by considerations of humanity and by their political interest in the re-establishment of a stable German régime, to subsidize

[1] Stettinius: *Roosevelt and the Russians*, p. 233.

[2] Until a record of Churchill's private conversations with Stalin at Yalta has been published it will be impossible to reconstruct the full story of the Conference. It is very likely that Churchill found occasion to champion France in private with Stalin, but what, if any, *quid pro quo* Churchill may have yielded must remain a matter for speculation. It may be that the British accepted the Russian formula for Poland in exchange for Stalin's acceptance of the British proposal for admitting France to the Allied Control Council of Germany. But this is merely a guess.

[3] See above, pp. 489–90.

[4] The figure was not chosen altogether at random. Russian experts had calculated that the national wealth of Germany at the end of the war would amount to $75 milliard of which about $22 or $23 milliard would be in mobile form, available for transfer to other countries. Subtracting $10 milliard worth of this mobile wealth would, they calculated, reduce the German standard of living to roughly the level of East European states (Stettinius: *Roosevelt and the Russians*, p. 155).

Germany if too heavy reparations were imposed? Thoughts such as these were presumably in Churchill's mind when he challenged the wisdom of trying to set any figure for the total reparations to be paid by Germany until after expert study had indicated how much could reasonably be expected. He dwelt upon the fiasco of reparations after the First World War and gave a warning against a repetition of that experience.

Roosevelt took no very decisive stand. He declared that the United States would not, as in the 1920s, lend money to Germany after the end of the war. He explained that Germany should not be made to starve by excessive removals of industry, but at the same time Russia and Britain should get as much reparations as possible. As far as the United States was concerned, Roosevelt declared, his Government wanted no reparations from Germany other than the confiscation of German property located in the United States itself.

After this preliminary exchange of views, the Big Three agreed that a Reparation Commission should be set up in Moscow to study the technical details, and they asked the Foreign Ministers to prepare instructions for the Commission.[1]

This proved a difficult task. Meeting with his colleagues, Eden continued to champion a moderate policy towards defeated Germany and raised the question of how reparations should be apportioned between the various countries which had suffered damage from the Nazis. Various subordinate issues proved amenable to compromise, but the central question of whether or not to fix a total value for reparations payments could not be answered to the satisfaction of both the British and the Russians. On this point, Stettinius personally felt that the Russians were not unreasonable in proposing a total of $20 milliard;[2] but on instructions from Roosevelt he backed Eden and urged that no sum should be fixed until after expert study.

The inability of the Foreign Ministers to agree led to a second discussion of the reparations problem at the plenary session of 10 February. Stalin spoke with great emphasis on behalf of the Russian demands, and said that if what the British really meant was that Russia should get no reparations at all, now was the time to say so openly. Churchill repudiated such an intention, but as before he opposed any mention of a specific sum, pending investigation of Germany's capacity to pay. Roosevelt, too, showed more openly his doubts about the practicability of imposing heavy reparations than he had done during the earlier discussion of the question. However, when the dispute between Stalin and Churchill showed no sign of terminating in agreement, Roosevelt decided to accept the Russian figure of $20 milliard 'as a basis for discussion', leaving the British to disagree.[3]

[1] Stettinius: *Roosevelt and the Russians*, pp. 123–7. [2] Ibid. p. 206.

[3] Leahy: *I Was There*, pp. 371–2; Sherwood: *Roosevelt and Hopkins*, p. 862; Eng. edition, ii. 851; Stettinius: *Roosevelt and the Russians*, pp. 234–6. The latter account describes Stalin as 'giving in',

Although agreement could thus not be attained on the question of the total amount of reparations to be demanded from Germany, on other aspects of the problem satisfactory formulae were arrived at. It was agreed that both the suffering endured at the hands of the Nazis and the contribution to Allied victory should be considered in apportioning reparations among the various claimant nations. It was also agreed that German reparations should take three forms: capital removals, payments from current production, and—a striking and somewhat chilling innovation in international practice—forced labour.

In general, these decisions concerning future Allied policy towards Germany were vague; and the failure to achieve complete agreement on reparations and other issues foreshadowed the situation which prevailed at the Potsdam Conference five months later. Yet the future of Germany was surely the most important single question confronting the Allies. While Germany remained undefeated the problem could be shelved or disguised by generalities: but it is clear at least in retrospect that one of the major failures at Yalta was the inability of the Big Three to arrive at any genuine meeting of minds as to their future policy for the administration of Germany. The machinery proposed by the European Advisory Commission was all very well, but it could not possibly work in practice unless the instructions given to each Allied High Commissioner ran parallel. The discussions at Yalta made it clear that such parallelism could not be expected.

One reason why the German question was handled so unsatisfactorily at Yalta was the pressure of other business. American attention was focused primarily upon the United Nations organization; and the problem of Poland usurped an entirely disproportionate amount of time. Both these issues came up for the first time at the third plenary session on 6 February.

Discussion of the voting formula for the Security Council was the first item on the agenda at the third plenary session. This had been the main point upon which the Dumbarton Oaks Conference had bogged down,[1] and Roosevelt regarded a solution of the impasse as his primary political aim at the Conference. The Americans had drawn up a compromise formula which they hoped the Russians would accept. It had been submitted to Stalin and Churchill for examination on 5 December 1944; and great was the consternation of the Americans when they discovered that Stalin had not found time to familiarize himself with the details of the new proposal.[2]

not Roosevelt; but Stettinius is not quite accurate, as the language of the protocol shows (ibid. p. 308).

[1] See above, pp. 507–8.

[2] Byrnes: *Speaking Frankly*, p. 37; Leahy: *I Was There*, p. 356; Stettinius: *Roosevelt and the*

Stettinius did his best to repair the situation with a careful and detailed exposition of the American scheme. He distinguished two categories of questions which might come before the Security Council. Some would require a unanimous vote of the permanent members of the Council—including such matters as admission and suspension of member nations, removal of threats to peace and suppression of breaches of the peace, regulation of armaments, &c. But there were certain other issues of a quasi-judicial nature which might be expected to come before the Security Council—for example, whether an international dispute was likely to threaten peace if long continued, whether the Council should call on the nations concerned to settle a dispute themselves or should pursue peaceable procedures suggested by the Council, whether a dispute should be referred to the International Court of Justice, or whether a regional association of nations should be asked to try to settle a quarrel. With respect to issues such as these the Americans suggested that the representatives of the permanent members of the Council should not be permitted to vote if their own nation were a party to the dispute.[1]

When Stettinius had finished his explanation, Churchill stated that he found the proposal entirely satisfactory. Stalin asked for more time to study it. In the ensuing discussion Stalin emphasized that the structure of the international organization should be such as to prevent disputes between the Great Allied Powers. Only so, he said, could renewal of German aggression be prevented. He recalled how the League of Nations had expelled Russia during the Finnish War of 1939, and made it clear that he feared any abrogation of the veto power might open the door to a similar mobilization of the moral, if not of the physical, power of the United Nations organization against Russia at some time in the future.

Despite these doubts, Stalin announced at the plenary session on the following day (7 February) that he was happy to accept the American proposal for voting procedure on the Security Council in its entirety, having become convinced that the necessary unity of the Great Powers was fully protected.[2] But there was still a fly in the ointment. The Russians asked that three or at least two of the Soviet Republics be invited to be charter

Russians, p. 140. Churchill, too, found it hard to get excited over the technicalities of the procedure of an organization yet to be born. On the eve of the Yalta Conference he inclined to the opinion that, since everything would depend upon continued agreement among the Big Three, it would be sensible to recognize the fact and accept the Russian argument for an absolute and unqualified veto power. Eden, on the other hand, supported the compromise proposal (cf. ibid. pp. 58–59, 64).

It is possible that Stalin's profession of ignorance on this occasion was a deliberate gambit, designed to give him more time for behind-the-scenes bargaining with Roosevelt. Stettinius did not so interpret the situation, but he was excluded from much of the inner workings of the Conference.

[1] Stettinius: *Roosevelt and the Russians*, pp. 132–7.

[2] This decision may have resulted from private consultations between Stalin, Roosevelt, and Churchill. At any rate, Churchill was able to inform Stettinius just before the session opened that 'Uncle Joe will take Dumbarton Oaks' (ibid. p. 161).

members of the new organization. This was a retreat from the demand made at Dumbarton Oaks for the admission of all sixteen Soviet Republics,[1] but it none the less embarrassed Roosevelt seriously.[2] The President tried to evade the issue by embarking upon irrelevancies. He then proposed that the Foreign Ministers should consider the whole matter of which nations should be invited to become charter members of the new international organization, and at the same time should set a time and place for an international conference that would establish the new world organization. Churchill, anxious to defend the right of India to representation in the Assembly of the United Nations organization, professed himself to be personally in sympathy with Stalin's proposal, but reserved official decision.[3]

When the Foreign Ministers met to discuss the problem, Eden made it clear that the British Government would support Russia's claim to multiple representation in the Assembly. Stettinius hedged, but immediately after the end of the meeting Roosevelt decided that he would have to swallow his scruples and agree to the Soviet claim on behalf of the Ukraine and White Russia. The Foreign Ministers also agreed that the proposed Conference should meet on 25 April 1945 in the United States, and on 10 February Roosevelt approved Stettinius's idea of locating the Conference at San Francisco.[4]

One more hurdle had to be crossed. Stalin wanted the two constituent Republics of the Soviet Union for which he was claiming separate representation to be invited to San Francisco; the Americans and British wished to leave the matter open for decision by the San Francisco Conference itself, with the understanding that they both would back the proposal for the admission of the Ukraine and White Russia to the Assembly of the United Nations organization whenever the Soviet Union chose to propose the step. Stalin conceded the point after some debate.

The whole matter of determining what nations should be invited to the Conference was awkward. Stalin and Molotov objected to inviting countries, mainly in Latin America, with which the Soviet Union did not maintain diplomatic relations, and which had not declared war against Germany. They also questioned the propriety of inviting Turkey and

[1] See above, p. 506.

[2] One of the arguments used against American participation in the League of Nations was that the U.S.A. would be outvoted by the British, because the overseas self-governing dominions of the Crown had been given separate representation side by side with the United Kingdom in that organization. The Soviet Union's demand for multiple representation in the Assembly of the United Nations organization might expose Roosevelt to a similar criticism, and he was always mindful of Wilsonian precedents.

[3] Churchill also tried to postpone decision upon the time and place of a conference for establishing the new organization—moved, the Americans thought, by considerations of internal British politics. Cf. Stettinius: *Roosevelt and the Russians*, p. 163; Sherwood: *Roosevelt and Hopkins*, p. 863; Eng. edition, ii. 852.

[4] Stettinius: *Roosevelt and the Russians*, pp. 178, 186.

Egypt to San Francisco. Roosevelt succeeded in disarming criticism by a frank admission of the situation in Latin America. The United States, he explained, had told these countries in 1942 that it would not be necessary for them to declare war, and he felt they should not be penalized for having followed American advice. The matter was resolved by deciding that all nations that declared war on 'the common enemy' before 1 March 1945 and that subscribed to the United Nations Declaration of January 1942 by the same date should be invited to San Francisco.[1]

One of the points which had been skipped over at Dumbarton Oaks was the question of how to deal with 'dependent areas' incapable of immediate self-government.[2] Stettinius proposed to Eden and Molotov that the five permanent members of the Security Council should consult each other before the San Francisco Conference in order to prepare recommendations for international trusteeship of such areas. He did not intend to raise the question of what areas might be placed under international trusteeship. What he wished was merely to repair a gap in the Dumbarton Oaks scheme by providing machinery for international trusteeship in the Charter of the new international organization. Eden and Molotov agreed; but when the matter came before the plenary session for ratification (9 February) Churchill exploded with wrath. He believed that the Americans were trying to introduce a device for establishing international control over colonial areas, including, presumably, British colonies. He calmed down a little when Stettinius explained that such international trusteeships would apply only to former League of Nations Mandates, territories taken from the Axis nations during the war, and any areas which might voluntarily be handed over by colonial Powers to international control. But even after this explanation Churchill remained indignant and suspicious. His explosive eloquence gave a dramatic demonstration of the strength of his attachment to the Imperial idea.[3] Nevertheless, it was settled that consultations should take place as Stettinius had suggested.

With Stalin's acceptance of the voting formula for the Security Council and the agreement to call a United Nations Conference at San Francisco on 25 April, Roosevelt could feel that he had attained the primary political

[1] Argentina was specifically excluded from the list of candidates. Stalin asked Roosevelt whether Argentina would be eligible to attend the conference, and the President replied in the negative, though he qualified his remarks by saying that a fundamental change in Argentine policy towards the United Nations would be necessary before admission (Stettinius: *Roosevelt and the Russians*, p. 180; Byrnes: *Speaking Frankly*, pp. 38–39). On the question of Argentina, see also pp. 585, 595 below.

[2] See above, p. 508.

[3] Churchill's wrath may partly have been a calculated piece of acting. Yet he had reason for his attitude. Roosevelt apparently suggested to Stalin at Yalta that Hongkong ought really to be turned over to China (Leahy: *I Was There*, p. 368; Sherwood: *Roosevelt and Hopkins*, p. 866; Eng. edition, ii. 854). But once the President had made his deal with Stalin over Dairen and Port Arthur he could hardly raise the question of Hongkong with Churchill in good countenance, and presumably he refrained from doing so.

goal he had set before himself. Unless some unforeseen stumbling-block arose, the war-born United Nations would be securely perpetuated in an international organization to which, if the matter were handled with due caution, the American public and Congress would in all probability adhere.

The only stumbling-block was Russia's demand for triple representation in the Assembly. Some of Roosevelt's most experienced political advisers at the Conference, men who were thoroughly familiar with American party affairs, were convinced that public opinion could easily be mobilized against any such inequality between the United States and Russia.[1] Accordingly on 10 February, as the Conference was nearing its end, Roosevelt wrote letters to Stalin and Churchill asking whether they would support an American request for three seats in the Assembly, if such a request should prove necessary. Stalin answered in the affirmative on the next day, and Churchill did the same.[2]

Even after this assurance had been received, Roosevelt was worried. He decided that his consent to back the Russian request for admission of the Ukraine and White Russia to the Assembly should be kept secret. This secrecy backfired a few weeks later when news of the arrangement leaked into the American press and compelled the President to confess the whole thing under very awkward circumstances.[3]

Despite his worry over the multiple vote for the Soviet Union, Roosevelt could feel generally content with the agreement which had been made about the United Nations organization. The same could not be said for the settlement of the Polish question, which, from the time it was broached during the latter part of the third plenary session on 6 February, dominated the work of the Conference until its end.

The Polish question was acute, and affairs in Poland did not stand still during the Conference. While the debates at Yalta were in progress, the Red Army completed the job of driving the Germans from Polish soil. Day by day the Provisional Polish Government, recognized and supported by Russia, consolidated its control over Polish affairs. Both the British and the Americans wanted to see a new Polish Government established, one which

[1] Byrnes: *Speaking Frankly*, p. 40; Stettinius: *Roosevelt and the Russians*, p. 249; Leahy: *I Was There*, p. 344.

[2] Byrnes: *Speaking Frankly*: p. 41; Stettinius: *Roosevelt and the Russians*, pp. 250–1.

[3] See below, p. 577. Why Roosevelt fell into this error of tactics is impossible to say. On the one hand he and his advisers certainly over-estimated the potential opposition among the public to joining the United Nations organization. On the other hand, it is possible that Roosevelt may have hoped somehow to persuade the Russians to drop the whole thing and settle for a single seat in the Assembly (cf. Stettinius; *Roosevelt and the Russians*, p. 249). The whole matter was absurdly unimportant from a practical point of view, for the Assembly was to have only limited authority, and, in a group of forty to fifty nations, two extra votes, one way or another, could make little or no difference.

would bring together all democratic parties, and, by inference at least, one in which the Polish Communists would have only a minority position. Stalin, on the other hand, was willing to consider a 'broadening' of the Provisional Government then in existence, but was not willing to start afresh or to establish a government in which the Communists would not have the leading part.

When the matter first came up on 6 February Stalin made what was for him a long and impassioned speech, stating that the Polish question was of vital importance for Russia since Poland constituted the great pathway by which Germany could invade the Soviet Union. He declared that a strong, independent, and democratic Poland was a vital necessity for Russia since only such a state could block the Germans: but though the men gathered round the table were certainly aware of the real issue at stake, no one chose to press the question of what Stalin meant by democratic and independent.

There were two aspects of the problem. On the matter of Polish boundaries, Roosevelt and Churchill were both willing to accept something close to the Curzon Line as the demarcation between Russia and Poland. Roosevelt, to be sure, still hoped to persuade Stalin to give Lwów and the nearby oil-wells to the Poles, but, when Stalin declined to do so, Roosevelt dropped the matter without more ado.[1] Poland's western boundaries were more in dispute. The Russians wished the Poles to annex German territory as far as the Oder and Neisse rivers; Churchill objected to 'stuffing the Polish goose' too full of German lands. In the end, it was decided to leave the matter open. Poland, according to the protocol and communiqué, was to receive 'substantial accessions of territory on the north and west', but the new German-Polish boundary was to be fixed only after consultation with the Polish Government itself.[2]

The question of boundaries was in every sense secondary to the question of what sort of government should be established in Poland. Discussions during the plenary sessions and the meetings of the Foreign Ministers rang the changes on various formulae presented by the three Powers for the solution of this problem. It is unnecessary to pursue the progress of the argument in detail. Elaborate circumlocution and sophistical appeals to Polish public opinion and sovereign dignity disguised but scarcely hid the real motives at play.

At first the Americans hoped that it would be possible to persuade the Russians to abandon their newly recognized Provisional Government by

[1] Stalin did, however, agree to allow deviations from the Curzon Line at Russian expense to the extent of five to eight kilometres to suit the boundary to local topography.

[2] A point of American constitutional law made it necessary for Roosevelt to alter the language of the agreement on Polish boundaries at the last minute. Instead of committing the three Allied Governments to territorial changes—a step which might infringe a prerogative of the American Senate—the agreement was put in the form of an expression of the will of the three Heads of Government (cf. Stettinius: *Roosevelt and the Russians*, p. 239).

creating some sort of reasonably neutral machinery for setting up a new Government of National Unity. On the night of 6 February Roosevelt sent a proposal to that effect to Stalin. It proved unacceptable and was withdrawn on 9 February.[1] From that time onward it seemed clear that Roosevelt wished to reach some sort of verbal agreement over Poland at almost any cost. He had come to recognize the tenacity with which the Russians clung to their position and, presumably, he gave up hope of reaching a real meeting of minds. Rather than sacrifice the United Nations organization and the prospect of long-term co-operation with Russia, Roosevelt was willing to give in. After all, as he observed at the plenary session of 8 February, the dispute over the Provisional Government concerned only a temporary situation. All were agreed on the necessity for early elections, free and democratic, which alone could establish the legitimacy of a Polish Government.[2] This did not imply that Roosevelt believed there would be no difficulties over agreeing upon what constituted a free and democratic election. But that was a problem for the future; and with characteristic optimism he could hope that the situation would change, especially when the end of the war against Germany removed the necessity for military security behind Russian lines—one of the most telling arguments which Stalin used on behalf of maintaining the Provisional Government.

Roosevelt presumably believed that he was simply putting first things first by subordinating the Polish question to the establishment of a United Nations organization and to the maintenance of good feeling between the West and Russia. Hence he was in a mood to compromise, quite apart from the growing weariness he must have felt under the exhausting schedule which the Conference imposed upon him.

The British attitude was more unbending; but as the Americans wavered, and sought to sink the difference between Russian and Anglo-American policy towards Poland in a Sargasso Sea of words, there was little that Churchill and Eden could do but reiterate their distrust and dissatisfaction with the Provisional Government as then constituted.

The final decision came on 10 February, the day when nearly all disputed issues were brought to some sort of rest. The declaration on Poland, subscribed to by all three Powers on that day, ran as follows:

> A new situation has been created in Poland as a result of her complete liberation by the Red Army. This calls for the establishment of a Polish Provisional Government which can be more broadly based than was possible before the recent liberation of [the] western part of Poland. The Provisional Government which is now functioning in Poland should therefore be reorganized on a broader democratic basis with the inclusion of democratic leaders from Poland itself and from Poles abroad. This new Government should then be called the Polish Provisional Government of National Unity.

[1] Ibid. pp. 148–50, 199.

[2] Ibid. p. 192.

M. Molotov, Mr. Harriman and Sir A. Clark Kerr are authorized as a commission to consult in the first instance in Moscow with members of the present Provisional Government and with other Polish democratic leaders from within Poland and from abroad, with a view to the reorganization of the present Government along the above lines. This Polish Provisional Government of National Unity shall be pledged to the holding of free and unfettered elections as soon as possible on the basis of universal suffrage and secret ballot. In these elections all democratic and Anti-Nazi parties shall have the right to take part and to put forward candidates.[1]

The declaration further stated that, as soon as the Government of Poland had been reorganized as prescribed, the three Allied Powers would extend diplomatic recognition to it.

The careful ambiguity of this declaration is apparent. Was the existing Provisional Government to be scrapped and a new one established? Or was it to constitute the basis of the reorganized Government of National Unity? The real question of the role of the Polish Communists in the new Provisional Government was left as it had been before the discussions started. Obviously, the Russians wished to keep the Communists in a dominant position, and, with the Red Army on the ground, were in a position to do so. Thus, for all the studiously vague wording of the Declaration, it was only realistic to regard it as a success for Stalin. The arguments and remonstrances of the Western Powers had not really changed the Russians' intentions nor had they altered the balance of forces within Poland one iota.

Churchill and Roosevelt realized this fact, whatever hopes they may have had for the Commission which had been set up to oversee future negotiations among the Poles.[2] Roosevelt privately remarked that he knew the agreement could be stretched by the Russians to fit their purposes, but declared: 'It's the best I can do for Poland at this time.'[3] Publicly, in his report to Congress about the Yalta Conference on 1 March, the President fell back upon faint praise. He said: 'I am convinced that the agreement on Poland, under the circumstances, is the most hopeful agreement possible for a free, independent, and prosperous Polish state.'[4] Churchill, too, in his report to the House of Commons on 27 February, did not disguise the fact that the agreement on Poland left still unsettled the most important matter of all: how representative of Polish opinion would the new Provisional Government be? And how free would the elections be? He consoled his hearers with the thought that on these matters the British Government retained full freedom of action, and would pursue a resolute policy.[5]

[1] Stettinius: *Roosevelt and the Russians*, pp. 309–10.
[2] For the meeting of the Commission see below, pp. 576 seqq.
[3] Leahy: *I Was There*, p. 370.
[4] Rosenman: *The Public Papers and Addresses of Franklin D. Roosevelt, 1944–45 volume*, p. 583.
[5] 27 February 1945, H.C.Deb. 5th ser., vol. 408, coll. 1280–4.

A factor which helped to sweeten the Polish pill for Roosevelt and Churchill was Stalin's acceptance of a Declaration on Liberated Europe. This document had been drawn up by the U.S. State Department, and was introduced into the Yalta deliberations on 9 February. By that time the Conference was drawing towards a close, and the Declaration stirred up only a very perfunctory debate. The text, as accepted, ran in part as follows:

> The establishment of order in Europe and the re-building of national economic life must be achieved by processes which will enable the liberated peoples to destroy the last vestiges of Nazism and Fascism and to create democratic institutions of their own choice. . . .
>
> To foster the conditions in which the liberated peoples may exercise these rights, the three governments will jointly assist the people in any European liberated state or former Axis satellite state in Europe where in their judgment conditions require (*a*) to establish conditions of internal peace; (*b*) to carry out emergency measures for the relief of distressed peoples; (*c*) to form interim governmental authorities broadly representative of all the democratic elements in the population and pledged to the earliest possible establishment through free elections of governments responsive to the will of the people; and (*d*) to facilitate where necessary the holding of such elections. . . .
>
> When, in the opinion of the three governments, conditions . . . make such action necessary, they will immediately consult together on the measures necessary to discharge the joint responsibilities set forth in this declaration.[1]

The Americans conceived this Declaration as a sort of antidote to the 'spheres of influence' deal which Churchill and Stalin had concluded in October 1944. Tripartite responsibility and action in all areas of Europe was to be the pattern for the difficult period after the end of hostilities, and special spheres in which one or another of the Allies would have pre-eminent influence were to be abandoned. Stalin clearly had no such thought in mind when he accepted the Declaration. Perhaps he felt it a harmless piece of rhetoric, soothing to the Americans. After all, three-Power action, by the terms of the Declaration, would occur only when all three of the Allies judged it necessary, and any one Power could always find any proposed action unnecessary if its own policies seemed to be called in question. Churchill's views have not been made public; but he was, and at Yalta declared himself to be, ready to submit British actions in Greece to the test of elections supervised by the three Great Powers.[2]

Discussion of the Polish problem took so much time at the Yalta Conference that other political problems got relatively little attention. The situation in Yugoslavia came under consideration formally on 9 February when Eden and Molotov agreed in the course of a crowded meeting of the

[1] Stettinius: *Roosevelt and the Russians*, pp. 305–6.

[2] Ibid. p. 218.

Foreign Ministers that the Tito-Šubašić Agreement of November 1944[1] should promptly be put into effect. At the plenary session on the same day, Churchill and Stalin ratified the agreement.[2] The British also submitted memoranda on the Austro-Yugoslav and the Italian-Yugoslav frontiers, but the Conference was so hurried in its final stages that these questions were relegated to future diplomatic settlement. British objections to the formation of a Yugoslav-Bulgarian federal state were similarly put on record at Yalta; but the question was referred for settlement to the British and American Ambassadors in Moscow who were to consult Molotov on the issue. Memoranda submitted by Eden dealing with the powers of the Western representatives on the Control Commission for Bulgaria, with Greek grievances against the Bulgars, and with British claims to Rumanian oil equipment met the same fate. The Russians did not want to discuss such questions, while Roosevelt had become anxious to bring the Conference to an end and was not willing to haggle over details which could be handled just as well through normal diplomatic channels.

The situation in Persia excited rather more attention. In September 1944 the Russians had tried to get oil concessions in northern Persia, but the Persian Government took the position that no concessions would be granted as long as foreign troops continued to occupy their country.[3] The Russians reluctantly acquiesced for the time being, but in the early months of 1945 Soviet occupation forces in northern Persia began to exercise a closer control over local governmental affairs and to encourage agitation for the autonomy of Azerbaijan, the north-westernmost province of Persia.[4] This seemed to the British a situation that needed airing, and Eden wished to reach an agreement for an early withdrawal of Russian, British, and American troops from the country.

Roosevelt, too, had a peculiar and personal interest in the country. When he had visited Persia for the Tehrān Conference, he had seen the poverty of the land. Soon thereafter he conceived the idea of bringing American technical skill to bear upon the problem of improving the agriculture and water-use of Persia as a sort of demonstration of the potentialities of international economic and technical co-operation in time of peace. This scheme he outlined at the plenary session of 7 February, but his colleagues did not choose to discuss the idea, and so it was dropped.

[1] See above, p. 529.

[2] The only point of disputation concerned two additions to the Tito-Šubašić agreement which the British wished to see made. These prescribed the co-option to Tito's Anti-Fascist Assembly of members of the pre-war Yugoslav legislature who had not exposed themselves to accusations of collaboration, and the submission of legislative acts passed by Tito's Assembly to ratification by a future Constituent Assembly. Stalin accepted these provisions without much argument (Stettinius: *Roosevelt and the Russians*, pp. 208, 214).

[3] This was simultaneously a rebuff to American oil companies which had also been seeking concessions from the Persian Government (Hull: *Memoirs*, ii. 1509).

[4] See *Survey* for 1939–46: *The Middle East in the War*, pp. 483–5.

The Russians were no doubt suspicious of the peculiar concern for Persia which the British and Americans expressed at Yalta. Molotov stubbornly refused to discuss Persian affairs, arguing that the problem was not a pressing one. Hence, no agreement about the withdrawal of troops or about the procedure for seeking oil concessions in the future was reached.[1]

On 10 February Stalin raised the question of revision of the Montreux Convention which governed Turkey's power over the Bosporus and Dardanelles.[2] He said that an agreement more favourable to Russia could and should be substituted for the existing one, but, since the Conference was by then in its last stages, he proposed simply that the Foreign Ministers should consider the question at their next meeting. Roosevelt and Churchill both agreed without demur.[3]

The multiplicity of problems which confronted the Yalta Conference was all too apparent to the men who participated in it. When Churchill suggested (8 February) that for the future the three Powers should arrange periodic meetings of the Foreign Ministers at intervals of not more than three months in order to handle the host of similar questions which victory would be sure to bring, all agreed with the proposal. London was chosen as the first place of assemblage. The meetings, it was agreed, would take place in the three capitals in rotation.[4]

A cursory discussion of the treatment to be accorded to major war criminals, introduced by Churchill at the plenary session of 9 February, was the only other matter of note considered at Yalta. There was, again, no decision, save to refer the matter to future meetings of the Foreign Ministers.[5]

The Yalta Conference came to a climax on 10 February when decisions were reached on Poland, the Declaration on Liberated Europe, the admission of France to the Allied Control Commission for Germany, the text of the telegram to be sent to Tito and Šubašić urging them to act upon their agreement of November 1944, and on the statement about reparations. All the threads of negotiation, compromise, and evasion came together on that day at the plenary session; and when it was over the real work of the Conference had come to an end.

That evening Churchill gave a dinner at which high spirits and a sense

[1] Stettinius: *Roosevelt and the Russians*, pp. 175, 230; Sherwood: *Roosevelt and Hopkins*, p. 865; Eng. edition, ii. 853.

[2] For the Montreux Convention, see *Survey* for 1936, pp. 584–645.

[3] Stettinius: *Roosevelt and the Russians*, pp. 237–8.

[4] This arrangement took the place of a plan which the State Department had urged upon Roosevelt for the establishment of a European High Commission. The President, however, had rejected the idea and consequently it was not brought before the Yalta Conference (ibid. pp. 42, 193–4).

[5] Ibid. pp. 219, 309.

of relief and relaxation prevailed. On the next day, all that remained was to sign the documents which the Conference had produced, and to agree upon the wording of the communiqué and protocol. The communiqué omitted mention of several points which had been discussed. It declared that military plans for the defeat of Germany had been concerted, and described arrangements for the occupation and control of Germany, omitting mention of dismemberment of the country on the ground that it might prolong Nazi resistance. Reparations, the San Francisco Conference, the Declaration on Liberated Europe, and statements on Poland, on Yugoslavia, and on future meetings of the three Foreign Ministers were all made public. The details of the voting formula for the Security Council were, however, withheld pending consultation with the two other permanent members of the Council, France and China. Likewise the agreement to give Russia multiple representation in the Assembly was kept secret.

The communiqué, released on 12 February 1945, ended on an optimistic note.

> Our meeting here in the Crimea has reaffirmed our common determination to maintain and strengthen in the peace to come that unity of purpose and of action which has made victory possible and certain for the United Nations in this war. . . .
>
> Only with the continuing and growing co-operation and understanding among our three countries and among all the peace-loving nations can the highest aspiration of humanity be realized—a secure and lasting peace which will, in the words of the Atlantic Charter, 'afford assurance that all the men in all the lands may live out their lives in freedom from fear and want'.
>
> Victory in this war and establishment of the proposed international organization will provide the greatest opportunity in all history to create in the years to come the essential conditions of such a peace.[1]

The American delegation, at least, fully believed these words. A mood of exultation prevailed on the ship as Roosevelt returned from Yalta, and when the communiqué reached the American press it was greeted with widespread approbation.[2] Some dubious voices were raised, particularly on behalf of Poland;[3] but in general such doubts and complaints were overwhelmed in a chorus of enthusiasm and confidence.

But, as though symbolic of the shadows that were soon to fall upon the Yalta agreements, the President's company in its passage across the

[1] Text of the communiqué and of the protocol of the Yalta Conference is published in *Documents on American Foreign Relations, 1944–1945*, pp. 348–55; also in Stettinius: *Roosevelt and the Russians*, pp. 293–312.

[2] Cf. editorials in *New York Times*, *New York Herald Tribune*, and *Chicago Daily News*, 13 and 14 February 1945; and a collection of extracts from seventeen leading newspapers published in *New York Herald Tribune*, 14 February 1945.

[3] e.g. remarks by Congressman O'Konski and Senator Wheeler, *New York Times*, 14 February 1945.

Atlantic was not a happy one. Hopkins, feeling desperately ill, left the ship in order to fly home, where he promptly went to a hospital. Roosevelt was annoyed at his departure, and the two men parted coolly, never to meet again. A similarly unhappy ending to a long companionship came when Roosevelt's military aide died of heart attack on board ship. Roosevelt was personally affected by this loss, and when he reached Washington and arranged to make a formal report to Congress, on 1 March 1945, upon the Yalta Conference his mood was no longer so confident, though his hopes for the future and for an eventual and satisfactory solution of the problems of peace remained bright.[1] His own death was only six weeks away as he spoke.

Churchill may not have shared to the full Roosevelt's sense of elation at the end of the Yalta Conference, but the reactions of the British press were as enthusiastic as those of the American.[2] As in America, there were misgivings about Poland, and the question of the severity of reparations demands upon Germany was also publicly mentioned as a possible flaw in the Yalta agreements. Yet these were minor matters compared with the assurances of Big Three harmony and an early end to the war against Germany.

How Stalin viewed the decisions of the Conference cannot be determined. That he thought well of the general outcome seems to be suggested by the blaze of publicity and laudation which was turned upon the Yalta communiqué in all the Soviet press. *Pravda*, for instance, published a special issue to describe the Conference, and said editorially that the Yalta Conference had proved that 'the alliance of the three big Powers possesses not only a historic yesterday and victorious today, but also a great to-morrow'; and *Izvestia* called the Conference the 'greatest political event of current times'.[3] The Russian radio was similarly turned over to information about and praise of the Conference.[4]

To many men in all the Allied countries it seemed as though the Grand Alliance had stood the difficult test of impending victory. Hopes for an enduring peace and for cordial co-operation among the Great Allies had

[1] Sherwood: *Roosevelt and Hopkins*, pp. 873–5; Eng. edition, ii. 861–3.

[2] See e.g. *Manchester Guardian, News Chronicle, Daily Telegraph, Daily Herald, Daily Express, Daily Worker*, leading articles, 14 February 1945.

[3] Quoted from *New York Herald Tribune*, 14 February 1945.

[4] Stalin's initial satisfaction with the Yalta decisions probably did not last long. His speech in celebration of Red Army Day (23 February 1945) conspicuously lacked any reference to Yalta and, indeed, all but the most fleeting reference to the Western Allies. This was in marked contrast to his speech of 6 November 1944 in which he dwelt upon the co-operation between Russia and the West (Stalin: *Great Patriotic War*, pp. 131, 137, 148–51). Difficulties with the Western Powers which had already broken out in Rumania (see below, p. 575) may account for this change, if change it was; it is also possible that members of the Politburo had objected to some of the concessions made at Yalta by the Russians and persuaded Stalin to see matters in a somewhat different light. Men like Hopkins tended to believe that the latter might be the case (cf. Sherwood: *Roosevelt and Hopkins*, p. 870; Eng. edition, ii. 859).

never been stronger. Yalta, as far as the Allied publics were concerned, had been a resounding success. The disputes which had threatened Allied unity in the autumn of 1944 seemed to have been solved satisfactorily. With the war in Europe obviously drawing towards an end, it was a time of high elation, when the fine sentiments of the Atlantic Charter, of the United Nations Declaration, and of speeches at Dumbarton Oaks seemed on the point of becoming something more than mere rhetoric.

In view of subsequent disillusionment, it is hard to recapture the mood of the days that followed the publication of the Yalta communiqué. Within a short time hesitation and doubts about the agreements reached in the Crimea began to assert themselves. The reversal of feeling which followed upon the inability of the Great Powers to make the Yalta agreements work brought the virtues of the agreements themselves into dispute. Yet at the time there was little hesitation or doubt, and it is in the light of the immediate situation of February 1945 that the agreements must in fairness be judged. Certainly there had been compromise on all sides. Stalin had conceded to Roosevelt a limitation on the Soviet veto power on the Security Council; Roosevelt had conceded territory and special rights in the Far East to Stalin. Stalin had conceded something to the British in Yugoslavia; and Churchill had yielded a good deal in Poland.

In trying to estimate whether Roosevelt and Churchill made a good bargain, one fact must always be borne in mind: the Red Army was already in possession of most of Eastern Europe, in a position to defy the West if Stalin chose to do so. And in Manchuria, the Russians would surely have been able to take all or more than all that Roosevelt had conceded as soon as Japanese power collapsed. Thus, unless one argues that the Western Powers should have prepared to fight Russia as soon as Germany collapsed, or to break off their battles against the Nazis and the Japanese short of victory—both of which would have been inconceivable at the time—it seems only fair to say that the concessions made at Yalta to Stalin were no more than recognition (and, in the case of Poland, only partial recognition) of the existing military balance of power.

Yet Yalta was for the Western Powers, and particularly for Roosevelt, a sort of Waterloo. The generous ideals which Roosevelt proclaimed and cherished accorded ill with Stalin's actions in Poland and Eastern Europe generally; and the deal over the Far East was surely a contradiction of Roosevelt's own principles. But having compromised his ideals to satisfy Stalin Roosevelt failed to win the Soviet dictator's support for what remained of them. Rooseveltian principles, even blunted and twisted to accommodate Russian interests, did not appeal to Stalin. What he wanted was an alliance against Germany, not a brave new world. If Stalin ever found time to try to unravel the intellectual and personal puzzle that Roosevelt put before him, he may well have felt a sort of amused scorn for the President's vision of humanity saved from its own evil passions by bath-tubs and democracy. As a Marxist, Stalin presumably believed that such a panacea overlooked the prime root of all social evil—capitalism; but this proposition, so axiomatic to a Marxist, was one that very likely never even crossed Roosevelt's mind.[1] He was a reformer, not a revolutionary; a humanitarian, not an ideologue; a politician, not a political scientist. Yet in Stalin's imagination capitalism was an ever present threat to his party and country, a threat which he could never entirely overlook nor long forget in any dealing with its leading representatives, whether Hitler, or Churchill, or Roosevelt.[2]

The fundamental failure at Yalta was not Roosevelt's resort to compromise but a failure of intellectual understanding. To be sure, Roosevelt did not cling consistently to his ideal world of the future. But practical compromise between principle and expediency, between the ideal and the possible, had been the keynote of Roosevelt's whole career in domestic American politics, and with the combination he had worked wonders. When he attempted to apply similar methods to international relations, however, his wonder-working power abruptly vanished. The reason was that Roosevelt failed to take adequately into account the enormous intellectual and moral gulf which divided him and the West generally from Stalin and Russia. Without a more extensive adherence to similar moral principles, without a common acceptance of conventional limits to the use of force, without a greater sympathy, a firmer consensus, and a more genuine community of mind, workable compromise was impossible. Only by accepting Stalin on his own terms, only by unreservedly espousing the amorality of power could more durable agreements have been reached. But that would have seemed to Roosevelt (and to the American and British publics as well) a cynical betrayal of the best hope of humanity.

At Yalta neither side fully recognized the difference in intellectual and moral climate which so divided them. Yet the difference made their most

[1] It would be interesting to know whether Roosevelt was in any degree acquainted with Bolshevik ideology. A man of his generation and upbringing may well have escaped all knowledge of Bolshevism, save as a caricature—the long-haired, bomb-throwing revolutionary of newspaper cartoons. Since Stalin obviously did not conform to such a caricature, Roosevelt may have concluded that the whole image was a fiction.

For an interesting example of how a well educated American could play a leading part in public affairs without knowing anything of Marxist ideology until it came to his attention with all the force of a new revelation in 1946, see *The Forrestal Diaries*, ed. Walter Millis (New York, Viking Press, 1951), pp. 127–8.

[2] Cf. Stalin's statement to Harold Stassen on 9 April 1947 in which he identified the German and American economic systems and asserted that the difference between Hitlerian and American forms of government was merely a 'temporary, political factor' (*Soviet News*, 9 May 1947).

honest efforts to reach agreement no more than a fumbling at cross purposes. Under the circumstances it is not strange that the Yalta agreements did not long endure, and that after Yalta the Grand Alliance, despite various ups and downs, showed ever increasing signs of rupture.

PART III

BREAKDOWN OF ALLIED CO-OPERATION

FEBRUARY 1945–DECEMBER 1946

CHAPTER I

PROBLEMS OF VICTORY

FEBRUARY–SEPTEMBER 1945

(i) Co-operation on Whose Terms?

(a) Military Events, February–May 1945

At the time of the Yalta Conference the Red Army had reached the Oder, the last barrier before Berlin, and while the Conference was in session the Anglo-American forces began the offensive which was to carry them to the Rhine by mid-March. The Allied armies were obviously moving in for the kill, but it remained to be seen how fast each front would be able to advance and where the Red Army would make contact with the forces under Eisenhower.

Against Japan, too, the fronts were in motion. In Burma the Japanese were in full retreat. With the capture of Rangoon on 3 May 1945 Japanese control over nearly all the country was broken, although numerous small bodies of dispersed Japanese troops remained in the rear of the victorious British Fourteenth Army. The onset of the monsoon in May made further operations very difficult; and in any case the strategic aim of the Burma campaign had been achieved. The main effort of the forces under Admiral Mountbatten was therefore directed towards preparations for an amphibious attack on Malaya, while operations in Burma were confined to mopping up—a not inconsiderable task.

In the Pacific, American forces assaulted Iwo Jima on 19 February and Okinawa on 1 April 1945. These islands, respectively 775 and 450 miles south of Japan, were defended by large Japanese garrisons which fought with heroic tenacity. As a result, the battle on Iwo Jima lasted for a month, and Okinawa was not conquered until 21 June 1945. Japanese use of suicide planes to attack Allied warships,[1] including a piloted rocket plane, led to very considerable naval losses; but the Japanese fleet had been so

[1] A British carrier task force reached the Pacific in the middle of March 1945, and took part in the battles off Okinawa, beginning 26 March. Despite Admiral King's unco-operative attitude in Washington (see above, p. 486 and n. 3), American naval authorities in the Pacific welcomed the addition to their forces and helped to supply the British fleet (cf. Cunningham: *A Sailor's Odyssey*, pp. 635–40).

damaged in the battle of Leyte Gulf in October 1944[1] that it could not hope to challenge Allied control of the sea any longer.

On 5 July 1945 General MacArthur announced that the Philippines had been completely freed from Japanese control, although, as in Burma, numerous detachments of Japanese troops remained at large in the islands. This victory, combined with the conquest of Iwo Jima and Okinawa, opened the way for a landing on the main Japanese islands. Two springboards for attack had been laboriously built; one string of island bases reached across the Pacific from Hawaii, a second stretched northward from Australia. Both now converged on Japan. Preliminary to the final landing itself, air attack on the Japanese home islands steadily mounted in intensity, and an increasingly effective air and sea blockade sapped Japan's economy by reducing or cutting off essential imports. Japan's situation was made even more hopeless when the Russians, on 5 April 1945, officially denounced the Neutrality Pact which they had signed with Japan in April 1941.[2]

While these events in the Pacific presaged disaster for Japan, the Allied campaigns against Germany moved rapidly to their climax. By the middle of March 1945 Eisenhower's troops had overrun the Siegfried Line and reached the Rhine from the Swiss border to the North Sea. Indeed, a lucky chance put the American First Army across the Rhine as early as 7 March at Remagen where it was able to establish a small bridgehead. During the last week of March the main crossings were made. In the north, the Twenty-first Army Group under Montgomery crossed in the neighbourhood of Wesel on the night of 23–24 March; to the south, the U.S. Third Army under Patton jumped off a day earlier.

Eisenhower's plan was to encircle the Ruhr in a great pincers movement, as a preliminary to a drive through central Germany aimed at the Leipzig area. After the crossing of the Rhine, the Anglo-American troops met with only light resistance. The Germans were thoroughly disheartened, and their supplies and communications had been cut to pieces by air attack. As a result, the Ruhr was encircled by 1 April, just a week after the crossing of the Rhine; and by 18 April the last of the 325,000 German soldiers thus cut off surrendered.[3]

[1] See above, p. 461.

[2] *Documents on American Foreign Relations, 1944–1945*, pp. 846–7. The Pact was to last for five years, and, unless denounced by one of the parties a year in advance of its expiry, automatically renewed itself for an additional five years. Thus, theoretically, the U.S.S.R. was not legally free to attack Japan until April 1946 even after the denunciation of the Pact. Stalin attempted to create legal cover for his infraction of treaty obligations at the Potsdam Conference (see below, p. 637, note 1). It is, incidentally, a striking demonstration of the bias of men's minds, that no American or British spokesman considered the scrapping of this treaty to be a problem. National advantage in this as in other cases altogether eclipsed consideration of international law, the sacredness of treaties, or moral principle. This was true not only of Stalin but of the American and British authorities who invited and urged him to join in war against Japan.

[3] Eisenhower: *Crusade in Europe*, pp. 387–93, 404–6.

Meanwhile, important gains for the Red Army in the south led to the capture of Vienna on 13 April; but, despite the fact that they had reached the Oder, no more than fifty miles from Berlin, before the end of January, the Russians did not make much forward progress on that sector of the front until after the middle of April. Two factors account for this three months' delay. One was the cautious military strategy which Stalin decided to adopt. Instead of thrusting ahead towards Berlin as rapidly as possible, the Red Army devoted several weeks to extending its front on the Oder northward until Stettin had been captured, thus giving a much broader base from which to launch the final attack.[1]

A second factor which slowed the Red Army's rate of advance was German fear of the Russians—a fear which impelled German soldiers to fight far more determinedly on the eastern than on the western front. Thus, while Eisenhower's armies plunged into the vitals of Germany and met with only scattered resistance, the Red Army found the going much more difficult. This German behaviour did not fail to sow seeds of distrust between Russia and the West. The speed and relative ease of Eisenhower's advance made Stalin suspect some sort of secret understanding between the Germans and the Western Allies. His suspicions soon came into the open. On 8 March 1945 German Headquarters in Italy sent a general to press on with surrender negotiations. Conversations had already been opened through clandestine channels, but now it seemed worth while to pursue them further. Accordingly, Field Marshal Sir Harold Alexander[2] proposed to send representatives from his headquarters to Switzerland to meet the German general.[3] After its approval by the Combined Chiefs of Staff, this step was made known to the Russians on 11 March.

Stalin's suspicions were, presumably, already lively, and he asked that Soviet officers should take part in the proposed conversations. The Combined Chiefs of Staff countered on 15 March with the proposal that Russian representatives should join only in subsequent conversations at Alexander's headquarters. But the Russians were not satisfied with the prospect of coming in perhaps to find an agreement already made. Molotov

[1] According to Kalinov (*Les Maréchaux soviétiques vous parlent*, pp. 160–1) this decision was taken only after a dispute between Marshal Zhukov, who wished to lunge forward to Berlin about the middle of February, and Marshal Sokolovsky, who urged greater caution and the preliminary conquest of the entire eastern bank of the Oder. Stalin's decision, according to the same authority, turned upon the agreement which had been reached through the European Advisory Commission dividing Germany into zones of occupation (see above, p. 481); a division that guaranteed Russia primacy in the area round Berlin. It is interesting to observe how the Zhukov-Sokolovsky dispute paralleled the Montgomery-Eisenhower dispute in the west. Substituting the Rhine for the Oder the arguments were almost exactly the same; and the political motivation—the desire to reach the German capital first—was operative both with Zhukov and with Montgomery.

[2] Alexander had succeeded Wilson as Allied Commander-in-Chief in the Mediterranean on 12 December 1944.

[3] Reports of this proposed meeting reached London and Washington from Berne.

therefore insisted in a cable of 16 March that the conversations in Switzerland be broken off. Actually, a meeting on 19 March at Locarno produced no results; but by now the Russians were thoroughly aroused, and, perhaps misled by secret service reports, refused to believe that a secret deal had not been arranged.[1] On 23 March Molotov protested in violent language against secret negotiations between the Anglo-Americans and the Germans. The next day Roosevelt intervened with a cable to Stalin assuring him of Anglo-American good faith. After an exchange of rather pointed telegrams, Stalin on 3 April fully revealed his suspicions:

> My military colleagues . . . do not have any doubts that the negotiations have taken place and they have ended in an agreement with the Germans, on the basis of which the German Commander on the Western Front—Marshal Kesselring—has agreed to open the front and permit the Anglo-American troops to advance to the east, and the Anglo-Americans have promised in return to ease for the Germans the peace terms.
>
> I think that my colleagues are close to the truth. . . . As a result of this, at the present moment the Germans on the Western Front in fact have ceased to wage war against England and the United States. At the same time, the Germans continue the war with Russia, the ally of England and the United States.[2]

Roosevelt, replying on 4 April, denied any such agreement, and said: 'Frankly, I cannot avoid a feeling of bitter resentment toward your informers, whoever they are, for such vile misrepresentations of my actions or those of my trusted subordinates.'[3] Churchill replied in a similar vein, and when Alexander recalled his representatives from Switzerland on 4 April 1945 the storm blew over.

This 'Berne incident' coincided with a final debate over military strategy between British and American authorities. Having crossed the Rhine and encircled the Ruhr, Eisenhower proposed to direct his main thrust through central Germany, aiming at the remaining industrial centre round Leipzig. Apart from further crippling German industry by such a move, Eisenhower sought to prevent German withdrawal into the mountains of Bavaria and western Austria—the National Redoubt of which German propagandists had spoken, but which existed only in their imagination. Eisenhower's plan called for a transfer of the U.S. Ninth Army from Montgomery's command to Bradley's, thus weakening the thrust along the coastal plain of northern Germany.

[1] It is possible that some German agents had discussed one-sided surrender with American or British agents in Switzerland and that reports of such offers reached Stalin; but it seems certain not only from the testimony but from the actions of the responsible Allied commanders that Russian fears were ungrounded.

[2] Leahy: *I Was There*, p. 391; cf. ibid. pp. 386–93 for an account of the whole incident.

[3] Ibid. p. 392.

Eisenhower's strategic plan was communicated to Stalin on 28 March without specific authorization from the Combined Chiefs of Staff. In doing this Eisenhower felt he was acting in accordance with the powers he had been given at Yalta to enter into direct contact with the Russians.[1] Churchill, however, felt otherwise. Troubles in Rumania and Poland had already arisen to shadow the apparent harmony which had been achieved at Yalta, and the Prime Minister thought that the time had come to push American and British troops into the most advantageous positions from which to bargain with the Russians after Germany's defeat. Specifically, he believed that Eisenhower should concentrate as much force as possible for a race to Berlin.[2] The political and psychological advantages of such a move, Churchill believed, were overwhelming; and, with German resistance already crumbling to dust, mere technical military considerations had lost their importance.[3]

Obviously, Eisenhower's action in communicating his plan to Stalin on 28 March prejudged the issue, and Churchill was furious. He felt that Eisenhower had taken upon himself decisions of the highest political significance without comprehending what he was doing. But the American Chiefs of Staff backed Eisenhower and rejected the British strategic proposal for concentration under Montgomery aimed at Berlin. Eisenhower explained on 30 March: '... Berlin itself is no longer a particularly important objective', and on the following day the U.S. Chiefs of Staff told their British colleagues and the Prime Minister:

> The battle in Germany is now at a point where it is up to the Field Commander to judge the measures which should be taken.... The single objective should be quick and complete victory. While recognizing there are factors not of direct concern to SCAEF [Supreme Commander, Allied Expeditionary Force], the U.S. Chiefs consider his strategic concept is sound and should receive full support. He should continue to communicate freely with the Commander in Chief of the Soviet Army.[4]

In the face of the American attitude, Churchill could only submit. Events were moving at such a pace that a reversal of the plan would have been a practical impossibility, for by the time the controversy ended, on 7 April, American and British troops were already streaking across Germany towards the Elbe and the Russian front line.

By 17 April 1945 the Russians were finally ready to attack Hitler's capital. Two powerful armies advanced from the Oder, and by 25 April

[1] See above, p. 543.

[2] One must remember that the Russian offensive across the Oder had not yet begun, and that the Red Army was still as far from the German capital as it had been in January.

[3] National feeling entered into the dispute, too, for Churchill's plan would have called for reinforcement of Montgomery's army group, whereas Eisenhower's strategy deprived the British commander of a part of the troops which had been assigned to him for the crossing of the Rhine.

[4] Eisenhower: *Crusade in Europe*, pp. 401–2.

Berlin was completely surrounded. On the same day American and Russian advance patrols encountered one another at Torgau on the Elbe.

As Anglo-American and Russian troops approached one another, it became imperative to arrange for a system of recognition signals, and it was convenient, if not absolutely necessary, to agree upon lines of demarcation beyond which neither side would advance. Eisenhower took the initiative on 14 April, when he proposed to halt his advance through central Germany at the Elbe and asked the Combined Chiefs of Staff to authorize him to so inform the Russians. The British, however, objected to stopping at the Elbe unless compelled to do so. Thus, in effect, the issue which had been debated at the beginning of the month was raised anew. It was no longer a question of a race for Berlin along the north German plain as against a drive through central Germany; instead it had become a question of how far Anglo-American troops would and could penetrate into Germany and Central Europe before meeting the Red Army.

The American Chiefs of Staff and the new President,[1] Harry Truman, approved Eisenhower's proposal for drawing a definite line of demarcation between Russian and Anglo-American spheres of military operation; and on 21 April Truman cabled to Churchill his opinion:

> The question of tactical deployment of American troops in Germany is a military one. It is my belief that General Eisenhower should be given certain latitude and discretion. . . . It is my thought that you and I might send a message to Stalin urging that the date and the procedure for withdrawal to different zones of occupation be fixed by mutual agreement between the three Governments.[2]

Eisenhower exercised his discretion by informing the Russians on 21 April that he would not send troops across the Elbe and Mulde rivers in the central (and most advanced) part of the front.[3]

Later the line of demarcation was extended northward to include Lübeck on the Baltic within the Anglo-American limits, and southward along an imaginary line running through Carlsbad, Pilsen, and Linz. When this proposal was submitted to the Russians, on 1 May 1945, they accepted it willingly enough; but when three days later the rapidly shifting military situation led Eisenhower to suggest that he might be able to advance his troops farther into Czechoslovakia as far as the bank of the Elbe, the Chief of the Russian General Staff took violent exception to the new proposal, and it was therefore not acted upon.[4] As a result, despite the fact that there were no Red Army troops in Bohemia, and despite

[1] For Roosevelt's death on 12 April see below, p. 578.

[2] Leahy: *I Was There*, pp. 410–11.

[3] Eisenhower: *Crusade in Europe*, p. 411. Actually Eisenhower's decision required the withdrawal of some detachments which had already established bridgeheads across the Elbe (cf. Wilmot: *Struggle for Europe*, p. 695).

[4] Eisenhower: *Crusade in Europe*, p. 418; Deane: *Strange Alliance*, pp. 159–60.

the fact that American forces reached the Carlsbad–Pilsen line with ease and could have advanced at least to Prague (where the Czechs had revolted against the Germans and needed succour), nevertheless the original line of demarcation was observed and the honour of liberating the Czech capital was left to the Red Army.

Meanwhile Germany's long awaited collapse became a fact in the first week of May. On 1 May the German radio announced Hitler's death. Admiral Dönitz succeeded to his position as head of the Third Reich. On 2 May what was left of Berlin surrendered to the Russians, and the German army in Italy surrendered to Field Marshal Alexander. On 4 May the German armies in Holland, north-west Germany, and Denmark surrendered to Field Marshal Montgomery. These surrenders were called 'tactical' in order to avoid the necessity of bringing Russian representatives into the negotiation;[1] but after the 'Berne incident' the British and American authorities realized how suspicious the Russians had become and fully intended to insist upon a formal surrender to all three Allied Governments.

Admiral Dönitz did what he could to evade surrendering to the Russians. Upon his accession to power, he announced that his task was to save Germany from Bolshevism. His method of doing so was to instruct German soldiers to surrender to the Anglo-Americans. This order, combined with German fear of Russian vengeance, resulted in a flight for refuge in Anglo-American prison camps. Various German commanders whose troops had been engaged against the Red Army tried to surrender organized forces; but Eisenhower and his subordinates punctiliously refused to accept such offers on the ground that 'tactical' surrender could be made only to the forces against which battle had been waged.

Dönitz held out as long as he could, but when Eisenhower threatened to close his front lines to Germans fleeing from the Red Army, the German admiral realized that the game was up and authorized his representatives to sign an Unconditional Surrender at Eisenhower's headquarters in Rheims. Russian and French representatives were on hand to take part in the ceremony, which occurred in the early morning hours of 7 May 1945.[2] Stalin, however, was ill content with a ceremony that gave primary

[1] Leahy says bluntly that 'tactical surrender' was 'a device adopted to avoid the Soviet insistence that we could not accept any surrender without all three powers participating in the negotiations' (*I Was There*, p. 417).

[2] There was considerable confusion at the last minute in drawing up the instrument of surrender. The European Advisory Commission had prepared a text which was approved by all the Allied Governments; after the Yalta decision about dismemberment of Germany (see above, p. 547) a modified text, secret from the French, came into existence. No one knew which of these texts to present to the Germans, but officers in SHAEF chose to disregard both documents and drew up a third text of their own which was the one actually used. General Smith states that he had forgotten about the existence of the European Advisory Commission's text (Walter Bedell

place to the Anglo-Americans. He was thoroughly suspicious of German 'tactical' surrenders to the West, and feared that the Germans might still in practice obey Dönitz's orders and surrender only to the Anglo-Americans. These considerations led him to refuse to recognize the validity of the surrender at Rheims. He insisted upon a second capitulation in Berlin. Accordingly on 9 May, the day after hostilities had ceased according to the terms of surrender signed at Rheims, a second ceremony was staged at Marshal Zhukov's headquarters in the shattered German capital. Only after this second surrender did Stalin consider the war at an end.

But news of the ceremony at Rheims could not be suppressed. The German radio told the world of what had happened within a few hours, and, of course, long before the Berlin ceremony could be arranged. Furthermore, an American reporter who had witnessed the surrender at Rheims broke the release date by putting the news on the Associated Press wire at 9.30 a.m. on 8 May. This put Churchill and President Truman in an embarrassing position. After failing to get Stalin's agreement to advance the date of the official proclamation of V-E day, they decided to go ahead independently.[1] Hence it happened that while Britain and America celebrated their victory over Germany on 8 May, the Russians held off until the following day. This discrepancy was symbolic of the disharmony which the last months of the war in Europe had brought to the Allies. Victory, as is usual with alliances, did not consolidate friendship. Despite all the heartfelt demonstrations of Russo-Anglo-American comradeship in arms provoked by the exhilaration of the moment, the three Governments found much to quarrel about behind the scenes.

(*b*) Disillusionment with Yalta, February–April 1945

The agreements made at Yalta concerning the future of Europe had been more apparent than real, and it was not long before the realities obtruded themselves upon even the most unwilling minds. Within two weeks of the close of the Yalta Conference disputes between Western and Russian diplomats became acute in Rumania, and by the first week in March, less than a month after Yalta, negotiations with respect to Poland reached a stalemate. In public, American and British officials tried to minimize

Smith: *Moscow Mission 1946–1949* (London, Heinemann, 1950), p. 8) but it seems probable that other factors were at work. Smith must have remembered the farce of the Italian armistice terms, drawn up far in advance and largely inapplicable to the situation as it developed (see above, pp. 286, 306–8); and that recollection must have tempted him to brush aside the E.A.C. document, which, like its Italian prototype, was long and detailed. Nevertheless, at the insistence of the American member of E.A.C., Ambassador Winant, the SHAEF text was amended to include a general enabling clause which became the basis for subsequent assumption of political control over Germany by the Allies. For a detailed account of these events, cf. Philip E. Mosely: 'Dismemberment of Germany', *Foreign Affairs*, April 1950, xxviii. 495–7.

[1] Leahy (*I Was There*, pp. 420–5) reproduces verbatim telephone conversations he held with Churchill in an effort to concert the announcement.

the clash between themselves and the Russians and took a forcedly optimistic view. Privately they realized that the future pattern of European politics was at stake.

Events in Rumania came to a crisis first. On 2 December 1944 the Government which had first been formed after the *coup d'état* of 23 August[1] was replaced by a new Cabinet under General Radescu. The change gave the Communists control of some important Ministries, chiefly the Ministry of the Interior and of the Police; but Radescu himself and the majority of his Ministers were far from being Communist stooges, and the Rumanian army remained a stronghold of opposition to Communism. This situation did not conform to Russian wishes. Early in January 1945 leaders of the Rumanian Communist Party visited Moscow, and presumably were there instructed to bring about a further change in the Rumanian Government. When they returned, agitation against Radescu was organized on an evergrowing scale, until rioting broke out in Bucharest on 24 February 1945. Two days later Andrei Vyshinsky, Russian Deputy Foreign Minister, arrived in the Rumanian capital and demanded the dismissal of Radescu and the appointment of Petru Groza in his stead as Prime Minister. Groza was leader of a peasant party called the Ploughman's Front which, despite an independent origin in 1933, had become no more than a rural disguise for the Rumanian Communists.

King Michael was reluctant to yield to Vyshinsky's demands, but, being unable to get more than verbal sympathy from American and British representatives in Bucharest, he felt compelled to accept the Russian nominee. Accordingly, on 6 March a new Government, thoroughly dominated by the Communists and headed by Groza, came to power.[2]

This thinly disguised *coup d'état* thoroughly displeased the Americans who felt that the Russians had wantonly disregarded the Yalta Declaration on Liberated Europe. The British Government, however, believed that Rumania did not offer a good test case. Churchill's deal with Stalin of October 1944 had, after all, assigned predominant influence to Russia in Rumania. Moreover, the American view that the Declaration on Liberated Europe superseded all previous engagements might endanger the British position in Greece.[3] Events in Rumania were sufficiently obscure

[1] See above, p. 467.

[2] The Russians tried to strengthen the Rumanian Communist Party by offering the new Groza Government the return of the part of Transylvania which Hitler had assigned to Hungary. Rumanian administration was extended to Transylvania by Stalin's fiat on 10 March 1945, just four days after Groza took office (*New York Times*, 11 March 1945).

[3] Byrnes: *Speaking Frankly*, pp. 50–53. The Groza Government included representatives of two insignificant 'bourgeois' splinter parties. One of them, Gheorghe Tatarescu, had as Prime Minister in 1936 sentenced Anna Pauker, a leading Communist, to jail. Their inclusion can best be explained as a pious gesture to honour the 80:20 percentage figure which Stalin and Churchill had fixed in October at Moscow. But cf. Roberts: *Rumania*, pp. 262–73.

and distant to pass without much notice by the American public; and, lacking active support from Britain, the American Government limited their action to ineffectual diplomatic protests.

Poland, however, was a different matter. There British and American views coincided, and the long history of the problem, combined with the existence of a numerous and well organized body of Polish-Americans, made the fate of Poland a matter of high public and governmental interest. The first meeting of the British and American Ambassadors with Molotov[1] in Moscow, instead of bringing about a smooth reorganization of the Polish Government, merely revealed how widely Russia and the West differed in their interpretation of the Yalta formula for Poland. The Russians insisted that only Polish leaders who supported the Yalta decisions should be consulted about reorganizing the Provisional Government. This excluded Mikolajczyk, who had publicly protested against the Big Three's action, and in effect limited the field to Communists and their sympathizers, since patriotic Poles could not bring themselves to approve the loss of the eastern provinces which had been sealed at Yalta. On 5 March, at the fourth meeting of the Ambassadors with Molotov, the whole negotiation seemed on the point of breakdown, when the Western representatives rejected Molotov's proposal to invite four leaders from the Provisional Government and three other Polish public figures to discuss the reorganization of the Government.[2]

The Rumanian crisis was then at its height. (The Groza Government took power on the following day.) It seems clear that the Russians decided to go ahead in Poland as they had in Rumania, whether or not the Western Allies approved. Their first step was to open negotiations with leaders of the Polish Underground who still recognized the authority of the exiled Government in London. After making various promises to these leaders, the Soviet authorities lured them to a meeting, arrested them, and packed them off to prison in Moscow. The arrests were made on 27 and 28 March. On 6 April the London Poles received somewhat jumbled news of what had occurred and announced it to the world. But their stories were not altogether consistent and lacked circumstantial detail. Consequently their complaints were discounted in many quarters as false propaganda. The Russians kept silence for more than a month, and the rush of other news connected with Germany's surrender tended to distract public attention from the woes of the Poles. By their duplicity and ruthlessness the Russians were thus able to decapitate the Polish underground organization which had so successfully withstood the Germans. In the following weeks

[1] For the appointment of this Commission of three at Yalta see above, pp. 557–8.

[2] Lane: *I Saw Poland Betrayed*, pp. 92–93.

vigorous police and para-military measures were taken to disperse and destroy what remained of the rank and file of the Polish underground. In this fashion the power of the Provisional Government was consolidated and their only rival reduced to impotence.

The Russians tried, equally, to strengthen the international standing of the Warsaw régime. Despite Soviet protests, the United States and Britain refused to invite the Provisional Government of Poland to the San Francisco Conference until after it had been reorganized according to the Yalta formula. The exiled Government in London was also excluded, so that Poland had no official representation when the Conference opened. Just on the eve of the Conference, however, the Russians signed a treaty of alliance with the Warsaw Government, on 21 April 1945. This Stalin did despite protests from the West; and in doing so seemed to imply the permanence of the Provisional Government.[1]

Meanwhile the consultations in Moscow concerning the reorganization of the Polish Government made no progress. The Russians would not consider 'reorganization' of a character likely to upset Communist predominance in the Polish administration, while Britain and America continued to insist upon a 'reorganization' which would allow non-Communist leaders to rally their supporters freely in preparation for an election which would determine Poland's future form of government. The personal intervention of Roosevelt and Churchill could do nothing to resolve this collision of policy, nor could appeals to the text of the Yalta Declaration on Poland budge either side from its chosen interpretation of the words.[2]

At the end of March the prestige of the Yalta agreements in the United States suffered a serious blow when news of Roosevelt's deal with Stalin to support Ukrainian and White Russian membership in the Assembly of the United Nations[3] leaked into the press. Roosevelt was forced rather lamely to confirm the accuracy of the first report, published on 29 March; and his effort to sweeten the pill by dwelling upon American rights to triple representation failed to win any important support. The American Government, therefore, dropped the matter and said no more about their claim to more than one seat in the Assembly.

[1] The treaty with Poland was paralleled by similar treaties concluded by the Soviet Union with Yugoslavia (11 April 1945, see below, p. 581), France (10 December 1944, see above, p. 530), Czechoslovakia (12 December 1943, see above, p. 429), and Great Britain (26 May 1942, see above, p. 179). It is likely that the Russians wished to sign the Polish treaty before the opening of the San Francisco Conference, since the legitimacy of bilateral security agreements could be better defended as *faits accomplis* than in any other way. The status of Soviet bilateral agreements became a minor stumbling-block at the San Francisco Conference. See below, p. 599. Texts of the Polish and Yugoslav treaties may be found in *Documents on American Foreign Relations, 1944–1945*, pp. 856–8, 860–2.

[2] Byrnes (*Speaking Frankly*, pp. 53–56) summarizes some of the cables exchanged between Roosevelt, Churchill, and Stalin over Poland in these weeks.

[3] See above, pp. 553 and 555.

The manner in which this news reached the American public made a very bad impression, quite apart from doubts which many Americans felt about the principle of admitting separate members of the Soviet Union to an assembly of supposedly sovereign states. Inevitably the question was raised: What other secret agreements were made at Yalta? Instead of the shining achievement which Yalta had once seemed, the Conference came to be associated with rather shady deals and sinister secrets.

Disillusionment had indeed set in, even though Allied difficulties over Rumania, Poland, and the 'Berne incident' were, on the whole, played down by the press in each country. Nevertheless, when on 29 March the Russians announced that Molotov would not attend the San Francisco Conference, the news came as something of a surprise to the public in America and Britain. Allied misunderstandings were moving from the secret recesses of diplomacy to the public forum, and the millions who had hoped for better things from the victory over Fascism were bewildered and dismayed.

This was the situation when Roosevelt died of cerebral haemorrhage on 12 April 1945. Roosevelt's sudden and unexpected death put an extraordinary strain upon the American system of government, for he had held the threads of foreign as well as of domestic policy in his own hands, and his successor, Harry Truman, had been completely excluded from the inner counsels of government.[1] More than that, Roosevelt's death removed a great symbol of Allied solidarity and deprived many millions of people all round the world of the chief single embodiment of their ardent hopes for a better future.

One immediate consequence of Roosevelt's death was a reversal of the decision not to send Molotov to San Francisco. Stalin made this gesture, on the advice of Ambassador Harriman, as a sign of his desire to continue co-operation with the United States under its new President; and made it despite Molotov's own protest.[2]

But gestures did not change policies, and when Molotov reached San Francisco he brought obstruction and controversy with him. As relations between Russia and the West became worse in the following months, many of Roosevelt's warmest supporters attributed the decay of the Grand Alliance to changes in American attitudes following Roosevelt's death. The fact that strained relations antedated Roosevelt's disappearance from the scene was not widely publicized at the time, since all concerned still hoped

[1] This was normal American practice. The Vice-President's main function was to act as chairman of the Senate, and Roosevelt undoubtedly had chosen the ex-Senator, Truman, as Vice-President mainly on the ground that he would be able to use his personal popularity in the Senate to help persuade that body to ratify the treaty bringing the United States into the new United Nations organization (cf. Sherwood: *Roosevelt and Hopkins*, p. 882; Eng. edition, ii. 870).

[2] Ibid. pp. 883–4; Eng. edition, ii. 872–3; Byrnes: *Speaking Frankly*, p. 60.

to repair the cracks in the Alliance. This made the charges of Truman's critics the more plausible.

In a very limited sense there may be some truth in the argument. Truman was, perhaps, personally less inclined to meet the Russians half way than Roosevelt had been.[1] But a much more important factor was a change in American military outlook. With victory so near in Europe overwhelming force could soon be brought against Japan, and Russia's assistance began to seem less important. Progress towards the establishment of American bases in the Russian Far East[2] had been almost nil. Meanwhile, newly won bases in the Pacific islands began to seem adequate to support the bombing offensive against Japan. As a result, on 24 April 1945, the U.S. Chiefs of Staff abandoned their plan for basing American planes in Siberia. They also decided not to divert naval strength to the task of opening sea lanes north of Japan unless pressed to do so by Moscow. This meant that the U.S. navy would not guarantee to continue the delivery of supplies to the Red Army in the Far East[3] after hostilities between Japan and Russia had started.

These decisions were of the utmost importance. In effect the Americans no longer were willing to make any great concession to secure Russian participation in the Japanese war. On 22 April Truman's advisers felt, according to Admiral Leahy, that 'no particular harm could be done to our war prospects if Russia should slow down or even stop its war effort in Europe and Asia'.[4] Thus the military basis of the Grand Alliance largely evaporated; only common political ends could be counted on to keep the conflicts between the Allies from reaching irreconcilable proportions.

Common political ends were not unimportant; each of the Big Three wanted peace and security and recognized that only their continued co-operation could secure these goals. But what seemed an elementary precaution to safeguard the security of the Soviet Union to the one side seemed Communist duplicity and aggression to the other; and, in the face of this stubborn contradiction of views, the Grand Alliance gradually dissolved into rival, hostile parts.

That events would have taken a slightly different course had Roosevelt lived is highly probable; but to believe that he would somehow have prevented the break-up of the Alliance or even have been able much to retard the pace at which it broke up is to take an absurdly superficial view of international relations. Truman depended on the same advisers as Roosevelt had depended upon, and so far as he could he followed Roose-

[1] Leahy says: 'The insulting language of the recent Stalin telegrams . . . was an affront to the solid, old-fashioned Americanism possessed by Harry Truman' (*I Was There*, p. 409).

[2] See above, p. 543.

[3] For the promise of supplies made by General Deane to Stalin in October 1944 see above, pp. 518–19.

[4] Leahy: *I Was There*, p. 412.

velt's policies. It was not Truman nor Churchill nor Stalin who broke up the Alliance but the disappearance of a common enemy whose power alone could lead the three Governments concerned to subordinate their differences and mutual fears to some larger fear.[1] Indeed, Roosevelt died at exactly the right time for the sake of his myth and for the sake of his own peace of mind. He died when the victory he had so greatly helped to contrive lay unmistakably at hand, and before the Alliance he had so hopefully nursed began definitely and irretrievably to disintegrate. He died when bright hopes were still possible, and up to the moment of his death he never despaired of achieving tolerable, if not perfect, harmony with Russia. The last cable he wrote, addressed to Churchill, said: 'I would minimize the general Soviet problem as much as possible because these problems, in one form or another, seem to arise every day and most of them straighten out as in the case of the Bern meeting. We must be firm, however, and our course thus far is correct.'[2] How could man die better, undismayed by the odds and sure his course had thus far been correct?

(c) The Test of Victory, May–July 1945

Roosevelt's death, as we have seen, brought Molotov to San Francisco. *En route* the Russian Foreign Minister stopped in Washington and had an uncomfortable interview with Truman during which the Polish question was vainly discussed. The changed relationship among the Allies quickly became manifest at San Francisco, where petty squabbles over such questions as the chairmanship of the Conference were combined with more serious disputes over Poland and Argentina.[3] But while these quarrels were to prove themselves portents of the future, at the time they did not seem especially significant. Instead, public attention was fixed upon the drama of Germany's collapse, and, despite the undercurrent of distrust which Russian officials so regularly made manifest, the men on the spot in Germany were proud of their common victory and in most things co-operated effectively.[4] Yet behind the scenes, Allied disagreement remained as troublesome as ever. In addition to the chronic question of

[1] It is a sad commentary on the intelligence and good will of mankind that no alliance of independent states, so far as the writer knows, has ever survived decisive victory; and that successful confederations have drawn their initial strength from the existence of a common enemy. Without an external threat to inspire fear, it seems that positive aims, no matter how good in themselves, will not suffice to bind together men whose loyalty is traditionally dispersed among different governmental units.

[2] Byrnes: *Speaking Frankly*, p. 59.

[3] See below, pp. 594–5.

[4] Accusations made by the Russians concerning American and British failure to abide by the agreement made at Yalta for the repatriation of Allied prisoners of war led to a public exchange of incivilities at the beginning of May. Cf. the official American statement of 3 May 1945 in *Documents on American Foreign Relations, 1944–1945*, pp. 849–50. For the general attitude of mind which prevailed in SHAEF Headquarters at the time of V-E day, cf. Eisenhower: *Crusade in Europe*, pp. 428, 438, 444.

Poland, Germany's defeat raised new difficulties in the Trieste region, in Austria, and, most importantly, in Germany itself.

When the German army in Italy surrendered to Field Marshal Alexander on 2 May 1945 Anglo-American and Yugoslav forces at once embarked upon a race for Trieste. The result was an intermingling of British and Yugoslav troops in Trieste and neighbouring districts. A bitter dispute at once arose over Tito's claim to administer Istria, as well as certain districts in Carinthia which had belonged to Austria before the war. At one time it seemed possible that open hostilities might break out between the Yugoslav and Allied troops,[1] but calmer counsels prevailed and by 9 June the American, British, and Yugoslav Governments were able to sign an agreement regulating military arrangements in the disputed districts. Definite determination of the frontier was reserved until peace treaties should be made with Italy and Austria.[2]

Tito's action on this and other questions put his Government definitely in the Russian as opposed to the Anglo-American camp. Despite the agreement Churchill had made with Stalin in October 1944 to share equally in influencing Yugoslav affairs,[3] and despite the fact that after Yalta Šubašić and two other 'western' candidates had been admitted to Tito's Government, it had become clear that Tito was firmly in control and had a will and policy of his own. On 11 April 1945 he signed a treaty of alliance with Russia directed against Germany, and his every action and utterance, as befitted a good Communist, expressed admiration for Russia and distrust of capitalist imperialism. Churchill was distressed at the miscarriage of his plans but could do nothing but fix a barrier to Tito's expansion by using the troops under Alexander's command.

Austria was involved in the Yugoslav controversy in the sense that Tito laid claim to former Austrian as well as to former Italian territory. There was another, and from a Western point of view, more serious aspect to Austrian affairs, however. The European Advisory Commission had divided Austria into occupation zones as it had Germany; but, when the German surrender brought fighting to a close, Anglo-American troops had not penetrated far into Austria whereas the Russians had captured Vienna and the eastern part of the country. On 29 April Moscow radio announced that the Russian commander in the field, Marshal Tolbukhin, had recognized a provisional Government of Austria under Karl Renner,

[1] Clark: *Calculated Risk*, pp. 443–8; Leahy: *I Was There*, p. 430.

[2] Text of the agreement may be found in *Documents on American Foreign Relations, 1944–1945*, p. 914. In this dispute Tito in effect tried to undo an agreement defining zones of military occupation which had been entered into by himself and Alexander in February 1945. British lines of communication into Austria were immediately at stake, but in the background was the dispute between Italy and Yugoslavia over their Adriatic boundary—a dispute which had distracted the Peace Conference at Paris in 1919.

[3] See above, p. 495.

a Social Democrat. This action was taken without prior consultation with the Western Powers, and, since Renner's Government consisted largely of Social Democratic and Communist representatives, it was easy to imagine that the Russians were trying to set up yet another puppet régime on the recent Rumanian model. Britain and the United States refused to recognize the Renner Government; the Russians refused to disavow it. As a result arrangements for carrying out the zonal occupation envisaged by the European Advisory Commission—in particular arrangements for quadripartite control of Vienna—threatened to break down.[1] The dispute was still in progress at the time of the Potsdam Conference[2] and the fate of the Renner Government was not settled until the autumn.

Nevertheless, agreement upon the machinery of Allied control in Austria was successfully negotiated by the European Advisory Commission on 4 July 1945. The German rather than the Italian and East European pattern was followed. In addition to the four zones of occupation into which Austria had been divided by the E.A.C. in March, Vienna was established as a joint zone. Allied policy for the country as a whole was to be determined by a Council consisting of the four Commanders-in-Chief. This agreement represented a concession on the part of the Russians, who had tried to win for themselves a primacy on the Allied Council for Austria analogous to the primacy they exercised in Rumania, Bulgaria, and Hungary.[3]

The situation in Germany was in a sense simpler, since none of the Allies chose to recognize or support the claims of any German group to act as a central government. But, as in Austria, the actual distribution of troops at the end of hostilities was very different from the zonal arrangements made in advance by the European Advisory Commission. Eisenhower's armies had penetrated far into the zone assigned to Russia and had crossed the Czech border by a few miles. In view of the numerous strains upon Allied fellow-feeling, it was not a simple matter to arrange withdrawals.

In particular, Churchill felt ill-content with the problems he saw opening before him. The British zone of Germany contained the most densely populated industrial regions of the country and could not hope to maintain its population from local food resources. But with the end of the German war, the scale of American Lend-Lease shipments was reduced, and the Americans would not agree at first that the requirements of German occupation constituted a legitimate demand upon Lend-Lease. Under the circumstances, since the British were not willing to run the risks of trying to control a starving population, they had either to find food sup-

[1] Holborn: *American Military Government: Its Organization and Policies*, pp. 78–81.

[2] See below, p. 619.

[3] Philip E. Mosely: 'The Treaty with Austria', *International Organization*, vol. iv, 1950, pp. 220–1.

plies for the Germans from their own straitened resources or try to come to definite agreements with the other occupying Powers by which they would provide some of the food required in the British zone from the production of other parts of Germany. Since the Soviet zone was the principal producer of agricultural surplus in Germany, this meant, in effect, coming to terms with the Russians.

Churchill conceived the possibility of bargaining with Stalin for food in exchange for Anglo-American retirement to the zonal boundaries. But such a proposal ran counter to the prevailing American attitude and assumptions about future relations with Russia. Indeed, once victory had been won in Germany the Americans were mainly interested in getting their troops into the battle against Japan as quickly as possible. The unexamined assumption upon which American strategy had largely been based—the assumption that as soon as the fighting finished things would return to normal more or less of themselves—only gradually weakened. For the moment, American policy was to press for the dissolution of SHAEF into its national components, to establish an occupation régime as promptly as possible, to get combat troops out of Europe as fast as ships could be found to carry them, and to leave the European countries to manage their own economic affairs with the help of UNRRA but without any further Lend-Lease. In the light of these American aims and attitudes, Churchill's effort to use the unexpectedly favourable distribution of Anglo-American troops as a bargaining counter in dealing with Stalin seemed little short of a betrayal of the Alliance and a potential trap to involve Americans in what by rights should be purely European affairs.[1]

For the moment, however, the question of Allied policies and machinery of control in Germany could be postponed. Each army had its hands full disposing of prisoners of war and displaced persons, restoring communications and essential services, sorting out its own units and, not least, celebrating victory and the end of the rigours of the battlefield. Winding up all the complicated business of SHAEF was itself a tremendous task since British and American administration had been intimately mingled at all levels; and the work of military government, which required the selection, to carry out local administrative tasks, of Germans who were at once reasonably capable and not too indelibly Nazi, exercised the best efforts of a considerable staff.

The Polish question, being less confused, was more difficult. When the British, American, and Russian Foreign Ministers had gathered at San Francisco, they undertook negotiations to try to break the deadlock which had arisen in Moscow in March. But their efforts were entirely unavailing,

[1] Leahy: *I Was There*, pp. 409–10.

and when on 3 May Molotov announced that Soviet authorities had indeed arrested leaders of the Polish underground for 'diversionist' activities in the rear of the Red Army,[1] Eden and Stettinius decided to break off further conversations pending full information and explanation.

After this failure, it seemed that only a meeting of the three Heads of Government could hope to save the Alliance from open rupture over Poland. At the same time, the multifold problems of Allied policy in Germany clearly called for consultation at the topmost level. As a preliminary to such a meeting, Truman decided to send two special envoys to feel out the ground. Accordingly, Hopkins flew off to Moscow on 23 May 1945 and Joseph E. Davies, former U.S. Ambassador to Moscow, left for London on the same day.

Davies found Churchill deeply depressed and anxious. His domestic political problems were serious, for the Coalition Government had dissolved on 23 May and Churchill had to face an election, scheduled for 5 July 1945. But the situation in Europe weighed even more heavily on Churchill's mind. The British Government were just entering upon a violent controversy with France over Syria, which led on 31 May 1945 to British military intervention against the French, who were attempting to suppress Syrian nationalists by force. The incident did not augur well for future Franco-British co-operation on the Continent; yet Churchill had championed de Gaulle and the French for years in the hope of building a strong counterweight to Russian power on the mainland of Europe with which to replace defeated Germany.

The American attitude, too, seemed to presage an early withdrawal from European affairs. American authorities were proposing to limit further Lend-Lease shipments to material for use against Japan. As a result, Britain faced economic disaster or something close to it. Yet if both the French and the Americans abandoned Britain, the continent of Europe would lie prostrate before the Russians. The British by themselves could hardly hope to counter Russian power and Communist propaganda. Churchill's undisguised fear and distrust of Stalin surprised and shocked Davies, who had become a leading exponent of friendship with Russia. He reported to Truman:

I said that frankly, as I had listened to him [Churchill] inveigh so violently against the threat of Soviet domination and the spread of Communism in Europe, and disclose such a lack of confidence in the professions of good faith in Soviet leadership, I had wondered whether he, the Prime Minister, was now willing to declare to the world that he and Britain had made a mistake in not supporting Hitler, for as I understood him, he was now expressing the doctrine which Hitler and Goebbels had been proclaiming and reiterating for the past four years in an effort to break up allied unity and 'divide and conquer'. . . .

[1] See above, pp. 576–7.

He heard me through, and with intentness. He said that he had been under very great pressure, that he had been just thinking out loud, and that the expressions might have been stronger than he had intended to convey.[1]

Churchill did, however, insist that American and British troops should not withdraw to their zonal boundaries without first securing concessions from the Russians; and his general attitude impressed Davies as putting the preservation of Britain's position in Europe above the preservation of peace.

Hopkins's mission to Stalin was a far more productive one. In his first interview with the Russian dictator on 26 May 1945 Hopkins explained that he wished to examine the whole gamut of issues which affected the fundamental relationship between the United States and Russia, and mentioned Poland, Germany, the Pacific War, and Soviet relations with China as topics he wished to consider. He invited Stalin to propose the questions that bothered him, and at the second interview, on 27 May, Stalin mentioned American support for Argentina's admission to the San Francisco Conference, the reparations negotiations, the Polish problem, the curtailment of Lend-Lease, and the disposition of the German navy and merchant marine as points of grievance against the United States.

Hopkins proceeded to try to reassure Stalin. He declared that the United States was willing to transfer a third of German shipping to Russia, and that the question could be easily disposed of at a meeting of the Big Three. He asserted that Lend-Lease for the Japanese war would continue in accordance with agreements already made; and argued that the abrupt termination of all shipments to Russia immediately after V-E day had been a mistake made by subordinates which had already been corrected.

Stalin's grievance over reparations was that the Americans and British had delayed the conversations agreed upon at Yalta by asking that France be added to the Reparations Commission. On this point Hopkins professed ignorance, but said that the United States would probably not insist upon French participation 'in an unyielding manner', and that in any case it had now been agreed that conversations should begin without the French.

American support of Argentina at San Francisco he attributed to the pressure of Latin American countries, whose representatives had, Hopkins explained, insisted upon Argentina's inclusion when Molotov demanded that the Provisional Polish Government should be invited.[2] Stalin brushed the matter aside, saying that it belonged to the past now anyway.

This brought Hopkins to the nub of all: Poland. The Polish question, he said, was not so much important in itself but as a barometer of Allied co-operation. What the United States wanted, he declared, was a government—any government—desired by the Poles themselves and at the same

[1] Leahy: *I Was There*, p. 442.

[2] Hopkins was not quite accurate in his explanation: see below, pp. 594–5.

time friendly to Russia. Stalin in reply said that he had no intention of exporting the Soviet system to Poland and recognized the right of the United States to take an interest in Polish affairs. He admitted that the Russians had taken unilateral action in Poland, action which 'would have been much better left undone' but which had been necessary because of the presence of the Red Army in Poland and its need for a secure and orderly rear.

The discussion then turned to the problem of how to constitute a satisfactory Provisional Government. Stalin suggested that out of the eighteen to twenty Cabinet seats in the existing Provisional Government four might be turned over to representatives of Polish parties which were excluded from the existing Government, and mentioned that Mikolajczyk would be acceptable as one of these new members.[1] Hopkins asked for time to consider this suggestion.

The third interview between Hopkins and Stalin was devoted to the Far East and Germany. Stalin informed Hopkins that the Red Army would be ready to attack in Manchuria on 8 August 1945. The two men agreed that the American Government should help to make arrangements for a conference between Stalin and the Chinese Foreign Minister at which the question of cession of special rights to Russia in Manchuria would be settled. Stalin repeated his assurances that he would support the unification of China under Chiang Kai-shek, and agreed that a quadripartite trusteeship over Korea—U.S.S.R., U.S.A., China, and Great Britain—should be established until that country became capable of self-government. These agreements Hopkins found very heartening, even when Stalin indicated that he expected to participate in the occupation of Japan on a zonal basis.

With regard to Germany, Stalin told Hopkins that he no longer favoured dismemberment of the Reich, and promised to appoint Marshal Zhukov as the Russian member of the Allied Control Council for Germany so that that body might begin to function.[2] He also spoke of Russian plans for prosecution of war criminals, and discussed with Hopkins the general economic policy which the Allies should pursue in Germany.

At the fourth meeting, on 30 May, arrangements for a conference with Truman and Churchill were discussed and settled. The date was set for mid-July and the area of Berlin was chosen as the site. Then the conver-

[1] Under strenuous pressure from the British, Mikolajczyk had publicly declared his support for the Yalta decisions in April 1945, thus conforming to the requirements the Russians had set forth for participation in the Provisional Government and in the commission which was to settle its composition (cf. Mikolajczyk: *Pattern of Soviet Domination*, p. 128).

[2] Russian delay in appointing a representative to the Allied Control Council had prevented handling of critical questions during the three weeks following V-E day. After waiting in vain to concert their action with Russia, the United States and Great Britain had appointed Eisenhower and Montgomery as their representatives on the Council by 22 May.

sation turned once more to Poland. Hopkins explained American conceptions of the fundamental political rights without which democracy was only a farce; Stalin, facing a rather awkward point, replied that these principles were well known but could only be applied in time of peace and then with certain limitations. Toleration of Fascists,[1] for example, could not be allowed under pretence of democratic freedom of speech. Hopkins 'thoroughly understood the Marshal's opinions' and reassured him by stating that the United States had no interest in seeing any member of the existing Government in Exile included in the reorganized Provisional Polish Government.

The fifth meeting turned to the consideration of the names of specific Polish leaders who might be invited to take part in the discussions preliminary to reorganizing the Provisional Government. After the meeting Hopkins attended a dinner in his honour. He there brought up with Stalin the question of the Polish underground leaders who had been arrested, suggesting that if they were released there would be no further difficulty in drawing up a list of Poles to consult about the reorganization of the Provisional Government. Stalin, however, was not willing to release his prisoners. He blamed the British for connivance with the exiled Government, and declared that he had no intention of allowing the British to run Polish affairs.[2]

During the following days Hopkins rested while Harriman and others negotiated with British and American home authorities and with subordinate Russian officials in an effort to draw up an acceptable list of Poles who would be invited to Moscow to reorganize the Provisional Government. The cables were numerous, but agreement was at length successfully reached. The names of the approved Polish leaders were announced on 12 June, a week after Hopkins's departure from Moscow.

Meanwhile, the San Francisco Conference seemed heading for disaster. A new dispute over Security Council procedure had arisen between the Russians and the Western Powers when the Russians insisted that the veto power should enable any permanent member of the Council to prevent

[1] On 26 May *Pravda* had defined the Russian attitude as follows: 'The Soviet people in their own vital interests demand of the provisional governments in the liberated countries merely that there should be no pro-fascist elements in the governments, or elements hostile to the Soviet Union. Fascism and hostility to the Soviet Union are concepts that coincide with each other' (reproduced from *Documents on American Foreign Policy, 1944–1945*, p. 853).

[2] The charge of 'diversionist activities' in the rear of the Red Army which was pressed against the arrested Poles centred upon their possession of radio sending sets which they had used to communicate with the Poles in London, and through them with the British. Stalin viewed the Polish leaders as agents of British espionage, or chose to pretend so to Hopkins. Throughout the negotiations Hopkins distinctly dissociated American from British policy in Poland, and passed over Stalin's attacks upon Great Britain without comment. The British were, of course, excluded from direct participation in the negotiations, but were kept informed of Hopkins's progress through the State Department, and to some degree by direct contact with the British Ambassador in Moscow.

discussion of any issue which it preferred not to bring into such a public forum.[1] Truman conceived the idea of asking Hopkins to try to settle this matter with Stalin, and on 6 June, the day before he left Moscow, Hopkins took the question up with Stalin and Molotov. In a side discussion with Molotov, Stalin showed that he had not understood the problem, and then turned to Hopkins and said that he thought the whole argument was insignificant and that the American view should be accepted. Thus in an almost casual manner Stalin reversed the Russian stand, and an issue on which torrents of words had been expended disappeared as if by magic.[2]

Hopkins's mission, and the settlement of the Polish issue which followed quickly thereafter, was like the breaking of a log-jam. Disputes which had seemed to threaten immediate breakdown of the Grand Alliance were patched up, the San Francisco Conference was able to proceed triumphantly to draw up the Charter of the United Nations, Allied administrative arrangements in Germany were regularized, agreement on Allied administration of Austria was reached by the European Advisory Commission, the Trieste dispute was temporarily shelved, and the ground for the Potsdam Conference prepared. Good feeling seemed to have been restored. Stalin even expressed gratitude for Lend-Lease.[3]

These results flowed centrally from the settlement of the Polish issue, and, though Stalin had yielded to the extent of admitting Mikolajczyk and some other non-Communist Poles within the pale, the Western Powers yielded far more. It was perhaps not perfectly clear at the time, but it was proved by subsequent events that Communist domination of the Polish Provisional Government survived the 'reorganization' for which Hopkins's mission had prepared the way; yet it was to prevent such domination that Britain and America had argued so long. Having won a clear path to his appointed goal—a 'friendly' government in Poland—Stalin was willing and anxious to conciliate the West on other issues, and it was doubtless this desire which accounted for the casualness with which he settled the dispute over the veto power on the Security Council. If the West would allow him to dominate Eastern Europe and Manchuria Stalin was willing to co-operate; but he clearly put Soviet interests in these border regions ahead of all other considerations.

During the weeks that followed Hopkins's departure from Moscow the Polish Government was quickly reorganized. On 17 June the invited

[1] See below, pp. 600–3.

[2] Sherwood (*Roosevelt and Hopkins*, pp. 887–912; Eng. edition, ii. 875–902) reproduces extensive extracts from Hopkins's record of these conversations and is the basis for the above account.

[3] On 12 June 1945, the third anniversary of the Lend-Lease agreement with Russia, Stalin sent a telegram to Truman saying: 'American arms, supplies, and food made a considerable contribution to the defeat of Germany' (*New York Times*, 12 June 1945).

Polish leaders met in the Russian capital. On 23 June they agreed upon the members of the Cabinet of the 'reorganized' Provisional Government; on 28 June the new Cabinet took office; and on 5 July 1945 the British and American Governments extended official recognition to the new Provisional Polish Government of National Unity. Of the twenty-one Cabinet seats, fourteen were held by veterans of the Lublin Committee; and the Communists, with their sympathizers, kept control of the Ministries most valuable for the internal control of the country.[1]

While the Polish problem was thus being resolved, the Allies made equally rapid progress in Germany. Zhukov's appointment as the Russian member of the Allied Control Council was announced on 30 May; and on 5 June the British, American, French, and Russian commanders met in Berlin and promulgated three declarations upon which the future Allied administration of Germany was to rest. The first of these asserted that, since there was no central authority in Germany capable of accepting responsibility for the administration of the country under the direction of the victorious Allies, the four Powers concerned 'hereby assume supreme authority with respect to Germany, including all the powers possessed by the German Government, the High Command and any state, municipal, or local government or authority'. After listing various acts immediately required of the Germans, the declaration continued:

> . . . the four Allied Governments will take such steps, including the complete disarmament and demilitarization of Germany, as they deem requisite for future peace and security.
>
> The Allied Representatives will impose on Germany additional political, administrative, economic, financial, military and other requirements arising from the complete defeat of Germany. . . . All German authorities and the German people shall carry out unconditionally the requirements of the Allied Representatives, and shall fully comply with all . . . proclamations, orders, ordinances and instructions.[2]

Thus Germany was bound hand and foot, but a positive Allied policy was not revealed because there had as yet been no agreement upon such policy.

The other two documents promulgated at the same time, however, did define the machinery of Allied administration. A statement on the zones of occupation described the four zones which had been agreed upon and put Greater Berlin under the joint authority of all four Powers. The third statement described the machinery for central government. A Control Council, whose members were to be the four zonal Commanders-in-Chief, was to deal with matters affecting Germany as a whole, and would assure

[1] Mikolajczyk: *Pattern of Soviet Domination*, p. 147. The Polish Underground leaders who had been arrested in March were tried before a Soviet military court while the consultations for the reorganization of the Polish Provisional Government were in progress. The trials resulted in prison sentences of varying lengths for the accused.

[2] *Documents on American Foreign Relations, 1944–1945*, pp. 217–22.

'appropriate uniformity of action by the Commanders-in-Chief in their respective zones of occupation'. Its decisions were to be unanimous.[1]

The next question to be solved was how and when each occupation force should take up its allotted zone. The Western Allies insisted that their entry into Berlin should coincide with their withdrawal from the Russian zone; and there were delays while minor details were settled. On 29 June, however, everything was arranged, and during a four-day period, beginning 1 July, the requisite troop movements took place.[2] Arrangements defining British, American, and French rights of access to Berlin, prescribing each nation's responsibility for supplying the sections of the city placed under its occupation, and regulating the procedure of the Allied Kommandatura for the city, were made during the following days. On 10 July the first meeting of the Allied Kommandatura took place.[3]

A corollary of the establishment of national zones of occupation was the dissolution of SHAEF. This took place on 14 July 1945, after which date Eisenhower's authority was confined to the command of American troops and limited to the American zone of occupation. With the dissolution of SHAEF the most successful Allied command the world had ever seen came to an end.

When the machinery of Allied control had thus been set up, the problem of what common policies should be enforced in Germany became pressing. American policy had been defined by a directive from the Joint Chiefs of Staff (J.C.S. 1067, as it was called). This document, issued on 14 May 1945, was kept secret until 17 October 1945. The British Government, too, prepared instructions for their representatives in the British zone. General principles were made public on 20 May 1945. Presumably French and Russian policy was similarly communicated to their respective Commanders-in-Chief; but clearly common policy for Germany as a whole, if there was to be any, could only be laid down after inter-governmental consultation. This was to be one of the main tasks of the Potsdam Conference.

The effect of Hopkins's mission to Stalin and of the subsequent steps taken

[1] *Documents on American Foreign Relations, 1944–1945*, pp. 222–4. The boundaries of the French zone of occupation, agreed to in principle at Yalta (see above, p. 548), were first defined by a document drawn up by the European Advisory Commission and accepted on 2 May 1945 (cf. Lucius D. Clay: *Decision in Germany* (London, Heinemann, 1950), p. 13).

[2] The American garrison of Berlin arrived in time to celebrate the American national holiday on 4 July with a parade through Berlin's shattered streets.

[3] General Clay, who was the American representative in these negotiations, says that he and his British colleague accepted 'as a temporary arrangement' the allocation of a main highway, a rail line, and two air corridors for their access to Berlin. But the agreement was left indefinite—with important consequences in 1948 (see *Survey* for 1947–8, pp. 242 seqq.)—because Clay 'did not want an agreement in writing which established anything less than the right of unrestricted access' (Clay: *Decision in Germany*, p. 26).

in Poland and Germany by the Allies was to make Germany rather than Poland the major barometer of Allied harmony or disharmony. Affairs in Austria and the Balkans were minor though not unimportant irritants to future relations between Russia and the West; and at a later date the tangled skein of Chinese and Far Eastern affairs began to loom large. But after June 1945 the fate of the Grand Alliance turned more decisively upon Germany than upon any other single issue; and it was when the Allies could no longer even pretend to agree upon a common course in Germany that the Grand Alliance finally and definitely collapsed.

Certainly Hopkins, Truman, and Churchill did not deliberately abandon Poland to the Russians in June 1945: they hoped that the Provisional Government would organize reasonably fair elections which would establish a reasonably free and independent Polish Government that would be acceptable to all the Allies. But when events moved in a contrary direction there was little or nothing the Western Powers could do. By the time the Polish elections took place, in January 1947, the problem of Germany had usurped first place, and the thinly veiled hostility between Russia and her former allies had reached such a pitch that there could be no hope of effective diplomatic intervention to swing Polish affairs more in the direction desired by Britain and America.

But the future course of events was hidden in June and July 1945, and to hopeful eyes it seemed that a workable compromise had at last been found for Poland and that Allied co-operation in Germany was, if not assured, at least made possible by the establishment of the Allied Control Council.

Reinforcing this optimistic view was the fact that the San Francisco Conference had been a success; from it the Charter of a new world organization had emerged, committing the nations of the world to the preservation of peace and to the ideals of democracy. To the achievements of that Conference we must now turn.

(ii) The San Francisco Conference, 25 April–26 June 1945

Agreement at Yalta on the voting formula for the Security Council cleared the way for the first full-dress gathering of the war-born United Nations. On behalf of the four sponsoring Powers,[1] the United States issued invitations on 5 March to a United Nations Conference on International Organization. Forty-six Governments had qualified for the honour of attending the Conference by declaring war before 1 March 1945; but the unresolved dispute over reorganization of the Provisional Polish Government meant that a forty-seventh, Poland, was not allowed to attend. The forty-six Governments were invited to 'prepare a charter for a general international organization for the maintenance of international peace and

[1] France was invited to join Britain, Russia, China, and America as a sponsor of the Conference, but de Gaulle, smarting under recent insults to his pride, declined.

security' on the basis of the Dumbarton Oaks proposals, supplemented by the Yalta voting formula. All accepted, and the delegates duly gathered at San Francisco on 25 April 1945 for the opening ceremonies.

The Conference was surrounded by an enormous apparatus of publicity. No less than 2,636 journalists were accredited, and the American Government organized a great propaganda campaign, before, during, and after the Conference, designed to convince the American and, to a lesser degree, the world public, of the importance and value of a new international organization. In addition, a great army of special pleaders assembled at San Francisco to try to advance their peculiar causes—including, among others, a delegation of Iroquois Indians protesting against the non-observance of treaties concluded between the Iroquois tribes and the United States Government.[1]

The Conference itself was conducted on a vast scale. A total of 282 delegates represented their various Governments, and were assisted by staffs and a secretariat totalling over 2,500 persons. A mountain of paper was turned out daily to record the deliberations of the Conference; and, as was inevitable with an undertaking so large and so hastily organized, confusion reigned at almost every level.[2]

The San Francisco Conference brought the Great Powers face to face for the first time with their smaller allies *en masse*, and one of the major lines of fission which dominated the Conference arose between the Governments which had drafted the Dumbarton Oaks proposals and those which were now for the first time having a chance to try their hand at constitution-making for the post-war world. Britain, America, Russia, and China were naturally inclined to defend their handiwork against the criticism and proposals for modification which other Governments put forward. Yet the Great Powers were not closely united among themselves. The haste with which the Conference had been organized prevented the Big Four from reaching agreement among themselves on such issues as trusteeships or the relation between regional organizations and the proposed world organization.

Further, there were important differences in prestige among the Great Powers. China occupied her position only by courtesy, and counted for relatively little at the Conference. The position of France was particularly delicate. The war-time eclipse of French national power did not correspond to the role which was assigned to France for the future. Moreover, the French Government had refused to become a sponsor of the Conference on the ground that France had not taken part in the preliminary consultation which had produced the Dumbarton Oaks proposals. These anomalies

[1] Clifford Hulme: *San Francisco Conference* (London, Kemsley Newspapers, 1945), p. 12.

[2] Cf. C. Eagleton: 'The Charter Adopted at San Francisco', *American Political Science Review*, October 1945, xxxix. 935.

were lessened when on 4 May the sponsoring Powers decided to admit the French to their private conversations at which most of the important issues before the Conference were thrashed out behind the scenes. This step soothed French pride, but did not entirely strip away the cloak of injured dignity with which the French enveloped themselves at the Conference.

A more important difference among the Great Powers was this: Britain and America were accessible to the pressure of lesser countries represented at the Conference in a way that Russia was not. The British Dominions and the Latin American countries held a special place in the orbit of the two Powers; and their wishes, often vigorously put forward, had to be taken into account. The Russians were under no comparable pressure, and as a general rule stuck rigorously to their own interpretation of the Dumbarton Oaks proposals.

Among the lesser Powers, there were two more or less well defined regional blocs: the Latin American and the Arab states. In addition, a grouping of 'middle Powers' existed with reference to some issues. Countries like Australia, Canada, and Brazil, which had contributed men and resources to the war on a substantial scale, felt that their voice in the new international organization should be commensurate with their new national power, and did not always believe that the Dumbarton Oaks proposals gave them their due.

Another line of fission which was of great importance at the Conference, and which sometimes split national delegations into different parts, arose from divergent views of the basic nature of the future organization. There were men who believed that abstract principles of justice, morality, and international law should govern the operation and structure of the organization; others tended to look upon it as a device for adjustment between rival states and for the application of overwhelming power against petty disturbers of the peace. Few if any delegates espoused either position to the exclusion of the other; everyone recognized that power and justice had somehow to be combined. But there were very great differences in emphasis. At one extreme, the Russians acted, though they did not always talk, as though they wanted an alliance of the Great Powers which would keep the lesser fry in order. Herbert V. Evatt, the chief Australian delegate, became the most prominent champion of the view that justice and equality between the nations came first, and that the special rights which the Great Powers had arrogated to themselves in the Dumbarton Oaks proposals should be reduced in order to bring them, too, under the rule of law.

For working purposes, the Conference was divided into twelve committees. Sections of the Dumbarton Oaks document were assigned to each committee for revision. The committees reported to four Commissions, and the Commissions to plenary sessions of the entire Conference. Co-ordination of the Conference as a whole was, in theory, entrusted to a

Steering Committee and a smaller Executive Committee. In practice, however, the most important work was done by an informal group consisting of the chief representatives of the four sponsoring Powers, together with France (after 4 May). This body thrashed out in private the main problems of the Conference as they arose, and then presented a common Great Power front to the other nations. Delegates from other Governments could protest against a decision so made, but the Great Powers could always round up enough votes to assure the acceptance of any measure supported by all of them.

Thus it turned out in fact, though not in form, that preliminary agreement among the Big Three (France and China hardly counted, though their representatives did have entrée to the inner counsels) was the *sine qua non* of any change in the Dumbarton Oaks proposals. In these private conclaves Britain and America in general played the role of intermediaries, pressing upon the Soviet delegates those arguments advanced by the lesser Powers of which they approved. The Russians, on the other hand, aware of the fact that they could seldom command support from the smaller Powers on controversial points, regularly adopted an intransigent attitude when challenged, trading upon the fact that neither Britain nor America dared to risk Russian withdrawal from the new international organization. The Russians, too, wanted to see the Conference succeed in the sense that they wanted an international organization; but, remembering the League of Nations, they were resolved to make it impossible for the new organization ever to become an alliance against the Soviet Union. The Security Council veto was the great safeguard against such an evolution. Consequently the Russians steadily resisted the efforts of the smaller Powers to reduce its scope. Controversy over the exact definition of the veto power, therefore, became the greatest single issue at the Conference.

The San Francisco Conference opened on 25 April 1945. On the same day Russian and American troops met on the Elbe. Rumours of victory in Europe were current from the start, and the atmosphere of the Conference was like that of the great peace conferences of the past. The first few days were devoted to ceremonial speeches and to the task of organizing the Conference. Snags soon developed. At the first business meeting, on 26 April, Molotov objected to assigning the chairmanship of the Conference to Stettinius. A three-hour wrangle ensued until the meeting adjourned without any decision. On the next day Molotov accepted a British compromise proposal to the effect that each of the sponsoring Powers should take the chairmanship in turn, but immediately the Russian Foreign Minister raised a new storm by demanding that the Provisional Government of Poland be invited to the Conference. It was Stettinius's turn to object. After a second lengthy wrangle, the decision not to invite Poland until after the reorganization of the Provisional Government was allowed to stand.

Molotov's tactics irritated the American and other delegates, and put the Conference behind schedule. Consequently, when on 30 April the question of the admission of Argentina to the Conference came up, Stettinius was in a hurry.[1] The Americans found themselves in an embarrassing position, since at Yalta Roosevelt had expressly excluded Argentina from eligibility,[2] but at the Inter-American Conference on Problems of War and Peace (Mexico City, 21 February–8 March 1945) Stettinius had agreed to support the admission of Argentina to initial membership in the United Nations organization.[3] When Argentina's admission was proposed, Molotov objected; Stettinius supported the proposal, and an all-day debate followed. Molotov put his case before the public by means of a special news conference and won considerable journalistic sympathy for his stand; but the votes were on Stettinius's side, and rather than see the business of the Conference still further delayed, the Americans pressed matters to an immediate decision. Only three nations voted with Molotov, and Argentina was admitted, along with the Ukraine and White Russia.[4]

The public clash between Russia and the United States over these preliminary issues boded ill for the smooth conduct of the Conference. Stettinius's steam-roller tactics, using the numerical weight of Latin American votes to push through Argentina's admission, were criticized by many liberal and leftist groups in the United States and in other countries. The result was paradoxical, for while the Russians certainly suffered overwhelming defeat in the vote on Argentina, the Americans suffered something of a moral set-back.

For the rest of the Conference, the voting power more or less at American disposal[5] was not used to settle disputes between the Great Powers. Only after matters had been decided behind the scenes and some sort of agreement had been reached among the sponsoring nations did they come before

[1] The admission of Argentina had been linked with the admission of Poland in behind-the-scenes bargaining (see above, p. 585). The Russians proposed to trade Argentina's admission for Poland's: the Americans refused to accept the bargain; and as a result Molotov took the matter on to the floor of the Conference (cf. *New York Times*, 2 May 1945).

[2] See above, p. 554 and note 1.

[3] This change of front was a concession to Latin American feeling. Partly, Stettinius felt compelled to concede something in return for the promise of Latin American support for the admission of the Ukraine and White Russia; partly, too, the United States wanted to conciliate Argentina and improve the strained relations which had arisen between the two countries during the war.

[4] Denmark, too, was admitted on 27 May when her liberation made possible the establishment of an 'Allied' Government there. This brought the number of Governments participating in the Conference up to fifty.

[5] Of the fifty nations which by its end attended the Conference, twenty were Latin American, and Liberia and the Philippines were equally if not more thoroughly open to United States pressure. Since decisions were by two-thirds vote, this gave the United States a veto power on the Conference floor as long as the bloc held together.

the Conference for formal action. Obviously, any other course would have risked Russian withdrawal: votes of countries like Panama or Haiti were not going to bind the Union of Soviet Socialist Republics to accept provisions of the Charter which the Russians disliked. Hence, after the Argentine affair had blown over, the Russians, too, in effect enjoyed a veto over the proceedings of the Conference; and when the Great Powers could not agree, the Conference simply reached a stalemate until a formula could be found to suit the Russian, American, and British delegations.

As the Conference got down to work on detailed revision of the text of the Dumbarton Oaks proposals, debates and compromises on thousands of minor points kept the delegates busy. The major outlines of the original proposals survived, but amplification, clarification, and minor alteration of the original resulted in a very considerable total change. Only a detailed commentary on the text of the Charter of the United Nations as it eventually emerged could do justice to this part of the Conference's work;[1] here we must content ourselves with describing a few of the major departures from Dumbarton Oaks which were made at San Francisco.

First of all, important sections were added to the Charter. Thus, a preamble, modified from a draft written by Field Marshal Smuts, struck a muted millennial note which had been absent from the Dumbarton Oaks proposals.

A second major addition to the original proposals was the provision of legal machinery for international trusteeship of dependent territories. This matter, side-stepped at Dumbarton Oaks,[2] had been briefly discussed at Yalta.[3] It had there been agreed that the sponsoring Governments would consult one another before the San Francisco Conference met with the aim of presenting to the Conference definite proposals for trusteeship. Actually, agreement had not been reached when the Conference began, and each of the Great Powers, together with Australia, presented their own separate trusteeship plan to the Conference. There were, of course, numerous disputes over details, and it proved particularly difficult to agree whether independence should be declared to be the ultimate goal for dependent territories or not. In the end 'progressive development towards self-government or independence as may be appropriate to the particular circumstances of each territory' was accepted as one of the basic objectives of trusteeship.[4]

This represented a not unambiguous compromise between the desires of

[1] Leland M. Goodrich and Edvard Hambro's *Charter of the United Nations: Commentary and Documents* (Boston, World Peace Foundation, 1946) is a rather legal-minded but none the less admirable commentary. See also *United Nations Documents, 1941–1945* (London, Royal Institute of International Affairs, 1946).

[2] See above, p. 508.

[3] See above, p. 554.

[4] U.N. Charter, article 76.

imperial Powers such as Great Britain and France and the wishes of such countries as China and the Soviet Union which championed the rights of colonial peoples.[1]

Trusteeship, of course, was not to apply to established colonial empires, save as colonies might voluntarily be put under the new system.[2] Article 73 of the Charter, however, set forth general principles to apply to all colonial areas governed by members of the United Nations. It declared that the 'interests of the inhabitants of these territories are paramount'

[1] The United States took an ambiguous position on the question of trusteeships. Influential elements in the State Department believed that a system of international trusteeships would be the best of all possible ways to raise colonial peoples to the level of equal participation in international life, and, indeed, men like Hull and Roosevelt had long played with the idea of transforming the old European colonial empires into international trusteeships. Opposition from the British had led to a postponement of this programme; and by 1944 opposition from military leaders at home, supported by influential Congressmen, had forced the Americans to think again. The U.S. navy was particularly insistent in pressing for annexation of former Japanese islands in the Pacific.

The solution of this conflict of views was a compromise. The Americans decided to argue for trusteeship over former League of Nations mandates and territories taken from the Axis Powers as a result of the Second World War, and to give up as impracticable the larger plan of transforming European colonial empires to the new pattern. Moreover, they decided that trusteeship territories should be divided into strategic and non-strategic areas: in the former, fortification and military garrisons would be authorized. Under this arrangement, it was hoped that the U.S. navy would be able to use some of the former Japanese islands of the Pacific as naval bases, occupying them under the authority of the Security Council. This idea was a rather watered-down version of Roosevelt's earlier vision of United Nations military bases scattered round the world (see above, p. 319). The important difference was that the Americans now looked forward to establishing only American forces in the ex-Japanese islands; and the project of trying to set up United Nations bases in other parts of the world was shelved until some future time when the military arrangements, projected in the Charter, had come into force.

On the issue of whether or not independence should be a declared aim of trusteeship, the Americans supported the British and French. After all, the U.S. navy did not want Okinawa, for instance, to have a legal claim to independence at some future time when American naval supremacy in the Pacific had been made to rest in part upon the possession of a base there.

The change in the American position on trusteeships between the time of the Moscow Conference of Foreign Ministers in October 1943 (when Hull first formally broached the idea—see above, p. 333) and the San Francisco Conference measured the growth of military influence in the determination of American post-war policy, and served, also, as an index of how the changed military position of the country reacted upon traditional views of imperialism. From 1944 onward American official opinion was far less critical of the British Empire than had been the case in the first years of the war. The possible advantages of being able to use British bases, scattered so conveniently over the world, had dawned on American military leaders; and their own ambitions in the Pacific made it illogical for them to voice criticism of analogous British arrangements in other parts of the world.

American civilian opinion, especially the liberal and leftist wings thereof, lagged behind the change in official policy, and a man like Hull felt deeply disappointed at the emasculation of his original trusteeship proposals (Hull, *Memoirs*, ii. 1598–1601, 1638, 1706). Roosevelt's death probably played an important part in effecting this shift in official American policy. He had been a leader of the anti-imperialists in the American Government, while Truman was less inclined to grand dreams of the future and more open to arguments for the need of protecting American national security.

On this, more than any other issue, the new post-war role of the United States as a great, though disguisedly, imperial Power, was forecast at San Francisco.

[2] It did apply to League of Nations mandates and to territory taken from the Axis nations.

and bound the imperial nations, among other things, 'to develop self-government' and 'to take due account of the political aspirations of the peoples'.

A third omission from the Dumbarton Oaks proposals was a definition of the jurisdiction of the International Court of Justice. A Committee of Jurists had met in Washington from 9 to 20 April to consider this question, and made recommendations to the San Francisco Conference. The Committee produced a draft statute of the Court, which, with few modifications, was accepted by the Conference.[1]

These additions to the Dumbarton Oaks proposals filled obvious gaps, and, except for trusteeship, did not provoke serious controversy. When it came to changes in the original proposals, however, the Great Powers in general resisted anything more than clarification of meaning; and the changes in substance which were made came only after much debate.

Nevertheless, the sections of the Dumbarton Oaks proposals which dealt with the powers of the General Assembly and of the Social and Economic Council were altered significantly as a result of the pressure of the smaller Powers. The description of the Assembly's powers was made more definite and interpretations of the Dumbarton Oaks text which might have limited its activities were made impossible by changes in wording.[2] The Assembly was given the right to make recommendations to the Security Council or to the members of the United Nations on any matter save when the Security Council was 'exercising in respect of any dispute or situation the functions assigned to it in the present Charter'.[3]

Similarly, the dignity of the Social and Economic Council was enhanced by classing it among the 'principal organs' of the new international organization. More important, perhaps, the members of the United Nations undertook 'to take joint and separate action' to raise standards of living, to solve 'international, economic, social, health, and related problems', and to promote 'universal respect for, and observance of, human rights

[1] The only matter of controversy was whether the existing World Court at The Hague should be allowed to continue, or whether a new one should be constituted. Since several countries excluded from the United Nations had accepted the jurisdiction of the Hague Court, it was decided to start afresh rather than try to unravel the legal tangle which would have resulted from the alternative course.

[2] In particular, it was provided that as soon as the Security Council ceased to deal with a question the Assembly would be notified thereof, thus throwing the issue open to recommendations from the Assembly again. This change was intended to prevent a sort of pocket veto by the Security Council, whereby the Council might, by taking a question under its consideration, prevent the Assembly from making recommendations for an indefinite length of time, even though the Security Council neglected to take active steps for the solution of the question (cf. Herbert V. Evatt: *The United Nations* (Cambridge, Mass., Harvard University Press, 1948), pp. 10, 19–21).

[3] U.N. Charter, articles 10, 12.

and fundamental freedoms for all without distinction as to race, sex, language, or religion'.[1]

Declarations of this sort, like the principles prescribed for colonial administration, appealed to the idealism of the delegates from some of the smaller nations. They were, however, pious gestures directed towards liberal world opinions rather than serious programmes for action, since effective enforcement would involve extensive intervention in the internal affairs of professedly sovereign nations.

It was the Security Council which, according to the Dumbarton Oaks proposals, was to exercise the main responsibility for keeping the peace, and inevitably the main contests at San Francisco arose over the exact definition of its powers. There were two principal problems: the definition of the veto power, and the definition of the relationship between the Security Council on the one hand and regional organizations (like the Pan-American Union) or local security arrangements (like the Russian system of bilateral alliances) on the other hand. The two problems were connected with one another, since, as the Dumbarton Oaks text stood, any one of the permanent members of the Security Council could veto an action undertaken by a regional international body designed to keep the peace. From the American point of view, this meant that European and Asiatic Powers could interfere in the Americas—a violation of the sacrosanct Monroe Doctrine; from the Russian point of view, it meant that the operation of the bilateral mutual aid pacts which had been concluded with France, Britain, Poland, Czechoslovakia, and Yugoslavia[2] could not legally come into force until after the Security Council had approved their operation against Germany. Neither the United States[3] nor Russia was satisfied with such a situation, since neither Power was ready to trust its future security entirely to the new international organization.

The Dumbarton Oaks text read: 'No enforcement action should be taken under regional arrangements or by regional agencies without the authorization of the Security Council.'[4] This blanket subordination of regional organizations to the Security Council was modified by two provisions of the new Charter. Article 51 asserted: 'Nothing in the present Charter shall impair the inherent right of individual or collective self-defense if an armed attack occurs against a Member of the United Nations, until the Security Council has taken the measures necessary to maintain

[1] U.N. Charter, articles 55, 56. [2] See above, p. 577 and note 1.

[3] The United States delegation was divided on this point, some wishing to do nothing to derogate from the supreme authority of the Security Council. But two considerations were decisive. The Latin American nations were emphatic in wishing to see their regional arrangements with the United States kept free from potential Russian or other veto; and competent political experts on the American delegation pointed out that any document that abrogated, or seemed to abrogate, the Monroe Doctrine would not be acceptable to the United States Senate (cf. *New York Times*, 10 May 1945).

[4] Chapter VIII (c) 2 (*United Nations Documents*, 1941–1945 (R.I.I.A.), p. 101).

international peace and security.' The right of collective self-defence against armed attack, thus guaranteed, satisfied the American nations that the operation of their mutual defence arrangements would not be subject to undue interference. The Russians, however, pointed out that aggressive action by Germany short of armed attack might require joint counter-action under the terms of their mutual aid pacts. To cover this contingency, the language of the Charter was made to read as follows: '... no enforcement action shall be taken under regional arrangements or by regional agencies without the authorization of the Security Council, with the exception of measures directed against any enemy state. ... The term enemy state ... applies to any state which during the Second World War has been an enemy of any signatory of the present Charter.'[1]

These two escape clauses in effect not only limited the authority of the Security Council but reduced the scope of the Great Power veto as well. American self-defence and Russian preventive action against Germany could proceed even in the face of disagreement among the permanent members of the Security Council as to the necessity of the action in question.

A second limitation on the power of the Security Council was written into the Charter in deference to the objections made by Canada and other 'middle Powers' to the provisions of the Dumbarton Oaks draft which gave the Council the right to call upon nations not represented on that body to provide troops for enforcing peace. On 30 May it was agreed that, if such a contingency should arise, the member whose forces were to be called upon for action would be invited to join in the discussions on the Security Council and would be entitled to vote on any question 'concerning the employment of contingents of that Member's armed forces'.[2]

These modifications of the power of the Security Council were certainly important, but they were overshadowed by the debate which arose over the meaning and detailed application of the Yalta voting formula.[3] Several of the smaller Powers, most prominently Australia, demanded that the Great Power veto over investigation and peaceful settlement of disputes should be eliminated from the Charter. Quite apart from this desire to reduce the privileges of the Great Powers, it soon became apparent that the interpretation of the Yalta voting formula offered all sorts of difficulties. As it stood no one could say with assurance in what circumstances and to what subjects the veto power would apply. In an effort to smoke out the Great Powers and clarify the whole problem, the delegates of all the lesser nations compiled a list of twenty-three questions, and presented their queries to the sponsoring Powers for answer on 22 May. The questions covered a large range: Would the veto apply to decisions to investi-

[1] U.N. Charter, article 53.

[2] Ibid. article 44.

[3] See above, pp. 551–2.

gate disputes? Would the decision whether a question were 'procedural' or not be subject to the veto? Would abstention from voting have the same effect as a negative vote? Would the veto apply to the election of a Secretary-General and to decisions to refer disputes to the International Court? &c.[1]

These, and like questions, were easier to ask than to answer. When the American, British, Chinese, and Russian delegates came to discuss them a deep disagreement opened between the Russian interpretation of the Yalta formula and that accepted by the other sponsoring nations. On 27 May Andrei Gromyko (who had succeeded Molotov as the senior Russian delegate on 9 May) let it be known that the veto applied to any decision as to whether a question were 'procedural' or not; and on 2 June he dropped a bombshell when he informed his colleagues that before a dispute could even be discussed by the Security Council all the permanent members should vote to put it on the agenda.

Actually, the wording of the Yalta formula was so ambiguous that almost any interpretation could be defended. It read:

> . . . Decisions of the Security Council on procedural matters should be made by an affirmative vote of seven members.
>
> Decisions of the Security Council on *all other matters* should be made by an affirmative vote of seven members including the concurring votes of the permanent members; provided that, in decisions . . . [pertaining to peaceful settlement] a party to a dispute should abstain from voting.[2]

The Russians now declared that among the 'all other matters' mentioned in the Yalta text was the matter of deciding whether or not a particular dispute should be discussed at all. This ran directly contrary to an interpretation which had been publicly made by the American State Department.[3] The British and Chinese supported the American view, while the delegates from the lesser nations who had so vigorously launched the hue and cry for relaxation of the veto power were aghast. The Russians had called in question a position which they thought was already secure: the right of any aggrieved party to get a hearing for its case.

For several days the Conference seemed on the point of failure. Gromyko was bound by his instructions from Moscow. The other delegates and their home Governments were determined not to accept the Russian interpretation, which would have deprived the Security Council of nearly

[1] The questionnaire is reproduced in Goodrich and Hambro: *Charter of the United Nations*, pp. 333–7.

[2] *Documents on American Foreign Relations, 1944–1945*, p. 360.

[3] On 24 March 1945 the Acting Secretary of State, Joseph C. Grew, issued the following statement: 'Could the projected international Organization be precluded from discussing any dispute or situation which might threaten the peace and security by the act of any one of its members? The answer is "No". . . . It is this Government's understanding that under these voting procedures there is nothing which could prevent any state from bringing to the attention of the Security Council any dispute or any situation which it believes may lead to international friction or may give rise to a dispute.' Full text may be found in *Documents on American Foreign Relations, 1944–1945*, p. 416.

all independent authority and made it into little more than a puppet stage on which solemnly to re-enact decisions made by the Great Powers through other channels. On 4 June Truman decided to appeal directly to Stalin, through Harry Hopkins, to reverse the Russian stand; and as we have seen Hopkins was easily successful.[1]

On 7 June news of Stalin's ruling reached the Conference. On the same day, the sponsoring Powers issued a statement defining their interpretation of the Yalta voting formula. The statement did not take up the twenty-three questions which had been put on 22 May by the smaller nations: instead it dealt with 'general attitudes towards the whole question of unanimity of permanent members in the decisions of the Security Council'. The key passage was the following:

> Further, no individual member of the Council can alone prevent consideration and discussion by the Council of a dispute or situation brought to its attention. . . . Nor can parties to such dispute be prevented by these means from being heard by the Council. . . .
>
> Beyond this point, decisions and actions by the Security Council may well have major political consequences and may even initiate a chain of events which might, in the end, require the Council under its responsibilities to invoke measures of enforcement. . . . This chain of events begins when the Council decides to make an investigation, or determines that the time has come to call upon states to settle their differences, or makes recommendations to the parties. It is to such decisions and actions that unanimity of the permanent members applies, with the important proviso, referred to above, for abstention from voting by parties to a dispute.[2]

The statement concluded by declaring that the Yalta formula was 'essential' for the operation of an effective international organization, and bluntly informed the smaller Powers that the decision whether a matter were procedural or not would have to remain subject to the veto. As for the other questions which had been put, 'it is clear what the answers . . . should be', but the Great Powers refrained from specifying.

Many delegates felt dissatisfied with this statement. In spite of the Great Powers' assurance, the answers to some of their twenty-three unanswered questions were not at all clear. They likewise protested that the veto had not been modified, as they had hoped;[3] but, in view of the

[1] See above, p. 588. When the veto problem first became acute, the Americans considered whether or not to appeal to Stalin to change the Yalta text on voting procedure in order to exempt mere investigation by the Security Council from the veto. It was decided not to do so on the ground that the American and British case in Poland rested on the sacrosanctity of the Yalta agreements, and any change in one part might provide a basis for a change in another part of the Yalta texts (cf. *New York Times*, 26 May 1951).

[2] Text of the Statement may be found in Goodrich and Hambro: *The United Nations Charter*, pp. 128–30.

[3] Herbert V. Evatt of Australia wrote a memorandum which said: '. . . without veto, the Council can only discuss whether a dispute can be discussed, and can only investigate whether

united front among the Great Powers, there was nothing the discontented delegates could do. On 12 June, Evatt's last attempt to restrict the veto by extending the definition of 'procedural' matters was defeated, and the long debate came to an end. The Yalta formula, with all its ambiguities, was incorporated unchanged in the Charter.

In the final stages of the discussion, the veto came to be tied up with the question of amendment to the Charter. As the inflexible attitude of the Great Powers became manifest, the men who hoped for a restriction in the special privileges accorded to the Great Powers came to pin their hopes upon some future revision of the Charter. As a concession to this point of view, it was provided that if after ten years the Charter had not been amended by the regular machinery—a two-thirds vote by both Assembly and Security Council, including all the permanent members—it would be possible to amend the Charter by calling a Conference authorized by a simple majority in the Assembly, combined with an affirmative vote by any seven members of the Security Council. Thus after ten years the veto power over amendment to the Charter would be suspended. This decision, reached on 15 June, ended the work of the Conference on the complicated matter of Security Council procedure.

A last alarum came on 18 June when the Russians challenged the definition of the powers of the Assembly to discuss international problems. By this time everyone was anxious to end the Conference, which had already run more than two weeks beyond the scheduled deadline. At the same time, no one wished to see the whole Charter fall to the ground by stumbling on this last hurdle. Consequently, a compromise proved possible after three days. The Assembly was granted the right to discuss 'any questions or matters within the scope of the present Charter'; and when this formula had been accepted, on 21 June, the only task remaining to the Conference was to approve the entire text.[1]

Finally on 26 June all was ready, and the assembled delegates signed the Charter they had so painfully drawn up. The occasion was solemnized by a speech from President Truman. He spoke with qualified optimism:

> The Charter of the United Nations which you have just signed is a solid structure upon which we can build a better world. . . .

it should be investigated.' This he felt was inadequate (Goodrich and Hambro: *United Nations Charter*, p. 131).

[1] The final wind-up was delayed by the task of arranging and phrasing the whole document, which had been drafted by separate committees with the results which could be expected from multiple authorship. A second problem was translation and careful collation of the texts in English, Russian, Chinese, French, and Spanish—all of which were declared to be equally authentic. The Chinese version of the Charter presented special difficulties owing to the limitations of established Chinese vocabulary. Several dozen new characters had to be invented to carry the meaning of the Charter into Chinese.

Upon all of us, in all our countries, is now laid the duty of transforming into action these words which you have written. Upon our decisive action rests the hope of those who have fallen, those now living, those yet unborn—the hope of the world of free countries—with decent standards of living—which will work and cooperate in a friendly civilized community of nations.

This new structure of peace is rising upon strong foundations.

Let us not fail to grasp this supreme chance to establish a world-wide rule of reason—to create an enduring peace under the guidance of God.[1]

Qualified optimism was, indeed, the general reaction among the delegates and journalists who had been present at the Conference. Few if any felt wholly satisfied with the Charter, but everyone felt that it was at least a start towards world order. Churchill telegraphed congratulations: 'You have made an invaluable contribution to the re-establishment of the hopeful basis for the future of peace, understanding and goodwill among men.'[2] Stalin, however, did not commit his views to the public prints.

Newspaper comment was similar in tone. The *New York Times* declared in an editorial (27 June 1945) that 'the great majority of the people of the country are satisfied that a good start and a true one has been made toward creating an organization that can rid the world of the curse of war'. The *Manchester Guardian* of the same date observed:

This will truly be, as the League of Nations never was, a world organization. But, like the League, the United Nations can never be more than an instrument of co-operation between the signatory States. If they have the will to use it, they will find it a better instrument than the League, stronger yet suppler, with a finer balance between power and responsibility. If they have not the will they will find it just as easy to ignore or to set aside.

Izvestia struck a similar note:

Perhaps the solution reached will not appear ideal to some, but it is the best possible at present. The establishment of eternal peace between the peoples, and the immediate elimination of the causes of conflicts and wars, is not the object of the new organization. Its objects are more realistic. The question is an organization able to prevent possible aggression or to curb the aggressor by the united forces of the peace-loving peoples. . . . One can say with conviction that the final text of the United Nations Charter leaves far behind all previously existing projects for the creation of a stable international organization.[3]

In general, Russian newspapers emphasized the importance of the unanimity of the Great Powers; British comment tended to dwell upon the significance of the abandonment of isolationism by the United States and the new place of the Soviet Union in the comity of nations; while

[1] *Documents on American Foreign Relations, 1944–1945*, pp. 450–5.

[2] *New York Times*, 27 June 1945.

[3] 27 June 1945, quoted from *Soviet Union and the San Francisco Conference* (London, Soviet News, 1945), pp. 3-4.

many American journalists were more hopeful than were their colleagues in the other countries for the future of law, justice, and moral principle among nations. But, despite these differences in emphasis, the cordial, if guarded, welcome extended to the Charter among the newspapers of all three nations augured well.

The Charter of the United Nations organization had, of course, to be ratified before coming into force; and to handle matters in the meanwhile a Preparatory Commission was established representing each of the signatories. It was charged with the duty of convoking the first General Assembly, preparing an agenda for that meeting, preparing suggestions for winding up the League of Nations and for incorporating into the new structure such pre-existing international bodies as the Food and Agriculture Organization, the World Bank, Monetary Fund, &c., as well as various organizations which had been subsidiary to the League.

The formalities of ratification went ahead speedily. President Truman submitted the Charter to the United States Senate on 2 July 1945, and it was approved by that body on 28 July by an almost unanimous vote. Only two Senators voted in the negative. This measured the difference in American sentiment between 1945 and 1920. It also reflected the impact of the administration's publicity campaign and the careful handling of Senatorial and party sensibility which had been a leading concern of the State Department and the Presidency from the time when plans for a future international organization were first adumbrated.

Britain deposited her instrument of ratification on 20 October; Russia on 24 October; and with Russia's action ratification by the required majority (including the concurrence of all permanent members of the Security Council) was complete. Accordingly, on 24 October 1945, the American Secretary of State formally declared that the Charter had come into effect.[1]

A new experiment in international organization had been launched, trailing clouds of glory more subdued than those which had attended the birth of the League of Nations twenty-six years before. Obvious differences between Russia and the West had troubled the San Francisco Conference almost throughout its work, and everyone realized, indeed emphasized, that the success or failure of the new organization would depend upon the future path of Great Power diplomacy. Yet agreement had been reached at San Francisco, as it had in earlier conferences between the Great Powers; and it seemed not impossible to hope that the Grand Alliance, now provided with a permanent machinery, would survive,

[1] Text of his declaration may be found in Goodrich and Hambro: *United Nations Charter*, pp. 385–6.

expand, and ramify until the nations of the world achieved an effective, semi-automatic subordination of international disputes to the processes of law.

For such an evolution to occur, day-to-day disputes and differences between the Great Powers would have to be amicably adjusted; and even before the San Francisco Conference came to an end it was clear that the problems presented by conquered Germany and liberated Europe required prompt and authoritative solution if the fissure between Russia and the West were not to become a chasm. Accordingly, another conference of the Big Three was arranged for mid-July at Potsdam. The fate of the Charter produced at San Francisco obviously depended on the outcome of this—and a long line of subsequent—conferences. To them we must now return.

(iii) The Potsdam Conference, 17 July–2 August 1945

(*a*) Rival Plans for European Settlement

The third and last meeting of the three great Allied Governments at Potsdam was the longest and least satisfactory of their war-time conferences. By July 1945 military questions had sunk to a merely marginal place, whereas the political issues, which had been marginal at Tehrān, had risen to dominate the entire Conference. Yalta stood midway: military bargains over the Far East at that Conference profoundly affected and in a sense counterbalanced disagreements over the political future of Europe. But at Potsdam the military cement to the Grand Alliance had almost entirely flaked away. Despite the fact that the U.S. Joint Chiefs of Staff officially recommended to Truman on the eve of the Potsdam Conference that American policy should be to 'encourage Russian entry into war against Japan',[1] some of the highest American military leaders were no longer eager to have Russian help in the war.[2] The American navy was unwilling to guarantee sea communications with Russia across the Pacific until after the American landing in Japan planned for November 1945 had taken place.[3] As far as the Americans were concerned, the Red Army would have to fight its own battles in Manchuria with the supplies already on hand until 1946. In general, American plans for the Pacific War were quite independent of Russian action or inaction in the Far East; and the same was true of British plans for the Japanese war.[4]

The disappearance of any imperative need for military co-operation between Russia and the Western Powers made the amicable and satisfactory settlement of the political issues which victory in Europe brought

[1] Harriman Statement, *Congressional Record*, 27 August 1951, p. A5669.
[2] Leahy: *I Was There*, p. 450.
[3] See below, p. 630.
[4] For an account of the military side of the Potsdam Conference see below, pp. 630–4.

in its train vastly more difficult. Despite the length of the Conference (Tehrān had lasted four days, Yalta eight, Potsdam sixteen—a curiously exact geometrical progression) many of the agreements published in the final communiqué were merely agreements to discuss disagreements further through a new Council of Foreign Ministers; and the genuine agreements which were reached, notably those pertaining to Germany, did not signify a real meeting of minds, but rather a bargain reluctantly concluded on either side in the face of urgent necessity to do something with the defeated enemy.

It is important to try to reconstruct the state of mind with which the leaders of the three Governments approached the Potsdam Conference; but, in the nature of the case, Russian attitudes can only be a matter of speculation. Stalin made two of his goals quite clear. For one thing, he wanted reparations from Germany on a large scale. This he had already made clear at Yalta,[1] and Soviet wishes with respect to reparations had not changed since February. Stalin's second objective at Potsdam was to secure British and American recognition of the new régimes which he had established in Eastern Europe. The 'People's Democracies' of Rumania, Bulgaria, Yugoslavia, Albania, Hungary, and Poland had still to face formidable opposition at home. If they were to prove a success, it was important that opposition elements should not be encouraged by Western support. As a sign and symbol of their disinterest in the opposition parties and groups of Eastern Europe, Stalin wanted the Western Powers to accord diplomatic recognition to the new governments—recognition analogous to that which he had extended to the French and Italian Governments in 1944.

A third object which Stalin set before himself was the rounding out of the Soviet security zone, especially to the south. Whether he hoped to get British and American agreement to this at Potsdam,[2] or whether he imagined rather that he would be able to present the Western Powers with a series of *faits accomplis* which they would be powerless to undo, cannot be said. Presumably Stalin would have preferred to act in agreement with the West; and, as the event showed, he was not willing to risk acting in defiance of the strenuous opposition of Britain and America. His programme of expansion at the time of Potsdam was, however, quite clear. On 25 June 1945, three weeks before the Conference met, the Soviet Ambassador in Ankara had approached the Turkish Government to suggest the terms on which a Russo-Turkish treaty could be renewed.[3] The

[1] See above, pp. 549–51.

[2] It is worth remembering that at Tehrān both Churchill and Roosevelt had shown nothing but sympathy for Russian wishes to have warm-water ports in the south (Sherwood: *Roosevelt and Hopkins*, p. 791; Eng. edition, ii. p. 786; Churchill, v. 336; U.S. edition, v. 381; see also above, p. 363). This may have led Stalin to expect little opposition to his plans in 1945.

[3] The Russo-Turkish treaty of 1925, which had previously regulated the relations of the two

terms were reported unofficially to be the granting of military bases to the Russians on the Bosporus and Dardanelles, cession of the two eastern provinces of Kars and Ardahan, and acceptance of unspecified changes in the Balkans.[1] Simultaneously the Russian efforts to stir up separatist feeling in northern Persia resulted in the establishment of an Azerbaijan National Committee of Liberation,[2] and the Russians pointedly failed to reply to a note from the Persian Government, on 31 May 1945, requesting withdrawal of foreign troops.[3] Had these plans borne fruit, Turkey in the south might have been reduced to the status of Finland in the north; and Azerbaijan have become a second Outer Mongolia.

In Europe, too, the rounding out of the Russian security zone required some territorial changes. The western boundary of Poland had been left indeterminate at Yaltà;[4] but the Russians did not hesitate to hand over to the Poles former German territory as far as the Oder and western Neisse rivers without waiting for the endorsement of the Western Allies.[5] This act established Polish administration over extensive German lands, and the Poles promptly began to treat the new territory as an integral part of their state, driving the German inhabitants from the soil and replacing them with Polish settlers.

A second change was the annexation of the easternmost portion of Czechoslovakia—Ruthenia, or Sub-Carpathian Ukraine—to the Soviet Union. This was effected on 29 June 1945 by agreement between the two Governments, perhaps in return for a Russian undertaking to support Czech claims against Poland to the district of Teschen. In any event, Teschen was occupied by Czech troops on or before 6 July.[6] The acquisition of Ruthenia by the Russians not only united all Ukrainians under Stalin's authority but gave the Red Army control of important passes over the Carpathians and a common frontier with Hungary. This obviously strengthened Russia's military position very considerably against any future troubles in the middle Danube region.

countries, was denounced by the Russian Government on 19 March 1945 (see *Survey* for 1939–46: *The Middle East in the War*, p. 465).

[1] *New York Times*, 28 June 1945; *The Times*, 28 June 1945. The last of these demands may have referred to plans for the creation of an autonomous Macedonia and the annexation of Thrace to Bulgaria. Stalin had certainly played with such projects in the last months of 1944 (cf. Barker: *Macedonia*, pp. 98–101).

[2] *Observer*, 1 July 1945.

[3] Harry N. Howard: 'The Soviet Union and the Middle East', *Annals of the American Academy of Political and Social Science*, May 1949, p. 185.

[4] See above, pp. 555–6.

[5] This transaction was not publicized at the time, and it is impossible to say exactly when the Russians assigned the new territory to the Polish Government. As early as 24 June 1945 a Polish spokesman announced that no power 'can tear us away from the Oder, the Neisse, and the Baltic', implying possession of the territories in question (*Manchester Guardian*, 2 July 1945). It is probable that the Russians had secretly fixed the western boundaries of Poland a whole year before by a treaty signed on 25 July 1944 with the Lublin Committee (cf. Mikolajczyk: *Pattern of Soviet Domination*, p. 159).

[6] Betts: *Central and South East Europe, 1945–1948*, pp. 177–8. For the Polish acquisition of Teschen in 1938 see *Survey* for 1938, iii. 45–68.

In view of Stalin's policy in Germany, Eastern Europe, and the Middle East one must ask whether he still hoped to maintain friendly relations with Britain and America. More generally, there is the problem of how Stalin conceived the relationship between his short-range policy and the spread of Communist revolution to Europe, if not to all the world. The condition of Western Europe after the overthrow of the Nazis was certainly one in which revolutionary sentiment might be expected to flourish; and Stalin's economic goals in Germany would, if fully met, have deepened and prolonged the economic suffering upon which revolutionary discontent could batten. Yet Communist parties in Western Europe did not raise the standard of revolution; instead they participated in the governments of such countries as France, Italy, and Belgium and refrained from violent agitation in the streets which their power and prestige would have made easily possible.[1]

The conduct of the Western Communist Parties certainly suggests that Stalin still hoped for a satisfactory *modus vivendi* with Britain and America; and various of his public statements both before and after the Potsdam Conference asserted the hope of continued co-operation.[2] In general, it seems reasonable to suppose that Stalin had not explicitly and definitely given up the idea of world revolution any more than he had definitely and explicitly abandoned hope of continued co-operation with Britain and America. Yet, as in the past, he put the security of the Soviet Union before all else. The contradictions of capitalist society could, perhaps, be trusted to ripen towards revolution of their own accord in due season; meanwhile the Russian frontiers needed strengthening, and to guard against rapid German revival it was necessary to come to an understanding with Britain and America for the military government of the defeated enemy. He may well have hoped that his actions in the borderlands between Russia and Germany would not stir up serious Western opposition; but if need be he was prepared to defend his gains in Eastern Europe even if it meant breaking with Britain and America.

It is possible that Stalin went to Potsdam secure in the belief that the United States would soon withdraw from Europe and that British power

[1] In April 1945 the beginning of a more actively revolutionary policy was adumbrated when Jacques Duclos denounced 'Browderism' in *Cahiers du Communisme*. Browderism had led to the formal abolition of the Communist Party of the United States in May 1944. This error was corrected in July 1945, and William Z. Foster replaced Earl Browder as the leader of the re-established Party. According to Duclos, the core of Browder's 'Right deviation' had been co-operation with finance capital, the material foundation of Fascism. This tempest in a teapot—and the American Communist Party was a rather small teapot—received considerable publicity in Communist journals all round the world but did not immediately lead to a shift in Communist policy away from co-operation with other parties in Western Europe.

[2] e.g. interview with the Dean of Canterbury, *The Times*, 9 July 1945; exchange of telegrams with Attlee, ibid. 21 August 1945; interview with U.S. Congressmen, *New York Times*, 18 September 1945, 1 October 1945.

would be inadequate to interfere with his plans.[1] At Yalta Roosevelt had told Stalin categorically that American troops would not remain in Germany for more than two years after the end of the fighting.[2] The frame of mind in which Truman and Byrnes came to Potsdam did nothing to change this outlook, since one of their principal concerns was to speed the conclusion of peace treaties so that American troops could get back home. Similarly, Russian economists may have taken an even stronger view of Britain's economic weakness than did Churchill and Attlee; and hope of an economic crisis in the United States itself, gorged with the profits of war and without an adequate market for the products of an expanded industry, may already have loomed large in Russian prognosis of the future. Whether or not Stalin had these thoughts in mind, it seems obvious that he regarded the Anglo-Russo-American alliance as an inadequate support for Russian security; stronger bonds with the satellite nations were necessary as supplement, or if necessary as replacement, for the unreliable Grand Alliance.

The two principal figures among the Americans who went to Potsdam, President Truman and the newly appointed Secretary of State, James E. Byrnes, were inexperienced in international dealings.[3] Aware of their inexperience, Truman and Byrnes took especial care to prepare definite agenda for the Conference and to brief themselves on all questions likely to come up. In their eyes the problems to be faced were straightforward enough, however complicated in detail. The Japanese war seemed well under control and needed little top-level attention. Europe, however, had to be set to rights, and this clearly required co-operation among the Great Powers on the lines laid down by the Yalta Declaration on Liberated Europe. Preparations for peace treaties needed to be begun by means of private consultations among the Great Powers—consultations like those

[1] Cf. Philip E. Mosely: 'Soviet-American Relations since the War', *Annals of the American Academy of Political and Social Science*, May 1949, pp. 207–8. Mosely makes the interesting suggestion that the change in Russian policy from co-operation with the West in Germany may be connected with a transfer of responsibility for German affairs from the Russian Ministry of Foreign Affairs to the M.V.D. and economic Ministries. In this connexion cf. Byrnes's remarks about Ivan Maisky's discomfiture at Potsdam (*Speaking Frankly*, pp. 84–85). Maisky, who was one of the most 'Western' of Russian officials, could not persuade his fellow members of the Reparations Commission to accept Russian demands. His failure may have discredited co-operative efforts, just as, for instance, a failure of Hopkins's mission to Stalin in May 1945 would probably have discredited the principle of co-operation with Russia in American circles.

[2] See above, pp. 532, 548.

[3] Byrnes had been at Yalta, but had not taken a leading part in the Conference. His previous experience had been domestic—Congressman, Senator, Supreme Court Justice, Director of Economic Stabilization, and, from April 1943, head of the Office of War Mobilization, in which position he won the nickname 'Assistant President', so sweeping were his powers over domestic affairs (see above, p. 228).

which had led to the establishment of the United Nations organization. Finally, economic and political principles to govern Allied administration in Germany had to be fixed.

The Americans were willing to go what seemed to them a long way in helping Europe to set its house in order. Economic assistance through UNRRA had been provided for; and Truman hoped that this would be enough. A long debate as to whether or not Lend-Lease assistance should and legally could be continued for such purposes as sustaining French and British occupation forces in Germany had apparently been decided in the negative when Truman ordered on 5 July 1945, the day before departing for Potsdam, that Lend-Lease should be 'limited to that which is to be used in the war against Japan'.[1] But the President's mind was not irrevocably made up, and, when the question was reopened by the Secretary of War on 11 July, Truman wavered.[2]

On the political level, the Americans were prepared in conjunction with Britain and Russia to send missions to observe and assist with the preparation of elections in the various countries of Europe whose political disorganization seemed to require such supervision. This seemed the quickest and surest way to establish democratic governments; and, if Russian and British missions collaborated in the effort, the Americans hoped that the resultant governments in such countries as Italy, Greece, Rumania, Hungary, and Bulgaria would be acceptable to all the Great Powers.[3]

It would be wrong to think that Truman and Byrnes were so naïve as to suppose that such a procedure would be likely to please the Russians. But they did hope that the Russians would be so tied by their frequent commitment to democratic elections as a sovereign cure for political ills that they would not be able in good conscience to refuse such an offer. In American eyes the proposal was no more than a practical method of acting upon the Yalta Declaration on Liberated Europe, a Declaration which Stalin, after all, had accepted only five months before. Moreover, elections and the consequent establishment of democratic governments would diminish or remove the many irritants to good relations between Russia and the West which recent events in the Balkans had provided; and the armistice régimes, which gave Russia primacy in the northern Balkans and Britain primacy in Italy, would come to an early end. If, incidentally, American prestige in these countries should increase, that would not be unwelcome; indeed, it would be a well-deserved reward for American disinterestedness and faithfulness to democratic principles.

Yet though Truman and Byrnes were willing to go this far towards involving the United States in European affairs, the guiding purpose

[1] Leahy: *I Was There*, pp. 439–40.

[2] See also below, p. 632.

[3] Byrnes: *Speaking Frankly*, p. 73.

behind the whole American policy was to permit an early withdrawal from Europe. To establish democratic governments as promptly as possible would simplify the making of peace treaties and permit the return of American soldiers within a short time. Similarly, limiting American financial assistance to Europe would save the taxpayer at home and force Europeans to stand on their own feet. American economic experts, of course, realized how far such a programme was from the realm of practical possibility unless the United States were willing to see Europe go through incalculable political convulsions and profound economic suffering; but American politicians and ordinary laymen felt quite definitely that with the end of the war it was time to get back to normal, and the quicker the better. Truman and Byrnes were both primarily politicians, and underestimated the potential generosity of the American public—especially when generosity had the effect of sustaining a boom economy at home. But in 1945 the possible benefits of foreign expenditure for the American domestic economy were only abstract calculations of economists: shortages at home were real and the idea of shipping vast quantities of goods abroad for nothing but a political return seemed nonsense.

Thus the general goal of the Americans at Potsdam was to get back to normal as quickly as possible. Difficulties in Europe seemed irritating trivialities rather than major matters of national concern. Europe was still foreign: a place where Americans did not belong, but where they had the moral obligation to do a bit of house-cleaning before the rightful tenants took over once again.

The British Government found themselves haunted by three great interconnected fears. One was economic collapse at home; a second was a too speedy American withdrawal from Europe; the third was continued Russian expansion in Europe and the Middle East.

Domestic issues had come to the fore in Great Britain with the break-up of the war-time coalition on 23 May and the general election of 5 July which followed. Owing to the time required for service votes to be counted, the results of the election were not announced until 26 July when the Potsdam Conference was in mid-career. Realizing that a change in government might result from the election, Churchill invited Clement Attlee, leader of the Labour Party, to attend the Potsdam Conference as an observer from the start; but, after the results had been made public and Attlee had taken over the office of Prime Minister, Churchill remained in England while Attlee and his new Foreign Minister, Ernest Bevin, returned to Potsdam to finish the Conference.

This change had an effect like, though perhaps less pronounced than, the change in the American Government which had followed Roosevelt's death. Attlee and Bevin had directed most of their energies during the war to domestic problems; and Bevin, particularly, was relatively inexperienced in foreign affairs. Nevertheless, the Cabinet system ensured that both Bevin and Attlee had at least a general acquaintance with all the major issues that came before the British Government, and in fact the continuity of British foreign policy surprised nearly all outsiders. Nevertheless, the coincidence between the British election and the Potsdam Conference probably damaged the British cause at the Conference. According to an American participant, Churchill was unusually ill-prepared in its first stages; and Bevin showed more aggressiveness than knowledge of details in its latter days.[1]

The paucity of published material makes it difficult to describe British goals at Potsdam with any assurance. Two points are clear. The British hoped to persuade the Americans to adopt a more generous Lend-Lease policy, particularly with regard to granting supplies to occupation forces. Secondly, the British were anxious to make an arrangement with the Russians whereby food from east Germany would become available to lighten the burden of feeding the dense industrial population in the British zone of occupation. These preoccupations reflected the difficult economic situation which abruptly confronted Britain after the end of the European war.

An acute consciousness of the precarious economic situation at home obviously weakened British foreign policy generally, and it does not appear that the British Government advanced any very important proposals for the general settlement of Europe at the Potsdam Conference. The deal with Russia about spheres of influence, which Churchill had concluded in October 1944,[2] had not worked well, and the British made no effort to reaffirm the bargain. Instead, one of the main themes of the Conference became an exchange of recriminations between the British and Russian leaders over recent events in Greece, Yugoslavia, and other countries, influence in which had been apportioned between the two Great Powers in the previous October. The British had lost their toehold in Yugoslavia and seemed likely to do so in Poland; and British control of a restless and impoverished Greece seemed a poor counterweight to the recent expansion of Russian power and influence. As long as there was hope of American support neither Churchill nor Bevin was willing to concede to the Russians the satisfaction of their newly enlarged ambitions. But there was very little to do but protest verbally. Protest the British did, and doing so merely provoked counterblasts from Stalin.

The result was that many of the meetings at Potsdam partook more of the nature of propaganda than of negotiation. A second consequence was that the opposition between Russia and Britain was more obtrusive

[1] Leahy: *I Was There*, pp. 465, 490.

[2] See above, p. 495.

than that between Russia and America. The British, naturally, were more vitally concerned with European affairs than were the Americans, and had come to realize more sharply than had the Americans that the economic recovery of Europe could not proceed without a modicum of German recovery. If nothing else, coal had to come from German mines; and that meant food for miners; and food had either to be paid for by German exports or secured from eastern Germany by agreement with the Russians. Thus the British were more stubborn in opposing Russian demands for reparations from Germany than were the Americans, among whom the idea of punishing the vanquished enemy still commanded some support.

It followed that the Americans found themselves once again in the middle: far closer to the British than to the Russians, but still in a position to act as compromisers so far as compromise could be made. When the Americans found that their general programme for European settlement displeased the Russians, they were willing to postpone matters and settled for a few pious phrases. They felt no direct responsibility for European affairs except in Germany; and if their offer failed to satisfy the Powers most directly concerned, there was nothing an honest broker could do but retire gracefully. Moreover, Truman and Byrnes quite genuinely wished to keep on tolerably good terms with the Russians, and could hope, as Roosevelt had regularly done, that something would turn up to improve relations in the future. Hence putting off disputed questions and referring them to the Council of Foreign Ministers seemed a good enough solution for the time being, and Byrnes left the Conference feeling that it had been on the whole a success.[1]

The American attitude tended to disguise the depth of the clash between their own programme for Europe and that espoused by the Russians. Stalin perhaps was encouraged to believe that the Americans would not try to act on their high-sounding principles and would leave him undisturbed with his security zone of client states. Britain seemed the chief opponent, and it was against Britain that Russian propaganda and diplomacy were consequently turned in the following months.

Yet in a very real sense the fundamental problem at the Potsdam Conference was not a contest between Britain and Russia so much as one between America and Russia. The Americans came to Potsdam with a general plan for European settlement; the Russians had their own and quite different idea of how Europe's future should be arranged. When the American proposals were not accepted, Truman and Byrnes withdrew them readily enough. But such withdrawal did not necessarily mean abandonment: and because the Americans had a far greater power to back their policies than had the British, their ideas about a proper European settlement mattered more in the long run than did the quarrels

[1] Byrnes: *Speaking Frankly*, p. 87.

between British and Russian representatives over one another's actions in the smaller European countries. But while the fundamental opposition which was to dominate international post-war politics became quite evident at Potsdam, it was not pursued nor developed to any logical conclusion.

(*b*) The Meeting at Potsdam[1]

The Potsdam Conference got off to a good start despite the fact that Stalin was a day late in arriving. On 17 July he paid a preliminary call on Truman and stayed for lunch. He surprised the Americans by asserting that he believed Hitler was still alive, hiding in Spain or Argentina: otherwise conversation was limited to pleasantries. When the first plenary session met in the afternoon, Stalin proposed that Truman should preside. The President wasted no time in getting down to business. He immediately presented four proposals which had been worked out by his advisers: the establishment of a Council of Foreign Ministers to prepare the peace treaties; an outline of Allied political and economic policy towards Germany; joint action in accordance with the Yalta Declaration on Liberated Europe to supervise elections in Italy, Greece, Rumania, Bulgaria, and Hungary; relaxation of the armistice terms and admission of Italy to the United Nations. Churchill was a little taken aback by Truman's brisk manner—a manner in striking contrast to Roosevelt's informal habits—and emphasized the necessity of careful study before acting on any of Truman's proposals. Stalin had ready a list of topics he wished to discuss, and presented his agenda in outline. The disposition of German ships; reparations; Russian claims to trusteeship over some of the former Italian colonies; diplomatic recognition of the Governments of Rumania, Bulgaria, and Hungary; Spanish Fascism; the status of Tangier; recent events in Syria and the Lebanon; and the elimination of Polish organizations in London: these were the items he mentioned. Churchill had no similar programme to present, but said one would be prepared for later submission to the Conference. After some preliminary discussion about the proposed Council of Foreign Ministers, the plenary session referred the matter to the three Foreign Ministers for further investigation and report. Then as briskly as it had begun, the first session ended.[2]

After this first encounter, Truman felt reassured by Stalin's courtesy and believed that he would have little difficulty in reaching agreements with the Russian leader. The course of the next day's proceedings did nothing to dispel this belief. The Foreign Ministers met in the morning and agreed upon the desirability of establishing a Council of Foreign

[1] See also below, pp. 630–3.

[2] Leahy: *I Was There*, pp. 463–5; Byrnes: *Speaking Frankly*, pp. 68–70.

Ministers. The new body was to prepare drafts of peace treaties with ex-enemy states in Europe and Asia. The question of its composition was resolved when the rule was accepted that each treaty should be drafted by the representatives of the nations which had signed the armistice with the particular enemy in question. It was additionally provided that France should be counted as a signatory of the Italian armistice. The European Advisory Commission was to be supplanted by the new body; but the consideration of current questions at periodic meetings of the Foreign Ministers, agreed to at Yalta, was not to be merged with the more restricted task of treaty drafting.

When this agreement was reported back to the plenary session on the afternoon of the same day, 18 July, it was accepted almost without discussion. Byrnes, the main sponsor of the scheme, was duly gratified. A paper precisely defining the task and ancillary organization of the Council of Foreign Ministers was submitted and approved on 20 July at the fourth plenary session. London was chosen as the permanent seat of the Council, and the first meeting was set for 1 September 1945. Thus the machinery for making peace was established, and the Americans, at least, hoped and believed that a few months would suffice for the legal pacification of Europe.[1]

The main attention of the second plenary session was directed towards the second of Truman's proposals: determination of Allied policy towards Germany. Political policy was distinguished from economic policy for purposes of convenience, and only the former came up for discussion on this occasion. But it was impossible to separate the two completely. This was shown when the first important collision arose over the demarcation of the eastern boundary of Germany. The British were not reconciled to the extension of Polish territory as far as the western Neisse. Their objections were both political and economic. On humanitarian grounds, Churchill deplored a policy which involved the uprooting of several million Germans. On economic grounds, he objected to the extra strain which millions of refugees would impose on the food and other resources of the western zones of Germany; and, even more important, he realized that without food supplies from the agricultural areas of eastern Germany, it would be impossible to feed the population of the British zone from German resources. The British were themselves short of food and could feed the German population under their control only by buying abroad, for the most part from the United States. Yet Britain already lacked

[1] Byrnes thought that two or three meetings of the Council of Foreign Ministers would probably be enough to draft the peace treaties. According to his plan the Foreign Ministers would merely agree upon general principles to be followed, and detailed drafting would be entrusted to deputies; then, with a draft accepted by all the Great Powers, the treaties would be submitted to a general conference of all the United Nations for final adoption—a procedure consciously modelled on that which had produced the United Nations Charter (*Speaking Frankly*, pp. 70–72).

dollars, and it seemed utterly inadmissible to the British leaders that Russian policy in eastern Germany should result in adding a serious further strain to Great Britain's difficult economic position *vis-à-vis* the United States.

On political grounds, Churchill believed that, if the Poles took over extensive German territory, the stage would be set for future wars. German national pride could not be expected to reconcile itself to the loss of so much territory which had for centuries been indisputably German; and a policy which would keep Germany permanently so weak as to be incapable of any *revanche* would have the incidental effect of making the general economic and political revival of Western Europe difficult if not impossible. In such a case Russian military predominance, which Churchill found so embarrassing at the moment, would not be temporary but permanent; and Britain would have to live under the shadow of Soviet hegemony—actual or potential—over the entire continent of Europe.

Stalin, of course, appreciated the political implications of the westward extension of the Polish boundary with equal clarity. What seemed dangerous to Churchill seemed a guarantee of Russian security to Stalin. So direct and serious a clash could not be settled out of hand. On Truman's suggestion, it was agreed that the 1937 boundaries of Germany should be taken 'as a basis for discussion'; but this agreement did not at once soothe the angry feelings which had been raised. Churchill's attack on Russian unilateral action in ceding German territory to Poland provoked Stalin to counter-attack by demanding the prompt liquidation of the Polish Government in Exile. In particular, he demanded the repatriation of the Polish army and navy, by force if need be. Churchill declared that he would never force Poles to return against their will; and after a rather warm debate, the whole Polish question was referred to the Foreign Ministers.

The Conference then returned briefly to the business of the day, Germany. All agreed that a uniform system of administration should be established in each of the four zones of occupation; and with this agreement the three Heads of Government referred to the Foreign Ministers the task of drawing up detailed instructions for the political conduct of the Allied occupation forces. The meeting then ended.[1]

Actually, the task of preparing political instructions for the Allied occupation forces in Germany was not as formidable as it might seem. The European Advisory Commission had already devoted a long effort to this task, and had reached agreement on nearly all points. The Foreign Ministers had only to endorse the work of their subordinates. It was therefore possible for them to report back on the following day, 19 July,

[1] Leahy: *I Was There*, pp. 466–7.

with a text which was accepted at the third plenary session after only perfunctory discussion.

The secret of this easy progress was that the provisions for political policy in Germany were largely negative. The purposes of the occupation government were defined as follows:

(1) The complete disarmament and demilitarization of Germany and the elimination or control of all German industry that could be used for military production. . . .

(2) To convince the German people that they have suffered a total military defeat and that they cannot escape responsibility for what they have brought upon themselves. . . .

(3) To destroy the National Socialist party and its affiliated and supervised organizations, to dissolve all Nazi institutions, to insure that they are not revived in any form, and to prevent all Nazi and militarist activity or propaganda.

(4) To prepare for the eventual reconstruction of German political life on a democratic basis and for eventual peaceful cooperation in international life by Germany.[1]

It is true that the declaration on Germany affirmed the principle of uniformity in all zones of occupation, and that it made provision for the restoration of local self-government. Similarly, freedom of speech, of the press, and of religion, the formation of trade unions and of democratic political parties were all approved, subject, however, to 'the necessity of maintaining military security'.[2] But such provisions as these did not disturb the overriding authority of the occupying forces; nor did they really commit anyone to a common positive policy. Words like 'democratic' were capable of various interpretations; and 'military security' could be stretched to cover any arbitrary action by the zone commanders.

Nevertheless, the rapid acceptance of this document at the Potsdam Conference signified progress of a sort. It was the last point on which the Allies found it easy to agree, and from 19 July until almost the end the Conference accomplished nothing. Indeed the third plenary session turned into a cat and dog fight between Churchill and Stalin. Churchill took the offensive at the beginning of the meeting, charging Bulgaria with hostile plans against Greek Macedonia. Stalin retorted that the matter was not on the Conference agenda and should be discussed privately.

Of the three items that were on the agenda, only the first, the political directive on Germany, could be disposed of. Questions relating to Poland were again laid aside for the Foreign Ministers to report upon; and a new

[1] Protocol of the Proceedings of the Berlin Conference reproduced in *Documents on American Foreign Relations, vol. viii, July 1, 1945–December 31, 1946*, ed. Raymond Dennett and Robert K. Turner (Princeton University Press for World Peace Foundation, 1948), p. 927.

[2] *Documents on American Foreign Relations, 1945–1946*, p. 928.

quarrel between Churchill and Stalin broke out over the third item, the disposition of German shipping. Churchill wished comparative losses to be considered in dividing the spoils; Stalin wished to have his full third of naval and merchant shipping, but was willing to postpone taking possession of the latter until after the end of the Japanese war. The Americans were prepared to support the Russians on this point, but the matter was referred to the over-worked Foreign Ministers.

Stalin next turned to Spain. He wished the Allies to withdraw diplomatic recognition from Franco, but both Churchill and Truman demurred. Next Churchill reproached Stalin over Tito's refusal to permit a genuine partnership between Communist and non-Communist political groups in Yugoslavia. This Churchill declared was a violation of the Yalta agreements, though he may well have had more in mind the 50–50 formula agreed to in Moscow in October 1944. Stalin denied that the Yalta agreement had been violated, and said he would not discuss the situation in Yugoslavia without bringing Yugoslav representatives to the Conference. Truman stepped into the ring to say that he had no intention of holding court to adjudge the grievances of all Europe: the Conference was to discuss matters upon which the Big Three could agree. The quarrel over Yugoslavia was thereupon dropped. Churchill immediately returned to the attack, complaining of Russian confiscation of British and American oil properties in Rumania. Stalin replied that this should be settled through normal diplomatic channels, but agreed to refer the matter to the Foreign Ministers. On this note the third plenary session broke up, having sat for only fifty minutes. It had scarcely been an encouraging encounter.[1]

The fourth plenary session, on 20 July, began with a consideration of the status of Italy. Stalin pointed out that while he had extended diplomatic recognition to Italy and France, the Western Powers had not reciprocated by recognizing the Governments of Rumania, Bulgaria, Hungary, and Finland. The matter was turned over to the Foreign Ministers for the usual investigation and report.

Then Churchill resumed his verbal offensive, and accused the Russians of obstructing the entry of British, American, and French officers into Vienna and of delaying the occupation of the zones of Austria assigned to Western forces. Stalin was able to catch Churchill out on this question, for, as he pointed out with pained surprise, it had just been agreed that the appropriate troop movements would begin in one or two days' time.

The contest shifted next to the matter of the disposal of Italian colonies in Africa. Stalin said that he wanted trusteeship over one of the Italian colonies in Africa, and it was Churchill's turn to assume an air of pained surprise. 'I had not considered the possibility of the Soviet Union desiring

[1] Leahy: *I Was There*, pp. 467–70.

to acquire a large tract of the African shore', he declared, and argued that the matter should not be discussed until the peace conference. Truman acted as pacifier, suggesting once again that the question should be referred to the Foreign Ministers.[1]

The next day, 21 July, attention shifted to Poland and the Balkans. It was agreed that all assets of the Polish Government in Exile should be transferred to the new Provisional Polish Government. But Churchill had refused to agree to forcible repatriation of Polish troops, and, when the question of the western boundary of Poland came up for the second time, the argument simply retraced old paths. The American proposal for holding elections in Italy, Greece, Hungary, Rumania, and Bulgaria under the supervision of joint missions sent by the Great Powers was also discussed briefly; but Stalin skilfully deflected the debate to the issue of recognition. Truman said the United States had no intention of recognizing the existing governments in the Russian-dominated area until after free elections; Churchill supported the President, and Stalin, obviously nettled, brusquely declared that such an attitude made agreement impossible.[2]

The sixth plenary session, on 22 July, continued fruitless debate over the Polish boundary. The full scope of Russian ambitions for trusteeship holdings became explicit when Stalin put in a bid for a share of former League of Nations mandates, and of Korea. Churchill then brought up the matter of Russian demands on Turkey, and the revision of the Montreux Convention to which he, Roosevelt, and Stalin had informally agreed at Yalta.[3] The debate over the Turkish Straits was resumed on the following day, when Truman attempted to solve the difficulty by broaching a general plan for establishing free and equal access to all the key international waterways of Europe: the Turkish Straits, the Rhine, the Danube, and the Kiel Canal. Stalin was not impressed, and declared that Russia's geographical position required special rights in the Straits. The British, too, were not enthusiastic, and nothing could be decided.[4]

So far, what was probably the most important single matter before the Conference had not been explicitly discussed in the plenary sessions: that is, economic policy towards Germany and especially German reparations. Both Britain and America were anxious that any agreement on reparations should not depress the German economy to such a point that it would become necessary to subsidize the Germans in the western zones. They were also anxious not so to damage the Germany economy as to

[1] Byrnes: *Speaking Frankly*, pp. 76–77; Leahy: *I Was There*, pp. 471–2.

[2] Ibid., pp. 472–5; Byrnes: *Speaking Frankly*, pp. 72–74.

[3] See above, p. 561.

[4] Leahy: *I Was There*, pp. 475–7.

induce revolution, civil disorder, or wholesale starvation. The Russians, on the other hand, stubbornly insisted upon their pound of flesh. They argued that Roosevelt had agreed to the figure of $20 milliard for German reparations at Yalta,[1] and would accept no less than half that amount as their share. The Americans, however, had been won over to the view championed by the British at Yalta, and the two Western Powers refused to accept any fixed total. Instead they argued for apportionment of reparations on the basis of percentages of surplus German capital plant—plant, that is, which would not be needed for maintaining the German standard of living at a level not higher than the European average without any assistance from abroad. Until this question could be solved, agreement on the principles for the economic administration of Germany was held up.

Since the Reparations Commission, established in accordance with the Yalta decisions, was primarily charged with the task of reaching agreement on the question, it did not come before the Conference formally until near the end. The members of the Reparations Commission had come to Potsdam, however; and since reparations probably constituted the most important single issue at stake, the disputes of the Reparations Commission tended to dominate the mood of the whole Conference.

There were a number of other, relatively minor, issues also. Withdrawal of troops from Persia, Russian claims to part of East Prussia, including the city of Königsberg, the prosecution of war criminals, the expulsion of Germans from the countries of Eastern Europe, the threat of 'Monarcho-fascism' in Greece, and Tito's expansionist aims in Istria and southern Austria were among the questions which had been put on the agenda of the Conference but had not yet been directly discussed at the plenary sessions.

In view of the total lack of progress towards agreement which had characterized the discussions after 19 July, the Conference seemed to face an impasse. The standard technique of referring contentious matters to the Foreign Ministers accomplished nothing. The Foreign Ministers were quite helpless in view of the conflicts between their superiors, and could only tire one another by talking round and about and back and forth. There were, in effect, two really major questions: economic policy towards Germany and Soviet policy in the Balkans. Each had a connected subordinate problem: the western boundary of Poland was linked with the future of the German economy; and Stalin resolutely tied British and American policy in Italy and Greece to any discussion of his own conduct in the northern Balkans. Only if the clash of views on these major points could somehow be compromised would the Conference have any hope of even apparent success. Lesser issues could be expected to fall into place fairly easily once decision on the key disputes had been reached.

[1] See above, p. 550.

Two more plenary sessions, on 24 and 25 July, did nothing to change the situation; and at that point it became necessary to suspend the formal meetings of the Conference to allow the British representatives to go home to receive and act upon the results of the election. Formal sessions were not resumed until the evening of 28 July, but the interim was not wasted. Byrnes, in particular, busied himself trying to find formulas with which to smooth over and postpone decisions on awkward points. Truman was anxious to bring the Conference to a close; and indeed the final sessions were conducted under the threat of imminent American departure, with or without agreement. Byrnes, an old hand at composing differences among American politicians, was more concerned to reach agreements than to defend any particular principles. He was thus ready enough to abandon the more ambitious parts of the original American programme: free waterways, supervised elections, guarantees of freedom of the press, &c. He clung tenaciously, however, to the principle that no economic arrangement should be made that would require American assistance to Germany or Italy. It was largely as a result of his persistence as a horse-trader that the Conference in the end was able to produce a series of verbal agreements which, at least on the surface, seemed to make the Conference a success.

Progress was slow, however, and at the first plenary session after Attlee returned to Potsdam with his new foreign Secretary, Ernest Bevin, on 28 July, the discussion was almost as fruitless as before. Italy and the Balkans were on the agenda; and the only agreement came when Stalin's claim to Italian reparations was allowed so long as the amount demanded did not reduce Italy to dependence on outside, i.e. Anglo-American, economic aid.

Stalin fell ill the next day, and the plenary sessions had to be postponed until he recovered. The Foreign Ministers were busy during the interval, and at last began to make some progress. After informal consultations with the Russians and the British, Byrnes drew up three papers dealing with German reparations, the Polish frontier, and the 'anomalous' positions of Italy, Bulgaria, Finland, Hungary, and Rumania. These he presented to the other two Foreign Ministers on 30 July. An all-day session seemed to promise agreement along the general lines Byrnes proposed, and, in the hope of hastening matters, Byrnes informed Molotov the next morning that, unless the Russians would accept all three papers at the ensuing plenary session, the Americans would leave the Conference on 1 August. Attlee and Bevin had already agreed 'in principle' to the American proposals.[1]

It was against this background that the log-jam finally gave way on 31 July at a four-hour plenary session. It opened with Byrnes's presentation

[1] Byrnes: *Speaking Frankly*, pp. 84–85.

of his three papers. They constituted, he emphasized, an interdependent whole. With regard to German reparations, he proposed that each Power should satisfy its claims to reparations by removal of capital equipment from its own zone of occupation. In addition, the Western Powers would undertake to transfer to Russia a quarter of the surplus capital plant located in their zones. Half of this amount would be transferred gratis; half in exchange for food and coal delivered from the Russian zone to western Germany. In this way, Byrnes tried to balance the British demand for food from the east against the Russian demand for half of all reparations from Germany.[1]

The key question in any such apportionment of reparations was the decision as to what constituted surplus capital equipment. This task was assigned to the Allied Control Council, acting under general instructions from the Reparations Commission. Obviously such a procedure would take months to come to completion, and the Russians badly wanted reparations right away. To meet this demand, Byrnes proposed that 'advance reparations' should begin at once by marking particular plants in the western zones for delivery to Russia. Such advance deliveries would in due course be credited against the totals worked out systematically by the Reparations Commission and the Allied Control Council. A most important principle, in the words of the final communiqué, was the following:

> Payment of reparations should leave enough resources to enable the German people to subsist without external assistance. In working out the economic balance of Germany, the necessary means must be provided to pay for imports approved by the Control Council in Germany.
>
> The proceeds of exports from current production and stocks shall be available in the first place for payments for such imports.[2]

Moreover, as was later agreed in the statement of economic principles to govern Allied administration in Germany, the German standard of living should not exceed (and by inference should not fall far below) the average living standard of continental Europe.

In general, this formula for German reparations came closer to American and British ideas than to Russian; but since the zonal arrangement gave the Western Powers most of Germany's heavy industry, there was really nothing Stalin could do to get more from the West. It was clear that the Americans at least were ready to leave Potsdam without any agreement at

[1] It was estimated that 40 per cent. of all German capital assets were located in the Russian zone of occupation. To make up the Russian percentage to half thus required shipments from the western zones. Byrnes's original proposal would have given the Russians only 47·5 per cent. of the presumed total reparations. But since it was already perfectly clear that the Western Powers would not imitate the thoroughness of Russian looting in the eastern zone of Germany, such calculations were almost meaningless.

[2] *Documents on American Foreign Relations, 1945–1946*, p. 930.

all. Hence Stalin had little leverage for bargaining, however ill-content he was to see the figure of $20 milliard vanish into the mists.

Byrnes's second proposal did something to redress the balance. With respect to the western Polish frontier, he was willing to agree to leave to the Poles the territory which had been assigned to them by Russia on an interim basis, but reserved the final delimitation of frontiers for the German peace treaty. This can have deceived no one: the Poles were already treating the territory in question as an integral part of Poland, expelling the German inhabitants and planting Polish settlers in their place. In effect, the Western Powers bowed to the *fait accompli*. This was, mainly, a concession by the British, who had most vigorously challenged the Russian action.

With respect to the status of Italy and the Russian satellite countries, Byrnes evolved an almost meaningless formula. The preparation of a peace treaty with Italy was declared to be the first task before the Council of Foreign Ministers. Preparation of peace treaties with the Russian satellites was put as the Council's second urgent task. With respect to diplomatic recognition, which Stalin had so strongly pressed: 'The three Governments agree to examine each separately in the near future, in the light of the conditions then prevailing, the establishment of diplomatic relations with Finland, Rumania, Bulgaria and Hungary to the extent possible prior to the conclusion of peace treaties with those countries.'[1]

When Byrnes had finished reading his three proposals to the plenary session, Stalin made a last attempt to get more reparations from Germany. He asked for a third of German foreign assets, a third of the gold captured in the western zones, and a third of the current stocks of German industry. Stalin also renewed a demand which he had made earlier in the Conference for the establishment of a tripartite Anglo-Russo-American authority to control the Ruhr industries.

Some very brisk bargaining now took place. The British and Americans protested vehemently against Stalin's new demands; and when, by way of a substitute, Stalin suggested an increase in the proportion of reparations to be transferred gratis to the Russians from the western zones, Byrnes leaped upon the idea, affirming that he would accept it if Stalin in turn accepted all the three proposals he had put before the Conference. The bargain was struck on these terms. The Russians were now to receive 15 per cent. of surplus German capital equipment from the western zones gratis; and the proportion to be exchanged for food and coal from the Russian zone was reduced accordingly to 10 per cent.[2] As a part of the

[1] Communiqué of the Berlin Conference, *Documents on American Foreign Relations, 1945–1946*, p. 934.

[2] This change raised the Russian share in total German reparations to 50 per cent., working on the assumption that 40 per cent. of total German capital assets fell within the Russian zone of

bargain, the Russians dropped their proposal for the establishment of a tripartite administration of the Ruhr.[1] The disposal of external German assets was left for further discussion; but on the next day it was agreed that the Russians should have the right to seize German assets located in the countries under their occupation, with the exception of Czechoslovakia. Poland's claims to reparations were to be satisfied by the Russians; and the claims of other Allied countries were to be met from the share allotted to the Western Powers. Finally, Stalin reluctantly agreed to the admission of a French representative to the Reparations Commission—a step made necessary by the existence of a French zone of occupation.[2]

With this agreement, the crisis was past. Two more days were required to wind up the Conference and prepare the communiqué and protocol. The most important action was formal approval of the statement of economic principles for Allied administration of Germany. This document, like its political counterpart, had been worked over by the European Advisory Commission, but, unlike it, committed the Allies to a number of positive policies. It declared that Germany should be treated as a single economic unit—a principle which the reparations agreement directly contravened and made almost nonsensical, since Russian policy was so much more drastic than any likely to be accepted by the Western Powers. In addition, the Allied administration was instructed to effect essential repairs to transport, to enlarge coal production, to maximize agricultural output, and to effect emergency repair of housing and public utilities. By provisions such as these the necessity of restoring the German economy to something approaching an even keel was at least partially recognized.

occupation. The new proportion thus conformed to the original Russian demand for half of all reparations.

[1] Four-Power (British, American, Russian, and French) administration of the Ruhr had been tentatively approved by Truman before the Conference opened (Leahy: *I Was There*, p. 455). There was, however, among the American delegation to the Conference much doubt and opposition to an action which would advance Russian power into the industrial heart of western Europe, and when the dispute over reparations arose and Russian intransigence became clear, Truman refrained from advancing the proposal. Meanwhile, the Russians had proposed three-Power administration of the Ruhr themselves (Mosely: 'Soviet-American Relations Since the War', *Annals of the American Academy of Political and Social Science*, May 1949, p. 208). It is worth remembering that the Morgenthau Plan, approved by Roosevelt and Churchill in September 1944 (see above, pp. 488–90), had provided that the Ruhr should be put under the international control of the Security Council. American ideas for the dismemberment of Germany and the administration of the Ruhr, as reported in Leahy, conform in considerable degree to Morgenthau's proposals; and it was not until the Potsdam Conference had begun that Truman definitely abandoned them. Thus the stubbornness shown by the Russians on the matter of reparations cheated them of American support for a much more radical and long-standing change in German affairs, the internationalization of the Ruhr.

[2] Leahy: *I Was There*, pp. 493–5; Byrnes: *Speaking Frankly*, pp. 81–85.

Equal distribution of the ships of the German navy and merchant marine between the three Allied Powers was also accepted, with the provision that distribution of the German merchant fleet would not take place until after the end of the Japanese war. This was a concession to the Russians. On the matter of war criminals, however, Stalin's wish to mention ringleaders by name was overruled. Instead, the communiqué simply took note of the discussion then taking place in London for the establishment of an international tribunal to try major war criminals whose offences had no special geographical location, and expressed the hope that prompt action would follow.

The communiqué similarly recognized that the expulsion of German inhabitants from Eastern European countries would 'have to be undertaken'. The hope was expressed that it would proceed in an orderly and humane fashion, and that further expulsions would be suspended until the Allied Control Council could make arrangements to receive the refugees in Germany. This phraseology was a concession to British and, to a lesser extent, to American humanitarianism and to Anglo-American concern over the refugee problem in the western zones of Germany. But it made no practical difference, for the expulsions continued, and were anything but orderly and humane.

Having struggled so long over the western boundary of Poland, the Western Powers made little or no objection to endorsing Russian claims to part of East Prussia, including the city of Königsberg—important to the Russians as the only ice-free port on the Baltic within their grasp.[1] A counter-concession on the part of the Russians was their agreement to 'improve' the procedure of the Allied Control Commissions in Hungary, Bulgaria, and Rumania now that the war had ended. Regular consultation between the Russian and other members of the Commissions was promised, and free movement of persons and mail was guaranteed.

Still another Russian concession was the promise to begin the evacuation of Tehrān immediately; but consideration of complete evacuation of foreign troops from Persia was put off until the first meeting of the Council of Foreign Ministers. A final concession was the Russian promise to participate in a conference to regulate access to European inland waterways.

Other points could not be settled in the rush of the final days of the Conference, or were dropped as trivial. Charges and counter-charges directed against Greece and Yugoslavia fell into the latter category. The knotty problem of the Turkish Straits and of the disposal of Italian colonies fell into the former.

Thus in a great flurry the Conference came to its end. On 2 August the

[1] This had been informally discussed at Tehrān (cf. Churchill, v. 357; U.S. edition, v. 403). See also above, p. 363.

final plenary session approved the communiqué and protocol. This done, the weary participants dispersed.

The decisions reached at Potsdam certainly did not constitute a long-term settlement of European affairs. Yet the Allies had been able to agree upon the most pressing of their problems: the treatment to be accorded to defeated Germany. And that seemed a considerable achievement.

But the achievement was less than appeared. One crying anomaly of procedure—the exclusion of the French—soon nullified most of the decisions which had been reached so painfully. Although France was represented on the Allied Control Council for Germany and had been assigned a zone of occupation in Germany, the French Government had neither been invited to participate in the Potsdam Conference nor had French approval been secured for the principles governing the treatment of Germany which the Big Three evolved among themselves. France, obviously, was not bound by the agreements; yet the French had the right to veto Allied action in Germany by virtue of their membership of the Control Council. This would have been of small importance if the French had been willing to accept the Potsdam decisions; but they were not. The French were even more afraid of German numbers and industrial power than were the Russians and hoped to see their powerful neighbour partitioned or, as a minimum, divided into semi-autonomous regions. To administer all Germany from Berlin and permit the establishment of central economic controls for the whole country, according to the pattern adumbrated by the Potsdam communiqué, ran directly counter to French ideas; moreover the wounded *amour-propre* which dominated so much of French behaviour in the period immediately after the liberation of their country impelled the French to defy, and take special pleasure in defying, the Big Three. As a result, the first rock upon which the Potsdam arrangements for Germany grounded was French intransigence.

The omission of France was a great and obvious defect. Yet Stalin's unwillingness to regard France as an equal, or anything like an equal, made any other course a practical impossibility. Had Britain and America insisted upon bringing de Gaulle to Potsdam, Stalin would probably have refused to come without a satellite of his own such as Poland: and that the West would not agree to. Thus the Great Allies found themselves in the awkward position of being unable to act either with or without the French.

The other great defect of the Potsdam agreements has already been sufficiently emphasized. There was no meeting of minds on European issues as a whole. For the time being, Russia successfully defended her domination of Eastern Europe from threatened interference by Britain and America; but neither of the Western Powers was willing to accept passively and without question the new order the Soviets had brought to their 'People's Democracies'. The dispute was simply postponed until the time came to draw up peace treaties; and if the Heads of Government could not agree at Potsdam in July there was small likelihood that the Foreign Ministers would be able to do so when they met for the purpose of drafting treaties in September.

But these difficulties were not perfectly evident at the time. Men whose hopes had fed upon the many expressions of war-time solidarity and whose hearts had been fired by the Charter of the United Nations could view the decisions of Potsdam as, in Byrnes's words, 'a basis for the early restoration of stability in Europe'.[1] The fact that the Russian radio and press evinced its usual enthusiasm for the results of the Conference seemed to prove that the Russians and the Western Powers had really agreed. *Izvestia* said: 'The Conference has strengthened the ties between the three Governments and widened the limits of their co-operation and understanding. . . . The results of the Conference create a new certainty that the Governments and peoples of the three great democratic Powers together with the other United Nations will ensure the creation of a just and firm peace.'[2]

The British and American press were far less enthusiastic. In the United States there was some disappointment at the failure of the communiqué to say anything about Russian participation in the war against Japan; and many journalists and Congressmen felt that Russia had got the best of the bargain. The *New York Times* wrote editorially (5 August 1945): 'It would be unwise to accept the economic part of this program without question, for it is nothing less than remaking the material civilization of a continent. . . . But a beginning has been made. . . .We may reserve judgment on certain practical matters, but the general spirit of the Potsdam decisions expresses the war aims of the American people.'[3] On 6 August, Senator Arthur H. Vandenberg, an influential leader among the Republicans, issued a statement in criticism of the vagueness of the communiqué, especially with respect to free elections and a free press in Eastern Europe;[4] and accurate reports of some of the unsolved difficulties which had come before the Conference made it clear that the omission of mention of Turkey and Persia from the communiqué reflected stubborn divergences between Russian and Western policies.[5]

[1] *Speaking Frankly*, p. 87.

[2] Quoted from *Manchester Guardian*, 4 August 1945.

[3] Cf. *Christian Science Monitor*, 6 August, *Chicago Daily News*, 7 August 1945. The anti-Roosevelt portion of the American press was far more critical, suspecting a sell-out to Russia: e.g. *Chicago Tribune*, 4 August 1945: 'The Conference should have brought Russia into the war against Japan. . . . Russia should have pledged herself unequivocally to demand neither territory nor concessions in Asia. . . . The conference should have recognized . . . that the first duty of statesmanship is to revive Europe's economy.'

[4] *New York Herald Tribune*, 7 August 1945.

[5] See e.g. James B. Reston in *New York Times*, 5 August 1945.

When Truman arrived back in the United States he thus had to face a somewhat half-hearted if not openly dubious public. On 9 August 1945 he made a radio report to the nation. By that time the Russians had declared war on Japan and the first atomic bomb had been dropped. Potsdam had already faded into the background. Nevertheless, the President recapitulated the main decisions of the Conference, defended the principle of compromise in international dealings, and affirmed, optimistically, that Rumania, Bulgaria, and Hungary 'are not to be spheres of influence of any one power'.[1]

The British reaction to the Potsdam Conference was almost the same as the American. Doubts about the economic treatment to be accorded to Germany and concern over the matters left unmentioned in the communiqué damped down enthusiasm for the outcome of the Conference.[2] When Parliament reassembled, Churchill made a vigorous speech on foreign affairs on 16 August, in which he did not disguise the numerous points of difference between British and Russian policy. With respect to Potsdam he said: 'We should not, however, delude ourselves into supposing that the results of this first Conference of the victors were free from disappointment or anxiety, or that the most serious questions before us were brought to good solutions.' He went on to a vigorous denunciation of the 'police governments' of Eastern Europe, and with reference to the expulsion of Germans from some of those countries produced a phrase destined to become a catchword: 'Sparse and guarded accounts of what has happened and is happening have filtered through, but it is not impossible that tragedy on a prodigious scale is unfolding itself behind the iron curtain which at the moment divides Europe in twain.'[3] When Bevin spoke in his turn, he too did not mince words, nor minimize conflicts with Russia. With respect to Bulgaria, Rumania, and Hungary he said: '. . . the impression we get from recent developments is that one kind of totalitarianism is being replaced by another. This is not what we understand by that very much overworked word "democracy". . . .'[4] Whatever their differences over domestic matters, Bevin and Churchill saw nearly eye to eye with respect to British foreign policy.

But before the new Parliament could get round to considering foreign affairs, drastic, unforeseen, and dramatic events in the Far East had, for the moment, dwarfed the troubles of Europe. Japan had capitulated, war had ended. Atomic warfare had thrown up its vast and sinister mushroom to shadow the earth. Decisions taken at Potsdam played their part in this drama; and it is the military aspect of the Conference and the sudden surrender of Japan which we must now consider.

[1] Text of Truman's speech may be found in *New York Herald Tribune*, 10 August 1945.

[2] e.g. *Manchester Guardian*, *Glasgow Herald*, 4 August, *Observer*, *Sunday Times*, 5 August 1945.

[3] 16 August 1945, H.C. Deb. 5th ser., vol. 413, coll. 82–84.

[4] Ibid. col. 291.

(iv) Victory over Japan

(a) Strategic Plans

The battle for Okinawa (1 April–21 June 1945) was in its final stages before the American Joint Chiefs of Staff were able to decide upon the next offensive move in the Pacific. The conjunction of General MacArthur's forces moving up from the South-West Pacific with those under Admiral Nimitz striking across the central Pacific created difficult problems of jurisdiction. Neither the U.S. army nor the U.S. navy wished to see its forces subordinated to a commander from the other service; and this dispute was enhanced by differing concepts of strategy. The navy emphasized the importance of blockade, and for many months naval strategists advocated closing the ring round Japan by establishing a base on the China coast before attempting any frontal assault. The U.S. army, on the contrary, believed in striking at the heart of the Japanese Empire as quickly as possible, and after the capture of Okinawa the time seemed ripe.[1]

The problem came to a head when approaching victory on Okinawa urgently raised the question: What next? On 18 June Admiral King finally agreed that an operation against Formosa or the south China coast should be by-passed in favour of a direct attack upon the southernmost of the main Japanese islands, Kyushu. President Truman approved the plan, and on 29 June the Chiefs of Staff set 1 November 1945 as the target date for the invasion of Kyushu. The delicate matter of command was solved by dividing it. Admiral Nimitz was to direct the initial landings, but after army forces had come ashore over beach-heads secured by the Marines, MacArthur would take over command of the operation.[2]

The Americans calculated that they had sufficient forces on hand to attack Kyushu without asking any help from Britain or Russia. But there were other aspects of the war. Japanese forces in Manchuria, China, South-East Asia, and the East Indies would have to be coped with; and, as the Americans already knew, the British and Russians had views of their own on these matters. The Potsdam Conference was therefore opportune. Over-all military arrangements against Japan could there be agreed and co-ordinated among the three Allies.

The military deliberations at Potsdam were not so much concerned with strategy as with administration and long-range policy, and by far the most important phase of the conversations was Anglo-American. The British Chiefs of Staff came to the Conference with a series of proposals which they believed would confirm and extend the Anglo-American military partner-

[1] It is interesting to observe how this debate paralleled the Anglo-American debate over strategy against Germany.

[2] Leahy: *I Was There*, pp. 488–50; Wilson: *Eight Years Overseas*, p. 254.

ship. For the immediate future, they wished to reorganize the commands against Japan on the pattern which had been so successful in Europe. In particular, they hoped to persuade the Americans to make the Pacific command into an Allied one, subordinated to the Combined Chiefs of Staff rather than to the American Joint Chiefs of Staff.[1] They had two arguments. First, a British naval force had been operating under American command in the Pacific since March 1945 and it seemed reasonable that an Allied body, the Combined Chiefs, should exercise supreme control over what was now in physical fact an Allied force. Second, although Mountbatten's South-East Asia Command came under the British Chiefs of Staff, he had made his staff bi-national, and it remained so despite the fact that almost no American forces remained under his command. For the sake of balance and easy co-ordination it therefore seemed reasonable to demand that a single body, the Combined Chiefs of Staff, should control both the Anglo-American theatres of war against Japan.

For the longer run and on the world stage, the British were anxious to maintain the Anglo-American military partnership. They proposed that the Combined Chiefs of Staff Committee should become a permanent institution, since it seemed obvious to them that the advantages of Anglo-American military co-operation would not end with Japanese defeat. Similarly, the British Chiefs of Staff were most anxious to persuade their American colleagues that Lend-Lease aid for British and French occupation troops in Germany should not be cut off despite the fact that active war in Europe had ended.[2]

The American Joint Chiefs of Staff were either opposed or dubious on all these points. They had no intention of relaxing their exclusive control over Pacific operations, and did not hesitate to say so. They were reluctant to agree to a continuation of the Combined Chiefs Committee. At Potsdam the Americans dodged the issue, saying that it was too early to discuss the future of the Combined Chiefs Committee. They did, however, agree to continue its operation until the peace treaties had been signed.[3] Finally, the American Joint Chiefs of Staff refused to recommend continuation of Lend-Lease for the use of British or other occupation forces. This was a matter of great importance to an economically prostrate Britain, and it was round Lend-Lease policy that the warmest debates of the Combined Chiefs of Staff centred at Potsdam.

The upshot as usual was compromise. The American Joint Chiefs retained untrammelled control of Pacific operations, and their strategic plan was accepted. However, the Americans promised to consult the

[1] The exclusive Pacific jurisdiction of the U.S. Chiefs of Staff had been first established in March 1942 and was confirmed formally at Casablanca at a time when the British had no forces to spare for the Pacific.

[2] Leahy: *I Was There,* pp. 448, 477.

[3] Ibid. p. 478; Wilson: *Eight Years Overseas,* p. 262.

British Chiefs of Staff regularly, and accepted 'in principle' the British offer of four divisions to participate in a land attack upon the main island of Japan, Honshu.[1] The British Chiefs of Staff remained as before in control of the South-East Asia Command, but its boundaries were enlarged to cover a part of MacArthur's old South-West Pacific theatre, including the East Indies, Malaya, Siam, and Indo-China. The Philippines and the important naval base at Manus in the Admiralty Islands remained under American control; and Australia became a rear area, excluded from either theatre of operations. Mountbatten was instructed to take over his enlarged theatre by 15 August 1945. General objectives for his further operations were assigned, but the task of working out detailed operational plans was left to the British, as was the delicate matter of adjusting Dutch, French, Australian, and native political and military aims in South-East Asia and the South-West Pacific.

The almost complete eclipse of China as an active factor in these military calculations was noteworthy. The report of the Combined Chiefs did pay lip service to China by listing all possible support to Chiang Kai-shek among the policies to be pursued;[2] but the Americans had at length come round fully to the view long held by the British: they no longer believed that the Chinese could play any important part in defeating Japan. Time was now too short to equip and train a powerful Chinese army, even had it been easy to deliver supplies. And the political and psychological obstacles to the creation of a modern Chinese army had become all too evident to the American commanders on the spot and in Washington. The Americans, therefore, no longer treated China as a Great Power in embryo. Instead of an ally, the Chinese had become a problem.

The Combined Chiefs of Staff could not agree upon Lend-Lease policy. The British were not willing to yield their claim to assistance for their occupation forces in Germany; the American Chiefs of Staff refused to sanction such diversion of American resources from the Japanese war. The dispute was unresolved when the Combined Chiefs met with Truman and Churchill on 24 July, to submit their report for final approval. At that meeting the President indicated his personal sympathy with the British request for continued Lend-Lease assistance. Four days later, on 28 July, he approved instructions to the American Joint Chiefs of Staff which gave the British what they wanted. Lend-Lease was to continue for the use of occupation troops until the end of the Japanese war.[3]

[1] Leahy: *I Was There*, p. 482; Wilson: *Eight Years Overseas*, p. 258. Acceptance of British land forces for the assault on Honshu was conditional upon the approval of MacArthur and Nimitz. The former was notoriously opposed to any British participation in his war against Japan (cf. Sherwood: *Roosevelt and Hopkins*, pp. 878–9; Eng. edition, ii. 867–8).

[2] Leahy: *I Was There*, p. 483.

[3] This, of course, contradicted Truman's own order of 5 July (see above, p. 611). The advice of

Military negotiation with the Russians was comparatively brief. There was only one tripartite meeting at Potsdam at which the Russian, American, and British Chiefs of Staff each described their intended operations against Japan. The Russians set the latter half of August as the time at which they would be ready to take the offensive against the Japanese in Manchuria. The senior Russian representative, General Antonov, said that the exact date would depend upon the satisfactory conclusion of negotiations then in progress in Moscow between the Chinese Foreign Minister and the Russian Government.[1]

At the end of the meeting, Admiral Leahy gave General Antonov a series of suggestions for the improvement of Russo-American military co-ordination. Establishment of two American weather stations in the Soviet Far East, delimitation of zones of naval and air action between American and Russian forces, direct liaison between Russian and American headquarters in the Far East, and reciprocal rights for the use of naval and air bases by battle-damaged craft were the proposals. A second meeting, on 26 July, was arranged between the American and Russian military authorities to settle these points. With minor changes the Russians accepted all the American suggestions.[2]

The military conversations with the Russians were generally limited to exchange of information. The only matter of strategic debate arose when Antonov asked for American action to open and safeguard the sea route north of Japan. This Admiral King said could not be undertaken until after the capture of Kyushu; in the meanwhile the Red Army would have to subsist upon supplies already stock-piled in the Far East.[3]

The net effect of the decisions taken at Potsdam was to reduce the Allied character of operations against Japan to rather small proportions. The Americans insisted upon dealing directly with the Russians in all matters of operational co-ordination without British participation; similarly they dealt with the British with respect to affairs in South-East Asia without Russian participation. The geographic fact that the American theatre of operations lay between the other two made this line of action possible; but the fact that both Russians and British depended in large part upon American supplies was of more importance in permitting the American Joint Chiefs of Staff to assert their power as they did at Potsdam.

Actually, it is hardly an exaggeration to say that the Russian, American,

Secretary of War Stimson was of decisive importance in persuading Truman to overrule the Joint Chiefs of Staff on this issue.

[1] The stumbling-block in these negotiations was the unwillingness of the Chinese to accept Russian interpretation of the rights in Manchuria and north China which had been promised by Roosevelt to Stalin at Yalta. A treaty was finally concluded, after more than six weeks' negotiation, on 14 August 1945. See below, pp. 646–8.

[2] Deane: *Strange Alliance*, pp. 272–5. It was apparently on this occasion that Korea was divided along the 38th parallel between Russian and American zones of action. See below, p. 643.

[3] Deane: *Strange Alliance*, pp. 274–5. See also above, p. 606.

cipal allied powers acting in the interests of the United Nations at war with Japan. For that reason, participation of the forces of other nations that have taken a leading part in the war against Japan will be welcomed and expected. The occupation forces will be under the command of a Supreme Commander designated by the United States.

Although every effort will be made, by consultation and by constitution of appropriate advisory bodies, to establish policies for the conduct of the occupation and the control of Japan which will satisfy the principal Allied powers, in the event of any differences of opinion among them, the policies of the United States will govern.[1]

With respect to the established government of Japan, it was laid down that:

. . . the Supreme Commander will exercise his authority through Japanese Governmental machinery and agencies, including the Emperor, to the extent that this satisfactorily furthers United States objectives. The Japanese Government will be permitted . . . to exercise normal powers of government in matters of domestic administration. . . . The policy is to use the existing form of Government in Japan, not to support it.

The economic policies enjoined upon MacArthur were generous. Demilitarization was not to lead to destruction of factories readily convertible to civilian use; occupation costs were to be met by Japan only 'to the extent that this can be effected without causing starvation, widespread disease and acute physical distress'; reparations were to be limited to seizure of Japanese property abroad and to 'the transfer of such goods and existing capital equipment and facilities as are not necessary for a peaceful Japanese economy'.[2]

While these major points of policy were under discussion, lesser but nevertheless awkward problems clustered round the ceremony of surrender. The U.S. navy, which had taken the leading part in the Pacific war, hated to see MacArthur take the Japanese surrender. Naval *amour propre* was salved when it was decided to stage the ceremony on board the U.S.S. Missouri, and when Admiral Nimitz was empowered to sign the instrument of surrender on behalf of the United States while MacArthur signed as Supreme Allied Commander.[3]

Russo-American relations were crossed by a series of misunderstandings and mutual suspicions, many of them arising from delays and difficulties in the transmission of messages from Manila, where MacArthur had his headquarters, to Moscow. Thus the Americans received a false report that Russian troops were landing on the northernmost Japanese island,

[1] *Occupation of Japan*, pp. 74–75.
[2] Ibid. pp. 78–81.
[3] Byrnes: *Speaking Frankly*, pp. 212–13.

Hokkaido, and protested.[1] Similarly, the Russians feared that the Americans were trying to deny them the Kuriles, and suspected that the Soviet representative would not be transported to Manila in time to take part in the surrender ceremony.[2]

These and similar complications, the need to assemble and transport an occupation force, and, finally, a typhoon delayed Japan's formal surrender until 2 September. On that day, after an Allied fleet had anchored in Tokyo Bay and American troops together with a few British Marines had set up a small bridgehead on the outskirts of Tokyo, at 9.08 a.m. local time, the instrument of surrender was signed. It took the form of an Imperial Proclamation of Unconditional Surrender, accepted by the United States, Britain, Russia, and China 'in the interests of the other United Nations at war with Japan'. Representatives of Australia, Canada, New Zealand, France, and the Netherlands were also present and signed.

Simultaneously the Imperial Japanese Headquarters issued a general order defining the procedures to be followed in surrendering the various elements of the Japanese armed forces, scattered as they were from the East Indies to the Kuriles and from Burma to the islands of the central Pacific. Five zones were marked out. Japanese forces in China (excluding Manchuria), Formosa, and Indochina north of the 16th parallel were directed to surrender to the Chinese. Those in Manchuria, Korea north of the 38th parallel, the Kuriles, and Sakhalin were ordered to surrender to the Russians. In Burma, Siam, Indochina south of the 16th parallel, the East Indies, Malaya, and the Bismarck and Solomon Islands the Japanese were instructed to surrender to the South-East Asia Commander or to the Australians—details to be arranged between the two. Japanese forces in the other Pacific islands were to surrender to the Commander-in-Chief, U.S. Pacific Fleet; and those in Japan itself, the Philippines, and Korea south of the 38th parallel were to surrender to the U.S. army.[3]

MacArthur intended that disarmament and repatriation of Japanese soldiers should go forward in an orderly manner, and tried to prevent any local surrenders from taking place before the general capitulation in Tokyo Bay.[4] The Chinese and British conformed to his plan. As a result, it was

[1] Stalin asked that Hokkaido should be assigned as Russia's zone of occupation in Japan. This was refused by the Americans (Deane: *Strange Alliance*, p. 281). On 16 August Truman stated in a press conference that separate zones of occupation would 'in his opinion' be unnecessary in Japan (*New York Times*, 17 August 1945). This was presumably a public reference to the Russian request.

[2] Deane, op. cit. pp. 280–4.

[3] For text of the order see the *New York Times*, 2 September 1945. The division of Korea along the 38th parallel seems to have originated with the demarcation of limits of air and naval operation which was agreed between the Americans and Russians at Potsdam (see above, p. 633). In general, the surrender instructions preserved existing boundaries of Allied theatres of operation, and there is no reason to suppose they were changed in this case. Korea's bisection had been presumed earlier by one of MacArthur's orders, dated 24 August: for text see *New York Times*, 27 August 1945.

[4] This caused Mountbatten some embarrassment, for he had to hold up plans for landing in

not until 12 September that Mountbatten received the formal surrender of the Japanese forces within the South-East Asia Command at Singapore. Similarly Japanese troops in China surrendered to a representative of Chiang Kai-shek at Nanking on 9 September.[1]

The Russians, however, were not bound by MacArthur's orders and instructions. Vasilievsky, the Russian Commander-in-Chief in the Far East, took the surrender of the Kwantung army in Manchuria on 21 August. Two days later Stalin was able to announce the complete occupation of that province. Having advanced so far, the Red Army stopped and did not enter China proper, leaving the Japanese forces there to be dealt with by others. The Red Army did, of course, proceed to occupy the northern half of Korea.

Thus by the middle of September 1945, the partition of the Japanese co-prosperity sphere was completed in practice and formalized by a series of military orders and agreements. But the traces of Japanese conquest and of the great Asiatic revolt against European domination which had been fostered by Japan's example and propaganda could not be eliminated by merely military methods. Except in Japan itself political upheaval, conflict, and uncertainty threatened from the start to overturn the legal and military situation established in the Far East by the last general order of Japanese Imperial Headquarters.

(*c*) Allied Difficulties in the Far East

The orderliness with which the surrender of Japanese forces was carried through did not prevent the rapid emergence of difficulties among the Great Powers over affairs in the Far East. During the war native nationalist and revolutionary organizations had arisen in Asia and in the East Indies which were sufficiently powerful to prevent any simple return to pre-war political conditions. Adjustments had to be made, but the Great Powers could not agree among themselves as to what exactly should be done. Moreover, neither Russia not Britain liked the American monopoly of control in Japan, while all three Powers, but especially Russia and the United States, found their interests and policies in China running counter to one another.

Yet, in general, Allied difficulties in the Far East were less vital than those which arose over the settlement of European affairs. Spheres of influence were clearly marked out by the surrender arrangements, and each Power

Malaya until after 2 September, even though landing craft were in some cases already at sea (Mountbatten: *Report*, pp. 182–3).

[1] The surrender at Nanking was a ceremonial gesture, since in most parts of China under the Japanese occupation there were no Nationalist forces near enough to take the surrender in detail. Only large-scale transport provided by the Americans permitted Chiang's forces to move into the main cities formerly under Japanese control; and despite this American help a few Japanese garrisons surrendered to the Chinese Communists.

was therefore able to pursue its policies within its own sphere, subject only to occasional protest from outside. Not until 1947 did the spheres of influence established by the pattern of surrender in the Far East suffer serious breach as a result of the spread of Communist power over China—a process not complete until 1949. A very summary sketch of the political problems in the Far East immediately after Japan's surrender is therefore all that is relevant to this history.

As far as Japan herself was concerned, one of the first problems that came up was whether and under what conditions Russian, Chinese, and British occupation forces would join the American garrison which had first taken over occupation duties. Negotiation on this point was connected with disputes over the political control to be exercised over General MacArthur. In September 1945, when Byrnes went to London for the first meeting of the Council of Foreign Ministers, he took up the matter of the Far Eastern Advisory Council with Bevin. By conceding a place on the proposed Council to India, and by agreeing that it should be authorized to meet in Tokyo as well as in Washington, Byrnes was able to win British consent to the establishment of a Council on the lines originally proposed by the United States on 21 August.

This apparent success turned out to be illusory. Molotov, although he had originally agreed to the American proposal, now refused to accept it, and entered a series of protests against MacArthur's actions in Japan. He demanded an Allied Council with mandatory powers, and objected to the manner in which the Russian representative at MacArthur's headquarters had been neglected. As a result, when the Far Eastern Advisory Council first met in Washington, on 30 October 1945, it met without a Russian member, and promptly adjourned to see whether a Russian could not be enticed into joining its deliberations. Not only Russia, but both Britain and Australia—not to mention the other states represented—were profoundly discontented with a merely advisory role in Japanese affairs.[1] Consequently, the United States Government at length decided that some concession would have to be made. A new proposal was drawn up which Byrnes presented at the gathering of Foreign Ministers in Moscow in December 1945.[2]

In the autumn of 1945 the Americans wanted British, Chinese, and Russian troops to share the burden of Japanese occupation duty. The American demobilization programme made it difficult to maintain adequate forces without such help. But at the same time the Americans did not want to divide Japan into separate zones of occupation on the pattern which had already shown serious defects in Germany. This created a

[1] Byrnes: *Speaking Frankly*, pp. 215–17. [2] See below, pp. 704–6.

stumbling-block, for as early as 30 October 1945 the Russians refused to send Red Army troops to Japan if it meant recognizing MacArthur's supreme command over them. This refusal caused the Americans to wonder whether sharing of the tasks of occupation with British or Australian troops would be wise, or would instead merely give the Russians grounds for their already lively suspicion that the Anglo-Americans were combining against them.[1]

The Australians, however, were particularly anxious to crown their part in the Pacific war by sharing in the occupation of Japan; and British policy encouraged the development of inter-Commonwealth defence arrangements for the Pacific, where, as the war had shown, the Royal Navy was no longer adequate by itself. As a result, after three months' negotiation, an agreement was signed on 30 January 1946 between Australia and the United States. It provided for the dispatch of a corps of Australian, New Zealand, and British-Indian troops to Japan, together with naval and air units, all gathered under the command of an Australian general, who in turn came under MacArthur. A prefecture of Japan was assigned to be garrisoned by the British Commonwealth Force, but military government was reserved for the Americans. In a public statement issued on the same day, the American Government announced:

> The participation of British Commonwealth forces in the occupation of Japan is in line with the policy made public by the President on 22 September [1945] which stated that the 'participation of the forces of other nations that have taken a leading part in the war against Japan will be welcomed and expected'.
>
> In accordance with this declaration, invitations were extended also to the Governments of China and the Union of Soviet Socialist Republics to send troops to participate in the occupation. The Chinese Government has informed this Government that, while it is willing to provide a contingent of troops, it is not in a position to do so at the present time. The Union of Soviet Socialist Republics has not accepted the invitation to participate.[2]

The result, clearly, was that militarily speaking MacArthur and the Americans retained their effective monopoly in Japan.

The situation in China at the time of Japanese surrender had apparently been stabilized by the conclusion of a Sino-Soviet treaty of Friendship and Alliance on 14 August 1945. Negotiation of this treaty had begun on 1 July when T. V. Soong arrived in Moscow for the purpose.[3] Soong came in obedience to American and Russian pressure: the two Powers were

[1] *Forrestal Diaries*, pp. 105–7.

[2] *Occupation of Japan*, pp. 93–94. Text of the U.S.-Australian agreement may be found ibid. pp. 89–93.

[3] Before the negotiation came to a conclusion Soong was replaced by Wang Shih-chieh as head of the Chinese delegation.

anxious to secure Chinese ratification of the Yalta agreement concerning special rights and concessions to Russia in Manchuria before the time came for the Red Army to attack the Japanese. Soong approached the negotiation in a stubborn mood, fearing and distrusting Russian intentions.[1]

Long-drawn-out haggling over the exact definition of Russia's prospective rights in Manchuria resulted. The departure of Stalin and Molotov for the Potsdam Conference interrupted the bargaining, and during that Conference (17 July–2 August 1945) the Americans did what they could to back up Soong's insistence that nothing more than the letter of the Yalta agreement should be allowed to the Russians.[2] But the Russians had two advantages: overwhelming military force and the political alternative of offering their support to the Chinese Communists. It followed that Soong had to yield on most disputed points.

The Treaty itself simply provided for military and economic co-operation in the war against Japan and afterwards. The meat came in a series of notes exchanged between the two Governments 'relating to the Treaty of Friendship and Alliance', and in a series of supplementary agreements defining the new status of Dairen, Port Arthur, the Manchurian railways, and relationships between Russian and Chinese authorities in Manchuria during the period of its occupation by the Red Army. In these documents, the Russians explicitly recognized China's full sovereignty over Manchuria, renounced any intention of interfering in Sinkiang, and agreed to render to China moral support and aid in the form of military supplies and other material resources. In addition, the Russians promised to give such support and aid only to the National Government of China, thus expressly repudiating the Chinese Communists.

In return, the Chinese agreed to recognize the independence of Outer Mongolia if a plebiscite indicated the desire of the population of that area for independence. They agreed further to establish Dairen as an international free port and to transfer half of its harbour facilities to Russian control; to accord the Russians joint use of the Liaotung peninsula (Port Arthur) as a naval base (the city of Dairen was excluded from the base area); and to operate jointly with the Russians all the railways of Manchuria.

Nominally, these agreements provided for equality between Russians and Chinese on the various controlling boards and councils which were set up, and reserved civil administration exclusively for the Chinese; but a number of provisions made clear which nation would in fact be supreme. Thus the Chinese entrusted the defence of the Port Arthur naval base to

[1] On the eve of his departure for Moscow he told Admiral Leahy that China could not agree to give Russia the stranglehold on Manchuria which the Yalta agreement would make possible, and suggested that military action—perhaps only after 500 years—would be necessary to drive the Russians back (Leahy: *I Was There*, pp. 445–6).

[2] Byrnes: *Speaking Frankly*, p. 205.

the Russian Government, and the Russians reserved the right to station any number of men within the base wherever they chose. Since the naval base was more than fifty miles in length from tip to base of the peninsula, there was plenty of room for an entire army.[1] There can have been little doubt in either Chinese or Russian minds that, as a result of these agreements, Russia would enjoy military supremacy in all Manchuria, and through control of the railways would also be in a position to dominate the whole economic life of the province.

Nevertheless, it was not a bad bargain from the point of view of the Chinese National Government. The Russians expressly undertook not to support the Chinese Communists, and it seemed likely that if they honoured their word the forces of Chiang Kai-shek would speedily be able to assert their power over all China proper. If he had effectively lost Manchuria, Chiang seemed to have gained China. It is not strange, therefore, that Chiang told the American Ambassador he was 'generally satisfied with the treaty'.[2]

The Americans, too, were at first well content with the bargain that had been struck. The point upon which Truman had especially insisted at Potsdam—that Dairen should be made a free port for vessels of all nationalities—was safely written into the agreements, and the Chinese had been able to parry some of the original Russian demands.[3] It was not long, however, before disturbing reports about Russian activities in Manchuria began to reach American authorities. In the last week in August 1945 the Russians began to seize machinery and other goods from the Manchurian factories, taking them into Siberia. This the Russians claimed to be quite legitimate: they were simply taking possession of war booty, for had not the factories been an essential element in the Japanese war effort? The Americans, however, objected to so loose a definition of war booty, and claimed that disposal of Japanese assets in Manchuria should be decided by joint consultation.[4] A second problem arose over the treatment of prisoners of war. The Potsdam Declaration had promised that Japanese soldiers would be demobilized and sent home as soon as disarmed. The Russians, however, refused to repatriate the Japanese they had taken prisoners, using them instead as forced labour in Siberia.

In China proper, however, the immediate effect of the Sino-Soviet agreement seemed to bear out the hopes of the Chinese and American Governments. Desultory negotiations which had been in progress since May 1944 between the Chinese Communists and the National Government[5] took on new life. The Communists yielded on a number of previ-

[1] Texts of the treaty and supplementary agreements may be found in *Department of State Bulletin*, 10 February 1946, pp. 201–8.

[2] *United States Relations with China*, p. 120.

[3] Ibid. pp. 121–3.

[4] *Department of State Bulletin*, 11 March 1945, p. 364.

[5] See above, pp. 516–18.

ously disputed points, and by 11 October 1945 it seemed as though a firm agreement between the rivals had been reached on all important points. Thereafter the situation rapidly changed. Communist and Nationalist troops began openly to threaten one another and negotiation stalled once again.

Two factors accounted for the change. First, American assistance was offered to the Chinese National army on a very considerable scale. This took the form of transporting Chinese troops both by air and sea into the areas of the country formerly under Japanese control.[1] The Americans conceived the operation as part of the process of repatriation of Japanese soldiers. After all, some authority with armed force at its command had to take over from the Japanese if anarchy were to be avoided. But everyone realized that the Americans by their action were helping the Chinese Nationalists against their Communist rivals; and, naturally enough, as they became more and more confident of American support, the Chinese Nationalists became less and less inclined to make terms with the Communists. As far as numbers went, the Nationalists enjoyed something like a 5:1 military superiority over the Chinese Red Army; and with American help they were able to occupy all important centres of population in China proper by the end of 1945.[2] With these advantages, Chiang did not feel it necessary to make concessions.

The other factor in the changed face of China was the growth of covert Russian assistance to the Communists. As early as 10 September 1945 the U.S. Government began to receive reports that Russian commanders in Manchuria were admitting Communist armed forces and assisting them to take over the local administration.[3] (The Communists had not operated in Manchuria on any significant scale during the war.) In proportion as the Chinese Communists could feel sure of Russian support, even on a comparatively small scale, they in their turn were less and less anxious to come to terms with the Nationalists. If civil war and an open clash between Russian and American policy in China were to be avoided, speedy and determined efforts were clearly necessary.

With the object of setting in train such efforts, Truman persuaded General Marshall, recently resigned from his war-time post as Chief of Staff of the U.S. Army, to undertake a special mission to China. His appointment was announced on 27 November 1945.[4] Shortly afterwards, Byrnes tried to meet the Chinese problem by seeking agreement with the

[1] In addition, a force of over 50,000 U.S. Marines landed in North China at the request of the Nationalist Government. Their professed mission was to hasten Japanese repatriation, but they also served as a very potent deterrent to Communist expansion in an area of China where the Communists were strongest.

[2] *United States Relations with China*, pp. 105–12, 311–13.

[3] Ibid. p. 122.

[4] See below, p. 709.

Russians at Moscow in December.[1] We shall have to return to these attempts later.

The political situation in South-East Asia which confronted Admiral Mountbatten on the morrow of Japan's surrender was even more chaotic than that which prevailed in China. The Japanese had established puppet governments in former European colonies, and these governments did not necessarily disintegrate when Japanese support was withdrawn. In addition, various guerrilla groups had formed during the war, sometimes under Communist leadership, sometimes with an anti-Japanese nationalist programme. Local, tribal, national, and personal rivalries confused and weakened the Asiatic revolt against European domination; yet the fact that discontented groups had arms in their hands and were well enough organized to be able to direct discontent into political channels presented a very delicate and difficult problem to the British commanders who were appointed to receive Japanese surrender in Malaya, southern Indochina, and the East Indies.

Moreover, the Europeans were divided against themselves. The French and Dutch wanted to resume their pre-war control over Indochina and the East Indies respectively, and were profoundly unwilling to trust the defence of their imperial interests to the British, even though they lacked troops of their own to enforce more drastic policies than those the British were prepared to support.

Finally, behind Mountbatten's back was the vast problem of India's future. Most of the troops at his disposal were Indian, and some of them were not unsympathetic with the nationalist and independence movements which had arisen in such areas as Java and Burma. On 15 August 1945 the Speech from the Throne opening the new Parliament had committed the Labour Government to 'do their utmost to promote in conjunction with the leaders of Indian opinion the early realisation of full self-government in India'.[2] Similarly, a White Paper of 17 May 1945 had declared with reference to Burma: 'The ultimate objective of His Majesty's Government will be that representatives of the Burmese people, after reaching a sufficient measure of agreement between the various parties and sections, should draw up a Constitution of a type which they themselves consider most suitable for Burma. . .'[3]

With such commitments to India and Burma, the British Government could not logically support the more rigorous policy demanded by the Dutch in the East Indies—a policy which could have been carried through

[1] See below, pp. 707–8. [2] 15 August 1945, H.C. Deb. 5th ser., vol. 413, col. 57.

[3] Great Britain: *Burma, Statement of Policy by His Majesty's Government*, Cmd. 6635 (London, H.M.S.O., 1945), p. 10.

only by resort to force on a considerable scale. Instead, the British regularly and persistently sought to avoid force and find a basis for political reorganization which would satisfy the more moderate nationalist ambitions of the local peoples and at the same time preserve some element of European influence. In their own possessions this British policy was on the whole successful, but in the East Indies violence soon broke out.

Looking at the conduct of the Great Powers in the Far East as a whole, one can see a rapid realignment taking place in the months immediately after Japan's surrender. During the war years the United States had been frequently critical of British imperialism; the British for their part were at first the main critics of the American assumption of sole authority in Japan, while Russo-American relations with respect to China seemed to have been satisfactorily adjusted by the Sino-Soviet treaty of 14 August 1945, and the Russians seemed willing to concede Japan to the United States' sphere. Within a few weeks, however, the Americans changed partners. American authorities when confronted with the complexities and difficulties of 'independence' in South-East Asia decided that it would be wise to make haste slowly, and found no important points upon which to quarrel with British policy, which was directed to the same ends. Similarly, agreement with British (and particularly Australian) officials over the administration of Japan proved possible; while the progress of events had already compelled the Americans to concur in the low estimate of China's power which British authorities had held from the beginning of the war.

On the other hand, American difficulties with Russia multiplied. Before the end of 1945 the danger of an open and head-on clash between the two Powers over the prostrate body of China had become painfully apparent; and the Russians soon took up the role, so recently vacated by the Americans, of critic-in-chief of colonial imperialism in Asia.

This striking diplomatic shift occurred only partly under the stimulus of events in the Far East. The affairs of Europe were on the whole more vital and more pressing. Consequently it was primarily events in Europe that set the Great Powers against one another—an antagonism which had in its turn vast subsequent repercussions in China and in the Far East generally.

CHAPTER II

QUARRELS OVER PEACE

SEPTEMBER 1945–DECEMBER 1946

(i) Changing Climates of Opinion

BETWEEN V-J day and the end of 1946 the Grand Alliance disintegrated. Allied co-operation was superseded by the emergence, at first dimly and haltingly, of global antagonism between the Soviet Union and the United States. This antagonism did not become sharp and definite until 1947 when the Truman Doctrine and Marshall Plan in Europe and the Chinese Communist offensive in Asia turned the earlier sporadic clashes of policy into cold war;[1] but before the end of 1946 Russo-American co-operation was unmistakably a thing of the past.

Allied relationships passed through two fairly distinct phases before the lines were finally drawn in 1947. Until about May 1946 Britain and Russia seemed protagonists in a contest for power and influence in Europe and the Middle East. The United States, during this period, stood relatively in the background, seeking to re-establish as soon as possible a 'normality' which in part had vanished from most of the world, and in part had never existed.

Two key events mark the shift in American and Russian attitudes which brought on the cold war. One was the open rupture between American and Russian policy in Germany. The issue was economic: on 3 May 1946 General Lucius D. Clay, head of the American Military Government in Germany, informed his Russian colleague on the Allied Control Council in Berlin that, except for 'advance reparations' already agreed to, deliveries of German surplus capital equipment from the American zone would be halted until the Russians agreed to administer Germany as an economic unit and to make an accounting of the reparations already withdrawn from the Russian zone of occupation.[2] In earlier disputes over Allied policy in Germany, the Americans had generally taken a middle position between the British and Russians. This was the first occasion upon which the Americans took the lead in opposing Russian claims. Clay's action provoked loud and violent protests in the Russian press, and for the first time American policy was exposed to full-throated Russian propaganda attack. The affair thus constituted an important landmark in Russo-American relations.

The second event was the decision of the American Congress to approve a loan of $3,750 million to Great Britain.[3] The British loan was first

[1] See *Survey* for 1947–8, pp. 11–61, 268–311.

[2] Clay: *Decision in Germany*, p. 122. This made no immediate difference, for only 'advance reparations' had actually begun, and they were to continue. See below, p. 725.

[3] See below, pp. 663, 685–8.

officially proposed on 6 December 1945 and was not finally approved by Congress until 13 July 1946. The importance of the loan and the accompanying debate, apart from its very great economic significance for Great Britain, was that it sealed Anglo-American political solidarity in the post-war world. It also put off the great American dream of returning to normal until some indefinite future when the Russians, presumably, would agree to mend their ways.

As a result of these two events, Stalin had to face a common Anglo-American front in the latter part of 1946.[1] More and more the intrinsic economic and potential military power of the United States thrust leadership of the coalition upon American shoulders.

These developments in the sphere of international economics and politics were accompanied by shifts in propaganda and opinion in Russia, the United States, and Great Britain. As usual, changes of opinion in part resulted from international developments, and simultaneously contributed towards further shifts in foreign policy. Domestic pressures and problems were also important factors contributing to the new climate of opinion which emerged gradually in Russia and in the United States.

The most striking change came in Russia. The end of the war was followed by a marked reaction. Bolshevik slogans and ideology were officially revived, while war-born patriotism of the traditional Great Russian variety was discreetly dropped. Glorification of Russian achievements in the Second World War was by no means neglected, but the official interpretation attributed Russia's success more and more to the Soviet system and to doctrinal orthodoxy which had allowed the great Stalin to foresee and prepare for capitalist attack.[2] Since channels of expression were thoroughly under central control, the change came rather abruptly. In August 1945 Mikhail Kalinin, President of the Supreme Soviet, sounded the new note: 'But even now, after the greatest victory known to history we cannot for one minute forget the basic fact that our country remains the one socialist state in the world. ... The victory achieved does not mean that all dangers to our state structure and social order have disappeared. Only the most concrete, most immediate danger, which threatened us from Hitlerite Germany, has disappeared.'[3] On 6 November 1945, after the failure of the first meeting of the Council of Foreign Ministers, Molotov told the Moscow Soviet: 'While we

[1] As early as 4 April 1946 Stalin expressed the opinion to the American Ambassador that the United States had 'definitely aligned itself with Great Britain against the U.S.S.R.' (Smith: *Moscow Mission*, p. 40).

[2] Cf. Stalin's election speech of 9 February 1946 and Molotov's speech of 6 February 1946 (*Stalin and Molotov Address their Constituents* (London, Soviet News, 1946)).

[3] Quoted from Frederick C. Barghoorn: 'The Soviet Union between War and Cold War', *Annals of the American Academy of Political and Social Science*, May 1949, p. 4.

are living in a "system of states", and while the roots of Fascism and imperialist aggression have not been finally extirpated, our vigilance in regard to possible new violators of peace should not slacken, and concern for the strengthening of co-operation between the peace-loving powers will continue to be our most important duty.'[1]

The possibility of future conflict between capitalism and Communism was made more explicit by Stalin in a speech of 9 February 1946. He said: 'Marxists have stated more than once that the capitalist system of world economy conceals in itself the elements of general crisis and military clashes. . . .' He went on to describe the war just ended as a great test of the Soviet system, and explained that the three Five-Year Plans had served to prepare the industrial base for the Russian victory. This cleared the way for his announcement of some of the goals of future Five-Year Plans, in the following words:

> We must achieve a situation wherein our industry is able to produce annually up to 50,000,000 tons of pig iron, up to 60,000,000 tons of steel, up to 500,000,000 tons of coal, up to 60,000,000 tons of oil.
>
> Only under such conditions can we regard our country as guaranteed against any accidents. This will require perhaps three new Five-Year Plans, if not more. But this task can be accomplished and we must accomplish it.[2]

Three days earlier Molotov had described the programme more briefly: 'To overtake and surpass economically the most developed capitalist countries of Europe and the United States of America . . . such is the task.'[3] These speeches, particularly Stalin's, made a deep impression on some of the leaders of the British and American Governments. In the United States William O. Douglas, a Justice of the Supreme Court and prominent figure in the liberal wing of the Democratic Party, privately called it the 'Declaration of World War III'.[4]

In the second half of 1946 the Communist Party initiated a thoroughgoing campaign against cultural and intellectual 'cosmopolitanism', i.e. admiration for or recognition of the West's achievements. This campaign, carried to absurd lengths in the following months, was part of a general effort by the Party to reassert its totalitarian control over Russian thought and behaviour. The fact that millions of soldiers had been exposed to the outward appearances of Western civilization, combined with war-weariness and the natural impatience of a population suffering from continued deprivation, presented an awkward challenge to Communist propaganda. Increasingly violent attacks upon Western culture,[5] glorification of all

[1] *Report by V. M. Molotov on the 28th Anniversary of the Great October Socialist Revolution* (London, Soviet News, 1945), p. 28.

[2] *Stalin and Molotov Address their Constituents*, pp. 3, 17.

[3] Ibid. p. 26.

[4] *Forrestal Diaries*, p. 134.

[5] Cf. Kalinin's speech to a congress of agitators in August 1945: 'There was talk here about people coming back from Germany who have seen "cultures" of German villages which made a

things Soviet, emphasis upon the dangers of capitalist encirclement and attack—these were the lines of propaganda which the Party fell back upon in an effort to overcome and erase doubts and apathy which had arisen among the people of Russia in the wake of the great victory. A widespread purge of the Party, the public eclipse of the military figures who had led the Red Army to victory, and renewed emphasis upon the importance of ideological training were complementary steps designed to strengthen the Party at the expense of its only possible rival in Russian society, the army.[1]

It is impossible to know what cross currents of hopes and fears led to this reaction in Russia. Perhaps Stalin and his advisers seriously believed in the dangers of capitalist attack, but it seems reasonable to assume that internal conditions within Russia also played a considerable part in determining the new Party line. By exaggerating the danger from outside, the Russian Government could justify new demands upon the Russian people for obedience, patience, and work. Spectral capitalist predators provided the Government with a convenient scapegoat for any failures to increase the supply of consumers' goods as rapidly as the population expected or hoped. Equally, a return to militant Marxism may have been needful in order to ensure the loyalty and enthusiasm of the body of men upon whom at bottom Stalin relied for the execution of his will in Russia—the rank and file of the Party. In proportion as they were enthusiastic doctrinaires they must have been troubled at the spectacle of co-operation and kind words between Soviet Russia and capitalist strongholds like Britain and the United States; and when victory removed the tactical justification for such conduct Stalin may have found himself under some pressure to change his course.[2]

Whatever the factors that influenced Stalin in shifting the Party line in 1945–6, it *was* shifted, and that very fact made co-operation among the erstwhile Allies more difficult. Doctrines of inevitable war tend to be self-validating: in proportion as men believe and act upon them, they do in fact become true. Thus in so far as the leaders of the Russian Government said, believed, and acted upon the conviction that capitalist hostility to the

certain impression on them. Our agitators must uncrown this German culture. . . . There are people both in towns and villages who hardly ever read and are really very little developed, who yearn to dress more fashionably, to wear hats, even smoking-jackets, and use toilet water. They want to seem to be educated people. But by themselves and from inside themselves they are not cultured. Such seems to me to be the culture of the German burgher or rich farmer. This is pure external culture, an empty one, not grasping the depths of the human soul. . . . All this may create an impression on inexperienced people with no aesthetic taste. In general, the German standardised way of life cannot blind a reasonable person' (quoted from Smith: *Moscow Mission*, p. 280). Molotov on 6 November 1945 renewed the theme: 'Not all of us have yet rid ourselves of obsequious worship of the West, of capitalist culture. . . . Unless one rids oneself of these shameful survivals, one cannot be a real Soviet citizen' (ibid. pp. 281–2).

[1] Cf. Deutscher: *Stalin*, pp. 555–64; Merle Fainsod: 'Postwar role of the Communist Party', *Annals of the American Academy of Political and Social Science*, May 1949, pp. 20–32.

[2] Andrei Zhdanov has sometimes been taken as the leading representative of this doctrinaire element in the Party, but such identification must remain speculative.

Soviet Union was inevitable, they helped to create that hostility, incidentally, of course, proving themselves good prophets and demonstrating to simple minds the truth of Marxist doctrine.

American opinion underwent a more gradual, confused, but equally great, change during the months between V-J day and the end of 1946. The first mood, as in Russia, was one of reaction: 'Let's get back to normal.' The rapid demobilization of the armed forces and the equally precipitate removal of governmental controls over the domestic economy were symptoms of this state of mind. The cancellation of Lend-Lease and efforts to hasten the making of peace treaties reflected the same attitude applied to the conduct of international affairs.

Quite soon, however, it became apparent that events were not moving in the expected direction. Europe's economic difficulties required extraordinary measures, of which the most important was the British loan. Moreover, Russia's conduct in Eastern Europe and at the conference table did not fit into the American pattern of normality, and, indeed, seemed a cynical repudiation of war-time promises. At first there was much confusion in American opinion. The conservative-minded were at one and the same time the most anxious to get back to normal and the most suspicious of Russia and of Communism. Liberals and Leftists, on the other hand, were more inclined to support continued American involvement abroad, but at the same time urged patience and understanding towards Russia. Two parallel processes gradually altered this alignment. By degrees many conservatives allowed their fear and dislike of Russia and of Communism to outweigh their dislike of foreign entanglement, and thus became supporters of an active foreign policy directed towards the 'containment' of Communism. At the same time, many liberals suffered disillusionment and gave up hope of any firm and successful understanding with Russia, at least for the time being. People of this persuasion tended to argue on behalf of economic help to European and other countries, but shrank, as did many conservatively-minded persons, from political, still more from military, action. As a result, a more forward American foreign policy developed first in the economic sphere.

These realignments of public opinion were greatly accelerated by the publicity which attended the activities of the United Nations. Debates over the control of atomic energy, over the Russian refusal to withdraw the Red Army from Persia, and over Anglo-Russian clashes concerning Greece and Indonesia dramatized the conflicts among the Great Powers and profoundly shook earlier optimism in the efficacy and adequacy of the new United Nations organization.

The change was none the less gradual. Thus, when Winston Churchill, speaking as a private citizen, called upon the United States to maintain a special relationship with the British Commonwealth in order to fend off the shadow of Communist aggression, his words came as a shock to most Americans. His famous speech, delivered on 5 March 1946 at Fulton, Missouri, in the presence of Truman and other dignitaries, seems relatively mild when read in the light of later developments. Churchill advocated 'the continuance of the intimate relationships between our military advisers' and 'joint use of all naval and air force bases in the possession of either country', and looked forward to an eventual common citizenship between Britain and America. He declared: 'We aim at nothing but mutual assistance and collaboration with Russia', but went on to paint a dark picture of events behind the 'iron curtain'—a phrase which this speech first made current in the United States. He said:

Nobody knows what Soviet Russia and its Communist international organization intends to do in the immediate future, or what are the limits, if any, to their expansive and proselytizing tendencies. . . .

From Stettin in the Baltic to Trieste in the Adriatic an iron curtain has descended across the Continent. . . . The Communist parties, which were very small in all these eastern states of Europe, have been raised to pre-eminence and power far beyond their numbers and are seeking everywhere to obtain totalitarian control. . . .

Whatever conclusions may be drawn from these facts—and facts they are—this is certainly not the liberated Europe we fought to build up. Nor is it one that contains the essentials of permanent peace. . . .

On the other hand, ladies and gentlemen, I repulse the idea that a new war is inevitable; still more that it is imminent. . . . I do not believe that Soviet Russia desires war. What they desire is the fruits of war and the indefinite expansion of their power and doctrines. . . .

From what I have seen of our Russian friends and allies during the war, I am convinced that there is nothing they admire so much as strength, and there is nothing for which they have less respect than for weakness, especially military weakness. . . .

If the Western democracies stand together in strict adherence to the principles of the United Nations Charter, their influence for furthering those principles will be immense and no one is likely to molest them. If, however, they become divided or falter in their duty . . . then indeed catastrophe may overwhelm us all. . . .

If we adhere faithfully to the Charter of the United Nations and walk forward in sedate and sober strength, seeking no one's land or treasure, seeking to lay no arbitrary control upon the thoughts of men, if all British moral and material forces and convictions are joined with your own in fraternal association, the high roads of the future will be clear, not only for us but for all, not only for our time but for a century to come.[1]

This speech attracted great attention all round the world. Truman

[1] *New York Times*, 6 March 1946.

declined to comment on what Churchill had said, but Stalin took the unusual step of publishing (on 13 March 1946) a rebuttal, cast in the form of an interview with a *Pravda* correspondent. Stalin's words were belligerent. He said:

> To all intents and purposes, Mr. Churchill now takes his stand among the warmongers. . . . A point to be noted is that in this respect Mr. Churchill and his friends bear a striking resemblance to Hitler and his friends. Hitler began his work of unleashing war by proclaiming a race theory. . . . Mr. Churchill begins to set war loose also by a racial theory, maintaining that only nations speaking the English language are fully-fledged, called upon to decide the destinies of the entire world.

After denying that Russia controlled the states of Eastern Europe and asserting that they were fully democratic, Stalin concluded: 'I do not know whether Mr. Churchill and his friends will succeed in organising. . . a new military expedition against Eastern Europe. But if they succeed in this, which is not very probable, since millions of common people stand on guard over peace, then one can confidently say that they will be beaten, just as they were beaten 26 years ago.'[1]

When issue had so resoundingly been joined between Stalin and Churchill, American officials hesitated to associate themselves publicly with the former Prime Minister[2] and refused to make any public comment. Uncertainty and unwillingness to join definitely in a coalition against Russia continued to exist among Americans for several months to come. Divergences of opinion between liberal and conservative elements in the United States remained strong, and a group of 'New Dealers', typified by Henry Wallace, Truman's Secretary of Commerce, felt increasingly restive against the course followed by the Secretary of State in his dealings with Russia. On 23 July 1946 Wallace wrote a letter to Truman in which he criticized the Government's military policy, its diplomatic policy, and, above all, its atomic energy policy. Taken together, Wallace declared, these American actions and proposals did much to justify Russian suspicion and non co-operation.[3]

This letter was not made public at the time, however, and it was not until mid-September that the issue came out into the open. The occasion was a speech made by Wallace on 12 September 1946 in which he criticized a 'get tough with Russia' policy, and said:

> . . . to make Britain the key to our foreign policy would be the height of folly. . . . We must not let British balance-of-power manipulations determine whether and when the United States gets into war. . . .

[1] *Daily Telegraph*, 14 March 1946.

[2] It was announced on 14 March that Dean Acheson, Under-Secretary of State, would not attend a public dinner for Churchill in New York, being 'too busy' (*New York Times*, 15 March 1946).

[3] *New York Times*, 18 September 1946, reproduced the entire letter.

We may not like what Russia does in eastern Europe; her type of land reform, industrial expropriation, and suppression of basic liberties offends the great majority of people in the United States—but, whether we like it or not, the Russians will try to socialize their sphere of influence just as we try to democratize our sphere of influence.

Russian ideas of social-economic justice are going to govern nearly a third of the world. Our ideas of free enterprise and democracy will govern much of the rest. Competition should be put on a friendly basis, and the Russians should stop conniving against us in certain areas of the world, just as we should stop scheming against them in other parts of the world.[1]

Wallace's speech was immediately interpreted as a criticism of Byrnes's conduct of foreign affairs. Byrnes himself so interpreted it, and demanded that Truman should either accept his resignation at once or make it clear to Wallace that he had no right to criticize publicly the foreign policy of the United States. For a week Truman tried to find some compromise between the two members of his Cabinet, but in vain. Finally, on 20 September 1946, he dismissed Wallace from his post as Secretary of Commerce.[2]

But though the policy of the American Government seemed to have been more definitely cast in an anti-Russian mould by this affair, Truman still continued to hope and hesitate. Moreover, public opinion was far from unanimous. Wallace had many sympathizers among old supporters of Roosevelt. To them it seemed as though an unholy coalition of conservative southern Democrats and conservative Republicans was dominating American foreign policy under the guise of bi-partisanship. But this group was a minority, and when Communists, both in the United States and abroad, came vigorously to Wallace's support, his cause was damaged and eventually doomed.

It is none the less true to say that the real hardening of American opinion against Russia did not come until 1947 and 1948 when the rejection of Marshall Aid was followed by the coup in Czechoslovakia and the success-

[1] *The Times*, 13 September 1946.

[2] The Byrnes–Wallace quarrel was embittered by the fact that both men had regarded themselves as potential successors to Roosevelt. Wallace had been Vice-President until 1944, and Byrnes had been a leading candidate for that office in 1944; and it was only Roosevelt's decision that had given the post to Truman. Roosevelt was not selecting a successor when he chose Truman; rather he was looking for a man personally popular in the Senate who would help to persuade that body to endorse American participation in a permanent United Nations organization. Hence both Wallace and Byrnes felt that he really should be in Truman's shoes. In addition, each represented an important wing of the Democratic Party—Wallace the liberal-leftist and Byrnes the southern-conservative. Truman's personal relations with each man were therefore difficult; and politically he felt it important to avoid antagonizing either of them. For these reasons, the President decided only reluctantly in Byrnes's favour.

At the beginning of the year, Byrnes himself had been the butt of Truman's criticism (see p. 718, note 2); and in his quarrel with Wallace Byrnes felt that the President had not backed him up properly. Relations between Truman and his Secretary of State did not mend in the following months, and on 7 January 1947 Byrnes resigned in a huff.

ful Communist offensive in China.[1] There had been a great change in 1946, and Americans had been compelled to reconsider their foreign policy. Events themselves and the discussion which centred round Churchill's and Wallace's speeches gradually undermined the war-time admiration and sympathy for Russia. Dislike, indignation, and distrust, together with puzzlement, profound uncertainty, and self-criticism, supplanted optimism and the expectation of a prompt return to 'normal'. But in 1946 Americans had not yet convinced themselves that Russia was definitely an enemy. Neither had they come to the conclusion that they ought to assume active leadership of the 'free world' and provide more than moral and economic help to the opponents of Communism. Cold war had not yet come; instead a spooky twilight troubled Russo-American, and therefore world, relations.

Changes in the climate of British opinion in 1945–6 were similar to those which occurred in the United States, but the fluctuations were not nearly so sweeping. Because war-time optimism had on the whole been less sanguine, disillusionment was less complete; because Conservatives had been nurtured in a concept of balance of power, they tended to think more of balancing Russian power than of stamping out Communism; because the Labour Party—at least in major part—accepted the traditions of British foreign policy, there was little partisan dispute on foreign affairs; and, finally, because the British people from long experience did not expect all nations to agree with them or to accept their good intentions at face value and without question, they did not leap to the conclusion that a nation that opposed them was *ipso facto* wicked and perverse. Long experience of international affairs in some measure armed the British public against excessive optimism and equally against excessive moral indignation when hopes were disappointed.

It is true that some of the supporters of the new Labour Government hoped and believed that because they were Socialists Attlee and his associates would be able to establish better relations with Stalin than any Conservative Government could hope to do. But this was more of an election argument than a serious article of belief. As it turned out, Attlee and Bevin did not much alter Churchill's foreign policy in Europe, and Stalin showed, if anything, less liking for English Socialism than he had for English Conservatism. To counter British and American protests against their actions in Eastern Europe, the Russians concentrated their propaganda against British actions in Greece, Indonesia, and elsewhere. Hence the Labour Government never had an opportunity to play a mediating role between capitalist America and Communist Russia as some of its supporters had hoped it would be able to do.

[1] See *Survey* for 1947–8, pp. 153–7.

In fact, the economic and other difficulties which faced the British Government were so great that there was relatively little margin for official choice and correspondingly little scope for public controversy. Economically, Britain had to have help from the United States or face incalculable disaster. Politically, British and Russian interests collided in Europe, and, unless the Government were willing to abdicate all pretension of ranking as a Great Power and submit to Russian hegemony on the European continent, there was no role but one of opposition to and protest against Russian expansion.

These hard facts were not always easy for the British public to swallow. Thus Harold Laski, one of the intellectual pillars of the Labour Party, was quoted on 12 May 1946 as saying that, if the necessity ever arose, Britain under a Labour Government would support Russia rather than the United States;[1] and die-hard imperialists, led on by Lord Beaverbrook's newspapers, protested against the loan from the United States on the ground that it would destroy the economic basis of the British Empire. But these were voices crying in the wilderness. Churchill's plea at Fulton, Missouri, for fraternal association with the United States, combined with Bevin's firm opposition to Russian expansion, corresponded far more closely to the prevailing mood of the British public. Foreign policy consequently provoked far less controversy than in the United States. Nearly everyone realized that American friendship had become a necessity while Russian friendship, however unfortunately, had become impossible at least for the immediate future. The important choices of post-war international politics rested with Russia and the United States. Consequently, it was the climate of Russian and American opinion that set the tone of world affairs. Caught with the rest of the world between the two giants, the British could only wait anxiously for American help and hope dubiously for a Russian change of heart.

(ii) Transformation of Allied Economic Relations

(*a*) The Post-war Economic Situation

The Second World War wrought two great, and in some measure contradictory, changes in world economic relationships. In the first place, the United States grew in wealth and productive capacity during the war years when the other major belligerents suffered greater or less loss and damage. As a result, the end of fighting revealed a world in which an extraordinary concentration of wealth in American hands confronted a vastly needy world—a world which for the most part could not possibly pay for goods delivered from America with anything but political support and, perhaps, gratitude.

[1] *Daily Mail*, 13 May 1946.

In the second place, the war had seen the subordination of economic activity to political and military ends on a scale which had no earlier parallel in European history. During the war years prices and calculations of profit or loss did not control decisions as to how to combine capital and labour to produce goods in any of the principal belligerent countries; and even in peripheral areas and neutral countries governmental control over prices, imports, exports, fiscal policy, &c., had been found necessary or desirable to cushion the impact of the war upon established economic patterns, and to direct economic activity into politically acceptable channels. A new sort of world economy emerged in which governments played a determining role and in which conscious policy overrode or supplanted the operations of free market economy.

The odd contradiction between these two great changes lay in the fact that, of all the leading countries of the world, the United States was least prepared, psychologically, to accept political control over economic relationships as a permanent or normal feature of social life. American foreign economic policy during and immediately after the war was largely inspired by a desire to lower political barriers to trade and financial dealings. Such a policy, of course, promised great advantages to American industry and agriculture, both of which had come to enjoy a considerable margin of technical superiority in large-scale production. But Americans did not believe that their advocacy of liberal policies was simply or purely selfish. They thought instead that free exchange of goods and services was the only sound basis for international peace, and believed that, whatever short-run difficulties other countries might have in adjusting themselves to American competition, in the long run all the peoples of the world would benefit.

The development of international economic relations in 1945 and 1946 may be interpreted as a conflict between these American ideas as to how economic affairs should be managed and the new institutions and habits which subordinated traditional financial and economic considerations to calculations of state power and policy. America's vast wealth gave great weight to American economic ideas, but it was not long before Americans themselves began to adjust their thinking to the unexpected political and economic realities which confronted them in the post-war period. A reversion of American policy towards politicalization of international economic relations was already clear by the end of 1946.

One must, therefore, deal with two fairly distinct periods. From the end of the fighting until the spring of 1946 American economic policy was intended to pave the way for prompt liberalization of international economic relations. This policy had two aspects. Negatively, it implied the abandonment of special war-time practices—the abolition of Lend-Lease, of the Anglo-American Combined Boards, and of the governmental economic operations which had been entrusted to the Foreign Economic Administration. On the positive side, the American Government supported the International Monetary Fund and the new International Bank which had been projected at the Bretton Woods Conference,[1] and in addition drafted proposals for the establishment of an International Trade Organization to function as a specialized agency under the United Nations.

The Americans realized, however, that no immediate and automatic liberalizing of world economic relations could occur while Europe and much of Asia were still suffering from the ravages of war. Special interim arrangements thus had to be resorted to: UNRRA, Export-Import Bank Loans, Lend-Lease 'pipe-line' credits, and the sale of surplus property to foreign governments on easy terms. These various devices were all conceived as temporary and extraordinary stop-gaps, but it was just such departures from the assumed norm that constituted the backbone of international economic relations in the immediate post-war period.

The second period was marked by the revival of international economic dealings which were motivated mainly by political considerations. For our purposes, the best marker of this new departure was the approval of the loan to Britain by the American Congress in the midsummer of 1946.[2] This loan was made not so much for economic as for political reasons. Yet one must not exaggerate the rapidity with which the new frame of mind came to prevail in the United States. When the British loan was first proposed to Congress the arguments used to support it were thoroughly in harmony with the ideal of liberalizing world economic relations; indeed, the loan was urged upon Congress as an indispensable means for ensuring such eventual liberalization. Even as late as June 1947, when the Marshall Plan was first proposed, it was presented to the American public as a means of re-establishing a viable European economy which would then permit the removal of political barriers to free economic exchange round the whole world.

But little by little arguments of this sort became in American mouths mere lip-service to ideals and ideas which the rapid changes of post-war international relations had outmoded. After about May 1946 the American Government decided to use their economic strength only to help their political friends, and went so far as to cancel loans which had already been made to such countries as Czechoslovakia[3] and Poland,[4] whose Governments could no longer be classed among America's friends. The complete breakdown of efforts to negotiate an economic settlement with Russia was a more important symptom of the same change.[5] The Russians never

[1] See above, pp. 449–52. [2] See below, pp. 685–8. [3] See below, p. 690, note 2.
[4] See below, p. 733. [5] See below, pp. 690–3, 733.

had any doubt about the subordination of economic to political policy: and, when American diplomats proposed that in return for a Lend-Lease settlement and a supplementary loan the Russian Government should relax its economic exploitation of Eastern Europe, Stalin viewed the proposal as thinly disguised American imperialism. If he could not get a loan with no strings attached, he preferred to do without.

By the summer of 1946 American economic policy abroad had become the handmaiden of political policy. Experience had shown that the ideal of world-wide freedom of economic exchange did not fit the political realities of the post-war world. It presupposed either universal harmony among the nations or indifference to the economic basis of national strength—an indifference which no statesman could maintain in the light of the experience of the twentieth century.

Yet in American eyes the measures they found themselves obliged to take seemed temporary and profoundly unsatisfactory. Hope of an eventual liberalization of international economic relations—if no longer globally, then at least within the circle of the non-Communist world—remained strong. Most Americans were not prepared to admit that governmental control over international economic dealings had come to stay, if only because such a situation would imply greater governmental power over domestic economic affairs than American tradition sanctioned. Thus it was with eyes more or less deliberately shut to the permanence of temporary expedients that the American Government and people returned to a modified war-time pattern of international economic relations in the last six months of 1946.

(*b*) Divergent Domestic Economic Policies among the Big Three

The futility of the American effort to liberalize international economic relations was partly due to the fact that each of the Big Three adopted a different domestic economic policy in the post-war period. But, without a basic community of economic institutions and attitudes in the major countries of the world, the establishment of a world-wide free international market for the exchange of goods, money, and services was almost, or perhaps altogether, impossible.

As soon as the war ended the American Government began dismantling the machinery of economic management which they had built up during the war. In doing so, the Government were responding to the will of the people. Governmental restraints on production and on consumption had galled business men and consumers during the war. Moreover, the tradition which valued free enterprise and the price mechanism of the free market as the principal regulator of production remained strong. This tradition was seldom challenged in principle even where special interest groups violated it in practice. To be sure, there were important difficulties, and the dismantlement of controls did not occur all at once. On 21 August 1945 the Controlled Materials Plan, which had guided American war production since 1943,[1] was abolished, and the priorities system was drastically reduced in scope. Restrictions on the production of consumers' goods were withdrawn bit by bit, and, when the War Production Board[2] was officially dissolved on 4 November 1945, its successor, the Civilian Production Administration, inherited controls over only a few branches of the economy, mainly textiles and leather goods, where critical shortages persisted.[3] Housing was a special problem, and in January 1946 a separate administrative agency was established with power to allocate scarce building materials and to establish housing priorities.

The cancellation of military orders and the inevitable delays while factories were converted for the production of civilian goods led to a sharp decrease in the total industrial production of the United States in August and September 1945. The corner was turned in October, however, and by November indices of production were within 20 per cent. of the war-time peak, and, in terms of current prices, amounted to more than double the pre-war figures.[4] This was a remarkable performance, facilitated, of course, by the enlarged labour supply which resulted from rapid demobilization and by the fact that firms had generally made advance preparations for a return to civilian production.

Nevertheless, a tremendous pent-up purchasing power created extensive shortages of goods. Consequently, it did not seem wise to remove price control as rapidly as production control had been withdrawn. The future of price control became a critical issue between the administration and Congress in 1946.[5] When Congress presented a Bill which would have weakened national price control drastically while nominally continuing it in operation, Truman vetoed it on 9 June 1946, thus temporarily ending governmental control of prices entirely. A compromise was agreed to on 25 July 1946, but the reimposition of price control was only partial and did not prevent a rapid rise in consumers' and wholesale prices.

The American Government took similarly drastic steps to disengage itself from economic operations abroad. On 27 September 1945 an executive order terminated the legal existence of the Foreign Economic Administration.[6] The task of winding up its affairs was entrusted to other branches of the Government, for the most part to the Department of State, which in its turn delegated responsibility for the sale of surplus Government property

[1] See above, pp. 226–7.
[2] For the establishment of the W.P.B. in January 1942, see above, pp. 125–7.
[3] *Industrial Mobilization for War,* i. 946–56.
[4] Ibid. i. 958–9.
[5] At this date the original bill establishing price control was about to lapse.
[6] For the establishment of F.E.A. in September 1943, see above, pp. 228–9.

abroad to a special commissioner.[1] This, indeed, was the main residual function passed on to F.E.A.'s successors. Governmental purchasing of raw materials and other goods, as well as governmental export of American products, was to stop. As far as the United States was concerned, international trade would henceforth be conducted by private firms and individuals.

Yet it would be a mistake to think that the experience of the war and of the depression years which had preceded it left no mark on the American economy or on governmental policy in economic matters. On the contrary, the extension of governmental control over the American economy was very great, and seemed small only in comparison with the practices of European countries. Atomic energy, the greatest single technical advance of the war, remained entirely in governmental hands. Some munitions factories, also, were not converted for civilian production but remained at the disposal of the Government on a stand-by basis. Moreover, the agricultural segment of American production throve upon an elaborate system of subsidies, guaranteed prices, crop quotas and governmental purchase, storage, and sale of 'surpluses'.

The scale of public expenditure remained at the end of 1946 more than four times as great as in 1940. This increase (exaggerated, of course, by the rise in prices) meant that governmental activity had bitten deeply into the general American economy. Governmental demands for goods and services and governmental fiscal and credit policies, together with governmental rules, regulations, and laws, exercised far greater influence over private business than before the war. Thus the operations of the free market were hedged and criss-crossed by new official activities. Even more important, a new conception of the responsibility and ability of government to assure full employment and prosperity had been fixed in the minds of the American people and was written formally into law by the Employment Act of 1946.

Though the United States was regarded as a capitalist country by foreigners, and though Americans themselves regarded their economic system as one dominated by free enterprise, the post-war system was really a mixture of old-fashioned capitalism and new-fashioned state control—a mixture in which governmental policy exercised extraordinarily far-reaching influence.[2] Thus even at home, where the Americans did not have to

[1] Extracts from the relevant official papers may be found in *Documents on American Foreign Relations, 1945–1946*, pp. 159–62.

[2] It would be possible to write an interesting essay on the long-range social and economic consequences of the inflow of business men to Washington during the war. It seems plausible to argue that the closer experience of governmental methods which came to thousands of the leaders of private industry during the war dissolved some of the suspicion and dislike of governmental regulation which had characterized American business men in the early years of the New Deal. Instead of fighting the Government and grumbling against new-fangled nonsense issuing from government offices, business men quite generally came to know their way round in the maze of Washington officialdom and realized that modern government was not merely a police-

consider socialist or other alien ideas, the return to 'normal' after the war was a very limited one, while the fresh encroachment of political control on economic processes was very great.

Unlike either America or Russia, Britain's domestic economic policy could never be dissociated from foreign economic relations. The country lived by export and import, and every other consideration had to be weighed and measured against that fact. Britain's overriding domestic economic problem was an international problem: to raise exports to a level that would pay for necessary imports and meet other foreign financial obligations of the British Government and people.

The economic agreement with the United States concluded in November 1944[1] had provided for the beginning of reconversion of British industry, revival of export trade, and a tapering off of Lend-Lease. But this agreement had been based on the assumption that the war against Japan would last into 1946, giving time for a gradual readjustment of the British economy before Lend-Lease terminated. The unexpectedly early end of the Japanese war led to the abrupt cancellation of Lend-Lease on 2 September 1945, before British industry was prepared for resumption of large-scale exports, and before the British economy as a whole could hope to be even nearly self-supporting. As a result, fresh conversations with the United States became imperatively necessary.[2]

The perilous international economic position of Great Britain made it entirely impossible for anyone to imagine that removal of war-time controls would lead to automatic resumption of pre-war economic patterns. Capital damage and deterioration at home made such a programme doubly impossible; and the fact that the election of 1945 installed a Labour and professedly socialist Government in power showed how far public sentiment had turned away from any desire to return to a pre-war 'normal'.

One may distinguish two fairly distinct aspects of the economic policy pursued by the Labour Government. Some of the measures it put into force stemmed from socialist ideas: for example, nationalization of certain basic industries, expansion of social services and insurance provided by the

man, but a very good customer and a soft-hearted banker as well. The resultant courtship between the traditional leaders of American society—the business men—and the ageing New Deal might be described as one of the most important by-products of the war-time experience.

[1] See above, p. 511. This agreement was based upon the Roosevelt–Churchill conversations at the Second Quebec Conference, September 1944. Although economic experts worked out a detailed programme for the period between V-E and V-J days, their efforts were never ratified by the two Governments (cf. D. N. Chester: *Lessons of British War Economy* (Cambridge University Press, 1951), p. 80). Thus the United States was legally free to cancel Lend-Lease immediately after V-J day without infringing any binding agreement with Britain. Hancock and Gowing (*British War Economy*, p. 533) rather unfairly fail to make this clear.

[2] See below, pp. 688–93.

Government, and a tax policy designed to reduce inequalities of income. On the other hand, there was a large number of practices pursued by the Government which bore little relation to socialist theory. The imperative need to restore a balance between exports and imports, between foreign assets and foreign obligations, could hardly be left to chance. A series of measures designed to restrict consumption at home, to limit foreign financial demands, and to increase exports had to be taken. Government control aimed at these ends was at least as important as were measures intended to bring the ideal of the welfare state closer to reality.

In general, the British Government retained most of the powers which they had acquired during the war. Allocation of materials to manufacturers, consumer rationing, price control, bulk buying of some essential commodities by the Government, and control of all dealings in foreign exchange continued in force. The one important field in which relaxation of control seemed possible was man-power. War-time regulations permitting the Government to direct labour to particular jobs were kept on the books, but a series of orders restricted the application of these extraordinary powers to special groups in the population, and compulsion was in practice almost entirely abandoned.[1] Labour shortage was, however, a serious problem for many industries and for agriculture. The British Government adopted the expedient of importing large numbers of prisoners of war to help fill the gap.[2]

The great change, of course, was that the Government no longer used its economic powers to increase war production and maintain the nation's armed forces at maximum strength, as during the war, but instead sought to boost exports and hasten reconstruction at home. To secure a balanced and prosperous economy, it was officially calculated that British exports would have to be increased to 175 per cent. of pre-war levels, a target which was all the more difficult because in the first nine months of 1945, up to V-J day, exports were running at only 42 per cent. of the 1938 rate.[3] A second important difference from war-time was that the amount of direct government orders for munitions and other goods decreased sharply when the fighting ended. Hence the Government's control of production became more indirect and in some cases allowed private industry a good deal more liberty of choice. But, as in the United States, Government expenditure remained in 1946 about four times as great as before the war;[4] and the

[1] Great Britain: *Ministry of Labour and National Service Report for the Years 1939–1946*, Cmd. 7225 (London, H.M.S.O., 1947), pp. 116 seqq.

[2] Repatriation of Italian prisoners of war began in December 1945, but they were replaced by Germans whose repatriation did not start until October 1946. The peak number of prisoners of war employed in Britain was reached in September 1946 and amounted to 301,000 (ibid. pp. 193–4).

[3] Great Britain, Treasury: *Statistical Material presented during the Washington Negotiations*, Cmd. 6707 (London, H.M.S.O., 1945), pp. 5, 8.

[4] The figures are as follows: 1938, £1,013 million; 1946, £4,209 million (Great Britain,

economic importance of the Government as a purchaser of goods and services was correspondingly enlarged.

It would be quite wrong to imagine that the Labour Government liked imposing all the regulations upon British industry and trade which seemed necessary in order to re-establish a secure balance of international payments. On the contrary, some of the regulations appeared to be necessary evils. Consumer rationing and the blockage of foreign exchange accounts, for example, were so regarded; and the Government hoped to be able to relax and eventually to remove them.

This attitude was not very different from that which prevailed in the United States. The major contrast arose from the fact that removal of controls was possible in America on a vastly greater scale than in Britain. Nor was the socialist ideal of universal welfare unfamiliar in the United States, though it was most emphatically not called 'socialist', and, of course, American social legislation fell short of British measures.

The fact that the British Government considered itself socialist while the word was anathema in the United States may easily obscure the fundamental likenesses between British and American reactions to the economic problems which confronted the two countries in the immediate post-war period. British Socialism was a moderate, piecemeal affair. Large sectors of British industry remained in private hands, and the Labour Government did not attempt or wish to eliminate private enterprise and the play of market prices entirely. Similarly, American private enterprise was cabined, cribbed, and confined by a Government anxious to assure the welfare (and the votes) of workmen and farmers. The difference was one of degree. Avowedly socialist ideas and the straitened economic circumstances of the country pushed the British Government farther, but in both countries governmental control of the economy was partial—an empirical response to circumstance; and in both countries it was primarily intended to improve the lot of the population as a whole, particularly that of the poorer classes.

The British export drive met with considerable success, but fell far short of achieving a balance of international payments. By 1946 the deficit in current transactions had been reduced to £344 million,[1] a sum which was probably less than half as great as the deficit for 1945.[2] The effort to restore

Treasury: *National Income and Expenditure of the United Kingdom 1946 to 1950*, Cmd. 8203 (London, H.M.S.O., 1951), table 20, p. 31).

[1] Great Britain, Treasury: *United Kingdom Balance of Payments 1946–1950*, Cmd. 8201 (London, H.M.S.O., 1951), table 1, p. 5.

[2] No official tabulation of the balance of payments for 1945 was published by the British Government. However, the Bank for International Settlements (*Seventeenth Annual Report* (Basle, 1947), p. 46) provides the following figures:

British current payments deficit for 1945: £875 million
,, ,, ,, ,, for 1946: £400 million.

This calculation obviously differs considerably from the official record, and it is not clear how the divergence arose. Presumably the Bank used preliminary and perhaps unofficial figures for its calculations.

international solvency was not, however, so successful as might appear at first glance. British exports found easiest ingress to soft currency countries, whereas it proved difficult to increase exports to countries in the dollar area. Actually, the deficit in current transactions with the dollar area in 1946 amounted to £330 million.[1] Only the passage of the British loan by the American Congress in July 1946 prevented the resultant dollar gap from paralysing Anglo-American trade.

For Soviet Russia the termination of Lend-Lease and Mutual Aid meant an abrupt return to an almost completely autarkic economic system.[2] The war, however, had extended Russian control over new territory, and the Russian Government did not hesitate to plunder Eastern Europe and Manchuria in order to relieve somewhat the terrible poverty which afflicted the Russian people themselves. The war had been a great disaster for the Russian economy. It has been estimated that about a quarter of Russia's pre-war capital equipment was destroyed or otherwise dissipated during the war.[3] Over-all production probably declined also during the war years; and the concentration of resources upon munitions production meant that production of civilian goods suffered drastically.[4] Acute privation, overwork, and desperate war-weariness among the population were natural consequences.

During 1945 the Soviet Government conducted their economic affairs without the benefit of a master plan. Presumably emergency reconversion and reconstruction absorbed the attention of the Government. War booty, reparations, and the forced labour of prisoners of war supplemented the normal resources of the Russian economy. The net importance of these

[1] Cmd. 8201, table 10, p. 22.

[2] UNRRA operations in the Ukraine and White Russia and a Lend-Lease 'pipe-line' credit from the United States constituted exceptions; but their scale was comparatively small. UNRRA deliveries to the Ukraine and White Russia were valued at $249 million, and the pipe-line credit was estimated at $244 million. By contrast, Lend-Lease deliveries in the first six months of 1945 alone had been valued at $2,169 million.

[3] Abram Bergson, James Horton Blackman, and Alexander Erlich: 'Postwar Economic Reconstruction and Development in the U.S.S.R.', *Annals of the American Academy of Political and Social Science*, May 1949, p. 53.

[4] An estimate of Russian industrial production shows the following changes:

	Gross value of output (in millions of 1926–7 roubles)	
	1940	*1945*
All industry	138,000	127,000
Munitions and heavy industry	84,000	96,000
Consumers' goods industries	54,000	31,000

(ibid. p. 59).

items cannot be estimated, but was certainly substantial and may have more than made good the stoppage of Lend-Lease supplies.[1]

As the immediate emergency of war and readjustment to peace passed, more systematic control of the economy and plans for the future expansion of production were drawn up by the State Planning Commission. On 9 February 1946 Stalin announced that a new Five-Year Plan would soon be ready, and it was presented to the Supreme Soviet on 13 March. Two days later Nikolai Voznesensky, chairman of the State Planning Commission, described the new Five-Year Plan to the members of the Supreme Soviet in a very interesting speech. He began by explaining that the victory which had been won by Soviet arms resulted from the pre-war policy of industrialization and the collectivization of agriculture. Now it was necessary to restore the damage of the war and to advance farther. Listing the goals of the fourth Five-Year Plan he put the development of heavy industry and railway transport first, while production of consumers' goods came second. This emphasis conformed to the pre-war practice of the Soviet Government, and presaged continued privation for the Russian people. In Voznesensky's words: 'The rate of growth of the output of means of production somewhat exceeds that of the output of articles of consumption.' This was necessary, because 'to slow down the pace of rehabilitation and the further development of the national economy of the U.S.S.R. means to fall behind, and those who fall behind are beaten. This is why we must achieve the pace of development envisaged by the Five-Year Plan.'[2]

What falling behind meant was, first and foremost, falling behind militarily. One of the five main goals of the new plan was 'to supply the armed forces of the Soviet Union with the most modern military equipment', since 'monopolistic capitalism is capable of breeding new aggressors'. Indeed military considerations underlay the whole plan, even though Voznesensky's speech and the text of the Plan itself[3] were designed to obscure the fact. Thus, atomic research was provided for in the plan, but Voznesensky explained that such work would be directed towards 'the needs of industry and transport'. Similarly the development of new

[1] In March 1947 the British Foreign Minister asserted that Soviet reparations from Germany alone had reached a value of $7,000 million. Other estimates are lower, but all must be guesses. Cf. Franz L. Neumann: 'Soviet Policy in Germany', *Annals of the American Academy of Political and Social Science*, May 1949, pp. 174–5; J. P. Nettl: *The Eastern Zone and Soviet Policy in Germany 1945–50* (London, Oxford University Press, 1951), pp. 237–8. If one adds the booty and reparations from the rest of Eastern Europe and from Manchuria, the total value becomes very great. No over-all estimate seems possible, however. Cf. Alexander Gershenkron: 'Russia's Trade in the Postwar Years', *Annals of the American Academy of Political and Social Science*, May 1949, pp. 88–90.

[2] These and subsequent quotations from Voznesensky's speech are taken from *Soviet Monitor*, bulletins nos. 7075, 7076 (Saturday, March 16, 1946) issued in London by Tass Agency in mimeographed form.

[3] *Law on the Five Year Plan, 1946–50* (London, Soviet News, 1946) is an official translation.

industry was to be concentrated in the Urals and Siberia, while industrial reconstruction in western and more exposed parts of the Soviet Union would not go much beyond restoration of pre-war capacity; but Voznesensky justified this policy on the ground that it would bring new enterprises to 'districts and towns possessing the requisite fuel, power, and raw material resources'.

Despite the obvious bias of the plan in the direction of heavy industry and armament, it did offer the hope of improved living conditions for the hard-pressed population. Voznesensky explained that bread and flour rationing would end in 1946 and promised that all other forms of civilian rationing would end in 1947. Wages were to rise and costs decline until pre-war living standards were surpassed.

The over-all goals of production embodied in the plan were very ambitious. Gross industrial output was to rise by 1950 to 148 per cent. of the pre-war figure, and this despite the fact that production in the devastated districts of the Soviet Union had not nearly recovered from the war at the time the plan was introduced. Moreover, this was to be achieved without foreign aid. In Voznesensky's words, the Government intended to maintain 'the well-tried policy of . . . ensuring the technical and economic independence of the Soviet Union'.

It seems clear that the fourth Five-Year Plan represented a return to the same principles of economic management which had inspired the earlier plans of the 1930s. The leading characteristic of Stalin's economic policy remained the ruthless subordination of welfare to national security conceived primarily in terms of military strength.[1] Just as the victory in 1945 was held to have justified the policy of the 1930s, so the danger of new war was held before the Russian people to justify the continuation of the policy in 1946. The Soviet Government regarded their people as instruments to be used first of all to secure the state against its potential enemies; and compared to this overriding goal their welfare had to take second place. Russia's age-old poverty made second place a very lean one indeed. Despite Voznesensky's rosy prognosis, it seemed probable that even the low pre-war living standards had not been recovered in the Soviet Union by 1949.[2]

Information about the Soviet economy is so scanty and imperfect that

[1] This is not to say that the whole Bolshevik movement was not sustained by a hope of future welfare; but such a millennial hope was ever subject to postponement. Industrialization and Communist world revolution, removing the danger from encircling capitalism, had to come to their appointed completion before welfare could supplant security as the primary goal of Soviet economic policy. Nevertheless the hope of better things to come, if not in this generation then in some future generation, can be a very powerful human motive, and may help to make otherwise intolerable conditions tolerable. It seems entirely likely that the Marxian vision of a stateless, classless, harmonious, and wealthy society played and continues to play this role in Russia for hundreds of thousands if not for millions of persons.

[2] Bergson and others, op. cit. p. 62.

it must be largely a matter of guesswork to estimate actual achievements. However, the following table may show something of the trend in 1945 and 1946.

Soviet Production[1]

	1940	*1945*	*1946*
Coal, million tons	166	113	124
Electric power, thousand million kilowatts	48·3	43·2	47·5
Pig iron, million tons	15	9·2	10·2
Steel, million tons	18·3	11·2	12·2
Cotton cloth, million meters	4,005	1,674	1,959
Woollen cloth, million meters	119·8	56·9	74·0
Grain, million tons	119	66	61
Cotton, million tons	2·7	1·2	1·7
Cattle, million head	54·5	47·0	46·8
Hogs, million head	27·5	10·4	8·6

If these figures are approximately accurate, it is obvious that Russian production had not recovered its 1940 level by the end of 1946. Recovery of heavy industry was far ahead of consumers' production, as would be expected from the war-pattern and from the bias of Soviet post-war policy. The almost catastrophic condition of agriculture reflected in the decline of grain production and the decrease of animal population was largely the result of severe drought in 1946. This unpredictable misfortune made it necessary to postpone the abolition of food rationing until after the time Voznesensky had promised. Crop failure must have brought hunger to many Russian households in 1946.

Russia's poverty and the determination of the Soviet Government to remain militarily strong at all costs dictated Russian economic policy. Britain's trade deficit and the wish of the British Government to improve and equalize the living conditions of the population determined the course of British economic policy. The policy of neither Government fitted with the American hope for freer international trade and financial exchange. Had the United States been willing to continue Lend-Lease into peace-time and divert American goods to assist the industrial reconstruction and advance of her two principal Allies, it is possible (though, in Russia's case, not likely) that something approximating the American liberal ideal could have been realized. But such a step was politically and psychologically out of the question. Facing shortages at home, Americans were not willing significantly to reduce their own standard of living to assist other nations; yet, given the devastated condition of the world, a drastic reduction of

[1] Bergson and others, op. cit. pp. 56–57.

American consumption would have been necessary to provide a more nearly equal base upon which to construct the liberal economic order of American dreams.[1]

(c) American Efforts to establish Liberal International Economic Relations

At Potsdam those among Truman's advisers who advocated a broad interpretation of the Lend-Lease Act won a victory when they persuaded the President to approve use of Lend-Lease for the provisionment of British and French occupation forces in Germany.[2] But the end of the Japanese war put a new complexion on the matter. Lend-Lease had been conceived as an extraordinary measure. The argument that extraordinary conditions did not evaporate with the cessation of the fighting could not countervail the general American belief that gifts to other countries should end with the war. In 1945 Congress had explicitly forbidden the use of Lend-Lease funds for post-war relief, rehabilitation, or reconstruction.[3] Therefore, even had he wished to do so, Truman would have found it difficult to continue Lend-Lease after V-J day.[4] He did not so wish, and on 21 August 1945 the President announced that from the time of Japan's formal surrender Lend-Lease would stop. Thus at one stroke Truman decreed the end of the principal link which had bound the national economies of the Grand Alliance together.

The impact of the blow was mitigated, however, by the concomitant offer to complete the delivery, on terms to be negotiated, of Lend-Lease goods already on order. Moreover, the idea of demanding repayment for Lend-Lease was dropped. In a message to Congress, on 6 September 1945, Truman declared: 'We must recognize that it will not be possible for our Allies to pay us dollars for the overwhelming portion of the lend-lease obligations which they have incurred.'[5]

It was equally impossible for most countries to pay cash for the Lend-Lease 'pipe-line', and in the following weeks the American Government negotiated a series of agreements whereby these deliveries were to proceed on credit. One of the earliest agreements was concluded with the Soviet Union on 15 October 1945. The Americans undertook to deliver a long list of goods which had been on order for the Russians at the time of V-J

[1] It is, perhaps, a universal trait of human nature to refuse any such self-sacrifice save in the face of a tangible enemy. Thus it was Hitler as much as Roosevelt who built Lend-Lease; one may surmise that it was the bogy of capitalist encirclement that made Stalin's fourth Five-Year Plan supportable; and it was the Communist threat that persuaded the United States Congress to make American goods available on credit or as gifts to non-Communist nations in 1946 and after.

[2] See above, p. 632.

[3] See above, p. 513.

[4] For the termination of Lend-Lease, see also Appendix II, pp. 784–6 below. A discussion of the question will also be found in the *Survey* for 1939–46: *The Realignment of Europe*, with special reference to the effect on Britain's economic position.

[5] *Documents on American Foreign Relations, 1945–1946*, p. 127.

day. The Russians promised to pay for these goods in dollars, beginning on 1 July 1954. The loan was to bear interest at the rate of $2\frac{3}{8}$ per cent. per annum, and its total amount was to be fixed only when the goods had been delivered and their cost determined.[1] The value of goods delivered under this agreement was estimated at the end of 1946 to be $244 million. By the end of 1946 similar pipe-line agreements had been concluded with thirteen countries, and the total value of the goods exported from the United States in accordance with the terms of these agreements was estimated at about $1,200 million.[2] In most cases deliveries were made on credit, but in some instances, e.g. Australia and New Zealand, an immediate cash settlement was arranged.

The American Government made two major exceptions to the policy of shutting off Lend-Lease with V-J day.[3] The economy of China was as chaotic as was her political and military condition. To expect repayment for any American aid provided to the Chinese Government was, under the circumstances, an absurdity; yet not to help Chiang Kai-shek would open the path to the Communists in the north and would hinder the disarmament and repatriation of Japanese troops located in China. Consequently, the American Government decided to continue Lend-Lease aid to China, and in fact the total value of supplies and services provided to the Chinese after V-J day was almost exactly equal to all Lend-Lease deliveries made during the war. It was not until 30 June 1946 that Lend-Lease to China was stopped, and a 'pipe-line' credit substituted to finance still further deliveries.[4]

The case of Italy also demanded special treatment. An allocation of $100 million from Lend-Lease funds was made on 15 June 1945 for civilian relief in Italy. When V-J day came this programme was not cancelled, but continued in operation until the end of the year. In addition, industrial machinery and supplies, worth $73 million, were shipped to Italy through Lend-Lease channels during 1945. This credit was made available to the Italian Government in compensation for the lire issued to American troops as pay.[5] From the beginning of 1946, however, responsibility for Italian relief and reconstruction passed to UNRRA.

By far the most important Lend-Lease account was, of course, the British. The intimate intermixture between British and American military supply systems in many parts of the world, and the fact that a large portion of Britain's civilian supplies had come through Lend-Lease channels made

[1] For text of the agreement see ibid. pp. 127–32.
[2] *Twenty-third Report on Lend-Lease Operations*, p. 5.
[3] See also Appendix II, p. 785 below.
[4] *Twenty-third Report on Lend-Lease Operations*, p. 17.
[5] Ibid. pp. 25–26.

it almost impossible to end Lend-Lease abruptly on 2 September; and in fact American aid and British Mutual Aid continued to operate until the end of the year. Negotiation to define the future economic relations between the two countries and simultaneously to settle the Lend-Lease and Mutual Aid accounts were undertaken without delay, beginning on 13 September 1945. A series of agreements resulting from the negotiation was announced on 6 December 1945.

By these agreements, an accounting was to be made of services and supplies delivered by either country to the other between V-J day and 31 December 1945, when all such transactions would end. A preliminary estimate showed that Britain would owe a total of about $118 million as a result of these exchanges. In addition, Britain's net obligation from Lend-Lease and Mutual Aid operations prior to V-J day was fixed at $532 million, making a sum total of $650 million owed by Great Britain.[1] This debt was to be paid off on the same terms as the new British loan of $3,750 million which was negotiated at the same time.[2]

The method by which the sum of $650 million was arrived at was complex and need not be described here in detail. In general, all supplies consumed or destroyed during the war were written off. Accounting was applied only to stocks of goods on hand at V-J day and to the pipe-line deliveries. Moreover, the United States retained title to munitions and military supplies which had been provided to Britain, and reserved the right to repossess such items, but on the understanding that the right would not be exercised generally. On this basis, the value of all military supplies was omitted from the calculation of the sum due to the United States. What *was* counted were civilian supplies—mainly food and raw materials, non-combat aircraft, petroleum stocks, and permanent installations located in the two countries.

In view of the fact that the total value of Lend-Lease supplies to Great Britain was calculated by the Americans at $31,393 million, while Mutual Aid to the United States was valued by the British at £1,201 million, a settlement for $650 million can properly be regarded as generous. As for the 'benefit to the United States' prescribed in the original Lend-Lease Act, it was the defeat of the enemy; and the Anglo-American Joint Statement which outlined the terms of settlement said so explicitly.[3] Roosevelt's determination to avoid war debts like those which troubled international relations during the 1920s and 1930s had borne fruit.

The settlement of the British Lend-Lease account provided a pattern for subsequent settlements with other countries. An agreement with India

[1] These figures were subject to subsequent adjustment, and the Lend-Lease/Mutual Aid account was not finally closed until after a number of detailed supplementary agreements had been concluded in March 1946 (see Appendix II, p. 786 below).

[2] For an account of the British loan, see below, pp. 682 seqq.

[3] *Documents on American Foreign Relations, 1945–1946*, pp. 132–4.

was reached on 16 May 1946, with France on 28 May; and with Australia, New Zealand, Belgium, and Turkey in the later months of 1946. Active negotiations with South Africa, Norway, Greece, and the Netherlands led to further settlements early in 1947; but throughout 1946 Russia and her satellites in Eastern Europe shied away from any effort to wind up Lend-Lease accounts by agreement.[1]

The net effect of the pipe-line agreements and of the negotiated settlements of Lend-Lease obligations was to reduce the amount of American aid provided to other countries very sharply, while at the same time nearly all past indebtedness arising from Lend-Lease operations was written off. A system of U.S. loans covered the obligations other governments accepted as a settlement for Lend-Lease help and financed the terminal Lend-Lease deliveries. Thus, in American eyes, things were brought back to normal. In time of peace foreign governments would be expected to pay for American goods, if not at once, then sometime in the future.

It was apparent, however, that foreign countries would continue to need American goods almost as much as during the war and on a scale much larger than that provided for by the Lend-Lease pipe-line agreements. The American Government tried to meet this need by authorizing the Export-Import Bank on 31 July 1945 to increase its foreign loans to as much as $3,500 million.[2] With the end of Lend-Lease pipe-line deliveries, this became a major channel through which the export of American goods was financed in the first six months of 1946.[3] By the middle of the year, however, nearly all the Bank's funds had been allotted, and, since no increase in its lending power was authorized by Congress, its further operations were much reduced in scope. The International Bank for Reconstruction and Development, provided for at Bretton Woods, began to organize itself for operations in June 1946; and it was that organization upon which, in the official American view, further responsibility for the financing of world trade should devolve.

[1] *Twenty-third Report on Lend-Lease Operations*, p. 7.

[2] The Export-Import Bank had been established in 1934 to make loans to promote the foreign trade of the United States. Its capital was provided by the Government, and its loans were normally issued for specific purposes, and granted more or less according to normal banking practice with an eye to the financial soundness of the borrower.

[3] As of 31 December 1946 credit totalling $3,492,680,678 had been authorized by the Export-Import Bank. This sum was distributed geographically as follows:

Europe	$1,938,995,894
Asia	432,894,939
Latin America	996,227,159
Other	70,890,000

The East European countries had a good share of these loans, but the Soviet Union was conspicuous by its absence. For a tabulation of the loans by country, see *Documents on American Foreign Relations, 1945–1946*, pp. 638–9.

The gradual transition from Lend-Lease to the International Bank as the device for financing American exports took place according to the pattern for which American officials had hoped. It was a transition from extraordinary war-time methods to new peace-time practices; and the only thing wrong with the scheme was that the International Bank's resources were inadequate to meet world needs, and the international political climate was unpropitious for the international financial and trade policies to which the International Bank's Charter committed that institution.[1] New 'extraordinary' measures had to be taken even in 1946, and the International Bank in fact never had more than marginal importance as a regulator of international dealings.

The dissolution of the Anglo-American Combined Boards[2] followed a similar pattern. On 25 September 1945 Truman approved a statement of American policy which called for the early abolition of the Boards, while at the same time foreseeing the desirability of creating a number of inter-governmental committees to allocate materials which remained in global short supply. In October Canada and Great Britain accepted the American statement and agreed that the Combined Raw Materials Board and the Combined Production and Resources Board should be abolished on 31 December 1945. The Combined Food Board, however, won a reprieve until 30 June 1946 owing to the serious food shortage which threatened Europe and the entire world.

The C.R.M.B. and C.P.R.B. were replaced by five international 'commodity committees' whose responsibility was the allocation of tin, hides and leather, cotton cloth, rubber, and coal. Membership varied, being designed to include the major national producers and consumers of each commodity. In due course the Combined Food Board was succeeded by an International Emergency Food Council, established under the aegis of the Food and Agriculture Organization of the United Nations. This new body took over on 1 July 1946. But, in proportion as Anglo-American domination of the raw materials and food exchanges of the world was relinquished to bodies with a wider representation, the effectiveness of inter-governmental consultation decreased. By the middle of 1946 co-operative action in these fields had largely come to an end, and each nation went its own way.[3]

[1] Russia's failure to ratify the Bretton Woods agreements symbolized the breakdown of the whole scheme. The participating nations tried to entice the Russians into joining by extending the deadline for adherence until the end of 1946, but without success. This meant, of course, that instead of being world-wide financial institutions the Bank and Monetary Fund were limited to the non-Communist world.

[2] See above, p. 129, for the establishment of the Combined Boards in January 1942.

[3] Rosen: *The Combined Boards in the Second World War*, pp. 64–70, 249–50.

The Combined Shipping Adjustment Board had met disaster earlier. It remained nominally in existence until 1946, but was moribund from the early months of 1943.[1] In August 1944 an effort, largely inspired by the British Government, was made to recover some of the lost ground. A new inter-governmental body, the United Maritime Authority, was set up for the specific purpose of regulating shipping after the end of the German war and for a period not exceeding six months after V-J day. This body, to which sixteen nations eventually adhered, faced the problems of the immediate post-war shipping shortage with some success; but when the big task of shipping soldiers home had been largely completed, it seemed possible for the various sea-faring nations to return to national control of their merchant marines as the United States and some other nations wished to do. Consequently, when, six months after V-J day, the United Maritime Authority was duly dissolved, on 2 March 1946, it was succeeded by a United Maritime Consultative Council with merely advisory and informational functions.[2]

The Combined Chiefs of Staff and the Munitions Assignment Board—by far the most significant and successful of the Combined Boards established at the Arcadia Conference in 1942—were not dissolved so hastily, though, of course, the Munitions Assignment Board ceased most of its activities with the end of hostilities. But even in the military sphere the Americans were not enthusiastic about a continuation of the special war-time partnership with Britain, and they agreed to keep the Combined Chiefs of Staff Committee in existence only until the peace treaties had been signed—an event which then seemed not far in the future.[3] In anticipation of an early liquidation of the Anglo-American military partnership, a growing reserve, especially on the American side, checked the free flow of information and reduced the frankness with which questions of military policy were discussed on the Combined Chiefs of Staff Committee.[4] It thus lost its war-time importance.[5]

The weakening of Anglo-American military co-operation was particularly notable in the field of atomic research. Even during the war Ameri-

[1] See above, pp. 132–4.

[2] For extracts from the relevant agreements see *Documents on American Foreign Relations, 1944–1945*, pp. 631–5; *1945–1946*, pp. 672–5.

[3] The demise of the Combined Chiefs of Staff Committee was announced on 28 September 1949. The body was never formally disbanded; rather, it lapsed as new channels for military consultation came to be established in connexion with the North Atlantic Treaty Organization; and the announcement of 28 September 1949 merely confirmed existing fact (cf. *Manchester Guardian*, 29 September 1949). The Munitions Assignment Board, presumably, underwent a similar dissolution.

[4] Wilson: *Eight Years Overseas*, pp. 261–2.

[5] The converse of this change was the reassertion within the American Government of the primacy of the State Department in all dealings with foreign countries. This in turn was partly a question of personalities. Byrnes was not the man to allow others to tread on his toes; and the resignation of men like Secretary of War Stimson (September 1945) and General Marshall (November 1945) weakened the prestige of the military in matters affecting foreign affairs.

can policy had been to keep some of the secrets of atomic bomb production in American hands, and when the war ended the British and Canadian share in American atomic work soon came to an end.[1] When Congress found time to define the future of atomic research and development by law, it confirmed and extended the policy of secrecy. Not only military but peaceable uses of atomic energy were put under secret seal.[2] Thus, the Atomic Energy Act of 1946 established a special Commission to control the development of atomic energy in the United States, and instructed the Commission 'that until Congress declares by joint resolution that effective and enforceable international safeguards against the use of atomic energy for destructive purposes have been established, there shall be no exchange of information with other nations with respect to the use of atomic energy for industrial purposes. . . .'[3] This did not mean that the United States intended to try to retain an indefinite monopoly of atomic power. But international participation in atomic development was, according to the American (and British) view, to be contingent upon the prior establishment of an effective system of international inspection and control under the United Nations.[4]

While the war-time forms of Allied economic co-operation were thus terminated, attenuated, or transmuted into what it was hoped might be permanent international institutions, UNRRA, conceived as a means for bridging the difficult post-war period, came into its own. When the United Nations Relief and Rehabilitation Administration was first established, in November 1943,[5] its projected task was to supply relief to liberated countries. At the second session of the UNRRA Council, in September 1944, the scope of UNRRA operations was enlarged by a resolution permitting operations in ex-enemy countries for the relief of displaced persons, and, in addition, UNRRA undertook to provide a limited scale of relief to the people of Italy. In August 1945 policy was further altered to accord equal status to Italy and to Austria, and in February 1946 Hungary was also made eligible for relief. Germany and Japan, however, remained without the pale, and maintenance of the population in those countries became the responsibility of the occupying forces.

Numerous administrative difficulties, including the not inconsiderable problem of shipping, delayed the beginning of large-scale UNRRA operations until 1946. The organization terminated its major activities by the

[1] Leahy: *I Was There*, p. 505.

[2] This, of course, overrode Roosevelt's assurances to Churchill on the subject. See above, p. 493.

[3] *Documents on American Foreign Relations, 1945–1946*, p. 443.

[4] For an account of negotiations for the international control of atomic energy see below, pp. 710–11, 744–5.

[5] See above, p. 314.

middle of 1947. Between these dates, however, UNRRA was an important factor in the international exchange of goods, and helped to stave off the worst suffering which would otherwise have visited the population of the war-devastated countries.

Altogether UNRRA handled resources valued at $3,968 million, and distributed commodities worth $3,683 million, the difference being devoted to administrative expenses and transfers to various successor agencies. By far the largest contribution of funds to UNRRA came from the United States Government—$2,668 million or nearly 65 per cent. of the total. The British Government was the second largest contributor, with $617 million (nearly 15 per cent.) and Canada came third with $139 million (3½ per cent.). Seventeen nations received UNRRA aid, but eight of these far outbalanced the remainder. The value of goods shipped by UNRRA to these eight principal recipients may be seen from the following table:[1]

	million $		*million* $
China	518	Greece	347
Poland	478	Czechoslovakia	261
Italy	418	Ukraine	188
Yugoslavia	416	Austria	136

The notable fact about these figures was the political neutrality with which relief and other supplies were distributed by UNRRA. This, of course, was a leading principle of the organization, and was the main reason why post-war relief had been entrusted to an international body in the first place. But as relations between the Anglo-Americans and Russia worsened, the United States and Great Britain found themselves in the position of providing supplies through UNRRA to unfriendly nations of Eastern Europe. This was not to the liking of Secretary of State Byrnes. American Congressmen disapproved even more strongly, and voted the second appropriations for UNRRA with reluctance and only after some months' delay. All proposals for the continuance of UNRRA's operations after midsummer 1947 met with growing American resistance. A full year before UNRRA ended its activities Byrnes had come to the conclusion that 'any new appropriations by Congress for foreign relief should be allocated by the United States'.[2] This American attitude was decisive, and the organization's operations came to an end in the course of the first half of 1947, not because rehabilitation had been achieved but because there were no more funds.

The UNRRA experiment had its place in the general American plan for international co-operation towards a liberal post-war economic system. Its hasty termination reflected the general failure of that dream. We must

[1] Woodbridge: *UNRRA*, iii. 428, 498–500.

[2] Byrnes: *Speaking Frankly*, p. 146.

now consider the leading manifestations of the pattern of international economic relations which supplanted the liberal blue-print of 1944 and 1945.

(d) Return to Political Economics

The major axis upon which international economic relations in 1946 turned was the American loan to Britain. Its fate nicely illustrates the change which came over American foreign economic policy. The loan was negotiated and first presented to the American Congress and public as a means of assuring the early establishment of freer international trade; it was finally passed by the House of Representatives as a means of stopping Russia. To be sure, political feeling was not absent from the early stages of the loan negotiation, nor did the Americans abandon their faith in the usefulness of the loan as a step towards the liberalization of international trade when it was finally approved by Congress. But the emphasis definitely and unmistakably shifted in the course of the seven months' debate which preceded Congressional ratification of the loan agreement.

The Anglo-American Financial and Trade Agreement, as it was called officially, was first announced on 6 December 1945. It was connected with, though legally independent of, the Lend-Lease/Mutual Aid settlement described above.[1] As the Lend-Lease settlement regulated the war-time economic dealings of Britain and America, so the new 'line of credit',[2] together with accompanying agreements on future trade and financial policies, was intended to regulate future economic relations between the two countries.

The famous economist, Lord Keynes, headed the British mission which negotiated the Financial and Trade Agreement. As he explained afterwards to the House of Lords, Keynes approached the negotiation with the hope that he could persuade the Americans to assist Britain's conversion to a viable peace-time economy 'by financial aid that approximated to a grant'. In particular, he hoped that no interest charges would be levied.[3] The sort of arrangement the British delegation had in mind would have amounted to a prolongation of Lend-Lease; and they were prepared to argue their case on the ground that Britain's economic sacrifices had been disproportionately great, especially during the years 1939–41 before Lend-Lease became operative. In effect, the British proposed that the principle of equal sacrifice, which American officials accepted as a general criterion for the settlement of Lend-Lease accounts, should be applied

[1] See above, pp. 674–8.

[2] So called because the American Government undertook to advance credit as needed by the British Government up to a total of $3,750 million, but did not at once transfer the total amount to Britain's account as would be the normal procedure with a loan. This, of course, reduced the incidence of interest charges, and was designed for that purpose.

[3] 18 December 1945, H.L.Deb. 5th ser., vol. 138, coll. 780, 784.

retrospectively to the 1939–41 period. As for the uses to which American aid should be put, and future British economic policy generally, Keynes and his colleagues hoped to avoid hard and fast commitments.[1]

The Americans, however, were not inclined to embark on invidious comparisons of past sacrifices. Too many other Allied nations could, on any such basis, demand American help. Instead, the Americans looked mainly to the future, holding before themselves an image of a prosperous, peaceful world; and they sought to use their economic power to forward their hopes. As Keynes put it: 'Our American friends were interested not in our wounds, though incurred in the common cause, but in our convalescence.' Convalescence to the Americans meant international co-operation to reduce political obstacles to trade, and the acceptance of international rules which would prevent economic warfare of the type which had been practised so effectively by the Nazis in the 1930s. *Vis-à-vis* Britain, this meant that in return for a loan the Americans demanded a definite undertaking from the British Government that Empire tariff preference and the blockage of sterling accounts would be eliminated or drastically modified. This seemed to the Americans to be a necessary first step towards the establishment of non-discriminatory multilateral world trade upon which, in turn, they believed the hope of stable peace and international prosperity rested. American experts agreed that to charge interest for the loan would put an unwise strain on British capacity to pay, but they felt that an interest-free loan would not prove acceptable to Congress. Consequently they insisted upon interest, but made the terms as favourable as they could.

Since the Americans were in a position to grant or withhold help, they held all the trumps in the negotiation. Failure to reach agreement would not have hurt the American economy very much; it would have come close to crippling Britain. It followed that on most disputed points the British delegation was compelled to yield, save when their arguments genuinely convinced the Americans. Thus the total finally agreed upon, $3,750 million, was smaller than the British had hoped for. It seemed to Lord Keynes a bare minimum with which to cover the anticipated trade deficits of the next five years during which the credit was to run. Secondly, the British negotiators yielded to the American demand for abrogation of special financial controls which hindered the conversion of pounds into dollars. In the words of the Agreement:

> The Government of the United Kingdom will complete arrangements as early as practicable and in any case not later than one year after the effective date of this Agreement, unless in exceptional cases a later date is agreed upon after consultation, under which . . . the sterling receipts from current transactions . . . will be freely available for current transactions in any currency area without

[1] Ibid. coll. 779–81.

discrimination; with the result that . . . each member of the sterling area will have its current sterling and dollar receipts at its free disposition for current transactions anywhere.[1]

As far as Empire tariff preference was concerned, the British commitment was far less definite. The Trade and Financial Agreement itself contained only a passing reference to 'the fact that an important purpose of the present line of credit is to promote the development of multilateral trade and promote its early resumption on a non-discriminatory basis'; but a Joint Statement issued by the two Governments on the same day, 6 December 1945, was rather more specific. The American Government made public a series of proposals for consideration by an International Conference on Trade and Employment.[2] These proposals, among other things, called for elimination of discriminatory tariffs; and the Joint Statement of 6 December declared that

. . . the Government of the United Kingdom is in full agreement on all important points in these proposals and accepts them as a basis for international discussion. . . .

The two Governments have also agreed upon the procedures for the international negotiation and implementation of these proposals. To this end they have undertaken to begin preliminary negotiations . . . for the purpose of developing concrete arrangements to carry out these proposals, including definitive measures for the relaxation of trade barriers of all kinds.[3]

This heavy verbiage boiled down to a British promise to consider favourably the elimination of Empire tariff preference as part of a general international agreement to reduce barriers to trade.

The loan terms were very favourable to Great Britain. Repayment was not to begin until 31 December 1951; it was to occur in fifty annual instalments, and interest was set at 2 per cent. Moreover, the Americans promised to waive interest whenever British trade balance fell below the levels of 1936–8; and interest so waived would not be added to the debt but simply written off. This clause meant that in bad times Britain would in effect enjoy an interest-free loan such as Lord Keynes had originally sought.

When the Agreement was first announced, reaction in both Britain and America was lukewarm to hostile. Many Americans felt that the time had come to stop foreign lending on so large a scale, and some felt that the British had no claim to specially favourable terms. The British, on the other hand, felt that the Americans had driven a very hard bargain and were taking advantage of Britain's economic prostration to undermine the economic ties of Empire. In particular, the British objected to the one-

[1] *Documents on American Foreign Relations, 1945–1946*, p. 647.

[2] A fuller discussion of these proposals will be found in the *Survey* for 1939–46: *The Realignment of Europe.*

[3] *Documents on American Foreign Relations, 1945–1946*, pp. 627–8.

sidedness of the promises embodied in the Agreement and related papers. Britain undertook to remove foreign exchange controls and promised to consider favourably removal of Empire preference; but the United States promised nothing, and, as British economists could very reasonably point out, the American tariff was a more serious obstacle to international trade than was Empire preference.[1] Lord Beaverbrook and other supporters of Empire were vocal in their objection to the Agreement, and the Beaverbrook press conducted a long campaign against it. Nevertheless the need for a continued flow of American goods to sustain the economy was urgent. Knowing this, the House of Commons ratified the Agreement, by 345 votes to 98, on 13 December 1945.[2]

When the Financial and Trade Agreement was drawn up, the two Governments assumed that it would come into effect at the beginning of 1946. Some delay due to the slowness of the American Congress had been expected, but no one imagined that seven months would pass before the House of Representatives finally approved the Agreement. The interim was an anxious time for Great Britain. All the financial and economic planning of the British Government depended on the loan.

Truman's administration did what was possible to hasten Congressional action. It was, however, necessary to wait until Congress returned from its Christmas recess before officially presenting the Agreement on 30 January 1946, when Truman sent a special message to Congress asking for its prompt ratification. In the meanwhile, a series of speeches by leading figures in the Government and a widespread propaganda effort inspired by the administration sought to overcome public and Congressional indifference and opposition to the loan. But Congress was in no mood to jump at Truman's command, and procedure was distinctly leisurely from the start.

The Senate acted first. Debate centred mainly round economic questions. Critics of the Agreement argued that so large a loan to Britain would increase inflation at home, would open the gates to similar large loans to other countries which the United States could not afford to give, would help a dangerous competitor to American business with taxpayers' money,

[1] The United States tariff was non-discriminatory in the sense that all countries with which 'most-favoured nation' treaties had been concluded enjoyed equal rights of access to the American market. British tariffs, on the other hand, discriminated in favour of the Dominions and colonies. Thus the American tariff was not explicitly and directly challenged by the proposals for the regulation of international trade set forth by the U.S. Government, though American officials certainly hoped to be able to persuade Congress to agree to reductions in tariff protection. Otherwise repayment of the British and other loans would be nearly or quite impossible.

[2] Churchill advised his Conservative followers to abstain from voting on the measure; in spite of this seventy-two Conservatives voted against accepting the terms, together with twenty-three Labour and three Independent M.P.s.

would help Socialism, could never be repaid, and was unbusinesslike since the loan had no tangible security. Counter-arguments stressed the interest of the United States in a prosperous, trade-enriched world, and pointed out that Britain's peculiar trading position meant that the loan would not constitute a precedent for others.

After preliminary hearings before a Senate committee, the measure reached the floor on 17 April 1946. There it ran into bitter opposition. A few Senators attempted a filibuster against the loan and succeeded in holding up business for several days. Other opponents adopted the tactic of presenting amendments to the Agreement with the intention of making it unacceptable to the British Government. The chief such amendment was one requiring Great Britain to sell some of the Caribbean Islands to the United States. This amendment came up for vote on 9 May and was defeated by a narrow margin, 40 votes to 45. A decisive step in the debate was taken by Senator Arthur Vandenberg, the leading Republican spokesman on questions of foreign policy. Just before starting off for the Paris meeting of the Foreign Ministers, which he attended as a special adviser to Byrnes, he told the Senate on 22 April 1946 that after long and perplexing consideration he had come to the conclusion that the loan should be approved.[1] His speech split Republican opposition to the measure, and helped to ensure its eventual passage. Finally, after heavy pressure from Truman, the Senate voted to approve the Agreement, by 46 votes to 30, on 10 May 1946.

During the Senate debate some voices had been raised to point out the political significance of the loan. Senator Wheeler, for example, was quoted as saying: 'The only reason I can find for making the loan is to bolster the British sufficiently to head off Communism in Europe. If that's the theory, we'll have to keep on making loans to them.'[2] Various journalists pointed out the same thing in more restrained language,[3] but the official argument for the loan remained strictly economic, and most of the public and senatorial attention was directed towards its economic aspects.[4]

When the Agreement came up for debate in the House of Representatives, however, emphasis shifted. The measure was taken up by a House committee on 14 May and was reported to the floor on 8 July 1946. The familiar ground already explored by the Senate was once again thoroughly gone over, but important new considerations were also added. Testifying

[1] *The Times*, 23 April 1946.

[2] *Daily Telegraph*, 3 April 1946.

[3] e.g. *Observer*, 17 March, *Wall Street Journal*, 19 March, *New York Times*, 18 April, *New York Herald Tribune*, 6 May 1946.

[4] The official title of the Congressional resolution that finally passed both Houses reflected this stage of the debate. It was styled 'Senate Joint Resolution 138, To Implement Further the Purposes of the Bretton Woods Agreements Act by Authorizing the Secretary of the Treasury to Carry Out an Agreement with the United Kingdom, and for Other Purposes'.

for the Agreement on 16 May, Secretary of the Treasury Vinson said that there was no alternative at the moment but a division of the world between Russian and Anglo-American economic blocs. This remark provided new ammunition for critics of the measure, who asserted that the United States would in effect be allying herself with Great Britain against Russia.[1]

From this time on the major issue of the loan debate was whether in fact it would commit America to the political support of Britain in opposition to the Soviet Union; and, if so, whether that was a good or a bad thing to do. On 17 June the House committee reported favourably on the Agreement, but a minority report signed by five members declared: 'This loan will give impetus to Anglo-American imperialistic elements. Later the American people will be told this loan was advance guarantee of American money, guns and boys for all future British Empire needs and desires.'[2]

But as American opinion hardened against Russia and came to see Stalin's Government as the great obstacle to prompt settlement of world problems, this sort of argument lost its effect. Perhaps, after all, Russian imperial Communism threatened the interests of the United States as well as those of Britain; perhaps the United States had a duty to lead the free world and strengthen it against Communism; perhaps the political gains to be secured by a loan to Britain were as important as economic ones; perhaps they were even more important. If so, the Financial and Trade Agreement had everything to recommend it. More and more Congressmen came to view the question in this light as the collision between American and Russian policy became public—first at the April meeting of the Council of Foreign Ministers,[3] then, in May, in Germany.[4]

At the last minute, however, the new view of the loan negotiation raised another obstacle. British policy in Palestine had roused the opposition of American Jews and of important elements in the American Government. Would the loan constitute an endorsement of British Palestine policy? Various Zionist organizations in the United States were not backward in deciding that it would, and brought pressure to bear on Congressmen accordingly.[5]

When debate began in the House, on 8 July, the Palestine issue was

[1] *New York Times*, 16 May, *The Times*, 17 May 1946. Vinson's remark was stimulated by the failure of the Soviet Union to adhere to the World Bank and International Monetary Fund, a failure which had just become apparent.

[2] Ibid., 18 June 1946.

[3] See below, pp. 717 seqq.

[4] See below, p. 725. There is historical irony in the fact that Russia's ruthless demand for German reparations, and the resultant open quarrel with General Clay, more than any other one single factor assured the passage of the loan to Britain and closed the doors to any American loan to Russia. Stalin's ruthlessness sometimes had most damaging by-products, and this was surely one of them.

[5] *New York Times*, 4 July, *Manchester Guardian*, 6 July 1946.

relaxed somewhat as a result of a statement by Congressman Sol Bloom, chairman of the House Foreign Affairs Committee. Bloom, himself a Jew, sharply criticized British policy in Palestine but asserted that the loan was a different question which should be considered separately. 'I know', he said, 'that this loan is going to help my country. As an American I am going to vote for that which is in the best interest of my country.'[1]

The debate on the floor of the House turned almost entirely upon the political issues; but a new note was apparent. Instead of arguing that the loan would support Britain against Russia, its champions now tended to see the world contest as one directly between the United States and Russia. In the words of the Majority Leader of the House, Representative John McCormack:

> Every country in the world is watching the outcome of this vote, because on it depends whether or not, so far as they are concerned, the United States will assume its place as leader, constructive leader, among the nations of the world, or fall back again to the isolationism following the days of World War I.
>
> If we close our eyes . . . if our public officials charged with the responsibility fail through indifference, uncertainty or fear, to do the things we ought to do in our own national interests, then we leave those countries who look toward Washington with friendly eyes no alternative but to be subjected to the sphere of influence of Moscow.[2]

It was largely on the strength of this line of argument that the loan passed by a vote of 219 to 155 on 13 July 1946. The Congressional Bill was signed by Truman two days later and the Financial and Trade Agreement went into effect immediately.

It is difficult to exaggerate the importance of this debate for American foreign policy. Until about May 1946 the American Government and people had been inspired primarily by a desire to get away from the extraordinary responsibilities which the war had thrust upon them. The official programme called for a gradual transition from war-time relationships to new international arrangements which, it was hoped, would secure peace and prosperity for all the world. American sentiment never regretted the United Nations; but in 1945 and the first months of 1946 it was generally hoped and believed that foreign economic policy should operate through the various subsidiaries of the new international organization, and that all other extraordinary commitments and involvements should be sloughed off as rapidly as possible.

The discussion of the British loan stimulated a basic change in American feeling. Here was a concrete issue: should extraordinary and specially favourable economic help be extended to Great Britain? Should the

[1] *Christian Science Monitor*, 8 July 1946. [2] *New York Times*, 13 July 1946.

operation of the new international economic bodies be supplemented by acts of national policy passing through other channels? Withdrawal within national boundaries and reliance upon the legal channels of the United Nations was not as easy as had been hoped: Britain needed help and Russia was non co-operative, even threatening. After much confusion and debate, the Congress in voting for the loan in effect voted to renew the special relationship with Great Britain which had been built up during the war, and decided to face the Russian challenge with active economic counter-measures.

The debate should be compared with the 1939–41 debate between isolationists and interventionists. In both cases the fundamental point at issue was the place of the United States in the world; in both cases traditional and deep-felt views were challenged by the proposals put before Congress by the President; in both cases the issue specifically concerned American support of Britain. But the debate in 1939–41 had been longer, and it was finally terminated by the Japanese. The effect of the war-time experience, and of the special hostility which Americans felt towards Communism,[1] was reflected in the fact that this time Congress decided by itself to embark on new commitments. Yet one should also remember that the commitment in 1946 was smaller. Not military but economic assistance was in question, and it was not until 1947 that American opinion

[1] It is perhaps worth asking why American opinion was so much more easily stirred against Communist Russia than against Nazi Germany. Certainly one important factor was the war itself, which had convinced many people that American isolation from the rest of the world could no longer work. Another factor was the idealism which Roosevelt had generated: its disappointment in the immediate post-war world could most easily be explained as the result of evil machinations by the Russians, and efforts to realize the ideal of a peaceful and prosperous world came inevitably to wear the guise of determined opposition to Russian policies which conflicted with the ideal.

There was, however, another aspect to the situation. Nazi ideas were by their very nature confined in their appeal to members of the appropriate racial groups. Communism, on the other hand, was universal. It followed that the Communist criticism of American institutions and practices was more direct and damaging than anything Nazi propagandists had been able to use. Moreover, during the 1930s Communist criticism of American life had attracted some important sympathizers in certain intellectual circles in the United States. A crusade against Communism abroad was thus intimately mixed up with a domestic political struggle to eliminate critics of capitalism from places of influence in American domestic affairs—in particular, from the Government.

In terms of practical politics, it was of the utmost importance that the groups among which residual isolationist sentiment was strongest were simultaneously the groups most opposed to Communism. As a result, no large and influential body of opinion could be mobilized against foreign policies designed to oppose Russia and Communism. Only out-and-out Communists—and they were so few as to be nearly negligible as a popular force—opposed the new direction of American policy in an organized fashion. Rooseveltian liberals who had aspired ardently to a world of universal law united with conservatives in believing that Russia was the main threat to their hopes for the future despite the wide difference in the substance of such hopes.

When Nazi aggression began no comparable complex of hopes and fears existed to mobilize American opinion against Hitler. The contrast between American policy in the 1930s and American policy in the late 1940s must be understood in terms such as these.

came round to support military and political action against Russian expansion.

The decision to support Britain marked a real turning-point in American policy. The idea of post-war withdrawal from Europe soon faded away after July 1946; American leadership of free Europe against Russia and her satellites came rapidly to the fore as a substitute goal of American policy. Inevitably faith in the United Nations as a cure for the world's ills faded too as the American Government decided to pursue national policies outside its framework. But all these changes came gradually, and at the time were not perfectly understood. Some who supported the loan to Britain hoped it would be a precursor to a similar loan to Russia.[1] Still others put the liberal economic goals embodied in the Agreement first, and regarded the political angle as subordinate or unfortunate.

Nevertheless, when due allowance is made for these confusions and misinterpretations of the significance of the decision, it seems fair to say that in voting for the loan the U.S. Congress half-knowingly reverted to the subordination of economic to political policy which had characterized international economic relations during the war years. It was not Britain's financial soundness, in the traditional bankers' sense, that most concerned Congress when it approved the loan; instead it was its political soundness against Communism; and after July 1946 this became more and more explicitly the criterion used by the United States Government in granting and withholding loans.[2]

The fate of the negotiation between the United States and Russia for the settlement of Lend-Lease accounts and for the advance of additional American credits to the Soviet Union reflected the gradual shift in American attitudes. Official records were not available in 1952, but according to newspaper reports the course of negotiation was as follows. As early as January 1945 Stalin opened the question of future American credits, suggesting that Russia would need a loan of about $6 milliard to tide over post-war reconstruction. This suggestion was met by American refusal on the ground that so large a sum was not available.[3] In August

[1] Henry Wallace, Secretary of Commerce, was the most prominent figure who took this position.

[2] A minor but illustrative instance of the policy in action was the cancellation, on 16 October 1946, of a loan made by the Export-Import Bank to Czechoslovakia. This resulted largely from the fact that Secretary of State Byrnes noticed Czech delegates at the Paris Peace Conference applauding a Russian reference to American dollar imperialism. If a Czech Government under Communist influence feared political domination as a result of American financial support, he determined to remove the cause of their alarm, and arranged for the cancellation of the loan (Byrnes: *Speaking Frankly*, pp. 143–4).

[3] This reply was something less than frank. High officials of the American Government opposed a policy of extending credits to Russia without attaching strings that would, in Ambassador Harriman's phrase, 'protect American vital interests' (*Forrestal Diaries*, p. 41).

1945 the Russians made a second approach, suggesting a total of \$1 milliard instead. This request was made to the Foreign Economic Administration, which shortly afterwards was abolished as part of the post-war administrative reorganization of the American Government.[1] Its records were transferred to the State Department, which thenceforward assumed responsibility for foreign economic policy. In the confusion, according to the official story, the papers pertaining to the Russian request for a credit of \$1 milliard were lost and forgotten until they happened to be rediscovered about the end of February 1946.[2]

When the long-standing Russian proposal was uncovered, the American Government sent off a note explaining the situation and suggesting that discussion of a loan should be connected with a settlement of Lend-Lease and a discussion of Russian foreign economic policy generally. This was the identical procedure which had been followed in the negotiation with Great Britain and other Allied countries; but the Russians chose to interpret it as a clear case of American financial aggression. The Americans were proposing to bring into question Russia's economic dealings with her satellites in Eastern Europe, where a series of treaties had assured Russia of especially favourable trade terms.[3] This was unacceptable, and the Russians said so in a reply delivered on 15 March.[4]

About a month later the United States sent a reply urging a prompt beginning of negotiations. Some effort was made to meet Russian objections to the original American proposal, but the State Department was still firmly committed to the ideal of non-discriminatory trade and would not agree to overlook Russian policies in Eastern Europe.[5]

This was the situation when the Export-Import Bank decided that there was no use in waiting any longer for agreement to be reached with Russia. On 9 May it was announced that the sum of \$1 milliard which had provisionally been earmarked for a loan to Russia would instead be used for loans to France, China, and Italy. But the American Government had

[1] See above, pp. 665–6.

[2] *New York Times*, 1 and 3 March, 21 April 1946. It may seem difficult to believe this story, yet it is impossible to explain on any other basis the public assertions made by the Secretary of the Treasury and others in the first months of 1946 that no request for a loan to Russia had been received by the American Government. The rapidity with which the war-time administrative machine was broken up and the speed with which key members of such a body as the Foreign Economic Administration returned to private life can alone account for such an amazing oversight; but one can imagine how the Russians interpreted the American action. It is quite possible that some officer of F.E.A., disliking the whole idea of a loan to Russia, quietly buried the relevant documents in the files and failed to notify his successor of their existence.

[3] For a description of Russian trade relations with these countries see Margaret Dewar: *Soviet Trade with Eastern Europe, 1945–1949* (London, Royal Institute of International Affairs, 1951).

[4] *Wall Street Journal*, 18 March, *New York Times*, 20 March 1946. Other conditions attached or at least suggested by the United States were Russian adherence to the World Bank and International Monetary Fund (cf. *New York Times*, 21 April 1946).

[5] Ibid. 20 and 21 April 1946.

not yet definitely and irrevocably decided against advancing credit to Russia, if only Stalin would come round and agree to American trade principles. What Truman proposed to do was to ask Congress to raise the legal limits of Export-Import Bank credit by an additional $1,500 million to provide a margin for Russian, and perhaps other, loans if satisfactory terms could be arranged.[1]

This was the time, however, when the British loan debate came to a climax in the Senate; and the administration decided that it would not be prudent to ask Congress for still more foreign lending authority while the British loan was in the balance. Consequently, nothing was done for the time being, although exchanges of diplomatic notes between the American and Russian Governments over the question of a loan and Lend-Lease settlement continued.

As time went on, the chances of any agreement with Russia rapidly dimmed. On 18 July 1946 Truman announced that he did not intend to ask Congress to raise the limit of Export-Import Bank credit during the current session, a decision which effectively ruled out any possibility of a loan to Russia before 1947, since the Bank had already committed nearly all its funds.[2] In October 1946 the United States once again invited the Russians to begin negotiations for settling Lend-Lease accounts; and in an interview with an American journalist on 26 October Stalin replied in the affirmative to the question: 'Is Russia still interested in obtaining a loan from the United States?'[3] But Russia stubbornly wished to have a loan with no strings attached and the United States with equal stubbornness insisted that any loan would have to come as part of a general economic settlement. With the steadily deteriorating political relationship between the two countries, no modification of either position could be expected. Consequently, Russia had to go without a loan, while the United States saw the hope of world-wide international trade and financial exchange on liberal principles go glimmering into the outer darkness.

Yet once again one must be on guard against exaggerating the rapidity and definiteness with which the new alignment of economic and political policy took place. Important elements in the American Government continued to hope that an understanding could be arranged with the Russians in spite of all that had transpired, and, when Secretary Marshall made his celebrated offer of American economic help to Europe in June 1947,[4] he did not exclude Russia and Eastern Europe; indeed, when asked at a subsequent news conference, he explicitly included Russia among the countries which might receive such aid. It was Russia's rejection of the Marshall Plan that sealed the economic and political opposition of East

[1] *Christian Science Monitor*, 9 May 1946.
[2] *New York Herald Tribune*, 19 July 1946.
[3] *Manchester Guardian*, 30 October 1946.
[4] See *Survey* for 1947–8, p. 22.

and West; until that time Americans had hesitated and hoped even while each successive act pushed them more and more definitely into open opposition to Russia.

(iii) Diplomatic Sparring among the Big Three, September 1945–April 1946

(a) Introduction

The seven months following V-J day showed a fairly definite pattern of ups and downs in Allied cordiality. The first meeting of the Council of Foreign Ministers in London (11 September–2 October 1945), instead of laying down the principles for peace treaties with Italy, Rumania, Bulgaria, Hungary, and Finland, broke up in stalemate, ostensibly over a question of procedure but really because Russian policies in Eastern Europe and in the Far East conflicted with Anglo-American policies. An effort to break the stalemate led to a meeting of the American, British, and Russian Foreign Ministers in Moscow, from 16 to 26 December. At that meeting Byrnes offered Russia some part in fixing policies for the occupation of Japan; and in return the Russians agreed to make a gesture to meet Anglo-American demands in Eastern Europe. Procedure for the conclusion of peace treaties with Italy and the Russian satellite states of Eastern Europe was agreed upon, and the path seemed clear for resumption of more cordial Allied co-operation.

But the cordiality soon broke down. The Persian Government took the initiative in bringing a dispute over the failure of the Red Army to evacuate the northern provinces of Persia before the Security Council of the United Nations in January 1946. Britain and America supported the Persian complaints. As a counter-measure, the Russians lodged charges against British policy in Greece and Indonesia and supported Syrian protests against Anglo-French military occupation of the Levant. The compromises agreed to at Moscow in December could not withstand the propaganda storms which these incidents stirred up. Efforts to concert action and policy became increasingly sporadic, while bitter words exchanged in the public forum provided by the United Nations made co-operation and compromise more and more difficult for both sides.

Nevertheless, when the first disputes over Persia, Greece, Indonesia, and the Levant had blown over, March 1946 brought something of a lull. An agreement fixing the level of German industry marked an important step towards a common four-Power policy in that country; and the withdrawal of Russian troops from Persia and from Manchuria in the course of March and April 1946 removed important sources of friction. But these moves did not spring from any fundamental meeting of minds. The immediate goals of Russian policy remained almost everywhere in contradiction to the goals of American and British policy. This situation was brought home during the efforts to negotiate peace treaties, efforts which were so nearly fruitless that the Council of Foreign Ministers had once again to be called in, on 25 April 1946.

The second meeting of the Council of Foreign Ministers differed from its predecessor in one significant respect. At the insistence of the American Secretary of State, efforts to maintain secrecy were abandoned in favour of open diplomacy. As a result, speeches and arguments before the Council of Foreign Ministers tended to become like those already current in the United Nations: propaganda designed for public, and especially for home, consumption. Serious efforts to arrive at agreement by compromise could not thrive under these circumstances.

Thus from the end of April 1946 it seems correct to recognize that the relations of the Great Powers entered a new phase. Rivalry replaced earlier efforts at co-operation; propaganda largely displaced diplomacy; and the pivot of international relations shifted from the conference tables to the actions of rival pro-consuls in Germany, where the largest stakes of the post-war world lay. By degrees, too, the United States emerged in Britain's place as the Soviet Union's main opponent. While the Russians consolidated their control over Eastern Europe, the United States, somewhat reluctantly, as we have seen, came to the financial rescue of non-Communist governments.

During the immediate post-war period one may distinguish three distinct critical areas of the world. First, and most prominent, were the Russian borderlands: the parts of Eastern and Central Europe which the Red Army had brought under Russian control, the parts of China which had been occupied by the Communists, Manchuria and northern Korea where the Red Army was in occupation, and the states on Russia's southern frontier—Turkey and Persia. Stalin's policy in these areas was not apparently uniform, at least in the short run; but in each of them he sought to expand Russia's power, using various measures short of military conquest and annexation. With varying degrees of success, the Anglo-Americans sought to limit the expansion of Russian influence into these areas. Consequently, moves and counter-moves accompanied by a noisy debate over the Russian borderlands constituted the major theme of world diplomacy.

The second critical area was Western Europe. There coalitions, including Communists, governed all the liberated countries. Economic problems—indeed, the elemental problem of finding food for the population—tended to dominate the life of Western Europe in the months which followed the end of hostilities. Politically, France was of course the most important

Power, and the French attempted, not without some success, to act as mediators between the Anglo-Americans and the Russians. Both the Russians and the Western Powers tried to win the sympathy and support of Western Europe, but the struggle in France, Italy, Belgium, the Netherlands, and Scandinavia was not nearly so acute as the parallel struggle in Eastern and Central Europe. The manœuvres of Communist and non-Communist Parties, American loans and Russian wheat deliveries, constitution-building, colonial policy: these were the stuff of French, Belgian, and Dutch politics, and, as long as the Communists refrained from attempting revolutionary action, developments in Western Europe did not impinge decisively on the relations of the Big Three. Fear of Communist revolution in Western Europe was certainly an important factor in American and British foreign policy; Russian policy may have been influenced by the parallel hope of revolution. But such hopes and fears were not immediate: the struggle over the Russian borderlands had first to be settled. Moreover, the political traditions of Western Europe encouraged national independence, and memories of the past encouraged politicians and the public to resist outside interference. As a result, the nations of Western Europe were able to work out their own affairs with only marginal intervention from the Great Powers.

The third critical area of the world was the great arc of formerly dependent territories, stretching from the eastern Mediterranean lands through India to South-East Asia and Indonesia. Here pre-war European political dominion was challenged by rising nationalism mixed with social revolt. The great imperial Powers—Britain, France, the Netherlands—found it necessary to give way, though in varying degrees and at varying rates. Arab-Jewish friction in the Near East and Muslim-Hindu friction in India added another dimension to the transformation of the political status of these regions; and minority problems in Persia, Malaya, Indo-china, and Indonesia were almost equally explosive.

Germany and China were each special cases of the highest importance. In Germany the Russian borderlands overlapped Western Europe. What happened to Germany would have enormous and very probably decisive repercussions over all the Continent. As Russia and America drifted apart, a contest for German support arose between them. The contest took devious paths at first, for war memories could not be wiped out at once, and gestures designed to attract Germans almost automatically alienated other European nationalities. But before the end of 1946 Molotov and Byrnes were rivalling one another with thinly disguised appeals for German favour.

In China, too, there was an overlap of two of the prime forces of the post-war world: Soviet expansion and the Asiatic revolt met and were embodied in the persons of the Chinese Communists. Any bid the Russians might make for alliance with the peoples of Asia would have its most immediate and greatest test in neighbouring China. But Russian policy was hesitant at first, perhaps because Stalin did not believe the Chinese Communists could possibly win a civil war. Similarly American policy until after the end of 1946 was aimed at securing some sort of pacification by negotiation between the Communists and Chiang Kai-shek. Hence it was not until after the period here under consideration that the lines came to be clearly drawn in China: in 1945 and 1946 confusion and profound uncertainty prevailed.

Since this book is concerned with the fate of the Grand Alliance, only the first of these great critical areas comes directly into the story. The Asiatic revolt and the crisis of Western Europe must be passed over lightly while attention is focused upon the Russian borderlands, and particularly upon affairs in Germany and China, for it was the conflict of Soviet with Anglo-American policy in these areas that dissolved the Grand Alliance of the Second World War.

(*b*) The Council of Foreign Ministers, London, 11 September–2 October 1945

According to the protocol of the Potsdam Conference, the Council of Foreign Ministers was established 'to do the necessary preparatory work for the peace settlements'; but a further clause stated: 'Other matters may from time to time be referred to the Council by agreement between the member Governments.' This latitude became a stumbling-block when the Council first assembled in London, on 11 September 1945. Molotov wished to discuss the arrangements made for the occupation of Japan; Byrnes wanted to limit the Council of Foreign Ministers to consideration of the peace treaties.[1]

There were other difficulties in agreeing upon the procedure and agenda —e.g. the French wished to consider Germany—which delayed the first discussion of the Italian peace treaty until two days after the Council began its meetings. Of these, the point which became critical later in the Conference seemed at first a very minor matter, and was agreed to without difficulty on the first day. The question was this: should all five Foreign Ministers who were members of the Council—U.S.A., U.S.S.R., U.K., France, and China—take part in the discussion of each treaty? The Potsdam protocol had said: 'For the discharge of each of these tasks [drafting the various peace treaties] the Council will be composed of the

[1] Byrnes: *Speaking Frankly*, p. 93. This did not mean that the American Secretary of State ruled out informal talks about arrangements for the occupation of Japan; indeed he hoped to be able to persuade both Bevin and Molotov to agree to the proposal for an advisory Allied council which the American Government had first made in August. See above, p. 641. Byrnes also had in mind a proposal for a treaty to guarantee the long-term demilitarization of Japan to which the American Government would be a party (Byrnes, op. cit. pp. 213–15).

members representing those states which were signatory to the terms of surrender imposed upon the enemy state concerned. . . . Other members will be invited to participate when matters directly concerning them are under discussion.' On 11 September it was unanimously agreed that the Council's procedure should be to allow all five Foreign Ministers to take part in preliminary discussion of each treaty, but when it came to voting on particular clauses then states which had not signed the armistices would not be allowed to vote.[1]

When these various preliminaries had been settled, the Council on 13 September at length began to consider the Italian treaty. A British draft was taken as the basis for discussion. Three important problems soon became apparent: the demarcation of the Italo-Yugoslav boundary, the disposal of Italian colonies, and the matter of reparations. France, Britain, and the United States were not united on the first two of these questions, but all dissented from the Russian proposals. Molotov wished to transfer the whole of Venezia Giulia, including the city of Trieste, to Yugoslavia, and wanted the Soviet Union to acquire the right to administer one of the Italian colonies, preferably Tripolitania, as a trustee under the United Nations. With respect to reparations, Molotov proposed that Italy be required to pay a total of $600 million, of which one-sixth should go to Russia. A week of argument led to almost no progress, except for a decision to send experts to investigate matters on the spot and recommend a line for the Italo-Yugoslav boundary.

On 18 September the Rumanian treaty came up for consideration. Before going any farther, Molotov wished the Western Powers to extend diplomatic recognition to the provisional government of Rumania, and to the other Russian-supported governments of Eastern Europe. In private conversation with Byrnes he pressed the demand, and when Byrnes tried to assure him that the United States wished to see governments in Eastern Europe that were both friendly to the Soviet Union *and* democratic, Molotov refused to believe him. The persistent refusal of the United States to recognize the existing governments, he declared, could only mean that America and Britain wished to see governments unfriendly to the Soviet Union in Rumania and elsewhere.[2]

For the next two days at the formal meetings of the Council the Foreign Ministers wrangled over details of the Rumanian treaty, and passed on to a preliminary debate over the Bulgarian and Hungarian treaties. But the official debates were all by-play. What really was at stake was whether America and Britain would willingly acquiesce in Russian dominance over Rumania and the other ex-enemy countries of Eastern Europe.[3]

[1] Philip E. Mosely: 'Peace-Making, 1946', *International Organization*, February 1947, i. 23.

[2] Byrnes: *Speaking Frankly*, pp. 98–99.

[3] It is not clear that Byrnes recognized the issues really at stake. His complete failure to under-

On 19 September Molotov made a new attempt to come to a private understanding with Byrnes, asking the American what it was he really wanted, what hidden motives lay behind the talk about democratic liberties in Rumania and Bulgaria as prerequisite to diplomatic recognition. Byrnes, for his part, thought that perhaps it was fear of renewed German aggression that underlay Soviet policy in Rumania and elsewhere. To try to solve the problem he suggested, tentatively, a twenty-five-year treaty, to which the United States would be a party, guaranteeing the demilitarization of Germany. This would be a twin to a similar treaty for Japan. Molotov declared himself 'interested', and promised to refer the proposal to Stalin. But his indignation at American and British 'interference' in Rumania and Eastern Europe was not changed.

On the following day, 20 September, Molotov brought the clash over Rumania before the Council of Foreign Ministers. He accused Britain and the United States of opposing the Groza Government because it was friendly to the Soviet Union; and when Byrnes and Bevin replied by referring to the Yalta Declaration on Liberated Europe with its guarantees of democratic government and tripartite intervention to assist in the establishment of such governments, Molotov angrily declared that the Anglo-Americans were 'conducting an offensive' against him.[1]

There was, indeed, much to worry the Russians in Rumania. On 21 August 1945 King Michael had appealed to the Big Three for assistance in remodelling the Government to make it more democratic. By this move he hoped to bring the machinery envisaged in the Yalta Declaration on Liberated Europe into operation. Simultaneously, the King asked the

stand Russian attitudes and suspicions is nicely illustrated by his own report in *Speaking Frankly*. One incident is typical. At Moscow, when Byrnes interviewed Stalin on 22 December 1945, he mentioned his difficulties in agreeing with Molotov over the Balkans. 'It is terribly important to settle this matter and to proceed with the peace treaties', Byrnes reports himself as saying, '*so that we can be in a position to render them economic assistance*' (ibid. p. 116). An argument less likely to persuade Stalin can hardly be imagined. He must have interpreted Byrnes's words to mean: 'We must have peace treaties to re-establish capitalist exploitation of Rumanian oil wells and Finnish nickel mines', but Byrnes apparently believed that the hard plight of East Europeans, deprived of UNRRA and other forms of international relief, would prey on Stalin's mind and make him eager to have American help to relieve the suffering. Byrnes's mind was profoundly parochial, as insensitive to Russian modes of thought as Stalin and Molotov were incapable of understanding the characteristic mixture of idealism and self-interest with which Americans approached international negotiation. It was surely a misfortune that the effort at world pacification in 1945–6 should have been entrusted to men so firmly rooted in their respective national backyards as Byrnes, Bevin, and Molotov were.

[1] Byrnes: *Speaking Frankly*, pp. 100–1. At some time during the meeting in London Byrnes proposed the appointment of a three-Power commission to give advice to Rumania and Bulgaria about the broadening of their governments and the improvement of conditions of civil liberty in those countries (ibid. p. 117). It was proposals such as this that Molotov viewed as constituting an Anglo-American diplomatic offensive against the Russian position in Eastern Europe.

Prime Minister, Groza, to resign, which he refused to do; and Michael then began a royal sit-down strike, declining to validate decrees of the Council of Ministers. The situation became very ticklish. The legality of Groza's Government was more than questionable, and hopes of a change ran high among the Rumanian groups which opposed the Communists. A large popular demonstration in Bucharest on the occasion of the King's birthday, 8 November 1945, proved how easily opposition to the Government could be stirred up and how precarious was the Government's power.

The Russians did what they could to stabilize the situation. On 12 September they announced a substantial relaxation of the economic clauses of the armistice; and on 18 September Molotov announced in a press conference that the Rumanian Government had full Russian support. British and American diplomats in Bucharest, however, hoping to be able to make a reality of the Yalta Declaration on Liberated Europe, and wishing also to help their friends in Rumania, encouraged resistance to the Government with vague and cautious words which hopeful Rumanian politicians interpreted to mean far more than they really did.[1]

The situation in other countries of Eastern Europe was almost as bad from the Russian point of view. In Poland opposition to the Communists was strong. Stanislaw Mikolajczyk's Peasant Party refused to co-operate with the Government by joining in a single electoral list with the other parties represented in the Cabinet. This meant that, until police measures had broken the power of the Peasant Party and had cowed all the various opposition elements that rallied to Mikolajczyk's side, the Government did not dare to hold elections. In Bulgaria and Hungary, too, peasant parties were in opposition to the governments backed by Russia, and there could be little doubt that elections conducted free of police terrorism would result in serious setbacks for the Communists and their fellow travellers. Economic suffering, partly due to Russian seizure of reparations and booty, was intense in the whole of Eastern Europe; and discontent inevitably turned primarily against the governments in power. As a result, the Russians and their local Communist supporters could retain their predominance in all these countries only by high-handed police methods.

The practical effect of Byrnes's and Bevin's demands for relaxation of police oppression, for greater civil liberties, and for free and prompt elections in Eastern Europe would have been to ensure the overthrow of the existing régimes. To suppose that successor governments would be friendly to Russia by any definition of the word (save, perhaps, in Bulgaria and Czechoslovakia) could only be the result of ignorance or of duplicity. Byrnes and Bevin may have been ignorant, but Molotov preferred to

[1] Roberts: *Rumania*, pp. 301 seqq.

believe them false. It does not appear that the Americans or British ever fully and frankly faced the contradiction between the two parts of their programme for Eastern Europe. Friendliness for Russia and 'democratic' government[1] were incompatible in most of the countries in question; but Byrnes and Bevin either did not know or preferred not to admit the fact. The Russians, for their part, could not face the embarrassment of frankly confessing their unpopularity with the peoples of Eastern Europe.[2] Instead they called the Opposition fascist.

Lack of frankness on both sides, combined perhaps with imperfect understanding of the facts of the case, made discussion of the affairs of Eastern Europe singularly profitless and altogether exacerbating. Each side felt indignant and morally in the right. Molotov detected a capitalist plot to deprive Russia of the fruits of victory; the Western Foreign Ministers saw in Russia's actions a cynical disregard of war-time promises. Certainly the legal case for the West was a good one. Byrnes and Bevin were only trying to realize the principle set forth in such documents as the United Nations Declaration and the Declaration on Liberated Europe. The real defect lay in these documents themselves; in the tacit assumption underlying them that it was possible to plant democracy in Eastern Europe by diplomatic fiat, and that such governments, if established, would be capable and responsible, peaceably inclined, and automatically acceptable to all the Great Powers. The Russian case was correspondingly bad from a legal point of view. But the Russians and the Communists were in a position to use force to establish their rule, and the very real abuses of pre-war government and society in Eastern Europe gave some colour to their propagandist claims to be the agents of reform and social progress.

Smarting under Byrnes's and Bevin's attack, Molotov characteristically decided to take the offensive himself. On 22 September he notified his

[1] Actually, democratic government could hardly be expected to arise from the social structure of the peasant countries of Europe, if by democratic government one means a government like that of Britain or France or the United States. The effort to import democratic Constitutions into peasant Europe after the First World War was not a success. The newfangled Western garb did not fit the body politic; and as long as the bulk of the population persisted in regarding officialdom as its natural enemy—and not without ample reason both past and present—then Western-style Constitutions could not be expected ever to correspond to political reality. This deeper dilemma of Anglo-American policy in Eastern Europe was demonstrated in Greece, where the machinery of parliamentary government did not suffice to create the fact. Yet Greece, on the whole, offered more favourable ground for the growth of Western political institutions than did the other countries of Eastern Europe.

[2] According to Philip E. Mosely ('Face to Face with Russia', Foreign Policy Association, *Headline Series*, No. 70, July–August 1948, p. 23) Stalin said at Potsdam: 'A freely elected government in any of these [East European] countries would be anti-Soviet, and that we cannot allow.' Such frankness was not, apparently, repeated in later negotiations.

colleagues that the Russian delegation would not be able to attend the scheduled meeting of the Council of Foreign Ministers, and asked instead to see Byrnes privately. When the two met, Molotov turned to the question of Japan, demanding that the Americans agree to establish an Allied Control Council to supervise MacArthur's occupation. Byrnes asked for time, and offered to discuss the question when the Foreign Ministers' meeting had ended.

After this conversation, Bevin joined the party, and Molotov lodged objection to the participation of China and France in the discussion of the treaties for Eastern Europe, which he claimed was a violation of the provisions of the Potsdam protocol. Later in the day he explained his new position to the French and Chinese Foreign Ministers at a formal meeting of the Council. They, of course, disliked the idea, and so did Byrnes and Bevin. For the next ten days the Council wrangled fruitlessly over the question of how the Potsdam protocol should be interpreted.

On 28 September Byrnes produced a compromise which he hoped would satisfy Molotov. He proposed that the drafting of the treaties should be limited to the representatives of the nations that had signed the armistices with the countries in question—a concession to the Russians —provided that the drafts should then be submitted to a peace conference at which all the members of the United Nations 'which supplied substantial military contingents against European members of the Axis' would be represented. But this did not satisfy the Russian Foreign Minister, who, indeed, made it clear that his tactics were deliberately obstructive.

Everyone tired of this fruitless quarrel, and on 2 October 1946 the Council broke up, having settled virtually nothing. It even proved impossible to agree upon a communiqué and protocol describing the meeting since Molotov insisted that all reference to the participation of China and France in the Balkan peace treaty discussions should be deleted from the record.[1]

The resounding failure of this first meeting of the Council of Foreign Ministers presented everyone with the problem of what to do next. This was especially acute for Byrnes, whose whole policy was designed to arrange peace treaties promptly in order to permit American withdrawal from active participation in European affairs. After his return to Washington, he initiated a number of conciliatory moves. In conjunction with Great Britain, the United States extended diplomatic recognition to the provisional Government of Austria on 20 October 1945 and to the provisional Government of Hungary on 2 November.[2] In each case recognition was extended after receipt of a promise to hold free elections in the near future.

[1] Byrnes: *Speaking Frankly*, pp. 102–6. [2] Ibid. p. 107.

Elections were duly held, in Hungary on 4 November and in Austria on 25 November; and in both countries the Communists won only a small minority of the votes. New governments in which they held only a subordinate position were organized.

In Bulgaria and Rumania the situation was more difficult. Byrnes decided to send a special representative to these countries, a man whose 'liberal' point of view would not be open to question. Mark Ethridge, publisher of the *Louisville Courier-Journal*, was chosen for this job. His duty was to discover whether American diplomatic representatives had allowed themselves to be misled into exaggerating the abuses of the Communist-dominated Governments of Bulgaria and Rumania.[1] His report was not published, but it was made clear that he generally agreed with the views of the American officials already on the scene.[2]

From the Russian side, there is some reason to suppose that the breakdown of the Council of Foreign Ministers in London excited dismay. Molotov's tactics may have been based on the belief that Byrnes and Bevin would recoil from the prospect of open rupture, and so give way. In earlier conferences, when disputed issues like Poland had come up, the Americans had always shown anxiety to arrive at agreement, even at the cost of concessions of principle. But in London things had not worked out that way and Molotov had nothing to show for his intransigence. It is possible that Stalin decided to try to conciliate Western opinion by allowing more or less free elections in Hungary and Austria in November 1945.[3] But the outcome of this experiment cannot have been reassuring to the Russians. Their friends had taken a bad beating at the polls, and Opposition groups in Poland and Rumania were correspondingly heartened.

In Bulgaria and Yugoslavia, on the other hand, the Communists achieved far better results, using only a modicum of strong-arm methods. Elections in Bulgaria on 18 November 1945 returned an overwhelming majority for the Fatherland Front, and thus gave a new legitimacy to Communist domination of the Government. Elections in Yugoslavia on 11 November 1945 were even more one-sided, establishing the power of Tito's People's Front against all comers. Soon after, on 29 November, Yugoslavia was proclaimed a republic and King Peter's rights to the

[1] Ethridge also looked over the situation in Greece where it had proved unexpectedly difficult to get all parties to agree to hold an election.

[2] Byrnes: *Speaking Frankly*, p. 115.

[3] It is also possible that Hungarian and Austrian Communists may have indulged in such wishful thinking as to convince themselves that they could retain and consolidate their power by means of relatively free elections. Stalin may have been misled by their reports, and have found the actual result in the two countries a most unwelcome surprise. So competent an observer as Ambassador Harriman attributed the Russians' decision to abandon the Yalta and Potsdam Agreements as a basis for co-operation with the West to Stalin's discovery of the hostility of East Europeans to the Red Army, together with his growing belief in the weakness of America and Britain (*Congressional Record*, 27 August 1951, pp. A5670–1).

throne were repudiated by the new Government. But the Bulgars and Serbs had a long tradition of friendship for Russia; the Communist Party of Bulgaria had always been relatively strong, and Tito had his war-time achievements to build upon. These special advantages did not apply in Rumania and Poland, yet Rumania and Poland were of prime importance for Stalin's conception of security. Hence elections in these countries were not attempted until Communist success could be assured in advance.

These events and gestures did not forward the process of peace-making nor do much to bring the Great Powers into better accord. After the London meeting of the Council of Foreign Ministers an oppressive silence emanated from Moscow. Towards the end of October 1945 Byrnes decided to take matters up directly with Stalin. Acting on the Secretary of State's suggestion, Truman wrote a letter to the Soviet dictator which Ambassador Harriman presented to him on 25 October. The letter dwelt on new details of the American plan for treaty-drafting procedure, and also went into the problem of Rumania and Bulgaria. When Stalin had read it, he said with some irritation that the question of Japan had been left out. He complained that the Russian representative at MacArthur's headquarters was handled 'like a piece of furniture', and asserted that in general Russia was being treated like a second-rate Power and not like an ally.[1]

Byrnes was, or claimed to be, surprised by Stalin's reaction. He had assumed that Molotov's animadversions on American behaviour in Japan were intended only to becloud the issue of Russian unilateral action in Eastern Europe. But now that Stalin had spoken, it seemed necessary to do something to meet Russian criticism or else to abandon American claims to influence affairs in Eastern Europe. The fact that the British, and particularly the Australian, Governments were also dissatisfied with the existing arrangements for controlling General MacArthur, and wished, like the Russians, to have a larger voice in deciding what should be done in Japan, made the problem all the more urgent. Consequently Byrnes and his assistants busied themselves during the following weeks with the preparation of proposals for the administration of Japan that would satisfy Russia and Australia and at the same time preserve an adequate scope to the American command. This was a difficult matter, for MacArthur did not wish to have any truck with outsiders generally (including for most purposes the leaders of the American Government itself), and in particular he did not wish to see his authority limited by any Allied political council.[2]

[1] Byrnes: *Speaking Frankly*, pp. 108, 216–17.

[2] MacArthur's attitude was largely a reflection of his masterful personality, but it stemmed

Nevertheless, after consultation with representatives of the U.S. armed forces, Byrnes was able to draw up proposals for the control of General MacArthur that accorded a larger role to the Allied Governments; and on Thanksgiving Day, 29 November 1945, he decided that it would be worth while to try to reopen negotiation with the Russians. He suggested a meeting limited to the Big Three Foreign Ministers at Moscow. The British and Russian Governments agreed. As a result on 16 December 1945 Byrnes, Bevin, and Molotov once again confronted one another, this time in the Russian capital.

(*c*) Compromise at Moscow, 16–26 December 1945

The fact that Byrnes went to Moscow not to draft peace treaties in isolation from other problems but to try to settle any and all differences between Russia and the West meant that a much more businesslike atmosphere prevailed from the start. The programme was very broad. Arrangements for the Japanese occupation, the situation in Korea and in China, in Greece and Indonesia, in Manchuria and Persia were all to be discussed in addition to control of atomic energy, procedure for making the peace treaties, and the conditions upon which Britain and America would recognize the Governments of Bulgaria and Rumania.[1] If agreement could be reached on all these points a comprehensive settlement among the Great Powers might result. Actually much was done, but one important issue—Russian activity in northern Persia—was dropped from the agenda without a decision. This failure proved almost immediately fatal to Great Power harmony.

The general lines of the compromises made at Moscow were these. First, the Russians accepted the American plan for a peace conference and agreed upon a list of twenty-one countries to be invited. In return, the Americans and British accepted the Russian contention that preliminary consideration of peace treaty terms should be confined to the signatories of the armistices. The deputies of the Foreign Ministers were instructed to resume immediately the task of drafting the five treaties already begun, and the date for the Peace Conference was set at not later than 1 May

also from the long-standing American military tradition of the separability of war from politics. If one started from the premiss that the occupation of Japan was a military operation, one could argue that mere civilians should therefore be subordinate to soldiers and should not have any superior policy-making power. By such a *tour de force* the military art could be made to engulf politics and economics—a curious inversion of the original thesis. U.S. army leaders in Germany arrived at the opposite conclusion, wishing to turn over responsibility for occupation government to civilian authorities as soon as possible, but Byrnes steadily refused to take on the task (cf. Eisenhower: *Crusade in Europe*, p. 441; Byrnes: *Speaking Frankly*, p. 244).

[1] Ibid. p. 111.

1946. After the Peace Conference had 'considered' the draft treaties, the final texts were to be drawn up by the armistice signatories, thus leaving the Great Powers with what amounted to a veto over any recommendations which might be advanced by other nations at the Peace Conference.[1] This agreement solved the procedural tangle that had strangled the London meeting of the Council of Foreign Ministers. It seemed, to Byrnes especially, a great step forward and was announced to the world in a special communiqué on Christmas Day 1945.

By the second major compromise the Americans conceded something to Russian, Australian, and British pressure with respect to Japan in return for Russian concessions with respect to Rumania and Bulgaria. The agreement about Allied control machinery for Japan closely followed the proposal Byrnes brought with him to the meeting. Briefly, two bodies were to be established: a Far Eastern Commission, sitting in Washington, and an Allied Council for Japan, operating from Tokyo. The Far Eastern Commission was to consist of representatives of eleven nations with important interests in the Pacific area; decisions were to be taken by 'less than unanimous vote' providing that the Big Four concurred. Its functions were defined as follows:

> To formulate the policies, principles, and standards in conformity with which the fulfillment by Japan of its obligations under the Terms of Surrender may be accomplished.
>
> To review, on the request of any member, any directive issued by the Supreme Commander for the Allied Powers or any action taken by the Supreme Commander involving policy decisions within the jurisdiction of the Commission.
>
> To consider such other matters as may be assigned to it by agreement among the participating Governments. . . .[2]

The Commission was explicitly forbidden any jurisdiction over military or territorial questions; and it could communicate with the authorities in Japan only through the official channels of the American Government. Moreover, in case the Commission should be slow to act, the American Government reserved the right to issue 'interim directives' to MacArthur. In view of the fact that the United States, like the other Great Powers, had a veto power over Commission decisions, this meant in effect that such interim directives could be maintained indefinitely, even against the wishes of all the other nations on the Commission if the American member were willing to defy them all. In case of persistent disagreement the Commission was sure to lapse into complete insignificance. This, of course, was what did happen.

[1] An official report of the Moscow meeting may be found in U.S.A., Senate Committee on Foreign Relations, and U.S.A., Department of State: *A Decade of American Foreign Policy, Basic Documents 1941-49* (Washington, U.S.G.P.O., 1950), pp. 58–66. [This volume is referred to hereafter as *A Decade of American Foreign Policy*.] Cf. Byrnes: *Speaking Frankly*, pp. 111–15.

[2] *A Decade of American Foreign Policy*, p. 60.

The second body, the Allied Council for Japan, was merely advisory. It comprised military representatives of China, Russia, America, and a fourth member jointly representing Britain, India, Australia, and New Zealand. All orders would continue to come from the Supreme Commander's headquarters, but by the terms of the agreement reached in Moscow MacArthur was obliged to 'consult and advise with the Council in advance of the issuance of orders on matters of substance, the exigencies of the situation permitting'.[1] The one real check on the authority of the Supreme Commander was the provision that, in case of disagreement among the members of the Council upon the course of action necessary for carrying out a decision made by the Far Eastern Commission, then 'the Supreme Commander will withhold the issuance of orders on these questions pending agreement thereon in the Far Eastern Commission'.[2]

It is obvious that the new machinery for Japan did not really trench seriously upon American control. The same was true of the arrangements made for Rumania and Bulgaria at Moscow: a nominal concession did not disturb Russian influence over those countries. When the three Foreign Ministers met in Moscow Rumania had only a provisional government, unsanctioned by elections; Bulgaria on the other hand had just completed her first post-war election. This difference led the Great Powers to distinguish between the two countries. For Rumania a three-Power Commission was set up 'to proceed to Bucharest immediately' and there satisfy itself that two 'truly representative' members of the leading Opposition parties were added to the Cabinet. These new Cabinet members were at the same time to be 'suitable' and willing to 'work loyally with the Government'. Finally, the Government so broadened should promise free elections in the near future, give assurances concerning civil liberties, and grant freedom of action to all 'democratic and anti-fascist parties' to prepare for the elections. When all this had been accomplished, the British and American Governments promised to recognize the remodelled and reformed Rumanian Government.[3]

As for Bulgaria:

. . . the Soviet Government takes upon itself the mission of giving friendly advice to the Bulgarian Government with regard to the desirability of the inclusion in the Bulgarian Government of the Fatherland Front, now being formed, of an additional two representatives of other democratic groups, who (*a*) are truly representative of the groups of the parties which are not participating in

[1] *A Decade of American Foriegn Policy*, p. 62.

[2] MacArthur's views of the new arrangement were made public on 30 December 1945 in an extraordinary statement to the press. He said he had told Byrnes on 31 October that the plan was not acceptable; that he had not been subsequently consulted; but would nevertheless 'try to make it work' (*New York Times*, 31 December 1945).

[3] *A Decade of American Foreign Policy*, p. 64.

the Government, and (*b*) are really suitable and will work loyally with the Government.[1]

In return, Britain and America once again promised to recognize the reorganized Bulgarian Government. This really committed the Russians to nothing; and in fact members of the Opposition parties in Bulgaria were not added to the Government.[2]

It is obvious that these agreements did nothing to face the fundamental problem. 'Truly representative' leaders of the Opposition in Rumania and Bulgaria were by definition unwilling to 'work loyally' with the existing Governments in those countries, and no three-Power Commission could change the fact. In Rumania, it is true, a relaxation of the tension between Communists and their rivals did take place. When the Commission arrived in Bucharest on 31 December 1945 King Michael broke off his royal strike against the Groza Government; and on 7 January two relatively minor political figures from the two major Opposition parties were admitted to the Cabinet. But Groza remained as Prime Minister and the Communist domination of the Government was in no way affected. Formal promises of civil liberties and early elections proved entirely empty in the months that followed; but, before the unregenerate behaviour of the Rumanian Government had become fully apparent, Britain and America, on 5 February 1946, fulfilled their part of the bargain, and extended diplomatic recognition to the remodelled Groza Government. In Bulgaria, where no change in the Government took place, Western recognition was withheld. Thus the agreement reached at Moscow in December had the effect of salving the inflamed situation in Rumania for the time being, but solved nothing.

The third major compromise reached by the Foreign Ministers at Moscow affected American and Russian policy in China and Korea. Since V-J day, suspicion, mistrust, and sporadic fighting between the Chinese Communists and the National Government had combined with difficulties between Russian and American military authorities in Korea to trouble the Asian mainland. But the proclaimed policies of the Russian and American Governments were not seriously at loggerheads. On 16 December 1945, the day the Foreign Ministers met in Moscow, Truman published a statement on American policy towards China. The President called for cessation of civil war and a conference among representatives of the 'major political elements' in China to arrange a permanent solution

[1] Ibid. pp. 64–65.

[2] It is possible that the failure to broaden the Bulgarian Government was connected with the refusal of the Greek Government to co-opt representatives of the Communist Front, EAM. An EAM delegation requested the formation of a representative Greek Government including themselves on 8 January 1946, and were refused. Four days later the negotiations for inclusion of the Bulgarian Opposition in the Government were broken off. The coincidence is at least suggestive.

to the internal strife. He reaffirmed American recognition of Chiang Kai-shek's Government as the only legal authority in China, but declared that the existing 'one party government' should be broadened to include representatives of other parties and groups. Truman also said that a necessary condition for the unification and democratization of China was the abolition of autonomous armies like those commanded by the Communists. He expressly denied that American arms would ever be used to affect the course of civil war, but offered the prospect of American economic aid to a unified and pacified China.[1]

When the question of China came before the Foreign Ministers in Moscow, Molotov found nothing to object to in the President's statement. But he pressed Byrnes for something more specific. In particular Molotov wanted to know what American troops were doing in north China and when they would be withdrawn. He proposed to fix a date for the simultaneous withdrawal of Russian troops from Manchuria and of American troops from China; but to this Byrnes would not agree, arguing that the Americans had to complete the job of repatriating the Japanese and could not set a term to the accomplishment of the task. After an amicable discussion of the question with Stalin, it was agreed to leave open the question of a schedule for the withdrawal of troops.[2] The communiqué contented itself with generalities. The three Foreign Ministers declared their agreement on the need 'for a unified and democratic China under the National Government, for broad participation by democratic elements in all branches of the National Government, and for a cessation of civil strife. They reaffirmed their adherence to a policy of non-interference in the internal affairs of China'.[3]

Thus, in effect, Molotov and Bevin endorsed American policy in China. In return, Byrnes accepted the Russian programme for Korea.[4] Specifically, the Foreign Ministers called for the early establishment of a 'provisional Korean democratic government'. To assist in its creation a joint Russo-American Commission was to be established. Urgent and immediate problems in Korea were to be taken up at a conference between representatives of the Russian and American zonal commanders to be convened within two weeks.[5]

These agreements were so general that they meant almost nothing. In practice, difficulties soon arose in both Korea and China. Deadlock in Korea came at the very beginning. After months of futile wrangling, Russo-American negotiations on the spot were broken off in May 1946. As in Germany, the Korean zones of occupation became separate com-

[1] Text of Truman's statement may be found in *Documents on American Foreign Relations, 1945–1946*, pp. 799–800.

[2] Byrnes: *Speaking Frankly*, pp. 226–8.

[3] *A Decade of American Foreign Policy*, pp. 63–64.

[4] Byrnes: *Speaking Frankly*, p. 222.

[5] *A Decade of American Foreign Policy*, p. 63.

partments, with independent systems of administration and with almost no economic exchange between them.

In China the course of events was far more complex. General Marshall arrived in China as special representative of the President[1] on 21 December 1945, and he used his great prestige to try to bring the Communists and Chiang Kai-shek to an agreement. At first he seemed to meet with some success. On 10 January 1946 a formal truce was proclaimed. Marshall was able to organize special teams comprising Communist and Kuomintang representatives together with American army officers to enforce the cessation of hostilities in the provinces. On 25 February Chiang and a Communist representative signed an agreement for the enfolding of Communist army units into the Chinese national army. During the same weeks plans for the reorganization of the Chinese Government and for the introduction of a new Constitution were elaborated.

Thus until April 1946 the American programme for China seemed to be working out reasonably well. The Russians remained relatively passive and their relations with Chiang Kai-shek were correct, if cool. In Manchuria, to be sure, the Russians continued their seizure of machinery and other movable wealth, shipping it off to the eastern provinces of Siberia. They also attempted to reach an understanding with the Chinese National Government for joint exploitation of mines and other immovable industrial wealth in Manchuria through the establishment of Sino-Soviet companies. But the Chinese rejected the proposal in March 1946, after the American Government had registered their disapproval of any such arrangement.[2] This setback to Russian hopes did not prevent the Soviet Government from continuing to deal with Chiang as head of the Chinese Government. Thus the withdrawal of the Red Army from Manchuria, completed by the end of April 1946, was made in agreement with the National Government and, indeed, in accordance with a Chinese request.

But the maintenance of officially correct relations with Chiang did not prevent the Russians from favouring the Communists in a variety of underhand ways. Communist troops were allowed, for example, to move into Manchuria and take up positions immediately outside towns garrisoned by the Red Army. As a result, when the Russians withdrew from Manchuria, the Chinese Communists were in a position to acquire large stores of Japanese arms which the Russians left behind them. The Russians also put a variety of petty obstacles in the way of the Nationalist troops—refusing to allow them to use the port of Dairen, for instance, and declining to co-ordinate the evacuation of Russian troops from Manchuria with the advance of Chinese nationalist forces. These acts had important consequences. Since the Red Army withdrew from Manchuria more rapidly than the Chinese nationalist armies could

[1] See above, p. 649.

[2] *United States Relations with China*, pp. 123–4, 596–8.

advance, the result was an interregnum during which the Chinese Communists, already on the ground in some force, were able to assert their control over large tracts of the country-side and in some important towns.[1]

Nevertheless, the help the Russians gave to the Communists was far smaller than the help Americans were giving to the armies of the National Government. This, and the fact that Communist armed forces were only about one-fifth as great as those at Chiang's disposal, probably convinced Stalin that Chiang and not the Communists would continue to dominate China in the foreseeable future.[2] While Stalin may not have liked this prospect, there seems to be no evidence to show that he was willing in 1945 or in the early months of 1946 to take active steps to prevent Chiang from establishing his power over all China.

But to return to the Moscow Conference. The three compromises—concerning peace treaty procedure, Japan and Eastern Europe, and China and Korea—constituted the backbone of the work accomplished by the three Foreign Ministers. A fourth matter seemed of great importance to the British and American Governments: the international regulation of atomic energy. On 10 November 1945 Attlee and Mackenzie King, Prime Minister of Canada, travelled to Washington to consult with Truman about what should be done to forward the peaceful use of atomic energy and to prevent its military application in the future. On 15 November the three Heads of Government issued a statement defining their policy. It said, in part:

In order to attain the most effective means of entirely eliminating the use of atomic energy for destructive purposes and promoting its widest use for industrial and humanitarian purposes, we are of the opinion that at the earliest practicable date a Commission should be set up under the United Nations Organization to prepare recommendations for submission to the Organization. . . .

In particular, the Commission should make specific proposals:

(*a*) For extending between all nations the exchange of basic scientific information for peaceful ends,

(*b*) For control of atomic energy to the extent necessary to ensure its use only for peaceful purposes,

(*c*) For the elimination from national armaments of atomic weapons and of all other major weapons adaptable to mass destruction,

(*d*) For effective safeguards by way of inspection and other means to protect complying states against the hazards of violations and evasions.

The work of the Commission should proceed by separate stages, the successful

[1] *United States Relations with China*, pp. 122, 147–8.

[2] Stalin and Molotov said as much to successive American interrogators: to Hurley in August 1944, to Hopkins in May 1945, to Byrnes in December 1945 (cf. *United States Relations with China*, p. 72; Sherwood: *Roosevelt and Hopkins*, p. 902; Eng. edition, ii. 891; Byrnes: *Speaking Frankly*, p. 228).

completion of each one of which will develop the necessary confidence of the world before the next stage is undertaken.[1]

When the three Foreign Ministers met in Moscow, the first meeting of the United Nations General Assembly lay only three weeks in the future. At that meeting the United States, Britain, and Canada intended to sponsor a resolution for the creation of a United Nations Atomic Energy Commission in conformity with the proposal of 15 November. At Moscow Byrnes and Bevin were anxious to persuade the Russians to join in sponsoring the resolution. Molotov, however, indicated that he did not consider the matter to be of great importance. He asked that atomic energy be placed last on the agenda of the Conference. When it came up he accepted the American and British proposal, though he did object at first to the 'stage by stage' principle.[2] Russian support assured the easy passage of the resolution when it was presented to the General Assembly. The United Nations Atomic Energy Commission was, accordingly, established on 24 January 1946;[3] but this auspicious beginning did not lead to fruitful work in the year that followed.

Only on one important matter did the Foreign Ministers find it impossible to agree at Moscow: Persia. Russian activities in northern Persia had encouraged the development of a separatist movement under Communist leadership in Azerbāījān. In November 1945, when the central Persian Government attempted to send a detachment of troops to the north to put down armed uprisings against its authority, the Red Army barred the road. The Persian troops prudently turned back.

This incident led to protests by the British and American Governments. The Western Powers argued that the Russians were violating the Declaration on Persia, issued at the conclusion of the Tehrān Conference, on 1 December 1943, which committed the Big Three to safeguard the 'sovereignty and territorial integrity' of Persia.[4] It seemed clear to the British and American Governments that Russian action in Azerbāījān was threatening to partition the country by establishing a Communist puppet régime in the northern provinces.[5]

When this delicate matter came up at Moscow, it proved impossible to reconcile the divergent views of the three Governments. In conversation with Byrnes, Stalin dwelt upon the danger to Baku oil wells which a weak and potentially hostile neighbour presented. He bluntly refused to evacuate the Red Army from Persian soil by 2 March 1946 (i.e. six months

[1] *Documents on American Foreign Relations, 1945–1946*, p. 548.

[2] Byrnes: *Speaking Frankly*, pp. 122, 267–8.

[3] See below, pp. 744–6.

[4] See above, pp. 365–6.

[5] A fuller account will be found in the *Survey* for 1939–46: *The Middle East, 1945–50*.

after the end of the war, as prescribed by an Anglo-Soviet treaty of 1942 which regulated the joint occupation of the country). Bevin attempted a compromise by suggesting the appointment of a three-Power commission to investigate the situation and make recommendations. He offered this as an alternative to a public airing of the dispute before the Security Council which he and Byrnes were both anxious to avoid. At one time Molotov gave the impression that he would agree to Bevin's proposal, but on 26 December he changed his tune, declaring flatly that the Persian problem was not properly on the agenda of the meeting and could not be considered. Feeling ran high, especially between Bevin and Molotov, and Byrnes feared that too many angry words would endanger the agreements already reached. He therefore suggested breaking the Conference off, with the understanding that informal consultation on outstanding problems would be resumed in London when the Foreign Ministers attended the opening sessions of the United Nations.[1]

Accordingly, early in the morning of 27 December 1945, the Conference at Moscow came to its close. The three Foreign Ministers had made a serious effort to come to an understanding with one another and had been able to reach a number of important compromises which saved appearances even if they did not much affect realities of power and conflicts of policy. But, significantly, the meeting had ended on a note of vehement dispute. In the months that followed dispute did not become less vehement. Instead it became public.

(*d*) Open Quarrels, openly arrived at, January–April 1946

The General Assembly of the United Nations met for the first time in London on 10 January 1946. Fifty-one nations were represented. The major business was to get the United Nations organization started. The various executive organs of the United Nations had to be launched through elections of members to the Security Council, the Social and Economic Council, the International Court of Justice, and the Trusteeship Council. Rules of procedure had to be adopted and numerous administrative and budgetary matters decided. Organizational problems of this sort kept the Assembly busy but did not directly affect or depend upon conflicts among the Great Powers. Progress was therefore relatively unimpeded, and by the time the Assembly adjourned a skeletal framework for the new international organization had been created. Not everything could be done at once, however, and the Assembly adjourned on 14 February 1946, having agreed to continue its first session in New York in September.[2]

[1] Byrnes: *Speaking Frankly*, pp. 118–21.

[2] A convenient summary of the activities of the United Nations in 1946 may be found in *International Organization*, February 1947, i. 46–116.

The Security Council met for the first time on 18 January 1946, as soon as the non-permanent members had been elected by the Assembly.[1] On 24 January the Persian Government initiated the first important business by lodging a complaint against the 'interference of the Soviet Union . . . in the internal affairs of Iran'. The matter came up for discussion on 26 January. Both Britain and America supported the Persian complaint. After some blunt exchanges, on 1 February 1946 the Security Council temporarily disposed of the matter by requesting the Russian and Persian Governments to try to solve their differences by direct negotiation and to inform the Council of the outcome.

The outcome of these bilateral negotiations was surprisingly satisfactory from the Western point of view. After prolonged negotiation, involving a second appeal to the Security Council by Persia in March, the Russian and Persian Governments reached agreement on 24 March 1946. According to the communiqué issued by the Persian Government on 4 April the Russians agreed to the following:

> Red Army troops will evacuate all Iranian territory within one and one-half months from Sunday, March 24, 1946. . . .
>
> An agreement for the formation of a joint Iranian-Soviet oil company and its terms will be submitted to the fifteenth Majlis [i.e. Persian Parliament] for its approval within seven months after March 24.
>
> With regard to Azerbaijan, since it is internal Iranian affair, peaceful arrangements will be made between the Iranian government and the people of Azerbaijan for carrying out of reforms, in accordance with existing laws and in a benevolent spirit toward the people of Azerbaijan.[2]

In accordance with this agreement, the Russians completed the evacuation of northern Persia by 6 May 1946, leaving behind them an autonomous Azerbāījān Government under Communist domination. The central Persian Government was at first afraid to act against this régime, but in December 1946, when regular Persian troops marched northward, the autonomous Azerbāījān Government collapsed like a house of cards. The Majlis, too, found courage to reject the oil agreement with Russia, and did so without provoking any effective Russian retaliation.

The course of events in Persia must be compared with what transpired between Russia and Turkey during the same months. In November 1945 the Great Powers began formal negotiations with Turkey for a revision of the Montreux Convention which regulated access to the Turkish Straits. The Turks, backed by Britain and America, refused to agree to Russian demands for special rights to garrison the Straits area. On 20 December 1945, while the Foreign Ministers were in session in Moscow, Russo-

[1] Egypt, Mexico, and the Netherlands were elected for one-year terms; Australia, Brazil, and Poland for two-year terms.

[2] *Documents on American Foreign Relations, 1945–1946*, p. 858.

Turkish relations took a new turn when the Russian press launched a noisy campaign for the retrocession of the eastern Turkish provinces of Kars and Ardahan. These public demands provoked resolute Turkish defiance.[1] Anglo-American support for Turkey was unwavering, and in the face of such a combination the Russians forebore from precipitate action. A war of nerves, conducted at fairly low intensity, continued throughout 1946 without bringing any nearer the realization of Russian ambitions.

Thus in both Persia and Turkey Russia's plans for reinforcing her military security and extending her influence came to a full stop. Turkish stubbornness and Persian suppleness, combined with the diplomatic action of the West, presumably persuaded Stalin that the gain was not worth what it might cost him—whether world opprobrium in connexion with Persia or open war with the Turks. After April 1946 the dispute with Persia no longer filled newspaper headlines, and Russia's relations with the two states on her southern frontier ceased to play a critical part in Great Power relations.

When the Persian question first came before the Security Council in January 1946, the Russians were, of course, on the defensive. But they did not wish it to appear that they alone were subject to criticism. Accordingly, the Ukrainian delegate lodged a complaint against the actions of British forces in Indonesia on 21 January; and on the same day the Russian delegate registered a similar complaint against British troops in Greece. On 4 February the Syrian and Lebanese delegates presented another complaint against the presence of British and French troops in their countries, and the Russians supported them. There is no profit in pursuing the ins and outs of legal argument and claim and counter-claim which arose during the discussion of these cases by the Security Council. The Syrian and Lebanese issue was solved by an agreement for the withdrawal of British and French troops; and in May 1946 both complainant countries expressed their satisfaction at the steps which had been taken. In Indonesia, the Security Council refused to send out an investigating commission as the Ukrainian delegate proposed; and with reference to Greece the Security Council on 6 February 1946 adopted a resolution 'taking note' of the views which had been expressed by the various governments and declaring the question closed.

The acid remarks and extravagant accusations exchanged among the Great Powers, and particularly between British and Russian representatives, in the course of these debates dramatized for the world public the conflicts which had arisen among the former Allies. The fact that Great Britain was the main butt of Soviet attack gave the American delegation a chance to play the role of mediator and pacifier on several occasions.

[1] *New York Times*, 21 and 22 December 1945.

The alignment also made it possible for many Americans to feel a smug superiority. Some, especially persons of liberal and Leftist views, felt there was little or nothing to choose between Russian and British policy: both showed the Old Adam of power politics, and of the Great Powers only the United States seem to bear true witness to the New Dispensation writ large in the United Nations Charter.

The fireworks of the Security Council constituted only one aspect of Big Power relationships during the first three months of 1946. Side by side with the propaganda war, a modicum of co-operation and agreement was preserved, almost behind the scenes. This was more or less the case in China, as we have seen; and it was equally true in Germany.

The Allied Control Council in Berlin had got off to a bad start owing to the fact that the French Government had not been invited to the Potsdam Conference, and did not accept the decisions of that Conference with respect to Germany.[1] Consequently, efforts to establish the rudiments of a central German administration met French opposition on the Control Council; and by 14 October 1945 these efforts were suspended. Thereafter, occupation authorities in each zone went their own way, establishing local administration according to various patterns and at various times.

As winter came on, economic problems loomed larger and larger. General disorganization and damage to machinery and communications combined with undernourishment among the miners to make it impossible to produce much coal from the German mines. Yet coal was the main commodity that Western Germany could hope to export in order to pay for food and other necessary imports; and coal was vitally needed by other countries of Europe to sustain their own damaged economies. Millions of German refugees from the east complicated the problem of feeding the population. As a result, in the autumn of 1945 both Britain and the United States found it necessary to import food for their zones of Germany, despite the fact that the Germans could not pay anything in return. The resulting drain on British resources was particularly heavy.

From the point of view of Allied relationships two points were of critical importance. Britain and the United States were anxious to make an agreement with the Russians which would assure the economic unity of Germany. Only thus could east German food become available for the needy west. The Russians were equally anxious to get their share of reparations from Western zones of Germany. But before reparations deliveries could begin on a regular basis, it was necessary to decide what factories would be 'surplus' to the peace-time German economy; and this in turn required a systematic survey to determine the appropriate industrial capacity

[1] See above, p. 627.

needed to maintain a peace-time German economy. Much detailed work and some close bargaining went into the preparation of an agreement defining the 'level of industry' which would be left to Germany. The agreement was accepted by the four members of the Allied Control Council on 26 March 1946.[1]

The calculations which had gone into making the level of industry plan were based on the assumption that the German economy would function as a single unit, as had been prescribed by the Potsdam agreement. Only if the production of the various zones became fully complementary would the agreed-upon level of industry suffice to maintain the population and make it possible for Germany to pay for necessary imports.

Having agreed to a level of industry, the next tasks before the Allied Control Council were to designate specific factories as 'surplus', thus making them available for removal as reparations; to allot the various plants among the recipient nations; and simultaneously to make the necessary administrative arrangements for unifying the economies of the four zones.

But how to proceed? Britain and America were increasingly concerned to get their zones on a self-supporting basis in order to eliminate the necessity for subsidies from their respective home treasuries. The Russians, on the other hand, were becoming impatient for the reparations from the Western zones which had been promised them under the Potsdam agreement, but which had not yet been forthcoming on any large scale. But the two goals were contradictory. Spoliation of the German industrial plant would make more difficult the establishment of German self-sufficiency; and the Western Powers were resolved that they would not start a large-scale reparations programme until the Russians took steps to put the resources of their zone of occupation at the disposal of the German economy as a whole. This the Russians were quite unwilling to do. They had uses of their own for surplus food and other goods produced in the Eastern zone and were not concerned about what it might cost the British and American Governments to coddle the West Germans.

It is conceivable that these differences might have been resolved if the general climate of Allied relations had been different; but, as things were, the tug-of-war over the German economy merely added fuel to the fire. The level of industry agreement of 26 March 1946 marked the high-water

[1] General Clay (*Decision in Germany*, pp. 106–19) provides some interesting side-lights on the work of the Council in drawing up the level of industry plan. The key figure was steel production capacity. This was fixed at 7½ million tons annually, a compromise between the Russian figure of 4½ million tons and the British figure of 9 million tons. Oddly enough, the State Department differed from the American authorities in Germany, and proposed limitation of German steel capacity to 3½ million tons, less than half the figure General Clay judged proper—7,800,000 (ibid. p. 108). It seems apparent that the advocates of something like the Morgenthau Plan for Germany were still active in the State Department in December 1945 when this question was debated.

mark of agreement over Germany; thereafter the policies and attitudes of Britain and America on the one side drifted farther and farther from those of the Russians, until an open break came early in May.[1]

In other regions of the world the agreements reached at the Moscow meeting of the three Foreign Ministers worked out as might have been expected. In Rumania the Communists kept control. The Western Powers were dissatisfied but forebore from active protests in the hope that the promised free elections would bring in a more acceptable régime. In Japan the nullity of the Far Eastern Commission's authority was conclusively demonstrated when its remonstrances against too hasty holding of elections, sent to General MacArthur on 21 March 1946, were briskly dismissed as groundless eight days later. The elections were held on 10 April, returning a rather conservative majority; and the Far Eastern Commission lapsed into futility.[2]

Meanwhile, the Foreign Ministers' deputies in London were privately at work trying to agree upon the details of the five peace treaties. The Russian deputy lacked any independent authority to negotiate, even over trivia; and the basic differences which had been revealed at the first meeting of the Council of Foreign Ministers had not been removed. As a result, progress was slow, and it soon became apparent that the Peace Conference, scheduled to assemble by 1 May 1946, would have to be postponed.

In April the Foreign Ministers decided to meet again to try to resolve the difficulties that beset their deputies. Accordingly the Council of Foreign Ministers assembled for a second time on 25 April, this time in Paris.

(iv) The Onset of the Cold War, April–December 1946

(*a*) The Five Peace Treaties

When the Council of Foreign Ministers met for the second time, on 25 April 1946, Molotov surprised his colleagues by blandly dropping the procedural argument which had wrecked the first endeavour at peace-making during the preceding September. Meeting in the French capital and operating under rules which permitted full newspaper publicity, Molotov no longer wished to exclude France from discussion of the East European treaties. But this volte-face was not a sign of any real change of policy; rather it was an adjustment to a new propaganda problem. Molotov did not wish unnecessarily to alienate French sympathy by offending the national *amour propre*, and it was exactly this calculation that had

[1] See below, pp. 724 seqq.

[2] Texts of the letters exchanged between the Commission and MacArthur may be found in *Documents on American Foreign Relations, 1945–1946*, pp. 280–3.

led Byrnes to propose meeting in Paris and to demand publicity for the Council's deliberations.[1]

Thus from the beginning the atmosphere of the second meeting of the Council of Foreign Ministers was dominated by a new spirit.[2] On both sides the desire to score a propaganda victory overbalanced any desire to reach agreement. Discussions consequently degenerated into tedious oratory. Real interests and intentions were frequently cloaked in fine words and high principles, while bluntness and imputation of evil motives to the other side became a prominent stock in trade. Byrnes excelled in using fine words, Molotov in bluntness; Bevin used both. The net result scarcely forwarded the peace treaties.

Intricacies of the debate need not be retraced here. Between 25 April and 16 May, when the Council went into recess for a month, some minor clauses of the proposed treaties were accepted; but the major conflicts remained completely unresolved. Molotov modified his claim for an outright trusteeship over Tripolitania, suggesting instead a joint Russo-Italian administration. But this did not quiet Bevin's fear of seeing Russian power clamped across the 'life-line' of the British Empire. Discussion of the Italian-Yugoslav boundary, of Italian reparations, and of economic clauses in the satellite treaties, showed no signs of getting anywhere, and

[1] Byrnes: *Speaking Frankly*, pp. 124, 251.

[2] A significant change in the relationship between President Truman and Secretary of State Byrnes took place immediately after the Moscow Conference in December 1945. This change seems to have affected American foreign policy both in the manner of its formulation and in its immediate aims.

During Truman's first months in the Presidency, he left foreign affairs almost entirely in Byrnes's hands. Byrnes, after all, had been one of Roosevelt's confidants and lieutenants, whereas Truman had been entirely excluded from high affairs. Hence Byrnes could justly claim to be an old hand, better able to pursue Roosevelt's policies than Truman could be. The presidential novice apparently agreed to give Byrnes a free rein.

But during the Moscow Conference Byrnes neglected to inform Truman of the deals he made until after they were accomplished. This nettled Truman, and when Byrnes returned to Washington the President chided him for failing to consult his superior and criticized some of the compromises Byrnes had made. For a semi-official account of what passed, as seen from Truman's personal point of view, see William Hillman, ed.: *Mr. President: the First Publication from the Personal Diaries, Private Letters, Papers and Revealing Interviews by Harry S. Truman* (New York, Farrar, Straus & Young, 1952), pp. 21–23.

Thereafter, it seems reasonable to surmise that Truman took a more active part in shaping American foreign policy, and that Byrnes's plenipotentiary powers in dealings with Molotov were correspondingly reduced. It also seems clear that compromise for the sake of compromise was abandoned. In Truman's own words: 'I do not think we should compromise any longer. I'm tired of babying the Soviets' (ibid. p. 23).

This was a new note in American foreign policy, and marked a break with Roosevelt's effort to seek an understanding with Stalin at almost any cost. It does not follow that Roosevelt himself, had he lived, might not have done the same; nor is it true to say that Truman kept strictly and constantly to the position he had taken in a moment of irritation against his over-mighty Secretary of State. Indeed, as we have already seen (above, p. 659), it was not until September 1946, when Wallace was dismissed from the Cabinet, that the policy of seeking compromise with the Russians by conceding at least a part of their demands was more definitely and publicly repudiated.

tempers were frequently strained by Molotov's uncompromising manner. Indeed, the American delegation concluded that the Russians did not want to see peace treaties which would end the military occupation of the countries of South-East Europe.[1]

The major new characteristic of the second meeting of the Council of Foreign Ministers was the direction of Molotov's propaganda attack. The United States replaced Great Britain as his primary target. The principal occasion for Molotov's onslaught was an American effort to write into the East European peace treaties provisions guaranteeing free navigation of the Danube and equality of treatment for all nations in economic and trade relations. In this Molotov professed to see sinister American capitalism attempting to fasten its claws into the weak economies of Eastern Europe. In reality, American policy in Germany was probably at least as important in provoking Molotov's wrath.[2]

Efforts to fix a date for calling the Peace Conference met with no success. Molotov insisted that the Council should first agree on all basic issues. Similarly, proposals to appoint special deputies to begin work on a peace treaty for Germany met with Russian veto. One of the few positive achievements was an agreement to modify the Italian armistice terms and abolish the Allied Commission in that country. This move, a sop to Italian national feeling, involved no loss to the Russians, whose share in the direction of Italian affairs had always been marginal, and Molotov therefore agreed.

Facing an apparent impasse, the Council took a recess on 16 May 1946. The Foreign Ministers reassembled a month later on 15 June, again in Paris, to continue their efforts. Old ground was once more canvassed during the first days, but by 27 June Molotov began to show signs of yielding on a number of points. On that day he accepted some of the economic provisions of the Rumanian treaty which he had previously opposed and suddenly agreed to the transfer of the Dodecanese Islands to Greece. The next problem to be solved was the delimitation of the Italian-Yugoslav border. In accordance with a French suggestion, the Council agreed that Trieste and its immediate environs should become an international zone; and, again following a French suggestion, the Council approved a new border between Italy and Yugoslavia which fell between the line advocated by the Russians, favourable to the Yugoslavs, and the line proposed by the Americans, more favourable to the Italians. But the Foreign Ministers were not able to agree on the details of the future international administration of Trieste, and this question remained open when the Peace Conference met. How to dispose of the Italian colonies likewise proved too difficult to decide; but Molotov did accept an American proposal to postpone decision for a year after the peace treaties

[1] Byrnes: *Speaking Frankly*, pp. 125, 129.

[2] See below, pp. 724 seqq.

came into effect, with the understanding that if private negotiation could not resolve the problem it should be referred to the United Nations General Assembly.

These agreements represented heartening progress. Two matters remained: Italian reparations and the summoning of a general Peace Conference. Molotov wished the other members of the Council to accept point-blank his demand for $100 million reparations from Italy before he would agree to call the Peace Conference. Byrnes and Bevin refused to 'buy' the Conference for such a price, but offered to reconsider the reparations question if Molotov would first agree to calling the Peace Conference. In the end, on 4 July, Molotov gave in. The Council fixed upon 29 July 1946 as the date for the assemblage of the Peace Conference, and on the next day Byrnes and Bevin in effect conceded Molotov's demand for $100 million reparations from Italy.

Further controversy over the rules of procedure to be applied at the Peace Conference delayed the invitations to the twenty-one nations whose eligibility had been agreed upon at Moscow in December. Molotov wished to bind the smaller Powers to a rigid procedure at the Conference, but in the end he agreed that the procedural recommendations drawn up by the Council of Foreign Ministers would be only 'suggestions'. When this had been settled, the invitations were duly issued on 9 July, even though the Council of Foreign Ministers had not yet agreed upon a régime for Trieste. The Council ended its meeting on 12 July 1946 after three days of discussion on German questions.[1]

The Paris Peace Conference (29 July–15 October 1946) accomplished more than might have been expected from the manner in which it had come to birth. Two reasons may be advanced to explain this fact. One was that the Great Powers had not agreed upon all the treaty clauses in advance, so that the smaller nations were not confronted with completed drafts when the Conference began. A second reason was that the Soviet Union could not command more than six[2] out of twenty-one votes, and under the rules of procedure which the Conference accepted the Russian minority was insufficient to block the adoption of recommendations upon which the other nations agreed.

The decisive struggle took place at the beginning, over the adoption of procedural rules. Russian efforts to require a two-thirds majority for all recommendations failed. Instead two classes of recommendations were recognized, those supported by two-thirds and those supported by a simple

[1] Byrnes: *Speaking Frankly*, pp. 131–7.

[2] The Ukraine, White Russia, Yugoslavia, Poland, and Czechoslovakia regularly supported the Soviet Union.

majority. Secretary Byrnes announced that the United States would accept any recommendations passed by a two-thirds vote, regardless of what the American position on the question had been at the Conference itself. This gave the opinions of the smaller Powers far more weight than would otherwise have been the case, and removed the Conference from the realm of farce.

Each nation had a chance to submit modifications or new proposals for inclusion in the five draft treaties which the Conference had been summoned to consider. Altogether more than three hundred amendments came under consideration. Fifty-three of them were passed by a two-thirds majority and forty-one by simple majority.

Many of the suggested changes in the treaty texts were of a minor nature, including improvements of legal phraseology which the painful nature of the preliminary negotiations had frequently left highly imperfect. The most important matters of substance which came up for consideration were the delineation of the Italo-Yugoslav border; the definition of the international régime for Trieste; provision for summoning a future international conference to regulate navigation on the Danube; and distribution of Italian reparations among claimants other than the Soviet Union.[1]

Many bitter words were publicly exchanged during the course of the Peace Conference. A marked feature was the mechanical discipline of the bloc of states under Soviet influence; and the existence of such a bloc tended to create a counter bloc of Western states, despite the fact that France and some other nations tried systematically to mediate and take an independent middle position on disputed points. Though a Peace Conference in name, the atmosphere of the Conference was certainly not one of peace and international concord.

The next step, according to the procedure agreed to at Moscow in December 1945, was to reconvene the Council of Foreign Ministers to consider the suggestions which had come from the Peace Conference and draw up final texts of the five treaties. Accordingly, the Council of Foreign Ministers met for a third time on 4 November 1946, this time in New York.[2]

The first discussions were not promising. Molotov refused to accept any of the Peace Conference recommendations which had been passed against the Soviet bloc's vote; and he was in no wise mollified when Bevin accepted with good grace a recommendation which the British dele-

[1] Byrnes: *Speaking Frankly*, pp. 139–49.

[2] This third session ran concurrently with the meetings of the United Nations General Assembly which had begun on 23 October.

gation had opposed at the Peace Conference itself. Complete deadlock seemed to have been reached.

After about four weeks, Byrnes told Molotov privately that there seemed no further use in trying to agree upon the peace treaties and suggested that the Council adjourn its meetings. This new attitude apparently took Molotov by surprise. The Soviet Union stood to gain a good deal by the conclusion of the five treaties that had been so long under negotiation. The Italian treaty prescribed the withdrawal of British and American troops from that country before the end of 1947. Such withdrawal might offer more scope for the Italian Communists; and at the least would reduce direct Western influence. On the other hand, the conclusion of the treaties with Rumania and Hungary required no parallel withdrawal of Russian forces, since as long as Austria remained under occupation it could plausibly be argued that 'line of communications troops' were required in those countries to support the Russian garrison of Austria. A similar argument applied to Germany and lines of communication through Poland. Thus until treaties could be drawn up with Austria and Germany the Russians could legally maintain troops in the three satellite countries whose loyalty to Russia and Communism was undependable. Bulgaria did not lie athwart any line of communication; but withdrawal of Russian troops from that country in accordance with the peace treaty would not seriously endanger Communist control since the Party was already strong. As for Finland, the treaty recognized Russia's rights to keep garrisons in Finland permanently.

A second gain which the treaties would bring to Russia was the abolition of the awkward Allied Control Commissions in the East European states. These bodies had been reduced to ineffectiveness, but so long as they and the armistice régimes remained the Western Powers had a good legal claim to share in Rumanian, Bulgarian, Hungarian, and (Britain alone) Finnish affairs.

On the other hand, the treaties guaranteed civil liberties and prescribed economic practices which the Russians disliked. Molotov presumably never intended to take these provisions seriously. Once the armistice régimes had come to an end, the sacred sovereignty of national governments could be invoked to assure a Communist interpretation of all such objectionable clauses.

Thus the prospect of a breakdown in the peace treaty negotiations could not please Molotov. Presumably he decided that concessions would have to be made; and having so decided he made them in a big way. With only a few face-saving changes in phraseology, Molotov surprised his colleagues by accepting in rapid succession forty-seven of the fifty-three recommendations which had been passed by a two-thirds vote in the Peace Conference, and twenty-four of the forty-one recommendations which had received a bare majority. The recommendations Molotov still would not accept were simply dropped. This sudden spurt made it possible to agree upon the final texts of the treaties for Italy, Rumania, Bulgaria, Hungary, and Finland by 6 December 1946, when the Council of Foreign Ministers ended its long travail over these documents. Signature of the treaties was scheduled for 10 February 1947.

Before it broke up, the Council of Foreign Ministers discussed the problem of drafting German and Austrian peace treaties, and agreed to instruct the deputies in London to start work on these far more difficult and important documents at once. A new meeting of the Council to handle these problems was set for March 1947. Moscow was chosen as the site for this, the fourth meeting of the Council of Foreign Ministers.[1]

By mid-December 1946 the process of peace-making had quite lost its original meaning. When Byrnes took office as Secretary of State he had imagined himself a new Wilson, bringing peace to Europe and the world in a matter of months. Instead, he had faced systematic obstruction and a barrage of hostile propaganda from Molotov, and in the end had very little to show for the high hopes with which he had launched his peace-making career. It seems right to say that Molotov out-manœuvred him. Molotov played one game and Byrnes had tried to play another. Liberal principles—equality of access of all nations to the trade of the world, civil liberties, democracy, disarmament of ex-enemy countries—these had been the goals which the American Government initially set themselves to realize through the peace treaties. Molotov on the contrary set out to protect Russia's special position in Eastern Europe. He succeeded, Byrnes failed—partly because of Molotov's tactics, partly because Byrnes's own approach to the problems of peace was so doctrinaire.

Appeals to democratic principles not backed by significant military force merely irritated the Russians without impressing them, the more so since the democratic principles which Byrnes and Bevin supported would have weakened or destroyed Russia's influence in the countries adjacent to the Soviet Union's western border. A 'spheres of influence' deal with the Russians might have been possible; and if Britain and America had been prepared to maintain large military forces in Western Europe they might have been able to compel the Russians to act with more restraint in Eastern Europe. But neither policy was tried; and the actual fruit of Byrnes's diplomacy—the five treaties—was rather a setback than a gain for the West.

Yet Molotov's apparent success was a larger defeat. His behaviour at the successive meetings of the Foreign Ministers had alienated public

[1] Byrnes: *Speaking Frankly*, pp. 150–4.

sympathy in America and Britain. More than that, Molotov's diplomacy had done much to persuade the American Government and people to adopt an actively anti-Russian policy and had prevented American withdrawal from Europe on the scale and time-table Byrnes originally imagined. Rudely awakening the American giant from dreams of easy peace, stirring old fears of Communism in American hearts, loosening American purse-strings for the support of non-Communist countries: these by-products of Molotov's diplomacy were not in accord with Russian long-range interests. By seeking to hold what had been won in the war, and by threatening to expand into new areas, the Russians began the creation of what they most feared—an anti-Russian coalition led by the United States. But these consequences were not fully apparent until later; in the short run Stalin and Molotov could congratulate themselves on having taken clever advantage of the peace negotiations to safeguard Russian predominance in Eastern Europe.

(*b*) The Struggle in Germany

From April 1946 to the end of the year the most immediate and critical problem confronting the Great Powers was what to do about Germany. Verbal battles before the Security Council and in the Council of Foreign Ministers contained a large element of make-believe, but the contest in Germany was very real and very serious. Germany's central position in Europe, the numbers and technical skill of the German people, the value of German coal and industrial products for the economy of Europe as a whole, and the potential military power of the German nation all combined to make Germany the chief prize to be won in Europe, or, indeed, in the world.

In September 1945, during the first meeting of the Council of Foreign Ministers in London, Byrnes proposed informally to Molotov that the Great Powers should conclude a treaty providing guarantees for the demilitarization of Germany.[1] At Moscow in December 1945 he mentioned the matter to Stalin, and got the impression that the Russians would welcome such a step. Accordingly, a draft was drawn up by experts in the State Department, and on 29 April 1946 Byrnes submitted the draft to his colleagues at the second meeting of the Council of Foreign Ministers.[2] The draft committed the four Governments—U.S.A., U.S.S.R., U.K., and France—to take steps to ensure the complete disarmament of Germany. A four-Power Commission of Control was to have powers of constant inspection to make sure that secret rearmament did not take place, and the four Powers undertook to intervene at once with military force if a

[1] See above, p. 698.

[2] The draft had been sent to the British, French, and Russian Governments for informal consideration in February.

future German Government contravened the provisions of the treaty. The treaty was to run for twenty-five years, with the possibility of renewal.[1]

From the point of view of traditional American diplomacy the offer to sign such a treaty was a new and radical departure. Byrnes hoped that such an instrument would reassure the Russians and the French against fear of some new Hitler, and would clear the way for the early conclusion of the European peace treaties. The treaty draft expressly looked forward to the end of Allied occupation of Germany, presumably in the near future; and when he presented it to the Council Byrnes simultaneously suggested that deputies be immediately appointed to begin work on a peace treaty with Germany.[2]

The French and British accepted the proposal, reserving the right to suggest modifications in the text Byrnes had presented to them. Molotov, however, objected on what can only be described as captious grounds. He said that the first task was to enforce the Potsdam agreements for German disarmament and demilitarization; then argued that the term of the treaty should be extended to forty years. When Byrnes pointed out a clause in the draft that stated explicitly that 'nothing shall prevent or delay completion of the process' of complete demilitarization of Germany, and agreed to extend the term to forty years, Molotov fell back upon the vaguer objection that the treaty Byrnes proposed was 'inadequate' and would not 'be a reliable guarantee of security in Europe and the world'. He objected, also, to the absence of provisions for ensuring the democratization of Germany—a matter Byrnes thought should be taken care of by the peace treaty—and finally objected that the proposed treaty omitted any guarantee of the $10 milliard reparations due to the Soviet Union from Germany.[3]

In mentioning reparations Molotov was coming closer to the heart of the matter. As he later said in a public speech, one of the aims of the Red Army in Germany was to 'assure reparations deliveries';[4] and when the Council of Foreign Ministers took up German questions in April and May 1946 new difficulties between American and Russian authorities had just arisen over the delivery of reparations to Russia. After fruitless efforts to get the Russian representative on the Allied Control Council to agree to submit an accounting of the reparations taken from the Eastern zone of Germany, and equally unsuccessful efforts to persuade the Russians to relax the economic barriers between their zone and the Western ones, General Clay decided to halt future deliveries of reparations from the

[1] Text may be found in *Documents on American Foreign Relations, 1945–1946*, pp. 205–8.

[2] Byrnes: *Speaking Frankly*, pp. 171–3.

[3] Ibid. pp. 174–5.

[4] *Molotov on the Future of Germany* (London, Soviet News, 1946), p. 7, a translation of Molotov's statement of 9 July 1946 (see p. 726 for this statement).

American zone until the Russians came round. This decision he announced to his colleagues on the Control Council on 3 May 1946.[1]

Molotov's rejection of the proposed demilitarization treaty and Clay's action in stopping future reparations deliveries from the American zone marked the end of all pretence of common policy in Germany on the part of the war-time Allies. The American action was provoked by an unwillingness to continue subsidizing the German economy while the Russians siphoned off German resources in the form of reparations. The Russian action in rejecting Byrnes's proffered treaty must be interpreted as a sign of unwillingness to prepare for an early termination of the occupation of Germany, and their attitude on economic questions made it clear that they did not desire the merger of their zone with the Western zones. These were far more fateful decisions than any taken in connexion with the five peace treaties, if only because of Germany's intrinsic importance in Europe.

When the Council of Foreign Ministers convened for the second time in Paris, the German question was again debated, beginning on 9 July 1946. Molotov attempted a remarkable *tour de force*. On 9 July he read a statement attacking Byrnes's proffered demilitarization treaty and the stoppage of reparations deliveries. The Russian Foreign Minister criticized the failure of the occupation authorities to take steps to eliminate 'German war and military-economic potential', and attacked the Western zonal authorities for failing to eliminate Fascism, especially for their failure to break up its economic base—the cartels and landed estates. He reasserted in most emphatic terms the Russian demand for $10 milliard reparations, which he declared should be exacted 'without fail' in spite of the recent 'unlawful statement' made by General Clay.[2]

On the next day, however, Molotov embarked on a new and startling tack. Having demanded his pound of flesh from Germany on 9 July, on 10 July he attacked the recent level of industry plan which had been promulgated by the Allied Control Council[3] on the ground that it unduly restricted German production. After some indirect references to the Morgenthau Plan, which Molotov suggested still inspired Western policy

[1] Clay: *Decision in Germany*, p. 122. Certain factories had been earmarked for advance delivery to Russia, and these were not affected by Clay's decision.

[2] *Molotov on the Future of Germany*, pp. 3–8. Molotov's revival of the figure of $10 milliard for the Russian share of German reparations was, of course, a return to a position the Russians had been compelled to abandon at Potsdam. He also blandly claimed the right to receive reparations from current German production which they had also abandoned at Potsdam in favour of a percentage of capital removals. Under the circumstances one can only assume that the Russians had given up all intention of co-operating with the Western Powers in Germany, and that Molotov's pronouncements were intended to justify the rejection of the demilitarization treaty in the eyes of the world. He sought especially to appeal to French opinion, which naturally sympathized with demands for heavy reparations from Germany. The American officials in Paris believed one of Molotov's main aims was to strengthen the position of the French Communists (Clay: *Decision in Germany*, p. 127).

[3] See above, p. 716.

towards Germany, he said: 'Germany should be granted the right to export and import and, if this right to foreign trade is to be effectual, we should not hinder Germany from increasing her output of steel, coal and manufactured products of a peaceful nature, naturally within certain bounds, and on the understanding that inter-Allied control is inevitably established over German industry, and over the Ruhr industries in particular.' And again:

Of course we stand in principle for the conclusion of a peace treaty with Germany, but before concluding this treaty there should be set up a single German Government sufficiently democratic to be able to extirpate all remnants of Fascism in Germany, and sufficiently responsible to be able to fulfil all its obligations towards the Allies, including more particularly those in respect of reparations deliveries to the Allies.

It goes without saying that we raise no objection to the setting up of a German central administration. . . . Before talking about a peace treaty with Germany, it is necessary to solve the question of setting up an all-German Government.

The main obstacle to this, he implied earlier in his speech, was the policy of the Western nations which favoured federalizing or dismembering Germany, or separating the Ruhr from the rest of the country. As for the Soviet Government, it would never 'stand in the way of the German people's rightful aspirations', provided that Germany remained disarmed.[1]

This was a direct and clever appeal to the national feeling of the Germans. Molotov appeared as the champion of German political unity and of the removal of economic restrictions which, if enforced, would doom Germany permanently to a lowered standard of living and to an artificial disadvantage in competition with British, French, or Belgian exporters. To be sure Molotov still wanted reparations and international control of the Ruhr, but the Germans already suffered under these disabilities and so stood to lose nothing new in return for the economic and political relief Molotov offered. Under the circumstances, Molotov's proposals were distasteful only to the Western Powers, who found themselves forced to take the defensive before the bar of German opinion.[2]

[1] *Molotov on the Future of Germany*, pp. 9–13.

[2] Molotov's statement was, of course, a startling contrast to the Russian position during the negotiations leading to the level of industry plan, when the Russians had pressed for a lower steel production total than the other Powers thought practicable or desirable. But it would perhaps be wrong to believe that the contradiction was simply an effort to win German support and sympathy, and to embarrass the Western Powers. The Russians had found that the seizure of capital goods as reparations, dismantlement of factories, and the transfer of machinery eastward, were not a very efficient way of getting much-needed goods for the Russian economy quickly. Machines were liable to damage in transit and there were delays in getting factories started up again in Russian territory, even when other problems—labour supply, power supply, raw material supply, &c.—did not hamper or prevent renewed production.

The Western authorities believed that Russian policy in the East zone of Germany altered in April or May 1946. Instead of proceeding further with removals German factories were set to work for the Russian market *in situ*. Among other things, it was reported to the British and

The British and American Foreign Ministers were taken aback by Molotov's new departure. Bevin replied briefly that the British would agree to putting the Ruhr under four-Power supervision as soon as all German industry was subjected to similar control, but not before. This was at best a negative retort; but Byrnes was able to do better. On the next day, 11 July, he proposed that a practical start be made towards unifying German economic life by offering to merge the American zone with any or all of the other zones.[1] On 20 July Byrnes's suggestion was formally presented to the Allied Control Council in Berlin and it was accepted by the British representative on 30 July 1946. The Russians, of course, refused to join their zone with the American and British, and so did the French.

Negotiation for the economic merger of the British and American zones was a rather long-drawn-out affair, not completed until 2 December 1946. The organizational side was not particularly difficult. The two Governments were anxious to avoid the appearance of creating a West German Government. They agreed to establish a series of executive committees to deal with separate aspects of the German economic problem—food and agriculture, transport, communications, civil service, finance, and a general one to handle 'economics' as a whole. These committees were German in personnel. Their seats were divided among the leading cities of the British and American zones. Such an arrangement was inherently clumsy, but was adopted to avoid the creation of a West German capital.

More important was the establishment of an Anglo-American Board which was charged with the task of working out common economic standards and practices for the two zones. This Board was to give instructions to the German committees, which would attend to detailed application of policies so laid down. The key matter of foreign trade was entrusted to a Joint Export-Import Agency, staffed by British and American officials. This agency was to receive the foreign exchange earned by

American authorities that substantial amounts of munitions were produced in Eastern Germany in 1946—an infraction of the demilitarization clauses of the Potsdam agreements (Clay: *Decision in Germany*, p. 128; Byrnes: *Speaking Frankly*, p. 177; Nettl: *The Eastern Zone and Soviet Policy in Germany*, pp. 204, 208 seqq.).

Obviously the new Russian policy would be more popular in Germany since it meant an end to dismantlement and it would guarantee employment to Germans.

Molotov's public pronouncement of 10 July was a logical extension of the policy. If Germany were to be made to produce for Russian requirements, limits on production were no longer desirable; and a unified Germany would be able to supply more. Both Russians and Germans stood to gain by such an arrangement; the more so since most German products were competitive with British and American export goods, while Russia and Eastern Europe could, if political decision inclined that way, provide Germany with food and important raw materials in exchange for manufactures. Hitler's dream of *Grossraumwirtschaft* would have been realized in reverse, with Russia, not Germany, politically dominant.

With such possible gains in view, the fact that the proposal would damage the political interests of the Western Powers may have seemed to Molotov as almost a subsidiary, though not unwelcome, consideration.

[1] Clay: *Decision in Germany*, pp. 130–1.

exports from the Western zones and to make contracts for necessary German imports. The foreign trade deficits anticipated during the immediate future were to be met equally by grants from the American and British Governments.

It was this latter point which constituted the main obstacle to the conclusion of the negotiations. The British Government were seriously alarmed at the drain upon their resources which resulted from the trading deficit of the British zone of Germany. In particular, the British Government did not wish to have to pay dollars for imports required by Germany. But the American Government did not wish to increase their obligations as a result of the zonal merger. Quite the opposite: the principal motive behind the whole negotiation was to reduce American costs by making Germany more nearly self-supporting. When British and American authorities in Germany proved unable to come to agreement on the share each country should contribute to the German trade deficit, the matter was brought before Byrnes and Bevin during the meeting of the Council of Foreign Ministers in New York in November 1946. Bevin made an appeal to Byrnes to accept responsibility for at least 60 per cent. of the cost of supporting the two zones; but Byrnes was not to be moved, and Bevin in the end agreed to accept an equal sharing of the burden. The final agreement was signed on 2 December 1946, and Bizonia, as the new arrangement soon came to be called, began operation with the new year, on 1 January 1947.[1]

While British and American officials were conducting their negotiations for the economic merger of their zones of Germany, the Allied Control Council continued its day-to-day operations as before. The Russian and French members of the Council were informed of the steps towards Anglo-American agreement; and the door was carefully kept open for the adhesion of the other occupying Powers at some time in the future. Neither the Russians nor the Anglo-Americans repudiated the formal commitment of Potsdam to treat Germany as an economic unit,[2] but each was resolved to unite the German economy only on its own terms.

During the second half of 1946, however, each side tended to believe

[1] Clay: *Decision in Germany*, pp. 163–73; Byrnes: *Speaking Frankly*, pp. 195–7. Text of the agreement may be found in *Documents on American Foreign Relations, 1945–1946*, pp. 218–21. It should be recognized that the American Government in accepting responsibility for half the German deficit were relieving Britain of some of the costs previously borne by the British Treasury. Because the British zone was more heavily industrialized, its deficit was greater than the American zone's. Thus it was calculated that for 1947 the deficit of the American zone would be $200 million and of the British zone $400 million. By the agreement the U.S. Government undertook to supply about $300 million, $100 million more than would have been the American share if the principle of separate responsibility for each zone's deficit had been accepted, as first proposed by the American negotiators.

[2] See above, p. 625.

that the other would eventually yield. The American decision to halt reparations deliveries to Russia did not prevent the Control Council from proceeding with studies and other preparations for the resumption of reparations payments—earmarking plants for dismantlement, valuing them, allotting them to the claimant countries, &c. This perhaps persuaded the Russians to believe that the Americans were really bluffing, and would eventually agree to carry out the reparations programme in return for some Soviet concession. Similarly, American officials hoped and tended to believe that a sufficient show of resolution on their part would make the Russians realize that the only way in which they could get their much desired reparations would be by agreeing to treat Germany as an economic whole, pooling the resources of their zone with those of the Western zones, and agreeing to an accountancy of German exports to Russia and Eastern Europe. It was this frame of mind which permitted the members of the Control Council to maintain reasonably friendly personal relations during the second half of 1946, and to agree upon a large number of relatively minor enactments—excise taxes, trade union policy, repeal of Nazi legislation, parcel post regulations, &c.[1]

Nevertheless, there was a series of incidents between Russian and other occupying forces. Kidnappings in the Western sectors of Berlin, apparently inspired by the Russians, provoked alarm among non-Communist Germans and stimulated protests from the Western Powers. Quarrels over disciplinary acts against members of one another's armed forces, and over seizure of such bits of property as railway rolling-stock, &c., showed how easily the Russians and the Western Powers might come to loggerheads. Moreover, a more or less constant propaganda war was fought in the newspapers, those of the Eastern zone criticizing the actions of the Western authorities and those in the West attacking Russian behaviour and policies.[2]

One of the themes of Communist propaganda, circulated usually not through the public press but by means of whispering campaigns—or what the Americans believed were whispering campaigns—was very effective. The rumour ran that the Americans would soon withdraw from Germany and from Europe, disgusted at the perils and costs of an active European policy.[3] It is even possible that the Russians seriously counted upon such a retreat. Roosevelt had said at Yalta that American troops could not be maintained in Europe for more than a couple of years after the end of the war,[4] and the policy of Byrnes and Truman was designed, among other things, to permit the early withdrawal of all or nearly all American

[1] Clay: *Decision in Germany*, p. 132.
[2] Ibid. pp. 133–9.
[3] Byrnes: *Speaking Frankly*, p. 187.
[4] See above, pp. 532, 548, 610.

occupation forces. Thus the Russians were not without some ground for hoping that American behaviour after the Second World War would conform to that of 1919–20.

Partly to counteract propaganda to this effect and partly to offer the Germans an attractive policy that would rival Molotov's pronouncement of 10 July, Byrnes decided to make a formal and public declaration of American policy towards Germany. Accordingly, on 6 September 1946, the Secretary of State addressed a mixed German and American audience at Stuttgart. The Paris Peace Conference was then in session, and exchange of bitter accusations between the Russians and the Americans had reached a cacophonous crescendo. Negotiations for the economic merger of the American and British zones were still in their initial stages; and, at the other end of Europe, the Greek guerrilla movement was just beginning to sprout for a second time. It was against this troublous background that Byrnes made his speech.[1] Every effort was made to invest the occasion with solemnity and to publicize the Secretary of State's remarks.

Byrnes began by emphasizing America's permanent and inescapable involvement in the affairs of the whole world. He went on to affirm American attachment to the principles of the Potsdam settlement, but declared that if they could not be translated into reality it would be necessary to revise upward the level of industry agreement, which presupposed German economic unity. Byrnes attacked Molotov's claim for reparations from current German production as being clearly incompatible with the Potsdam agreement, and came out flatly for the complete obliteration of economic barriers and differences between the zones of Germany. 'The time has come', he said, 'when the zonal boundaries should be regarded as defining only the areas to be occupied for security purposes by the armed forces of the occupying powers and not as self-contained economic or political units.' As for the long-term economic future, he declared: 'Germany must be given a chance to export goods in order to import enough to make her economy self-sustaining. Germany is a part of Europe, and recovery in Europe, and particularly in the states adjoining Germany, will be slow indeed if Germany with her great resources of iron and coal is turned into a poorhouse.' On the political side, Byrnes announced:

> It is the view of the American Government that the German people throughout Germany, under proper safeguards, should now be given the primary responsibility for the running of their own affairs. . . .
>
> All that the Allied governments can and should do is to lay down the rules under which German democracy can govern itself. The Allied occupation

[1] In Washington, too, the dispute between Wallace and Byrnes was on the point of coming out into the open with Wallace's speech of 12 September. See above, pp. 658–9.

forces should be limited to the number sufficient to see that those rules are obeyed. . . .

The United States favors the early establishment of a provisional German government for Germany. . . .

. . . We do not want Germany to become the satellite of any power or powers or to live under a dictatorship, foreign or domestic. The American people hope to see peaceful, democratic Germans become and remain free and independent.

He went on to call in question the Neisse river boundary with Poland—'the heads of government did not agree to support at the peace settlement the cession of this particular area'—but stated that the Saar should be transferred to France and Königsberg to Russia—the latter in accordance with the agreement reached at Potsdam.[1]

In these economic and political declarations there was nothing radically new, although to have such an authoritative spokesman proclaim them under such formal circumstances was a novelty. What was new was Byrnes's emphatic declaration: 'I want no misunderstanding. We will not shirk our duty. We are not withdrawing. We are staying here. As long as there is an occupation army in Germany, American armed forces will be part of that occupation army.' This, of course, was designed to rebut rumours to the contrary, and it did mark an important shift in the official American point of view.[2] Moreover the general tone of the speech was far more friendly towards the Germans than earlier official pronouncements from the United States had been. This was particularly apparent in the peroration:

The United States cannot relieve Germany from the hardships inflicted upon her by the war her leaders started. But the United States has no desire to increase those hardships or to deny the German people an opportunity to work their way out of those hardships so long as they respect human freedom and follow the paths of peace.

The American people want to return the government of Germany to the German people. The American people want to help the German people to win their way back to an honorable place among the free and peace-loving nations of the world.[3]

With this speech the Morgenthau Plan was well and truly buried as far as official American thinking was concerned, and a new phase of relations with Germany was opened. Byrnes had become Molotov's rival as a suitor for German support. Economic recovery, political unification, self-

[1] See above, p. 626.

[2] Yet Byrnes's bold statement was not backed by effective force. U.S. troops in Germany had lost nearly all combat value by September 1946, being largely administrative personnel. Thus only three days before the Stuttgart speech, the Secretary of the Navy recorded his opinion that in case of Russian attack the 'most important problem' would be to arrange the evacuation of U.S. army forces from Germany (*Forrestal Diaries*, p. 198).

[3] Text may be found in *Documents on American Foreign Relations, 1945–1946*, pp. 210–18.

government, reduction of the occupation forces: these were goals nearly all Germans would welcome; and Byrnes was able to score heavily against Molotov with his remarks about reparations and the Polish boundary.

One may perhaps guess that this speech, together with the progress of the zonal merger and the continuance of General Clay's intransigence on the reparations issue, combined to induce Molotov to agree at the third meeting of the Council of Foreign Ministers to begin work on the drafting of a German peace treaty. Whatever his motives, on 12 December 1946 the Russian Foreign Minister withdrew his earlier objections to the appointment of deputies to begin detailed consideration of a draft treaty, and the Council of Foreign Ministers agreed to assemble again in March 1947 to consider the deputies' work. At the end of the year it looked as though perhaps agreement might yet be reached. Events in Greece and Turkey leading to the proclamation of the Truman Doctrine in March 1947[1] were to blast this hope, though one may doubt whether the intrinsic difficulties of a German settlement would not have prevented agreement in any case.

(*c*) The Fate of Europe

The developing struggle between the Anglo-Americans and the Russians for command of Germany gained some of its importance from the fact that Germany was the pivot of the entire European continent. Whichever grouping of Powers succeeded in establishing its influence over Germany could expect to attain a dominating position in all Europe. Hence action in Germany was a sort of touchstone for policy in Europe as a whole.

It seems possible to trace the marks of a new departure in both Russian and American policy towards Europe after April–May 1946. At about that time each Power gave up the idea of compromising its own purposes for the sake of agreement with the other. As we have seen,[2] the Americans began to restrict their economic help to nations whose governments were politically 'sound'. The cancellation of an Export-Import Bank credit to Poland on 10 May, and similar action with respect to Czechoslovakia on 18 October 1946 stand as signposts; and American loans and subsidies to Great Britain, France, Italy, and Western Germany constitute the other side of the same policy.

The Russians, for their part, sought to consolidate Communist control over the states of Eastern Europe which had already fallen within their sphere of influence. This took the form partly of a series of trade agreements which tended to bind the satellite states to the Russian economy, and partly of political steps designed to validate Communist-led provisional governments through rigged elections. After the disillusioning

[1] See *Survey* for 1947–8, p. 14.

[2] See above, p. 663.

experiences the Russians had had with free elections in Hungary and Austria in November 1945,[1] they were careful not to expose themselves to any repetition of the setback. Accordingly, in Rumania and Poland police action was carefully and systematically directed to cripple opposition parties, and elections were postponed until the police had had time to ensure Communist victory at the polls. As a result, Rumanian elections were not held until 19 November 1946, and the Polish elections were put off until 19 January 1947. In each case the Communists and their supporters secured a handsome majority. Diplomatic protests from the Western Powers fell on deaf ears.

In Western Europe, Communist parties remained relatively quiet. Coalitions in which the Communists played a subordinate part governed Italy, France, and Belgium throughout 1946, but there were indications, particularly in Italy, that the Communists were prepared and might be able to seize power by a *coup d'état*. Arms which had been cached by partisan units, both Communist and non-Communist, were discovered in several parts of northern Italy during the autumn of 1946; and no one could tell what might happen when British and American troops withdrew in 1947 in accordance with the peace treaty. In France the Communists were not so strong as they were in Italy and the economic circumstances of the country were not so depressing. Nevertheless it was his inability to reach agreement with the Communists that led General de Gaulle to resign from the French Government on 20 January 1946. In May rumours of Communist plans for a *coup d'état* seriously alarmed the American Government,[2] and throughout the year successive French Cabinets rose and fell with disturbing rapidity as a by-play of party politics.

Between Eastern and Western Europe lay a zone of uncertainty. Czechoslovakia, Hungary, and Austria belonged to neither side of Churchill's iron curtain. After the withdrawal of American and Russian troops from Czechoslovakia in December 1945 the Czechs became masters in their own house. Elections on 27 May 1946 returned the Communists with the largest vote, and a coalition Government under a Communist Prime Minister took office on 1 June. But the pattern of Communist conduct in Czechoslovakia was more like that in Western Europe than like that in Russian-occupied countries. The Government was a genuine coalition, and the leading place occupied by the Communists reflected the sentiment of the population with reasonable accuracy.

In Hungary the victory of the Smallholders' Party at the polls in November 1945 led to the establishment of a government in which the

[1] See above, pp. 701–2.

[2] *Forrestal Diaries*, p. 157.

Communists had only a minority part. Despite the fact that Russian troops remained in occupation, the leaders of the Hungarian Government clearly associated themselves with the West on a number of controversial issues—e.g. regulation of the Danube shipping—but, as events in the spring of 1947 were to show, the Government had no profound roots among the people which would allow effective defiance of Russian wishes. Nevertheless, throughout 1946 the Smallholders remained in office, and the Russians postponed decisive action against them until the peace treaty had put an end to the Allied Control Commission.

Austria was a meeting place, like Germany, for the occupation forces of the four principal Allied Powers. Unlike Germany, however, Austria had a national Government and, after the elections of November 1945, the Government was definitely anti-Communist. With the support of the Western occupation authorities, the Austrian Government did what it could to make its authority real throughout the country; and, in spite of Russian seizure of 'war booty' on a considerable scale, the Austrian Government succeeded in keeping the country from the fate of Germany and Korea. The zones of occupation did not become separate worlds, and, however badly torn between rival occupation armies, Austria became a social and political reality.[1]

Greece occupied a special position. She alone of the countries of Europe became the scene of a practical test of the American plan for implementing the Yalta Declaration on Europe. American initiative resulted in the organization of an international mission to supervise the Greek elections. Russia refused to participate in this mission on the ground that such a procedure was an improper violation of national sovereignty. Thus Stalin avoided setting a precedent that would have been highly embarrassing in such countries as Poland and Rumania. Russia's refusal meant that when the elections took place, on 31 March 1946, only American, British, French, and South African observers were on hand to certify to the democratic orthodoxy of the result.[2]

The election turned out to be a sweeping victory for the Populists—a conservative royalist party. The new Greek Government immediately

[1] The major landmark in Austria's internal development was the adoption by the four occupying Powers of a new control machinery on 28 June 1946. For text see *A Decade of American Foreign Policy*, pp. 614–20. By its terms the Austrian Government were given the power to make binding laws for all the country which could not be vetoed except by unanimous vote of the Control Council. Thus the principle of unanimity which so paralysed Allied efforts in Germany was made to operate in reverse in Austria. Cf. Philip E. Mosely: 'The Treaty with Austria', *International Organization*, May 1950, iv. 221.

[2] AMFOGE (Allied Mission for Observing Greek Elections), as it was called, marked an important change in the American official attitude towards Greek affairs. Before the spring of 1946 American officials and the public, too, tended to criticize British behaviour in Greece as smacking of imperialism; after the elections the U.S. Government felt impelled to defend the democratic legitimacy of the Greek Government, and resented Russian attacks upon the 'monarcho-fascists' who had come to power.

busied themselves in organizing a plebiscite on the future of the monarchy, which resulted in the recall of King George II. The Government's policy towards the Communists was certainly oppressive, and the economic hardships which faced the population were disheartening. These facts prepared the ground for a revival of Communist-led guerrilla action in the summer of 1946; but there is every reason to suppose that the guerrilla movement did not start a second time spontaneously. Rather, international Communism, and ultimately the Russian Communist Party and Government, made use of the explosive human material available to them in Greece to start civil war. Men who had retreated across the Yugoslav and Bulgarian frontiers when the war-time ELAS was disbanded in 1945 reappeared in the summer of 1946 to form the nucleus of new bands; and they were able to get important help from across the northern border, though in absolute terms the quantity of arms and supplies that could be delivered over mountain trails was small.[1]

During the last months of 1946 the renewed Communist guerrilla forces went from strength to strength, and the Greek Government, at first overconfident, rapidly began to lose their morale. More important, the army and police were often undependable. Soldiers disliked shedding the blood

[1] This statement is based upon the writer's residence in Greece, 1944–6, and a visit in the spring of 1947. Documentary evidence of the Russian hand behind the revival of Greek guerrilla war cannot be advanced by anyone excluded from the inner circles of international Communism. One should not discount the possibility that Yugoslav, Bulgar, and Greek Communist wishes perhaps counted for a good deal in determining high policy. Yet it is impossible to doubt that the Russians could have vetoed the resumption of guerrilla war in Greece had they wished to do so. They had no reason to regret the new embarrassment which guerrilla fighting would create for the British and for the 'monarcho-fascist' Greek Government. The alleged misdeeds of the British troops in Greece and the abuses, regularly magnified, permitted by the Greek Government provided the Russians with very helpful propaganda material in the United Nations and elsewhere. The affairs of Greece could be effectively used to distract attention from Communist actions in Eastern Europe. Moreover, the Russians may have calculated that the guerrilla movement might so discourage the British as to lead them to withdraw and so open the path to a Communist victory in Greece. Such was, in fact, very nearly the actual course of events in the first months of 1947 when the British Government decided that the cost of maintaining their own and the Greek Government troops was too great for the Treasury to bear any longer.

It would be very interesting to know exactly when the decision to resume guerrilla action in Greece was taken. The first reports of the existence of the bands reached Athens at the end of May 1946; but for some time it was not apparent that the movement was an organized one. Presumably the decision to send Greek guerrillas back to their mountains must have been taken a few weeks before the news reached Athens, which would place the decision early in May 1946. If this reasoning is sound, it provides one of the best indications of a change in Russian policy about that time. Instead of making any further efforts at co-operation the Russians began unscrupulous jockeying for advantage against the Western Powers. Indeed, the revival of the Greek guerrilla may have been Russia's manner of retaliating for the attitude taken by the Western Powers to German reparations deliveries at the beginning of May.

Another aspect of the situation was the Ukrainian complaint against the Greek Government lodged with the Security Council in August 1946. This move may well have been calculated to blacken the international reputation of the Greek Government before the guerrilla movement gained much notoriety—to make the guerrilla war seem a popular rising against intolerable tyranny and not a product of foreign manipulation and secret intervention.

of fellow Greeks and feared vengeance if the Communists should win after all; consequently pursuit of the guerrillas was often half-hearted and some desertions took place.

The problem which the Greek situation in its new aspect presented to British and American policy was very serious. First resort was to the United Nations. In December 1946 the Greek Government registered a complaint against its northern neighbours, Albania, Yugoslavia, and Bulgaria.[1] When the United Nations did not succeed in stopping civil war in Greece or even in preventing assistance to the guerrillas from over the frontier, more drastic steps were decided upon. On 12 March 1947 President Truman proclaimed his belief that 'it must be the policy of the United States to support free peoples who are resisting attempted subjugation by armed minorities or outside pressures' and recommended to Congress that special help, military and economic, should be extended to Greece and Turkey in order to enable those countries to stop Communist expansion.[2] With the Truman Doctrine a new and far more definite phase of the 'cold war' opened and the fate of Europe took a new turn.

(*d*) The Far East

By a remarkable coincidence, the months of April and May 1946 marked changes in the political aspect of the countries of the Far East quite as great as the changes which occurred at about the same time in Europe. Two events alone need here be mentioned. They were of commanding importance and set the stage for the future development of the whole Asiatic area.

The first was the issuance on 16 May 1946 of a British White Paper on India. This paper presented a plan for summoning an Indian Constituent Assembly to draft a Constitution for the future governance of the country. In addition, the paper stated that the immediate task of governing India would be entrusted to an 'interim Government in which all the portfolios, including that of War Member, will be held by Indian leaders'.[3] Speed and dispatch in establishing Indian independence was the dominant note of the entire White Paper. The influence of the British Government in determining the future form of Indian government was systematically minimized. The last section of the document reflects its general tone:

> To the leaders and people of India, who now have the opportunity of complete independence, we would finally say this. We and our Government and countrymen hoped that it would be possible for the Indian people themselves to agree upon the method of framing the new Constitution under which they will live.

[1] See below, pp. 742–3.

[2] *Department of State Bulletin*, 23 March 1947, pp. 534–47; *Documents* (R.I.I.A.) for 1947–8, pp. 2–7. For the Truman Doctrine, see *Survey* for 1947–8, p. 14.

[3] Great Britain: *India, Statement by the Cabinet Mission and His Excellency the Viceroy*, Cmd. 6821 (London, H.M.S.O., 1946), p. 8.

Despite the labours which we have shared with the Indian parties and the exercise of much patience and goodwill by all, this has not been possible. We, therefore, now lay before you proposals which . . . we trust will enable you to attain your independence in the shortest time and with the least danger of internal disturbance and conflict. . . .

We hope that the new independent India may choose to be a member of the British Commonwealth. We hope, in any event, that you will remain in close and friendly association with our people. . . . Whatever that choice may be, we look forward with you to your ever-increasing prosperity among the greatest nations of the world and to a future even more glorious than your past.[1]

The decision of the British Government embodied in this document must surely rank among the most fateful of recent history. Instead of disintegrating in violence between rulers and ruled, the British empire over India was to end by negotiation and legal process, and leave a residue of real respect on the part of Indian leaders for their former imperial masters. The rest of the year was consumed with attempts on the part of the Muslims and Hindus to come to an understanding with one another in order to advance along the path laid out in the White Paper of May. Quarrels between the rival communities were endless, but the British Government never altered their decision to abdicate. This determination, coupled with a similar policy in Burma, brought a new era to one great segment of Asia.

The second great change in Asia occurred in China. Its quality was very different. On 15 April 1946 the truce between the Chinese Communists and the National Government which had been signed on 10 January 1946[2] was broken when the Communists attacked and occupied the city of Changchun in Manchuria. Large-scale fighting promptly broke out. On 23 May the forces of the National Government succeeded in driving the Communists from Changchun, after which they continued to advance northward towards Harbin—thereby themselves breaking the line of demarcation which had been drawn by the truce agreement of 10 January.

General Marshall made strenuous efforts to check the spread of civil war, and at first he met with some success. A new short-term truce was arranged early in June, and an agreement for ending hostilities in Manchuria was successfully negotiated on 26 June. But the events of April–May had hardened mutual suspicion between the two rival Chinese groups. Efforts to reach a permanent settlement and real unification of China no longer promised success. During July new fighting broke out in North China, and the Communists began an open and bitter propaganda

[1] Cmd. 6821, p. 9. [2] See above, p. 709.

campaign against American intervention in Chinese affairs. Nor did they content themselves with words: two brushes between Chinese Communist troops and U.S. Marines stationed in North China occurred during the second half of July, resulting in fifteen American casualties.

During the rest of 1946 civil war spread and intensified. Negotiations languished as Communists and Kuomintang officials refused to make any concessions to one another; and by the beginning of August it became apparent that Chiang Kai-shek had decided to settle accounts with the Communists once and for all by military means. The troops of the National Government, being more numerous and in general better equipped than the Communist armies, were able to advance against their enemies, and by November 1946 they had seized nearly all the important cities of China. But the Communists had not been beaten. Instead they resumed guerrilla tactics, occupying the country-side round towns held by Nationalist garrisons, interfering with transport, cutting off small detachments, and generally threatening the lines of communication upon which Chiang's advanced forces depended. Nationalist military successes in the autumn of 1946 were thus largely illusory, and at the end of the year Chiang found that many of his best troops had fought their way into a very precarious position.

In August 1946 General Marshall considered the wisdom of withdrawing from Chinese affairs; but, when Chiang Kai-shek offered new conditions upon which he would renew the truce, Marshall changed his mind and decided to try once again to pacify the country by diplomacy. But efforts at negotiation between the Communists and Chiang Kai-shek proved as fruitless as before. They were broken off on 19 November 1946 by the departure of the Communist delegation from Nanking; and with this breakdown the prolonged American effort to mediate between the two parties came finally to an end.

General Marshall felt that both sides were to blame for the failure of his efforts. He did not want to identify the United States with either party in the civil war; and, if impartial mediation were no longer possible, then Marshall favoured American withdrawal and non-intervention. But such a policy ran athwart a variety of commitments made to Chiang Kai-shek's Government—credits for the purchase of surplus war material, an agreement to send an American military mission to train the Chinese army, and promises of various forms of economic assistance. Moreover, American opinion, both within the Government and outside it, was vastly confused by the new situation in China. Some criticized American support for Chiang and demanded withdrawal of American troops still stationed in North China. Others pressed for a more resolute anti-Communist policy.

On 18 December 1946 President Truman issued a new statement on China in an effort to quiet some of the criticism which had arisen and to make clear to the world what official American policy hoped to accomplish in China. He reviewed the events of the preceding year and reaffirmed the goals he had set for American policy in December 1945: unity and democracy, internal peace, a broadening of the National Government, and economic recovery with American help. Truman laid considerable stress on the repatriation of nearly 3 million Japanese soldiers and civilians which had been completed during the year. He explained that American forces stationed in China had already been decreased from a peak strength of 113,000 men to a mere 12,000, and would be further decreased in the future now that the job of repatriating Japanese had been completed.

As for the future, Truman declared:

> It is a matter of deep regret that China has not yet been able to achieve unity by peaceful methods. . . . We are ready to help China as she moves toward peace and genuine democratic government.
>
> The views expressed a year ago by this Government are valid today. . . . China is a sovereign nation. We recognize that fact and we recognize the National Government of China. We continue to hope that the Government will find a peaceful solution. We are pledged not to interfere in the internal affairs of China. Our position is clear. While avoiding involvement in their civil strife, we will persevere with our policy of helping the Chinese people to bring about peace and economic recovery in their country.[1]

But what if 'involvement in their civil strife' were an inescapable corollary of 'helping the Chinese people to bring about peace and economic recovery'?[2] Truman offered no answer to this problem, nor did General Marshall's recall from China on 7 January 1947 do anything to clarify the American reaction to the choice which events had, in reality, already presented to them. The question was to become an increasingly disputed one in American political circles, and no clear-cut decision was ever made. American policy hesitated between complete withdrawal from China and large-scale support of Chiang against the Communists. The result was that half-hearted support to the Nationalist Government, accompanied by numerous injunctions to reform, effectively alienated the affections of both sides in the Chinese civil war.

It may well be asked whether the breakdown of the negotiations between the Chinese Communists and the National Government resulted from some secret change in Russian policy. Did Stalin decide to promote civil war in China at the same time that he decided to promote it in Greece? Was the Communist attack on Changchun a consequence of

[1] The text of Truman's statement may be found in *United States Relations with China*, pp. 689–94. The above narrative account is based on pp. 149–216 of the same work.

[2] This dilemma was recognized by some of the American officials concerned: cf. General Wedemeyer's remarks reported in *Forrestal Diaries*, p. 111.

some sign from Moscow? Such questions cannot be answered. Chinese Communist commanders in the field may well have been influenced more by local situations than by instructions from the distant Kremlin; yet the coincidence in time is suggestive. Whether the initiative for the infraction of the truce came mainly from Moscow or mainly from local commanders, it seems probable that by the second half of 1946 the Russians had decided that prolonged civil disturbance in China would be worth while, if only to embarrass the United States and keep a Chinese Communist buffer between Soviet Asia and the central Chinese Government.[1]

Whatever Stalin's appreciation of the new Chinese situation may have been, a direct clash between Russian and American interests had unmistakably begun to develop during 1946. China was to rival Germany as a bone of contention between the two giant Powers during the following years.

(*e*) The United Nations

From one point of view the United Nations and the Security Council had achieved a great success in helping to bring about Russian withdrawal from northern Persia in May 1946.[2] But it was a success that contributed to the broadening of the gulf between Russia and the West. Instead of realizing the hopes of men like Roosevelt, and becoming a quasi-governmental body with world-wide authority sustained by the harmonious agreement of the Great Powers, the Security Council became a sounding board for rival propaganda, while many of its meetings degenerated into petty haggling over legal and procedural points. This evolution fundamentally affected all the parts and branches of the United Nations. It both reflected prevailing international tensions and at the same time contributed to the sharpening of the growing polarity between Russia and America.

The meetings of the Security Council during the last nine months of 1946 conformed to the pattern established at the beginning of the year. Four main items of business came up for discussion: Spain, Greece, admission of new members to the United Nations, and armaments. In each case no serious effort to arrive at satisfactory compromise was made. Instead the Great Powers sought to score off one another and to mobilize home and world opinion against the rival camp.

On 9 April 1946 the Polish delegate notified the Council that 'the activities of the Franco Government have already caused international friction and endangered international peace and security' and asked that

[1] According to Kalinov (*Les Maréchaux soviétiques vous parlent*, pp. 132–3), a Russian military mission, headed by Marshal Simon Timoshenko, was secretly sent to train the Chinese Communist armies at some indeterminate date 'after the war'.

[2] See above, p. 713.

the matter be considered and appropriate action taken.[1] Long and involved debates followed, in the course of which the Russians and their supporters attacked Franco vigorously while Britain and the United States tried to soft-pedal the issue. In the end no decision was reached. Instead, the matter was referred to the General Assembly on 4 November 1946.

The Spanish question was not particularly acute; but the situation in Greece was, and debate over the affairs of Greece consumed more time than any other issue during 1946. The first round, arising from the Soviet complaint against the presence of British troops in Greece (January 1946)[2] had been declared closed on 6 February, but Greek problems would not stay buried. On 24 August the Ukrainian delegate complained to the Security Council that the Greek Government's policy was a threat to peace. He charged that frontier incidents on the Albanian border had been caused by Greek authorities with the 'obvious object of provoking armed conflict with Albania'.[3] The Ukrainian delegate further alleged that the Greeks were persecuting the Albanian and Slavic minorities in northern Greece, and asserted that ultimate responsibility for the misconduct of the Greek Government rested on the shoulders of the British troops stationed in that country.

This complaint provoked a long wrangle over its admissibility. When that had been settled in the affirmative an even longer and more bitter debate followed over the substance of the charge. No decision was reached. Russia vetoed any action acceptable to Britain and the United States, and the Western Powers were equally adamant in refusing to approve any proposal supported by the Russians or their satellites. On 20 September the matter was dropped from the agenda of the Security Council.

Greek affairs came up for a third time when on 3 December the Greek Government informed the Council that Albania, Yugoslavia, and Bulgaria were 'lending their support to violent guerrilla warfare now being waged in Northern Greece against public order and the territorial integrity' of the state.[4] The discussion this time was shorter. An American resolution calling for the appointment of an investigating commission to examine the situation on the spot was accepted by the Security Council on 19 December.[5] Further consideration of Greek and Balkan affairs was then postponed until the commission could report its findings. This step was no sign of real agreement between the rival Great Powers. On the contrary, the Russians hoped to use the commission to publicize abuses in Greece, whereas the British and Americans hoped to prove that the Greek

[1] United Nations, Security Council: Document S/34, 10 April 1946.

[2] See above, p. 714.

[3] United Nations, Security Council: *Official Records, First Year, Second Series, Supplement No. 5*, Document S/137.

[4] Ibid. *Supplement No. 11*, Document S/203.

[5] Ibid. *Supplement No. 28*, pp. 700–1.

case against Albania, Yugoslavia, and Bulgaria was well founded by sifting evidence on the spot. The quarrel was thus simply transferred to new ground.

The stalemate on the Security Council was illustrated by the inability of that body to approve applications for admission to the United Nations. When the matter was considered, on 28–29 August 1946, the Russians vetoed admission of nations outside their sphere of influence, and the Western Powers reciprocated by refusing to admit Soviet satellites. A similar spirit prevailed during a debate on a Russian proposal submitted on the same day which called for a report on all United Nations forces stationed in foreign lands. This came up for discussion on 23 September and led to some brusque exchanges when the Russians suggested that American forces in Iceland and China and British forces in Greece, Indonesia, Egypt, and 'Irāq prejudiced international peace. American and British representatives indignantly pointed out that the Russian proposal would omit from the reckoning a vast army in Russia which lay within easy striking distance though not in actual occupation of other countries. Once again, nothing was decided.

One of the most important failures of the Security Council was that it did not get the Military Staff Committee into action. This Committee was conceived by the U.N. Charter as a sort of counterpart of the war-time Combined Chiefs of Staff, with the duty of concerting military policy among the Big Five and preparing plans for international enforcement of peace. But in 1946 the general climate of international relations made such an effort a clear impossibility. Although the Military Staff Committee was formally organized on 25 January 1946, it accomplished nothing. It could not even reach agreement on its own rules of procedure. The Military Staff Committee very quickly disappeared from public view, yet the conception of an international police force directed by an international military committee had been the bone and marrow of Roosevelt's original idea of the United Nations.[1]

The poor record of the Security Council in 1946 blasted the optimistic hopes which had been so general at the time of the San Francisco Conference. World co-operation was certainly not to be had as a result of bitter public disputes among the Great Powers. The General Assembly, however, was able to do rather better. Harsh accusations and stinging rebuttals distinguished its proceedings also, but when the Assembly met for the second part of its first Session, from 23 October to 16 December 1946, Russian obstruction did not prevent the accomplishment of a number of potentially important things. The Assembly's proceedings could not be paralysed by any Great Power veto, and as a result the Assembly tended to become more important, more independent, and more useful as a

[1] See above, p. 356.

channel for reaching international decisions than would have been the case had the Security Council functioned harmoniously. Confronted by open rivalry among the Great Powers, lesser nations were able to affect international decisions far more than they could have done if they had faced a solid front among the Great Powers.

On some points the Assembly debates paralleled those of the Security Council, and were equally ineffective. Admission of new members, disarmament, and policy towards Spain were canvassed, and the only definite step which resulted was a resolution, passed on 12 December 1946, calling upon the members of the United Nations to break off diplomatic relations with Franco.[1] Discussion of the world food shortage, of the uses and abuses of the veto on the Security Council, and of the status of Indians in South Africa drew attention to these problems but accomplished little else.

More tangible results were achieved in the organizational field. The Assembly ratified agreements made with such bodies as ILO (International Labour Office), UNESCO (United Nations Educational, Scientific, and Cultural Organization), FAO (Food and Agriculture Organization), IRO (International Refugee Organization), and WHO (World Health Organization). These 'specialized agencies', some newly set up, some inherited from the League of Nations or from war-time negotiations, were provided with funds and authorized to try to relieve problems or improve international co-ordination within their respective fields of activity. A similar accomplishment was the establishment of the Trusteeship Council and the approval of trusteeship agreements governing the administration of old League of Nations Mandates.

In one important sphere—control of atomic energy—matters remained in the balance throughout 1946. The Atomic Energy Commission, established on 24 January 1946,[2] met for the first time on 14 June. At this meeting the Americans and the Russians submitted their proposals for the international regulation and control of atomic energy. The two differed markedly, but it was not immediately apparent that successful compromise could not be reached.

The Americans proposed the establishment of an International Atomic Development Authority which would have managerial control over all atomic work with potential military uses. In addition, the Authority would have power to inspect and license all other uses of atomic energy, and the duty of furthering research and development designed to make atomic energy available for peaceful uses. An important point was the American demand that any national veto power should be abolished in

[1] United Nations: *Resolutions adopted by the General Assembly*, 39 (i), 12 December 1946, pp. 63–64.

[2] United Nations: *Official Records, First Part, First Session of the General Assembly, Plenary Meetings 1946*, pp. 258–9. See also above, pp. 710–11.

order to make possible prompt and automatic punishment of any nation that violated its agreements by producing atomic weapons. As for U.S. atomic bombs, they would be put at the disposal of the new International Authority and further manufacture would cease as soon as an adequate system of international control had been established.[1]

The Russians proposed an international agreement which would prohibit the production or use of atomic weapons, and commit its signatories to destroy atomic bombs already in existence. The Russians further proposed that two international committees should be set up: one to supervise the exchange of scientific information about atomic research among the nations; the second to prevent the use of atomic energy in ways detrimental to humanity. This second committee was to devise an adequate system of sanctions to be employed against a nation which turned the new resource to military purposes.[2]

Apart from the question of priority—should atomic bombs be outlawed and destroyed *before* international control was established, or vice versa—the main problem seemed to be what sort of sanctions against military manufacture of atomic weapons the Russians would accept. After some preliminary discussion, the Atomic Energy Commission decided to refer the question of the feasibility of international control of atomic energy to a technical sub-committee. This body considered the methods by which it might be possible to detect and prevent the military use of atomic energy. After some months of investigation it decided that effective control would be technically possible and suggested methods of achieving it.

This returned the discussion to the political arena. What sort of international control would the Soviet Union accept? In December 1946 Andrei Gromyko, the Soviet member of the Commission, made it clear that the veto would, in the Soviet view, have to extend to the activities of any international atomic authority,[3] while Bernard Baruch, the American representative, insisted upon the elimination of the veto 'even if we stand alone'.[4]

Despite this direct collision of views, at the end of the year the Atomic Energy Commission was able to submit a report to the Security Council which embodied recommendations for the international control of atomic energy substantially like those advanced by the United States. When the report was voted upon, on 30 December 1946, the Soviet and Polish members of the Commission did not vote against it, but merely abstained. This seemed to suggest that Russian opposition to the American plan was not so great as to prevent further discussion on the basis of the American

[1] United Nations: *Atomic Energy Commission, Official Records, No. 1*, 14 June 1946, pp. 10–13.

[2] Ibid. *No. 2*, 19 June 1946, pp. 26–29.

[3] Ibid. *No. 10*, 30 December 1946, pp. 143–8.

[4] Ibid. *No. 7*, 5 December 1946, pp. 89–92.

proposals. While agreement had not been reached, the possibility of agreement seemed still open. Definite impasse was not reached until 1947 when the cold war had extended to the whole gamut of Russo-American and world relations.[1]

[1] See *Survey* for 1947–8.

PART IV

REFLECTIONS AND GENERAL OBSERVATIONS

WHILE the war lasted the demands of military security and the prudence of official policy minimized the conflicts which divided the Grand Alliance. After the war quite opposite views gained wide currency both in Russia and in the West—interpretations of the war-time experience which ascribed systematic deceit and treachery to the other partner of the Alliance. The truth clearly lay somewhere between these extremes. Neither Machiavellian conspiracy nor open-hearted camaraderie dominated the inner counsels of the three great Allied Powers during the war. But in 1952 it was still too soon after the event for any man to be able to grasp adequately the real workings and historic significance of the Grand Alliance. This was so partly because of gaps in available information, particularly the absence of reliable information from Russia. It was also true because the time perspective was still short. Only with the benefit of hindsight could the place of the Grand Alliance in world history be clearly appreciated.

Meanwhile a preliminary estimate was possible. With the help of official publications and private memoirs one could penetrate some, perhaps most, of the distortions which official reticence and policy had presented to the public during the war itself; and an examination of the records which had been published by 1952 permitted the correction of over-simplified interpretations which had become current since Russia and the West had ceased even to pretend to co-operate. That is what this book has attempted, risking all the errors and inadequacies of interpretation which must be expected in contemporary history.

An effort, in conclusion, to fit the story of the Grand Alliance into the framework of world history presented a fascinating though particularly treacherous intellectual challenge. Yet it seems worth while to make a preliminary effort to distinguish what was merely temporary and what was more enduring in the relationships which were established among the great Allied Powers during the war.

It is easy enough to see what was temporary. In 1945 and 1946 most of the international machinery of the Grand Alliance was dismantled, and replaced, if at all, by relatively ineffective bodies working under the United Nations. Indeed, in one sense the Grand Alliance, lock, stock, and barrel, was a fleeting alignment of national states directed against common enemies; an alignment which was promptly altered when common enemies ceased to threaten. The life history of the Alliance conformed exactly to the pattern set by hundreds if not thousands of earlier coalitions which had formed and passed away in the long course of history, beginning in the days of the Mesopotamian city states. It was indisputable that the Grand Alliance had been formed in response to German and Japanese attacks; and that when those countries had been defeated it dissolved, leaving behind, like an echoing shell, the United Nations organization which had once been designed to house the Alliance permanently.

Any estimate of Allied co-operation that failed to stress the importance of common enemies must be far from the truth. In Russia's case, the course of events after 1946 made the reality obvious; but the renewal of the Anglo-American alliance after 1946 might tend to obscure the importance of common enemies in keeping British and American policy in harmony. Yet a consideration of the course of Anglo-American relations in the autumn of 1944 and the spring of 1945, when Germany's defeat was already certain and before the Americans recognized any definite threat from Russia, suggests how easily Anglo-American friendship and co-operation could be interrupted by lack of common danger.

But when all due importance had been given to the roles of Hitler and Tojo in creating and sustaining the Grand Alliance, and when its kinship with the vanished alliances and coalitions of history had been fully appreciated, something more remained. The Alliance did not fail to leave deep marks on international relations which promised to be if not permanent at least enduring. These might conveniently be considered under five heads: (1) the development of supra-national administration; (2) the changed relationship between Great Britain and the United States; (3) the changed scale of international politics; (4) the formulation and promulgation of a potent international myth; and (5) the promotion of what may perhaps be called the 'social revolution' of our time. Of these, (2) was really a special case of (3), but its peculiar significance for the world at large perhaps justifies separate consideration. In addition, all might be considered manifestations of (5), for we are anatomizing what is in truth an inseparable whole.

(i) The Development of Supra-national Administration

The Grand Alliance of the Second World War was a far better articulated organization of power than earlier alliances had ever been. This was partly due to technological improvements in communication. With radio, telegraph, telephone, teletype, mechanical coding and scrambling devices, and the rest, a tremendous volume of secret communication between the Allied capitals and with all the battlefronts became possible. The major war-time conferences could hardly have taken place without the aeroplane, and these were only the most prominent of thousands of meetings between Allied officials whose travel to and fro depended on the speed and ease of air transport.

The density of communication made possible by new techniques was supplemented in a most significant way by the development of new bi-national and international administrative practices. Anglo-American administrative consolidation reached a far higher pitch than did any consolidation between Russia and the Western Powers; but even in Russia's case much was accomplished.

This was especially true in the sphere of economic relations. A large Russian supply mission in Washington and another in London worked on a day-to-day basis with American and British officials to translate the paper agreements of the successive Soviet Supply Protocols into shiploads of supplies for Russia. To be sure, the Russians were always chary of giving information about their internal economy to foreigners, and jealously maintained their independence in matters of economic policy. Yet the needs of their situation were such as to force them to depend for certain essentials on supplies available from the West.

Even a cursory examination of the texts of the successive Soviet Supply Protocols will show how complex and vast the operation became. Thousands of items, in definite amounts and often made to Russian specifications, were listed for delivery in these protocols; items not only of finished munitions but of industrial materials at all stages of fabrication as well as of industrial machinery and parts. However one-sided the relationship, however little the Russians gave either by way of information or of material in exchange, it was none the less true that Russian production came to be integrated with that of the Western Powers through conscious planning and scheduling of production and deliveries. Rationalization between as well as within the Allied economies reached a very considerable pitch.

The military advantages of such economic integration were enormous. Without American help through Lend-Lease neither Russians nor British could possibly have maintained their fighting forces at the strength and level of equipment at which they in fact did maintain them. The elementary matter of food for the Red Army was an obvious case. Without the Lend-Lease shipments Stalin would have had to direct far more man-power and other resources to the reconstruction, expansion, and intensification of Russian agriculture than he did; and, if he had, the result would have been a serious subtraction from Russia's military strength. Britain's case was even more extreme. Without food from America, Canada, and elsewhere the whole fabric of British society would have collapsed—or else mobilization would have had to be largely undone in order to produce goods for export on a sufficient scale to permit payment for imports.

Economic rationalization on an international scale had existed in earlier times, but never to anything like the same degree. In the Napoleonic wars British subsidies had helped nations like Prussia to support armies against the French, and in the First World War the complex structure of private and inter-governmental war loans had served a similar purpose against Germany. But in these cases the relationship between nations was largely confined to the financial level. Dealings were in terms of money rather than in terms of goods, and little or no conscious effort was made to plan the most efficacious application of available productive resources among the Allied nations.

In the other spheres of military strategy and political aims the Grand Alliance achieved a far less significant degree of co-ordination. Russia's war remained essentially separate from the one fought by the Anglo-Americans. This was symbolized by the fact that the Russians refrained from declaring war against Japan until the Japanese had already been beaten. Yet Stalin's voice was not unimportant in fixing the strategy of the Western Powers in their war against Germany. And at the beginning of 1945 the Russians agreed to advance the date of their final attack upon Berlin in order to help relieve German pressure on the western front at the time of the 'Battle of the Bulge'.

But these sporadic instances of strategic integration were not sustained by any regular administrative channels for free exchange of plans and military capabilities. Only Stalin could talk freely with British and American representatives, and he was seldom available. Almost endless delays and petty difficulties beset efforts to co-ordinate military undertakings on a subordinate level. This was illustrated, for example, by the slow frustration of American efforts to establish air bases in the Far Eastern provinces of Siberia.

One of the most peculiar characteristics of the Grand Alliance was the divergence in national attitudes towards the proper relation between military and political strategy. The Americans tended to separate military from political ends by an all but impassable barrier. Indeed, American generals often seemed to regard war as a game after which, when it had been won and lost, the players would disperse and go home. Their constant resort to figures of speech derived from the American game of football was both characteristic and symptomatic.[1] The British and the Russians, on the other hand, seldom if ever lost sight of the intimate connexion between military movements and the future balance of power which was bound to emerge from the war. The result was that the strategy of the war in Europe resembled an Alice in Wonderland game of four-handed chess, a game which the Russians and Nazis played according to traditional

[1] Clark (*Calculated Risk, passim*) offers one of the clearest examples of this habit of mind and speech.

rules, while the British attempted to do so, but suffered constant interference from the Americans who wished to play according to rules of their own manufacture—rules according to which Russian chessmen could take only Nazi pieces from the board.

Perhaps it is unfair to the Americans to put the matter so baldly. They believed that the rules of international politics as between the members of the Grand Alliance had been changed by such declarations as the Atlantic Charter, and, of course, if words were taken for facts, they were right. Thus it is perhaps wrong to accuse the Americans of failing to recognize the relation between military strategy and political power. Rather, they pinned their faith to a new conception of power: to a world order in which the nations would combine to enforce international law; a world order which would therefore no longer turn upon balance of separate national powers and spheres of influence. In so far as American military policy was based upon these political presuppositions, the strategy advocated by Marshall and Roosevelt made good sense: the earliest elimination of the Nazis and the Japanese with the least cost in men and material would in such a view open the way to a new and better world. Manœuvring for national advantage as against other members of the Grand Alliance would then be both unnecessary and wicked, for it would amount to an incipient betrayal of the future.

But American efforts to convert the British and Russian Governments to such a view of international politics were not successful. Political co-ordination between the members of the Grand Alliance, and particularly between Russia and the West, never transcended a purely verbal plane. The Soviet Union's adherence to such documents as the Atlantic Charter and the United Nations declaration of January 1942 had importance from a propagandist point of view, but Stalin presumably regarded them as no more than that. They were certainly no guide to his policy. The Dumbarton Oaks proposals and the United Nations Charter were of greater significance because they established new and lasting international institutions; but Russia's signature of these documents did not signify the elimination of any of the standing political differences between East and West.

Yet in spite of the disagreements between the Great Powers which hampered the United Nations from the time of its establishment, the efforts of the Grand Alliance to achieve some sort of international political administration were not completely fruitless. The United Nations, with its thousands of officials, committees, boards, councils, secretaries, and the rest, came into existence; and some of the United Nations specialized agencies were able to pick up the threads of international economic administration which were first developed by the members of the Grand Alliance during the war. In 1952 the United Nations almost totally lacked executive power; but the personnel and monetary resources which allowed the accumulation of information and attracted publicity to the results of international investigation of social and political problems had their importance. National action might sometimes be influenced by data and advice provided by United Nations bodies—sometimes, but perhaps not often, unless national interest or the veiled influence of one of the Great Powers urged in the same direction.

But it was not supra-national administration combining all three of the Great Allies that had the greatest and most enduring significance. Rather, it was the special linkage between Great Britain and the United States, extending over economic and military matters, that promised to provide the principal model for post-war innovation. The North Atlantic Treaty Organization (NATO) and Economic Co-operation Administration (ECA) could trace their ancestry directly to the Anglo-American experience of the war.

Anglo-American economic co-operation covered wider ground, involved an exchange of a much greater quantity of goods, and implied a closer interdependence than was ever the case *vis-à-vis* Russia. The most novel thing in the co-operation between the two countries was the bi-national administration of their armed forces. Success in this most delicate field of co-operation was really confined to the European theatres of war. Attempts to transplant the pattern of combined military administration elsewhere were never very successful. Mountbatten in South-East Asia made the most serious attempt; but he never had enough Americans under his command to make his a genuinely bi-national command. The same was true in the Pacific theatres, where the American commanders disposed of forces overwhelmingly American. In China, political and personal feuds together with difficulties of supply made the attempt at combined command an utter failure.

But these contrasts only served to underline the extraordinary quality of Anglo-American co-operation in North Africa and Europe. British and American armies fought almost as one. All the chances and disappointments which might have led to bitter national recrimination were successfully lived down, and common endeavour developed a common spirit among most of the men who worked together on the staff of SHAEF and AFHQ.

This spirit was neither British nor American but a combination, and in some measure independent of either national component. In this respect the Allied staffs were quite like any branch of a great national government. Groups of men organized to work together regularly develop a greater or less common front against outsiders. But the significant thing in the experience of SHAEF and AFHQ was that the barrier of nationality was on the whole broken through.

The military administration of the First World War hardly offered an analogy. Even after a single commander for the western front had been appointed, national barriers were not relaxed very greatly between the British, French, and later the American armies. Supply systems were kept separate, and to a considerable degree the operational employment of each national army remained a matter of diplomatic negotiation rather than of unified command. Of course Eisenhower's and Wilson's commands were never removed from the sphere of diplomacy entirely. Divergent national plans and wishes had seriously to be taken into account, and the decisions of each Allied commander regularly bore the marks of compromise between opposing national pressures. But national pressures were limited by two factors: the unwillingness of either Government to risk the break-up of combined command, and the resistance offered by the combined staffs themselves to outside interference with their plans. In actual fact, most of the major Anglo-American strategic decisions of the war were the product of a triangular negotiation between the two Governments and the Allied commander on the spot. Consultation with the commanders in the field was constant, and gave the Allied staffs in each theatre of operations a quasi-autonomy.

Yet one should not exaggerate. Anglo-American co-operation in the spheres of economic and military administration was very real and extended from the topmost levels of government to the very bottom. But this success was only partly a product of good sense, goodwill, and good management. It was also the product of a fundamental change in the power relationship between Britain and America, a second enduring feature of the war-time experience.

(ii) The Changed Relation between Britain and America

From Nelson's victory at Trafalgar until the last decade of the nineteenth century, the Royal Navy enjoyed a relatively easy supremacy on the high seas. On that material basis, supplemented by British' industrial prowess and by a great outpouring of colonists from the home islands into underpopulated British possessions, a world-girdling empire was built, partly by consolidation of earlier acquisitions, partly by new annexation. British commercial and financial dominion reached far beyond the bounds of British political rule, extending over most of China and South America and, for a few decades in the middle of the century, penetrating the broad expanse of the Ottoman Empire as well.

After about 1870 this imposing structure underwent more or less steady erosion. British economic supremacy was the first buttress of Empire to fall. The industrial rise of Germany and of the United States after 1870 and the industrialization of Japan after about 1890 deprived Britain of her earlier advantages in many markets. Even more telling was the rise of German, American, and Japanese naval power, which by the end of the century made the Royal Navy no longer an unlimited sovereign of the seas but first among equals. As it happened, the First World War brought two of the three new naval Powers into war at Britain's side; but in the Second World War Japan joined Germany, and their combined naval, military, and air power far outclassed what Britain alone could bring against them.

In the circumstances, the survival of the British Empire and of the British Government itself depended on the action or inaction of the United States. British sovereignty had become severely restricted; the choices open to the British Government had been narrowed; the possibility of conducting affairs without urgent and anxious consideration of probable American reaction to each step had been removed.

Had the United States become hostile, Britain would have been helpless to continue the war against Germany. But that possibility could safely be ruled out, since sentiment and national interest alike drew the United States to the British side. But American neutrality, if it had been indefinitely maintained, would have been almost equally shattering to the British war effort. One can only imagine the consequences if Lend-Lease assistance had not been extended to Great Britain in the spring of 1941. Without American supplies and munitions, Britain would have been compelled to restrict her war effort by diverting men and supplies to the task of keeping the population alive. Production for export would have taken priority over production for war; and the margin left for military effort might or might not have sufficed to keep the North Atlantic open and the Channel clear of invaders. Without American help Britain's best prospect would have been a precarious defensive.

Actually, of course, American help was forthcoming on a significant scale even before the fall of France, and in the years that followed the amount of material and military help from across the Atlantic mounted steadily until 1944, when the peak of preparation for the great attack was at last reached. The gradualness with which the United States came to Britain's rescue, the hesitation and uncertainty which surrounded Roosevelt's first moves in the direction of support for the Allies, the long-drawn-out anxiety of the British Government and people lest the Americans come with too little and arrive too late tended to disguise from both nations the irrevocable quality of America's new adventure. Throughout the rush of the war most Americans preserved the idea that when victory came things would revert to something like the pre-war pattern; and many Englishmen felt that Britain's traditional place in the world as ruler of a great Empire and exemplar to all Europe would be preserved. Instead, the United

States became heir to Britain's world position, a change that brought considerable embarrassment to most Americans and regret to most Englishmen.

The steps by which this transformation came about can be seen clearly enough. The shifting balance of power between Britain and America may be illustrated, for example, by considering how the successive strategic decisions of the war were made. In 1942, when America's mobilization was still in its initial stages and when British armed strength available against Germany still overbalanced that of the United States, Churchill with difficulty persuaded the Americans to accept his strategy of attacking North Africa. During 1943 American armed strength came to surpass the British, and the tug of wills between Churchill and Marshall over the advantages and disadvantages of an invasion of Italy turned into something like stalemate which was decided in Churchill's favour partly by Eisenhower's advice and partly by circumstance—Badoglio's offer of surrender and the lack of time to prepare an invasion of Normandy before bad weather set in.

But by November 1943 American dominance of the Anglo-American partnership became definite. At Cairo and Tehrān and again at Malta just before the Yalta Conference, Churchill and the British Chiefs of Staff had to give way to American views on the critical issues in dispute. By then American armed forces had swollen in numbers until they far exceeded British strength, and American commanders had taken over the principal theatres of war in both Europe and the Pacific.

The growing disparity of power between the two countries cannot have been easy for British leaders to adjust themselves to. But the sharp edges of the new American power were blunted and in some measure hidden by forbearance and good comradeship. Churchill regularly made the best of the situation by throwing himself with full vigour and enthusiasm into whatever operation had been agreed to, even when he had resisted the original proposal with all his might. And the Americans were not totally insensitive to British arguments and cautions. When disputes arose, it was nearly always possible to find a compromise whereby the Americans conceded something to the British in return for more fundamental British concessions to the American point of view.

Personalities were undoubtedly important in shaping the Anglo-American partnership throughout the war years. Churchill and Roosevelt set their individual mark upon the conduct of affairs; so did Eisenhower and Alexander, Marshall and Dill, Hopkins and Eden, each in his own sphere. A common, or almost common, language was of fundamental importance; and the community of belief and traditions which historical affiliation had created between the two countries entered into the amalgam in a way that can only be compared to the relation between Britain and the Dominions.

But these factors, however much they facilitated Anglo-American co-operation, cannot be held fundamentally responsible for its unique success. The Anglo-American success depended at bottom on the fact that the British Government *had* to agree with the Americans, and, realizing their position, yielded gracefully before dispute had gone so far as to disturb day-to-day administrative co-ordination between the two Governments. The British voice was heard on all critical occasions, and sometimes it modified the Americans' decisions; but there was always an ultimate authority whose decision was binding. When the leaders of the American Government—chiefly the President and the Chiefs of Staff—said yes or no, action was undertaken accordingly; but the British yes and no was always subject to review.

This did not result from a voluntary abdication on Churchill's part. He simply recognized that, if he insisted upon a course of action distasteful to the United States Government, the Americans could always afford, however reluctantly, to quarrel openly with him, and then bring economic pressure to bear against which no British Government could stand. Britain could afford no such luxury, and had always therefore to stop short of any action that promised to alienate American sympathy and support.

Stalin's position was much more independent. He could ill afford the loss of American supplies, perhaps; but he could at a pinch afford it none the less. His despotic control of internal propaganda and police meant, among other things, that the option of a renewed agreement with Hitler was never entirely closed while the war lasted; and, when it ended, Stalin soon demonstrated that the Soviet Union could survive as a Great Power in open opposition to the United States and Great Britain combined. To be sure, Stalin purchased his sovereignty at the price of the toil and suffering of his subjects, whose lives were made strenuous and impoverished by the demands of the Bolshevik state. But, though the cost was high, Russian sovereignty and freedom of international action were preserved against all outside pressure, an achievement which lay beyond the desire and beyond the power of the British Government.

The psychological adjustment to the new balance of power between America and Britain came slowly in each country, and indeed had not been by any means completed in 1952. The British Government and the British public were loath to abdicate their inherited world position. Throughout 1945 and 1946 the British tried with growing difficulty to sustain the economic costs of empire in the Mediterranean and of occupation in Germany. But the strain proved too heavy, and in 1947 a considerable part of the burden was transferred to the United States.

In the United States the mantle of sea and air power which the war had transferred from one side of the Atlantic to the other required equally drastic, though perhaps more welcome, psychological adjustments. Until the end of 1946 few Americans had accepted the full weight of the responsibility that power conferred. The Government and most of the American people still hoped that a generous financial policy would be enough to restore Europe in general and Britain in particular to their old position in the world, or something like it, thus relieving the United States from the sticky job of trying to arbitrate and smooth over the quarrels and upheavals that war had brought to the globe.

It was principally naval and air force circles which welcomed and moved forward into the vacuum created by Britain's weakness. The U.S. navy wished to annex strategic islands in the Pacific, and managed to restrain other elements of the American Government from making such a consummation impossible. The navy also decided to send a fleet to the Mediterranean and maintained most of the island bases in the Atlantic which had been built during the war. The U.S. air force pursued parallel policies, maintaining and even building new airfields in many far-flung corners of the earth. The two services were exactly following the policy of the Royal Navy after the Napoleonic wars, and for similar reasons.

One of the most striking changes in American official and, less markedly, in American public attitudes was the new view of the British Empire which rapidly gained ground after the war had ended. Roosevelt and his friends had been severely critical of British and other brands of European colonialism and had made no secret of their belief that native peoples should have their freedom after the war. But events in China, India, and elsewhere soon showed that liberation and the establishment of peaceable self-government were not an easy thing that could always be accomplished at will or by a simple act of abdication. As some of the complexities of the problem dawned upon the American public, a more cautious and sympathetic attitude towards British colonial policy gained ground; and when, later still, the fear of Communism and the extent of its hold upon native liberation movements became apparent, official and popular sympathy in the United States tended to come round to the side of the European colonial nations. But this reversal was not completed until after 1946.

(iii) The Changed Scale of International Politics

The eclipse of British sea power by that of the United States was only part of a general transformation of the scale of world politics. In the largest sense the United States found herself after the Second World War in Britain's traditional geopolitical position. North America might be considered as a great island lying against the world continent of Eurasia-Africa, just as in the smaller sense Britain was an island set against the land mass of continental Europe.

The eclipse of Germany and France as great military Powers resulted in a shift of the centre of land power eastward into Russia. The vast man-power, the growing industrial strength, the rigorous military organization of Russian society, and not least the mere space enclosed within the Soviet state, with the natural resources and the military advantages which went with it, combined to make the Soviet Union a giant which no single nation of Western Europe could hope to match on the battlefield.

The change in political scale brought about during the war was very striking. The war began in 1939 as a struggle between old and famous nation states of Western Europe, while both the Russians to the east and the Americans to the west remained officially neutral. But Hitler had so increased the intensity of domestic organization for war as to raise Germany's power far above that of his opponents. The rapid and easy victories of 1939–40 resulted. Germany thereupon became the centre of a Europe-wide economic-political unit whose military effectiveness far outmatched that of any single nation state. In 1941 Hitler attacked the Soviet Union and later in the year the United States joined Britain and Russia to form the Grand Alliance. Thus by the end of 1941 the war was no longer an affair of national units in the old sense: rather continent-wide aggregations of power were locked in mortal combat.

In the Far East the transformation was less marked. Japan's co-prosperity sphere was trans-national, embracing the coastal and island areas of South-East Asia and the South-West Pacific. But the articulation of its parts was limited by the comparative backwardness of most of the territory that the Japanese had conquered. The industrial core of the Japanese power complex remained as it had been at the beginning: Japan proper supplemented by Manchuria and northern Korea. Japan gained space and some important raw materials, but did not acquire much in the way of added industrial-military strength through her conquests. For this reason the Japanese war retained more nearly traditional proportions than did the war in Europe.

One can find interesting historical parallels to the change in political scale which the Second World War brought in its train. The irruption of Macedon into the Greek city state system and the subsequent rise of the Hellenistic monarchies was one instance. The fate of the Italian city states at the end of the fifteenth and throughout the sixteenth centuries, when the French and Spanish monarchies intervened in Italian politics, was another. In both these cases an old established civilization was invaded and turned upside down by new Powers which had arisen on its periphery. The fate of Western Europe seemed, midway through the twentieth century, strictly comparable. In both cases, too, the wealth and culture of the city states which had made them leaders of civilization were damaged by wars fought among the new giant Powers for control of the old centre of civilization; while a simultaneous process of economic and cultural development brought the new giant states more nearly to a level with the old centre of civilization. That the world might undergo a similar evolution in the second half of the twentieth century was surely possible.

The change in the international status of Europe seemed to come rather suddenly with the war, but in a very real sense the dramatic changes of 1939–45 were the product of centuries of development. The spread of European civilization to new regions, in particular the rise of industrial systems in the peripheral areas of America and Asia, must be regarded as the fundamental cause of Europe's mid-twentieth-century plight.

On the frontiers of European civilization, where Europeans came into contact with weak and backward peoples, it was easy to build great states covering most of a continent. Such was the first achievement of the Americans and the Russians. Having done so, new advantages came to them when modern industrialism penetrated to these vast outliers of the European state system. Taking advantage of European experience, it was possible to plan and build factories, dig mines, &c., on a more nearly rational model, unhampered by obsolescent plant and unimpeded by the variety of restrictive social practices which had grown up *pari passu* with the development of industrialism in Europe. Even more to the point, a large political unit permitted easy combination of natural resources on a vast scale—the sort of combination which was beset by serious if not altogether insurmountable obstacles in a Europe divided between small, mutually distrustful national units. The result was the rise of potentially enormous military Powers beyond the confines of Western Europe. The Second World War provided the stimulus which transformed the potentiality into actuality, confronting Europe overnight with new giants in the earth with which the established nation states could never hope to compete singly.

The effect upon the spirit of European peoples might be profound, though in 1952 it was perhaps too early yet to tell exactly what it would be. Before 1939 Frenchmen or Englishmen or Germans could think themselves more or less masters of their own fate, operating within familiar and well worn patterns of political behaviour. After 1945 these nations found themselves reduced to the status of second-class Powers, as they had earlier reduced such nations as Sweden and the Netherlands to relative impotency. All too clearly the acts of others—of strangers from distant parts whose acquaintance with European civilization and habits of thought was incomplete in the case of the Americans and grossly distorted in the case of the Russians—came to control what happened in Europe.

From being prime movers in world politics, European nations had become pawns in someone else's game, and, with the change, some of the savour went out of life, some of the energy, enterprise, and derring-do which had distinguished European civilization from its inception leaked away to be replaced by passivity and fear.

Whether Europe would be able to recover from the blows dealt to its traditional organization by the First and Second World Wars remained one of the great questions to be answered by the history of the following fifty or one hundred years. Only a great internal revolution, transforming established political and economic modes of organization and introducing a continental scale of social organization, seemed likely to redeem European sovereignty in a world dominated by such super-Powers as Russia and America; and the whole weight of centuries, of vested interests, and of ancient hates and fears, stood in the way of such renovation. Technically it would certainly be possible, but socially and politically it might prove impossible. Reason, insight, and the technique of administration in which Europeans as individuals and as nations often excelled would have a difficult struggle against tradition, sentiment, and atavistic emotion; and such a struggle could never be dissociated from the prodding, pushing, pulling of the super-states already established on Europe's margins. The struggle between Russia and America to deny Europe's resources to each other was not likely to prove helpful to the cause of European reorganization.

(iv) The Formulation of a Great Myth

If one by-product of the Grand Alliance was the creation or enlargement of an international administrative structure, and a second was the enlargement of the political scale, there was a third change which, while much less tangible, might prove in the long run far more important. This was a change in public attitude, especially in the United States, towards international affairs. Other countries, notably Great Britain and the other members of the Commonwealth, shared in the change; but since America alone had the power in the post-war world to act upon new convictions, and since the change was generally more marked in the United States than elsewhere, it seems best to limit this discussion to the American scene.

Briefly, Roosevelt embodied a myth and persuaded many if not most Americans to believe in it. The myth was an optimistic one. Roosevelt repeatedly said and apparently fully believed that, when once victory had been won and the forces of fascist aggression had been trodden into the dust, an era of international peace, prosperity, freedom, and justice could be inaugurated, and surely would be if men of goodwill strove manfully to that end.

Such a millennial hope had deep roots in American history. The missionary impulse to civilize a wilderness had been mingled from the early days of the Republic with the firm belief in American moral superiority to the Old World. As far as international affairs were concerned, Americans could and did point with satisfaction to the relative peace and good neighbourliness which prevailed in the New World in contrast to the wars and bitterness of the Old. American diplomatic experience before the Second World War had been profoundly parochial. Active American policy had been almost confined to Latin America, where the United States enjoyed an easy superiority of power and could exercise a loose hegemony. With no rivalry to fear from Canada to the north and with wide oceans on east and west, the problems of military security and political balances of power which so dominated European diplomacy hardly touched American conduct of foreign affairs.

Yet the traditional American assumption of moral superiority towards Europe was mingled with a sense of inferiority and helplessness in the face of European diplomatic guile. The whole attitude can be compared with that of Bunyan's Christian beset with the deceits of Vanity Fair. Like Christian, American statesmen and people generally felt that the only safe policy was to refuse to deal with untrustworthy men, and this feeling constituted an important element in American isolationism.

America's intervention in European affairs, first in 1917 and again in 1941, was only superficially a contradiction of this tradition. More truly, it was a fulfilment. With Wilson and Roosevelt the parallel with Bunyan's hero was complete. For Wilson from 1917 to 1919 and Roosevelt from 1941 until his death launched the United States on a pilgrimage to a Heavenly City—the city where peace, justice, and good neighbourliness would surely reign. War became not a political instrument but a crusade, and victory became a new Pisgah from which sight of the Promised Land would first be granted to the weary people of the world.

Such idealism was a potent force inasmuch as it focused a desire which was almost universal among the peoples of the world, shared in by all sorts and conditions of men. Wilson and after him Roosevelt became prophets and teachers, able to conjure up in the minds of millions a hope and confidence that they sorely needed. In Wilson's case, the American people turned against their leader when the first rapture faded. But there lingered a sense of self- and world-betrayal; and when Roosevelt came to preach a similar doctrine the American public rallied to the new standard more soberly but perhaps more resolutely than before.

In time of disillusionment, after the break-up of the Grand Alliance, one might be tempted to dismiss as naïve the high professions of the war years. Yet such a judgement would be over-hasty. Quite apart from the immediate use of the myth for sustaining Allied morale and damaging that of the enemy, the hope of a new and better world, which Roosevelt so regularly held before himself and all men, had helped to change popular attitudes towards world affairs in a manner which might yet have profound consequences.

This was especially true in Roosevelt's own country. The leading novelty of international relations in the years 1947–52 had been the new role played by the United States; and an important addition to national interests, which of course operated to affect American foreign policy, was the moral crusade which Americans generally believed themselves to have undertaken—a crusade against tyranny and aggression, wearing, this time, a Communist mask. This idealistic streak in American attitudes towards international affairs was not without very practical effect. One can hardly believe, for instance, that the people of America would have supported a war in Korea had it not been undertaken on behalf of world ideals, however much transformed and hardened since they left Roosevelt's hands.

Now self-righteousness and moral indignation may not be perfectly reliable guides to national policy in a multi-national power system. They are, indeed, fundamentally subversive of any such system, pressing always towards the establishment of some supreme authority with the power to declare the right and to enforce it. But to a very significant degree just such attitudes came to dominate American foreign policy after the establishment of the United Nations; and if the consequence turned out to be that in the second half of the twentieth century the power of the United States would be directed towards the modification and eventual overthrow of the system of plural state sovereignty, Roosevelt (and, before him, Wilson) would have to be held responsible in large measure.

Wise men have said that myths as much as facts move mankind and govern human history. The war-time hope of peace and prosperity for all once victory had been won was certainly a myth; a myth which defied history and the realities of the political relationship between Russia and the Western Powers. But when myths can appeal to profound human impulses and desires, as this one did, and when myths succeed in stirring a new loyalty in human hearts, as this one might eventually do, then they can rise above fact and survive disappointment to create great institutions and bring about revolutions in the affairs of men—not, of course, exactly in the form intended or foreseen from the beginning, nor in isolation from other motives of self-interest, ambition, hate, and fear.

In 1952 it was still too early to tell whether the myth which Roosevelt wrote into the history of the Grand Alliance would come to rival such tremendous engines of human change as the Christian or Marxian myths; but to dismiss it from the running altogether and call it nothing but folly would be to misunderstand the human heart and misjudge the most potent of all methods of political leadership.

Even in 1952 one could say this much. Just as the expansion and consolidation of Russian state power at home and abroad had, since the Bolshevik Revolution, drawn strength and justification from Marxian doctrine, so the expansion and consolidation of American power seemed to have found an intellectual—or, if you will, verbal—justification in the myths associated with the names of Wilson and Roosevelt. Peace, justice, freedom, and plenty, if one believes them attainable, are powerful and positive goals for which to strive; goals which may sustain an active foreign policy and lead to actions in places where national self-interest alone would never venture.

Of all the elements which held the Grand Alliance of the Second World War together, the professed war aims were apparently the most fragile. Before the fighting had ended, Roosevelt himself betrayed much of his own principle in dealing with Stalin over Poland and Manchuria; and the co-operation among the Great Allied Powers, for the sake of which he made these concessions, did not survive the destruction of their common enemies. Yet in the long run it is possible that the ideals professed and proclaimed to all the world by the leading statesmen of the Grand Alliance might turn out to be one of the most pregnant of all their actions.[1]

(v) The Promotion of the Social Revolution

One of the greatest changes in human beliefs in the twentieth century had been the growth of the conviction that social and economic relations were at least potentially subject to rational control and conscious management. Roosevelt's confidence in the possibility of creating a good world by the action of the human will reflected such a belief; it equally dominated the Marxian vision of Communism. The growth of supra-national administration was but an example of the practical effort to control human affairs by taking conscious thought. The rise of new super-Powers, likewise, had been made possible by the successful co-ordination of the social energies of great numbers of men spread over large areas of the earth's surface: co-ordination by means of a governmental bureaucracy which attempted to manipulate men and things to create military strength and, perhaps, to secure other goals. Thus all the enduring changes brought about by the Grand Alliance (and by the enemy) during the war could be viewed as aspects of a great change in human thought and conduct which might be called the Social Revolution of the twentieth century.

[1] The myth should be compared with the idea of the brotherhood of man—a myth which some scholars believe Alexander of Macedon first officially promulgated—which was largely renounced as a basis of policy by his successors, but which survived to become a powerful prop to the Roman Empire and a basic ingredient of Christianity. The political myth associated with the name of Roosevelt might yet have a similarly distinguished, world-transforming career.

The conviction that men might deliberately control and manipulate their social and economic relations had a long intellectual history which might be traced back at least to Plato; but it was only in the twentieth century that the idea began to take root outside intellectual circles and became no longer a matter of unpractical day-dreams but the warp and woof of national and international politics.

The First World War marked a great inroad of conscious management upon traditional social and economic patterns. After the war, the Bolsheviks began to make social and economic planning a normal condition in Russia. After some false starts the new system really got under way only in 1928; and soon after, beginning in 1933, Hitler introduced something essentially similar in Germany. Both Stalin and Hitler built upon the experience of controlled society which had been gained during the war mobilization of 1914–18; and, preparing for a new war, they succeeded in extending and perfecting the system. The nations of the West lagged far behind, but when the Second World War broke upon them, something similar happened. With important modifications and with some significant self-restraint, the Governments of Britain and America established controlled societies of their own.

The two World Wars of the twentieth century might thus be seen as midwives to a new type of social organization. Precedents and rudiments were easy to find in peace-time development, but war, both in 1914–18 and in 1939–45, brought a great acceleration to changes already under way. The threat of foreign danger and the hope of victory drove or persuaded men to introduce new methods of social control; and, when the new methods produced great and impressive results, men's minds were changed. New power and new wealth seemed suddenly within men's grasp when social energies were successfully bent to a common end by the operation of a more or less rationally controlled administrative machine.

This social revolution might be compared with the two cardinal revolutions of modern European history, the Industrial and French Revolutions. Indeed it was of a piece with them both. The Industrial Revolution resulted from the application of science to engineering. By taking thought men were able to harness the forces of physical nature to their own purposes, thereby vastly increasing the wealth and power at their disposal. Things were subjected to rational manipulation, not for the first time, of course, but on a new scale and with awe-inspiring results.

The French Revolution, among other things, applied or tried to apply reason to political institutions. By taking thought men believed they could adjust political relationships according to their desires and make them responsive to their needs and purposes. The same human reason, which when applied to things produced the goods of the new factories, when applied to politics might produce (or was this an illusion?) the goods of liberty, equality, and fraternity.

There was, however, a very important difference. The goods produced industrially were easily and all but universally recognized as good: cheaper cloth, cheaper and more rapid transport, &c., served ends of material comfort and convenience which few persons could repudiate. But the question of the ends to which political institutions should be directed was much more dubious and controversial, involving emotions and interests which were scarcely amenable to rational calculation and adjustment.

This problem was even more acute in connexion with the social revolution of the twentieth century. As in the case of the Industrial and French Revolutions, rational control and manipulation had been applied to new sectors of human activity. Social and economic institutions which had arisen haphazardly through the centuries were remodelled and adjusted to make them serve a single end: victory. Under the pressure of war or preparation for war, this end might suffice. But the garrison state in which social energies and material resources are all directed towards maintaining maximum military strength cannot be very attractive in itself, if only because it suppresses or neglects so much of the variety of human experience and values. The welfare state, which Marxians and Western democrats alike professed to be their ultimate goal, had only partially been tried, and it did not escape the problem of ends: whose welfare among the often conflicting welfares of separate social groups, classes, nations, and races? and what sort of welfare?

The logical extreme of either the garrison or the welfare state, both based on the principle of deliberate manipulation of human and material resources to achieve agreed ends, would be to establish two groups: human cattle and the managers who tend and use them. In such a case the political problem would become one of maintaining agreement among the managers as to the ends to be served; and this might require dictatorship. Russian society, indeed, had by 1952 approached this extreme already.

Anyone who values individuality must recognize and fear the consequences of such an evolution. Fortunately, logical extremes are seldom if ever realized in practice. Survivals of the old, irrational, but oddly attractive past might confidently be expected despite any further advances of the social revolution that we have been considering. Fears and qualms were most unlikely to undo what had already been accomplished. Men had seen what could be done, and they wished for at least some of the products of conscious social management; and, as long as rival sovereign states continued to exist in the world, fear of the enemy would always prod the laggards to new efforts at planned co-ordination and co-operation to achieve greater military strength and an ever-illusory 'security'.

It is worth while to emphasize how great were the war-time achievements in applying conscious manipulation to social action. Even with improvised and rough and ready methods of rational calculation, such as those brought into use in Britain and America, impossible production goals, impossible logistical operations, impossible military undertakings rather abruptly became possible. Traditional limits to human activities were removed through the abolition of financial and other obstacles to the full employment of labour, machinery, and human ingenuity.

Such a bursting through of old and unconsidered social limits was a tremendous victory for instrumental rationality. In one sphere of activity after another men took deliberate thought as to how best to achieve a particular result, and then were able to dispose human and material resources in such a way as to secure something close to, if seldom identical with, the foreseen and desired end.

Not only did managed economies become universal among the leading nations of the world, but, as we have seen, management was extended to international economic and military action. In addition, techniques of propaganda and 'war information' were applied in every belligerent country to control, within limits, the thoughts and feelings of men. Russia and Germany went much farther in this direction than did Britain and America, for this was one field in which old liberal scruples continued to interfere with the new techniques of social control.

The expansion of the armed forces occasioned still a third great extension of rational control of human resources. Soldiers were fed, housed, clothed, disciplined, taught, transported to distant parts, assigned an enormous variety of tasks, and in the end brought home or buried by an abstraction known as 'the government', or more concretely, by officers and officials who took their orders in an unbroken chain of command from a few men at the top of the governmental hierarchy.

This was not new, of course. But the numbers of men concerned, and the length of time during which they experienced the military life, was greater than ever before. The armed forces transformed themselves from a marginal body of specialists into a substantial segment of the entire adult male population, and took large numbers of women into the ranks also. The impact of such an experience was hard to estimate, but by any standard it was tremendous. The daily lives of millions were reduced to a pattern, shaped by deliberate planning to achieve certain ends: and the force of such a disciplined mass became something only dreamed of earlier.

Civilians, too, experienced something of the new power of the state. Rationing, price and wage control, direction of labour, priorities, military encroachment upon the amenities and in many countries upon the necessities of life: these and similar practices profoundly affected the daily lives of everyone, though of course the transformation was far less drastic than that which came to the men in uniform.

There were two notable by-products of the social upheaval brought by the war. One was the blurring of the normal, traditional distinction between civil and military. Economic planning could not be neatly divided into military and civilian compartments, and was not. The distribution of man-power between military and civilian employment was a single problem. The service of the civilian as much as of the soldier was subordinated to the general task of winning the war—or such, rather, was the ideal which governmental planners and administrators strove to realize.

In a similar fashion the historical distinction between war and peace came to be blurred and diminished. The formal matter of concluding peace treaties presented unsuspected difficulties after the fighting had ended, and the Second World War had scarcely ended before the aptly named cold war began. Even more significant was the discovery that extraordinary measures like those introduced during the war could not be given up, at least not right away. Social and economic practices had been so transformed by deliberate planning that automatic return—indeed any return—to pre-war conditions could not take place. The social order that had been cunningly contrived to wage war had to be consciously readjusted and transformed to meet new conditions.

If one probes to the root of the matter, two factors which combined to make the social revolution possible may be distinguished. One was the progress of administrative technique—the development of communication, of statistics, of competent bureaucratic personnel, of concepts like national product, mobility of man-power, component scheduling, and of devices for mass training in new skills. These developments were the work of the managers: of governmental officials, of economists and other social scientists, and of army officers. The other contributory factor was the erosion of social tradition among the mass of the population. This phenomenon had in its turn many causes which can hardly be argued here. But it should be observed that the war vastly hastened the process. In the course of the war, millions of people in Europe, Asia, and America were uprooted, and the hold of national, religious, and personal traditions upon their lives was weakened as a result. The population of advanced industrial countries tended to become a malleable mass, offering less and less systematic resistance to the manipulation of officialdom.

But, however much traditional obstacles to social control were weakened, a stubborn residuum of human psychology continued and doubtless would always continue to limit the managers. Gross appeals to elemental fear and greed are usually more suited to mobilize mass support than are finely reasoned arguments. Planners and managers run the risk of finding themselves chained to a great angry beast—a mass population divested of most traditional restraints upon the passions, amenable only to wheedling and threats, controllable only by police and propaganda.

The social revolution of the twentieth century had certainly not solved the universal problem of human society: the problem created by the inadequate goodness and rationality of mankind at large. Yet it was an amazing thing: reason and foresight, planning and discipline, industrial and social technique had won power and wealth beyond the dreams of earlier ages. However frail the reed, human reason, applied to things and to the actions of men, had won its victories; and the Second World War marked a great chapter in the adventure. The knowledge and the power men now possessed provided the means for transforming the world; but the questions of the end for which they might be used and of the goodness of that end became all the more problematic as tradition and habit lost their power to maintain agreement about social values.

However fleeting the details of organization, however unstable the alignment of Powers which together constituted the Grand Alliance of the Second World War, these great changes promised to endure for a considerable time to come. Supra-national administration, Britain's decline as a Great Power, the change of political scale, the myth of peace on earth through human planning, and the social revolution caused by the application of reasoned calculation to social activity were none of them begun during the Second World War, but each received a new impulsion. The co-operation of the Great Allied Powers forwarded these changes as they could not have been forwarded had each nation conducted its affairs in isolation. In this, and in the fascination of a story of great deeds, great dangers, great men, and great victories, lay the permanent significance of the Grand Alliance of the Second World War.

APPENDIX I

MAJOR ALLIED CONFERENCES AND MEETINGS

7 DECEMBER 1941–31 DECEMBER 1946

Date	*Place*	*Name or Code-name*	*Chief Participants*	*Main Matters dealt with*
22 December 1941–14 January 1942	Washington	Arcadia	Churchill, Roosevelt, Hopkins, Beaverbrook, U.S. Joint Chiefs of Staff, British Chiefs of Staff.	Strategy: hold Japan, attack Germany first; Anglo-American Combined Boards; Combined Chiefs of Staff; Combined Commands in Far East; U.N. Declaration.
April 1942	London	..	Hopkins, Marshall, Churchill, British Chiefs of Staff.	U.S. plans for attack on Germany: Sledgehammer and Round-up.
20 May–2 June 1942	London and Washington	..	Molotov, Churchill; Molotov, Roosevelt, U.S. Chiefs of Staff.	Second front in 1942. Shipments to Russia; Anglo-Soviet Treaty.
18–25 June 1942	Washington	..	Churchill, Roosevelt, Combined Chiefs of Staff.	Second front; atomic research (interrupted by Tobruk news).
18–25 July 1942	London	..	Hopkins, Marshall, King, Churchill, British Chiefs of Staff.	Decision to invade North Africa—Torch.
12–15 August 1942	Moscow	..	Churchill, British Chiefs of Staff, Stalin.	Breaking news of Torch to Russians.
14–25 January 1943	Casablanca	..	Churchill, Roosevelt, Combined Chiefs of Staff.	Offensive in Mediterranean; Unconditional Surrender.
12–25 May 1943	Washington	Trident	Churchill, Roosevelt, Combined Chiefs of Staff.	Overlord for 1944; Burma; shipping; atomic energy.
14–24 August 1943	Quebec	Quadrant	Churchill, Roosevelt, Combined Chiefs of Staff.	Italy; Burma; Overlord; South-East Asia Command.
18–30 October 1943	Moscow	..	Molotov, Eden, Hull, Deane, Ismay.	Post-war planning; international organization; military co-ordination with Russia.
10 November–1 December 1943	Atlantic City	UNRRA Council First Session	..	Post-war relief.
22–26 November 1943	Cairo	Sextant	Roosevelt, Churchill, Chiang Kai-shek, Combined Chiefs of Staff.	Strategy in Far East; post-war settlement in Far East.

Date	Place	Name or Code-name	Chief Participants	Main Matters dealt with
28 November–1 December 1943	Tehrān	Eureka	Roosevelt, Churchill, Stalin, Combined Chiefs of Staff, Eden, Hopkins, Molotov.	Strategy: Mediterranean versus Overlord; exploratory conversations on post-war settlement.
3–6 December 1943	Cairo	..	Roosevelt, Churchill, Combined Chiefs of Staff, Inönü.	Strategy: Burma versus Mediterranean; effort to bring Turkey into war.
1–22 July 1944	Bretton Woods	U.N. Monetary and Financial Conference	..	Monetary Fund; International Bank.
21 August–9 October 1944	Dumbarton Oaks	..	U.S.A., U.K., U.S.S.R., Chinese delegations.	Post-war international organization.
11–19 September 1944	Quebec	Octagon	Roosevelt, Churchill, Combined Chiefs of Staff, Morgenthau.	Policy towards defeated Germany; British economic future.
5 October–23 November 1944	Washington	..	Keynes, Morgenthau.	Lend-Lease between V-E and V-J days.
9–20 October 1944	Moscow	..	Churchill, Stalin, Harriman (observer only).	Balkans; spheres of influence; Polish problem.
31 January–3 February 1945	Malta	..	Combined Chiefs of Staff, Churchill, Eden, Stettinius.	Strategy on western front; shipping; Anglo-American zones of occupation in Germany.
4–11 February 1945	Yalta	..	Stalin, Roosevelt, Churchill, Chiefs of Staff, Molotov, Stettinius, Eden, Hopkins.	Terms for Russia's entry into war with Japan; Security Council voting formula; Polish problem; policy towards Germany; Declaration on Liberated Europe.
25 April–26 June 1945	San Francisco	Conference on International Organization	Delegations from 50 nations.	U.N. organization.
26 May–5 June 1945	Moscow	..	Hopkins, Stalin.	Poland.
17 July–2 August 1945	Potsdam	..	Truman, Churchill, Stalin, Attlee, Byrnes, Eden, Bevin, Molotov.	Germany, reparations; terms to Japan; peace-making procedure.
11 September–2 October 1945	London	Council of Foreign Ministers, First Session	Byrnes, Bevin, Molotov, Bidault, Wang Shih-chieh.	Peace treaties for Italy, Rumania, Bulgaria, Hungary, Finland.
16–26 December 1945	Moscow	Conference of Foreign Ministers	Byrnes, Bevin, Molotov.	Peace treaty procedure; China; Japanese occupation; Korea; Balkan Governments; Persia; atomic energy.

10 January–14 February 1946	London	U.N. General Assembly First Session, first part	..	Organizational work: establishment of Security Council, &c.
25 April–15 May 1946	Paris	Council of Foreign Ministers, Second Session, first part	Byrnes, Bevin, Molotov, Bidault.	Five peace treaties; Peace Conference; German policy.
15 June–12 July 1946	Paris	Council of Foreign Ministers, Second Session, second part	Byrnes, Bevin, Molotov, Bidault.	Five peace treaties; Peace Conference; German policy.
29 July–15 October 1946	Paris	Paris Peace Conference	Delegations from 21 nations.	Amendment of peace treaties with Italy, Rumania, Bulgaria, Finland, Hungary.
23 October–14 December 1946	New York	U.N. General Assembly, First Session, second part	..	Completion of establishment of U.N. subsidiary organs.
4 November–11 December 1946	New York	Council of Foreign Ministers, Third Session	Byrnes, Bevin, Molotov, Maurice Couve de Murville.	Final amendment of five peace treaties.

APPENDIX II

LEND-LEASE

by SIR DAVID WALEY

(i) The Philosophy of Lend-Lease

PRESIDENT ROOSEVELT at his Press Conference on 17 December 1940 said:

Suppose my neighbor's house catches fire, and I have a length of garden hose four or five hundred feet away. If he can take my garden hose and connect it up with his hydrant, I may help him to put out the fire. Now what do I do? I don't say to him before that operation, 'Neighbor, my garden hose cost me $15; you have to pay me $15 for it'. . . . I don't want $15—I want my garden hose back after the fire is over.[1]

This was the origin of the system of Lend-Lease and Mutual Aid. Within the following five years the United States gave Lend-Lease aid to a total of $50,244 million and received reverse Lend-Lease to a total of $7,817 million; the United Kingdom gave Mutual Aid to the total of over $8,000 million and received Mutual Aid to the total of over $27,000 million; Canada gave Mutual Aid to a total of over U.S. $4,000 million.

In the event, the original metaphor proved wholly inappropriate. With minor exceptions, the fire hose was not given back after the fire was over.[2]

After Pearl Harbour, Lend-Lease was based on a different philosophy—the pooling of resources to a common end by partners in a common effort. This philosophy was repeatedly and vigorously expressed in the President's quarterly *Reports to Congress on Lend-Lease Operations* (Washington, U.S.G.P.O.). 'We must use the weapons from the arsenal of the democracies where they can be employed most effectively.'[3]

The real costs of the war cannot be measured, nor compared, nor paid for in money. They must and are being met in blood and toil. But the financial costs of the war can and should be met in a way which will serve the needs of lasting peace and mutual economic well-being.

All the United Nations are seeking maximum conversion to war production, in the light of their special resources. If each country devotes roughly the same fraction of its national production to the war, then the financial burden of war is distributed equally among the United Nations in accordance with their ability to pay. Such a distribution of the financial costs of the war means that no nation will grow rich from the war effort of its allies. The money costs of the war will fall according to the rule of equality in sacrifice, as in effort.[4]

This theme was repeatedly developed in subsequent reports, particularly the *Fourteenth Report* and the *Twentieth Report*.

[1] Stettinius: *Lend-Lease*, p. 1.

[2] Formally the 'fire-hose' principle was carried out in the settlement since ships were returned and food and materials on hand were paid for. But in fact most of the 'fire hose' had been eaten up or shot away.

[3] *Third Report on Lend-Lease Operations*, dated 12 December 1941, Letter of Transmittal, p. 5.

[4] *Fifth Report on Lend-Lease Operations*, dated 11 June 1942, pp. 22–23.

From 1939 when the war broke out in Europe until we were attacked at Pearl Harbor in 1941, the principal nations of the British Commonwealth and the U.S.S.R. were spending much larger portions of their national income for war purposes than the United States was spending for defense purposes. By 1943, the United States, the principal nations of the British Commonwealth and the U.S.S.R. were spending about one-half of their income on war, including their spending for lend-lease and reverse lend-lease. Thus, after 1942 the relative financial costs of the war contributions of the United States and our principal allies were, for practical purposes, approximately equal. . . . On this basis each ally fulfills its responsibility to contribute its full measure to the defeat of the enemy, and the money costs of war will fall according to the rule of equality of sacrifice and equality in effort.[1]

In fact Lend-Lease did not achieve equality of sacrifice. The U.S.S.R. and all the countries whose territory was devastated and occupied suffered appalling losses which were wholly or partly escaped by the United Nations whose territories were not occupied. The United Kingdom incurred financial obligations, for the most part to others of the United Nations, to a total of some £4,000 million. No attempt was made to apply retrospectively the principle of equality of sacrifice by bringing under Lend-Lease British pre-Lend-Lease expenditure, which in April 1943 amounted to some £1,500 million ($6,000 million).[2]

The result was that Britain's gold and dollars dwindled to $12 million in April 1941. But they were built up again from mid-1942 onwards, largely because the United States Government bought with dollars from the sterling area the sterling currencies for the pay and allowances of United States forces stationed in the sterling area.[3]

Thus 'Lend-Lease' was a misnomer. It suggested that the fire hose would be returned after the war, whereas in the event it was neither lent nor leased, but freely contributed to a common purpose. 'The overwhelming portion of lend-lease aid, which now totals over $42 billion, has been directly consumed by our allies in the war.'[4]

The Lend-Lease Act began with the words: 'Further to promote the defense of the United States'. This was the simple, straightforward, and convincing justification of the policy which the name of Lend-Lease disguised rather than emphasized. Equality of sacrifice, though repeatedly advocated, was in fact not attained.

(ii) The Lend-Lease Solution of the Dollar Problem of the Sterling Area

The sterling area at the outbreak of war in September 1939 had dollar assets worth some $4,400 million. Purchase of munitions in the United States was

[1] *Twentieth Report on Lend-Lease Operations*, dated 30 June 1945, p. 42.

[2] Sir Kingsley Wood in the Budget Speech on 12 April 1943 (H.C.Deb., 5th ser., vol. 388, col. 938).

[3] The total amount paid on this account was estimated at $1,200 million during the war period, see D. F. McCurrach: 'Britain's U.S. Dollar Problems 1939–45', *The Economic Journal* (Quarterly Journal of the Royal Economic Society), September 1948. The sterling area's dollar balances were also replenished from 1942 onwards by the reduction in payments due under pre-Lend-Lease contracts. Net gold and dollar reserves, which stood at $395 million at the end of 1941, increased to $1,710 million at the end of 1944, and to $1,897 million at the end of 1945.

[4] *Twentieth Report on Lend-Lease Operations*, p. 43.

suspended till the Arms Embargo imposed under the Neutrality Act had been repealed on 4 November 1939. Until the fall of France the policy was to husband the dollars of the sterling area for essential defence needs on the basis that reserves might have to cover the Allies for a three-year war—to behave, indeed, 'as if we were on a desert island, on short rations which we must stretch as far as we can.'[1] But with the fall of France Britain's non-dollar sources of supply were cut off by enemy occupation or restricted by shipping difficulties. The British Government took over the French contracts in the United States lock, stock, and barrel. After the fall of France Britain could not hope to make her resources last for years and had to gamble on using up her dollar reserves within a few months in the hope that some solution would be found thereafter.

By the end of 1940 Britain had spent $4,500 million, and had reduced her reserves by $2,500 million; she had outstanding liabilities for payment in 1941 of $1,274 million, and the estimated dollar deficit of the sterling area in the year 1941 was $1,464 million. 'By the middle of December, new British contracting in the United States had practically stopped'.[2]

The problem before President Roosevelt was to find a means of enabling the British Commonwealth to continue the fight without departing from the technical neutrality of the United States and without repeating the system of international War Loans which had led to such disastrous results after the first World War. Stettinius[3] recorded that a suggestion was made by President Roosevelt in the summer of 1940 that the drain on the British reserve of dollars should be reduced by hiring ships to Britain instead of selling them. This idea had first been proposed by the United States Treasury Department, whose lawyers found that army property could, under a statute of 1892, be leased by the Secretary of War 'when in his discretion it will be for the public good'. This pointed the way to a solution in the form of lending and leasing.

Roosevelt told his Press Conference on 17 December 1940: 'What I'm trying to do is to eliminate the dollar sign.' His proposal was that the United States Government should place all the contracts for munitions to be manufactured in the United States. If the United States decided that they 'would be more useful to the defense of the United States if they were used in Great Britain than if they were kept in storage here', the American Government could 'either lease or sell the materials, subject to mortgage, to the people on the other side'.[4]

The President's Press Conference on 17 December 1940 was followed by a 'fireside chat' in which Roosevelt first used the oft-repeated phrase: 'We must be the great arsenal of democracy.' This was followed on 6 January 1941 by the President's annual message to Congress on 'The State of the Union'.

On 10 January 1941 the Lend-Lease Bill—HR 1776[5]—which had been drafted by Oscar Cox of the Treasury Department and discussed with the Cabinet Members and Congressional leaders was introduced in the Senate and the House of Representatives.

[1] A. B. Purvis (who was chairman of the British Supply Council in North America at the time of his death in 1941), quoted by Stettinius: *Lend-Lease*, p. 60.

[2] Ibid. p. 61. [3] Ibid. p. 62. [4] Ibid. p. 66.

[5] See *Documents on American Foreign Relations, 1940–1941*, pp. 715–23, for the text of the Bill as originally introduced and subsequently amended.

The Lend-Lease Act,[1] as finally approved, was officially entitled 'An Act to Promote the Defense of the United States'. It provided that the President, when he deemed it in the interest of national defence, might authorize, to the extent to which funds were made available, the production or procurement of any defence article for the government of any country whose defence the President deemed vital to the defence of the United States and might 'sell, transfer title to, exchange, lease, lend, or otherwise dispose of' any such defence article to any such government. The terms and conditions of such aid 'shall be those which the President deems satisfactory and the benefit to the United States may be payment or repayment in kind or property, or any other direct or indirect benefit which the President deems satisfactory.' Provisos were inserted that the Act did not authorize convoying by naval vessels of the United States nor entry of any American vessel into a combat area.

The Foreign Affairs Committee of the House of Representatives heard twenty-nine witnesses from 15 January to 29 January 1941. The Foreign Relations Committee of the Senate heard forty-one witnesses from 27 January to 8 February. The case put forward for the Bill was, in essence, that it was necessary to 'promote the defense of the United States'. It was argued by the Secretary of State that, if British resistance collapsed, Germany could, and would, attack the United States. 'Were Britain . . . to lose command of the seas, Germany could easily cross the Atlantic—especially the South Atlantic—unless we were ready and able to do what Britain is doing now. . . . Subversive forces are hard at work in many American countries. . . .' Assistance to Great Britain 'is a vital part of our national self-defense. . . . The great problem of democracy is to organize and use its strength with sufficient speed and completeness. The proposed legislation is an essential measure for that purpose.'[2]

Morgenthau, the Secretary of the Treasury, put his case thus:[3]

> The British Government owes American manufacturers $1,400 million on orders already placed. It has enough gold and dollar exchange assets to meet these outstanding commitments, but the British just haven't got the dollars to take care of their additional needs . . . . They will not place orders that they cannot pay for. Therefore, the ordering has practically ceased. . . . I am convinced that they do not have dollar assets beyond those which they have disclosed to me . . . and lacking a formula being worked out by Congress . . . by which Great Britain can buy supplies here, I think they will just have to stop fighting, that is all.

The arguments against the Bill were that the fear of an easy or early invasion of the United States by Germany was groundless and that the right way to promote the defence of the United States was to increase the output of 'defense articles' and to keep them at home; that the policy underlying the Bill, in the light of Roosevelt's fireside chat and message to Congress, would inevitably lead the United States first into convoying ships carrying war supplies and then into war; that the United States had been cleverly beguiled by the smart Europeans

[1] Ibid. pp. 712–15.

[2] U.S.A., House of Representatives, Committee on Foreign Affairs: *Hearings on the Lend-Lease Bill* (Washington, U.S.G.P.O., 1941), Statement by Secretary of State Cordell Hull, pp. 6, 7.

[3] U.S.A., Senate, Committee on Foreign Relations: *Hearings on the Lend-Lease Bill* (Washington, U.S.G.P.O., 1941), Statement by Morgenthau, pp. 9, 43, 47.

into taking part in the First World War, and that it was her overriding interest to keep out of the Second World War. In Colonel McCormick's words: 'The experiences of the Athenians at Syracuse, the Romans in Germany, Napoleon in Egypt, the Russians in Manchuria show that the greatest catastrophes come to navies, armies and nations when they embark on distant military adventures. I pray to God that hysteria, propaganda, and ambition will not become strong enough to immolate our present generation of young men.'[1] As Colonel Lindbergh put it: 'What we are doing in following our present policy is giving up an ideal defensive position in America for a very precarious offensive position in Europe. If we are ever invaded in America, the responsibility will lie upon those who send our arms abroad.'[2]

The most widespread criticism of the Bill was that it gave to the President dictatorial powers: this criticism was expressed by Americans who wished to give all and any aid to Great Britain; by others who wished to give all aid short of war; and by others who were opposed to the whole policy of aid to Britain.

'The debate went on all over the country—on the radio, on street corners, around the stoves in country stores, at Grange and Rotary club and labor union meetings, in college rooms, and in the churches. . . . We were divided on the issue of Lend-Lease without regard to party, profession, background, or creed. . . .'[3] There were ex-Presidential candidates, college presidents, students' societies, labour organizations, and business associations on each side of the controversy.

Eventually the House of Representatives approved the Bill by 260 to 165 votes and the Senate by 60 votes to 31. It was signed by the President on 11 March 1941, and next day Congress was asked for the first Lend-Lease appropriation which, after strenuous debate, was passed on 27 March 1941.

One of the criticisms frequently made in the Hearings in Congress was that the British controlled valuable businesses in the United States and had no claim to Lend-Lease aid until these had been sold. Morgenthau had said to the Senate Foreign Relations Committee in January 1941: 'Every dollar of property, real property, or securities, that any English citizen owns in the United States, they have agreed to sell during the next twelve months, in order to raise money to pay for the orders they have already placed.'[4]

The sale of these businesses was regarded in the United Kingdom as an unreasonable proposal, since inevitably they were deprived of a great part of their value when severed from their original ownership. The British felt that they were not only being asked to sell their shirts to enable them to continue 'to promote the defense of the United States', but also to sell them at a bargain-basement price. But the United States administration regarded the sacrifice as necessary.

And so while the Debate on the first Lend-Lease Appropriation was at its height, the sale of American Viscose Corporation was rapidly arranged. . . . We received over $54 million. This was widely regarded in Britain as a rubbish price, a view reinforced by the award of compensation of over £27 million to Courtaulds, the former British

[1] U.S.A., Senate, Committee on Foreign Relations: *Hearings on the Lend-Lease Bill*, p. 479.
[2] Ibid. p. 492.
[3] Stettinius: *Lend-Lease*, pp. 74–75.
[4] U.S.A., Senate, Committee on Foreign Relations: *Hearings on the Lend-Lease Bill*, p. 66.

owners. But it was a rubbish price only in the sense that any sale of a direct investment could not possibly realise the full value of the business to its British owners. American Viscose was unknown to the American investing public. A great advertising campaign had to be undertaken including not only the highest efforts of brokers' salesmen, and mountains of printed matter, but even the use of films.[1]

The Lend-Lease Act solved the problems of 1942–4, but meanwhile the pressing problem of 1941 was to pay for deliveries under pre-Lend-Lease munitions contracts and to pay for other goods not covered by Lend-Lease. The case which Morgenthau had put before Congress was that the assets which Britain held on 1 January 1941 were sufficient, though not more than sufficient, to pay for deliveries under these pre-Lend-Lease contracts. But this assumed that Britain could realize $900 million on 'Direct Investments'. The forced sale of American Viscose showed how wide of the mark this estimate would prove. In April 1941 Britain's net available gold and dollar reserves were reduced to a low level and she still had to meet some $1,000 million on pre-Lend-Lease contracts.

Happily, means appeared to halt this Clearance Sale in depressed markets. Legislation was passed authorising loans by American Government departments to foreign governments provided these loans were adequately secured by collateral. Negotiations with The Reconstruction Finance Corporation resulted in July 1941 in an Agreement for a loan of $425 million secured by marketable securities, direct investments, insurance companies and the income of insurance branches. In the event we required to draw only $390 million.[2]

The loan bore interest at 3 per cent. and was repayable in fifteen years, within which period it would be amortized from the income on the collateral.[3] The necessary United Kingdom legislation was passed by the House of Commons on 25 July 1941.[4]

At first the principal part in administering Lend-Lease was taken by Harry Hopkins and a small staff drawn mainly from the President's Liaison Committee, which had been appointed on 6 December 1939 to co-ordinate domestic and foreign purchases of war supplies. On 2 May 1941 this staff was given formal status as the Division of Defense Aid Reports, with Major-General James H. Burns as Executive Officer.

On 28 August 1941 the President asked Edward Stettinius, Jr. to take over the administration of the Lend-Lease programme.[5] On 28 October 1941 the President issued an Executive Order creating the Office of Lend-Lease Administrator and delegating to the Administrator all the President's powers under the Lend-Lease Act and the Lend-Lease Appropriation Acts, except the designation of Lend-Lease countries (reserved for the President) and the negotiation of Master Agreements (delegated to the State Department).

After the appointment of Stettinius as Under-Secretary of State the 'Foreign Economic Administration' (F.E.A.) was established on 25 September 1943. It took over a number of functions, including Relief, Economic Warfare, and Lend-Lease. Leo T. Crowley was appointed Administrator. The F.E.A.

[1] McCurrach: 'Britain's U.S. Dollar Problems', *Economic Journal*, September 1948, pp. 360–1.
[2] Ibid. p. 362.
[3] 22 July 1941, H.C.Deb. 5th ser., vol. 373, col. 799.
[4] Ibid. col. 1173.
[5] Stettinius: *Lend-Lease*, p. 105.

was abolished, and its functions handed over to the State Department on 20 October 1945.

Having recorded these administrative arrangements, the writer must pause to pay humble tribute to Henry Morgenthau, the father (under the President) of Lend-Lease and thus a chief architect of the Allied victory, and to Edward Stettinius, who won universal admiration for the way in which he presided over the formative period of Lend-Lease.

By 1944 Lend-Lease Aid represented 17 per cent. of American war expenditure and the cost in that year to the United States was valued at $15,000 million. In 1944 Lend-Lease covered 27·2 per cent. of British Empire supplies of munitions. The United States was devoting between 4 and 5 per cent. of her national income to Lend-Lease to the British Empire, while the United Kingdom was devoting about the same proportion of her national income to reciprocal aid to the United States. (Australia and New Zealand were devoting nearly 7 per cent. and 10 per cent. respectively of their national incomes to reciprocal aid).[1]

But these immense results were only reached gradually. In 1941, the first year of Lend-Lease, while food began to flow at once and plant was created on a large scale for future deliveries of munitions, less than 100 aeroplanes, and 786 tanks, were sent to the United Kingdom under Lend-Lease.[2] But the proportion of Lend-Lease deliveries to all countries which consisted of munitions increased from 21·5 per cent. in 1941 to 46·7 per cent. in 1942 and to 61·5 per cent. in 1944. A similar evolution is seen in the following analysis of Lend-Lease aid to the British Empire:[3]

Per cent.	*1941*	*1942*	*1943*	*1944*	*Jan. to Aug. 1945*
Munitions (and ships)	31·7	53·6	70·3	67·5	64·3
Industrial materials and products	13·2	13·3	9·4	8·0	10·4
Agricultural products	37·1	17·5	11·9	14·1	16·4
Services	17·9	15·5	8·4	10·6	9·0
Total Excluding Petroleum ($ million)	999	4,525	8,659	9,967	3,781

It is curious in the light of these figures to remember that some people in 1941 argued that it was to Britain's interest that the United States should remain neutral, since she would be able to spare Britain less help if she were herself at war.

After Pearl Harbour it was agreed in principle that each partner should contribute all it could, and as best it could, to winning the war, though the final decision on the nature and amount of the contribution of the United States continued to rest with the U.S. Government. After Churchill's visit to Washington in December 1941 the Combined Chiefs of Staff Committee,[4] the Combined

[1] As estimated by Professor R. G. D. Allen ('Mutual Aid', pp. 260–2). [This paper is referred to hereafter as Allen: 'Mutual Aid'.]

[2] Stettinius: *Lend-Lease*, p. 94.

[3] See Allen: 'Mutual Aid', p. 263. For the period 2 September 1945 to 30 June 1947 the total was $442 million, of which munitions comprised 24 per cent., agricultural and industrial products comprised 74 per cent., and services comprised 2 per cent. (See the *Twenty-fifth Report on Lend-Lease Operations*, p. 13.)

[4] See above, pp. 109–16.

Raw Materials Board, and the Combined Shipping Adjustment Board were created in January 1942. The Combined Production and Resources Board and the Combined Food Board were set up in June 1942.[1]

A different system was adopted in regard to supplies to Russia. Lists of items and quantities were discussed and the agreement to ship such items and quantities was embodied in successive Protocols.[2] The Russians were not asked to disclose their gold and dollar assets, as the United Kingdom and other United Nations were required to do as a condition of Lend-Lease aid.

(iii) The Lend-Lease Agreements

(*a*) The White Paper of 10 September 1941

After the introduction of Lend-Lease, American critics alleged that materials supplied on Lend-Lease were being used by British exporters in the manufacture of goods which competed with American exports. The matter was raised in July 1941 by the American Ambassador in London, Winant, and as a result of his insistent demands[3] an agreement was reached at the end of July, and this was embodied in a White Paper[4] dated 10 September 1941.

This was in form a unilateral statement by the United Kingdom Government, but it was for the following four years treated by the United States authorities as a contractual obligation on the part of the British Government and sometimes interpreted in a legalistic spirit. The rules governing what was and was not properly eligible for Lend-Lease, including those based on the White Paper, 'developed with changing conditions and probably became the instrument of keeping the amount of our reserves in check. . . . They were varied from time to time by administrative edict and became a highly formalized tangle of rules and interpretations.'[5]

The White Paper of September 1941 covered not only Lend-Lease materials, but also materials similar to those being provided under Lend-Lease and materials in short supply obtained from the United States (whether under Lend-Lease or for cash). The United Kingdom Government undertook not to use Lend-Lease materials for exports, not to apply materials similar to those supplied under Lend-Lease in such a way as to enable their exporters to enter new markets or to extend their export trade at the expense of the United States exporters, and not to use materials subject to restrictions in the United States on the ground of short supply for export except in special cases, in particular for the supply of 'material which is needed overseas in connexion with supplies essential to the war effort for ourselves and our Allies which cannot be obtained from the United States'.

The White Paper dealt not only with export policy, but also with the distribution in the United Kingdom of Lend-Leased goods. An assurance was given

[1] See above, pp. 129–37. [2] See above, pp. 144–6, 236–41.

[3] See John G. Winant: *A Letter from Grosvenor Square* (London, Hodder & Stoughton, 1947), p. 105.

[4] Great Britain, Foreign Office: *Correspondence respecting the Policy of His Majesty's Government in the United Kingdom in Connexion with the Use of Materials received under the Lend-Lease Act*, Cmd. 6311 (London, H.M.S.O., 1941).

[5] McCurrach: 'Britain's U.S. Dollar Problems', *Economic Journal*, September 1948, p. 362.

that the distribution of such goods would result in no remuneration over and above a 'fair return for the services rendered in the work of distribution'. In most cases the distributors would be agents of His Majesty's Government, and not principals. Food would be sold to wholesalers, but neither wholesalers nor retailers would receive 'any greater remuneration than is adequate to cover the cost of the services performed'.[1] The Ministry of Food having established a close control over all distributive margins, the assurance did not give rise to difficulties comparable with those which resulted from the assurance about exports.

(*b*) The Master Agreements

On 23 February 1942 the Master Agreement[2] between the United Kingdom and the United States was signed after 'many months of study and negotiation' and was hailed as 'the first important milestone on the road toward achievement of the objectives set forth in the Atlantic Charter'.

Section 3 (*b*) of the Lend-Lease Act had provided that the terms and conditions upon which foreign governments received aid 'shall be those which the President deems satisfactory, and the benefit to the United States may be payment or repayment in kind or property, or any other direct or indirect benefit which the President deems satisfactory'.[3] Congress had been told that this Section 'implies that some quid pro quo will always be called for'. At various times it was suggested that the quid pro quo should be the transfer of the West Indies or British Empire raw materials. Eventually in 1945 an agreement was reached by which the 'quo'—which amounted to perhaps $20,000 million[4]—was settled by a 'quid' which involved no payment in cash or kind. Infinite pains had been taken to educate American opinion to recognize the wisdom and justice of such an 'unsordid' settlement; the Master Agreement of 23 February 1942 was the first step to this end.

The Agreement deferred the final determination of the terms and conditions of Lend-Lease, but provided (Article VII) that they

> shall be such as not to burden commerce between the two countries, but to promote mutually advantageous economic relations between them and the betterment of world-wide economic relations. . . . To that end, they shall include provision for agreed action . . . directed to the expansion . . . of production, employment, and the exchange and consumption of goods, which are the material foundations of the liberty and welfare of all peoples; to the elimination of all forms of discriminatory treatment in international commerce, and to the reduction of tariffs and other trade barriers.[5]

By 1945 thirty-five Master Agreements on similar lines had been concluded; Australia and New Zealand had accepted the principles of the Lend-Lease Agreement with the United Kingdom as applicable to their relations with the

[1] Cmd. 6311, pp. 3–4.

[2] Great Britain, Foreign Office: *Agreement between the Governments of the United Kingdom and the United States of America on the Principles applying to Mutual Aid*, Cmd. 6341 (London, H.M.S.O., 1942); *Documents on American Foreign Relations, 1941–1942*, pp. 235–7.

[3] *Fourth Report on Lend-Lease Operations*, dated 11 March 1942, p. 31.

[4] U.S.A., House of Representatives, Committee on Foreign Affairs: *Hearings on the Lend-Lease Bill*, Statement by Stettinius, p. 137.

[5] For a fuller summary of the Agreement see above, pp. 140–1.

United States; and Canada had accepted the underlying principles of Article VII.

By these agreements the dollar sign was eliminated and promises to pay to Bearer were replaced by promises to reduce trade barriers and eliminate discriminations after the war—a process which no doubt seemed in 1942 easier to achieve than it seemed some years after the war had ended.

(c) The Reciprocal Aid Agreements

Immediately after Pearl Harbour the United Kingdom supplied barrage balloons and anti-aircraft guns for the defence of the United States coasts and the Panama Canal. This was christened 'Reverse Lend-Lease'. In Article II of the Master Agreement of 23 February 1942 the United Kingdom undertook to continue to contribute to the defence of the United States and to 'provide such articles, services, facilities or information as it may be in a position to supply'.

The position was further defined in the Reciprocal Aid Agreement of September 1942,[1] by which the United Kingdom undertook to provide (1) munitions, (2) other supplies and services for the U.S. forces (except pay and allowances), (3) supplies and services for capital works in the United Kingdom or in the British Colonial Empire, and (4) supplies and services elsewhere, in so far as the United Kingdom or Colonial Empire was the most practical source of supply.

Similar Reciprocal Aid Agreements were signed with Australia and New Zealand on the same date, and with France, Belgium, and the Netherlands in 1945 after their liberation. Reciprocal Aid was received from India without a formal agreement. The total Reciprocal Aid received by the United States to 30 June 1947 is estimated in the *Twenty-fifth Report*[2] at $7,819 million, of which over 86 per cent. was from the British Empire.

The types of Reciprocal Aid which the United Kingdom undertook to provide excluded supplies of raw materials and food imported into the United States. In the *Fourth Report*, dealing with the first year of Lend-Lease operations, it was explained[3] that 'we will of course continue to pay dollars for many things we receive today. If we did not, the seller countries would lose what little dollar exchange they now have available to use for cash purposes in our markets. Since they would have no other source of dollar exchange, they would be even more dependent on lend-lease aid than they are now.'

This was a cogent argument. But, by the summer of 1943, the British Government had completed dollar payments on most of their pre-Lend-Lease contracts (amounting in value to $3,600 million); and they then 'agreed to extend the principle of Reverse Lend-Lease to include many raw materials and foodstuffs

[1] Great Britain, Foreign Office: *Exchange of Notes between the Governments of the United Kingdom and the United States of America on the Principles applying to Reciprocal Aid*, Cmd. 6389 (London, H.M.S.O., 1942); *Documents on American Foreign Relations, 1942–1943*, pp. 234–6. See above, p. 142, for a summary of the Agreement.

[2] *Twenty-fifth Report on Lend-Lease Operations*, p. 77.

[3] *Fourth Report on Lend-Lease Operations*, p. 33.

shipped to the United States'.[1] By 1 April 1945 materials (including tea, cocoa, palm kernels, palm oil, sisal, hides, and copra) to a total value of $164 million had been received by the United States under this arrangement.[2]

(iv) Analysis of Mutual Aid

It was always difficult for either country to appreciate at its full measure the magnitude of the British Empire's Reciprocal Aid to the United States. It was less dramatic than the supply of aircraft, guns, and tanks under Lend-Lease. As Stettinius put it:[3] 'Carrying our troops and guarding them across the ocean, and providing all the buildings and other construction we need in Britain, is only the beginning of Reverse Lend-Lease. The rest consists chiefly of ten thousand and one bits and pieces.'

The United States Administration spared no pains to 'write up' Reverse Lend-Lease. The *Twelfth* and *Seventeenth Reports on Lend-Lease Operations* were devoted solely to the Reverse Lend-Lease received from the United Kingdom, Australia, New Zealand, and India.[4]

No less than 31 per cent. of the supplies for the invasion of Europe were obtained by the United States forces as Reverse Lend-Lease. 'It would have taken 1,000 loaded ships to send from the United States the supplies provided to our forces by the United Kingdom. We and they used these thousand ships to bring over from America 6,800,000 tons of tanks, trucks, bombs, and other supplies. . . .' The new construction involved in the bases, camps, supply, and repair depots for the United States forces employed almost one-third of the United Kingdom's building labour force. Existing facilities were handed over 'equivalent to 1,000 city blocks'.[5]

The third report on Mutual Aid by the United Kingdom Government, published in October 1946,[6] after making it clear that the available figures could not give a complete evaluation of Mutual Aid, contained an analysis of British Reciprocal Aid to the United States, which (subject to the above reserve) was valued at £1,241,402,000. British Mutual Aid to Russia during the war period was valued at £318 million and aid to other countries at £519 million—a total over £2,000 million. The report stated that these arrangements for the most part had ceased by October 1946, and that the agreements were then 'being terminated in the spirit which gave birth to them and in strict accordance with the principles on which they were concluded. The vast flow of commodities and services exchanged and consumed in fighting the common enemy are not to be left standing as monetary liabilities, but cancelled by common consent.'

The conduct of the war provided a striking example of the 'division of labour'

[1] Stettinius: *Lend-Lease*, p. 284. This arrangement was announced to the House of Commons on 11 November 1943 (H.C.Deb. 5th ser., vol. 393, col. 1298).

[2] *Twentieth Report on Lend-Lease Operations*, p. 19. According to the *Twenty-fifth Report*, p. 77, the total value of agricultural, industrial, and other commodities received up to 2 September 1945 was $1,877 million.

[3] Stettinius: *Lend-Lease*, p. 277.

[4] The United Kingdom and the Indian Government were both concerned in Reverse Lend-Lease from India.

[5] *Seventeenth Report on Lend-Lease Operations*, dated 24 November 1944 (reprinted London, H.M.S.O.), pp. 6–7.

[6] Great Britain, Treasury: *Mutual Aid, Third Report*, Cmd. 6931 (London, H.M.S.O., 1946).

between the United States and the British Commonwealth countries. The United Kingdom, Australia, New Zealand, and India were mobilized for war to a higher degree than the United States. For example, the United Kingdom had 55 per cent. of her labour force in the armed forces and war employment in June 1944, whereas the United States had 40 per cent. The British countries were able to supply more than their proportionate share of fighters and war-workers because a part of the munitions, raw materials, and food for the British fighters and war-workers was supplied by the United States and Canada as Mutual Aid. The dollar statistics cannot measure the respective contributions of the fighters in getting on with the job, but indicate how the tools were provided. Of all Lend-Lease aid to the British Empire, munitions accounted for 65 per cent., and shipping and other war services for 10 per cent. Of the remaining 25 per cent., half was for food. The United States Lend-Leased to the British Empire in 1944 13½ per cent. of the American output of aircraft, 29½ per cent. of the American output of tanks and vehicles, and 5 per cent. of the American food and agricultural produce.

The composition of Reciprocal Aid from the United Kingdom to the United States varied even more than Lend-Lease Aid with the successive stages of the war. As between the years ending 30 June 1943 and 30 June 1945, construction fell from 41·7 per cent. of the total to 6·7 per cent., while foodstuffs and raw materials rose from 2·8 per cent. to 15·6 per cent. and services (including building maintenance) from 19·2 per cent. to 43·7 per cent.[1]

Lend-Lease from the United States to the British Empire and Reverse Lend-Lease from the United Kingdom to the United States could be compared in various ways. From 1942 to mid-1945:

> U.S. lend-lease aid to the British Empire represented 11 per cent. of U.S. war expenditures, and the corresponding proportion was nearly 9 per cent. for the U.K. At the peak rate of flow of mutual aid, the U.S. was devoting not far short of 15 per cent. of all her war expenditures to lend-lease aid to the British Empire (first half of 1944), while the U.K. spent about 12 per cent. of the total cost of the war on reciprocal aid to the U.S. (late in 1944). . . . In the whole period of mutual aid, almost identical proportions of national income, about 4¾ per cent., were devoted to lend-lease in the U.S. and to reciprocal aid in the U.K. At peak, late in 1944, the proportions were nearly 7 per cent. in each country. . . . About 4 per cent. of total domestic output in the U.S. was directed to the British Empire under lend-lease in the whole period of operation, and at peak the proportion was nearly 6 per cent. The corresponding proportion for the U.K. was about 3 per cent. in the three years from mid-1942 to mid-1945, with a peak of about 4 per cent. in the spring of 1944 before D Day.
>
> The conclusion, therefore, is that all measures point to the same general result. Relative to her resources the U.K. contribution in the form of reciprocal aid to the U.S. may have been rather less, but certainly it was not much less, than the U.S. contribution in the form of lend-lease aid to the British Empire.[2]

These conclusions would not be much altered if the Reciprocal Aid given by the United States and by the United Kingdom to Russia were included in the calculations, since the proportions of Lend-Lease and of Reciprocal Aid to third countries were roughly the same.

[1] See Allen: 'Mutual Aid', p. 265. [2] Ibid. pp. 261–2.

In short, while the United Kingdom, Australia and New Zealand,[1] and India did more than their proportionate share of mobilization for fighting and war-work, and the United Kingdom made a unique sacrifice of overseas financial resources, the United Kingdom also did roughly its proportionate share of Mutual Aid and Australia and New Zealand much more than their proportionate shares.

(v) Termination of Lend-Lease

On 30 November 1944 the Prime Minister announced to the House of Commons[2] the revised Lend-Lease arrangements for the period after the defeat of Germany and before the defeat of Japan. Britain expected to reduce her needs for Lend-Lease aid to not much more than a half of what she had been receiving in 1944. After the defeat of Germany, some release of man-power to increase the supplies available for civilian consumption would be justifiable and necessary. This would be effected without the British Commonwealth ceasing to bear her due share in the defeat of Japan.

The new situation also brought relief as regards freedom to export. The United Kingdom Government had on 11 November 1943 announced in the House of Commons that in view of changes in the world situation, including the supply of food and raw materials as reverse Lend-Lease, the unilateral undertaking given in the White Paper of 10 September 1941 not to use Lend-Lease materials for exports should be replaced by a new statement.[3] But negotiations on this most thorny of topics over a period of twelve months had hitherto borne no fruit.

It had, however, now been decided as from 1 January 1945 to exclude from Lend-Lease manufactured articles for civilian use which entered the export trade and many raw and semi-fabricated materials, such as iron and steel and some non-ferrous metals, including aluminium.[4] Thus Britain would be free to export a wide range of goods made from those materials. By this decision the Lend-Lease embargo on exports was largely removed, though scarce materials had still to be reserved for essential war purposes.

In a further statement on 21 December 1944[5] the Chancellor of the Exchequer reiterated: 'We hope that there are no potential exports of any importance likely to be affected by any restrictions arising out of Lend-Lease.' He added that the arrangements were not expected to cause an increased drain on British gold and dollar resources.

The atomic bombs dropped on Hiroshima and Nagasaki on 6 August and 9 August 1945 brought the war with Japan to an unexpectedly rapid end, and when Japan capitulated on 14 August no plans had been agreed upon to deal

[1] See above, p. 778.
[2] H.C.Deb. 5th ser., vol. 406, coll. 69–74.
[3] Ibid. vol. 393, col. 1312.
[4] Some items had already been removed from the list of goods eligible for Lend-Lease. Tobacco for civilian use had been excluded in May 1943 (ibid. vol. 389, col. 949) and capital goods in November 1943 (ibid. vol. 396, col. 38). Civilian supplies of all kinds to British colonies not actually forming battle fronts had also been removed from the list. These decisions had no doubt been influenced by the increase in the sterling area's dollar balances.
[5] H.C.Deb. 5th ser., vol. 406, col. 1977.

with the world's dollar problem. A week later, on 21 August, President Truman directed the Foreign Economic Administration to take steps immediately to discontinue Lend-Lease operations. This decision was logical, since the need to 'promote the defense of the United States' had come to an end. But it undoubtedly came as a shock to the recipients of Lend-Lease.

In general 'straight' Lend-Lease was stopped and the goods in the pipe-lines were offered for delivery only if the recipient governments had undertaken to pay for them on terms to be mutually agreed.[1] As exceptions, 'straight' Lend-Lease was continued (1) to China to help her to expel the Japanese forces; (2) in the form of shipping for two months; (3) to Belgium, which had furnished reverse Lend-Lease to the United States troops in excess of Lend-Lease aid received by her; and (4) to complete deliveries covered by an allocation from Lend-Lease funds of $100 million for civil supplies in Italy.

Within a month of V-J day negotiations had begun for the settlement of Lend-Lease and Mutual Aid accounts between the United States and the United Kingdom, but when a settlement was reached it attracted comparatively little notice, since it was announced at the same time as the agreement for an American loan to Britain on 6 December 1945.[2]

President Roosevelt in his annual message to Congress in January 1941 had said: 'For what we send abroad we shall be repaid within a reasonable time following the close of hostilities in similar materials or at our option in other goods of many kinds which they produce and we need.' But this, wisely, was not written into the Lend-Lease Act.

The way for an 'unsordid' settlement was, after Pearl Harbour, prepared in many of the President's quarterly *Reports to Congress on Lend-Lease Operations*, particularly in the *Fifth Report*. This recognized that 'the real costs of the war cannot be measured, nor compared, nor paid for in money. They must and are being met in blood and toil.'[3] The *Twentieth Report* pointed out that to treat the sum total of $42 milliard as a debt would be disastrous for the debtors and the United States alike.

The joint statement issued by the United States and United Kingdom Governments on 6 December 1945[4] referred both to the 'benefits already received by them in the defeat of their common enemies' and to the understandings reached upon commercial policy. The essence of the settlement was that 'no financial obligation was created on the part of either country in respect to the goods furnished under lend-lease or reverse lend-lease which were lost, destroyed, or consumed in defeating our enemies. These goods and services were used in winning the war and neither country benefits financially from such use at the expense of the other.'[5]

Some $26 to $27 milliard of Lend-Lease aid by the United States to the

[1] For the pipe-line agreements see above, pp. 674–5.

[2] See above, pp. 682–5, for the negotiation and terms of the Loan Agreement.

[3] *Fifth Report on Lend-Lease Operations*, p. 22.

[4] Great Britain, Treasury: *Financial Agreement between the Governments of the United States and the United Kingdom dated 6th December, 1945*, Cmd. 6708 (London, H.M.S.O., 1945); *Documents on American Foreign Relations, 1945–1946*, pp. 132–4.

[5] *Twenty-second Report on Lend-Lease Operations*, dated 31 December 1945, p. 9.

United Kingdom, and reverse Lend-Lease which at comparable prices might be valued at $6 milliard, were wiped off the financial slate—the largest wiping of the slate in the pages of history.

The joint statement of 6 December 1945 was followed on 27 March 1946 by the signature of a Joint Memorandum and nine agreements 'regarding settlement for Lend-Lease, Reciprocal Aid, Surplus War Property and Claims'.[1] The nine 'Specific Agreements' of 27 March related to supplies which had not been consumed in winning the war. They provided that the net liability of the United Kingdom, estimated at $650 million, should be paid off within fifty years on the same terms as the American Loan.

This $650 million was made up as follows:

	$ million
Goods in the pipe-lines, net, and settlement of hitherto disputed claims on both sides	118
U.S. Government surplus stocks in the U.K.	60
Redistributing petroleum stocks	90
Lend-Lease goods held for civilian use in the U.K.: non-combat aircraft: and the Lend-Lease constituent of installations in the U.K. and Colonies	382
	650

The general effect of the nine Specific Agreements has been summarized by Professor R. G. D. Allen.[2] His conclusions were that: (1) there were no financial obligations for Mutual Aid goods destroyed or consumed during the war; (2) naval vessels and merchant ships of 100 gross tons and over were returnable; (3) the title to Lend-Lease munitions and other supplies held by United Kingdom forces at V-J day were subject to recapture by the United States, though the right was not generally to be exercised (their financial value did not enter into the settlement); (4) goods in the pipe-lines, the 'civilian holdings', surplus stores, petroleum, and other items listed above were bought and sold by the two sides and this resulted in the net debt of $650 million charged to the United Kingdom.

Thus the system of pooling resources and Mutual Aid, which was built up by unprecedented efforts in 1942 and reached its peak in 1944, was brought to an end on V-J day on its financial side and by 31 December 1945 on its supply side. The method of disentangling the accounts for post-V-J day supplies was settled by March 1946, and the chapter brought to a satisfactory and surprisingly little noticed close.

(vi) Canadian Mutual Aid

Canada, having in 1913 been almost wholly an agricultural country,[3] had by 1944 become the fifth largest industrial country in the world, and by this date 80 per cent. of her national income was derived from industry. The Canadian Index of Industrial Production rose from 100 in the first half of 1939 to 275 at the end of 1943.[4]

[1] Great Britain, Foreign Office: *Joint Memorandum and Agreements*, Cmd. 6813 (London, H.M.S.O., 1946).

[2] Allen: 'Mutual Aid', pp. 244–6.

[3] Bank for International Settlements: *15th Annual Report* (Basle, 1945), p. 20.

[4] Ibid. *16th Annual Report* (Basle, 1946), p. 16.

Thus Canada was both a granary and an arsenal of the United Kingdom and others of the United Nations. During the period September 1943 to September 1945, 57 per cent. of Canada's production of munitions, to the total value of $5,000 million, was for Mutual Aid (mainly to the United Kingdom), 29 per cent. for Canada's own fighting forces, and 14 per cent. for the United States.[1]

The financial problems involved by this very great contribution were difficult. Canada had, both before and still more during the war, a credit balance with the sterling area and a debit balance with the United States. Before the war the credit balance was met in convertible sterling: a gold payment of U.S. $250 million was made by the United Kingdom in 1940, but gold payments could not be continued after the exhaustion of the sterling area's gold and dollar reserves. Eventually the sale of Canadian munitions to the U.S.A. helped to solve the problem.

The cardinal principle of Canadian policy, as stated by the Minister of Finance on 20 March 1941, was 'to see that United Kingdom purchases in this country are not hampered by reason of any lack of Canadian dollars'.[2] This policy was also applied to the rest of the sterling area, the U.S.S.R., China, France, and Greece.

Further principles were: (1) not to create unmanageable international War Debts 'which did so much to prevent recovery from the effects of the war of 1914–18'; and (2) not to ask for Lend-Lease aid from the United States.

In pursuance of this general policy, Canada adopted the following measures: (1) Canadian securities (mainly Government and National Railway securities) were repatriated to the value of $800 million.[3] (2) Early in 1942 the Canadian Government made to the United Kingdom Government a loan of $700 million which bore no interest during the war. The proceeds of the loan were used to reduce Canadian sterling balances, which had been allowed to pile up as a temporary stop-gap measure. The United Kingdom agreed to use, for repaying this loan, the proceeds of the sale in Canada or redemption of Canadian securities held in the United Kingdom. (3) During 1943 Canada repaid to the United Kingdom more than $200 million which the United Kingdom had spent on building plants in Canada to produce war supplies, and thus Canada obtained ownership of these plants. (4) Canada under the War Appropriation (United Kingdom Finance) Act of 1942 made a free gift of $1,000 million to the United Kingdom and this enabled the Canadian dollar earnings of the United Kingdom to be used for the rest of the sterling area.

Thus during the war period, up to 31 March 1943, $2,700 million (about £600 million) were provided from

		$ million
(1)	Repatriation	800
(2)	Loan	700
(3)	Plants	200
(4)	Gift	1,000
		2,700

[1] *Canadian Mutual Aid Board Final Report, 1946* (Ottawa, 1947), p. 16. [2] Ibid. p. 6.

[3] $ in this section means Canadian dollars. The rate during the war was about 4·5 Canadian dollars to £1.

The Canadian Mutual Aid Agreement took effect from 1 September 1943. The expenditure on Mutual Aid account was:

	$ million		$ million
In 1943–4	772	including for the U.K.	723
In 1944–5	932	,, ,,	719
In 1945–6	767	,, ,,	670
	2,471		2,112

The system of Mutual Aid, which prevailed from 1 September 1943 to 1 September 1945, was based on the Canadian Acts of 20 May 1943 (which made available $1,000 million), and 23 June 1944 (which made available a further $800 million), and the Mutual Aid Agreement of 11 February 1944.

The Agreement provided for aid in 'war supplies', not in cash. War supplies would not as a general rule have to be returned to Canada, except in the case of ships and supplies required for relief.

Canada did not ask for 'Reverse' Mutual Aid.

> It was arranged with the United Kingdom that their receipts of Canadian dollars—including payments by Canada for the maintenance of Canadian Forces overseas, exports from the United Kingdom to Canada etc., insofar as they exceeded the amount required for the direct expenditures in Canada of United Kingdom missions, and agencies, and other current requirements, would . . . be used by the Mutual Aid Board to meet the cost of war supplies for the United Kingdom and thereby keep to a minimum the supplies required to be paid for out of Mutual Aid funds.[1]

Thus the United Kingdom, besides receiving the free gift of $1,000 million and war supplies delivered as Mutual Aid to the amount of $2,112 million, paid from 1 April 1943 to 31 March 1946 some $4,000 million in cash for munitions, foodstuffs, and raw materials including the net deficit of the rest of the sterling area (namely $360 million).

In round figures the deficit of the sterling area with Canada during the war was over $7,300 million (roughly £1,640 million) which was covered as follows:

	$ million
Free gift and Mutual Aid	3,100
Cost of Canadian forces overseas	2,200
Sale of securities, and plants	1,000
Sale of gold (400), and Loan (700)	1,100

Whereas the Lend-Lease settlement with the United States reached an 'unsordid' conclusion after months of negotiations, the Mutual Aid Agreement with Canada was 'unsordid' from the outset, since no 'consideration' was envisaged and goods delivered as Mutual Aid were not, generally speaking, to be returned to Canada.

Agreements concluded on 6 March 1946[2] provided simply that all inter-governmental war claims would be settled by the payment of $150 million from the United Kingdom to Canada. An amount of $425 million owing to Canada

[1] *Canadian Mutual Aid Board Final Report*, p. 32.

[2] H.C.Deb. 5th ser., vol. 420, coll. 510–20.

with respect to the British Commonwealth Air Training Scheme was waived. The two Governments agreed to discuss before 1 January 1951 the question of interest on the loan of $700 million and the repayment of any balance of the loan then outstanding.

The writer wishes in conclusion to pay a tribute to the friendship and sympathetic understanding with which these problems were dealt with at all times by Messrs. Ilsley, Minister of Finance during the War; Clark, Deputy Minister of Finance; and Graham Towers, Governor of the Bank of Canada.

INDEX[1]

[1] In the cross-references in this index, references in small capitals are to other main headings, while references in ordinary type are to subdivisions of the same main heading.

WORLD POLITICAL
1939

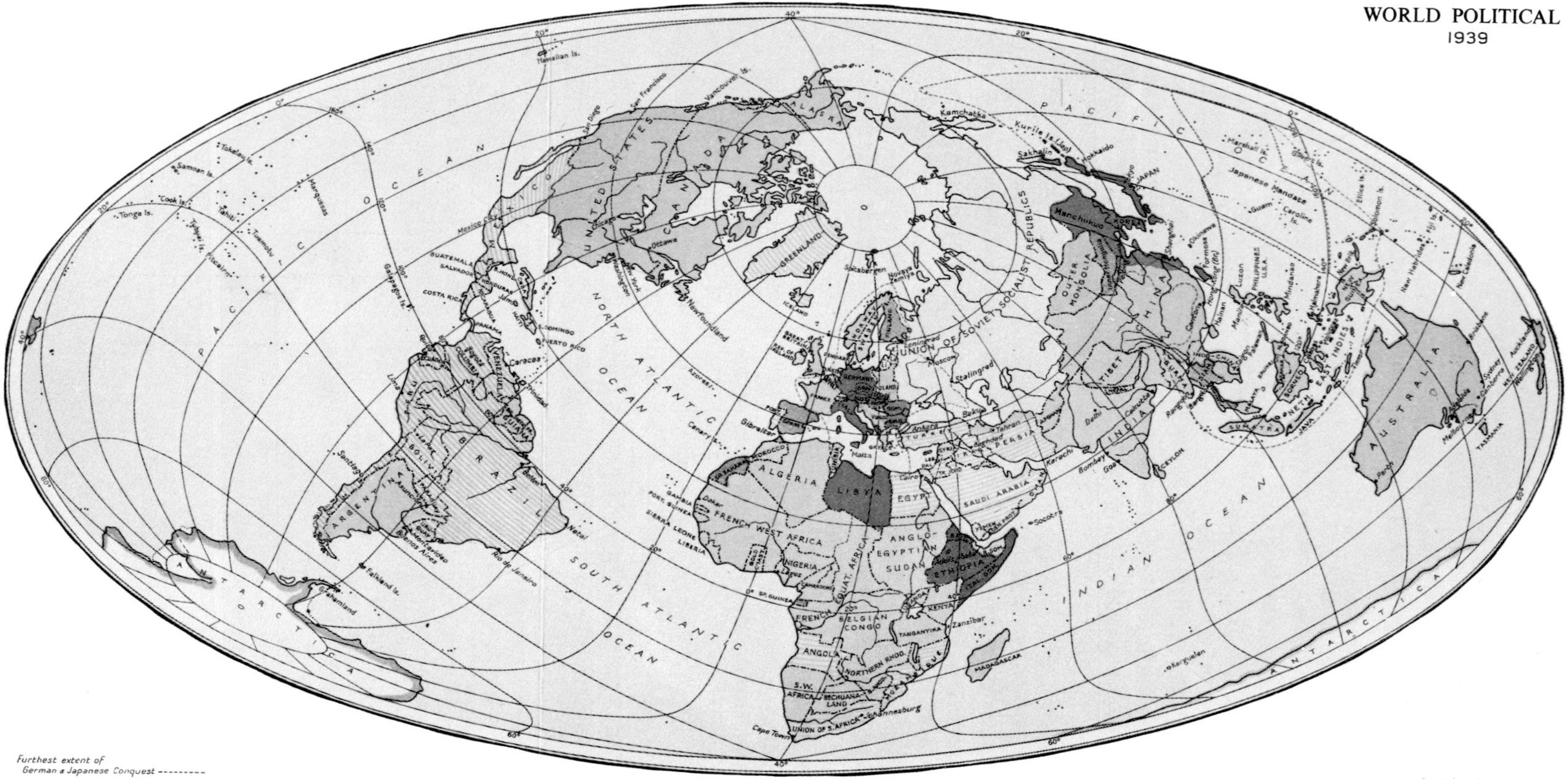

Furthest extent of
German & Japanese Conquest ---------

WORLD POPULATION

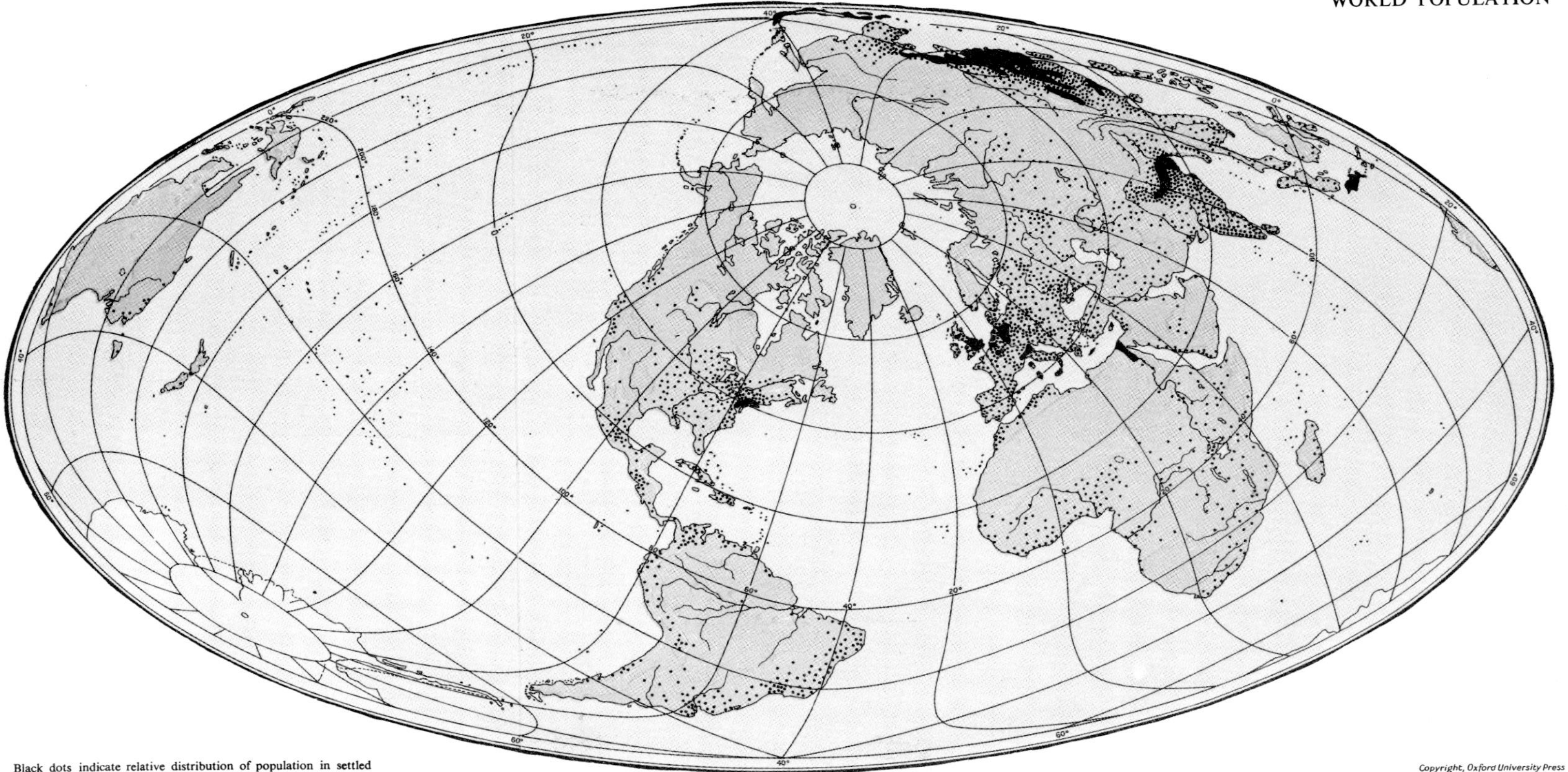

Black dots indicate relative distribution of population in settled areas which are coloured green.

WORLD PHYSICAL